WASHINGTON
HANDBOOK

WASHINGTON HANDBOOK

FIFTH EDITION

DON PITCHER

MOON
PUBLICATIONS INC.

WASHINGTON HANDBOOK
FIFTH EDITION

Published by
Moon Publications, Inc.
P.O. Box 3040
Chico, California 95927-3040, USA

Printed by
Colorcraft Ltd., Hong Kong

ISBN: 1-56691-045-5
ISSN: 1085-2646

Editor: Gina Wilson Birtcil
Copy Editor: Nicole Revere
Production & Design: Rob Warner and David Hurst
Cartographers: Bob Race and Brian Bardwell
Index: Diane Wurzel and Nicole Revere

Front cover photo: Robert K. Olejniczak

Distributed in the USA by Publishers Group West
Printed in Hong Kong

Please send all comments,
corrections, additions,
amendments, and critiques to:

**WASHINGTON HANDBOOK
MOON PUBLICATIONS, INC.
P.O. BOX 3040
CHICO, CA 95927-3040, USA
e-mail: travel@moon.com**

Printing History
1st edition — March 1989
2nd edition — June 1990
3rd edition — July 1992
4th edition — October 1994
5th edition — February 1997

For Karen

CONTENTS

MAPS

(continues on next page)

MAPS
(continued)

MAP SYMBOLS

——	EXPRESSWAY	―)―(―	TUNNEL	——	NATIONAL BOUNDARY
——	MAIN HIGHWAY	⟨⟩	BRIDGE	—·——·—	STATE BOUNDARY
——	SECONDARY ROAD	≈	PASS	—··——··—	COUNTY LINE
– – –	UNPAVED ROAD	— —	STATE FERRY	—···——···—	OTHER BOUNDARY
· · · · ·	FOOT TRAIL	·············	OTHER FERRY	■	POINT OF INTEREST
INTERSTATE HIGHWAY		○	LARGE CITY	●	HOTEL / ACCOMMODATION
U. S. HIGHWAY		○	MEDIUM CITY		N. P. = NATIONAL PARK
STATE HIGHWAY		○	TOWN		S. P. = STATE PARK
COUNTY / OTHER ROAD		▲	MOUNTAIN		C. P. = COUNTY PARK
WATER		▲▲	CAMPGROUND		CG. = CAMPGROUND

ABBREVIATIONS

B&B—bed and breakfast	DNR—Department of Natural Resources	km—kilometer
CCC—Civilian Conservation Corps	F—Fahrenheit	PCT—Pacific Crest Trail
d—double occupancy	4WD—four-wheel drive	RV—recreational vehicle
		s—single occupancy

ACCOMMODATION CHARTS

SPECIAL TOPICS

ACKNOWLEDGMENTS

This is the fifth edition for *Washington Handbook,* and my first time at the helm. Most books in print this many times around are fairly set in their ways, and you can expect only incremental changes. But this version proves that you *can* teach an old dog new tricks. Readers will note several obvious changes—particularly the increased weight, which makes it doubly useful as a doorstop. I hope they will also notice that the coverage is much more thorough (and considerably more opinionated). I drove 14,000 miles in my travels around Washington to research this update, and attempted to get at least a taste of nearly every corner and crevice of this diverse and scenic state. I've certainly missed much, but will try to make the next edition even more complete.

This book is the product of a team of folks that includes my pencil-packing editor, Gina Birtcil, mapmaker Bob Race who cringes every time he sees another of my jam-it-all-in base maps, designer and layout guru Dave Hurst, and all the other folks at the Moon office in the fair city of Chico (where Velveeta is considered a gourmet food product). Thanks to all of them for their dedicated work in getting this volume out.

Much of the information found within these pages was provided by ever-patient tourism

folks at the various chambers of commerce, along with Forest Service and Park Service employees, museum workers, and other dedicated Washington boosters. The following people within this group were especially helpful: Nancy Batt, Rhonda Beckman, Douglas Buell, Jill Carlos, Kathy Cocus, Jim Conomo, Diane Cooley, Roylene Crawford, Trina Dice, Sharon Eklund, Pamela K. Fabela, Susan Harder, Diane Holz, Ella Houston, Kris Kelley-Watkins, Rick Leenstra, Jr., Cindy Len, Lin Leon, Steve Levin, Melissa Main, Laurie Medlicott, Tami Peitersen, Patricia A. Perry, Amy Pfeiffenberger, Mary Priñe, Jean Raupp, Kay Ritchie, Dick Roller, Marian Ross, Melodé Sapp, Diane Schostak, Linda K. Smith, Joan Stern, Barb Thompson, Mary Thomsen, Irene Thornton, Mary Vermillion, Myra Wentworth, Martha Lou Wheatley, Linda Wilton, and Louann Yager. Thanks to everyone!

A number of folks deserve a special commendation for their help in making this book possible: Sue Hildreth in Seattle, Fred Euphrat in California, and my friends in Washington, Alaska, and California who provided help along the way. A very special thank you goes to Karen Shemet for helping me get through this big project with at least a modicum of sanity left. Her support made all the difference in the world.

TELL US ABOUT YOUR TRIP

Is this book out of date? Of course it is. By the very nature of the publishing business, words in print were always written at some earlier time and based upon information gathered even earlier, usually sometime during the last Ice Age. Things change fast in Washington, and you're bound to find new (or old) places that I missed, motels that are dives (but I said they were great), noteworthy restaurants with 10 secret herbs and spices, incorrect phone numbers for the nudist colonies, and the names of top-secret military bases where they store all those UFOs that crashed. So send those cards and letters, especially if you know something offbeat that I missed. I attempt to update this book every two years, and always appreciate any hot tips, criticisms, or compliments you may wish to contribute. I try to respond to all letters, but because I'm often on the road you may have to wait awhile for a response. Please write me with your suggestions and comments:

Don Pitcher
Washington Handbook
Moon Publications, Inc.
P.O. Box 3040
Chico, CA 95927-3040
USA

BOB RACE

INTRODUCTION

The 1990s have seemed a coming-of-age for the state of Washington, as Americans and international travelers discover what locals have long known: that the state contains some of the most diverse and fascinating country in the Lower 48. The state's forests are no secret—they don't call it the "Evergreen State" for nothing—but the abundance of other attractions are astounding. These include the city of Seattle, one of the nation's most enjoyable and sophisticated metropolitan areas; the dramatic Cascade Mountains with glacier-clad summits and active volcanoes; the arid plains, giant dams, and rolling wheat fields of eastern Washington; the long sandy beaches and rugged rocky coastline bordering the Pacific; the justly famous gorge of the mighty Columbia River; hundreds of islands of all sizes and shapes in Puget Sound; and, of course, the lush rainforests of the Olympic Peninsula for which the state is so famous. For the visitor, the state offers almost too much to see.

Travelers to Washington will quickly learn that they aren't the first to discover its wonders. The state's population has grown rapidly in the last decade and shows no signs of slowing. Part of this is due to increased jobs in high technology, but it

also has been fueled by favorable publicity. More and more, the national media spotlight lands on the state, acclaiming it for cutting-edge entrepreneurship, magnificent scenery, abundant outdoor adventures, and culinary treats to rival those anywhere. Washington's proclaimed livability has also made it a favored destination for American, European, and Asian visitors. Increased tourism has been a boon to some of the smaller towns in the Cascades and along the Olympic Peninsula, where the drastic reduction in timber harvesting has cost thousands of jobs. Tourism hasn't replaced logging and sawmill work, but it has provided new options.

Washington may be tucked away in the northwest corner of America, but it stands at the front door of the Pacific. The state's access to major Asian markets—Washington is closer to Asia than any of the contiguous states—has made it a major player in the Pacific Rim. Boeing and Microsoft especially have major stakes here; Boeing airplanes are one of the nation's most important exports, and Microsoft's computer software programs sell to a global market—and have made Bill Gates the richest human on the planet.

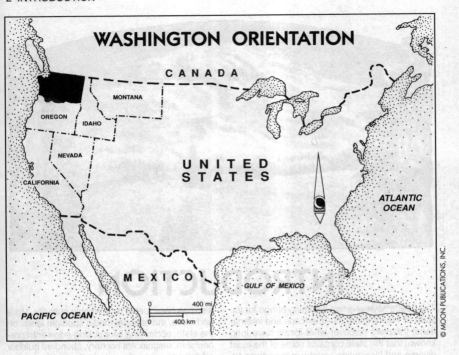

THE LAND

GEOGRAPHY AND CLIMATE

Washington is a bit isolated from the rest of the country. The Pacific Ocean forms its western boundary, the Columbia River separates the state from Oregon for most of its southern border, and Idaho is its eastern neighbor. Unlike the East Coast, where major cities are only an hour or two apart by car, Seattle and Spokane are six hours apart, and Seattle and Vancouver/Portland are almost four hours apart.

A State Divided

To the surprise of many first-time visitors, instead of having only evergreen forests, natural lakes, and lots of saltwater with snowcapped mountains towering over it, Washington has a dual personality. It is divided into the dramatically

different eastern and western halves by the Cascade Range, which extends 600 miles from Canada through Washington and Oregon before flattening out and disappearing in northern California. The Cascade Range has a powerful effect on the state's climate and scenery. The mountains wring moisture from the clouds, dumping rain and snow on the western flanks, but leaving little for the dry and sunny east side. Those who expect to see only the evergreen land of the state's promotional campaigns are surprised when they travel through the treeless hills of eastern Washington that are covered with wheat and row crops. This country has its own beauty, and in places resembles the wide open spaces of Wyoming or Montana—not an image commonly associated with Washington.

Much smaller but with an equally dramatic silhouette, the Olympic Range is quite different from the ancient and volatile Cascades. The Olympics (the backbone of Olympic National Park) are some of the world's youngest mountains, just one or two million years old. Though not exceptionally tall (Mount Olympus is the highest at 7,965 feet, and it can't be seen from Puget Sound), the Olympics produce dramatically varied weather. Storms spawned over the Pacific dump 70-100 inches of annual rainfall on the coastal plains, and 150 inches or more (with a record of 184 inches at Wynoochee oxbow) in the rainforests on the western and southwestern slopes—the heaviest precipitation in the contiguous United States. But on the northeast slopes of this range, Port Angeles, Sequim, Port Townsend, Whidbey Island, and the San Juans are in the driest area of western Washington, receiving only 12-20 inches annually. The most familiar example of this is Sequim, which has become a retirement haven because it sits in the rain shadow of the Olympics and is so dry that farmers must irrigate their crops.

Western Washington
Aside from the Olympic rainforests, most of the "wet side of the mountains" actually isn't all that wet: Seattle's annual rainfall of 38 inches is less than that of Chicago or New York. Winter snowfalls are generally light and melt quickly; a real snowstorm paralyzes the city for days due to the lack of snow-removal equipment and snow-driving expertise among natives.

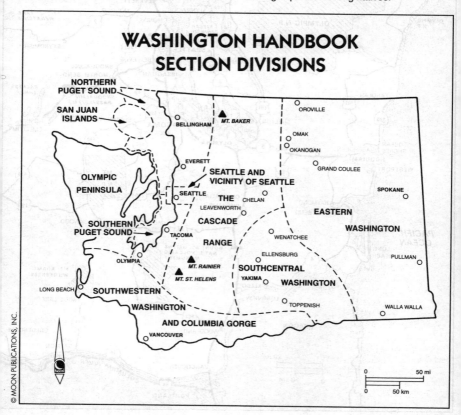

WASHINGTON HANDBOOK SECTION DIVISIONS

© MOON PUBLICATIONS, INC.

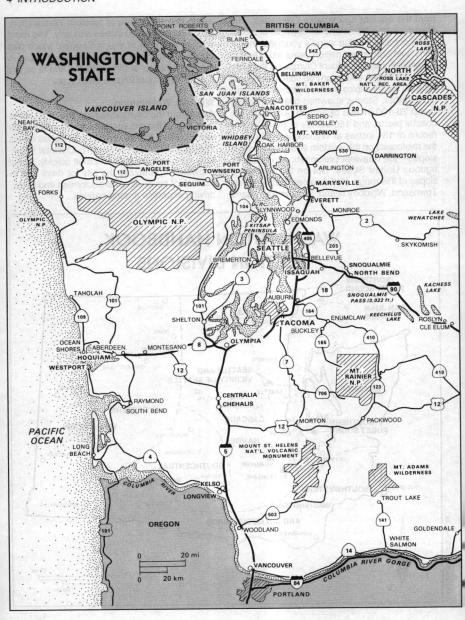

STATE FACTS

Nickname: The Evergreen State
Entered the Union: November 11, 1889; the 42nd state
Population, 1995: 4.9 million
Population rank: 18th of 50 states
Ethnic breakdown:
  White 88.5%
  Black 3.1%
  Native American 1.6%
  Asian and Pacific Islanders 2.4%
  Spanish origin 4.4%
Area: 68,192 square miles
Area rank: 20th of 50 states
Median household income: $31,183
Median income rank: 19th of 50 states and D.C.
Largest cities:
  Seattle 520,000
  Spokane 187,000
  Tacoma 184,000
  Bellevue. 87,000
  Everett 75,000
  Yakima 58,000
  Bellingham 55,000
  Renton 43,000
Leading industries: aerospace, forest products, food processing
Number of farms: 38,000
Total trade, 1988: $54.9 billion
Leading trade partner: Japan, $21.8 billion
State bird: willow goldfinch
State flower: Coast rhododendron
State tree: western hemlock
State motto: alki (Chinook word meaning by-and-by)

Typical western Washington weather is mild and wet in the winter, warm and dry in the summer. Semipermanent high- and low-pressure systems in the North Pacific create predictable patterns of clouds and light rain beginning in October, with daytime temperatures in the 40s throughout most of the winter; December and January are the region's wettest months. In spring, the clouds give way to partly sunny days, and it's not unusual to have six weeks of cloudless skies in July and August. Summer daytime temperatures are usually in the 70s and 80s, with perhaps half a dozen 90° days each year. Thunderstorms are rare, tornadoes even more rare, and, oddly, given that Washington gets a lot of moisture, the humidity is low.

Seattle averages about an inch of snow per month in winter, though many winters are snow-free; the record snow depth is 29 inches. Mount Rainier is the place to go for snow—in the winter of 1955-56, the Paradise ranger station (elev. 5,500 feet) received 1,000 inches (83 feet) of snow. Winters with at least 70 feet are the norm. Cascade ski areas usually open in November and remain open through early spring, beginning and ending with Mt. Baker's eight-month ski season.

Western Washington's skiing may be good, but the swimming is not. Water temperatures along the Pacific Coast and in the Strait of Juan de Fuca average 45° in January, rising to 53° in July, with some secluded coves and bays getting into the 60s. Puget Sound stays around 55° year-round, though again some protected areas warm up to the mid-60s and become swimable. Most swimming and waterskiing is done in the region's numerous lakes.

Eastern Washington

Compared with western Washington, the "dry side of the mountains" has hotter summers, colder winters, more snow, and less rain. The area from the Cascade Range east across the Columbia Basin to the Palouse hills has hot, dry weather with an average of only seven to 15 inches of annual rainfall. Summer daytime temperatures are in the 90s, with many days each year over 100°; the state's record high of 118° occurred at Ice Harbor Dam (near Pasco) in 1961. The bonus is that it's not humid. July and August are the driest months, often devoid of any precipitation at all; what rain they do receive generally comes packaged in thunderstorms. Winters bring 10-35 inches of snowfall and daytime temperatures in the 20s and 30s.

The Okanogan and Methow Valleys, in the north-central part of the state, are a cross-country skier's paradise. Annual winter snowfalls range from 30 to 70 inches, beginning in November and staying on the ground through March or April. January maximum temperatures hover around 30°, with some nighttime below-zero temperatures recorded each year. In summer, the Okanogan Valley is another eastern Washington hot spot, with average temperatures from 85° to 90° and several 100s each season, plus occasional thunderstorms and hailstorms.

Much of this part of Washington, from the Columbia River east to the Spokane area and the Palouse hills south of Spokane, is technically a desert because the rainfall is less than 12 inches a year; in a few places no more than eight inches are measured. In fact, this is the northern end of the Great American Desert that runs from the Mexican border north almost to the Canadian border. Except for an occasional spot high enough to turn clouds into rainfall, the area hasn't had trees in several million years. Today

it doesn't look like the Sahara or Death Valley because of the vast irrigation systems that have been built there, turning the desert into a cross-hatched garden.

The largest irrigation project, of course, is the massive Columbia Basin Project, created by Grand Coulee Dam, which puts water on a half-million acres of farms and vineyards. The mighty Columbia—second biggest river in America—drains an area of 259,000 square miles within parts of seven states and Canada. With the dams backing water over the river's rapids, barges can now travel all the way to Clarkston and Lewiston along the Washington/Idaho border. The remainder of the irrigation water comes from smaller rivers, such as the Yakima, or from deep wells. Most of eastern Oregon, which has

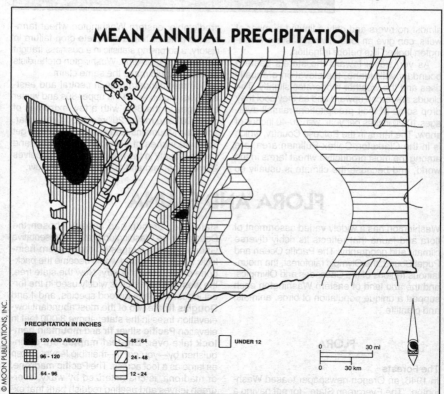

MEAN ANNUAL PRECIPITATION

PRECIPITATION IN INCHES

- 120 AND ABOVE
- 96 - 120
- 64 - 96
- 48 - 64
- 24 - 48
- 12 - 24
- UNDER 12

0   30 mi

0   30 km

Grand Coulee
at Dry Falls

DIANNE BOULERICE LYONS

almost no rivers and only a limited number of wells, can give an idea of what eastern Washington looked like before irrigation.

As you travel toward the state's eastern boundary with Idaho, the elevation gradually rises and the weather moderates slightly. The clouds are forced upward and as they cool they drop some of their precipitation: rainfall averages 10-20 inches per year, with 20-40 inches of snow. The farms in the Palouse Country, which is in the Clarkston-Colfax-Pullman area, are among the most productive wheat farms in the world, and because the climate is usually so predictable, eastern Washington wheat farmers have never had a complete crop failure in history, a surprising statistic in a business fraught with weather problems. Washington orchardists wish they could make the same claim.

Summer temperatures in central and eastern Washington are in the upper 80s and winter averages in the 30s, with a few extremes of plus 100° and minus 20° recorded every year. The Blue Mountains in the southeast corner get up to 40 inches of precipitation, while Pend Oreille County in the northeast corner receives 28 inches of rain and 40-80 inches of snow.

FLORA AND FAUNA

Washington has a widely varied assortment of flora and fauna that reflects its richly diverse climate and geography. The Pacific Ocean and Puget Sound, the Olympic rainforest, the mountainous regions of the Cascades and Olympics, and the arid land of eastern Washington each support a unique population of birds, animals, and plantlife.

FLORA

The Forests
In 1946, an Oregon newspaper teased Washington, "The Evergreen State," for not having a state tree. Oregon had already chosen the Douglas fir, so Washington State Representative George Adams suggested the western hemlock, which he claimed would become the backbone of the forest industry. Now the state tree, the **western hemlock** is widely used in the forest industry as a pulpwood species, and it and **Douglas fir** are two of the most abundant low-elevation trees in the state; above 3,000 feet in elevation **Pacific silver fir** and **mountain hemlock** take over. **Big-leaf maples** are distinguished by—you got it—their big leaves, often as large as a foot across. The **Pacific madrone**, or madrona, is characterized by waxy, evergreen leaves and peeling reddish bark that ex-

poses a smooth underskin. Other common trees are the **western red cedar, Sitka spruce, grand fir, black cottonwood, red alder,** and **vine maple.** Northeast Washington and parts of the Cascades have other species, including lodgepole pine, western larch, western white pine, ponderosa pine, and Engelmann spruce.

Olympic Rainforest

At Olympic National Park, the Hoh, Queets, and Quinault River Valleys constitute the better part of the Olympic rainforest, an area unique in the world. Purists would say that 150 or more inches of annual rainfall doesn't qualify this region as a rainforest, a term usually reserved for the steamy jungle tropics. Whatever it's called, this area produces some of the world's largest trees. The largest known western hemlock and Sitka spruce grow in the Quinault Valley, the largest Douglas fir is in Queets, and the largest red alder is in the Hoh. The four major species here—the Sitka spruce, western red cedar,

Hoh Rain Forest in Olympic National Park

Douglas fir, and western hemlock—all grow very tall: trees average 200 feet, with many topping 300 feet.

The height of the trees isn't the only fascinating aspect of the rainforest: the visitor is immediately struck by how green everything is, and how pristine. These areas have never been logged; what you see is nature, pure and simple. Enormous trees spring out of the long-since-decayed "nurse logs" that gave them life, with club moss eerily draping the branches; ferns and mosses cover nearly every inch of available ground in a thick carpet. Though most rainfall occurs from fall to spring, even summer days feel damp from high humidity and ocean fog. And it isn't just trees that one finds in these rainforests, but an incredible diversity of ferns, mosses, shrubs, herbs, and other plants, along with many kinds of birds, mammals, insects, and amphibians.

Old-Growth Forests

Old-growth forests are defined as being at least 250 years old, though some stands are actually far older, approaching 1,000 years. Other terms one commonly hears for old-growth forests are: virgin timber (this term is out of favor in the P.C. world), mature forests (loggers prefer the term over-mature, implying that they need to be cut), or ancient forests (preferred by some environmentalists because ancient is a venerable term commonly associated with wisdom).

Because of the tall overstory trees that moderate temperatures and hold much of the snow, original forests are more stable than cutover areas and less susceptible to climatic extremes. This helps the survival of forest animals by allowing them to browse at all times of the year. It also allows for a multilayered understory of trees, bushes, and herbs that can support a larger variety of animal life. In addition, defects in the old trees and standing dead trees—called snags—provide nesting sites for birds, flying squirrels, and other animals, while the fallen trees create nutrient-rich mulch as they decay. In many old-growth forests, these fallen giants become "nursery logs" with new trees sprouting in a straight line along the trunk.

This heterogeneous structure differs markedly from the second- and third-growth tree farms where an even-aged monoculture of trees (usually Douglas fir) rises over a depauperate forest floor. Tree plantations achieve fast growth and produce marketable timber, but they are a poor substitute for a more diverse natural forest where many plants and animals coexist.

Going, Going, Gone?

When the first Anglo settlers reached western Washington, they found immense forests that seemed to roll on forever, forests so dense that they severely slowed transportation. The wilderness represented an abundant source of wood to feed the demands of a growing society, particularly when gold sent thousands of miners to California and the Klondike. Logging was a dangerous but financially rewarding way to survive, and the cleared land created productive farmland for later settlers. After a century and a half of this, barely 15% of the original forests survive in the Pacific Northwest, and nearly half of these are within Olympic and Mt. Rainier National Parks. Most of Washington's private timberlands are operated as tree farms. On Forest Service lands, a moratorium on the logging of old-growth stands has been in effect for several years because of environmental concerns, most notably the preservation of spotted owl habitat (see below). The closure to logging has caused major disruptions in timber-dependent communities, forcing many loggers and millworkers to look for other employment. The anti-greenie sentiment runs strong in these towns. Sierra Club bumper stickers are ill-advised.

Rhododendrons

In 1892, Washington needed a flower to represent the state at the Chicago World's Fair. Many flowers were nominated, but the contest came down to two: the coast rhododendron and the common clover. While it doesn't seem that clover would offer much competition, it was a close call—the rhody won with just 53% of the vote. The region from British Columbia south to northern California and east to the foothills of the Cascades is prime rhody-growing territory. There are about 500

rhododendron

pure species hardy to the climate and several hundred more greenhouse varieties, which are combined and cross-pollinated to produce thousands of hybrids.

Rhodies are standard equipment in western Washington gardens, relatively easy to grow and beautiful to behold, in colors from yellows to pinks to bright reds and whites. The well-known rhododendron gardens on Whidbey Island, Federal Way, Bainbridge Island, Brinnon, and smaller gardens in area parks have impressive displays in spring and early summer.

MARINELIFE

Killer Whales

The orca, or killer whale, is the largest member of the family Delphinidae, a classification that includes toothed whales and dolphins. The males are significantly larger than the females of the species: up to 32 feet long, weighing five to six tons, with dorsal fins up to six and a half feet high and four feet wide and tail flukes spanning nine feet. Unencumbered by its size, the orca frequently travels at speeds upward of 30 mph. Named "killer whales" because they take warm-blooded prey, these cetaceans eat anything from harbor and ringed seals to seabirds, otters, dolphins, fish, and squid, depending on the local food supply. In Puget Sound, they generally eat only fish—mostly salmon, rockfish, and cod—and leave the other species alone.

Reports of killer whale attacks on humans and boats have been recorded as far back as 1911. In that year, H.G. Ponting, a photographer for the Scott expedition to the South Pole, was reportedly standing on ice within six feet of the water when eight whales broke through the ice and threw him into the sea. Reports such as these are so rare that one can only surmise that in those situations the orcas mistook people for marine mammals. The fact that whales and dolphins do not attack humans is one of the mysteries of

BOB RACE

nature. The orca is much more famous in this country for kissing spectators at Sea World.

Orcas are highly social, traveling in packs or "pods" of two to 40 individuals. Families stay together, protecting the young (who, at eight feet long and 400 pounds at birth, would seem to require little protection) and mourning their dead. There are three resident pods in Puget Sound and along the Washington coast, with a total of about 80 members; other transient pods occasionally swim into the area but don't stay long. The most frequent sightings are around the San Juan Islands, especially at Lime Kiln State Park on the west side of San Juan Island—the only park in the U.S. dedicated exclusively to whale-watching.

gray whale

Gray Whales

Every spring, tour boats leave the docks at Westport and a few other coastal towns for a close-up look at the migrating California gray whales. These enormous whales—ranging up to 42 feet in length and upward of 30 tons—migrate from the Bering and Chukchi seas to the warm breeding lagoons off Baja California in winter, passing the Washington coast southbound in November and December and northbound from April to June.

Occasionally a group of gray whales comes into Puget Sound, and several have beached themselves and died for thus-far unknown reasons. Most, however, follow the outer coastline. The gray is a baleen whale: it feeds by stirring up mud in shallow water, sucking in the water, mud, and organisms, and using its baleen—a fringelike sieve in its mouth—as a filter to trap its prey while forcing the mud and water back out. Gray whales are easily identified by their gray color, the absence of a dorsal fin, and bumpy ridges on their backs; their faces are generally covered with patches of barnacles and orange whale lice. Unconcerned with their appearance, gray whales often lift their faces out of the water up to about eye level in a motion referred to as "spy-hopping." Although gray whales aren't aggressive and are often even friendly, whalewatchers in small boats should keep a respectful distance, since a whale may "breach," or jump completely out of the water, creating one heck of a wave as 30 solid tons splash back into the water.

Porpoises

Visitors often think that the black-and-white sea creatures riding the bow waves of their ferry or tour boat are baby killer whales, but these playful characters are Dall's porpoises. Commonly seen in the Strait of Juan de Fuca alongside the ferry *Coho* from Port Angeles to Victoria, B.C., the porpoises frequently travel south through the Admiralty Inlet and, on rare occasions, as far south as Tacoma. Dall's porpoises reach lengths of six and a half feet and weights of up to 330 pounds; they feed primarily on squid and small fish.

The harbor porpoise is Puget Sound's smallest cetacean, ranging to nearly six feet in length and 150 pounds. Although similar in appearance to the Dall's porpoise, the harbor porpoise is much more shy and rarely spotted in the wild. Accurate counts are impossible, but the population around the San Juan Islands has been estimated at fewer than 100; none live in Puget Sound, though resident populations were spotted there in the 1940s.

In summer and early fall, schools of up to 100 Pacific white-sided dolphins enter the Strait of Juan de Fuca, traveling as far inshore as Port Angeles but rarely any farther east. Reaching up to seven feet in length and 200 pounds, these dolphins are common off the shores of Japan, where their numbers are estimated at 30,000-50,000, and along the continental shelf from Baja California to the Gulf of Alaska. These dolphins have black backs, white shoulders and bellies, and hourglass-shaped streaks that run from their foreheads to their tails; the rear halves of their dorsal fins are light gray. Like the Dall's porpoise, white-sided dolphins enjoy riding bow waves and often leap full-length out of the water alongside a boat.

Seals and Sea Lions

Harbor seals are numerous throughout Puget Sound and the Strait of Juan de Fuca, with their statewide population estimated at 7,000. They can be seen at low tide sunning themselves on rocks in isolated areas, but they will quickly return to the water if approached by humans. Though they appear clumsy on land, these 100- to 200-pound seals are poetry in motion underwater; they flip, turn, and glide with little apparent effort, staying underwater for as long as 20 minutes. (You can see harbor seals up close at the underwater viewing tank at Point Defiance Zoo in Tacoma.) Harbor seals have a bad reputation with area salmon fishermen, although studies of the seals' stomach contents and fecal material indicate that they feed primarily on flounder, herring, pollock, cod, and rockfish, as well as some mollusks and crustaceans.

The California sea lion is a seasonal visitor to the Strait of Juan de Fuca and northern Puget Sound, though on some mornings in winter and early spring their barking can be heard in shoreline communities as far south as Tacoma. These dark brown sea lions breed off the coast of California and Mexico in the early summer, and then some adventurous males migrate as far north as British Columbia for the winter. A large group of them collects just offshore from Everett, where a commercial tour boat takes visitors out for a closer look. A group of them discovered how easy it is to capture salmon and steelhead trout as they mill around in front of the fish ladder at Hiram Chittenden Locks in Seattle's Ballard District. Given a group nickname of Herschel, the sea lions have thus far evaded every attempt by wildlife biologists to keep them from the easy pickings, including being shipped back to California; in only a matter of days the sea lions made the swim from the San Francisco area and were back at the locks.

The lighter-colored northern sea lions are more numerous in the Puget Sound area, numbering up to several hundred in winter, primarily around Sucia Island in the northern Sound. The males of the species are much larger than the females, growing to almost 10 feet in length and weighing over a ton, while the females are a dainty six feet long and 600 pounds. Both are almost white when wet; the male has a yellow mane.

Other Marine Creatures

Puget Sound is home to the largest species of **octopus** in the world. Though it grows to 12 feet across the arms and weighs 25-30 or more pounds, it's not dangerous and, in fact, often plays with divers. These octopi can make themselves incredibly flat to get where they have to go: according to a local octopus legend, one of these giants slid out of its tank and under a door into its owner's bedroom.

Another peculiar Puget Sound inhabitant is the **geoduck** (pronounced "GOO-ey-duck," from the Indian *gweduck,* meaning "dig deep"). These large, phallic-shaped clams can dig as deep as five feet, weighing in at four or five pounds with reports of some clams exceeding 15 pounds. The fleshy part of the body is so large that neither the entire body nor the siphon can be completely withdrawn into the shell. (Stop by Pike Place Market in Seattle to see what these creatures look like.) Geoducks are generally cut up and used in chowder, but some quality restaurants serve them as regular menu items or specials.

The **horse clam** is the second-largest Pacific Northwest clam, weighing up to five pounds; they can't completely withdraw their siphons, but at least their bodies fit inside their shells. Horse clams only dig about two feet deep, so they're much easier to gather and can be found in Cultus and Useless bays at the south end of Whidbey Island. Both geoducks and horse clams prefer sandy or sand-gravel beaches. For information on clamming, contact the Washington State Department of Fisheries, tel. (360) 753-6600. Before digging, it's always a good idea to call the Red Tide Hotline at (800) 562-5632 for the latest on the safety of clams.

DIANNE BOUERICE LYONS

geoduck, the Pacific Northwest's most revolting clam

LAND ANIMALS

Washington is home for a wide variety of land mammals, some of which have been brought back from the edge of extinction. Federal and state wildlife agencies alike have worked to preserve habitats for all forms of wildlife, and the state has become a richer place to live as a result.

Mule deer, the rare Columbian white-tailed deer, Rocky Mountain and Roosevelt elk, bighorn sheep, mountain goats, black and grizzly bears, and a wide variety of smaller mammals, such as marmots, beaver, badgers, muskrat, nutrias, rabbits, and squirrels, are some of the animals you can expect to see, especially in the numerous wildlife refuges scattered across the state. Present but less likely to be seen are woodland caribou and moose, occasional visitors in the far northeast corner of the

state. Even the timber wolf—exterminated from Washington in the 1930s—has made a comeback. The first wolf call was heard in the summer of 1990, and small numbers have now moved into the North Cascades from British Columbia.

Columbian White-Tailed Deer
Lewis and Clark were the first explorers to comment on this subspecies of mule deer, which evolved along the lower Columbia River between the Willamette River and the Pacific Ocean. By the time 5,200 acres were set aside for them in the 1960s, their numbers had dwindled into the dozens. Now they are thriving and number in the hundreds. They look very much like their larger cousins, but they are smaller and have a slightly longer tail and a white underside. The Columbia White-tailed Deer National Wildlife Refuge is just west of Cathlamet on Hwy. 4. Part of it is farmland still in use on the mainland, and the remainder is a group of islands in the Columbia River, where the deer often swim to browse on the willows and other low-growing plants.

Roosevelt Elk
Another subspecies, the Roosevelt elk live on the Olympic Peninsula, mostly inside the boundaries of Olympic National Park, and are thus given adequate protection to prevent them from being hunted to extinction. They are a subspecies of their Rocky Mountain relatives, which were almost killed off in the Cascades. They look similar to their relatives, but their antlers aren't as spectacular as those coveted by trophy hunters. Roosevelt elk are named for President Theodore Roosevelt, who was instrumental in their preservation.

Cougars
This big cat doesn't make any of the endangered or threatened species lists because its numbers are increasing in Washington, as evidenced by the number that have been killed by humans recently. In 1993 a total of 14 were killed. A sheriff in Jefferson County on the Olympic Peninsula shot a cougar that was eating a family's pet dog. A rancher in Stevens County in the Okanogan Highlands shot one

that he said was chasing two of his children. As frightening as it is to be stalked by a big cat, wildlife experts say it is very unlikely that the cougar has mayhem in mind when following or watching humans. Like all cats, they are unusually curious animals. Few people have been attacked by cougars: between 1890 and 1990 only 58 documented attacks occurred in the U.S. and Canada. If you come face to face with one, maintain eye contact while backing slowly away. Try to appear larger than you are by raising your arms or by spreading a jacket or shirt. If you have children with you, pick them up. Talk loudly. But never, never run. Wildlife officials say compressed-air horns are effective against cougars, as they sometimes are against bears.

Bears

Black bears are fairly widespread in Washington, with large populations on the Olympic Peninsula and in Pend Oreille County. All of the black bears on the Olympic Peninsula are black; in other areas they may be black, brown, or honey-colored. They'll eat anything, from carpenter ants to berries to dead elk to salmon, plus anything you pack in from the supermarket. Black bears are so numerous that 400 of them are "harvested" each year in northeastern Washington.

Grizzly bears are rare in Washington, but there may be a few in the North Cascades and in the northeast corner of the state, spilling over from Idaho's Selkirk Mountains. Grizzlies once roamed throughout the western states, but now they are a threatened species with just a handful in Washington, and a total population of fewer than 1,000 in the Lower 48. Most of these survive in remote parts of Wyoming, Idaho, and Montana. A female grizzly must be five to eight years old before reproducing, and she cares for her cubs for two to three years before having any more offspring, so her reproductive capacity is low. The best way to protect both the grizzly bear population and yourself is to avoid encounters with them.

Avoid unexpected encounters with bears by letting them know you're there. If you walk with a breeze hitting your back, any bears ahead of you will know you are coming. If you're unable

SLUGS

If western Washington had an official creature, it could easily be the common slug: the region is famous for them. The damp climate is just what slugs need to thrive: not too wet, because slugs aren't waterproof (they will absorb water through their outer membranes until their bodily fluids are too diluted to support them), and not too dry, because insufficient humidity makes them dry up and die. Optimum humidity for slugs is near 100%, which is why you'll see them crossing the sidewalk very early in the morning, at dusk, or on misty days.

During the dry parts of the day, they'll seek refuge under the pool cover you casually tossed onto the lawn, or under the scrap lumber piled in the back of your lot.

Slugs look like snails that have lost their shells, or little green or brown squirts of slime about three to five inches long. Though more than 300 species of slugs exist worldwide, the Northwest is home to little more than a dozen. The native **banana slug,** light green or yellowish with dark spots, has been rapidly outnumbered by the imported European

banana slug

FLORENCE BOULERICE

black slug, which is now far more common in area gardens than the native variety. Slugs can curl up into a ball to protect themselves, or flatten and elongate themselves to squeeze into tight places. They move on one long foot by secreting mucus that gets firm where the foot must grab hold and stays slimy under the part that must slide. They see (probably just patterns of light and dark) with eyes at the ends of a pair of tentacles; they have a mouth and eat primarily plants and mushrooms.

Getting rid of slugs is no easy matter. Traditional home remedies include saltshakers and beer traps; both require a strong stomach. Most residents just try to avoid stepping on them.

to see everything around you for at least 50 yards, warn any hidden animals by talking, singing, clapping your hands, tapping a cup, rattling a can of pebbles, or wearing a bell. Safety is also in numbers: the more of you hiking together, the more likely a bear is to sense you and stay away. Don't let your dog run free—it may sniff out a bear and lead it back to you. When camping in the backcountry, store all food, soaps, garbage, and clothes worn while cooking in a sack hung from a tree branch at least 10 feet up and four feet out from the tree trunk. In an established campground, keep those items in your car's trunk. Don't sleep where you cooked dinner, and keep sleeping bags and gear away from cooking odors. Stories are sometimes heard about grizzlies attacking women during their menstrual period, though nobody knows for sure if the scent actually causes an attack. Cautious women may choose to hike in grizzly country at another time.

If you do encounter a bear, here's how to identify it: a grizzly is generally lighter in color than a black bear, though color alone can't be used for identification. Look for the grizzly's shoulder hump (behind its head) and a "dish face" profile, with a distinct snout. (Black bears have no hump and a straight profile.) While you're looking for identifying marks, slowly detour out of the bear's path and stay upwind so the bear will know you're there; don't make abrupt noises or movements. While retreating, look for a tree to climb—one in which you can get at least 12 feet up and stay there until you're certain that the bear has left the area. Don't try to outrun the bear—grizzlies can hit 40 mph in short bursts, and you can't beat that, no matter how scared you are.

If you encounter a bear and it sees you, try to stay calm and not make any sudden moves. If no tree is close, your best bet is to back slowly away. Sometimes dropping an item such as a hat or jacket will distract the bear, and talking also seems to have some value in convincing bears that you're a human. If the bear sniffs the air, or stands on its hind legs it is probably trying to identify you. When it does, it will usually run away. If a bear woofs and postures, don't imitate, as this is a challenge. Keep retreating! Most bear charges are a bluff; the bear will often stop short and amble off.

If a *grizzly* bear actually does attack, curl up face-down on the ground in a fetal position with your hands wrapped behind your neck and your elbows tucked over your face. Your backpack may help protect you somewhat. Remain still even if you are attacked, since sudden movements may incite further attacks. It takes a lot of courage to do this, but often a bear will only sniff or nip you and leave. The injury you might sustain would be far less than if you had tried to resist.

Many authorities now recommend against dropping to the ground if you are attacked by a *black* bear, since they tend to be more aggressive in those situations. You're better off fighting back with whatever weapons are at hand if attacked by a black bear.

Recently, cayenne pepper sprays such as "Counter Assault" (available at camping stores) have proven useful in fending off some bear attacks. These "bear mace" sprays are effective only at close range and in non-windy conditions, and are not a cure-all or a replacement for being careful in bear country. Pocket skyblazer flares are also sometimes effective. Be careful with these in dry country—you might scare the bear away and end up starting a forest fire.

BIRDS

Eagles

Approximately 300 pairs of bald eagles make their year-round home in Washington, primarily west of the Cascades. In winter that number swells to over 1,600 birds, drawn to rivers throughout the state by the carcasses of spawned-out salmon. Several whitewater-rafting companies operating in the North Cascades offer midwinter Skagit float trips just for the thrill of seeing these majestic birds; see "Bald Eagle Viewing and Whitewater Rafting" in the Cascade Range chapter for more information.

In past times the bald eagle was often blamed for the deaths of sheep and other domestic animals. Actually, eagles much prefer dead and dying fish to anything running around on hooves; their common fare, aside from dead salmon, is sick or injured waterfowl or rabbits that didn't make it across the road. An aggressive bird, the eagle will often purloin the catch of an osprey

DIANNE BOULERICE LYONS

bald eagle wintering on the Skagit River

or other bird in favor of finding its own. Occasionally a pair of eagles will team up to catch a gull or diving bird, with each eagle taking a turn at striking the bird when it surfaces from its dive and following above it as it attempts to escape underwater. When the prey eventually becomes exhausted from the diving and dodging, it is snatched from the water and carried off.

The adult bald eagle's distinctive white head and tail make it easy to spot. But it takes four years for it to acquire distinctive markings, making the immature eagle confusing to identify, as it may show whitish markings anywhere on its body. In contrast, the somewhat similar golden eagle has distinct white patches on its tail and underwings.

Bald eagles are sensitive to disturbances in their environment; the Dept. of Fish and Game recommends that an undisturbed circle 660 feet in diameter surround a nest during the breeding season to preserve the nest site. Their large nests, sometimes measuring over eight feet wide and 12 feet high, are often found in old-growth spruce and fir; snags are popular for sunning, resting, and watching for their next meal.

The state's heaviest concentration of breeding bald eagles can be seen on the San Juan Islands, enjoying the warm updrafts around Mt. Constitution on Orcas Island and Mt. Findlayson and Mt. Dallas on San Juan Island, and along the Strait of Juan de Fuca. The annual "salmon festival" brings the resident and migrating birds to the inland reaches of the Skagit, Sauk, Nooksack, and Stillaguamish rivers, with some enterprising pairs seen along southern Puget Sound and the lower Columbia River.

Owls

The bird of the hour in western Washington is the **northern spotted owl,** which nests in old-growth forests along the Pacific Coast—forests that are filled with snags and broken trees that provide ideal nesting spots and smaller, sheltered trees for young owls who can't yet fly properly and must use their feet to climb from tree to tree. These forests are full of spotted-owl food: flying squirrels, snowshoe hares, and wood rats. They are big eaters and quite territorial: 2,200 acres of old-growth forest will support but a single pair of owls. Because suitable forest is being greatly reduced by logging, the spotted owls' numbers are diminishing—only an estimated 2,500 pairs remain in the Pacific Northwest's old-growth forests, and researchers believe they could be gone in 30 years if logging continues at its present rate.

Other Birds

Other noteworthy birds in western Washington include the **great blue heron,** frequently seen along harbors or suburban lakes. The **belted kingfisher** is a common year-round resident of Puget Sound and the Strait of Juan de Fuca. **Red-tailed hawks** are often perched along I-5 and other highways, waiting for a meal. Noisy **Stellar's jays,** blue with a black head, are common in picnic areas and neighborhoods.

In the Cascades and east of the mountains, the beautiful **mountain bluebird** is sometimes spotted in snags in open areas, and the town of Bickleton in the Horse Heaven Hills of southern Washington maintains hundreds of bluebird houses that stand on fence posts, in trees, and in front of the church. East of the mountains, striking black-and-white **magpies** are frequently seen flitting over the highway.

ENDANGERED SPECIES

Washington's forests, coastlines, and waterways host literally thousands of wildlife species. For millennia wolves slipped through forest undergrowth, deer grazed in the eastern Palouse, and otters dove for oysters among the San Juans. But they're disappearing now.

European trappers took out beaver and otter pelts, ranchers grazed wild species out of existence, and a host of other animals couldn't compete against farmers and developers with plows, pesticides, and shotguns.

Endangered Species

Today, at least 21 species are listed as endangered (being eliminated from portions of or all of its former range) in the state of Washington, and seven are considered threatened (not now endangered, but could become so in the foreseeable future). Among them are the following:

White Pelican: The last time these birds nested in Washington, Calvin Coolidge was president and the Great Crash was still three wild years away. Land reclamation and irrigation projects steadily eroded their habitat. Although nearly 2,000 white pelicans were counted in the Columbia Basin during September 1990, and they were spotted all across eastern Washington, white pelicans still don't nest here.

Brown Pelican: A record 4,980 brown pelicans were counted along the Washington coast during 1990 with the greatest numbers in Grays Harbor, and Pacific, Clallam, and Jefferson Counties. The bird is on the federal endangered list because chemical pollutants drastically reduced the population in the 1970s. They do not breed in Washington but have always migrated to the state. As their numbers increase, the Fish and Wildlife Service is considering reclassifying brown pelicans from endangered to threatened.

Aleutian Canada Goose: These geese originally nested on several small islands in Puget Sound, but after the introduction of foxes, immature goslings, unable to escape, were easy prey. During a 20-year recovery program the wild population has increased from a known 800 in 1975 to more than 6,300 in 1990. Today Aleutians primarily use Washington habitats during migration and are found mostly in Willapa Bay and along the lower Columbia River.

Peregrine Falcon: By 1975 pesticides and hunters had left only one pair of these falcons in Washington, but in 1990, 15 pairs were known. Nine of the nesting sites were along the coast, four were in the San Juan Islands, and two were in the Columbia River Gorge. Few bird species have been the subject of such intensive recolonization programs; they have partially adapted to urban living, with some spotted in Seattle and Tacoma.

Sandhill Crane: Both the lesser and the greater sandhill cranes occur in Washington, although the latter's numbers are dismally small. Breeding cranes were virtually absent in Washington by 1941, but more than 5,500 lesser cranes were seen in October 1990 in the Columbia National Wildlife Refuge area in the Columbia Basin.

Snowy Plover: This small, darting creature is in trouble. Plovers nest only on sandy or gravelly beaches and spits; for developers, this is prime beachfront property. Drastically reduced habitat has sent plover populations spiraling down.

spotted owl

BOB RACE

In 1987 nesting areas were closed to off-road vehicles, but the closure resulted in more camping and fishing in the area. The garbage left behind by campers and fishermen attracted more seagulls and crows, which prey on plover eggs. By 1990,

(continues on next page)

ENDANGERED SPECIES

(continued)

with only two known breeding areas in the state and an estimated adult population of 17, the Fish and Wildlife Service finally listed the snowy plover as *threatened*—not endangered.

Upland Sandpiper: Washington is on the western edge of this bird's breeding range; the only known nest is in eastern Spokane County. Sandpipers once flourished in several places in eastern Washington. Their decline has been attributed to habitat loss due to farming, overgrazing, and land development.

Spotted Owl: This is the bird of the 1990s. More hoopla surrounded the listing—and management proposals—of this species than any other in recent history. Logging interests called it the beginning of the end for the Pacific Northwest's timber industry; environmental interests saw it as a long-overdue plan to save the last islands of old-growth forest (to date, less than 15% of the Pacific Northwest *hasn't* been cut at least once already). Tempers flared. Battle lines were drawn.

In July 1991 the Fish and Wildlife Service listed the northern spotted owl as a threatened species throughout all three West Coast states and set forth guidelines recommending that habitat within at least a 1.8-mile radius of nests in the Cascade Range and a 2.2-mile radius on the Olympic Peninsula be maintained. Under tremendous political pressure, the plan is now under review.

The Endangered Species Act was specifically written to prevent economic considerations from derailing its intent. If the spotted owl controversy succumbs to logging, it will be the first time since the act's passage that neither the letter nor the intent of the law was followed.

Gray Wolf: Early in this century trappers had virtually wiped out wolf populations in the Western United States. But in 1990, breeding gray wolves were back in Washington. Wolf pups and adults have been seen and heard in North Cascades National Park and in the Okanogan and Wenatchee National Forests.

Grizzly Bear: Six ecosystems have been identified by the Fish and Wildlife Service in the Selkirk Mountains and the North Cascades as recovery areas for bringing grizzlies into the forests. The state's population is estimated at about 30.

Sea Otter: These amazing creatures, whose scruffy faces originally inspired sailors to spin mermaid tales, once ranged the breadth of Washington's coastline. By the early 1900s trapping had almost completely depopulated the western North American coast.

In 1990, biologists counted 212 sea otters off the Olympic coast, where a group was transferred from Alaska in 1969 and 1970. Most live in the area protected by both the Olympic National Park and the Washington Islands National Wildlife Refuge.

Mountain Caribou: The Selkirk Mountain caribou herd had dwindled to only 29 animals at one point, but the herd had grown to about 90 by 1990. All but this small herd had disappeared from the continental U.S., and the mountain caribou was listed as endangered by the state in 1982; in 1984 it was placed on the federal list. To increase the herd, 12 mountain caribou were trapped in British Columbia and brought to the Selkirk herd.

Threatened Species

Oregon Silverspot Butterfly: The first silverspot butterfly seen in Washington since 1986 was spotted on the Long Beach Peninsula in 1990. The site where it was found is under consideration for purchase or management agreement by the state Department of Wildlife. The butterfly is wholly dependent on blue western violets—it is the only plant on which the larvae feed and develop.

Western Pond Turtle: These methodical fellows once roamed, however slowly, throughout the southern Puget Sound around lowland lakes and ponds. Development has since swallowed almost all their habitat whole, and nonnative predators—bullfrogs and bass—finished off the rest. Currently they are found only in three locations within Klickitat and Skamania counties.

It is believed that only about 40 remain after a 1990 outbreak of pneumonia killed 36. Twenty more were treated at Woodland Park and Point Defiance

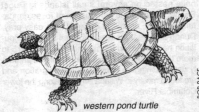

western pond turtle

BOB RACE

BOB RACE

pygmy rabbit

Ferruginous Hawk: Wildlife officials believe that the population of these hawks is holding steady, and most of the management problems involve protecting nest sites from human disturbance. An extensive survey in 1987 found 62 nesting pairs. Nesting poles and tree platforms have been built for them in the Juniper Forest of eastern Washington.

Pygmy Rabbit: This species is found in only five locations in an eastern Washington county, with a population estimated at about 300. Two of the five known sites are on state land and the other three on private land. A land exchange was arranged to allow game biologists three years to study the site and develop a plan to protect it. Habitat loss was the major factor in the pygmy rabbit's decline: Pygmys prefer dense sage where the soil is soft enough to dig burrows. These were the first lands to come under agricultural use when eastern Washington was settled.

zoos and survived. They were moved to the South Puget Wildlife Area. A "head start" program at the Woodland Park Zoo is getting populations moving, ahem, a little more quickly.

Birders will find Eugene S. Hunn's *Birding in Seattle and King County* an invaluable guide to birding sites from Seattle to Snoqualmie Pass.

Included are maps, charts, bird lists, and additional information on mammals and plantlife.

HISTORY

PREHISTORY

Although Washington is one of the more recent additions to the U.S., archaeological evidence suggests that the Pacific Northwest was one of the first populated areas in North America. In recent years, animal and human remains as much as 13,000 years old have been found across the state.

In the late 1950s and early 1960s, archaeologists uncovered numerous artifacts and partial skeletons of people known as Marmes Man in a cave overlooking the Palouse River near its confluence with the Snake River. Dated at more than 10,000 years old, this is one of the earliest known human occupation sites in North America.

At Ozette in the northwest corner of the state, an ancient village was covered by a mudflow, perhaps triggered by an earthquake some 500 years ago. More than 50,000 well-preserved artifacts have been found and cataloged, many of which are now on display at the Makah Museum in Neah Bay. Other sites have also revealed how long people have been here: thumbnail-sized quartz knife blades found at the Hoko River site near Clallam Bay are believed to be 2,500 years old.

One of the most fascinating discoveries occurred in 1977, when Emanuel Manis, retired on a farm outside of Sequim, was digging a pond on a back corner of his land and found two enormous tusks. A Washington State University archaeological team, led by zoologist Carl Gustafson, concluded that these were mastodon tusks between 12,000 and 14,000 years old. The group discovered other mastodon bones, including a rib that contained the bone point of some prehistoric weapon used to kill the animal. These bones are now on display at the Sequim-Dungeness Museum in Sequim.

Native Americans

According to one theory, Native Americans originally crossed over to Alaska from Asia at the end of the last Ice Age, when the sea was 300 or more feet below present levels and the strait was a walkable passage. As these Native Americans spread throughout the Pacific Northwest, they adopted significantly different lifestyles on each side of the Cascades.

West of the mountains, salmon, shellfish, whales, and other seafood made up a large part of the Indian diet; western red cedars provided ample wood for canoes, houses, and medicinal teas and ointments. A mild climate and plentiful food allowed these coastal tribes to stay in one place for most of the year, and in fact the north coast Indians were among the wealthiest in America. They often built longhouses—wooden structures up to 100 feet long and 40 feet wide that housed several families.

Coastal tribes were skilled canoe carvers and could travel up the Columbia as far as The Dalles, where rapids prohibited further progress. Inland tribes would meet them here for an annual fair with trading, dancing, gambling, and general hell-raising. Haidas and Tlingits from Alaska and British Columbia thought nothing of paddling hundreds of miles to trade—or raid.

East of the Cascades, particularly near the Columbia River, salmon was an important part of the diet, though dependence on deer, elk, bear, squirrel, and rabbit led these tribes to live seminomadic lives. The introduction of the horse to eastern Washington in the mid-1700s made hunting, especially for large bison, much easier. Indians in eastern Washington lived in caves or rock shelters while hunting, as well as in well-insulated pithouses that could hold several families.

The Pacific Northwest tribes were introduced to the by-products of white man's culture, such as knives, guns, and the deadly smallpox virus, before ever laying eyes on a white explorer. One leader in northeast Washington, Chief Charles Goosmus, went blind from crying after his twelve children all died within a month.

The Europeans' arrival was met with reactions ranging from tolerant acceptance to swift murder. Relations between the races are still strained today; the interpretation of peace treaties signed in the 1850s is being hotly debated in the 1990s, with many lawsuits concerning property, water, and especially fishing rights pending. Tribes have also caused considerable consternation among some local and state governmental agencies by building casinos on their reservations and earning millions of dollars each year for their members. Though they make up only 1.3% of the Pacific Northwest's total population, today's Native Americans are a growing force: there were nearly 100,000 Indians in Washington, Idaho, and Oregon in 1980, representing an 88.5% increase since 1970. Most of them do not live on reservations, though there are 22 reservations scattered throughout the state, the largest being the Yakima and Colville.

A NEW WORLD

The first foreigners to land on Washington's shores were Chinese and Japanese fishermen who arrived weeks or months after they were blown off course. None of the Asian nations was interested in expanding across the Pacific in those days, and nobody particularly cared about the land to the east. Records, if any, were skimpy and ignored. That was definitely not the case in southern Europe.

Spanish Explorers

In 1592, exactly a century after Columbus made his landfall in the Caribbean, a Greek explorer sailing along Washington's coast under the Spanish name Juan de Fuca claimed to have discovered the fabled "Northwest Passage," an inland waterway crossing North America from the Pacific to the Atlantic. Later explorers did find a waterway close to where de Fuca indicated, but it led only into today's Puget Sound, not all the way to the Atlantic Ocean.

Spain, hoping to regain some of its diminishing power and wealth, sent an expedition out in the 1700s to explore the Northwest Coast. In 1774, Juan Perez explored as far north as the Queen Charlotte Islands off Vancouver Island and was the first European to describe the Pacific Northwest coastline and Olympic Mountains before being forced to turn back by sickness and storms.

Totem poles such as this are common throughout Washington.

In 1775, a larger Spanish expedition set out, led by Bruno de Heceta and Juan Francisco de la Bodega y Quadra. Heceta went ashore at Point Grenville, just north of Moclips on the Washington coast, and claimed all the Northwest for Spain. Farther south, Quadra sent seven men ashore in a small metal craft for wood and water; they were quickly killed and their boat torn apart in the whites' first encounter with coastal Native Americans. The two ships sailed away without further incident; Quadra named the island Isla de Dolores ("Isle of Sorrows"), today's Destruction Island. Quadra continued his explorations as far north as present-day Sitka, Alaska, while Heceta sailed north to Nootka Sound. Heceta failed to note the Strait of Juan de Fuca, but he did come across "the mouth of some great river," presumably the Columbia, though the death or illness of much of his crew prevented further exploration and robbed Spain of an important claim.

Russian Voyages

Russian exploration of the Pacific Northwest began in the mid-1700s, when Vitus Bering led two expeditions to determine whether a land bridge connected Russia with North America. Bering sailed as far south as the Columbia River before turning back. The abundance of sea otters and beavers led Russian fur traders to establish posts from Alaska to northern California, which posed a serious threat to other nations hoping to stake a claim.

The Russians were quite active along the coast for several years and this led to one of the Northwest's most poignant tragedies, the result of a shipwreck near the Strait of Juan de Fuca in 1808, four years after the Lewis and Clark party had visited the Columbia estuary. The Russian ship, the *Saint Nicholas,* ran aground on Destruction Island and the crew tried to walk down the coast to Grays Harbor. Accompanying them was Anna Petrovna Bulygina, wife of Nikolai Bulygina, commander of the ship. The trip was a disaster in every way. Anna was captured, tortured, and raped by the Indians; she committed suicide. Coincidentally, she was the first Caucasian woman to set foot on the West Coast. An English ship rescued the other survivors, who were signaling the boat with a kite that had twisted gut for a string.

Early English and American Exploration

England was the force to be reckoned with in the battle for the Northwest. In 1776, Captain James Cook took two ships, the *Discovery* and the *Resolution,* and 170 men on an expedition that brought him to the Hawaiian Islands, the Oregon coast, and Vancouver Island's Nootka Sound. Though he charted the coastline from Oregon to the Bering Sea, he made no mention of the Columbia River or the Strait of Juan de Fuca. Cook was killed by hostile Hawaiians in a dispute over a boat in 1779, and his crew returned to England.

Other English sailors continued in Cook's footsteps. In 1787, Charles Barkley and his wife Frances explored and named the Strait of Juan de Fuca. In 1788, John Meares named Mount Olympus and other features of the Olympic Peninsula.

An American, Robert Gray sailed out of Boston to explore and trade along the Northwest Coast in the 1792. Stopping first at Nootka Sound—the hot spot to trade on Vancouver Island—Gray worked his way south and spent three days anchored in today's Grays Harbor. Continuing south, Gray discovered the mouth of the Columbia River and traded there with the Chinook Indians before heading home.

Best known today, however, is the expedition led by George Vancouver in 1792. His goal was to explore the inland waters and make one last attempt at finding the Northwest Passage. The names of Vancouver's lieutenants and crew members are like a list of Washington place-names: Baker, Rainier, Whidbey, Puget. (Many of the place-names were attached to curry political favor back home; almost anyone in a position of power had his name stuck on something.) The expedition carefully charted and thoroughly described all navigable waterways and named every prominent feature. When Vancouver heard of Gray's discovery of the Columbia River, he sent William Broughton upriver to a point east of Portland to strengthen England's claim on the land.

Until 1792, only the coastal areas of the Pacific Northwest had been explored. The first explorer to cross North America north of Mexico was a British trader, Alexander Mackenzie. In 1788, he traveled as far as the Arctic in search of the fabled Northwest Passage. In 1792-93,

Mackenzie followed the Bella Coola River from the Canadian Rockies to just north of Vancouver Island. His two expeditions proved that there was no Northwest Passage, at least north of the 50th parallel.

Lewis and Clark Expedition

The best-known overland expedition began in St. Louis in 1804, led by Meriwether Lewis and William Clark. President Thomas Jefferson sent these men and their party to study the geology, animals, and plantlife of the 827,000 square miles acquired in the Louisiana Purchase, which extended as far west as the Rocky Mountains, and to explore and map the rivers and lands west of the Rockies that were still more or less up for grabs as the new country competed with England, Russia, and Spain for all the land between the two oceans.

Lewis and Clark's group left St. Louis in canoes and keelboats, heading north on the Missouri River to present-day North Dakota. After wintering there with the Mandan Indians, the party, whose numbers were reduced to 28 for the final push, set out again on the Missouri River, crossed the Rockies on foot, and headed down the Clearwater River to the Snake River, in search of the Columbia River they knew would lead them to the ocean. In October 1805, the party got their first view of the Columbia, and followed it downriver for many a "cloudy, rainey, disagreeable morning" until they reached the Pacific Ocean.

They built a winter camp, Fort Clatsop, south of the river and spent a cold, wet winter there, plagued by sickness. In spring they headed for home. The two leaders split up, with Lewis returning much the way they had come and Clark exploring the Yellowstone River to the south. They met up again in North Dakota where the Yellowstone enters the Missouri and returned to St. Louis in September 1806.

Fur Traders

Wilson Price Hunt, partner in the fur-trading business with John Jacob Astor, led the second American overland expedition in 1811. His party joined others who arrived by ship—first the *Tonquin,* in 1811, and then the *Beaver,* arriving a year later—to establish Astoria, a fort on the south side of the Columbia River. Hunt was instructed to follow Lewis and Clark's route through Montana, but aggressive Blackfeet Indians changed his mind. Instead he traveled through present-day Wyoming, taking to canoes—a poor choice for the wild Snake River. One canoe was smashed and its experienced navigator killed, leading to Hunt's decision to divide the expedition into three groups and continue overland.

Donald McKenzie's team reached Astoria in January 1812; Hunt's group arrived a month later. The last third of the expedition straggled in a year after the first, in January 1813.

British overland exploration was accomplished mainly by David Thompson, a fur trader and chief cartographer for the North West Company in the early 1800s. In 1810, under Thompson's direction, Finan McDonald and Jacques Finlay built Spokane House, the first trading post in the state of Washington. Thompson traveled extensively throughout the Canadian Rockies, south into Kettle Falls and downriver to the mouth of the Columbia in 1811, where he found that the Americans had already established a fort at Astoria—Astor's men had arrived four months earlier. Though he was disappointed, Thompson's detailed maps and sketches of the Columbia were used for many years by settlers and traders.

The First White Settlers

During the time between the early exploration and the permanent settlement of the Northwest, British and American trading posts emerged to take advantage of the area's abundant supply of beaver and sea-otter pelts. Two English companies, the North West Company and Hudson's Bay Company, merged in 1821; American fur-trading outfits included many small, independent companies as well as John Astor's Pacific Fur Company and the Rocky Mountain Fur Company.

The most influential of them, the Hudson's Bay Company, built its temporary headquarters on the north side of the Columbia, 100 miles inland at Fort Vancouver, across the river from the confluence with the Willamette.

The settlers planted crops (including the apples and wheat that are so important to Washington's economy today), raised livestock, and made the fort as self-sufficient as possible. At its

THE WHITMAN MASSACRE

Following the Lewis and Clark expedition of 1805-06, American interest in the "Oregon Country" began to rise exponentially. Some of the earliest to travel westward as settlers were missionaries seeking to convert the Indians to Christianity, and one of the first of these pioneers was a young medical missionary, Dr. Marcus Whitman. Whitman had been lured west in part by new reports (mostly fraudulent) that the northwest Indians were seeking men to teach them about the Bible. In 1835, he and another missionary, Samuel Parker, headed west to locate sites for Protestant missions in the Oregon Territory. Convinced of a need, Whitman hurried back, married Narcissa Prentiss, and recruited three other missionaries. By 1836, this small entourage was heading westward in covered wagons; it was the first time white women ventured across the continent overland.

The success of this trek helped establish the Oregon Trail as a way westward. Whitman played another crucial role in 1843 when he led the largest wagon train ever assembled—the 1,000 person Applegate Wagon Train—from Independence, Missouri, to the mouth of the Columbia River. This six-

WASHINGTON STATE HISTORICAL SOCIETY/2

Dr. Marcus Whitman

Narcissa Whitman

month trip fired the public's imagination and helped open the gates to a flood of some 350,000 later emigrants. But this is not why he is remembered today, though it certainly had an impact on what followed.

The Mission

The Whitmans settled along the Walla Walla River in a spot the Cayuse Indians called Waiilatpu (wy-EE-la-poo), "Place of the Rye Grass." The home they built was the first permanent home whites had built in the Northwest, and their new daughter was the first white girl born west of the Rockies and north of California. Their new mission was intended to convert the Cayuse Indians, but these efforts met with minimal success; the Cayuse had little interest in religious worship, books, schooling, or farming. They did, however, appreciate Dr. Whitman's medical knowledge and assistance. Despite setbacks, the Whitmans persevered, and their mission became a vital Oregon Trail stopping point until 1844 when most emigrants shifted to a more southerly route. One day a wagon train arrived carrying the seven Sager children whose parents died on the way west; the Whitmans took them in as their own.

Historians have forever after argued over the attitude the Whitmans and other missionaries had toward the Indians. Some say Marcus Whitman whipped them and treated them like childlike savages of inferior mental capacities. Others say both Whitmans treated them with courtesy. One basic fact remains: the missionaries of that era showed little respect for the natives' culture and beliefs, an attitude that led to suspicion and distrust. To compound matters, some Indians became ill from the laxatives the Whitmans gave them, while others ate some of the poisons Whitman used to keep animals away from his gardens.

End of a Dream

The Indians of Oregon Territory lived in relative peace with the emigrants, although there were scattered raids on wagon trains, along with thefts of equipment, horses, and cattle. But as the trickle of wagons turned to a westward deluge, and as settlers began to occupy their ancestral lands, an anger began to boil inside. The breaking point came in 1847 when a devastating measles epidemic—brought by the emigrants—swept through the region, killing fully half of the Cayuse. Doctor Whitman's medicines worked for whites, but not for the Indians, who had no natural resistance to the disease. Cayuse leaders feared that it was all a ruse, and that Whitman was poisoning their people to make room for more Anglo settlers.

On November 19, 1847, a band of Cayuse Indians raided the mission, killing Marcus and Narcissa Whitman, two of the Sager children, and nine others. They then took 50 people captive; most of them were eventually ransomed for $500 worth of trade goods, but two more children died of measles while in captivity. The murders provoked a war between the Cayuse and emigrant settlers, and when news of the massacre reached Washington, D.C., it created a national uproar that led to the official establishment of Oregon Territory the following year and the closure of the country to settlers until 1859. Thus in life—as a leader in establishing the Oregon Trail—and in death—as the inspiration for the first territorial government west of the Rockies—Marcus Whitman changed American history. Three years after the massacre, five Cayuse warriors were turned over to Washington territorial officials; all five were baptized, given Christian names, and quickly hanged.

---

peak, 500 people lived at or near the fort. Fort Vancouver served as a model for other Hudson's Bay Company posts at Spokane, Okanogan, and Nisqually. When settlers began arriving in droves and the beaver population diminished in the late 1840s, the Hudson's Bay Company was crowded out and moved its headquarters north to Fort Victoria on Vancouver Island. The demise of Fort Vancouver came in large part because its chief factor, Dr. John McLoughlin, was a humane man and helped new arrivals by giving them food and seed grain for planting crops on land the Hudson's Bay Company thought should be owned by England.

Missions were another important method of establishing white settlements in the Washington Territory. The first missionary, Jason Lee, was sent by the Methodist Church in 1834 to introduce Christianity to the Native peoples, but instead he spent much of his time and resources ministering to whites at Fort Vancouver.

In the 1840s, "Oregon Country" north of the 42nd parallel was jointly occupied by the U.S. and England. The westward movement gained momentum when a New York editor coined the phrase "Manifest Destiny" to symbolize the idea that all of the land west of the Rockies rightfully belonged to the United States. If you exclude trappers, prior to 1843, there were barely 40 white settlers west of the Rocky Mountains.

Between 1840 and 1860, 53,000 settlers moved west to Oregon Country to take advantage of the free land they could acquire through the Organic Act of 1843 and the Donation Land Law of 1850. Under the Organic Act of the Provisional Government, each adult white male could own a 640-acre section of land (one square mile) by simply marking its boundaries, filing a claim, and building a cabin on the land. The Donation Land Law put additional restrictions on land claims: 320 acres were awarded to white or half-white males who were American citizens and had arrived prior to 1851; another 320 acres could be claimed by his wife.

These and other restrictions effectively eliminated claims by blacks, Asians, single women, non-U.S. citizens, and Native Americans, thereby giving pioneers the legal right to take Indian land. These land grants were too large for most families to farm and prevented towns and industries from growing as quickly as they might have; people were simply too far apart. By 1855, all the land in the Willamette Valley had been claimed.

The promise of free land fueled the "Great Migration" of 1843, in which 875 settlers traveled to the Oregon Country, six times the number of the previous year. More pioneers followed: 1,500 in 1844 and 3,000 in 1845. Most settlers came by way of the Oregon Trail from St. Joseph, Missouri, along the North Platte River, through southern Wyoming and southern Idaho into Oregon, then north to the Columbia River. Soon the route looked like a cleared road; traces of it can still be seen where the wagon tires dug ruts in stone and where the ground was packed so hard by the wheels that grass still cannot grow. Washington's early settlers congregated around five fledgling cities: Seattle, Port Townsend, Oysterville, Centralia, and Walla Walla; other smaller communities developed at Tumwater, Steilacoom, Olympia, and Fairhaven, now part of Bellingham. In eastern Washington the major communities were Spokane and Walla Walla.

Settling the Claims

By 1846, only the U.S. and England retained claims to the Oregon Country; Spain and Russia had sold or lost their North American possessions. Negotiators brought the U.S. and England to agreement on a division at the 49th parallel from the Rockies to the main channel between Vancouver Island and the mainland, running through the center of the Strait of Juan de Fuca to the Pacific Ocean.

The unspecified "main channel" was viewed to be either the Rosario Strait or the Haro Strait, leaving the San Juan Islands in the middle of the disputed waterway. Both nations claimed the islands. The British maintained a Hudson's Bay Company fort, but American settlers began moving in and establishing farms. In 1859, one of the Americans shot and killed a British-owned pig that had repeatedly rooted in his garden, and the resulting uproar nearly started a war. The British demanded payment for the pig; the American refused, and soon both sides began bringing in soldiers and heavy weapons. Within three months the English had a force of 2,140 troops, five warships, and 167 heavy guns arrayed against the American army's 461 soldiers and 14 cannons. Fortunately, calmer heads prevailed, and no further shots were fired in the "Pig War" (see the special topic "The Pig War"). Soldiers of both nations remained on the islands for the

Fort Vancouver, one of the Pacific Northwest's most successful settlements

TACOMA PUBLIC LIBRARY

next 13 years, and in 1872, Germany's Kaiser Wilhelm was chosen to conduct arbitration. He awarded the islands to the Americans and pronounced the Haro Strait the dividing channel.

In spite of all this arbitration, one small piece of real estate managed to be overlooked. A peninsula hung down from the Canadian mainland into the Strait of Georgia south of the 49th parallel, making it American land. Rather than settling the matter when it was discovered, the appendix still dangles there and is known as Point Roberts, a bit of America attached to Canada.

Growth of a New State

In 1848, President Polk created Oregon Territory and appointed Joseph Lane as the first territorial governor a year later. In the early 1840s, most Americans lived south of the Columbia River. By 1849, only 304 people lived north of the river, but in the next year that number tripled as more and more settlers ventured northward. As they moved farther away from the territorial government, the settlers felt left out of governmental matters and decided to separate from Oregon. Delegates met at the Monticello Convention in 1852 to list reasons for the proposed separation, and Congress found little opposition to the bill. Washington Territory—named, of course, for George Washington—was created in 1853. The initial territory included much of present-day Idaho and Montana. In 1863, Idaho Territory was carved off the whole, followed by Montana Territory in 1864, giving the territories much the same boundaries that the states now occupy.

When Washington became a territory, its population was under 4,000 people; by 1880 it had grown to over 125,000 and was considered a serious candidate for statehood. Washington was admitted as the 42nd state in 1889, with Olympia as its capital and a growing population of over 173,000. When the news was telegraphed to Washington officials in Olympia, they discovered one problem; the telegraph had been sent collect, and they could not read it until the cost was paid. Welcome to the United States!

Into the Twentieth Century

The 40 years between 1870 and 1910 marked a period of tremendous growth in Washington. In

Seattle's Space Needle, a legacy from the 1962 World's Fair

1870, the territory's population was just shy of 24,000; in 1910, the new state, created with the same boundaries, had 1,142,000 residents. Much of this growth was a direct result of the arrival of the Northern Pacific and Great Northern railways in the late 1880s, bringing industry and settlers to Puget Sound and creating new towns all along their routes. Spokane saw rapid economic growth during the 1880s, outfitting miners for the gold, silver, and lead rush in Idaho.

The 1880s also spelled disaster for Spokane, Ellensburg, and Seattle, when major portions of these cities' thriving downtown areas were destroyed by fire. Though the cities were rebuilt quickly in brick, the state was hit hard by a nationwide depression, the Panic of 1893, when growth slowed on both sides of the mountains and businesses failed. A gold rush in the Yukon and the emergence of hydroelectric power helped get the state back on its feet. At the end of this period of growth, the Alaska-Yukon-Pacific Exposition of 1909 brought nationwide attention and over 3.7 million visitors to what is now the University of Washington campus in Seattle to promote the ties between Washington, the far north, and Pacific Rim countries.

The Great Depression slowed Washington's population growth to just 11% between 1930 and 1940. Seattleites were the first to call makeshift "towns" of boxes and crates "Hoovervilles," named in honor of President Herbert Hoover, whom they blamed for the nation's ills. One of the largest covered nine acres about where the Kingdome stands today.

The first and second world wars changed Washington's economy from one based largely on mining, farming, logging, and fishing to manufacturing and ship and airplane building, highlighted by Boeing's B-17: over 13,000 of the "Flying Fortresses" were built for WW II. Boeing continues to be one of the state's largest employers and most important industries and in the 1990s became America's biggest exporter.

Seattle's 1962 World's Fair was the first such exposition to be an economic success, drawing more than 9.6 million people during its six-month run and creating a permanent addition to the city's culture with the Seattle Center. Spokane followed suit 12 years later with Expo '74, emphasizing environmental concerns and cleaning up its own Spokane River in the process.

Too Much?

Perhaps all of this self-imposed media attention was a mistake: Washington, especially west of the Cascades, continues to grow at a rate that many residents find alarming. Today, the state is rapidly approaching five million people. The trend has accelerated in the 1980s and '90s, particularly around Puget Sound. The city of Bellevue has grown from a cowtown when it was incorporated in 1953 to a booming city of almost 90,000 people today, complete with high-rise buildings, mega malls, an ever-spreading suburbia, and traffic snarls. Nearby Redmond—where Microsoft employs thousands of workers in a two-million square foot corporate campus—grew by 25% in the four years between 1989 and 1993. Cities and suburbs alike are beginning to suffer from overcrowding, pollution, traffic jams, increased crime, and other big-city problems as more and more visitors are opting to stay for good, putting stress on water, refuse, and highway systems that were designed for smaller populations. Today all too many Washington towns and cities seem bent upon joining the strip-mall frenzy that is turning many places into what one book called "The Geography of Nowhere." The challenge of the '90s and beyond will be to preserve the state's unsurpassed natural resources and beauty while allowing controlled growth.

TACOMA PUBLIC LIBRARY

INDUSTRY AND ECONOMY

Washington's earliest industries—fishing, mining, farming, and logging—depended upon the abundant natural resources that the pioneers found here. Today only farming and logging are major industries, although logging took a severe hit when large tracts of land were set aside to protect the habitat of spotted owls and other potentially endangered animals (see the special topic "Endangered Species" for more details). Farming remains the basis for much of Washington's economy, and hydroelectric power creates jobs and low electric rates from the state's plentiful resources (unfortunately, these same dams have had a devastating impact on salmon runs, particularly in the Columbia River). Over the years, though, manufacturing, shipping, and other industries have become increasingly important to the state's economy, particularly the trio of Boeing, Microsoft, and Weyerhaeuser.

Mining

Coal was first discovered east of Bellingham in 1849, and mining began in 1855. Discoveries of coal in the Cascades in the late 1800s gave rise to a number of small mining towns (such as Black Diamond, Carbonado, Wilkeson, Newcastle, Cle Elum, and Roslyn) on both sides of the Cascades. Though coal was plentiful—ge-

ologists today believe there are from six to 65 billion tons in the state—it was soft and therefore limited in its uses. Often found in steep ravines or streams, it was also difficult to extract and transport. Underground explosions and other accidents gave Washington more mining fatalities per number of miners than any other state for several years in the late 1800s. By the turn of the century, coal from the Rocky Mountains had become a cheaper and more practical fuel source, and by 1930 coal mining had virtually disappeared. Today, coal mining is seeing a minor revival: for the past several years, over five million tons of coal per year have been strip-mined near Centralia for use in a thermal-electric power plant there.

Other minerals begat industries that met with varying degrees of success. Discoveries of gold and silver in the mountains of Washington's northeastern corner caused short-lived rushes—and Indian wars, as whites crossed onto reservation lands—but outfitting miners for the gold rushes of Idaho and the Yukon yielded a better return for Seattle and Spokane. Silver, gold, and lead mines in Monte Cristo were to have been the economic basis of Everett, John D. Rockefeller's city on Port Gardner Bay, until the depression of 1893 forced him to withdraw

Miners at the Carbonado mining disaster of 1930—Washington led the country in mining fatalities for many years.

TACOMA PUBLIC LIBRARY

his support. A steel mill in Kirkland, an iron refinery outside Port Townsend, and a copper mine in Holden either never got started or met with limited success. A successful silver, gold, and lead refinery in Tacoma was started in 1890 by William R. Rust; he later sold the plant to the American Smelting and Refining Company (ASARCO) for processing copper.

Recent mining at Wenatchee's Asamera's Cannon gold mine could yield over a million ounces of gold over the next decade, and a gold mine still operates in Republic. However, Washington's most valuable minerals are the least exotic: 60% of the money made from mineral production is derived from cement, stone, and gravel pits in the western half of the state.

Lumber

The Pacific Northwest states of Washington, Oregon, and Idaho supply about 60% of the total lumber in the United States. Washington is generally the third- or fourth-largest producer of the 50 states, with Oregon taking the lead since 1938. Douglas fir, western hemlock, and western red cedar are some of the commercially important trees native to the area west of the Cascades.

Wood and wood products have been a vital part of Washington's economy ever since the coastal Indians first began using cedar for long-houses, totem poles, canoes, and even clothing made from cedar bark. The first white settlers and missionaries used wood for construction of their forts, homes, and blockhouses, and British explorer John Meares was the first to ship lumber to the Orient in 1788. Seattle's founding fathers depended on shipments of lumber to San Francisco for much of their income; Yesler's waterfront sawmill was an important part of the city's early economy. The lumber business boomed with the cheaper transportation provided by the arrival of the railroads in Puget Sound in the late 1880s and '90s.

In 1900, Frederick Weyerhaeuser purchased 900,000 acres of prime forest land from the Northern Pacific Railroad for $6 an acre, later increasing his holdings to over two million acres by 1913. With over six million acres today, the Weyerhaeuser Corp. is now the largest lumber company in the country.

Forests cover over 23 million Washington acres, 18 million of which are commercial forests. It's difficult to look at the shaved hillsides of the Cascades and not think it offensive, but all of us use wood, the trees are replanted, and until the recent cutbacks the logs and wood products produced $5-7 billion annually and employed a large proportion of Washington's workers.

Farming

Washington's Native Americans relied on hunting and food gathering rather than agriculture to supply their families' needs. It wasn't until Fort Vancouver was established in the 1820s that commercial agriculture took hold in Washington, as Hudson's Bay Company acquired a surplus of cattle to sell to the early settlers. Farming developed slowly west of the Cascades, as the heavily forested land first had to be cleared, and the acidic soils produced minimal yields. As settlers spread east of the Cascades, the wide-open spaces were perfect for cattle ranching, sheep herding, and grain growing.

Agriculture grew rapidly through the turn of the century due to the arrival of the railroads that created markets, irrigation projects, and the free land provided by the Organic Act of 1843 and the Donation Land Law of 1850. Agriculture flourished during the first and second world wars and quickly rebounded after the Depression when refrigeration allowed Washington farmers to compete on a national scale.

More recently, the 1952 Columbia Basin Irrigation Project opened up a half-million parched acres for farming around Ephrata and Moses Lake. Today, Washington farmers and ranchers produce more than $3.3 billion annually, over 80% of which is derived from agriculture east of the Cascades. The biggest money crop is wheat, grown on three million acres in eastern Washington, especially in the famous Palouse hills near Pullman. Nearly all the state's wheat is shipped overseas to Japan, Korea, Taiwan, the Philippines, and other Asian markets. Other important crops are hay, potatoes, livestock, apples, pears, cherries, grapes, onions, and other fruits and vegetables. Washington is one of the few states that grows cranberries; these are grown in the southeast corner on bogs near Willapa Bay.

Washington is probably best known for its apples, some 10 *billion* of which are grown annually, fully 60% of the nation's total apple production. The center of apple growing is between Wenatchee and Chelan, but orchards can be found in many parts of the state. More than two-thirds of the apples grown in Washington are of the red delicious variety, though many other varieties are also produced.

One of the state's fastest-growing crops is wine grapes. In 1972, Washington had just six wineries; today there are almost 80, and visitors come to tour the Columbia and Yakima Valleys much as they would California's wine-producing regions. Washington is now recognized as one of the prime wine producers in the country, with many award-winning wines, and three official wine-growing regions: Columbia Valley, Yakima Valley, and Walla Walla Valley. Washington boosters point out that these valleys lie at the same latitude as the France's Burgundy and Bordeaux regions. The state's largest producer of wines is Chateau Ste. Michelle, with wineries in both the Yakima Valley and in Woodinville (near Seattle).

Fishing

Fishing is one of the state's oldest industries, as the original Native Americans on both sides of the Cascades depended on Columbia River salmon and other fish for much of their diet, and coastal Indians from the Neah Bay area were whalers. Commercial fishing, less important to the early settlers than logging and other industries, wasn't firmly established until the 1860s, when canneries, new salmon-fishing techniques, and new markets at home and abroad led to the industry's rapid expansion.

Until the mid-1990s, the Pacific Northwest salmon industry harvested more than 250,000 pounds of salmon annually, worth about $100-150 million. In the early 1990s, the run collapsed due to a combination of warm oceanic currents, the destruction of spawning habitat due to dams and logging, and droughts. Ocean fishing was banned off the coast of Washington and Oregon, and except for certain tribal fisheries and a few short openings, it has remained closed. Washington's many state and private hatcheries produce all five species of Pacific salmon, but there is evidence that hatchery-grown fish are part of the problem since they compete with natural populations and are more susceptible to diseases due to a lack of genetic diversity. Also, commercial fisheries targeted on hatchery-raised fish often take large numbers of the wild fish populations at the same time. Restoring the salmon will require habitat preservation and restoration, mitigation of the devastating effects of hydroelectric dams, less emphasis on hatchery-raised fish, and stronger controls on the number of fish that can be caught.

Hydroelectric and Nuclear Power

Washington's first hydroelectric power was generated in the late 1880s in Spokane, when Spokane Falls were used to power a saw to cut wood for a local hotel. Uses multiplied to include street lighting, trolley lines, and more, and in 1889 Spokane's Washington Water Power Company was established as one of the first hydroelectric power companies in the country. Tacoma was the first major city to produce its own power when, in 1898, it took over a local utility company and later built dams on the Nisqually and Skokomish Rivers.

Franklin D. Roosevelt's New Deal paved the way for the construction of the first federally built dam on the mighty Columbia River: the Bonneville Dam, completed in 1938. It was quickly followed by the Grand Coulee Dam and others, until 14 Columbia River dams produced electricity to power much of the Pacific Northwest and California. They also provided water to irrigate much of central Washington. By the 1970s, 96% of the state's power was hydroelectric in origin.

Inexpensive hydroelectric power has been taken for granted since its inception; Tacoma City Light has been boasting for years that it offers the cheapest electric rates in the nation. But the state's recent drought years demonstrated that even in the soggy Pacific Northwest, low electric rates are not guaranteed, and other energy alternatives must be considered. Even with the abundance of dams, the Pacific Northwest has to import energy from Canada to supply the growing demand. The other factor that has come into play is fish, or rather the lack of fish. Plummeting salmon runs in the 1990s have pushed some salmon populations to the brink, and much of the blame is being laid upon the dams that block the upstream migration of adults and kill young salmon heading out to sea.

Public outrage, way-over-budget construction costs, and safety concerns have made nuclear power a poor second choice. In 1968, the Washington Public Power Supply System (WPPSS, commonly called "Whoops") began work on five nuclear generators, three at the Hanford site near Tri-Cities and two at Satsop in Grays Harbor County. The $6 billion budget stretched to $24 billion, and public outcry over the inevitable rate hikes to pay for the construction resulted in approval of an initiative limiting such groups' spending and the mothballing of all but the reactors at Hanford and Satsop. Customers are paying for these white elephants through the Bonneville Power Administration's substantial rate hikes, and citizens of the world will be paying for centuries to come as they grapple with the deadly waste that they create.

What's left? Coal-fired plants, such as the Centralia Steam Plant, may become more important if coal reserves can be efficiently and economically mined. Solar energy, wind farms, geothermal energy, and other alternatives will require years of research and economic support before they can become any more than token energy producers. Conservation is probably the best alternative, but cheap power has made too many folks wasteful of energy.

Aircraft Manufacturing

Washington's economy is closely tied in with the success of the Boeing Company, the state's largest employer and manufacturer of both commercial and military aircraft. Its founder, William E. Boeing, started his fledgling aircraft business in a hangar on Lake Union, then moved to a shipyard on the Duwamish River in 1916. World War I brought orders for training planes, and the company held on after the war by producing boats, furniture, and other items, plus U.S. Post Office transport planes and Army fighter planes. World War II brought over 13,000 orders for its B-17 bomber, and at the end of the war, B-29 bombers dropped the infamous atomic bombs on Nagasaki and Hiroshima.

After the war, William Allen took over as president of Boeing, and the company produced its first jet-powered passenger plane, the 707, in 1958. In the late 1960s, Boeing's 747 plant opened in Everett in the world's largest building, and Boeing was established as the world leader in aircraft manufacturing. The late '60s and early '70s were hard times for Boeing, as government contracts for the SST and other military aircraft fell through; employment fell from 110,000 to 38,000 workers. The company had to diversify to survive, so it created subdivisions in commercial aircraft, military aircraft, hydrofoils, and helicopters. In the '80s, Boeing's employment was stabilized at 68,000 to 80,000

Seattle and Tacoma economies depend heavily on containerized shipping.

workers, and the company is still the world leader in commercial aircraft production, making Boeing the country's major exporter in an era of enormous trade deficits.

The end of the Cold War hurt Boeing, but not as much as it did other defense contractors. Fortunately, Boeing relies almost entirely on sales to commercial airlines. However, as the world economy faltered in the early 1990s, Boeing had to reduce its workforce again, but not nearly as drastically as the big 1969 reduction—when someone put up a billboard reminding the last person to leave Seattle to turn out the lights. Boeing also changed its sales technique by inviting airline executives in to help design new airplanes rather than sticking to the old way of simply telling the customers what they were going to get.

Shipping

From the time Seattle's earliest settlers dropped a horseshoe on a clothesline into Elliott Bay to determine its depth, shipping has played an important role in the development of Puget Sound communities. Today, Seattle and Tacoma are among the most important seaports in the world, and other seaports and riverports along the Columbia as far inland as Clarkston helped to establish waterborne trade as one of the state's largest industries.

The first goods shipped from Seattle were logs that would be used as dock pilings in San Francisco. Lumber and wood products still account for a good portion of the area's exports, particularly from smaller ports such as Everett, Port Gamble, Port Angeles, Hoquiam, Olympia, and Bellingham. Seattle and Tacoma are important containerized shipping ports, where bulk and manufactured goods from airplanes to wheat are exported to Japan, China, Taiwan, Canada, and Australia. Telecommunications equipment, cars and trucks, clothing, and petroleum products are the primary imports, arriving from Canada, Japan, Taiwan, and Hong Kong. As the port of Tacoma plans a major expansion and Seattle continues to be a national trade leader, the future for containerized shipping in Washington looks very bright. Oil tankers also arrive from Alaska to supply four oil refineries in Anacortes and Ferndale.

While Seattle and Tacoma get most of the shipping attention, Columbia River ports have been doing very well, thank you, especially the Port of Longview and the Port of Kalama, which do a big business as a terminal for grain coming down the Columbia River from the Snake River and Tri-Cities bound for Pacific Rim nations, and imports headed inland from Japan and other Far Eastern ports. Farther upriver, agricultural and wood products are shipped from Lewiston/Clarkston and the Tri-Cities area.

BOB RACE

ON THE ROAD

ACCOMMODATIONS, CAMPING, AND FOOD

LODGING

Lodging in Washington covers the complete spectrum, from five-star luxury accommodations where a king would feel pampered all the way down to seedy motels so tawdry that even folks on the tightest of budgets think twice. The law of supply and demand holds fairly true when it comes to motel rates. You'll pay the least at motels in rural areas away from the main tourist track, and the most at popular destinations in peak season. This is especially true on midsummer weekends for such places as the San Juan Islands, Chelan, Leavenworth, Whidbey Island, or Long Beach, and for Seattle year-round. At many of the resort towns, you may need to reserve months ahead of time for the peak season, and a minimum stay of two or more nights may be required. It always pays to call ahead. If you don't smoke and can't stand the stench of tobacco in motel rooms, be sure to

ask about nonsmoking rooms. Many motels and nearly all B&Bs have them.

Throughout this book I have listed only two prices for most lodging places: one person (single, or s) and two people in one bed (double, or d). The lodging charts list peak-season prices and are arranged from least to most expensive. They do not include local or state taxes (eight percent), which can sometimes be substantial. These prices are not set in concrete and will certainly head up over time. If a convention is in town or the motel is nearly full, they may rise; if the economy is tight, or it's the off-season at a seasonal area, you may pay considerably less. Always ask to see the room before deciding to stay at one of the less expensive motels—places that I consider more than adequate may be beneath your standards. If in doubt, you may want to choose one that gets the AAA seal of approval.

For a complete listing of motels, hotels, and bed and breakfasts in Washington, request a copy of the free *Washington State Lodging & Travel Guide,* available from the Washington State Tourism Development Division, tel. (800) 544-1800. It's also available at larger visitor centers around the state. The annual *TourBook* for Washington and Oregon (free to members of the American Automobile Association) is a helpful guide to the better hotels and motels, offering current prices and accurate ratings. Folks who aren't members of AAA may want to purchase a copy of the very helpful *Traveler's Affordable Accommodations: Washington State,* by Elaine Ingle (Wenatchee: Cottage Computer Publishing). It's sold in bookstores throughout the state.

Hostels

Hostels offer the least expensive lodging options in Washington, with bunkbed accommodations for just $10-15 per person. They are a good choice for single travelers on a budget, or anyone who wants to meet other independent travelers. Although they are commonly called youth hostels, these really are not just for high school and college folks; you're likely to meet adventurous people of all ages (though the 20-something crowd is in the majority). The official versions are managed by **Hostelling International** (better known as AYH), with statewide headquarters at the Seattle hostel, tel. (206) 281-7306. In addition to Seattle, they operate hostels in Bellingham, Birch Bay, Fort Columbia (near Long Beach), Fort Flagler (near Port Townsend), Fort Worden (in Port Townsend), Spokane, and Vashon Island. At these hostels, guests stay in dormitory-style rooms, have access to a kitchen, and generally do a cleanup chore. You'll need to bring your own sleeping bag or linen, and an annual membership fee is required (nonmembers can sometimes pay a higher overnight rate, but members get priority). A variety of restrictions may put a crimp in things, including that most hostels kick you out in the morning and remain closed till 5 p.m. or so, and that no alcohol is allowed. Some also have a curfew. Most have a few spaces for couples who want their own room, but you may need to reserve these in advance. The benefits of hostelling include the chance to meet fellow travelers and a sense of camaraderie and adventure that one would never get at a cheap motel. Instead of turning on the TV set, you'll meet travelers from all over the world and discover must-see sights and great out-of-the way cafes.

Private hostels are less predictable, with fewer rules. Alcohol is generally allowed, and you won't have to be back before the witching hour, but they can be more chaotic and noisy at times. These range all over the place, from the rambling old school at Bingen that is now a destination for windsurfers, to the funky Doe Bay Village Resort where the clothing-optional hot tub is filled most evenings. Seattle has three such places: Vincent's Backpackers Guest House, American Backpackers' Hostel, and Green Tortoise Backpacker's Guest House. Three other private hostels are the small and friendly Rain Forest Hostel south of Forks, Triangle J Ranch Hostel near Republic, Mike's Beach Resort near Eldon on Hood Canal, Grays Harbor Hostel in Elma, and Whittaker's Bunkhouse, a favorite of climbers and backpackers in Ashford (near Mt. Rainier). All these official and unofficial hostels are described in appropriate sections of this book.

Motels and Hotels

The largest cities—Seattle, Spokane, Tacoma, Bellevue, Olympia—obviously have the greatest range of accommodations, from Motel 6's $28 rooms, to Sheratons, Hyatts, Red Lions, and Olympic Four Seasons, charging $100 and up per night. All of these cities, without exception, have very inexpensive lodging just outside city limits, so you can stay a half-hour or less away and spend the extra money having fun. If you're staying at the pricier chains, be sure to always ask about discounts such as AAA member rates, senior discounts, corporate or government rates, business travel fares, military rates, or other special deals. Try not to take the first rate quoted at these places, especially if you're calling their 800 number; these "rack rates" are what they charge if they can get away with it. You may also get better prices sometimes by bargaining with clerks who are more likely to be able to dicker over price than the 800 number operators who are sitting in Alabama. Of course, if it's a big convention or festival weekend, you may have no choice.

In Seattle or Spokane, you can stay at the budget chains near the airport; in Tacoma, stay up the road in Fife. Call ahead for reservations whenever possible; the least expensive rooms fill up fast. Finding a room—any room—can be extremely difficult in summer (even on weekdays) at popular resort areas such as Lake Chelan, the San Juan Islands, the national parks, or along the ocean. Staying a half hour from the action can save you money—try the motels in Wenatchee when Lake Chelan is filled up, or stay in Forks or Port Angeles instead of at Olympic National Park lodges.

Bed and Breakfasts

Approximately 400 bed and breakfasts are scattered around the state of Washington. Some parts of the state, particularly Port Townsend, are filled with restored turn-of-the-century Victorian homes that have been converted to B&Bs. Other B&Bs are old farmhouses, lodges, cottages, or modern homes with private entrances. In most cases, a room at a B&B will cost as much as a moderately priced motel room. You may miss the cable TV, pool, and room service, but you'll get breakfast (ranging from coffee and cinnamon rolls to a gourmet feast), often complimentary evening wine or tea, and peace and quiet.

Many B&Bs don't allow kids, and almost none allow pets or smoking; probably half the rooms won't have a private bath (though one is probably just a few steps away). If you plan to pay by credit card, make sure they will accept it when you make reservations—many don't. B&Bs are a fine way to get acquainted with a new area and a good choice for people traveling alone, since you'll have opportunities to meet fellow travelers in the library, over tea, or at breakfast. Note however, that there is often little or no difference between the price a single person pays and that paid by a couple.

One problem with B&Bs is that they sometimes seem a bit too homey and lack the privacy afforded by motels. I've been in ones where the owner sits by your table in the morning, feeling it his duty to hold a conversation. This may be fine sometimes, especially if you want to learn more about the local area, but not so great if you want a romantic place or just want to read the newspaper. Honeymooners in search of privacy may prefer B&Bs that offer separate cottages.

For a wide selection of B&Bs, contact **Pacific Bed and Breakfast,** tel. (206) 784-0539, a reservation service for more than 200 B&Bs in Washington. The **Washington State B&B Guild,** tel. (800) 647-2918, will send you a brochure describing their members.

CAMPING

State Parks

Washington maintains more than 80 state parks with campgrounds, offering clean and scenic accommodations across the state. Tent sites are $10, RV hookups (not available in all of these) cost $15. Some state parks also offer more primitive campsites for $5-7 that attract hikers and cyclists. Most park sites include a picnic table, barbecue grill, nearby running water, garbage disposal, a flush toilet, and, in most parks (except Horsethief Lake, Wallace Falls, Mount Spokane, and Spencer Spit), coin-operated hot showers. Many state parks are closed Oct.-March; those that remain open often have limited winter camping facilities. See the individual park descriptions for specifics on seasons.

The state also maintains 17 marine state parks in the San Juan Islands and 23 in Puget Sound. Moorage occupancy is limited to 72 hours and cannot be reserved in advance. An annual moorage permit for vessels under 26 feet is $50, and nightly fees are $8; annual permits for vessels longer than 26 feet cost $80 with a nightly fee of $11. Moorage buoys cost $8 per night for all sizes.

In 1996, Washington began a reservation line for approximately half of the state parks, with the rest coming on line in 1997. Reservations are available as little as two days in advance, or as much as 11 months ahead of time. A $6 reservation fee is charged in addition to the first night's campground fee and can be paid by credit card or check. For the complete story, including current space availability at various state parks, call (800) 452-5687 Mon.-Fri. 8 a.m.-5 p.m. year-round. Call (800) 233-0321 for other park information.

Other Public Campgrounds

See individual national forest and park listings for details on camping there; camping is good but generally more primitive, and none of them have showers. Some of these are free, but most campgrounds charge a $7-10 fee. More than

40 Forest Service campgrounds are reservable for an extra fee of $7.50. Reservations may be made up to four months ahead, or as late as 10 days prior to your arrival. Call (800) 280-2267 for more information. On most national forests (except along major routes) dispersed camping is allowed at no charge; simply find an off-the-road place to park for the night. This is not allowed in the national parks. Park Service campgrounds are also not reservable; get there early on busy summer weekends!

Washington's Department of Natural Resources (DNR) manages millions of acres of public lands in the state, primarily on a multiple-use (some call it multiple-abuse) basis. The emphasis is on timber harvesting. Not everything has been logged, however, and campsites are located at DNR forests throughout the state. For a helpful map showing more than 80 free public campgrounds on their land, stop by their offices in Castle Rock, Chehalis, Colville, Ellensburg, Enumclaw, Forks, or Sedro-Woolley, or call the statewide DNR office in Olympia: (360) 902-1000, or (800) 527-3305 in Washington.

For a fairly complete listing of campgrounds in Washington, with detailed descriptions, get *Pacific Northwest Camping* by Tom Stienstra (San Francisco: Foghorn Press). Members of AAA should pick up a copy of the *CampBook* for the Northwest states, which lists tent and RV sites throughout Washington.

Private RV Parks

Every town of any size has at least one private RV park and so-called campground. Many of these are little more than vacant lots with sewer and electrical hookups, showers, and toilet facilities. Not great for tents, but just what the doctor ordered for the RV crowd. These private campgrounds generally charge $2-4 for showers if you're not camping there. A better deal in many towns is to use the shower in the local public swimming pool, where you get a free swim thrown in for the entrance charge.

FOOD AND WINE

As all parts of the country do, Washington places an emphasis on certain kinds of food, an emphasis that has gained the name "Northwest cuisine." Definitions of this vary, but "fresh" is the operative term in most of these. Fresh salmon is popular and can be found on virtually every restaurant's menu, from Ivar's fish bars to Black Angus steakhouses. Red snapper, halibut, and cod are also served fresh almost everywhere in western Washington. Less common are the local Olympia oysters and geoduck clams.

As far as restaurants covered in this book, assume all to be moderately priced for the type of food or drink offered unless otherwise noted.

As you head east, the seafood is generally frozen, though some restaurants pride themselves on their fresh fish and will mention it in

Turtlebrook Farm Inn, Orcas Island

ARCHIE SATTERFIELD

their ads. Steaks are often imported from the Midwest and are generally very good. Western Washington is also known for its strawberries, blackberries, and various other kinds of berries. The King County Cooperative Extension Service publishes lists of U-Pick vegetable and berry farms, and the tabloid can be found at nearly all public libraries and some tourist information bureaus. For a detailed directory of organic farms, natural foods grocers, and organic restaurants, and a listing of farmers markets throughout the state, contact Washington Tilth, tel. (206) 527-9216.

Eastern Washington is the place to go for fresh fruit and produce. Washington apples are mostly of the red and golden delicious, rome beauty, and Granny Smith varieties. Many other kinds of fruit are grown along the central corridor—cherries, peaches, apricots. The Walla Walla sweet onion is reputedly mild enough to bite into raw, like an apple, and it is sold in gift packs. Asparagus, pears, and berries of all kinds are also big eastern Washington crops.

Wine grapes are a large part of the Yakima and Columbia River Valleys' agriculture. Wineries line the highway between Yakima and the Tri-Cities and into Walla Walla; others are scattered east to Spokane. Washington wines have become world-class in just a few years, winning awards and gaining in popularity across the country. Visit at least a few wineries (western Washington also has a number of them, though the grapes are usually grown in eastern Washington), or stop by the local grocery store for a wide selection of Washington and other Northwest wines. The Washington Wine Commission publishes a free guide to the state's 80 wineries, including descriptions of the state's viticultural regions, recent vintages, and a glossary of wine terms. It's available for free in many tourist offices.

RECREATION AND PUBLIC LANDS

When it comes to recreation, Washington pretty much has it covered. You can surf on a Westport beach one day, go horseback riding the next, and be on the edge of a Mt Rainier glacier the following day. The Pacific coast has long beaches for play in the sand, fishing, or beachcombing; the various national parks and forests offer backcountry hiking at its finest in the Olympics, Cascades, and northeast Washington; Puget Sound is a haven for sea kayaking and sailing; Columbia Gorge offers some of the finest windsurfing on the planet; anglers love the countless lakes, reservoirs, and rivers; river rafters and kayakers head down the state's whitewater rivers throughout the summer; and cyclists discover roads and trails of every description. In the winter, the options shift to snow sports, and Washington has 'em all, including skiing of all types, snowboarding, sledding, skating, and snowmobiling. See "Campgrounds," above, for info on state park and other public campgrounds in Washington.

The Mountaineers
Established in 1906, The Mountaineers is a 15,000-member organization of outdoor enthusiasts with a strong environmental bent. Based in Seattle, the club organizes hiking, climbing, cycling, skiing, snowshoeing, sea kayaking, and many other activities and events throughout the year. They even have a singles group to meet others with similar interests. This is a great organization with a dedication to preserving the wild places; they were instrumental in the establishment of both Olympic National Park and the Alpine Lakes Wilderness. Membership is $42 per year, with an initiation fee of $33, and members receive The Mountaineer, a monthly listing of activities, along with 20% discounts on their many excellent books. In addition to Seattle, The Mountaineers have branches in Olympia, Tacoma, Everett, and Bellingham. For more info, contact the main office at 300 3rd Ave. W in Seattle, tel. (206) 284-6310. For a catalog of the 300 books and other publications they produce, call (800) 284-8554; many of these are available in bookstores throughout the Northwest.

Environmental Education
The Northwest Interpretive Association, in Seattle at 909 1st Ave., Suite 630, tel. (206) 220-4140, is a nonprofit organization that supports environmental education and sells books, topographic maps, and other publications

through gift shops in many National Park Service, U.S. Forest Service, and other governmental offices throughout Washington. They sponsor an impressive range of natural history field seminars, from photographic ski tours to discussions of open pit leach mining to nature writing workshops. Call them for a catalog of current offerings available by mail.

Other nonprofit organizations with similar missions are the **North Cascades Institute** in Sedro-Woolley, tel. (360) 856-5700, ext. 209 (see "North Cascades Highway" in the Cascade Range chapter); and the **Olympic Park Institute** at Lake Crescent in Olympic National Park, tel. (360) 928-3720 or (800) 775-3720 (see "Olympic National Park" in the Olympic Peninsula chapter).

American Alpine Institute

The American Alpine Institute, the nation's top climbing school, is located in Bellingham at 1515 12th St., tel. (360) 671-1505. The staff includes accomplished mountain climbers and educators and offers courses starting with the basics and going all the way to advanced monthlong mountaineering programs. Classes are taught all over the world—from the Himalayas to Alaska—with beginning mountaineering classes taught in the North Cascades.

Fishing

Fishing licenses are available from sporting goods and other stores throughout the state. Residents pay $17, nonresidents $48, license, or $9 and $17 respectively for three-day fishing licenses. Contact the Washington State Dept. of Fisheries in Olympia for a copy of current game fish regulations; tel. (360) 753-6600. Clamming is a very popular activity in many parts of coastal Washington, especially along the beaches near Long Beach, Westport, and Ocean Shores. The season changes each year, so check with the State Fisheries Office in Olympia for specifics. Clamming licenses are $5 for Washington residents, $20 for nonresidents.

SNOW SPORTS

Downhill Skiing

The best ski areas in Washington are stretched along the Cascades from Mt. Baker to Mt. Rainier. Snow on the western slopes of the Cascades is usually wet and heavy, while some ski areas on the eastern slopes, such as Mission Ridge, have powdery snow. The following is a list of Washington downhill ski areas: **Alpental, Ski Acres, Snoqualmie,** and **Hyak** (all four of these are at Snoqualmie Pass), **Ski Bluewood, Crystal Mountain, Echo Valley, Hurricane Ridge, Loup Loup Ski Bowl, Mission Ridge, Mount Baker, Mount Spokane, Sitzmark, Stevens Pass, Leavenworth Ski Bowl,** and **White Pass.** See the travel chapters for details, and pick up the *Washington State Winter Recreation Guide,* published by the ski industry, at visitor centers throughout the state.

Cross-Country Skiing

Cross-country, or Nordic, skiing is particularly popular on the eastern slopes of the mountains, in part because the snow is more powdery and the weather is usually sunny and clear. Some of the best is in the Methow Valley, where 150 km of trails are marked, the majority of which are groomed. The **Methow Valley Ski Touring Association** provides a hotline for ski-touring information, (800) 422-3048, and a brochure showing the major trails. Other popular cross-country skiing areas include Mount Tahoma Trails (near Mount Rainier National Park), Echo Valley (near Lake Chelan), Hurricane Ridge (Olympic National Park), Leavenworth Winter Sports Club, Stevens Pass Nordic Center, White Pass Nordic Center, and Ski Acres Cross-Country Center. See the travel chapters for details on these. Most of these areas groom trails for both traditional and skate-skiing.

The state maintains more than 50 **Sno-Parks** in the Cascades and eastern mountains, with nearby skiing trails (sometimes groomed, sometimes not). Permits are required to park at these plowed areas, and are available from retail outlets throughout the state. The cost is $7 for a one-day pass, $10 for three days, or $20 for the entire winter season, with the money helping to pay for plowing, signs, trail grooming, and maintenance. The State Parks and Recreation Commission, tel. (800) 233-0321, sells Sno-Park permits and maps of groomed cross-country ski trails in the state ($4), and it offers a free brochure/map showing the areas. For the current snow avalanche danger in the backcountry, call the Forest Service at (206) 526-6677.

Snowmobiling

The state maintains over 2,200 miles of groomed snowmobile trails, primarily in the Cascades and northeast part of the state. For a map showing snowmobile trails, and a publication on snowmobile use in the state, contact Washington State Park Recreation Division, tel. (800) 233-0321.

PUBLIC LANDS

Almost 45% of Washington's 42.6 million acres are publicly held. The largest landholding agencies are the U.S. Forest Service, Bureau of Indian Affairs, National Park Service, U.S. Fish and Wildlife Service, and various branches of the military, but the state (primarily the Dept. of Natural Resources) owns almost 3.5 million acres of land.

National Parks

Washington's three major national parks attract millions of visitors each year, and offer mustsee sights. **North Cascades National Park** covers a half-million acres of wild mountain country that includes more than 300 glaciers, hundreds of miles of hiking trails, and the 55-mile long Lake Chelan. **Mount Rainier National Park** contains the state's tallest and best summit, the 14,411-foot Mt. Rainier. Hiking trails encircle the peak, and scenic mountain roads provide lingering views of the mountain meadows, subalpine forests, and glaciers that make this one of the nation's crown jewels. **Olympic National Park** is famous for the lush west-side rainforests that include enormous old-growth trees, but it also has dramatic mountainous country and the incomparable Pacific coastline. In addition to these areas, the Park Service manages a small part of the **Klondike Gold Rush National Historical Park** in Seattle's Pioneer Square (the main part is in Skagway, Alaska), the **Coulee Dam National Recreation Area** on Lake Roosevelt in eastern Washington, **San Juan Islands National Historic Park** on San Juan Island, **Ebey's Landing National Historical Reserve** on Whidbey Island, **Fort Vancouver National Historic Site** in Vancouver, and **Whitman Mission National Historical Site** near Walla Walla. All of these are described in depth elsewhere in this book.

National Park Service offices in Washington are:

Coulee Dam National Recreation Area, P.O. Box 37, Coulee Dam, WA 99116, tel. (509) 633-9441

Fort Vancouver National Historic Site, 612 E. Reserve, Vancouver, WA 98661, tel. (360) 696-7655

Klondike Gold Rush National Historical Park, 117 S. Main St., Seattle, WA 98104, tel. (206) 553-7220

Mount Rainier National Park, Tahoma Woods, Star Route, Ashford, WA 98304, tel. (360) 569-2211

North Cascades National Park, 2105 Hwy. 20, Sedro-Woolley, WA 98284, tel. (360) 856-5700

Olympic National Park, 3002 Mount Angeles Rd., Port Angeles, WA 98362, tel. (360) 452-0330

San Juan Island National Historical Park, P.O. Box 429, Friday Harbor, WA 98250, tel. (360) 378-2240

Whitman Mission National Historic Site, Route 2, Walla Walla, WA 99362, tel. (509) 522-6360

Forest Service Lands

United States Forest Service lands cover more than nine million acres in Washington state within seven national forests. These forests are managed for multiple uses, but the emphasis has—until recently at least—been on logging. Concerns over spotted owl survival led to a moratorium that has nearly halted timber harvesting in many areas. The National Forests of Washington also contain 24 wilderness areas that cover more than 2.5 million acres. Over half of the total acreage falls within the three largest: Glacier Peak Wilderness (576,900 acres), Pasaytan Wilderness (530,000 acres), and Alpine Lakes Wilderness (393,360 acres). The wilderness areas are described in appropriate chapters of this guide. For an excellent overview of these and other natural areas, get *Exploring Washington's Wild Areas* by Marge and Ted Mueller (Seattle: The Mountaineers). The Forest Service also manages Mount St. Helens National Volcanic Monument, and the Columbia River Gorge National Scenic Area, two of the state's most interesting natural areas.

U.S. Forest Service offices in Washington are:

Colville National Forest, Supervisor's Office, 675 S. Main St., Colville, WA 99114, tel. (509) 684-3711

Gifford Pinchot National Forest, 6926 E. 4th Plain Blvd., Vancouver, WA 98668, tel. (360) 750-5000

Columbia River Gorge National Scenic Area, 902 Wasco Ave., No. 200, Hood River, OR 97031, tel. (541) 386-2333

Mount St. Helens National Volcanic Monument Headquarters, Gifford Pinchot National Forest, 42218 Northeast Yale Bridge Rd., Amboy, WA 98601, tel. (360) 750-3900

Mount Baker/Snoqualmie National Forest, Supervisor's Office, 21905 64th Ave. W, Mountlake Terrace, WA 98043, tel. (206) 775-9702

Okanogan National Forest, Supervisor's Office,1240 South 2nd Ave., Okanogan, WA 98840, tel. (509) 826-3275

Olympic National Forest, Headquarters Office, 1835 Black Lake Blvd. SW, Olympia, WA 98512, tel. (360) 956-2400

Wenatchee National Forest, Supervisor's Office, 301 Yakima St., Wenatchee, WA 98801, tel. (509) 662-4335

Umatilla National Forest, 1415 W. Rose Ave., Walla Walla, WA 99362, tel. (509) 522-6290

State Parks

The state of Washington manages more than 100 state parks covering over 232,000 acres. These are scattered in almost every corner of the state. Most are quite small, encompassing a few hundred acres or less, but some, such as Moran State Park in the San Juan Islands and Deception Pass on Whidbey Island are several thousand acres each and attract throngs of visitors each year; Deception Pass State Park is visited by more than three million folks annually. State park facilities are surprisingly diverse, including several historic forts (Fort Townsend, Fort Flagler, Fort Ebey, Fort Worden, and others), many miles of sandy ocean beaches (including Grayland Beach, Fort Canby, Long Beach, Ocean City, and Pacific Beach), one of the largest public telescopes in the region (Goldendale Observatory), a park devoted to whale-watching (Lime Kiln), a campground where Lewis and Clark spent a night (Lewis and Clark

Trail), and an incredible waterfalls surrounded by desolate eastern Washington land (Palouse Falls). In addition, the state park system includes numerous historic sites, 10 environmental learning centers for school kids, and 40 marine parks, many of which are accessible only by boat. All of the developed state parks are described elsewhere in this volume; see above for a description of camping in the parks.

A fine source for state park information is the definitive *Washington State Parks* by Marge and Ted Mueller (Seattle: The Mountaineers). If you don't want to pay anything, request the helpful *Parks Guide* produced by Washington State Parks. For this publication, brochures on the parks you plan to visit, or reservations contact the Washington State Parks and Recreation Commission in Olympia, tel. (360) 902-8563 or (800) 233-0321.

BACKCOUNTRY SAFETY

Beaver Fever

Although Washington's backcountry lakes and streams may appear clean, you may be risking a debilitating sickness by drinking the water without treatment. The protozoan *Giardia lamblia* is found throughout the state, spread by both humans and animals (including beaver). Although the disease is curable with drugs, it's always best to carry safe drinking water on any trip or to boil water taken from creeks or lakes. Bringing water to a full boil is sufficient to kill Giardia and other harmful organisms. Another option is to use water filters, available from backpacking stores. Note, however, that these may not filter out other organisms such as Campylobactor bacteria that are just 0.2 microns in size. Chlorine and iodine are not always reliable, taste foul, and can be unhealthy.

Hypothermia

Anyone who has spent much time in the outdoors will discover the dangers of exposure to cold, wet, and windy conditions. Even at temperatures well above freezing, hypothermia—the reduction of the body's inner core temperature below 95° F—can prove fatal. Hypothermia is a problem during the Northwest summers more often than winters because people often mistakenly believe that the bright, sunny morning weather is going to last. In the higher elevations of the Cascades and Olympics the weather is unpredictable, and the temperature can drop dramatically in a matter of hours or even minutes.

In the early stages, hypothermia causes uncontrollable shivering, followed by a loss of coordination, slurred speech, and then a rapid descent into unconsciousness and death. Always travel prepared for sudden changes in the weather. Wear clothing that insulates well and that holds its heat when wet. Wool and polypropylene are far better than cotton, and clothes should be worn in layers to provide better trapping of heat and a chance to adjust to conditions more easily. Always carry a wool hat, since your head loses more heat than any other part of the body. Bring a waterproof shell to cut the wind. Put on rain gear *before* it starts raining; head back or set up camp when the weather looks threatening; eat candy bars, keep active, or snuggle with a friend in a down bag to generate warmth.

If someone in your party begins to show signs of hypothermia, don't take any chances, even if the person denies needing help. Get the victim out of the wind, strip off his clothes, and put him in a dry sleeping bag on an insulating pad. Skin-to-skin contact is the best way to warm a hypothermic person, and that means you'll need to also strip and climb in the sleeping bag. If you weren't friends before, this should heat up the relationship! Do not give the victim alcohol or hot drinks, and do not try to warm the person too quickly since it could lead to heart failure. Once the victim has recovered, get medical help as soon as possible. Actually, you're far better off keeping close tabs on everyone in the group and seeking shelter before exhaustion and hypothermia set in.

Frostbite

Frostbite is a less serious but quite painful problem for the cold-weather hiker; it is caused by direct exposure or by heat loss due to wet socks and boots. Frostbitten areas will look white or gray and feel hard on the surface, softer underneath. The best way to warm the area is with other skin: put your hand under your arm, your feet on your friend's belly. Don't rub it with snow or warm it near a fire. In cases of severe frostbite, in which the skin is white, quite hard, and numb, immerse the frozen area in water warmed to 99° to 104° until it's thawed. Avoid refreezing the frostbitten area. If you're a long way from medical assistance and the frostbite is extensive, it is better to keep the area frozen and get out of the woods for help; thawing is very painful, and it would be impossible to walk on a thawed foot.

Other Safety Tips

Dealing with bears is discussed under "Flora and Fauna" in the Introduction chapter. The most important part of enjoying—and surviving—the backcountry is to be prepared. Know where you're going; get maps, camping information, and weather and trail conditions from a ranger before setting out. Don't hike alone. Two are better than one, and three are better than two; if one gets hurt, one person can stay with the injured party and one can go for help. Bring more than enough food so hunger won't cause you to continue when weather conditions say stop. Tell someone where you're going and when you'll be back.

Always carry the **Ten Essentials:**

• map
• compass—and know how to use it
• water bottle
• first-aid kit
• flashlight
• matches (or lighter) and fire starter
• knife
• extra clothing (a full set, in case you fall in a stream), including rain gear
• extra food (Some hard-core hikers carry dog food so they won't be tempted to dip into the emergency rations.)
• sunglasses—especially if you're hiking on snow

Check your ego at the trailhead; stop for the night when the weather gets bad, even if it's 2 p.m., or head back, and don't press on when you're exhausted—tired hikers are sloppy hikers, and even a small injury can be disastrous in the woods.

INFORMATION AND COMMUNICATIONS

INFORMATION

For a free travel packet that includes the *Washington State Lodging and Travel Guide* (very helpful), along with a seasonal *Washington State Field Guide,* call the Washington State Department of Tourism at (800) 890-5493. Their Internet address, http://www.tourism.wa.gov, provides the same info online, plus comprehensive details on travel to Washington, and links to many related home pages. You can also use it to order copies of state tourism publications, or pick them up in person at the larger visitor centers around Washington, along with free state maps. The state has seven "gateway" visitor information centers at various points around its borders: Blaine, Maryhill, Oroville, Megler (across from Astoria, Oregon), Ridgefield, Spokane, and Vancouver. The Vancouver office is open year-round; the others generally May-September.

Every city or town has a chamber of commerce. Most have offices that are filled with free brochures, maps, and information on lodging and restaurants. Some on busy highways are diligent about stocking brochures and other tourist publications from areas all over the state and into other states and Canadian provinces. Take advantage of the help they offer. See "Information and Services" under each place for the chamber's address and phone.

Ranger stations at the national parks and forests can sell you forest and topographic maps, campground and trail information, and other printed material. See above for a listing of the main Forest Service and Park Service offices, and below for state offices.

For books, maps, and pamphlets on Washington's federal lands, visit the **National Forest and Parks Outdoor Recreation Information Center,** 915 Second Ave., Room 442, Seattle. You can also call them for a list of publications available by mail order; tel. (206) 220-7450.

Get more specific information on your destination by writing or phoning one of the offices listed below.

STATE GOVERNMENT OFFICES

Washington Department of Natural Resources, P.O. Box 47001 Olympia, WA 98504, tel. (360) 902-1000, or (800) 527-3305 in Washington

Washington State Parks and Recreation Commission, 7150 Cleanwater Lane, Olympia, WA 98504, tel. (360) 753-2027 or (800) 233-0321

Washington Department of Fish and Wildlife, P.O. Box 43135, Olympia, WA 98504, tel. (206) 902-0200

Washington State Department of Tourism, 101 General Administration Bldg., P.O. Box 42500, Olympia, WA 98504, tel. (800) 544-1800

Washington State Ferries, Pier 52/Coleman Dock 801 Alaskan Way Seattle, WA 98104, tel. (800) 843-3779, outside Washington (206) 464-6400

COMMUNICATIONS

Post Offices

Post offices generally open between 7 a.m. and 9 a.m. and close between 5 p.m. and 6 p.m.; only a few are open on Saturday. Their outer doors are usually open, so you can go in to buy stamps from the machines. Some drug or card stores also operate a postal substation where you can buy stamps or mail packages within the U.S. (you'll have to go to a real post office for mailing to foreign addresses or other special services). Many grocery store checkout counters also sell books of stamps with no markup.

Phone Service

Washington's three telephone area codes—206 in the Seattle area, 509 in eastern Washington, and 360 elsewhere—lead to some initial confusion, but are not that hard to keep straight (except for the wandering dividing line along the Columbia Gorge). To help, I have listed the local area code under "Information and Ser-

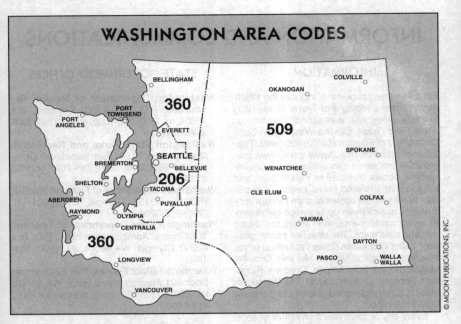

WASHINGTON AREA CODES

BELLINGHAM

COLVILLE

OKANOGAN

360

PORT TOWNSEND

PORT ANGELES

EVERETT

509

SPOKANE

WASHINGTON

SEATTLE

WENATCHEE

BELLEVUE

BREMERTON

206

SHELTON

TACOMA

CLE ELUM

COLFAX

ABERDEEN

PUYALLUP

YAKIMA

RAYMOND

OLYMPIA

CENTRALIA

DAYTON

360

LONGVIEW

PASCO

WALLA WALLA

VANCOUVER

© MOON PUBLICATIONS, INC.

vices" for each city, as well as with each telephone number.

In most of Washington, dial 911 for medical, police, or fire emergencies. More remote areas have separate numbers for all three, and they're listed under "Information and Services" in each section of this book; as a last resort, dial 0 for the operator. Most hospitals have 24-hour emergency room service; some cities have dial-a-nurse services that offer free medical advice.

TRANSPORTATION

BY AIR

Washington's two major airports are Seattle-Tacoma International (Sea-Tac) and Spokane International, served by most major carriers and a handful of smaller airlines. United, tel. (800) 241-6522; Continental, tel. (800) 525-0280; Delta, tel. (800) 221-1212; American, tel. (800) 433-7300; TWA, tel. (800) 221-2000 or (206) 447-9400 (Seattle); USAir, tel. (800) 428-4322; Northwest, tel. (800) 225-2525, among others, provide national and international service. Alaska Airlines, tel. (800) 426-0333, serves the Western states; America West, tel. (800) 382-6517, flies to California, Las Vegas, and the Southwest and Midwest states. Horizon Air (a subsidiary of Alaska Airlines), tel. (800) 547-9308, is the big "little" airline, connecting many medium-to-large Washington cities, including Seattle, Spokane, Bellingham, Lewiston, Moses Lake, Pasco, Port Angeles, Pullman, Walla Walla, Wenatchee, and Yakima.

Try for a south-side window seat (on an east-west route) when flying into or out of Sea-Tac for a spectacular close-up view of Mt. Rainier and, in the distance, Mt. St. Helens. On the north-south routes the plane usually flies within a mile or two, on either side, of Mt. St. Helens.

BY TRAIN

Amtrak serves Washington with four major routes, though the current political climate may lead to service reductions in the near future. The north-south route along the West Coast is aboard the **Coast Starlight,** which has daily service to Seattle, Tacoma, Olympia/Lacey, Centralia, Longview/Kelso, and Vancouver, through Oregon and south to San Francisco and Los Angeles. The **Mount Baker International,** provides daily train connections north to Vancouver, B.C., via Edmonds, Everett, Mount Vernon, and Bellingham.

Amtrak's east-west route, aboard the **Pioneer,** departs Seattle, passing through Tacoma, Olympia/Lacey, Centralia, Longview/Kelso, and Vancouver as it continues through Portland and Idaho to Salt Lake City and Chicago. Four times a week, the east-west route to Chicago is on the **Empire Builder,** which stops at Spokane, then turns southwest to Portland with stops at Pasco, Wishram, Bingen/White Salmon, and Vancouver, or to Seattle through Ephrata, Wenatchee, Everett, and Edmonds.

For route, schedule, and fare information, phone Amtrak at (800) 872-7245. Be forewarned, though: Amtrak requires advance reservations; you can't just go down to the station and climb aboard.

BY CAR

Washington is a part of America, and as such, the car is king here. Despite their negative impacts on the environment, cars do make it easy to reach remote areas that are not served by any air, rail, or bus lines. Numerous car rental agencies operate at or near Sea-Tac and Spokane International Airports, as well as in all large cities.

Washington's major interstates are I-5, running north to south from the Canadian border through Blaine, Bellingham, Mount Vernon, Everett, Seattle, Tacoma, Olympia, Centralia, Longview/Kelso, Kalama, and Woodland to Vancouver; I-90, running west to east from Seattle through Issaquah and North Bend over Snoqualmie Pass to Cle Elum, Ellensburg, Moses Lake, Ritzville, and Cheney to Spokane; I-82 heads south from Ellensburg through the Yakima Valley almost to the Tri-Cities.

From late fall to early spring, expect snow at I-90's Snoqualmie Pass (between North Bend and Cle Elum in central Washington), Stevens Pass on U.S. Hwy. 2 and White Pass on State Hwy. 12. Cayuse Pass on State Hwy. 410 and Rainy and Washington Passes on State Hwy. 20 (the North Cascades Hwy.) are closed after the first snowfall each winter.

Snow tires or chains are frequently required, and the passes are sometimes closed during storms because of hazardous road conditions, blocking accidents, or avalanche danger. Skiers and other winter travelers passing through the Cascades should always carry a set of chains and emergency equipment (flares, shovel, blankets, and food). Before you set out, phone (900) 407-7277 (35 cents per minute) or (206) 434-7277 for the Department of Transportation's **Mountain Pass Reporting Service;** they give road and weather conditions for all of the Cascade passes from October through April 15. AAA Washington also has a free 24-hour recorded message on major highways within a day's drive of Puget Sound: tel. (206) 646-2190.

Out-of-state visitors may be surprised by the abundance of wide-open spaces, particularly in the mountains and the eastern half of the state—and the long distances between gas stations, restrooms, and other niceties. Worse yet, some little towns close up tight after 5 p.m. and on Sunday. Play it safe and fill the tank whenever you pass through a moderately populous area; stock a cooler with drinks and sandwiches; be sure your destination motel has a room ready and waiting for you.

A warning to Washington newcomers: The state seems to have more cops per capita than anywhere else in the nation. They all have radar guns and aren't afraid to use them. Watch your speed!

BY BUS

Longhaul Buses
Greyhound, tel. (206) 628-5526 (Seattle) or (800) 231-2222, serves most major cities in Washington, providing nationwide connections. Their main routes are along I-5 from Canada to Oregon and along I-90 from Seattle to Spokane, with additional service on the Oregon side of the Columbia Gorge and west to Astoria.

Trailways has a bus station at 1936 Westlake Ave. in Seattle, tel. (206) 728-5955 or (800) 366-3830, and offers service along the I-5 corridor, with stops in Portland, Vancouver, Longview, Centralia, Olympia, Tacoma, Seattle, Everett, Mount Vernon, and Bellingham. They also have service connecting Spokane with Seattle, stopping in Issaquah, Ellensburg, Yaki-

ma, Moses Lake, and Ritzville en route. Other buses run from Spokane south through Colfax, Pullman, and Lewiston, Idaho, and from Walla Walla to Pasco, Ritzville, and Spokane. The Trailways network continues through Idaho, Oregon, and Nevada, but you'll need to transfer to Greyhound for other destinations.

Other, more localized bus companies are **Borderline Stage,** tel. (509) 684-3950, serving northeastern Washington, and **Empire Lines,** tel. (509) 624-4116, in eastern Washington.

Perhaps the most unusual wheeled transportation company is **Green Tortoise Alternative Travel,** which some call a "traveling commune" or a "road show on wheels." The Green Tortoise has twice-weekly buses from Seattle to Los Angeles that take 48 hours to reach Los Angeles, including a sightseeing stop in San Francisco and a rest stop for a vegetarian feast, sauna, and entertainment at the operation's digs in southern Oregon. It also has tours all over the hemisphere, from Alaska, to Yellowstone National Park, to Costa Rica. This is a fun and inexpensive way to explore the country. Call (206) 324-7433 or (800) 867-8647 for details on all their trips. The Green Tortoise also runs a private hostel in Seattle.

Public Transit Buses
Washington's public buses offer a remarkably comprehensive system, with low-priced service throughout all of western Washington. The coverage is less complete east of the Cascades, but still quite good. Some of these services—such as the Link in the Chelan/Leavenworth/Wenatchee area, Skagit Transit in Mount Vernon, and East Jefferson Transit on the Olympic Peninsula—are entirely free, paid for through local sales taxes. A number of the bus systems also have bike racks. The Washington State Department of Transportation publishes a helpful *Passenger Transportation Options* booklet detailing all public and private buses in the state; call (360) 586-2401 for a copy.

Seattle's **Metro Transit,** tel. (206) 553-3000 or (800) 542-7876, has extensive service within the city and regular daily routes throughout most of King County. **Pierce Transit,** tel. (206) 581-8000 or (800) 562-8109, serves Tacoma and Pierce County. **Intercity Transit,** tel. (360) 786-

1881 or (800) 287-6348, has daily routes throughout Olympia and Thurston County. **Grays Harbor Transportation Authority,** tel. (360) 532-2770 or (800) 562-9730, connects Olympia with Hoquiam, Ocean Shores, Westport, and Lake Quinault in Olympic National Park. Public buses operate throughout the Olympic Peninsula, making it possible to easily reach towns surrounding the park for a minimal fare. **West Jefferson Transit,** tel. (800) 436-3950, has free bus service continuing north from Lake Quinault to Forks, where you can transfer to **Clallam Transit,** tel. (360) 452-4511 or (800) 858-3747, for the northern end of the Olympic Peninsula, including Port Angeles, Sequim, Neah Bay, and Olympic National Park's Sol Duc Hot Springs and Lake Crescent. Connect with **Jefferson Transit,** tel. (360) 385-4777 or (800) 773-7788 in Sequim for Port Townsend, Port Ludlow, Quilcene, and other east Jefferson County points. **Kitsap Transit,** tel. (360) 373-2877, serves the Kitsap Peninsula, including Bremerton, Port Orchard, and Bainbridge Island.

The Long Beach Peninsula is served by **Pacific Transit,** tel. (360) 875-9418 or 642-9418, with connections to Raymond, South Bend, and Astoria, Oregon. **C-TRAN,** tel. (360) 695-0123, serves Vancouver and surrounding towns (including Amboy, Yacolt, La Center, and Washougal), with connections to Portland. Longview, Kelso, Castle Rock, Kalama, and Woodland are served by Community Urban Bus Service (CUBS), tel. (360) 577-3399. In Chehalis, **Twin Transit,** tel. (360) 330-2072, has local service in Chehalis and Centralia, and in Centralia you can catch Grays Harbor Transit for points on the Olympic Peninsula.

Northern Puget Sound is served by several transit agencies. **Community Transit,** tel. (360) 353-7433 or (800) 562-1375, has service throughout Snohomish County, including Everett, Lynnwood, Snohomish, Monroe, Granite Falls, and Darrington. **Skagit Transit,** tel. (360) 428-8547 or (800) 488-5477, covers Mount Vernon and Burlington. **Island Transit,** tel. (360) 678-7771, serves Whidbey Island, and **Whatcom Transit,** tel. (360) 676-7433, has buses to Bellingham, Ferndale, Lynden, and Blaine.

The bus line coverage in eastern Washington isn't as thorough. In Spokane, take **Spokane Transit,** tel. (509) 328-7433, throughout Spokane and Cheney. In Pullman, **Pullman Transit,** tel. (509) 332-6535, provides local bus service, and the **Wheatland Express Commuter Bus,** tel. (509) 334-2200 or (800) 334-2207, has shuttle service between Pullman and Moscow, Idaho. **Link Transit,** tel. (509) 662-1155 or (800) 851-5465, has free bus service in Chelan, Wenatchee, Leavenworth, and Manson. **Valley Transit,** tel. (509) 525-9140, serves Walla Walla and College Place. **Yakima Transit,** tel. (509) 575-6175, has routes throughout Yakima and the surrounding area. The Tri-Cities have **Ben Franklin Transit,** tel. (509) 735-5100, has service to Kennewick, Pasco, and Richland.

WASHINGTON STATE FERRIES

The Washington state ferry system is the largest mass transit system in the state, carrying more than 23 million passengers each year across Puget Sound. This is by far the most scenic way to see the Sound, but the system also serves many commuters who ride the ferry to work each day in Seattle, Tacoma, or Everett. Many longtime residents take rides on them, sometimes simply as a way to get away from the office for an hour with a brown-bag lunch.

The Routes
Washington has the largest ferry fleet in the United States, with 25 different vessels, ranging from a 94-foot passenger boat to jumbo-class 440-foot-long ships capable of carrying more than 200 cars and 2,000 passengers. The ferries call at 20 different ports around Puget Sound, from Tacoma to Vancouver Island.

The best sightseeing is on the Anacortes-San Juan Islands route, which once a day continues to Sidney, British Columbia Ferries also connect Port Townsend with Keystone (Whidbey Island); Clinton (Whidbey Island) with Mukilteo (southwest of Everett); Edmonds with Kingston (on the Kitsap Peninsula); Seattle with Winslow (Bainbridge Island) and Bremerton; Fauntleroy (southwest Seattle) with Southworth (southeast of Bremerton) and Vashon Island; and Tacoma (at Point Defiance) with Tahlequah (at the south end of Vashon Island). All of these routes are described in detail elsewhere in this book.

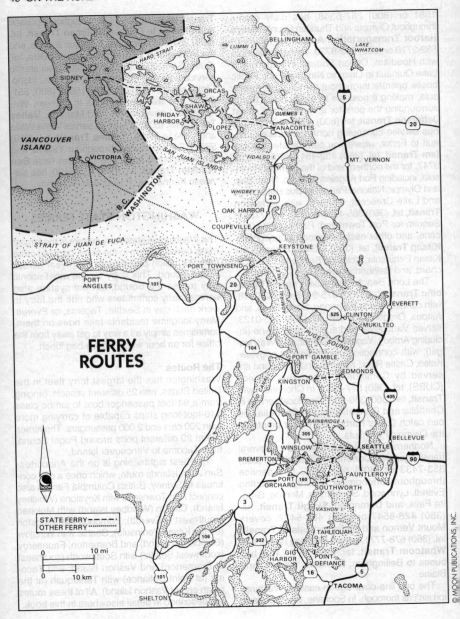

FERRY
ROUTES

STATE FERRY ----
OTHER FERRY ....

0   10 mi

0   10 km

© MOON PUBLICATIONS, INC.

Practicalities

The ferry system operates on a first-come, first-served basis, with reservations only available for the routes from Anacortes to Sidney, B.C., and from Orcas Island or San Juan Island to Sidney. The ferries operate every day, including holidays. Fares range widely, depending upon your destination, whether you are on foot or in a vehicle, and the season—there's a 20% surcharge from the second Sunday in May through the second Sunday in October. Senior citizens receive a 50% discount, applied only to the passenger or driver portion of the fare (not the vehicle). Fares must be paid with cash, traveler's checks, or personal checks (Washington residents only); no credit cards.

The larger ferries have food service, vending machines dispensing candy bars and junk food, and beer; the smaller boats have vending machines only. Brochure racks are usually packed with flyers from local B&Bs, real estate firms, and restaurants. Pets on leashes are allowed on the car decks or in carrying containers on passenger decks. Bikes, kayaks, and canoes are also allowed onboard for a small surcharge.

For more information about the state ferry system, along with fares and sailing schedules, call (206) 464-6400 (Seattle) or (800) 843-3779 (in Washington only).

Avoiding the Crowds

Washington State Ferries are especially busy during the commute hours, when thousands of people head eastward to Seattle, Everett, and other cities each weekday morning, and back home again in the evening. Pleasure traffic increases on weekends, especially during the summer. Friday afternoons and Saturday mornings see crowded ferries heading westbound, especially to Whidbey Island and the San Juan Islands. Many of these same folks return on Sunday afternoons and evenings. Unless you don't mind waiting in long lines—up to two hours or more sometimes—avoid travel at these times (or head in the opposite direction of the crowds). Foot passengers never need to wait, but those in vehicles may find themselves watching several ferries come and go before they can get on board at peak hours.

OTHER FERRIES

Other Washington Ferries

Other Washington ferries include the Anderson Island Ferry, tel. (360) 581-6290, which has daily service between Steilacoom, Anderson Island, and Ketron Island. **Horluck Transportation Co.,** tel. (360) 876-2300, has a daily route between Bremerton and Port Orchard for foot traffic only. Various counties operate ferries, including the ferry to Lummi Island near Bellingham (tel. 360-676-6730), the ferry between Anacortes and Guemes Island (tel. 360-293-6356), between Puget Island near Cathlamet and the Oregon side of the river (tel. 360-795-3301), the two free ferries across the upper Columbia River at the Keller crossing just above Grand Coulee Dam (no phone), and between Gifford and Inchelium (tel. 509-684-4335) on the Colville Indian Reservation.

Ferries to British Columbia

The Washington State Ferry connects Anacortes, the San Juan Islands, and Sidney, B.C.; see above for details. In addition to this, several private companies offer ferry connections to Vancouver Island. All of these are described in depth elsewhere in this book.

Take the MV *Coho,* tel. (360) 457-4491 or (206) 622-2222, from Port Angeles to Victoria, B.C., across the Strait of Juan de Fuca. From Seattle the *Victoria Clipper,* tel. (206) 448-5000 or (800) 888-2535, has passenger-only service to Victoria daily in summer. The *Royal Victorian* sails between Seattle and Victoria from mid-May to late September, offering passenger and vehicle transport Thurs.-Sun. only; tel. (206) 625-1880 or (800) 668-1167.

Independent tour and charter boat companies in Seattle, Tacoma, Everett, Bellingham, San Juan Island, Westport, and other coastal cities offer sightseeing, fishing, and whale- and sea lion-watching tours throughout the year.

BY BICYCLE

Washington, and particularly Seattle, is among the most bicycle-friendly places in America. At least 10,000 persons commute to work by bicycle in Seattle. Puget Sound's numerous islands provide great scenery, some of the state's best weather, and little automobile traffic: Whidbey Island, for instance, gets only a third of the rainfall Seattle gets and offers spectacular vistas from little-traveled back roads, plus plenty of camping at the state parks.

The beauty of the San Juan Islands is best experienced on a bike, and you'll save $10 or more on the ferry toll to Friday Harbor when traveling without the cumbersome automobile. Vashon, Bainbridge, Mercer, and Camano Islands are also easy to get to and have little automobile traffic.

The urban areas have ample opportunities for cyclists. Seattle has received the blessings of *Bicycling* magazine as the "Best North American City for Bicycling," crediting the city's friendly atmosphere and the many miles of scenic and safe paths. Seattle adopted a comprehensive policy toward biking that led to more signs, more bike racks, Metro buses with bike racks, special bike lanes, and so forth. An example of this enlightened attitude toward self-propulsion is the Burke-Gilman Trail, a 14-mile paved bike path from Gasworks Park to Kenmore at the north end of Lake Washington. There, it connects with the Sammamish River Trail, which runs another 10 miles to Redmond's Marymoor Park, passing just east of Woodinville's Ste. Michelle and Columbia wineries—great places to stop for lunch with a bottle of wine.

In West Seattle, the road and bike path from Alki Beach to Lincoln Park is a popular 12-mile loop. Five Mile Drive in Tacoma's Point Defiance Park is open to cars as well, but cyclists are given a wide berth; the road passes through an impressive old-growth forest.

For information on bicycling in Washington, check with the chambers of commerce for maps of bike routes throughout their city or county. These are available in Seattle, Bremerton, the Tri-Cities, Tacoma, Spokane, Bellevue, and Kirkland. The Washington State Department of Transportation in Olympia, tel. (360) 705-7000, publishes bicycle maps and guidelines, including a very helpful statewide map showing traffic data and road widths to help determine which roads are the safest. The Seattle Engineering Department, tel. (206) 684-7583, will send you a detailed bicycle map of Seattle.

Bike Tours

A number of companies offer cycling tours across parts of Washington. The largest is California-based **Backroads,** tel. (800) 462-2848, with trips to Whidbey Island, the Olympic Peninsula, the San Juan Islands, and the north Cascades, along with dozens of other places worldwide. Call them for a catalog; these are some of the most elaborate publicity brochures you'll ever see! These trips aren't cheap: starting at $698 for a five-day trip include lodging, food, and a sag wagon. **Bicycle Adventures,** tel. (360) 786-0989 or (800) 443-6060, is an Olympia-based company with trips throughout the Northwest, including Puget Sound, the San Juan Islands, and Columbia Gorge. Trips start at $696 for a four-day pedal around the San Juans. **Scenic Cycling Adventures,** tel. (541) 385-5257, has San Juan Island rides for $649. As with Backroads, both of these companies include food, lodging, and a support vehicle in the rate.

BOB RACE

SEATTLE

By now you've probably heard all the monikers applied to Seattle: America's Most Livable City, Emerald City, Latte Land, and City of Niceness. For the last decade or so, the media have "discovered" (with a population of more than 520,000 people) Seattle as a lively and enchanting place to explore and live. The obvious charms of Seattle and the Puget Sound region draw more tourists each year, many of whom come back to stay.

Throughout its history Seattle has been a gateway: first to Alaska and western Canada, today to Asia as planes refuel here for their destinations and shipping companies gain an extra day's travel by shipping through Puget Sound, and of course to the beauty of the Pacific Northwest. Three of the country's most spectacular national parks and moody Mount St. Helens National Monument are within two hours' driving time from the city; skiing, hiking, year-round boating, swimming, and fishing are less than an hour away.

Seattle's charm isn't just a function of what it's near, but also what it is—and was. Oddly shaped towers and preserved historical districts stand alongside modern skyscrapers and the busy waterfront in a jaunty kind of disharmony. Every major event in the city's short life span, from Yesler's 1850s sawmill to the 1962 World's Fair, has left its legacy; the resulting mishmash of periods gives the city a flavor absent in showpieces of urban renewal.

History doesn't make a city livable. No one event or attraction here can ever take that credit. Rather, it's a thousand incidents, enjoyed daily: dining at the waterfront, watching the sun set behind the Olympics as sailboats head home; reading the *Seattle P.I.* on your early-morning ferry commute, accompanied by a lively porpoise escort service; listening to a free outdoor lunchtime concert at Freeway Park; stopping for fresh vegetables or fish at Pike Place Market; cleansing your lungs with fresh, rain-rinsed air as you dodge slugs and puddles on your morning run; attending a summertime office party on a harbor tour boat; being surprised by a clear view of bashful Mt. Rainier from the highway or the QFC parking lot.

The People

A New York friend of mine who spent time in Seattle found it a difficult adjustment. The kind of

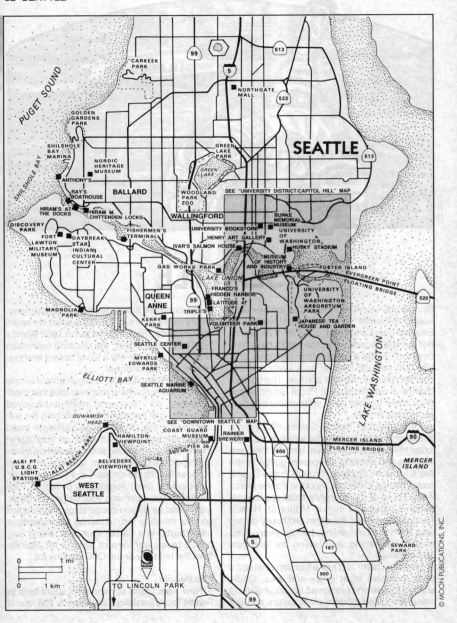

© MOON PUBLICATIONS, INC.

things that drive aggressive New Yorkers over the edge in seconds seem to roll right off a Seattleite's back. It was the little things that stuck out: drivers waiting for other cars to pull out ahead of them, the almost total lack of horn-honking, the easy acceptance of long lines at an espresso bar, the friendly bus drivers who didn't charge for a short ride, and the pedestrians waiting for the "Walk" sign before crossing a deserted street. Sometimes this laid-back nature approaches the annoying stage—such as the times clerks stop to chat with a customer about her kids while a long queue waits patiently—but Seattleites take it all in stride. (One writer complained of being unable to get in an argument on any subject, calling it being "stoned to death with popcorn.") Maybe it's the strong Scandinavian heritage of acceptance and community; maybe it's the on-again off-again rain that teaches patience; or maybe it's something they put in the espresso. . . .

Climate

Okay, it's true. In 1898, a boy actually drowned on a downtown Seattle city street. Apparently he was trying to cross an enormous sinkhole on a raft, fell off, and couldn't swim. Despite what you may have heard, however, it doesn't normally rain enough to drown folks in Seattle. The city actually gets less annual rainfall than New York City—it just falls more slowly. Gray and drizzly skies are standard fare from October to May; when it does rain, it's frequently a who-needs-an-umbrella sprinkle. One of Seattle's oddest facts is that more pairs of sunglasses are sold there per capita than any other American city, yet umbrella and raincoat sales are no higher than any other city. The winter weather pattern remains nearly constant; storms off the Pacific coast send swirling clouds over Seattle for months, leading you to believe that the TV weather forecaster uses the same satellite photo all season.

Nearly all of the precipitation is rain; less than an inch of snow per month is the average, so plows are few . . . and generally in disrepair. When snowstorms dropped 17 inches on Seat-

tle in November of 1985, only four of the city's seven snowplows worked. Commuters, few of whom had much experience driving on snow, relied on chains to traverse the I-5 snowfield and some actually reached their destinations; most simply abandoned their cars and turned the freeway into a disorderly parking lot. Automobile insurance companies hated that storm.

Seattle and other western Washington residents have learned to expect these three seasonal events: a windstorm on Thanksgiving that knocks out electrical power while the turkey is in the oven; floods on the Snohomish and Skagit Rivers around Christmas and New Year's that force farmers to evacuate their homes built on the floodplain; and perfect Santa Barbara weather the weekend of July 4. You could almost make a living betting on these meteorological events.

When spring arrives the clouds move more quickly; rain comes in unpredictable spurts. Summer convinces many visitors to move here: low humidity, temperatures in the high 70s to 80s, and cloudless skies; sometimes two entire months pass without a drop of rain. It makes natives restless and irritable. Then, as suddenly as it began, summer ends: clouds and smiles return, temperatures go down, and residents stockpile firewood, books, hot chocolate, and party invitations for the soggy season ahead.

Getting Oriented

See the "Seattle" map to get an idea of the major neighborhoods and thoroughfares. The city's street numbering system takes a little time to understand. Avenues run north and south, streets run east and west, but street names get more complex than this. Example: N.E. 63rd St. is in the Ravenna District east of 1st Ave. NE, and 63 blocks north of Yesler Way; 63rd Ave. SW is in West Seattle, south of Yesler Way and 63 blocks west of the Duwamish Waterway. Fortunately, the system starts to make a bit of sense after awhile and is used throughout King County (named for Martin Luther King Jr.), making it easier to find streets in neighboring cities such as Bellevue or Renton.

HISTORY

The First Inhabitants

The original settlers around present-day Seattle were the Duwamish and Suquamish tribes. They were semi-nomadic people who sustained on salmon and other seafood, along with seasonal plants. The Suquamish called the entire Puget Sound basin something that sounded like "Whulge," and the name stuck with early European explorers until Capt. George Vancouver named the sound for his friend, Peter Puget.

The city was named after Chief Sealth (or "Seattle"—Indian names didn't translate well into English), and both spellings are used on his tomb. The son of a Suquamish tribal leader and a Duwamish woman, Sealth became the chief of both tribes around 1810, and witnessed Capt. George Vancouver's visit in 1792. Fifty years later he befriended early settlers, encouraging a policy of peace between Indians and white newcomers. The Suquamish tribe was eventually allotted land on the Kitsap Peninsula, but the Duwamish were relegated to land on other reservations. Many of these first residents eventually moved to Seattle.

Most Indians feared the consequences of the utterance of their names after death; historians debate whether the chief was happy that the city was to be named in his honor. Some claim it was against his will; others hold that Sealth was paid handsomely by the city's founders for his name. In any case, the name stuck, and certainly sounded better than the settlement's original name, Duwamps. Today a bronze sculpture of Chief Seattle stands at the corner of Fifth and Denny Way; his burial site, a peaceful Suquamish cemetery across the Sound, overlooks his namesake's skyscrapers.

Early Settlers

Although some white men were in the Duwamish River Valley not far from Puget Sound, David Denny and Lee Terry were the first white men to arrive at what became Seattle. Twenty-two pioneers had left Cherry Grove, Illinois, in wagons bound for Portland, Oregon; they then boarded the schooner *Exact* and sailed to Alki Point in 1851. The settlers ambi-tiously planned to develop "the New York of the Pacific Coast" at their landing site.

Lumber was the focus of their early economy, beginning with the arrival of the *Leonesa* from San Francisco in 1852. The ship's captain had been wandering northward when he stumbled across the Alki settlement. The settlers sold the skipper 35,000 board feet of logs. Seeing an economic future in shipping lumber, the pioneers took to the waters in Indian canoes and, with the help of Mrs. Denny's clothesline and Lee Terry's horseshoes, took soundings along the Puget Sound shoreline. Discovering that the deepest waters were in today's Elliott Bay, the group relocated to Pioneer Square. Interestingly, this was the same bay about which Lt. Charles Wilkes wrote, "I do not consider the bay a desirable anchorage."

Logs were skidded down the original "Skid Road," now Yesler Way, to Henry Yesler's steam-powered sawmill. Yesler enjoyed such success that by the 1880s Yesler's Wharf was a town unto itself, with saloons, warehouses, shops, homes, and offices built on pilings extending 900 feet over the mudflats. The mill remained one of the city's economic pillars for two decades.

Women were scarce in Seattle's early years, so in the 1860s Asa Mercer made two trips to New England to find refined, educated, single women willing to endure a little hardship to get a husband. The "Mercer Girls" (see the special topic "An Unlikely Hero") brought culture and class to the rowdy pioneer town.

Railroad

Until the 1880s, most transport to and from Seattle was by boat. Hopes for alternative methods were dashed when the Northern Pacific Railroad chose Tacoma as its Northwest terminus, citing unstable and steep terrain in Seattle. Though they received intermittent service via Tacoma by 1883, Seattleites wanted to be part of a regular, mainline route. As James J. Hill began expanding the Great Northern Line westward, rumors of a Seattle terminus resulted in a population boom and rising real estate values; the rumor became fact in 1893.

AN UNLIKELY HERO

One of the most respected pioneer names in Seattle is Mercer, and one of the most famous incidents in early Seattle was engineered by Asa Shinn Mercer.

Asa Mercer graduated from Lafayette College, Pennsylvania, in 1861 and immediately set out for Seattle to join his elder brother, Judge Thomas Mercer, who was busy settling the new city. He became the first president of the University of Washington before it even existed; he helped clear the site on a hillside overlooking the village of Seattle and put up classrooms, and then he scouted the region for students. For the first two terms, he not only was president of the university, he was the entire faculty.

As he toured the region, he heard the same complaint repeatedly: not enough women. Interracial marriages were common, alcoholism was high, and morale was low. Mercer believed the area could not thrive until it had a firm family footing.

Asa Shinn Mercer

He tried to get the territorial government to subsidize female immigration, but while the men who ran the government were sympathetic, the treasury was empty. The disgruntled would-be marriage broker packed a suitcase and caught a ship back to Boston. The Civil War was creating thousands of young widows; many women of marrying age were willing to go. But when sailing time came, only 11 showed up. Mercer was probably disappointed, but it wasn't bad for a start. They arrived in Seattle on May 16, 1864. Within only a few months all the women were married, and Mercer was a local hero.

Mercer left again in 1865, this time promising to enlist no less than President Lincoln's assistance. But when his ship arrived in New York from Panama, he found almost the entire nation hung in black crepe paper; President Lincoln had been assassinated the night before Asa's arrival.

Mercer was almost crushed by this news, but he made a quick recovery and went down to Washington, D.C., to talk to President Andrew Johnson and his cabinet. Another strikeout.

Feeling more hopeless by the minute, he took a chance and called on General Ulysses Grant and found an unlikely ally. Grant had been assigned to Fort Vancouver not too long before the war; he remembered the excruciating loneliness men suffered in the settlements that were hardly more than clearings in the dark, damp forests. He promised to do what he could.

Grant persuaded the president to donate a steamboat to Mercer's cause and ordered the quartermaster of the Army to provide it. Believing the ship was his, Mercer went on a recruiting mission all over the East Coast, speaking at churches in New York, Boston, and Washington, D.C., and in only a short time he had more than 500 women signed on.

When he returned to claim his ship, there was a hitch. He could have it, but he would have to buy it at a bargain-basement price: $80,000 in cash, only one-third its value. Mercer, of course, had no money and neither did the territorial treasury. And the women began arriving in New York to sail west to matrimony.

No railroads ran coast to coast yet, but a tycoon named Ben Holladay had a stagecoach and a ship line, and he cut Mercer a deal: Holladay would buy the ship and in return he would haul 500 of Mercer's brides-to-be for a very low price.

Mercer quickly agreed, and the end finally seemed in sight. But no. The *New York Herald* newspaper caught up to the story and began printing accusations that Mercer was little more than a white slaver. The headlines were imaginative and painful:

HEGIRA OF SPINSTERS
PETTICOAT BRIGADE
CARGO OF HEIFERS
MERCER-NARY ADVENTURE

(continues on next page)

UNIVERSITY OF WASHINGTON/2209/3392

AN UNLIKELY HERO
(continued)

More than half of the women returned home and Holladay canceled his offer, but he offered to haul the remainder at the regular fare. Then Mercer saw what had really happened: it was Holladay who had planted the white-slave stories, to get the vessel at the bargain price without having to keep his end of the deal.

Still, on January 6, 1866, the *Continental* cast off from New York with more than 300 women aboard, bound for the frontier. It wasn't a cruise-ship crossing. By the time they reached South America, the first mate was in chains for murdering a seaman. The food was horrible; for a 17-day stretch the menu was boiled beans and tea made of salt-water.

But it wasn't such a terrible crossing that romance was impossible. Mercer fell for one young lady, who promptly rebuffed the luckless hero. So he transferred his intentions to another woman, who accepted his proposal; they were married as soon as they arrived in Seattle.

When the ship called in San Francisco it almost caused a riot. Hundreds of lonely or curious men rowed boats out for a look at the women—one really anxious fellow climbed up a rope hanging over the side, but Mercer knocked the man back into San Francisco's cold bay. Ministers and do-gooders,

believing the newspaper stories that had preceded the ship, tried to talk the women into leaving.

And Ben Holladay wasn't through with his piracy—he refused to take the women on to Puget Sound. Mercer was again on the street without any money; desperately, he wired the territorial government for money and in return he received a rather long—collect—telegram of congratulations.

Everyone finally booked passage aboard the schooner *Tanner,* and at each stop on the way north rumors of lynch parties awaiting Mercer grew. A minister suggested that he hide in the hold of the ship and stay there until the excitement of their arrival died down.

But Mercer instead stood on the bow of the ship as it docked, and his bluff worked: everyone was too engrossed in the arrival of the brides to bother with Mercer; all except one of the women were married within months.

But the debtors caught up with Mercer, and although they didn't lynch him, they excluded him from the city's social and business community. Feeling old, cold, and very poor, Asa Mercer left Seattle shortly thereafter and showed up at various other cities around the West, his enthusiasm back at full throttle, his belief in the future of the West always strong.

The intermittent railroad service of the '80s and highly successful lumber and coal export businesses encouraged a phenomenal population boom: from 3,500 in 1880 to 43,000 in 1890. The city's quality of life also improved rapidly, with the grading and planking of streets and sidewalks, the installation of sewer systems, electric lights, and telephones, and home mail delivery. Horse-drawn streetcars were quickly replaced by the electric variety.

Chinese workers began arriving in the 1860s; by the mid-1880s they numbered more than 500. Anti-Chinese sentiment rose as whites feared that cheap Chinese labor would cost them their jobs; the ensuing riots convinced most of the Asian laborers to flee. Judge Thomas Burke and others tried to maintain control and ultimately some Chinese remained.

The Great Fire
On June 6, 1889, 58 city blocks—the entire downtown area—were destroyed by the Great Seattle Fire. When a burning pot of glue tipped over inside a cabinet shop about 2 p.m., flames spread within minutes to an adjoining wooden liquor storeroom. Within a half-hour the entire city was threatened. Then, just when the flames were nearly under control, the hydrants abruptly dried up; firefighters tried to stop the blaze by blasting structures in the fire's path, to no avail. Jacob Levy refused to surrender his house; his 70-man bucket brigade repeatedly doused it, while a man in the street laid 10-to-one odds that the house would burn down. Levy won.

Firemen threw burning sidewalks over the cliff, ripped up roadway planking, and fought the flames with bucket brigades; the fire was finally contained by 8:30 that night. The next morning it was decreed unanimously that wooden structures would be forever prohibited in the burnt district. Business was conducted under canvas tents until the rebuilding—in brick—was completed a year later.

Seattle always had problems with drainage: streets were mudflows much of the year, and toilets backed up when the tide came in (leading some entrepreneurial souls to construct two-level toilets). While rebuilding, a clever solution was suggested: raise the sidewalks! First-floor storefronts became basements, creating Seattle's Underground.

Despite Seattle's misfortune, its pioneers were a selfless group. On May 31, only a week before the big fire, Johnstown, Pennsylvania, was struck by a disastrous flood when a dam broke above town. More than 2,000 persons, of a population of 30,000, were killed. Seattle had voted to send a gift of $558 to the survivors. After the fire was contained, the city upheld its vote to send the money, believing Johnstown was worse off.

The Klondike Gold Rush

On August 16, 1896, George Washington Carmack and two Indian friends, Skookum Jim and Tagish Charley, discovered gold deep in Canada's Yukon on a creek that fed into the Klondike River near its confluence with the Yukon River. Word reached Fortymile, an Alas-

ka settlement on the Yukon River, and the town was almost entirely evacuated as the miners hurried to stake a claim. A year later, when the first 68 wealthy prospectors and their gold arrived in the Lower 48, the "Klondike Gold Rush" began.

The first ship to return, the *Excelsior,* arrived in San Francisco on July 15, 1897, and created some interest, but Californians knew all about gold rushes and weren't enthusiastic; the coastal steamer *Portland* arrived in Seattle two days later. Beriah Brown, a reporter on the *Seattle Post-Intelligencer,* hitched a ride on a tug and met the ship when it cleared customs at Port Townsend. He wrote that the ship was laden with "a ton of gold"; actually more than two tons left the ship in suitcases, crates, and coffee cans. Brown's words were electrifying. The rush was on: fathers left their families and even Seattle's mayor resigned to seek his fortune in the Klondike.

The Klondike trip wasn't an easy one: a 1,000-mile sea voyage to Skagway, Alaska, then an arduous hike over the snowy 33-mile Chilkoot Pass and White Pass to Lake Bennett, where would-be prospectors slapped together all manner of craft for floating down the Yukon to the Klondike. The North West Mounted Police required that each prospector carry a year's supply of food plus necessary tools and clothing, leading to the catchphrase, "a ton of gold, a ton of goods."

turn-of-the-century Seattle

SEATTLE/KING COUNTY CONVENTION AND VISITORS BUREAU

Erastus Brainerd, a former newspaperman, formed a publicity committee for the Seattle Chamber of Commerce and promoted Seattle as *the* place to get outfitted for the Klondike. Tacoma, Seattle, Vancouver, and Portland competed for the gold-rushers' dollars, but Brainerd ensured that Seattle received five times as much advertising as the other cities by writing feature articles, sending stacks of special newspaper editions to every postmaster in America, and encouraging citizens to write "letters to the editor" for papers worldwide.

Brainerd was enormously successful and Seattle emerged as the undisputed outfitting leader. The streets became open markets: clothing, condensed milk, dehydrated potatoes, and tools were piled high. Anything named "Klondike" was a potential big-seller, giving rise to "Klondike underwear" and "Klondike milk." Shady operators capitalized on their customers' eagerness: the Trans-Atlantic Gopher Company sold gophers allegedly trained to dig for gold. Siberian Huskies and other rugged breeds were enlisted to help pull dogsleds through the Alaskan snowfields. As the supply dwindled, families had to keep a close eye on their pets—dogs of every breed and size were stolen.

Though a handful of prospectors did strike it rich, the best claims had been staked long before most treasure-hunters arrived—leaving thousands of men worse off than when they began. Seattle emerged as the real winner, though: many of those who found gold returned to the city to establish businesses, while Seattle's "gold" was gained from outfitting the prospectors. It's said that half the $200 million in Klondike gold ended up in Seattle. More than any other event in the city's history, the Klondike Gold Rush made Seattle the major city in America's Northwest corner. From 1897 onward Seattle's future was closely allied with the north, leading one observer to say that Seattle was the only city in America to own a state (Alaska). But don't try convincing an Alaskan of that claim unless you're ready for a fight.

The Denny Regrade
One of the prominent features of Seattle is its steep hills that make walking and driving difficult. Many schemes were hatched to eliminate them, but only one ever came to fruition: the Denny Regrade project. Beginning in 1902, the city engineer directed high-pressure hoses that pumped water from Lake Union onto the steep slopes of Denny Hill near present-day Seattle Center, washing the soil into Elliott Bay and creating the waterfront of today. It took eight years to complete the project, but this is now one of the few relatively level parts of this otherwise hilly city.

Modern Seattle
At the start of WW II the Boeing Airplane Company employed only about 4,000 workers, manufacturing planes on a subcontract basis for the Douglas Company of California. Orders for Boeing's B-17 bomber, developed in the mid-'30s, swelled their employment to 30,000 by 1942. Sales peaked in 1944 at $600 million, while employment figures topped 50,000.

After the war, Boeing's sales fell sharply to $14 million in 1946, when 11,000 workers were laid off. Business picked up again during the Korean conflict and the U.S./U.S.S.R. Cold War with the sale of B-47s and, later, B-52s. William M. Allen, Boeing's postwar president, sought to end this roller-coaster economy by gambling all of the company's reserves on a commercial jet-powered plane, the 707, which permanently changed civilian air travel. Later successful developments—the 727, 737, and jumbo 747—helped establish Boeing as a worldwide leader in aviation.

Civic leaders decided to throw a party to celebrate Boeing's—and, simultaneously, Seattle's—success. City Councilman Al Rochester was a leading advocate of "Century 21," the 1962 World's Fair. Rochester wanted something very special; "not just another showcase for the state seal done in corn tassels, milk cans, and steers' rears." Senator Warren G. Magnuson somehow maneuvered $9 million out of the Pentagon for the event—which became the first world's fair to show a profit.

Century 21 drew over 9.5 million people and left the entire Seattle Center—the Space Needle, Monorail, Pacific Science Center, Opera House, Coliseum, Arena, etc.—as a legacy to the event. Today, the Seattle area is vibrant and prosperous, supported in part by such major corporations as Boeing, Microsoft, and Weyerhaeuser, but also by thousands of smaller businesses.

SIGHTS

Seattle is big enough to keep an intrepid visitor busy with weeks of explorations, and even residents who have spent years here still have not ventured into all it's nooks and crannies. Like most other large American cities, Seattle is a conglomeration of neighborhoods, each with an individual character that reflects both its inhabitants and its history. Because of this, you'll find sights organized respective of these neighborhoods. The attractions listed below include all of the better-known, along with several that stretch the envelope a bit. Whatever you do, try to see at least several of the following: Pike Place Market (this should be number one on every list), Pioneer Square, the Seattle Art Museum, the Seattle Marine Aquarium, the Space Needle, Pacific Science Center, Ballard Locks, Woodland Park Zoo, the Burke Museum, and the Museum of Flight. For even more fun, add in a tour of the Rainier Brewery, the ever-popular Underground Tour in Pioneer Square, a stroll around Green Lake or through the arboretum in Volunteer Park, or a visit to one of the city's funky and delightful neighborhoods: best bets are Capitol Hill (Broadway Ave.), University District, and Fremont, all discussed within this section.

DOWNTOWN

Downtown Seattle is a busy, almost frenetic place, with the expected mix of stuffed shirts, fashion-conscious men and women, and confused tourists. In recent years it has been transformed as tall skyscrapers fill its center. Tallest of all is the **Columbia Seafirst Center,** a sleek black structure that climbs 76 stories over downtown from the corner of 5th Ave. and Columbia Street. It dwarfs every other building in town. A glassed-in viewing deck on the 73rd floor provides a panorama of the entire region, but it will cost you $3.50 ($1.75 for seniors and kids). Ask at the information desk in the lobby for access. Also here is Metro Traffic Control, the nerve center for traffic reports on 19 local radio stations. With a view like this, it's hard to imagine a better locale to watch the traffic.

Another attention-grabbing skyscraper is the **Security Pacific Tower** at 4th Ave. and University St., a surprising structure that seems to balance on the tip of an upside-down pyramid. Two of the more attractive newer skyscrapers are the **Washington Mutual Tower** at 3rd and Seneca, and the **US Bank Centre** at 5th Ave. and Union Street. The latter of these contains a marvelous collection of colorful glass art, including a 12-foot-high piece by Dale Chihuly, America's best-known glass sculptor.

One of the primary downtown shopping areas centers around the intersection of 4th Ave. and Pine St., the location for Westlake Center, Nordstrom, and The Bon Marché (see "Shopping," below). The central plaza here is a gathering place for musicians and the lunch-hour crowd, though it is somewhat shrunken now that Pine St. is again open to traffic (Nordstrom demanded that the city re-open it in exchange for a major reworking of the old Frederick and Nelson store nearby—the voters agreed in 1995). The **Phoenix Rising Gallery**, 2030 Western Ave., tel. (206) 728-2332, is one of the finest in Seattle; you'll find many tables packed with jewelry, gifts, and artwork.

The **Paramount Theater** sits on Pine St. near the 9th Ave. intersection; in 1994-95, this dowdy 1929 theater was transformed into one of the grandest theaters on the West Coast. It provides a venue for Broadway plays, concerts, and other productions.

Downtown Transportation
Getting around downtown is easy—all Metro buses here are free every day between the hours of 6 a.m. and 7 p.m. The boundaries for this free area are S. Jackson St., I-5, Pine St., Battery St., and Alaskan Way. A bus tunnel runs through the center of the city, with downtown stops at Convention Place (9th and Pine), Westlake Center (4th and Pine), University Street (3rd and University), and the International District (5th and S. Jackson). The Monorail connects Westlake Center with Seattle Center.

At Sixth Ave. and Seneca over I-5, the aptly named **Freeway Park** is a solution to the blight

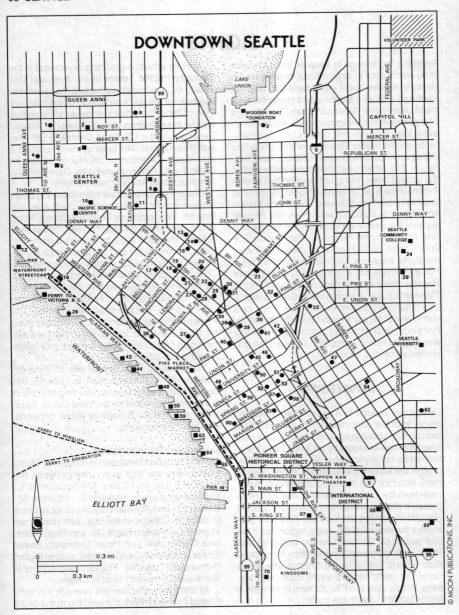

DOWNTOWN SEATTLE

© MOON PUBLICATIONS, INC.

DOWNTOWN SEATTLE

1. Green Tortoise Backpackers Guesthouse
2. Bahn Thai
3. Residence Inn by Mariott
4. Inn at Queene Anne
5. Coliseum
6. Opera House
7. AAA Auto Club of Washington
8. Tropics Motor Inn
9. Hampton Inn
10. Space Needle
11. Best Western Executive Inn
12. Myrtle Edwards Park
13. Best Western Loyal Inn
14. Seattle Travelodge
15. Days Inn Town Center
16. Old Spaghetti Factory
17. Two Bells Tavern
18. Regency
19. Ramada Inn
20. Jazz Alley
21. King's Inn
22. Sixth Ave. Inn
23. Greyhound Bus Depot
24. Intiman Theatre Co.
25. Egyptian Theatre
26. Edgewater Inn

27. Warwick Hotel
28. Claremont Hotel
29. Westin Hotel
30. Trailways Station
31. Vance Downtown Hotel
32. West Coast Camlin Hotel
33. West Coast Plaza Park Suites
34. Mayflower Park Hotel
35. Roosevelt Hotel
36. Cutters Bay House
37. St. Regis Hotel
38. Monorail Terminal/ Westlake Center
39. Nordstrom
40. Century Square
41. Sheraton Seattle Hotel
42. visitor information/ Convention Center
43. public fishing pier
44. Victoria Clipper to Victoria, B.C.
45. Rainier Square
46. Seattle Hilton Hotel
47. Sorrento Hotel
48. Seattle Marine Aquarium and Omnidome
49. Seattle Art Museum

50. Four Seasons Olympic Hotel
51. Holiday Inn Crowne Plaza
52. Pacific Plaza Hotel
53. Hotel Vintage Park
54. Frye Art Museum
55. Gray Line Water Sightseeing and public fishing pier
56. Hotel Seattle
57. public library
58. Stouffer Madison Hotel
59. Seattle Harbor Tours, and public fishing pier
60. Alexis Hotel and Arlington Suites
61. YMCA
62. Executive Court Suites
63. Argosy Tours and Ivar's Acres of clams
64. Washington State Ferry Terminal
65. Ye Olde Curiosity Shop
66. Comedy Underground
67. Amtrak
68. House of Hong
69. Nikko
70. F.X. McRory's

of a freeway roaring through the heart of a city. Located just outside the Convention Center, the park was built on a lid over part of that freeway and has greenery, waterfalls, fountains, and free summertime lunch concerts.

Seattle Art Museum

The Seattle Art Museum (SAM) opened its impressive new downtown building in December 1991 at a cost of $62 million. Located at 100 University St., SAM has 155,000 square feet of gallery space, a 299-seat auditorium, a 109-seat lecture hall, a gift shop, and a cafe. Out front is the distinctive 48-foot-high *Hammering Man* sculpture by Jonathan Borofsky; it fell over during installation in 1991 and had to be rebuilt. Inside, you climb a flight of marble steps past Chinese statuary to three floors filled with artwork. The second level contains exhibits that change every two months or so, while the two

top floors feature more permanent displays. The third floor is filled with works from Asia (a Japanese wood and paper house adds new meaning to the term "paper-thin walls"), Africa (wonderful beaded and feathered hats, a Mercedes Benz coffin, and several sexually explicit carvings), and Native American culture (incredible bentwood boxes, Chilkat robes, and shaman objects). On the fourth floor are works by American and European artists, including pieces by Georgia O' Keeffe, Claude Monet, Willem de Kooning, Henri Matisse, Rembrandt, Andy Warhol, and others. The Northwest Modern room here contains more avant-garde works, from the frivolously fun to the freakish.

SAM is open Tues.-Sun. 10 a.m.-5 p.m., and Thursday 10 a.m.-9 p.m., (closed Monday). Admission is $6 for adults, $4 for seniors and students, and free for kids under 12. The first Tuesday of every month is free, and your ticket always gets you into both the Seattle Art Museum and the Seattle Asian Art Museum in Volunteer Park, tel. (206) 654-3100 (see "Capitol Hill" later in this chapter for more information). Free docent-led tours of SAM are offered daily; see the information board in the lobby for the next tour. The museum also has an interactive CD-ROM tour that adds a new dimension to the museum. For $4, you get a Walkman-style CD player and CD disk with descriptions of the various pieces in the permanent collection, along with music, interviews, poetry, and more. You can either set it up as a standard tour, or punch in numbers below individual works for a description of the art. The museum also sponsors a lecture series, classes, programs on the arts, music, and films. Pick up their quarterly program guide for specifics, or call (206) 654-3100 for more information on the museum and upcoming exhibitions.

Frye Art Museum

This private museum was endowed by Charles and Emma Frye, who made some of their millions selling lard to the Germans after WW I and taking oil paintings as partial payment. The collection they amassed is—not surprisingly—heavy on works by late 19th century German artists, though it also has pieces by Edouard Manet, Louis-Eugène Boudin, and even Pablo Picasso's *Vase de Fleurs*. Each winter the Frye exhibits the finest works of the American Watercolor Society, with other shows every six weeks or so.

The Fryes had a meat packing plant along Seattle's waterfront—but no heirs. Their wills established a trust that would fund a free public art museum; no need to leave a donation here since the trust still owns extensive and highly profitable parcels along Seattle's waterfront. Lots of free parking across the street, too. The museum underwent major renovations in 1995. It is located near Capitol Hill at 704 Terry Ave., tel. (206) 622-9250; open Mon.-Sat. 10 a.m.-5 p.m., and Sunday noon-5 p.m.

PIKE PLACE MARKET

Every large city seems to have its iconographic symbols. In New York they include the Statue of Liberty and the Empire State Building, in San Francisco the Golden Gate Bridge and the cable cars, in Paris the Louvre and Eifel Tower. For Seattle, it's the Space Needle and Pike Place Market. The Space Needle is a place to take out-of-town visitors, but Pike Place is—as more than one writer has called it—the true heart and soul of Seattle, a sensory and social statement of why the city is such a livable place. Here visitors and locals buy the freshest fish and produce in town, listen to the mixed bag of street musicians, enjoy the parade of humanity, and explore a myriad of shops; it's hard not to love it.

History

Pike Place Market began in 1907, when the city set aside an area along the waterfront where

The monorail carries passengers to and from Seattle Center and downtown.

SEATTLE/KING COUNTY CONVENTION AND VISITORS BUREAU

Shoppers are drawn to Pike Place Market and stores along the hillclimb.

DIANNE BOUERICE LYONS

farmers could sell their products directly to consumers, cutting out the middlemen. That first day—August 17—only a half-dozen farmers showed up, but word quickly spread, and the market was an immediate hit. By 1937, more than 600 farmers, fish-mongers, and others were hawking their wares at the market. At least half of these merchants were Japanese-Americans. Consequently, when they were sent to internment camps in the 1940s, the market also suffered greatly.

After the war, the market continued to struggle; by the late '60s the numbers had dwindled to 60 or so old-timers. Developers salivated at this piece of choice downtown real estate, promising to level the ancient buildings and construct modern high-rises and parking garages. Fortunately, the people of Seattle had more sense than this. In a 1974 election, they voted two-to-one to not only keep the market, but also to turn it into an historic district. Today, the buildings are managed by Pike Place Market Preser-

vation and Development, and all vendors must pass a stringent set of rules that keeps the market in the hands of owner-operators, especially those offering traditional market services (unless they originated in the market, such as Starbucks). You'll never see a McDonald's here. The smaller temporary spaces are rented out on a daily basis, while the larger, more established businesses have leases with the management.

The Market

Initial appearances can be deceiving in the Pike Place Market. It's much larger than you might think, spreading over three levels in the Main Arcade, and up several blocks to include half a dozen other large buildings, each filled with additional shops. All told, the market contains more than 250 businesses spread over nine acres. For a market map and newsletter, head to the **information booth** near the market entrance on the corner of Pike St. and 1st Ave.; you can also purchase half-price tickets here for concerts and plays on the day of the show. The booth is open daily 10 a.m.-6 p.m. all year; the market itself is open Mon.-Sat. 9 a.m.-6 p.m., and Sunday 11 a.m.-5 p.m. Things are pretty slow early in the morning, giving you more time to explore without having to fight your way through the crowds. Just a few feet from the info booth is **Read All About It** newsstand, where you'll find all sorts of magazines, along with papers from such diverse locations as Tulsa, Fairbanks, New Zealand, and even Tacoma. Continue down this corridor to **Crêpe de France** for a quick and delicious spinach and cheese crepe, or drop into **DeLaurenti Market** for imported foods and wines, plus a gourmet deli.

The main focal point is beneath the famous "Public Market Center" neon sign. Enter here to meet **Rachel,** the fat bronze market pig/piggy bank that has been here since 1986. Drop a coin in to help support local charities; at last count Rachel had collected more than $35,000 for seniors, children, and the homeless. Check out the tiles covering the floor; they're imprinted with the names of those who donated money in the early 1980s to replace the worn old wooden floor. Even Ronald Reagan got a tile, though he never gave one thin dime; some local benefactor paid for his tile.

Follow the throngs of tourists to **Pike Place Fish,** right behind Rachel. You can't miss the famous flying fish (watch your head!), the raucous repartee, and the clowning around. It helps to be part showman to work here. Despite a competitor's complaint that "I can't see how throwing fish makes them taste any better," everything here is very fresh. For a bit less flair, but equally high quality, try one of the other three stalls selling fresh seafood in the market.

The building you're standing in is called the **Main Arcade,** and was the original market structure. Across the street are the Corner Market and the Sanitary Market buildings (the sanitary market received its name because horses were kept out). Several other buildings are also part of the market, but these are the core, and you could easily spend hours exploring their shops.

Be sure to walk downstairs in the Main Arcade to the "DownUnder Shops" that cover three less-touristy levels. You'll find all sorts of places lining the alleys: a magic shop, a comic book store, a tiny barber shop, and several antique shops, one of which sells museum-quality pieces from Asia.

Back on the main level, wander around to find **Tenzing Momo Herbal Apothecary** and **Market Spice,** or visit the **Athenian Inn,** tel. (206) 624-7166, one of the old market stalwarts and the place where several scenes in "Sleepless in Seattle" were filmed. Open since 1909, it still cranks out great red-flannel hash for breakfast and good seafood and burgers for lunch and dinner. Elliott Bay views are an added bonus. Another old-time favorite (it opened in 1908) is **Lowell's Restaurant,** where market locals still come for coffee every morning.

As you head north from here, you'll enter the **North Arcade,** where small tables are crowded with peddlers hawking artwork, jewelry, dried flowers, jams and jellies, T-shirts, fresh produce, and a myriad of other goods. More booths continue outside along the street.

The three connected buildings across the street—**Corner Market, Sanitary Market,** and **Post Alley Market**—are filled with many more shops. The **Three Girls Bakery,** in existence since 1912, is one of the market institutions, serving some of the best baked goods in town. A few other noteworthy shops in this group of buildings are: **Pike Place Market Creamery** with its old-fashioned coolers and fresh milk products; **Rasa Malaysia** with fresh and spicy Malaysian

meals to go; **Milagros,** selling Mexican folk art and handicrafts; **Sisters** with great grilled focaccia-bread sandwiches; the **Crumpet Shop** with English teas, soft crumpets, and sweet jams; **Left Bank Books** with leftist tomes strewn about; and the **Pike Place Flowers** stall that adds a splash of color to the corner of Pike and 1st.

Continue north from these buildings past Pine and Stewart Streets to the Stewart House and the Soames-Dunne Building, where the scents and sights will pull you inside. Here you'll find several delightful eating places: **Emmett Watson's Oyster Bar,** serving some of the finest oysters on the half shell; **Piroshky, Piroshky,** where you can watch them assemble delicious Russian treats; and **Cuchina Fresca,** with out-of-this-world garlic bread and big square chunks of Sicilian pizza.

This sampling barely touches on the variety of shops in the market; you'll also discover a high-quality butcher shop, a Birkenstock dealer, a parrot and reptile house, a Kosher deli, and even an ongoing rummage sale with old clothes and shoes.

Directly across from the market on the corner of 1st and Pike is **Fantasy Unlimited,** tel. (206) 682-0167. Tourists often wander in thinking this is another card shop but quickly discover that the cards (among other items) go well beyond the risqué. Inflated condoms cover a back wall (to show the various styles), sex toys and gag gifts crowd the shelves, and (upstairs) leather and chain fetish items share space with a body-piercing salon. There are lots of sleazy porn shops along 1st Ave., but this bright place is probably the only one where the seemingly mainstream public shops in the company of the tattooed, black leather, and nipple-ring crowd.

Tours and Parking

One-and-a-half-hour **Market tours** are available daily for $5; call (206) 682-7453 for more info. Leave your car in the parking lot below; it's nearly impossible to drive up Pike Place with lunch-hour pedestrians overflowing the sidewalks, and parking spaces are harder to find than an honest lawyer. Your best bet is to take the bus around town—it's free throughout downtown Seattle—but you can always find parking in the Market Parking Garage downhill from the Pike Place. Get your ticket validated at one of the merchants in the market.

THE WATERFRONT

Generally a sightseer's first waterfront stop, Elliott Bay's Piers 48-70 represent the main waterfront: restaurants, gift shops, museums, the aquarium, and harbor-tour departure points, connected by a sidewalk and the Waterfront Streetcar. The waterfront was made famous in Murray Morgan's *Skid Road,* written in 1951 about a rather different place. He called it:

A good, honest, working waterfront with big gray warehouses and trim fishing boats and docks that smell of creosote and seagulls and tugs and seafood restaurants and beer joints and fish stores—a waterfront where you can hear foreign languages and buy shrunken heads and genuine stuffed mermaids. . . where you can stand at an open-air bar and drink clam nectar, or sit on a deadhead and watch the water, or go to an aquarium and look at an octopus.

Getting Around

The **Waterfront Streetcar** consists of 1927 Australian-built trolleys that run along the waterfront from Pier 70 at the north end, past the Washington State Ferry Terminal at Pier 52, through Pioneer Square, and on to the Metro tunnel station in the International District. They operate every 20 minutes; weekday hours are 7:11 a.m.-11:10 p.m., weekend hours are 9:10 a.m.-11:40 p.m. Get a ticket for 85 cents ($1.10 in the commute hours) at the self-serve ticket machine at any of the nine streetcar stations along the route. It is valid for 90 minutes, and you can also use Metro passes and transfers. Call (206) 553-3000 for more information.

Park your car under the Alaskan Way Viaduct and try for a meter; as a last resort, pay the exorbitant fees at parking lots. The meters cost $1 an hour, which alone is cause enough to leave your car at a suburban park-and-ride.

Aquarium and Omnidome

A visit to Pier 59's **Seattle Marine Aquarium,** tel. (206) 386-4320, will give you an appreciation of the incredible diversity of sealife. The traditional part of the aquarium leads you past a "touch tank" filled with various tidepool creatures, and aquariums of various sizes containing everything from an octopus to an electric eel. Displays tell about the creatures and how humans are affecting their survival. A tropical reef exhibit makes you want to hop on a plane for Fiji. The real treat is outside, where you'll find large tanks containing harbor seals, sea otters, and northern fur seals, along with a salmon ladder and hatchery. Check the board to see when the next feeding time comes for the sea mammals. Ducks and shorebirds occupy another noisy section, but the star feature is an underwater dome where you sit surrounded by fish from the Sound. It's as if the tables have been turned and the humans are in a giant fishbowl looking outward at salmon, skates, halibut, rockfish, and other creatures. The Seattle Aquarium is open daily 10 a.m.-8 p.m. Memorial Day to Labor Day, and daily 10 a.m.-6 p.m. the rest of the year; admission is $7 adults, $5.50 seniors and disabled, $4.50 ages six to 18, $2.25 ages three to five, and free for ages two and under. The last entrance ticket is sold an hour before closing time.

Upstairs from the Aquarium is **The Museum of Sea & Ships,** tel. (206) 628-0860, a small collection of navigation instruments, ship models, nautical equipment, and various artifacts. It is open daily 9 a.m. to 7 p.m. Memorial Day through Labor Day and daily 10 a.m.-5 p.m. the rest of the year.

The **Omnidome,** also on Pier 59, tel. (206) 622-1868, lets you experience erupting volcanoes, outer space, foreign countries, and ocean excursions on their incredible 180-degree dome screen with six-channel sound. The 45-minute-long programs run continuously from 10 a.m. every day; admission is $6 for adults, $5 for seniors and ages 13-18, $4 for ages three to 12, and children under three get in free. They always have two different films; see both for an extra $2, or get a combination pass to both the Aquarium and Omnidome for $11 adults, $8.25 seniors and ages 13-18, $7.50 for ages six to 12, and $6.50 for ages three to five.

More Pier Peering

Public fishing is allowed at **Waterfront Park** on Pier 57, but have a look at the water before you decide to eat what comes out of it. Worth a stop is **Creative Northwest** at Pier 55; everything they carry has been caught, grown, or hand-crafted in the Northwest. Pick up Anacortes smoked salmon, Oregon glass and ceramic goblets, Mt. St. Helens ash ornaments and oil lamps, and gift packs with teas, jams, and chocolates. **Ye Olde Curiosity Shop,** a combination museum/gift shop on Pier 54, tel. (206) 682-5844, specializes in the bizarre: shrunken heads, mummies, the "Skinny Stubbs" human skeleton, a two-headed calf, plus inane souvenirs and tacky curios. Very touristy, and not nearly as interesting as Marsh's Free Museum in Long Beach.

The Edgewater, Pier 67, tel. (206) 728-7000, is Seattle's only hotel right on saltwater. It was recently renovated, and a good restaurant, Ernie's Grill, has been added. Pier 70 has more stores and restaurants, including **Whales World Gift Shop,** with whale-related T-shirts, books, toys, and more. **Myrtle Edwards Park,** at Alaskan Way and Broad St., has a one-mile path along the bay to Grain Terminal.

At the other end, Pier 36 hosts the **Puget Sound Vessel Traffic Service,** tel. (206) 286-5650, providing 24-hour weather and marine traffic information for boaters in Puget Sound and the Strait of Juan de Fuca. See a free slide show and take the 15-minute guided tour. Open daily 8 a.m.-4 p.m. The **Coast Guard Museum,** tel. (206) 217-6992, also on Pier 36, has nautical artifacts, models of Coast Guard cutters, historic photographs, and a 15-minute slide show. Open Monday, Wednesday, and Friday 9 a.m.-3 p.m., and Sat.-Sun. 1-5 p.m.; free. The Coast Guard has two 400-foot icebreakers and two 378-foot cutters that are homeported at Pier 36. They are generally open to tours on weekends 1-4:30 p.m.

Washington State Ferries depart Pier 52 for Winslow and Bremerton across the sound. The *Victoria Clipper* docks at Pier 63 between trips. Argosy tour boats leave from Pier 55. See "Transportation" later in this chapter for more information.

Coming to Pier 66 in 1996 is a new museum, **Odyssey Contemporary Maritime Museum,** which will be home for tour ships operating out of Seattle as well as a museum housing historic boats and exhibits reflecting Seattle's rich maritime history.

PIONEER SQUARE

If Pike Place Market is eclecticism gone mad, then Pioneer Square is eclecticism gone upscale: boutiques, art galleries, Oriental-carpet stores, and sidewalk cafes are nestled between corner missions; executives in tailored suits pass Occidental Park's homeless residents. In spite of frequent complaints about the aggressiveness of the panhandlers and drunks who reside in nearby flophouses and missions (or on the street), the 20-block restored historical district along 1st Ave., Yesler Way, and S. Main St., south of downtown, is one of Seattle's most varied areas. Get here from town center by riding one of the free buses along 1st Ave., or taking the waterfront trolley.

One of the more unusual sightings you're likely to make in Pioneer Square is police patrolling the area on mountain bikes—Seattle boasts the first bike cops in the nation. The southern edge of the Pioneer Square area abuts the International District and the Kingdome. The tall Venetian-style clock tower of Amtrak's **King Street Station** occupies the intersection of S. King St. and 3rd Ave. South. Other sights in the area include: **Waterfall Park** at 2nd Ave. S and S. Main St., where a cascade of water provides a break from the street noise (this was the site of the first UPS office, established in 1907) and the rather depressing **Occidental Park,** a cobblestone space with several totem poles and park benches occupied by men and women who survive on the streets or in nearby missions.

History
Pioneer Square itself is actually a triangle of land at the angled intersection of 1st Ave. and Yesler Way, with a beautiful turn-of-the-century iron and glass pergola, and a small park centered around a totem pole and a monument to Chief Seattle. The Tlingit totem is a replica of an original pole that was destroyed by an arsonist in 1938. The original pole was stolen on a fateful night in 1890 from Southeast Alaska's Tongass Island by a group of the city's leaders. After the original was burned, the city sent a check for $5,000 to carve a new one. The Tlingits reportedly cashed the check, and then sent a note

saying, "Thanks for finally paying for the first one. A new pole will cost another $5,000."

This is the oldest section of Seattle, although the center of activity has long since migrated north a half-mile or so. After the great fire of 1889, the area was rebuilt in brick buildings, many of which still stand here. Over the years, as businesses moved to newer places north of here, Pioneer Square became a center for cheap flophouses, drunks, and prostitutes. At its center was Yesler Ave., originally called Skid Road because it was used to drag logs to the shoreline—hence the term "skid row." By the 1960s, business leaders proposed cleaning up the mess in a massive urban renewal project that would flatten the old buildings to provide parking spaces for downtown. Fortunately, saner folks recognized the potential of the area, and in 1970 it was designated the Pioneer Square Historic District.

Klondike Gold Rush Park
The Klondike Gold Rush National Historical Park, 117 S. Main St., tel. (206) 553-7220, is Seattle's portion of a two-part national historical park commemorating the gold rush; the other section is in Skagway, Alaska. Housed in the 1901 Union Trust Annex, the Seattle portion of the park traces Seattle's role in the 1897 gold rush with films on the event—including Charlie Chaplin's *Gold Rush*—informative exhibits, wonderful old photos, and gold rush and natural history books. During the summer, there's always something going on here: ranger talks, gold-panning demonstrations, films, and guided walks on summer weekends (assuming the budget isn't axed more). Open daily (except Christmas, New Year's Day, and Thanksgiving) 9 a.m.-5 p.m.; free. Be sure to pick up the interesting map/brochure on the gold rush, with descriptions of historic buildings in Pioneer Square.

Visiting the Underground
Bill Speidel's Underground Tour is one of the city's most distinctive tours. From Doc Maynard's Public House at 1st Ave. and James St., you roam the Pioneer Square area above and below; a guide provides humorous anecdotes (often at the expense of Tacoma residents), along with local history. You'll learn about the speakeasies, gambling parlors, illegal lotteries,

and opium dens that once occupied this section under the streets. You'll also hear how the city's tidewater location created all sorts of problems for early residents, particularly those who tried to flush toilets on an incoming tide, and how the "seamstress tax" was applied to single women working out of the Sweet Home Boarding House in the red-light district. The tour ends shamelessly in a museum/gift shop where you're encouraged to purchase such practical items as deluxe rubber rats and cockroaches. These very popular one-and-a-half-hour tours leave several times daily; $5.50 for adults, $4 for students, $4.50 for seniors, $2.50 for kids. Reservations recommended; phone (206) 682-1511 for a schedule, or 682-4646 for reservations.

Smith Tower
At 42 stories, this was the tallest building west of the Mississippi when completed in 1914 and remained Seattle's tallest building for several decades. Now dwarfed by neighboring skyscrapers, you can still view Pioneer Square and downtown from its 35th-floor outdoor observation deck. The Chinese Room here contains a chair that was a gift from the Empress of China. Get here by riding the handsome antique elevator ($2 for adults, $1 for seniors and kids), the only one in Seattle with a real live elevator operator. Atop the tower, look for the fish-shaped windsock, a tradition begun by Ivar Haglund, the founder of Ivar's Acres of Clams, who owned this building at one time. It caused quite a stir in the 1970s when he put the windsock up in place of an American flag.

Shops
Get a free brochure on Pioneer Square at the park office or at the cash register of almost any area merchant; it will have a map pointing out historical buildings in the area. The best known shop in the area is the spacious **Elliott Bay Book Company,** 101 S. Main St., tel. (206) 624-6600, with its downstairs cafe. This Pioneer Square bookstore, incidentally, is *the* quintessential place for Seattle bibliophiles. Other intriguing shops include: **Merchants Cafe,** 109 Yesler Way, tel. (206) 624-1515, the city's oldest restaurant (it opened in 1890); **Foster/White Gallery,** 311 1/2 Occidental S, tel. (206) 622-2833, featuring works by the world famous glass

artist Dale Chihuly, along with the paintings of Mark Tobey and Morris Graves; **Iris Fine Crafts,** with handcrafted jewelry, pottery, glassware, and gifts at 317 1st Ave. S; **Sound Winds Air Arts,** a colorful windsock showcase at 206 1st Ave. S; and **Northwest Gallery of Fine Woodworking,** 202 1st Ave. S, exhibiting wood sculpture and furniture produced by Northwest artists.

One of the best ways to enjoy the collection of art galleries in Pioneer Square is to join the art crowd for the **First Thursday Gallery Walk.** All galleries hold their openings on the evening of the first Thursday of each month.

INTERNATIONAL DISTRICT

Sometimes called "Chinatown," this part of Seattle has long been home to people from all over Asia, including those of Japanese, Korean, Chinese, Filipino, and Vietnamese ancestry. The International District is easy to reach; just catch one of the free buses and ride through the tunnel to the International District bus tunnel station, where outsized origami pieces decorate the walls.

All roads lead to **Hing Hay Park,** a small city park with a colorful pagoda-style Chinese pavilion donated by the city of Taipei. Watch out for the hundreds of pigeons that get fed all the time here, and coat the pavilion with their droppings.

Wing Luke Memorial Museum at 414 Eighth St. S, tel. (206) 623-5124, has changing exhibits of Asian folk art displayed Tues.-Fri. 11 a.m.-4:30 p.m., and Sat.-Sun. noon-4 p.m.; admission $2.50 for adults, $1.50 for seniors and kids. Free on Thursday.

The International District lacks the crowded intensity of San Francisco's Chinatown, but the streets are lined with hole-in-the-wall restaurants, shops selling imported goods, and Asian grocers. You can easily find a filling lunch for under $5; walk around to see what looks interesting. **Kobe Terrace Park,** a community garden, lines the hillside above the International District; it is capped by a concrete lantern given to Seattle by its Sister City of Kobe, Japan. (The devastating 1995 Kobe earthquake hit home in Seattle; many people in the International District have relatives there.)

King St. is the heart of the district; Chinese shops line both sides. The largest Asian supermarket in the Northwest, **Uwajimaya,** at King and Sixth Streets, tel. (206) 624-6248, sells everything from high-quality groceries to Japanese furniture. Step inside for an eye-opening venture across the Pacific and excellent light meals in the Japanese deli.

SEATTLE CENTER AND BELLTOWN

The flat section of land just north of downtown was originally a steep bluff, but the Denny Regrade washed the hill away, allowing for its development. Now called Belltown, the mixed commercial and residential neighborhood is rapidly becoming a funky center for the city's music and arts scene. The biggest attraction for visitors here is Seattle Center, a 74-acre legacy of the 1962 World's Fair that is home to the Space Needle. Seattle Center is an odd mishmash of attractions, designed with the Jetson's-era architecture of the early '60s. The best way to venture into this space-age world is aboard the dated but fun **Monorail,** the elevated train (of sorts) that connects trendy Westlake Center at 5th and Pine with passé Seattle Center. This strange contraption was considered a model for transportation in its day, but Seattle's is the only one to ever make it beyond the amusement park (Disneyland has one, of course). The Monorail costs adults 90 cents for the 90-second ride; it runs each way every 15 minutes and is open daily 9 a.m.-midnight in the summer, and Sun.-Thurs. 9 a.m.-9 p.m., Fri.-Sat. 9 a.m.-midnight, the rest of the year.

Although it attracts many adults, Seattle Center is evolving into a major place for children. In addition to the carnival rides and a fast trip up the Space Needle, the area includes a fantastic Children's Museum, the Pacific Science Center with hands-on displays, and the Seattle Children's Theatre. For general information about Seattle Center and upcoming events, call (206) 684-8582.

Space Needle

The Space Needle is one of Seattle's trademarks, a 605-foot tower topped by a flying saucer viewing deck and restaurant. Elevators blast you to the top where you can walk out on the observation deck for a 360-degree view of downtown Seattle, of planes flying by, and of the Cascades, Mt. Rainier, and the Olympics on a clear day. On a rainy day you'll most likely be able to make out downtown. Detailed signboards describe the buildings and other surrounding features.

The Space Needle is privately owned and highly commercialized. Nobody is here to act as a guide or answer questions. Two mediocre restaurants are a level below, and the main observation deck is crowded with tacky gift shops, a pricey lounge, video games for the kids, penny-mashing machines, and a bland print gallery. Be sure to purchase the official snack food of the Space Needle (M&M's) and official ice cream bar (Dove) while here. But the spectacular view is hard to beat. The elevator ride up and back costs a sky-high $7 adults, $6.50 for seniors, $3.50 for ages five to 12, and free for younger kids. (If you have restaurant reservations, the ride is free.) Call (206) 443-2111 or (800) 937-9582 for more information. The observation deck is open daily 8 a.m. to midnight. Get here on most Thursdays between 9 a.m. and 10 a.m. to watch "Halo Man" Mark Puchalski change the light bulbs 500 feet above the ground. And yes, he does have a safety line.

Pacific Science Center

The Pacific Science Center, tel. (206) 443-2001, began as the U.S. Science Pavilion at the 1962 World's Fair. Its distinctive white concrete arches over pools and fountains are a landmark. This hugely popular museum (over 1.2 million visitors a year) is a family favorite, with more than 200 hands-on exhibits of all sorts (including the chance to play virtual basketball or hang glide over a virtual city), a colony of naked mole rats (cold-blooded mammals that live in ant-like colonies with a breeding queen and lots of workers), a planetarium, and a ménage of memorable mechanized Mesozoic dinosaurs. The fountains outside are filled with fun water toys that blast jets of water at all sorts of objects; there's even a spinning two-ton granite ball with a small nozzle. Also here is the high-rail bike with demonstrations most days. The big IMAX theater at Pacific Science Center—one of 100 in the world—uses large-format film to create dramatic and detailed movies. The Science Center

The Pacific Science Center attracts almost one million people every year

ERIN HOGAN

also has a changing series of exhibits and special events, including a popular **Model Railroad Show** in late November and the kids-favorite **Bubble Festival** in mid-August.

Admission to the Pacific Science Center is $6 adults, $5 ages six to 13 and seniors, $3.50 ages two to five, free under age two. Admission to the IMAX Theater or the popular laser shows are an additional $2 each. (Free to seniors on Wednesday.) Pacific Science Center is open daily 10 a.m.-6 p.m. mid-June through Labor Day, and Mon.-Fri. 10 a.m.-5 p.m., Sat.-Sun. 10 a.m.-6 p.m. the rest of the year. Closed only for Thanksgiving and Christmas. If you don't want to wait in long lines for the featured attractions (such as virtual reality), try to come Sunday morning or Mon.-Wed. afternoons when things tend to be a bit quieter.

Seattle Children's Museum

Downstairs in Center House is the delightful Seattle Children's Museum, tel. (206) 298-2521. After a major expansion in 1994, the museum now covers almost the entire bottom level with wacky and fun exhibits that manage to simultaneously educate children. Each year, 200,000 kids drag their parents through the 32,000 square feet of play space. Favorites include a theater where children can dress up in costumes, a maze of pipes and pulleys to play with, a pretend doctor's office, a time machine to go back to ancient Greece or a Mayan village, a mountain wilderness where they can climb a mountain or dress up as an animal, and an Imagination Station where kids work with artists on murals, puppets, masks, or tiles. Every day there's some sort of hands-on workshop, and the gift shop sells educational toys. Do kids like this place? The average stay is three hours; try getting any child to do anything for three hours! This magical place is open Tues.-Sun. 10 a.m.-5 p.m. Admission is $4.50 for adult or kids. Adults must accompany children under 12.

Other Sights

Fun Forest, Seattle Center's amusement park, is open late spring to early autumn. Nothing special here, but kids like it; call (206) 728-1585 for details. Popular with a slightly older set is **Skateboard Park** with ramps for all sorts of stunts. On the grounds are two **dinosaur topiaries,** life-sized creatures composed of 7,000-plus ivy plants and 11,000 pounds of sphagnum moss. The larger of the two is said to be the largest topiary in the world.

The **Center House,** a former armory that was reborn as a shopping and fast-food mall for the World's Fair, is lined on two levels with fast-food restaurants. A major renovation in 1995 should vastly improve this space, along with the nearby **International Fountain,** formerly a laughingstock. The basement of Center House is home to the hugely successful Seattle Children's Museum (described above). A three-ton slab of the **Berlin Wall** stands near Center House, a gift from a German businessman in 1991.

Seattle Center also contains the completely remodeled **Coliseum,** home of the NBA's Seattle SuperSonics; the **Bagley Wright Theater** where the Seattle Repertory Theater performs; and the **Opera House,** home of the Seattle Opera, Seattle Symphony, Seattle Youth Symphony, and Pacific Northwest Ballet (see "Performing Arts," later in this chapter).

Coming in the future is the **Jimi Hendrix Museum,** a high-tech $50 million structure to be built on Broad St. near the Space Needle in memory of the Seattle-born musician who died in 1970. The project will feature Hendrix artifacts (including his Fender Stratocaster used to play "The Star-Spangled Banner" at Woodstock), a 500-seat theater, a professional recording studio, a multimedia library, and interactive hands-on technology to create your own music. The museum is the brainchild of Paul Allen, the billionaire cofounder of Microsoft, who is also putting a large amount of money into the venture. Jimi Hendrix is buried in his family plot in Renton (see the Southern Puget Sound chapter).

LAKE UNION

Lake Union is a natural lake that was transformed early in this century when canals were dug linking Lake Washington, Lake Union, and Puget Sound. The Chittenden Locks provide boat access from Puget Sound into Lake Union. For many years Lake Union was treated mostly as an industrial area that floated. On the north shore stood a glum plant that manufactured gas. The south shore was dominated by boatyards and a Navy Reserve station, and parts of the east shore were (and still are) used by the federal government for its research vessels. The east shore also originally included a clutter of extremely modest cottages and some shacks that rested atop barrels, logs, and anything else that floated.

The western shore was devoted to boatyards and a seaplane base—it wasn't much then, but you oughta see it now. The lake's potential as an urban neighborhood is almost completely realized. The old gas plant has become Gasworks Park, one of the most imaginative parks in America. Most of the debris has been removed from the shores, and where once you saw only greasy clutter you now see people, lots of people. The only drawback to its success is that ordinary folks and creative types, who invented the houseboat neighborhoods, can no longer afford to live there. It has become one of the trendiest addresses in Seattle. Houseboats, some nearing the $1 million price tag, have taken over most of the eastern shore and part of the northwestern end. The extreme southern end is a mixture of expensive docks, a shopping center called Chandler's Cove, the Center for Wooden Boats, and the Maritime Heritage Center.

The remainder of Lake Union has been improved enormously with several restaurants, an occasional art studio (the world-renowned glass artist **Dale Chihuly** has his studio and workshop here (see "Stanwood" in the Northern Puget Sound chapter for information on his famous Pilchuck Glass School), and a series of tiny street-end parks. **Chandler's Cove** has several restaurants. **Cucina! Cucina! Italian Cafe** is the largest and intentionally one of the noisiest restaurants in Seattle. Other restaurants in Chandler's Cove include Duke's Chowderhouse, Benjamin's, I Love Sushi, and Opus Too.

Maritime History

The south end of Lake Union is home to a number of history-oriented organizations. The **Center for Wooden Boats,** tel. (206) 382-2628, restores and maintains a fleet of historic rowboats and sailboats. Take a class here to learn about wooden boat building, or rent one of the boats to sail or row around the lake for an afternoon. The 1922 steamer, *Virginia V,* last of Puget Sound's "Mosquito Fleet" (so named because they looked like mosquitoes on a puddle) and a National Historic Landmark, has taken up residence next-door at Chandler's Cove. She is available for cruises and charters, tel. (206) 624-9119. Chandler's Cove also has historic maritime photos and ship models on display.

The small **Maritime Heritage Center,** tel. (206) 447-9800, displays vintage wooden boats that you can look over while volunteers are at work on restoration projects. The star here is the *Wawona,* built in 1897, and the first ship in America to be listed as a National Historic Site. This was the largest three-masted sailing schooner built in North America and one of only two such vessels still in existence (the other is in San Francisco). The *Wawona* is open for self-guided public tours daily ($1 adults, 50 cents kids). The restoration process is slow, partly because it is nearly impossible to get wood of the same quality; nearly all the virgin forests are gone. (You don't see planks six inches by eight inches and up to 120 feet long today!)

Built on the site of a former gas plant, **Gasworks Park** at N. Northlake Way and Meridian Ave. N is the world's only industrial site conversion park. Amidst a great deal of controversy, architect Richard Haag incorporated much of the original rusting gas equipment into the park's landscaping, including a play barn kids (and the homeless) love. Enjoy the views of Seattle and Lake Union from the industrial equipment and fly a kite from the hills built into the park. The paved and very popular **Burke-Gilman Trail,** begins west of Gasworks, skirts Lake Washington, connects to the Sammamish River Trail, and ends in Redmond's Marymoor Park, 24 miles away.

CAPITOL HILL

Capitol Hill is a study in sharp contrasts. The hill itself is one of the most prestigious old neighborhoods in Seattle, with countless mansions and stately older homes, quite a few of which are now elaborate bed-and-breakfast inns. The campuses of Seattle Central Community College and Seattle University sit on the south end of Capitol Hill, providing a youthful flavor to the area. There are two commercial centers for the area: a small, fairly quiet strip along 15th Ave. E, where you'll find several excellent eateries and shops, and the busy, on-the-edge Broadway Ave. E stretch. Because of a strong gay and lesbian presence, Broadway has been likened to San Francisco's Castro District, but it could also be Berkeley's Telegraph Avenue. It's a great place to people-watch, and to catch up on the latest fashion statements for the youthful art crowd. You're guaranteed to see more black leather skirts and jackets, frenzied florescent green hair, nose rings, tattoos, and pink triangles here than anywhere else in Seattle. The center of this buzz is **Broadway Market,** a thriving set of offbeat shops with—for some reason—a big Fred Meyer store occupying the back half. Buy magazines at Bulldog News, get a glass of wheatgrass juice at the arty Gravity Bar, pick up an out-of-the-closet T-shirt or silver nipple ring at the Pink Zone, buy half-price concert tickets at Ticket/Ticket, or get a blast of latte at B&O Espresso. Interesting artworks are displayed on the upper level. Walk down the street in either direction and you'll discover artist Jack

Mackie's amusing **Dancers Series: Steps,** bronze footprints of various dances embedded in the sidewalk.

Volunteer Park
This Capitol Hill park (enter from 14th or 15th Ave. E) has 44 acres of lawn, a concrete reservoir, and a number of interesting attractions. A 75-foot brick **water tower** is open daily; climb its long spiral staircase for a great view of town. On the other side of the park is the glass **Conservatory,** built in 1912 and filled with colorful plants of all kinds. One room houses cacti, others contain ferns, bromeliads, and seasonal displays. The central space contains a gorgeous collection of orchids. There's always something in bloom at the Conservatory, making this a great, steaming-warm place to visit on a rainy winter day. The Conservatory is open daily 10 a.m.-7 p.m. from May to mid-September, and daily 10 a.m.-4 p.m. the rest of the year.

The centerpiece of Volunteer Park is the **Seattle Asian Art Museum,** tel. (206) 654-3100, a recently opened center for works from China, Japan, Korea, and south Asia. (This 1933 artdeco building was the location of the Seattle Art Museum until it moved downtown in the early 1990s.) Exhibits cover two spacious wings, including rooms with Japanese folk art, Indian Mughal art, Quing dynasty Chinese art, and Korean art. Of particular interest are the beautiful Japanese screens, the bronze Buddhist sculptures, and the collection of intricate Chinese snuff bottles. The museum is open Tuesday, Wednesday, and Fri.-Sun. 10 a.m.-5 p.m., Thursday 1-9 p.m. Free tours are offered daily at 2 p.m., except Thursday, when the tour is at 7 p.m. Admission costs $6 for adults, $4 for seniors and students, and free for kids under 12. This fee lets you in both the Asian Art Museum and the Seattle Art Museum downtown on the same day. The first Tuesday of each month is free for both of these. A small gift shop sells books and other items, and a cafe has light meals.

Just north of Volunteer Park is **Lakeview Cemetery,** tel. (206) 322-1582, where many of the city's early residents are buried, including Doc Maynard, and the daughter of Chief Seattle. Most folks come here, however, to visit the gravesite of martial artist and actor **Bruce Lee,** who died in 1973. His son, Brandon Lee, also a martial artist and actor, is buried here as well. He died in 1993 while filming *The Crow.*

QUEEN ANNE AND MAGNOLIA

Queen Anne is a small neighborhood crowning the tallest hill in Seattle. Given the commanding vistas from this location, it comes as no surprise that the captains of industry built mansions here at the turn of the century. Many of these spacious and pretentious old homes are still here, along with a few cobblestone streets, but alongside are other, less ostentatious homes that give Queen Anne a comfortable atmosphere. Mount Rainier, downtown Seattle, the Olympics, and the harbor can all be seen from tiny **Kerry Park** at W. Highland Dr. and 2nd Ave. W on the south slope of Queen Anne Hill. Especially popular with photographers in search of picture-postcard shots of Seattle. The upscale **Queen Anne Thriftway,** 1908 Queen Anne N., tel. (206) 284-2530, has to be one of the friendliest grocery stores anywhere; it's hard to get down the aisles without getting a smile from an employee or patron.

West of Queen Anne is the similar Magnolia neighborhood, with a wonderful shoreside route (Magnolia Dr.) along the north edge of Elliott Bay to Discovery Park. **Magnolia Park,** perched upon a high bluff, is a great place for views of Puget Sound and the Olympics and a favorite place to watch the ships sailing by and the sun setting over the Sound.

Discovery Park
Located five miles northwest of downtown in the Magnolia District, the 535-acre Discovery Park juts out into Puget Sound. In Discovery—Seattle's largest city park—you'll discover an "urban wilderness" with a wild feeling that belies its location next to two million people. The park features a 2.8-mile **loop trail** through forest and meadow, with access to two miles of Puget Sound beaches, plus the half-mile interpretive **Wolf Tree Nature Trail.** Discovery Park's West Point is reputedly Seattle's best birding spot, with more than 150 kinds of birds, including frequent sightings of loons, grebes, cormorants, terns, and other marine birds.

Discovery Park is located on what was originally **Fort Lawton,** a defensive base begun in the late 1890s as a place to protect Puget Sound. It served mainly as a shipping center early in this century, and in WW II as a vital processing base for more than a million troops en route to the Pacific, the second busiest point of embarkation on the West Coast. At it's peak, the fort contained a small city's worth of buildings, and the mess hall bragged that it could feed 12,000 troops in an hour. Things slowed down after WW II and the Korean War, and the fort was declared surplus property and given to the city of Seattle. In March of 1970, 500 Indians invaded the grounds, claiming the old fort site as a Native American cultural center. It took two battalions of Army troops and 119 arrests (including actress Jane Fonda) to quell the protest. Eventually, the city agreed to set aside 20 acres for what is now the **Daybreak Star Arts and Cultural Center,** tel. (206) 285-4425. A small collection of art is inside, but the building is mainly used for Native American events, including a **salmon bake and art market** the second Saturday of each month.

The rest of Fort Lawton became Discovery Park in 1972. Quite a few of the fort's structures remain, including more than a dozen from the earliest days. An interesting walking tour booklet detailing the fort and its history is available at the park's **visitor center,** open daily 8:30 a.m.-5 p.m. all year. They offer free Saturday afternoon nature walks at 2 p.m., along with a variety of classes and special events; call (206) 386-4236 for details.

BALLARD AND SHILSHOLE BAY

The section of Seattle called Ballard was established in the 1880s by Capt. William R. Ballard, and had grown to more than 15,000 people by the early part of this century. After a long battle over access to drinking water (Seattle had it, Ballard didn't; Seattle wanted to annex Ballard, Ballard wanted to stay independent), the citizens finally gave up and voted to join Seattle in 1907.

Ballard and nearby Shilshole Bay were the Nordic section of Seattle when immigration from Norway and Sweden peaked from 1890 to 1910.

By the turn of the century, Nordic immigrants made up a quarter of Seattle's wood industry workforce and also significantly contributed to mining, farming, fishing, and shipbuilding. Sivert Sagstad established his Ballard Boat Works in Shilshole Bay four months after his arrival and built more than 300 wooden boats. Ballard still retains much of its Scandinavian heritage, although like most of the city, the ethnic lines are becoming more and more blurred. Downtown Ballard has Norwegian and Swedish flags along the street, plus several Nordic shops: **Norse Imports Scandinavian Gift Shop,** 2016 N.W. Market St., tel. (206) 784-9420; **Olsen's Scandinavian Foods,** 2248 N.W. Market St., tel. (206) 783-8288; and **Scandie's,** 2301 N.W. Market St., tel. (206) 783-5080 (real lutefisk and Swedish pancakes). But you'll also find teriyaki and burrito places from newer immigrants.

Nordic Heritage Museum

A spacious old red brick grade school (built in 1907) has been transformed into the Nordic Heritage Museum, 3014 N.W. 67th St., tel. (206) 789-5707, the only museum of its kind in the nation. The first floor opens with a lengthy and educational exhibit on the "Dream of America," including the factors that pushed people to emigrate here in the 19th century. Upper levels cover the new life—in tenement slums, logging camps, and aboard fishing boats, with more exhibits on explorations by the Vikings, changing art and craft displays, and a gift shop with books on the homeland. The world's longest tapestry (295 feet) stretches through several second-floor rooms. The third floor has individual spaces for each of the Nordic countries: Norway, Sweden, Finland, Denmark, and Iceland. (Did you know Reykjavik, Iceland is a Sister City to Seattle?) Also in the building are a research library and the **Scandinavian Language Institute,** where you can join classes in Danish, Norwegian, or Swedish. The museum is open Tues.-Sat. 10 a.m.-4 p.m., Sunday noon-4 p.m.; admission is $3 for adults, $2 for seniors and students, $1 for kids six to 16 years, and free for kids under six.

Come to the museum in July for the **Tivoli festival** with a pancake breakfast, food and craft booths, entertainment, and beer garden. Another very popular event is the **Syttende Mai** parade on May 17, Norwegian Constitution Day; this is the largest Syttende Mai parade outside Norway.

Chittenden Locks

At the west end of Ballard, on N.W. 54th St., the **Hiram M. Chittenden Locks,** tel. (206) 783-7059, connect saltwater Puget Sound with freshwater Lake Washington via Lake Union. The locks (also known as the Ballard Locks) serve various functions: as a passageway for some 90,000 ships each year, as a way to prevent saltwater intrusion into the lakes, and as a fish ladder. Built between 1911 and 1917, the locks are managed by the U.S. Army Corps of Engineers, who have a visitor center here, tel. (206) 783-7059, open daily 10 a.m.-7 p.m. in the summer, and Thurs.-Mon. 11 a.m.-5 p.m. in the winter. Films are shown here every half-hour. They offer free hour-long guided tours every day at 1 p.m. and 3:30 p.m. in the summer, and on Saturday and Sunday at 2 p.m. in the winter months, or join the throngs and figure it out for yourself. The locks are one of Seattle's most heavily visited attractions; over a million people come here each year to watch container ships, tugs, tour boats, fishing boats, and pleasure craft make the transition between salt- and freshwater. They also come to see the salmon return home to spawn via big underwater windows along the fish ladder—best time to look for the salmon is late June to early September.

The locks are home to the controversial California sea lions, collectively named Herschel, who get much of the blame for sharply declining salmon and steelhead runs over the last decade. The sea lions do indeed eat fish heading up the fishpass, and all sorts of tricks have been attempted to keep them away. When they were trapped and flown to California, it took them only a few days to swim the 1,000-plus miles back to Salmon Bay. Environmentalists point out that the real culprit is not the sea lions, but the loss of spawning streams where development and logging have damaged much of the original habitat. They also note that most of the sea lions are here in the winter, affecting the steelhead, but not the summer salmon migration. Finally, in 1995 the U.S. Fish and Wildlife Service gave permission to kill a few sea lions at the locks to protect steelhead and salmon runs.

On the bank overlooking the locks are the **Carl S. English Jr. Botanical Gardens,** with more than 500 species of plants that English collected from around the world, plus native Northwest species. Included are pines, palms, oaks, dawn redwood, swamp flowers and trees, and a great collection of rhododendrons. The locks and gardens are free and are open daily 7 a.m.-9 p.m. A brochure details a self-guided tour through the gardens.

Along the Water

Across the Ballard Bridge in Salmon Bay is the **Fishermen's Terminal,** a bustling marina—largest in the Northwest—packed with some 700 commercial fishing boats. Ask around to buy seafood directly from the fishermen, or head to **Wild Salmon Fish Market,** 1900 W. Nickerson St., tel. (206) 283-3366, on the water's edge.

West of the Chittenden Locks, Seaview Ave. curves north along the shore past Shilshole Bay with several popular seafood restaurants—most notably Ray's Boathouse and Anthony's Homeport—and Seattle's major pleasure boat moorage, **Shilshole Marina.** Continue north to the enormously popular **Golden Gardens Park,** with one of the Sound's best bathing beaches.

North beyond this is **Carkeek Park,** N.W. 110th St., where you'll find a beautiful picnic area and playground, enjoyable hiking trails, and walks and talks at the Environmental Education Center, tel. (206) 684-0877. Puget Sound is accessible via a footbridge over the railroad tracks. If the tide's in, chances are the beach will be out.

FREMONT

The "Republic of Fremont" is Seattle's most offbeat neighborhood, a place with everything from a troll to a Russian rocket, and an attitude embodied in the official motto, the "Freedom to be Peculiar." The best way to reach Fremont is across the **Fremont Drawbridge,** according to the *Guinness Book,* the world's most active drawbridge, with over 500,000 openings. Be ready to wait; on busy weekends it often opens every 10 minutes or so.

Sights

Once you cross the bridge, you'll meet the city's most famous piece of public art, Richard Beyer's life-size group of commuters and a dog, *Waiting For The Interurban*. They are often decked out in used hats, balloons, or umbrellas contributed by passersby. Head one block east and turn up the road beneath the Aurora Bridge that towers above you. Two blocks uphill you'll meet the locally famous **Aurora Bridge Troll** in the act of devouring a VW bug. From here, walk to the official "Center of the Universe" at the corner of N. 35th St. and Evanston Ave., where a 53-foot-high **Russian rocket** prepares to blast off from one building. Inside the building you'll discover more weirdness. **Ah Nuts,** tel. (206) 633-0664, is packed with the bizarre—ghoulish dental tools, a wax version of Vincent Price, old cards, small caskets, neon lights, and all sorts of other junk. The **Almost Free Outdoor Cinema** brings B movies and cartoons to the wall behind here on Saturday nights in the summer; call (206) 282-5706 for details.

The monthly **First Saturday Gallery Walk,** showcasing artists at work, is one of Fremon's many attractions for art lovers. One of the most interesting is the **Edge of Glass Gallery,** 513 N. 36th St., tel. (206) 547-6551, where you can watch students and teachers blowing glass Thurs.-Sat. 11 a.m.-3:30 p.m. and Sunday noon-4 p.m. (The Seattle area is now considered an international center for glassblowing, rivaled only by Venice, Italy.)

Glamorama, 3414 Fremont Ave. N, tel. (206) 632-0287, is a must-see shop with strange and wacky toys (including voodoo dolls), retro garb, gifts, and cards from all over. It even has a walk-in wedding chapel (look up for the overhead cake) for those who want a ceremony with less pomp and more weirdness. **Fremont Hemp Co.,** on the corner of Fremont Place and N. 36th St., tel. (206) 632-4367, has clothing, paper, and other items made from the plant that also produces marijuana. Edible seeds (sterilized, alas) are also sold here. The **Fremont Sunday Market** brings a farmers market, jewelry, flea market, and live music to Fremont between May and Christmas. Other attractions include a big basement-level **Antique Mall** at Fremont Place and N. 35th St., tel. (206) 548-9140; **Tribe's** at 704 N. 34th St., tel. (206) 632-8842, with Native American arts and teas; and a fine new **Puget Consumers' Co-op** market on N. 34th Street.

Breweries

The **Redhook Ale Brewery,** 3400 Phinney Ave. N, tel. (206) 548-8000, offers fascinating 45-minute tours of their state-of-the-art brewery in Fremont, located in an old trolley car barn. The company has only been in existence since 1981, but it has become one of the most successful microbreweries in America—so successful, in fact, that they've actually outgrown the label and could better be called a mid-level brewery. In 1994, Anheuser-Busch bought 25% of the company, and they are planning a massive $30 million brewery in Portsmouth, New Hampshire. Redhook is best known for pub-style English bitter called Ballard Bitter, with the slogan "Ya sure ya betcha" on the label. This is where they brew Redhook draft beers; the bottled beers are now made in a sparkling new facility in Woodinville (see the Vicinity of Seattle chapter). Tours of the Fremont plant are given Mon.-Thurs. at 1 p.m. and 4 p.m., Friday at 1, 4, and 6 p.m., Sat.-Sun. at noon, 1:30, 3, and 4:30 p.m.; tasting is $1 (includes souvenir glass). The **Trolleyman Pub** here has excellent light meals and all their brews on tap. Reservations are not needed.

Hale's Ales, originally located in Kirkland, opened a new brewery next door to the Redhook brewery in 1995, and has an English-style pub, tours, and classes. All their beer goes into barrels, not bottles.

WALLINGFORD AND GREEN LAKE

Wallingford consists of a busy strip of shops just west of I-5 along N. 45th Street. This attractive neighborhood is close enough to the university to have a strong student flavor, but far enough away to mix in a more upscale atmosphere. Just north of Wallingford is Green Lake, almost a mile wide, and the center for recreation in the area. A small neighborhood shopping area centers around the intersection of N.E. Ravenna Blvd. and E. Green Lake Way North, with other places scattered around the shore. On the south side of the lake is the Woodland Park Zoo.

Woodland Park Zoo

Ranked among the nation's best, the Woodland Park Zoo has in recent years undergone a transformation from the old bars-and-cages version of zoos to a far more interesting place with re-created wildlife habitats from around the world. A five-acre "African savanna" has zebras, lions, and giraffes roaming freely (but not together, to the lions' chagrin). The nocturnal house is home to bats, sloths, and other creatures of the night. Also included are a new tropical Asia habitat and elephant forest where you can watch daily elephant logging demonstrations during the summer. Be sure to spend time at the Northern Trail section that leads past brown bears, river otters, bald eagles, mountain goats, gray wolves, and snowy owls, all in a relatively realistic setting (even the plants are native to Alaska). The sod-roofed Tundra Interpretive Center here has a video on Athabaskan village life and a re-created scientific research camp. Raptor demonstrations are given on summer weekends, and the big field in the middle is a good place for a lunch break. Anyone who has seen animals in the wild knows how cramped they must feel in any zoo, but things are much better than before, and the zoo does serve a vital educational function for the vast majority of people whose only other contact with wild animals is on a *National Geographic* special. A few disturbing cages filled with paranoid cats and monkeys remain from the bad old days, offering a stark contrast to the more spacious modern exhibits.

Situated between Phinney and Aurora, N. 50th and N. 59th, tel. (206) 684-4800, the zoo is open daily 9:30 a.m.-6 p.m. from mid-March to mid-October, and daily 9:30 a.m.-4 p.m. the rest of the year. You can remain on the grounds after the gates close, but you need to be out by 7:30 p.m. Admission is $7.50 for adults, $5 for ages six to 17, $5.75 for seniors and college students with valid ID, $2.25 for kids three to five years, and toddlers two and under are free. Parking is $3.50 parking fee ($2.50 in winter).

Next to the zoo is the **Woodland Park Rose Garden,** tel. (206) 684-4880, with hundreds of rose varieties spread over two acres.

Green Lake

An extremely popular three-mile paved bicycle, jogging, and skating loop—watch out for errant skateboards—encompasses Green Lake, where you can also sail and swim or rent a paddle-boat, canoe, kayak, sailboard, or rowboat. A kids-only fishing pier is at the east end of the lake. Crocodile hunting was popular here in 1986 when assorted reports of a lake creature took on the proportions of a Loch Ness Monster. The "monster" turned out to be a three-pound, 28-inch caiman that was shipped to a private breeder in Kansas City, and the lake was unofficially declared crocodile-free.

UNIVERSITY DISTRICT

The University District (better known as "The U District") is the center for student activity near the University of Washington's campus. The U District covers several blocks near the intersection of University Way NE ("The Ave") and N.E. 45th St., with inexpensive restaurants, CD and book stores, boutiques, coffeehouses, and other student-oriented places. This is probably the best place in Seattle to get a quick lunch or an ethnic dinner for just a few bucks. There are so many good places (especially Asian) that all you need to do is find one packed with students. Several shops are noteworthy along University, including the **Folk Art Gallery,** 4138 University Way NE, tel. (206) 632-1796, for items from around the world; the **University Bookstore,** 4326 University Way NE, tel. (206) 634-3400, for one of the largest bookstores in Washington; **Beauty and the Books,** 4213 University Way NE, tel. (206) 632-8510, a used book shop jammed with thousands of old volumes, along with four friendly cats; and **Bulldog News,** 4208 University Way NE, tel. (206) 632-6397, the largest magazine and newspaper seller in town.

University of Washington

The University of Washington is the largest and best-known university in the state and home to 35,000 students (8,000 of these are graduate students) during the school year, plus some 13,000 staff and 3,500 faculty members.

The university began on a 10-acre downtown site in 1861, when Seattle was little more than a cow town. It had a fitful time at first, and it closed several times before finally getting established. After statehood in 1889, the school began to

the Fine Arts building constructed for the 1909 Alaska-Yukon Pacific Expo

TACOMA PUBLIC LIBRARY

grow rapidly, and the campus was relocated to the present site. (The original location on University St. downtown is still university property.) The Alaska-Yukon-Pacific Exposition of 1909 was held on the UW campus, and in exchange for use of the campus, the fair's promoters constructed several permanent buildings and landscaped the grounds, making UW one of the nation's most beautiful campuses.

Today, UW is a major center for research in the fields of Asian languages, zoology, astronomy, cell biology, forestry, fisheries, physics, and many other areas of study. The school is highly competitive; incoming freshmen collectively have a 3.56 grade point average, and the graduate programs are widely acknowledged as some of the strongest in America. The UW library system contains more than five million volumes spread over two dozen campus libraries, making it one of the largest in the nation. The university's football and basketball teams often rank in the nation's top 20. Walk down University Way on the day of a football game, and you'll quickly learn that the team colors are purple and gold, and the mascot for the Huskies is an Alaskan Malamute. (By the way, the shorthand term for the Huskies is "Dawg," but never "Dog.")

The campus is an attractive place, with tall brick buildings, a central square (Red Square), fountains, views of Lake Washington, and shady, landscaped grounds. The **UW Visitors Information Center** at 4014 University Way NE, tel. (206) 543-9198, is open Mon.-Fri. 8 a.m.-5 p.m. all year. Stop here for information on campus tours, bus schedules, campus maps, upcoming sporting events, and other activities. On campus, the center of activity is the **Student Union Building.** For a taste of the good life, head to wide-open **Red Square** on a sunny spring day and join the throngs of sunseekers, Frisbee players, musicians, and brown-baggers. The square, by the way, is named for the color of its bricks, not the politics of its denizens.

Museums

The **Burke Museum** stands just inside the north entrance to the campus near the intersection of N.E. 45th St. and 17th Ave., and features an incredible collection of North American Indian artifacts and natural-history displays. The main floor focuses on Native peoples from the Northwest coast and includes some of the finest carved canoes and masks, woven cedar bark and grass baskets, and painted artifacts in existence. Especially notable are items from Chief Shakes, including his killer whale hat. Downstairs are exhibits of various fossils (including a dinosaur and an Ice Age ground sloth), colorful rocks and minerals, brilliant moths and butterflies, plus informative displays on old-growth forests. The museum also has changing exhibits on both floors, a museum store, and totem poles out front. Downstairs is a fine little coffeehouse—it becomes a study hall many afternoons during the school year. The Burke is open daily 10 a.m.-5 p.m., tel. (206) 543-5590. Entrance costs $3 for adults, $2 seniors or students, $1.50 ages six to 18, and free to kids under six, as well as UW students and staff.

Washington's oldest art gallery, the **Henry Art Gallery** on the west edge of the campus, is undergoing a massive $16.5-million expansion that will result in more than 47,000 square feet of exhibition space. Construction began in 1995, and the museum is expected to reopen early in 1997. In the past, the gallery has been a major facility for traveling exhibits of 19th- and

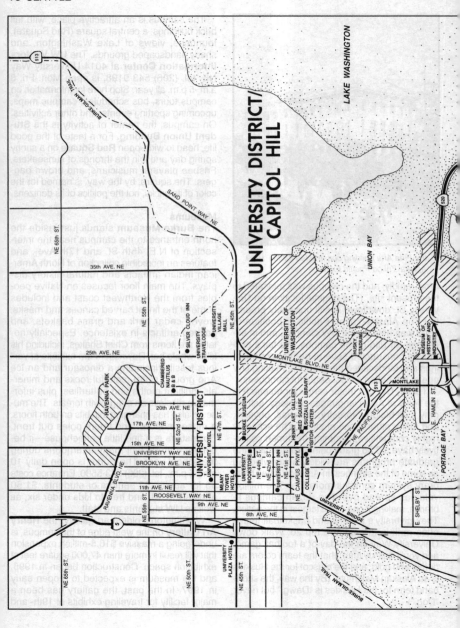

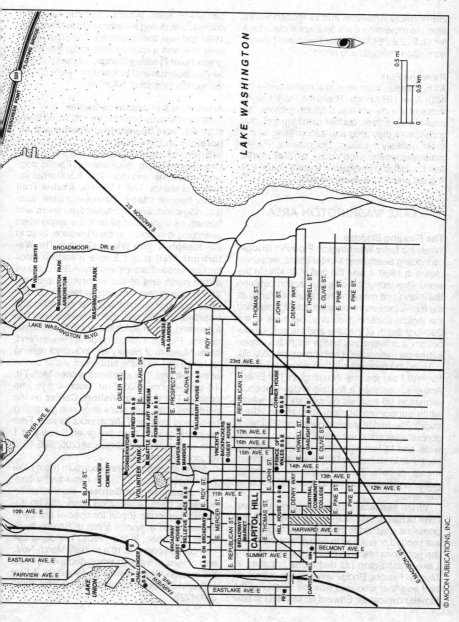

20th-century American and European works; after the expansion it will be a world-class facility. Call (206) 543-2280 for the current status, admission charges, and hours.

Ravenna Park

All but hidden from view in a ravine under the 15th Ave. NE bridge, Ravenna Park has 52 acres of woodlands and a babbling brook, accessible via a three-quarter-mile loop trail, plus a children's play area and soccer field, all in a most unlikely location. Douglas fir, Pacific madrone, western red cedar, big-leaf maple, and English and Pacific yew line the nature trail. A great place for a weekend stroll.

LAKE WASHINGTON AREA

The Floating Bridges

When the **Lake Washington Floating Bridge,** connecting Seattle and Mercer Island, was completed in 1939, it was the first of its kind in the world. Previously, the only connection between the island and mainland had been via ferry; as the ferries grew more crowded, a bridge seemed the logical solution. However, because of the 200-foot depth of the lake and the soft, mucky bottom, a conventional bridge would have been extremely expensive, if not impossible, to build.

Using the concrete cell technology developed for WW I barges, the Washington Toll Bridge Authority designed a floating bridge that could withstand 90-mph winds with six-foot waves while supporting bumper-to-bumper 20-ton trucks. The bridge was supported by 25 floating concrete sections, each 350 feet long, 59 feet wide, and 14 feet high; each concrete pontoon contains 96 watertight 14-foot-square compartments, or cells. The pontoons are cabled together and connected to stationary fixtures at either end.

When seasonal variations cause the lake level to rise or fall (as much as three feet), the pontoons attached to the stationary approaches are flooded or emptied to ensure that the rest of the pontoons maintain their flotation level. The Lake Washington (its real name is Lacey V. Murrow Floating Bridge in honor of a prominent civil engineer who also was the brother of the famed newscaster Edward R. Murrow) is now part of I-90 traffic. While being refurbished, the original sank during a winter storm in November 1990 and was then replaced. The span is just over one and a quarter miles long; the **Evergreen Point Floating Bridge,** connecting Seattle with Bellevue and Kirkland on Route 520, is the world's longest at 1.4 miles.

Arboretum and Japanese Garden

Trees and shrubs from all over the world thrive at the 267-acre **University of Washington Arboretum** on Lake Washington Boulevard. A half-mile trail leads visitors past lodgepole pine, Oregon crabapple, huckleberry, Pacific dogwood, madrone, and more than 5,500 other varieties of plants. The 1.25-mile **Azalea Trail** winds through cherry, Japanese maple, azalea, dogwood, and rhododendron trees and bushes; it's a gorgeous place in the spring when everything is in bloom. In the off-season, head to the **Joseph A. Witt Winter Garden.** The **Waterfront Trail** is a 1.5-mile roundtrip stroll through wooded islands and Union Bay's shores at the north end of the arboretum, passing through the largest remaining wetland in Seattle (duck sightings guaranteed). The woodchip and boardwalk trail is level, with numerous benches for resting, but wheelchairs or strollers are not options. Pick up a nature guide at the west end, at the Museum of History and Industry's parking lot (or inside), or at the arboretum visitor center at the east end. The arboretum is open Mon.-Fri. 10 a.m.-4 p.m., Sat.-Sun. noon-4 p.m., no charge. The **Graham Visitors Center** on the north end of the park has a shop with gardening books and gardening knickknacks for sale. Free hour-long guided tours are given Sunday at 1 p.m. (except in December); call (206) 325-4510 for more information.

At the south end of the arboretum (near Lake Washington Blvd. E) is the three-and-a-half-acre **Japanese Tea Garden**—manicured ornamental trees, a secluded pond, and an authentic teahouse (open for special tea ceremonies once a month) given to Seattle by its sister city, Kobe, in the 1960s. The Japanese Tea Garden opens at 10 a.m. daily March-Nov., and closes at varying times depending upon the season. Admission is $2 for adults, $1 for kids and seniors, kids under six free; tel. (206) 684-4725.

Museum of History and Industry

Located at 2700 24th Ave. E—on the south side of Union Bay and just across the Montlake Bridge from the university—this is the city's finest museum for local history. Some features include an interesting exhibit on the great fire that destroyed much of downtown in 1889, ornately carved figureheads from old sailing vessels, a mansion-sized dollhouse that makes young girls envious, and Boeing's B-1 flying boat—the company's first commercial plane. There are many other exhibits that change periodically, and shows that last just a few months before moving on. The museum is open daily 10 a.m.-5 p.m. (except Thanksgiving, Christmas, and New Year's); admission is $5.50 for adults, $3 for seniors and kids (ages six to 12), $1 for ages two to five, and free for kids under two. No charge on Tuesday. Call (206) 324-1126 for more information.

Other Sights

The **Northwest Puppet Center,** 9123 15th Ave. NE, tel. (206) 523-2579, is a fun place for kids, with weekend shows all year and a puppet museum offering changing exhibits of puppets from around the globe. The over-18 crowd will want to come here for the **Adult Puppetry Festival** held in May.

Jutting into Lake Washington on a forested peninsula is **Seward Park** on Lake Washington Blvd. S and S. Juneau Street. It features trails, picnic areas, fishing, swimming, and Mt. Rainier views. A one-mile loop trail takes you past Douglas firs six feet in diameter, madrones, big-leaf maples, and the shores of Lake Washington.

WEST SEATTLE

West Seattle is a neighborhood of simple homes and apartments with views west across Puget Sound. Take Spokane St. to West Seattle where viewpoints, a scenic drive, a beach, parks, and a bike path await. For photography buffs, **Hamilton Viewpoint** at California Way SW provides a panoramic view of Seattle's skyline, the Cascades, and Elliott Bay, as does **Belvedere Viewpoint** at S.W. Admiral Way and 36th Ave. SW.

For a leisurely scenic drive, head along the water on Harbor Ave. SW to Duwamish Head, then west on Alki Ave. to **Alki Beach Park,** a long, narrow, sandy stretch—as close to a real beach (outside Golden Gardens) as you'll find on this part of Puget Sound. In warm weather a whole beach culture emerges here—cruising cars, illegally parked vehicles, bonfires, suntan goop, the works—even though the water rarely gets above 55° F. Keep going on Alki Ave. to the **Alki Point Lighthouse,** tel. (206) 286-5423. Tours of the station are available Mon.-Fri.; a day's notice is required.

Continue south on Beach Dr. SW to **Lincoln Park's** trails and beach. A bike path follows the same scenic route.

SOUTH SEATTLE

The south end of Seattle is dominated by industrial developments, especially an enormous Boeing plant. The area is not especially attractive but does contain one of Seattle's most enjoyable sights, the fabulous Museum of Flight, along with Rainier Brewery and the Kingdome.

Museum of Flight

This world-class museum, at 9404 E. Marginal Way S, tel. (206) 764-5720, is one of the premier Seattle attractions, a place rivaled only by the National Air and Space Museum in Washington, D.C. The main focal point is the dramatic steel and glass **Great Gallery** packed with dozens of planes, many of which appear to be flying in formation. Everything here has been meticulously restored. Suspended overhead are a Douglas DC-3, a replica of the Wright Brothers' glider, and another 18 aircraft. An additional 40 planes sit on the tarmac below, including a Russian MiG-21 and the famous M-12 Blackbird, officially the fastest plane ever to fly (this is disputed by many sources). Also on the ground level is an F/A-18 Hornet mockup—guides let you sit inside as they describe its complex features—and even a '50s-era Aerocar III. Built by Moulton B. Taylor for the fly-and-drive crowd, the Aerocar III could fly at 105 mph and convert into a car in 10 minutes. Highly knowledgeable docents lead free 20-minute and hour-long tours; stop by the desk to see when the next one begins. Throughout the day, the theater screens *The Dream of Flight,* an award-winning film narrated by Walter Cronkite, and other films about flying.

A second large exhibit space at the Museum of Flight is the **Red Barn,** a lovingly restored structure that was the Boeing Company's original manufacturing plant. It was moved here in 1975 and traces the history of flight through fascinating exhibits on two floors, including a restored 1917 Curtiss Jenny biplane and a replica of the Wright Brothers' wind tunnel. Also at the Museum of Flight are a hands-on area where kids pretend to pilot their own miniature aircraft, a Challenger Learning Center where school groups launch the space shuttle into orbit, a gift shop selling aviation paraphernalia and books (including a model of the top-secret Aurora pulse jet), a library with an extensive collection of aviation volumes, and the Wings Cafe with light meals. More planes are arranged outside the museum. Set aside at least three hours for this extraordinary museum, especially if you're a pilot! And yes, it's okay to take photos.

Get to the museum by taking exit 158 from I-5, turning right on E. Marginal Way, and following the signs, or by taking the No. 174 bus from downtown or the airport. The museum is open daily 10 a.m.-5 p.m., and Thursday till 9 p.m. (closed Christmas); admission $6 adults, $3 seniors and kids ages six to 15, free for kids under six. Get in free to the museum between 5 and 9 p.m. on the first Thursday of each month. A second Museum of Flight store, along with a restored Ryan M-1, can be found at Sea-Tac Airport. The Museum's Restoration Center is located at Paine Field in Everett (near the Boeing Plant); call (206) 745-5150 for tour information. In late June and early July, the museum hosts **Emerald City Flight Festival,** a family airshow that has brought such attractions as the B-2 Stealth bomber, the Concorde, and the Canadian Snowbirds.

Kingdome

Built in 1976, the Kingdome is Seattle's largest sports facility. This is where you can watch the Seahawks football games or Mariners baseball games, or attend boat shows, tennis matches, basketball playoffs, and other events. The Kingdome is housed under the world's largest concrete roof, a roof whose collapsing tiles caused major embarrassment in 1994. The stadium can house up to 66,000 football or 60,000 baseball fans. The Kingdome is just south of the International District and is pretty hard to miss; get here by Metro bus—many lines stop here—or park outside in the many acres of parking spaces. Tours of the Kingdome are given Mon.-Sat. all year (except during events), for $4 adults, $2 seniors and ages six to 12, free under age six. All tours begin at Gate D, on the northwest side, call (206) 296-3128 for more info and reservations.

Rainier Brewery

Take a free tour of Rainier Brewery, 3100 Airport Way S, tel. (206) 622-2600, Mon.-Sat. 1-6 p.m. all year. Kids must be accompanied by an adult. Take the Airport Way South exit from I-5; the brewery is on the left side. This is where they make not just Rainier ("Vitamin R"), but also many other labels of suds, including Henry Weinhard's, Black Label, Schmidt's, Heidelberg, Yakima Red, Yakima Honey Wheat, and Emerald City. Rainier was purchased in 1996 by Stroh Brewing Company. The 30-minute tour begins with a peppy 10-minute video on the company and ends in the Mountain Room, a pub (of sorts) dominated by a 12-foot wide romantic 19th-century oil painting by James Everett Stuart, *Sunset Glow—Mount Rainier.* (The gold-gilded frame alone weighs 500 pounds!) The adjacent gift shop sells beer mugs and T-shirts, but the real attraction is the beer. Visitors get three big glasses full, and can choose from nine different brands on tap; a great deal for cheapskates and boozers. Nonalcoholic beers and root beer are also available. The tasting room closes at 6 p.m., so folks leaving on the last tour won't get a brew unless they do their tasting before heading out. Be prepared to wait up to 45 minutes for tours in the peak tourist season.

Hart Brewery

Located at 1201 1st Ave. S, this microbrewery/pub has proven an immediate success since opening in 1995. The brewery combines the production of Thomas Kemper Lagers (also brewed in Polsbo) and Pyramid Ales (also brewed in Kalama). Tours are offered every day, call (206) 682-8322 for times, or stop by the pub for one of their 14 beers on tap and delicious pub grub, including pizzas and shepherd's pie.

ACCOMMODATIONS

See the accommodations charts for a relatively complete listing of lodging options in Seattle. Cheaper places are available, but they generally are cheap for a reason. If you're on a tight budget, stay near the airport on Pacific Hwy. S (Hwy. 99) or north of the Ship Canal on Aurora Ave. (Hwy. 99), rather than in run-down city-center hotels. Note that both of these "motel rows" are on heavily traveled roads with chain restaurants and ugly strip malls; try to get a room facing away from the street if you're a light sleeper. From either area it's a quick Metro bus ride to downtown. A recommended budget place not too far from downtown is **Park Plaza Motel.**

For lodging in neighboring areas such as Bellevue, Kent, and Redmond, see the Vicinity of Seattle chapter.

Many of the more luxurious hotels and motels offer special discount rates for business travelers or members of various organizations, so be sure to ask about them, or stop by the Convention and Visitors Bureau for a copy of the calendar of events booklet, filled with discount coupons. The bureau also offers a **Seattle Hotel Hotline,** tel. (800) 535-7071, through which you can make reservations at local hotels at no charge. For some reason, many of these pricey lodging places insist upon charging extra for local calls, even when you are already paying over $100 a night! Note also that parking at most downtown hotels is an extra charge, often $9 or more per day.

CAMPING

There are no public campgrounds in the immediate vicinity of Seattle, but **Fay-Bainbridge State Park** has year-round campsites on Bainbridge Island, just a short ferry ride away. You'll need a car or bike to get to the park from the ferry dock (it's six miles away). Other state park campgrounds around Seattle are in Federal Way (Dash Point State Park), Enumclaw (Kanaskat-Palmer Recreation Area), and Des Moines (Saltwater State Park). See appropriate sections for complete descriptions. The clos-

est Forest Service campgrounds are in the Cascades at least 35 miles to the east on I-90.

The closest private RV parks are: **Holiday Park Resort,** 19250 Aurora Ave. N, near Kenmore, tel. (206) 542-2760; **KOA Seattle South Campground,** 5801 S. 212th, in Auburn, tel. (206) 872-8652; **Trailer Inns RV Park,** exit 11A off I-90 in Eastgate, tel. (206) 747-9181; **Bryn Mawr Beach,** 11448 Rainier Ave. S, in Renton, tel. (206) 772-3000; and **Vasa Park Resort,** on Lake Sammamish near I-90, tel. (206) 746-3260.

HOSTELS

As every young traveler knows, youth hostels are generally the cheapest places to stay, offering clean and safe lodging at flophouse prices. The **Hostelling International Seattle** is in the heart of town at 84 Union St., tel. (206) 622-5443, and just steps away from Pike Place Market. The hostel beds in 20 small dorm rooms cost $16 for AYH members, or $19 for nonmembers. Only members can stay here during July and August, though anyone can pay the fee to join up when they register. There are a couple of private rooms that cost $37-43 d; reserve these three months ahead for summer visits. Reservations are also imperative for dorm rooms from June through September; be sure to make reservations at least a week or two ahead. The hostel has no curfew, though you'll need to ring the bell if you come in after 2 a.m. It has a full kitchen; no alcohol allowed. Be sure to ask about discounts to many local attractions, including the Aquarium, Omnidome, and Museum of Flight. Travelers sometimes complain that the hostel's small rooms and bustling atmosphere give it a sterile feeling, but it is cheap, clean, and perfectly located.

Three private hostels offer alternatives to the AYH, but are similarly popular; make reservations at least a week ahead for the summer. **Vincent's Backpackers Guest House;** tel. (206) 323-7849 or (800) 600-2965, has a boardinghouse atmosphere and marginally clean dorms, but is in a good neighborhood on Capitol Hill. The rules are lax, and alcohol is allowed.

SEATTLE ACCOMMODATIONS

These accommodations are listed from least to most expensive within each category. Rates may be lower during the winter months. The area code is 206.

HOSTELS AND YMCA

Vincent's Backpackers Guest House; 527 Malden Ave. E (Capitol Hill); tel. 323-7849 or (800) 600-2965; $12 pp in dorm rooms, $30-35 d private rooms; free airport and ferry pickup, free continental breakfast, full kitchen, storage lockers, no curfew, a bit seedy

Commodore Motor Hotel; 2013 2nd Ave.; tel. 448-8868; $12 pp for bunk rooms (AYH card required); $33-46 s, $37-49 d for private rooms; local calls 50 cents

Green Tortoise Backpacker's Guest House; 715 2nd Ave. N (Queen Anne); tel. 282-1222; $13 pp in dorm rooms, $24 in shared rooms, $30 d in private rooms; full kitchen, garden with view, quiet location, no curfew

American Backpackers' Hostel; 126 Broadway Ave. E (Capitol Hill); tel. 720-2965; $13 pp in dorm rooms, $28 s or $35 d in private rooms; sauna, library, pool table, free continental breakfast

Hostelling International—Seattle; 84 Union St.; tel. 622-5443; $16 pp AYH members, $19 pp nonmembers in dorm rooms, $37-43 d in private rooms; AYH hostel, complete kitchen, storage lockers, laundry room, close to Pike Place Market, no curfew, parking $7

Downtown YMCA; 909 4th Ave.; tel. 382-5000; $33-35 s, $37-39 d; bath down the hall, complete exercise facility with pool, sauna, jacuzzi, and weight room, parking $7

BED AND BREAKFASTS

Beech Tree Manor B&B; 1405 Queen Anne Ave. N; tel. 281-7037; $49-79 s or d; Victorian mansion on Queen Anne Hill, seven guest rooms, private or shared baths, full breakfast, kids welcome

Capital Hill House B&B; 2215 E. Prospect (Capitol Hill); tel. 322-1752; $50-65 s or d; nicely furnished 1932 brick home, full breakfast

College Inn Guest House; 4000 University Way NE; tel. 633-4441; $25 pp for hostel-type dorm rooms, $32-45 s, $55-65 d; European-style hotel, historic 1909 University District building, bath down the hall, all rooms include free continental breakfast

Corner House B&B; 102 18th Ave. E (Capitol Hill); tel. 328-2865; $50 s, $65 d; light breakfast, children welcome

Queen Anne Hill B&B; 1835 7th Ave. W; tel. 284-9779; $55-85 s or d; 1907 Queen Anne home with English gardens, panoramic vistas, five guest rooms, shared or private baths, continental breakfast, kids welcome

Villa Heidelberg; 4845 45th Ave. SW (West Seattle); tel. 938-3658; $55-85 d; 1909 home, wraparound porch with mountain vistas, gourmet breakfasts

Landes House; 712 11th Ave. E (Capitol Hill); tel. 329-8781; $59-90 s or d in 1906 Victorian house, or $150 d for two-bedroom apartment; clothing-optional hot tub, continental breakfast, gay owned and operated, mixed clientele

Pensione Nichols B&B; 1923 1st Ave., No. 300; tel. 441-7125; $60 s, $85 d, suites $160 d; near Pike Place Market, 12 guest rooms, shared or private baths, continental breakfast, parking $8, kids welcome

Prince of Wales B&B; 133 13th Ave. E (Capitol Hill); tel. 325-9692 or (800) 327-9692; $60-85 s or d; full breakfast, four guest rooms, private or shared baths, children over three welcome, two-night minimum stay

Gaslight Inn B&B; 1727 15th Ave. E (Capitol Hill); tel. 325-3654; $62-98 s or d; historic home, outdoor pool, nine guest rooms, private or shared baths, continental breakfast, no kids, AAA approved

Hill House B&B; 1113 E. John St. (Capitol Hill); tel. 720-7161 or (800) 720-7161; $65-95 s or d; turn-of-the-century Victorian home, five guest rooms, private or shared bath, gourmet breakfast, no kids, AAA approved

Broadway Guest House/Bacon Mansion B&B; 959 Broadway Ave. E (Capitol Hill); tel. 329-1864 or (800) 240-1864; $65-125 s, $74-125 d; 1909 Tudor mansion, grand piano, six guest rooms, shared or private baths, light breakfast, kids welcome

Green Gables Guesthouse; 1503 2nd Ave. W (Queen Anne); tel. 282-6863 or (800) 400-1503; $65-125 s, $75-125 d; antique-filled Frank Lloyd Wright home, solarium, full breakfast

Tugboat *Challenger;* 1001 Fairview N (Lake Union); tel. 340-1201; $55-125 s, $75-145 d; unique on-the-water lodging in tugboat and yacht, full breakfast

Shafer-Baillie Mansion Guest House; 907 14th Ave. E (Capitol Hill); tel. 322-4654 or (800) 922-4654; $69-115 s or d; luxurious 1914 English Manor mansion, 14 guest rooms, most with private baths, continental breakfast

B.D. Williams House B&B; 1505 4th Ave. N (Queen Anne); tel. 285-0810 or (800) 880-0810; $74-94 s, $79-99 d; antique-filled Victorian home, dramatic views, full breakfast, children okay, AAA approved

Chambered Nautilus B&B; 5005 22nd Ave. NE (University District); tel. 522-2536; $72-98 s, $79-105 d; 1915 Colonial home with antique furnishings, large library, six guest rooms, private or shared baths, full breakfast, kids okay

Mildred's B&B; 1202 15th Ave. E (Capitol Hill); tel. 325-6072; $75 s, $85 d; luxurious Victorian home, three guest rooms, private baths, fireplace, grand piano, full breakfast, free airport shuttle, kids welcome

Bed & Breakfast on Broadway; 722 Broadway E (Capitol Hill); tel. 329-8933; $75 s, $85 d; 1906 mansion, stained glass, antique furnishings, grand piano, full breakfast

Bellevue Place B&B; 1111 Bellevue Place East (Capitol Hill); tel. 325-9253 or (800) 325-9253; $75 s, $85 d; 1905 Victorian house, shared baths, solarium, full breakfast, no kids

Salisbury House B&B; 750 16th Ave. E (Capitol Hill); tel. 328-8682; $75-95 s, $85-105 d; 1904 home with garden, wrap-around porch, four guest rooms, private baths, full breakfast, no kids under 12

Roberta's B&B; 1147 16th Ave. E (Capitol Hill); tel. 329-3326; $75-95 s, $80-105 d; turn-of-the-century home, full breakfast, AAA approved

University Inn; 4140 Roosevelt Way NE; tel. 632-5055 or (800) 733-3855; $75-86 s, $85-95 d; outdoor pool, jacuzzi, fitness room, free continental breakfast, free newspaper, local calls 25 cents, AAA approved

Scandia House B&B; 2028 34th Ave. S (Lake Washington); tel. 725-7825; $85 s or d; unique modern home, panoramic views, private baths, king-size bed, full breakfast

Hainsworth House B&B; 2657 37th Ave. SW (West Seattle); tel. 938-1020; $85-95 s or d; 1907 Tudor mansion, two guest rooms, private baths, decks, full breakfast, no children

Capitol Hill Inn B&B; 1713 Belmont Ave.; tel. 323-1955; $85-175 s, $90-175 d; 1903 Victorian home, antique furnishings, five guest rooms, private or shared baths, full breakfast, espresso bar, two-night minimum stay, no kids under 12, AAA approved

Chelsea Station B&B; 4915 Linden Ave. N (Green Lake); tel. 547-6077 or (800) 400-6077; $89-104 d; elegant 1920 Colonial home near Woodland Park Zoo, full breakfast

Colonial Manor; 4432 42nd Ave. SW (West Seattle); tel. 938-3381; $95 s or d; 1911 Colonial box home, fireplace, two-night minimum stay, light breakfast

(continues on next page)

SEATTLE ACCOMMODATIONS

(continued)

SEA-TAC AIRPORT AREA MOTELS

Note: Pacific Hwy. is also called Hwy. 99. The airport entrance is at 178th and Pacific Hwy., so addresses nearest 17800 Pacific Hwy. are closest to the airport. The numbers increase as you head south.

Ben-Carol Motel; 14110 Pacific Hwy. S; tel. 244-6464; $31-50 s or d; kitchenettes available, local calls 30 cents, small pool, basic but clean

Motel 6, Sea-Tac South; 18900 47th Ave. S; tel. 241-1648 or (800) 466-8356; $32 s, $38 d; outdoor pool

Travelers Choice Motel; 3747 S 146th St.; tel. 246-3100; $33 s or d

King's Arm Motel Motor Inn; 23226 30th Ave. S; tel. 824-0300; $35 s or d; outdoor pool, kitchenettes

Motel 6, Seattle South; 20651 Military Rd. (I-5 exit 51); tel. 824-9902 or (800) 466-8356; $33 s, $39 d; outdoor pool

Motel 6, Sea-Tac Airport; 16500 Pacific Hwy. S; tel. 246-4101 or (800) 466-8356; $33 s, $39 d

Mini-Rate Motel; 20620 Pacific Hwy. S; tel. 824-6930; $35 s, $42 d; kitchenettes available, free airport shuttle, clean

Legend Motel; 22204 Pacific Hwy. S; tel. 878-0366; $36-40 s or d; kitchenettes

Tac-Sea Motel Park-Fly; 17024 International Blvd.; tel. 241-6511; $37 s, $43 d; free airport shuttle, AAA approved

Shadow Motel; 2930 S. 176th St., Sea-Tac; tel. 246-9300; $39-43 s, $42-47 d; local calls 25 cents

Spruce Motel; 14442 Pacific Hwy. S; tel. 244-9930; $40-43 s or d; kitchenettes

Sea-Tac Crest Motor Inn; 18845 Pacific Hwy. S, Sea-Tac; tel. 433-0999 or (800) 554-0300; $42 s, $45 d; free airport parking, free airport shuttle, AAA approved

Jet Inn Motel; 3747 S. 142nd St., Tukwila; tel. 431-0085; $43 s, $47 d; newer motel, local calls 35 cents

Jet Motel Park 'n Fly; 17300 Pacific Hwy. S, Sea-Tac; tel. 244-6255 or (800) 233-1501; $43-50 s, $52-56 d; outdoor pool, free airport shuttle, local calls 54 cents, AAA approved

Towne & Country Suites; 14800 Interurban Ave., Tukwila; tel. 246-2323 or (800) 545-2323; $45 s, $48 d; country location, outdoor pool, sauna, kitchenettes available

Sea-Tac Airport Travelodge; 2900 S. 192nd St., Sea-Tac; tel. 241-9292 or (800) 578-7878; $45-50 s, $50-55 d; sauna, free airport shuttle, local calls 30 cents, AAA approved

New Best Inn; 23408 30th Ave. S; tel. 870-1280; $45-65 s or d

Travelodge Sea-Tac North; 14845 Pacific Hwy. S, Tukwila; tel. 242-1777 or (800) 578-7878; $48 s, $53 d; free airport shuttle, local calls 30 cents, AAA approved

Sandstone Inn; 19225 Pacific Hwy. S, Sea-Tac; tel. 824-1350 or (800) 223-4476; $48-58 s, $52-62 d; kitchenettes available, free airport shuttle and seven-day airport parking, local calls 40 cents, AAA approved

Thriftlodge; 17108 Pacific Hwy. S, Sea-Tac; tel. 244-1230 or (800) 525-9055; $49-54 s, $54-59 d; full breakfast, free airport shuttle, AAA approved

Continental Court All Suite Motel; 17223 32nd Ave. S, Sea-Tac; tel. 241-1500 or (800) 233-1501; $50 s, $55 d; outdoor pool, free airport shuttle, quiet location, AAA approved

Howard Johnson at SeaTac Airport; 20045 Pacific Hwy. S, Sea-Tac; tel. 878-3310 or (800) 872-0202; $50-60 s, $55-60 d; free airport shuttle and parking, local calls 35 cents, AAA approved

Airport Plaza Hotel; 18601 Pacific Hwy. S, Sea-Tac; tel. 433-0400; $60 s, $65 d; free airport shuttle, local calls 40 cents, AAA approved

Econo Lodge-SeaTac Airport; 13910 Pacific Hwy. S; tel. 244-0810 or (800) 446-6900; $55 s, $65 d; free continental breakfast, jacuzzi, weight room, free airport shuttle, free airport parking, local calls 30 cents, AAA approved

Silver Cloud Inn at Tukwila; 123050 48th Ave., Tukwila; tel. 241-2200 or (800) 551-7207; $56 s, $64 d; outdoor pool, jacuzzi, exercise facility, free continental breakfast, AAA approved

La Quinta Inn; 2824 S. 188th St., Sea-Tac; tel. 241-5211 or (800) 531-5900; $58-64 s, $65-71 d; outdoor pool, jacuzzi, exercise facility, free airport shuttle, AAA approved

Sea-Tac Super 8 Motel; International Blvd. at 192nd St.; tel. 433-8188 or (800) 800-8000; $59 s, $65 d

Georgetown Inn; 6100 Corson Ave. S; tel. 762-2233; $59-64 s, $69-72 d; newer motel, free continental breakfast, sauna, exercise room, kitchenettes available, local calls 25 cents, AAA approved

Hampton Inn-Seattle Southcenter; 7200 S. 156th St., Tukwila; tel. 228-5800; $63-71 s, $73-81 d; outdoor pool, jacuzzi, fitness center, free airport shuttle, AAA approved

Heritage Inn; 16838 International Blvd.; tel. 248-0901 or (800) 245-2968; $54-64 s, $64-70 d; free airport shuttle, AAA approved

WestCoast Gateway Hotel; 18415 Pacific Hwy. S.; tel. 248-8200 or (800) 426-0670; $69 s, $79 d; free continental breakfast, weight room, free airport shuttle, local calls 50 cents

Hampton Inn Hotel Seattle Airport; 19445 International Blvd., Sea-Tac; tel. 878-1700 or (800) 426-7866; $69-71 s, $79-81 d; outdoor pool, free continental breakfast, free airport shuttle, AAA approved

Holiday Inn, Boeing Field; 11244 Pacific Hwy. S, Tukwila; tel. 762-0300 or (800) 465-4329; $69-72 s, $77-83 d; outdoor pool, courtyard, free airport shuttle, local calls 60 cents, AAA approved

Comfort Inn at Sea-Tac; 19333 Pacific Hwy. S., Sea-Tac; tel. 878-1100 or (800) 228-5150; $69-75 s, $80 d; exercise room, jacuzzi, free continental breakfast, free airport shuttle, local calls 35 cents, AAA approved

Days Inn at Sea-Tac Airport; 19015 International Blvd. S, Sea-Tac; tel. 244-3600 or (800) 325-2525; $69-92 s, $79-105 d; free airport shuttle, free continental breakfast, AAA approved

Holiday Inn, Seattle Sea-Tac; 17338 Pacific Hwy. S, Sea-Tac; tel. 248-1000 or (800) 465-4329; $79-124 s, $79-134 d; indoor pool, jacuzzi, exercise room, free airport shuttle, AAA approved

Nendel's Seattle at Southcenter; 15901 West Valley Hwy., Tukwila; tel. 226-1812 or (800) 547-0106; $75 s, $85 d; outdoor pool, wading pool, jacuzzi, sauna, exercise room, free airport shuttle, AAA approved

Rodeway Inn Sea-Tac; 3000 S. 176th St.; tel. 242-0200; $76 s or d; pool, exercise room, local calls 25 cents, AAA approved

WestCoast SeaTac Hotel; 18220 Pacific Hwy. S.; tel. 246-5535 or (800) 426-0670; $83 s, $93 d; outdoor pool, sauna, jacuzzi, free airport shuttle, AAA approved

Quality Inn SeaTac; 17101 Pacific Hwy. S, Sea-Tac; tel. 246-7000 or (800) 221-2222; $84 s, $94 d; outdoor pool, sauna, exercise facility, free airport shuttle, free continental breakfast, AAA approved

Courtyard by Marriott; 400 Andover Park W, Tukwila; tel. 575-2500 or (800) 321-2211; $87 s, $97 d; indoor pool, jacuzzi, exercise room, AAA approved

Doubletree Inn; 205 Strander Blvd.; tel. 575-8220 or (800) 528-0444; $88-108 s or d; indoor pool, sauna, jacuzzi, breakfast buffet, evening beverages, racquetball and exercise rooms, free airport shuttle, AAA approved

Radisson Hotel Seattle Airport; 17001 Pacific Hwy. S, Sea-Tac; tel. 244-6000 or (800) 333-3333; $89-129 s or d; outdoor pool, exercise room, sauna, concierge, massage available, free airport shuttle, AAA approved

(continues on next page)

SEATTLE ACCOMMODATIONS

(continued)

Doubletree Suites; 205 Strander Blvd., Tukwila; tel. 246-8220 or (800) 222-8733; $89-143 s or d; two-bedroom suites, indoor pool, jacuzzi, sauna, racquetball courts, exercise room, AAA approved

Best Western Airport Executel; 20717 Pacific Hwy. S, Sea-Tac; tel. 878-3300 or (800) 528-1234; $80-95 s, $85-101 d; indoor pool, exercise room, atrium, jacuzzi, sauna, local calls 40 cents, free airport shuttle, free airport parking, AAA approved

Seattle Marriott Hotel, Sea-Tac; 3201 S. 176th St., Sea-Tac; tel. 241-2000, (800) 643-5479, or (800) 228-9290; $93-134 s or d; atrium with pool, sauna, jacuzzi, health club, buffet breakfast, free airport shuttle, AAA approved

Homewood Suites; 6955 Southcenter Blvd., Tukwila; tel. 433-8000 or (800) 225-5466; $109-129 s, $119-139 d; one- and two-bedroom suites with kitchens, outdoor pool, jacuzzi, exercise facility, free breakfast, free airport shuttle, local calls 50 cents, AAA approved

Wyndham Garden Hotel Seattle-Tacoma; 18118 Pacific Hwy. S, Sea-Tac; tel. 244-6666 or (800) 822-4200; $110 s; $120 d; indoor pool, jacuzzi, AAA approved

Seattle Airport Hilton; 17620 Pacific Hwy. S, Sea-Tac; tel. 244-4800 or (800) 445-8667; $114-125 s or d; outdoor pool, exercise room, jacuzzi, free continental breakfast, free airport shuttle, local calls 65 cents, AAA approved

Embassy Suites Hotel; 15920 West Valley Hwy., Tukwila; tel. 227-8844 or (800) 362-2779; $119-134 s or d; large suites, outdoor pool, jacuzzi, sauna, exercise room, atrium, free continental breakfast, free airport shuttle, local calls 75 cents, AAA approved

Red Lion Hotel Seattle Airport; 18740 Pacific Hwy. S, Sea-Tac; tel. 246-8600 or (800) 547-8010; $120-135 s, $125-140 d; outdoor pool, exercise room, concierge, free airport shuttle, AAA approved

Residence Inn by Marriott-Seattle South; 16201 West Valley Hwy., Tukwila; tel. 226-5500 or (800) 321-2211; $125 s or d; suites, outdoor pool, jacuzzis, kitchens, free continental breakfast, free airport shuttle, AAA approved

DOWNTOWN AND VICINITY MOTELS AND HOTELS

St. Regis Hotel; 116 Stewart St.; tel. 448-6366; $30 s, $38 d with bath down the hall, $38 s, $44 d with private bath; clean older hotel, no children, $8 parking

Moore Hotel; 1926 2nd Ave.; tel. 448-4851 or (800) 421-5508 (U.S. and Canada); $34 s, $39 d; turn-of-the-century Pike Place Market area hotel, plain rooms with private baths, local calls 50 cents, $8 parking fee

Sandpiper Villas Family Motel; 11000 1st Ave. SW; tel. 242-8883; $39 s, $44 d; one-bedroom suites with kitchens, outdoor pool, phones $3 extra

West Seattle Travelodge; 3512 S.W. Alaska St.; tel. 937-9920; $43-70 s or d; kitchens available, free continental breakfast

City Center Motel Seattle; 226 Aurora Ave. N; tel. 441-0266; $45 s or d, local calls 30 cents

Sixth Avenue Inn; 2000 6th Ave.; tel. 441-8300 or (800) 648-6440; $48-84 s, $58-96 d; local calls 50 cents, free parking, AAA approved

Seattle Inn; 225 Aurora Ave. N; tel. 728-7666 or (800) 255-7932; $49-68 s, $52-82 d; indoor pool, jacuzzi, exercise room, sundeck, game room, free continental breakfast, local calls 50 cents, free parking

King's Inn; 2106 5th Ave.; tel. 441-8833 or (800) 546-4760; $50-85 s, $55-90 d; kitchenettes available, local calls 30 cents, free parking

Eastlake Inn; 2215 Eastlake Ave.; tel. 322-7726; $59 s or d; kitchenettes available

Tropics Motor Inn; 225 Aurora Ave. N; tel. 728-7666; $59-72 s or d; indoor pool, free continental breakfast, local calls 50 cents

Econo Lodge by the Space Needle; 325 Aurora Ave.; tel. 441-0400 or (800) 446-6900; $69 s or d; outdoor pool, local calls 25 cents; kitchenettes available, AAA approved

Seattle Downtown Travelodge; 2213 8th Ave.; tel. 624-6300 or (800) 578-7878; $60-85 s, $75-85 d; free parking and local calls, AAA approved

Hotel Seattle; 315 Seneca; tel. 623-5110 or (800) 426-2439; $66-70 s, $72-76 d; local calls 35 cents, $11 parking fee

Inn at Queen Anne; 505 1st Ave. N; tel. 282-7357 or (800) 952-5043; $70 s, $80 d; studio apartments with kitchens, local calls 50 cents, $6 parking

Pacific Plaza Hotel; 400 Spring St.; tel. 623-3900 or (800) 426-1165; $77-97 s or d; free continental breakfast, local calls 50 cents, $8 parking fee, AAA approved

Quality Inn City Center; 2224 8th Ave.; tel. 624-6820, (800) 437-4867 (WA), or (800) 228-5151 (U.S); $80-165 s, $87-175 d; jacuzzi, sauna, kitchenettes available, free continental breakfast, newspaper, and parking, AAA approved

Days Inn Town Center; 2205 7th Ave.; tel. 448-3434 or (800) 648-6440; $82 s, $85 d; free parking, local calls 50 cents, AAA approved

Best Western Loyal Inn; 2301 8th Ave.; tel. 682-0200 or (800) 528-1234; $84 s, $90 d; jacuzzi, sauna, kitchenettes available, local calls 35 cents, AAA approved

Travelodge by the Space Needle; 200 6th Ave. N; tel. 441-7878 or (800) 578-7878; $85-104 s, $91-110 d; outdoor pool, jacuzzi, free continental breakfast, AAA approved

Executive Court Suites; 300 10th Ave.; tel. 223-9300; $85-95 s or d; one and two bedroom suites, full kitchens, jacuzzi, free downtown shuttle, free parking, local calls 25 cents

WestCoast Vance Hotel; 620 Stewart St.; tel. 441-4200 or (800) 426-0670; $85-105 s, $95-105 d; classic hotel, local calls 50 cents, $9 parking, AAA approved

WestCoast Camlin Hotel; 1619 9th Ave.; tel. 682-0100 or (800) 426-0670; $94 s or d; outdoor pool, parking $9, AAA approved

Best Western Executive Inn; 200 Taylor Ave. N; tel. 448-9444 or (800) 528-1234; $99 s, $109 d; jacuzzi, exercise room, free downtown shuttle, free parking, local calls 50 cents, AAA approved

Pioneer Square Hotel; 77 Yesler Way; tel. 340-1234; $99 s, $109 d; beautifully restored 1914 hotel on Pioneer Square, continental breakfast, local calls 40 cents, $5-15 parking, AAA approved

Inn at Virginia Mason; 1006 Spring St.; tel. 583-6453 or (800) 283-6453; $100 s, $125 d; remodeled European hotel, courtyard, quiet location, local calls 35 cents, $5 parking, AAA approved

Hampton Inn; Roy St. at 5th Ave. N; tel. 282-7700 or (800) 426-7866; $110-150 s or d; new motel, exercise room, kitchenettes available, king-size beds, full breakfast buffet, free underground parking

Edgewater Inn; 2411 Alaskan Way; tel. 728-7000 or (800) 624-0670; $119-195 s, $119-210 d; Pier 67 overlooking Puget Sound, parking $6, local calls 81 cents, AAA approved

Residence Inn by Marriott-Seattle Downtown; 800 Fairview Ave. N; tel. 624-6000 or (800) 331-3131; $125-170 s or d; suites with kitchens, indoor pool, sauna, jacuzzi, exercise room, free local shuttle, free newspaper, buffet breakfast, central atrium, local calls 50 cents, AAA approved

WestCoast Roosevelt Hotel; 1531 7th Ave.; tel. 621-1200 or (800) 426-0670; $125-170 s or d; parking $10, local calls 75 cents, AAA approved

Mayflower Park Hotel; 405 Olive Way; tel. 623-8700, (800) 426-5100 (U.S. and Canada), or (800) 562-4504 (in WA); $130 s, $140 d; $9 parking fee, AAA approved

(continues on next page)

SEATTLE ACCOMMODATIONS
(continued)

The Westin Hotel, Seattle; 1900 5th Ave.; tel. 728-1000 or (800) 228-3000; $135-195 s, $149-215 d; indoor pool, jacuzzi, saunas, sundeck, fitness center, parking $14, AAA approved

Inn at the Market; 86 Pine St.; tel. 443-3600 or (800) 446-4484; $135-300 s or d; free shuttle service, health club, parking $14, local calls 75 cents, AAA approved

Sorrento Hotel; 900 Madison St.; tel. 622-6400 or (800) 426-1265; $145-220 s, $160-235 d; four star luxury hotel, free downtown shuttle service, concierge, parking $12, local calls 80 cents, AAA approved

Sheraton Seattle Hotel & Towers; 1400 6th Ave.; tel. 621-9000 or (800) 325-3535; $148-215 s, $168-235 d; indoor pool, jacuzzi, concierge, parking $14, local calls 75 cents, AAA approved

Ramada Inn Downtown; 2200 5th Ave.; tel. 441-9785 or (800) 272-6232; $150 s, $160 d; parking $10, AAA approved

Stouffer Madison Hotel; 515 Madison St.; tel. 583-0300 or (800) 468-3571; $154-234 s or d; indoor pool, jacuzzi, health club, concierge, free newspaper, parking $13, AAA approved

Holiday Inn Crowne Plaza Seattle; 1113 6th Ave.; tel. 464-1980, (800) 521-2762, or (800) 858-0511 (in WA); $159-200 s or d; jacuzzi, sauna, exercise facilities, parking $14, local calls 50 cents, AAA approved

WestCoast Plaza Park Suites; 1011 Pike St.; tel. 682-8282 or (800) 426-0670; $170-230 s or d; outdoor pool, suites with kitchens and fireplaces, jacuzzi, exercise room, free continental breakfast, parking $9, AAA approved

Houseboat Hideaways; Lake Union; tel. 323-5323; $155 for 28-foot houseboat (sleeps four), or $175 for 40-foot houseboat (sleeps six); unique Lake Union accommodations with kitchenettes

Holiday Inn Crowne Plaza; 6th & Seneca; tel. 464-1980 or (800) 521-2762; $180 s or d; jacuzzi, sauna, exercise room, impressive views, local calls 50 cents, parking $13

Seattle Hilton Downtown; 6th Ave. & University St.; tel. 624-0500 or (800) 445-8667; $174-184 s, $189-199 d; parking $12, local calls 75 cents, AAA approved

The Warwick Hotel; 401 Lenora St.; tel. 443-4300 or (800) 426-9280; $175 s, $185 d; four-star luxury hotel, indoor pool, jacuzzi, sauna, exercise room, parking $11, free downtown shuttle, AAA approved

Hotel Vintage Park; 1100 5th Ave.; tel. 624-8000 or (800) 624-4433; $185-215 s or d; luxury four-star hotel, parking $14, local calls 75 cents, health club, wine reception, free newspaper, AAA approved

Alexis Hotel; 1007 1st Ave.; tel. 624-4844 or (800) 426-7033; $185-355 s or d; four-star luxury hotel, free continental breakfast, evening sherry, health club, steam room, free newspaper, concierge, condominium suites with kitchens at adjacent Arlington Suites (same management) for $165-265, valet parking $15, AAA approved

Four Seasons Olympic Hotel; 411 University St.; tel. 621-1700 or (800) 332-3442, (800) 268-6282 (WA), or (800) 223-8772 (outside WA); $200-265 s, $230-295 d; grand luxury hotel, indoor pool, jacuzzi, sauna, health club, valet parking $15, local calls 75 cents, AAA approved (five diamond)

NORTH END MOTELS

Most of these hotels are on North Seattle's "motel row," Aurora Ave. (Hwy. 99). See the rooms first at the cheapest motels to make sure they meet your standards.

Shoreline Motel; 16526 Aurora Ave. N; tel. 542-7777; $28-34 s, $32-34 d; kitchenettes available, local calls 35 cents

Bridge Motel; 3650 Bridge Way N (off Aurora Ave.); tel. 632-7835; $32 s, $36 d

Park Plaza Motel; 4401 Aurora Ave. N; tel. 632-2101; $32-35 s or d; phone calls 25 cents, friendly and clean, AAA approved

Aurora Motor Inn; 8820 Aurora Ave. N; tel. 527-3090; $33 s or d

Villa Del Mar Motel; 3938 Aurora Ave. N; tel. 632-2550; $35 s or d; small rooms

Thunderbird Motel; 4251 Aurora Ave. N; tel. 634-1213; $35 s, $39 d; kitchenettes available, local calls 20 cents

Nites Inn; 11746 Aurora Ave. N; tel. 365-3216; $38 s or d

Georgian Motel; 8801 Aurora Ave. N; tel. 524-1004; $40 s or d; kitchenettes

Marco Polo Motel; 4114 Aurora Ave. N; tel. 633-4090 or (800) 295-4090; $40-44 s, $44-48 d; recently remodeled, kitchenettes available, AAA approved

La Hacienda Motel; 5414 1st Ave. S; tel. 762-2460 or (800) 553-7531; $42-46 s, $45-55 d; kitchenettes available, free continental breakfast, local calls 25 cents, AAA approved

Black Angus Motor Inn; 12245 Aurora Ave. N; tel. 363-3035; $44-48 s or d; local phone calls 30 cents

Casabel Motel; 3938 Whitman N (off Aurora Ave.); tel. 632-8200; $48 s or d; kitchenettes available, quiet location, local calls 50 cents

Quest Inn; 14817 Aurora Ave. N; tel. 367-7880; $49 s, $53 d; newly remodeled, kitchenettes available, AAA approved

Days Inn North Seattle; 19527 Aurora Ave. N; tel. 542-6300 or (800) 329-7466; $49 s, $54 d; free continental breakfast, kitchenettes

University Motel; 4731 12th Ave. NE; tel. 522-4724 or (800) 522-4720; $49 s, $55 d; kitchenettes available, local calls 25 cents, AAA approved

Emerald Inn Motel; 8512 Aurora Ave. N; tel. 522-5000; $50-60 s, $54-65 d; kitchenettes available, new motel, AAA approved

Rodeside Lodge; 12501 Aurora Ave. N; tel. 364-7771 or (800) 227-7771; $50-65 s or d; outdoor pool, sauna, jacuzzi, pool table, AAA approved

Max Ivor Motel; 6188 4th Ave. S; tel. 762-8194; $50-100 s or d; kitchenettes available, AAA approved

Seafair Inn; 9100 Aurora Ave. N; tel. 522-3754 or (800) 445-9297; $55-65 s, $58-68 d; kitchenettes available, local calls 25 cents, AAA approved

University Travelodge; 4725 25th Ave. NE; tel. 525-4612 or (800) 578-7878; $60 s, $65 d; outdoor pool, jacuzzi, kitchenettes available

Claremont Hotel; 2004 4th Ave.; tel. 448-8600 or (800) 448-8601; $69-89 s, $79-99 d; historic hotel, kitchenettes available, $9 parking fee

Silver Cloud Inn—University District; 5036 25th Ave. NE; tel. 526-5200 or (800) 551-7207; $69-99 s, $75-106 d; new motel, indoor pool, jacuzzi, exercise room, free continental breakfast, AAA approved

Best Western Continental Plaza; 2500 Aurora Ave. N; tel. 284-1900 or (800) 528-1234; $70-79 s, $70-80 d; outdoor pool, free continental breakfast, Lake Union vistas, kitchenettes available, AAA approved

Meany Tower Hotel; 4507 Brooklyn Ave. NE; tel. 634-2000 or (800) 648-6440; $78 s, $88 d; University District 15-story hotel, exercise room, free newspaper, local calls 35 cents, AAA approved

Best Western Evergreen Inn; 13700 Aurora Ave. N; tel. 361-3700 or (800) 213-6308; $80 s, $88 d; free continental breakfast, jacuzzi, sauna, exercise room, AAA approved

University Plaza Hotel; 400 N.E. 45th St.; tel. 634-0100 or (800) 343-7040; $82 s, $92 d; outdoor pool, fitness room, AAA approved

Seattle Ramada Inn at Northgate; 2140 N. Northgate Way; tel. 365-0700 or (800) 272-6232; $99-116 s, $105-124 d; outdoor pool, AAA approved

Dorm beds go for $12 per person, or stay in a private room for $30 s or $35 d. A free continental breakfast is included.

American Backpackers' Hostel, tel. (206) 720-2965, is a newly opened and very popular hostel on Capitol Hill with a kitchen, sauna, library, and pool table, plus a free continental breakfast. They offer free pickup from the airport and downtown (minimum of three people). Dorm beds are $13 per person, while private rooms cost $28 s or $35 d.

Green Tortoise Backpacker's Guest House, tel. (206) 282-1222, is a friendly and funky place in a quiet Queen Anne neighborhood with a back patio and fine views of the Space Needle. As with the other private hostels, there is no curfew and alcohol is okay. It can be a bit noisy at night, with lots of folks coming and going, so bring your earplugs. Guests get a make-your-own breakfast of sorts (eggs and toast). Dorm rooms cost $13-15 per person, private rooms go for $30-35 d. As with other Seattle lodging places, the Green Tortoise fills up quickly in the summer; call ahead for reservations. The hostel is connected with the one-and-only Green Tortoise Bus, tel. (800) 867-8647, a great and inexpensive way to explore the country. The bus has a regular run connecting Seattle, San Francisco, and Los Angeles, and all points along the way. It also has tours all over the hemisphere, from Alaska to Costa Rica.

Another relatively inexpensive lodging option is the **Downtown YMCA,** tel. (206) 382-5000, where rooms cost $33-35 s, $37-39 d. Stay here and get free use of all the Y's facilities, including a pool, sauna, jacuzzi, and weight room. The **Commodore Motor Hotel,** tel. (206) 448-8868, has dorm spaces for AYH members at $12 per person in bunk rooms. Free parking.

BED AND BREAKFASTS

Seattle has quite a number of outstanding B&Bs, particularly in the Capitol Hill neighborhood, where many of the places are historic mansions. See the accommodations chart for a complete list of local B&Bs; see the Yellow Pages for a listing of B&B reservation services. The **Seattle B&B Association,** tel. (206) 547-1020, keeps tabs on who has space at a dozen of the nicer B&Bs in town. Some of the cities surrounding Seattle have less expensive B&Bs; check them out in "Vicinity of Seattle" below.

In the heart of Pike Place Market, **Pensione Nichols,** tel. (206) 441-7125, is a European-style B&B with views of Puget Sound and the Market. Eight antique-furnished guest rooms share three baths; continental breakfast included. **The College Inn,** tel. (206) 633-4441, is a budget-priced European-style B&B with 25 rooms featuring period furnishings, sinks, shared baths, and a deli, pub, and cafe on the first floor. Continental breakfast is included; children are welcome. **The B.D. Williams House** atop Queen Anne Hill, tel. (206) 285-0810 or (800) 880-0810, is a family B&B—most of their five rooms command city and mountain views. The stately **Gaslight Inn,** tel. (206) 325-3654, has nine rooms, a library, outdoor pool, and continental breakfast. It frequently books up far ahead, so reserve early for the summer.

Green Gables Guesthouse, tel. (206) 282-6863 or (800) 400-1503, is a 1904 Foursquare home in Queen Anne designed by Frank Lloyd Wright. The home is filled with antiques, and the owners are very hospitable. **Bed & Breakfast at Mildred's,** tel. (206) 325-6072, is an attractive Capitol Hill Victorian home right across the street from Volunteer Park. It has three guest rooms, and is filled with antiques. **The Beech Tree Manor,** tel. (206) 281-7037, is a turn-of-the-century mansion that sits atop Queen Anne Hill. The four-bedroom, three-bath inn features English decor, a period fireplace, and wicker rockers on the shady porch.

The **Prince of Wales B&B,** tel. (206) 325-9692 or (800) 327-9692, on Capitol Hill has four guest rooms, three of which offer excellent views of Puget Sound and the Olympics. There's a two-night minimum stay in the summer months. Capitol Hill's **Hill House B&B,** tel. (206) 720-7161 or (800) 720-7161, is in a classic turn-of-the-century Victorian home with five tastefully appointed rooms.

Chelsea Station, tel. (206) 547-6077 or (800) 400-6077, is directly across from the rose gardens at the south entrance to Woodland Park Zoo, within walking distance of Green Lake. Enjoy an endless supply of cookies, all-day coffee and tea, and a library of books to help with your sightseeing. Three guest rooms, each with private baths, and three spacious suites, also with private bath, offer uncommon comfort.

Chambered Nautilus, tel. (206) 522-2536, offers Cascade views on a hill within walking distance of UW. The Georgian colonial home was built in 1915 by Dr. Herbert Gowen, founder of the university's Department of Oriental Studies, and is the only B&B close to the campus. It often fills up far ahead, so book early.

The **Corner House B&B** on Capitol Hill, tel. (206) 328-2865, is one of the less expensive B&Bs in Seattle and welcomes children. It has just two guest rooms.

Built in 1914, the stately **Shafer-Baillie Mansion Guest House,** tel. (206) 322-4654 or (800) 922-4654, sits along "Millionaire's Row" on Capitol Hill, with 14 attractively decorated guest rooms. This is also a popular place for weddings and receptions.

The most unusual B&B in Seattle is the "Bunk & Breakfast" **Tugboat *Challenger,*** tel. (206) 340-1201. This is a retired 96-foot oceangoing tug that has been cleaned up and only slightly redecorated. Tied up permanently at the west end of Lake Union, it has seven cabins, including the two-room Captain's Cabin with many amenities—private bath, stereo, refrigerator, desks, and a view of the skyline.

The **Capitol Hill Inn,** tel. (206) 323-1955, has four rooms decorated in authentic Victorian-era furnishings, including hand-screened wallpaper, European antiques, and original woodwork. A friendly mother-daughter team runs this old Victorian that was once a brothel. **Scandia House B&B,** tel. (206) 725-7825, is located in a distinctive modern home with panoramic views across Lake Washington to the Cascades. **Villa Heidelberg,** tel. (206) 938-3658, is a West Seattle B&B built in 1909, with a wraparound porch, four guest rooms, pleasant gardens, and impressive views of Puget Sound and the Olympics.

Bellevue Place B&B, tel. (206) 325-9253 or (800) 325-9253, is a Capitol Hill home built in 1905, with a solarium and nicely landscaped grounds. **Roberta's B&B,** tel. (206) 329-3326, has five guest rooms in a turn-of-the-century home across the street from beautiful Volunteer Park on Capitol Hill. **Salisbury House B&B,** tel. (206) 328-8682, is another historic Capitol Hill mansion, with four guest rooms, a paneled library, and a flowery backyard. The **University Inn,** tel. (206) 632-5055 or (800) 733-3855, bills itself as a small, neighborhood hotel that has grown from a 42-room motel to more than 140 rooms. Continental breakfast is included.

FOOD AND DRINK

Entire books are available on dining in Seattle; the best restaurant guides to Seattle are *Seattle Best Places* and *Seattle Cheap Eats,* both published by Sasquatch Books, the book-publishing arm of *The Seattle Weekly. Cheap Eats* is the more practical of the two if you aren't on an expense account, but *Best Places* offers more complete coverage of the city beyond the restaurants. What follows here is only a minuscule sampling of what's available. Assume all to be moderately priced for the type of food or drink offered, unless otherwise mentioned. See also "Entertainment and Events" later in this chapter for places and events offering meals and fresh-brewed beer.

BREAKFAST

The team of Peter Levy and Jeremy Hardy has managed to tap into the perfect recipe for success on the Seattle breakfast scene, with several eateries scattered around town: Capitol Hill's **Coastal Kitchen,** 429 15th Ave. E, tel. (206) 322-1145; Wallingford's **Beeliner Diner,** 2114 N. 45th St., tel. (206) 547-6313; and Queen Anne's **5 Spot,** 1502 Queen Anne Ave. N, tel. (206) 285-7768. Each of these has it's own character—Coastal Kitchen has a more varied fare and out-of-this-world pancakes, Beeliner delivers the smart-ass commentary one expects in a diner (plus *lots* of noise), and the 5 Spot emphasizes all-American comfort food. You will not go wrong at any of these, but be ready for a mob scene if you wake up after 9 a.m. on Sunday morning. All of these also offer down-home American cooking for lunch and dinner.

14 Carrot Cafe, 2305 Eastlake Ave. E, tel. (206) 324-1442, is located along a busy industrial street, but cranks out delicious breakfasts in a spacious atmosphere.

Yoo Hoo, 607 N. 35th St. (Fremont), tel. (206) 633-3760, is a fun place with a funky, arty decor one expects in Fremont. Incredible waffles are the main treat here, topped with real maple syrup, but everything else is perfection, from the fresh OJ to the salads and sandwiches for lunch. Not far away is **Mae's Phinney Ridge Cafe,** 6412 Phinney Ave. N, tel. (206) 782-1222, a cow-infested place complete with a "Moo Room" for milk shakes and displays of cow paraphernalia. The food is all made from scratch and includes big, sticky cinnamon rolls and scrumptious hash browns. And yes, it gets jammed on weekends.

Another great place (actually two of them) where you'll have to fend off the weekend brunch crowds is **Julia's,** 4401 Wallingford Ave., tel. (206) 633-1175, and 5410 Ballard Ave. NW, tel. (206) 783-2033. The food is tasty, with lots of vegetarian items and a lively atmosphere. **Surrogate Hostess,** 746 19th Ave. E (Capitol Hill), tel. (206) 324-1944, is also popular for breakfast and lunch, or just to sip a cappuccino. It's a great place to relax and discuss the problems of the world with other folks.

COFFEE AND TEA

Latteland

It's hard to know where to begin when it comes to coffee in this place where coffee consumption tops that of any other American city. With literally hundreds of espresso bars, carts, and drive-ups all over Seattle, you would be hard-pressed to *not* find a great cup of java. The best known, of course, is **Starbucks,** with 27 shops (at last count) scattered all over the city, including the original shop in the Pike Place Market (the most spacious and enjoyable Starbucks is in University Village). Named for the coffee-drinking first mate in *Moby Dick,* Starbucks is considered by many the godfather of quality coffee in the Northwest. That first store opened in 1971, offering perfectly roasted beans and a commitment to quality; roasted beans more than a week old are given to charities. The employees of Starbucks also have a reputation for being very knowledgeable about coffee and can help neophytes with the intricacies of the various espresso drinks. In recent years the company has be-

come a national phenomenon, expanding into major cities throughout the U.S. and Canada. You can even order it by phone; call (206) 447-1575 or (800) 445-3428. (Seattleites will be shocked to learn that espresso was a fixture in the Bay Area in Northern California years before it migrated north; Berkeley's Caffe Mediterraneum has been pouring the brew since the 1950s.)

After Starbucks, most of the espresso shops are small operations with just one or a handful of locations. **Cafe Septieme,** 2331 2nd Ave., tel. (206) 448-1506, has the charm of a Parisian cafe and is a romantic place to enjoy a big bowl of cappuccino. Four other great places to sip espresso are: **B&O Espresso,** 204 Belmont E, tel. (206) 322-5028, 401 Broadway Ave. E, tel. (206) 328-3290, and 103 Cherry St., tel. (206) 621-9372; **Uptown Espresso,** 525 Queen Anne N, tel. (206) 281-8669; **Torrefazione Italia,** 320 Occidental S, tel. (206) 624-5773, and 622 Olive Way, tel. (206) 624-1429; and **Cafe Paradiso,** 1005 E. Pike St. (Capitol Hill), tel. (206) 322-6960.

One of the more unique coffeehouses is **Temple Cafe,** located on the second floor of the historic Odd Fellows Hall at 915 E. Pine St., tel. (206) 324-2035. The atmosphere is Bohemian, with an arty crowd, along with folks who wander down from the Metaphysical Library (described below under "Information and Services") two flights up.

Still Life in Fremont, 709 N. 35th St., tel. (206) 547-9850, is a wonderful coffeehouse with healthy sandwiches, rich soups, chocolate desserts, and espresso served in a bright and oft-crowded cafe. Another distinctive place is **The Virtual Commons,** 200 Roy St. in Queen Anne, tel. (206) 281-7339, where the espresso mixes with talk of web pages, computer games, and Internet software. Each table has computer terminals where you can surf the Internet (for a fee).

Most Seattle coffeehouses are entirely smoke-free, but the **Last Exit on Brooklyn,** 5201 University Way NE, tel. (206) 526-9155, violates this with a vengeance. The main room is always a dense cloud of fumes, and is jammed with a noisy mix of aging longhaired beat-generation poets, tie-dyed college kids, and frumpy street folks. The cluttered, mismatched furnishings and hippie-style art on the wall fit the crowd. The coffee is always great, and you can escape the smoke in the back room, where you're likely to meet folks playing chess or the addictive game of Magic. Last Exit on Brooklyn opened in 1967 (the first real coffeehouse in Seattle) and was on Brooklyn St. (hence the name) until a couple of years ago when it was forced to relocate. Another old favorite—it opened in 1975—is just a few blocks down: **Cafe Allegro,** 4214 ½ University Way NE (it actually faces the alley on 15th St.), tel. (206) 633-3030. It's still a popular sit-down-and-stay-awhile espresso house with three rooms spread over two floors.

Teahouses

The **Teacup,** 2207 Queen Anne N, tel. (206) 283-5931, sells almost a hundred varieties of teas from all over the globe and always has something interesting to taste. The Chinese-style **Teahouse Kuan Yin,** 1911 N. 45th St., tel. (206) 632-2055, is connected to Wide World Books and offers a taste of Asian teas, along with light meals. For a taste of old England, don't miss **The Crumpet Shop,** tel. (206) 682-1598, in Pike Place Market, where you get delicious fresh crumpets and a steaming pot of tea.

DELIS AND LIGHT MEALS

There are countless places around Seattle for quick lunches, and the U District, Capitol Hill, and Pike Place Market are all packed with eateries for folks on the run, from pizza-by-the-slice to sushi. The better grocery market chains (PCC, QFC, and Larry's) all have excellent delis inside. Downtown, don't miss **DeLaurenti Market,** tel. (206) 622-0141, in Pike Place Market. Wander through the aisles for gourmet imported groceries and wines, or stop by the deli (Cafe Mangia Bevi) for salads and outstanding panini (grilled sandwiches). The garlic bread and eggplant dishes at **Cuchina Fresca,** 1904 Pike Place, tel. (206) 448-4758, are some of the best you'll ever find. **Cafe Panini,** 807 1st Ave., tel. (206) 340-5966, makes some of the best paninis this side of New York (they also supply these to several Starbucks locations). **Kosher Delight,** 1509 1st Ave., tel. (206) 682-8140, is a true

Jewish deli near the Pike Place Market. Philly cheesesteak lovers will want to visit another Pike Place delicatessen, **Philadelphia's Deli,** tel. (206) 464-1899.

For a deli with a New Orleans flavor, head to **La Mediterranean Deli,** 528 Broadway Ave. E (Capitol Hill), tel. (206) 329-8818, where spicy Cajun gumbo, barbecued chicken, and fresh corn bread await. A wonderful Italian deli with fresh pastas, breads, and salads, is **Pasta & Co.,** in University Village Mall, tel. (206) 523-8594. **Take It From Us,** 2904 1st Ave., tel. (206) 448-3442, offers fast and delicious take-away sandwiches, plus more substantial items for a to-go dinner.

AMERICAN

Looking for the best burger in town? The argument rages, but the public votes with their feet (and mouths) for **Dick's Drive-In,** 111 N.E. 45th St. (Wallingford), tel. (206) 632-5125. The food at this straight-from-the-'50s joint consists of greasy fries, fat burgers, and wonderful chocolate milk shakes. There's almost always a line out front on a summer evening. Dick's also can be found at 115 Broadway Ave. E (Capitol Hill), tel. (206) 323-1300, 9208 Holman Rd. NW (Crown Hill), tel. (206) 783-5233, and 12325 30th Ave. NE (Lake City), tel. (206) 363-7777. Another very popular place for burgers and BLTs (along with delightful breakfasts and famous cinnamon rolls) is **Hi-Spot Cafe,** 1410 34th Ave. (Madrona), tel. (206) 325-7905.

Two Bells Tavern, 2313 4th Ave., tel. (206) 441-3050, is an offbeat place jammed at lunchtime with artists, wanna-be artists, and folks on the fringe, along with the button-down set. They all come here for some of the best and biggest burgers in Seattle, served on sourdough rolls and topped with fried onions. The menu expands to include tasty soups, salads, and other well-prepared pub grub.

For "comfort food" in a no-frills setting, it's pretty hard to beat **The Bells,** 8501 5th Ave. NE (Northgate), tel. (206) 524-3100. They've been here for over 45 years and still serve the all-American favorites the way your mom made them, including meatloaf, beef stew, baked potatoes, homemade soups, and tapioca pudding.

Delcambre's Ragin Cajun, 1523 1st Ave., tel. (206) 624-2598, serves a delicious Cajun lunch or dinner of red beans and rice, spicy gumbos, sausage, and jalapeno cheese bread. For genuine soul food with a Louisiana touch, head to **Thompson's Point of View,** 2308 E. Union St., tel. (206) 329-2312. The menu includes catfish, big meaty burgers, and gumbos.

Belltown Billiards, 2201 1st Ave., tel. (206) 448-6779, is one of Seattle's newest "in" spots in the hip Belltown District near Seattle Center. It's on the floor below **Queen City Grill,** another popular eatery. The billiards parlor is so popular that major corporations sometimes book it for private parties. The 12 custom tables attract pool sharks, and the food parade is led by pizzas, pastas, and fish.

The two **13 Coins** are Seattle's classiest 24-hour restaurants and gathering places for both the famous and the infamous. They offer more than 130 menu items in two locations: 125 Boren Ave. N (downtown), tel. (206) 682-2513; or 18000 Pacific Hwy. S, tel. (206) 243-9500, near Sea-Tac Airport (entertainment nightly here).

Metropolitan Grill, 2nd and Marion, tel. (206) 624-3287, is one of the best places in town for steak and has been rated by some critics as one of the top 10 in America. Seafood (including great clam chowder), pork, lamb, and pastas are also on the menu. Expensive. Another favorite steakhouse, Hiram's at the Locks, is described under "Dining with a View" below.

NORTHWEST CUISINE

The Painted Table in the Alexis Hotel at 92 Madison St., tel. (206) 624-3646, serves Northwest cuisine with a flair that has gained a national following and the accolades of critics. The innovative menu changes, but always includes outstanding seafood and pastas, plus unusual salads. Each place setting has handpainted plates from local artists (you can buy them for a "mere" $65 each).

Marco's Supperclub, 2510 1st Ave., tel. (206) 441-7801, is a bright and arty Belltown place with a menu that bumps from grilled salmon to Jamaican jerk chicken to fried sage leaf appetizers (much better than it sounds). The food is always creative, and the atmos-

phere is relaxed. Entrees cost around $10-14.

Georgian Room, in the Four Seasons Olympic Hotel at 411 University St., tel. (206) 621-7889, is an elegant dining room with a Renaissance look and Northwest cuisine. The food is expensive but much lighter than what you might expect in a luxury hotel. The salmon, sturgeon, rabbit, lamb, veal, and steaks are cooked to a creative perfection, and the menu also includes a five-course vegetarian dinner that has garnered national praise. Expect to pay around $100 for a dinner for two with wine and dessert.

Fuller's, in the Sheraton Hotel at 1400 6th Ave., tel. (206) 447-5544, has cuisine that consistently receives national awards, including such flavorful specials as Ellensburg lamb, gorgonzola and pear stuffed beef tenderloin, and sautéed salmon. The modernistic artwork here is equally gorgeous, including glass by Dale Chihuly and a collection of paintings by Mark Tobey and Morris Graves.

SEAFOOD

Given its waterfront location, it should come as no surprise that Seattle's specialty is fresh seafood of all types. The city is jammed with seafood restaurants of all levels, from the takeaway fish-and-chips joints to luxury dining that will set you back $30 per person and more.

With five species of oysters grown in Puget Sound waters—including the native Olympia oyster—Seattle is becoming known as one of the best places to slurp fresh oysters on the half-shell. **Emmett Watson's Oyster Bar,** tel. (206) 448-7721, is one of the best of these, a relaxed little place in the Soames-Dunn Building at Pike Place Market. Reasonable prices and ultrafresh oysters, plus great salmon soup or fish and chips. **Elliott's Oyster House & Seafood Restaurant,** Pier 56, tel. (206) 623-4340, is one of the finest seafood restaurants on the waterfront, with crab, clams, and freshly shucked oysters. Expensive.

Ray's Boathouse, 6049 Seaview Ave. W, tel. (206) 789-3770, is north of the Ship Canal along Shilshoe Bay, with outstanding views over Puget Sound at sunset (be sure to reserve a window table) and perfectly prepared oysters, fish, and other fresh seafood. This large and attractive place has a slightly nautical design with wooden floors and beams like an old boat shed, and it is a bit expensive (expect a bill of $25 per person), but the seafood is great. Reservations are a must. You can save money and avoid the crowds by arriving weeknights 5-6 p.m. A complete "early bite dinner" with clam chowder, entree, and dessert costs just $13. Upstairs is a spacious and equally popular cafe serving a lighter menu, including oysters and fish and chips.

Anthony's Homeport, 6135 Seaview Ave. W, tel. (206) 783-0780, is just up the road, with moderately priced fresh fish and a saucy cioppino; Sunday brunch, too. Delightful vistas from the windows across Lake Union.

One of the city's best-known (and most expensive) seafood restaurants is **McCormick's Fish House and Bar,** 722 4th Ave., tel. (206) 682-3900. The menu changes, depending upon what's fresh that day, and the bar is a favorite place to hobnob after work. Reservations recommended.

Ivar's Acres of Clams, on the waterfront at Pier 54, tel. (206) 624-6852, was folksinger Ivar Haglund's original restaurant (open since 1938). Prior to his restaurateur days, Haglund sang a ballad called "Acres of Clams" telling of the Sound's then-lonely beaches resting atop a wealth of clams. The restaurant is an unpretentious, cavernous seafood place with a take-out bar on the sidewalk that attracts lines of business folks at lunch. The Ivar's chain now has several other locations, the most notable one being **Ivar's Salmon House** on Lake Union at 401 N.E. Northlake Way, tel. (206) 632-0767; it's located in a cedar facsimile of an Indian longhouse with historic photos and Tlingit carvings on the walls, and dugout canoes hanging from the rafters. This is a fantastic waterside location with an outside deck (summers only) looking across the lake to downtown Seattle. Unfortunately, the food at both these Ivar's is good, but not great. A better bet may be to stop by the Whale Maker Lounge at the Salmon House for happy hour (free hors d'oeuvres Mon.-Fri. 4-6:30 p.m.), and to check out the rather intimidating (for males at least) killer whale "whalemakers." You're more likely to get a window seat here than in the restaurant.

DINING WITH A VIEW

The **Space Needle Restaurant,** tel. (206) 443-2100 or (800) 937-9582, is a top-of-the-world dining experience at 500 feet, very popular with tourists, visiting relatives, and teens on prom night. The food is so-so (but expensive), but the view is unsurpassed, as the revolving restaurant completes a 360-degree turn by the time you get to dessert. A second restaurant here, **The Emerald Suite,** has a more elaborate (and even more expensive) menu, plus more intimate dining.

Cafe Sophie, 1921 1st Ave., tel. (206) 441-6139, is just up from Pike Place, inside an old funeral chapel (lots of ghost stories here). Don't let that put you off, the food here is wonderful (including a seared swordfish salad, grilled lamb chops, beef tenderloin, herb crepes, and out-of-this-world desserts), and the rooms are fascinating. The library offers panoramic vistas across the Sound. A bit pricey, but not bad for lunch, and they offer jazz on Friday nights. The **Cloud Room** atop the Camlin Hotel at 1619 Ninth Ave. has great cityscape and Lake Union views.

Cutter's Bay House, 2001 Western Ave., tel. (206) 448-4884, just up the street from Pike Place Market, has a lively bar with a long list of hors d'oeuvres; their specialties—mako shark, fresh Northwest fish, and regular pasta and prime rib dishes—are moderately priced and accompanied by an extensive wine-by-the-glass and imported beers list. This is one of Seattle's prime check-out-the-studs/babes places for the yuppie crowd. Sunsets over the Olympics are striking.

Franco's Hidden Harbor, 1500 Westlake Ave. N, tel. (206) 282-0501, has a mellow water-level view of Lake Union through a forest of boat masts and rigging. Their main claim to fame is fresh Dungeness crab served in 19 different menu choices. **Chandlers Crabhouse and Fresh Fish,** 901 Fairview Ave. N, tel. (206) 223-2722, is on the south shore of Lake Union with views north across the lake. Expensive (but fairly standard) seafood, chicken, and steaks.

Salty's on Alki, 1936 Harbor Ave. SW, tel. (206) 937-1600, claims to have the best view of the Seattle skyline from its Lake Union location.

The expensive menu features seafood and steaks but isn't particularly notable.

Hiram's at the Locks, 5300 34th Ave. NW, tel. (206) 784-1733, has an industrial look to it and serves steak and seafood, plus a popular Sunday brunch. This is a fun place to watch the Chittenden Locks in action.

Other places with great views include Adriatica (see "Middle Eastern and Indian" below), Copacabana Bolivian Restaurant (see "South of the Border" below), and Maximilien in the Market (see "French" below). Anthony's Homeport, Ivar's Salmon House, and Ray's Boathouse are seafood restaurants (described above) with over-the-water vistas.

PIZZA

Seattle's best quick pizza place is **Pizzeria Pagliacci,** with four sit-down locations around town: 4529 University Way NE, tel. (206) 632-0421; 426 Broadway Ave. E, tel. (206) 324-0730; 4003 Stone Way N, tel. (206) 632-1058; and 550 Queen Anne Ave. N, tel. (206) 285-1232. This is about as close as you can get to real New York style pizzas: perfect thin crusts and distinctive toppings (including the pesto primo with olive oil, garlic, fontina, mozzarella, and ricotta cheeses, pesto, and red peppers). They always have several types of pizzas available by the slice, as well as calzones and lasagna, or order a full one with your favorite toppings.

Another pizza place with a loyal following and several Seattle locations is **Romio's Pizza,** 616 1st Ave. (Pioneer Square), tel. (206) 621-8500, or 2001 W. Dravus (Queen Anne), tel. (206) 284-6878. A special favorite are pizzas on a garlic crust. Other Romio's are 3242 Eastlake Ave. E (Eastlake), tel. (206) 322-4453; 8523 Greenwood Ave. N (Greenwood), tel. (206) 782-9005; and 917 Howell St. (downtown), tel. (206) 622-6878.

For incredible Chicago-style stuffed pizza that's guaranteed to please, visit **TestaRossa,** 210 Broadway Ave. E (Capitol Hill), tel. (206) 328-0878. It isn't cheap, but the arty creations are all delightful, and they're open till midnight on weekends.

Zeek's Pizza, 41 Dravus St. (Queen Anne), tel. (206) 285-6046, is a small pizzeria with unusual pizzas—including Organic Drift (fresh oregano, spinach, red onion, and feta)—and crowds of students. They also sell pizza by the slice. Another very good pizza operation is **Guido's Pizzeria,** 7902 E. Green Lake Dr. N (Green Lake), tel. (206) 522-5553, and 2108 N.E. 65th St., tel. (206) 525-3042 (Ravenna).

The **Original Pioneer Square Pizza Co.,** 614 1st Ave. (next door to Doc Maynard's), tel. (206) 343-9103, has great thin crust pizzas, including pizza by the slice. **Nicolas Pizza & Pasta,** 1924 N. 45th, tel. (206) 545-9090, is a fine Wallingford sit-down pizza place with a spacious dining area and an open kitchen.

EUROPEAN

Italian
The Old Spaghetti Factory, across from Pier 70 at 2801 Elliott Ave., tel. (206) 441-7724, is always noisy, good, and inexpensive—a popular place to bring the kids.

You can have a pricey Italian feast on Pioneer Square at **Umberto's,** 100 S. King St., tel. (206) 621-0575. **Paparazzi,** 2202 45th St. N, tel. (206) 547-7772, has more moderately priced Italian meals. If you have $55 or so to drop, the prix fixe dinner at **al Boccalino,** 1 Yesler Way (Pioneer Square), tel. (206) 622-7688, has one of the finest and freshest Italian meals anywhere. Especially notable are the prawns and garlic served over a bed of sautéed spinach, and the saddle of lamb. Good Italian wine list, too.

For an outstanding southern Italian eatery, visit **Salvatore Ristorante Italiano,** 6100 Roosevelt Way NE (U District), tel. (206) 527-9301. Specials include veal dishes, linguine with clams, and pasta with red hot peppers, tomatoes, capers, anchovies, and olives. They also have a fine choice of antipastas and Italian wines.

French
For impressive French cuisine, **Le Gourmand,** fairly expensive, is at 425 N.W. Market St. in Ballard, tel. (206) 784-3463. And certainly try **Crêpe de Paris,** Rainier Square, 1333 Fifth Ave., tel. (206) 623-4111, which was one of the first French restaurants in Seattle. It's very popular for lunch and has a cabaret show some evenings that requires reservations. **Un Deux Trois,** 1329 1st Ave., tel. (206) 233-0123, features a changing menu of French dishes, in-

cluding reasonably priced take-out specials. The chocolate tarts with fruit are famous. Another good place is **Maximilien in the Market,** in Pike Place Market, tel. (206) 682-7270, with views across Elliott Bay and lamb, fish, veal, and beef entrees.

Other European

For a light Greek meal, try Capitol Hill's **El Greco,** 219 Broadway Ave. E, tel. (206) 328-4604. Out in the U District, the **Continental Restaurant,** 4549 University Way NE, tel. (206) 632-4700, is a longtime favorite for inexpensive Greek meals. They also have a fine deli here. The **Lakeside Cafe,** 7419 Greenwood Ave. N (near Green Lake), tel. (206) 783-6945, is a small neighborhood cafe with spanakopita, moussaka, and other inexpensive and surprisingly good Greek specialties. If you're just looking for a fast gyro, stop by **Mr. D's** in Pike Place Market, tel. (206) 622-4881.

Try **Kaleenka Russian Cafe,** a homey, lace-curtained change of pace at 1933 1st Ave., tel. (206) 728-1278. The piroshkis, chicken Kiev, and borscht are all excellent. Not far away is **Labuznik,** 1924 1st Ave., tel. (206) 441-8899, with rich, meaty dishes from Eastern Europe. Expensive.

SOUTH OF THE BORDER

El Toreador, 47 Fourth Ave. NW, tel. (206) 784-4132, is a justly popular Mexican spot with perfectly prepared dishes, handmade tortillas, delicious guacamole, and *enchiladas verdes* that make you think you've gone to heaven. **Casa-U-Betcha,** 2212 1st Ave., tel. (206) 441-1026, is a vastly different sort of place, with only a passing resemblance to traditional Mexican cookery. The food here is sort of a Southwest-meets-Northwest style, with blue margaritas and offbeat food combinations such as coyote moon carnitas, marinated and charbroiled prawns, and an enthusiastic, very noisy crowd. The neo-industrial decor has won national design awards.

Seattle is jammed with dozens of take-away shops selling burritos, tacos, and other standard south-of-the-border fare. For a healthy alternative, be sure to try the **Macheezmo Mouse** shops at 1815 N. 45th, tel. (206) 545-0153; 211 Broadway Ave. E, tel. (206) 325-0072; 701 5th

Ave., tel. (206) 382-1730; and 425 Queen Anne Ave., tel. (206) 282-9904. The menu goes light on the sauces, cheese, and sour cream, but without sacrificing taste.

Copacabana Bolivian Restaurant, tel. (206) 622-6359, is a wonderful place on a sunny day, with a patio overlooking Pike Place Market. It's easy to find, just walk down the street through the market and look up to find folks sitting back for a beer in the sun. The spicy Bolivian food is flavorful and hearty.

ASIAN AND MIDDLE EASTERN

Chinese

As you might guess, the International District is laden with Asian restaurants. Among the best is **House of Hong,** 409 Eighth Ave. S, tel. (206) 622-7997, with dim sum, seafood, chicken, and Hong Kong barbecue (inexpensive to moderate). Things get crowded in the evening, but the dim sum carts always have something appealing on board. **Tai Tung,** 655 S. King St., tel. (206) 622-7372, is the real thing, packed with Chinese from the neighborhood and longtime Seattleites who consistently rate it an International District favorite. The food can be inconsistent, so your best bet is to look around and see what others are eating for a clue on what to order.

Sea Garden, 509 7th Ave. S, tel. (206) 623-2100, serves Cantonese meals, but the food isn't the bland chow mein you might expect. Instead, the menu offers a wide range of soups, many seafood specialties, and perfectly cooked vegetables. It's also open till midnight most nights.

For Chinese food with a difference, head to the always-crowded **Panda's,** at 7347 35th Ave. NE (Wedgewood), tel. (206) 526-5115, or 1625 W. Dravus St. (Magnolia), tel. (206) 283-9030. Watch the busy cooks in the open kitchen, and enjoy the friendly service and distinctive dishes such as a battered eggplant fried with vegetables, or green onion and smoked salmon pancakes. But be ready for a wait most evenings. Save time and order out; they have free delivery to the north end of town. The U District has a big cluster of cheap student-oriented places with heaping helpings of Chinese food. Just walk up University Way NE to see what looks good.

Japanese
Musashi's Sushi & Grill, 1400 N. 45th St. (Wallingford), tel. (206) 633-0212, is an always-crowded, friendly little place with inexpensive fresh sushi (the main attraction), chicken teriyaki, and *bento* box lunches.

HaNa Restaurant, 219 Broadway Ave. E, tel. (206) 328-1187, on Capitol Hill is another very popular place for *bento* box lunches, salmon teriyaki, sushi, sashimi, tempura, and other simple meals. Just up the street is a fine Japanese noodle house, **Kitto,** 614 Broadway Ave., tel. (206) 325-8486, with simple but tasty bowls of *yakisoba,* teriyaki, and *udon.*

Kiku Tempura House, 5018 University Way NE, tel. (206) 524-1125, is one of the most popular student eateries on the "Ave." The tempura and teriyaki are quick and delicious, and you get huge portions. Great for a quick lunch or evening meal.

Another popular student place with made-to-order sushi and huge portions of teriyaki is **Tokyo Garden Teriyaki,** 4337 University Way NE, tel. (206) 632-2014. Order at the counter and wait for your number to be called. You'll get a big side of rice topped with teriyaki sauce, and a bowl of miso soup to go with the delicious teriyaki chicken or beef. Recommended.

Kamon on Lake Union, 1177 Fairview Ave., tel. (206) 622-4665, is a big place along the east side of Lake Union, with a splashy yuppified decor and excellent fresh sushi.

Out in Lake City (north of the U District) is **Toyoda Sushi,** 12543 Lake City Way NE, tel. (206) 367-7972, with some of the freshest and most succulent sushi anywhere around. This immaculately clean little shop also has excellent meat dumplings *(gyoza),* vegetable rolls, and fresh fish entrees. It gets crowded most nights.

For an upscale meal, **Nikko,** in the Westin Hotel at 1900 5th Ave., tel. (206) 322-4641, is best known for its outstanding sushi bar—considered by many to be the finest in Seattle—accompanied by a rather pricey Japanese menu that includes sukiyaki, teriyaki, tempura, and *kaiseki* dinners. Stop by earlier in the day for the *bento* box lunches.

Thai
For Thai cuisine, try the **Thai Restaurant** near the Seattle Center at 101 N. John St., tel. (206) 285-9000, **Jai Thai,** 3423 Fremont Ave. N, tel.

(206) 632-7060, or **Bahn Thai,** 409 Roy St., tel. (206) 283-0444; all three are inexpensive and popular with the locals. **Bangkok Cafe/Araya Places,** 4730 University Way NE, tel. (206) 524-3220, is split into two halves, Bangkok Cafe, offering a full range of dishes, and Araya Places, cooking up vegetarian specialties from the same kitchen (but separate cooking surfaces). Prices are reasonable, and the food is artfully prepared and excellent. They also have a $6 all-you-can-eat lunch buffet.

Thai Thai Restaurant, 11205 16th Ave. SW, tel. (206) 246-2246, is out of the way, but well worth the drive. The food is spicy hot, with great Thai noodles, soups, and chicken angel wings.

Middle Eastern and Indian
The U District and nearby Wallingford have a corner on the market for the best in Indian and Middle Eastern restaurants. You won't go wrong at **Cedars Restaurant,** 1319 N.E. 43rd St., tel. (206) 632-7708, or the larger Cedars a few blocks away at 4759 Brooklyn Ave. NE, tel. (206) 527-5247. Great Lebanese meals (especially the falafels), plus Indian specialties and an Indian grocery at the Brooklyn location.

Neelam's Authentic Indian Cuisine, 4735 University Way NE, tel. (206) 523-6830, lives up to its name with outstanding and very spicy East Indian meals. It has Tandoori and vegetarian specialties (but no beef), plus wonderful curries. The onion *kulcha* bread is hard to beat. Another extremely popular and reasonable U District student hangout is **Tandoor Indian Restaurant,** 5024 University Way NE, tel. (206) 523-7477.

Kabul, 2301 N. 45th St. (Wallingford), tel. (206) 545-9000, creates reasonably priced Afghan cuisine, including quite a few vegetarian dishes such as sautéed eggplant with a tomato, yogurt, and mint sauce. The food has obvious Indian influences but is distinctively different. The basmati rice spiced with saffron and pepper and topped with raisins and nuts is a treat in itself. Kabul has live sitar music on midweek evenings.

Adriatica, 1107 Dexter Ave. N, tel. (206) 285-5000, is an eastern Mediterranean restaurant on the west side of Lake Union with a grand view across the lake and skyline. The food is pricey but wonderful, especially the fried calamari and the chocolate espresso soufflé. Another fine Middle Eastern restaurant is **Mediterranean Kitchen,** 4 W. Roy St. (Queen Anne), tel. (206) 285-6713, where the food is always packed with garlic, and the portions are enormous. Excellent and reasonable. They also have a take-out place, **The Oven,** at 213 Broadway Ave. E, tel. (206) 328-2951.

Other Asian
Wild Ginger, 1400 Western Ave., tel. (206) 623-4450, gets rave reviews from local food critics, and jumps all over Asia; Vietnamese, Thai, Indonesian, and Sichuan Chinese dishes all come out of this creative kitchen. Wild Ginger is best known for its *satay* bar that features skewered and grilled seafood, chicken, pork, and vegetables, but also offers delicious curries, soups, and crab. The menu changes seasonally.

For an inexpensive but tasty Vietnamese lunch, head to **My's Restaurant,** 4220 University Way NE, tel. (206) 634-3526. This immensely popular student eatery dishes up huge portions of soups and fried noodle specials, including several vegetarian specialties. **Viet Nam Vietnamese Cuisine,** 660 S. King St. (International District), tel. (206) 467-6426, has a wide-ranging Vietnamese menu that includes several spicy soups.

Rasa Malyasia is now a small chain, with five local take-away shops; the largest (and the original) is in Pike Place Market, tel. (206) 624-8388. Stop here for Malaysian noodle dishes topped with meats, shrimp, or vegetables, along with a spicy peanut sauce.

NATURAL AND VEGETARIAN FOOD

Juicebars
Ed's Juice & Java, 7907 Wallingford N, tel. (206) 524-7570, is a shoebox-sized shop that often has a line out front on summer weekends. Located along Green Lake, they squeeze all sorts of fresh juices and also offer espresso drinks. In the University District, **Ricardo's Juice Bar,** 4217 University Way NE, tel. (206) 633-1327, makes all sorts of fresh juices and smoothies, along with healthy sandwiches, veggieburgers, hearty soups and stews, and more.

Vegetarian Restaurants
The **Gravity Bar,** 113 Virginia St. (downtown), tel. (206) 448-8826, and 415 Broadway Ave. E (Capitol Hill), tel. (206) 325-7186, has a gleaming 21st-century decor and attracts a noisy and

trendy DIB (dressed-in-black) art crowd. The food is all healthy and well prepared, with fresh-squeezed juices (over 75 juice combinations offered), flavor-packed steamed veggies with brown rice, great salads, and espresso. If you're feeling adventurous, try the wheat grass shots, also available from your nearby lawnmower.

Blue Planet Cafe, 2208 N. 45th St. (Wallingford), tel. (206) 632-0750, is the complete antithesis of the Gravity Bar. Blue Planet seems straight out of the Age of Aquarius, where recycling and conservation are emphasized, the crowd is laid-back and long-haired, and the menu is filled with simple and nutritious foods using no milk or egg products.

Cafe Flora, 2901 E. Madison St., tel. (206) 325-9100, is one of the city's best-known vegetarian restaurants. Everything is fine, but the rustic polenta is especially notable. They also offer offbeat pizzas (Blatjang pizza has a chutney-like topping of apricots, chili, fig, and ginger, with feta cheese) and portabello Wellington (grilled portabello mushrooms with pecan pâté and leeks in a puff pastry).

For more vegetarian eats, see also the Georgian Room, described above under "Northwest Cuisine," plus Araya Places, Kabul, and Neelam's Authentic Indian Cuisine, described above under "Asian and Middle Eastern."

MARKETS, GROCERS, AND BAKERIES

Fish Markets
Everyone knows about the fish-mongers in Pike Place Market, where the fish are always fresh and the entertainment comes at no extra charge, but Seattle also has several other fine places to buy fresh seafood. **Mutual Fish Company,** 2335 Rainier Ave. S, tel. (206) 322-4368, has old-time service and the quality you'd expect from Japanese owners. Another place with a long heritage and excellent fresh fish, crabs, and chicken is **University Seafood & Poultry,** 1317 N.E. 47th St., tel. (206) 632-3900, in the U District.

Farmers Markets
Everyone's favorite place to buy fresh produce is **Pike Place Market** (described above), where the produce is always beautifully presented. Unfortunately, prices are not any cheaper than in the grocery stores, and many of the stalls in-

sist upon selecting items for you. Another option in the summer is the **University District Farmers Market,** held Saturday 9 a.m.-2 p.m. from June to mid-October. It takes place in the University Heights yard on the corner of 50th St. NE and University Way NE.

Other farmers markets are in the **International District** at the Metro Station Plaza, 401 S. Jackson, on Saturday 10 a.m.-4 p.m., mid-June to mid-October; in the **Catholic Community Services Facility** at 23rd and Yessler, Saturday 10 a.m.-3 p.m., late June through October; and on **Capitol Hill** at 10th Ave. and Pike St., Saturday and Sunday 10 a.m.-5 p.m., mid-May to mid-October.

Grocers and Wineshops

As might be expected, Seattle has quite a few high-quality natural and organic grocers. The best-known is **Puget Consumers' Co-op,** a.k.a. "PCC," with seven stores around Seattle offering bulk foods, organic produce, and other healthy edibles. You don't have to be a member to shop here, though your prices are a bit lower if you join this 35-plus year old cooperative. Several of the markets—notably the Ravenna and Fremont stores—have fine delis with both vegetarian and meat dishes. For membership information and store locations, call (206) 547-1222. Two other excellent natural foods stores in Capitol Hill are the nonprofit **Central Co-op** at 1835 12th Ave., tel. (206) 329-1545, and **Rainbow Grocery,** 409 15th Ave., tel. (206) 329-8440.

Seattle has most of the major West Coast chains—Albertson's, Safeway, Red Apple, and Thriftway—along with several local grocery chains that rival Nordstrom's in service and presentation of products. **QFC** stands for Quality Food Stores, and they do indeed stress service. Another local favorite is **Larry's Markets,** a small chain with gourmet foods, artfully designed stores, big delis, and fresh breads and produce. At least one of their stores even has valet parking. **Uwajimaya,** at King and Sixth Streets in the International District, tel. (206) 624-6248, is a large store selling high-quality Asian groceries. **DeLaurenti Market,** tel. (206) 622-0141, in Pike Place Market is filled with gourmet imported groceries and wines from Europe. Other excellent places for wines include the tiny brick **Esquin Wine Merchants** shop at 1516 1st Ave. S, tel.

(206) 682-7374. They are big on Italian wines but also carry Northwest varieties and offer tastings, classes, and reasonable prices. **Pike and Western Wine Merchants** at the Pike Place Market has groceries, along with a diverse choice of Northwest wines. Another noteworthy shop is **La Cantina Wine Merchants,** tel. (206) 525-4340, in the University Village Mall.

Bakeries and Sweets

When it comes to chocolates, it is pretty hard to beat **Dilettante Chocolates,** 416 Broadway E (Capitol Hill), tel. (206) 329-6463, and 1603 1st Ave. (downtown), tel. (206) 728-9144. Both shops have wonderful chocolate truffles, tortes, and other sweets, and the Broadway shop also has a light menu with soups, salads, and sandwiches.

One of the finest places for rich and rustic breads is **Grand Central Baking Company,** 214 1st Ave. S, tel. (206) 622-3644. They also crank out perfect pastries and exquisite espressos.

The Urban Bakery, 7850 E. Greenlake Dr. N, tel. (206) 524-7951, is another great spot for fresh-from-the-oven baked goods, including scrumptious chocolate cakes, cheesecakes, and pies. The espresso bar is a favorite stopping place for the Green Lake post-jogging crowd. **Honey Bear Bakery,** 2106 N. 55th St. (Wallingford), tel. (206) 545-7296, is a favorite neighborhood place for an espresso and pastry (try the white chocolate brownies) with the groovy crowd.

Great Harvest Bread Co., 5408 Sand Point Way NE, tel. (206) 524-4873, bakes deliciously seasoned whole-wheat breads and always has free slices to taste with a dollop of butter. Another fine bakery is **Standard Bakery on Queen Anne,** 1835 Queen Anne Ave. N, tel. (206) 283-6359, with not just breads and pastries, but a deli with sandwiches, soups, and incredible pumpkin pies. **Three Girls Bakery,** in existence since 1912, is one of the Pike Place Market institutions, serving some of the finest croissants and sweets in town. A small inside counter offers a more relaxed setting.

Five Loaves and Fishes, 2719 E. Madison St. (Broadmoor area), tel. (206) 726-7989, has big, dense loaves of spelt (wheatless) bread, along with more traditional breads, sweets, and healthy vegetarian lunches and fresh vegetable juices. You'll get a dose of Seventh-Day Adventist literature with your meal; closed Saturday. For something completely different, stop by the QFC, Larry's, or PCC markets to try a loaf of bread made by the **Spent Grain Baking Co.,** made from the sweet grains left behind in the beer brewing process at local microbreweries.

Lots of bagel places in Seattle, but none of these come close to the caliber of what you'll find in New York or the Bay Area. Worth a try is **Bagel Oasis,** 2112 N.E. 65th St., tel. (206) 526-0525, and 462 N. 36th St., tel. (206) 633-2676, with distinctive baked (not boiled) bagels and other baked goods. Another local favorite is **Seattle Bagel Bakery,** 1302 Western Ave., tel. (206) 624-2187.

ENTERTAINMENT AND EVENTS

Seattle has gained a reputation as a major center for alternative music, particularly in the genre known as "grunge" (Seattleites prefer to call it "the Seattle sound"). The best entertainment guides are several free papers that show up every week at stores or in paper boxes throughout the city. *The Seattle Weekly* has articles on politics and Seattle goings-on, along with concert information, club dates, restaurant reviews, movie, lecture, sports, dance, and theater listings. Another freebie, *The Stranger,* has a generation-X edge, and is the best source for upcoming music; all the nightclubs advertise here. Farther from the mainstream is *The Rocket,* with music reviews written from a decidedly cynical perspective. Enough teen angst to fill a bathtub. The *Seattle Times* Thursday edition and *Seattle Post-Intelligencer* Friday edition also have weekly entertainment sections packed with details on dance, dining, theater, movies, and literary events.

NIGHTLIFE

Brewpubs and Hangouts
In recent years the Northwest has become a production center for high quality handcrafted ales made in the English and German traditions. True, most folks still swill down Rainier or Budweiser, but the microbrewed specialty beers are growing rapidly as people discover the difference between quantity and quality. Three of the largest places are described above: Hart Brewery, Hales Ales Brewery, and Redhook Ale Brewery. All of them, described below, have popular brewpubs with hearty pub fare.

Out in the U District is **Big Time Brewery and Alehouse,** 4133 University Way NE, tel. (206) 545-4509, with several fresh-brewed ales on tap and an 80-year-old backbar where you can enjoy the passing scene through the big front windows.

Pike Place Brewery, 1432 Western Ave., tel. (206) 622-3373, is a popular place in the heart of the market, with some of the best micros around (including XXXXX Stout), plus one of the best home brew supply places in America right next door, **Liberty Malt Supply Company.**

Join the loud sporting crowd at **Pacific Brewing Co.,** 322 Occidental S, tel. (206) 621-7002, near the Kingdome. Good beers that change with the seasons, a trendy atmosphere, and a menu that includes sandwiches, oysters on the half shell, bratwurst, and other light meals. It really hops after football or baseball games. Another place with a similar atmosphere, but a bigger menu, is **F.X. McRory's** across the street from the Kingdome's parking lot at 4199 Occidental Ave. S, tel. (206) 623-4800. They don't brew their own here, but they do offer 25 different Northwest microbrews on tap and some of the best fresh oysters on the half-shell anywhere.

Other pubs that brew on the premises and offer bar food include: **McMenamins Pub & Brewery,** 200 Roy St. (Queen Anne), tel. (206) 285-4722, **Maritime Pacific Brewing Co.,** 1514 N.W. Leary Way (Ballard), tel. (206) 782-6181, and **California and Alaska St. Brewery,** 4720 California St. SW (West Seattle), tel. (206) 938-2476.

The U District's **Blue Moon Tavern,** 712 N.E. 45th St. (no phone), is one of the most famous old-time hangouts in Seattle, the sort of place that once attracted the likes of Allen Ginsberg,

THE SEATTLE SOUND

Mention grunge to Seattleites and they'll probably roll their eyes and try to change the subject. It's part of the grunge mystique that it shrinks from attention. But the youthful look and sound that in the early 1990s won Seattle the moniker "The New Liverpool" (another groaner to locals) has enjoyed more popularity and commercial success than its tattooed and ear-ringed devotees ever bargained for.

Too slow and deliberate to be called punk rock, but as loaded with angst and despair as anything their underground predecessors put out a decade before, grunge music began in the 1980s by Seattle bands like Green River, Skin Yard, Alice in Chains, and Nirvana, enjoying substantial local popularity.

Wailing vocals, prominent guitar lines, and grim sensibilities were among the bands' similarities. But an aversion to glamorous "anthem rock," the kind put out by '80s superstars Van Halen and Journey, is perhaps their greatest shared characteristic.

Buoying the bands early on were Seattle's Sub Pop record label (their CD and tape store is at 1928 2nd Ave., tel. 209-443-0322), and The Rocket, a free semimonthly newspaper.

The band Mudhoney had an early local hit called "Touch Me I'm Sick"; it epitomized the dreary mood the bands affected. It also exemplified the tainted sexuality expressed in many grunge songs, a theme that, to date, marks grunge as the most striking musical reflection of the AIDS epidemic.

Stars of college radio in the '80s and early '90s, it was only a matter of time before one of the grunge bands made it big. Nirvana took the honors when their single "Smells Like Teen Spirit" broke onto commercial radio late in 1991, propelling the band's album sales into the millions and opening the door to the most controversial development in the grunge movement: success.

Seattle music fans watched in horror as their bands, whom they once saw live at clubs like The Vogue for a $3 cover charge, signed contracts with major Hollywood record labels, appeared on the cover of Rolling Stone, toured with names like Neil Young, and, of course, made millions and millions of dollars. Even Sub Pop made plans to open a retail store (on 2nd Ave. between Virginia and Stewart Streets) for the young disciples who began crowding their offices.

Meanwhile, across the country, middle-class teenage kids began dressing like impoverished young Seattleites: baggy pants, flannel shirts, and clunky, black boots made by Doc Marten. They grew their hair long but shaved it above the ears and around the back, died it red or green or some odd combination. Oh, yes, and tattoos. Tattoos on the arm, tattoos on the back, tattoos around the ankle, tattoos across the chest. Then came the body-piercing wave that started with multiple earrings, migrated to nose rings, lip rings, eyebrow rings, nipple rings, and even rings in certain areas not commonly exposed to passersby.

A Hollywood movie set in Seattle (Singles, starring Matt Dillon and Bridget Fonda) even had a grunge soundtrack and depicted several romances between Northwest young people—though only one character, Pearl Jam singer Eddie Vedder, could really be identified with the grunge scene.

One of the biggest shocks to the grunge world came on April 2, 1994, when Kurt Cobain, Nirvana's singer/guitarist/songwriter, was found dead in his Seattle home. After battling a heroin habit and intense stomach pain, the man whose words, voice, and Fender Stratocaster had brought grunge music to a mass audience shot himself in the head. He left a wife, baby daughter, and millions of fans behind.

Deeming the suicide a consequence of success would be oversimplifying. However, it's true that Cobain and Nirvana were (in)famous for resisting the slick, big-money culture of the recording industry, and the hordes of what they saw as superficial fans. ("We'd like to thank our true fans," Cobain once said as he accepted an MTV award.)

While no one really set a date—maybe it was the day Kmart introduced its grunge clothing line—aficionados eventually declared grunge dead.

The bands still made albums; Soundgarden's 1993 CD Superunknown got rave reviews. They still sold millions of albums; Nirvana's 1993 release, In Utero, went double-platinum within four months. And the long-hair, baggy-clothes look is, if anything, more popular then ever.

But for those who saw the scene in its infancy, the spotlight of mainstream media like MTV and even Newsweek has withered the dark Northwest moss that once seemed to carpet the bass lines and turn the dire lyrics into something vaguely poisonous. And the sight of their flannel shirts on department store rounders troubles them.

While grunge rockers rarely used words like "integrity," the issue of selling out had always been topical in the grunge scene; it was reportedly the reason for Green River's break-up in the '80s. Nor was it accidental that the cover of Nirvana's breakthrough CD *Nevermind* depicts a baby swimming after a dollar bill on a fishhook.

Perhaps the two bands that came out of the Green River separation, Pearl Jam and Mudhoney, epitomize the dilemma of subculture turned pop culture. By early 1994 Pearl Jam had become perhaps the most successful grunge band of all, with two multiplatinum albums; Mudhoney, meanwhile, was making do with a much smaller, more devoted following and record sales that had yet to reach the golden number of half a million. In recent years, even the term "grunge" has fallen out of favor; now it's "the Seattle sound," at least to folks in Seattle.

—Jason Ross

Jack Kerouac, and Tom Robbins. It still brings in the Deadheads on Sunday nights for a jukebox jam.

Pioneer Square Bars

Nine bars in the Pioneer Square area have banded together to charge a flat rate of $8 ($5 on weekdays) that lets you into all of the clubs that night. Because of this, the area is abuzz with people sampling the various acts and strolling along the sidewalks. This wonderful concept fosters listening to other types of music; several places offer blues or R&B, while others have grunge, jazz, or reggae. Probably the most popular places in this group are the **Fenix,** 323 2nd St., tel. (206) 343-7740, and the adjacent **Fenix Underground.** Both of these attract a younger crowd of local trendsetters and are owned by actor John Corbett, who played the DJ in the recently deceased TV show *Northern Exposure.* A sampling from other members of the Pioneer Square shared-cover group includes: **Colourbox,** 113 1st St. S, tel. (206) 340-4101, a cavernous, smoky place filled with grunge devotees; **New Orleans Restaurant,** 114 1st St., tel. (206) 622-2563, serving up spicy Creole meals plus Dixieland jazz, R&B, and zydeco; **Bohemian Cafe,** 111 Yesler Way, tel. (206) 447-1514, with great blues bands (including the phenomenal Isaac Scott Band); and **The Central,** 207 1st Ave., tel. (206) 622-0209, with the oldest bar in Seattle, here for over a century.

Other Rock Clubs

The Belltown industrial/commercial area north of downtown has several more popular nightclubs. The **Off Ramp,** 109 Eastlake E, tel. (206) 628-0232, has lots of space for jamming to some of Seattle's hottest bands. **Crocodile Cafe,** 2200 2nd Ave., tel. (206) 441-5611, is another great club that attracts the bigger acts on the alternative scene. **Backstage,** 2208 N.W. Market, tel. (206) 781-2805, hosts a range of music, including top national acts. **The China Club,** 1471 N.W. 85th St., tel. (206) 789-6903, mixes Chinese food and rockin'-out music, attracting both local and national acts. **Vogue,** 2018 1st Ave., tel. (206) 443-0673, is a center for the fringe crowd, with fetish night on Sunday, plus reggae, industrial, and alternative music or CDs other nights. **Victor's Sports Bar & Nightclub,** 75 Marion, tel. (206) 622-1969, is more than a noisy place to watch the game; also here are rock bands and hip-hop DJs with a young crowd. **O.K. Hotel,** 212 Alaskan Way, tel. (206) 621-7903, has two rooms, one with jazz or unusual performance pieces, and the other with rock bands. Other popular live music and DJ clubs are **The Weathered Wall,** 1921 5th Ave., tel. (206) 448-5688; **Under the Rail,** 5th and Battery, tel. (206) 728-7149; **Ballard Firehouse,** Russell and Market in Ballard, tel. (206) 784-3516; **DV8,** 131 Taylor N, tel. (206) 448-0888; **Moe,** 925 E. Pike St., tel. (206) 324-2406; and **Lockstock,** 4552 University Way NE, tel. (206) 634-3144.

Re-Bar, 1114 E. Howell St., tel. (206) 233-9873, is a fun dance club with a mixed gay, lesbian, and straight crowd, and DJs spinning all sorts of music. The city's biggest gay/lesbian bar is **Timberline,** 2015 Boren, tel. (206) 622-6220, with a huge maple dance floor and C&W music. Drop by on Tuesday nights for free two-step lessons. Also popular is the **Romper Room,** 106 1st. Ave. N, tel. (206) 284-5003, with a music mix that romps all over the place, from country to Grateful Dead. One of Seattle's most unusual nightspots is **Sit & Spin,** 2219 4th Ave., tel. (206) 441-9484, a laundromat where you can watch the clothes go round while dancing, eating, or playing board games.

Jazz and Blues

The most popular place for Seattle jazz buffs is **Dimitriou's Jazz Alley,** Sixth and Lenora, tel. (206) 441-9729, where big-time national acts and up-and-coming talent can be heard. For blues music, head to **Larry's,** 209 1st S, tel. (206) 624-7665, or one of the Pioneer Square clubs. **Paragon Bar & Grill,** 2125 Queen Anne Ave. N, tel. (206) 283-4548, features live jazz and blues most nights with no cover. A nice setting for dinner, too.

Comedy Clubs

Seattle's biggest comedy club is **Comedy Underground,** 222 S. Main St., tel. (206) 628-0303, where local and national talents perform for capacity crowds. **Giggles,** another comedy club at 5220 Roosevelt Way NE, tel. (206) 526-5653, has cheap food and beer with local, smaller-time acts. **Market Theater,** in Pike Place Market, tel. (206) 781-9273, has well-known and beginning comics, along with improvisational theater performances.

Film

Seattle has earned an international reputation among filmmakers as having one of the most discriminating audiences in America. Nobody quite knows why live theater and movies are taken so seriously, but movies are sometimes tested on Seattleites before being released, and Seattle viewers have often made a little-known film a winner.

For rainy-day moviegoing, **Cinerama** at 2100 4th Ave., tel. (206) 443-0808, and **UA Cinema 150** at 6th and Blanchard, tel. (206) 728-1622, offer first-run movies in a standard moviehouse atmosphere, as do the cinemas at Northgate and Southcenter malls. For off-the-beaten path films, try the **Egyptian Theatre,** 801 E. Pine, tel. (206) 323-4978; **Pike Street Cinema,** 1108 Pike St., tel. (206) 682-7064; **Grand Illusion,** 50th and University Way NE, tel. (206) 523-3935; **911 Media Arts Center,**

117 Yale Ave. N, tel. (206) 682-6552; **The Weathered Wall,** 1921 5th Ave., tel. (206) 448-5688; and **The New Varsity,** 4329 University Way NE, tel. (206) 632-3131. You'll also want to participate in the **Seattle International Film Festival,** held from late May to mid-June, the largest of its kind in America. It attracts more than 100,000 filmgoers. If you're just looking for a cheap flick, try the **Crest Theater,** 16505 5th Ave. NE, tel. (206) 363-6338, where all shows are only $2 (the movies may be slightly out of date).

PERFORMING ARTS

Given its size and vibrancy, you'd expect an active cultural scene in Seattle. Those expectations are exceeded by an extraordinary range of activity, especially in live theater. Much of the cultural action—at least when it comes to live theater, classical music, opera, and ballet—centers around Seattle Center (better known as "that place with the Space Needle"). For up-to-date info on arts events in Seattle, call (206) 447-2787 (24 hours). The Friday edition of both the *Seattle Times* and *Seattle Post-Intelligencer* newspapers have a complete listing of upcoming productions.

Get tickets for upcoming events from **Ticketmaster,** tel. (206) 628-0888. For half-price concert, comedy, and dance tickets the day of the show, stop by the **Ticket/Ticket,** booths at Pike Place Market and in Broadway Market at 401 Broadway Ave. E, tel. (206) 324-2744.

Live Theater

Nobody is quite sure why—maybe it really is the weather—but live theater has always done well in Seattle. Consequently, if you don't see a good movie, you will have a wide choice of plays and musicals to try. **Seattle Repertory Theatre** produces six plays (classic and contemporary) from October through May in the Bagley Wright Theater at Seattle Center, tel. (206) 443-2222. The company received a Tony Award in 1990. **ACT** (A Contemporary Theatre) fills out the other half of the year, performing at 100 W. Roy; tel. (206) 285-5110. **Pioneer Square Theater's** Mainstage, a former burlesque joint at 512 2nd Ave., and two smaller stages host local and national dramas and comedies; phone (206)

622-2016 for tickets. The **Intiman Theatre Company** brings classic dramatic theater to Seattle from May through November at Seattle Center's Intiman Playhouse, tel. (206) 626-0782. **The Group** is called the nation's premier multicultural theater, with performances in Seattle Center House from September through June, tel. (206) 441-1299.

Seattle Children's Theater, tel. (206) 441-3322, is the largest (and perhaps finest) children's theater in the U.S. and is located in the impressive Charlotte Martin Theatre at Seattle Center. Productions and classes run Sept.-May and include both the silly and the serious. The **Bathhouse Theatre,** on the shore of Green Lake in an old bathhouse, tel. (206) 524-9108, also presents a wide range of plays all year, from Shakespeare to musical revues.

Music and Dance

Seattle Center Opera House hosts the **Seattle Opera Association,** whose Sept.-May regular season is almost always a sellout, tel. (206) 389-7676. They present five productions annually, including Wagner's famous four-opera Ring cycle every four years; next time is 1999.

The Opera House is also home to the **Seattle Symphony** from September through May, tel. (206) 443-4747. The symphony has been gaining international attention under conductor Gerard Schwartz, a leading proponent of modern American composers and promoter of the Mostly Mozart series. The symphony performs more than 100 concerts a year, covering the spectrum from Bach to Frank Zappa. A "Musically Speaking" series features a Sunday afternoon mix of the classics with interesting commentary about the music and the composers. The **Seattle Youth Symphony,** tel. (206) 362-2300, which will make you wish you'd practiced more, also plays in the Opera House several times a season.

The **Pacific Northwest Ballet,** whose season is Oct.-May., produces the

BOB RACE

traditional *Nutcracker* for Christmas with sets by illustrator Maurice Sendak; tel. (206) 628-0888. Six contemporary dance companies help fill out the repertoire of dance in Seattle.

EVENTS

Chinese New Year is celebrated in late January or early February when the International District comes alive with parades and colorful displays; call (206) 623-8171 for info. **Fat Tuesday** is Seattle's weeklong Mardi Gras celebration at Pioneer Square in February with jazz and Cajun music, a Spam-carving contest ("works" from the contest are placed in the Spam Museum, or at least that's what they say), arts and crafts, and a parade.

In May the celebrations get serious, and one of the first is the **University Street Fair,** which brings more than 500 artists to display their wares on University Way NE on the third weekend in May. Also here are food booths and live music. More than 5,000 musicians (Nigerian, Chinese, Appalachian, Indonesian, and bluegrass, among others), dancers, and craftspeople display their talents while enormous amounts of food are consumed at the **Northwest Folklife Festival** held at Seattle Center on Memorial Day weekend; tel. (206) 684-7300. Also in May, the **Pike Place Market Festival** has free entertainment on three stages, strolling clowns and musicians, and a kids' area; tel. (206) 587-0351.

In June the **Pioneer Square Fire Festival** celebrates Seattle's great fire of 1889 (any excuse for a party, right?) with free activities in the park, a parade of classic firefighting equipment, contests, and free entertainment; tel. (206) 682-4648. Also in June, the **Dixieland Jazz Festival** is held at four sites in West Seattle; tel. (206) 932-4044. Each June, the funky "Republic of Fremont" holds the **Fremont Street Fair,** with booths, live music, ethnic food and drink, and assorted street performers and residents of the lunatic fringe. Call (206) 548-8376 for details. In late June and early July, the Museum of Flight hosts **Emerald City Flight Festival,** an air show that has brought such attractions as the B-2 Stealth bomber and the Concorde.

July begins with twin fireworks displays, one on Lake Union, and the other on Elliott Bay. The latter of these is sponsored by Ivar's Acre of Clams and is said to be one of the largest in America. Shortly afterward, the **Lake Union Wooden Boat Festival** is held at the south end of the lake, where you'll see some of the most beautiful boats on Puget Sound. In mid-July the **Bite of Seattle** is held in the Seattle Center, which gives restaurants, wineries, microbreweries, and coffeemakers an opportunity to show their products; tel. (206) 232-2982. Across the way in Ballard, **Seafoodfest** arrives on the second weekend of July, with a street festival, salmon barbecue, food and crafts booths, beer garden, and children's games. Later in the month more than 1,500 runners participate in the **Emerald City Marathon,** tel. (206) 285-4847.

Seattle's biggest fair of the year, **Seafair,** tel. (206) 623-7100, is a three-week-long extravaganza of crafts, parades, triathlons, ethnic festivals, and demonstrations by the Navy's Blue Angels, culminating in the unlimited **hydroplane races** on Lake Washington in early August.

New restrictions on alcohol consumption have made the infamous rowdy, beer-guzzling hydroplane crowds a thing of the past, but the notorious Seafair Pirates still wreak their own version of havoc.

A Labor Day weekend arts extravaganza, **Bumpershoot,** brings together writers, musicians, and craftspeople for a big end-of-summer party at Seattle Center. Bumpershoot attracts more than a quarter-million visitors annually, and features such performers as B.B. King, Bonnie Raitt, and the Neville Brothers. In early August the **Pacific Northwest African-American Festival** celebrates black heritage with a parade, arts and crafts, and music; tel. (206) 224-2511. One of the more unusual events is the **Bubble Festival** held in mid-August at the Pacific Science Center. Professional bubble blowers show how to blow square bubbles and how to freeze them; tel. (206) 443-2001.

King 5 Winterfest is a five-week holiday festival with decorations, children's entertainers, choirs, an ice rink, lighting ceremony, Santa Claus, and New Year's Eve celebration at Seattle Center.

The last festival of the year is the **Christmas Ships Parade,** a lighted flotilla that cruises Lake Washington in mid-December; the Seattle/King County Convention & Visitors Bureau, tel. (206) 461-5840, has route and viewing information.

SPORTS AND RECREATION

Spectator Sports

Major league sports are thoroughly represented in Seattle. The American League's **Mariners,** who didn't have a winning season until 1991, play at the Kingdome. Call (206) 622-4487 for tickets. The National Football League's **Seahawks,** tel. (206) 628-0888, frequently draw capacity crowds at the Kingdome, as do the National Basketball Association's **SuperSonics** at the Seattle Center Coliseum; tel. (206) 281-5850. The building was completely rebuilt in 1994-95, at a cost of $74 million (the original cost $4.5 million in 1962), transforming it into a state-of-the-art facility with room for 17,000 screaming basketball fans. Seahawks tickets are scarce—most are sold to season-ticket holders—but the Sonics are generally not sold out until the day of the game. (The Seahawks have been the object of a bitter custody battle over whether they will move to Southern California or stay in Seattle. As of this writing, Paul Allen—the multibillionaire cofounder of Microsoft—had an option to purchase the team. He has promised to keep them in Seattle if improvements are made to the Kingdome or a new stadium is constructed. Stay tuned.)

The Seattle **Thunderbirds,** tel. (206) 728-9124, play minor-league hockey from October to May at the Seattle Center Arena for the Western Hockey League. College sports are big here too, particularly the University of Washington's Husky football (tel. 206-543-2200) and basketball (tel. 206-543-2200) teams. That also applies to the women's basketball team that has been gaining in national prominence of late.

Another big Seattle-area sporting event nearly year-round is auto and motorcycle racing at **Seattle International Raceway,** 31001 144th in Kent, tel. (206) 631-1550.

More than 10 million Japanese people play the 3,000-year-old sport called Go, and the game has a devoted following on college campuses in America. The **Seattle Go Center**—the only one in America—opened in 1995 at 700 N.E. 45th Street. Funded by a one-time national champion Japanese Go player, Kaoru Iwamoto, the center has tables for 18 players at once and is used for national and international tournaments.

Boating

Rent wooden rowboats and sailboats at the **Center for Wooden Boats,** 1010 Valley St., tel. (206) 382-2628, on the south end of Lake Union. Or, rent sea kayaks from **Northwest Outdoor Center,** 2100 Westlake Ave. N, on the west side of the lake. NWOC is an outstanding place to learn about sea kayaking from the experts. They offer classes at all levels—from short introductory classes to six-day total-immersion whitewater kayak programs—sell many brands of kayaks, and provide guided tours to more than 25 destinations around Washington State. Call (206) 281-9694 for a detailed booklet describing all these options.

Sailboat Rentals and Yacht Charters, 1301 N. Northlake Way, tel. (206) 632-3302, has boats on the north end of Lake Union, or rent sailboards from **Bavarian Surf,** 711 N.E. Northlake Way, tel. (206) 545-9463.

In the summer you can rent kayaks, rowboats, paddleboats, sailboards, and canoes to play around the warm waters of Green Lake at **Green Lake Boat Rentals,** 7351 E. Green Lake Dr., tel. (206) 527-0171.

Over on Lake Washington, head to **University of Washington Waterfront Activities Center,** just east of the Montlake Bridge, tel. (206) 543-9433, for canoe or rowboat rentals. Take windsurfing lessons on Lake Washington from **Mount Baker Rowing and Sailing Center,** 3800 Lake Washington Blvd., tel. (206) 386-1913.

Let's Go Sailing, tel. (206) 624-3931, has relaxing sailing trips from Pier 56 on the downtown waterfront. A two-and-a-half-hour sunset sail around Elliott Bay is $35.

Cycling and Running

Bikes are a favorite way to get around Seattle, even on rainy winter days. For an easy and level ride, walk, run, or skate, join the throngs at **Green Lake,** where a 2.8-mile paved path circles the duck-filled lake. On sunny spring weekends you're likely to meet hundreds if not thousands of other folks out for fun in the sun.

The city's engineering department produces an excellent free map detailing the various cycling routes around Seattle, available from their office at 600 4th Ave., tel. (206) 684-7570. The most popular bike path is an old railroad route, the **Burke-Gilman Trail.** This 14-mile-long paved path begins in Fremont at 8th Ave. NW, cuts through Gasworks Park on the north shore of Lake Union, and then follows along Lake Washington all the way to the north end in Kenmore. From here, the 10-mile-long **Sammamish River Trail** continues to Marymoor Park in Redmond for a total of 24 miles of bike riding, rollerblading, running, or walking pleasure.

Another favorite ride is the six-mile **Alki Trail** that follows right on the shore of Puget Sound at Alki Point. It begins at the intersection of Harbor Ave. SW and S.W. Florida St., and curves around the north tip and then west to Alki Point Lighthouse.

Lake Washington Blvd. through the Arboretum and south along Lake Washington to Madrona Park makes for a very scenic bike ride, but traffic can get heavy. Other popular cycling places include Bainbridge Island, Mercer Island, Seward Park (in south Lake Washington), and Elliott Bay Trail (just northwest of downtown off Alaskan Way).

Rent bikes and rollerblades from a variety of local shops (see the Yellow Pages); one of the best and biggest is **Gregg's Greenlake Cycle,**

7007 Woodlawn Ave. NE, tel. (206) 523-1822. Bike tours of the Seattle area are offered by **Terrene Tours,** tel. (206) 325-5569.

Swimming

Swimmers will find eight city-run indoor pools around town: **Ballard,** 1417 N.W. 67th St., tel. (206) 684-4094; **Evans,** 7201 E. Green Lake Dr. N, tel. (206) 684-4961; **Helene Madison,** 13401 Meridian Ave. N, tel. (206) 684-4979; **Meadowbrook,** 10515 35th Ave. NE, tel. (206) 684-4989; **Medgar Evers,** 500 23rd Ave., tel. (206) 684-4766; **Queen Anne,** 1920 1st Ave. W, tel. (206) 386-4282; **Rainier Beach,** 8825 Rainier Ave. S, tel. (206) 386-1944; and **Southwest,** 2801 S.W. Thistle St., tel. (206) 684-7440. The very popular outdoor **Colman Pool,** 8603 Fauntleroy Way SW, tel. (206) 684-7494, is open summers only with saltwater bathing. The pools at Evans, Queen Anne, and Southwest have saunas, and the Ballard and Southwest pools have jacuzzis.

Green Lake is a favorite summertime swimming hole, but the water gets a bit rank by the end of the season with algal growth. (Lots of nutrients from all the duck and goose poop.) Other beaches with lifeguards in the summer include: Madison Park, Madrona Park, Magnolia Park, Magnuson Park, Mount Baker Park, and Seward Park.

SHOPPING

Shopping Centers

Unlike most other cities around the Sound, Seattle's downtown shopping district has not died out under the pressure of surrounding suburban malls. In fact, downtown shopping is more alive than ever, with the addition of **Westlake Center** at 5th Ave. and Pine St. and **Century Square** at 4th Ave. and Pike Street. Top-shelf jewelry, perfume, art, leather goods, and clothing stores abound in these two small centers. Westlake is also the endpoint for the Monorail from Seattle Center, and it has an information booth with an adjacent Ticketmaster booth with discounted day-of performance tickets. Downstairs, you'll find the entrance to the bus tunnel; upstairs are many quick food shops.

Two giants remain downtown: **Nordstrom** at 5th between Pike and Pine, is the national chain's flagship store and exemplifies all that is right about the chain; and the **Bon Marché**, at 4th and Pine, has stepped up its marketing and image after the demise of Frederick and Nelson. For generations Frederick's was Seattle's best department store but it went out of business a few years ago. The old store is being refurbished by Nordstrom in return for the reopening of Pine St. to cars.

Another downtown shopping center, this one underground, is **Rainier Square** between 4th and 5th Avenues and Union St., with small shops, including the **Lynn McAllister Gallery,** with a fine collection of Northwest paintings, prints, glass art, and sculptures. On 5th near University, **Wild Wings** specializes in wildlife and Western art, with limited edition prints by Bateman, Parker, Maass, and more, plus duck stamp prints and woodcarvings. The underground concourse has bookstores and restaurants and serves as an entrance to **Eddie Bauer,** another store founded in Seattle that became global.

The **waterfront** and, up the hillclimb, **Pike Place Market** are loaded with tiny wine shops, boutiques, and craft stores, plus the big, obvious produce stands and tourist traps; see "The Waterfront" and "Pike Place Market" above, for a detailed description of these areas. **Pioneer Square,** also discussed earlier, offers some of the city's finest galleries, antiques, and book and clothing stores.

Shopping malls abound in the Seattle area, the biggest being the **Northgate Shopping Mall,** seven miles north of Seattle (exit 173 from I-5); the **Southcenter Mall,** down I-5 into Tukwila (see "Southern Puget Sound"); and **Bellevue Square** (see "Vicinity of Seattle").

Outdoor Gear

When it comes to outdoor recreation, Seattle's famous **Recreation Equipment Inc.,** better known as REI, is in a class of its own. Easily the most successful cooperatively run company in America—it has 1.4 million members—REI has 30 stores scattered all over the country but is especially strong on the West Coast and in Seattle where it originated in 1938. A lifetime REI membership costs $15 and entitles you to yearly revates of around 10%. Built at a cost of $30 million, REI's sparkling new 99,000-square-foot flagship store on Eastlake between John and Thomas Streets opened in 1996 and is a center for backpackers, climbers, and other adventurers. The building features a 65-foot central climbing wall—tallest in the world—a 250-seat auditorium where you can watch outdoor presentations of all sorts, a deli and juice bar, kids' play area, a "rain room" to test waterproof gear, and three levels of parking below the store. Computer terminals throughout the store provide access to the Internet where you can get info on outdoor destinations worldwide. Rent all sorts of gear from their rental department, including backpacks, climbing shoes, tents, sleeping bags, ice axes, and skis of all types. REI stores offer evening clinics on everything from backcountry avalanche awareness to Costa Rican rainforests. Call (206) 323-8333 for more information.

Swallows' Nest 2308 6th Ave., tel. (206) 441-8151, is another fine outdoor and climbing shop with rental gear of all types. They often carry brands not available at REI. Other major outdoor rec places include: **The North Face,** 1023 1st Ave., tel. (206) 622-4111; **Eddie Bauer,** 5th and Union, tel. (206) 622-2766; **Patagonia,** 2100 1st Ave., tel. (206) 622-9700;

and **Warshal's Sporting Goods,** 1000 1st Ave., tel. (206) 624-7300. Warshal's is the most distinctive of these, an old-fashioned place that caters more to the fishing, camping, and hunting crowd than to the trendy pacesetters at North Face. They also have a big selection of photographic equipment.

Books and Magazines
Seattleites spend more money on books per capita than any other American city, $107 a year per person at last count (almost twice the national average). Given this, you can be assured that the city has lots of choices when it comes to buying books.

With more than 150,000 titles on the shelves, a comfortable atmosphere and knowledgeable staff, plus a cafe and almost nightly readings by acclaimed authors and poets, the **Elliott Bay Book Company,** 101 S. Main St., tel. (206) 624-6600, is a local legend. This Pioneer Square bookstore is *the* quintessential place for Seattle bibliophiles. Pick up their quarterly *Elliott Bay Booknotes* for detailed book reviews and articles about the craft of writing.

The **University Bookstore,** at 4326 University Way NE, tel. (206) 634-3400, competes with Harvard for the nation's largest university bookstore, carrying an impressive array of titles, plus office supplies, "go-Huskies" clothing, cameras, CDs, and more. Just down the block is a place at the opposite end of the spectrum, **Beauty and the Books,** 4213 University Way NE, tel. (206) 632-8510. This rambling used book shop is jammed with thousands of old titles and is a great place to plop down on one of the funky couches. Four affectionate black-and-white cats rule this place. Also on "the Ave" is **Bulldog News,** 4208 University Way NE, tel. (206) 632-6397, the largest magazine and newspaper store in town, with over 2,000 titles, including quite a few foreign magazines. Almost any night you're bound to find several dozen folks scanning the issues (and doing quite a bit of reading). Bulldog also has a smaller shop at

Broadway Market in Capitol Hill. The other excellent place for magazines and out-of-town newspapers is the **Read All About It** newsstand at Pike Place Market, tel. (206) 624-0140.

For a great selection of travel books, visit **Wide World Books and Maps,** 1911 N. 45th Ave. (in Wallingford), tel. (206) 634-3453. The tea shop next door is a fine place to read about Asia while sipping fresh Chinese tea. For gay and lesbian titles (plus much more) drop into **Bailey/Coy Books** in Capitol Hill at 414 Broadway Ave. E, tel. (206) 323-8842. Unrepentant liberals, socialists, and radicals love **Left Bank Books** in the Pike Place Market, tel. (206) 622-0195. You can get an idea of the orientation at the collectively run **Red & Black Books,** 432 15th Ave. E (Capitol Hill), tel. (206) 322-7323, from their credo: "Capitalism is Organized Crime."

East West Book Shop, 1032 N.E. 65th St., tel. (206) 523-3726, is the place for the crystal, channeling, and pyramid-power crowd. For something more down to earth (literally), be sure to visit **Flora and Fauna,** 121 1st Ave, tel. (206) 623-4727, the biggest local purveyor of natural history volumes in the West. Lots of other bookstore choices in town, including a big **Barnes and Noble** store that opened in University Village in 1995.

Photography
Photographers can stock up on supplies at **Cameras West,** 1908 Fourth Ave., tel. (206) 622-0066, or **Warshal's,** 1000 1st Ave., tel. (206) 624-7300. Professionals head to **Glazer's Camera Supply,** 430 8th Ave. N, tel. (206) 624-1100, where the shelves are stocked with lighting gear, darkroom supplies, tripods, and other supplies. A few doors down the street is **Ivey-Seright Photo Lab,** 424 8th Ave. N, tel. (206) 623-8113, the best Seattle place for professional quality processing and cutting-edge digital imaging work. **Photographic Center Northwest,** 2617 5th Ave., tel. (206) 441-7030, has classes for all levels of ability.

INFORMATION AND SERVICES

Exchange foreign currency at **First Interstate Bank,** 1215 4th Ave., tel. (206) 292-3111, or **Rainier Bank,** 1301 5th Ave., tel. (206) 621-4111.

For information on Seattle attractions and events, plus maps and other assistance, contact the **Seattle/King County Convention and Visitors Bureau,** located at 800 Convention Place in the Washington State Convention and Trade Center, on the Galleria level. They are open Mon.-Fri. 8:30 a.m.-5 p.m., Sat.-Sun. 10 a.m.-4 p.m. in the summer; and Mon.-Fri. 8:30 a.m.-5 p.m. in the winter. While here, be sure to pick up the *Seattle Visitors Guide,* a compendium of local entertainment, restaurants, shopping, and sights. Call them for a big packet of Seattle information at (206) 461-5840. Also in the convention center are various shops, changing displays of fine artwork along the walls, and access to **Freeway Park,** built over part of I-5, with greenery, waterfalls, and fountains. The Convention and Visitors Bureau also maintains small visitors centers next to the Space Needle (summers only). At Sea-Tac Airport, the Travelers Aid stations have limited local info and brochures.

The **National Forest and Parks Outdoor Recreation Information Center,** 915 2nd Ave., room 442, tel. (206) 220-7450, has information on Forest Service and Park Service lands throughout Washington. Open Mon.-Fri. 8:30 a.m.-4:30 p.m. year-round.

If you're a member, the **AAA Travel Store** at 330 6th Ave. N is a good source of maps and area information plus travel guidebooks, luggage, and other travel-related accessories.

Another excellent guidebook to the area is *Seattle Access,* published by Harper Perennial and available in local bookstores. *Seattle Best Places,* published by Sasquatch Books, also details many of the finer aspects of the city.

Libraries

The main branch of the **Seattle Public Library** is at 1000 4th Ave., tel. (206) 625-4952, with another 23 neighborhood libraries scattered around town. The main library is open Sunday 1-5 p.m., Mon.-Thurs. 9 a.m.-9 p.m., and Fri.-Sat. 9 a.m.-6 p.m. The University of Washington has collections of more than five million volumes spread in its various campus libraries, the majority of which are housed in the enormous **Suzzallo and Allen Libraries** near the center of campus. (This includes the original Suzzallo building, plus the connected Allen building added in the 1980s.) Call (206) 543-0242 for more information.

As-You-Like-It Library, 915 E. Pine, tel. (206) 329-1794, is the most unusual library in Seattle. Located on the fourth floor of the historic Odd Fellow's Hall, this collection of 12,000 metaphysical books fills two rooms and is open Mon.-Sat. 11 a.m.-9 p.m. Books cover the spectrum, including astrology, magic, hermetics, parapsychology, telepathy, and tarot. Anyone can come here to read, but to check out books you'll need to pay a $20 annual fee. They even offer mail-order service.

TRANSPORTATION

AIRPORT ACCESS

Seattle's airport is 12 miles south of town and midway between Seattle and Tacoma, hence the name, **Sea-Tac Airport.** All the major domestic, and many international airlines fly into Sea-Tac. The airport's underground monorail makes it easy to get to the various terminals, and a state-of-the-art luggage transport system means you usually won't wait long for your bags. Call (206) 431-4444 or (800) 544-1965 for updates on airport parking, weather and traffic conditions, ground transportation schedules and rates, and other airport services. Get Metro bus schedules and details on shuttle bus and limo service from counters in the baggage claim areas.

The least expensive way to reach Seattle is aboard one of **Metro's** city buses. Numbers 174, 184, and 194 run between Sea-Tac and downtown Seattle about every half-hour; one-way fare is $1.10 off-peak, $1.60 peak; tel. (206) 447-4800. The buses leave from outside the lower-level baggage claim area of the domestic terminal (turn right as you exit), or catch them downtown if you're headed out. It takes approximately 50 minutes to reach downtown. Make sure you catch the bus heading north to Seattle, not south to Federal Way! Metro buses travel along the Pacific Highway and provide the cheapest access for the many motels close to the airport.

To do it the easy (and expensive) way, grab a cab on the airport's second level; they recently went through an image change, cleaned up the cabs (and in some cases, themselves), and now all are required to charge the same rates—$18-25 one-way to Seattle, depending on destination and number of passengers.

Gray Line Airport Express, tel. (206) 626-6088, has airport pick-up service to and from eight downtown hotels about every half hour from 5 a.m. to midnight; $7.50 adults, $5.50 kids. No reservations needed, just board the bus outside the baggage claim area.

Shuttle Express, tel. (206) 622-1424 or (800) 942-7433, has door-to-door van service between Sea-Tac to Seattle ($14-19), Everett ($19), Belle-

vue ($18), and other cities around Seattle, including Issaquah, Kirkland, Bothell, and Mercer Island. Make reservations ahead of time for a pickup at your lodging place in town.

Port Angeles-Seattle Bus Lines, tel. (206) 681-7705 or (800) 764-2287, operates buses from Sea-Tac to Tacoma and Port Angeles, along with various points in between, including Bremerton, Poulsbo, and Gig Harbor. The fare to Port Angeles is $16, or $6 to Tacoma.

A similar service is run by **Airporter Shuttle,** tel. (800) 235-5247, with connections between Sea-Tac and Marysville, Mount Vernon, Anacortes, Oak Harbor, Bellingham (including the Alaska Ferry terminal), and Blaine on the Canadian border. Direct service to the Alaska Ferry is $29 for adults, $26 for seniors, and $15 for kids under 16.

Quick Shuttle Service, tel. (800) 665-2122, provides connections between Sea-Tac and Vancouver, B.C., for $29. **Olympic Van Service,** tel. (360) 452-3858, has shuttle service to Port Angeles, Sequim, and other areas along the way.

TRAINS AND LONG-HAUL BUSES

Amtrak
Amtrak serves Seattle at its historic King Street Station (Third Ave. S and S. King St.), tel. (206) 464-1930 or (800) 872-7245. The **Coast Starlight** has daily service connecting Seattle with Tacoma, Olympia, Centralia, Kelso-Longview, Vancouver, Portland, and south to Oakland and Los Angeles. The **Empire Builder** connects Seattle with Edmonds, Everett, Wenatchee, Ephrata, and Spokane, continuing to Minneapolis and Chicago; service is four times a week. The **Mount Baker International** provides daily train connections to Vancouver, B.C., via Edmonds, Everett, Mount Vernon, and Bellingham.

Bus Service
Greyhound, tel. (800) 231-2222, provides daily bus service throughout the lower 48 and to Van-

couver, B.C., from their bus terminal at 9th and Stewart. **Northwest Trailways,** tel. (206) 728-5955 or (800) 366-3830, operates from their station at 1936 Westlake Ave., with service throughout the Northwest, and on to Vancouver, B.C.

The most unusual bus transportation from Seattle is the **Green Tortoise,** tel. (800) 867-8647, a twice-weekly bus ride from Seattle to Los Angeles that takes 48 hours. The comfortable old bus stops at Green Tortoise's creekside park in southern Oregon for a vegetarian feast ($3), and a chance to swim or enjoy the sauna. This is a great and fun way to travel if you don't mind sleeping on a foam pad and hanging out with youthful hostelers. One-way tickets are $49 to San Francisco, or $69 to Los Angeles. Green Tortoise also operates trips to the East Coast from San Francisco, plus all sorts of voyages, including monthlong treks to Alaska, 16-day tours of the national parks, and even trips around Mexico and Central America.

METRO TRANSIT BUSES

Seattle is still in search of a light-rail transit system that will be acceptable to the voters—they rejected an ambitious proposal in 1995—but the Metro bus system provides efficient connections throughout the area. Metro buses run 6 a.m.-1 a.m. every day, about every 30 minutes on the city routes. The Metro customer service offices are at 821 2nd Ave. and in the Westlake Station. Fares are 85 cents off-peak, $1.10 peak within the city; $1.10 off-peak or $1.60 peak, outside city limits. For $3, you can purchase a visitor pass that gives you unlimited rides on Metro buses and the streetcars, and a roundtrip ride on the Monorail. Buy them at the Convention and Visitors Bureau, the youth hostel, the Westlake Metro station, Monorail stations, and other places around town. Call (206) 684-1716 or (800) 542-7876 for route info and details on bus passes. All Metro buses have bike racks on the front and carry bikes at no extra charge. Bikes are not carried within the Ride Free area of downtown.

Ride Free Zone
Metro has a Ride Free Zone for downtown riders. You can simply hop onto a bus anywhere in the zone and ride free. The boundaries are S. Jackson St., I-5, Pine St., Battery St., and Alaskan Way, and the buses are free between 6 a.m. and 7 p.m. Rides on the waterfront streetcars are not included in the zone.

A 1.3-mile **bus tunnel** cuts through the center of downtown along Pine St. and 3rd Ave., with stops at Convention Place (9th and Pine), Westlake Center (4th and Pine), University St. (3rd and University), and the International District (5th and S. Jackson). This unique tunnel was built with the future in mind: tracks are already in place for a light rail system (if voters ever support it), and the buses switch from diesel outside, to electric power inside the tunnel. The tunnel is decorated with several pieces of art commissioned for the project (part of the state's One Percent for the Arts program). But the best part of the whole thing is that it is within the Ride Free Zone.

Waterfront Streetcar
The Waterfront Streetcar is a very popular Metro-operated trolley that follows along the waterfront and up to Pioneer Square and the International District—it costs 85 cents ($1.10 in commute hours). See "The Waterfront" earlier in this chapter for a complete description.

Other Public Transit
Pierce Transit, tel. (800) 562-8109, has southern Puget Sound bus service connecting downtown Seattle with Tacoma. **Community Transit,** tel. (800) 562-1375, provides commuter bus service connecting Everett and other Snohomish County cities with downtown Seattle and the University District.

FERRY SERVICE

Washington State Ferries
One of the best ways to see Seattle is from the water, and one of the cheapest ways to do so is aboard the Washington State Ferries that operate almost continuously from before sunrise to after 1 a.m. daily. The ferries leave from the main terminal at Pier 52 for **Bainbridge Island** and **Bremerton.** To either destination, car-and-driver fares are $7.10 one-way; passengers and walk-ons pay only $3.50 roundtrip. A passenger-only **Seattle-Vashon Island** ferry ($3.50

roundtrip) has daily departures from Pier 50 in the summer, and Mon.-Sat. departures in the winter.

The Fauntleroy ferry dock in west Seattle serves Southworth on the Kitsap Peninsula and Vashon Island about every 20-50 minutes daily. Car-and-driver fares to **Southworth** are $7.10 one-way; passengers and walk-ons pay $3.50 roundtrip; the crossing takes approximately 35 minutes. A 15-minute **Fauntleroy-Vashon Island** crossing costs $9.55 roundtrip for car and driver, $2.30 roundtrip for passengers and walk-ons. Get to the Fauntleroy dock by heading south on I-5 to exit 163; follow the signs from here.

There is a 50 cent surcharge to carry bikes on all these ferry runs. Fares for vehicles are a bit lower in the off-season (mid-October to mid-May), and discounts are available for seniors, children, and people with disabilities. If you're going to be traveling a lot on the ferries, ask about frequent-user coupon books. There are no ferry connections from Seattle to the San Juan Islands; you'll need to get to Anacortes or Sidney, B.C., to begin a San Juans trip (or see "Victoria and San Juan Ferries" below). For more information on Washington State Ferries, call (206) 464-6400 or (800) 843-3779.

Victoria and San Juan Islands Ferries

For a daylong excursion to Canada, take the **Victoria Clipper** from Pier 63 to Ogden Point in Victoria. Reservations are required for the cruise, tel. (206) 448-5000 or (800) 888-2535, and it takes two hours to reach Victoria. The roundtrip cruise can be completed in one day (8:30 a.m. departure and 9:30 p.m. return) while allowing a brief stay in Olde English Victoria. Roundtrip fares for adults are $89 mid-May to mid-October, with lower off-season fares and discounts for seniors and kids. For variety, take the *Clipper* to Victoria and fly back on Kenmore Air (see below). They also offer optional one- or two-night stays in Victoria, or a "Triple Play" that includes a night each in Victoria and Vancouver, plus a wide range of other tours into British Columbia. In addition, Their *San Juan Explorer* commutes between Seattle and the San Juan Islands, or Victoria and the San Juans. Roundtrip runs from Seattle to the San Juans costs $49 for adults; from Victoria it's $44. For something simpler, try a two-hour sunset cruise from Seattle for $16.

The **Royal Victorian** sails between Seattle and Victoria from mid-May to mid-October, offering passenger and vehicle transport. The ferry leaves Pier 48 at 1 p.m., arriving Ogden Point, Victoria, at 5:30 p.m. From Victoria, the ferry sails at 7:30 a.m., arriving in Seattle at noon. The boat operates Thurs.-Sun. only and has a buffet, espresso bar, duty free shopping, lounge, children's play area, and gift shop on board. One-way fares are $21 for passengers, $46 for a car and driver. Bikes are an extra $5, and private day rooms are available for $25 more. Reservations are advised. Call 625-1880 or (800) 668-1167 for reservations, or (800) 683-7977 for recorded info.

BY CAR

Note: For mountain pass conditions, call the State Department of Transportation at (206) 976-7623 (for 35 cents) from November to March; in the Seattle area, try **AAA**'s free number, tel. (206) 448-8611.

Like most other large cities, Seattle has far too much automobile traffic, creating major traffic jams during the weekday commute hours. If possible, try to stay on public transit, both for your own sanity and for the environment. By all means avoid the 3-6 p.m. weekday rush hour, when I-5 and the floating bridges are often virtual parking lots. According to one recent study, Seattle's traffic was the fifth worst in the United States. One of the more difficult aspects of Seattle city driving isn't getting there, but getting back: finding an I-5 entrance ramp can be frustrating, especially after you zigzag over and under the highway a few times. One sure cure: Head down Fifth Ave. because entrances to both north- and southbound traffic are along it. Another good, although very busy, way to approach the freeway is on Mercer St.: get in the right lanes for southbound, northbound to the left.

Driving around downtown Seattle is much more difficult than walking, and is almost as expensive as flying to Portland, because at some point you've got to park the car. Parking downtown is difficult on weekdays—and costly: meters (if you can find one) are $1 an hour, and private lots cost $7-12 a day. Be warned that the vigilant meter maids seem always to be waiting for the "expired" flag to pop up so they can stick you with a $20 ticket. That can buy a lot of bus fares!

TOURS

When it comes to tours, Seattle has every possible option, from the standard drive-'em-around-in-the-bus type to the goofy, tongue-planted-firmly-in-cheek version.

Bill Speidel's Underground Tours

Bill Speidel's tour falls in the latter category. It covers the Pioneer Square area while a guide provides humorous anecdotes (often at the expense of Tacoma residents), along with local history. You'll learn about the speakeasies, gambling parlors, illegal lotteries, and opium dens that once occupied this section under the streets, among other interesting facts. (See "Pioneer Square," earlier in this chapter, for a complete description.) These very popular one-and-a-half-hour tours leave several times daily; $5.50 for adults, $4 for students, $4.50 for seniors, $2.50 for kids. Reservations recommended; phone (206) 682-1511 for a schedule, or 682-4646 for reservations.

Air Tours

To see the city from about 1,500 feet, try one of **Chrysler Air's** 20-minute scenic floatplane rides over Seattle; only $33 per person, two-person minimum. Longer flights are available to Mt. St. Helens, Mt. Rainier, or the San Juan Islands. Flights take off and land at Lake Union seven days a week, year-round; reservations are recommended but not required; tel. (206) 329-9638.

The world's largest seaplane operation, **Kenmore Air,** tel. (206) 486-1257 or (800) 543-9595, has year-round scheduled floatplane flights from Lake Union or Lake Washington. Destinations include the San Juan Islands ($79 one-way; $109-139 roundtrip), Poulsbo ($79 one way), Victoria ($83-93 one-way; $139-159 roundtrip), and onward to several Vancouver Island destinations in the summer. Note, however, that a 24-pound baggage weight limit is in effect for these flights, with excess baggage charged at 50 cents/pound. Kenmore Air also offers scenic flights over the San Juans on a standby basis for $30 (you ride along on the

roundtrip flight if they have seat space that day), but you aren't allowed to use this for one-way transportation to the islands. This is a real bargain since the flights normally last over two hours! In addition, they offer more standard flightseeing trips over Seattle at $90 (up to three people) for a quick 20-minute flight.

Sound Flight at the Renton Airport runs numerous flightseeing tours around the entire state and north into British Columbia. A half-hour flight over Seattle costs $45 per person; a one-hour flight over Puget Sound costs $69 per person; a one-and-a-half-hour flight over Mt. Rainier is $89; and a four-hour flight to the San Juan Islands with a two-hour stop is $129 per person. They can also take you on a six-hour trip to Victoria for $149, to Ross Lake in the North Cascades for $169 per person, and to many other destinations. For information call (206) 255-6500.

West Isle Air, tel. (206) 671-8463 or (800) 874-4434, has daily service from Boeing Field in Seattle to the San Juan Islands for $60-80 per person one-way.

Scenic Air, tel. (206) 764-1175 or (800) 995-3332, flies out of Boeing Field, five miles south of Seattle, with flightseeing trips around Puget Sound for $49.

Bus and Van Tours

Gray Line, tel. (206) 626-5208 or (800) 426-7532, offers a number of Puget Sound tours. Discover Seattle with a three-hour tour highlighted by the Ballard Locks, Kingdome, UW, and the waterfront for $21 adults, or $11 ages two to 12. A three-and-a-half-hour "Gold 'n' Wings" tour includes Pioneer Square, West Seattle, and the Museum of Flight for $25 adults, or $13 kids. Combine these two tours for an all-day visit to Seattle for $41 adults, or $21 kids. If you are ready for a whirlwind trip, add in an Argosy boat cruise of the Chittenden Locks to this to total 10 hours of sightseeing for $61 adults, or $31 kids. Gray Line has several other sightseeing trips, including day trips to Mt. Rainier ($40 adults, $20 kids), and overnight trips to Mt. Rainier ($106 per person, including lodging at historic Paradise Inn). Other Gray Line trips include one-day jaunts to Victoria ($89) and Vancouver, B.C. ($67-79), the San Juan Islands ($59 adults, $30 kids), the Spirit of Washington Dinner Train ($75-87), and Everett's Boeing plant ($30). (See "Airport Access," above, for Gray Line's airport express buses.)

Show Me Seattle Tours, tel. (206) 633-2489, offers more individualized attention on their van tours and emphasizes the offbeat and quirky places that make Seattle unique. Three-hour tours cost $28 and cover such sights as an outdoor Jello-mold collection, the Aurora bridge troll, microbreweries, Bainbridge Island, or the city's neighborhoods.

Customized Tours, tel. (206) 878-3965, has van tours of Seattle for $25, tours of Seattle's outskirts (including the UW campus, arboretum, Volunteer Park conservatory, Ballard Locks, and more) for $25, tours of Snoqualmie Falls area for $25, Boeing plant tours for $20, and trips to Snoqualmie Pass and Roslyn (of *Northern Exposure* fame) for $45. All these trips last approximately three hours.

Seattle Tours, tel. (206) 660-8687, offers three-hour van tours ($28) that depart major downtown hotels several times a day.

Seattle Name-Droppers Tour, tel. (206) 625-1317, is a three-hour tour of Seattle showing where the rich and famous, and usually dead, former Seattleites worked, lived, and sometimes killed. These include such diverse figures as Bruce Lee, Carol Channing, Ted Bundy, Tom Robbins, and Ray Charles, plus many others.

Chinatown Discovery, tel. (206) 236-0657, provides educational tours of the International District, including a three-hour trip ($30) that features a seven-course dim sum lunch.

Scenic Bound Tours, tel. (206) 433-6907, takes you on all-day van trips to the wild places around Puget Sound, including both Mt. St. Helens and Mt. Rainier for $55, or Mount Rainier National Park for $47. These tours provide a chance to explore forested hiking trails, high mountain lakes, and scenic passes.

Adventure Outdoors, tel. (206) 842-3189, provides day trips to Mt. Rainier, the Olympics, Mt. St. Helens, Leavenworth, or Vancouver for $99, as well as two- and three-day trips that include all meals and overnight accommodations. Prices for the overnight versions depend upon the number of people involved, the length of time, and the destination; count on around $300 per person for four people on a two-day trip to Mt. Rainier.

Boat Tours

A number of boat tours and ferry services depart from Seattle's waterfront, providing a relaxing, scenic change of pace for the foot-weary traveler. The most popular is offered by **Argosy Cruises,** tel. (206) 623-4252 (recording) or 623-1445, with a fleet of eight tour and charter cruise vessels. Their one-hour informative tour of Elliott Bay and the waterfront describes the hows and whys of containerized shipping along with historical background. The tours depart daily from Pier 55; $13 for adults, $6 for kids, free for kids under age five. No reservations necessary. Argosy also has a 90-minute Lake Washington cruise for $17.50 adults, $16 seniors, $8 kids, free for under five. These take place onboard the historic MV *Kirkland,* a 110-foot wooden ferry built in 1924. One of their most popular tours takes you from Elliott Bay through the Chittenden Locks into Lake Union, and then back by bus. This two-and-a-half-hour narrated tour costs $20 adults, $11 kids, free for under five; tours offered daily April-Oct., and Fri.-Mon. the rest of the year. Reservations are required; call (206) 623-4252 for departure times. Argosy also has charter fishing trips around Puget Sound, cruises to Tillicum Village (see below), and special event cruises throughout the year, including a series of "Christmas Ship" tours with on-board choirs singing carols.

Explore Nature's Aquarium, at Pier 55, tel. (206) 623-6364, offers a unique boating experience. Two hour cruises take you out into the Sound where divers carry underwater video cameras hooked up to monitors on the boat, providing a fascinating way to see fish, octopus, sea cucumbers, crabs, and other creatures on the seafloor. The divers have two-way radios that allow them to provide commentary along the way. These tours cost $28 for adults, $20 for kids under 12.

The ***Spirit of Puget Sound*** is a three-deck tour boat with a dance floor, a cafeteria-style dining room, and plenty of upper-deck space for fresh air. The boat has lunch cruises ($26-27), dinner cruises ($45-48), and moonlight party cruises ($17); call (206) 443-1442 for details. It departs from Pier 70.

For something different, take a guided tour by sea kayak of Lake Union ($20), or a sunset trip through the Ballard Locks to Puget Sound and back ($30). No experience necessary. These are offered by **Northwest Outdoor Center** on Lake Union, 2100 Westlake Ave. N, tel. (206) 281-9694. **Outdoor Odysseys,** tel. (206) 361-0717, offers sea kayak tours around various parts of the Sound, as well as the San Juans and other places.

Alaska Sightseeing Cruise West, 4th and Battery Building, Suite 700, Seattle, tel. (206) 441-8687 or (800) 426-7702, offers all-inclusive "Island Discoveries" tours of the San Juan Islands and Puget Sound each September and October. These seven-night voyages aboard the 165-foot *Spirit of Discovery* depart Seattle and include visits to Victoria, the San Juans, Whidbey Island, Hood Canal, Port Townsend, La Conner, and Mt. Rainier. Not for the budget crowd: The cost is $1,159-2,186 per person.

Callahan Capers, tel. (206) 322-9157, offers specialized tours of Lake Union houseboats—from the funky to the fabulous—including the home where *Sleepless in Seattle* was filmed. Jeri Callahan can match your interests, whether it is by kayak, sailboat, or motorboat.

Tillicum Village Tour

This village has been one of Washington's premier experiences for tourists for many years, and can be visited as part of a full-day trip including dinner with Argosy's **Tillicum Village Excursion,** leaving from Piers 55 and 56. The village is on Blake Island, a state park accessible only by boat. The trip includes a salmon

bake in a cedar longhouse, dances, nature trails, Indian artifacts, and a gift shop. Departing from the Seattle waterfront, the four-hour tour is available daily from May through mid-October, with reduced tours the rest of the year; fares are $50 for adults, $47 for seniors, $33 for ages 13-19, $20 for ages six to 12, $10 for ages four to five. Infants free. Reservations are required; tel. (206) 443-1244. For those who want more time to explore the hiking paths around the island, the company offers six-and-a-half-hour trips on Saturday from mid-June to early September, plus Sunday in July and August.

Walking Tours

Seattle Walking Tours, tel. (206) 885-3173, are led by Duse McLean, author of *The Pocket Guide to Seattle.* Tours begin from Westlake Park and end in the International District, with an emphasis on the city's architecture and history. She also offers customized tours that concentrate on your own interests. The similarly named **See Seattle Walking Tours,** tel. (206) 226-7641, offers comfortably paced treks around town, including a guided walk that covers Pike Place, the Space Needle, Monorail, Pioneer Square, and lots more. Half-day tours are $15; $25 for all day. Another company with well-done walking tours is **Above and Beyond Tours,** tel. (206) 516-2919. Take an introductory tour of downtown, Pike Place Market, and Pioneer Square, or neighborhood tours through Queen Anne or Capitol Hill for $18.

BOB RACE

VICINITY OF SEATTLE

Lake Washington creates an eastern boundary for Seattle, separating the city from its suburban city cousins across the famous floating bridges. Completion of these bridges made it possible for commuters to live in the suburbs and work in Seattle. Now, many workers commute from homes in Seattle to high-tech jobs on the Eastside. In recent years, this area has seen an incredible population growth—over 50% in the 1980s—fueled by high-tech industries such as Microsoft, Boeing, and Nintendo. This expansion has led Eastside to rival the Bay Area as a national technology center, and has pushed cities such as Bellevue and Redmond to the bursting point with growth beyond their wildest dreams (or nightmares, depending upon your perspective). Eastside cities now total 500,000 people, more than live in Seattle. For the traveler, these cities are not even fractionally as interesting as Seattle, but each has something unique. And a few of the places—notably Kirkland, Edmonds, and Issaquah—are actually worth visiting.

BELLEVUE

Across Lake Washington, Bellevue (pop. 86,000) has grown from a Seattle suburb to Washington's fourth-largest city. When the city was incorporated in 1953, the surrounding land was primarily agricultural and Bellevue's downtown streets were simple gravel roads. As the home to many rapidly expanding high-tech industries, Bellevue now has its own high-rise downtown and the biggest shopping mall in the area.

Bellevue is often accused of attracting people concerned about living in the "right" neighborhood, driving the "right" automobile, sending their children to the "right" schools—in other words, Bellevue is considered, by people who don't live there, the Southern California of Puget Sound. It *is* upscale, even though the homes are often no nicer than many other Seattle suburbs. But you can add about $50,000 to the price for the pleasure of saying that you live in Bellevue.

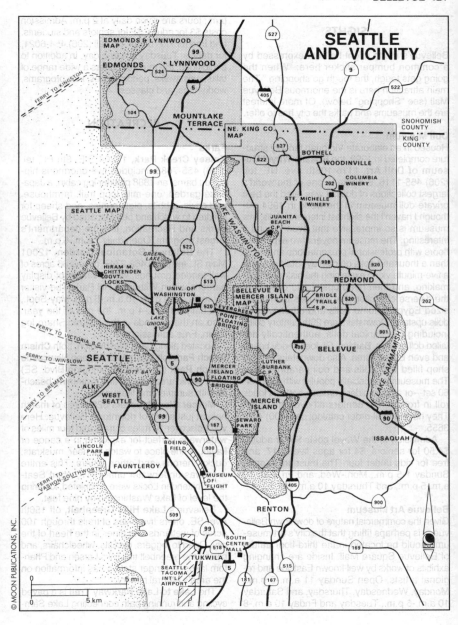

SEATTLE AND VICINITY

EDMONDS & LYNNWOOD MAP

EDMONDS · LYNNWOOD

SEATTLE MAP

BELLEVUE & MERCER ISLAND MAP

NE. KING CO. MAP

SNOHOMISH COUNTY

KING COUNTY

MOUNTLAKE TERRACE

BOTHELL

WOODINVILLE

COLUMBIA WINERY

STE. MICHELLE WINERY

JUANITA BEACH C.P.

REDMOND

BRIDLE TRAILS S.P.

HIRAM M. CHITTENDEN GOVT. LOCKS

GREEN LAKE

UNIV. OF WASHINGTON

LAKE UNION

SHILSHOLE BAY

EVERGREEN POINT FLOATING BRIDGE

BELLEVUE

LAKE WASHINGTON

LAKE SAMMAMISH

FERRY TO KINGSTON

FERRY TO VICTORIA, B.C.

FERRY TO WINSLOW

SEATTLE

ELLIOTT BAY

ALKI

WEST SEATTLE

MERCER ISLAND FLOATING BRIDGE

LUTHER BURBANK C.P.

MERCER ISLAND

SEWARD PARK

ISSAQUAH

FERRY TO BREMERTON

LINCOLN PARK

FAUNTLEROY

BOEING FIELD

MUSEUM OF FLIGHT

RENTON

FERRY TO VASHON-SOUTHWORTH

SOUTH CENTER MALL

TUKWILA

SEATTLE TACOMA INT'L AIRPORT

0   5 mi
0   5 km

SIGHTS

Bellevue's motto might best be expressed by a common bumper sticker here: "When the going gets tough, the tough go shopping." The main attraction here is the enormous Bellevue Mall (see "Shopping" below). Of more interest are the museums and parks the city has to offer.

Doll Museum

Housed in an elaborate Victorian fantasy structure completed in 1992, the **Rosalie Whyel Museum of Doll Art,** 1116 108th Ave. NE, tel. (206) 455-1116, is home to one of the world's largest collections of dolls. It was rated the best private doll museum in the world in 1994. Although I haven't the slightest interest in dolls, this museum is so impressive that even I found it interesting. The museum covers two expansive floors with professional presentations and more than a thousand dolls on display. Start out with a five-minute video explaining the history of doll-making, and then head upstairs to check out the diverse collection that includes thumbnail-sized Egyptian tomb dolls and other antique dolls upstairs. Downstairs are 20th-century dolls, including mechanical dolls, authentically detailed doll houses, Barbies, GI Joes, teddy bears, and even Elvis figures. Also downstairs is a gift shop filled with dolls and doll paraphernalia. The museum is especially popular with the over-60 set—or at least older women—and bus loads roll in from senior centers all over the state. They have a mail-order catalog; call (800) 440-3655.

Admission to the Whyel costs $5 for adults, $4.50 for seniors, $4 for ages five to 17, and free for kids under four. The museum is open Sunday 1-5 p.m., Mon.-Wed. and Fri.-Sat. 10 a.m.-5 p.m., and Thursday 10 a.m.-8 p.m.

Bellevue Art Museum

Given the commercial nature of downtown Bellevue, it is perhaps fitting that the city's art museum should be located in the third-floor atrium of Bellevue Square Mall. Inside are changing exhibits of works by well-known Eastside and regional artists. Open Sunday 11 a.m.-5 p.m., Monday, Wednesday, Thursday, and Saturday 10 a.m.-6 p.m., Tuesday and Friday 10 a.m.-8

p.m.; tours are given daily at 2 p.m. Admission costs $3 for adults, $2 for seniors and students, and free for kids under 12; call (206) 454-6021, for details. Tuesday is a free day. In addition to exhibitions, the museum offers a wide range of talks, artist walks, performances, kids programs, workshops, and classes.

RECREATION

Parks

Kelsey Creek Park, 13204 S.E. 8th Pl., tel. (206) 455-7688, includes two enormous hip-roofed barns, an 1888 pioneer log cabin, a Japanese garden, one-mile loop trail, farmhouse, and cows, rabbits, pigs, ponies, and sheep for children to watch and pet. Managed by Bellevue Parks and Recreation, it is the department's largest program. Open daily 7 a.m.-6 p.m.

The **Bellevue Botanical Garden,** 12001 Main St., tel. (206) 462-2749, covers 36 acres of well-tended grounds, with a variety of display gardens within Wilburton Hill Park. The visitor center is open daily 10 a.m.-6 p.m. May-Sept., and daily 10 a.m.-4 p.m. the rest of the year. Also on the grounds is the historic Sharp log cabin. Free admission.

Located along Lake Washington, both **Chism Beach Park** (off 100th Ave. SE) and **Newcastle Beach Park** (off Lake Washington Blvd. SE) have picnic areas, trails, and swimming beaches with summertime lifeguards.

Mercer Slough covers 320 acres of marsh habitat just south of downtown Bellevue. Here you'll discover 10 miles of trails and four miles of waterways perfect for exploring in a canoe or kayak. A fine place to watch for deer, muskrats, ducks, herons, and other critters. This entire area was underwater until 1917, when Seattle's Chittenden Locks were completed, lowering the level of Lake Washington by nine feet.

Bellevue's **Lake Hills Greenbelt,** off 156th Ave. SE, offers five miles of trails through 100 acres of wetlands and pines in the heart of the city. Open to joggers, cyclists, wheelchairs, and hikers, the greenbelt trail links Larsen and Phantom lakes. A ranger station has information on the area's natural history.

The **Lake to Lake Parkway Trail** is a paved cycling and running path connecting Lake Sam-

BELLEVUE AND MERCER ISLAND ACCOMMODATIONS

Accommodations are arranged from least to most expensive. Rates may be lower during the winter months. The area code is 206.

Kanes Motel; 14644 S.E. Eastgate Way; tel. 746-8201 or (800) 746-8201; $34 s, $38 d; kitchenettes available

Eastgate Motel; 14632 S.E. Eastgate Way; tel. 746-4100; $36 s, $42 d; kitchenettes available, AAA approved

Holiday Court Hotel; 10 100th Ave. NE; tel. 454-7018; $45-55 s or d; outdoor pool, local calls 25 cents, kitchenettes available

Mercer Island Travelodge; 7645 Sunset Hwy., Mercer Island (exit 9 off I-90); tel. 232-8000 or (800) 578-7878; $47 s, $58 d; jacuzzi, AAA approved

Bellevue Travelodge; 11011 N.E. 8th St.; tel. 454-4967 or (800) 578-7878; $49 s, $54 d; outdoor pool, kitchenettes available, AAA approved

Days Inn; 3241 156th Ave. SE; tel. 643-6644 or (800) 325-2525; $44-74 s, $49-79 d; jacuzzi, continental breakfast, AAA approved

Bellevue B&B; 830 100th Ave. SE; tel. 453-1048; $55-100 s or d; homey atmosphere, city and mountain views, two guest rooms, private baths, full breakfast, no kids under 10

West Coast Bellevue Hotel; 625 116th Ave. NE; tel. 455-9444; $58-77 s, $68-87 d; outdoor pool, exercise room, AAA approved

Petersen Bed and Breakfast; 10228 S.E. 8th St.; tel. 454-9334; $60 s or $65 d; comfortable home, hot tub on deck, two guest rooms, atrium kitchen, shared bath, full breakfast, kids welcome

Silver Cloud; 10621 N.E. 12th St.; tel. 637-7000; $69 s, $75 d; outdoor pool, jacuzzi, kitchenettes available, AAA approved

Bellevue Hilton; 100 112th Ave. NE; tel. 455-3330 or (800) 445-8667; $79-129 s, $89-139 d; indoor pool, jacuzzi, sauna, exercise room, AAA approved

Best Western Bellevue Inn; 11211 Main St.; tel. 455-5240 or (800) 421-8193; $80-85 s, $90-95 d; outdoor pool, exercise room, local calls 60 cents, AAA approved

Courtyard by Marriott; 14615 N.E. 29th Place; tel. 869-5300 or (800) 443-6000; $84 s, $94 d; indoor pool, jacuzzi, AAA approved

Hyatt Regency Bellevue; N.E. 8th St. and Bellevue Way; tel. 462-1234 or (800) 233-1234; $89-145 s, $89-170 d; 24-story tower, AAA approved

Red Lion Inn/Bellevue Center; 818 112th Ave. NE; tel. 455-1515 or (800) 733-5466; $91-120 s, $101-131 d; indoor pool, kitchenettes available, AAA approved

Duck-In B&B; 4118 100th Ave. SE; tel. 232-2554; $95 s or d; historic two-bedroom cottage on Lake Washington, kitchen, continental breakfast, kids welcome

Red Lion Hotel; 300 112th Ave. SE; tel. 455-1300 or (800) 733-5466; $120-140 s, $135-155 d; outdoor pool, jacuzzi, exercise room, AAA approved

Embassy Suites; 3225 158th Ave. SE; tel. 644-2500 or (800) 362-2779; $129-149 s, $149-189 d; suites, indoor pool, jacuzzi, sauna, exercise room, full breakfast, AAA approved

Residence Inn by Marriott; 14455 29th Place NE; tel. 882-1222; $135-195 s or d; one- and two-bedroom suites with kitchens and fireplaces, outdoor pool, jacuzzis, sports court, AAA approved

mamish with Lake Washington. Call the Bellevue Parks and Recreation Dept., tel. (206) 455-6881, for details.

Other Recreation

Swim at the **Bellevue pool,** 601 143rd Ave. NE, tel. (206) 296-4262, or in Lake Washington at Chism Beach and Newcastle Beach Parks (described above). **Outer Limits Kayak School,** 15600 N.E. 8th St., tel. (206) 781-6650, has river kayaking classes for all levels, from the basics to rolling and river rescue. They also offer guided river trips in the U.S. and Europe.

ACCOMMODATIONS AND CAMPING

See the "Bellevue and Mercer Island Accommodations" chart for a complete listing of area motels and B&Bs. Lodging is nearly impossible to find during the Arts and Crafts Fair in late July; book three months ahead if you're planning a visit then. The East King County Convention and Visitors Bureau can provide lodging information during the fair.

In spite of its reputation for being upscale, Bellevue has some of the most reasonably priced B&Bs in the Puget Sound region. **Bellevue Bed and Breakfast,** tel. (206) 453-1048, offers a homey atmosphere, kitchen and laundry privileges, and city and mountain views. **Petersen Bed and Breakfast,** tel. (206) 454-9334, welcomes kids in their comfortable home just five minutes from Bellevue Square. A home-style breakfast and use of the hot tub on the deck are included.

Campgrounds

Although the nearest public campground is many miles away in the Cascades, Bellevue does have tent and vehicle spaces at two private RV parks: **Trailer Inns RV Park,** exit 11 west from I-90, tel. (206) 747-9181, and **Vasa Park,** 2560 W. Lake Sammamish Rd. SE, tel. (206) 746-3260.

FOOD AND DRINK

Cafe Fresco, 10246 Main St. (Old Bellevue), tel. (206) 462-4744, is a European-style coffeehouse with the best local espresso, plus delicious gourmet sandwiches and soups. **Azalea's Fountain Court,** 22 103rd Ave. NE, tel. (206) 451-0426, is another notable Old Bellevue restaurant, with light gourmet fare and fresh seafood from an ever-changing menu. The restaurant has outside seating for summer days, and live jazz on Friday and Saturday nights. Recommended.

Located 21 floors up in the Seafirst Building at Bellevue Place (10500 N.E. 8th St.), **Daniel's Broiler,** tel. (206) 462-4662, has good seafood chowder and steaks, and extraordinary views. The lounge here offers wines by the glass, oysters on the half shell, and a variety of light meals and desserts, plus live guitar, jazz, or piano music nightly.

Jake O'Shaughnessey's in the Bellevue Square Mall, tel. (206) 455-5559, is popular for prime rib and steak. The bar has 27 different beers on tap in a convivial pub setting (if you can forget you're in a mall).

European and African Food

Pogacha, 119 106th Ave. NE, tel. (206) 455-5670, is certainly one of the more unusual Bellevue restaurants, with flavorful toppings on Croatian-style pizzas, and delightfully crunchy breads. **Cuchina! Cuchina!** 800 Bellevue Way NE, tel. (206) 637-1178, is very popular with downtown yupsters, offering foccacia, pizzas from the wood-burning oven, and fresh pasta.

Sprazzo offers impressive vistas from the top of the Key Bank Building at 10655 N.E. 4th St., tel. (206) 454-8255. The Mediterranean menu includes well-prepared food from North Africa, Turkey, and Greece. This contrasts rather sharply with the strip-mall location of **Giuseppie's,** 144 105th Ave. NE, tel. (206) 454-6868, but you'll be pleased to discover authentic Italian cooking.

Tosoni's, 14320 N.E. 20th St., tel. (206) 644-1668, serves big portions of hearty and delicious Eastern European fare. For something really different, **Kokeb,** 926 12th Ave., tel. (206) 322-0485, has inexpensive but delicious Ethiopian cuisine.

Asian Food

Raga Cuisine of India, 555 108th Ave. NE, tel. (206) 450-0336, offers classical Indian food, with tandoori, lamb, and vegetarian specialties, plus a popular luncheon buffet. **King and I Thai Cuisine,** 10509 Main St., tel. (206) 462-9337, comes recommended by locals for dependably great Thai dinners at a reasonable price.

The best local Chinese restaurant is **Noble Court,** 1644 140th Ave. NE, tel. (206) 641-6011, said to have the tastiest dim sum around, along with many unusual offerings. Another favorite—especially with Chinese customers—is **Ming Place,** 13200 Northup Way, tel. (206) 643-3888. For authentic Korean meals, head to **Seoul Olympic Restaurant,** 1200 112th Ave. NE, tel. (206) 455-9305. Good Japanese restaurants include: **I Love Sushi,** 11818 N.E. 8th St., tel. (206) 454-5706, and **Kampai Japanese Cuisine,** 201 106th Ave. NE, tel. (206) 451-8777.

Bellevue has the standard grocers, including two excellent upscale Larry's Markets, but one store really stands out: **Uwajimaya,** 15555 N.E. 24th, tel. (206) 747-9012. This is the other half of a two-store operation (the original is in Seattle's International District) and features fresh seafood, high-quality produce, a deli with sushi and other Japanese specialties, plus Japanese books and gifts.

EVENTS AND ENTERTAINMENT

Events
The Bellevue Art Museum sponsors the annual **Pacific Northwest Arts and Crafts Fair,** held in Bellevue Square the last weekend of July. It is one of the state's largest such fairs, and many artists' careers have been helped along by the juried show and the enormous crowds. As a climatological aside, it is an oddity of history that rain has never fallen on the fair, and it has been going for decades. As a result, some locals always plan picnics for that weekend.

Other Bellevue events include **Japan Week** in October, and a **Summer in the Park** concert series.

Entertainment
See the free *EastsideWeek* paper, available throughout Bellevue, for this week's nightlife and theater action. You won't find anything approaching the Seattle scene in staid Bellevue, but several places are worth checking out:

Spencer's Restaurant, 148th and Hwy. 520, tel. (206) 881-8888; **Joseph's Bistro Bar,** 11211 Main St. (in the Best Western Bellevue Inn), tel. (206) 455-5240; **Hunan Chef,** 425 116th NE, tel. (206) 451-8398; **Daniel's Broiler,** 10500 N.E. 8th, tel. (206) 462-4662; and **Azteca,** 150 112th NE, tel. (206) 454-8359. In addition to these, **Crossroads Shopping Center,** 15600 N.E. 8th Ave., tel. (206) 644-1111, has free live music of all types on Friday and Saturday nights.

For additional information on Bellevue and the surrounding area, contact the East King County Convention and Visitors Bureau, 520 112th Ave. NE, Ste. 101, tel. (206) 450-3630 or (800) ...

THE ARTS

Bellevue boasts the **Bellevue Philharmonic Orchestra,** tel. (206) 455-4171, with classical and pop concerts performed at *Westminster Chapel* (13646 24th St. NE), and the new **Meydenbauer Center** on the corner of 112th Ave. NE and N.E. 6th Street. The latter is a state-of-the-art facility with a 410-seat theater and spacious facilities for conventions and exhibitions. The Meydenbauer also hosts theatrical and musical productions from a variety of east-side companies, including the **Bellevue Chamber Chorus,** tel. (206) 881-0445, a group of 30 singers who perform Oct.-May.

See celebrity international artwork and openings at **Universal Fine Art Gallery,** 2032 148th St., tel. (206) 454-2484.

SHOPPING

At N.E. 8th St. and Bellevue Way NE, **Bellevue Square** is one of the Northwest's largest shopping malls—more than 200 stores (including Nordstrom, The Bon Marché, JCPenney, and FAO Schwarz) and a dozen restaurants, plus the Bellevue Art Museum in the third-floor atrium and glass-enclosed elevators for added panache. Locals crow that this upscale shopping center attracts more visitors than Disneyland.

For a glimpse into Bellevue's past, visit the shops and galleries in **Old Bellevue's** restored business district on Main St. between 100th and Bellevue Way. These include **Cuttysark,** 10237 Main St., tel. (206) 453-1265. The store is almost a museum, with intricate old ship models, marine antiques of all sorts, and flags from around the globe.

Bellevue also is home to several surprisingly large bookstores, including: **Barnes and Noble Bookstore,** 626 106th Ave. NE, tel. (206) 451-8463; **Tower Books,** 10635 N.E. 8th St., tel. (206) 451-1110; and **University Book Store,** 990 102nd Ave. NE, tel. (206) 632-9500.

INFORMATION AND SERVICES

For additional information on Bellevue and the surrounding area, contact the **East King County Convention and Visitors Bureau,** 520 112th Ave. NE, Suite 101, tel. (206) 450-5633 or (800) 252-1926. Open Mon.-Fri. 8:30 a.m.-5 p.m., and Sat.-Sun. 10 a.m.-4 p.m. in the summer, and Mon.-Fri. 8:30 a.m.-5 p.m. the rest of the year.

Bellevue's spacious and modern **Public Library,** at 11501 Main, tel. (206) 455-6889, is the

largest in King County (which includes Seattle).

The **area code** for Bellevue and the rest of the Seattle vicinity is 206.

TRANSPORTATION

Metro Transit, tel. (206) 553-3000 or (800) 542-7876, has several buses serving Bellevue from Seattle, plus numerous local routes. The main stop is the Bellevue Transit Center, on N.E. 6th St. downtown.

Shuttle Express, tel. (206) 622-1424 or (800) 487-7433, provides frequent direct service between several Bellevue hotels and Sea-Tac Airport for $11, along with door-to-door connections. **VIP Airport Shuttle,** tel. (206) 277-8211, also has airport service. **Suburban Airporter,** tel. (206) 455-2353, also serves the east side from Sea-Tac.

VICINITY OF BELLEVUE

MERCER ISLAND

Mercer Island (pop. 21,000) is primarily an upper-middle-class Seattle suburb, connected to the city only at its north end by I-90's floating bridge. The island has stringent growth regulations that help preserve its rural character and severely limit both the size of its commercial district and the height of buildings. Partly because of these limitations, the cost of a home has approached stratospheric levels; the average home on Mercer Island sells for over $355,000!

Sights

Mercer Island is approximately five miles long and two miles wide, with scenic roads that make for delightful bike tours. **Luther Burbank Park** at 2040 84th Ave. SE is the island's best waterfront park, with a beach, hiking trails, a picnic area, and fishing in Lake Washington. Start here for a 15-mile loop bike tour of the island: first go east on N. Mercer Way, then south on E. Mercer Way to the island's southern tip, then back up north on W. Mercer Way. At S.E. 68th St. and Island Crest Way, **Pioneer Park** has equestrian and hiking trails in a natural, wild setting (no

restrooms), including a three-quarter-mile interpretive nature trail.

Practicalities

Mercer Island Travelodge, 7645 Sunset Hwy. (exit 9 off I-90), tel. (206) 232-8000 or (800) 578-7878, has rooms for $47 s or $58 d, including access to a hot tub. Homier accommodations can be found at **Duck-In B&B,** 4118 100th Ave. SE, tel. (206) 232-2554, a romantic two-bedroom cottage with a big grassy lawn right on the shore of Lake Washington.

Mercer's small business district is located on the north end of the island and just off I-90. Here you'll find most of life's necessities: chocolates, espresso, books, booze, bike repairs, and Thai food. In fact there are actually two good Thai restaurants here: **Thai on Mercer,** 7691 S.E. 27th St., tel. (206) 236-9990, and **Pon Preom Restaurant,** 3039 78th Ave. SE, tel. (206) 236-8424. For excellent Italian meals and pizzas, head to **Caffe Italia,** 2448 76th Ave. SE, tel. (206) 232-9009. Swim at the **Mercer Island Pool,** 8815 S.E. 40th, tel. (206) 296-4370.

The **Mercer Island Chamber of Commerce,** 7601 S.E. 27th, tel. (206) 232-3404, has local information.

Getting There

The only way to drive to Mercer Island is to take I-90 over the Mercer Island (Lacey V. Murrow) Floating Bridge. The bridge was built in honor of a prominent civil engineer who also was the brother of the famed newscaster Edward R. Murrow. While being refurbished, the original sank during a winter storm in November 1990 and was then replaced. The span is just over 1.25 miles long.

Metro Transit, tel. (206) 553-3000 or (800) 542-7876, has regular service to the island from either Seattle or Bellevue, along with a number of on-island routes.

Shuttle Express, tel. (206) 622-1424 or (800) 487-7433, provides frequent direct service from the Mercer Travelodge to Sea-Tac Airport for $14, along with door-to-door connections.

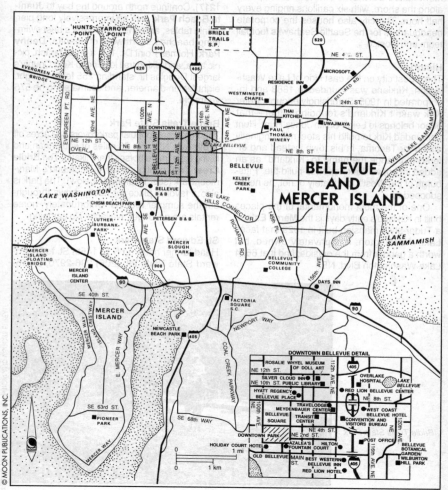

KIRKLAND

Kirkland (pop. 42,000) is a gentrified bedroom community that has managed to retain much of its original charm in spite of the boutiques, art galleries, cafes, and condos lining Lake Washington. A waterfront business development called **Carillon Point** is a centerpiece along the shore, with six carillons ringing every half hour. The city also houses the corporate headquarters for the Seattle Seahawks football team and Costco.

History

The oldest city on the east side of Lake Washington, Kirkland was founded in 1888 and incorporated in 1905. Surprisingly enough, Peter Kirk wasn't Kirkland's founding father—that honor belongs to Leigh Smith Jones Hunt. Hunt persuaded Kirk to build his steel mill, originally slated for Tacoma, in his town instead and offered to change the name to "Kirkland" as an added incentive. Kirk hoped to build the "Pittsburgh of the West"; fortunately or not, he never succeeded.

One of the most monumental of the places built in Kirkland's early days is the **Marsh Estate,** a Tudor-style mansion built in 1929 that faces Lake Washington. It is privately owned, but worth a gander from the outside; find it at 6604 Lake Washington Blvd. NE.

City Parks

A cluster of city parks provide much-needed open space on the shore of Lake Washington. **Marina Park** and **Waverly Beach Park** are right downtown, and provide great across-the-lake views. Just north of downtown along Lake Washington is **Juanita Bay Park,** an old golf course now transformed with scenic hiking trails and guided walks in the summer (call 206-828-1217). Continue north around the bay to **Juanita Beach Park,** with an impressively long pier, picnic tables, and one of the area's best swimming beaches. Northwest of Juanita, **Denny Park,** Holmes Point Dr., has a small beach, picnic area, and hiking trail leading to King County's largest Douglas fir, standing 255 feet in height, eight feet in diameter, and estimated to be 575 years old.

Bridle Trails State Park

This immensely popular park covers 482 acres off 116th Ave. NE, with 28 miles of equestrian and hiking trails (more horses than hikers). The **Bridle Crest Trail** continues on to Redmond's Marymoor Park (see "Redmond," below). The park is also a favorite place for riding shows throughout the summer months. Unfortunately, horse rentals are no longer available. No camping.

St. Edward State Park

Head farther north on N.E. 145th St. to St. Edward State Park, tel. (206) 296-2970, a 316-

Bridle Trails State Park

EAST KING COUNTY CONVENTION AND VISITORS BUREAU

KIRKLAND AND REDMOND ACCOMMODATIONS

Accommodations are arranged from least to most expensive within each city. Rates may be lower during the winter months. The area code is 206.

KIRKLAND

Motel 6; 12010 120th Pl. NE; tel. 821-5618 or (800) 466-8356; $33 s, $39 d; outdoor pool

Silver Cloud Inn; 12202 N.E. 124th St.; tel. 821-8300 or (800) 551-7207; $53-58 s, $59-64 d; outdoor pool, jacuzzi, exercise room, continental breakfast, kitchenette available, free airport shuttle, AAA approved

La Quinta Inn; 10530 N.E. Northup Way; tel. 828-6585 or (800) 531-5900; $57-63 s, $64-70 d; outdoor pool, AAA approved

Best Western Arnold's Motor Inn; 12223 N.E. 116th St.; tel. 822-2300 or (800) 332-4200; $62-78 s, $62-81 d; outdoor pool, jacuzzi, continental breakfast, free airport shuttle, AAA approved

Shumway Mansion B&B; 11410 99th Place NE; tel. 823-2303; $65-95 s or d; historic mansion near Juanita Beach, eight antique-furnished guest rooms, private baths, water views, full buffet breakfast, evening snacks, health club access, AAA approved

Clarion Inn; 12233 N.E. Totem Lake Way; tel. 821-2202 or (800) 221-2222; $95 s, $105 d; stocked mini-bar, large rooms, outdoor pool, sauna, jacuzzi, exercise room, AAA approved

The Woodmark Hotel on Lake Washington; 1200 Carillon Pt.; tel. 822-3700 or (800) 822-3700; $110-180 s, $120-195 d; elaborate hotel, lake views, grand piano, stocked minibars, TV in the bathroom, terry robes, full breakfast, AAA approved (four diamonds)

REDMOND

Silver Cloud Inn; 15304 N.E. 21st St.; tel. 746-8200 or (800) 551-7207; $59-63 s, $65-69 d; jacuzzi, exercise room, AAA approved

Cottage Creek Manor; 12525 Avondale Rd. NE; tel. 881-5606; $65 s or d; Tudor-style manor, attractive country setting, two guest rooms, private bath, continental breakfast, no kids under 12

Best Western Redmond Inn; 15304 N.E. 21st St.; tel. 883-4900 or (800) 528-1234; $68-91 s, $78-101 d; outdoor pool, jacuzzi, kitchenettes available, AAA approved

Lilac Lea Christian B&B; 21008 N.E. 117th St.; tel. 861-1898; $85 d; modern cottage suite, private bath, antique furnishings, continental breakfast, no alcohol, no kids

acre retreat from civilization. This quiet piece of property was part of a Catholic seminary until 1977; when the seminary closed, the diocese sold the land to the state and the park opened the following summer. Saint Edwards boasts three-quarters of a mile of forested, undeveloped Lake Washington shoreline and five miles of hiking and mountain biking trails, plus picnic areas, a gymnasium, and an indoor pool. tel. (206) 296-2970. The separate St. Thomas Cen-

ter nearby is still owned by the archdiocese and is used as a conference center and for various recovery programs.

Accommodations
See the "Kirkland and Redmond Accommodations" chart for a complete listing of places to stay in the Kirkland area.

The **Shumway Mansion,** tel. (206) 823-2303, a 23-room B&B and reception center, is a three-minute walk from Juanita Beach. The antique-furnished inn was built in 1909; it was bought in 1982 by the Harris family and moved down the hill to its present location on spacious grounds overlooking Juanita Bay. This is a favorite place for weddings.

The **Woodmark Hotel,** tel. (206) 822-3700 or (800) 822-3700, doesn't look that impressive from the outside but is actually one of the finest lodging places in the area, with every possible amenity and rooms overlooking Lake Washington. This is the only hotel on the shores of the lake.

Food and Drink

Kirkland is blessed with an abundance of fine restaurants, many of which are right downtown.

Good breakfast places are **Cousins of Kirkland,** 140 Central Way NE, tel. (206) 822-1076, where cheese blintzes are a specialty, and **Hector's Restaurant,** 112 Lake St., tel. (206) 827-4811, with home-style breakfasts and a tasty lobster bisque at lunch.

Coyote Coffee Company, 111 Main St., tel. (206) 827-2507, is a funky and relaxed place with art-filled walls and excellent sandwiches, salads, soups, pastries, and espresso coffees.

Head to Moss Bay Marina for moderately priced, consistently good steak or seafood at **Anthony's Homeport,** tel. (206) 822-0225. This is a great place to watch the sun go down across Lake Washington. Just up the way at the marina is **Third Floor Fish Cafe,** tel. (206) 822-3553, a yuppified place specializing in seafood. Another place with lake vistas and seafood specials is **Yarrow Bay Grill and Beach Cafe,** 1270 Carillon Point, tel. (206) 889-9052.

Coyote Creek Pizza Co., 228 Central Way NE, tel. (206) 822-2226, bakes excellent and distinctive pizzas, including a "Northwest Delight" with hazelnuts, mushrooms, green apples(!), and red onions.

The **Ristorante Paradiso,** 120 A Park Lane, tel. (206) 889-8601, offers outstanding nouvelle cuisine with an Italian twist, including fresh seafood, lamb chops, and veal. **Cafe Juanita,** 9702 N.E. 120th Place, tel. (206) 823-1505, is another fine Italian restaurant with dependably great meals and an extraordinary choice of Italian wines.

La Provençal, 212 Central Way, tel. (206) 827-3300, is the oldest French restaurant operating in a single location in the Puget Sound area; it's owned by Philippe Gayte, who learned to cook in his native Rhone Valley. Very expensive, but outstanding.

Izumi, in the Totem Lake West Shopping Center, tel. (206) 821-1959, has very good Japanese sushi, tempura, teriyaki, and other specialties. Another treat is the extremely popular **Shamiana,** 10724 N.E. 68th St., tel. (206) 827-4902, a great place for Indian and Pakistani food, including a number of vegetarian specials.

For spicy Hunan and Sichuan cooking, head to **Asian Wok,** 1720 Market, tel. (206) 827-4117. **City Thai Restaurant,** 134 Parkplace Center, tel. (206) 827-2875, is the place to go if you can't afford a visit to Thailand, with food that wins top honors in the *EastsideWeek* readers' polls year after year. **Las Margaritas,** 12821 N.E. 85th St., tel. (206) 827-4422, has the best Mexican meals in town. Also of note is **Azteca Mexican Restaurant,** 12015 124th Ave. NE, tel. (206) 820-7997, a kid-friendly place with a fun gas-fired tortilla machine.

Join the raucous, upscale crowd at the **Kirkland Roaster and Ale House,** 111 Central Way, tel. (206) 827-4400, to sample the 19 microbrews on tap, including several of Hale's Ales made in the adjacent brewery. The menu covers quite a range, from fresh fish to nachos. But the featured attraction is a huge spit where they roast chicken, lamb, and other meats.

Events

Kirkland Arts Festival, the second weekend in July, attracts crowds of people for local arts and crafts; call (206) 822-8444 for details. In late September, **Taste Kirkland** is another very popular fair with food booths lining the main thoroughfare and live music at Marina Park. The **Kirkland Jazz Festival** comes to town the second weekend of August. The second Thursday of each month, the art galleries open up from 6 to 9 p.m. for an **Art Walk.**

Entertainment

Waldo's Tavern, 12657 N.E. 85th St., tel. (206) 827-9292, is a big place with live rock bands on weekends and pool tables all the time. **Kirkland Roaster and Ale House,** 111 Central Way, tel. (206) 827-4400, is the place for live music on Wednesday and Thursday nights, and comedy on Friday and Saturday nights. More music and dancing at **Davinci's Flying Pizza and Pasta,** 89 Kirkland Ave., tel. (206) 889-9000. **Coyote Coffee Company,** 111 Main St., tel. (206) 827-2507, has poetry on Monday nights, and music or comedy on Friday nights.

Shopping

More than a dozen different art galleries can be found in Kirkland, including the **Kirkland Arts Center,** tel. (206) 822-7161, with exhibits and classes in the historic Peter Kirk Building (1891) at 620 Market Street. Many of the galleries are right downtown on Central Way NE and Park Lane. The second Thursday of each month, the galleries open for **Art Walk,** featuring artist receptions and show 6-9 p.m.

The **Old Heritage Place** is a collector's paradise. Located at 151 3rd St., this antique mall has 72 shops filled with collectibles. **Eastside Trains,** 217 Central Way, tel. (206) 828-4098, is a surprisingly large place where 40-something men play with model trains and pretend to be kids again (or pretend to be buying trains for their kids).

Information and Services

For maps and a limited amount of other information, drop by the **Kirkland Chamber of Commerce,** 356 Parkplace Center, tel. (206) 822-7066. Open Mon.-Fri. 9 a.m.-5 p.m. year-round. Find the **Kirkland Public Library** at 406 Kirkland Ave., tel. (206) 822-2459. The local **area code** is 206.

Transportation and Tours

Metro Transit, tel. (206) 447-4800 or (800) 542-7876, provides daily bus service to Kirkland from Seattle and other points in King County.

Shuttle Express, tel. (206) 622-1424 or (800) 487-7433, has frequent direct service from several Kirkland motels to Sea-Tac Airport for $13-16, along with door-to-door connections.

Argosy Cruises, tel. (206) 623-4252 (recording) or 623-1445, offers scenic 90-minute boat tours of Lake Washington, departing from Kirkland's Marina Park May-October. These narrated cruises feature the lake and surrounding sights (including homes of the famous), and cost $17.50 adults, $16 seniors, $8 kids, free for kids under five.

REDMOND

Redmond began as a boat landing along the Sammamish Slough, the slow-moving stream that links Lake Washington and Lake Sammamish. Foot travel in pioneer days was virtually impossible due to the dense forests and extensive marshland, so most inland travel was accomplished via river. Today the city is the self-proclaimed bicycle capital of the Northwest, holding regular bicycle races at its Velodrome in Marymoor Park.

In recent years, the city of Redmond has been transformed from a Seattle suburb to a city in its own right—with traffic jams to match. A number of large companies now call Redmond home, including Nintendo, Eddie Bauer, and software giant Microsoft. The Microsoft campus now encompasses almost two million square feet of office space in Redmond, and it has additional facilities in Bothell, Bellevue, and Kirkland. (Bill Gates, the multibillionaire founder of Microsoft, lives in nearby Medina; his mansion faces Lake Washington.) Because of Microsoft and other high-tech firms, Redmond grew by an incredible 25% between 1989 and 1993 and is now home to over 40,000 people.

Parks and Recreation

Marymoor Park on the West Lake Sammamish Pkwy. has 533 acres of open space on Seattle banker James Clise's 1904 estate. Half of the furnished 28-room mansion is now the **Marymoor Museum,** tel. (206) 882-6401, featuring photos and exhibits of local history; open Sunday and Tues.-Thurs. 11 a.m.-4 p.m., donation. The other half is used for weddings, receptions, parties, and other gatherings. Marymoor Park is better known for its **Velodrome,** with a banked 400-meter bike-racing track that draws competitors from across the United States. This is one of the only such facilities in the nation. Bike races are held Thursday and Friday evenings from May to September; tel. (206) 389-5825. The park also features a one-mile interpretive trail, soccer fields, tennis courts, a model airplane field, dog training grounds, and picnic shelters.

Idylwood Park is south of Marymoor Park along the west shore of Lake Sammamish, with a swimming beach and picnicking grounds.

Sixty-eight-acre **Farrel-McWhirter Park,** 10400 192nd Ave. NE, has horse and hiking trails, picnicking, a barnyard zoo, and horse arena. Charlotte's Trail is a paved path that extends the length of the park, ideal for disabled visitors.

Swim at the **Redmond Pool,** 17535 N.E. 104th, tel. (206) 296-2961.

Sammamish River Trail

The paved 13-mile Sammamish River Trail begins in Marymoor Park and follows the river through Redmond, Woodinville, and on to Kenmore. There it connects with Seattle's Burke-Gilman Trail, which continues all the way to Fremont, a total distance of approximately 27 miles. This immensely popular path provides Mt. Rainier and Lake Washington views, and passes the Chateau Ste. Michelle and Columbia wineries, favorite stopping places. The **Puget Power-Redmond Trail** is a three-mile gravel path (great for mountain bikes) that connects the Sammamish River Trail to Farrel-McWhirter Park.

Lodging

See the "Kirkland and Redmond Accommodations" chart for a listing of places to stay in the Kirkland area. **Cottage Creek Manor,** tel. (206) 881-5606, is a Tudor-style manor home in an attractive country setting. **Lilac Lea Christian B&B,** tel. (206) 851-1898, has a comfortable and attractive cottage suite with a Christian emphasis (no alcohol allowed) that may put some folks off.

Food

For the best local breakfasts, visit **Village Square Cafe,** 16150 N.E. 85th, tel. (206) 885-7287. **Cornerstone Desserts & Espresso,** on the corner of Cleveland and Leary Way, tel. (206) 883-3871, is a pleasant little place with coffees and sweets in an historic brick building. Famous locally for their espresso shakes.

Two good lunch places are: **Fill Yer Belly Deli & Grill,** 8461 164th Ave. NE, tel. (206) 883-1080, and **Mikie's Brooklyn Bagel Deli,** 16640 Redmond Way, tel. (206) 881-3344. Mikie's has fresh-baked breads and deli meats from New York; locals call their bagels the most authentic on the Eastside.

Kikya, 8105 161st Ave. NE, tel. (206) 881-8771, is a wonderful small Japanese restaurant with friendly service and high-quality food. Don't come here on a weekend evening unless you're ready to wait. **Peking Chinese Restaurant,** 16875 Redmond Way, tel. (206) 883-2681, has some of the finest Mandarin and Sichuan food on the Eastside. **Redmond Thai Cuisine,** 16421 Cleveland, tel. (206) 869-6131, serves Thai meals.

il Bacio, 16564 Cleveland St., tel. (206) 869-8815, has delicious and authentic Italian cuisine and a wonderful bakery. Get homemade pizzas and calzones at **Big Time Pizza,** 7281 W. Lake Sammamish Pkwy. NE, tel. (206) 885-6425.

Bonne Sante Restaurant, 16564 Cleveland, tel. (206) 869-2280, mixes exercise with meals. The restaurant offers healthy gourmet cuisine and vegetarian specials at reasonable prices; next door, the owners operate a Tai Chi Chuan martial arts studio.

The **Redmond Saturday Market** brings fresh veggies, flowers, crafts, fruit, honey, and more to 7730 Leary Way. It's held downtown May to early October on Saturday 8 a.m.-2 p.m.

Events

Redmond's spring season begins with **Artsplash,** featuring plays, music, and art exhibitions in mid-April; call (206) 556-2331 for details. Head to Marymoor Park on the Fourth of July weekend for the very popular annual **Heritage Festival,** tel. (206) 296-2964, with arts and crafts, music, ethnic dancing, and food booths. It's followed by fireworks next to the Redmond High School.

The **Redmond Derby Days Festival** in mid-July is a major cycling event with street criterion bike races, a carnival, an antique car show, parades, arts and crafts, and plenty of food. It has been going on since 1939. Call (206) 885-4014 for details. The **Evergreen Classic Horse Show**—one of the top 10 equestrian shows in the nation—is held at Marymoor Park each August.

Shopping

The **Antique Connection,** 16701 Cleveland St., tel. (206) 882-3122, has 65 antique dealers under one roof. For more antiques, try **Days**

Gone Bye Antique Mall on the lower level of the Ethan Allen Bldg., 2207 N.E. Bel-Red Road.

Information and Services

The **Greater Redmond Chamber of Commerce,** 16210 N.E. 80th St., tel. (206) 885-4014, has local information, and is open Mon.-Fri. 9 a.m.-5 p.m. year-round. The local **area code** is 206. Swim at the **Redmond Pool,** 17535 N.E. 104th, tel. (206) 296-2961.

Transportation

Metro Transit, tel. (206) 553-3000 or (800) 542-7876, has daily bus service around Redmond, on to Seattle and Bellevue, and throughout King County.

Shuttle Express, tel. (206) 622-1424 or (800) 487-7433, provides frequent direct service from Redmond's Silver Cloud Inn and Redmond Inn to Sea-Tac Airport for $16, along with door-to-door connections.

ISSAQUAH

At the foot of the "Issaquah Alps," Issaquah (pop. 7,800) offers an escape to country-fresh air in a fast-growing town loaded with history. Just two exits east of Renton on I-90, Issaquah's hills are within a half-hour drive of Seattle and Tacoma. These are very old, worn-down mountains; their lower elevation keeps them mostly snow-free—and hikeable—virtually year-round. The town itself is a pleasant place to enjoy the blend of old and new; but get here soon, because shopping malls and suburbs are quickly devouring the remaining open space.

HISTORY

Members of the Snoqualmie tribe inhabited the land around present-day Issaquah for centuries, subsisting on the rich fish resources in Lake Sammamish, Lake Washington, and nearby rivers. They called this place "Squak," after the sound made by the thousands of ducks and cranes that passed through each spring and fall. To the whites, the Indian word sounded something like "Issaquah." The earliest Anglo settlers arrived here in the 1860s, opening coal mines, logging the dense evergreen forests, and starting farms. Originally called "Gilman" when it was established in 1889, the town was later given the Indian word. Coal discoveries brought a flood of miners to the area, and coal remained the economic mainstay till the 1920s. The town was a rough place at first: rioters sent Chinese workers fleeing for their lives, and the state militia was later brought in to shut down a coal strike by union activists from the Wobblies. Nearly every one of the first 70 town ordinances

enacted dealt with liquor, misconduct by public officials, and out-of-control animals.

The coal mines closed in the 1920s, but lumber mills replaced them as loggers stripped away the surrounding forests. Issaquah puttered along for the first half of this century, but completion of the Lake Washington Floating Bridge in 1940 and the opening of Interstate 90 in the 1970s made commuting easy. This sudden influx of new people has led to the construction of many new homes and businesses, transforming this once-sleepy burg into a bustling place. Today, the largest local employers are high-tech industries: Boeing Computer Services, Siemens Medical Systems, Egghead Software, and Microsoft. But there still are vestiges of the farming past: the creamery in town produces all the Darigold yogurt sold in the Northwest.

SIGHTS AND TOURS

Museums

The **Gilman Town Hall Museum,** 165 S.E. Andrews, tel. (206) 392-3500, is open Saturday and Monday 10:30 a.m.-2:30 p.m.; free. Built in the 1890s, this building served as the original town hall, back when Issaquah was known as Gilman. Railroad tools, children's toys, a pioneer kitchen and grocery store, artifacts, and many historical photographs are on display inside. Out back is the old two-cell town jail, built in 1914.

The **Lobberegt's Auto Museum,** 1504 228th SE, tel. (206) 392-3690, is a small privately owned collection of classic cars. Call ahead to arrange a visit.

TO REDMOND

LAKE SAMMAMISH

TO PINE LAKE

PUBLIC BEACH

228th AVE. SE

SE 43rd Way

LAKE SAMMAMISH STATE PARK

E. LAKE SAMMAMISH PKWY. SE

TO VASA PARK RESORT

ISSAQUAH

ISSAQUAH-PINE LAKE RD.

ISSAQUAH-FALL CITY RD.

NW SAMMAMISH RD.

MOTEL 6
HOLIDAY INN

EXIT 15

NEWPORT WAY

HERITAGE SQUARE

TOWN & COUNTRY SQUARE
THE COMMONS MALL

NW GILMAN BLVD.

GILMAN STATION

GILMAN VILLAGE

SE NEWPORT WAY

CHAMBER OF COMMERCE

NE GILMAN

TO SNOQUALMIE VALLEY HOSPITAL

RAINIER BLVD.

BOEHM'S CHOCOLATES

NEWPORT BLVD.

WASHINGTON ZOOLOGICAL PARK

900

RENTON-ISSAQUAH RD.

VILLAGE THEATRE

BUS STATION

SALMON HATCHERY

AQUATIC CENTER

MINE SHAFT

WILDWOOD BLVD.

RAILROAD DEPOT
E. SUNSET WAY

ISSAQUAH HISTORICAL SOCIETY MUSEUM

FRONT ST.

2nd AVE. SE

RENTON-HOBART RD.

COUGAR MOUNTAIN PARK

0   0.5mi

0   0.5km

SQUAK MOUNTAIN STATE PARK NATURAL AREA

© MOON PUBLICATIONS, INC.

Gilman Village

Issaquah's Gilman Village is a collection of 40 or so turn-of-the-century homes, all moved and restored to form a quaint cluster of boutiques selling clothing, crafts, gifts, kitchenware, and jewelry. If you're into lacy frou-frou, you'll love these boardwalk-linked places. Several shops do offer something more substantial, including a number of restaurants listed below. Be sure to drop by **Evolution,** tel. (206) 392-6963, an artists cooperative that sells high quality works, including many pieces made from recycled products. **Northwest Gallery of Fine Woodworking** has museum-quality furniture and carved pieces (priced to match), while the **Chukar Cherries** shop sells their sweet cherry concoctions, with free samples for the tasting.

Boehm's Chocolates

Another place to purchase sweets (no freebies, alas) is Boehm's Chocolates at 255 N.E. Gilman Blvd., tel. (206) 392-6652, offering free candy factory tours July to mid-September; call ahead for reservations. If you can't get on a tour, just walk outside and peek in the side windows. Boehm's makes all sorts of chocolate pieces, even chocolate turkeys and dolphins. Open daily 9 a.m.-6 p.m.

Washington Zoological Park

Issaquah's Washington Zoological Park 19525 S.E. 54th, began as an elementary school project in 1972, and still maintains a teaching orientation, but has now grown into one of the finest zoos in the state. No elephants or giraffes here, but you will find a wide range of threatened or endangered animals from around the globe, including the hyacinthine macaw and the Hawaiian nene goose. The real attractions, however, are the cats, including cheetahs, and the world's largest cougar facility. Visitors to the zoo are treated to detailed and highly informative tours by the docents and staff. Many of the animals were born here and enjoy interacting with visitors. The zoo is open Sunday 11 a.m.-5 p.m., and Wed.-Sat. 10 a.m.-5 p.m. April-Sept.; Sunday 11 a.m.-4 p.m., and Thurs.-Sat. 10 a.m.-4 p.m. the rest of the year. The ticket booth closes a half-hour before closing time. Admission is $4.50 for adults, $4 for seniors, $3.50 for ages four to 15, $2.50 for ages two to three, and free

for younger kids. Washington Zoological Park is entirely self-supporting, receiving no governmental assistance.

Issaquah State Salmon Hatchery

The Issaquah State Salmon Hatchery, 125 W. Sunset Way, tel. (206) 392-3180, raises five million Chinook and one million coho salmon annually for release into Issaquah Creek. In existence since 1936, the hatchery is a good place to learn about the life cycle of salmon and how they are raised. The grounds are open daily dawn to dusk, with tours in late summer. The hatchery is also a center of activity during the Salmon Days Festival each October (see "Events," below).

Historical Tour

Several buildings from Issaquah's turn-of-the-century glory days are still in use; remains from the mine are also evident. Go down Newport Way to Park Blvd. and turn right onto Wildwood for a look at the original miners' homes, preserved and still occupied. At the end of the block, a depression in the ground near a grove marks the entrance to the mine's first shaft; to the right is the concrete bulkhead used to anchor the mine's hauling machinery.

Downtown, a number of historically significant buildings face Front Street. **Odd Fellows Hall** is the oldest, built in 1888. The second-oldest commercial building is the **Grand Central Hotel,** dating from 1903; today it houses offices and apartments. Adjacent to the railroad tracks on Sunset Way, the lovingly restored **Railroad Depot** was built in 1889 (the year Washington became a state), out of Washington Territory timber—note the "W.T." symbol. Issaquah's downtown streets have been planted with all sorts of fruit trees and berry bushes; get here in late summer to pick apples, cherries, pears, plums, or blueberries as you stroll along.

Another notable old building, the enormous **Pickering Barn**—once owned by Washington's first territorial governor, William Pickering—has been completely restored as part of the new Pickering Place Shopping Center. Ironically, the old barn is now an environmental center for the city, despite the fact that the agricultural past it represents is now a shopping mall! For more information on Issaquah's historical sights, head to the visitor information center or pick up a self-guiding tour map from the museum.

RECREATION

The Issaquah Alps

As the "Trailhead City," Issaquah takes pride in a chain of nearby mountains—the "Issaquah Alps"—a range older than the Cascades that includes Tiger, Cougar, and Squak Mountains. The Tiger Mountain area is Washington's most popular hiking area, attracting hundreds of hikers and mountain bikers on a sunny summer day. Also here are many shallow talus caves that are fun to explore. Eventually, a series of greenbelts will connect all the nearby parks, making it possible to head out from downtown onto a myriad of paths.

The **Issaquah Alps Trails Club** organizes hikes every Saturday and Sunday, plus twice during the week, all year, to points of interest along 200 miles of trails in these mountains. No membership or previous registration is necessary; just meet the group at the south end of the Issaquah Park and Ride lot on Hwy. 900, and join a carpool to the trailhead. Call (206) 328-0480 for recorded information on upcoming hikes.

If you want to step out on your own, stop by the city-run **Trails Interpretive Center** at 110 S.E. Bush St. for maps and hiking information, or purchase *Guide to Trails of Tiger Mountain* by William K. Longwell Jr., published by the Issaquah Alps Trails Club. Topographic maps and hiking equipment are available from **High Mountain Adventures,** 670 N.W. Gilman Blvd., tel. (206) 391-0130.

Tiger Mountain State Forest covers 13,500 acres of forested lands and is capped by 3,004-foot **East Tiger Mountain,** the highest peak in the range. The hike up East Side Rd. to the summit provides spectacular views of the surrounding country. To reach the trailhead, take I-90 exit 25; go right onto Hwy. 18 and drive three miles to a dirt road on the right; proceed to the power line and park. Start your seven-mile hike on the uphill road under the power line.

Tiger Mountain is also home to one of the more unique local parks, **Fraternity Sno-**qualmie Nudist Park, tel. (206) 392-NUDE, a 40-acre family place to let it all hang out, so to speak. This is the oldest (in existence since 1931) and largest nudist park in the Northwest. They sponsor a clothing-optional "Bare Buns Fun Run" in early July, followed in mid-August, by a summer music festival—called, what else, **Nudestock.** Thousands of nudists show up. Fun for the whole naked family.

Cougar Mountain Regional Wildland Park encompasses second-growth forests surrounding this 1,595-foot peak, with well-marked trails climbing past an old mining camp and waterfalls.

Squak Mountain State Park covers 613 acres of forested land just south of Issaquah and contains a maze of poorly maintained trails. Access is a bit tricky; ask locally for directions. No camping at Squak Mountain.

Horseback Riding

Even with no prior experience, riding a horse along wooded trails can be a relaxing, enjoyable way to view the scenery. **Tiger Mountain Outfitters,** 132nd Ave., tel. (206) 392-5090, offers guided three-hour trips in Tiger Mountain State Forest. **Kelly's Ranch,** 7212 Renton-Issaquah Rd., tel. (206) 392-6979, has guided trips around Squak Mountain, while **High Country Outfitters,** 23836 S.E. 24th, tel. (206) 392-0111, offers trail rides and overnight trips into the Cascades.

On the Water

A mile and a half northwest of Issaquah, **Lake Sammamish State Park** is one of the more popular Puget Sound area parks, attracting over 1.5 million visitors each year. Facilities include a big sandy beach for sunbathing and swimming, a swimming float, bathhouses, boat ramps, picnic tables, hiking trails, and a concession stand selling fast food. The area is popular with boaters and water-skiers. Get here on a sunny weekend morning and you'll find long traffic jams at the boat launch. Call (206) 455-7010 for more information. No camping.

Owners of smaller motorboats, canoes, and rafts may prefer **Pine Lake,** a county park off 228th SE with a five-mph speed limit on the lake.

ACCOMMODATIONS

Lodging

Standard, inexpensive motel rooms are available at **Motel 6,** 1885 15th Pl. NW at I-90 exit 15, tel. (206) 392-8405 or (800) 466-8356, for $34 s or $40 d, including an outdoor pool. You'll find more luxurious accommodations at **Issaquah Holiday Inn,** 1801 12th Ave. NW (I-90 exit 15), tel. (206) 392-6421 or (800) 465-4329. Amenities include a salmon-shaped outdoor pool, sauna, and jacuzzi; rooms cost $72 s or $82 d.

Homier quarters can be found at **Mountains & Planes B&B,** 100 Big Bear Place NW, tel. (206) 392-8068. The home is a traditional cedar structure with a garden and three guest rooms (shared or private baths) for $38 s, $49-55 d. A two room suite ($70 for up to four) is also available. A full breakfast is served.

The Country Inn, at 685 N.W. Juniper St. in downtown Issaquah, tel. (206) 392-1010, has two guest rooms in a century-old estate. Rates are $55 s, $65 d, with a full breakfast.

Campgrounds

Although there are no public campgrounds near Issaquah, privately run RV parks are available, including: **Issaquah Village RV Park,** 50 1st Ave. NE, tel. (206) 392-9233 or (800) 258-9233; **Issaquah Highlands Camping Club,** 10610 Renton-Issaquah Rd. SE, tel. (206) 392-2351; **Blue Sky RV Park,** 9002 302nd Ave. SE, tel. (206) 222-7910; and **Vasa Park Resort,** on the west side of Lake Sammamish at 3560 W. Lake Sammamish Rd., tel. (206) 746-3260.

FOOD AND SHOPPING

Issaquah has a wide diversity of restaurants serving everything from fast food to gourmet fare. Several of the best are in Gilman Village, where the lovingly restored old buildings add to the ambience. Notable Gilman Village eateries include: **Tantalus Restaurant,** tel. (206) 391-6090, for Greek specialties; **Ristorante Nicolino Italiano,** tel. (206) 391-8077, for deliciously authentic southern Italian dinners; and **The Art House Cafe,** tel. (206) 392-2648, for

espressos and panini. For lunch, join the crowds at **The Sweet Addition,** tel. (206) 392-5661, where the salads and sandwiches are always well prepared, and the decadent cakes, truffles, and pies are a real temptation. Not recommended if you're on a diet. Also good for breakfast and lunch is **Snow Goose Cafe,** tel. (206) 391-4671.

Fine restaurants can also be found elsewhere in Issaquah. Start the day with a breakfast at **12th Ave. Cafe,** 1235 12th Ave., tel. (206) 392-5975. Housed in the Village Theatre building at 303 Front St. N, **Stage Right Cafe,** tel. (206) 392-0109, is a delightful, airy cafe with yuppie nouvelle meals and coffees for reasonable prices. A block up the street is **The Nutcracker Tea Room,** 157 Front St. N, tel. (206) 392-3424, with a big choice of fresh-from-the-oven European pastries.

Tasty Chinese food—but the atmosphere is rather plain—at **Mandarin Garden,** 40 E. Sunset Way, tel. (206) 392-9476.

Jay-Berry's Gourmet Pizza & Pasta & Lounge, 385 N.W. Gilman Blvd., tel. (206) 392-0808, bakes the best pizzas in town, and the lounge overlooks quiet Issaquah Creek.

American Eats

Looking for an all-American meal? Look no farther than **The Roost Restaurant,** 120 N.W. Gilman Blvd., tel. (206) 391-8077, for thick steaks and spicy ribs. The **XXX Drive-In,** 98 N.E. Holly St., tel. (206) 392-1266, is a real old-time favorite, with burgers, shakes, and the best root beer around. On summer weekends, their parking lot fills to overflowing with dozens of vintage cars, from Hudsons to Mustangs. Another very popular burger joint is **Gulliver's,** 1640 N.W. Gilman Blvd., tel. (206) 392-4822.

Markets and More

The **Issaquah Farmers Market,** located at 150 W. Newport Way, attracts shoppers on Saturday 9 a.m.-3 p.m. from late April to late November. In addition to fresh produce, the market features all sorts of handicrafts.

Get quality cuts of meat and fresh smoked salmon at **Fischer's Meats & Seafoods,** 85 Front St. N, tel. (206) 392-3131, in existence since 1910. **Suncrest Bread Co.,** 1175 N.W.

Gilman Blvd. (next to Safeway), tel. (206) 392-8983, bakes earthy and delicious fat-free breads, cinnamon rolls, and muffins using organically grown wheat.

Hedges Cellars, 1105 12th Ave. NW, tel. (206) 391-6056 or (800) 859-9463, is unique in its focus on producing just one wine: a blend using cabernet sauvignon and merlot grapes from the Yakima Valley. The tasting room is open Thurs.-Sat. noon-6 p.m.

See "Sights," above, for details on Issaquah's most interesting place to shop, Gilman Village.

In historical downtown Issaquah, the **Issaquah Gallery** has paintings, photography, stained glass, pottery, and prints by Northwest artists at 49 N. Front St., tel. (206) 392-4247.

ENTERTAINMENT AND EVENTS

Theater

After many years in cramped quarters, the semi-professional **Village Theatre** moved into lush new digs in 1995, including a 488-seat theater and a soundproof family room for screaming babies. Theatrical productions are generally on the light side, with a heavy dose of musical favorites. For tickets and performance information contact the theater at 120 Front St. N, tel. (206) 392-2202 (or call Ticket Master at 206-292-2787).

Events

Issaquah's **July 4th Parade** is fun for everyone, with all the usual events. Every fall, salmon return to their birthplace at the state salmon hatchery, and Issaquah doesn't miss the opportunity for a celebration. The two-day **Salmon Days Festival** is held the first weekend in October with a parade, kids fair, 350 arts and crafts booths, live music, a pancake feed, fun run, and hatchery tours. More than 200,000 people crowd downtown Issaquah for the festival. Another very popular event, with a rather unique clientele, is Nudestock, described above under "Recreation."

INFORMATION AND TRANSPORTATION

For maps and information contact the **Issaquah Visitor Information Center,** 160 N.W. Gilman Blvd., tel. (206) 392-7024. Open Mon.-Fri. 9 a.m.-5 p.m., Sat.-Sun. 10 a.m.-4 p.m. Find the **library** at 120 E. Sunset Way, tel. (206) 392-5430. Issaquah's **area code** is 206.

You can get to and from Seattle, North Bend, Redmond, and other points in King County via **Metro Transit,** tel. (206) 447-4800 or (800) 542-7876.

To connect to virtually anywhere in the country, take **Greyhound** from 55 Sunset Way, tel. (206) 392-7142. **Northwestern Trailways,** tel. (800) 366-3830, also has bus connections throughout the Northwest from their stop at 91 1st Pl. NW.

Shuttle Express, tel. (206) 622-1424 or (800) 487-7433, provides frequent direct service from Issaquah's Holiday Inn and Motel 6 to Sea-Tac Airport for $16, along with door-to-door connections.

NORTH FROM SEATTLE

WOODINVILLE

Woodinville (pop. 26,000), barely far enough from Seattle to have its own identity, is a rapidly growing town that was just incorporated in 1993. It has many stables and bridle trails and is becoming a very popular cycling destination, with easy access from Seattle via the Burke-Gilman and Sammamish River trails that pass right by several wineries and a big brewery. This is also the destination of the Spirit of Washington dinner train, described below.

Chateau Ste. Michelle Winery
Woodinville is home to the state's largest winery, Chateau Ste. Michelle, off Hwy. 202 at 14111 N.E. 145th St., tel. (206) 488-1133. Though the wine grapes are grown in eastern Washington, this winery is among the nicest to visit. The original 1912 residence—once owned by Seattle lumber baron Fred Stimson—is surrounded by 87 acres of manicured grounds that include experimental vineyards, an arboretum, and trout ponds. An amphitheater is used for a full summer season of music and arts events with picnics on the lawn; get tickets from Ticket Master, tel. (206) 292-2787. The crowds gather at the impressive French-chateau winery building, built in 1967. Very informative cellar tours and free tastings are offered every half-hour daily 10 a.m.-4:30 p.m., except Christmas and New Year's Day. Avoid the summer mob scene by visiting on Monday or Tuesday; weekends can get pretty hectic. Those who take the tours can taste four different wines, but if you don't take a tour you can sample a wider variety. The gift shop sells wines, books on wine, cheese, and more. By the way, it may come as a surprise to learn that Chateau Ste. Michelle is owned by U.S. Tobacco.

Columbia Winery
A modern Victorian-style building directly across the road from Chateau Ste. Michelle houses the Columbia Winery, tel. (206) 488-2776. This is Washington's oldest winery, founded in 1962 by 10 friends—six of whom were University of Washington professors. Columbia produces award-winning chardonnay, semillon, cabernet sauvignon, merlot, among others. Their winemaker, David Lake, holds the prestigious title "Master of Wine," and is the only one in America so honored. The tasting room is open Sunday 10 a.m.-5 p.m., and Mon.-Sat. 10 a.m.-7 p.m. (except holidays), with tours daily in the summer, but only on weekends in the winter. The winery gets very crowded during the daily visits of the Spirit of Washington train (see below); avoid coming here on Saturday 1:30-2:30 p.m., and Sunday 12:30-1:30 p.m., unless you want to join the throngs in the dining room. (Besides, they only give train passengers a quick-and-dirty 10-minute version.) The best time to visit is during the grape crush each September and October.

Other Wineries
Another nearby winery is **Silver Lake Winery,** 17616 15th Ave. SE, No. 106B, tel. (206) 485-2437; open Mon.-Fri. noon-5 p.m. They also have a tasting room in the Country Village Mall at 23732 Bothell-Everett Hwy., tel. (206) 485-6041, open Sunday 11 a.m.-5 p.m., and Mon.-Sat. 10 a.m.-6 p.m. **Facelli Winery,** 16120 Woodinville-Redmond Rd, tel. (206) 488-1020, is a small family operation with a tasting room that opens on weekends noon-4 p.m. The **Paul Thomas Winery** (owned by Columbia Winery) has a tasting room near the intersection of N.E. 175th St. and Hwy. 202; tel. (206) 747-1008.

Brewery
The Pacific Northwest has the highest per capita consumption of draft beer in America, so it should come as no surprise that microbreweries are immensely popular. **Redhook Ale Brewery,** tel. (206) 483-3232, opened a new brewing and bottling plant right next door to the Columbia Winery in 1994 and has rapidly grown beyond the "micro" stage. This huge facility is one of two owned by the company (the second is in Ballard, see the Seattle chapter). All beer made here follows the German *Reinheitgebot*

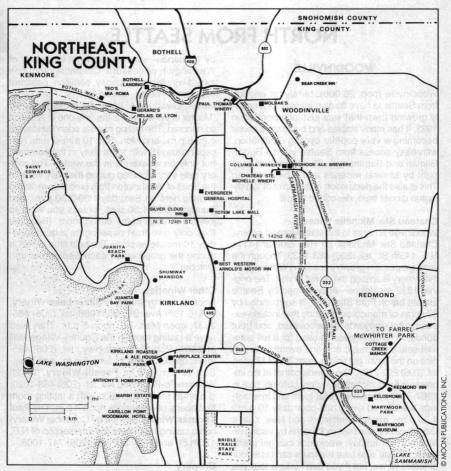

NORTHEAST KING COUNTY

© MOON PUBLICATIONS, INC.

purity law, which mandates that only four ingredients be used in beer: malted barley, hops, yeast, and water.

Tours ($1, including the glass) are offered several times a day, and include a sampling of several brews. The pub here, **Forecasters Public House,** has a half-dozen beers on tap, a limited menu of light and tasty meals (not the standard pub grub), and live music on Monday and Saturday nights. Get T-shirts in the gift shop.

Nursery

Molbak's, an impressive nursery at 13625 N.E. 175th St., tel. (206) 483-5000, is far larger than it looks—more than 2,000 varieties of indoor and outdoor plants, cut flowers, garden tools, trees, bulbs, and a conservatory/aviary fill the numerous greenhouses here. Molbak's is as popular with browsers as serious gardeners; an espresso bar and gift shop add to the fun. Open daily.

Spirit of Washington Dinner Train

Fine food and wine, plus Lake Washington scenery, are the highlights of this train ride. The 1935 diesel engines pull the passenger cars between Renton Depot and Columbia Winery in Woodinville, a 45-mile roundtrip run that takes three and a half hours. A quick tour of the winery and tasting room is included. Passengers have a choice of several entrees and desserts on the dinner train, which costs $57 for the parlor car, $69 for the dome. Lunches and brunches are $47 and $59. The train operates year-round. For details, call (206) 227-7245 or (800) 876-7245.

From June to mid-September, **Gray Line of Seattle,** tel. (206) 626-5208 or (800) 426-7532, offers package tours that include roundtrip transportation between Seattle and the train station in Renton.

Outdoor Recreation

For a bit of fresh Woodinville air try the **Tolt Pipeline Trail,** an 11-mile hiking and horse trail that passes through town and extends to Snoqualmie Valley near Duvall. Find the trailhead just around the corner from Chateau Ste. Michelle. The paved **Sammamish River Trail** (see "Redmond," above) passes through on the other side of Ste. Michelle on its way north and west to Bothell and Seattle, or south to Redmond.

Hot air ballooning is a popular attraction in Woodinville; contact **Climb on a Rainbow,** tel. (206) 364-0995, for details.

Bed and Breakfasts

Bear Creek Inn B&B, 19520 N.E. 144th Pl., tel. (206) 881-2978, features river-rock fireplaces, patios, fluffy comforters, a hot tub, and a sunken tiled bathtub (shared by two guest rooms), all surrounded by an acre of lawn and firs. Rooms are $65 s or d, including a full breakfast.

Food

Woodinville has a wide variety of dining experiences, including the Forecasters Public House at Redhook Ale Brewery, described above. At **Armadillo Barbecue,** 13109 N.E. 175th St., tel. (206) 481-1417, you may not find armadillo on the menu, but you will find real Texas-style barbecued ribs, chicken, baked beans, and

more, plus wine and beer in a fun atmosphere; open for lunch and dinner daily.

Feast on Mexican food at **Las Margaritas,** 13400 N.E. 175th, tel. (206) 483-5656; or head to **Sushi Kuma,** 17321 140th Ave. NE, tel. (206) 820-7676, for out-of-this world fresh sushi. **Chin's Palace,** 175th Station, 13317 N.E. 175th St., tel. (206) 486-6252, serves Mandarin, Sichuan, and Cantonese dishes. Good pizzas, pasta, and veal at **Italianissimo,** 17650 140th Ave. NE, tel. (206) 485-6888.

Out in the nothing place called Maltby (approximately five miles northeast of Woodinville on Hwy. 522), is **Maltby Cafe,** tel. (206) 483-3123, where the outstanding breakfasts and lunches are well worth the trip.

The **Woodinville Farmers Market** comes to the Sorenson School at 13209 N.E. 175th on Saturday 9 a.m.-4 p.m. from mid-June through October.

Events

Local events include the bizarre **All Fool's Day Parade and Basset Bash,** and the very popular **Washington Food And Wine Festival and Grape Stomp** in August. Music and arts events are staged in the amphitheater at Chateau Ste. Michelle. Contact the winery at (206) 488-1133 for information; to obtain tickets call Ticket Master at (206) 292-2787 or stop by the amphitheater box office.

Shopping

Visit **Hollywood Schoolhouse,** Hwy. 202 and 120th Pl. NE (head east from Ste. Michelle), for a novel shopping experience. You'll find antiques, arts and crafts shops, and galleries in this old-time country school. At the same intersection (across the street), **Emerald City Antiques,** tel. (206) 485-5555, features 150 shops with antiques, collectibles, jewelry, prints, glassware, and more.

Pennsylvania Woodworks, 17601 140th Ave. NE, tel. (206) 486-9541, sells furniture, quilts, woven rugs, wooden toys, and more handmade items by Amish craftsworkers.

Information and Transportation

Get local information from the **Woodinville Chamber of Commerce,** 17630 140th Ave.

NE, tel. (206) 481-8300. The local telephone **area code** is 206.

Metro Transit, tel. (206) 553-3000 or (800) 542-7876, has daily bus service to Seattle and environs from Woodinville.

BOTHELL

Bothell (pop. 13,000) was founded in 1884 by David Bothell and his family. Apparently without competition, they logged the area, built a hotel, platted the town, and sold lots to pioneers who wanted to get away from the bustle of the city. Northeast of Lake Washington on the Sammamish River, Bothell is about a half hour from Seattle. The town straddles the line separating King and Snohomish counties, creating an odd political situation for local elections.

The featured attraction is **Bothell Landing,** 18120 N.E. Bothell Way, where a park, small shopping complex, and the **Bothell Historical Museum** mark the original steamboat berth. The museum, tel. (206) 486-1889, housed in the 1893 William Hannan cabin, is open Sunday 1-4 p.m. March-December. Cross the footbridge behind the museum to pick up the paved **Sammamish River Trail** and follow it east to Marymoor Park in Redmond, or head west on the **Burke-Gilman Trail** to Seattle.

Country Village, between Bothell Landing and I-405 at 23714 Bothell Hwy. SE, has 45 antique, food, jewelry, clothing, and gift shops. Stop by the Carriage House Museum here for a sampling of local history.

Swim at the **Northshore Pool,** 9815 N.E. 188th St., tel. (206) 296-4333.

Accommodations and Campgrounds

Wyndham Garden Hotel, 19333 Northcreek Parkway, tel. (206) 485-5557, has rooms for $79-84 s or d, including an outdoor pool, jacuzzi, and exercise room. Luxury accommodations are found at **Residence Inn by Marriott,** 11920 N.E. 195th St., tel. (206) 485-3030 or (800) 228-9290, where two-bedroom suites go for $108 s or d, including an outdoor pool and jacuzzi.

Open year-round, **Lake Pleasant RV Park,** 24025 Bothell-Everett Hwy., tel. (206) 483-9436, has lakeside RV pads and campsites.

Food

Bothell's best restaurant is **Gerard's Relais de Lyon,** an elegantly classic French restaurant in a remodeled home at 17121 N.E. Bothell Way, tel. (206) 485-7600; open for dinner only, Tues.-Sun. evenings. Exquisite meals, but priced accordingly. Other European tastes can be satisfied at **Teo's Mia Roma,** an Italian restaurant at 7614 N.E. Bothell Way in Kenmore, just west of Bothell. Open for dinner only; tel. (206) 486-6200.

Events and Entertainment

Local events include an **Arts and Crafts Fair** in August, and **Music in the Park** on Friday evenings in July and August. Country Village has all sorts of minor festivals and open houses that draw in shoppers throughout the year. Bothell's **Fourth of July** celebration is also a fun event.

For live music Wed.-Sat. nights, head to **B.C. McDonald's,** 17917 Bothell-Everett Hwy., tel. (206) 481-9227.

Information and Services

Get information at **Northshore Chamber of Commerce,** 10410 Beardslee Blvd., tel. (206) 486-1245. The local telephone **area code** is 206. Swim at the **Northshore Pool,** 9815 N.E. 188th St., tel. (206) 296-4333.

Transportation

Metro Transit, tel. (206) 553-3000 or (800) 542-7876, has bus service between Seattle and Bothell. Once in Bothell you can travel to Lynnwood, Edmonds, or Everett on **Community Transit,** tel. (206) 353-7433 or (800) 562-1375.

Shuttle Express, tel. (206) 622-1424 or (800) 487-7433, provides frequent direct service from Bothell's Wyndham Garden Hotel and Residence Inn to Sea-Tac Airport for $18, along with door-to-door connections. **Kenmore Air,** tel. (206) 486-1257 or (800) 543-9595, has floatplane service from the nearby town of Kenmore on the north end of Lake Washington. They fly to Victoria, B.C., and the San Juan Islands on a daily basis.

LYNNWOOD

Lynnwood (pop. 30,000) sprouted along Hwy. 99 before the Interstate era, but has made its pres-

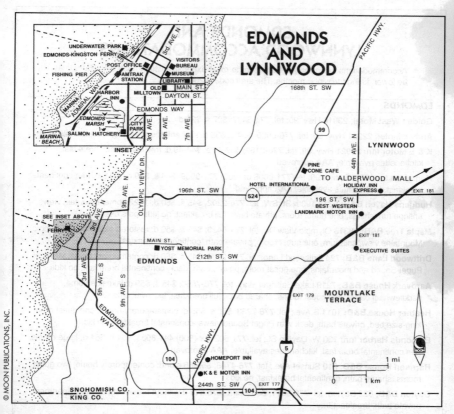

ence known, thanks to the enormous **Alderwood Mall** on the east side of town. It hosts The Bon Marché, Nordstrom, JCPenney, Sears, Lamonts, and many smaller stores; the mall is surrounded by other, smaller shopping plazas. Most businesses are stretched along Hwy. 99; here you'll find the discount stores and auto dealerships. The other main drag is 196th St. SW, which runs from Puget Sound in Edmonds through the heart of Lynnwood, past yet more shopping centers and auto-repair places.

For a taste of a slower era, drop by **Keeler's Korner,** at 164th and Hwy. 99, where you'll find two old gas pumps in front of an aging two-story building now on the National Register of Historic

Places. The surroundings are typical of the area (and of much of America): cheesy developments, condos, fast food, cheap motels, and strip malls.

Accommodations and Food

See the "Edmonds and Lynnwood Accommodations" chart for a complete list of local lodging options.

Fine dining is at a minimum in Lynnwood, but several ethnic places are worth a visit. **Papazanni,** 18415 33rd Ave. W, tel. (206) 776-9551, is a good Italian restaurant, and **Pio Pio's,** 18620 33rd Ave. W, tel. (206) 776-3580, has authentic Mexican meals and free happy-hour munchies seven days a week. Get Thai cuisine at

EDMONDS AND LYNNWOOD ACCOMMODATIONS

Accommodations are arranged from least to most expensive within each city. Rates may be lower during the winter months. The area code is 206.

EDMONDS

Golden West Motel; 23916 Hwy. 99; tel. 771-3447; $27 s, $29 d

Andy's Motel; 22201 Hwy. 99; tel. 776-6080; $34 s, $38 d; kitchenettes available, local calls 25 cents

K & E Motor Inn; 23921 Hwy. 99; tel. 778-2181; $39-44 s, $44-49 d; free continental breakfast, kitchenettes available, AAA approved

Homeport Inn; 23825 Hwy. 99; tel. 771-8008 or (800) 771-8009; $44 s, $49 d; hot tub, free continental breakfast, kitchenettes available, AAA approved

Hudgens Haven B&B; 9313 190th St. SW; tel. 776-2202; $45 s, $50 d; 1922 home, mountain views, antique furnishings, one guest room, private bath, full breakfast, no kids, pets okay

Maple Tree B&B; 18313 Olympic View Dr.; tel. 774-8420; $45 s, $50 d; restored older home, Olympic Mountains view, solarium, one guest room, private bath, continental breakfast

Driftwood Lane B&B; 724 Driftwood Lane; tel. 776-2686; $45 s, $50 d; contemporary home, views of Puget Sound and mountains, one guest room, private bath, deck, continental breakfast, no kids

Aardvark House B&B; 7219 Lake Ballinger Way; tel. 778-7866; $45 s, $55 d; lakeside home, paddlewheel barge, two guest rooms, shared bath, full breakfast, kids welcome

Heather House B&B; 1011 B Ave.; tel. 778-7233; $50 s, $55 d; contemporary home, one guest room, king-size bed, private bath, deck with Puget Sound views, continental breakfast, no kids

Edmonds Harbor Inn; 130 W. Dayton St.; tel. 771-5021 or (800) 441-8033; $54 s, $64 d; large rooms, free continental breakfast, kitchenettes available, AAA approved

Harrison House B&B; 210 Sunset Ave.; tel. 776-4748; $55-65 s or d; contemporary home, two guest rooms, shared bath, continental breakfast, no kids

Dayton B&B; 522 Dayton; tel. 778-3611; $85 s or d ($75 s or d without breakfast); upstairs apartment, private bath, breakfast tray

---

Thai Cuisine, 1120 164th St. SW, tel. (206) 742-9155; Chinese food at **Jemmy's Wok,** 16212 Bothell-Everett Hwy., tel. (206) 742-8858; teriyaki at **Toshi's Teriyaki,** 20829 Hwy. 99, tel. (206) 771-5320; and breakfast, burgers, and sandwiches at **Jimbo's,** 196th at Hwy. 99, tel. (206) 778-1111. Popular for lunch is **Mill Creek Cafe,** 16430 9th Ave. SE, tel. (206) 743-2333. A decent chain restaurant is **Olive Garden Italian Restaurant,** 4221 196th St. SW, tel. (206) 670-2977.

A place of particular interest makes no claim on fine dining, but it is just the kind of place every town needs: good food, lots of it, and no nonsense about calories, fat, and all that healthy stuff. **Pine Cone Cafe,** 18929 Hwy. 99, tel. (206) 776-0788, serves generous portions of all-American fatty foods at a not-so-fat price, and your coffee cup never runs dry. You'll get a patty melt here without the waitress wrinkling her nose, and you'll get hash browns so crunchy and tasty that you'll almost forget the country sausage and squeeze-bottle of ketchup. They'll cook anything they have on the menu anytime of day. It isn't elegant, but it is nice. **Warning:** If you don't smoke, you may not appreciate the Smokers Yes! sign inside.

Recreation and Events

The **Lynn-Swim Recreation Center,** tel. (206) 670-6288, has a sauna, plus an indoor pool that

LYNNWOOD AND MOUNTLAKE TERRACE

Court of Monte Cristo; 16003 Hwy. 99; tel. 743-0312; $27 s, $29 d.

Lynnwood Motor Inn; 18109 Hwy. 99; tel. 778-2808; $42 s or d; kitchenettes available, local calls 25 cents, no kids

Holiday Inn Express; 4117 196th St. SW; tel. 775-8030 or (800) 465-4329; has rooms for $50-55 s, $55-60 d; jacuzzi, free continental breakfast, AAA approved

Silver Cloud Inn; 19332 36th Ave. W; tel. 775-7600 or (800) 551-7207; $54-68 s, $60-74 d; outdoor pool, jacuzzi, exercise room, kitchenettes available, free continental breakfast, AAA approved

Hotel International; 5621 196th St. SW; tel. 771-1777 or (800) 626-5750; $58 s, $68 d; jacuzzi, kitchenettes available, local calls 40 cents, AAA approved

Best Western Landmark Motor Inn; 4300 200th SW; tel. 775-7447; $59-69 s, $63-73 d; indoor pool, jacuzzi, exercise room, kitchenettes available, AAA approved

Residence Inn by Marriott; 182000 Alderwood Mall Blvd.; tel. 771-1100 or (800) 228-9290; $120 for up to four; two-bedroom suites, outdoor pool, jacuzzis, sports court, kitchens, free continental breakfast, free local shuttle, AAA approved

Executive Suites Hotel; 20610 44th Ave. W; tel. 775-2500 or (800) 628-0611; $169 s or d; suites, outdoor pool, jacuzzi, exercise room, game room, free full breakfast in the atrium, reception with cocktails and snacks, kitchenettes available, AAA approved

---

opens up during the summer. **Scriber Lake Park** includes this small pond, encircled by a half-mile nature trail. Lynnwood also has an **REI** store with all sorts of outdoor gear at 4200 194th St. SW, tel. (206) 774-1300.

Mountlake Terrace (pop. 20,000), a bedroom community just south of Lynnwood, calls itself the "city of parks" and features a recreation pavilion housing an Olympic-sized pool, weight room, and racquetball courts. **Ballinger Park Golf Course,** 23000 Lakeview Dr., tel. (206) 774-4940, is also in Mountlake Terrace.

The **Lynnwood Heritage Festival** in late September features arts and crafts, food booths, and entertainment.

Information and Services
The **South Snohomish County Chamber of Commerce,** 3400 188th St. SW, tel. (206) 774-0507, has local info; open Mon.-Thurs. 8:30 a.m.-5 p.m., and Friday. 8:30 a.m.-4 p.m. year-round.

Headquarters for the **Mt. Baker-Snoqualmie National Forest** is in Mountlake Terrace at 21905 64th Ave. W, tel. (206) 775-9702; open Mon.-Fri. 8 a.m.-4:30 p.m. year-round. Stop by for information on this 1.7-million-acre national forest that covers the west side of the Cascades from Snoqualmie Pass to the Canadian border.

Transportation
Community Transit, tel. (206) 353-7433 or (800) 562-1375, provides bus connections to other parts of Snohomish County for just $1, and on to Seattle for $1.50.

EDMONDS

Edmonds, 15 miles north of Seattle on Puget Sound, is a small, florally enhanced city (pop. 31,000) surrounded by rolling hills and pine forests that some Californians—older ones, of course—say looks like Sausalito did before the deluge of humanity. In spite of its spurt of growth since the mid-1980s, downtown Edmonds has retained its small-town appearance, and if you live there you can walk to everything, including the auto mechanic. The town is best known as the gateway to the Olympic Peninsula; the state ferry shuttles constantly between Edmonds and Kingston on the Kitsap Peninsula.

The first white settlers found the shores of Puget Sound crowded with dense forests. By the turn of the century, Edmonds was at the center of the action with 10 shingle mills working at full tilt along the waterfront. The trees, of course, didn't last forever, and when the last mill closed in 1951, Edmonds was gradually transformed into a suburb of Seattle. Today it is such a quiet, end-of-the-road place that each generation of teenagers calls it Deadmonds; then they can't wait to move back when they become adults. Although it is illegal to play a radio or tape player on Sunset Ave. loud enough be heard 30 feet away, quiet doesn't mean uninteresting—and a walk along Edmonds' mile-and-a-half waterfront makes a pleasant afternoon outing.

Sights

A good way to see Edmonds is to begin with a stroll on the half-mile-long **Sunset Ave.** with its Victorian homes and views of Puget Sound and the Olympic Mountains. If the tide is out you can walk back along the beach.

At the foot of Dayton St., **Olympic Beach Park** has a life-size bronze sculpture of a father and children looking at sea lions. The park has picnic tables and a small beach. Two restaurants, a deli, and a fish market adjoin the park.

A 950-foot lighted public **fishing pier** runs out into the Sound, where anglers cast for salmon and bottom fish and jig for squid. Walkers and joggers like the new boardwalk that runs a quarter of a mile along the Port of Edmonds marina from the fishing pier to **Anthony's Homeport Restaurant.** Try the shrimp cocktail; they serve it in a milkshake glass. The marina itself is home to 1,000 boats, including the largest charter fishing fleet on Puget Sound. It is only a short walk down to the small **Edmonds Marina Beach Park,** a perfect place to fly kites, cook a dinner over a beach fire, and watch ferries crossing the sound into the sunset.

A dozen or more shops and restaurants in a former automobile agency remodeled into old-time atmosphere make up **Old Milltown** at 5th Ave. S and Dayton. Step inside to check out the historic photos of Edmonds. For a more modern flavor, try **Harbor Square's** boutiques and galleries near the waterfront on W. Dayton.

The **Edmonds Museum,** 118 5th Ave. N, tel. (206) 774-0900, has a working shingle mill model, a marine room, and other displays depicting Edmonds's past. Open Sunday, Tuesday, Thursday, and Saturday 1-4 p.m. year-round. No charge.

The shoreline drive north from Edmonds along Olympic View Dr. leads through comfortable neighborhoods, and eventually reaches **Picnic Point County Park,** approximately seven miles north of town. This is a popular place for a beach picnic, with Puget Sound and the Olympics as a backdrop. Access is a bit quicker from Hwy. 99; go west on Shelby Rd. for 1.3 miles, bear right onto Picnic Point Rd. at the "Y," and continue another 1.5 miles to the park. A closer place is **City Park** on 3rd Ave. S at Pine Street. The park has picnic shelters and a bandstand for summertime concerts. Just south of here is a small king salmon hatchery run by a group of local anglers.

Outdoors and Underwater

Just two blocks from downtown is the **Edmonds Marsh,** a haven for wildlife of all kinds. It's an amazing little piece of the natural world where blackbirds, herons, ducks, and crows feed in an enclave surrounded by a boatyard, abandoned oil tanks, an athletic club, and creeping development. A boardwalk overlooks the marsh.

Off the shoreline of Brackett's Landing (the little beach next to the ferry dock) is the 27-acre **Underwater Park.** It was the first underwater park in Washington and is used by scuba divers year-round to explore the 300-foot DeLion dry dock, sunk there in 1935 to serve as a breakwater and marinelife habitat. Since then, other underwater structures—including old tires, steel shelving, a model of the Evergreen Point Floating Bridge, and two tugboats—have been added for the enjoyment of both fish and diver, resulting in one of the Pacific Northwest's most popular underwater parks. From the shore, you'd never know anything was down there. You can rent diving equipment or find a dive buddy at **Underwater Sports,** 264 Railroad Ave., tel. (206) 771-6322, two blocks south across the street from the Amtrak depot.

If you aren't into scuba diving, try the swimming pool in **Yost Memorial Park** at Bowdoin and 96th Ave. W. Call (206) 775-2645 for details.

Accommodations

See the "Edmonds and Lynnwood Accommodations" chart for a complete list of local lodging options. There are no nearby public campgrounds. Edmonds has several surprisingly inexpensive B&Bs. **Heather House B&B,** tel. (206) 778-7233, is a large modern home with a king size bed in the single guest room, and decks offering spectacular views of Puget Sound. Stay along the shores of Lake Ballinger at **Aardvark House B&B,** tel. (206) 778-7866, where guests can play around on a paddle wheel barge. Kids are welcome. **Maple Tree B&B,** tel. (206) 774-8420, is located within an older restored home, and is notable for the fine views of the Olympics. More great views at **Driftwood Lane B&B,** tel. (206) 776-2686, a contemporary home where you can sit on the deck overlooking Puget Sound.

Food
Brusseau's, 5th and Dayton, tel. (206) 774-4166, is Edmonds's trendiest restaurant (this means you'll find Lycra-clad cyclists at the outdoor tables) and serves three moderately priced meals daily. Outstanding breads and pastries—including monstrous cinnamon rolls—or try the soups, salads, quiche, or sandwiches for lunch. Highly recommended.

Enjoy Northwest seafood for lunch, dinner, or Sunday champagne brunches at **Arnie's,** 300 Admiral Way, tel. (206) 771-6533, two blocks south of the ferry terminal beside the city park. Their popular end-of-the-day bar overlooks the marina and is a great place to watch the ferries come in.

Provinces Asian Restaurant & Bar, upstairs inside Old Milltown (201 5th Ave. S), tel. (206) 744-0288, serves up a diverse and eclectic selection of Asian cuisine, covering the spectrum from Japanese to Cambodian. **Cafe International,** offers an equally diverse menu; the plates arrive sizzling hot with tempura, Louisiana rock shrimp tortellini, and many other entrees.

El Puerto Mexican Restaurant, 423 Main St., tel. (206) 672-2469, has quality south-of-the-border meals. **Chantrelle,** 316 Main St., tel. (206) 774-0650, is a popular downtown bistro with three dependably fine meals a day.

Edmonds has a good French restaurant, **Cafe de Paris,** 109 Main St., tel. (206) 771-2350, near the ferry landing, with entrees in the $15-20 range. For Italian meals and pizza, you won't go wrong at **Ciao Italia,** 5133 25th Ave. NE, tel. (206) 524-6989.

Shopping
Edmonds has several large antique and collectibles stores, including the **Waterfront Antique Mall,** inside an antique Safeway building at 190 Sunset Ave. S, tel. (206) 670-0770, and **Edmonds Antique Mall** with dealers on the upper level of Old Milltown at Dayton and 5th, tel. (206) 771-9644. The Waterfront Antique Mall is the better of the two. **Gallery North,** an artists' cooperative inside Old Milltown, tel. (206) 774-0946, is the finest local gallery.

Entertainment and Events
Local events of note include the **Edmonds Art Festival** on the third weekend of June, with a juried art show, artists in action, arts and crafts booths, and live music. The old-fashioned **Fourth of July** brings the usual parades, a chicken barbecue, fireman's water fights, live music, and fireworks. The **Taste of Edmonds Festival** on the third weekend of August is a very popular street fair with ethnic foods, cooking demonstrations, a carnival, music, and beer garden. **Concerts in the Park** are held at city park on Sunday afternoons during July and August. End the season with something decidedly different, the self-explanatory **Underwater Pumpkin Carving Contest,** held at Bracketts Landing.

Cascade Symphony, a 90-piece orchestra in existence for more than 30 years, features winter concerts at Puget Sound Christian College Auditorium, 410 4th Ave. N, tel. (206) 778-4688.

Information and Services
The friendly folks at the log cabin **Edmonds Visitors Bureau,** 120 5th Ave. N, tel. (206) 776-6711, will be happy to provide you with maps and current information. The office is open Mon.-Fri. 9 a.m.-4 p.m., and Saturday 11 a.m.-3 p.m. in the summer, and Mon.-Fri. 9 a.m.-4 p.m. winters. Pick up local brochures inside the Waterfront Antique Mall if the visitors bureau is closed. Find the **Edmonds Public Library** at 7th and Main, tel. (206) 771-1933. The **area code** for Edmonds is 206.

Transportation
Community Transit, tel. (206) 353-7433 or (800) 562-1375, provides bus connections to other parts of Snohomish County for just $1, and on to Seattle for $1.50.

Take the **Washington State Ferry** from Edmonds to Kingston, the Olympic Peninsula's drop-off point. The crossing takes 30 minutes and leaves Edmonds about every 40 minutes during the day. Summer fares are $7.10 one-way car and driver, $3.50 for passengers or walk-ons; tel. (206) 464-6400 or (800) 843-3779.

Edmonds is one of the few towns its size to still have train service. **Amtrak's Empire Builder** heads south to Seattle and east to Spokane and Chicago. The **Mt. Baker International** provides daily train connections to Vancouver, B.C., via Everett, Mount Vernon, and Bellingham. For information on Amtrak, call (206) 778-3213 or (800) 872-7245.

BOB RACE

NORTHERN PUGET SOUND

EVERETT

Everett (pop. 75,000) is a largely industrial city that once had a row of pulp and paper mills with their distinct, unpleasant odors. Most of them have closed, and today Everett is best known as the place where Boeing's 747, 767, and 777 jets are assembled. Located on Puget Sound 27 miles north of Seattle, it could be a sister city to Tacoma in terms of geography, distance from Seattle, and industrial base.

The city's historic downtown core is undergoing a minor rebirth as buildings are restored and the streets are spruced up. Unfortunately, the main commercial drag, Evergreen Way (Hwy. 99) offers another side to the city; here you'll find used car lots, pizza joints, tire and auto parts dealers, storage lockers, fast-food and discount stores of all types, and mile after mile of stoplights, backed-up traffic, and exhaust fumes.

The Setting

Everett is flanked by distant mountains, with Mt. Baker to the north, Mt. Rainier to the south, and 5,324-foot Mt. Pilchuck to the east. Puget Sound's Port Gardner Bay is at its front door, and the view across the Sound includes Whidbey Island, Gedney Island, and Camano Island. The Snohomish River curves north on the edge of town and creates a maze of islands and sloughs before emptying into Puget Sound.

Coupled with its waterfront location, Everett is surrounded by recreational opportunities, as well as more indoor fun than most cities its size. It is close to the skiing at Stevens Pass—the Cascades begin virtually at the city's back door—the rivers and lakes have excellent boating and fishing, and the Sound is speckled with small boats during salmon runs.

HISTORY

Everett is one of the few Puget Sound areas that prompted Capt. George Vancouver to get off his boat. After coming ashore in 1792, Van-

couver named the area "New Georgia" for King George III, and the English claim to this land lasted for more than 50 years.

Eastern Money

The city of Everett was established in 1891 in boomtown fashion by a group of influential East Coast promoters that included John D. Rockefeller, Charles Wetmore, Henry Hewitt Jr., and Charles Colby. They envisioned it as the "New York City of the West," and based their dreams on the expectation that the Great Northern Railroad would make Port Gardner its western terminus, and that the nearby Monte Cristo mines would bring unparalleled wealth. Instead, Seattle was chosen as the end point for the railroad, and the gold and silver mines never lived up to expectations. In addition, the Silver Panic of 1893 led to a devastating national depression that lasted until the Klondike gold rush of 1898 helped lift the nation out of its financial doldrums.

It was Charles Colby who named the town—in honor of his infant son Everett—but downtown streets also bear the names of the others whose financing got the city started: Rockefeller, Wetmore, and Hewitt. The new town was aided significantly by the Monte Cristo mines, and a smelter was built to serve them. However, the ore did not last, and it was eventually timber that guaranteed the city's success.

Lumber Years

As much or more influential than Rockefeller in Everett's development was a man named Frederick Weyerhaeuser. Born in Germany in 1834, he immigrated to the U.S. in 1852, where he worked in an Illinois lumber mill and married a

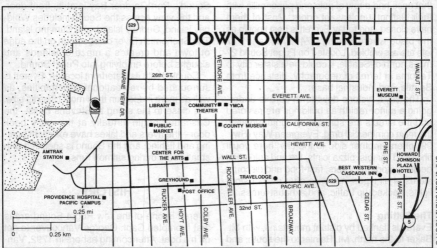

Boeing 747-400s await final assembly at the Everett factory.

BOEING

German woman, Elizabeth Bloedel. Weyerhaeuser was so hardworking and thrifty that he was able to buy the mill a few years later, and then expanded his operation westward. His main Pacific Coast lumber mill was built in Everett in 1903, becoming—and long remaining—the city's most important industry. When he died, Weyerhaeuser's lumber company was the biggest in the country. Weyerhaeuser is now headquartered in Tacoma.

By the early 1900s, lumber, paper, and shingle mills—along with other factories producing everything from nails to barges—had given Everett the moniker, "the city of smokestacks." Everett was also known for its labor unrest during the first two decades of this century, and the Industrial Workers of the World (Wobblies) congregated in Everett with their then-radical ideas that included worker ownership of factories. The worst fears of all were realized on November 5, 1916, when two boatloads of Wobblies from Seattle arrived. The Everett Massacre that followed resulted in the death of at least seven men.

BOEING PLANT

A tour of Boeing's astounding 747-767 assembly plant is *the* highlight of a visit to the Everett area, and for many technology and aviation buffs, it's the highlight of a visit to the whole state. The plant itself—11 stories high—has the largest capacity of any building in the world, containing 291 million cubic feet and covering an incredible 62 acres. (For trivia buffs, the largest building by floor surface is the West Edmonton Mall in Canada; the Boeing assembly plant comes in second.) A total of eight 747s or 767s can be assembled at one time, and it takes eight months to complete each plane. They roll outside through football-field sized doors. Boeing's new 777s are assembled in another Everett building (not generally open to the public), while their 737s are put together in the Renton facility.

Tours

Free 90-minute tours of the Everett Boeing plant are available hourly in the summer months, Mon.-Fri. 9 a.m.-3 p.m., and at least twice a day (9 a.m. and 1 p.m.) on winter weekdays. No kids under age 10, and no tours on Thanksgiving, the day after Thanksgiving, or between December 23 and January 9. The tours begin with three short films (including the star attraction, where a 777 is assembled in a few brief moments). Then you head out, take a shuttle to the building, and get a guided tour of the plant. No bathrooms along the way, so make a pit stop before departing. No still or video cameras are permitted, and the tours are offered on a first-come, first-served basis; reservations are available only for groups of 10 or more.

Because of the tours' popularity, get to the Boeing Tour Center two or three hours ahead of time during the mid-summer peak season, and be sure to arrive before 11 a.m. to make sure of getting on a tour that day. (Tip: Try arriving by 7:30 a.m. since Boeing sometimes offers an 8 a.m. tour that is less crowded. The least crowded days are Tues.-Thurs.) Avoid the wait entirely by plunking down $20 for a three-hour tour that leaves Seattle daily in the summer. These are offered by both **Gray Line of Seattle,** tel. (206) 626-5208 or (800) 426-7532, and **Customized Tours,** tel. (206) 878-3965. **Mosquito Fleet,** tel. (206) 252-6800 or (800) 325-6722, offers tours of Boeing and Everett's historic sites for $19; these depart from Everett.

The Tour Center—where you begin and end your visit—has all sorts of aircraft-related gifts, perfect for any pilot friends. Call (206) 342-4801 for a recording with more details on the Boeing tours. To reach the Tour Center, take I-5 exit 189 west onto Hwy. 526 and follow the signs.

OTHER SIGHTS

Museums and Art
One of Everett's oldest commercial buildings, constructed in 1906, houses the **Everett Museum,** 2915 Hewitt Ave., tel. (206) 259-8849. The museum covers two floors and includes changing exhibits on the city's history. Open

Wed.-Sun. 1-4 p.m.; free. While at the museum, pick up a Hewitt Ave. historical brochure and take a walking tour of downtown Everett's many turn-of-the-century businesses.

Also of interest is the **Snohomish County Museum and Historical Association** at 2817 Rockefeller Ave., tel. (206) 259-2022. Here you'll find historical photos and artifacts from throughout the county, and a museum store selling local history books. Open Wed.-Sun. 1-4 p.m. At the 13th St. dock, see a collection of firefighters' equipment in the **Firefighters Museum** any time; the museum was designed for through-the-window viewing.

The **Everett Center for the Arts** at 1507 Wall, tel. (206) 259-0380, exhibits works of regional artists and includes a permanent glass collection and monthly art displays. Open Mon.-Fri. 10 a.m.-5 p.m., and Saturday 11 a.m.-3 p.m.

Additional Sights
In its early years, Everett was home to some of the timber industry's most successful entrepreneurs. These lumber barons built elaborate mansions in the north end of town on Grand and Rucker Avenues, many of which still stand.

Everett's newly opened **Naval Station** is home port to an aircraft carrier battle group headed by the **USS Abraham Lincoln** and five support ships. Ship tours are available during Salty Sea Days in June and on the Fourth of July weekend.

Everett's lumber barons lived in exquisite mansions.

DIANNE BOUERICE LYONS

Paine Field is home to the **Museum of Flight Restoration Center,** where aircraft are restored for this outstanding Seattle museum. The restoration center is located in Building C-72, and is open Tues.-Sat. 10 a.m.-5 p.m.; no charge. Call (206) 764-5720 for more information. Get here from the Boeing Tour Center by returning to Hwy. 526 eastbound, and taking the first exit (Airport Rd.). Head south on Airport Rd. for a mile, and turn right onto 100th St. SW. Building C-72 is on the right side.

If you're really desperate for something to do, tour the **Millstone Coffee Roasting Plant**—the largest such facility in the Northwest—Mon.-Thurs. 8 a.m.-5 p.m.; advance reservations required. Call (206) 347-3995, ext. 232, for details.

Parks

Located on Alverson Blvd., **American Legion Park** features a par course, tennis courts, and baseball field. **Forest Park** on Mukilteo Blvd. has a popular summertime children's animal farm and an indoor public pool. **Howarth Park,** just west of Forest Park on Mukilteo Blvd., has tennis courts and a fine view of Possession Sound from an observation tower.

The best-known local park is **Jetty Island,** just off the mouth of the Snohomish River. This two-mile long narrow stretch of sand is composed of spoils from dredging the harbor and river mouth and is very popular with birders, sea mammal watchers, or people just out for a picnic and a bit of beachcombing. It is served by a free passenger ferry that runs every half-hour during the summer months from Marina Park. For information call (206) 259-0304.

ACCOMMODATIONS AND CAMPING

See "Everett Accommodations" chart for a complete listing of local motels, hotels, and B&Bs.

Located south of town at 11621 W. Silver Lake Rd., **Silverlake RV Park,** tel. (206) 338-9666, has swimming and fishing in addition to the standard RV hookups. **Lakeside RV Park,** 12321 Hwy. 99 S, tel. (206) 347-2970 or (800) 468-7275, is on a three-acre lake with all hookups and facilities.

FOOD

Breakfast and Lunch

Start the day at **The Sisters Restaurant,** 2804 Grand Ave. (inside the Everett Public Market), tel. (206) 252-0480, a friendly place with great breakfast specials and espresso coffees, along with lunches of homemade soups, salads, veggie burgers, and quiche. The **41st St. Bar & Grill,** 1510 41st St., tel. (206) 259-3838, also makes good home-cooked breakfasts, as well as gourmet burgers and salads for lunch.

City Cafe, 2801 Colby Ave., tel. (206) 259-5090, serves breakfasts, and the deli cranks out good sandwiches on home-baked bread. Several other popular lunch places can be found downtown along Colby Ave. near Wall Street.

American

Everett Marina Village has a couple of popular waterfront restaurants with views to match the food: **Anthony's Homeport,** tel. (206) 252-3333, has fresh Northwest and imported seafood flown in fresh daily, and tasty fish-and-chips for a simpler meal. **Confetti's,** tel. (206) 258-4000, serves steak, prime rib, pasta, and seafood.

Gerry Andal's Ranch Restaurant, 620 S.E. Everett Mall Way, tel. (206) 355-7999, features a full American ranch-style menu. For the best local burgers, head to **Sparky's Watering Hole & Eatery,** 3201 Rucker Ave., tel. (206) 252-4444. **Sporty's Beef & Brew,** 6503 Evergreen Way, tel. (206) 347-1733, has more burgers and beer, plus three large-screen televisions for sports fans.

International

Passport Restaurant, 1507 Wall St., tel. (206) 259-5037, offers an eclectic mix, from Thai mint noodles with shrimp to Greek steak salad to vegetarian specials. They also operate the nearby **Pave Specialty Bakery,** 2613 Colby, tel. (206) 252-0250, with earthy breads and European pastries.

Find authentic Mexican meals and a friendly atmosphere at **Tampico Restaurant,** 2303 Broadway, tel. (206) 339-2427.

Spice of Thai, 607 Everett Mall Way SE, tel. (206) 290-7900, is one of those unexpected

EVERETT ACCOMMODATIONS

Accommodations are arranged from least to most expensive. Rates may be lower during the winter months. The area code is 206.

Motel 6; 10006 Evergreen Way; tel. 347-2060 or (800) 466-8356; $30 s, $36 d; outdoor pool

Waits Motel; 1301 Lombard Ave.; tel. 252-3166; $30-32 s, $35-37 d; kitchenettes available

Royal Motor Inn; 952 N. Broadway Ave.; tel. 259-5177; $32 s, $35 d; outdoor pool

Topper Motel; 1030 N. Broadway Ave.; tel. 259-3151; $32 s, $35 d; kitchenettes available

Motel 6; 224 128th St. SW; tel. 353-8120 or (800) 466-8356; $32 s, $38 d

Cherry Motel; 8421 Evergreen Way; tel. 347-1100; $35 s, $38 d

FarWest Motel; 6030 Evergreen Way; tel. 355-3007; $37-50 s or d; kitchenettes available, AAA approved

Welcome Motor Inn; 1205 N. Broadway Ave.; tel. 252-8828; $40 s, $48 d; kitchenettes available, AAA approved

Travelodge; 3030 N. Broadway Ave.; tel. 259-6141 or (800) 255-3050; $44 s, $49 d; AAA approved

Days Inn; 1122 N. Broadway Ave.; tel. 252-8000 or (800) 845-9490; $45 s, $50 d; jacuzzi, continental breakfast, kitchenettes available, AAA approved

Comfort Inn; 1602 S.E. Everett Mall Way; tel. 355-1570 or (800) 221-2222; $49-60 s, $54-64 d; outdoor pool, jacuzzi, continental breakfast, AAA approved

Ramada Inn; 9602 19th Ave. SE; tel. 337-9090 or (800) 228-2828; $49-65 s, $59-70 d; outdoor pool, jacuzzi, kitchenettes available, AAA approved

Cypress Inn; 12619 4th Ave. W; tel. 347-9099 or (800) 752-9991; $59-64 s, $66-69 d; outdoor pool, AAA approved

Best Western Cascadia Inn; 2800 Pacific Ave.; tel. 258-4141 or (800) 448-5544; $61-69 s, $69-77 d; outdoor pool, jacuzzi, exercise room, continental breakfast, AAA approved

By the Bay B&B; 821 4th St., Mukilteo; tel. 347-4997; $65 s or d; 1914 home, one guest room, private bath, antiques, porch and patio, continental breakfast

Holiday Inn Hotel; 101 128th St. SE; tel. 745-2555 or (800) 221-9839; $74-95 s, $75-100 d; indoor pool, jacuzzi, exercise room, business center, game room, free local shuttle, AAA approved

Howard Johnson Plaza Hotel; 3105 Pine St.; tel. 339-3333 or (800) 556-7829; $79 s or d; indoor pool, sauna, jacuzzi, exercise room, free airport or railroad shuttle, AAA approved

Marina Village Inn; 1728 W. Marine View Dr.; tel. 259-4040 or (800) 281-7037; $82-179 s or d; very nice rooms facing Gardiner Bay, private jacuzzis, telescopes, AAA approved (four diamond)

---

gems. Located in a strip mall, this small restaurant cranks out great curries, Thai eggplant, and other specialties. Find more very good Thai food at **Orchid Thai Cuisine,** 9506 19th Ave. SE, tel. (206) 338-1064.

South of town along Silver Lake (exit 186 from I-5), **Athenian Gourmet Pizza Greek & Italian Cuisine,** 11223 19th Ave. SE, tel. (206) 337-4134, lives up to its name with great pizzas and authentic Greek dishes. Another place for very good pasta and pizza is **Gianni's Ris-**

torante Italiano, 5030 Evergreen Way, tel. (206) 252-2435. Get pizza by the slice at **Genovese Italian Kitchen,** 4019½ Colby Ave., tel. (206) 252-9294.

EVENTS

Held on the first weekend in June, **Salty Sea Days** features a parade, Navy ship tours, an arts show, plus kayak and sailboard races.

Everett's **Freedom Festival U.S.A.** blasts into town for the Fourth of July weekend, with a parade, fireworks, and ship tours. It's followed on the third weekend of July by the **Washington State International Air Fair,** featuring civilian aerobatics, military jet demonstrations, and other flying displays in an exciting two-day air show; tel. (206) 355-2266. Also held in August, **Kidleidoscope/Art in the Park,** tel. (206) 259-0300, features craft booths, live performances, and hands-on activities and classes for children.

A summer-long recreational event from July to September sponsored by the parks department, the annual **Jetty Island Days** celebration includes free scenic ferry rides to the island departing from the Marina Village Visitors Dock, guided nature walks, sailing and rowing regattas, concerts, and campfire programs, as well as picnicking, beachcombing, and birdwatching on a saltwater beach. For a program of events, call Everett Parks and Recreation, tel. (206) 259-0300.

Return to Everett on the second and third Saturdays of December for the **Christmas Boat Parade** around Port Gardner Bay.

ARTS AND ENTERTAINMENT

The Arts
Theatrical performances are held throughout the year in the new showpiece **Everett Community Theater,** 2710 Wetmore, tel. (206) 259-8888. The theater features touring musicals, concerts, and regional performing arts groups. The **Everett Symphony** performs at the Everett Civic Auditorium on Colby Avenue. Concerts are scheduled Nov.-May; call (206) 259-0382, for more information. For something less formal, the **Music in the Parks** program brings live music on Sunday afternoons June-Aug. to local parks; tel. (206) 259-0300.

For those more inclined toward the visual arts, visit the **Everett Center for the Arts** (described above), **Northlight Gallery,** at 810 Wetmore in Everett Community College, tel. (206) 388-9363, or **Sheldon James Gallery,** 1724 W. Marine View Dr., tel. (206) 252-6047.

Nightlife
Everett has a disproportionate number of dancing and drinking establishments for a city this

small. **Club Broadway Entertainment Center,** 1611 Everett Ave., tel. (206) 259-3551, includes **The Country Club,** with hot bands and the largest C&W dance floor in the area. Dance lessons are given Tues.-Sun. evenings. The same building houses **Starlight Dance Club** for Top-40 tunes, **Olympic Sports Bar** for classic-rock bands, darts, and pinball, and **Bourbon Street** for live blues music.

Hardy's Bar & Grill is a popular happy-hour spot, with a piano bar and dance floor at the WestCoast Everett Pacific Hotel. **Filibeck's Chuck Wagon Inn,** 6720 Evergreen Way, also has live entertainment and dancing Tues.-Sat. nights. **Casbah Restaurant & Lounge,** 2222 Everett Ave., tel. (206) 259-1750, has live rock music Wed.-Sat. nights. **Gerry Andal's Ranch Restaurant,** 620 S.E. Everett Mall Way, tel. (206) 355-7999, features country and rock music, along with dance lessons Wed.-Sun. nights. Other places with live music include: **Portobello at the Marina,** 1728 W. Marine View Dr., tel. (206) 258-6254; **Petosa's on Broadway,** 3121 Broadway, tel. (206) 258-1544; and **The Everett Underground,** 1212 California, tel. (206) 339-0807.

SPORTS AND RECREATION

Spectator Sports
The San Francisco Giants' Class-A farm team, the **Everett Giants,** plays at Everett Memorial Stadium from mid-June to September; weekdays and Saturday games start at 7 p.m.; Sunday at 6 p.m. Call (206) 258-3673 for schedule information.

Recreation
The **Everett Marina** is the second largest in Puget Sound and a fun place to watch the boating action. Swim or sunbathe at **Silver Lake,** where a lifeguard is on duty between late June and Labor Day, or enjoy the saltwater and two miles of sandy beach at **Jetty Island.** Local swimming pools include the summer-only **McCollum Park Pool,** 600 128th St. SE, tel. (206) 337-4408, or the year-round **Forest Park Swim Center,** tel. (206) 259-0300. **Paine Field Recreation Center,** at Paine Field on the south side of Everett, tel. (206) 353-4944, has basketball, racquetball, tennis, volleyball, and weightlifting facilities, plus a sauna.

Health-conscious vacationers may be interested in a one-day membership at the **Everett YMCA,** 2720 Rockefeller, tel. (206) 258-9211; for $10 you can use the rooftop track, racquetball and squash courts, weight room, jacuzzi, and indoor pool.

Rent bikes from **Bicycle Center,** 4718 Evergreen Way, tel. (206) 252-1441. In the summer, you can rent canoes, rowboats, sailboats, and paddleboats from **Everett Parks and Recreation Dept.** at Silver Lake, tel. (206) 337-7809.

There are three public 18-hole golf courses in the Everett area. In Everett proper, visit the **American Legion Memorial** at 144 W. Marine View Dr., tel. (206) 259-4653, and the **Walter E. Hall Golf Course** at 1226 W. Casino Rd., tel. (206) 353-4653. Up north a bit is the **Kayak Point Golf Course,** 13 miles west of Marysville at 15711 Marine Dr., tel. (206) 652-9676 or (800) 562-3094. Mukilteo is home to the **Harbour Pointe Golf Course,** 11817 Harbour Pointe Blvd., tel. (206) 355-6060.

SHOPPING

The area's largest shopping center is **Everett Mall,** with over 140 small shops, giant department stores including The Bon Marché, Mervyn's, PayLess, Sears, and 10 movie theaters under one roof. Along the bay at **Everett Marina Village** is an 1890s-style waterfront marketplace with restaurants, gift shops, and clothing stores, to name a few.

The **Everett Public Market,** 2804 Grand Ave., has more than 100 antique dealers, plus fresh fish and produce, the Sisters Restaurant, and the Underground nightclub. **Washington Gift Baskets,** 2227 Broadway, tel. (206) 252-7241 or (800) 942-2753, sells gourmet foods and souvenirs from Everett and the surrounding state.

For discount shopping, it's hard to beat Evergreen Way (Hwy. 99), where all the big stores can be found, complete with acres of paved parking spaces. Not the most attractive place, but it serves the purpose. Of interest is a surprising cluster of thrift stores around Evergreen at 52nd St., including Value Village, St. Vincent de Paul's, Salvation Army, and Children's Hospital Thrift Store.

INFORMATION AND SERVICES

For maps and brochures, stop by the **Everett Area Chamber of Commerce,** on the first floor of the historic Weyerhaeuser office building at 1710 W. Marine View Dr., tel. (206) 252-5181. Open Mon.-Fri. 9 a.m.-5 p.m. year-round. The **Snohomish County Visitor Information Center,** 101 128th St. SE (at I-5 exit 186), is open daily 9 a.m.-5 p.m. (longer in the summer). Call (206) 338-4437 for more information.

The **area code** for Everett and the Seattle vicinity is 206.

Local hospitals include **Providence General Hospital's** two campuses: the **Colby Campus** at 14th and Colby, tel. (206) 258-6301; and **Pacific Campus** at 916 Pacific, tel. (206) 258-7555.

TRANSPORTATION AND TOURS

Bus Service
Everett Transit's buses and trolleys provide local transportation for 80 cents; call (206) 353-7433 for schedule. To get out of town, **Community Transit** goes south to Edmonds and Seattle, north to Stanwood and Darrington, and east to Snohomish, Lake Stevens, and Granite Falls for only a buck ($1.50 to Seattle); call (206) 778-2185 or (800) 562-1375 for information.

Northwestern Trailways, tel. (800) 366-3830, and **Greyhound,** tel. (206) 252-2143 or (800) 231-2222, have bus connections throughout the Northwest, stopping in Everett at 1503 Pacific.

If you're flying into Sea-Tac airport, **Shuttle Express,** tel. (206) 622-1424 or (800) 942-7433, has door-to-door van service between Sea-Tac and Everett for $20 one-way. Make reservations ahead of time for a pickup in Everett.

Train Service
Amtrak trains serve the Everett area from their 2900 Bond St. station; tel. (206) 258-2458 or (800) 872-7245. The **Empire Builder** heads south to Seattle and east to Spokane and Chicago. The **Mt. Baker International** provides daily train connections to Vancouver, B.C., via Mount Vernon and Bellingham.

Ferry Service

The Mukilteo-Clinton ferry connects the Everett area to the south end of Whidbey Island every half-hour (no service between 1 a.m. and 5 a.m.). Fares are $4.80 one-way for car and driver ($4 in winter), $2.30 roundtrip for passengers or walk-ons, and $2.80 one-way for bicycles with rider. Call (206) 355-7308 or (800) 843-3779 for a schedule.

Tours

The **Mosquito Fleet**, 1724-F W. Marine View Dr., tel. (206) 252-6800 or (800) 325-6722, offers year-round boat tours that take travelers through Deception Pass to Friday Harbor on San Juan Island, where they can spend several hours enjoying the sights, or stay on board to watch for whales before returning to Everett. You can take your bike along for no extra charge. The total trip length is approximately 10 hours. Fares are $69 for adults, $59 for seniors, or $49 for kids (lower rates in the winter). The company also has boat tours of the new Naval base and its ships, and a "sea lion encounter" around Everett Harbor. Both of these trips last 75 minutes and cost $15 for adults, $14 for seniors, and $10 for kids ages three to 17. The sea lion tour is only offered Oct.-April. Four-hour historical tours of Everett, with a visit to the Boeing plant, cost $19.

VICINITY OF EVERETT

MUKILTEO

The name Mukilteo (muck-il-TEE-o) comes from an Indian term meaning "good meeting place"; for centuries the site served as a location for councils and potlatches. In 1855, this was where the Point Elliott Treaty was signed, in which the leaders of 22 Indian tribes handed over their land to white settlers. (Tribal chiefs were unaware that they were trading all their lands for tiny reservations that they wouldn't see for many years.) The first Anglos settled here three years later, and by 1861, Mukilteo had been designated the county seat, a title it later lost to Everett. In the 1920s, Mukilteo was home to the Puget Sound and Alaska Powder Company, a manufacturer of dynamite. The plant blew up in 1930, at the same time the local lumber mill was shutting its doors. Since then, Mukilteo (pop. 13,000) has gradually become an attractive suburb of Everett, with a perfect little lighthouse, views across Puget Sound to Whidbey Island, and a busy ferry terminal. Travelers or commuters en route to Whidbey aboard the state ferries frequently find themselves stuck in long lines of traffic.

Sights

Adjacent to the ferry terminal, **Mukilteo State Park** has a large picnic area, a popular beach for sunbathing (but the water can be treacherous), and a boat launch with excellent fishing in Possession Sound; open for day use only. Because of consistent winds, the park is a favorite with kite flyers and windsurfers. Not far away is the wooden **Mukilteo Lighthouse**, built in 1905 and still functional. It's open for free tours April-Sept., Sat.-Sun. 1-4 p.m.; call (206) 355-4141 for details.

Behind the Rosehill Community Center at the corner of 4th St. and Lincoln Ave., the tiny **Mukilteo Historical Museum**, tel. (206) 355-2514, has photos, artifacts, and rotating exhibits on local history. Open Saturday 1-3 p.m., Oct.-March only; free.

Other historical structures in town include two churches that face off against each other at 3rd and Loveland: the **First Presbyterian Church** (1907) and the **St. John Catholic Church** (1919). Head up Mukilteo Blvd. for a scenic drive through older residential neighborhoods along the water, and past a string of parks as you head into Everett, including Edgewater Park, Harbor View Park (excellent views), Howarth Park, and Forest Park.

Food

Mukilteo has one of the Ivar's chain of seafood restaurants, but you're better off heading uphill to **Arnie's**, 714 2nd St., tel. (206) 355-2181, for water views from two levels. Enjoy reasonably priced and very good lunches and dinners of salmon and other seafood, along with chicken, steaks, and a Sunday champagne brunch.

EVERETT AND MUKILTEO

LEGION MEMORIAL
GOLF COURSE

LEGION
PARK

JETTY
ISLAND

ROYAL MOTOR INN
TOPPER MOTEL
DAYS INN

13th ST.

WAITS
MOTEL

WELCOME
MOTOR INN

PROVIDENCE GENERAL
HOSPITAL - COLBY CAMPUS

FIREFIGHTERS MUSEUM
MARINA PARK

EVERETT

19th ST.

CHAMBER OF COMMERCE
EVERETT MARINA VILLAGE
NAVAL STATION

24th ST.

POSSESSION SOUND

PORT GARDNER

HEWITT AVE.

PACIFIC AVE.

529

SEE "DOWNTOWN EVERETT" MAP

FRIDAY
AVE.

35th ST.

41st ST.

EVERETT
MEMORIAL
STADIUM

HOWARTH PARK

HARBOR VIEW PARK

FOREST
PARK

EXIT 192

BLVD.

MUKILTEO

LIGHTHOUSE AND MUKILTEO S.P.
ARNIE'S / MUKILTEO
HISTORICAL MUSEUM

FARWEST MOTEL

MUKILTEO
CLINTON
FERRY

MUKILTEO

5

BOEING
ASSEMBLY
PLANT

526

CASINO RD.

CHERRY
MOTEL

EXIT 189

WALTER E. HALL
GOLF COURSE

MUKILTEO SPEEDWAY

RAMADA INN

COMFORT INN

EVERETT MALL

99

PAINE
FIELD

100th ST. SW

SW
EVERETT
MALL
WAY

525

MOTEL 6

99

BROADWAY

19th AVE.
SE

527

SILVER LAKE RV PARK
AND SILVER LAKE PARK

TO SEATTLE

SILVER
LAKE

128th ST. SW EXIT 186

HOLIDAY INN

MOTEL 6

EVERGREEN WAY

PACIFIC HWY.

529

TO
MOUNT
VERNON

5

SNOHOMISH RIVER

W MARINE VIEW DR.

GRAND AVE.

WETMORE

BROADWAY

COLBY

0   1 mi

0   1 km

© MOON PUBLICATIONS, INC.

The **Seahorse Restaurant** at 707 Front St., tel. (206) 353-6477—in existence for more than 40 years—has seafood, steak, prime rib, and pasta (and captive sea horses) with dancing on the weekends. More dancing on Friday and Saturday nights at **The Ponderosa Tavern,** 12701 Mukilteo Speedway, tel. (206) 355-3811.

La Cascada Acapulco Mexican Restaurant, 801 2nd St., tel. (206) 348-9569, cooks up tasty and authentic south-of-the-border meals. Get freshly ground coffee beans or espresso at **Mukilteo Coffee Co. Cafe,** 619 4th Ave., tel. (206) 348-4825.

Just west of the intersection of Highways 525 and 526, **Charles at Smuggler's Cove,** 8310 53rd Ave. W, tel. (206) 347-2700, serves highly praised French dinners in elegant surroundings. The name comes from its original owners, including the 1920s gangster Al Capone, who distilled whiskey here, shipping it out via a tunnel that led to the waterfront.

For fresh garden produce and crafts, head to the **Mukilteo Marketplace,** held at 4th and Lincoln on Friday noon-8 p.m. from June to early October.

Events
Held at the state park downtown, the mid-August **Mukilteo Festival** has a pancake breakfast, parade, salmon barbecue, fishing derby, arts and crafts display, and country music and dancing.

Recreation
Swim at the **Mukilteo YMCA,** 9600 Holly Dr., tel. (206) 290-5834, or **Kamiak High,** 10801 Harbour Pointe Blvd., tel. (206) 356-6620. The local **library** is at 304 Lincoln Ave., tel. (206) 355-2542. Rent boats and fishing gear from **McConnell's Boathouse** on Front St., tel. (206) 355-3411.

Transportation
The Washington State Ferry has service between Mukilteo and the town of Clinton on the south end of Whidbey Island every half-hour from 5 a.m. to 1 a.m. Fares are $4.80 one-way for car and driver ($4 in winter), $2.30 roundtrip for passengers or walk-ons, and $2.80 one-way for bicycles with rider. Call (800) 843-3779 for schedule information. You only pay on the westbound leg of the trip (leaving Mukilteo). Call (206) 355-7308 or (800) 843-3779 for a schedule.

Community Transit covers nearly all of Snohomish County, with service south to Seattle, and east as far as Snohomish and Darrington for only $1 ($1.50 to Seattle); call (206) 778-2185 or (800) 562-1375 for information.

MARYSVILLE

Founded in 1872, Marysville (pop. 15,000) grew up on logging and farming. Both remain economic mainstays—along with manufacturing enterprises and gambling jobs at the nearby Tulalip Casino—but the city is best known for its berry farms that produce delicious strawberries, raspberries, and blueberries. Marysville has experienced rapid growth in recent years, due in part to its proximity to Everett and the relative affordability of homes here.

Sights
In addition to nature trails, a duck pond, and a petting zoo (tel. 360-659-8581; open daily 11 a.m.-7 p.m. from mid-May to mid-August), the 50-acre **Jennings Memorial Park/Jennings**

Nature Park at 6915 Armar Rd., tel. (360) 659-3005, is home to the Gehl House Historical Museum. **Mother Nature's Window** is a unique private park on 100th St. NE at 55th Ave. NE, with an outdoor amphitheater and various carved objects amid a second-growth forest.

The **Children's Museum of Snohomish County,** 105 Marysville Mall, tel. (360) 659-1483, is a popular center where kids can learn through hands-on exhibits of all types. Open Tues.-Sat. 10 a.m.-4 p.m.

Tulalip

Learn the rich history of the Tulalip (too-LAY-lip) tribe along the 1.5-mile-long **Walk with the Ancestors Interpretive Trail** that begins at St. Anne's Church in the village of Tulalip (five miles west of Marysville). St. Anne's is on the site of the oldest Catholic mission on Puget Sound.

Operated by the Tulalip Tribes, **Tulalip Casino,** right off I-5 at exit 199, has bingo, blackjack, craps, roulette, baccarat, poker, and pulltabs. Open Mon.-Thurs. 6 p.m.-2 a.m., and Fri.-Sun. 10 a.m.-2 a.m. For information call (360) 651-1111.

Accommodations

The **Best Western Tulalip Inn** offers moderately priced luxury at 6128 33rd Ave. NE (exit 199), tel. (360) 659-4488 or (800) 528-1234, with an indoor pool, jacuzzi, free airport shuttle, and rooms for $63-68 s, or $71-76 d. **Village Motor Inn,** 235 Beech St., tel. (360) 659-0005, has rooms for $52 s or $57 d. Local calls are 25 cents. Budget lodging at **City Center Motel,** 810 State Ave., tel. (360) 659-2424, for $27 s or $29 d.

Recreation and Campgrounds

Twelve miles north of Marysville, **Wenberg State Park,** tel. (360) 652-7417, on Lake Goodwin has a very popular sandy swimming beach, excellent fishing for rainbow and cutthroat trout, waterskiing, a concession stand for fishing supplies and snacks, plus campsites ($11; $16 with hookups) and RV sites ($16) on 46 acres. Open year-round. Get here early on summer weekends to find a space, or call (800) 452-5687 for campsite reservations ($6 extra fee), available up to 11 months ahead of time.

Covering 650 acres, **Kayak Point Regional Park,** approximately 15 miles west of Marysville on Marine View Dr., is home to a popular swimming beach, picnic area, and boat launch. Camp here year-round for $14, including electrical hookups for RVs. No showers, and the bathrooms are closed in the winter months.

Nearby is the 18-hole **Kayak Point Golf Course,** tel. (360) 652-9676 or (800) 562-3094, considered one of Washington's finest public courses.

Food

Marysville's **Village Restaurant,** 220 Ash St., tel. (360) 659-2305—in business since 1937—is famous for its "mile-high" meringue pies and other all-American fare. More burgers, steaks, and salmon at the **Longhouse** next to the Tulalip Casino, tel. (360) 651-1111.

The best place to eat in Marysville is **Fanny's Restaurant,** 505 Cedar St., tel. (360) 653-8164, where the diverse and eclectic menu includes international and vegetarian dishes. For Italian food and pizza, head to **Conto's,** 314 State Ave., tel. (360) 659-9222.

Get great espresso coffees at the friendly **Ed'spresso** stand, tel. (360) 659-8665, inside the Sno-Co Berry Pak Building at 4th and Cedar Streets. During June and July, you can purchase fresh raspberries and strawberries here, though most of the packing is for wholesale customers.

Henry's Lady, in the Best Western Tulalip Inn, 6128 Ave. NE, tel. (360) 659-4488, has a popular Sunday brunch that features omelettes, Belgian waffles, and strawberry desserts. Stop by Tues.-Sat. nights for dancing to live music. And if you just want to pig out, head to **Royal Fork Buffet,** 319 Marysville Mall Way, tel. (360) 653-1435, for lunch ($6) or dinner ($7).

Entertainment and Events

Stop by Jennings Memorial Park on Friday evenings during July and August for live concerts of all sorts. The third week in June brings the **Strawberry Festival,** the town's tribute to one of its major crops. This is the area's biggest summer event, with parades, a carnival, car show, art and food booths, and adult trike races. The festivities last 10 days; call (360) 659-7664 for details. The second weekend of July brings

Sights and Bites, with an art show, demonstrations by artists, gourmet foods, and live music. It is followed by the **Homegrown Arts & Crafts Fair,** held the first weekend of August. On the first Saturday in December, Santa Claus heads down festively adorned State Ave. for a torchlight **Christmas Parade.**

Information and Services

Get local information from the small **visitor center** located next to Donna's Truck Stop on 116th St., tel. (360) 653-2634. Open daily 9 a.m.-5:30 p.m. in the summer, and daily 9 a.m.-4 p.m. the rest of the year. Marysville's **chamber of commerce** 4411 76th St. NE, tel. (360) 659-7700, isn't of much use to travelers, but for $10(!) they will give you a relocation booklet on the town. Name freaks will want to visit **Amen! Christian Bookstore** on the corner of State and 4th Streets.

The **area code** for Marysville is 360.

Transportation

Community Transit, tel. (206) 353-7433 or (800) 562-1375, offers bus service to other parts of Snohomish County for just $1, and on to Seattle for $1.50. **Greyhound,** tel. (360) 252-2144 or (800) 231-2222, has long-distance bus service.

SeaTac Airporter Shuttle, tel. (800) 448-8443, has direct service from Marysville to SeaTac for $16.

LAKE STEVENS

The settlement of Lake Stevens (pop. 4,200) borders the north shore of this attractive lake located five miles east of Everett and acts as a bedroom community for that city. The town centers around Frontier Village Shopping Mall. Stop by the small **Lake Stevens Historical Museum** at 1802 124th Ave. NE, tel. (206) 334-3944, for a glimpse of the past. Open Fri.-Sat. 1-4 p.m. The library occupies the same building.

Lundeen Park covers eight acres of shoreline just west of town, with a roped-off swimming beach, playground, picnic tables, and grand views across the water to the Cascade Range. Another Snohomish County park—**Wyatt Park**—occupies the west shore of Lake Stevens with a dock, boat launch for fishermen and water-skiers, picnic area, plus a sandy beach

for sunbathing and swimming. No camping at either of these parks.

Scenic Drive

The drive northwest from Lake Stevens on Hwy. 92 to Granite Falls cuts through a big open valley created by the Pilchuck River. Enjoy the old farm homesteads with junk-covered yards, the U-pick berry farms, horse pastures, and tree farms while you can; it won't be long before the rapidly encroaching city pushes Wal-Marts, 7-Elevens, and split-level homes over all of this. See the Cascade Range chapter for details on the scenic "Mountain Loop" that begins in Granite Falls.

Practicalities

The main event in Lake Stevens is **Aquafest,** held on the last weekend of July, featuring a parade, arts and crafts, music, food, and a race. Get information from the **Lake Stevens Chamber of Commerce,** 9327 4th NE, tel. (360) 334-0433. Open Tuesday, Thursday, and Friday 10 a.m.-2 p.m.

Community Transit, tel. (206) 353-7433 or (800) 562-1375, offers bus service to other parts of Snohomish County for just $1, and on to Seattle for $1.50.

ARLINGTON

Just three miles from busy I-5, quiet Arlington (pop. 4,400) offers a delightful slice of small town America without the shopping-"mall-itis" blighting so much of the Puget Sound area. Downtown is a healthy mix of clothing stores, auto parts stores, and restaurants.

Lodging

Smokey Point Motor Inn, 17329 Smokey Point Dr. at Arlington exit 206 off I-5, tel. (360) 659-8561, has rooms from $40 d, plus an outdoor pool, jacuzzi, and kitchenettes. The **Arlington Motor Inn,** 2214 Hwy. 530 (exit 208), tel. (360) 652-9595, has rooms for $39-44 s or $44-49 d, and includes use of a jacuzzi.

Campgrounds and RV Parks

Year-round camping ($10) is available at **River Meadows County Park,** tel. (360) 435-3441, located several miles east of town on the South

Fork of the Stillaguamish River. Drive east on Hwy. 530 for three quarters of a mile, turn right onto Arlington Heights,. and continue two miles. Turn right on Jordan Rd., and drive another three miles to the park. River Meadows Park also offers enjoyable hiking trails, picnic grounds, and a mile of river shoreline for fishing. The surrounding area is filled with farms with all sorts of critters, from longhaired Scottish cattle to Peruvian horses. Lots of horses are pastured around here, and Byle's Tit Farm (hey, I don't name these places) makes a great place to pose for a comical photo.

Smokey Point & Ponderosa Hill RV Park, 17019 28th Dr. NE, tel. (360) 652-7300 or (800) 662-7275, has RV spaces.

Food
Amazingly enough, Arlington has none of the national fast food chains; hopefully they won't arrive any time soon. **Islands Bakery,** 19224 62nd Ave. NE, tel. (360) 435-2100, has delicious fresh-baked breads and pastries.

Two restaurants right off I-5 at the Hwy. 530 exit, **Weller's Chalet Inn** and **O'Brien Turkey House,** are remarkably good considering their location. Weller's has good sandwiches and steak and seafood dinners. O'Brien's has sandwiches, salads, and light dinners (heavy on the turkey). **John Petosa's,** just west of exit 206, is a good Italian restaurant.

Get fresh produce at the downtown **farmers market** held on Saturday 9 a.m.-2 p.m. June-September. Enjoy a picnic lunch at **Two Rivers Park** along the South Fork of the Stillaguamish River just east of town.

Events
Arlington's airport is the third largest general aviation facility in Puget Sound and calls itself the world's largest ultralight airport. In late July, it is home to the **Northwest Experimental Aircraft Association Fly-In,** America's third largest fly-in. It includes experimental planes, military aircraft, hot air balloons, and an air show. The weekends around the Fourth of July bring **Frontier Days,** the town's annual celebration, with parades, an auto show, triathlon, and rubber duck race. And be sure to return to Arlington in December to see why they call it the "Christmas tree city."

Information and Transportation
Stop by the **Arlington Chamber of Commerce,** tel. (360) 435-3708, in the trailer on N. Olympic Ave. for local information; open Mon.-Fri. 10 a.m.-4 p.m. year-round.

Community Transit, tel. (360) 353-7433 or (800) 562-1375, offers bus service to other parts of Snohomish County for just $1, and on to Seattle for $1.50.

STANWOOD

Founded in 1865, Stanwood started as a center for the transport of logs floated down the Stillaguamish River. Located just east of the bridge to Camano Island, this compact farming village of 2,000 people prides itself on having as its chief employer the largest independent frozen-pea processor in the world: Twin City Foods. The town hosted the world's shortest railroad—seven-eighths of a mile—until it shut down in 1938.

Sights
Many of Stanwood's early residents were Scandinavian, a heritage that is still apparent in the Norwegian rosemaling (floral designs) on a handful of local buildings. Visit the **Scandia Bakery-Lefse Factory,** tel. (360) 629-2411, where you'll find fresh potato lefse and other treats.

The **Pilchuck Glass School** near Stanwood, tel. (360) 445-3111, was begun in 1971 by Dale Chihuly, now recognized as one of the world masters in the creation of glass sculptures. Today Pilchuck has 25 teachers and attracts artists from all over the world for its intensive sessions.

The **D.O. Pearson House Museum,** on the corner of 102nd Ave. NW and 271st St. SW, tel. (360) 629-3352, houses local historical items in a home built in 1890; open Sunday 2-5 p.m.

For an delightful country drive, head southeast from Stanwood on the road to the tiny burg called **Silvana.** Along the way, you'll wind along wooded Prestliens Bluff, overlooking big dairy farms, haystacks, and aging barns.

Practicalities
Park RVs at the Stanwood Fairgrounds, where the **Stanwood-Camano Community Fair** is held in late July and early August. Call (360) 445-2806 for specifics.

Eat at **Cafe Bistro** for Italian fare, or **Jimmy's Pizza,** tel. (360) 629-6565, for surprisingly good pizzas. Get fresh produce at the **Stanwood-Camano Family Garden Market,** in downtown Stanwood, Saturday 9 a.m.-4 p.m., May-October.

For local information, drop by the **Stanwood Chamber of Commerce,** 8705 271st St. NW, tel. (360) 629-4912.

Community Transit, tel. (360) 353-7433 or (800) 562-1375, provides bus connections to other parts of Snohomish County for $1, and on to Seattle for $1.50. The **SeaTac Airporter Shuttle,** tel. (800) 235-5247, has daily shuttles from Stanwood to Sea-Tac for $19.

CAMANO ISLAND

Primarily a residential island of vacation homes separated from the mainland by the shortest of bridges, Camano Island was originally inhabited by the Kikialos and Snohomish Indians and later, in the mid-1850s, by European loggers and settlers. Like Whidbey Island to the west, Camano receives fewer than 20 inches of rain annually because of the Olympic rain shadow effect. It is a quiet, bucolic place.

Camano Island State Park
Located 14 miles southwest from Stanwood, this state park covers 134 acres along Saratoga Passage. The picnic tables on the park's west side provide striking views of Whidbey Island and the Olympics. Hiking trails, including a half-mile interpretive loop, wind through 600-year-old

Douglas firs with possible sightings of bald eagles, deer, raccoon, and opossum. Other activities here include fishing from the Point Lowell boat launch and sunbathing along the cliff-backed beaches. The park's two camping areas have tent sites ($10; no hookups) and coin-operated showers. Open year-round. Call (800) 452-5687 for campsite reservations ($6 extra fee), available up to 11 months ahead of time.

Lodging
Stay at **Wilcox House B&B,** 1462 Larkspur Lane, tel. (360) 629-4746, a Victorian-style home offering great vistas to Mt. Baker on sunny days. Four guest rooms with private baths are available, and a full breakfast is served. Rates are $55 s, $65 d. No kids under age 10. **Salal Hill B&B,** 850 N.W. Camano Dr., tel. (360) 387-3763, is a Tudor-style home with three guest rooms (shared or private baths), a jacuzzi, game room, and spacious park-like grounds. Rooms are $50-70 s or d; no kids under age 10. The **Inn at Barnum Point B&B,** 464 S. Barnum Rd., tel. (360) 387-2256 or (800) 910-2256, has two spacious guest rooms with private baths in a modern Cape Cod-style home overlooking the water. A century-old orchard is nearby. This is a fine place for a quiet and romantic getaway. Rates are $85 s or d, including a full breakfast.

Transportation
Community Transit, tel. (360) 353-7433 or (800) 562-1375, offers bus service from Camano Island to other parts of Snohomish County for $1, and on to Seattle for $1.50.

MOUNT VERNON AND VICINITY

The rich bottom land of the Skagit (SKAJ-et) Valley near Mount Vernon produces peas, potatoes, cabbage, cauliflower, broccoli, cucumbers, strawberries, raspberries, spinach, corn, vegetable seeds, and the area's best-known crops: daffodils, tulips, and irises. More than half the world's cabbage and spinach seeds are grown in the valley.

With a fast-growing population of more than 20,000, the city of Mount Vernon is largest in the county, and in spring is certainly among the prettiest: tulips and daffodils are *everywhere,* from fields to yards to gas stations. The attractive downtown features brick-fronted buildings, planters filled with flowers, and a prosperous mixture of stores. Unfortunately, just a mile to the north, the city shows another side—the shopping frenzy of Skagit Mall and other car-infested commercial havens.

Downtown Burlington (pop. 4,800) is just a few minutes north of Mount Vernon, so close that it's difficult to tell where the borders are. It's hard to come up with any reason to spend much time in Burlington, unless you're heading to the shopping malls, a cheap motel, or home to suburbia.

The Skagit River is the second largest in the western U.S.; only the mighty Columbia River has more water. The Skagit reaches all the way to Manning Provincial Park in British Columbia and was an important access route into the Cascades during the early years of settlement. Today the river's main attraction is not transportation but recreation such as whitewater rafting or float trips down upper reaches of the river. Several large dams on the upper Skagit provide large amounts of power to the Pacific Northwest.

History

Mount Vernon was named after George Washington's plantation, both to honor him and because the town was founded on his birthday in 1877. It was established along a big bend in the Skagit River where an enormous log jam prevented the upstream passage of steamships. Settlers were forced to stop here to portage

around the jam before continuing overland or upstream in smaller boats. After the logjam was finally cleared in 1879, Mount Vernon became a refueling stop on the way upriver—it grew rapidly. In 1884 it was chosen as the county seat, and by 1900 its population exceeded that of neighboring La Conner. Construction of a lumber mill, and the arrival of the railroad, followed by the routing of old Hwy. 99 and modern-day I-5, helped establish Mount Vernon as a crossroads city.

SIGHTS

Flowers

With its rich loamy soil and mild weather, the Skagit Valley is Washington's primary bulb-growing region and home to Washington Bulb Co., the largest producer of bulbs in America (and maybe the world). From late March through April, more than 2,000 acres of the valley are carpeted with flowering daffodils, tulips, irises, and lilies; more than 41 million bulbs are produced annually. The first commercial tulips were test-planted here in 1908, but commercial success did not come until after WW II, when Dutch immigrants brought their bulb-growing skills to the valley.

After March 1, get maps of the floral fields from the Mount Vernon Chamber of Commerce Office or by calling (800) 488-5477. Or, just head west from Mount Vernon toward La Conner; most of the fields are in an area bounded on the north by Memorial Hwy. 536, on the west by La Conner-Whitney Rd., on the south by Chilberg Rd., and on the east by the Skagit River. Crops are rotated to preserve the soil and to keep insect pests down, so last season's field of yellow daffodils may be home to a crop of flowering broccoli this year—more nutritious, but not nearly as photogenic.

The farm country of Skagit Valley is a great place to bicycle—nice, flat roads and very little traffic—except when the flowers are in bloom. During the Skagit Valley Tulip Festival (described below), these same back roads are

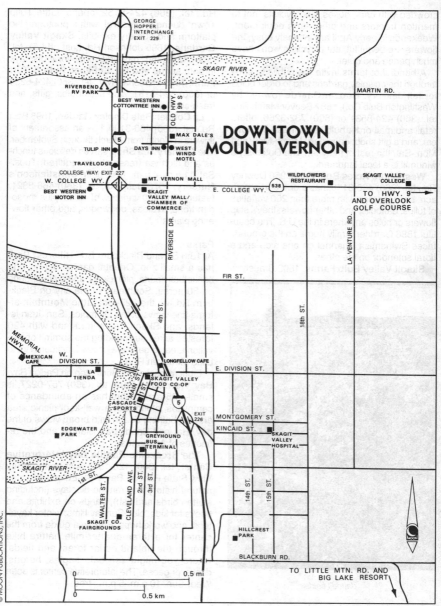

DOWNTOWN MOUNT VERNON

© MOON PUBLICATIONS, INC.

crowded with cars, buses, and cyclists, not to mention tractors and other farm equipment. Weekends in early April are insanely busy; the flowers are beautiful, but bicyclists won't have much peace and quiet.

A handful of farms invite the public to stroll through their display gardens and to order bulbs for fall delivery. **RoozenGaarde** (owned by Washington Bulb Co.), 1587 Beaver March Rd., tel. (360) 424-8531 or (800) 732-3266, offers retail and mail-order bulb sales, fresh-cut flowers, and a gift shop; open daily March-May, and Mon.-Sat. the rest of the year. The Dutch-style windmill is a local landmark.

West Shore Acres Bulb Farm, 956 Downey Rd., tel. (360) 466-3158, has a one-and-a half-acre show garden with more than 200 varieties of tulips, daffodils, and other flowers; they'll ship flowers or bulbs anywhere in the U.S. The beautiful 1886 Gardner family home on the grounds faces Swinomish Channel on one side and a floral splendor on the other.

Skagit Valley Bulb Farms, 1502 Bradshaw

daffodil fields

DIANNE BOUERICE LYONS

Rd., tel. (360) 424-8152, opens "Little Tulip Town" during the festival, with a photographic platform and nursery exhibits. **Skagit Valley Gardens,** 1695 Johnson Rd. (just off I-5), tel. (360) 424-6760, has additional floral displays in both spring and fall. **LeFeber Bulb & Turf Farm,** 1335 Memorial Hwy., tel. (360) 424-6234 or (800) 524-3181, also sells bulbs, gifts, and fresh-cut flowers.

La Conner Flats Display Garden, 1598 Best Rd., tel. (360) 466-3190, has an assortment of flowers in bloom from March through September. The **Granary Tea Shop** serves delicious lunches and high tea (reservations required) Tues.-Sat. 11 a.m.-4 p.m. Next door, **Christianson's Nursery,** 1578 Best Rd., tel. (360) 466-3821, features the 600 varieties of roses, plus rhododendrons, azaleas, dogwoods, and other flowering plants.

Parks

At 13th St. and Blackburn Rd., **Hillcrest Park** has a small zoo, Oriental garden, tennis and basketball courts, picnicking, and a playground on 30 acres. Southeast of the city on Blackburn Rd. W, the 927-foot **Little Mountain** affords fine views of the Olympics, San Juan Islands, and Skagit Valley farmland with 490 forested acres surrounding the summit observation area; to get there, follow Blackburn Rd. to Little Mountain Road.

Eight miles west of Burlington on Padilla Bay, **Bay View State Park,** tel. (360) 757-0227, is small—25 acres—but has an abundance of campsites, along with a well-kept picnic area and sunbathing beach with broad views of the bay, Hat and Saddlebag Islands, and the refineries of Anacortes.

The **Breazeale-Padilla Bay Interpretive Center,** tel. (360) 428-1558, just north of Bay View State Park on Bay View-Edison Rd., has natural history and marine displays (including stuffed birds and fish), hands-on exhibits and books for kids, plus Sunday films, winter kayak trips, and workshops. Borrow a guide from the center for a three-quarter-mile nature hike through the upland cedar forest and fields, where you might see bald eagles, herons, ducks, or geese. The interpretive center is open Wed.-Sun. 10 a.m.-5 p.m.; free.

ACCOMMODATIONS

See the "Mount Vernon and Burlington Accommodations" chart for a complete list of places to stay. Local motels and B&Bs fill up for the Tulip Festival; be sure to make reservations at least a month ahead if you plan to visit at that time. Also see "La Conner Accommodations" chart and "Chuckanut Drive" below for nearby places to stay.

Snuggled in the midst of 250 private wooded acres, **Whispering Firs B&B,** tel. (360) 428-1990 or (800) 428-1992, offers shaded seclusion, wooded hiking trails and private fishing, along with a large hot tub, a water wheel, and a big country-style breakfast. This modern 4,000-square-foot home has a stone fireplace in the living room and terraced lands containing small ponds and views of the San Juans. Dinners ($15 per person) are available by advance reservation.

Located northwest of Burlington in farming country, **Benson Farmstead B&B,** (360) 757-0578, is a beautifully restored 1914 home with four antique-filled guest rooms. A big breakfast is served, plus evening desserts, and guests can relax in the hot tub.

CAMPING

Eight miles west of Burlington on Padilla Bay, **Bay View State Park,** tel. (360) 757-0227, has year-round campsites for $11 ($16 for RVs) across Bay View-Edison Rd. from the waterfront. Call (800) 452-5687 for campsite reservations ($6 extra fee), available up to 11 months ahead of time.

Conway County Park, below the bridge over Skagit River in Conway (just off I-5), has campsites open June to mid-October. **Skagit County Fairgrounds** on the corner of Hazel and Virginia in Mount Vernon has additional public campsites.

Private RV parks include **Riverbend Park,** 305 W. Stewart Rd. (off I-5 exit 227), tel. (360) 428-4044; and **Big Lake Resort,** 1785 W. Big Lake Blvd., tel. (360) 422-5755. The latter also rents boats and has a swimming beach. **Burlington/Cascade KOA,** 646 N. Green Rd., tel. (360) 724-5511, is open year-round with full hookup sites, grassy tent sites, an indoor heated pool, sauna, and weight room.

FOOD

Mount Vernon is blessed with more than its share of excellent places to eat, from the oddball (**Chuck Wagon Drive-In,** 800 N. 4th St., tel. 360-336-2732, has to be seen to be believed) to elegant establishments offering some of the finest meals in the region. For all-American steak and seafood—plus a pub offering 100 types of beer and wine—stroll into **Gentleman Gene's,** 1400 Parker Way, tel. (360) 424-4363. **Max Dale's Restaurant,** 2030 Riverside Dr., tel. (360) 424-7171, serves fine steak, seafood, and prime-rib dinners, with entertainment and dancing in the lounge Tues.-Sat. nights.

International

Pacioni's Pizzeria, 606 S. 1st St., tel. (360) 336-3314, bakes outstanding thin-crust, crunchy pizzas with tasty toppings, along with calzone and panini. Inexpensive too; less than $4 buys a one-person cheese version, or $5.50 for one topped with feta cheese, garlic, sun-dried tomatoes, and olives.

For inexpensive, terrific Mexican food try **La Tienda,** tel. (360) 336-2304, a combination grocery store/restaurant (featuring homemade tamales) at 602 Division Street. Another noteworthy south-of-the-border eatery (great margaritas and *chile verde* dishes) is **Mexico Cafe,** 1320 Memorial Hwy., tel. (360) 424-1977.

China Wok Restaurant, 854 Burlington Blvd., tel. (360) 757-0074, has authentic Mandarin and Sichuan food, but the service can be on the slow side.

Northwest Cuisine

The Longfellow Cafe, tel. (360) 336-3684, in the historic Granary Building at 120 1st St., serves excellent seafood, pasta, sandwiches, and steaks, accompanied by an impressive selection of wines and beers, in an informal setting.

Enjoy moderately priced fresh seafood, delicious baked goods, and other highly creative preparations at **Wildflowers,** located in a 1934-vintage house with gardens at 2001 E. College

MOUNT VERNON AND BURLINGTON ACCOMMODATIONS

Accommodations are arranged from least to most expensive within each city. Rates may be lower during the winter months. The area code is 360.

MOUNT VERNON

Hillside Motel; 2300 Bonnie View Rd.; tel. 445-3252; $36 s or d

Tulip Valley Inn; 2200 Freeway Dr.; tel. 428-5969; $38 s, $42 d; kitchenettes available

West Winds Motel; 2020 Riverside Dr.; tel. 424-4224; $38 s, $44 d

Dutch Treat B&B; 1777 W. Big Lake Blvd. (on Big Lake); tel. 422-5466; $55 s or d; comfortable, simple home, one guest room, private bath, sandy beach on Big Lake, canoe, rowboat, and sailboat for guests, full breakfast

Days Inn; 2009 Riverside Dr.; tel. 424-4141 or (800) 325-2525; $55 s, $60 d; outdoor pool, AAA approved

Best Western College Way Inn; 300 W. College Way; tel. 424-4287 or (800) 528-1234; $55-61 s, $60-66 d; outdoor pool, jacuzzi, kitchenettes available, AAA approved

Travelodge; 1910 Freeway Dr.; tel. 428-7020 or (800) 578-7878; $59 s, $64 d; indoor pool, jacuzzi, exercise room, continental breakfast, kitchenettes available, AAA approved

Best Western Cottontree Inn; 2300 Market Place; tel. 662-6886 or (800) 662-6886; $64 s, $69 d; outdoor pool, AAA approved

Fulton House B&B; 420 Fulton St.; tel. 336-2952; $65-85 s or d; 1908 farmhouse, three guest rooms, private baths, full breakfast

Whispering Firs B&B; 1957 Kanako Lane (three miles south of Mount Vernon); tel. 428-1990 or (800) 428-1992; $60-90 s, $65-95 d; large modern home on 250 acres, views of the San Juans, three rooms, private baths, hot tub, cedar deck, gourmet breakfast, children welcome

The Inn at Thirteen Firs B&B; 2329-B Hwy. 9 (five miles southeast of Conway); tel. 445-3571; $75 s or d; large contemporary home on Lake McMurray, one guest room, private bath, sundeck, continental breakfast, no kids

BURLINGTON

Mark II Motel; 805 Goldenrod Rd.; tel. 757-4021; $31 s, $38 d

Sterling Motor Inn; 866 S. Burlington Blvd.; tel. 757-0071; $35-40 s, $40-43 d; kitchenettes available, AAA approved

Cocusa Motel; 200 W. Rio Vista; tel. 757-6044 or (800) 628-2257; $60 s or d; outdoor pool, kitchenettes available, AAA approved

Benson Farmstead B&B; 1009 Avon-Allen Rd.; tel. 757-0578; $70-80 s or d; 1914 farmhouse, hot tub, four guest rooms, shared or private baths, antiques, full breakfast, evening desserts

---

Way, tel. (360) 424-9724. This is a fine place for a romantic gourmet dinner. Highly recommended.

Produce and More

You don't have to be a member to shop at the Skagit Valley Food Co-op, 202 S. 1st. St., tel. (360) 336-3886; they just charge you more if you aren't. The market has a wide selection of bulk foods, locally baked bread, wine and beer, fresh produce, plus an all-natural deli for a take-out lunch or dinner. This is really the best (and most nutritious) quick meal deal in town—a whole lot better than the fast food joints that line Riverside Drive. On Friday evenings, they offer a very reasonable all-you-can-stuff-in spaghetti or burrito feed. Open till 7 p.m.

Another place for fresh produce (and flowers, of course) is the **Mount Vernon-Skagit Valley Farmers Market,** held in downtown Mount Vernon on Saturday 9:30 a.m.-1:30 p.m. between early June and late September. On Wednesday afternoons June-Sept. the **Burlington Farmers Market** can be found at Lion's Park. Lots of organic fruits and vegetables here. At other times, stop by Burlington's **Country Farms Produce Market,** 101 Orange Ave., tel. (360) 755-0488, for fresh locally grown fruits and vegetables.

SKAGIT VALLEY TULIP FESTIVAL

The 10-day Tulip Festival, held annually in early April by Mount Vernon, La Conner, and Anacortes, corresponds with the blooming of the tulip and daffodil fields and includes bus tours, Skagit River trips, bike rides, street fairs, antique shows, a salmon bake, volleyball and basketball tournaments, and an art show. The main attraction, of course, is the fields of flowers. Tour buses dump hundreds of sightseers on the area, and many more drive up from Seattle to photograph the colorful fields. There are bus shuttles on weekends and tours on weekdays to help alleviate some of the congestion, but with several hundred thousand visitors, it still gets crazy, especially on weekends between 11 a.m. and 4 p.m. Be sure to stop at the visitor's booths for a map of local bike lanes if you're pedaling around during the festival. Kodak sponsors an official photo platform at **Little Tulip Town** (Skagit Valley Bulb Farms), 1502 Bradshaw Rd., tel. (360) 424-8152, along with music, art, pony rides, kite flying, espresso coffee, cut flowers, and refreshments. In addition, RoozenGaarde, West Shore Acres, and Skagit Valley Gardens all have paths that wind through flower gardens. You can, of course, purchase cut flowers or buy bulbs at these or other local places. Call (800) 488-5477 for a detailed map and description of the fields and Tulip Festival activities.

In Mount Vernon itself, the Tulip Festival action centers on the downtown **Street Fair** that includes more than 130 art and craft vendors, plus live entertainment and food.

Festival Transportation
During the first two weeks of April, the *Victoria Clipper,* tel. (360) 448-5000 or (800) 888-2535, offers a special 12-hour voyage to La Conner from Seattle's Pier 69. This includes the cruise and a guided bus tour of the tulip fields for $55 on Sat.-Sun., $44 on weekdays; seniors and kids pay $45 on Sat.-Sun., $34 on weekdays.

On weekdays during the festival, **Tulip Transit** buses depart Burlington on two-to-four hour tours of the valley's flower fields. The cost is $8 for adults, $4 for kids, and free for children under three. Weekends bring out the **Skagit Transit** (SKAT) buses that loop through the valley for just $1 for adults or $3 for families. Call (360) 428-8547 or (800) 488-5477 for details.

OTHER EVENTS AND ENTERTAINMENT

Berry Dairy Days celebrate Burlington's agricultural roots (especially strawberry and milk production), with an arts and crafts show, salmon barbecue, softball tournament, and plenty of strawberry shortcake. The second weekend of August brings the **Skagit County Fair** to the fairgrounds on the southwest side of Mount Vernon off Blackburn Road. Fair activities include live entertainment, pig races, agricultural exhibits, food, and lots more.

On Memorial Day weekend, the **Skagit River Festival** features a parade, fireworks, miniature hydroplane races on the river, a 10-km race, plus various sporting events.

The Arts
Historic **Lincoln Theatre Center,** 712 S. 1st St., tel. (360) 336-2858, is the place for films, plays, and musical productions throughout the year. The original Wurlitzer organ—used for silent films and vaudeville shows in the 1920s—still works.

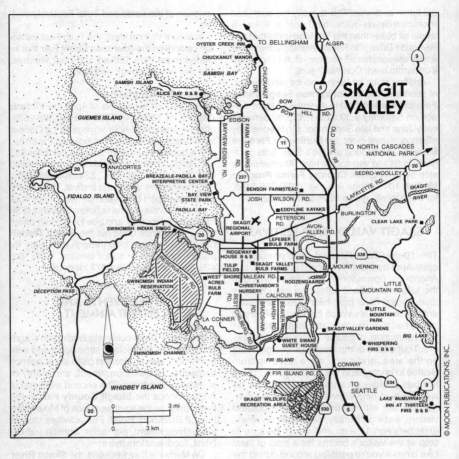

SKAGIT VALLEY

RECREATION

Swim at the **Skagit Valley Family YMCA**, 215 E. Fulton St., tel. (360) 336-9622.

If you're headed for the mountains, **Cascade Sports,** 509 S. 1st St., tel. (360) 336-6641, has backpacking, bicycle, and ski equipment plus outerwear and equipment rentals.

Six miles east of Mount Vernon on Hwy. 9, **Overlook Golf Course,** tel. (360) 422-6444, is a nine-hole course with views of Big Lake.

SHOPPING

Park your car to browse through the shops in downtown Mount Vernon, particularly along 1st Street's bakeries, gift and clothing stores, and cafes. You'll also discover four different bookstores here, including the spacious **Scott's Bookstore,** at 120 N. 1st St., tel. (360) 336-6181, a great place to linger.

If you prefer to shop in a mall, Mount Vernon and Burlington have several to choose from, including **Cascade Mall,** with Sears, JCPenney, Bon Marché, and Emporium, and **Pacific Edge Outlet Center,** 234 Fashion Way, tel. (360) 757-3549, with more than 50 outlet stores. **Eddyline Kayaks** are manufactured next to Bay View Airport, three miles west of Burlington. Drop by to tour the factory or for a test-paddle around their adjacent pond. Call (360) 757-2300 for details.

INFORMATION AND SERVICES

For maps, brochures, and festival information, contact the **Mount Vernon Chamber of Commerce,** tel. (350) 428-8547, located on the back side of Skagit Valley Mall behind the Ernst Store. Hours are Mon.-Fri. 8:30 a.m.-5 p.m., and Sat.-Sun. 9 a.m.-5 p.m. in the summer, or Mon.-Fri. 8:30 a.m.-5 p.m., Saturday 9 a.m.-4 p.m. the rest of the year.

The **area code** for Mount Vernon and points north to the Canadian border is 360.

For medical emergencies, Mount Vernon has **Skagit Valley Hospital,** 1415 Kincaid, off 15th, tel. (360) 424-4111.

TRANSPORTATION

Skagit Transit, tel. (360) 757-4433 (better known as SKAT), offers free bus service in the communities of Burlington and Mount Vernon. Just hop on board their state-of-the-art buses. Buses run seven days a week.

The **Airporter Shuttle,** tel. (800) 235-5247, has daily shuttles from Mount Vernon to Sea-Tac for $23. Both **Greyhound,** tel. (360) 336-5111 or (800) 231-2222, and **Evergreen Trailways,** tel. (800) 366-3830, connect nationwide from the Mount Vernon terminal at 1101 S. 2nd Street.

LA CONNER AND VICINITY

West of Mount Vernon, the broad Skagit Valley is carpeted with fields of vegetables and flowers, with a sprinkling of old barns and homesteads. This nearly level country is a favorite place for a spring or summer bike ride, especially when the tulips are blooming. After all this farmland, La Conner comes as quite a surprise; you might think you'd stumbled upon a transplanted Vermont town. The operative term here is cute, with more frills and lace than a Victoria's Secret catalog. La Conner is the most touristy town in Skagit County—too much so to suit the locals. But there's no denying it's a fun place to visit. Park your bike or car and browse the old buildings, shops, restaurants, and bakeries all jammed into a tiny downtown area along the saltwater Swinomish (SWIN-o-mish) Channel. You probably won't be alone. Crowds are likely on summer weekends and during the Tulip Festival, when La Conner looks like a California beachfront tourist trap in July, with standing traffic, cyclists, mobs of pedestrians, full parking lots, and sidewalk hot-dog stands. If you're driving here, don't bother looking for a space downtown on such days; just head north up 2nd St. to the big parking lot.

HISTORY

The Swinomish
The Swinomish Indians, the Skagit River Valley's original inhabitants, spent their winters in villages dominated by long cedar houses with central firepits, and their summers in temporary structures made from cattail reeds. They lived off the bounty of this verdant land, eating from the abundant natural larder of fish, fowl, and game. As with many other tribes, introduced diseases brought by early European explorers—especially smallpox—quickly spread through the villages, killing nearly everyone in their path. Only a single Swinomish family survived, and their descendants alone represent the Swinomish tribe of today. When white settlers moved into the Skagit Valley, they found only a fraction of the native people still alive, and, as elsewhere, they were increasingly marginalized and forced to sign away their land in the Point Elliott Treaty of 1855. Today, the **Swinomish Indian Reservation** occupies less than 5,000 acres of land on Fidalgo Island just across Swinomish Channel from La Conner.

From Trading Post to Tourist Central

The oldest town in Skagit County, La Conner's first white settlers arrived shortly after the Civil War. They built dikes to tame the annual floods on the Skagit River and planted crops in the fertile soil that proved to be some of the most productive in the world. The town grew up along Swinomish Channel—the protected slough that separates the mainland from Fidalgo Island. In 1876, John Conner purchased a trading post and named the site after his wife, Louisa A. Conner (L.A. Conner eventually became La Conner).

La Conner flourished as a fishing and shipping port—by the turn of the century more than 1,000 people lived here—but overfishing and the Depression of the 1930s combined to send it into decline. Fortunately, the area's beauty began attracting artists looking for an interesting but inexpensive place to live. Guy Anderson was one of the first to arrive. Others followed, and as a group, they came to be known as the Skagit Valley School. Sometime in the 1970s, Seattle art critic Tom Robbins moved here and began writing novels such as *Another Roadside Attraction, Even Cowgirls Get the Blues,* and *Skinny Legs and All.* Locals started promoting the town as a quaint place to escape city life, and the tourists have been flooding in ever since.

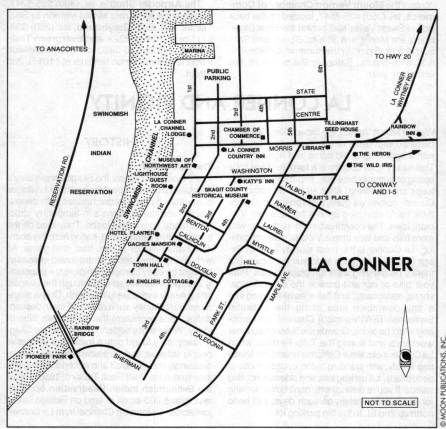

LA CONNER

NOT TO SCALE

© MOON PUBLICATIONS, INC.

DIANNE BOULERICE LYONS

Gaches Mansion

Today La Conner is home to barely 700 people but is one of Washington's most loved destinations. More than 160 local buildings in La Conner are on the National Register of Historic Places. Its galleries, gift shops, restaurants, museums, and 19th-century homes make for enjoyable exploring, and the bright-orange **Rainbow Bridge,** crossing the Swinomish Channel, is a good spot for photographers to get a shot of the La Conner waterfront with a Mt. Baker backdrop.

SIGHTS AND SHOPS

Museums

Skagit County Historical Museum, 501 4th St., tel. (360) 466-3365, sits high on a hill, with a panoramic view from the observation deck across the fields and farms of Skagit Valley. Inside are pioneer artifacts from the days of mining, logging, and fishing, historical photos, old farm equipment, horse-drawn carriages, Indian baskets, and even a moonshine still from the 1930s. Watch the 14-minute video for a taste of local history, or stop by the gift shop for books and crafts. Open Tues.-Sun. 11 a.m.-5 p.m. all year; admission is $2 for adults, $1 for seniors and kids ages six to 12, $5 for families, and free for under five.

The **Gaches Mansion** at Second and Calhoun was constructed in 1891 by George and Louisa Gaches and later served various pur-

poses, including a hospital and apartment building. A devastating 1973 fire gutted the structure, but local citizens raised the money to restore this majestic three-story Victorian mansion to its original beauty. The first floor is filled with turn-of-the-century furnishings, while the second floor contains hospital exhibits. Tours are offered Fri.-Sun. 1-5 p.m. in the summer, and Fri.-Sun. 1-4 p.m. in the winter; closed from late December through January. Admission is $2 for adults, $1 for kids, or $5 for families; call (360) 466-4288 for information.

Just around the corner from the Gaches Mansion at 2nd and Commercial, you'll find an 1869 log cabin that was moved here in 1959 from the Skagit River. Next door is the old brick city hall from 1886.

The new **Museum of Northwest Art,** 121 S. 1st St., tel. (360) 466-4446, features paintings and sculptures by well-known Northwest artists, including Guy Anderson, Mark Tobey, Morris Graves, and Kenneth Callahan. They also have changing contemporary art exhibits. Open Tues.-Sun. 10 a.m.-5 p.m. year-round.

The little **Fireman's Museum** on 1st St. contains a horse-drawn handpump that was used to put out fires in San Francisco following the 1906 earthquake. It was later used by the La Conner Fire Department; peek in the window to see it.

Pioneer Park, is a quiet riverside place for a picnic beneath tall Douglas fir trees next to Rainbow Bridge. No camping here.

LA CONNER AREA ACCOMMODATIONS

Accommodations are arranged from least to most expensive. Prices may be lower in the winter months. The telephone area code is 360.

BED AND BREAKFASTS

Wilma's Guest House B&B; 328 Washington St.; tel. 466-4289; $55 s or d; simple home, one guest room, continental breakfast

Art's Place; 511 E. Talbot; tel. 466-3033; $60 s or d; modern two-story home, balcony bedroom, spiral staircase, jacuzzi tub, continental breakfast

Katy's Inn B&B; 503 S. 3rd; tel. 466-3366 or (800) 914-7767; $69-85 s or d; 1876 Victorian home along Swinomish Channel, four luxurious guest rooms, shared baths, wraparound porch, library, gazebo with jacuzzi, full breakfast, no kids

An English Cottage; 832 S. 4th; tel. 466-2067; $75-95 s or d; beautiful old home with impressive flower gardens, one guest room and one suite, private baths, full English breakfast

Rainbow Inn B&B; 1075 Chilberg Rd.; tel. 466-4578; $75-95 s or d; 1908 farmhouse surrounded by tulip fields, eight guest rooms, shared baths, jacuzzi, gourmet breakfast

White Swan Guest House B&B; 1388 Moore Rd. (Fir Island); tel. 445-6805; $75 s or d; 1898 farmhouse with English garden, three guest rooms, shared baths, woodstove, large continental breakfast; garden cottage ($125 for up to four) has its own bath, kitchen, and sundeck, no young kids

Ridgeway B&B; 1292 McLean Rd.; tel. 428-8068 or (800) 428-8068; $75-125 s or d; 1928 Dutch Colonial brick farmhouse in tulip fields, six guest rooms and private cottage, shared or private baths, full breakfast and evening dessert, no young kids, AAA approved

MOTELS AND HOTELS

Lighthouse Guest Room; 512 S. 1st St.; tel. 466-3147; $60 s or d; one upstairs guest room, private bath, deck

The Heron Inn; 117 Maple St.; tel. 466-4626; $65-125 s or d; newer Victorian-style country inn, fireplace, jacuzzi, continental breakfast, no kids under 12, AAA approved

Hotel Planter; 715 1st St.; tel. 466-4710 or (800) 488-5409; $70-110 s or d; renovated 1907 hotel, very attractive rooms, garden courtyard, hot tub and gazebo, no kids on weekends, AAA approved

La Conner Country Inn; 107 S. 2nd St.; tel. 466-3101; $81-130 s or d; two-bedroom units, fireplaces, AAA approved

Wild Iris Inn; 121 Maple Ave.; tel. 466-1400 or (800) 477-1400; $85-130 s or d; luxurious new Victorian-style inn, jacuzzis, fireplaces, outside decks, breakfast buffet

La Conner Channel Lodge; 205 N. 1st St.; tel. 466-1500; $132-209 s or d; large and modern waterfront hotel, fireplaces, small decks, continental breakfast, AAA approved

Esteps' Residence in La Conner; 1st St.; tel. 466-2116; $135 for up to four; condominium on Swinomish Channel, kitchen, deck

Shopping

The most fun way to shop in La Conner is to simply meander through the downtown shops, stopping for lunch or a beer and heading out again. Art galleries, gift shops, antique dealers, espresso and sweets places, and restaurants line 1st and Morris Streets. Most of these sell cloyingly dolled-up tourist crap, but there are several notable exceptions. The tiny **Gallery Tenaski,** 710 S. 1st, tel. (360) 734-8017, is an artists' cooperative with unique jewelry and ceramics. A few doors away is **The Stall,** tel. (360) 466-3162, selling imports from all over the globe. **Rose & Thistle Tea Room & Antiques,** 606 E. Morris, tel. (360) 466-3313, has an odd mix: delicious English teas and quality vintage clothing. The **Joel Brock Studio,** 109 E. Commercial St., tel. (360) 766-6448, exhibits Brock's ethereal oil paintings.

Established in 1885, the **Tillinghast Seed Company,** 623 E. Morris St., tel. (360) 466-3329, is the oldest operating retail seed store in the Northwest, with flower and vegetable seeds and plant paraphernalia of all types. Even brown thumbs will enjoy this shop!

ACCOMMODATIONS AND CAMPING

La Conner is blessed with a number of delightful inns and historic B&Bs; see the "La Conner Area Accommodations" chart for a complete rundown. "Mount Vernon and Burlington Accommodations" chart lists additional places (these tend to be cheaper) just a few miles east of La Conner.

Several local lodging places are especially noteworthy. The newly renovated **Hotel Planter,** tel. (360) 466-4710 or (800) 488-5409, has nicely decorated rooms in this 1907 building, with a hot tub in the garden courtyard. For another taste of the past, **Katy's Inn B&B,** tel. (360) 466-3366 or (800) 914-7767, is an 1876 Victorian farmhouse facing Swinomish Channel with a wraparound porch, gazebo, and hot tub. Guests staying at **An English Cottage,** tel. (350) 466-2067, are treated to a beautiful old home with extraordinary flower gardens and a big English breakfast. **White Swan Guest House,** tel. (360) 445-6805, is an 1898 farmhouse with three guest rooms and a large English-style garden. A separate cottage has its own bath, kitchen, and sundeck.

Built from yellow bricks, **Ridgeway B&B,** tel. (360) 428-8068 or (800) 428-8068, stands midway between La Conner and Mount Vernon near the tulip fields. This grand three-story farmhouse is filled with antiques and collectibles and is surrounded by a flower-filled lawn and orchard. Another historic farmhouse next to the tulip fields has been turned into **Rainbow Inn**

B&B, tel. (360) 466-4578. Guests can enjoy the gourmet three-course breakfast, explore the surrounding floral bouquet, or just relax in the jacuzzi.

Campgrounds
Bay View State Park, eight miles north of La Conner, has year-round campsites for $11 ($16 for RVs). Call (360) 757-0227 for details, or (800) 452-5687 for campsite reservations ($6 extra fee), available up to 11 months ahead of time.

Campers and RVers are welcome at the **Potlatch RV Resort,** 415 Pearle Jensen Way, tel. (360) 466-4468, where you can relax in one of two hot tubs or the indoor pool while you're "roughing it." Head south to Fir Island for **Blakes RV Park & Marina,** 1171-A Rawlins Rd., tel. (360) 445-6533.

FOOD

Breakfast and Lunch
Start your day at **Calico Cupboard Cafe & Bakery,** 720 S. 1st St., tel. (360) 466-4451, for great homemade country breakfasts, plus healthy lunches and wonderful pastries. Arrive early to avoid a lengthy wait on summer weekends. Get excellent sandwiches, salads, and soups in the bright and airy **Hungry Moon Delicatessen,** 110 N. 1st St., tel. (360) 466-1602, located on the north end of town, away from the hordes. **The Granary in the Garden,** east of La Conner at 1592 Best Rd., tel. (360) 466-3190, serves delicious lunches and high tea (reservations required). **La Conner Tavern,** 702 S. 1st St., tel. (360) 466-9932, serves burgers and baskets of fish and chips.

Dinner
On the Swinomish Channel waterfront, **The Lighthouse Inn,** 512 S. 1st St., tel. (360) 466-3147, has outdoor-barbecued salmon, prime rib, steak, and fresh seafood. When the weather is nice, come here for outdoor dining. They also have live music on weekends. **La Conner Seafood & Prime Rib House,** 614 1st St., tel. (360) 466-4014, has waterfront dining emphasizing—as might be expected given the name—seafood and prime rib.

Palmer's Restaurant & Pub, 2nd and Washington at the La Conner Inn, offers an extensive wine list to complement its outstanding Northwest and European cuisine. Open for lunch and dinner; call (360) 466-4261 for reservations. Palmer's hilltop location makes it a popular place to watch the sun go down.

Seven miles west of La Conner, on Hwy. 20 between Anacortes and Mount Vernon, the **Farmhouse Restaurant,** 1376 La Conner-Whitney Rd., tel. (360) 466-4411, is a large and busy family spot with all the usual American specials. It attracts the crowds with low prices and ample servings, but the food isn't especially noteworthy.

China Pearl, 505 S. 1st St., tel. (360) 466-1000, has deliciously spicy Mandarin and Sichuan favorites.

The newly opened **La Conner Brewing Co.,** 117 S. 1st. St., tel. (360) 466-1415, has brewed-on-the-premises beer and tasty brick-oven pizzas and other pub fare.

Produce
In the summer, be sure to stop at the **Hedlin's Farm Fruit Stand** on the east edge of town for fresh corn, tomatoes, peas, honey, strawberries, and other produce from their nearby farm.

EVENTS
The event season kicks off each year with an early February **Smelt Derby.** La Conner's main event is also Mount Vernon's: the **Skagit Valley Tulip Festival** each April (see "Mount Vernon and Vicinity," above). It attracts thousands of folks to town, especially on festival weekends. Head to La Conner on the **Fourth of July** for a big fireworks display over Swinomish Channel. In mid-July the **Puget Sound Painters** are out in force, producing paintings that can be purchased at the Northwest Art Museum. Then comes the **Pioneer Picnic** in early August and the **Pumpkin Festival** with contests for the biggest and best-carved pumpkins. The season winds down with the **Art's Alive!** celebration in early November featuring demonstrations by painters, jewelers, potters, and others, and the **Christmas Ships Parade** up the Swinomish Channel each December.

RECREATION AND ENTERTAINMENT

Recreation
The Swinomish Channel is a peaceful body of water for paddling or rowing; rent a boat from **La Conner Rent-a-Boat,** 612-C N. Dunlap St., tel. (360) 466-3300. Several other companies offer charter fishing trips; see the chamber of commerce for specifics. **Viking Cruises,** 109 N. 1st St., tel. (360) 466-2639, has jet boats that depart La Conner for tours of Deception Pass. Rent bikes from **Boater's Discount Center,** 601 N. Dunlap St., tel. (360) 466-3540.

Take a hot air balloon ride ($105 per person) with **Vagabound Balloons,** tel. (360) 466-1906 or (800) 488-0269. They have daily flights April-September.

The state's **Skagit Wildlife Recreation Area,** a refuge south of La Conner on Fir Island, is a good place to look for wintering snow geese and trumpeter swans.

Gambling
Swinomish Indian Casino and Bingo has gambling (bingo, craps, roulette, blackjack, poker, sic bo, and pull-tabs, but no slots) at their new casino just across the Hwy. 20 bridge on Fidalgo Island; call (360) 293-4687 or (800) 877-7529 for details. A gift shop here sells native arts and crafts.

INFORMATION AND TRANSPORTATION

For local info, visit the **La Conner Chamber of Commerce** at 4th and Morris, tel. (360) 466-4778, open Mon.-Sat. 11 a.m.-3 p.m. year-round. The town **library** can be found at 614 E. Morris, tel. (360) 466-3352. La Conner's **area code** is 360.

No local bus service to La Conner, but **Sea-Tac Airporter Shuttle,** tel. (800) 448-8443, has transportation to Sea-Tac for $23. **Rainbow Van Service,** tel. (360) 466-5324 or (800) 733-5320, has a similar service and may be a better deal if you have several folks, since the rate is by the van load, not on a per-person basis.

CHUCKANUT DRIVE

Heading north up the coast from the Skagit Valley, one enters one of the most scenic stretches of highway in the state—Chuckanut Drive. This 11-mile portion of Hwy. 11 was the first route designated a scenic drive by the state. Built as part of the now-extinct Pacific Highway, it leaves I-5 just north of Burlington and heads straight as a cue stick across the black, flat soil of the Skagit Valley, passing the **Rhododendron Cafe** at the Bow-Edison intersection. The cafe serves good food and wine and is populated on weekends by bicyclists and weekend-drive aficionados. The tiny towns of **Bow** and **Edison** have recently begun attracting artists, and several studios are open for weekend visits. Not far away in the dinky place called Alger (just off I-5), is **Skagit Speedway,** tel. (360) 568-2529, with auto racing between mid-April and late September.

A short distance north of Bow, the highway runs head-on into the mountains that hover over Puget Sound; it's here that the fun begins. The road doesn't have a straight stretch for seven miles as it swoops and swerves along the face of the cliff with grand views across to Anacortes, Guemes Island, and, farther north, the San Juan and Lummi Islands. With no shoulder, a narrow strip of pavement, and tight corners, its a bit dicey for bikes, but the views are stunning.

As you drive north, you'll pass three more good places to eat. Overlooking Samish Bay and the San Juans at 302 Chuckanut Dr., **Chuckanut Manor,** tel. (360) 766-6191, at the southern end of the drive, specializes in fresh seafood and continental dishes, Friday night smorgasbord, and Sunday Champagne brunch. The bar has the best and usually quietest seats in the house and serves 26 different single malt scotches. The oyster-sized **Oyster Bar,** 240 Chuckanut Dr., tel. (360) 766-6185, is a small and expensive place clinging to the side of the mountain; it serves oysters (of course) and has a limited, mostly seafood menu. Every table overlooks the San Juan Islands. Specializing in Northwest food and wine, **Oyster Creek Inn,** 190 Chuckanut Dr., tel.

(360) 766-6179, in the heart of the mountainous section, serves seafood, chicken, lamb, and other dishes. This is a must-stop place right in the trees and ferns overlooking a cascading creek. Head a half-mile down the canyon to **Samish Bay Shellfish Farm,** tel. (360) 766-6002, for locally raised fresh oysters, clams, scallops, mussels, and Dungeness crabs (cooked while you wait).

Accommodations

Both **Chuckanut Manor** and **Oyster Creek Inn** have overnight accommodations, and although the restaurants are some distance apart, their lodgings are only yards apart. Chuckanut Manor, tel. (360) 766-6191, has two rooms upstairs over the restaurant that costs $95 s or d, including a jacuzzi, private deck, and continental breakfast. They also offer lodging at **Kristy's Cottage B&B,** with a hot tub, private deck, kitchen, and antiques for $95 s or d.

Oyster Creek Inn has a small cabin no more than a hundred yards south of Chuckanut Manor overlooking the bay. The Japanese-style cabin is furnished with lots of black lacquer, glass and brass, and a futon; $88 s or d, including champagne and breakfast.

Alice Bay B&B, 982 Scott Rd. on Sammish Island just west of Edison (actually a peninsula, not an island), tel. (360) 766-6396, has a contemporary two-story guest cottage in a seaside setting. This is a unique B&B where you can soak in the hot tub on the deck overlooking Alice Bay, take the rowboat out, watch nesting great blue herons, borrow a bike, or check out the owners' ostriches or oyster pens. Rates are $85 s or d, including a full breakfast; gourmet dinners are available by arrangement. Kids are welcome.

Parks and Beaches

Seven miles south of Bellingham on Chuckanut Dr., **Larrabee State Park** (tel. 360-676-2093) was the state's first, created in 1923 when Charles Xavier Larrabee's family donated 20 acres in his honor. The park contains a popular campground with tent sites ($11) and RV hookups ($16), plus coin-operated showers. Open year-round. Call (800) 452-5687 for campsite reservations ($6 extra fee), available up to 11 months ahead of time. Covering more than 2,500 acres of mountainous land, the park borders Samish Bay, with a boat launch, a sandy beach for sunning, and tidepools for marine explorations. Nine miles of hiking trails include the southern end of the **Interurban Trail** connecting the park with Bellingham. Other trails lead to scenic Fragrence and Lost Lakes for trout fishing, and to dramatic vistas from the 1,941-foot summit of **Chuckanut Mountain** (also accessible via a gravel road).

Continue north from Larrabee State Park to **Teddy Bear Cove,** located at the foot of the cliff just before you enter the Fairhaven District. This is one of the state's few nude beaches. No sign marks it on the highway, but the line of parked cars is like a pointing finger to the cove.

BELLINGHAM

With a population of more than 55,000, Bellingham is no longer a town, but it still maintains a friendly small-town feel. The city is an almost perfect blend of the old and the new, with stately homes and extraordinary museums, an abundance of cultural events, plus many fine shops and restaurants. Bellingham has managed to hold onto both its blue-collar paper mill jobs and white-collar university positions, while attracting increasing numbers of tourists. The city is a jumping-off point for northbound travelers aboard the Alaska Marine Highway's ferries; the terminal is in the historic Fairhaven section of Bellingham. With the addition of Amtrak service in 1995, plus easy access from I-5, it seems well positioned for the next century.

HISTORY

The original inhabitants of what is now Bellingham—the Lummi Indians—lived in wooden houses built of cedar planks that were placed seasonally around a permanent frame. They lived off the land, harvesting shellfish, fish, wild plants, deer, and other game animals. When Capt. George Vancouver sailed into Puget Sound in 1792, he found a community of nearly 3,000 native people living along these productive shores. He named it Bellingham Bay for Sir William Bellingham, the British Admiralty controller who provided Vancouver with supplies for his explorations.

European Settlement
Captain Henry Roeder and Russell V. Peabody established the first permanent settlement here in 1852; they came north from San Francisco in search of a sawmill site to supply their hometown's growing demand for lumber. When Roeder and Peabody met Lummi Chief Cha-wit-zit in Olympia, they asked him if he knew of any place with "falling water all the time from a high hill." Cha-wit-zit apparently understood the Americans' broken English and, speaking in kind, suggested "at Whatcom, noise all the time." With the aid of Lummi tribe members, Roeder and

Peabody built a mill at the foot of Whatcom Falls in 1853, producing lumber until it burned down in 1873.

William H. Prattle, another of Bellingham's earliest settlers, responded to Native American tales of local coal outcroppings by opening a marginally successful coal mine in the settlement called Unionville in 1853. The same year, San Francisco investors opened the Sehome Mine, adjacent to the Whatcom settlement, and it became one of the two largest employers in the area until the mine was flooded in 1878. Coal mining ceased until the Bellingham Bay Co. opened the largest mine in the state in the city's north end in 1918; it operated until 1951, when decreased demand led to its closure.

The 1850s also brought to Bellingham the aborted Fraser River Gold Stampede. About 10,000 people, most of whom had traveled north from California, came to Whatcom to await the opening of a trail to British Columbia's newfound gold. The trail was never completed, and an order from Vancouver Island's governor James Douglas that all gold diggers obtain permits in Victoria before entering the province further squelched the would-be gold rush. One remnant from the gold boom is a brick building on E St.; the first brick building in the territory, it first served mercantile purposes and later as the Whatcom County Courthouse for 25 years.

Fairhaven
The boomtown of Fairhaven grew to prominence in the late 1880s when rumors circulated that it would be the western terminus for the Great Northern Railroad. At its peak, the town hummed on 35 hotels and boardinghouses, seven saloons, an opera house, and 11 real estate offices. Despite the large number of hotels, many men were forced to sleep in tents along the beach.

The selection of Tacoma as the Great Northern's terminus sent Fairhaven into a tailspin, but the arrival of a smaller line—the Fairhaven and Southern Railroad—brought service from

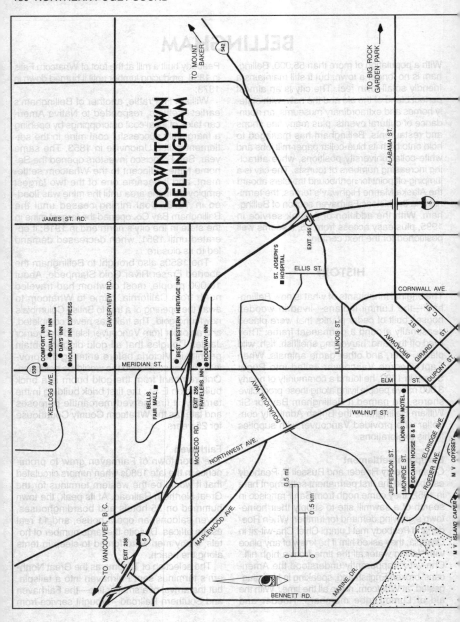

DOWNTOWN
BELLINGHAM

TO MOUNT BAKER

542

TO BIG ROCK
GARDEN PARK

ALABAMA ST.

5

JAMES ST. RD.

EXIT 255

ST. JOSEPH'S
HOSPITAL

ELLIS ST.

CORNWALL AVE.

C ST.

F ST.

ST.

GIRARD

BROADWAY

ILLINOIS ST.

DUPONT ST.

BAKERVIEW RD.

Comfort Inn
Quality Inn
Days Inn
Holiday Inn Express

Best Western Heritage Inn
Rodeway Inn

MERIDIAN ST.

539

KELLOGG AVE.

BELLIS
FAIR MALL

EXIT 256
TRAVELERS INN

McLEOD RD.

NORTHWEST AVE.

ELM
ST.

WALNUT ST.

SOCIALCURVE WAY

JEFFERSON ST.

MONROE ST.

LIONS INN MOTEL

DECANN HOUSE B & B

ELDRIDGE AVE.

ROEDER AVE.

M V ODYSSEY

MAPLEWOOD AVE.

EXIT 253

5

TO VANCOUVER, B.C.

0.5 mi

0.5 km

M V ISLAND CAPER

MARINE DR.

BENNETT RD.

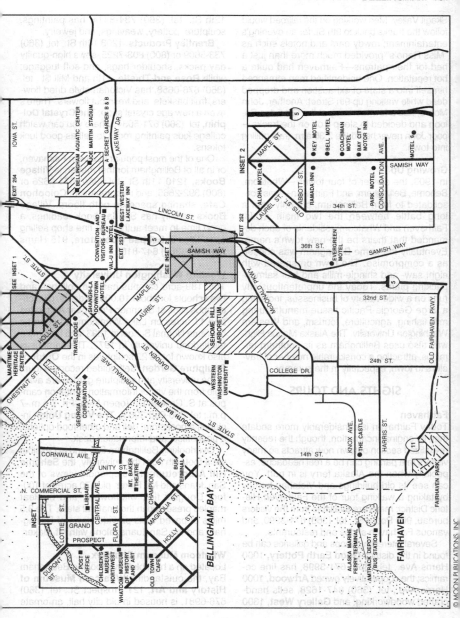

FAIRHAVEN

Skagit Valley. Men working on the railroad would follow the tracks back to 9th St. for an evening's entertainment; rowdy bars and hotels such as "Miss Reno's" provided much more than just a bed for their patrons—Fairhaven had quite a hot reputation. One unidentified man romanced himself into a state of exhaustion and dropped dead while walking up 9th Street. Another, John Moore, had a few too many at the Gilt Edge Saloon and decided to sleep it off on the tracks—poor John never heard the 2:30 a.m. train pulling into town.

Growing Up

In 1903, the cluster of four towns—Whatcom, Sehome, Bellingham, and Fairhaven—was consolidated to form Bellingham, but only after a long battle between the two main rivals, Fairhaven and Whatcom; residents of each demanded that theirs be the new town's name. Eventually the name Bellingham was chosen as a compromise. The town prospered with eight saw- and shingle-mills and four salmon-packing plants. Today the unpretentious city runs on a wide variety of businesses, including a large Georgia-Pacific tissue manufacturing mill, fishing, agriculture, tourism, and Western Washington University. The Alaska Marine Highway also uses Bellingham as its southern terminus, attracting a considerable number of travelers to town, especially in the summer.

SIGHTS AND TOURS

Fairhaven

Today Fairhaven is considerably more sedate than its original incarnation, though the recently revitalized section of town now attracts so many visitors that parking can be a real headache, especially when the Alaska ferry is in port. You can see its old buildings and Victorian homes by taking a walking tour of the Fairhaven Historic District; maps are available from the visitors bureau, 904 Potter St., tel. (360) 671-3990, and various Fairhaven shops and restaurants.

Several interesting shops and galleries can be found in the district. **Good Earth Pottery,** 1000 Harris Ave., tel. (360) 671-3998, has fine ceramics; the cooperatively owned **Artwood,** 1000 Harris Ave., tel. (360) 647-1628, sells handcrafted woodworking; and **Gallery West,** 1300 12th St., tel. (360) 734-8414, has paintings, sculpture, pottery, weavings, and jewelry.

Brentley Products, 1208 10th St., tel. (360) 733-5609 or (800) 803-7225, sews high-quality day packs, shoulder bags, and soft luggage; while **Rose and Thistle,** 11th and Mill St., tel. (360) 676-0658, has Victorian-style dried flowers, fruit baskets, and fresh-cut flowers. There's even a new age crystal shop, **The Crystal Dolphin,** tel. (360) 671-5034, where you can watch college kids painting rocks to sell as good luck tokens.

One of the most popular places in Fairhaven, or in all of Bellingham for that matter, is **Village Books,** 1210 11th St., tel. (360) 671-2626 or (800) 392-2665, and its companion, **Colophon Cafe,** sharing space on both floors. Village Books usually has Sunday book readings, a good time to meet authors. A fine shop selling used titles is **Eclipse Bookstore,** 915 Harris Ave., tel. (360) 647-8165.

Western Washington University

This 189-acre campus has five colleges and two schools for about 10,000 students, plus off-campus sites at Shannon Point near Anacortes and 11 acres on Lake Whatcom. It began as the State Normal School in 1893, and became a full-fledged university in 1977. The campus is also known for its 22 sculptures in the **Outdoor Sculpture Garden.** Self-guided recorded tours of the university and sculpture garden are available from the visitor information center on campus at S. College Dr. (open Mon.-Fri. 7 a.m.-7 p.m.; tel. 360-650-3963). **The Viking Union** includes a bookstore, deli and other food options, a post office, and information desk.

Overlooking Bellingham Bay and accessible via a footpath from the university, the **Sehome Hill Arboretum** offers splendid views of the San Juans and Mt. Baker, plus 70 acres of 100-foot Douglas firs, wildflowers, and big-leaf maples preserved in their natural state. The 3.5 miles of paved trails provide views of Bellingham and the San Juans, along with Mt. Baker.

Whatcom Museum Complex

Located on a high bluff overlooking Bellingham Bay, the outstanding **Whatcom Museum of History and Art,** 121 Prospect St., tel. (360) 676-6981, is housed in old city hall, an ornate red-brick building capped by a four-corner cupola and a tall clock tower. Built in 1892 as the New Whatcom City Hall, it remained in use until 1939 when the present city hall was completed on Lottie Street. Today, the museum has grown to include the old city hall, along with three nearby structures. A single entrance charge gets you in all four buildings: $3 for adults, or $2 for seniors and students. Hours for all but the Children's Museum are Tues.-Sun. noon-5 p.m. year-round.

The main building contains historical displays (complete with sound effects), changing exhibits, Victorian clothing, woodworking tools, toys, and contemporary art. Also here is a small gift shop with unusual items from around the globe. The **Syrie Education Center,** 201 Prospect, right next to old city hall, features many beautiful native baskets, bentwood boxes, reed mats, and even a Chilkoot blanket, plus a large number of stuffed birds. Also here are fascinating displays on the early days of Northwest logging—including the famous Darius Kinsey collection of images. These and thousands of other historical photographs make the archives one of the finest in Washington. Two nearby structures house separate collections that are also part of the Whatcom Museum "campus": the Children's Museum Northwest, and the Arco Building.

The **Arco Exhibits Building,** across the street at 206 Prospect, houses changing fine-art and historical exhibits. The **Children's Museum Northwest,** 227 Prospect St., tel. (360) 733-8769, has many participatory exhibits for kids of all ages, including an infant/toddler exploration center and puppet theater. Open Sunday and Tuesday noon-5 p.m., Wednesday noon-8 p.m., Thurs.-Sat. 10 a.m.-5 p.m.

Something Fishy
Bellingham's **Maritime Heritage Center,** 1600 C St., tel. (360) 676-6806, is an urban park where you can fish for salmon and steelhead

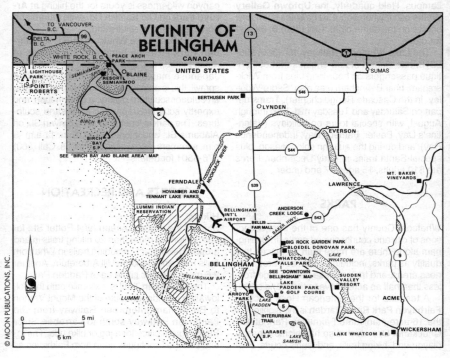

on Whatcom Creek, watch salmon spawning in mid-October, and learn about hatchery operation. Admission is free; open dawn to dusk. Kids will enjoy the marinelife touch tank where they can pet intertidal creatures. It's located inside the Harbor Center Mall at Squalicum Harbor off Roeder Avenue.

Tours

Maps of historic walking tours are available from the visitors bureau at 904 Potter Street. Walking tours include tours of stately Victorian mansions in the **Eldridge** and **Sehome** districts, and of **Fairhaven,** with its 1880s mansions and old brick storefronts. The **Squalicum Harbor** tour is along the two-mile promenade past pleasure and commercial boats and ships. This is the second-largest marina in the state; only Shilshole Marina in Seattle is bigger. The **Outdoor Art Walk,** takes you past works in downtown and on the Western Washington University campus. Held quarterly, the **Uptown Gallery Walks** occur when about 10 galleries open new shows on the same night. Call (360) 676-6981 for dates.

The **Lake Whatcom Railway,** tel. (360) 595-2218, has classic steam engines that pull antique passengers on hour-long trips from Wickersham, near Bellingham (see also "Sedro-Woolley" in the Cascade Range chapter). Trains depart on Saturday and Tuesday mid-June through August, with special tours on holidays (Valentine's Day, Easter, Father's Day, Independence Day), and during the autumn color season, plus special Santa trains in early December. Fares are $10 adults, $5 ages 17 and under.

PARKS

Whatcom County has one of the best collections of city and county owned parks. In Bellingham alone there are more than 35 places that qualify as parks, including green belt areas, fitness areas, and trails. These parks range from less than half an acre to over a thousand acres.

A test site for the American Rose Society, **Fairhaven Park Rose Garden** is the highlight of the 16-acre manicured Fairhaven Park at 107 Chuckanut Dr., which also has picnic areas, a playground, hiking trails, and tennis courts. Best

time to see it is July, when a hundred varieties of roses are in bloom at once.

Samish Park, 673 N. Lake Samish Dr., tel. (360) 733-2362, is a 39-acre county park with 1,500 feet of Lake Samish shoreline for swimming, fishing, boating, picnicking, hiking, and a children's play area. Rent canoes, paddleboats, rowboats, sailboats, or sailboards.

Whatcom Falls Park, near Lake Whatcom at 1401 Electric Ave., has 5.5 miles of hiking trails, tennis courts, a playground, a picnic area, and a state fish hatchery on 241 acres. With 12 acres on the lake itself, **Bloedel Donovan Park** has a swimming beach, boat launch, playground, and picnic area at 2214 Electric Avenue.

Lake Padden Park, 4882 Samish Way, has over 1,000 acres of hiking and horse trails, a golf course, picnic areas, and a playground, plus swimming, fishing, and nonmotorized boating on the lake.

Thirty-eight acres of practically untouched canyon wilderness is yours for the hiking at **Arroyo Park** on Old Samish Rd., with nature and horse trails and creek fishing.

Overlooking Lake Whatcom, **Big Rock Garden Park** includes hundreds of varieties of rhododendron and azaleas, along with dozens of Japanese maples. Surrounded by suburban sprawl, this is an oasis of tranquillity, with forests, an outdoor sculpture gallery, a greenhouse, and expertly sculpted Japanese-style sand sculptures. The park is located at 2900 Sylvan St., off Alabama St., and is open Wed.-Sun. 11 a.m.-5 p.m. summers, and winter weekends. Call (360) 676-6801 for details.

SPORTS AND RECREATION

Hiking

Stop by the visitors bureau (904 Potter St.) for descriptions of more than 20 hiking trails in and around Bellingham, including trails in Whatcom Falls Park and Sehome Hill Arboretum. Another 2.6 miles of paths circle Lake Padden Park.

The **Interurban Trail** is a six-mile path that follows the abandoned route of the Mount Vernon to Bellingham Interurban Railway from Old Fairhaven Parkway south to Larrabee State Park. A great place for a jog or bike ride. The Interurban Trail continues north from Fairhaven as the partially completed **South Bay Trail,** which will eventually connect Larrabee State Park with Lake Whatcom.

Equipping for the Outdoors

Rent sea kayaks, rowboats, and sailboats during the summer from **Fairhaven Boatworks,** near the Bellingham Cruise Terminal at 501 Harris Ave., tel. (360) 647-2469. **Bellingham Boat Rentals,** 3034 Silvern Lane, tel. (360) 676-1363, has canoes, kayaks, and pedal boats for rent on Lake Whatcom; open May-August. **The Great Adventure,** 201 E. Chestnut, tel. (360) 671-4615, rents all sorts of outdoor gear, from boots and packs to kayaks and skis. Rent bikes, skis, and snowboards from **Fairhaven Bicycle & Ski,** 1103 11th St., tel. (360) 733-4433.

Swimming

Newly opened in 1995, the **Bellingham Aquatic Center,** 1414 Potter St., tel. (360) 657-7665, has an indoor pool and water slide. A second pool is available at the local **YMCA,** 4600 Guide Meridian, tel. (360) 671-4378. In the summer months you can also swim at **Lake Padden Park** at 4882 Samish Way, tel. (360) 676-6985; **Lake Samish,** 673 N. Lake Samish Dr., tel. (360) 733-2362; and **Bloedel Donovan Park,** 2214 Electric Ave., tel. (360) 676-6985.

Golf

Golfers will find 16 different private and public courses within Whatcom County. Local public courses include: **Action Golf,** 1066 Lakeway, tel. (360) 676-5766; **Lake Padden Golf Course,** 4882 Sammish Way, tel. (360) 676-6989; **New World Pro Golf Center,** 5022 Guide Meridian, tel. (360) 398-1362; and the semi-private **Sudden Valley Gold & Country Club,** 2145 Lake Whatcom Blvd., tel. (360) 734-6435.

Baseball

The **Bellingham Mariners**—the Seattle Mariners Class A affiliate—play minor league baseball May-Sept. at Joe Martin Stadium on Lakeway Dr.; call (360) 671-6347 for ticket information.

American Alpine Institute

Bellingham is home to the American Alpine Institute, the nation's preeminent center for moun-

taineering education. Located at 1515 12th St., tel. (360) 671-1505, the school has a staff that includes accomplished mountain climbers and educators, and courses from the basics to advanced monthlong programs. Classes are taught all over the world—from the Alps to the Andes—with beginning mountaineering classes in the North Cascades. Prices start at $730 for a six-day alpine mountaineering class, or $650 for 10 days of advanced wilderness first-aid training.

On the Water

The visitors bureau has a complete listing of local sailing and fishing charter operators. **Island Mariner Cruises,** No. 5 Harbor Esplanade, tel. (360) 734-8866, has all-day whalewatching cruises on Saturday late May to early September, plus Monday and Wednesday in July and August at $45 for adults, $40 for seniors, and $35 for kids. Two-and-a-half-hour evening historical voyages narrated by Whatcom Museum storytellers are offered on Wednesday evenings from early July to mid-August. The cost is just $15.

The *Snow Goose* is a 65-foot fully equipped research vessel operated by two local marine biologists. They offer a range of trips, from four hours to five days. On all of these you'll get a firsthand look at marinelife and how researchers learn about life in Puget Sound. Call (360) 733-9078 for details on this unique opportunity.

More whalewatching aboard the **MV Odyssey,** tel. (360) 734-2292, a 64-foot vessel docked at Squalicum Harbor. Their trips are offered on Sunday in the summer.

San Juan Island Shuttle Express has a foot ferry to the San Juans, along with daily whalewatching. Victoria-San Juan Cruises offers daily excursions to Victoria, British Columbia. See "Transportation" below for details on these last two options. For information on other cruises to the islands, see the San Juan Islands chapter.

ACCOMMODATIONS

See the "Bellingham Accommodations" chart for a complete listing of local lodging options. The city's summertime rates seem to change with demand, so use these prices only as a guide. The **Bellingham and Whatcom County Convention and Visitors Bureau,** 904 Potter

BELLINGHAM ACCOMMODATIONS

Accommodations are arranged from least to most expensive within each category. Rates may be lower during the winter months. The area code is 360.

HOSTEL

Bellingham Hostel; 107 Chuckanut Dr.; tel. 671-1750; $10 pp for AYH members, $13 pp for nonmembers; dorm facilities, kitchen access, free pancake breakfasts

BED AND BREAKFASTS

The Castle; 1103 15th St.; tel. 676-0974; $45-95 s, $85-95 d; historic Fairhaven mansion, four antique-furnished guest rooms, shared or private bath, full breakfast, no kids under 12

DeCann House B&B; 2610 Eldridge Ave.; tel. 734-9172; $52-62 s, $59-69 d; Victorian-era home, bay views, stained glass, antiques, two guest rooms, private baths, full breakfast, free airport and ferry shuttle, no kids under 12

North Garden Inn B&B; 1014 N. Garden St.; tel. 671-7828, (800) 922-6414 (U.S.), or (800) 367-1676 (Canada); $59-79 s or d; ornate three-story Victorian home built in 1897, bay views, 10 guest rooms, private or shared baths, grand piano, full breakfast, AAA approved

A Secret Garden B&B; 1807 Lakeway Dr.; tel. 671-5327 or (800) 671-5327; $60-85 s or d; beautiful 1902 Victorian home, Bellingham Bay views, two guest rooms, private baths, grand piano, full breakfast, kids welcome

Sudden Valley Resort; 2145 Lake Whatcom Blvd.; tel. 734-6430 or (800) 734-6903; $70-155 s or d; on Lake Whatcom, studios to three-bedroom condos on 1,500 acres, outdoor pools, golf course, play barn for kids, sauna, tennis courts, boating, swimming, fishing

Big Trees B&B; 4840 Fremont St.; tel. 647-2850 or (800) 647-2850; $70-110 s or d; elegant 1907 craftsman home overlooking Lake Whatcom, wooded grounds, veranda, garden, three guest rooms, private baths, full breakfast, no kids under 12, AAA approved

Anderson Creek Lodge B&B; 5602 Mission Rd.; tel. 966-2126 or (800) 441-5585; $90-175 s or d; large contemporary home on 65 acres, indoor pool, fireplace, llamas, five guest rooms, private baths, continental breakfast

Schnauzer Crossing B&B; 4421 Lakeway Dr. (three miles east of Bellingham); tel. 734-2808 or (800) 562-2808; $110-180 s or d; luxurious contemporary home, glassed-in central room, two guest rooms and a cottage, private baths, hot tub, fresh fruit and flowers, gourmet breakfast, two-night minimum on weekends and holidays, kids okay

MOTELS

Evergreen Motel; 1015 Samish Way; tel. 734-7671 or (800) 821-0016; $30 s, $35 d; quiet motel near Lake Padden, free airport and ferry shuttle, kitchenettes available

Shangri-La Downtown Motel; 611 E. Holly St.; tel. 733-7050; $32 s, $35 d; kitchenettes available

Shamrock Motel; 4133 W. Maplewood; tel. 676-1050; $33 s, $37 d; kitchenettes available, free airport shuttle

Motel 6; 3701 Byron St.; tel. 671-4494 or (800) 466-8356; $34 s, $40 d; outdoor pool, avoid freeway side due to truck noise

Bell Motel; 208 N. Samish Way; tel. 733-2520; $35-43 s or d; kitchenettes available

Lions Inn Motel; 2419 Elm; tel. 733-2330; $38-45 s, $42-45 d; kitchenettes available, local calls 25 cents, AAA approved

Aloha Motel; 315 N. Samish Way; tel. 733-4900; $40 s or d; kitchenettes available

Bay City Motor Inn; 116 N. Samish Way; tel. 676-0332 or (800) 538-8204; $45 s, $50 d; outdoor pool, exercise room, continental breakfast, kitchenette available, AAA approved

Coachman Inn; 120 N. Samish Way; tel. 671-9000, (800) 962-6641 (Washington), or (800) 543-5478 (Canada); $45 s, $50 d; outdoor pool, jacuzzi, sauna, continental breakfast, AAA approved

Travelodge; 202 E. Holly St.; tel. 734-1900 or (800) 578-7878; $45 s, $50 d; AAA approved

The Traveler's Inn; 3570 Meridian St.; tel. 671-4600 or (800) 633-8300; $45 s, $52 d; outdoor pool, jacuzzi, AAA approved

Key Motel; 212 N. Samish Way; tel. 733-4060; $48 s or d; outdoor pool, sauna, jacuzzi, local calls 30 cents

Val-U Inn Motel; 805 Lakeway Dr.; tel. 671-9600, (800) 443-7777 (U.S.), or (800) 451-7767 (Canada); $51-55 s, $55-60 d; jacuzzi, continental breakfast, free airport and ferry shuttle, AAA approved

Park Motel; 101 N. Samish Way; $54 s, $59 d; tel. 733-8280 or (800) 732-1225; jacuzzi, sauna, continental breakfast, AAA approved

Rodeway Inn; 3710 Meridian St.; tel. 738-6000 or (800) 728-7230; $55 s or d; jacuzzi, AAA approved

Comfort Inn; 4282 Meridian St.; tel. 738-1100 or (800) 221-2222; $56 s, $61 d; indoor pool, jacuzzi, exercise room, continental breakfast, free airport and ferry shuttle, AAA approved

Hampton Inn; 3985 Bennett; tel. 676-7700 or (800) 426-7866; $59-64 s, $64-74 d; outdoor pool, fitness room, continental breakfast, free airport and ferry shuttle, AAA approved

Days Inn; 125 E. Kellogg Rd.; tel. 671-6200 or (800) 831-0187; $60 s or d; outdoor pool, jacuzzi, continental breakfast, kitchenettes available, AAA approved

Best Western Lakeway Inn; 714 Lakeway Dr.; tel. 671-1011 or (800) 528-1234; $61-70 s, $72-78 d; indoor pool, exercise room, jacuzzi, sauna, free airport shuttle, AAA approved

Quality Inn; 100 E. Kellogg Rd.; tel. 647-8000 or (800) 900-4661; $62-90 s, $72-96 d; outdoor pool, jacuzzi, exercise room, business center, kitchenettes available, breakfast buffett, free airport and ferry shuttle, AAA approved

Holiday Inn Express; 4160 Guide Meridian; tel. 671-4800 or (800) 465-4329; $63-85 s, $69-85 d; indoor pool, jacuzzi, continental breakfast, free airport and ferry shuttle, AAA approved

Best Western Heritage Inn; 151 E. McLeod Rd.; tel. 647-1912 or (800) 528-1234; $64-77 s, $69-82 d; outdoor pool, jacuzzi, free airport shuttle, AAA approved

Ramada Inn; 215 N. Samish Way; tel. 734-8830 or (800) 368-4148; $70-110 s or d; outdoor pool, continental breakfast

St., tel. (360) 671-3990 or (800) 487-2032 (recorded message), keeps track of local lodging availability during the summer months. Stop here for brochures on local places, discount coupons, or to check out their books with photographs of local B&Bs.

Hostels

Bellingham has a friendly and cozy 10-bed **AYH Hostel** in historic Fairhaven next to the Rose Garden with dorm spaces ($10 AYH members, $13 nonmembers); sorry, no private rooms. Like most hostels, it is closed during the day (9:30

a.m.-5 p.m.) and open for registration 5-10 p.m. Call (206) 671-1750 for advance reservations (strongly advised May-Sept.). The hostel is open year-round, with no curfew, though the common areas are locked after 11 p.m. They serve an all-you-can-eat pancake breakfast each morning.

Bed and Breakfasts

Several of Bellingham's B&Bs offer classic accommodations. **The Castle,** tel. (360) 676-0974, is one of these, with old-world grandeur and antique-furnished rooms in a century-old hilltop mansion. **North Garden Inn,** tel. (360)

671-7828, (800) 922-6414 (U.S.), or (800) 367-1676 (Canada), is an ornate four-story Queen Anne Victorian home with bay views from its rooms and a Steinway grand piano in the sitting room.

DeCann House B&B, tel. (360) 734-9172, is a Victorian B&B adorned by stained glass, etchings, family heirlooms, and fine views of the San Juan Islands. More fine views from **A Secret Garden B&B,** tel. (360) 671-5327 or (800) 671-5327, a gorgeous turn-of-the-century Victorian home with two guest rooms and a grand piano. **Big Trees B&B,** tel. (360) 647-2850 or (800) 647-2850, is a 1907 craftsman home with a stone fireplace, fir woodwork, and a big veranda. Located three miles east of town, the home sits in the trees overlooking Lake Whatcom.

Above Lake Whatcom and surrounded by tall evergreens is the modern **Schnauzer Crossing,** tel. (360) 734-2808 or (800) 562-2808, where you'll find luxurious and spacious accommodations, very friendly owners, a hot tub, and two standard (not the high-strung miniature version) schnauzers. Recommended.

For something different, **Sudden Valley Resort,** tel. (360) 734-6430 or (800) 734-6903, is located on 1,500 beautiful acres, with condos, an 18-hole golf course, kid's play barn, tennis courts, plus boating, swimming, and fishing on Lake Whatcom.

In a pinch, call **B.A.B's,** tel. (360) 733-8642, a reservation service specializing in B&Bs. Call **Whatcom County B&B Guild,** tel. (360) 676-4560, for details on the finest local B&Bs. See also "Lummi Island and Reservation," "Ferndale," and "Chuckanut Drive" in this chapter for nearby places.

CAMPING

The closest public campsites ($11 for tents, $16 for RVs) are seven miles south of town at **Larrabee State Park.** Call (800) 452-5687 for campsite reservations ($6 extra fee), available up to 11 months ahead of time. See "Chuckanut Drive," above, for details on the park. Additional campsites are approximately 14 miles north in **Birch Bay State Park,** 5105 Helwig Road. Year-round tent sites ($11) and RV hookups ($16) in the trees. Call (360) 371-2800

for information, or (800) 452-5687 for campsite reservations ($6 extra fee), available up to 11 months ahead of time. The privately run **Sudden Valley Resort,** 2145 Lake Whatcom Blvd., tel. (360) 734-6430, has tent and RV sites near Lake Whatcom.

FOOD

Bellingham has an amazing variety of creative eating establishments. Head to Fairhaven and just walk around to see what looks interesting, or check out the places below.

Breakfast

Great breakfasts and lunches at **Old Town Cafe,** an earthy place where the waitress is likely to have a nose ring and the queue of customers is out the door on a weekend morning. The atmosphere is laid-back and noisy; open till 3 p.m. most days.

A completely different dining experience can be found at **The Little Cheerful Cafe,** a minuscule place with a counter plus a handful of tables at 133 E. Holly, tel. (360) 738-8824. The cook has barely enough room to turn around. The food is genuine home-cooked all-American; be ready to wait a long time if you get here after 10 a.m. on weekends.

Lunch

Don't bother with all the standard fast-food grease pits; head instead to **Wok 'n' Roll Restaurant,** right across from the visitors bureau at 1400 King St., tel. (360) 733-0503. This friendly little cafe has American breakfasts and pastries, and very good Chinese lunches. Another place with healthy quick eats at reasonable prices is **Casa Qué Pasa,** 1415 Railroad Ave., tel. (360) 738-8226, where the burritos are the best in town. In Fairhaven, **The Yellow Submarine,** 1200 Harris Ave., tel. (360) 676-7500, puts together very good subs.

Head to **The Bagelry,** 1319 Railroad Ave., tel. (360) 676-5288, for fresh bagels and lox, bagel sandwiches, or other light brunch fare. **Swan Cafe** inside the Community Food Co-Op at 1059 N. State, tel. (360) 734-8158, serves hearty salads and sandwiches. This is a fine place for an inexpensive downtown lunch.

If you're in Fairhaven and want great sandwiches, bagels, quiche, or just a scoop of Ben & Jerry's, drop by **Colophon Cafe** inside Village Books at 1210 11th St., tel. (360) 671-2626.

International
Bel Porto, 1114 Harris Ave., tel. (360) 676-1520 or (800) 203-1520, has Mediterranean cuisine—especially pasta and seafood—and fair prices. Live jazz here on Sunday nights. **Il Fiasco,** 1309 Commercial, tel. (360) 676-9136, is another recommended Italian place. A bit expensive, but outstanding food.

For pizzas, **Stanello's Restaurant,** 1514 12th St. (Fairhaven), tel. (360) 676-1304, is the place to go; in business for more than 20 years. **Cascade Pizza,** 2431 Meridian, tel. (360) 671-0999, is also on local folks' recommended list.

At Fairhaven's **Dos Padres,** 1111 Harris Ave., tel. (360) 733-9900, has an extensive menu of Mexican dishes with a Southwest twist. Dos Padres is locally famous for their margaritas and nachos. Come here for lunch when prices are lower. Another very good Mexican restaurant with more traditional fare is **Gloria's,** 3040 Northwest, tel. (360) 647-1534. Some of the area's best New Mexican-style food can be found at **Pepper Sisters,** 1055 N. State St., tel. (360) 671-3414.

Get authentic Cantonese cuisine at **Hong Kong Garden Restaurant,** 2527 Meridian, tel. (360) 734-1124. **Taste of India,** 3930 Meridian (across from Bellis Fair Mall), tel. (360) 647-1589, is the place for Indian dinners.

American and Eclectic
Dirty Dan Harris' at 1211 11th St., tel. (360) 676-1011, in the Fairhaven District has prime rib, steaks, and fresh seafood dinners in an 1800s-style saloon. It's named for Daniel Jefferson Harris, a feisty eccentric best known for his bathing habits—or lack thereof—who platted the town's streets, built a dock, and sold lots to the thousands of folks who rolled into Fairhaven in 1883. He made a small fortune in the process.

Get gourmet burgers, steaks, chicken, and fresh seafood at **Bullie's,** 1200 Harris (Fairhaven), tel. (360) 734-2855. A bit on the pricey side. Then head upstairs for a brewski—lots of microbrews available—in Bullie's Beer Emporium. If you aren't looking for the gourmet

variety burger, **Boomer's Drive In,** 310 N. Samish Way, tel. (360) 647-2666, has the best anywhere around.

The Marina, 985 Thomas Glenn Dr., tel. (360) 733-8292, has a terrific harbor view, indoor-outdoor lounge, and reasonably priced meals. You'll find some of the best local fish and chips here.

Cobblestone Cafe, in Fairhaven down a cobblestone path at Harris Ave. and 11th St., is well-known for gourmet steak, poultry, pastas, and seafood. Entrees run around $20. **Blue Water Bistro,** 1215 Cornwall Ave., tel. (360) 733-6762, serves all three meals, plus espresso and fresh baked goods, and has jazz during Sunday brunch.

The Pacific Cafe, downtown at 100 N. Commercial, tel. (360) 647-0800, serves moderately priced "East-meets-West/Northwest" cuisine including steak, seafood, pasta, and teriyaki dishes in a warm atmosphere. Very good.

Espresso
Yes, you can get espresso in Bellingham; your best bet is **Tony's Coffee & Teas,** 1101 Harris Ave. (Fairhaven), tel. (360) 733-6319, where the smell of roasting coffee wafts through the air (and gets a bit too strong at times). They have another one downtown, but this is the real hangout for the long-hair and leather-jacket crowd. Read the newspaper, sample the carrot cake, play a chess game, or just lean back and enjoy the scene. This is as close to Berkeley as you'll get this far north.

Microbreweries and Pubs
Orchard St. Brewery, 709 W. Orchard Dr., tel. (360) 647-1614, opened in 1995 to rave reviews from locals, and it continues to draw the crowds. You might expect great fresh brews—and that you'll get—but the surprisingly sophisticated restaurant goes far beyond pub-grub fare, with filet mignon, king salmon, spot prawns, stone-oven pizzas, and other superb dishes. Reasonable prices, too. Open for lunch and dinner; don't miss this place. Other local brewpubs include **Mount Baker Brewing Co.,** 1408 Cornwall Ave., tel. (360) 671-2031, with live in-house brews on tap, an upstairs dance floor with live entertainment, and a downstairs lounge with a pool table and darts. **Boundary Bay Brewing Co.,** 1107 Railroad Ave., tel. (360) 647-5593,

features a large restaurant and four styles of beer on tap.

Located in Fairhaven downstairs at 1212 10th St., **Anchor's Ale House,** tel. (360) 647-7002, is an English-style pub with an antique oak bar, 10 microbrews on tap, a dart board, and absolutely no smoking. The menu includes deep-dish pizza by the slice, vegetarian specials, and British pasties (decidedly not vegetarian). At **Quarterback Pub & Eatery,** in Sehome Village Mall, tel. (360) 647-8132, you can watch a game on the big-screen TV while munching on pub fare.

Grocers and Bakeries

Bellingham's **Community Food Co-Op,** 1059 N. State, tel. (360) 734-8158, is a spacious natural foods market; nonmembers pay more, or join for just $4 if you're buying in quantity. Check out the **Swan Cafe** for a nutritious lunch or light dinner.

Haggen Foods has two large gourmet markets at 210 36th, tel. (360) 676-1996, and 2814 Meridian, tel. (360) 671-3300, with fine delis offering Chinese food, pizza by the slice, sandwiches, and a salad bar. A good deal for fast and tasty meals.

The **Bellingham Farmers Market** is held in the parking lot at Chestnut St. and Railroad Ave. from early April to late October. It runs Saturday 10 a.m.-3 p.m.

ARTS AND ENTERTAINMENT

The Arts

The **Whatcom Museum of History and Art** (see "Sights and Tours," above) is recognized as one of the finest regional museums on the West Coast with changing exhibits of regional history and contemporary art, plus occasional evening lectures and performances.

Western Washington University hosts a number of musical and theatrical groups in its auditorium, and the campus features 22 outdoor sculptures from the whimsical to the monumental. The **Performing Arts Center** series on campus features local productions as well as internationally known performing companies Oct.-May.

The historic **Mt. Baker Theatre**—built in 1927 as a vaudeville and movie palace—hosts the **Whatcom Symphony Orchestra,** plus other

musical and theatrical performances at 106 N. Commercial. Don't miss the weekly double features—shown on the largest screen in the Northwest—for just $3. For ticket information call (360) 734-6080. The two-week-long **Bellingham Festival of Music** each August brings world-class classical and jazz musicians to town, and the **Brown Bag Music Series** features concerts on the public library lawn each Friday mid-June to mid-August; tel. (360) 676-6985.

Staffed and performed entirely by local volunteers, the **Bellingham Theatre Guild** produces five plays a year from fall to spring in the old Congregational Church building at 1600 H St.; for ticket information call (360) 733-1811. More plays are presented Nov.-May in the **Theatre Arts** series at Western Washington University; call (360) 650-6146 for tickets.

Galleries

At 1603 N. State, **Hamann's Gallery,** tel. (360) 733-8898, features original artwork, etchings, and limited-edition prints. **The Elements Gallery,** 304 W. Champion St., tel. (360) 734-0308, is a cooperative fine arts gallery with paintings, stained glass, pottery, jewelry, and other pieces. **Chuckanut Bay Gallery,** 700 Chuckanut Dr., tel. (360) 734-4885, is also of note, featuring the works of potter Don Salisbury. Other galleries are found in Fairhaven, see "Sights" above for details.

Nightlife

Speedy O'Tubbs, 11th and Harris in Fairhaven, tel. (360) 734-1539, has a variety of live music—including rock, reggae, and blues. The place is said to have a resident ghost, who has appeared to a number of people between 3 and 4 a.m. in the foyer. Reputedly a woman, this spirit may have once been joined to the skeleton they found in a wall during reconstruction.

For live jazz, rock, or reggae, try **Bellingham Bay Brewing Co.,** 1226 N. State St., tel. (360) 734-1881; **Mount Baker Brewing Co.,** 1408 Cornwall Ave., tel. (360) 671-2031; **Beech House Pub,** 113 E. Magnolia, tel. (360) 733-3331; or **Black Angus Lounge,** 165 Samish Way, tel. (360) 734-7600. **Bel Porto,** 1114 Harris Ave., tel. (360) 676-1520, has jazz on Sunday nights. **Harry O's,** at Best Western Lakeway Inn, has piano entertainment nightly.

Out near Lake Whatcom, the **Sudden Valley Lounge,** 100 Sudden Valley, tel. (360) 734-6430, has rock music on the weekends. **Three B Tavern,** 1226 N. State St., tel. (360) 734-1881, has contemporary rock bands on Friday and Saturday nights. **Elephant & Castle Pub & Restaurant,** at Bellis Fair Mall, tel. (360) 671-4545, has a comedy night, dancing, and karaoke.

EVENTS

Bellingham's **Ski to Sea Race,** held Memorial Day weekend, tests the physical endurance and athletic skills of its participants over an 85-mile course that includes a downhill ski leg, running, bicycling, canoeing down the Nooksack River, and sailing across Bellingham Bay to the finish in the Fairhaven District. In existence for over 75 years, the race is the highlight of a weeklong festival that includes parades, a street fair with crafts, live music and dancing, food, and a beer garden on Sunday after the race. For specifics and dates, call (360) 734-1332.

The **Lummi Stommish Water Festival** is an annual mid-June event held at the Lummi Indian Reservation on Gooseberry Point. It includes 11-man war-canoe races, arts and crafts shows, Indian dancing, gambling, and a salmon bake; tel. (360) 734-8180. In late August, Western Washington University is the home of the two-week **Bellingham Festival of Music,** where outstanding classical and jazz musicians perform. Call (360) 676-5997 for ticket info. Around the same time, the **Bellingham Chalk Art Competition and Festival** attracts a wide range of talent, from kids to serious artists. Great fun as everyone gets to draw on the city's sidewalks and not get arrested.

Like other Puget Sound cities, Bellingham sponsors a Christmas **Lighted Boat Parade** in Bellingham Bay in early December; tel. (360) 733-7390.

SHOPPING

Bellingham's 900,000-square-foot regional shopping mall, **Bellis Fair** (I-5 exit 256B), was built mainly for Canadian shoppers who save money by buying in Bellingham rather than Vancouver (but the lower Canadian dollar has hurt sales in recent years). The mall has five anchor stores—The Bon Marché, Target, Mervyn's, JCPenney, and Sears—in addition to 150 smaller shops, a 14-restaurant food court, and a six-plex theater. Keep going out Meridian St. to enjoy the frenzy of shopping even more; here you'll find all the big discount chain stores, fast-food joints, new motels, and hundreds of B.C. license plates.

Sehome Village, on Samish Way at I-5 exit 252, has stores selling apparel, jewelry, fabrics, candy, and services from hairstyling to tickets for area events. The downtown **Parkade** at Holly and Commercial has covered parking for a number of small shops along Commercial Street. Head to Railroad Ave. for specialty shops and restaurants.

Antiques

Whatcom County has a number of antique shops and malls. In Bellingham proper, **Bellingham Antique Mall,** 202 W. Holly St., tel. (360) 647-1073, has a wide selection of collectibles from 20 dealers. **Bristol Antiques and Books,** 310 W. Holly St., tel. (360) 733-7809, has small collectibles and hundreds of new books on antiques. Several other antique shops are located along W. Holly Street.

INFORMATION AND SERVICES

For maps, brochures, and general information, contact the **Bellingham and Whatcom County Convention and Visitors Bureau,** 904 Potter St. (exit 253 off I-5), tel. (360) 671-3990 or (800) 487-2032 (recording). Open daily 9 a.m.-6 p.m. in the summer, and daily 8:30 a.m.-5:30 p.m. the rest of the year. They keep track of local lodging availability during the summer. A second visitor center can be found inside Bellis Fair Mall; open daily. In the summer, the Bellingham Cruise Terminal (where the Alaska ferry docks) also has an information booth. Open Thursday and Friday only.

For 24-hour emergency care, contact **St. Joseph's Hospital,** 2901 Squalicum Parkway at exit 255, tel. (360) 734-5400.

TRANSPORTATION

By Car
Bellingham is about 85 miles due north of Seattle via I-5. If you're not in a big hurry, get off the highway near Burlington and head north on Hwy. 11, a.k.a. Chuckanut Dr., for some breathtaking views of Puget Sound.

Downtown Bellingham makes up for its relatively small size with odd street intersections that send you off in the opposite direction you intended. It's as if someone laid out a grid, and then took the central (downtown) section and twisted it at a 45-degree angle. Newcomers are guaranteed to get lost at least once.

By Ferry
The **Bellingham Cruise Terminal,** located several blocks downhill from Fairhaven, is where you can catch ferries to the San Juans, Victoria, and Alaska. The terminal has reservation and ticketing booths for the **Alaska Marine Highway,** which provides passenger and vehicle ferry service to Prince Rupert and Southeast Alaska destinations. Alaska ferries usually depart on Friday evenings year-round; call (360) 676-8445 or (800) 642-0066 for details and a schedule. The terminal is open Thursday and Friday each week, in time for Alaska ferry arrivals and departures, and has a restaurant (but you're better off heading to Fairhaven) and gift shop.

Victoria-San Juan Cruises, 355 Harris Ave., tel. (360) 738-8099 or (800) 443-4552, offers ferry service between Bellingham and Victoria from late May to mid-October. You'll sail aboard the *Victoria Star,* a 300-passenger boat; the cost is $42 one-way, $74 roundtrip for adults, or $37 one-way and $21 roundtrip for kids. They also have overnight package tours and a "Triangle Tour" that includes bus transport from Seattle, ferry to Victoria, and a floatplane trip back to Seattle.

San Juan Island Shuttle Express, tel. (360) 671-1137, operates a 49-passenger ferry—the *Squito*—connecting Bellingham with Orcas Island and San Juan Island. Fares are $20 one-way, $33 roundtrip ($27 roundtrip for seniors, students, and kids ages three to 17), daily from late May through September. They also provide three-hour whalewatching cruises at $50 for adults, and $40 for kids under 12.

See "Sports and Recreation" above for information on local cruises and boat charters.

By Air
Bellingham International Airport has service to Seattle and other West Coast cities via **Horizon Air** and **United Air Express.** Many Canadians use the airport because they can get more convenient flights to some U.S. destinations, cheaper tickets, and the parking, $1 a day, is a big savings, too. **West Isle Air,** tel. (360) 671-8463 or (800) 874-4434, has scheduled service to the San Juan Islands, plus charter flights and flightseeing trips.

The Alaska Marine Highway ferry system docks its ships in Bellingham.

SEATTLE/KING COUNTY CONVENTION AND VISITORS BUREAU

If you're flying into Sea-Tac Airport and can't make good connections, **Airporter Shuttle** offers nine trips daily for $29 one-way, $52 roundtrip, tel. (360) 733-3600 or (800) 235-5247. **Quick Shuttle,** tel. (800) 665-2122, has shuttle service to Vancouver and Seattle destinations, including Sea-Tac.

By Bus

Locally, **Whatcom Transit,** tel. (360) 676-7433, provides bus service Mon.-Sat. to Bellingham, Ferndale, Sudden Valley, Lynden, Blaine, and the Lummi Indian Reservation. Fares are just

25 cents. They also offer a free Meridian shuttle in the Bellis Fair Mall area.

Both **Greyhound,** tel. (360) 733-5251 or (800) 231-2222, and **Northwestern Trailways,** tel. (800) 366-3830, provide nationwide bus connections from the Amtrak depot in Fairhaven.

By Train

Amtrak, tel. (800) 872-7245, provides daily train connections north to Vancouver, B.C., and south to Mount Vernon, Everett, Edmonds, and Seattle aboard the Mt. Baker International. Trains stop at the new Fairhaven depot, which opened in 1995.

NORTH TO CANADA

LUMMI ISLAND AND RESERVATION

Lummi (pronounced "LUM-ee," as in "tummy") is only an eight-minute ferry ride from the mainland, but since it is some distance from the other islands (the San Juans), it doesn't get a lot of attention or heavy automobile traffic. The peanut-shaped island's southern end is a steeply wooded mountain that slopes down abruptly to more or less level land on the north end, which is where nearly all the residents live. Most of the island is private property with no public access, but you can ride the roads to a few public areas.

Lummi Indians were the first inhabitants of the island, but they abandoned it after northern Indians raided their village to capture slaves. By the time the first Anglos arrived in the 1870s, the Lummi had moved to the mainland. Today 3,100 people live in scattered homes on the 13,000-acre Lummi Reservation at Gooseberry Point. This is where the ferry terminal and Lummi Tribal offices are located, along with the **Lummi Casino,** tel. (360) 758-7559 or (800) 776-1337, where gamblers can play blackjack, pai gow, poker, or bingo. There's also an inexpensive restaurant on the premises, but no alcohol. Open 24 hours a day.

Touring the Island

Lummi is a quiet island, home primarily to weekenders and a few salmon fishermen, some of whom fish with reef-nets in the style of the original Indians. This ingenious way of fishing is

unique to this area, and the state of Washington issues only about 50 commercial fishing licenses. You can see the reef boats on the western shore along Legoe Bay. Basically, two reef boats, which aren't much more than small barges, are anchored side by side over a reef where salmon are known to swim during their migration from the Pacific Ocean and between the islands on their way back to the Fraser River in British Columbia. The boats have a net suspended between them that directs the salmon into the end, and fishermen watch from a tower to tell when to close the nets, trapping the fish.

Lummi Island has a church, school, library, grocery store, espresso joint, post office, and community hall. It has no taverns, gas stations, or motels, but it does have several nice B&Bs.

Accommodations

Lummi Island is blessed with several terrific B&Bs. Located on the west side of the island at 2579 W. Shore Dr., **The Willows Inn,** tel. (360) 758-2620, has B&B accommodations for $110 s or d in seven guest rooms within a 1910 home. They also have a two-bedroom guest house for $145 d, and a honeymoon cottage for $145 d. All include a full three-course breakfast, private baths, and a jacuzzi. The honeymoon cottage provides additional privacy and a magnificent view of the islands. Dinners by advance reservation.

Located on a 21-acre spread, **West Shore Farm B&B,** 2781 West Shore Dr., tel. (360) 758-2600, offers accommodations in a unique octagonal home with sweeping Georgia Strait views. The two guest rooms with private baths are $80 s or $90 d, including a full breakfast, often made with fresh vegetables and herbs from the kitchen garden. Kids are welcome, but call for specifics. Dinners are available by reservation.

Sunnyhill B&B, 4080 Sunny Hill Lane, tel. (360) 758-2927, has an upstairs apartment with a private deck overlooking Rosario Straits and the San Juan Islands, and a kitchen stocked for a full make-it-yourself breakfast. Rates are $97 s or d for the first night, $75 s or d for two nights or more; kids welcome.

Artworks Gallery B&B, 2241 Tuttle Lane, tel. (360) 758-7668, is a one-bedroom apartment on the second floor with a kitchen and bath. Rates are $110 s or d (less for two nights or more); no kids.

Campgrounds and Recreation
The Washington Department of Natural Resources maintains a small kayak-accessible campground on the east side near the south end of the island. This is the only place on Lummi Island where you can camp. For details, see *North Puget Sound Afoot & Afloat,* by Marge and Ted Mueller (Seattle: The Mountaineers).

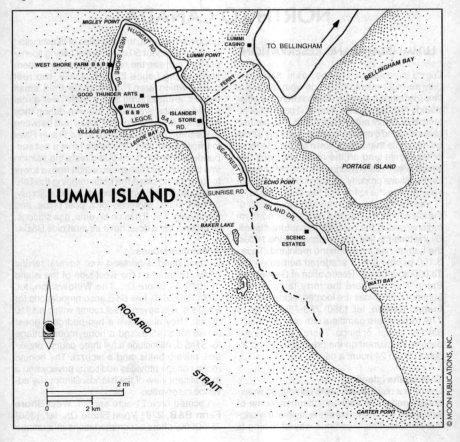

Food and Shopping

Just south of the ferry dock, the **Islander Store** tel. (360) 758-2190, has a deli, beer, pop, ice cream, and other necessities of life; open daily. A great place to stop for fresh-baked breads and pastries, or to sit down to a light meal or coffee with the locals. **Java the Hut,** tel. (360) 758-2509, is a mile south of the ferry (turn left), and offers espresso coffee, bagels, pastries, chili, quiche, and soups.

Buy fresh produce, flowers, and baked goods at the **Lummi Island Farmers Market,** held on summer Saturday 10:30 a.m.-12:30 p.m. in front of the Beach Store Cafe (currently closed, but it may reopen).

Good Thunder Arts, on Centerview Rd., tel. (360) 758-7121, has handcrafted pottery and other art work. Fresh shrimp, crab, and scallops are available at **Leo's Live Seafoods,** on Legoe Bay Rd., tel. (360) 758-7318.

Events

The **Lummi Stommish Water Festival** in mid-June is held on the Lummi Indian Reservation and features competitive war-canoe races over a five-mile course, with up to 11 people in a canoe (these attract participants from many other tribes). Other activities include arts and crafts sales, Indian dancing, a salmon bake, and a complex form of Indian gambling called slahal. For details, call the tribal office at (360) 734-8180.

Transportation

From I-5, go west on Slater Road to Haxton Way on the Lummi Indian Reservation and follow it to the **ferry landing.** The county-owned ferry makes eight-minute trips back and forth from Gooseberry Point on the mainland to Lummi Island every hour from 6 a.m. to midnight (more frequently during the commute period). Cost is $2 for cars, $1 for passengers (free for kids). For information call (360) 676-6730.

Because Lummi is nearly all in private hands, access is quite limited.
You can ride bikes or cars on the island's roads, but the undeveloped mountainous southern end of the island is off limits. The only readily accessible public beach is just north of the ferry dock. Rent bikes from **Island Rentals,** tel. (360) 758-2907, next to the Islander Store.

FERNDALE

Ferndale (pop. 5,700) sits on the west side of the Nooksack River north of Bellingham. High bluffs over the river provide fine views of the rich farmland, the Cascades, and Mt. Baker. In addition to agriculture, the town is supported by Arco and Tosco oil refineries, plus an enormous Intalco aluminum reduction plant, which employs more than 1,100 people. The bauxite ore arrives by ship from Australia and is processed into aluminum ingots for shipment to other mills. Aluminum production uses prodigious amounts of electricity (supplied by the Columbia River dams) since the anodes must be kept at 2,100° F for two weeks(!).

Parks

Pioneer Park, two blocks south of Main on 1st Ave., contains an extraordinary collection of a dozen hand-hewn log buildings. Many of these date from the late 19th century and were made with massive cedar logs—evidence of the trees that once stood here. This is one of the finest collections of log structures in Washington. Several of the cabins contain historical exhibits, including everything from postal relics to historical photos and a Linotype machine. The two-story Shields house, built in 1885, is the most elaborate. The cabins were moved here from the surrounding country by the Old Settlers Association, who recognized their value even in the 1930s. Tours of the buildings are available daily noon-6 p.m. May-September.

Head south from town on Hovander Dr. to **Hovander Homestead Park** where you'll find a restored turn-of-the-century Victorian home and farm on the Nooksack River, a big red barn, milk house, treehouse, children's petting zoo, flower gardens (including 30 varieties of dahlias), fruit orchard, hayfields, and antique farm equipment. Bring your picnic basket for a lunch along the river. Now a National Historic site, the park is open daily, but the homestead is open only on summer weekends. Admission is $3 per car. Tours are available in the summer Thurs.-Sun. 12:30-4:30 p.m.; call (360) 384-3444 for details.

Take a walk around a bog and interpretive displays at **Tennant Lake Natural History In-**

terpretive Center, at the end of Nielsen Rd. (just south of the turnoff to Hovander Homestead), tel. (360) 384-3444. The 200-acre park is a former homestead that has been adapted as an interpretive center for Tennant Lake, with a system of trails, a half-mile boardwalk along the marsh, and a birdwatching tower. One of the park's highlights is the **Fragrance Garden,** designed so that people who are visually impaired, and anyone else, can experience more than 60 varieties of plants by scent.

Lake Terrell Wildlife Preserve, four miles west of Ferndale, tel. (360) 384-4723, covers 11,000 acres and is operated by the state. It has restrooms, picnic areas, trails, fishing, and three boat launches.

Accommodations
The **Slater Heritage House B&B,** 1371 W. Axton, tel. (360) 384-4273 or (800) 815-4273, has beautifully landscaped grounds and four guest rooms with private baths in a restored 1904 Victorian home. Lodging, including a jacuzzi and full breakfast, is $60-85 s or d. Children welcome.

Scottish Lodge Motel, 5671 Riverside Dr., tel. (360) 384-4040, has an outdoor pool and rooms for $33-35 s or $38 d.

Campgrounds
Public campsites ($11) and RV hookups ($16) are just a few miles northwest of Ferndale at Birch Bay State Park (see "Birch Bay," below). Call (800) 452-5687 for campsite reservations ($6 extra fee), available up to 11 months ahead of time. The privately run **Ferndale Campground and RV Park,** 6335 Portal Way, tel. (360) 384-2622, has full hookups, showers, and laundry facilities.

Food
Sherry's Grill, 2012 Main St., tel. (360) 384-5404, serves breakfast all day, plus hamburgers and other all-American meals. No smoking. Also popular with locals are **Cedar's Cafe,** 2038 Main St., tel. (360) 384-1848, and **Ferndale Bakery,** 5686 3rd Ave., tel. (360) 384-1554. Eat authentic Mexican food at **Chihuahua,** 5694 3rd Ave., tel. (360) 384-5820.

Dirty Dan's Ferndale, 2254 Douglas Dr., tel. (360) 384-5262, is run by the same folks who have the popular Bellingham eatery (see

"Bellingham" for the lowdown on the name). They offer a similar menu featuring prime rib, steaks, and fresh seafood.

Events
Ferndale has several of the county's best festivals. The **Scottish Highland Games** take place in early June, with bagpipe music, Highland dancing, and the caper toss. In mid-July, the **International Folk Dance Festival** arrives at the park, with dancers of many nationalities, plus an arts and crafts fair, food, and music. Call (360) 384-3444 for details on these very popular events, both of which are held in Hovander Homestead Park. Then comes the **Whatcom County Old Settlers Picnic** at Pioneer Park on the last weekend of July. More than an old-timers picnic, this century-old festival includes country music, dancing, parades, and a carnival; call (360) 384-1866 for more info.

Information and Services
The **Ferndale Chamber of Commerce,** 5640 Riverside Dr., tel. (360) 384-3042, is the place to go for brochures and descriptions of local cycling or driving tours; open daily 9 a.m.-5 p.m. Play golf at **Riverside Golf Club,** 5799 Riverside Dr., tel. (360) 384-4116.

LYNDEN

Lynden (pop. 6,500) is the sort of town where dense pots of flowers hang from store eaves, kids ride bikes down wide, shady streets, and the big events are parades and old-time threshing bees. Ignore Mt. Baker and the Cascade Range east of town and it's easy to imagine yourself in a small Dutch town. Originally settled by people from Holland, Lynden still counts half its residents as from the "Old Country." The flat, green pastures surrounding town—some are just two blocks from town center—are dotted with dairy cattle so fat they look as if they've overindulged in their own products. Thousands of dairy cows, chickens, berries, hops, potatoes, and—borrowing from the town's Dutch heritage—bulbs are all raised or grown in this fertile agricultural region. (All this agriculture means, of course, that the odor of manure sometimes wafts through downtown.)

Little Holland

Add Lynden to the growing list of small towns in Washington that attract tourists by redecorating themselves to reflect an ethnic or historical heritage. Since most of its settlers were dairy farmers from The Netherlands, Lynden turned itself into a Dutch treat for people driving on Hwy. 539 between Bellingham, 12 miles south, and British Columbia, three miles north.

Several downtown buildings have been outfitted with Dutch false fronts painted caramel, chocolate, cheese-yellow, or sea blue. Front Street, the main drag, is dominated by a four-story, 72-foot-tall windmill that is part of the Dutch Village Mall, which also has a 150-foot indoor "canal," a theatre, and shops along a simulated Dutch cobblestone street. Many of these are cloyingly sweet, with places selling fudge, books, cards, kitchenware, knickknacks, and heart-shaped doormats.

The Dutch theme includes provincial flags flapping in the breeze, Dutch food and gifts (yes, wooden shoes) sold in stores, and costumed clerks on special holidays such as Holland Days (the first weekend in May). Residents in costumes sweep the immaculate streets that are normally clean anyway—just like in Holland.

Lynden is very conservative and religious; the Christian rest home and school are two of the largest local employers. The town has an unofficial ban on Sunday business, and a town ordinance prohibits dancing wherever drinks are sold—leading to Saturday-night 12-mile pilgrimages to Bellingham's hot spots. Be especially careful while driving busy Hwy. 539 on weekends.

Lynden Pioneer Museum

Lynden is home to one of the finest small museums in Washington, the Lynden Pioneer Museum at 217 W. Front St., tel. (360) 354-3675. On the main floor is a re-created turn-of-the-century Lynden town and a collection of Indian artifacts from the Queen Charlotte Islands. The basement is a must-see, centering around the forty or so buggies, wagons, sleighs, carts, and other horse-drawn vehicles that were donated by Fred K. Polinder. Also here are antique tractors and farm machinery, and a big antique car and truck collection. The museum is open Mon.-Sat. 10 a.m.-4 p.m.; $2 for adults, $1 for seniors or students.

Berthusen Park

This gorgeous city park is located northwest of town; get here by heading a mile west of town to Guide Meridian (Hwy. 539), then north to W. Main Road. Follow the signs to the park, located in a tall stand of old-growth Douglas fir and western red cedar. The park has picnicking, camping, a small fishing stream, and walking trails, but it is best known for its enormous barn (built in 1913) that contains old boats, sleds, and other memorabilia; outside are antique steam-powered tractors, along with the farming equipment they pulled or operated.

Accommodations

Spend a night in a windmill at the **Dutch Village Inn**, 655 Front St., tel. (360) 354-4440. Six hotel rooms (three are in the windmill and two have hot tubs) feature Dutch furnishings, antiques, and Dutch-style breakfast for $65-95 s or d. Higher-priced rooms have private hot tubs.

The clean and modern **Windmill Inn Motel**, 8022 Guide Meridian, tel. (360) 354-3424, has rooms for $37 s, $47 d. Hook up RVs outside for $15.

Century House B&B, 401 South B.C. Ave. (13th St.), tel. (360) 354-2439, has three elegant guest rooms with private or shared baths, a piano, fireplace, bay windows, and chandeliers in an 1888 home, plus a full breakfast. Rates are $60-80 s or d.

Three miles north of the little town of Everson (pop. 1,700), **Wilkins Farm B&B,** 4165 S. Pass Rd., tel. (360) 966-7616, may have the least expensive B&B accommodations in the state: just $22 s or $35 d in a 120-year-old farmhouse surrounded by cattle pastures. Three guest rooms share a bath, and a full breakfast is served. Kids okay, too.

Campgrounds

Berthusen Park, about a mile north on Guide Meridian, has shady campsites under the tall Douglas fir trees; $9 tents, $13 RVs. RV hookups are available at **Lynden KOA Kampground,** 8717 Line Rd. (three miles east of Lynden), tel. (360) 354-4772, and **Hidden Village RV Park,** 7062 Guide Meridian, tel. (360) 398-1041 or (800) 843-8606. In addition, the **Northwest Washington Fairgrounds** are open to RV parking with full hookups during the off-season; call (360) 354-4111 for details.

Food

You'll find Dutch specialties, soups, and a buffet, at **Dutch Mothers Restaurant,** 405 Front St., tel. (360) 354-2174. **Lynden Dutch Bakery,** tel. (360) 354-3911, is a good place for sandwiches and pastries, including excellent Dutch apple pie.

Not everything is from Holland in Lynden. **Syro's** has Greek and Italian fare, while **El Toreador,** 1710 Front St., tel. (360) 354-4478, serves authentic Mexican meals.

Events

The Queen Juliana Theatre in Dutch Village Mall is home to productions by the Lynden Performing Arts Guild Oct.-May. Call (360) 354-4425 for upcoming plays.

Holland Days, held the first weekend of May, brings wooden shoe races, Klompen dancing, and costumed Lyndenites scrubbing down Front Street. A parade and draft horse plowing show are the highlights of Lynden's **Farmer's Day Parade,** held the first weekend of June. In early August, an old-time **Threshing Bee** attracts visitors to view the puffing steam engines and old farm equipment at nearby Berthusen Park. Mid-August brings the largest event: more than 240,000 people come to the **Northwest Washington Fair,** with farm animal exhibits (from dog shows to best-decorated swine events), carnival rides, a tractor pull, demolition derby, and musical entertainers. The **Dutch Sinterklaas Celebration** in early December is a Christmas parade with lighted farm equipment, antique vehicles, horses, and floats, plus Sinterklaas (Santa Claus) atop a white horse.

Information and Services

The **Lynden Chamber of Commerce,** tel. (360) 354-5995, is upstairs in the back of the Delftst Mall on Front St.; open Mon.-Fri. 9 a.m.-4:30 p.m. Lynden's telephone **area code** is 360.

SUMAS

The bustling border town of Sumas (SOO-mass) is right on Hwy. 9 and is one of the main crossing points in Washington. You'll find plenty of cheap gas stations that Canadians can sneak across the border to for a tankful, a couple of gal-lons of milk, and a pull-tab or two from the mini-mart—the border crossing is open 24 hours a day. Also here are big grocers and duty-free shops.

The name Sumas comes from the Cowichan Indian word, "Sm-mess," meaning land without trees—an obvious reference to the surrounding prairie country.

Food, Lodging, and Entertainment

Stay at the modern **Sumas Mountain Village,** 819 Cherry St., tel. (360) 988-4483, for $60-110 s or d. Several of the rooms have hot tubs, and two have stone fireplaces. Lodging includes a $5 credit at the downstairs restaurant. The food is quality all-American, including homemade pies. Mexican meals can be found at **El Nopal Dos,** 120 Front St., tel. (360) 988-0305. More lodging at **BB Border Inn Motel,** 121 Cleveland, tel. (360) 988-5800, where rooms are $35 s and $40 d. **J.J. Fryes,** 625 Cherry St., tel. (360) 988-3797, has a DJ or rock bands on weekends.

Events and Information

Sumas Community Days in late June has a bed race (part of which is down a local creek), a car show, and fireworks. The **Sumas Junior Rodeo** on Labor Day weekend in September features bucking bulls at a "bullarama." Call the Sumas City Hall, tel. (360) 988-5711, for other local information.

BIRCH BAY

Birch Bay (pop. 2,000) is one of western Washington's oldest resort towns, the kind of place families go for generations, always renting the same cabin. The "Bay Area" has managed to keep its calm in spite of numerous housing and condominium developments going on nearby, and its only street still is designed for pedestrians instead of cars. Most of the cabins along the main street are modest beach cabins, and many are owned by Canadians; they constitute half the population here on a summer day.

The moon-shaped bay is one of the most shallow in the area, and during the summer the water heats up enough for comfortable swimming. It's said to be the warmest and safest

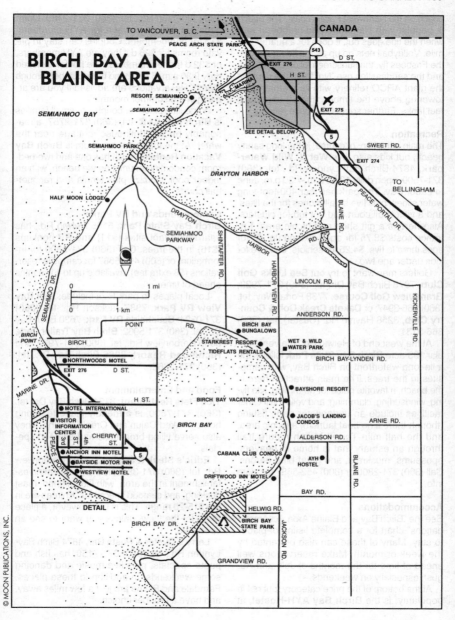

BIRCH BAY AND BLAINE AREA

CANADA

TO VANCOUVER, B.C.

PEACE ARCH STATE PARK

EXIT 276

D ST.

H ST.

543

MARINA

EXIT 275

SEE DETAIL BELOW

RESORT SEMIAHMOO

SEMIAHMOO SPIT

Semiahmoo Bay

SEMIAHMOO PARK

SWEET RD.

EXIT 274

5

DRAYTON HARBOR

TO BELLINGHAM

PEACE PORTAL DR.

HALF MOON LODGE

SEMIAHMOO PARKWAY

SEMIAHMOO DR.

DRAYTON HARBOR RD.

SHINTAFFER RD.

0   1 mi

0   1 km

MOON

LINCOLN RD.

HARBOR VIEW RD.

KICKERVILLE RD.

BLAINE RD.

BIRCH POINT

POINT RD.

BIRCH BAY BUNGALOWS

ANDERSON RD.

STARKREST RESORT

TIDEFLATS RENTALS

WET & WILD WATER PARK

BIRCH BAY-LYNDEN RD.

BIRCH BAY VACATION RENTALS

BAYSHORE RESORT

JACOB'S LANDING CONDOS

ARNIE RD.

BIRCH BAY

ALDERSON RD.

CABANA CLUB CONDOS

AYH HOSTEL

DRIFTWOOD INN MOTEL

BAY RD.

BIRCH BAY DR.

HELWIG RD.

BIRCH BAY STATE PARK

JACKSON RD.

GRANDVIEW RD.

DETAIL

NORTHWOODS MOTEL

EXIT 276

D ST.

MARINE DR.

H ST.

MOTEL INTERNATIONAL

VISITOR INFORMATION CENTER

3rd ST.

4th ST.

CHERRY ST.

5

PEACE PORTAL DR.

ANCHOR INN MOTEL

BAYSIDE MOTOR INN

WESTVIEW MOTEL

© MOON PUBLICATIONS, INC.

beach on the Northwest Pacific coast. The beach is popular with clammers and crabbers, and when the tide goes out, it goes for a quarter of a mile. Volleyball nets go up as the tide goes out, the Frisbees fly, the sunscreen lotion comes out, and the sandcastles rise. Not far to the south is the giant ARCO refinery with its eternal flame towering above the timber, and 50 enormous fuel tanks. Farther south is a Tosco refinery.

Recreation
The main attraction, of course, is the long sandy beach, but kids also love **Wet N' Wild Waterpark,** 4874 Birch Bay-Lynden Rd., tel. (360) 371-7500; open daily 10:30 a.m.-7:30 p.m. June to Labor Day. The park has four 400-foot-long water slides, plus five smaller ones for the tikes, and a volleyball court and hot tub for oldsters. Also here is a gift shop and picnic area. Entrance costs $8.75 for ages six and up, $5 for ages three to five, $4.25 for seniors, and free for kids under age two.

Golfers may want to try out **Sea Links Golf Club,** 7878 Birch Bay Dr., tel. (360) 371-7933; **Grandview Golf Course,** 7738 Portal Way, tel. (360) 366-3947; or **Dakota Creek Golf & Country Club,** 3258 Haynie Rd. (Custer), tel. (360) 366-3131.

At the west end of Helwig Rd., the very popular 193-acre **Birch Bay State Park** follows the mile-long waterfront on Birch Bay, with campsites in the trees. The main attraction here is the beach, a favorite place for swimming, kite flying, windsurfing, clamming, and volleyball. Other facilities include an underwater park, fishing (though there's no boat launch), a picnic area, and the half-mile Terrell Marsh nature trail through an estuary that is home to beavers, opossums, muskrats, and great blue herons. Call (360) 371-2800 or (800) 452-5687 for more info.

Accommodations
See the "Birch Bay and Blaine Area Accommodations" chart for a complete listing of places to stay. Many of these can also be rented by the week or month. Make reservations well ahead of time for the months of July and August, especially on weekends.

At the bottom of the price category, but not in popularity, is the **Birch Bay AYH-Hostel,** at 4639 Alderson Rd., tel. (360) 371-2180. Dorm beds are $10 per person for AYH members, $13 for nonmembers. Couples can stay in private rooms for $26 d if they are AYH members, or $32 d for nonmembers. The hostel is closed daily 9:30 a.m.-5 p.m., and from October through March. Reservations are advised if you are arriving in the summer months.

A fine little place for couples or small families is **Birch Bay B&B,** tel. (360) 371-2757, a reasonably priced "dollhouse" cottage near the water. At the top of the spectrum is **Birch Bay Vacation Rentals,** which has one and two-bedroom condominium units on the beach, with an indoor pool, jacuzzi, plus tennis and racquetball courts.

Campgrounds and RV Parks
Birch Bay State Park, 5105 Helwig Rd., has year-round tent sites ($11) and RV hookups ($16) in the trees. Call (360) 371-2800 for information, or (800) 452-5687 for campsite reservations ($6 extra fee), available up to 11 months ahead of time.

Local places to park RVs include: **Ball Bay View RV Park,** 7387 Jackson Rd., tel. (360) 371-0334; **Beachside RV Park,** 7630 Birch Bay Dr., tel. (360) 371-5962; **Birch Bay Trailer Park,** 8080 Harborview Rd., tel. (360) 371-7922; and **Richmond Resort,** 8086 Birch Bay Dr., tel. (360) 371-2262.

Food and Entertainment
Tide Flats Restaurant, 8124 Birch Bay Dr., tel. (360) 371-7800, is a friendly place featuring home-cooked Cajun and Creole cuisine. They also serve filling breakfasts and seafood specials.

Edric's Steak & Seafood, 8394 Harborview Rd., tel. (360) 371-3838, is the finest eating establishment in the area, with filet mignon, roast duckling, and seafood specialties. Entrees are in the $15-20 range. This is not, however, a place to go for the view, unless you want to see an open field.

Larry's Oyster & Pasta Bar, 4874 Birch Bay-Lynden Rd., tel. (360) 371-7150, has fish and pasta specials, plus live music and dancing some weekends. In addition to these places, Ferndale and Blaine are just a few miles away, and have a broader choice.

BIRCH BAY AND
BLAINE AREA ACCOMMODATIONS

Accommodations are arranged from least to most expensive for each town. Rates may be lower during the winter months. The area code is 360.

BIRCH BAY

Birch Bay AYH Hostel; 4639 Alderson Rd.; tel. 371-2180; dorm rooms: $10 pp for AYH members, $13 pp for nonmembers; private rooms: $26 d for AYH members, $32 d for non-members; open April-Sept. only, full kitchen, local calls 25 cents

Driftwood Inn Motel; 7394 Birch Bay Dr.; tel. 371-2620; $48-75 s or d; motel units, apartments, or rustic cottages, outdoor pool, beach access, kitchenettes available, canoe rentals, three-night minimum stay

Bayshore Resort; 7930 Birch Bay Dr.; tel. 371-7667; $63 for up to five; two-bedroom cottages, kitchenettes

Landlubber Cottages; 8036 Birch Bay Dr.; tel. 371-7200; $75 s or d; two older cabins, kitchenette

Birch Bay B&B; 8068 Birch Bay Dr.; tel. 371-2757; $75 for up to four; cute cottage with patio, kitchen, tandem bike, continental breakfast, friendly owners, available July and August only, kids welcome

Cabana Club Condos; 7503 Birch Bay Dr.; tel. 371-2511; $80-110 for 4-8 people in condos, $400-530/week; three-night minimum stay, fireplaces, kitchens, outdoor pool, jacuzzi, sauna

Birch Bay Vacation Rentals; 7824 Birch Bay Dr.; tel. 371-7633 or (800) 382-1199; $80-175 s or d; indoor pool, jacuzzi, racquetball courts, tennis courts, two-night minimum stay

Tideflats Rentals; 8124 Birch Bay Dr.; tel. 371-7800; $110-150 s or d; attractive studios, one- and two-bedroom units, full kitchens

Starcrest Resort Cabins; 4797 Cottonwood St.; tel. 371-7899; $210-250/week; one and two-bedroom cottages, kitchenettes

Birch Bay Bungalows; 8226 Birch Bay Dr.; tel. 371-2851; $400/week for up to six; two-bedroom cottages, private beach, kitchenettes

Jacob's Landing Condominiums; 7806 Birch Bay Dr.; tel. 371-7675 or (800) 382-1199; $510-1000/week; one-, two-, and three-bedroom units, indoor pool, jacuzzi, racquetball and tennis courts, fireplaces, kitchens

BLAINE

Westview Motel; 7080 Peace Portal Dr.; tel. 332-5501; $29-33 s, $33-37 d; kitchenettes available

Motel International; 758 Peace Portal Dr.; tel. 332-8222; $33 s or d

Anchor Inn Motel; 250 Cedar St.; tel. 332-5539; $34-45 s, $36-45 d; kitchenettes available, nice place

Bayside Motor Inn; 340 Alder; tel. 332-5288; $36 s or d; outdoor pool, kitchenette available

Northwoods Motel; 288 D. St.; tel. 332-5603; $37 s, $40 d; newly remodeled, outdoor pool

The Inn at Semiahmoo; 10 miles west of Blaine; tel. 371-2000 or (800) 770-7992; $135-273 s or d; elaborate coastal resort, indoor/outdoor pool, athletic club, sauna, steam room, jacuzzi, racquetball and tennis courts, beach, AAA approved (four diamonds)

Half Moon Lodge; Semiahmoo Dr.; tel. 371-2256; $150 s or d; three-bedroom modern log home, jacuzzi, fireplace, sauna, kitchen, one-week minimum stay June-Aug. ($900)

Events

Birch Bay Discovery Days is the main summer event, with a "clampetition" clamming contest, parade, golf tournament, and arts and crafts show. It's held in mid-July; call (360) 371-0334 for details. For something different, come here on January 1 for the annual **Polar Bear Swim** with other hardy fools.

Information and Transportation

The **Birch Bay Chamber of Commerce,** 7806 Birch Bay Dr., tel. (360) 371-5004, has local information.

Birch Bay is almost to the Canadian Border. From I-5, take exit 266, Grandview, west to road's end at Birch Bay State Park and turn right. Also, take exit 270, the Birch Bay-Lynden Rd. west to Harbor View Rd., and turn south. Harbor View Rd. goes north to Drayton Harbor and Blaine.

BLAINE

Known to most travelers as the town at the international border and the site of the Peace Arch, Blaine (pop. 2,900) faces out onto protected Drayton Harbor. It is just 35 miles from Vancouver, British Columbia. Interstate-5 cuts through town, bringing 70,000 folks a day, and traffic sometimes backs two or three miles; unless you're crossing into Canada, be prepared to turn off I-5 before the main part of Blaine. Traffic is worst on the Dominion Day/Independence Day weekend in July, when it can take you three hours to cross. Not surprisingly, Blaine depends upon all this cross-border traffic, though a small fishing fleet also provides jobs. Many of the town's post office boxes belong to Canadians who use them for business in the States. Blaine has cheap gas, grocery stores, a shopping mall, duty-free shops, five banks, and a couple of pretty good seafood restaurants. For some reason, it also has not just one, but two psychic readers.

Gasoline is considerably cheaper in the U.S. than in Canada, so thousands of Canadians drive across the border to Blaine each day just to fill their tanks. Many continue on to Bellis Fair Mall in Bellingham, although the gap between U.S. and Canadian prices is narrowing. There was a time when the garbage cans at the last rest area before Blaine would be filled to overflowing with old clothes Canadians had worn to the U.S., then discarded when they put on their new clothing to wear across the border and avoid paying duty.

History

The original peoples inhabiting this corner of Washington were the Semiahmoo Indians. Anglo settlers began arriving in the 1850s during the Fraser River gold rush, and the town of Blaine was platted in 1884 by James Cain. He

Peace Arch at the U.S.-Canadian border

ARCHIE SATTERFIELD

named his town for James G. Blaine, the Republican candidate for president that year (he lost to Grover Cleveland), and future Secretary of State. The town grew up on fishing, logging, and cross-border trade and served as a major shipping port for lumber.

Sights

Open for day use only, the 40-acre **Peace Arch State Park** at the Canadian border has beautifully landscaped grounds and gardens surrounding the Peace Arch, a symbol of friendship between the U.S. and Canada that stands with one "foot" in each country. The park was constructed in 1921 by American and Canadian volunteers and funded by Washington and British Columbia schoolchildren, who contributed from one to 10 cents each for the project. A piece of the *Mayflower* along with the Hudson's Bay Company steamer *Beaver* are included in the monument, and the inscription "Children of a Common Mother" dominates the facade. Facilities include a picnic area, playground, and game sanctuary. The floral displays include some 27,000 flowering plants, with rhododendrons and azaleas the stars in late spring, and dahlias the featured attraction in late summer. Get to the Peace Arch by heading north on 2nd St. into the parking lot; they don't like folks stopping at customs to enter the park.

East of town is one of the more vivid statements about the relationship between the U.S. and Canada. As you drive east toward Sumas and Lynden, you can turn north off the main road and follow it until it makes a sharp right turn to the east again. Here you will notice two, two-lane blacktop highways running east and west, side by side, with a ditch separating them. That ditch is the international boundary between Canada and America. That is all the international boundary is for more than 3,000 miles, the longest unprotected boundary in the world. When the boundary goes through forests, a swath is kept cleared by crews from both countries. But in Washington, it is separated from British Columbia by a ditch that any child can toddle across.

Semiahmoo County Park on the 1.5-mile-long Semiahmoo Spit has restored salmon cannery buildings and a gift shop and art gallery, plus a museum that depicts early fishing and cannery operation; open Wed.-Sun. 1-5 p.m.,

March through Labor Day; Wed.-Sun. 1-4 p.m. in the fall; closed mid-December through February. The park itself is open daily year-round. Call (360) 371-5513 for details. The Raven-Salmon Woman Totem Pole stands outside. A paved bike path parallels the road along Semiahmoo Spit.

Accommodations and Campgrounds

See the "Birch Bay and Blaine Area Accommodations" chart for a listing of places to stay. Several motels of questionable quality are not included here, but they might be acceptable if you're on a tight budget. Additional lodging places can be found just across the border in White Rock, British Columbia.

Located at the end of a long sandspit guarding Drayton Harbor, **The Resort Semiahmoo** is a planned community for the elite—don't even think about moving in if you're a commoner. The Inn at Semiahmoo is a part of this massive development with elaborate facilities such as a 300-slip marina, athletic club, indoor/outdoor pool, hot tub, racquetball and tennis courts, steam room, 18-hole golf course designed by Arnold Palmer, restaurants, lounges, and plenty of Puget Sound beachfront. The old buildings from the Alaska Packers Association cannery—in business till 1965—have been restored and developed into a conference center. The entire complex is not my cup of tea; it's one of those places with lots of flash (and cash) but absolutely no soul.

See "Birch Bay" above for nearby public and private campgrounds.

Food and Entertainment

The most popular local restaurant is **Harbor Cafe,** 295 Marine Dr., tel. (360) 332-5176, where you'll find oyster stew, cod fish and chips (big servings; go for the half-order), and clam chowder. Get fresh crab, salmon, and oysters at the friendly **Dakota Fisheries Seafood Market** next door.

The best local burgers are at **Nicki's Restaurant,** 1700 Peace Portal Dr., tel. (360) 332-7779. More burgers and seafood, plus "health-conscious" dinners at **Maritime Inn,** 1830 Peace Portal Dr., tel. (360) 332-3663. They also have excellent prime rib on Friday and Saturday nights.

Out on the end of Semiahmoo Spit, the Inn at Semiahmoo, tel. (360) 371-2000, has a formal restaurant, **Stars,** featuring pricey Northwest cuisine, plus a pair of lesser eateries.

Get decent pizzas and reasonably priced steaks at **Vista Pizza,** 442 Peace Portal Dr., tel. (360) 332-5155. Bob's Tavern, 1434 Peace Portal Dr., tel. (360) 332-6789, has C&W music and line dancing on weekends.

Lots more restaurants (including Thai and Greek places) in the pretty town of White Rock, just across the border. **Clancy's Tea Cosy,** 15223 Pacific Ave. in White Rock, tel. (604) 541-9010, is a fun place to relax with tea and a scone.

Shopping

The **Peace Arch Factory Outlets** are located just off I-5 at exit 270, six miles south of the border. Here you'll find 28 outlet stores open daily, including Levi's, Woolrich, Van Heusen, Bass, Helly-Hansen, and Mikasa.

Events

The annual **Hands Across the Border Peace Arch Celebration,** held at the Peace Arch the second Sunday in June, brings together veterans and boy scouts from the U.S. and Canada to celebrate our friendly relations. The **Skywater Festival** in late June is Blaine's main community event, featuring live music, a beer garden, and other activities. The first Saturday in August is **Windwords Day,** a kite flying festival at Semiahmoo Park.

Information and Services

The **Blaine Visitor Information Center,** 900 Peace Portal Way, tel. (360) 332-4544 or (800) 624-3555, is open summers Mon.-Fri. 9 a.m.-5 p.m., and Sat.-Sun. 9 a.m.-4 p.m.; plus Sunday 10 a.m.-4 p.m., and Mon.-Sat. 9 a.m.-4 p.m. the rest of the year. Blaine's telephone **area code** is 360.

Nelson Air Services, tel. (360) 332-6346, offers scenic flights and air charters from Blaine Municipal Airport.

Crossing into Canada

Citizens of the U.S. crossing the Canadian border generally have little trouble; all you need is a driver's license or birth certificate. Because of Canada's sane gun laws—in sharp contrast to America's anything-goes attitude—you aren't allowed to bring in firearms. Pitted fruits are also prohibited, though they aren't likely to be used as a weapon. If you're planning to make any large purchases, pick up a brochure describing what you can bring back without being charged extra duties. Americans are entitled to refunds on the seven percent GST tax paid in British Columbia; save your receipts.

POINT ROBERTS

Bounded on three sides by water and on the fourth by British Columbia, it's only by political accident that Point Roberts belongs to the United States. Nobody knew this appendix of land dangled below the international boundary when it was drawn at the 49th parallel. Rather than giving it to Canada, as it should have been, the U.S. kept Point Roberts and now everyone is glad. The local population is just 900 year-round, but in the summer months it swells to 4,500 as Vancouverites come down to enjoy summer homes along the beach and the boating from the protected marina.

Most businesses at Point Roberts discount Canadian dollars even though the signs claim prices are "at par." Local bars are the exception; drinks cost the same in greenbacks or the colorful version of dollars. The border itself is open 24 hours a day. You'll find the highway to Point Roberts clogged almost continually by Canadians driving down for cheap gasoline (sold by the liter), booze, cigarettes, and other American goods. Point Roberts also serves as a shipping point for Canadians, who maintain cross-border mailboxes at Point Roberts, as they do in Blaine, Sumas, and other border towns. Several businesses offer UPS and FedEx drop-offs. (By the same token, some American couples arrange to have their children born in Canada because it is cheaper, even for aliens, and the children will have dual citizenship until the age of 18, and access to Canada's almost-free health-care system.) Americans living in Point Roberts year-round like the steady income. It is the best kind of income because it doesn't involve having any infrastructure beyond good roads to bring the Canadians to town.

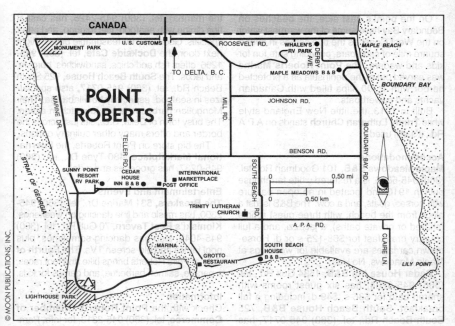

There isn't a lot to see here, but the shoreline is lined with summer homes. You'll find a smattering of restaurants, shops, gas stations, and other businesses, but Point Roberts is primarily a rural parcel of land with a slow-paced country feel.

The Border

Monument Park at the north end of Marine Dr. marks the 49th parallel that separates the U.S. and Canada. Not much here, just a small obelisk (border monument number one) erected in 1861 inscribed with the latitude and longitude at the westernmost point along the border. The road makes a sharp right here so you can't drive across, but Canadian homes are inches from the unguarded border, marked by a shallow ditch.

The border has had incidents that would cause wars between less friendly people. Several years ago a bulldozer owner from one side of the border did some work on the other side, and when he sent the bill, the recipient of his labor refused to pay. So the dozer owner cranked up his dozer, drove it across the border, and proceeded to demolish the work he had done. This upset the client, who fired shots at the dozer, which lumbered back across the border. Authorities on both sides of the border discussed the matter, took it under advisement, and apparently decided that justice had already been done; the incident faded into legal obscurity.

Parks, Recreation, and a Church

Located on the southwest tip of Point Roberts, Whatcom County's **Lighthouse Marine Park** has 22 acres and a half-mile beach, highlighted by a boardwalk with a 30-foot lookout platform. This is a great place to watch the white British Columbia ferries crossing the Strait of Georgia to Vancouver Island, and to look for killer whales (orcas) in the summer. The boat launch here sees a lot of use, with some of the Puget Sound's finest salmon fishing right off the point. The beach is a favorite place to build sandcastles, dig clams, fly kites, or enjoy the sunset. The park is open all year and charges a $3 day-use fee.

On the point's east side, the beaches on Boundary Bay have some of the warmest water on the West Coast as the tide comes in over a square mile of sand bars, providing safe fun for kids and waders. The **Point Roberts Marina** was carved out of the peninsula as a protected harbor with 1,000 slips filled with Canadian yachts and powerboats.

Built in 1913, the little New England-style white **Trinity Lutheran Church** stands on A.P.A Rd.; it's still used.

Accommodations
Maple Meadows B&B, 101 Goodman Rd., tel. (360) 945-5536, is a restored white farmhouse built in 1910 and located in an open pasture with horses, goats, and a cow. The B&B is just a block from the beach, with three guest rooms (shared or private baths), a jacuzzi, and a full country breakfast for $68-125 s or d. Horse-drawn carriages are available for weddings at Maple Meadows. No kids.

Cedar House Inn B&B, 1534 Gulf Rd., tel. (360) 945-0284, has six guest rooms with shared bath for $36 s, $49 d, including a full breakfast. **South Beach House B&B,** 725 South Beach Rd., tel. (360) 945-0717, has seven guest rooms in a large white house along the beach for $47 s or d including a continental breakfast.

Additional lodging places can be found just across the border in Delta, British Columbia.

Campgrounds
Camp at **Lighthouse Marine Park** for $12; no RV hookups; open all year. For camping reservations, call (360) 945-4911. Both **Sunny Point Resort RV Park & Campground,** on Gulf Rd., tel. (360) 945-1986, and **Whalen's RV Park & Campground,** near Maple Beach, tel. (360) 945-2874, have tent and RV spaces.

Food and Shopping
Grotto Restaurant, 713 Simundson Dr. (next to

the marina), tel. (360) 945-2425, has casual fine dining with seafood, filet mignon, and other specials. Good food for reasonable prices. Right next door, the **Dockside Cafe,** tel. (360) 945-1206, offers fish and chips, sandwiches, burgers, and tacos. The **South Beach House,** 725 South Beach Rd., tel. (360) 945-0717, also specializes in seafood, especially bouillabaisse. Their Mongolian barbecue is fun to watch in action. The busy town of Delta, B.C., sits just across the border and offers many other culinary options.

The big store on Point Roberts, the **International Marketplace,** 480 Tyee Dr., tel. (360) 945-0237, has groceries and a deli.

Entertainment and Events
The Breakers, 531 Marine Dr., tel. (360) 945-2300, has music and line dancing on weekends. **Kioniski's Reef Tavern,** 70 Gulf Rd., tel. (360) 945-4042, also has dancing sometimes, plus pool tables and big-screen TVs. The **Fourth of July** at Point Roberts brings bike and foot races, a parade, salmon barbecue, and cedar for kids.

Information
Check with the **Point Roberts Chamber of Commerce,** tel. (360) 945-2313, for info. Pamphlets describing Point Roberts are available from a kiosk near International Marketplace. The local **area code** for Point Roberts is 360, the same as the rest of northwest Washington.

Getting There
Point Roberts is 23 road miles from the rest of Washington state. Access is via I-5 to the Canadian border at Blaine, then north on Hwy. 99 to Delta, and south on Hwy. 17 to the B.C. town of White Rock and the American settlement at Point Roberts. The Tsawwassen ferry terminal is just a few miles from here, providing a **British Columbia Ferries** link to Sidney on Vancouver Island; call (604) 669-1211 for a schedule. No reservations are available for this ferry, and there's always room for walk-on passengers.

WHIDBEY ISLAND

INTRODUCTION

The longest island in the lower 48 states (New York's Long Island was declared a peninsula by a U.S. Supreme Court ruling in 1985), Whidbey Island encompasses 208 square miles in its 45-mile length—no spot of which is more than five miles from the water. The island is one of western Washington's biggest tourist attractions; attendance at Deception Pass State Park rivals that of Mount Rainier, and the quaint towns of Coupeville and Langley seem a step back in time.

History

When the first European explorers reached Whidbey Island, they found it one of the most densely populated places in the Northwest. The original inhabitants, the Salish Indians, depended upon the rich resources of both the sea and the land and used fire to keep the prairies open. The praries in southern Whidbey attracted settlers in the 1850s, who took advantage of the homestead act to carve out farms.

Credit for the 1792 "discovery" of Whidbey Island goes to Joseph Whidbey, master of George Vancouver's flagship, the HMS *Discovery*. Whidbey explored the island in a small vessel, although he apparently wasn't the first one there: while exploring the island's west side, Whidbey stumbled upon the rotted remains of another ship, too weather-beaten to identify.

Seeing the Island

Whidbey is one place in Washington that seems to invite use of the word "motoring," and on weekends you'll often see couples out with their most prized possessions—ancient Jaguar convertibles, classic MGs, and old Thunderbirds—cruising the length of Whidbey with mandatory stops in Langley and Coupeville. It is a perfect destination for a day-trip or a weekend outing, with a wide variety of places to stay, from hotels to B&Bs.

One nice aspect of the island is that its picturesque towns of Langley and Coupeville are natural; the charm of the two towns is a result of their history, not a theme created to attract tourism. Langley has always stood at cliff's edge with false-front buildings, and so has Coupeville. Besides being a center of tourism and a place where Everett commuters live, Whidbey Island's economy is supported by the Whidbey Naval Air Station in Oak Harbor (easily the largest local employer) and farming.

For a fast day tour, take the Mukilteo-Clinton ferry to the south end of the island (see "Getting There," below). Then take a leisurely drive up the island, with stops in each town and park. At about the halfway point, walk onto the Keystone-Port Townsend ferry and have lunch in Port Townsend. Afterward, ferry back to Whidbey and continue driving north to Coupeville, Penn Cove, Oak Harbor, Deception Pass, and off the island via Deception Pass Bridge. If the day is almost over, drive up to Chuckanut Dr. for dinner, then home via I-5. A good alternate route back home is through La Conner and to I-5 at Conway.

To really see Whidbey right you'll need more than a hurried day trip. Take the time to explore the many natural areas and historic sites, camping out in one of the excellent state parks or staying in a local B&B. Be warned, however, that lodging rates can approach the stratosphere, and that reservations are needed for summer weekends. If you're on a budget, your best bet is to camp out since lodging costs are at least $45 d in even the simplest places. Oak Harbor has the least expensive motel rooms, but is also the least interesting city on the island.

Weather

The climate is mild year-round: temperature ranges from 40° to 60° F 80% of the time; temperatures above 75° and below 20° are rare. Autumn brings late-evening and early-morning fog; winter comes with light rain or mist every other day, though the total annual rainfall ranges from less than 20 inches in Coupeville and points north, to 30 inches on the south end of the island.

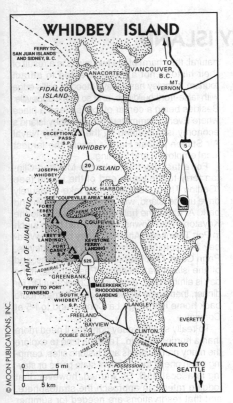

WHIDBEY ISLAND

FERRY TO
SAN JUAN ISLANDS
AND SIDNEY, B.C.

TO
VANCOUVER,
B.C.

ANACORTES

MT.
VERNON

FIDALGO
ISLAND

DECEPTION
PASS

DECEPTION
PASS
S.P.

WHIDBEY

5

JOSEPH
WHIDBEY
S.P.

ISLAND

20

OAK HARBOR

SEE "COUPEVILLE AREA" MAP

FORT
EBEY
S.P.

PENN COVE

COUPEVILLE

EBEY'S
LANDING

KEYSTONE
FERRY
LANDING

FORT CASEY
S.P.

STRAIT OF JUAN DE FUCA

525

MOON

ADMIRALTY BAY

GREENBANK

MEERKERK
RHODODENDRON
GARDENS

FERRY TO PORT
TOWNSEND

SOUTH
WHIDBEY
S.P.

LANGLEY

EVERETT

FREELAND

BAYVIEW

CLINTON

DOUBLE BLUFF

MUKILTEO

USELESS BAY

POSSESSION
PT.

TO
SEATTLE

0   5 mi

0   5 km

© MOON PUBLICATIONS, INC.

Getting There

To drive onto Whidbey Island, you've got only one option: the Deception Pass Bridge at the island's north end. To get there, go west on Hwy. 20 from I-5. Otherwise, you'll have to go by **Washington State Ferry** from Mukilteo or Port Townsend.

The Mukilteo ferry leaves for Clinton about every half-hour from 5 a.m. to 2 a.m. The 20-minute crossing costs $2.30 roundtrip for passengers, 50 cents extra roundtrip for bikes, and $4.80 one-way for car and driver ($4 in winter). Busiest times are during the weekday commute periods, Saturday mornings, and Sunday evenings (particularly during the summer).

From the Olympic Peninsula, board the ferry in Port Townsend to arrive at the Keystone landing next to Fort Casey State Park approximate-

ly 30 minutes later. These operate about every 45 minutes between 7 a.m. and 10 p.m. in the summer. Ferries leave about every 50 minutes, and fares are $1.75 one-way for passengers, 25 cents extra one-way for bikes, or $7.10 one-way for car and driver ($5.90 in winter). For information on the state ferry system call (800) 843-3779 statewide.

Getting Around

Island Transit, tel. (360) 678-7771 or 321-6688, is a free (!) bus system that offers Mon.-Sat. service all across Whidbey Island, from Clinton on the south to Deception Pass on the north.

Backroads, tel. (800) 462-2848, has six-day cycling tours of Whidbey Island and Kitsap Peninsula during the summer. These are offered as either camping trips ($750 per person including meals) or trips where you stay at local inns and B&Bs ($1300 per person including meals). A sag-wagon carries your gear, and you can choose your own pace. Bike rentals are also available.

CLINTON

Clinton (pop. 1,600) sits on the bluff looking south across Possession Sound to Mukilteo and Everett. The ferry traffic lines up for as much as a mile on Sunday and at the end of holiday weekends. For most folks, Clinton—named for Clinton, Michigan—is a get-through-it place with a handful of restaurants, coffeehouses, grocers, and other commuter services.

Driving or biking around Clinton's rural, wooded back roads provides fresh air and great views. Take Deer Lake Rd. (watch the signs—the road takes 90-degree turns without notice) to **Deer Lake Park** for swimming, boating, and fishing in a secluded, wooded area. From Hwy. 525, go left onto Campbell Rd., then left again on Maxwelton Rd. to **Dave Mackie County Park,** where you'll find the island's best Dungeness crabbing, along with shallow water for swimming. **Possession Beach County Park** covers just two acres at the southern tip of Whidbey Island, but is a fine place to enjoy the views.

The **North Star Trading Co.,** 6571 S. Humphrey Rd. (next to the ferry parking lot), produces ultra-soft sheepskin slippers and hats. Open Tues.-Sat. 10 a.m.-4 p.m.; call (360) 341-5426 or (800) 446-9276. The **Warm Winds Bookstore,**

WHIDBEY ISLAND ACCOMMODATIONS

Accommodations are arranged from least to most expensive within each town. Rates may be lower during the winter months. The area code is 360.

CLINTON

Marsh House; 6436 Maxwelton Rd.; tel. 579-7774; $75-100 s or d; contemporary studio unit, large garden, one guest room, private bath, kitchen, continental breakfast, kids okay

Northwest Vacation Homes; tel. 321-5005 or (800) 544-4304; $80-275 s or d; homes and cottages by the day or week

B's Getaway B&B; 4750 Orr Rd.; tel. 321-4721; $95 s or d; large older home, two guest rooms, private bath, full breakfast, no kids

Kittleson Cove B&B; 4891 E. Bay Ridge Dr.; tel. 221-2734; $125 in suite with kitchen, $175 s or d in cottage with fireplace, jacuzzi tub, kitchen; continental breakfast, kids welcome

Room with a View; 6369 S. Bayview Rd.; tel. 321-6264; $150 s or d Sun.-Thurs., $175 s or d Fri.-Sat.; honeymoon suite on six acres with views, private bath, jacuzzi on deck, king-size bed, continental breakfast, kids by arrangement

Home By The Sea B&B; 2388 E. Sunlight Beach Rd.; tel. 321-2964; $155-165 s or d; luxurious house on 10 acres, or cottage and suite near beach; views of the Olympics, jacuzzis, woodstoves, full breakfast, two-night minimum stay, children welcome

LANGLEY

Drake's Landing; 203 Wharf St.; tel. 221-3999; $45-55 s or d; five simple rooms, private baths, no TV, friendly owner

Inverness Inn; 2479 E. Hwy. 525; tel. 321-5521; $65 s, $74 d; three two-room duplex cottages, kitchenettes

Island Palms; 619 1st St.; tel. 221-8173; $65-90 s or d; Victorian home, two guest rooms, private baths, woodstove, continental breakfast

Cascade Sunrise B&B; 5730 S. Summerhill Dr.; tel. 341-8501 or (800) 473-7823; $75 s or d; country log home, panoramic views, two-room private suite, bikes, continental breakfast, kids okay

Pine Cottage B&B; 3827 McKeay Dr.; tel. 730-1376; $75 s or d; cottage on water, hot tub, woodstove, full breakfast, kids welcome

Fox Spit Farm B&B; 3527 S. Fox Spit Rd.; tel. 730-1337; $75-195 s or d; 1923 farmhouse on 10 country acres, gardens, porch, library, four guest rooms, shared or private baths, antique furnishings, continental breakfast, no kids

Garden Path Inn B&B; 111 1st St.; tel. 321-5121; $80-150 s or d; two downtown suites, kitchens, private baths, continental breakfast, no kids

Maxwelton Manor B&B; 5278 S. Maxwelton Rd.; tel. 221-5199; $85 s or d; colonial-style home, wooded setting, three guest rooms, private baths, llamas and peacocks, full breakfast, no kids under 12

Saratoga Sunrise Guest House B&B; 3770 S. Bells Beach Rd.; tel. 730-8407; $85 s or d; cottage, water views, full breakfast, fireplace, kitchen, no kids under 12

Eagles Nest Inn B&B; 3236 E. Saratoga Rd.; tel. 221-5331; $85-105 s, $95-115 d; custom four-story home, views across Saratoga Passage, hot tub, library, gourmet breakfast, no kids under 12, AAA approved

Twickenham House B&B Inn; 5023 Langley Rd.; tel. 221-2334 or (800) 874-5009; $85-120 s or d; modern country house, six large guest rooms, private bath, decks, fireplace, pub, gourmet breakfast, no kids, AAA approved

(continues on next page)

WHIDBEY ISLAND ACCOMMODATIONS

(continued)

Island Tyme B&B Inn; 4940 S. Bayview; tel. 221-5078; $85-135 s or d; new Victorian-style home on 10 acres, fireplaces, outside decks, five guest rooms, private baths, billiard table, children okay

Log Castle B&B; 3273 E. Saratoga Rd.; tel. 221-5483; $90-115 s or d; unique waterfront log home, four guest rooms, private baths, porch, water and mountain views, stone fireplace, canoe, full breakfast, no kids under 10

Whidbey Inn B&B; 106 1st St.; tel. 221-7115; $95-150 s or d; mountain and water views, six guest rooms, private baths, sundecks or fireplaces, continental breakfast, no kids

Country Cottage B&B; 215 6th St.; tel. 221-8709; $95-165 s or d; 1904 home (two guest rooms with jacuzzis), three separate cottages, water views, gazebo, private baths, fireplaces, full breakfast, no kids, two-night minimum stay

Gallery Suite B&B; 301 1st St.; tel. 221-2978; $100 s or d; apartment suite, overlooks water, kitchen, two-night minimum stay on summer weekends, continental breakfast, no kids

Sea Breeze; 5122 S. Bayview Rd.; tel. 321-5900; $100 s or d; three-bedroom home on beach, two bedrooms, fireplace, kitchen

Tara Vacation Rentals; tel. 331-6300 or (206) 624-3951 in Seattle; $100-250 d; homes and condos, weekly rates available, children welcome

Lone Lake Cottage B&B; 5206 S. Bayview Rd.; tel. 321-5325; $110 s or d in two cottages, suite, or small paddlewheel houseboat along Lone Lake; kitchens, jacuzzi tubs, fireplaces, canoes, rowboat, bikes, aviary, continental breakfast, two-night minimum stay on weekends

Primrose Path B&B; 3191 E. Harbor Rd.; tel. 730-3722; $110 s or d; 1920s cottage in the woods, water views, hot tub, kitchen, continental breakfast, kids welcome

Christy's Country Inn and Cottage B&B; 2891 Meinhold Rd.; tel. 321-1815; $135-150 s or d; Olympics views, penthouse suite and guesthouse, hot tub on deck, kitchens, fireplaces, full or continental breakfast, children welcome

Harrison House Inn; 201 Cascade Ave.; tel. 221-5801; $135-275 s or d; elaborate modern inn, large rooms, library, fireplaces, continental breakfast, no kids

Boat Yard Inn; 200 Wharf St.; tel. 221-5120; $145-165 s or d; modern studio or loft units, kitchens, two-night minimum stay, AAA approved

The Inn at Langley; 400 1st St.; tel. 221-3033; $165-245 s or d; overlooks Saratoga Passage, elegant rooms, fireplaces, decks, jacuzzis, continental breakfast, two-night minimum stay on weekends, AAA approved

Galittoire Contemporary Guest House; 5444 S. Coles Rd.; tel. 221-0548; $175-245 s or d; immaculate Japanese-style home on 11 acres, hot tub, gazebo, two guest rooms, king beds, private baths, jacuzzi tubs, exercise room, sauna, gourmet breakfast, evening hors d'oeuvres, two-night minimum stay on weekends, kids by arrangement, dinners available

Edgecliff Cottage B&B; tel. 221-8857 or (800) 243-5536; $195-235; one honeymoon cottage and one penthouse apartment, cliff location with view and private beach, jacuzzis, fireplaces, kitchens, private baths

FREELAND

Harbour Inn Motel; 1606 E. Main St.; tel. 321-6900; $47-70 s, $53-69 d; kitchenettes available, continental breakfast, AAA approved

Mutiny Bay Resort & Motel; 5856 S. Mutiny Bay Rd.; tel. 331-4500; cabins for $60 s or d with kitchenettes and shared bath; chalets for $115 s or d with kitchenettes, fireplaces, kids welcome

Seaside Cottage B&B; 213 E. Sandpiper Rd.; tel. 331-8455; $95 for up to four in cottage with kitchen, fireplace, deck, continental breakfast; $60 d in suite with kitchenette, kids okay

Double Bluff B&B; 6378 S. Double Bluff Rd., tel. 321-0502; $85-115 for up to four; shoreside cottages, beach, jacuzzi, fireplaces, continental breakfast

Uncle John's Cottage; 1762 E. Lancaster Rd.; tel. 331-5623; $90 s or d; two cottages, fireplaces, hot tub, kitchens, kids welcome

Bush Point Wharf B&B; 229 E. Main St.; tel. 331-0405; $95 s or d; remodeled house along beach, two guest rooms, private baths, jacuzzi, continental breakfast, kids okay

Villa Isola B&B Inn; 5489 S. Coles Rd.; tel. 221-5052; $95-105 s or d; country location, lawn bowling court, bikes, full bath, continental breakfast, evening desserts, no kids

Cliff House B&B; 5440 Windmill Rd.; tel. 331-1566; $425 d, $165 d for honeymoon cottage with kitchenette and fireplace; luxurious award-winning home, beach access and water views, large central atrium, jacuzzi, stone fireplace, king-size bed, continental breakfast, extensive video library, kitchen, two-night minimum stay, no kids

GREENBANK

Smugglers Cove Haven B&B; 3258 Smugglers Cove Rd.; tel. 678-7100 or (800) 772-7055; $95 s or d; apartment, private bath, king-size bed, fireplace, kitchen, continental breakfast, kids okay

Guest House B&B Cottages; 3366 S. Hwy. 525; tel. 678-3115; $135-185 s or d in cottages, $285 s or d in luxurious log lodge; on 25 acres, marine and mountain views, fireplace, kitchens, in-room jacuzzis, outdoor pool, pond, exercise room, two-night minimum stay, continental breakfast, no kids, AAA approved (four diamonds)

COUPEVILLE

Tyee Motel; 405 S. Main St.; tel. 678-6616; $43 s or d

Coupeville Inn; 200 N.W. Coveland St.; tel. 678-6668 or (800) 247-6162; $54-85 s or d; views of Penn Cove and the Cascades, continental breakfast, AAA approved

Countryside Inn; 487 W. Hwy. 20 (two miles south of Coupeville); tel. 678-5610; $57-95 s or d; kitchenettes available

The Inn at Penn Cove B&B; 702 N. Main; tel. 678-8000 or (800) 688-2683; $60-120 s, $60-125 d; two historic Victorian homes, six guest rooms, fireplace, kids okay, gourmet breakfast, AAA approved

Compass Rose B&B; 508 S. Main St.; tel. 678-5318 or (800) 237-3881; $65 s or d; historic Victorian home with antiques, two guest rooms, shared bath, gourmet breakfast, AAA approved

The Victorian B&B; 602 N. Main St.; tel. 678-5305; $65 s, $80-100 d; 1889 Victorian home, cottage and two guest rooms, private baths, full breakfast, AAA approved

Colonel Crockett Farm B&B; 1012 S. Fort Casey Rd.; tel. 678-3711; $70-95 s or d; 1855 Victorian farmhouse overlooking Admiralty Bay, on National Register of Historic Places, large lawn and flower beds, library, five guest rooms, private baths, buffet breakfast, no kids under 14

Anchorage Inn B&B; 807 N. Main St.; tel. 678-5581; $75-90 s or d; large and luxurious new Victorian-style inn, five guest rooms, private baths, full breakfast, closed Dec. 20-Feb. 20, no kids under 14, AAA approved

Fort Casey Inn B&B; 1124 S. Engle Rd.; tel. 678-8792; $75-125 s or d; two-bedroom units in 1909 officers' quarters, kitchens, private baths, continental breakfast, kids welcome

Captain Whidbey Inn; 2072 W. Captain Whidbey Inn Rd.; tel. 678-4097 or (800) 366-4097; $75-195 s, $85-195 d; beautiful grounds on Penn Cove, historic 1907 madrone log inn with rooms (shared baths), cottages, and houses (private baths, kitchens), breakfast buffet, AAA approved

(continues on next page)

WHIDBEY ISLAND ACCOMMODATIONS

(continued)

Garden Isle Guest Cottages B&B; 207 N.W. Coveland St.; tel. 678-5641; $85-95 s or d; two cottages, kitchens, private bath, light breakfast, AAA approved

Old Morris Farm B&B; 105 W. Morris Rd.; tel. 678-6586; $85-125 s or d; older home on 10 forested acres, gardens, hot tub, fireplace, four guest rooms, private baths, gourmet breakfast, evening snacks, no kids under 12

OAK HARBOR

Queen Ann Motel; 1204 W. Pioneer Way; tel. 675-2209; $44-49 s, $47-53 d; indoor pool, jacuzzi, kitchenettes available, AAA approved

North Whidbey Inn; 1175 Midway Blvd.; tel. 675-5911; $45-65 s, $50-70 d; kitchenettes available, local calls 25 cents

Acorn Motor Inn; 8066 80th NW; tel. 675-6646; $48-58 s, $52-64 d; continental breakfast, AAA approved

Coachman Inn; 5563 Hwy. 20; tel. 675-0727 or (800) 635-0043; $54-100 s or d; outdoor pool, jacuzzi suites, exercise room, continental breakfast, AAA approved (four diamonds)

Auld Holland Inn; 5861 Hwy. 20; tel. 675-2288 or (800) 228-0148; $55-85 s or d; Dutch-style motel, outdoor pool, jacuzzi, sauna, tennis court, exercise room, lawn games, kitchenettes available, AAA approved

Best Western Harbor Plaza; 5691 Hwy. 20; tel. 679-4567 or (800) 927-5478; $63-94 s, $68-102 d; outdoor pool, jacuzzi, exercise room, kitchenettes available, free continental breakfast, AAA approved (four diamond)

A Country Pillow B&B; 419 E. Troxell Rd.; tel. 675-4608; $75 s or d in house on water, antique decor, two guest rooms, shared bath, continental breakfast; $95 s or d in cottage, kitchen, no breakfast

Harbor Pointe B&B; 720 W. Bonnie View Acres Rd.; tel. 675-3379; $80-135 s or d; large contemporary home, private beach, gazebo-covered hot tub, four guest rooms, shared or private bath, full breakfast

---

tel. (360) 341-5922, is a new age/spiritual store in Clinton. **Island Greens,** 3890 E. French Rd., tel. (360) 321-6042, has a nine-hole golf course.

Accommodations and Food

See the "Whidbey Island Accommodations" chart for a complete listing of local lodging places.

For Chinese food, **Hong Kong Gardens,** tel. (360) 221-2828, is a half mile from the ferry landing on Hwy. 525 and has a view of Saratoga Passage. Try **Clinton Landing** at the ferry terminal for seafood.

Information

Clinton Chamber of Commerce, 6231 Galbreath Rd., tel. (360) 321-4545, has local information.

The telephone **area code** for Clinton and the rest of Whidbey Island is 360.

Transportation

The state ferry departs Clinton for Mukilteo approximately every half-hour throughout the day. See "Getting There," for specifics on fares. **Island Transit,** tel. (360) 321-6688, offers free bus service Mon.-Sat. throughout Whidbey Island.

LANGLEY

This town of fewer than 1,000 is six miles from the Clinton ferry landing, and a world away in style. The ritzy shops lining the streets of this tiny waterfront artists' community make for good browsing, and several of its lodging establishments have views across Saratoga Passage to Camano Island and beyond. You'll find an abundance of gourmet food shops, boutiques, B&Bs, bookstores, and art galleries.

History

Langley is probably the only Washington town founded by a teenager. In 1880, an ambitious 15-year-old German immigrant, Jacob Anthes, settled here. Because he was too young to file for a homestead, Anthes spent $100 to buy 120 acres of land, adding to his holdings with a 160-acre homestead claim when he reached 21. He later built a store and post office and teamed up with Judge J.W. Langley to plat the new town.

Sights

The main attraction in Langley is simply the attractive town itself with its setting right along Puget Sound. A favorite downtown stopping place for photos is the life-size bronze *Boy and Dog* by Georgia Gerber, a local sculptor. The 160-foot fishing pier offers great views and a chance to pull out your fishing pole, and the beach here is a popular place for picnicking and swimming. The **South Whidbey Historical Museum,** 312 2nd St., has local memorabilia (but no phone). Open Sat.-Sun. 1-4 p.m.

Whidbey Island Vineyard and Winery, 5237 S. Langley Rd., tel. (360) 221-2040, is a family operation, producing wines from estate-grown vinifera grapes, along with surprisingly good rhubarb wines. The tasting room is open Fri.-Sun. noon-5 p.m. Stop for a picnic overlooking the adjacent vineyard and apple orchard. Their wines are only available here or in local stores and restaurants.

Accommodations

See the "Whidbey Island Accommodations" chart for a complete listing of local lodging places. The local chamber of commerce has a reservation line, tel. (360) 221-6765, for local B&Bs and inns.

The rambling **Twickenham House B&B Inn,** tel. (360) 221-2334 or (800) 874-5009, is one of the more distinctive local places, with a country location, six guest rooms, and sheep grazing out front, plus ducks and chickens. Five-course gourmet dinners are available by advance reservation. Also worthy of notice are **Eagles Nest Inn B&B,** tel. (360) 221-5331, with its octagonal home and magnificent vistas, **Log Castle B&B,** tel. (360) 221-5483, a beautiful log home, and **Lone Lake Cottage B&B,** tel. (360) 321-5325, with an aviary, plus cottages and a tiny sternwheel houseboat along the shore of this scenic lake. Overlooking Saratoga Passage, **The Whidbey Inn,** tel. (360) 221-7115, has rooms and fireplace suites with a sundeck.

Probably the most elaborate local B&B is **Galittoire Contemporary Guest House,** tel. (360) 221-0548. Designed by the owner-architect, this beautiful Japanese-style home sits on 11 acres and is very popular for summer weddings. The two guest suites have everything you might want: king-size beds, jacuzzi tubs, an exercise room and sauna, plus gourmet breakfasts and evening hors d'oeuvres. They also offer sumptuous dinners.

Edgecliff Cottage B&B is another of the island's luxury spots, with a romantic cliffside cottage and a comfortable penthouse apartment. Each place has its own jacuzzi and fine views of Saratoga Passage and the Cascades. A stairway leads to a private beach. Very romantic.

The Langley area is home to two unique spiritual retreats that emphasize the need to reconnect with the natural world. One of these, **Marsh House,** (360) 579-8861, is an attractive contemporary home used by both groups and individuals. (Not everyone comes here on a spiritual quest; accommodations may also be available for families, especially during the winter months.) Lodging is available in a studio apartment, or in dorms when groups use the space. The neighboring **Whidbey Institute,** tel. (360) 341-1884, is a long-established retreat center with respected workshops. They operate the new age Warm Winds Bookstore in Clinton.

Campgrounds

Island County Fairgrounds, 819 Camano Ave., tel. (360) 321-4677, has year-round camping sites and RV hookups. Coin-operated showers can be found at the marina.

Food

Langley is blessed with an abundance of fine but surprisingly reasonable restaurants. It's almost a challenge to get a bad meal in this town! A personal favorite, **Star Bistro,** serves burgers, soups, fish and chips, salads, and more upstairs at 2011/2 1st St., tel. (360) 221-2627. The warm pasta salad with grilled chicken, toasted almonds, and tomato vinaigrette is a real treat. Downstairs, the **Star Market** has gourmet and imported items.

Down the street a bit at 113 First, **Cafe Langley,** tel. (360) 221-3090, has a big local following. Greek is the word: lamb kabobs, pita bread, soups, and other Middle Eastern dishes. Open for lunch and dinner. Less pretentious, but noteworthy nonetheless, is **Village Pizzeria,** right across the street at 108 1st St., tel. (360) 221-3363. All sorts of distinctive toppings, including clams and garlic.

Don't miss the **Dog House Tavern and Backdoor Restaurant,** tel. (360) 221-9996, corner of 1st and Anthes on the waterfront. Nothing fancy—just a fun and funky place to have burgers, fish and chips, or chili, or perhaps just a drink while enjoying the view. They sometimes have live music.

Mike's Place, 215 1st St., tel. (360) 221-6575, is another popular spot, serving breakfast and lunch daily from an international menu, complete with home-baked bread and pastries.

Get light breakfasts and lunches—plus espresso drinks and fresh juices—at **Raven Cafe,** 197 2nd St., tel. (360) 221-3211. **Village Bakery,** tel. (360) 221-3525, bakes out-of-this-world breads and sweets.

Whidbey Island Brewing Co., 630 2nd St., tel. (360) 221-8373, has a tasting room open daily noon-6 p.m., plus hot dogs, pretzels, and focaccia on the menu.

The **South Whidbey Tilth Farmers' Market** offers organic fruits and vegetables, plus fresh eggs, flowers, baked goods, and seafood on Saturday 10 a.m.-2 p.m. late May through October. It's held next to Bill's Feed & Tack at the intersection of Bayview Rd. and Hwy. 525.

Events

Langley's popular **Choochokam Festival of the Arts** is held in mid-July with food, arts and crafts displays, a children's theater, and music and dancing; call (360) 221-7494 for details. Don't miss Langley's **Island County Fair,** a four-day event in late August that includes a logging show, carnival, parade, music, and 4-H exhibits. Call (360) 221-4677 for details. Return here in mid-November for **A Country Christmas at the Fair,** a popular arts and crafts show.

Arts and Entertainment

A local theater group performs regularly in the old-fashioned theater on the short main drag. The **Clyde Theatre** on 1st St., tel. (360) 221-5525, is the only place to watch movies on the south end of Whidbey Island.

The **Artists' Cooperative of Whidbey Island,** tel. (360) 221-7675, has high quality arts and crafts in their gallery at 197 2nd Street.

Recreation

South Whidbey Island was seemingly designed for biking. The rolling hills, clean air, and beautiful weather are inspiring enough, but occasional whale and eagle sightings add to the pleasure. Rent a bike for a day (or week) from **The Pedaler,** 56031/2 S. Bayview Rd., tel. (360) 321-5040.

Information and Services

Langley Chamber of Commerce is located at 1241/2 2nd St. (in the alleyway between 1st and 2nd), tel. (360) 221-6765. The **Langley Public Library** is at 105 Cascade Avenue. The local telephone **area code** is 360.

Transportation

Island Transit, tel. (360) 321-6688, is a free bus system that offers Mon.-Sat. service throughout Whidbey Island.

Island Air at Langley Airport, tel. (360) 341-1505 or (800) 473-7823, offers scenic flights, plus charter service to Sea-Tac.

FREELAND

Freeland (pop. 1,300) was founded in 1900 by a utopian group of socialists. They formed a cooperative, the Free Land Association, and each contributed $10 toward five acres of land; the balance was to be paid off through cooperative labor. Their experiment didn't last long, but the name stuck.

Today Freeland has a handful of businesses (none of them cooperative) and is home to many folks who commute to Everett for work. A boat launch and small sunny picnic area are found at **Freeland Park** on Holmes Harbor, about two streets over from "downtown" Freeland—just look for the water. **Double Bluff Point,** three miles south of Freeland, is an interesting place to explore and a good place to find big chunks of soft coal that eroded from the cliff.

South Whidbey State Park
Easily the island's most underrated park, South Whidbey State Park on Smuggler's Cove Rd. has outstanding hiking and picnicking, plus clamming and crabbing on a narrow sandy beach (accessed via a steep path), campsites, and striking Olympic views. The 85 acres of old-growth Douglas fir and red cedar protect resident black-tailed deer, foxes, raccoons, rabbits, bald eagles, ospreys, and pileated woodpeckers. Late summer means salmon in the Admiralty Inlet; a public boat launch is located two miles south of the park at Bush Point. Be sure to hike the **Wilbert Trail,** a 1.5-mile path that climbs the tallest hill on Whidbey Island, providing panoramic vistas from the summit. Get to the park by heading east from Freeland on Bush Point Rd.; it becomes Smugglers Cove Rd. and continues past the park, a distance of seven miles.

Accommodations and Campgrounds
See the "Whidbey Island Accommodations" chart for a complete listing of local lodging places. Recommended is **Double Bluff B&B,** with two cottages overlooking a quiet white-sand beach. A good place to watch eagles, herons, and other birds, or to simply enjoy the quietude.

Camp at **South Whidbey State Park,** tel. (360) 331-4559, for $10; no RV hookups. Open late February to October. Call (800) 452-5687 for campsite reservations ($6 extra fee), available up to 11 months ahead of time. Park RVs at **Mutiny Bay Resort,** 5856 S. Mutiny Bay Rd., tel. (360) 331-4500.

Food
Main Street's **Island Bakery,** tel. (360) 331-6282, has breads, cookies, pastries, and deli lunches. **Freeland Cafe,** 1642 E. Main St., tel. (360) 331-9945, is an old-time establishment with breakfast served anytime, plus Hawaiian and Asian specialties.

Recreation
The Mutiny Bay Co., just north of Freeland, tel. (360) 331-2313, rents water skis, wetsuits, tents, kites, and other outdoor gear. Play golf at the 18-hole **Holmes Harbor Golf Course,** 50232 Harbor Hills Dr., tel. (360) 331-2363.

Information and Services
Freeland Chamber of Commerce, 1474 E. Hwy. 525, tel. (360) 331-1980, has local info. The **Freeland Public Library** is at 1614 E. Main Street. The telephone **area code** for Freeland and the rest of Whidbey Island is 360.

GREENBANK

Don't be surprised if you never see Greenbank center—the turn-of-the-century general store, restaurant, and post office are easy to miss—but you can't miss the acres and acres of loganberries growing just north of town on Hwy. 20. A big red barn marks **Whidbeys Greenbank Berry Farm,** tel. (360) 678-7700, one of the largest loganberry farms in the U.S., now owned by Chateau Ste. Michelle (which is in turn owned by U.S. Tobacco, something they don't publicize). The berries grown here are used in their Whidbey Island Liqueur, Washington's only cordial. Stop by the tasting room for a short self-guided tour and a taste of the liqueur and other Ste. Michelle wines. There's also a U-pick flower garden and gift shop; open daily 10 a.m.-5 p.m.

Meerkerk Rhododendron Gardens
This impressive garden boasts more than 1,500 varieties of rhododendron species and hybrids, plus other plants such as Japanese cherries, maples, and magnolias on a 53-acre site just south of Greenbank off Resort Road. Begun by Max and Anne Meerkerk in the 1960s, the gar-

dens are now maintained by the Seattle Rhododendron Society. Peak season for rhododendrons is in late spring. The gardens are open daily 9 a.m.-4 p.m.; tel. (360) 321-6682.

Practicalities

See the "Whidbey Island Accommodations" chart for a complete listing of local lodging places. If you have the bucks, the **Guest House B&B Cottages** are four-star accommodations with a homey feel.

At **Whidbey Fish Market and Cafe,** 3078 Hwy. 525, tel. (360) 678-3474, you won't find white linen tablecloths, but the fish is as fresh as it gets. Stop here on Monday and Saturday for their popular and filling all-you-can-eat fish feeds. Reservations are advised.

Greenbank's **Loganberry Festival** in July features a pie-eating contest, along with arts and crafts, live music, and food stands; call (360) 678-7700.

Island Transit, tel. (360) 321-6688, is a free bus system that offers Mon.-Sat. service throughout Whidbey Island.

FORT CASEY STATE PARK

Fort Casey State Park, an historic Army post three miles south of Coupeville next to the Keystone ferry dock, has two miles of beach, an underwater park, a boat ramp, hiking trails, picnic areas, spectacular Olympic views, and campsites, plus good salmon and steelhead fishing in remarkably clear water.

History

Fort Casey was one of the "Iron Triangle" that guarded the entrance to Puget Sound and the Bremerton Naval Shipyard at the turn of the century. This deadly crossfire consisted of Fort Casey, plus Fort Worden at Port Townsend and Fort Flagler on Marrowstone Island; fortunately, they never proved necessary, and the guns were never fired at an enemy vessel. Fort Casey's big weapons were the ingenious 10-inch disappearing carriage guns; the recoil sent them swinging back down out of sight for reloading, giving the sighter a terrific ride. By 1920, advances in naval warfare had made them ob-

solete, so they were melted down. During WW II, Fort Casey was primarily a training site, although anti-aircraft guns were mounted on the fortifications. The fort was closed after the war and purchased by Washington in 1956 for a state park.

Sights

If you're arriving on Whidbey Island by ferry from Port Townsend, get to Fort Casey by taking an immediate left onto Engle Rd. as soon as you exit the ferry terminal. Much of the fort is open for public viewing, including ammunition bunkers, observation towers, underground storage facilities (bring your flashlight), gun catwalks, and the main attraction—two disappearing guns. Because the originals were long gone, in 1968 these were brought here from an American fort in the Philippines.

Be sure to visit the **Admiralty Point Lighthouse Interpretive Center,** where you can learn about coast artillery and the 1890 defense post. The lighthouse has not been used since 1927, but you can climb to the top for a view of Puget Sound and the Olympic Mountains. Open Thurs.-Sun. 10 a.m.-4 p.m.

Many of the fort's old buildings are now used as a conference center run by Seattle Pacific University, and the turn-of-the-century officers' quarters have been turned into Fort Casey Inn B&B. Also nearby is shallow **Crockett Lake,** a good place to look for migratory and resident birds. The **Crockett Blockhouse,** one of four remaining fortifications built in the 1850s to defend against Indian attacks, stands on the north shore of the lake. An offshore underwater park is popular with divers. Northeast of Crockett Lake is Outlying Landing Field, used by Navy pilots to simulate aircraft carrier landings.

Campgrounds

The small and crowded campground ($10) at Fort Casey is open year-round, and has coin-operated showers, but no RV hookups. Get here early to be assured of a site on summer weekends; a better bet may be to head to Fort Ebey State Park (see "Coupeville," below) instead. A couple of pleasant hiking trails lead through the wooded grounds of the fort.

EBEY'S LANDING NATIONAL HISTORICAL RESERVE

Ebey's Landing, two miles southwest of Coupeville center, has easily the most striking coastal view on the island. As the roads wind through acres of rich farmland, the glimpses of water and cliff might remind you of the northern California or Oregon coastline; the majestic Olympics add to the drama.

Managed by the National Park Service and covering 17,400 acres, the Ebey's Landing National Historical Reserve helps keep this land rural and agricultural through scenic easements, land donations, tax incentives, and zoning. Approximately 90% of the land remains in private hands. Created in 1978, this was America's first national historic reserve. Headquarters are located at 908 N.W. Alexander St. in Coupeville, tel. (360) 678-6084.

History

The native Skagit Indians were generally friendly toward the white settlers, but their northern neighbors were considerably less forgiving of the invaders. Alaska's Kake tribe of Tlingit Indians had a fierce reputation as exemplified by the following incident recorded by Richard Meade (1871):

In 1855 a party of Kakes, on a visit south to Puget Sound, became involved in some trouble there, which caused a United States vessel to open fire on them, and during the affair one of the Kake chiefs was killed. This took place over 800 miles from the Kake settlements on Kupreanof Island. The very next year the tribe sent a canoe-load of fighting men all the way from Clarence Straits in Russian America to Whidby's Island in Washington Territory, and attacked and beheaded an ex-collector—not of internal revenue, for that might have been pardonable—but of customs, and returned safely with his skull and scalp to their villages. Such people are, therefore, not to be despised, and are quite capable of giving much trouble in the future unless wisely and firmly governed.

The man so beheaded was Col. Isaac Ebey, the first settler on Whidbey Island; his head was eventually recovered and reunited with his body before being buried at Sunnyside Cemetery. To fend off further attacks (they never came), the pioneers built seven blockhouses in the 1850s, four of which still stand.

The Anglo settlers were attracted to this part of Whidbey Island by the expansive prairies and fertile black soil. These prairies occupy the sites of shallow Ice-Age lakes; when the water dried up, the rich, deep soil remained. Indian burning helped keep them open over the centuries

DIANNE BOUERICE LYONS

Ebey's Landing

that followed, and the white settlers simply took up residence on this prime land.

Sights

The main attraction at Ebey's Landing National Historical Reserve is simply the country itself: bucolic farmland, densely wooded ridges, and steep coastal bluffs. Pick up an informative tour brochure describing a detailed tour of Ebey's Landing at the Coupeville museum.

For a very scenic bike ride or drive, turn onto Hill Rd. (two miles south of Coupeville) and follow it through the second-growth stand of Douglas fir trees. It emerges on a high bluff overlooking Admiralty Inlet before dropping to the shoreline at tiny **Ebey's Landing State Park.** From the small parking area at the water's edge, hike the 1.5-mile trail along the bluff above **Parego Lagoon** for a view of the coastline, Olympics, and the Strait of Juan de Fuca that shouldn't be missed. The lagoon is a fine place to look for migratory birds. Return along the beach, or continue northward to Fort Ebey State Park (three miles from Ebey's Landing). Along the way, keep your eyes open for gem-quality stones such as agate, jasper, black and green jade, plus quartz and petrified wood.

Another trail leads 1.4 miles from Ebey's Landing to **Sunnyside Cemetery,** where you can look north to snowcapped Mt. Baker and south to Mt. Rainier on a clear day. The cemetery is also accessible from Cook Rd. (see "Coupeville Area" map). The **Davis Blockhouse,** used to defend against Tlingit and Haida attacks, stands at the edge of the cemetery; it was moved here in 1915. Colonel Isaac Ebey is buried here.

COUPEVILLE

The second oldest town in Washington, the "Port of Sea Captains" was founded and laid out in 1852 by Capt. Thomas Coupe, the first man to sail through Deception Pass. The protected harbor at Penn Cove was a perfect site for the village that became Coupeville (pop. 1,500), and timber from Whidbey was shipped from here to San Francisco to feed the building boom created by the gold rush. Today, modern businesses operate from Victorian-era buildings amidst the nation's largest historical preservation district.

Downtown has an immaculate cluster of false-fronted shops and restaurants right on the harbor and a long wharf that was once used to ship local produce and logs to the mainland.

Historical Sights

The **Island County Historical Society Museum** at Alexander and Front Streets, tel. (360) 678-3310, has displays of pioneer relics—including a shadow box with flowers made from human hair and an interesting video on Whidbey Island history—and changing exhibits. Be sure to see the 1903 Holsman horseless carriage (one of just two in the world) and several fine Indian baskets in the basement. The museum is open Mon.-Fri. 11 a.m.-5 p.m., Sat.-Sun. 10 a.m.-5 p.m. May-Sept.; Fri.-Mon. 11 a.m.-5 p.m. the rest of the year. Entrance is $2 for adults, $1.50 for seniors, students, and military personnel, $4.50 for families, and free for kids under six.

While at the museum, pick up their brochure describing a short walking tour of the town's beautiful Victorian buildings. It lists some 40 buildings in Coupeville that are of historical significance and tells the family histories of many owners of the buildings, past and present. Ninety-minute guided tours are offered Saturday and Sunday at 1:30 p.m. May-Sept., departing from the museum.

One of the original Whidbey Island fortifications, the **Alexander Blockhouse,** built in 1855, stands outside the museum, along with a shelter housing two turn-of-the-century Indian racing canoes. Also out front are attractive gardens with herbs and drought-tolerant plants. Additional blockhouses can be found at the Sunnyside Cemetery, just south of town, and Crockett Lake within Fort Casey State Park.

Chief Snakelum's Grave, in a grove two miles east of Coupeville, commemorates the chief of the Skagit Tribe and one of the town's last Indian residents.

For something with a longer history, head south from downtown on Main St. to the house-sized boulder. Called a glacial erratic, this enormous rock was deposited here by the Vashon Glacier during the last ice age.

Penn Cove

For a very scenic drive, head northwest from Coupeville along Madrona Way, named for

© MOON PUBLICATIONS, INC.

COUPEVILLE AREA

the Pacific madrone (a.k.a. madrona) trees whose distinctive red bark and leathery green leaves line the roadway. Quite a few summer cottages and cozy homes can be found here, along with the gorgeous Captain Whidbey Inn. Offshore are dozens of floating pens where mussels grow on lines hanging in Penn Cove. On the northwest corner of Penn Cove, Hwy. 20 passes scenic **Grasser's Hill** where hedgerows alternate with open farmland. Development restrictions prevent this open country from becoming a mass of condos. Just north of here is the historic **San de Fuca schoolhouse.**

Fort Ebey State Park

Fort Ebey State Park, tel. (360) 678-4636, southwest of Coupeville on Admiralty Inlet, has campsites, a large picnic area, three miles of beach, and two miles of hiking trails within its 644 acres. The fort was constructed during WW II, though its gun batteries were never needed. The concrete platforms remain, along with cavernous bunkers, but the big guns have long since been removed. Due to its location in the Olympic rain shadow, the park is one of few places in western Washington where numerous varieties of cactus can be found; it also has stands of second-growth forests and fine views across the Strait of Juan de Fuca.

Although not as well known as other parks on Whidbey, it is still a favorite summertime spot. Much of Fort Ebey's popularity stems from tiny **Lake Pondilla,** formed by a glacial sinkhole—a bass-fisherman's and swimmer's delight. Follow the signs from the north parking lot for a two-block hike to the lake; half a dozen picnic tables and a camping area are reserved for hikers and bicyclists. Other trails lead along the bluffs south from here, and down to the beach. Adventurous folks (after consulting a tide chart and a bit of care) can continue all the way to Fort Casey State Park, eight miles away.

Accommodations

See the "Whidbey Island Accommodations" chart for a complete listing of local lodging places. The town is blessed with many historic buildings, several of which have been turned into delightful B&Bs and inns. Unfortunately, they are priced accordingly, and equally likely to be full on summer weekends. Be sure to make advance reservations.

One of the most striking places is **Compass Rose B&B,** tel. (360) 678-5318 or (800) 237-3881, a Stick-Eastlake Victorian home built in 1890 and packed with antiques. The building is on the National Register of Historic Places and has very friendly owners. **The Inn at Penn Cove B&B,** tel. (360) 678-8000 or (800) 688-2683, spreads across two lovingly restored Victorian homes built in 1887 and 1891.

Also of note is **Colonel Crockett Farm B&B,** tel. (360) 678-3711, an 1855 Victorian farmhouse with a large lawn and flower beds overlooking Admiralty Bay. The renovated home is on the National Register of Historic Places and is furnished with antiques. Right next to Fort Casey State Park, **Fort Casey Inn B&B,** tel. (360) 678-8792, consists of 10 restored Georgian revival homes that served as officers' quarters during WW I. These large two-story homes are divided into two duplex units each, with full kitchens and private baths. The basements were built to be used as bomb shelters in case of attack, and some still have the original steel-shuttered windows.

Captain Whidbey Inn, tel. (360) 678-4097 or (800) 366-4097, has rooms inside this classic two-story inn built in 1907 from madrone logs, plus modern cottages and houses. The expansive wooded grounds (with Pacific madrone trees) face onto Penn Cove. Even if you aren't staying here, be sure to stop and take in the scenery or sip a drink in the bar. The lodge operates a 52-foot wooden ketch, the *Cutty Sark,* with regularly scheduled sailing trips.

Campgrounds

Camp year-round at **Fort Casey State Park,** three miles south of Coupeville, for $10 (no RV hookups). **Fort Ebey State Park,** approximately five miles west of Coupeville, has campsites ($11; no RV hookups) and a camping area reserved for hikers and bicyclists ($5); open late February to October. Call (800) 452-5687 for campsite reservations ($6 extra fee), available up to 11 months ahead of time.

Rhododendron Park, a Department of Natural Resources-managed park is two miles east of Coupeville on Hwy. 20. Here you'll find free in-the-woods campsites in a second-growth stand of Douglas fir trees, with an understory that includes blooming rhododendrons in late spring.

Food

Captain Whidbey Inn, 2072 W. Captain Whidbey Inn Rd., tel. (360) 678-4097 or (800) 366-4097, has a restaurant emphasizing local seafood, especially Penn Cove mussels. Dinner reservations are needed if you aren't a guest. Get coffee and sweets at **Great Times Espresso,** tel. (360) 678-5860.

The **Coupeville Farmers Market** is held Saturday 10 a.m.-noon at 8th and Main Streets April-October.

Events

The **Penn Cove Water Festival** on the third weekend of May includes Indian canoe races, arts and crafts, and other activities. The **Coupeville Arts and Crafts Festival** on the second weekend in August features a juried art show that attracts participants from across the Northwest, plus arts and crafts exhibits, food, music, and entertainment.

On Sunday throughout the summer, **Concerts on the Cove** are held in the Town Park pavilion, featuring a wide variety of music; call

(360) 678-4684 for dates and tickets. If you're here the first weekend in October, don't miss the **Harvest Festival,** with music, food booths, a scarecrow contest, art and antique auction, and flea market.

Information and Services
The **South Whidbey Chamber of Commerce,** tel. (360) 678-5434, has a visitor center at the junction of Hwy. 20 and Main Street. Open daily 10 a.m.-5 p.m. June-Oct., and Mon.-Fri. 10 a.m.-5 p.m. the rest of the year. Get local info from the bike shop next door or Coupeville Inn at other times. The **Coupeville Arts Center,** tel. (360) 678-3396, offers a wide range of workshops throughout the year, from photography to papermaking to woodcarving.

The **Coupeville Public Library** can be found at 788 N.W. Alexander. **Whidbey General Hospital,** Main St. and Hwy. 20, tel. (360) 678-5151, provides emergency care.

Transportation
Island Transit, tel. (360) 678-7771, is a free bus system that offers Mon.-Sat. service throughout Whidbey Island. **All Island Bicycles,** 302 N. Main St., tel. (360) 678-3351, has bikes for rent or sale.

OAK HARBOR

Settled first by sea captains, then the Irish, and at the turn of the century by immigrants from Holland, Oak Harbor (pop. 19,000) takes its name from the many ancient Garry oak trees that grew here; those remaining are protected by law. The city was founded by three men in the early 1850s: a Swiss named Ulrich Freund, a Norwegian named Martin Tafton, and a New Englander named C.W. Sumner. The arrival of the military during WW II transformed this town, making it a busy place.

The city's historic downtown faces the water and retains a bit of local character, but the main drag—Hwy. 20—is yet another disgusting example of the malling of America. This is the only place on the island where you'll find burger joints, shopping malls, traffic jams, and noise. It's on a far smaller scale than many Puget Sound

cities, but comes as a rude shock if you've just driven in after visiting genteel Coupeville and Langley. One good aspect of this, however, is that Oak Harbor has the cheapest gas on the island. Be sure to fill up.

Whidbey Island Naval Air Station
The largest naval air base in the Northwest was placed here in 1941 because the area has some of the best flying weather in the U.S.: it gets only 20 inches of annual rainfall, is out of the path of commercial flight routes, and is virtually isolated with little electrical interference. So the Navy built a seaplane base just outside Oak Harbor, which is now home to tactical electronic warfare squadrons of EA-6B carrier-based jets, and A-6 Intruder attack bombers. The Whidbey Naval Air Station accounts for a payroll of 7,500 military personnel. For information, call (360) 257-2286.

Parks
City Beach Park on 70th SW, has a sandy beach with piles of driftwood, swimming, wading pool, gazebo, tennis and baseball facilities, campsites, and a Dutch windmill. There's a nice view of the peaceful and protected harbor from here, and a "Flintstone" car—popular with kids—just up from the beach. Look for ducks along the shore. **Smith Park** at Midway Blvd. has a fine collection of old Garry oak trees and a large boulder left behind by the last Ice Age.

Joseph Whidbey State Park, just south of the Naval Air Station on Swantown Rd., is largely undeveloped, with picnic tables, pit toilets, and a few trails. The real attraction here is the long and scenic beach, one of the finest on the island.

Holland Gardens, 500 Ave. W and 80th NW, site of the annual Holland Happening festival (see below), has shrub and flower gardens surrounding its big white and blue windmill—one of three in town.

Accommodations and Campgrounds
Oak Harbor has some of the least expensive lodging places on Whidbey Island. See the "Whidbey Island Accommodations" chart for a complete listing.

City Beach Park at the end of 70th St. SW, tel. (360) 679-5551, has campsites and RV sites along the lagoon for $15. RVers head to **North Whidbey RV Park,** 565 W. Cornet Bay Rd., tel. (360) 675-9597.

Food and Entertainment

As might be expected given the strong military presence in Oak Harbor, most eating places fall in the traditional all-American food groups: McDonald's, pizza joints, and steak houses. A better bet is **Kasteel Franssen** at the Auld Holland Inn, 5681 Hwy. 20, tel. (360) 675-2288 or (800) 228-0148, where they specialize in seafood, European cuisine, and excellent desserts, plus cocktails and entertainment in the lounge. Try to ignore the faux-Dutch trappings. For sandwiches, burgers, salads, and other lunch fare, visit **Dave's Bakery,** 116 W. Pioneer Way, tel. (360) 679-4860. **Pioneer Natural Foods,** 2135 200th Ave. W, tel. (360) 679-2646, has health foods and a juice bar.

Get authentic Mexican fare—including delicious *chiles rellenos* and "turbo godzilla margaritas"—at **Lucy's Mi Casita Mexican Restaurant,** 1380 W. Pioneer Way, tel. (360) 675-4800. Head to **China Harbor,** 1092 W. Pioneer Way, tel. (360) 679-1557, for Sichuan and Cantonese dishes.

L'Approdo Cucina Italiana, Hwy. 20 at 700 Ave., tel. (360) 679-8942, has Napolitano cuisine, along with blues and jazz bands nightly. For live rock 'n' roll on the weekends, head to the Blue Dolphin Restaurant.

Whidbey Playhouse, 1094 Midway Blvd., tel. (360) 679-2237, has plays throughout the year.

Events

The last weekend in April, Oak Harbor's Dutch roots appear as it hosts **Holland Happening**— a folk parade, arts and crafts show, international dance fest, Dutch dinner, and tulip show in Holland Gardens. The month of July kicks off with a **Fourth of July** parade and fireworks, followed by **Whidbey Island Race Week,** held in mid-July, and one of the top 20 yachting regattas in the world; tel. (360) 675-1314. **Sea & Sky Fest** celebrates the Navy's presence the third weekend of July with Blue Angels demonstrations, a 10-km run, pancake breakfast, and other activities; tel. (360) 675-3535. Then comes the **Dixieland Jazz Festival** the third weekend of August; call (800) 678-5519 for details. In early

December, the **Christmas Boatlight Parade** departs from Oak Harbor, proceeding around Penn Cove to the Coupeville Wharf and back.

Recreation

Swim at City Beach Park in the summer time, or the indoor **Vanderzicht Memorial Swimming Pool,** 2299 5th St. NW, tel. (360) 675-7667, the rest of the year. This facility includes a sauna, two jacuzzis, and a wading pool. The city is home to the 18-hole **Gellery Golf Course,** west of town on Clover Valley Rd., tel. (360) 257-2295.

Information and Services

The **Greater Oak Harbor Chamber of Commerce Visitor Information Center,** 5506 Hwy. 20, tel. (360) 675-3535, is open Mon.-Sat. 9 a.m.-5 p.m. summers, and Mon.-Fri. 9-11:30 a.m. and 12:30-5 p.m. the rest of the year.

The **public library** is located at 7030 70th St. NE, tel. (360) 675-5115.

Transportation

Island Transit, tel. (360) 321-6688, is a free bus system that offers Mon.-Sat. service throughout Whidbey Island.

Harbor Airlines, tel. (360) 675-6666 or (800) 359-3220, offers daily service from Oak Harbor's Ault Field to Sea-Tac and the San Juan Islands. **SeaTac Airporter Shuttle,** tel. (800) 448-8443, has direct bus service from Oak Harbor to Sea-Tac for $30.

DECEPTION PASS STATE PARK

Washington's most popular state park, Deception Pass, has facilities that rival those of national parks: swimming at two lakes, four miles of shoreline, 28 miles of hiking trails, fresh- and saltwater fishing, boating, picnicking, rowboat rentals, boat launches, viewpoints, an environmental learning center, and several hundred campsites. The park, nine miles north of Oak Harbor on Hwy. 20, covers almost 3,600 forested acres on both sides of spectacular Deception Pass Bridge.

History

When Capt. George Vancouver first sighted this waterway in 1792, he called it Port Gardner.

THE MAIDEN OF DECEPTION PASS

The Samish Indians told the story of the beautiful Maiden of Deception Pass, Ko-Kwal-Alwoot. She was gathering shellfish along the beach when the sea spirit saw her and was at once enamored; as he took her hand, Ko-Kwal-Alwoot became terrified, but the sea spirit reassured her, saying he only wished to gaze upon her loveliness. She returned often, listening to the sea spirit's declarations of love.

One day a young man came from the sea to ask Ko-Kwal-Alwoot's father for permission to marry her. Her father, suspecting that living underwater would be hazardous to his daughter's health, refused, despite the sea spirit's claim that Ko-Kwal-Alwoot would have eternal life. Miffed, the sea spirit brought drought and famine to the old man's people until he agreed to give his daughter away. There was one condition: that she return once every year so the old man could be sure she was properly cared for. The agreement was made, and the people watched as Ko-Kwal-Alwoot walked into the water until only her hair, floating in the current, was visible. The famine and drought ended at once.

Ko-Kwal-Alwoot kept her promise for the next four years, returning to visit her people, but every time she came she was covered with more and more barnacles and seemed anxious to return to the sea. On her last visit her people told her she need not return unless she wanted to; and since that time, she's provided abundant shellfish and clean spring water in that area. Legend has it that her hair can be seen floating to and fro with the tide in Deception Pass.

Today this Samish legend is inscribed on a story pole on Fidalgo Island. To get there, follow Hwy. 20 to Fidalgo Island; go west at Pass Lake, following the signs for Bowman Bay and Rosario Beach, and hike the trail toward Rosario Head.

But when he realized the inlet was actually a tidal passage between two islands, he renamed it "Deception Pass." Because of the strong tidal currents that can reach nine knots twice a day, the passage was avoided by sailing ships until 1852, when Capt. Thomas Coupe sailed a fully rigged three-masted vessel through the narrow entrance. Others quickly followed, and his namesake town—Coupeville—became a major shipping port.

Deception Pass Bridge

Completed in 1935, Deception Pass Bridge, a steel cantilever-truss structure, links Fidalgo, Pass, and Whidbey Islands. Much of the work was done by the Civilian Conservation Corps (CCC), who also built many other structures in the park. The bridge towers 182 feet above the water. It's estimated that each year more than 3.5 million people stop at the bridge to peer over the edge at the turbulent water and whirlpools far below, or to enjoy the sunset vistas.

Other Sights

Bowman Bay is just north of the bridge on the west side of the highway and has campsites, a boat launch, and a fishing pier, plus a **Civilian Conservation Corps Interpretive Center** inside one of the attractive structures that they built. Three rooms contain displays on the CCC and the men who worked for it in the 1930s. You may find one of the original CCC workers on duty, ready to talk about the old times. Open Thurs.-Mon. summers only.

Rosario Beach, just north of Bowman Bay, features a delightful picnic ground with CCC-built stone shelters. A half-mile hiking trail circles Rosario Head, the wooded point of land that juts into Rosario Bay (technically this is part of the 75-acre Sharpe County Park). The shoreline is a fine place to explore tidepools. The **Maiden of Deception Pass** totem pole commemorates the tale of a Samish Indian girl who became the bride of the water spirit (see the special topic for more). The Walla Walla College Marine Station is adjacent to Rosario Beach, and the underwater park offshore is very popular with scuba divers.

A mile south of the Deception Pass bridge is the turnoff to Coronet Bay Road. This road ends three miles out at **Hoypus Point,** a popular place to fish for salmon or to ride bikes. Great views of Mt. Baker from here.

Lakes and Hikes

Only electric motors, canoes, or rowboats are allowed on the park's lakes. You can observe beaver dams, muskrats, and mink in the marshes on the south side of shallow **Cranberry Lake**, which also hosts a seasonal concession stand. Good fishing for trout here, and the warm water makes a favorite swimming hole. North of the bridge is **Pass Lake**, another place to fish or paddle.

A 15-minute hike to the highest point on the island, 400-foot **Goose Rock**, provides views of the San Juan Islands, Mt. Baker, Victoria, and Fidalgo Island, and possibly bald eagles soaring overhead. The trail starts at the south end of the bridge, heading east from either side of the highway; take the wide trail as it follows the pass, then take one of the unmarked spur trails

uphill to the top. Other hiking trails lead throughout the park, ranging from short nature paths to unimproved trails for experienced hikers only.

Campgrounds

The primary campground along Cranberry Lake has year-round sites ($11 for tents; $5 for bikes) with hot showers and trailer dump stations, but no RV hookups or reservations. This is one of the finest campgrounds in this part of Washington, with tall Douglas fir trees and a gorgeous lakeside setting. Unfortunately, it's also one of the most popular; be ready for a multitude of fellow visitors. More campsites (summers only) at Bowman Bay, just north of the bridge. Call (360) 675-2417 for additional park information. Call (800) 452-5687 for campsite reservations ($6 extra fee), available up to 11 months ahead of time.

DIANNE BOUERICE LYONS

ANACORTES

Many visitors know Anacortes (ah-nah-KOR-tez) only as the jumping-off point for the San Juan Islands, but this city of more than 12,000 is far more than a ferry dock on the tip of Fidalgo Island. It is one of the more pleasant cities of that size in the Puget Sound basin and has a casual end-of-the-road atmosphere. Anacortes has become a highly desirable place to live—fortunate for real estate agents and property-tax collectors, but unfortunate for those who are thinking of moving here. Recent years have seen the town take pride in its heritage as buildings are renovated to house new shops.

Although it's hard to believe, Anacortes is legally on Fidalgo Island because it is surrounded by saltwater. The Sammamish Slough cuts a sluggish, narrow swath from the La Conner area around the hills known as Fidalgo Head. The slough is kept open for boaters, and it is spanned by a beautiful curving arc of a bridge.

HISTORY

Anglos first resided on the island in the 1850s, but William Munks, who liked to call himself "The King of Fidalgo Island," claimed to be the first permanent settler and opened a store in 1869. A geologist named Amos Bowman tried to persuade the company he worked for, the Canadian Pacific Railroad, to establish their western terminus at Fidalgo—despite the fact that Bowman had never seen the island. When they refused, Bowman came down to check out the property himself, bought 168 acres of it, and opened a store, a wharf, and the Anna Curtis Post Office—named after his wife—in 1879. Bowman was so determined to get a railroad—any railroad—into Anacortes, that he published a newspaper, *The Northwest Enterprise,* to draw people and businesses to his town.

He was so convincing that the population boomed to more than 3,000 people, even though, by 1890, the town's five railroad depots had yet to see a train pull up. The Burlington Northern Railroad eventually came, and residents found financial success in salmon canneries, shingle factories, and lumber mills. Anacortes grew to prominence as a shipping and fishing port; by its heyday in 1911 it was home to seven canneries and proclaimed itself "salmon canning capital of the world." Workers were needed for all these plants, and Anacortes became a major entry point of illegal laborers from China and Japan; several outlaws made a prosperous living

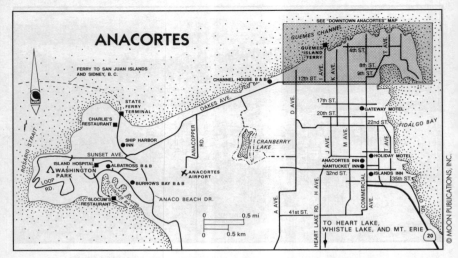

smuggling in both workers and opium. Anacortes' title as salmon canning capital of the world has long since been lost as salmon stocks dwindled in Puget Sound due to overfishing (and particularly the use of fish traps), but the city still maintains a strong seaward orientation.

Anacortes Today
The city of Anacortes relies on its Texaco and Shell oil refineries, the large Dakota Creek shipyard, two seafood processing plants (including the Trident Seafoods plant where they process Alaskan pollack for fish burgers used by Burger King and Long John Silver's), and tourists en route to the San Juan Islands. A fleet of gillnetters and seiners supplies salmon for local markets, and many of the boats here head north to Alaska each summer. In recent years the city has experienced surprising growth as retirees move in to enjoy the mild and relatively dry weather, and as tourism increases in importance.

SIGHTS AND TOURS

Museums and Historic Buildings
At 1305 8th St., the **Anacortes Museum,** tel. (360) 293-1915, has local historical exhibits including a doctor's and dentist's office, pho-

tographs, and period furniture. Open Thurs.-Mon. 1-5 p.m.; donation.

Get another taste of the past in a walk around Anacortes to see almost 50 historic murals on local buildings. The visitor center has descriptions of each and their location. Don't miss the mural of Anna Curtis across the street from the center.

Causland Park covers a city block at 8th St. and N Ave.; its colorful and playfully ornate mosaic walls and gazebo were built in 1920 with stones from area islands. Also here is a small amphitheater.

Other remnants of earlier days are scattered throughout town, including the historic sternwheeler *W.T. Preston*—now a National Historic Landmark—on display at 7th St. and R Ave. (next to the marina). The *Preston* operated as a snagboat for the U.S. Corps of Army Engineers snagboat from 1914 till she was finally retired in the 1970s and given to the city of Anacortes; it was the last sternwheeler operating on Puget Sound. The *Preston* kept the waterways clear of debris by towing off snags, logs, and stumps that piled up against bridge supports. Entrance to the *Preston* is $2 for adults, $1 for kids and seniors, and free for kids under eight. Call (360) 293-1916 for information.

Right next to the *Preston* is another historic structure is the 1911 Burlington Northern Railroad Depot at 7th and R, now refurbished as the **Depot Arts Center.** Inside is the nonprofit Northwest Departures Gallery, tel. (360) 293-3663. Open Sunday 1-4 p.m., Tues.-Fri. 1-4 p.m., and Saturday 10 a.m.-4 p.m.

Speaking of railroads, don't miss the **Anacortes Railway.** Over a 20-year period, longtime resident Tommy Thompson restored a 1909 narrow-gauge steam locomotive that pulls three passenger cars from the depot on a three-quarter-mile scenic train ride every summer weekend. Rides cost $1 for everyone; call (360) 293-2634 for more info.

The **Causland Park** area has a number of 1890s homes and buildings, many restored to their original splendor. The home owned and built by Amos and Anna Curtis Bowman in 1891 stands at 1815 8th St.; at 807 4th St., an architect's office is now housed in what was probably the finest bordello in the county in the 1890s. The little church at 5th and R was built by its Presbyterian congregation in 1889 and is undergoing restoration as a Croatian center; still in use is the Episcopal Church at 7th and M, built in 1896.

Founded in 1913 and now on the National Register of Historic Places, **Marine Supply & Hardware Co.,** 2nd and Commercial Ave., tel. (360) 293-3014, is the oldest continuously operating marine supply store west of the Mississippi. The original oiled wood floors and oak cabinets are still here, along with a potpourri of supplies. A fascinating place to visit. Friendly cat, too.

Viewpoints

Five miles south of Anacortes, 1,270-foot **Mt. Erie** is the tallest "mountain" on Fidalgo Island. The steep and winding road leads 1.5 miles to a partially wooded summit where four short trails lead to dizzying views of the Olympics, Mt. Baker, Mt. Rainier, and Puget Sound. Don't miss the two lower overlooks, located a quarter mile downhill from the summit. Get to Mt. Erie by following Heart Lake Rd. to Ray Auld Dr. and Mount Erie Road. Trails lead from various points along the Mount Erie Rd. into other parts of Anacortes Community Forest Lands.

For an impressive, low-elevation viewpoint of the Cascades and Skagit Valley, visit **Cap Sante Park** on the city's east side, following 4th St. to West Avenue. Scramble up the boulders for a better look at Mt. Baker, the San Juans, and the Anacortes refineries that turn Alaskan oil into gasoline. Not far away, a short trail leads to **Rotary Park** next to Cap Sante Marina, where you'll find picnic tables overlooking the busy harbor.

Washington Park

Three miles west of Anacortes, Washington Park is a strikingly beautiful picnic spot with 200 waterfront acres on Rosario Strait affording views of the San Juans and Olympics. Walk, bike, or drive the 2.3-mile paved scenic loop, and pull in to one of many waterfront picnic areas. Other facilities include a boat launch, several miles of hiking trails offering views of

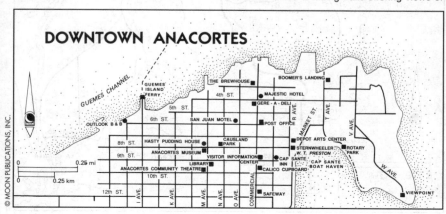

DOWNTOWN ANACORTES

VICINITY OF ANACORTES

YOUNG PARK

GUEMES ISLAND

EDENS RD.

GUEMES ISLAND PLAYGROUND

GUEMES ISLAND RD.

SOUTH SHORE RD.

SOUTH SHORE DR.

PUBLIC SHORELINE

FERRY TO SAN JUAN ISLANDS AND SIDNEY, B.C.

ROSARIO STRAIT

GUEMES ISLAND FERRY

STATE FERRY TERMINAL

CITY OF ANACORTES

12th ST.

32nd ST.

OAKES AVE.

D AVE.

COMMERCIAL AVE.

FIDALGO BAY

MARCH POINT BEACH

SHELL REFINERY

WASHINGTON PARK

CRANBERRY LAKE

ANACO BEACH RD.

HAVEKOST RD.

H AVE.

FIDALGO ISLAND

ROSARIO RD.

MARINE DR.

HEART LAKE RD.

HEART LAKE

LAKE ERIE

WHISTLE LAKE

OLD BROOK INN B & B

20

TEXACO REFINERY

MT. ERIE

CAMPBELL LAKE RD.

20

LAKE CAMPBELL

SWINOMISH CHANNEL

RESERVATION RD.

PASS LAKE

DECEPTION PASS S.P.

DECEPTION PASS

INDIAN RD.

CRANBERRY LAKE

20

WHIDBEY ISLAND

SKAGIT BAY

SNEE OOSH RD.

LA CONNER

0 — 2 mi

0 — 2 km

© MOON PUBLICATIONS, INC.

KING OF THE SMUGGLERS

Smuggling along the United States-Canadian border has always been a fact of life, and the items being transported back and forth have always been the same: liquor (particularly during the United States' foray into prohibition), illegal drugs, and illegal immigrants.

An Irishman named Larry Kelly was probably the best of all the smugglers. He even managed to die outside of prison. Kelly arrived in America simply by jumping ship in New Orleans and heading as far from there as possible. He fought in the Civil War on the Confederate side, but it wasn't long after the war that he arrived in Seattle because he heard about the "hole in the fence," meaning smuggling across the Canadian border. He also heard of the good fishing in Puget Sound for "bottle fish, poppies, and chinks," or liquor, opium, and Chinese laborers.

Kelly bought an old sailboat in 1872 and sailed north to Guemes Island, where he set up shop and learned it was easy to hide from the revenue cutters because they ran on a set schedule. Kelly made a nice profit smuggling opium, which he bought at $15 a pound in Britain and sold for $45 in the U.S.

The opium was packed in watertight tin cans, and to each can Kelly tied a chunk of salt as a sinker in case he was caught—after the salt dissolved, the can would float to the surface so Kelly could go back out and retrieve it. Kelly charged about $50 for smuggling a Chinese laborer out of Canada into the United States. Although he denied he ever killed one, other smugglers weren't adverse to chaining all of them together and dumping them overboard to drown if a revenue cutter approached. It is likely he did some of the things other smugglers did, such as putting them down on a beach in British Columbia and telling them they were in America.

Kelly was caught in 1882 with 40 cases of Canadian whiskey, and fined. He wasn't caught again for another four years, but that time he had 567 tins of opium. For this he was sent to McNeil Island Federal Penitentiary. And in 1891 he was caught for the final time, on a train with opium in his traveling bag. He was put away again, and while in prison decided to change his life. He wrote to the Louisiana Chapter of the Daughters of the Confederacy to see if any of his old friends from the Civil War were still alive. He found some in a Confederate old soldiers' home in New Orleans, and it was there he went on his release from prison, never to smuggle again.

At least he was never caught at it.

---

the San Juans and the Olympics, a playground, and campsites. The original park acreage was donated by one of Fidalgo Island's earliest pioneers, Tonjes Havekost, who said, "Make my cemetery a park for everybody." His grave stands on the southern edge of the park, overlooking Burrows Channel. Additional acreage was bought by the Anacortes Women's Club in 1922 from the sale of lemon pies—they paid just $2,500 for 75 beachfront acres.

Guemes Island

Skagit County operates ferry service to residential Guemes (GWEE-mes) Island from 6th St. and I Ave.; see "Transportation," below for details. Take your bicycle along for a scenic tour of this rural island. No stores on the island, but you'll find a mile-long public shoreline on the southwest end, plus two small county parks. Guemes Island Resort on the north end of the island has a country store and boat rentals.

RECREATION

Hiking

Stop by the visitor center and spend $3 for a guide to trails within the 2,200-acre **Anacortes Community Forest Lands** around Mt. Erie and Cranberry, Whistle, and Heart Lakes. More than 25 miles of trails are here, with mileage, elevation, and highlights. Many of these paths can be linked into loop hikes for folks of varying physical ability.

The 3.5-mile **Whistle Lake Shore Loop** circles this small body of water, offering water views, lots of birdlife, and old-growth stands of Douglas fir and cedar. An easy and almost-level path is the **Erie View Trail,** which departs from Heart Lake Rd. and follows a seasonal creek to a fine view of Mt. Erie a mile out. Return the same way.

From the trailhead at the intersection of Mount Erie and Heart Lake Roads, hike the half-mile **Pine Ridge Loop Trail,** for more views of Mt.

Erie and Sugarloaf. This moderately difficult hike takes from one to two hours. Another short hike is the 1.6-mile **Sugarloaf Trail,** starting on Ray Auld Dr. six miles from its intersection with Heart Lake Road. Follow the trail from the marshy trailhead straight up, ignoring side trails, to views to the west of Port Townsend, the San Juan Islands, and the Strait of Juan de Fuca, and north to Bellingham.

The Cranberry Lake area also has a number of hiking paths, including the mile-long **John M. Morrison Loop Trail** that starts at the end of 29th Street. This easy loop hike provides blufftop views of Cranberry Lake and old-growth Douglas fir forests, where some trees are seven feet wide. For experienced hikers, the 1.5-mile **Cranberry Lake Loop** circles the lake, starting from the parking lot at the end of Georgia Avenue. The narrow trail's difficulty lies in its poor footing and its disappearance into the lake in several spots. Allow two to three hours.

Biking and Boating
Rent bikes from **Ship Harbor Bicycle Rental** near the ferry terminal at Ship Harbor Inn, tel. (360) 293-5177 or (800) 852-8568. You can roll them aboard the ferry and head out as soon as you get to the San Juan Islands. (Bikes are also available for rent on the three main islands.)

Northwest Sea Ventures, tel. (360) 293-3692, has sea-kayak tours, from a quick sunset trip for $30 per person, to three-day tours of the San Juans for $260. They also offer all-day kayaking classes ($60) and rentals ($30 for singles or $40 for doubles). Several companies offer powerboat or sailboat charters; see the visitors center for a listing.

Other Recreation
Scimitar Ridge Ranch, 527 Miller Rd., tel. (360) 293-5355 or (800) 798-5355, has horseback riding, camping, and other family adventures. **Similk Beach Golf Course,** tel. (360)

ANACORTES ACCOMMODATIONS

Accommodations are arranged from least to most expensive. Rates may be lower during the winter months. The area code is 360.

BED AND BREAKFASTS

Channel House; 2902 Oakes Ave.; tel. 293-9382 or (800) 238-4353; $59-85 s, $69-95 d; turn-of-the-century home, San Juan Islands views, six guest rooms, private baths, hot tub, full breakfast

Hasty Pudding House B&B; 1312 8th St.; tel. 293-5773 or (800) 368-5588; $65-85 s or d; elegantly restored 1913 Edwardian home, antique furnished, fireplace, four guest rooms, private or shared baths, no kids under 10, full breakfast

Sunset Beach B&B; 100 Sunset Beach; tel. 293-5428 or (800) 359-3448; $69-79 s or d; beachfront setting, views of the San Juan Islands, three guest rooms, jacuzzi, full breakfast, AAA approved

Old Brook Inn B&B; 530 Old Brook Lane; tel. 293-4768; $70-80 s or d; modern Cape Cod style home on nine acres, Fidalgo Bay views, old orchard and babbling brook, two guest rooms, private baths, children welcome, continental breakfast

Blue Rose B&B; 1811 9th St.; tel. 293-5175; $75-80 s or d; 1910 craftsman home, two guest rooms, full breakfast

Albatross Bed and Breakfast; 5708 Kingsway W; tel. 293-0677 or (800) 484-9507; $80 s, $85 d; 1927 home with period furnishings, four guest rooms, private baths, fireplace, full breakfast and evening dessert, free airport and ferry transportation, kids okay, AAA approved

Outlook B&B; 608 H Ave.; tel. 293-3505; $85 s or d; 1910 home on Guemes Channel, two guest rooms (one with jacuzzi), private baths, woodstove, full breakfast

Burrows Bay B&B; 4911 Macbeth Dr.; tel. 293-4792; $95 s or d; luxurious contemporary home sleeps six, fireplace, large private deck, patio, sweeping view of the San Juans, full breakfast, free ferry transport

293-3444, has a nine-hole course with Puget Sound vistas.

ACCOMMODATIONS AND CAMPING

Lodging

See the "Anacortes Accommodations" chart for a complete listing of local motels and B&Bs. Anacortes is blessed with an abundance of cozy B&Bs and fine hotels; several of the nicest are also described below. Make reservations far ahead for the summer months; some places fill up by March for the peak summer season (July and August).

Within walking distance to downtown and the Cap Sante waterfront, the **Hasty Pudding House,** tel. (360) 293-5773 or (800) 368-5588, is an elegantly restored 1913 Edwardian B&B furnished in antiques and lace. Home-baked full breakfasts, hot apple cider, and a cozy fireplace add to the charm.

The Majestic Hotel, (360) 293-3355, is a European-style country inn in an historic building that was lovingly restored at a cost of several million dollars. The work shows in this four-story hotel with European antiques, view decks, and wet bars. Guests can relax in the cupola that caps the building, offering outstanding views in all directions. A big continental breakfast is included in the lodging charge.

The **Albatross Bed and Breakfast,** tel. (360) 293-0677 or (800) 484-9507, is a well-kept home with views of the marina and access to a 46-foot sailboat (extra charge). **Burrows Bay,** tel. (360) 293-4792, is a contemporary B&B with a luxury suite that features a fireplace, library, and a private deck with a sweeping view of the San Juans.

Channel House, tel. (360) 293-9382 or (800) 238-4353, is a 1902 home that also overlooks the San Juans. The four guest rooms have traditional and antique furnishings and private baths; outside is a hot tub, and a cottage with two additional rooms.

MOTELS, HOTELS, AND CABINS

Lake Campbell Motel & Apartments; 1377 Hwy. 20 (four miles south); tel. 293-5314; $35-60 s or d; kitchenettes available

San Juan Motel; tel. 293-5105 or (800) 533-8009; $40 s, $45 d; kitchenettes available, local calls 25 cents

Gateway Motel; 2019 Commercial Ave.; tel. 293-2655 or (800) 428-7583; $40 s, $45 d; kitchenettes available

Nantucket Inn; 3402 Commercial Ave.; tel. 293-6007; $48 s, $54 d; 1925 home, three guest rooms, private or shared baths, antique furnished

Holiday Motel; 2903 Commercial Ave.; tel. 293-6511; $50 s, $60 d; AAA approved

Anacortes Inn; 3006 Commercial Ave.; tel. 293-3153 or (800) 327-7976; $55-75 s, $60-85 d; outdoor pool, kitchenettes available, AAA approved

Cap Sante Inn; 906 9th St.; tel. 293-0602 or (800) 852-0846; $56 s, $60 d; AAA approved

Ship Harbor Inn; 5316 Ferry Terminal Rd.; tel. 293-5177, (800) 852-8568 (U.S.), or (800) 235-8568 (Canada); $59-65 s, $65-75 d; cabins and lodge, fireplaces, kitchenettes available, continental breakfast, AAA approved

Marina Inn; 3300 Commercial Ave.; tel. 293-1100; $65-89 s, $71-95 d; kitchenettes available, jacuzzi, continental breakfast, AAA approved

Islands Inn; 3401 Commercial Ave.; tel. 293-4644; $75-110 s, $80-110 d; island views, outdoor pool, jacuzzi, fireplaces, AAA approved

The Majestic Hotel; 419 Commercial Ave.; tel. 293-3355; $89-189 s or d; historic European-style country inn, guest rooms and suites with antiques, view decks, private baths, continental breakfast, cupola with views

Town Cottages; 1219 18th St.; tel. 293-1252; $450/week for turn-of-the-century cottages (sleep two) with kitchens, $590/week for two-bedroom condos (sleep four) with kitchens

Outlook B&B, tel. (360) 293-3505, is a classic 1910 craftsman home overlooking Guemes Channel and the San Juans. The attractive yard is landscaped with rhododendrons, camellias and azaleas. Inside, find two guest rooms (one with jacuzzi), private baths, and a wood stove. Another B&B from the same era is **Blue Rose B&B,** tel. (360) 293-5175, in a quiet neighborhood west of downtown.

Old Brook Inn, tel. (360) 293-4768, is an attractive modern home set in an old orchard (planted in 1868); nearby, find trails through nine acres of forest and a stocked pond. There are fine Fidalgo Bay views from the home. **Sunset Beach B&B,** tel. (360) 293-5428 or (800) 359-3448, has sweeping views of the San Juan Islands from its beachfront setting next to Washington Park.

In addition to these places, **Guemes Island Resort,** 325 Guemes Island Rd., tel. (360) 293-6643, has cabins and a house available on a weekly basis.

Campgrounds

Three miles west of Anacortes, the city-run **Washington Park,** tel. (360) 293-1918, has wooded campsites available year-round ($8 for tents, $12 for RVs), with coin-operated showers, laundry facilities, and boat launches. Two popular state parks with campsites are within 20 miles of Anacortes: Deception Pass State Park (see above), and Bay View State Park (see "Mount Vernon and Vicinity" earlier in this chapter.

Park RVs at **Anacortes RV Park Campground,** 1225 Hwy. 20, tel. (360) 293-3700; **Fidalgo Bay Resort,** 1107 Fidalgo Bay Rd., tel. (360) 293-5353; **Guemes Island Resort,** 325 Guemes Island Rd., tel. (360) 293-6643; **Lighthouse RV Park,** 1900 Skyline Way, tel. (360) 293-0618; and **Scimitar Ridge Ranch,** 527 Miller Rd., tel. (360) 293-5355 or (800) 798-5355. Scimitar Ridge even has covered wagons for family camping.

FOOD

Breakfast, Bakeries, and Lunch

Start your day at **Calico Cupboard Cafe & Bakery,** 901 Commercial Ave., tel. (360) 293-7315, for great homemade country breakfasts, plus healthy lunches and pastries. The cinnamon rolls and apple dumplings are particularly notable.

Fidalgo Bay Roasting Co., 710 Commercial Ave., tel. (360) 293-0243, is the place to go for fresh-roasted coffee or to relax with an espresso (or is that a contradiction in terms?).

La Vie en Rose, 416½ Commercial Ave., tel. (360) 299-9546, has wonderful French pastries, plus delicious soups and sandwiches for lunch. If you're heading out on the ferry, call ahead to have them put together a box lunch special.

For take-out food or casual eat-in dining, stop by **Gere-a-Deli,** 502 Commercial Ave., tel. (360) 293-7383. In addition to sandwiches, salads, soups, and homemade desserts, they also offer a big Friday evening pasta dinner with a wide range of choices.

Surf and Turf

On the waterfront at 209 T Ave., **Boomer's Landing,** tel. (360) 293-5108, specializes in lobster, steak, and seafood. Another nice steak and seafood place is **Slocum's Restaurant,** Skyline Way at Flounder Bay, tel. (360) 293-0644, with views of Skyline Marina. Slocum's is open for Sunday brunch and has an outdoor patio. **Charlie's Restaurant,** next to the ferry terminal, tel. (360) 293-7377, has a moderately priced menu with water and dock views; it's a convenient place to stop for a drink while you're waiting for your ship to come in.

Brewpub

You definitely won't go wrong with a lunch or dinner at **Anacortes Brewhouse,** 320 Commercial Ave., tel. (360) 293-3666; very good meals for reasonable prices, and fresh suds from the on-the-premises brewery.

Northwest Cuisine

La Petite Restaurant, 3401 Commercial Ave., tel. (360) 293-4644, serves some of the best dinners in Anacortes, plus a hearty Dutch breakfast; open daily for breakfast, dinner except Monday. Be ready to drop $30 per person or more for a dinner.

The Majestic Hotel's **Courtyard Bistro,** 419 Commercial Ave., tel. (360) 299-2923, serves excellent but pricey Northwest cuisine with a gorgeous garden setting, or save a bit by going for lighter fare in the **Rose & Crown Pub** on the premises.

Foreign Affairs

La Hacienda, 1506 Commercial Ave., tel. (360) 299-1060, serves Mexican lunches and dinners, and **Tokyo Japanese Restaurant,** tel. (360) 293-9898, has fresh sushi. **Hong Kong Restaurant,** 2501 Commercial Ave., tel. (360) 293-9595, offers Sichuan, Cantonese, and American meals.

Markets

Anacortes has a big Safeway, but for the freshest produce head to the **Saturday Market,** held summers inside the old depot at 611 R Street. For seafood, stop by two longtime favorites: **Thibert's Crab Market,** 697 Stevenson Rd., tel. (360) 293-2525, or **Knudson's Crab Market,** 2610 Commercial Ave., tel. (360) 293-3696.

ENTERTAINMENT AND EVENTS

The Arts

The **Depot Arts Center,** tel. (360) 293-3663, houses Northwest Departures Gallery, showcasing a wide range of locally produced art, plus the **Vela Luka Croatian Dancers,** a local group that performs all over the world. You can see them perform during the Skagit Valley Tulip Festival, and at several other times during the year. This is the most obvious example of Anacortes' active Croatian community; a cultural center is in the works at 801 5th Street.

The **Anacortes Community Theatre,** or ACT, stages six plays and musicals each year, plus annual Christmas performances in a 112-seat theater at 10th and M. For ticket information call (360) 293-6829.

Hang out in the book stacks at the **Anacortes Library** at 1209 9th St., tel. (360) 293-1910, or meet the authors during book and poetry readings at **Watermark Book Co.,** 612 Commercial Ave., tel. (360) 293-4277.

Nightlife

Head to **Anacortes Brewhouse,** 320 Commercial Ave., tel. (360) 293-3666, for live jazz on weekend evenings.

Festivals

Held the first three weekends in April in Anacortes, La Conner, and Mount Vernon, the ever-popular **Skagit Valley Tulip Festival,** tel. (360) 293-3832, offers everything from boat rides to fireworks; see "Mount Vernon and Vicinity" earlier in this chapter for details. The **Anacortes Waterfront Festival,** held at Cap Sante Boat Haven the weekend before Memorial Day each May, celebrates the city's maritime heritage with boat rides, entertainment, craft booths, farmers and seafood market, boat show and regatta, and art show.

Anacortes, like every other town in America, has a parade and fireworks on the **Fourth of July.** The last weekend in July brings the self-explanatory **Anachords Annual Barbershop Concert and Salmon Barbecue.**

The **Anacortes Arts and Crafts Festival,** held the first weekend of August, attracts more than 50,000 people and includes a juried fine art show, high-quality arts and crafts booths, a children's fair, ethnic foods, antique cars, and plenty of live music and entertainment. No charge; call (360) 293-6211 for details. If you missed this one, shoot for the **World's Largest King Salmon Barbecue** on the third weekend of August. Catch the holiday spirit, Puget-sound style: watch for the annual **Lighted Ships of Christmas Boat Parade,** held the second Saturday in December.

INFORMATION AND SERVICES

For maps, brochures, and up-to-date information, contact the **Anacortes Visitors Information Center,** 819 Commercial Ave., tel. (360) 293-3832. Open daily 9 a.m.-5 p.m. May-Oct., and Mon.-Sat. 9 a.m. -4 p.m. the rest of the year. Across the street is a mural of Anna Curtis, for whom the town was named. The Anacortes **area code** is 360.

For a tumble and spin-dry, try **Econo-Wash Laundry,** tel. (360) 293-2974, at 2022 Commercial. If you get hurt while tumbling and spinning, head to **Island Hospital** at 24th and M, tel. (360) 293-3183.

TRANSPORTATION

Ferry Service

To reach the San Juan Islands via state ferry, you have no choice but to leave from Anacortes—and ferry traffic keeps a good portion of local businesses in business. Be prepared for a lengthy wait on summer weekends. Avoid the waits by leaving your car in the free lot and walking aboard; there's always space for walk-on passengers. The Anacortes ferry terminal is four miles west of downtown on Oakes Ave. (12th St.) and has a small cafe with espresso, along with two nearby restaurants. For fares and other vital information see "San Juan Islands" below or phone the Washington State Ferry System at (360) 293-8166 in Anacortes, or (800) 843-3779 statewide.

Skagit County operates a small ferry to residential **Guemes Island** from 6th St. and I Avenue. The five-minute crossing costs $6.25 roundtrip for car and driver, and $1.25 roundtrip for passengers or walk-ons. The boat departs daily on the hour or better, from 6:30 a.m. most days to at least 6 p.m. Call (360) 293-6356 for details.

By Air

Departing from Anacortes Airport, **West Isle Air,** tel. (360) 293-4691 or (800) 874-4434, offers commuter flights year-round to San Juan Islands, plus flightseeing trips and air charters.

By Bus

Anacortes is one of the few cities in this part of Washington without local buses. To get to or away from Anacortes, **Evergreen Trailways/Gray Line,** tel. (800) 426-7532, and **Greyhound,** tel. (360) 336-5111 or (800) 231-2222, offer bus service. **SeaTac Airporter Shuttle,** tel. (800) 235-5247, has daily shuttles between Anacortes and Sea-Tac for $27 one-way, $49 roundtrip.

BOB RACE

SAN JUAN ISLANDS

Nestled between the Washington mainland and Vancouver Island, the San Juan archipelago consists of 172 named islands. In actuality, there are more than 786 at low tide and 457 at high tide. Four of the largest—Orcas, Lopez, Shaw, and San Juan—are served by state ferry and are home to approximately 12,000 people. These numbers swell to 30,000 at the peak of summer tourism. The pace is slow and the dress is casual, so leave your ties at home, but don't forget your binoculars (for watching whales and birds), camera, and bike.

More than any other part of Washington, the San Juans will give you a sense of being *away*. When the ferry pulls away from the Anacortes dock, it is almost like departing on a cruise ship. The islands have become one of the state's favorite places to get away, and each summer more visitors arrive, and the demand for facilities goes higher. In recent years the numbers have approached 1.7 million ferry passengers, along with many more folks who arrive by plane.

It isn't just tourists who travel to the San Juans. In the last two decades they have been discovered as a place to escape the fast pace of city living, and as a retirement haven. But any land deals are long gone. Anyone wanting to buy shoreline property will soon discover that the going rate is $1000 a foot! San Juan County has an assessed per-capita property valuation more than three times the state average. Another measure of the importance of land is this: there are 30 different real estate dealers on the islands, one for every 333 residents!

An oddity of the islands is that all of the three islands with heavy population manage to have their distinct personalities. Generally speaking (very generally), Lopez Island attracts low-key people who care less than most about an extravagant lifestyle, people who are comfortable alone or in a small community. San Juan is the county seat so that's where the lawyers and promoters and political hangers-on go. Friday Harbor is a hotbed of environmentalists vs. developers, a struggle that has been going on for decades. Fortunately, the **San Juan Preservation Trust,** a local nonprofit organization, has been able to protect a considerable amount of the remaining open space on San Juan Island through conservation easements.

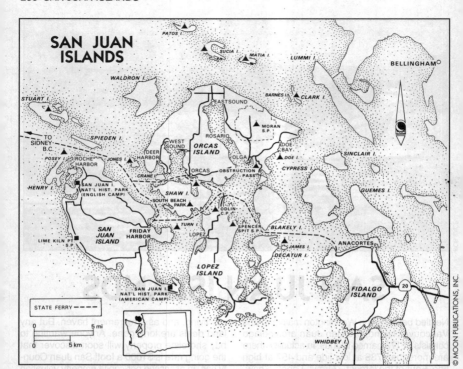

Orcas is something of the Kiwanis Club of the islands. Several industrialists have built homes there, including members of the Kaiser family and several Northwest industrial powers. The island also continues to attract those with less cash, particularly artists and writers.

CLIMATE

The San Juans do most of their tourist business between Memorial Day and Labor Day when the weather is warm—rarely above 85°—and sunny, but for the locals September and October are the nicest months of the year: the tourists are gone, and the weather is still warm and dry, with highs in the 60s and lows in the 40s or 50s, and the salmon are running. Because the islands are shielded by the Olympic and Vancou-

ver Island mountains, rainfall amounts to less than 25 inches per year; December is the wettest month, with 4.5 inches of rain on the average and temperatures in the low 40s. The sun shines an average of 247 days a year on the islands, much of that during the mostly dry summer months. It rarely snows in the San Juans, and when it does it lasts but a few days.

Water—or the lack thereof—is a serious problem on the islands, particularly during the all-too-frequent drought years. There are few permanent creeks and even fewer lakes on the islands, but there's heavy demand due to increasing development. Most B&Bs and other lodging places use low-flow showerheads and other means to conserve water. Do your part by not wasting a drop. This means avoiding long showers, not leaving the water running while brushing your teeth, and not flushing the toilet as often.

SPORTS AND RECREATION

The San Juans abound with outdoor pleasures of all kinds: cycling, sea kayaking, camping, hiking, scuba diving, sailing, windsurfing, whale-watching, and fishing to name a few. Specifics on these are listed in descriptions for the various islands below.

Sea Kayaking

The protected waters, diverse landscapes, rich wildlife, and a myriad of bays and coves make the San Juans a marvelous place to explore in a sea kayak. This is one of the finest ways to see the islands, as more and more folks are discovering each year. A number of companies offer such trips, and several will also rent kayaks to you. Kayaking companies are listed below under the "Sports and Recreation" headings for the three main islands. No experience is necessary on these kayak tours, but it certainly helps to be in good physical condition.

Elakah! Expeditions, tel. (360) 734-7270, is a Bellingham-based company with guided sea-kayaking trips in the San Juans lasting one to four days ($69-316 per person). Other trips head to destinations as far away as Baja and Alaska, and the company also offers unusual kayak trips with a spiritual tone, including African drumming, yoga retreats, mother-daughter camps, and storytelling adventures.

Outdoor Odysseys, tel. (206) 361-0717, has one-day ($65 per person), two-day ($210 per person), and three-day trips ($290 per person) to the San Juans, plus popular sea kayaking trips to other parts of Puget Sound.

Cycling

The San Juans seem to have been made for bike riding—mild weather, a wide diversity of terrain, gorgeous scenery, excellent facilities, and not a lot of traffic (except on San Juan). If you have a family in tow or aren't in great shape, head to slow-paced Lopez; Shaw is small but fun to explore; Orcas has more rugged terrain (including a tough ride to the top of 2,409-foot Mt. Constitution); while San Juan offers the most services.

You can bring your own bike on the ferry for an extra $2.75—a lot cheaper than hauling your car, and you won't have to wait—or rent one when you arrive. Bike rentals are available in Anacortes and on the three major islands by the day, hour, or week. Most shops rent touring and mountain bikes, panniers, child carriers, and helmets. See the individual islands for specifics on bike rental companies.

Backroads, tel. (800) 462-2848, has six-day cycling tours of the San Juans many times each summer. These are offered as either camping trips ($749 per person including meals), or trips where you stay at local inns and B&Bs ($1298 per person including meals). A sag-wagon carries your gear, bike rentals are also available, and you can choose your own pace.

Whalewatching

The waters around the San Juans are famous for the whales that come here during the summer months, so it's no surprise that the movie *Free Willy II* was filmed here. The most exciting of these are the orca, or "killer" whales that pursue migrating salmon and seals. What some visitors think are baby orcas are actually full-grown black-and-white Dall's porpoises. Other marine mammals commonly seen around the islands include minke whales, harbor porpoises, harbor seals, and even elephant seals.

Watching whales is a favorite activity around the San Juans, with daily tours offered from both San Juan and Orcas Islands throughout the summer. Most trips last five to six hours. Three resident pods, or families, of orcas are frequently spotted along these trips, along with a few strays. The whales are here in pursuit of migrating salmon. They have been extensively studied for more than 20 years; individual males are identifiable from distinctive markings on their tall dorsal fin. The excellent Whale Museum in Friday Harbor (see "San Juan Island") has a pamphlet with drawings showing these markings, and they also maintain a **Whale Hotline** for sightings and stranding information: (800) 562-8832. If you're heading out in your own kayak or other vessel, be sure to stay at least 100 yards from whales (it's the law) and even farther from seal and sea lion haul-out areas since the animals are easily spooked. The best time to see orcas is mid-June to mid-July, but they are periodically visible from mid-May to mid-September.

For local companies offering whalewatching voyages, see "Sports and Recreation" under San Juan Island and Orcas Island (below). In the peak season, be sure to make advance reservations for these popular trips. During the winter—when the whales are elsewhere—many of these companies offer wildlife viewing cruises.

ACCOMMODATIONS AND CAMPING

The San Juans are immensely popular in the summertime, particularly during the peak season of July and August. If you plan a visit at these times, there may well be no room in the inn, and not a lot of mangers available either. Save yourself a lot of headaches by making reservations far in advance. At the older and more established B&Bs this means calling at least four months ahead of time for a mid-summer weekend reservation! If you're looking for space on Memorial Day, the Fourth of July, Labor Day, or during the Jazz Festival in late July, make reservations up to a year in advance. Do *not* arrive in Friday Harbor on a July Saturday afternoon expecting to find a place; you won't. Many of the resorts, inns, and cottages also offer weekly rates and require a minimum summertime stay of at least two nights (sometimes a week). Also note that most B&Bs on the San Juans cater almost exclusively to couples and do not allow kids. Families may want to head instead to Birch Bay (see the Northern Puget Sound chapter), where the facilities are lower-key and more kid-proof.

There are not a lot of motels on the San Juans—and none of the big motel chains; most places on the islands have just a few rooms, so space is at a premium. It also costs a premium, and only a few lodges are less than $70 d. Hostel accommodations are available at Doe Bay Village Resort on Orcas Island. Dorm accommodations are also available at Orcinus Inn on San Juan Island. Several real estate companies on the islands offer weekly and monthly home rentals. Check the Seattle newspapers or the two local weekly papers—*The Journal of the San Juan Islands* and *The Islands' Sounder*—for vacation rentals.

In the winter months you'll find fewer fellow travelers, lower lodging rates (often 30% less), and less of a problem getting a room, but the weather won't be quite as inviting and things won't be as green. Winter holidays (especially Christmas to New Year's) are likely to be booked well in advance. See the accommodations charts for complete listings of places to stay on the three main islands.

Public campsites are most abundant on Orcas Island, but even these fill up; San Juan Island has only a handful, and they are generally completely reserved by the end of May (though private RV parks often have space).

INFORMATION AND SERVICES

For maps and information before you arrive, call the **San Juan Islands Visitor Information Service** at (360) 468-3663. Each of the three main islands has its own chamber of commerce office. Two books by Marge and Ted Mueller are the best sources for detailed information on the San Juans: *The San Juan Islands Afoot & Afloat* and *The Essential San Juan Islands Guide.* Both are published by The Mountaineers (Seattle).

The **area code** for the San Juan Islands is 360. All calls among the various San Juan islands are local calls.

Fuel and Food
If you're driving around the islands, be sure to fill your tank in Anacortes before getting on the ferry. Because of the extra cost of shipping fuel here (and because they can get away with it) gas stations on the islands charge at least 30% more for gas than on the mainland. Similarly, prices for food are also higher. Save by stocking up in Anacortes.

FERRY SERVICE

If you can only take one ride aboard a **Washington State Ferry**, the trip from Anacortes to the San Juans should be the one. The scenery is so beautiful that even amateur photographers can get spectacular sunset-over-the-islands shots. Ferries leave Anacortes at least a dozen times a day from 4:30 a.m. to 12:20 a.m. stopping at Lopez, Shaw, Orcas, and Friday Harbor, in that order; it takes roughly two hours from Anacortes to Friday Harbor. Not every ferry stops on each island, but nearly all of them stop at Friday Harbor on San Juan Island. Ferries between Anacortes and Sidney, B.C., run twice a day in the summer and once a day the rest of the year. The ferries have food and booze onboard, and a duty-free shop can be found on ferries heading to British Columbia. For more information, call (360) 293-8166 in Anacortes, (206) 464-6400 in Seattle, (604) 381-1551 in Victoria, or (800) 843-3779 statewide.

When to Travel

During the peak summer season for travel to the San Juans, it's wise to arrive at least two hours early on weekends, or an hour early on weekdays. On holiday weekends you may find yourself in line for up to five hours! Free parking is available at the Anacortes ferry terminal if you're heading over on foot or by bike. Both San Juan and Orcas Islands have excellent bus services, so you really don't need a car there anyway. The terminal usually has information on current campsite availability at parks on the San Juans (meaning they often say none are available) to help in planning where to stay that night. Avoid the crowds by traveling in midweek, early in the morning, late in the evening (except Friday evenings), or better yet, by foot, kayak, or bike.

The ferry system operates on a first-come, first-served basis, with reservations only available for the routes from Anacortes to Sidney, B.C., and from Orcas Island or San Juan Island to Sidney. No reservations for travel to the San Juans; just get in line and wait like everyone else.

Fares

Fares to Friday Harbor, the last American stop, are $4.95 for passengers, $20.30 car and driver ($16.80 in the winter), and a $2.75 surcharge for a roll-on bicycle. Carry-on kayaks cost $8.75 extra ($7.30 in winter). Car-and-driver fares to the other islands from Anacortes are a few dollars less. Interisland ferries are free for passengers and bikes, and $8.25 ($7 in the winter) for cars and drivers.

Ferry travelers are only charged in the westbound direction; eastbound travel within the San Juans or from the islands to Anacortes is free. (The only exception to this is for travelers leaving from Sidney, B.C.). If you're planning to visit all the islands, save money by heading straight to Friday Harbor, and then working your way back through the others at no additional charge.

Once a day a ferry continues on to Sidney, B.C.; fares are $6.90 for passengers, $35.65 for car and driver ($29.70 in the winter), and $4.50 for bicycle and rider.

Private Ferries

The *San Juan Explorer,* tel. (360) 448-5000 or (800) 888-2535, is a popular way to reach the islands from either Seattle or Victoria. The boat departs from Seattle's Pier 69 on daily cruises to the San Juans in the summer, less frequently the rest of the year. Roundtrip rates for adults are $54 to Friday Harbor (San Juan Island), and $62 to Rosario Resort (Orcas Island). Transportation between Friday Harbor and Victoria is $44 roundtrip for adults. Lower rates in the off-season and for seniors and kids. A variety of travel-and-lodging packages are also available for trips to the islands on the *Explorer.*

San Juan Island Express, tel. (360) 671-1137, operates a 49-passenger ferry—the *Squito*—connecting Bellingham with Orcas and San Juan Islands. Fares are $20 one-way, $33 roundtrip ($29 for seniors, students, and kids ages three to 17), and the boat operates on a daily basis from late May through September. They also provide three-hour whalewatching cruises from Friday Harbor for $45 adults, or $35 kids under 12, and from Friday Harbor for $32 adults, or $25 kids.

Island Transport Ferry Service has private water-taxi service to all the San Juan islands aboard a small catamaran; call (360) 293-6060 for details.

P.S. Express, tel. (360) 385-5288, provides passenger-only service between Port Townsend and Friday Harbor on San Juan Island. The boat leaves Port Townsend daily, May-Oct., and stays in Friday Harbor long enough for a quick three-hour visit, or you can overnight there, and return to Port Townsend later. The charge is $31.50 one-way, $45 roundtrip; bikes and kayaks $10 extra.

OTHER TRANSPORTATION

Boat Tours

The San Juans are famous as a boater's paradise, with relatively protected waters, good wind conditions, an abundance of coves and shoreline to explore, numerous state parks only accessible by boat, and gorgeous scenery. Many sailing charters and motorboat charters operate from the San Juans; see the specific islands for details. In addition, you'll find boat tours of the San Juans from Bellingham and Anacortes; see visitor centers in these cities for specifics.

The **Mosquito Fleet,** tel. (206) 252-6800, has jet catamaran tours that take travelers from Everett to San Juan Island, where they can spend several hours enjoying the sights around Friday Harbor, or stay on board to watch for whales before returning to Everett. The total trip length is nine hours. The boat runs year-round and costs $69 for adults, $59 for seniors, and $49 for kids (lower winter rates).

One of the more interesting boats is the **Snow Goose,** a Bellingham-based 65-foot research vessel operated by two marine biologists. They offer a range of trips, including five-day voyages around the San Juans where you'll get a firsthand look at marinelife and how researchers study life in Puget Sound. Call (360) 733-9078 for details.

The **Sacajawea** is a 59-foot motor yacht offering excellent tours of the San Juans and British Columbia's Gulf Islands. It carries up to eight passengers and offers more personalized trips than the larger tour boats. Fares are $1400 for a seven-day cruise around the San Juans, or $1755 for a nine-day cruise of the San Juans and Gulf Islands. This includes all meals and onboard accommodations. Trips depart from Seattle; call (206) 621-7623 for details.

Alaska Sightseeing Cruise West, tel. (206) 441-8687 or (800) 426-7702, offers all-inclusive "Island Discoveries" tours of the San Juans and Puget Sound in September and October. These seven-night voyages aboard the 165-foot *Spirit of Discovery* depart Seattle and include visits to Victoria, the San Juans, Whidbey Island, Hood Canal, Port Townsend, La Conner, and Mt. Rainier. Not for the budget crowd: The cost is $1159-2186 per person.

By Air

Kenmore Air, tel. (206) 486-1257 or (800) 543-9595, has scheduled floatplane flights from Lake Union in Seattle and Lake Washington in Kenmore to Friday Harbor and Roche Harbor on San Juan Island, to Fisherman Bay on Lopez Island, and to Rosario Resort and West Sound on Orcas Island. The fare is $70 one-way or $130 roundtrip. Kenmore Air also offers charter service to other destinations in the San Juans.

West Isle Air, tel. (360) 293-4691 or (800) 874-4434, has daily wheeled-plane flights from Anacortes or Bellingham to most of the San Juan Islands, including Lopez, Orcas, San Juan, Waldron, Stuart, Decatur, Blakely, Center, Spieden, and Sinclair for $25-35 per person one-way. Flights from Boeing Field in Seattle to these same destinations are $60-80 per person one-way. They also offer 40-minute flightseeing trips over the San Juans ($75 for three people) from Bellingham or Anacortes, charter service, and freight deliveries.

Harbor Airlines, (360) 675-6666 or (800) 359-3220, offers daily wheeled-plane service from Sea-Tac ($75 one-way; $130 roundtrip) and Oak Harbor ($25 one-way; $48 roundtrip).

Charter service is offered by **Aeronautical Services Inc.,** tel. (360) 378-2640. If several folks are flying together, they may offer your least expensive air-travel option.

SAN JUAN ISLAND

The largest island in the archipelago, San Juan Island is about 20 miles long and seven miles wide, covering 55 square miles. Friday Harbor, the only incorporated town in the chain, is also the county seat, the commercial center of the San Juans, and home to half of the island's 5,300 residents. Picturesque Friday Harbor sits along the west side, its marina protected by Brown Island. This is a U.S. Customs port of entry.

SIGHTS

Museums

The Whale Museum, 62 1st St. N in Friday Harbor, tel. (360) 378-4710, has whale and porpoise displays including full skeletons of a baby gray whale, plus adult killer and minke whales. Watch a fine 26-minute video on orcas, learn about snoring whales on an interactive video, examine whale fetuses, and learn how whales use echolocation, and how they mate. You can also "adopt" a whale for $25; you get the whale's photo and ID number. The museum is open daily 10 a.m.-5 p.m. from Memorial Day through September, and daily 11 a.m.-4 p.m. the rest of the year. Admission costs $3 for adults, $2.50 for students and seniors, $1.50 for kids five to 12. There's also a gift shop in the museum with games, T-shirts, and jewelry. If you spot a whale anywhere around the San Juans, swimming or stranded, call the museum's 24-hour hotline: tel. (800) 562-8832.

San Juan Historical Museum, 405 Price St. in Friday Harbor, tel. (360) 378-3949, is open Wed.-Sat. 1-4:30 p.m. May-Sept., and Thurs.-Fri. 1-4:30 p.m. the rest of the year. Located in an 1890s farmhouse, the museum includes fascinating antiques and historical artifacts, plus old farm equipment outside. No charge.

Roche Harbor Resort

Located on the north end of San Juan Island, Roche Harbor Resort is a delicious step into the past. In 1886, John S. McMillin established the Roche Harbor Lime & Cement Co., mining lime deposits from 13 hillside quarries and processing the lime in brick-lined kilns along the shore. By the 1890s this was the largest lime works west of the Mississippi and required 4,000 acres of forest just to keep the kilns running (each kiln burned 10 cords of wood every six hours!). McMillin built a company town for his employees, had warehouses that extended hundreds of feet into the bay, and operated a general store on the wharf. His Hotel de Haro began as a log bunkhouse, but later grew into the distinctive three-story wood structure of today. It was twice visited by President Theodore Roosevelt, in 1906 and 1907, and his signature can still be seen on the guestbook. The limestone quarries operated till 1956, when they were essentially mined out. The beautiful white-clapboard hotel has been restored and is fronted by a formal garden with rose trellises. McMillin's home is now a waterside restaurant, facing the protected harbor filled with sailboats. The old general store is still in use, the remains of several kilns are visible, and the simple cottages of McMillin's employees are now rented out to guests. The only affronts to this slice of living history are the ugly condos that have sprouted nearby.

Stop by the hotel to pick up a brochure describing the rich history of Roche Harbor. Take some time to explore the area around the hotel (now on the National Register of Historic Places), and the little New England-style Our Lady of Good Voyage Chapel—built in 1892, and the only privately owned Catholic church in the nation. The bizarre family mausoleum ("Afterglow Vista" no less) is approximately a mile from the hotel. Located north of the cottages and a quarter-mile hike up a dirt side road, the mausoleum's centerpiece is a stone temple packed with Masonic symbology, and containing the family's ashes in chairs around a limestone table. There's even a broken column symbolizing the "unfinished state" of life, but the planned bronze dome was never added to this once-grandiose mausoleum. Step out of the past at the fly-in aviation community nearby, with planes taxiing down Cesna Ave. and parked in hangers next to nearly every house.

SAN JUAN ISLAND

SPIEDEN CHANNEL

POSEY ISLAND STATE PARK

LONESOME COVE RESORT

ROCHE HARBOR

MAUSOLEUM

ROCHE HARBOR RESORT

WESTCOTT BAY

ROULEAU RD.

LIMESTONE POINT RD.

ROCHE HARBOR RD.

SAN JUAN CHANNEL

MT. YOUNG

ENGLISH CAMP

HARBOR RD.

LAKEDALE

MITCHELL BAY

SNUG HARBOR RESORT

STATES INN B & B

MITCHELL BAY RD.

WEST VALLEY RD.

LAKE RD.

EGG LAKE RD.

BEAVERTON VALLEY RD.

UNIVERSITY OF WASHINGTON MARINE BIOLOGY LAB

BROWN ISLAND

TURN ISLAND STATE PARK

MOON & SIXPENCE B & B

FRIDAY HARBOR

MARIELLA INN

SAN JUAN COUNTY PARK

WEST SIDE RD.

TRUMPETER INN B & B

SAN JUAN VALLEY RD.

TURN POINT RD.

PEAR POINT RD.

DUFFY HOUSE B & B

LIME KILN POINT STATE PARK

LIGHTHOUSE

WOLD RD.

DOUGLAS RD.

THE FARM B & B

THE MEADOWS B & B

WESTWINDS B & B

TOWER HOUSE B & B

BAILER HILL RD.

FALSE BAY RD.

CATTLE POINT RD.

GRIFFIN BAY

FALSE BAY

HARO STRAIT

MAR VISTA RESORT

PEDAL BAY BICYCLE PARK

OLYMPIC LIGHTS B & B

AMERICAN CAMP

JACKLE'S LAGOON

VISITOR CENTER

SOUTH BEACH

MT. FINLAYSON (290 ft.)

CATTLE POINT

0   1.5 mi

0   1.5 km

© MOON PUBLICATIONS, INC.

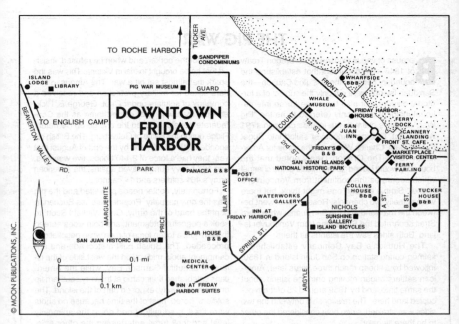

Lime Kiln Point State Park

A good spot to watch for whales is from Lime Kiln Point State Park along Haro Strait on the island's west side; it's the only park in the country dedicated exclusively to whalewatching. Sit here long enough on a summer day (it may be quite a while) and you're likely to see killer whales (orcas), and possibly minke and pilot whales, Dall's porpoises, or harbor porpoises. Rangers are usually at the park in the summer and fall and can answer your questions. The small white lighthouse was built in 1914 and has a fog horn that announces its presence constantly. Researchers use the lighthouse to watch for whales and to determine if boats are affecting their behavior. If there aren't any whales to watch, you can just take in the vistas that stretch to Victoria. No camping at the park.

Wildlife Viewing

Bald eagles live on the island year-round; look for them between Eagle Cove and Cattle Point on the island's east side. **Wolf Hollow Wildlife Rehabilitation Centre,** 240 Boyce Rd., treats

orphaned and injured wild animals, from hummingbirds to elephant seals. They are not generally open to the public; call (360) 378-5000 for information on guided tours.

Winetasting

Sample San Juan Cellars' wines at **The Island Wine Company,** next to the ferry dock in Friday Harbor, tel. (360) 378-3229 or (800) 248-9463; open daily 10 a.m.-6 p.m. This is the only place they are sold. (The wines are produced and bottled by other wineries using grapes grown in eastern Washington.)

PIG WAR SIGHTS

In one of the stranger pieces of history, the killing of a pig by an American settler nearly set off a war between the U.S. and Britain; see the special topic for details on this bizarre incident. Fortunately, conflict was averted and the San Juan Islands were eventually declared American territory. One doesn't have to look far to find

THE PIG WAR

Because of vague wording in the Oregon Treaty of 1846—the document that established the boundary between the U.S. and Canada—the San Juan Islands were not only the subject of a territorial dispute, but also the stage for an international incident commonly referred to as the "Pig War." Britain's claim to the islands came in 1791 when Capt. George Vancouver sailed into Puget Sound; Capt. Charles Wilkes did the same for America in 1841. The Oregon Treaty noted that the boundary would extend "to the middle of the channel which separates the continent from Vancouver's Island." Simple enough one might think, but there were actually two channels. Rosario Strait went between the mainland and the San Juans, while Haro Strait separated the San Juans from Vancouver Island. Both sides saw the islands as theirs.

The Hudson's Bay Company established a salmon-curing station on San Juan Island in 1850, followed by a sheep ranch three years later. American settlers began moving onto the island about the same time, and by 1859 around 25 of them occupied land here. The relationship between the two sides was strained, since both considered the other to be there illegally.

Porker Trouble

In June of 1859 one of the American settlers, Lyman A. Cutler, got tired of a Hudson's Bay Company-owned hog rooting in his potato patch, so he shot and killed it. English authorities insisted that Cutler pay for the porker, and when he refused, insisted that he be brought to trial in Victoria. This was the spark that almost set off a war. The American settlers asked for military protection and received a company of soldiers under Capt. George E. Pickett—the man who later gained fame as the Confederate general who led the charge up Cemetery Ridge during the Battle of Gettysburg. The British responded with quickly, and by the end of August that year they had a force of 2,140 troops, five warships, and 167 heavy guns arrayed against the American army's 461 soldiers and 14 cannons.

Fortunately, cooler heads prevailed and the pig was the only casualty. President James Buchanan sent the head of the army, Gen. Winfield Scott, to seek a peaceful settlement, and both sides agreed to leave just a token force of men while negotiations proceeded. The British built a stockade and encampment about midway on the west side of the island in beautiful Garrison Bay, while the Americans established their camp at the very southern tip on the most windy, exposed part of the island. The soldiers, bored most of the time because no shots were fired, gradually turned down the animosity level and took turns entertaining the other side. The troops remained there until the matter was settled by arbitration 12 years later by Kaiser Wilhelm I of Germany, who gave the San Juans to the United States.

Both the English and American camps are now part of the San Juan Islands National Historic Park.

how similar minor incidents set off dramatic consequences: in 1854 an emigrant's cow was butchered near Wyoming's Fort Laramie by a Miniconjou Indian; when he refused to surrender to the U.S. Army, a battle ensued that left 29 soldiers dead.

The small, privately run **Pig War Museum,** on the corner of Tucker and Guard, tel. (360) 378-6495, is open Mon.-Sat. noon-6 p.m. from Memorial Day through Labor Day. Admission is $3 for adults, $2 for seniors and students, free for kids under five.

San Juan Islands National Historic Park

The sites where the American and British forces were based are now part of the San Juan Is-

lands National Historic Park, with headquarters on Spring St. in Friday Harbor, tel. (360) 378-2240. Open daily 8 a.m.-5 p.m. Memorial Day through Labor Day, and Mon.-Fri. 8 a.m.-4 p.m. the rest of the year. The office houses a small exhibit about the so-called Pig War. The park itself is in two sections on different ends of the island: American Camp and English Camp. Both sites have picnic areas and beach access for day use only. The grounds are open year-round but do not have campgrounds.

American Camp

Located on the southeast corner of San Juan Island, American Camp sits on a windswept grassy peninsula five miles from Friday Harbor.

This is a wonderful place on a sunny summer afternoon, with both the Cascades and Olympics in view. It's a deliciously lonely place to explore on a rainy winter day.

Two buildings remain at American Camp—a barracks building and a laundress' house—along with a defensive fortification (redoubt) that was constructed by Henry M. Roberts, of *Roberts' Rules of Order* fame. A long white picket fence circles the grounds, and a trail leads downhill past the old Hudson's Bay Company Farm site on Grandma's Cove. Other nature trails take off to Mt. Finlayson (hardly a mountain at just 290 feet) and through the forests along **Jackle's Lagoon,** or you can explore driftwood-jammed **South Beach,** a wonderful place for a sunset walk on the sandy shores. This is the longest public beach on the island. The park is also home to thousands of rabbits whose ancestors were brought to the islands as a food source, but the inevitable happened and they keep multiplying. Birders come to American Camp to see the only nesting Eurasian skylarks in the U.S.; they were introduced to Vancouver Island early in this century and a small number ended up here.

The **American Camp Visitor Center** is open daily 8 a.m.-6 p.m. in the summer, and Thurs.-Sun. 8:30 a.m.-4:30 p.m. in winter. It houses historical exhibits, and you can watch a slide show on the conflict. During the summer, join in ranger-led "Pig War Story" walks most days, or watch historical reenactments and demonstrations on the weekends 12:30-3 p.m.

The tip of the peninsula is **Cattle Point Interpretive Area,** where you'll find a picnic shelter housed in an old powerhouse, and trails to a nearby lighthouse and beach.

English Camp

Ten miles from Friday Harbor on the northwest side of the island, English Camp (also known as British Camp) includes a restored hospital, a picturesque blockhouse right on the waters' edge, commissary, an ornamental garden, and small white barracks. The buildings are open daily 8 a.m.-6 p.m. in the summer, but closed the rest of the year. The location is a beautiful one, with protected waters on both sides of Bell Point—a sharp contrast to American Camp—and spreading maple trees overhead. The mile-long **Mt. Young Trail** leads from English Camp to the old British cemetery and then up through second-growth forests to 650-foot Mt. Young, the highest point on San Juan Island. Fine vistas of the archipelago from the top. An almost-level nature path also heads a mile out to the tip of Bell Point.

SPORTS AND RECREATION

Bikes and Moped Rentals

Although many folks bike around San Juan Island, it isn't as bike-friendly as slower-paced Lopez. Be ready for narrow roads and speeding cars; skinny-tire bikes are probably not a good idea for most folks here. Rent bikes to cruise around San Juan Island from **Island Bicycles,** 380 Argyle, tel. (360) 378-4941. **Zzoomers,** across from the ferry landing in Friday Harbor, tel. (360) 378-8811, rents both bikes and mopeds. **Suzie's Mopeds** in Churchill Square, Friday Harbor, tel. (360) 378-5244 or (800) 532-0087, rents mopeds March to October. Expect to pay around $25 a day for mountain or cross bikes and $45 a day for mopeds (less for more than one day). Helmets are included.

Sea Kayaking

Local companies offering kayak tours from San Juan Island include: **Crystal Seas Kayaking** in Friday Harbor, tel. (360) 378-7899; **San Juan Kayak Expeditions** in Friday Harbor, tel. (360) 378-4436; **Sea Quest Expeditions** in Friday Harbor, tel. (360) 378-5767; and **Roche Harbor Guided Tours** in Roche Harbor, tel. (360) 378-2155. San Juan Kayak Expeditions offers two- to five-day trips in the San Juans, and Sea Quest Expeditions is a nonprofit company that emphasizes environmental education during its one- to five-day paddling trips. Expect to pay around $210 for a two-day cruise, or $450 for five days on the water. Do-it-yourselfers can rent sea kayaks from **Emerald Seas Aquatics,** 180 1st St., tel. (360) 378-2772.

Whalewatching

The best time to look for whales around the San Juans is during the summer months, especially in June and July. Local companies that provide scheduled whalewatching trips from Friday Har-

Sailboats provide photographic opportunities in the San Juans.

bor include: **Bon Accord Charters,** tel. (360) 378-5921; **Fairweather Tours,** tel. (360) 378-2826; **San Juan Boat Tours,** tel. (360) 378-3499 or (800) 232-6722; **San Juan Excursions,** tel. (360) 378-6636 or (800) 809-4253; and **Western Prince Cruises,** tel. (360) 378-5315 or (800) 757-6722. San Juan Boat Tours also rents skiffs.

Sailing and Fishing Charters
Sailing charters (and bareboat charters—where you do the sailing) are available in Friday Harbor from **Charters Northwest,** tel. (360) 378-7196, and **Trophy Charters,** tel. (360) 378-2110.

Three local companies offer fishing charters from Friday Harbor: **Alaskan Dawn,** tel. (360) 378-6773; **Buffalo Works,** tel. (360) 378-4612; and **Trophy Charters,** tel. (360) 378-2110.

Diving
Emerald Seas Aquatics, 180 1st St. in Friday Harbor, tel. (360) 378-2772, is a full-service dive center with dive boat charters, training, equipment, and scuba tank filling. Open year-round. Locals claim that the San Juans offer the finest cold water diving on earth, and note that Jacques Cousteau called them his second-favorite place to dive.

Golf
The **San Juan Golf & Country Club,** 2261 Golf Course Rd., tel. (360) 378-2254, is a nine-hole public course.

Other Sports
Fitness fanatics might want to take advantage of one-day memberships offered by **San Juan Fitness and Athletic Club,** tel. (360) 378-4449, open daily in Friday Harbor. Facilities include an indoor pool, racquetball courts, exercise equipment, sauna, steam room, jacuzzi, and juice bar. **States Ranch Equestrian Center,** 2039 West Valley Rd., tel. (360) 378-4243, offers hour-long horseback rides ($25) on their 44-acre ranch.

ACCOMMODATIONS

See the "San Juan Island Accommodations" chart for a complete listing of local places to stay. During the summer it's a good idea to make reservations several months ahead of time to be assured of a space, particularly on weekends. **San Juan Island Central Reservations,** tel. (360) 378-8887 or (800) 836-2176, makes reservations for lodging places on the island and will help you with other details of a visit, including whalewatching tours, boat and kayak rentals, scenic flights, and fishing charters. Their office is next to the Friday Harbor ferry in the Cannery Landing Building.

Many of the resorts, inns, and cottages also offer weekly rates, and many require a minimum summertime stay of at least two nights (sometimes a week). For additional places with

SAN JUAN ISLAND ACCOMMODATIONS

Accommodations are listed from least to most expensive. Rates are often lower during the winter months. The area code is 360.

BED AND BREAKFASTS

Olympic Lights B&B; 4531-A Cattle Point Rd.; tel. 378-3186; $70-105 s or d; 1895 Victorian farmhouse surrounded by fields, five guest rooms, shared or private baths, Olympic views, full breakfast, no kids

Friday's B&B; 35 First St., Friday Harbor; tel. 378-5848 or (800) 352-2632; $70-155 s or d; restored 1891 inn with antiques, downtown location, 10 guest rooms, shared or private baths, continental breakfast, kids welcome

Duffy House B&B; 760 Pear Point Rd., Friday Harbor; tel. 378-5604 or (800) 972-2089; $75-85; 1926 Tudor home overlooking Griffin Bay, beach access, flower and vegetable gardens, five guest rooms, shared baths, full breakfast, two-night minimum stay in July and August, no kids under eight

Argyle House B&B; 685 Argyle St., Friday Harbor; tel. 378-4084; $75-90 s or d; 1910 craftsman, hot tub, three guest rooms and cottage, private baths, no kids under 10

Blair House B&B; 345 Blair Ave., Friday Harbor; tel. 378-5907; $75-125 s or d in six guest rooms with shared baths; $95-125 in cottage with private bath; 1906 home on attractive grounds, veranda, outdoor pool, hot tub, full breakfast, no kids under 12

San Juan Inn B&B; 50 Spring St., Friday Harbor; tel. 378-2070 or (800) 742-8210; $75-135 s or d; charming 1873 Victorian lodge, 10 guest rooms, shared or private baths, central garden, light breakfast

Hillside House B&B; 365 Carter Ave., Friday Harbor; tel. 378-4730 or (800) 232-4730; $75-145 s, $85-155 d; large contemporary home, aviary, wooded location, seven guest rooms, private or shared baths, full breakfast, no kids under 10, AAA approved

The Meadows B&B; 1980 Cattle Point Rd. (three miles east of Friday Harbor); tel. 378-4004; $80 s or d; 1892 farmhouse, country location, two large guest rooms, shared bath, full breakfast, AAA approved

Wharfside B&B; Slip K-13, Friday Harbor Marina; tel. 378-5661; $80-85 s or d; 60-foot sailing vessel *Jacquelyn*, two cabins, shared bath, full breakfast, two-night minimum stay July-September, kids welcome

Trumpeter Inn B&B; 420 Trumpeter Way (two miles west of Friday Harbor); tel. 378-3884 or (800) 826-7926; $80-110 s or d; impressive bay views, five guest rooms, private baths, full breakfast, kids by arrangement, AAA approved

States Inn B&B; 2039 W. Valley Rd. (seven miles northwest of Friday Harbor); tel. 378-6240; $80-110 s or d; historic home, working horse and sheep ranch, nine guest rooms, private baths, full breakfast, horseback rides available, no kids under 10, AAA approved

Tower House B&B; 1230 Little Rd.; tel. 378-5464; $90-125 s or d; Queen Anne-style country home on 10 acres, two guest suites, private baths, full breakfast, no kids

Tucker House B&B; 260 B St., Friday Harbor; tel. 378-2783 or (800) 965-0123; $90-135 s or d; 1898 Victorian house, three guest rooms with shared bath, three cottages with private baths (two with kitchens), woodstove or fireplace; full breakfast, jacuzzi, kids welcome in cottages

Harrison House Suites B&B; 235 C St., Friday Harbor; tel. 378-5587 or (800) 407-7933; $100-150 for up to four; 1910 craftsman home and 1930s cottage, five private suites with baths, attractively furnished, full breakfasts, kids welcome

Panacea B&B; 595 Park St., Friday Harbor; tel. 378-5848 or (800) 352-2632; $110-135 s or d; 1907 craftsman home, four guest rooms, private baths and entries, jacuzzi, free airport and ferry pickup, no children, continental breakfast

(continues on next page)

SAN JUAN ISLAND ACCOMMODATIONS

(continued)

Jensen Bay Pines B&B; Jensen Bay Rd.; tel. 378-5318; $125 s or d; entire 1920s country home, large front porch, one bedroom, kitchen, fireplace, continental breakfast, children okay

Westwinds B&B; 4909 H Hannah Highlands Rd.; tel. 378-5283; $145-245 s or d; entire house on 10 acres, kitchen, patio, private bath, panoramic views, horse pasture, continental breakfast, kids by arrangement

HOTELS, MOTELS, AND RESORTS

Orcinus Inn; 3580 Beaverton Valley Rd.; tel. 378-4060; $25 pp in dorm, $55-65 s or d in private rooms; rustic 1912 farmhouse, casual atmosphere

Sandpiper Condominiums; 570 Jenson Alley, Friday Harbor; tel. 378-5610; $65 s or d; reasonable studio apartments, kitchens, no phones

The Inn at Friday Harbor; 410 Spring St., Friday Harbor; tel. 378-4351 or (800) 752-5752; $70 s, $75 d; indoor pool, sauna, jacuzzi, exercise room, kitchenettes available, free ferry and airport shuttle, AAA approved

Roche Harbor Resort/Hotel de Haro; Roche Harbor; tel. 378-2155 or (800) 451-8910; $70-125 s or d in rooms with shared or private bath, $115-165 s or d in cottages with kitchens, $138-220 in condos with kitchens; historic 19th-century Hotel de Haro, outdoor pool, cottages, condos, marina, tennis courts, boat rentals, closed Nov.-March

The Inn at Friday Harbor Suites; 680 Spring St., Friday Harbor; tel. 378-3031 or (800) 552-1457; $78-108 s or d; suites with kitchenettes, three-night minimum stay, free ferry and airport shuttle, AAA approved

Mar Vista Resort; 2005 False Bay Dr.; tel. 378-4448; $80-125 s or d; beachfront one-, two- and three-bedroom cabins on 20 acres, kitchens, private beach, open mid-April to mid-October

Island Lodge; 1016 Guard St., Friday Harbor; tel. 378-2000 or (800) 822-4753; $85 s or d for motel rooms, $110-140 for one- and two-bedroom suites; on three acres with llamas, jacuzzi, sauna, sundeck, kitchens available, free ferry or airport shuttle, flower gardens, kids okay

Lonesome Cove Resort; 5810 Lonesome Cove Rd.; tel. 378-4477; $85-140 s or d; six attractive waterfront cabins on Lonesome Cove, kitchens, pond with ducks, boat rentals, five-night minimum stay in summer, kids okay

Moon & Sixpence; 3021 Beaverton Valley Rd.; tel. 378-4138; $95-105 s or d; historic turn-of-the-century farmhouse on 15 acres, three-room family flat or water tower suite, private baths, kids welcome

Snug Harbor Resort; 2371 Mitchell Bay Rd.; tel. 378-4762; $100 s or d in motel, $125 d in treehouse, $150 for up to four in two-bedroom unit; cozy resort on Mitchell Bay

Mariella Inn & Cottages; 630 Turn Point Rd., Friday Harbor; tel. 378-6868; $100-160 s or d in luxurious 1902 waterfront home, four guest rooms, shared bath, full breakfast; $100-225 for up to six people each in seven cottages, private baths, kitchens, fireplaces, continental breakfast; waterfront location, hot tub, four-night minimum stay in summer, no kids under 10

Friday Harbor House; 130 West St., Friday Harbor; tel. 378-8455; $165-325 s or d; fireplaces, jacuzzi tubs, picture windows, continental breakfast, two-night minimum stay on weekends, AAA approved

weekly rates, contact: **San Juan Island Vacation Rentals,** (360) 378-5060 or (800) 992-1904, or **Lighthouse Properties,** tel. (360) 378-4612.

The least expensive lodging on San Juan Island (at least for singles) is **Orcinus Inn,** tel. (360) 378-4060, a rustic 1912 farmhouse with a casual atmosphere and dorm beds.

B&Bs and Inns

Call the **Bed & Breakfast Association of San Juan Island** hotline at (360) 378-3030 for lodging availability at a dozen of the finest local establishments. **San Juan Inn B&B,** tel. (360) 378-2070 or (800) 742-8210, just a half block from the ferry, has been in the lodging business since 1873 and still retains its original Victorian charm. It's especially popular with cyclists. **Friday's B&B,** tel. (360) 378-5848 or (800) 352-2632, is one of the newer places to stay, but it's in one of Friday Harbor's oldest buildings. Great if you want to be close to the restaurants and shops, but it can be a bit on the noisy side at times.

For a real waterfront room, **Wharfside B&B,** tel. (360) 378-5661, has two cabins aboard the 60-foot sailing vessel *Jacquelyn,* docked at the Friday Harbor Marina.

Blair House B&B, tel. (360) 378-5907, is a beautifully restored turn-of the-century home on wooded grounds with antique furnishings, an outdoor pool, hot tub, and full breakfast. Guests can stay in either the house or a separate cottage.

Mariella Inn & Cottages, tel. (360) 378-6868, has an elegantly restored 1902 waterfront home with seven adjacent cottages. Located on a nine-acre rocky point, the home overlooks Friday Harbor. They rent bikes, kayaks, and sailboats, and offer gourmet dinners for guests and others Wed.-Sun. nights in the summer.

Built in 1910, **Argyle House B&B,** tel. (360) 378-4084, is a craftsman home just a short distance from downtown. Located on an acre of land, the B&B has three guest rooms, a private cottage, and a hot tub.

Hillside House B&B, tel. (360) 378-4730 or (800) 232-4730, a spacious contemporary home with four guest rooms, is notable for its full-flight aviary with a pheasant, quail, doves, and ducks.

The **Moon & Sixpence,** tel. (360) 378-4138, has a family suite and a three-level water tower that has been converted into a cozy space. The home (not a B&B) has an arty feeling supplemented by the adjacent weaver's studio.

Next to American Camp, **Olympic Lights B&B, tel. (360) 378-3186,** is housed within an 1895 Victorian farmhouse offering Olympic Mountains views, five guest rooms, and full breakfast with eggs from the farm hens.

Tucker House, tel. (360) 378-2783 or (800) 965-0123, within walking distance from the ferry, has rooms and cottages furnished in turn-of-the-century charm. Guest get a full breakfast and use of the hot tub.

The 1920s Tudor-style **Duffy House B&B,** tel. (360) 378-5604 or (800) 972-2089, overlooks the Olympics and the Strait of Juan de Fuca from its lonely location along Griffin Bay. There's a private beach and even a resident bald eagle nest tree that is active most summers.

Harrison House Suites B&B, tel. (360) 378-5587 or (800) 407-7933, offers privacy in the form of nicely appointed suites that sleep up to four (including kids), plus a gourmet breakfast. A good deal for families, and right in town.

At **Westwinds B&B,** tel. (360) 378-5283, guests get an entire house with extraordinary views from the deck, and a soaking tub in the bathroom. Perfect for honeymooners or folks trying to escape the crowds. Another favorite of the just-married set is **Lonesome Cove Resort,** tel. (360) 378-4477, nine miles north of Friday Harbor. Here are six pretty little cabins with delightful scenery and plenty of private space.

Roche Harbor Resort & Marina

Set on 150 acres of forested terrain, Roche Harbor Resort, tel. (360) 378-2155 or (800) 451-8910, is practically a living museum (see "Sights," above, for details). If you want to visit one of President Teddy Roosevelt's old haunts, stay in room 2A. The rooms themselves are on the slightly frumpy side in the hotel, but the cottages may be more to your liking. Avoid the ugly condos that have destroyed the view in this historic harbor. Facilities at the resort include a restaurant, an Olympic-sized outdoor pool, seaside tennis courts, motorboat, canoe, kayak, and paddle-boat rentals, and an historic walking tour. The lounge has live music and dancing nightly in the summer. Roche Harbor is also a U.S. Customs port of entry for boaters coming in from Canada.

CAMPING AND RV PARKS

Pitch a tent at the 12-acre **San Juan County Park,** a mile north of Lime Kiln State Park along West Side Rd., for $15; open year-round. Because this is the only public campground on the island, you'll need to make reservations far ahead if you plan a summer visit. Call (360) 378-2992 for reservation applications; reservations must be postmarked between January 1 and June 1, but you may find space on a summer weekday, or if someone doesn't show up on a weekend (and you arrive early). August is the most difficult time to find space. The park has a boat ramp and drinking water, but no showers or RV hookups. It is located along **Smallpox Bay,** so-named when a ship left two sailors with the disease on the island to prevent them from contaminating the rest of the crew. When they were helped by local Indians who had no immunity to the disease, smallpox spread quickly across San Juan Island. The feverous victims jumped into the bay to cool off and died of pneumonia. The few survivors fled the island.

Park that RV or pitch a tent at the spacious **Lakedale Campground,** 2627 Roche Harbor Rd., tel. (360) 378-2350 or (800) 617-2267, with secluded waterfront tent, bike, and RV sites, plus rentals of bikes, boats, and camping gear. Located 4.5 miles from Friday Harbor, and open mid-March to mid-October. Cyclists can pedal in to **Pedal Inn,** 1300 False Bay Dr. (five miles from Friday Harbor), tel. (360) 378-3049, where wooded campsites around a pond are just $4.50. Open May-Oct., with showers, a small store, and a laundromat. No cars allowed.

More campsites and RV hookups are available at **Snug Harbor Marina Resort,** 2371 Mitchell Bay Rd., tel. (360) 378-4762, plus skiff, sailboat, fishing tackle, and crab pot rentals, and a small store. **Town and Country Trailer Park,** 595 Tucker Ave. N (one mile from Friday Harbor), tel. (360) 378-4717, has tent sites and RV hookups, with showers and a laundry. Coin-operated showers are also available at the **Friday Harbor Marina** and **Roche Harbor Resort.** During the Jazz Festival, RVs can park in the fairgrounds parking lot for a fee.

FOOD

Given the enormous numbers of visitors to Friday Harbor, it comes as no surprise that the town has a wide range of restaurants and eateries, including some real gems. Head up almost any street and you're likely to find something of interest. Unless otherwise noted, all the restaurants listed below are located in Friday Harbor.

Breakfast, Lunch, and Baked Goods
Front Street Cafe, 101 Spring St., tel. (360) 378-2245, is *the* hangout place in town, with a fun atmosphere, espresso and pastries, and a ferry-side location. This is one of the best local places for breakfast, and their lunches (homemade soups, salads, sandwiches, and more) are also of note. Hang out with the old-timers and catch up on local gossip at Friday Harbor's **San Juan Donut Shop** on Spring St., tel. (360) 378-2271. Very good full breakfasts, too.

For coffee, **Stewart's Cajun/Creole Cafe & Used Bookstore,** 395 Spring St., tel. (360) 378-6071, is a fun place with used books, espresso, and breakfasts. Open summers only. **Madelyn's Bagel Bakery & Espresso,** tel. (360) 378-4545, has a perfect location on A St. above the ferry parking area. Slip out of your vehicle for a fresh bagel and cream cheese, the cinnamon rolls and cookies, or a Starbucks latte.

Located behind Funk & Junk, **Katrina's,** 65 Nichols St., tel. (360) 378-7290, doesn't offer much in the way of atmosphere or size, but makes up with delicious lunches (closed Sunday and Wednesday) that change every day. There's always freshly baked bread, salads, and vegetarian specials, but you never know what else will appear.

Seafood and American
Springtree Cafe, Spring St., tel. (360) 378-4848, serves a varied menu including fresh seafood and vegetarian specials in a simple setting with checked tablecloths and a heated patio. Open daily for lunch, dinner, and Sunday brunch (in summer).

The **Duck Soup Inn,** five miles north of Friday Harbor on Roche Harbor Rd., tel. (360) 378-4878, specializes in superbly done local seafood, along with a constantly changing and eclectic menu with an international flavor. This is where locals go for a celebration night. Entrees are in the $15-20 range; open summers only.

If you are simply in search of a great all-American burger, fries, and shake, head to **Vic's Driftwood Drive Inn,** 25 2nd St., tel. (360) 378-2120. **Papa Joe's,** 680 Spring St., tel. (360) 378-6955, serves big quantities of inexpensive all-American meals, including seafood and steaks.

Cafe Bissett, 170 West St., tel. (360) 378-3109, has elegant dinners and outstanding desserts in a tiny side-street location. Portions are on the small side.

Downrigger's, tel. (360) 378-2700, at the ferry landing, is open for lunch and dinner with fairly standard seafood, steak, burgers, and pasta, but the service is great and the waterside views even better.

Westcott Bay Seafood Farm, 4071 Westcott Dr. (a mile east of Roche Harbor), tel. (360) 378-6388, supplies local restaurants with gourmet oysters and clams; get them at the source for the freshest available.

International

Roberto's Italian Restaurant, 205 A St., tel. (360) 378-6333, consistently cranks out distinctive and delectable homemade Italian dishes, including some with a very spicy kick (notably the "prawns from hell"). Reservations required.

For very good deep-dish pizza, big salads, and Italian food in a family atmosphere, try **The Friday Harbor Bistro** at 35 1st St.; call (360) 378-3076 for orders to go.

The **Front St. Ale House,** 1 Front St., tel. (360) 378-2337, sits next door to the San Juan Brewing Company, and their ales are all on tap here. The menu emphasizes heavy English pub grub; get here at happy hour (4-6 p.m.) for the best meal deals.

Amigo's, 40 B Spring St., tel. (360) 378-5908, is the place for excellent, reasonably priced Mexican meals in a nothing-fancy atmosphere. Eat on the patio on a sunny day, but don't bother showing up in the winter; the owners are in Mexico.

Produce and Markets

Friday's Marketplace, directly across from the ferry terminal, is an open-air summer market with arts and crafts, fresh crab, espresso, and fish and chips. A **farmers market** is held on summer Saturdays 10 a.m.-2 p.m. at the county courthouse, and it features lots of organic fruits, vegetables, berries, and flowers.

Giannagelo Farms, on the north end of the island, grows impressive produce and makes herbal vinegars, dried herbs, and other natural treats.

Waterfront Deli & Market, on the corner of Front and Spring, tel. (360) 378-8444, has good sandwiches and salads to go. The island's largest grocer is **King's Market,** 160 Spring St., tel. (360) 378-4505, with fresh meats and fish, a fine deli, fishing tackle, and sportswear. **Way of Life,** 35 1st St., tel. (360) 378-5433, is a natural-foods market with organic produce and a vegetarian deli.

EVENTS

Jazz Festival

Each year thousands of people crowd into Friday Harbor for the main event—the Dixieland Jazz Festival. Held the third weekend in July, it features a dozen different bands and begins with a parade down Spring Street. Concerts are held at four locations in Friday Harbor and Roche Harbor, with shuttle bus service among the sites. If you plan to attend, make lodging reservations many months ahead of time (up to a year ahead for the fanciest B&Bs), and leave your car in Anacortes. Entrance to these concerts isn't cheap: starting around $10 per event. Call (360) 378-5509 for details on this year's Jazz Festival events.

Other Events

The **Pig War Barbecue Jamboree** in mid-June features barbecue contests with celebrity judges, a 10-km race, music, and dancing. The **Fourth of July** brings a parade and fireworks to Friday Harbor. (The best local Fourth of July fireworks, however, are over at Roche Harbor Resort.) The season ends with more fun at the four-day **San Juan County Fair** in mid-August, featuring a sheep-to-shawl race, chicken and rabbit races, music, livestock judging, and, of course, carnival rides.

THE ARTS

San Juan Community Theatre & Arts Center, 100 2nd St., tel. (360) 378-3211, has music, dance, and theatrical productions in Friday Harbor, including some surprises (the Alvin Ailey dancers as well as the San Francisco Opera and Ballet come here often). For something a bit more mundane, the **Royal Theatre,** 209 Spring St. in Friday Harbor, tel. (360) 378-4455, has first-run flicks.

Galleries

Sunshine Gallery, 85 Nichols St., tel. (360) 378-5819, is a cooperatively run gallery with excellent local artwork. A large, contemporary gallery in Friday Harbor, **Waterworks Gallery,** 315 Argyle at Spring St., tel. (360) 378-3060, has paintings, prints, watercolors, and sculpture by island and international artists. An **Artists Studio Open House** on the first weekend of June allows you the chance to meet local painters, sculptors, jewelers, and other artists in their studios.

INFORMATION AND SERVICES

The **San Juan Island Chamber of Commerce Visitor Centre** is directly across from the ferry terminal in the Friday's Marketplace complex, tel. (360) 378-5240. Stop by in the summer for local info; closed winters. **San Juan Island Central Reservations,** located upstairs in the Cannery Landing building (next to the ferry), tel. (360) 378-8887 or (800) 836-2176, makes lodging reservations and has information on local tours, transportation, and more when the visitor center is closed. Store bags in the coin-operated lockers on the other side of the street from the ferry terminal.

You can do your laundry at **Wash Tub Laundromat,** in Friday Harbor, tel. (360) 378-2070, or **Sunshine Coin-Op Laundry,** 210 Nichols Street.

Boardwalk Books, upstairs from Front St. Cafe, tel. (360) 378-2787, has a good choice of local and regional titles.

TRANSPORTATION

By Ferry

The **Washington State Ferry** stops right in Friday Harbor on San Juan Island; call (360) 378-4777 or (800) 843-3779 for details. See "Ferry Service," above, for details on ferry service and fares to the islands, including the private ferries.

Shuttle Bus

There is no need for a car on San Juan Island. **San Juan Transit,** tel. (360) 378-8887 or (800) 887-8387, operates 21-passenger shuttle buses around San Juan Island year-round. The cost is $4 one-way, $7 roundtrip, or just $10 for an all-day pass. Buses operate every 40 minutes from 8 a.m. to 8 p.m. on a daily basis (less frequently in the winter months) and can carry bikes and luggage.

Tours, Car Rentals, and Taxi

Car rentals and tours of the island are offered by the **Inn at Friday Harbor,** tel. (360) 378-3031. More car rentals from **M&M Auto Rentals,** tel. (360) 378-2794, and **Practical Rent a Car,** tel. (360) 378-2440. Call **Primo Taxi,** tel. (360) 378-3550, for local rides. Water taxi service is provided by **Fairweather,** tel. (360) 378-8029.

ORCAS ISLAND

Known as "The Gem of the San Juans," Orcas Island is considered the chain's most beautiful island. It is definitely the hilliest—drive, hike, or bike to the top of 2,409-foot Mt. Constitution for a panoramic view from Vancouver, B.C., to Mt. Rainier. Orcas's most prominent mansion, Rosario Resort, regularly graces the pages of national travel magazines and employs almost 200 people, making it San Juan County's largest private employer. The island—named by a Spanish explorer in 1792 for the viceroy of Mexico, not for the orca whales common in neighboring waters—is home to 3,200 people.

Towns

The ferry docks at the cluster of cafes and gift shops called **Orcas Village,** located on the south end of this horseshoe-shaped island. The tiny settlement of **West Sound** is eight miles northwest of the ferry landing, and has a large marina, along with a couple of stores. Approximately four miles west of here is another little gathering place, **Deer Harbor,** with a handful of resorts and B&Bs, a couple of restaurants, charter sailboats, and kayak rentals. It's appropriately named for the many black-tailed deer in the area and throughout the San Juans. Orcas Island is almost cut in half by East Sound, and the town of **Eastsound** sits at its head. This is the main village on the island, and the place to go for groceries, gas, and a wide choice of gift shops, cafes, and galleries.

SIGHTS

Moran State Park

Near Eastsound, 4,605-acre Moran State Park is most popular for its steep paved road to the 2,407-foot summit of **Mt. Constitution,** where you'll discover a 52-foot stone tower constructed by the Civilian Conservation Corps in the 1930s. This is the highest point on the San Juans and offers a commanding view in all directions, from Mt. Rainier to British Columbia. If you've ridden to the top by bike, it's an exciting ride back down. Another popular attraction is **Cascade Falls,** where Cascade Creek drops into a deep pool 100 feet below. A quarter-mile path leads to the falls, and you can continue uphill to two less impressive falls.

The park has more than 30 miles of other hiking trails, from easy nature loops to remote and rugged out-of-the-way hikes. Get a park map for details on all of these. A four-mile loop trail circles Mountain Lake, offering a chance to see black-tailed deer, particularly in the morning and early evening. You can climb to the summit of Mt. Constitution from Mountain Lake on a 3.7-mile path, or save your legs by catching a ride to the top and hiking downhill instead.

Moran State Park has several lakes that are popular for fishing, motorless boating, and swimming in the cold water. Rent rowboats at the largest of these, Mountain and Cascade Lakes, where you'll find good trout and kokanee fishing. Both also have boat ramps and fishing supplies. Cascade Lake has swimming in the summer, and the park is one of the most popular camping places in the state; see below for details.

Museums

Located in a cluster of six pioneer log buildings, the **Orcas Island Historical Museum** on North Beach Rd. in Eastsound, tel. (360) 376-4849, has a collection of relics from 1880s pioneer homesteads, Chinese immigrants, and philanthropist Robert Moran. Of particular note is a fine collection of Indian artifacts that includes carvings and baskets. Open Mon.-Sat. 1-4 p.m. June-Sept., Fri.-Sat. in May and the first half of October.

The small **Crow Valley School Museum,** tel. (360) 376-4260, three miles southwest of Eastsound on Crow Valley Rd., is open Thurs.-Sat. 1-4 p.m. from Memorial Day to mid-September. Built in 1888, this classic one-room school has old desks, class photos, report cards, school clothes, toys, and other pieces from a bygone era. No Internet access here.

SPORTS AND RECREATION

Bike and Moped Rentals

Rent bikes to cruise around Orcas Island from **Dolphin Bay Bicycles** near the ferry terminal in Orcas, tel. (360) 376-3093, or **Wildlife Cycles** in

ORCAS ISLAND

POINT LAWRENCE

DOE ISLAND STATE PARK

DOE BAY VILLAGE RESORT

DOE BAY RD.

BUCK BAY FARM B&B

ORCAS ISLAND ARTWORKS

OLGA

OBSTRUCTION PASS COUNTY PARK

LIEBER HAVEN MARINA RESORT

SPRING BAY INN

MORAN STATE PARK

MT. CONSTITUTION (2,407 ft.)

MOUNTAIN LAKE

CASCADE FALLS

CASCADE LAKE

HWY.

ROSARIO RESORT

HORSESHOE

EAST SOUND

BARTWOOD LODGE

MT. BAKER RD.

EASTSOUND

DOLPHIN BAY RD.

SMUGGLER'S VILLA RESORT

KANGAROO HOUSE B&B

ENCHANTED FOREST RD.

DOUBLE MT. B&B

JOY'S INN

ORCAS HOTEL

ORCAS

FERRY TO SHAW AND LOPEZ ISLANDS

BEACH HAVEN RESORT

WEST BEACH RESORT

WALKING HORSE COUNTRY FARM

CROW VALLEY SCHOOL MUSEUM

TURTLEBACK FARM INN

CROW VALLEY RD.

WEST SOUND

HORSESHOE HWY.

WEST SOUND

DEER HARBOR

DEEP MEADOW FARM B&B

DEER HARBOR

FERRY LANDING

FERRY TO SAN JUAN ISLAND

HARNEY CHANNEL

2 mi

2 km

© MOON PUBLICATIONS, INC.

Eastsound, tel. (360) 376-4708. Expect to pay around $20 a day, including helmet and lock. **Key Mopeds** in Eastsound, tel. (360) 376-2474, rents mopeds in the summer.

Sea Kayaking

Shearwater Sea Kayak Tours in Eastsound, tel. (360) 376-4699, is a long-established company offering three-hour kayak tours ($35 per person) departing from Rosario Resort, Deer Harbor Resort, and Eastsound, plus all-day tours for $65. In addition, they have three-day classes at the beginning and intermediate levels, and overnight trips for groups.

Osprey Tours in Eastsound, tel. (360) 376-3677, is a distinctive company that uses hand-built traditional Aleutian-style kayaks and offers half-day ($35) and all-day tours ($75). Kayakers get in the spirit of the adventure by wearing woven Native-style hats.

Rent single or double kayaks from **Crescent Beach Kayaks,** in Eastsound, tel. (360) 376-2464. If you're planning on launching your own kayak, be forewarned that you may be subject to a launching fee ($5 at Deer Harbor) if you aren't on public lands.

Spring Bay Inn, near Obstruction Pass, tel. (360) 376-5531, is a beautiful and modern B&B where your lodging rate includes a guided kayak tour.

Whalewatching

Local companies that provide scheduled whale-watching trips from Orcas Island include: **Deer Harbor Charters** in Deer Harbor, tel. (360) 376-5989 or (800) 544-5758; and **Orcas Island Eclipse Charters** in Orcas, tel. (360) 376-4663 or (800) 376-6566. Expect to pay around $45 for adults, $30 for kids, for a four-hour whalewatching cruise. Be sure to bring your binoculars, camera, and warm clothes.

Sailboat Charters

Deer Harbor is the main center for skippered sailboat charters on Orcas Island, with four companies: **Amante Sail Tours,** tel. (360) 376-4231; **Custom Designed Charters,** tel. (360) 376-5105; **Deer Harbor Charters,** tel. (360) 376-5989 or (800) 544-5758; and **Eclipse Charters,** tel. (360) 376-4663. Deer Harbor Charters also rents skiffs. Skippered sailing charters

(and bareboat charters) are also available from **Orcas Sailing Charters** in Orcas, tel. (360) 376-3080; **Sharon L. Charters** in Orcas, tel. (360) 376-4305; and **Valkyrie Sailing Charters** in Eastsound, tel. (360) 376-4018.

Other Recreation

Walking Horse Country Farm, tel. (360) 376-5306, offers guided trail rides ($40/hour) on their distinctive Tennessee walking horses, as well as carriage rides. The **Orcas Island Country Golf Club,** tel. (360) 376-4400, is a nine-hole public course on the Horseshoe Hwy. southwest of Eastsound.

ACCOMMODATIONS

See the "Orcas Island Accommodations" chart for a complete listing of local places to stay. During the summer it is a good idea to make reservations several months ahead of time to be assured of a space, particularly on weekends. Call the Orcas Island Chamber of Commerce **lodging hotline** at (360) 376-8888 for availability. It's updated on a daily basis in the summer.

Many of the resorts, inns, and cottages also offer weekly rates, and many require a minimum summertime stay of at least two nights (sometimes a week). For additional homes available by the week, contact **Lindholm Real Estate,** tel. (360) 376-2202, or Teri Williams at (360) 376-5938.

Bed and Breakfasts

The beautiful **Orcas Hotel** in Orcas, tel. (360) 376-4300, is a three-story Victorian built in the early 1900s that overlooks the ferry landing, Shaw Island, and Harney Channel. Extensively restored, it's on the National Register of Historic Places, and includes a range of rooms, from modest older ones with shared baths to luxurious honeymoon rooms with private bath and jacuzzi. Breakfast is served downstairs.

Situated on 80 acres in the shadow of Turtleback Mountain, **Turtleback Farm Inn,** on Crow Valley Rd., tel. (360) 375-4914, has seven rooms, all with private baths, in a comfortable, farmhouse atmosphere. On warm days the full country breakfast is served outdoors on the valley-view deck.

ORCAS ISLAND ACCOMMODATIONS

Accommodations are listed from least to most expensive. Rates are often lower during the winter months. The area code is 360.

BED AND BREAKFASTS

Kangaroo House B&B; N. Beach Rd.; tel. 376-2175; $60-100 s, $70-110 d Fri.-Sat.; $45-75 s, $55-85 d Sun.-Thurs.; 1907 craftsman home on two acres, porches, gardens, five guest rooms, private or shared baths, large sitting room, fireplace, period furnishings, big gourmet breakfast, AAA approved

Orcas Hotel; Orcas; tel. 376-4300; $69-170 s or d; classic three-story Victorian overlooking Harney Channel, 12 guest rooms, shared or private baths, antiques, full breakfast, kids by arrangement

L'Aerie B&B; Rosario Rd.; tel. 376-4647; $75-95 s or d; modern home, impressive views, full breakfast, kids by arrangement

Buck Bay Farm B&B; Olga; tel. 376-2908; $75-100 s or d; farmhouse on five acres, kids by arrangement

Turtleback Farm Inn B&B; Crow Valley Rd.; tel. 376-4914; $80-160 s or d; historic farmhouse on 80 acres, seven guest rooms, private baths, valley-view deck, gourmet breakfast, pond, two-night minimum stay May-Oct., no kids under eight, AAA approved

Hazelwood B&B; Victoria Valley Rd.; tel. 376-6300; $85-95 s or d; contemporary hilltop home on 12 acres, impressive vistas of Olympics and Sound, jacuzzi, three guest rooms, private bath, continental breakfast, two-night minimum stay in summer, no kids

Deep Meadow Farm B&B; Cormorant Bay Rd.; tel. 376-5866; $85-95 s or d; restored historic farmhouse, quiet 40-acre farm, two antique-furnished guest rooms, private baths, jacuzzi, two-night minimum stay in summer, full breakfast, kids by arrangement

Double Mountain B&B; west of Eastsound; tel. 376-4570; $85-125 s or d; contemporary home on 600-foot hill, dramatic vistas, three guest rooms, private baths, full breakfast, no kids under 10

Sand Dollar Inn B&B; Olga; tel. 376-5696; $88-115 s or d; historic home, good views of Buck Bay, four large guest rooms, private baths, full breakfast, no kids

Windsong B&B; West Sound; tel. 376-2500; $95-115 s or d; historic 1917 school house on three acres, three large guest rooms, shared or private baths, fireplaces, gourmet breakfast, no kids under 12

Chestnut Hill Inn B&B; Orcas; tel. 376-5157; $95-135 s or d; Victorian farmhouse in the country, fireplaces, private baths, free ferry shuttle, no kids

Spring Bay Inn B&B; near Obstruction Pass; tel. 376-5531; $135-155 s, $155-175 d; new shoreside lodge on 60 acres, four guest rooms, private baths, stone fireplaces, free kayak tours, hot tub, full breakfast, kids okay, AAA approved

MOTELS, LODGES, CABINS, RESORTS, AND RETREATS

Doe Bay Village Resort; Doe Bay; tel. 376-2291; $15 s, $30 d in hostel dorm, $40-92 s or d for rustic cabins, tent cabins, and yurts with shared or private baths; quiet setting on Otter Cove, unique and funky place, mineral springs and sauna ($3), communal kitchen

Palmer's Chart House; Deer Harbor; tel. 376-4231; $50 s, $60-70 d; contemporary home, water views, big garden, two guest rooms, private baths, private entrance deck, full breakfast, sailing trips available

Lieber Haven Marina Resort; near Olga; tel. 376-2472; $60-110 s or d; cabins and apartments, protected bay, boat rentals, kids okay

Outlook Inn; Eastsound; tel. 376-2200 or (800) 767-9506; $64 s or d with shared baths, $94 s or d with private baths; $99-225 s or d for modern suites; beautifully restored 1888 hotel, period furnishings, bay view, shared baths, free airport shuttle, AAA approved

Joy's Inn; Horseshoe Hwy. near golf course; tel. 376-4292; $65-75 s or d; spiritual retreat, relaxing country setting overlooking Crow Valley, two guest rooms, shared bath, woodstove, jacuzzi, art studio, four-night minimum stay, kids okay

North Beach Inn; Eastsound; tel. 376-2660; $65-175 s or d; rustic beachfront cottages, fireplaces, kitchens, kids okay, seven-day minimum stay in summer, closed December to mid-February

Deer Harbor Resort; 200 Deer Harbor Rd.; tel. 376-4420; $69-225 s or d; historic marina resort, cottages and villas, water views, outdoor pool, boat rentals

West Beach Resort; three miles west of Eastsound; tel. 376-2240; $80-110 s or d; beachside cottages, kitchens, fireplaces, private baths, free shuttle to ferry, boat rentals, one-week minimum stay in July and August

Bartwood Lodge; tel. 376-2242; $80-140 s or d; waterfront lodge, tennis court, fishing charters, kayak trips

Sandcastle Guest House; two miles north of Eastsound; tel. 376-2337; $85 s or d; contemporary one-bedroom house, deck overlooking Strait of Georgia, private beach, continental breakfast, two-night minimum stay, kids welcome

Liberty Call B&B; Orcas; tel. 376-5246; $85 s or d; two guest suites, private baths, kids okay

Beach Haven Resort; Enchanted Forest Rd.; tel. 376-2288; $85-110 for up to six in 12 rustic log cabins or lodge with kitchens, $175 for up to eight in A-frame; along beach with old-growth forest, seven-day minimum stay in summer, row boat and canoe rental, kid-friendly

Cabins on the Point; Eastsound; tel. 376-4114; $85-130 s or d; 1910 Cape Cod-style cabins near beach, kitchen, private bath, woodstove, two-night minimum stay, kids okay

Deer Harbor Inn; eight miles southwest of ferry terminal; tel. 376-4110; $89 s or d; modern log house, decks overlooking Deer Harbor, indoor pool, continental breakfast, no kids, AAA approved

West Sound Cottage; West Sound; tel. 376-2172; $95 s or d; six guest rooms in two buildings on the water, private baths, antique furnishings, kids okay

Rosario Resort & Spa; five miles south of Eastsound; tel. 376-2222 or (800) 562-8820; $95-220 s or d Fri.-Sat.; $65-150 s or d Sun.-Thurs.; historic resort on 22 acres, three pools (one indoor), sauna, jacuzzi, tennis courts, marina, exercise facilities, kitchenettes available, AAA approved

Landmark Inn; Eastsound; tel. 376-2423; $100-130 s, $110-130 d; condo units, private decks, kitchenettes, AAA approved

North Shore Cottages; Eastsound; tel. 376-5131; $120 s or d; two cottages along shore, fireplace, private decks, hot tubs, kids okay, two-night minimum stay

Smuggler's Villa Resort; Eastsound; tel. 376-2297 or (800) 488-2097; $145-185 for up to four people; condos with Haro Strait views, outdoor pool, hot tub, sauna, fireplaces, kitchens, tennis and basketball courts, private beach, kids welcome

Carriage House Vacation Cottage; Walking Horse Country Farm, West Beach Rd.; tel. 376-5306; $200 d; contemporary two-bedroom home, antiques furnishings, 27 acres of pastures, horse rides available, kitchen

The **Kangaroo House,** north of Eastsound Village and right next to the airport, tel. (360) 376-2175, was built in 1907 and bought in the '30s by a sea captain, Harold Ferris, who picked up a young female kangaroo on one of his Australian voyages. The kangaroo is long gone, but the name remains in this attractive old home with a big fireplace, period furnishings, and friendly owners. Be prepared for a stuff-yourself breakfast.

Over in Deer Harbor, **Palmer's Chart House,** tel. (360) 375-4231, was the first B&B on Orcas Island when it opened for business more than 20 years ago. Experienced world travelers, owners Majean and Don Palmer offer some of the most reasonable rates on the island, and provide sailing trips aboard their 33-foot yacht ($30 per person).

Sand Dollar Inn, tel. (360) 376-5696, near the ferry landing and once owned by a ferry boat captain, is an historic home with four large upstairs rooms offering good views of the water, private baths, and a hearty breakfast. **Deep Meadow Farm B&B,** tel. (360) 375-5866, is a nicely restored historic farmhouse on 40 quiet acres with two antique-furnished guest rooms, private baths, and an outdoor jacuzzi.

Sandcastle Guest House, tel. (360) 376-2337, is a contemporary waterside home on the north end of the island with fine views across the water from the upstairs deck. Kids are welcome.

Joy's Inn, tel. (360) 376-4292, is not a B&B, but a country retreat with a spiritual orientation and an art studio overlooking Crow Valley. The owners offer charters aboard their 41-foot sailboat.

Doe Bay Village Resort

This wonderfully funky small resort stands alone on the San Juan Islands, a throwback to the '70s with its rustic cabins, yurts, tent-cabins, and coed hostel (with a separate couple's room) set on scenic Doe Bay. There's even a treehouse for the really adventurous. In most of these you'll need to use the central shower house and communal kitchen. Located on a 50-acre spread, the resort stands in marked contrast to others on the islands; no dolled-up rooms, pseudo-Victorian architecture, antique vases, or lavish breakfast spreads here. Known as the Polarity Institute for several years, Doe Bay still maintains a relaxed new-age flavor, but the main emphasis is on relaxation, with a friendly aura (pun intended) that brings couples and families back again and again.

Featured attractions at Doe Bay are the sauna and creekside mineral-spring jacuzzis ($3 per person each day for guests; $6 per person for others), both decidedly clothing-optional. You can sit inside the wood-fired sauna with its octagonal stained-glass windows, and then head to one of three mineral baths with sulfurous water pumped from the ground. Two are heated, the third is refreshingly cold. The jacuzzis are covered and overlook a sandy beach.

The restaurant cooks vegetarian dishes and seafood three meals a day, and tent and RV hookups are available. Sea kayak tours and bike rentals are available; ask about renting a bike here and dropping it off at the ferry (or vice versa). Also ask about meditation activities and professional massages.

Other Resorts

Rosario Island Resort & Spa, tel. (360) 376-2222 or (800) 562-8820, is a nationally known getaway five miles south of Eastsound—the largest resort on the islands. The resort is housed in a turn-of-the-century mansion that once belonged to shipbuilder and Seattle mayor Robert Moran. Moran wasn't blessed with musical talent, so he played the 1,972-pipe organ like a player piano and none of his guests were the wiser; organ concerts are still held frequently. The historic building—on the National Register of Historic Places—has been beautifully restored, offering fine dining, a spa, exercise equipment, and massage (extra fee).

Beach Haven Resort, tel. (360) 376-2288, east of Eastsound, contains rustic log cabins, a lodge, and a private A-frame cabin along a pebbly private beach backed by a 10-acre stand of old-growth forest. This is a wonderful place for families on a relaxing vacation. There's a seven-day minimum stay in the summer.

CAMPING

Orcas Island's finest campsites are at **Moran State Park,** where campers can stay in four different campgrounds along Cascade and Mountain Lakes, plus a separate bike-in campground. Tent sites are $11 with coin-operated showers; no RV hookups. All sites are pre-assigned, so check in at the pay station across from Cascade Lake when you first arrive. Due to the park's popularity, reservations are required in the summer months. Call (800) 452-5687 for campsite reservations ($6 extra fee), available up to 11 months ahead of time. The campground is open year-round.

Obstruction Pass County Park is a tiny place with a boat ramp, a beach, and several walk-in campsites a half-mile from the road. No reservations or water. The park is located at the end of Obstruction Pass Rd., 2.5 miles southeast of Olga.

The decidedly funky **Doe Bay Village Resort,** near Olga, tel. (360) 376-2291, has tent and RV sites in an open field. Access to the resort's delightful jacuzzis and sauna costs an extra $3 per person per day for guests.

West Beach Resort, three miles west of Eastsound, tel. (360) 376-2240, has campsites and RV hookups (reservations accepted) along a scenic beach. Also here is a marina with boat rentals, fishing and scuba supplies, and groceries.

FOOD

The "big city" on Orcas—Eastsound—has the best choice of food on the island, though you'll find a scattering of fine restaurants and cafes elsewhere.

Orcas Landing and Deer Harbor
When you step off the ferry at Orcas, the grand old **Orcas Hotel** faces you. Inside is an excellent little cafe and bakery for light meals, pastries, and espresso, and a larger dining room/pub for sumptuous seafood dinners and other fare. Open for all three meals; call (360) 376-4300 for today's specials.

Deer Harbor Inn, at Deer Harbor (of course), tel. (360) 376-4110, is a spacious place with a comfortable atmosphere and outstanding meals. You can get something as simple as freshly baked bread and homemade soups, or choose a full dinner from the blackboard listing today's specials. There's always something from the sea, and a vegetarian entree.

Eastsound Area
Roses Bakery Cafe in Eastsound, tel. (360) 376-4220, is a very popular hangout, with outside tables to enjoy a big pastry and espresso on a sunny day. They also serve light breakfasts and lunches.

For Mexican food, **Bilbo's Festivo** on north beach in Eastsound, tel. (360) 376-4728, is something of a local legend. They're open daily for lunch and dinner, with tasty Mexican/Southwest fare, mesquite grilled meats, seafood, and fresh-fruit margaritas. Outside dining is available in the courtyard.

Get inexpensive but well-prepared traditional Italian meals and fresh seafood at **La Famiglia Ristorante,** also in Eastsound, tel. (360) 376-2335.

Ship Bay Oyster House, a short ways east of Eastsound, tel. (360) 376-5886, may be the best place to get fresh oysters in the San Juans. Located in an old farmhouse overlooking Ship Bay, the restaurant also cooks up a variety of fresh-from-the-sea daily specials, along with steak, chicken, and other meats.

Enjoy excellent Northwest cuisine at **Christina's** in Eastsound, tel. (360) 376-4904, located upstairs and directly behind the gas station. The menu changes daily, and there's a patio out back overlooking East Sound. Stop by at lunch for lighter and more reasonably priced meals.

The East End
Cafe Olga, inside the Orcas Island Artworks building south of Moran State Park, has inexpensive and delicious home-style lunches. The food covers a broad spectrum: sandwiches, vegetarian dishes, quiche, pasta, seafood curry, ethnic dishes, espresso, and their justly famous blackberry pie. Guaranteed to please. You also won't want to miss the adjacent cooperative gallery. For more vegetarian meals, head to **Doe Bay Village Resort,** tel. (360) 376-2291; see "Accommodations," above, for more on this unique place.

Rosario Resort & Spa, five miles south of Eastsound, tel. (360) 376-2222 or (800) 562-8820, has fine dining nightly, plus a very popular Friday night seafood buffet and Sunday champagne brunch.

Markets
For groceries, film, and other essentials, stop by the **Island Market** in Eastsound. This is the largest grocery store in the islands, with an in-store bakery and deli.

The **Orcas Island Farmers Market** is held at Eastsound's Village Square Saturday 10 a.m.-3 p.m., April to October. Come here for local produce, flowers, crafts, and clothing. More fresh organic produce is available on Wednesday near the ferry landing in Orcas Village. **Homegrown Market** in Eastsound, tel. (360) 376-2009, has natural foods and an organic deli with daily specials and salads.

EVENTS AND ENTERTAINMENT

Eastsound—like nearly every small town in the U.S.—has a fun parade on the **Fourth of July,** followed by boat races, music, and fireworks. The town also features sailboat races on Friday nights in the summer, and a **Pioneer Craft Day** in late July at the museum. Every Thursday at noon during July and August, head to Emmanuel Episcopal Church in Eastsound for a free **Brown Bag Concert.**

The **Orcas Theatre & Community Center,** which was built entirely with donated funds, hosts a variety of events nearly year-round in Eastsound, from concerts by nationally known musicians (Taj Mahal and Wynton Marsalis have both performed here), to theatrical performances and productions for kids. For ticket and schedule info, phone (360) 376-2281. Check out the latest movies at **Sea View Theatre,** tel. (360) 376-5724, in Eastsound.

SHOPPING

Orcas has a number of craft shops and galleries kept well supplied by the artists and craftspeople who live there. Olga's artist co-op is **Orcas Island Artworks,** tel. (360) 376-4408, with an assortment of locally made arts and crafts in an old barn at the junction of Horseshoe Hwy. and Doe Bay Rd. (south of Moran State Park).

Darvill's Rare Print Shop in Eastsound, tel. (360) 376-2351, sells rare prints from the 18th and 19th centuries, plus limited-edition prints by contemporary Northwest artists. **The Right Place** on West Beach, tel. (360) 376-4023, offers an assortment of local crafts, from pottery to blown glass. Next door is **The Naked Lamb,** tel. (360) 376-4606 or (800) 323-5262, where you'll discover hand-spun yarns, one of the largest selections of dyed-in-the-wool yarns in the nation, plus hand-knit sweaters, socks, and other goods. Not far away is **Orcas Island Pottery,** tel. (360) 376-2813, the oldest pottery studio in the Northwest.

The **Orcas Wine Company,** tel. (360) 376-6244 or (800) 934-7616, has small shops in Eastsound (below Christina's Restaurant) and at the Orcas ferry landing where you can sample their wines (made in eastern Washington).

INFORMATION AND SERVICES

Darvill's Bookstore in Eastsound, tel. (360) 376-2135, has a wide selection of books on the San Juans. Get local information from a rack inside **Pyewacket Books** in Eastsound, tel. (360) 376-2043; while you're here check out the new and used books. Call the **Orcas Island Chamber of Commerce** at (360) 376-2273.

Airport Center Self Service Laundry is located at the southwest end of the airport and just north of Eastsound, tel. (360) 376-2478.

TRANSPORTATION

By Ferry

The **Washington State Ferry** docks at Orca Village on the south end of the island; call (360) 376-2135 or (800) 843-3779 for details. For fare and schedule information see "Ferry Service" at the beginning of this chapter.

Other Transport and Tours

San Juan Transit, tel. (360) 376-8887 or (800) 887-8387, operates shuttle buses around Orcas Island April to November. The cost is $4 one-way, $7 roundtrip, or just $10 for an all-day pass. Buses meet all ferries and run hourly from 8 a.m. to 7:30 p.m. on a daily basis. They can carry bikes and luggage, and will even take you to the summit of Mt. Constitution—leave your car in Anacortes.

Orcas Taxi, tel. (360) 376-8294, offers cab service on the island, and **Practical Rent a Car,** tel. (360) 376-4176, has rental cars. **Magic Air Tours,** tel. (360) 376-2733, has scenic biplane tours from Eastsound Airport. See "Sports and Recreation," above, for details on bike and moped rentals on Orcas.

LOPEZ ISLAND

Because of its gently rolling hills and lack of traffic, Lopez (pop. 1,500) is very popular with cyclists; views of the surrounding islands and mountains to the east and west poke out from every turn. Despite being one of the largest San Juan islands, Lopez is probably the friendliest—waving to passing cars and bicycles is a time-honored local custom, and failure to wave will label you a tourist as surely as a camera around your neck and rubber thongs.

The business center for the island is **Lopez Village,** where you'll find a scattering of cafes, shops, a museum, stores, and especially real estate offices—which should tell you something about the island's newfound popularity. A few more businesses can be found along pretty Fisherman Bay—filled with sailboats and other craft—but the rest of the island is essentially undeveloped.

SIGHTS

Lopez's main attraction is its rural, pastoral countryside. The long stretches of hills, pastures, orchards, and woods might just as well be New England. Cows and sheep are a common sight, including some exotic long-haired breeds at **Cape St. Mary Ranch** on the southeast end of the island. Also of interest are the bright fields of daffodils, tulips, lilies, gladiolus, and delphiniums at **Madrona Farms,** near the intersection of Richardson and Davis Bay Roads. Bucolic Lopez Island is a delightful place to explore; unfortunately many of the beaches are privately owned and closed to the public.

Lopez Island Vineyards on Fisherman Bay Rd., tel. (360) 468-3644, is a small family winery that grows organic grapes and produces wines from these, along with grapes from eastern Washington. Open summers Wed.-Sun. noon-5 p.m., and weekends only for fall and spring; closed Christmas to mid-March.

A Taste of History
Lopez Historical Museum on Weeks Rd. in Lopez Village, tel. (360) 468-2049, is open Wed.-Sun. noon-4 p.m. during July and August; and Fri.-Sun. in May, June, and September. Closed the rest of the year. The museum contains local flotsam and jetsam: the first car driven on the island, old farm equipment, and historical photos. Outside, find a reef net boat and an aging tractor.

A couple of other buildings are worth a gander on the island. The **Lopez Library** is housed in a bright red and white 19th century schoolhouse

Fisherman's Bay,
Lopez Island

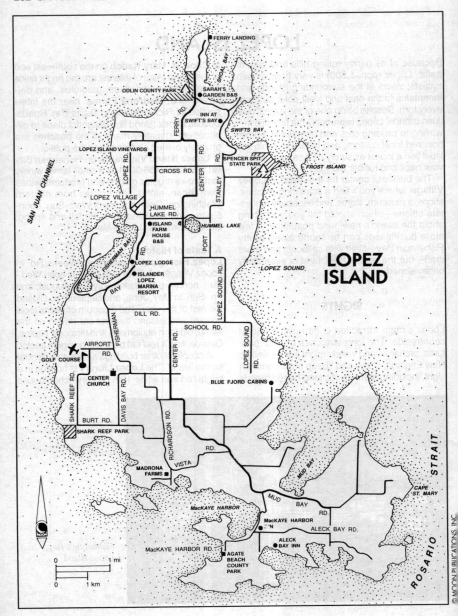

LOPEZ
ISLAND

FERRY LANDING

SHOAL BAY

SARAH'S
GARDEN B&B

ODLIN COUNTY PARK

INN AT
SWIFT'S BAY

SWIFTS BAY

SPENCER SPIT
STATE PARK

FROST ISLAND

LOPEZ ISLAND VINEYARDS

CROSS RD.

FERRY RD.

CENTER RD.

STANLEY RD.

LOPEZ VILLAGE

HUMMEL
LAKE RD.

ISLAND
FARM
HOUSE
B&B

HUMMEL LAKE

FISHERMAN BAY

PORT RD.

LOPEZ SOUND RD.

LOPEZ SOUND

LOPEZ LODGE

ISLANDER
LOPEZ
MARINA
RESORT

SAN JUAN CHANNEL

DILL RD.

FISHERMAN BAY

SCHOOL RD.

CENTER RD.

LOPEZ SOUND RD.

AIRPORT RD.

GOLF COURSE

CENTER
CHURCH

DAVIS BAY RD.

BLUE FJORD CABINS

SHARK REEF RD.

BURT RD.

RICHARDSON RD.

SHARK REEF PARK

VISTA RD.

MADRONA
FARMS

MUD BAY

CAPE
ST. MARY

MacKAYE HARBOR

MUD BAY RD.

MacKAYE HARBOR

ALECK BAY RD.

ALECK
BAY INN

MacKAYE HARBOR RD.

AGATE BEACH
COUNTY PARK

ROSARIO STRAIT

0   1 mi

0   1 km

MOON PUBLICATIONS, INC.

just east of Lopez Village. The **Lopez Island Community Church** in Lopez Village was built in 1904 and is notable for its steeple that splits into four cupolas. **Center Church,** built in 1887, is a simple white wood structure surrounded by a picket fence and next to a hilltop cemetery. The church is home to both Catholics and Lutherans (what would Martin Luther think of this?) and is approximately two miles south of Lopez Village on Fisherman Bay Road.

Parks

On the east side of the island, the 130-acre **Spencer Spit State Park,** tel. (360) 468-2251, has a mile-long beach for good year-round clamming, beachcombing, hiking, and picnicking. Also here are seasonal campsites, mooring buoys, and an RV dump station. A brackish lagoon frequently has ducks and shorebirds, and black-tailed deer are a common sight in the evening.

Other campsites and a boat launch are available at **Odlin County Park** at the north end of the island, just a mile from the ferry landing.

Very few of Lopez's beaches are open to the public. One exceptional exception is **Agate Beach,** located on the south end of the island at the end of MacKaye Harbor Road. This little park provides access to a beach filled with colorful wave-rounded stones. Another fine small park is **Shark Reef Recreation Area,** located at the south end of Shark Reef Rd. on the southwest side of the island. An easy half-mile path takes you through one of the few old-growth stands of trees left on Lopez to the rocky coastline. This is a good place to look for harbor seals, sea lions, and bald eagles.

SPORTS AND RECREATION

Biking

A favorite local activity is pedaling the 30-mile loop around Lopez Island. Once you get beyond the steep initial climb from the ferry dock, the rest of the island consists of gently rolling hills, a perfect place for families.

Rent bikes to tool around the island from **The Bike Shop on Lopez,** on School Rd. in the center of the island, tel. (360) 468-3497; **Cycle San Juans,** tel. (360) 468-3251; or **Lopez Bike Works,** along Fisherman Bay just south of Lopez

Village, tel. (360) 468-2847. Rates are around $25 a day. For a small fee, Cycle San Juans will deliver bikes to you at the ferry terminal as you arrive, or at your lodging place. They also offer bike tours starting at $35 for a half-day trip.

Sea Kayaking

Lopez Kayaks, tel. (360) 468-2847, has half-day ($37) and sunset ($28) kayak tours, plus kayak rentals for $50 per day for a single, and $75 per day for a double. Inquire at Lopez Bicycle Works on Fisherman Bay Road. They can deliver the kayak to you anywhere on the island. **MacKaye Harbor Inn,** MacKaye Harbor Rd., tel. (360) 468-2253, also rents kayaks.

Other

Sailboat charters are available from **Harmony Sailing Charters,** tel. (360) 468-3310, or **Kismet Sailing Charters,** tel. (360) 468-2435. **Lopez Island Golf Club,** tel. (360) 468-2679, is a nine-hole public course on Airport Road.

ACCOMMODATIONS

See the "Lopez Island Accommodations" chart for a complete listing of local places to stay. During the summer it is a good idea to make reservations a month or more ahead of time to be assured of a space, particularly on weekends. Many of the resorts, inns, and cottages also offer weekly rates. For additional places with weekly rates, contact: **Island House Realtors,** tel. (360) 468-3401, or **Village Guest House** in Lopez Village, tel. (360) 468-2191.

Located a mile south of the ferry, the **Inn at Swifts Bay,** tel. (360) 468-3636, is a brick Tudor-style home with guest rooms and suites, plus a private beach and hot tub (reservable for privacy). The big gourmet breakfast is guaranteed to please. Even closer to the ferry is **Sarah's Garden B&B,** tel. (360) 468-3725, which offers a single large room in a comfortable modern home at reasonable rates. This is one of the few places that accepts kids.

Edenwald Inn B&B, right in Lopez Village, tel. (360) 468-3238, is a contemporary inn with Victorian styling and comfortable rooms. The inn is surrounded by floral gardens, and meals are available downstairs.

LOPEZ ISLAND ACCOMMODATIONS

Accommodations are listed from least to most expensive. Rates are often lower during the winter months. The area code is 360.

Island Farm House B&B; Hummel Lake Rd.; tel. 468-2864; $50 s or d in room with private bath, $75 s or d in cabin with kitchenette, private bath, two-night minimum; 12-acre farm with animals, pond, continental breakfast

Sarah's Garden B&B; Ferry Rd. at Port Stanley Rd.; tel. 468-3725; $65 s or d; contemporary home near ferry, quiet location, large garden, one guest room, king-size bed, private bath, light breakfast, kids welcome

Blue Fjord Cabins; Elliott Rd.; tel. 468-2749; $68-78 s or d; two chalet cabins on Jasper Bay, secluded location, kitchens, decks, three-night minimum stay in July and August, kids okay

Lopez Lodge; Fisherman Bay Rd.; tel. 468-2500; $69-99 s or d; shared or private bath, kitchens, kids okay

Inn at Swifts Bay; Port Stanley Rd.; tel. 468-3636; $75-155 s or d; Tudor-style home, three guest rooms, two suites, private or shared bath, private beach, hot tub, gourmet breakfast, no kids

Islander Lopez Marina Resort; Fisherman Bay Rd.; tel. 468-2233 or (800) 736-3434; $80-275 s or d; outdoor pool, jacuzzi, marina, kids okay

Aleck Bay Inn B&B; Alec Lane; tel. 468-3535; $85-139 s or d; hot tub, private beach, sundeck, fireplaces, four guest rooms, private baths, full breakfast

Edenwald Inn B&B; Lopez Village; tel. 468-3238; $85-140 s or d; modern Victorian inn, eight guest rooms, private baths, full breakfast, free ferry or airport shuttle, kids welcome, AAA approved

MacKaye Harbor Inn B&B; MacKaye Harbor Rd.; tel. 468-2253; $87-140 s or d; stately 1904 home, four antique-furnished guest rooms, shared or private baths, beachfront location, full breakfast, bike and kayak rentals, no kids under nine

MacKaye Harbor Inn, tel. (360) 468-2253, is a turn-of-the-century farmhouse on the south end of the island. The five antique-furnished rooms are just a stone's throw from the water, where you can rent kayaks to explore protected MacKaye Harbor.

Blue Fjord Cabins, tel. (360) 468-2749 offer contemporary cabins in a wooded setting near Jasper Bay—a fine place to relax and soak up the quietude.

Aleck Bay Inn B&B, tel. (360) 468-3538, has a sundeck overlooking Aleck Bay and all sorts of amenities, including a hot tub, pool table, and private beach.

CAMPING

Campsites ($10) are available at **Odlin County Park,** just a mile south of the ferry landing. Call (360) 468-2496 for reservations (two-night min-

imum). No RV hookups, but the park does have a boat ramp. Open year-round.

Spencer Spit State Park, five miles from the ferry landing on the east end of Baker View Rd., tel. (360) 468-2251, has campsites for $10; no RV hookups, showers, or reservations. Open late Feb.-Oct., this very popular campground seems perpetually filled in the summer. Get here early to be assured of a place on a mid-summer weekend.

Coin-operated showers are available at the public restrooms near the Lopez Village Market, and at Fisherman Bay Marina.

FOOD

Gail's Restaurant in Lopez Village, tel. (360) 468-2150, serves good breakfasts, fresh-baked muffins, and other treats, and has a deli for lunch sandwiches. During the summer months,

Gail's has a full dinner menu that changes weekly, and a fine wine selection at fair prices. The food is Northwest cuisine with splashes from Thailand, Malaysia, China, and Mexico. Much of the produce in the summer comes from their own organic garden. They also cater special events, including the engagement party for Bill Gates and Melinda French.

Holly B's Bakery in Lopez Village, tel. (360) 468-2133, is the place to go for Starbucks coffee and a cinnamon roll. Open summers only. **Lopez Island Pharmacy,** tel. (360) 468-2616, has an old fashioned soda fountain.

The Bay Cafe in Lopez Village, tel. (360) 468-3700, opens daily in the summer for Mexican, Indonesian, Thai, American—you name it—lunch and dinner. Meals come complete with homemade soups and salad. Recommended. **Bucky's Lopez Island Grill,** also in Lopez Village, tel. (360) 468-2595, has great fish and chips, plus burgers, barbecued ribs, salads, and chicken.

The Galley Restaurant and Lounge, tel. (360) 468-2713, on Fisherman Bay, is best known for its enormous omelettes, prime rib, and abalone.

Groceries and Produce

Get groceries from **Village Market** in Lopez Village, tel. (360) 468-2266, the biggest on the island. The **Lopez Farmers Market** is open on Saturday 10 a.m.-1 p.m. in Lopez Village June to September. Stop by for fresh garden produce and flowers, along with arts and crafts. In the summer months, get fresh-cut flowers, jams, and jellies at the **Madrona Farms** stand on the

south end of the island at the corner of Richardson and Davis Bay Roads, tel. (360) 468-3301.

EVENTS AND SHOPPING

The big event in Lopez Village is—not surprisingly—the **Fourth of July,** where you'll find a parade, fun run, barbecue, and fireworks.

Don't miss **Chimera** in Lopez Village, tel. (360) 468-3265, a cooperatively run gallery with unusual blown glass pieces, sweaters, pottery, and jewelry.

INFORMATION AND SERVICES

The **Lopez Chamber of Commerce,** tel. (360) 468-3800, has local information. Pick up a free *Map and Guide of Lopez Island* from the museum or local real estate offices.

You can do your laundry at **Keep it Clean** on Fisherman Bay Rd. north of Lopez Village.

TRANSPORTATION

The **Washington State Ferry,** tel. (360) 468-2252 or (800) 843-3779, docks at the north end of Lopez Island, approximately four miles from Lopez Village. See "Ferry Service" at the beginning of this chapter for details on service and fares to the San Juan Islands.

There is no public bus service on Lopez Island, but **Angie's Cab Courier,** tel. (360) 468-2227, offers taxi service and car rentals.

OTHER ISLANDS

In addition to the three main islands, the San Juans contain a myriad of smaller ones. Shaw Island is served by the ferry system but has limited services. None of the others are visited by the ferries, and of the remaining islands, only Blakely Island has a store and marina. The rest are either marine state parks, part of the San Juan Islands National Wildlife Preserve, or private property.

SHAW ISLAND

The least visited of the ferry-served islands, Shaw (pop. 190) is primarily residential and known mostly for the nuns who operate the ferry dock and general store, **"Little Portion."** The four nuns are members of the Franciscan Sisters of the Eucharist, a Catholic order that takes vows of chastity, poverty, and obedience. Tours are available by appointment, and you are welcome to see the beautiful little chapel—with a nautical theme—where mass is held each Sunday. A half-dozen other nuns from the cloistered Benedictine order live at Our Lady of the Rock, where they operate a big dairy farm on the island.

Shaw Island remains essentially undeveloped, with second-growth forests covering most of the land. Access to all but a few beaches is limited by No Trespassing signs. You won't find any B&Bs, cottage industries, or bike rental places on the island; by law, the Little Portion store is the only business allowed. The store itself sells groceries, along with beer, wine, and chocolate for decadence.

Sights
The **Shaw Island Historical Museum** is housed in a small log cabin at the intersection of Blind Bay and Hoffman Cove Roads. It's open Tuesday 2-4 p.m., Thursday 10 a.m.-noon, and Saturday 2-4 p.m. (the same hours as the adjacent library). Out front is a reef-netting fishing boat similar to those still used to fish for salmon in the San Juans. Across the way is the **Little Red Schoolhouse,** one of the few one-room schools still in use.

South Beach County Park, two miles south of the ferry landing, has a dozen in-the-trees campsites ($10), a picnic area, boat launch, and limited drinking water. No reservations or showers. Get here early for a space on summer weekends since there are no other camping or lodging options on Shaw. The 65-acre park is best known for its long beach where you'll often find sand dollars.

The University of Washington's **Cedar Rock Biological Preserve** is a quiet off-the-beaten-path place on the south end of Hoffman Cove Road. A trail leads through fields, woods, and past small coves.

ISLAND STATE PARKS

A number of the smaller islands in the San Juan archipelago are preserved as marine state parks, accessible only by private boat and largely undeveloped. The parks have primitive campsites, no drinking water (bring plenty with you), and no garbage collection. Sea kayaks are a popular island-hopping mode of transportation, but since some of the smaller islands are several miles out, be careful not to overestimate your ability. Sailboats and motorboats can tie up at mooring buoys in these marine parks for a fee. The parks listed below all have camping. In addition, many other islets are open to day use, but islands within the San Juan Islands National Wildlife Refuge are off limits to protect nesting birds and other animals. For information on the marine parks and the wildlife refuge, talk with folks at Lime Kiln State Park on San Juan Island, tel. (360) 378-2044.

Blind Island State Park
This three-acre grassy island just north of Shaw Island in Blind Bay is a great place to watch the ferries pass by. The shoebox-sized park has mooring buoys and four primitive campsites ($5).

Doe Island State Park
Located just southeast of Orcas Island, Doe Island has five primitive campsites ($5) on a small, secluded island with a rocky shoreline. No moor-

ing buoys, but just a short kayak paddle from the hot tubs at Doe Bay Village Resort.

James Island State Park
Less than a half-mile east of Decatur Island and just four miles from the Anacortes ferry terminal, James Island has 13 primitive campsites ($5) on a small, cliff-faced and forested island with sunny beaches on the Rosario Strait. The island also has short hiking trails, mooring buoys, and a dock.

Clark Island State Park
Two miles northeast of Orcas Island, this island park has eight primitive campsites ($5), and beautiful beaches on the south end for walking, sunbathing, fishing, or diving offshore. Nearby is privately owned Barnes Island, plus a cluster of rocky islets called The Sisters; they are frequently crowded with seabirds.

Matia Island State Park
This marine park is three miles northeast of Orcas Island, with six primitive campsites ($5) near the dock and a large population of nesting puffins and other seabirds on a nearby rocky island. Most of Matia Island is managed as part of the San Juan Islands National Wildlife Refuge. It was also once home to a hermit who got a regular workout rowing the three miles to Orcas and walking another two miles to Eastsound to buy his groceries. On his last trip in 1921, he headed out from Eastsound in rough seas and was never seen again.

Sucia Island State Park
Covering 564 acres, Sucia Island State Park is the largest and most popular marine state park, and with good reason. The U-shaped park sits three miles north of Orcas Island and contains numerous protected anchorages, 50 mooring buoys, 55 primitive campsites ($5), and six miles of trails. The shoreline has delightful sandy beaches for sunbathing, exploring, clamming, and crabbing, plus bizarre water-carved sandstone formations. Offshore, you can scuba dive on sunken wrecks. Don't expect to be the only visitor on Sucia Island; on a summer weekend the waters around the island are jam-packed with U.S. and Canadian vessels of all description.

Patos Island State Park
Patos is northernmost of the San Juans, located six miles north of Orcas Island and two miles northwest of Sucia Island. The park has four mooring buoys, four primitive campsites ($5), and a trail that circles the forested island. You'll find great beaches to explore on the north side, good salmon and bottom fishing offshore, and a lighthouse (built in 1908 and now automated) at the northwest tip of the island.

Jones Island State Park
One of the most overused of the San Juan state marine parks, this 188-acre island is just a mile west of Orcas Island near Deer Harbor. The park has 10 primitive campsites ($5), seven mooring buoys, and a public dock. Hiking trails cross the island, passing places where a 1990 storm knocked down magnificent old-growth trees.

Turn Island State Park
Turn Island, just a quarter-mile from San Juan's east shore and within easy kayaking distance of Friday Harbor, is a very popular place for picnickers and campers. It features 10 primitive campsites ($5), three mooring buoys, two beaches, and three miles of wooded hiking trails.

Posey Island State Park
This pinprick of an island covers just one acre and is located a quarter-mile north of San Juan Island's Roche Harbor. Shallow waters and a single primitive campsite ($5) make this a favorite spot for folks on kayaks and canoes in search of their own little island.

Stuart Island State Park
Stuart Island, five miles northwest of Roche Harbor, has two well-protected harbors for boats and 19 primitive campsites ($5) with drinking water. The park covers only a small portion of this 3.5-mile-long island; much of the rest is private. A county road leads past a number of homes, an airstrip, and a white one-room schoolhouse now used as a library. A newer school building is nearby, along with a small cemetery. Also worth checking out is **Turn Point Lighthouse,** built in 1936, a seven-mile roundtrip hike from the park. Great views from here across to Vancouver Island and the nearby Gulf Islands in British Columbia.

PRIVATE ISLANDS

The rest of the San Juan Islands are home to a few hundred individuals. Some islands have only a single home, others a few dozen residences occupied seasonally. None have more than 80 or so people. Privacy is closely guarded on most of these islands, and visitors are not appreciated.

As the state ferry heads west from Anacortes to the San Juans, it threads its way between two privately owned islands, **Blakely** and **Decatur.** Blakely Island has a public marina with a store, post office, fuel, laundry, and showers on the north end, but the rest of the island is private and off limits. Decatur is even more private, with no stores or other facilities.

Located north of San Juan Island, tiny **Spieden Island** covers just 480 acres, and is home to a wild game farm with various species of exotic deer, wild goats, and antelope. The animals were brought here in the 1970s with the intention of attracting hunters; now they attract folks who just want to see them. For details on access, call San Juan Central Reservations at (360) 378-8887 or (800) 836-2176.

Waldron Island, northwest of Orcas, is nearly all private land, though Cowlitz Bay on the west side contains 273 acres of Nature Conservancy land with public access for day use only; this is primarily a bird refuge. Much of the island is flat and marshy, though the north end rises to 600 feet near Point Disney.

BOB RACE

© MOON PUBLICATIONS, INC.

SOUTHERN PUGET SOUND

TACOMA

Tacoma (pop. 184,000), a city in transition from an industrial past to a diversified future, is the next logical benefactor of western Washington's phenomenal growth. "The City of Destiny"

SOUTHERN PUGET SOUND

[Map showing Southern Puget Sound region with locations including Kitsap Peninsula, Vashon I., Federal Way, Tacoma, Sumner, Puyallup, Enumclaw, Buckley, Parkland, Spanaway, Olympia, Lacey, and highways 303, 16, 5, 90, 405, 18, 167, 512, 164, 410. Scale 0-15 mi / 0-15 km]

has several things to be proud of: a world-class zoo system, a revitalized downtown centering around a vibrant theater district, outstanding museums of history and art, numerous historic buildings, a large and diverse 700-acre city park, top-quality hotels and waterfront restaurants, two excellent universities and established community colleges, and new business dollars to provide a healthy base for what is becoming one of the state's fastest-growing cities.

Tacoma has long suffered from a sibling rivalry with its big sister to the north, Seattle. Despite considerable progress in recent years, Tacoma remains the butt of jokes and is regarded in the same way San Franciscans view Oakland—a place where, as Gertrude Stein said, "there is no there, there." The stench from the big Weyerhaeuser mill often wafts through downtown, and the city has more than its share of run-down and abandoned structures. Despite this, the citizens of Tacoma have made a concerted effort to turn things around. Truth be told, Tacoma is far better than Seattle snobs will admit. The city isn't likely to become a major tourist attraction, but it does have some delight-

© MOON PUBLICATIONS, INC.

ful aspects, especially several fine museums and the extraordinarily diverse Point Defiance Park.

The Port of Tacoma has been a leader in the containerized shipping business for many years and has often taken business away from Seattle (just as Oakland did to San Francisco). Today it is one of the largest container ports in the world, with gantry cranes, straddle carriers, and the latest in container-handling equipment. Tacoma also relies on wood products, shipbuilding, primary metal and chemical plants, health care,

and a growing high-tech industry. Agriculture is a big business in more rural parts of Pierce County.

HISTORY

English sea captain George Vancouver and his entourage first stumbled across the Puget Sound area in 1792 when Peter Puget, under Vancouver's orders, sailed by Point Defiance and the Narrows. Members of Hudson's Bay Company later came along and built Fort Nisqually in 1833,

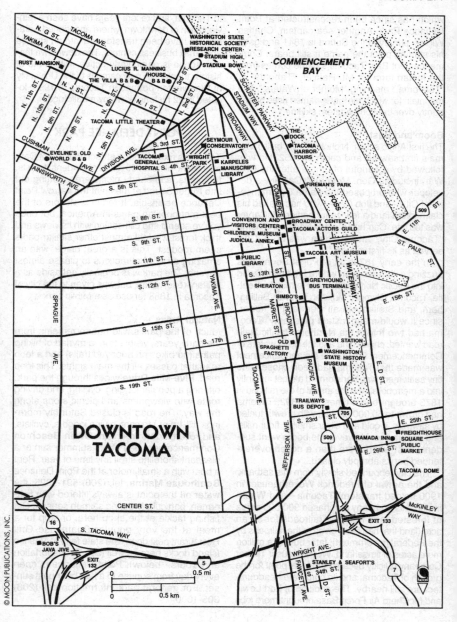

DOWNTOWN TACOMA

COMMENCEMENT BAY

N. G ST.
TACOMA AVE.
YAKIMA AVE.
RUST MANSION
N. 11th ST.
N. 10th ST.
N. 9th ST.
N. 8th ST.
N. 7th ST.
N. 6th ST.
LUCIUS R. MANNING HOUSE
THE VILLA B & B
B & B
N. 3rd ST.
N. 2nd ST.
N. I ST.
N. J ST.
WASHINGTON STATE HISTORICAL SOCIETY RESEARCH CENTER
STADIUM HIGH
STADIUM BOWL
TACOMA LITTLE THEATER
N. 5th ST.
CUSHMAN
EVELINE'S OLD WORLD B & B
AVE.
DIVISION AVE.
AINSWORTH AVE.
N. 3rd ST.
SEYMOUR CONSERVATORY
WRIGHT PARK
KARPELES MANUSCRIPT LIBRARY
SCHUSTER PARKWAY
BROADWAY
THE DOCK
TACOMA HARBOR TOURS
FIREMAN'S PARK
TACOMA GENERAL HOSPITAL S. 4th ST.
S. 5th ST.
S. 8th ST.
S. 9th ST.
S. 11th ST.
CONVENTION AND VISITORS CENTER
CHILDREN'S MUSEUM
JUDICIAL ANNEX
PUBLIC LIBRARY
COMMERCE
BROADWAY CENTER
TACOMA ACTORS GUILD
TACOMA ART MUSEUM
509
E. 11th ST.
ST. PAUL
FOSS
WATERWAY
SPRAGUE
AVE.
YAKIMA AVE.
S. 12th ST.
S. 13th ST.
SHERATON
BIMBO'S
MARKET ST.
BROADWAY
GREYHOUND BUS TERMINAL
E. 15th ST.
S. 15th ST.
S. 17th ST.
OLD SPAGHETTI FACTORY
UNION STATION
WASHINGTON STATE HISTORY MUSEUM
E. D ST.
S. 19th ST.
TACOMA AVE.
JEFFERSON AVE.
PACIFIC AVE.
TRAILWAYS BUS DEPOT
S. 23rd ST.
705
509
E. 25th ST.
RAMADA INN
E. 26th ST.
FREIGHTHOUSE SQUARE PUBLIC MARKET
TACOMA DOME
CENTER ST.
16
BOB'S JAVA JIVE
EXIT 132
5
0   0.5 mi
0   0.5 km
S. TACOMA WAY
WRIGHT AVE.
STANLEY & SEAFORT'S
S. 34th ST.
FAWCETT AVE.
D ST.
EXIT 133
McKINLEY WAY
7

© MOON PUBLICATIONS, INC.

which has since been reconstructed at Point Defiance Park. Another sea captain, Charles Wilkes, surveyed the Sound in 1841 and gave his starting point the name it still bears: Commencement Bay. Tacoma's name comes from the Indian term for Mt. Rainier, "Tahoma" or "Takhoma," meaning "Mother of Waters." The mountain for which the city is named rises prominently over the southeastern skyline.

Boom and Bust

The first Anglo settler, Nicholas Delin, built Tacoma's first sawmill and cabin in 1852. He was followed by a handful of others after the Civil War, including Gen. Morton McCarver—a developer who proposed the name Commencement City—and Job Carr—who had staked his claim to the land a few years earlier. McCarver was too late, Carr had already filed for the name "Tacoma City," and Tacoma was born; Carr served as its first mayor.

In the early 1870s all of Puget Sound was buzzing with rumors on where the first railroad into the Pacific Northwest would terminate. Seattle, Tacoma, Olympia, Mukilteo, Everett, Bellingham, and Steilacoom all vied for the honor, since it would mean instant prosperity. Tacoma had two things the Northern Pacific Railroad wanted: cheap land and the deep waters of Commencement Bay. Once the announcement was made that Tacoma had been chosen, the tiny settlement was transformed almost instantly into a metropolis, and the arrival of the railroad in 1873 brought boom times. By 1892, Tacoma had grown to 50,000 people, with growth fueled by sawmills, a gold and silver smelter, flour mills, and coal mines. However the boom went suddenly bust when more than a dozen overextended banks abruptly closed.

The city rebounded slowly from this setback, and the arrival of Frederick Weyerhaeuser in 1900 helped transform Tacoma—and Washington. His company purchased 900,000 acres of forested land from the railroads for $6 an acre (land that had been given to the railroads by the Federal government), later buying a million more acres of timberland. Weyerhaeuser Timber Company quickly became the focal point for the growth of Tacoma, and its corporate headquarters are still nearby. The addition of Fort Lewis and McChord Air Force Base brought more jobs to Tacoma, and recent years have seen a reinvigoration of downtown, where abandoned warehouses have been transformed into art studios and small business centers. The downtown theater scene is particularly active, with a trio of historic theaters. A new campus of the University of Washington opened in Tacoma in 1995, located in 22 historic downtown buildings.

POINT DEFIANCE PARK

Tacoma's most famous attraction is Point Defiance Park, almost 700 acres of gardens, forests, footpaths, and shady picnic areas jutting out into Puget Sound at the tip of the narrow Point Defiance peninsula. It reminds visitors of the best metropolitan parks in America, but once you've seen it, the cliff setting with its views and thick forest will make most other similar parks seem modest. This is a great place, with an amazing array of attractions to please almost anyone. The park was originally set aside as a military reservation, but was given to the city of Tacoma in 1888 for use as a public park.

Natural Areas

Much of the park's wild nature remains from the early years, visible from a myriad of hiking paths (no bikes on unpaved trails) and a loop road that passes all the main sights. This loop road, **Five-Mile Drive** winds through the park, offering a popular jogging, cycling, and driving route with viewpoints and picnic stops along the way. The road is closed Saturday mornings (till 1 p.m.) to cars, giving joggers, cyclists, and rollerbladers free rein. **Owen Beach** on Commencement Bay offers summer sun or a pleasant shoreline stroll any time of year. Rent a boat with a small motor at the Point Defiance **Boathouse Marina,** tel. (206) 591-5325; the water off the point is always littered with fishermen, particularly during salmon season. Get fishing tackle at the shop here, or stop for a meal at the very popular Boathouse Grill Restaurant next door. The state ferry to Vashon Island docks here as well (see "Transportation and Tours," below). Point Defiance is open every day from sunrise to a half-hour past sunset. For general park information call (206) 305-1000.

Gardens

In addition to the natural areas, Point Defiance Park is home to several beautifully maintained gardens. The **Japanese Garden** features a pagoda built in 1914, plus pools, a waterfall, and immaculate landscaping. A **Rhododendron Garden** covers almost five acres and is especially striking in the spring when the 115 varieties of rhododendrons bloom. The **Rose Garden** contains a rustic gazebo and some 1,500 rose bushes that are flowering June through September. Other featured gardens at Point Defiance are the **Iris Garden,** the **Dahlia Trial Garden** (best time to see these is August), and the **Northwest Native Garden** with plants from all six biotic zones in the Northwest.

Zoo and Aquarium

The biggest attraction at Point Defiance is the excellent Zoo and Aquarium—one of the finest zoos on the West Coast—home of beluga whales, polar bears, sharks, walrus, red wolves, elephants, and much more. The real attractions here are the ocean exhibits. You'll discover a tropical reef filled with brilliantly colored fish, a 160,000-gallon cold-water aquarium with fish, jellyfish, eels, and other critters from the Puget Sound area, and the main event: a large tank where you can look through the glass windows at more than 30 sharks, reaching up to 10 feet long. (Get here on Sunday and Thursday at 11 a.m., and Tuesday at 3 p.m. to watch the feeding frenzy.) Fascinating displays describe the lives of sharks, stingrays, and skates, and you will even get to see shark egg cases with living embryos. The Rocky Shores exhibit includes tufted puffins, harbor seals, Pacific walrus, beluga whales, and wonderfully playful sea otters. Another favorite attraction is the polar bear area, which features a deep pool where you can watch them swimming from behind a thick glass wall.

The zoo has cafes and gift shops. In August and September, the Friday evening Zoosounds concerts are fun for the whole family. In December, come in the evening to see the twinkling animal Zoolights. Zoo admission is $6.75 for adults, $6.25 for seniors, $5 for ages five to 17, $2.50 for ages three to four, and free for kids under two. The zoo is open daily 10 a.m.-7 p.m. Memorial Day to Labor Day, and daily 10 a.m.-4 p.m. the rest of the year; closed only on Thanksgiving and Christmas. Call (206) 591-5335 for recorded info, or 591-5337 for the office.

Fort Nisqually

Fort Nisqually Historic Site, on the southwest side of Point Defiance Park, has a half-dozen historic and reconstructed buildings inside log bastions. Fort Nisqually was a Hudson's Bay trading post in the mid-1800s and was originally located 17 miles to the south on the Nisqually delta near present-day Fort Lewis. The buildings were moved here in the 1930s and carefully restored. Of particular interest is the working blacksmith shop where you can learn how tools and hardware were fabricated for trade. Also on the grounds are the factor's house, a trade store, and a storehouse originally built in 1851. This is considered the oldest standing building in Washington. The staff is clad in period costumes from the 1850s and offer living history demonstrations on everything from spinning to black powder shooting. Come here in May to celebrate Queen Victoria's birthday, in August for a mountain man encampment, or in the fall for a candlelight tour. Entrance to the fort costs $1, or 50 cents for kids. Hours are daily 11 a.m.-6 p.m. June-Aug., and Wed.-Sun. 1-4 p.m. the rest of the year. Call (206) 591-5339 for more information.

Never Never Land

The strangest sight at Point Defiance is Never Never Land, where 10 acres of woods are sprinkled with 32 life-size scenes from favorite children's stories: Humpty-Dumpty, Hansel and Gretel, Goldilocks and the Three Bears, Peter Rabbit, and Mother Goose. Costumed characters delight the kids with these and other tales. Never Never Land is open daily 11 a.m.-5 p.m. (till 7 p.m. in mid-summer) May through Labor Day, and weekends only in April and September. Closed Oct.-March. Entrance is $2.50 for adults, $1.25 for kids, and free for youngsters age two and younger. Call (206) 591-5845 for details. Older children have fun at the Go Kart track in another part of Point Defiance Park.

Camp 6 Logging Museum

Camp 6 is a reconstructed logging camp with steam equipment from the late 1800s and early 1900s, when most Northwest logging was done from railroads. Featured attractions (everything still runs) include a 90-ton logging locomotive specially built to handle steep grades and sharp curves, a steam-powered 1887 Dolbeer Donkey engine that was used to yard logs, and various high lead, skidders, and other logging equipment from the heyday of timber harvesting in the Northwest. Also here are loggers' bunkhouses, including turn-of-the-century bunkhouses on rails that could be moved as the trees were cut. The bunkhouses contain photos and artifacts from life in the logging camps.

Kids love the 1929 steam-powered **P.D.Q. & K. Railroad,** which includes log cars, cabooses, speeders, and other railcars. It offers rides on weekend afternoons April-September. There's also a special **Santa Train** the first three weekends of December. Camp 6 is open Wed.-Sun. 10 a.m.-4 p.m. (till 7 p.m. in the summer); closed November and December. Call (206) 752-0047 for details.

OTHER SIGHTS

Historical Museums

Tacoma has long had a fine historical museum, but it is now home to the biggest and most impressive such facility in the state, the **Washington State History Museum,** which opened in 1996. This 100,000 square-foot building—

built at a cost of $40 million—sits adjacent to historic Union Station and repeats its rounded design in a series of three gracefully vaulted arches. The exhibits follow a progression through time that leads past a Salish Indian plank house, dioramas of mining and logging towns, exhibits on the arrival of the railroad and the effect of Depression of the 1930s, and a grand finale featuring a colossal map of Washington and a full-scale replica of a power transmission tower as the centerpieces of a high-tech interactive visit to Washington's past and present. Side galleries offer a chance to explore other topics, including the natural setting, and how the Klondike gold rush and WW II transformed the state. The museum is joined to the restored Union Station by a scenic courtyard and amphitheater, a fine place for a lunch break. Also inside the museum is a cafe and gift shop with books on Washington's history. Located at 1911 Pacific Ave., tel. (206) 593-2830, the museum is open Sunday 11 a.m.-5 p.m., and Mon.-Sat. 9 a.m.-5 p.m. (Thursday till 8 p.m.) from Memorial Day to Labor Day, and Sunday 11 a.m.-5 p.m., Tues.-Sat. 10 a.m.-5 p.m. (Thursday till 8 p.m.) the rest of the year. Admission is $7 for adults, $6 for seniors, $5 for ages 13-17, $4 for ages six to 12, $3 for ages three to five, and free for tots.

The **Washington State Historical Society Research Center,** 315 N. Stadium Way, tel. (206) 597-3642—where the museum was for-

downtown Tacoma and the 11th Street Bridge

TACOMA PUBLIC LIBRARY

merly housed—now contains a research library that includes thousands of historic photos, old posters (including many ship bills from the Klondike gold rush), and other archives. The rooftop patio provides a fine view of Stadium High School, the city of Tacoma, and Mt. Rainier.

Historic Buildings

Completed in 1911, Tacoma's copper-domed **Union Station** was designed by the same firm that built New York's Grand Central Station and has a similar sense of grandeur. The depot originally served as the terminus of the Northern Pacific's rail line and was later used by the Great Northern and Union Pacific railroads before falling into disuse. A multimillion dollar restoration project in 1989 transformed the distinctively domed building into a federal courthouse for all of western Washington—its magnificent central space filled by the works of the renowned Tacoma-born glass artist, Dale Chihuly. An 18-foot cobalt-blue chandelier hangs from the high center, and many other pieces provide bright accents. Union Station is open Mon.-Fri. 10 a.m.-4 p.m.; closed weekends. No charge.

Old City Hall, on the corner of S. 7th St. and Pacific Ave., is another distinctive downtown building. Patterned after an Italian town hall, the dominant feature is a tall free-standing clocktower. The building was built in 1905 and is now used for commercial offices.

Tacoma Art Museum

In recent years Tacoma has undergone something of an artistic renaissance as old warehouses are transformed into studios and galleries. The focal point of all this is the Tacoma Art Museum, 1123 Pacific Ave., tel. (206) 272-4258, a four-story building that is best known for its paintings and other pieces from 19th- and 20th-century American artists, and its permanent exhibitions of Dale Chihuly glass sculptures. New exhibits come to the museum almost monthly, and there are frequent lectures and other activities, plus two fine museum shops with gifts, art books, and jewelry (the larger one is across the street). The Artworks gallery is a fun space where kids (and adults) can create their own artistic masterpieces in the museum. Tacoma Art Museum is open Sunday noon-5 p.m., and Tuesday, Wednesday, Friday, and Saturday 10

a.m.-5 p.m., and Thursday 10 a.m.-7 p.m. Admission is $3 for adults, $2 for students and seniors, $1 for ages six to 12, and free for under age six. No charge on Tuesday.

For the Kids

The **Children's Museum of Tacoma,** 925 Court C (between Market St. and Broadway), tel. (206) 627-2436, is a fun and educational place for kids, with changing exhibits. When I visited (hey, they didn't say you have to be under age 10), kids were playing doctor and nurse as they operated on life-size cloth dummies. The museum is open Tues.-Sat. 10 a.m.-4 p.m. from mid-June through August, and Sunday noon-4 p.m., Tues.-Fri. 10 a.m.-5 p.m., and Saturday 10 a.m.-4 p.m. during the school year. Closed the first two weeks of September. Admission is $3.25 for kids and adults.

Tacoma Dome

Completed in 1983, this blue, geometric-patterned structure off I-5 is one of the largest wood-domed structures in the world. Spanning 530 feet in diameter, and 115 feet tall (as high as a 15-story building), the Dome is owned by the city and is used for various sporting and musical events (U2, Frank Sinatra, and Garth Brooks have all performed here), as well as trade shows. It can seat up to 22,000 persons, and its concert seating can go up to 28,000. For upcoming events at the Dome, call (206) 591-5318. Tours are not currently available, but a small museum of local sports history is open during events.

Stadium District

One of Tacoma's most historic sections is the Stadium District, located near **Stadium High School** on Tacoma Avenue. Built on the top of a hill in the style of a French chateau, this extraordinary high school was begun in 1891 and was intended to be a grandiose seven-story railroad hotel. The depression of 1893 left it vacant for several years until it was transformed into a high school in 1906. Next door is the Stadium Bowl, the West Coast's first stadium, and the site of visits by three presidents (Theodore Roosevelt, Warren Harding, and Franklin Delano Roosevelt), along with such sports legends as Babe Ruth and Jack Dempsey. More

DISASTER OVER THE SOUND

The windy Tacoma Narrows presented an obstacle to the linking of Tacoma with Kitsap Peninsula. During the buildup to WW II, the link became more crucial, since the shipyards of Bremerton were just 20 miles north on the peninsula. The ferry service was being overworked, and after many attempts backers finally got the 5,939-foot-long bridge built; in 1940 it was the third-longest suspension bridge in the world.

It was quite an undertaking, and the construction process was exciting for sidewalk superintendents from both shores. The towers stood 500 feet above the swift currents below, and more than 19,000 miles of wire were wound into the cables that supported the roadbed.

When it was finished in 1940, the workmen reported that the roadbed didn't behave properly; it rippled. A professor of engineering at the University of Washington, F. Bert Farquarson, was commissioned to make wind-tunnel tests, and he urged a much more comprehensive study. His warnings went barely heeded, and the insurance agent who sold the bridge insurance pocketed the premium—after all, who had ever heard of a new bridge falling?

In the meantime, the bridge earned its nickname of Galloping Gertie from its great rippling effect, and motorists in search of a thrill could pay their toll on a windy day, drive onto the bridge, and watch the car ahead completely disappear in the ripples.

It all ended on the morning of November 7, 1940, when a strong wind came up and held steady at about 40 mph. The bridge began a corkscrew twist so severe that it was closed. But Leonard Coatsworth, editor for the Tacoma *News Tribune*, was driving across at the time with his cocker spaniel, Tubby. Coatsworth found that he couldn't drive.

Before I realized it, the tilt from side to side became so violent that I lost control of the car . . . I jammed on the brakes and got out of the car, only to be thrown onto my face against the curb. I tried to stand and was thrown again. Around me I could hear concrete cracking. I started back to the car to get the dog, but was thrown before I could reach it. The car itself began to slide from side to side of the roadway.

On hands and knees most of the time, I crawled 500 yards to the towers . . . My breath was coming in gasps; my knees were raw and bleeding, my hands bruised and swollen from gripping the concrete curb . . . Finally my breath gave out completely and I lay in the roadway clutching the curb until I could breathe again, and then resumed my progress. Toward the last I risked rising to my feet and running a few yards at a time . . . Safely back at the toll plaza, I saw the bridge in its final collapse and saw my car plunge into the Narrows.

On that same morning a college student named Winfred Brown walked out onto the bridge a short distance, but returned when the bridge twisted so far that he seemed to be looking straight down at the water.

Professor Farquarson had heard of the contortions and drove down from Seattle to film the event. He went out onto the bridge to try and save Tubby but wasn't able to walk upright, so he retreated to the shore.

The twisting became worse; lampposts began snapping off and chunks of concrete were flying. Finally, about 100 feet of roadway with Coatsworth's car and Tubby fell into the Narrows. Soon most of the roadway was gone. The towers that had been supporting the concrete snapped back toward each shore until the cables stopped them, humming in the wind, and finally the whole twisted mess fell into Puget Sound.

The Narrows was without a bridge for almost exactly a decade while engineers designed, and redesigned, a new bridge that did not act like a sail every time a gale blew through. The new $14 million bridge was opened on October 14, 1950.

In 1992 the remains of Galloping Gertie were added to the National Register of Historic Places to protect her from salvagers. Only fish, marine mammals, and scuba divers visit her now.

than 100 turn-of-the-century mansions and stately homes can be found in the area around the stadium, including several of the city's best B&Bs. Be sure to see the **Rust Mansion** at 1001 N. I St., a Classical Revival structure built in 1905.

Wright Park at S. 3rd and G Streets is a shady place with gardens, paved paths, stone lions, lawn bowling greens, and a delightful surprise: the **W.W. Seymour Botanical Conservatory.** Built in 1908 and on the National Register of Historic Places, this Victorian-style conservatory—one of just three on the West Coast—hosts a bright array of tropical plants and cacti beneath 12,000 panes of glass. This is a great place to visit on a rainy winter day (or any time for that matter). The conservatory is open daily (except Christmas and Thanksgiving) 8 a.m.-4:20 p.m.; no charge. The small gift shop has botanical gifts, and the friendly cat will come up to greet you; call (206) 591-5330 for more information.

One of Tacoma's strangest sights is the **Karpeles Manuscript Library Museum,** 407 S. G St. (across from Wright Park), tel. (206) 383-2575. Located in an old Carnagie Library, the museum displays changing exhibits of rare and unique documents from all over the world, from D-Day defense plans signed by Adolf Hitler to letters written by Charles Manson. Open Tues.-Sun. 10 a.m.-4 p.m.

Yet More Sights

If you're in Tacoma on a semi-clear day, there are few places you can be without a view of 14,411-foot **Mt. Rainier.** It dominates the landscape with its permanent whitecap and looks particularly dramatic from the Cliff House parking lot (6300 Marine View Dr. at Browns Point in Federal Way), the 11th St. bridge, Ruston Way, and Gig Harbor.

Freighthouse Square on 25th and East D (a block north of Tacoma Dome) is Tacoma's version of Pike Place Market, though it isn't nearly as successful. More than 70 small shops and restaurants can be found inside the turn-of-the-century Milwaukee/St. Paul Railroad freighthouse. You can get everything from pet supplies to clothes to fettuccine here. It's worth a look if you're in town, and a couple of the ethnic cafes are quite good.

For a view of the action at the Port of Tacoma, head to the **observation tower** just off E. 11th St., where descriptive signs describe the port's history. Continue north to **Browns Point Lighthouse Park,** a sunny spot for picnicking, shipwatching, or launching your own boat. Here you've got a great view of downtown Tacoma and Point Defiance, Vashon and Maury Islands, the Olympics, and of course, the Sound. The trick is to find it (see the maps "Tacoma" and "Federal Way"). The lighthouse is open on weekends and contains an exhibit on the building of a Coast Guard boat; free. Call (206) 925-1111 for details.

Tacoma's **University of Puget Sound** has an attractive campus with older brick buildings on wooded grounds. The small Museum of Natural History, room 337 Thompson Hall, houses specimens in cases, but no exhibits. Cheap eats at the Student Center cafeteria.

Connecting Tacoma with the Olympic Peninsula, the **Tacoma Narrows Bridge** is the second bridge to cross the sound at this location, and the fifth largest suspension bridge in the world. The first was the famous "Galloping Gertie" (see the special topic "Disaster Over the Sound").

Other Parks

Fireman's Park is a small downtown park at S. 8th and A Streets with an Alaskan totem pole, outstanding views of Mt. Rainier and the harbor, and great whiffs of the pulp mill.

A two-mile cycling and jogging path runs along Ruston Way, good for a breezy post-lunch or -dinner walk. Follow Ruston to Tacoma's best known park, Point Defiance (described above), or stop at two smaller beachfront parks on the way: **Commencement Park,** with a fishing pier and large sundial, and **Marine Park,** a long narrow strip of shoreline with open grassy areas, picnic tables, a fishing pier, bait shop, and snack stand. Fishing may not be such a smart idea, however, since Commencement Bay is one of Puget Sound's "hot spots," where the bottom fish and even salmon have shown unhealthy levels of toxins.

Tucked away where you'd least expect it is the **Snake Lake Nature Center,** 1919 S. Tyler St., tel. (206) 591-5939. The 54 acres of marshland and evergreens are just a stone's throw from busy 19th St., but this is a fine place to watch ducks and other birds. They've got two miles of self-guiding nature trails for the do-it-yourselfers. Don't let the name scare you off—the lake was named for its shape, not its inhabitants. Trails are open daily from 8 a.m. until dark; the interpretive center (filled with hands-on exhibits) is open Mon.-Sat. 8 a.m.-5 p.m. year-round. No charge.

Wapato Lake is a good practice pond for novice rowboaters. Located at S. 72nd St. and Sheridan Ave., the park also has picnic tables, some small flower gardens, and boat rentals.

Lakewold Gardens, south of Tacoma off exit 124 at 12317 Gravelly Lake Dr., tel. (206) 584-4106, is a 10-acre collection of rare plants, including blue poppies from Tibet. The gardens feature one of the largest collections of rhododendrons and Japanese maples in the Northwest and were designed by noted landscape architect Thomas Church. A lovely Georgian-style brick home on this country estate is also open to the public. Hours are Thurs.-Mon. 10 a.m.-4 p.m., April-Sept., and Monday, Thursday, and Friday 10 a.m.-3 p.m. the rest of the year. Admission is $6 for adults, $5 for seniors and kids under 12.

ACCOMMODATIONS AND CAMPING

Lodging

See the "Tacoma Area Accommodations" chart for lodging in and around Tacoma. See also the "Auburn, Kent, and Federal Way Accommodations" chart for additional motels just a few miles north of Tacoma, and the "Gig Harbor Accommodations" chart for places just across the Tacoma Narrows bridge.

Many of Tacoma's motels are strung along Pacific Hwy. Southwest/South Tacoma Way/ Pacific Hwy. East; this is essentially a continuation of the same route with changing names. More motels are located near the various I-5 exits and along Pacific Ave. (east of I-5). South Tacoma Way/Pacific Hwy. Southwest is not the most inviting place to stay, but it does provide fast food, 7-Elevens, Chinese restaurants, strip malls, strip joints, and plenty of used car dealers. The Tacoma area has some of the least expensive motel rates in Washington, but not all of

these budget places may be acceptable. I've eliminated the worst ones, but for the cheapest of these you may still want to check the rooms to make sure they meet your standards.

Bed and Breakfasts

For reservations at local B&Bs, give a call to **Greater Tacoma B&B Reservation Service,** tel. (206) 759-4088. **Commencement Bay B&B,** tel. (206) 752-8175, in North Tacoma is an elegant large home built in 1937 and overlooking the bay. Guests have access to the deck, secluded hot tub, and game room.

The **Lucius Manning House B&B,** tel. (206) 272-8031, an 1889 Victorian in the historic Stadium District, is probably the finest B&B in Tacoma. Included in your lodging cost is admission to the art and history museums and to the local YMCA. Also in the Stadium District, **Villa B&B,** tel. (206) 572-1157, is a Mediterranean-style mansion built in 1925 and on the National Historic Register. The Villa features four large guest rooms, verandas, and gardens.

Built in 1906, **Eveline's Old World B&B,** tel. (206) 383-0595, is a spacious and quiet home with a large room and separate guest suite with a private entrance. The Austrian owner has furnished the B&B with country antiques from her home country. With reduced rates for longer stays, this is a good option if you plan to stay in Tacoma several days or weeks. **Oakes St. Barn B&B,** tel. (206) 475-7047, has two guest rooms in a large contemporary home with a hot tub.

Campgrounds

Camping is not allowed at Point Defiance Park, but head north to the city of Federal Way (see "Southeast King Country") for **Dash Point State Park** with year-round sites for both tents ($10) and RVs ($15). More campsites are located at **Kopachuck State Park,** 12 miles northwest of Tacoma (see "Gig Harbor" below), and **Penrose Point State Park** (see "Key Peninsula" below), approximately 20 miles west of Tacoma on the Key Peninsula. Call (800) 452-5687 for state park campsite reservations ($6 extra fee), available up to 11 months ahead of time.

Local RV parks include: **Cedars Trailer Park,** 5303 Pacific Hwy. E, Fife, tel. (206) 922-5172; **Fir Acres RV Park,** 12623 Bridgeport Way SW, Tacoma, tel. (206) 588-7894; **Karwan Village,**

TACOMA AREA ACCOMMODATIONS

Accommodations listed include Tacoma and Fife, arranged from least to most expensive. At the least expensive motels, see the rooms first to make sure they are up to your standards. The area code is 206.

BED AND BREAKFASTS

Eveline's Old World B&B; N. 8th and Cushman; tel. 383-0595; $50-55 s or d; turn-of-the-century home, one large guest room and one suite, private baths, Austrian antiques, full breakfast, kids welcome

Oakes St. Barn B&B; 5814 S. Oakes St.; tel. 475-7047; $65 s or d; contemporary home, hot tub, two guest rooms, shared bath, full breakfast

Villa B&B; 705 N. 5th St.; tel. 572-1157; $75 s or d; unique 1925 Stadium District mansion, verandas, four guest rooms, private baths, full breakfast, evening refreshments and dessert, no kids under 12

Lucius Manning House B&B; 302 N. Tacoma Ave.; tel. 272-8031; $75-100 s or d; beautifully restored antique-filled Victorian home, three guest rooms, private or shared bath, continental breakfast, no kids

Commencement Bay B&B; 3312 N. Union Ave., Tacoma; tel. 752-8175; $85-105 s or d; view home, hot tub on secluded deck, three guest rooms, private or shared bath, fireplace, game room, full breakfast, no kids under 12, AAA approved

MOTELS

Vagabond Motel; 10005 S. Tacoma Way, Tacoma; tel. 581-2920; $24-30 s, $27-35 d

Budget Inn; 9915 S. Tacoma Way, Tacoma; tel. 588-6615; $24-32 s, $32-36 d; kitchenettes available

Glacier Motel; 3401 Pacific Hwy. E, Fife; tel. 922-5882; $27 s or d; adult movies

Valley Motel; 1220 Puyallup Ave., Tacoma; tel. 272-7720; $29 s, $33 d; kitchenettes available

Enkay's Lakewood Lodge Motel; 11747 Pacific Hwy. SW, Tacoma; tel. 588-4443; $30 s or d

Grove Motel; 10202 Pacific Ave., Tacoma; tel. 531-7258; $30 s or d; kitchenettes available

Calico Cat Motel; 8821 Pacific Ave. S, Tacoma; tel. 535-2440; $30 s, $33 d; kitchenettes available, airport shuttle

Stagecoach Inn; 4221 Pacific Hwy. E, Fife; tel. 922-5421; $30 s, $33 d

King's Motor Inn; 5115 Pacific Hwy. E, Fife; tel. 922-3636 or (800) 929-3509; $30 s, $34 d; kitchenettes available

Blue Spruce Motel; 12715 Pacific Ave., Tacoma; tel. 531-6111; $30 s, $35 d; kitchenettes available

Motel 6; 5201 20th St. E, Fife; tel. 922-1270 or (800) 466-8356; $30 s, $36 d; outdoor pool

Golden Lion Motel; 9021 S. Tacoma Way, Tacoma; tel. 588-2171; $30-45 s or d; kitchenettes available

Home Motel; 11621 Pacific Hwy. SW, Tacoma; tel. 584-1717; $32 s or d; kitchenettes available

Fort Lewis Motel; 12215 Pacific Hwy. SW, Tacoma; tel. 588-7226; $32 s or d; kitchenettes available

Traveler's Inn; 3100 Pacific Hwy. E, Fife; tel. 922-9520; $32 s, $39 d; outdoor pool, AAA approved

Econo Lodge; 3518 Pacific Hwy. E, Fife; tel. 922-0550 or (800) 424-4777; $33 s, $37 d; AAA approved

Morgan Motel; 7301 Pacific Ave., Tacoma; tel. 472-5962; $34 s or d

Motel 6; 1811 S. 76th St., Tacoma; tel. 473-7100 or (800) 466-8356; $34 s, $40 d; outdoor pool

Madigan Motel; 12039 Pacific Hwy. SW, Tacoma; tel. 588-8697; $35-40 s or d; kitchenettes available

Redwood Motel; 17023 Pacific Hwy., Spanaway; tel. 531-0355; $35 s or d; kitchenettes available

(continues on next page)

TACOMA AREA ACCOMMODATIONS
(continued)

Travelodge; 3520 Pacific Hwy. E, Fife; tel. 922-0555 or (800) 578-7878; $36 s, $40 d; outdoor pool, AAA approved

Rothem Inn; 8602 S. Hosmer, Tacoma; tel. 535-0123; $36-49 s, $42-53 d; new motel, kitchenettes available

Econo Lodge; 9325 S. Tacoma Way, Tacoma; tel. 582-7550; $37 s or d; kitchenettes available, AAA approved

Western Inn; 9920 S. Tacoma Way, Tacoma; tel. 588-5241; $40 s, $44 d; kitchenettes available, AAA approved

Days Inn Tacoma South; 6802 Tacoma Mall Blvd., Tacoma; tel. 475-5900 or (800) 325-2525; $40-55 s, $45-55 d; outdoor pool, AAA approved

Days Inn; 3021 Pacific Hwy. E, Fife; tel. 922-3500 or (800) 325-2525; $40-55 s, $50-70 d; outdoor pool, kitchenettes available

Sherwood Inn; 8402 S. Hosmer, Tacoma; tel. 535-2800; $44-59 s, $49-64 d; outdoor pool, free airport shuttle, AAA approved

Travelodge; 8820 S. Hosmer, Tacoma; tel. 539-1153 or (800) 578-7878; $50-55 s, $55-60 d; outdoor pool, jacuzzi, free airport shuttle, free continental breakfast, kitchenettes available, AAA approved

Best Western Lakewood Motor Inn; 6125 Motor Ave. SW, Lakewood; tel. 584-2212 or (800) 528-1234; $50-60 s, $57-67 d; outdoor pool, free airport shuttle, AAA approved

Comfort Inn; 5601 Pacific Hwy. E, Fife; tel. 922-2301 or (800) 228-5150; $51 s, $56 d; jacuzzi, exercise facility, free continental breakfast, kitchenettes available, AAA approved

Royal Coachman Motor Inn; 5805 Pacific Hwy. E, Fife; tel. 922-2500 or (800) 422-3051; $56 s, $62 d; jacuzzi, health club, kitchenettes available, AAA approved

Corporate Suites; 3571 B St. E, Tacoma; tel. 473-4105 or (800) 255-6058; $58 s or d; one-room suites, kitchens, jacuzzi tubs

Best Western Tacoma Inn; 8726 S. Hosmer, Tacoma; tel. 535-2880 or (800) 528-1234; $58-70 s, $64-76 d; outdoor pool, jacuzzi, exercise room, playground, kitchenettes available, AAA approved

Holiday Inn Express; 34827 Pacific Hwy. S; tel. 838-3164 or (800) 465-4329; $59 s, $65 d; outdoor pool, AAA approved

Best Western Executive Inn; 5700 Pacific Hwy. E, Fife; tel. 922-0080 or (800) 528-1234; $59-69 s, $69-85 d; indoor pool, jacuzzi, sauna, exercise room, lounge, restaurant, free airport shuttle, AAA approved

La Quinta Inn; 1425 E. 27th St.; tel. 383-0146 or (800) 531-5900; $62 s, $70 d; outdoor pool, jacuzzi, exercise room, free continental breakfast, AAA approved

Shilo Inn; 7414 S. Hosmer, Tacoma; tel. 475-4020 or (800) 222-2244; $68-79 s or d; indoor pool, jacuzzi, sauna, exercise room, kitchenettes available, free continental breakfast, AAA approved

Howard Johnson Lodge; 8702 S. Hosmer, Tacoma; tel. 535-3100 or (800) 446-4656; $69 s, $74 d; outdoor pool, kitchenettes available, AAA approved

Ramada Hotel; 2611 East E St.; tel. 572-7272 or (800) 272-6232; $72 s, $77 d; sauna, exercise room, two-night minimum stay, AAA approved

Sheraton Tacoma Hotel; S. 1320 Broadway Plaza, Tacoma; tel. 572-3200 or (800) 845-9466; $105-115 s, $115-125 d; jacuzzi, sauna, airport shuttle, AAA approved

2621 84th St., Tacoma, tel. (206) 582-1197; and **Oak Knoll Trailer Park,** 10404 Pacific Hwy. SW, Tacoma, tel. (206) 588-8867.

FOOD

Breakfast, Lunch, and Coffee
Behind the Bavarian facade at **Busy Bee Cafe,** downtown at 317 S. 7th St., tel. (206) 272-9420, is a casual, homey place with a big breakfast menu, plus hefty burgers and other fare for lunch and dinner. Downtown Tacoma offers a number of lunch spots. **The Judicial Annex,** at 311 S. 11th (right at the corner of the Plaza), is an extremely popular place with speedy service, reasonable prices, and tasty soups, salads, sandwiches, and espresso. Drop by at lunch to talk legalese with students from nearby Norton Clapp Law Center. A good place to try out your repertoire of lawyer jokes.

Grounds for Coffee, 764 Broadway, tel. (206) 627-7742, is a sprawling and comfortable downtown coffeehouse with a limited menu of sandwiches, bagels, salads, and soup. This is the place to read the newspaper or hang out with friends.

Located in north Tacoma near Point Defiance Park, the **Antique Sandwich Company,** 5102 N. Pearl, tel. (206) 752-4069, seems a throwback to the early '70s. The atmosphere is earthy; the menu that includes good soups, clam chowder, salads, espresso, and sweets. Come back in the evening for live acoustic or folk groups.

Cicero's Old Town Coffee House, 2123 N. 30th St., tel. (206) 272-2122, is a small place with espresso drinks, pastries, and desserts.

American and Northwest Cuisine
Get outstanding Northwest cuisine with Asian influences at **Pacific Rim Restaurant,** 100 S. 9th St., tel. (206) 627-1009. Wonderful desserts, too. The lounge features rhythm and blues acts on weekends.

Fife City Bar & Grill, 3025 Pacific Hwy. E, tel. (206) 922-9555, gets kudos from Tacoma locals for its highly creative meals at surprisingly low prices. Open for three meals a day. The menu includes a wide diversity: shrimp Caesar salad, linguine with fresh basil and sundried tomato pesto, grilled reuben on rye, and hali-

but, salmon, and shrimp lasagna are a few of the lunch and dinner choices.

Ram American Grill & Fish House, 3001 Ruston Way, tel. (206) 756-7886, has a waterfront location and homemade pizzas, gourmet burgers, and Tex-Mex specialties.

Yankee Diner, 6812 Tacoma Mall Blvd. (south Tacoma), tel. (206) 475-3006, serves three solid all-American meals a day, including huge portions of pot roast, and a turkey dinner served year-round. Another place to fill yourself is **Southern Kitchen,** 1716 6th Ave., tel. (206) 627-4282, where the menu of home-cooked meals includes catfish, pork chops, collard greens, barbecued ribs, and sweet potato pie. This is a longtime Tacoma favorite, still run by Lessie Smith from south Alabama.

Pubs
Established in 1913, **The Spar Tavern,** 2121 N. 30th, tel. (206) 627-8215, has great pub grub: burgers, sandwiches, chili, and homemade soups, but it is a bar, so no kids. **Katie Downs Tavern,** 3211 Ruston Way, tel. (206) 756-0771, sits on a pier and attracts a good-sized crowd with a big selection of beer and wine, deep-dish pizza, a jeans-and-sneakers atmosphere, with outdoor seating in the summer; over age 21 only.

Located in a turn-of-the-century firehouse **Engine House No. 9,** 611 N. Pine, tel. (206) 272-3435, stocks nearly 50 local and imported beers and features a pub menu of pizza, tacos, soups, and salads.

Seafood
The **Lobster Shop Dash Point,** 6912 Soundview Dr. NE, tel. (206) 927-1513, sister to the Lobster Shop South across the bay on 4015 Ruston Way (tel. 206-759-2165), is the original, more rustic version, where the steaks, seafood, and wine list are unequaled. Great waterside views, too. Open for dinner only, and reservations are a good idea. The Lobster Shop South is open for lunch and dinner, and it serves a substantial Sunday brunch.

Located right on the water at 2761 Ruston Way, **Harbor Lights,** tel. (206) 752-8600, is a very popular, moderately priced seafood restaurant with a boisterous atmosphere, heaping helpings, and some of the tastiest fish and chips in town. Recommended.

Johnny's Dock, on 1900 E. D St. (near the Dome), is in one of Tacoma's less attractive parts of town, but the view of the city and the boats docked outside is spectacular (particularly at night). The basic steak-and-seafood menu is reasonably priced and good; the service is friendly, not overbearing.

Johnny's Ocean Fish Co., 2201 Ruston Way, tel. (206) 383-4571, in Old Town right alongside the fishing pier, is a friendly market with fresh and smoked seafood of all kinds. A good place to pick up fish recipes, too.

For the View

If you want a sweeping Sound view plus a look at Mt. Rainier, try the **Cliff House,** 6300 Marine View Dr. at Browns Point, tel. (206) 927-0400. The steak and seafood are very good—though not cheap; the downstairs lounge offers the same view and a sandwich menu.

Overlooking the Dome and busy I-5 is **Stanley and Seafort's Steak, Chop, and Fish House** at 115 E. 34th, tel. (206) 473-7300, with another view that gets better as the sun goes down. Part of a small chain of similar restaurants, Stanley and Seafort's is one of those dependably good places with fine meats, seafood, and desserts.

C.I. Shenanigan's, 3017 Ruston Way, tel. (206) 752-8811, is a spiffy waterside restaurant with outdoor seating, a seafood menu, and long waits on weekends. Reservations advised.

Asian

Two local places stand out if you're searching for ultra-fresh Japanese sushi: **Kabuki,** 2919 S. 38th St., tel. (206) 474-1650, in south Tacoma, and downtown at **Fujiya,** 1125 Court C., tel. (206) 627-5319. **Wendy's Vietnamese Restaurant** inside Freighthouse Square, 430 E. 25th, tel. (206) 572-4678, serves authentic and delicious Vietnamese meals. They have a second shop in the Tacoma Mall, tel. (206) 471-0228. **Mandarin on Broadway** is a fine downtown Chinese restaurant, at 1128 Broadway Plaza, tel. (206) 627-3400.

Italian

Bimbo's, 1516 Pacific Ave., tel. (206) 383-5800, has been serving old-time Italian specialties at this location for over 75 years—the food's still

great, but the run-down locale leaves something to desire. **Luciano's,** 3327 Ruston Way, tel. (206) 756-5611, has a much nicer location—right on the water—with trendier Italian fare.

Lorenzo's, 2811 6th Ave., tel. (206) 272-3331, is a local favorite with its real Italian food at moderate prices. An upscale place with fine northern Italian cuisine is **Grazie Ristorante,** 2301 N. 30th St., tel. (206) 627-0231. The **Old Spaghetti Factory** at 1735 S. Jefferson, part of a small national chain, can fill you to capacity with an assortment of low-priced pasta dishes and some terrific sourdough bread. This is a good spot to take noisy kids, but be prepared for a wait on the weekends.

Mexican

La Fondita, inside Freighthouse Square, tel. (206) 627-7326, has fresh and authentic Mexican food for a good price. A charming, casual, and inexpensive Mexican restaurant is **Casa Bonita,** at 6104 6th Ave., tel. (206) 565-1546. Another of the city's best Mexican restaurants is **Moctezuma's,** 4102 S. 56th St., tel. (206) 474-5593.

Produce

The **Tacoma Farmers Market** comes to 9th and Broadway ("Antique Row") every Thursday 10 a.m.-3 p.m. from early June to mid-September. Stock up on fresh fruits and vegetables, along with arts and crafts.

EVENTS

Kick the year off in a nonalcoholic way at Tacoma's **First Night** celebration, with all sorts of events: theater, gallery openings, live music, comedy, mimes, and more. Activities start at noon on December 31; call (206) 591-7205 for details.

The **Daffodil Festival** in mid-April features a parade of floral floats through downtown Tacoma, a marine parade with daffodil-decorated boats, plus live entertainment and other events.

Tacoma's big **Seafirst Freedom Fair** on the Fourth of July includes arts and cultural events, and live entertainment along the waterfront. A huge fireworks display is the feature when dusk arrives, but the main attraction is the airshow—

one of the largest in the nation—featuring both civilian and military aircraft over Commencement Bay. The **Taste of Tacoma** takes place at the same time, with dozens of local restaurants providing food, two concert stages with live music and entertainment, and a beer garden.

Several weekend **Salmon Bakes** are held July through September at Owen Beach in Point Defiance Park; call (206) 756-7336 for dates. The **Pacific Rim Wildlife Art Show,** tel. (206) 596-6728, comes to the Tacoma Dome in late September; it's the largest wildlife art show on the West Coast. Everything here is for sale. The zoo in Point Defiance Park has periodic summertime concerts ("Zoo Sounds"), and a holiday "Zoo Lights" for fun; tel. (206) 591-5358.

ENTERTAINMENT AND THE ARTS

Nightlife

There's plenty of nightlife in Tacoma. For an exhaustive list of night spots, plays, concerts, etc., check the Tacoma *Morning News Tribune*'s TGIF section on Friday, or *Puget Sound Choices,* a free weekly publication available around town.

Drake's, 734 Pacific, tel. (206) 572-4144, is the best place for dancing in town, with acoustic music on Wednesday, jazz on Thursday, and DJ hits on the weekend. Over on South Jefferson are two popular clubs: **The Wedge,** 1920 S. Jefferson, tel. (206) 272-1221, with alternative rock bands, and **The Swiss,** 1904 S. Jefferson, tel. (206) 572-2821, with rhythm and blues music. Also try **Kellys Restaurant,** 1101 Tacoma, tel. (206) 627-6425, for jazz; **Victory Club,** 2803 6th Ave., tel. (206) 272-8085, for alternative rock and blues; or **Elliott's,** inside the Sheraton Tacoma at 1320 S. Broadway Plaza, tel. (206) 572-3200, for blues rock bands.

Christie's at the Executive Inn in Fife has dancing to Top-40 bands, as does **Captain Nemo's,** 4020 Bridgeport Way W, tel. (206) 564-6460, and **Leslie's Restaurant and Night Life Lounge,** 9522 Bridgeport Way SW, tel. (206) 582-4118. For Top-40 DJ tunes, try **Black Angus,** 9905 Bridgeport Way SW, tel. (206) 582-6900.

Country music fans should head to **Baldy's Tavern,** 2501 Milton Way E, tel. (206) 927-9943,

or **Club North,** at North Fort Lewis, tel. (206) 964-0144.

For something different, the **Antique Sandwich Co.,** 5102 N. Pearl St. (right outside Point Defiance), offers acoustic and folk music in a family, no-alcohol setting.

Taverns

A neighborhood favorite is the distinctive **Bob's Java Jive,** 2102 S. Tacoma Way, tel. (206) 475-9843, a teapot-shaped bar on S. Tacoma Way with a neon-decorated handle and spout. Inside is a jukebox with classics from the '60s, and all-American meals. Built in 1927, this place is a classic inside and out. Not to be missed.

The **Ale House Pub & Eatery,** 2122 Mildred West, tel. (206) 565-9367, has one of the largest selections of draught beer in the state, with an incredible 63 different beers on tap. The menu is reasonable and good, and the big-screen TV is popular for sporting events. See also "Pubs" under "Food," above, for more places with booze and food.

Theater

Tacoma's **Broadway Center for the Performing Arts** contains a trio of outstanding theaters downtown near the intersection of 9th and Commerce Streets. The newest is **Theater on the Square,** a $12-million facility completed in 1993. This 302-seat theater is home to the nationally acclaimed **Tacoma Actors Guild,** who perform nightly (except Monday) through the winter season. Call (206) 272-2145 for ticket information. An adjacent spot of green contains a waterfall park, a fine place on a hot summer day. Also nearby are bronze performance masks representing various cultures.

Two lovingly restored 1918 buildings, the **Pantages Theater** and **Rialto Theater** offer a taste of Tacoma's glory days in the Broadway district. Pantages is a large and ornate vaudeville palace that was restored in 1983. There's always something going on at the Pantages— plays, acrobats, concerts—but be prepared to buy tickets early because many events sell out fast. A 1991 restoration of the Beaux-Arts style Rialto transformed it into a setting for films, concerts, lectures, and touring troupes. Call (206) 591-5894 to see what's on the agenda for both of these places. Also check the 1,650-seat **Tem-**

ple **Theatre** at 47 St. Helens, tel. (206) 272-2042, for more theatrical events, including Broadway plays, comedy shows, and concerts. Built in 1926, the Temple is one of the grandest halls in the Northwest.

In existence for more than 75 years, the **Tacoma Little Theater,** 210 N. I St. in the Stadium District, claims to be the oldest continuously performing theater west of the Mississippi. For upcoming programs, call (206) 272-2481.

Music and Dance
The **Tacoma Philharmonic,** tel. (206) 272-0809, brings symphony music to the Pantages Theater five times a year. The **Tacoma Symphony,** tel. (206) 756-3396, brings in several guest artists each year; enjoy classical music in the theater and free pops in the parks during the summer. The **Tacoma Youth Symphony,** tel. (206) 627-2792, has 250 musicians from 85 different schools and gives several concerts each year.

BalleTacoma offers several performances each year, including the annual *Nutcracker;* call (206) 272-9631 for more information. The **Tacoma Opera,** tel. (206) 627-7789, has English-language performances at the Pantages Theater.

SPORTS AND RECREATION

Point Defiance Park (described above) has many of Tacoma's best recreation opportunities, particularly on Saturday mornings when the roads are closed to cars. For outdoor gear, head to **Backpackers Supply & Outlet,** 5206 S. Tacoma Way, tel. (206) 472-4402, where you can also rent all sorts of outdoor supplies, including kayaks and canoes. This is the place to find out about **Tahoma Outdoor Pursuits,** tel. (206) 474-8155, a group that offers classes in kayaking, canoeing, rock climbing, mountaineering, skiing, and snowshoeing, along with a summertime kids' camp. In addition to the classes, they give sea kayak tours and whitewater kayak trips down nearby rivers.

Spectator Sports
The Pacific Coast Baseball League is represented by the **Tacoma Rainiers,** a AAA farm

club for the Oakland A's that plays at Cheney Stadium, 2525 Bantz Blvd. (off Hwy. 16), and sometimes outdraws the Seattle Mariners. For information, call (206) 752-7707. The **Tacoma Rockets** are a Western Hockey League franchise; their season is from September to March, and they play in the Tacoma Dome, tel. (206) 627-3653.

Swimming
Tacoma has five public swimming pools: **Eastside Community Pool,** 3424 E. L St., tel. (206) 591-2042; **People's Center Pool,** 1602 Martin Luther King Jr. Way, tel. (206) 591-5323; **South End Pool,** 402 E. 56th St., tel. (206) 474-3821; **The Centre at Norpoint,** tel. (206) 591-5504; and **Titlow Pool,** 8355 6th Ave., tel. (206) 564-4044. South End and Titlow are outdoor pools open only in the summer months.

Public swimming beaches can be found at **Titlow Park,** just south of the Narrows Bridge, and **Wapato Lake Park,** where a lifeguard is present in the summer. **American Lake Park,** south of Tacoma near Fort Lewis, also has swimming.

Golf
Local public golf courses include: **Allenmore Golf Course,** 2125 S. Cedar, tel. (206) 627-7211; **Meadow Park Golf Course,** 7108 Lakewood Dr. W, tel. (206) 473-3033; **North Shore Golf & Country Club,** 4101 North Shore Blvd. NE, tel. (206) 927-1375 or (800) 447-1375; **Brookdale Golf Course,** 1802 Brookdale Rd. E, tel. (206) 537-4400; **Classic Country Club,** 4908 208th St. E in Spanaway, tel. (206) 847-4440; and **Ft. Steilacoom Golf Course,** 8202 87th Ave. SW, tel. (206) 588-0613.

SHOPPING

Freighthouse Square on 25th and East D is the public market, with all sorts of specialty food shops, arts and crafts merchants, galleries, gift shops, knick-knack places, and a visitor center. Located in the block-long Milwaukee Railroad freighthouse, it's Tacoma's version of Pike Place Market (minus the fresh fish and produce). Not nearly as interesting as Pike Place, but well worth a visit nevertheless. Open seven days a week.

Browse through several antique shops along "**Antique Row**" near the old city hall in downtown Tacoma, and check out the native arts and crafts at **Curtright Gallery,** 759 Broadway, tel. (206) 383-2969.

A great place to explore for used books is just a block away from the Tacoma Dome: the **Tacoma Book Center,** 324 E. 26th St., tel. (206) 572-8248.

The **Tacoma Mall** has 140 stores, including Sears, JCPenney, The Bon Marché, and Nordstrom, all on one level. From I-5 follow the signs for Tacoma Mall Blvd. at the S. 56th St. exit. Smaller shopping centers line S. 38th St. just north of the mall; closer to the center of town, 6th Ave. has Kmart, Drug Emporium, and numerous other discount stores and small plazas. Another similar shopping area is **The Lakewood Mall** at 10509 Gravelly Lake Dr. SW, with 170 stores, including Mervyn's, Emporium, Target, Ernst, Gottschalks, and Lamonts as anchor stores. **South Hill Mall** has 100 stores, including The Bon Marché, Sears, JCPenney, Lamonts, Mervyn's, and Target.

A small, mostly upscale cluster of shops called the **Proctor District** runs along the 2700 block area of N. Proctor. It has several shops, including the Proctor District Antique Mall with more than 40 dealers, and the Pacific Northwest Shop, which stocks only goods produced in the region.

INFORMATION AND SERVICES

For more information on Tacoma and the surrounding area, head to **Tacoma-Pierce County Visitor and Convention Bureau** at 906 Broadway, tel. (206) 627-2836 or (800) 272-2662. Open Mon.-Fri. 8:30 a.m.-5 p.m. year-round. A second visitor center can be found inside Freighthouse Square at 442 E. 25th St., tel. (206) 272-7801. Open daily 9 a.m.-5 p.m. in the summer, and daily 10 a.m.-4 p.m. the rest of the year. (Follow the signs from I-5 exit 133, the Tacoma Dome exit.) The **area code** for Tacoma is 206.

The main **Tacoma Public Library,** tel. (206) 591-5666, is at 1102 Tacoma Ave. South. Open Mon.-Thurs. 9 a.m.-9 p.m., and Fri.-Sat. 9 a.m.-6 p.m. Be sure to head upstairs to the North-

west Room to check out the stained glass dome ceiling. Tacoma's main **post office,** at 1102 S. A St., tel. (206) 471-6122, has a small museum with a mail sleigh and other philatelic memorabilia, along with historic stamps.

Plenty of hospitals in the area have 24-hour emergency room service: **Humana Hospital,** S. 19th and Union, tel. (206) 383-0011; **Tacoma General,** 315 S. K St., tel. (206) 594-1050; and **St. Joseph Hospital,** 1718 S. I St., tel. (206) 591-6660.

TRANSPORTATION AND TOURS

The Street Maze
Tacoma's street numbering system is relatively easy to follow. The system would work much better on flat terrain with straight roads; as it is, some streets change names seven or more times as they move in and out of boxes on an imaginary grid. But as a general rule, anything prefixed or suffixed by a "Northeast" is between Browns Point (Marine View Dr.) and Federal Way; "North" is up by Point Defiance; "South" is the tricky one, as it takes up the whole midsection of Tacoma, and sometimes looks more west or north than south; "East" is in the Dome area; and "West" is over by the University Place section, south of the Narrows Bridge. But pay attention: the "Avenue" or "Place" or "Street" appended to the number is critical; for example, there's a 42 St. S, a 42 Pl. S, and a 42 Ave. S, and as a general rule such streets never intersect or even come near each other.

Bus Service
Pierce Transit, tel. (206) 581-8000 or (800) 562-8109, has daily bus service to Puyallup, Gig Harbor, Lakewood, Steilacoom, Spanaway, Fife, Buckley, and every other town in Pierce County, along with commuter service to Seattle and Olympia.

Greyhound, tel. (206) 383-4621 or (800) 231-2222, and **Northwestern Trailways,** tel. (800) 366-3830, connect Olympia to Seattle, Tacoma, Portland, and other cities along its north-south I-5 corridor, with access to virtually anywhere in the country. The bus station is located at 1319 Pacific Avenue.

Train Service

Amtrak, tel. (800) 872-7245, serves Tacoma from its passenger station at 1001 Puyallup Ave., between the tide flat area and I-5 in the eastern part of the city. The Coast Starlight provides daily service to the Puget Sound area from Portland, San Francisco, and Los Angeles; the Pioneer also serves Seattle, Tacoma, and Olympia from Salt Lake City.

Ferry Service

The **Washington State Ferry** system is a heavily used method of everyday transportation around the Puget Sound region. From Tacoma, however, it can only get you to Tahlequah on Vashon Island departing from Point Defiance; fares are $2.30 roundtrip for walk-ons, $9.55 roundtrip for car and driver. Fares are collected only on the way to Vashon, not when you return. For information on the ferry system call (206) 464-6400 from Seattle, (800) 843-3779 from elsewhere in the state.

Seattle-Tacoma International Airport

If you're flying into Tacoma, you'll probably arrive at the Seattle-Tacoma International Airport. As the name suggests, it's about halfway between

Seattle and Tacoma. Sea-Tac is small enough so you can make all your connections, but big enough to be a respectable international airport. For information on airport parking, ground transportation schedules and rates, and weather and traffic conditions, call (206) 431-4444 or (800) 544-1965. **Shuttle Express,** tel. (800) 487-7433, and **Capital Aeroporter,** tel. (206) 754-7113, offer door-to-airport service.

Tours

Tacoma Harbor Tours, 821 Dock St., provides dinner cruises and dancing aboard the historic MV *Silver Swan,* a 65-foot boat that was once part of the famed "Mosquito Fleet" that delivered mail, passengers, produce, and seafood to isolated parts of Puget Sound in the first half of this century. One-and-a-half-hour historical tours of Tacoma Harbor depart on Friday and Saturday. Call (206) 572-1001 or (800) 974-8007 for details.

Cascade Trailways Tours, tel. (800) 824-8897, has bus tours of the surrounding area, including Mt. Rainier, Mt. St. Helens, the San Juan Islands, and others. Also check with **Totem Tours,** tel. (800) 845-7291, for day trips and longer bus or plane tours all over the nation.

VICINITY OF TACOMA

PARKLAND/SPANAWAY, LAKEWOOD, AND FORT LEWIS

Technically separate towns, but in reality an extension of the Tacoma metropolitan area, the Parkland/Spanaway area hosts a few good restaurants and a beautiful park. Fort Lewis and McChord Air Force Base reside in neighboring Lakewood, appropriately named for its three lakes: American, Gravelly, and Steilacoom. Established in 1917 when the citizens of Tacoma passed a bond measure to donate land for a military post, Fort Lewis was a vital training center during WW I. Today, it is still one of the Army's largest permanent posts, with 18,000 rangers, Special Forces, and other soldiers, along with the Madigan Army Medical Center, a recently opened $200 million facility that is the largest on the West Coast. Nearby McChord Air Force Base has been here since 1938, and today employs more than 7,500 personnel in a variety of military and civilian roles.

Sights

Take exit 120 from I-5, 16 miles south of Tacoma, to the **Fort Lewis Military Museum,** tel. (206) 967-7206, located in a Swiss-style building originally used as a Salvation Army center. The museum emphasizes Northwest military history, including displays of the dress uniforms from various eras, the history of the I Corps, and such oddities as Gen. Norman Schwartzkopf's jeep (he was base commander here in the early 1980s). Obtain a pass at the visitors office on the east side of the freeway near the main gate. Open Wed.-Sun. noon-4 p.m.; free.

Another military collection you can see is the **McChord Air Museum,** tel. (206) 984-2485, one mile east on exit 125. The museum contains aircraft, flying gear, uniforms, and other Air Force memorabilia from the 1930s through the 1960s. Open Tues.-Sun. noon-4 p.m., closed holidays.

One of Spanaway's main summertime attractions is the **Spanaway Speedway,** which

has racing on Sunday afternoons, plus Wednesday, Friday, and Saturday nights March to October. The speedway is located at 159th and 22nd Ave. E; call (206) 537-7551 for the week's schedule.

Located off Pacific Ave., **Spanaway County Park** is an ideal place to take a walk, go for a swim, or take out the boat. Back to back with Spanaway Lake Golf Course, the park has a beach, trails, lots of trees, and picnic areas.

Accommodations, Food, and Nightlife

See the "Tacoma Area Accommodations" chart for Lakewood area motels.

Maxey's Restaurant, 10727 Pacific Hwy. SW, tel. (206) 588-5503, serves breakfast 365 days a year from 6 a.m. on. **La Palma,** at Lakewood Mall, tel. (206) 582-8349, has authentic Mexican dishes.

Marzano's, 516 Garfield S, tel. (206) 537-4191, is a wonderful little restaurant with perfectly prepared Italian meals. **Stuart Anderson's Black Angus** restaurants are consistently good; there's one in Lakewood at 9905 Bridgeport Way SW, tel. (206) 582-6900.

Leslie's Too, 11521 Bridgeport Way, tel. (206) 582-1531, has prime rib and seafood, plus live music nightly. You'll find Top-40 DJ tunes at **Lakewood Bar & Grill,** 10009 59th SW in Lakewood, tel. (206) 582-1196.

Events

Lakewood's main summer event is **Summerfest** at Lakewood Mall, where the streets are taken over by arts and crafts vendors, food vendors, live entertainment, a beer garden, and amusement park rides. It is held July 19-21. Call (206) 584-6191 for details. In mid-September, the **Spanaway Hydroplane Regattas** take place at Spanaway Lake; tel. (206) 565-3206.

Information and Services

The **Lakewood Area Chamber of Commerce,** 9523 Gravelly Lake Dr. SW, tel. (206) 582-9400, has local info. The telephone **area code** for Lakewood, Spanaway, and Parkland is the same as Tacoma's and Seattle's, 206.

STEILACOOM

The state's second oldest incorporated town (after Tumwater) had established itself as the busiest port on Puget Sound by 1854. Today the quaint town of Steilacoom still clings to and respects its historic heritage. More than 30 local buildings are on the National Register of Historic Places, including the state's first jail (1858), first Protestant church (1853), and first library north of the Columbia River (1858).

Sights
Bair Drug and Hardware, at 1617 Lafayette, tel. (206) 588-9668, is an 1895 shop with a sampling of historic items on display and a 1906 soda fountain where you can still get a soda or sundae, along with something you wouldn't find in 1906, espresso coffees. Great baked goods and pies here as well. Open Mon.-Thurs. 9 a.m.-5 p.m., Friday 9 a.m.-9 p.m., and Sat.-Sun. 8 a.m.-5 p.m.

The **Steilacoom Town Hall and Museum,** tel. (206) 588-0011, focuses on the town's pioneer period. Pick up their *Guide to Historic Steilacoom* for a walking tour. Located downstairs in the white New England-style Town Hall on Main and Lafayette, the free museum is open Tues.-Sun. 1-4 p.m. in the summer, and Fri.-Sun. 1-4 p.m. in November, December, and February.

The Historical Society also owns the **Nathaniel Orr Home and Orchard,** 1811 Rainier St., tel. (206) 584-4133, a two-story clapboard home built by its owner, who constructed wagons, coffins, and cabinets. The well-tended orchard includes apple, cherry, and plum trees. Open Sunday 1-4 p.m. April to October.

Located in a turn-of-the-century Congregational Church building, **Steilacoom Tribal Cultural Center and Museum,** 1515 Lafayette St., tel. (206) 584-6308, documents the history of the Steilacoom tribe with exhibits that feature the prehistory of the Tacoma Basin, historical artifacts, and contemporary artistry. The Steilacoom were one of the eight Washington tribes that were never allotted a reservation. The gift shop sells native crafts, and the snack bar serves light breakfasts and lunches, including homemade clam chowder. Open Tues.-Sun. 10 a.m.-4 p.m. year-round; admission is $2 for adults, $1 for seniors and kids, children under six free, and $6 for families.

East from the town of Steilacoom is **Fort Steilacoom,** tel. (206) 584-2368, right next to the massive Western State Hospital (a mental institution). Four small frame houses remain from this fort, established in 1849. One of the buildings has an interpretive center and small museum open for summertime tours on Saturday 1-4 p.m.

Fort Steilacoom County Park on Steilacoom Blvd. has game fields plus good-sized Waughop Lake (drive down Dresdon Lane, then park by the barns and take a walk around the Waughop Loop). **Sunnyside Beach Park** off Lafayette St. and **Salters Point Park** off 1st St. are both small waterfront parks with picnic facilities.

Food
Crystal chandeliers, antiques, and a wonderful Queen Anne Victorian home overlooking the Sound provide an elegant setting for some of the best food around Puget Sound, at **E.R. Rogers,** 1702 Commercial, tel. (206) 582-0280. The prime rib and seafood entrees are in the $15-30 range, but well worth the money. If you can't get reservations, at least have a drink in the cozy, upstairs-bedroom bar with a couple of outside tables. Open daily for dinner only, plus a very popular Sunday brunch.

Less ostentatious—and considerably cheaper—is **Bair Drug and Hardware** (see above) where the old soda fountain has sundaes, ice cream sodas, and fresh pies and sweets from the bakery. They also serve Friday night dinners.

Events
The **Fourth of July Parade and Street Fair** features food vendors, art booths, and live entertainment, with a fun small town parade. Be sure to sample the Tribal Museum's delicious smoked salmon and Indian fry bread. Other events include a popular **Salmon Bake** on the last Sunday in July, and the **Apple Squeeze Festival** in early October. Call (206) 584-4133 for details.

Ferry Service

Pierce County operates the small **Anderson Island-Steilacoom Ferry,** which leaves Steilacoom Dock about every two hours 6 a.m.-6 p.m. Roundtrip summer fares are $11.40 for car and driver, $2.70 for passengers and foot passengers, and $3.50 for a bicycle and rider for the 20-minute run. Call (206) 591-7250 for more information. The ferry also visits tiny Ketron Island (no public facilities). A separate ferry takes corrections officers and prisoners to McNeil Island, home of a state prison.

ANDERSON ISLAND

Miles of roads and rural bike paths are the primary attractions to draw mainlanders to quiet Anderson Island. The restored **Johnson Farm,** founded by John Johnson in 1881, has tours weekend afternoons in the summer. Also here is the pilothouse from the *Tahoma,* the island's ferry from 1943 to 1954. **Anderson Island Historical Museum,** tel. (206) 884-2135, has local historical items on display.

Lodging

There are two places to stay on the Anderson. **The Inn at Burg's Landing B&B,** 8808 Villa Beach Rd., tel. (206) 884-9185, is a modern log home featuring views of Mt. Rainier, a private beach, jacuzzi, and full breakfast. Rooms are $64-90 s or d. More exclusive is **Anderson House on Oro Bay,** 12024 Eckenstam-Johnson Rd., tel. (206) 884-4088, a beautiful 1920s farmhouse at the head of Oro Bay. Stay at one of four rooms in the house or in separate cabins, with rates ranging from $50 to $240 d. Kids are allowed in the cabins. A full breakfast is included, and gourmet lunches and dinners are available.

Ferry Service

The **Anderson Island-Steilacoom ferry,** tel. (206) 591-7250, leaves Steilacoom Dock about every two hours from 6 a.m. to 6 p.m. on a 20-minute run to the island. Roundtrip fares are $9.60 for car and driver, $2.30 for passengers and foot passengers, and $3.50 for a bicycle rider.

GIG HARBOR

Just across the Narrows Bridge from Tacoma, the prosperous town of Gig Harbor definitely warrants a visit. The harbor is one of the finest and most scenic on Puget Sound, with hundreds of sailing and fishing boats, tall pine trees, and a circle of seaside houses, all against the picture-perfect backdrop of Mt. Rainier—a photo that graces many calendars and magazine covers.

Gig Harbor was named by Commander Charles Wilkes who sent out a captain's gig (a small boat) for a survey of the area. When a sudden storm blew up, the protected waters—almost entirely circled by land—proved an excellent harbor for his gig. Today, Gig Harbor is home to many commercial fishing and pleasure craft. Boatbuilding was an important part of Gig Harbor's history, and hundreds of purse seiners, gill netters, tenders, yachts, and other vessels were constructed here over the decades. The town itself is tiny, with a population of only 3,300 (probably 3,298 of them boat owners) and an upscale touristy flavor. The shops, galleries, good restaurants, and at least one great tavern will keep you busy.

Sights and Shopping

The **Puget Sound Mariners' Museum,** tel. (206) 858-7258, features marine artifacts, historic photos, and memorabilia—including treasure from the wreck of the Spanish galleon *Atocha*—all with a touch of humor. Entrance costs $3 for adults and kids, $2 for seniors, and $5 for the whole family. Open Mon.-Fri. noon-4 p.m., and Sat.-Sun. noon-5 p.m. The **Peninsula Historical Society Museum** has more local items in the old St. Nicholas Church; call (206) 858-6722 for details.

Downtown Gig Harbor is strung out along the water, with shops and restaurants luring browsers. Head to the head of the harbor for **Ebb Tide Gallery & Gifts,** tel. (206) 851-5293, a cooperative gallery with the works of local artists, and **Gallery Row,** tel. (206) 851-6020, both at 8825 N. Harborview Drive.

Kopachuck State Park

You'd never expect so much solitude so close to a major city. Located 12 miles northwest of Tacoma off Hwy. 16 (just follow the signs),

TACOMA/PIERCE COUNTY VISITOR AND CONVENTION BUREAU

Kopachuck State Park

Kopachuck has a campground and picnic areas. The 103-acre park is shaded by skyscraping pines and has a beach for swimming, clamming, and fishing. It is also one of Puget Sound's most beautiful parks, and even includes the small (5.5 acres) Cutts Island, which is a marine park only a short distance offshore with mooring buoys. Scuba divers come here to explore an underwater park with a sunken barge. For more information, call (206) 265-3606.

Fox Island
Fox Island is five miles southwest of Gig Harbor and is connected by a bridge over Hale Passage. The island is home to a number of B&Bs, along with the **Fox Island Historical Society and Museum,** tel. (206) 829-1533.

Accommodations
Gig Harbor has a number of bed and breakfast establishments as well as the more private motels. See the "Gig Harbor and Fox Island Accommodations" chart for a complete listing. **The**

Fountains B&B, tel. (260) 851-6262, is an elaborate contemporary home in the country north of Gig Harbor. The guest suite has a private bath and entrance, and a fine view. **Davenport Hotel B&B,** tel. (206) 851-8527, is a spacious home on four acres of land, where breakfasts are a three-course affair. **Rosedale B&B,** tel. (206) 851-5420, is a contemporary Victorian-style home with a spacious guest suite and private bath, fireplace, and deck. **The Parsonage B&B,** tel. (206) 851-8654, was built in 1901 by volunteers for the First Methodist Episcopal Church and has two guest rooms, one with a king-sized bed.

No **Cabbages B&B,** tel. (206) 858-7797, is a comfortable beachside home with three guest rooms and a delicious full breakfast. **The Pillars B&B,** tel. (206) 851-6644, offers a plantation-style home with views of Puget Sound and Mt. Rainier, plus an indoor pool and jacuzzi.

Twelve miles north of Gig Harbor on Glen Cove, the **Old Glencove Hotel,** tel. (206) 884-2835, built in 1896 and now on the National Register of Historic Places, has been restored and transformed into a waterside bed and breakfast.

Over on Fox Island, three B&Bs provide cozy lodging choices: the **Beachside B&B,** tel. (206) 549-2524, has a gorgeous waterfront studio with fireplace, beach, kitchen, and buoy for boaters. **Island Escape B&B,** tel. (206) 549-2044, is a contemporary suite with a king-size bed, jacuzzi bath, and private deck affording a view of the Sound. **Sylvan on the Sound,** tel. (260) 549-2955, is a 1902 country home with two guest rooms and a full breakfast. Kids are welcome.

Campgrounds
Camp in the tall pines at **Kopachuck State Park** (described above), seven miles northwest of Gig Harbor, tel. (206) 265-3606. Tent spaces are $10; no RV hookups; open from late April to early October. Call (800) 452-5687 for campsite reservations ($6 extra fee), available up to 11 months ahead of time. The private **Gig Harbor Campground,** 9515 Burnham Dr., tel. (206) 858-8138, has RV and tent sites.

Food
At the immensely popular **Tides Tavern,** 2925 Harborview in Gig Harbor, you can arrive by car or boat (public dock right outside), and they've got a small deck for outdoor drinking and boat-watching. Besides burgers, the Tides

offers pizza, sandwiches, soup, nachos, cheap beer, and live music on Friday and Saturday nights. Nobody under 21 allowed.

Neville's Shoreline Restaurant, 8827 N. Harborview Dr., tel. (206) 851-9822, features a waterside location and excellent fresh seafood specials, including real English-style halibut fish and chips. Save a few bucks by ordering from their deli.

Harbor Inn Restaurant, 3111 Harborview Dr., tel. (206) 851-5454, has a great view of the harbor on three levels and serves lunch and dinner every day and breakfast on Sunday.

Get fiery hot Chinese food at **Harbor Monsoon Restaurant,** 4628 Pt. Fosdick Dr. NW, tel. (206) 858-9838, and all the Mexican standards from **Moctezuma's,** 4803 Pt. Fosdick Dr., NW, tel. (206) 851-8464. Also try **North by Northwest,** 9916 Peacock Hill Ave. NW, tel. (206) 851-3134, for Northwest cuisine, and **W.B. Scott's,** 3108 Harborview Dr., tel. (206) 858-6163, for steak, seafood, and rabbit.

GIG HARBOR AND FOX ISLAND ACCOMMODATIONS

Accommodations are arranged from least to most expensive within each category. Rates may be lower during the winter months. The area code is 206.

BED AND BREAKFASTS

The Parsonage B&B; 4107 Burnham Dr., Gig Harbor; tel. 851-8654; $50-75 s or d; 1901 parsonage, two guest rooms, shared bath, full breakfast, kids by arrangement

No Cabbages B&B; 7712 Goodman Dr., Gig Harbor; tel. 858-7797; $50-80 s or d; beach house, three guest rooms, shared or private bath, full breakfast, kids welcome

Sylvan on the Sound; 440 Sixth Ave., Fox Island; tel. 549-2955; $65 s or d; 1902 country home, two guest rooms, shared bath, full breakfast, kids welcome

Davenport Hotel B&B; 7501 Artondale Dr., Gig Harbor; tel. 851-8527; $65-75 s or d; contemporary country home, Victorian-style home, three guest rooms, shared or private bath, full breakfast, kids welcome

Old Glencove Hotel B&B; 9418 Glencove Rd.; tel. 884-2835; $85 s or d; historic landmark hotel, four guest rooms, shared or private baths, full breakfast, kids okay

The Pillars B&B; 6606 Soundview Dr., Gig Harbor; tel. 851-6644; $90 s, $120 d; plantation-style home, water and mountain views, indoor pool, jacuzzi, three guest rooms, private baths, full breakfast, no kids under 10

Beachside B&B; 679 Kamus Dr., Fox Island; tel. 549-2524; $95 s or d; waterfront studio, fireplace, kitchen, continental breakfast, kids okay

Island Escape B&B; 210 Island Blvd., Fox Island; tel. 549-2044; $95 s or d; contemporary suite, water views, king-size bed, jacuzzi bath, private deck, no kids

Rosedale B&B; 7714 Ray Nash Dr., Gig Harbor; tel. 851-5420; $95 s or d; contemporary home, one guest suite, private bath, fireplace, deck, full or continental breakfast, kids welcome

The Fountains B&B; 926 120th St. NW, Gig Harbor; tel. 851-6262; $95 s or d; contemporary home in the trees, one guest suite, private bath and entrance, no kids

MOTELS

Westwynd Motel-Apartments; 6703 144th St. NW, Gig Harbor; tel. 857-4047 or (800) 468-9963; $45-75 s or d; kitchenettes available

Gig Harbor Motor Inn; 4709 Pt. Fosdick Drive NW, Gig Harbor; tel. 858-8161; $52-56 s or d; attractive wooded location, kitchenettes available, weekly rates available

Harbor Bread Co., 8812 N. Harborview Dr., tel. (206) 851-4181, bakes wonderfully earthy breads, including several spicy versions and tasty pastries. The bakery is hidden behind Finholm's Market and Grocery at the head of the harbor. **Le Bistro,** 4120 Harborview Dr., tel. (206) 851-1033, is a small espresso place overlooking the harbor.

For the freshest local produce, head to the **Gig Harbor Farmers Market,** held on Saturday 9 a.m.-1 p.m. from May to October behind the United Methodist Church at 7400 Pioneer Way.

Events

Gig Harbor events include a **Community Parade** on the first weekend of June, **Cruzin' the Gig,** a car show in mid-May, and a couple of arts and crafts fairs: the **Summer Art Festival,** and **Christmas Tidefest.** Gig Harbor's **Lighted Boat Parade** the second Saturday of December is another enjoyable event. For information on any of these events, call the chamber of commerce at (206) 851-6865.

Arts and Entertainment

Gig Harbor's **Performance Circle Theater** has performances in Celebrations Meadow during the summer months and at Burton Park Theater, 6615 38th Ave. NW, on winter weekends. Celebrations Meadow is on the left side of Peacock Hill Ave., about one-half mile up from Harborview; the Burton Park theater is at the extreme north end of 38th Ave. NW. For information, call (206) 851-7529 or 549-2661.

Tides Tavern, 2611 Harborview Dr., tel. (206) 858-3982, has live rock or blues bands on the weekends, or head to **Cimarron,** 3211 56th St. NW, for folk or C&W bands.

Information and Services

The **Gig Harbor/Peninsula Area Chamber of Commerce,** 3125 Judson St., tel. (206) 851-6865, can provide you with local brochures and info. Open Mon.-Fri. 10 a.m.-5 p.m. year-round. Gig Harbor's telephone **area code** is 206.

Rent powerboats, jet skis, skippered sailboats, sea kayaks, pedal boats, and other on-the-water vessels from **Rent-a-Boat & Charters,** 8827 N. Harborview Dr., tel. (206) 858-7341.

Transportation

Pierce Transit, tel. (206) 581-8000 or (800) 562-8109, has daily service from Gig Harbor, Fox Island, Key Center and Longbranch to Tacoma and other parts of Pierce County, with connections from there to Seattle and Olympia.

The **Bremerton-Kitsap Airporter,** tel. (206) 876-1737 or (800) 562-7948, and **Port Angeles-Seattle Bus Lines,** tel. (800) 764-2287, both offer shuttle bus connections to Sea-Tac Airport.

KEY PENINSULA

West of Gig Harbor and across Carr Inlet is another fingerlike appendage reaching into the southernmost end of Puget Sound: Key Peninsula. The peninsula has a small commercial center called **Home,** but is essentially a haven for retirees and commuters.

Parks

Penrose Point State Park covers 152 acres of shoreline two miles south of Home. No RV hookups, but the park has tent spaces in the trees for $10 a night; open late April through Labor Day. Also here are a couple miles of hiking trails and a boat dock. Call (206) 884-2514 for more information, or (800) 452-5687 for campsite reservations ($6 extra fee), available up to 11 months ahead of time.

Purdy Spit, located at the head of Henderson Bay (the upper end of Carr Inlet), is bisected by Hwy. 302 and is a favorite place to beachcomb, dig for clams, and windsurf.

Events

Local summertime events include **Key Peninsula Pioneer Days** in August, and **Autumn Apple Squeezing** in mid-October.

VASHON ISLAND

Vashon Island is not the place to go if you're expecting a hot time on the ol' town; cows and horses probably outnumber humans. This rural, slow-paced, homey environment is fine for bike tours but not bar-hopping. The main attractions on Vashon are the bucolic countryside and the enjoyable small shops and B&Bs. There are no

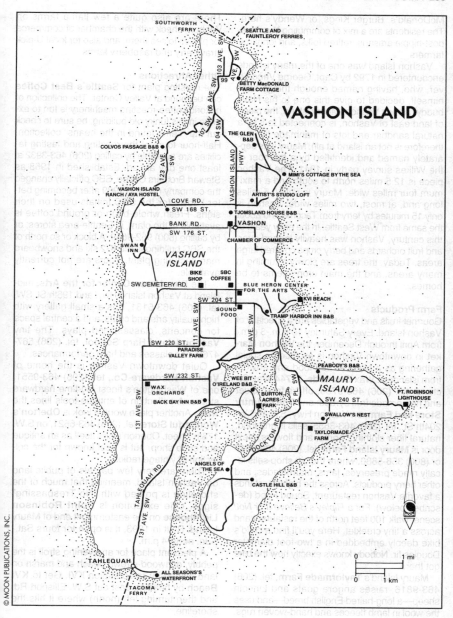

VASHON ISLAND

SOUTHWORTH
FERRY

SEATTLE AND
FAUNTLEROY FERRIES

103 AVE. SW
99
106 SW
104 AVE. SW
107 SW

BETTY MACDONALD
FARM COTTAGE

THE GLEN
B&B

COLVOS PASSAGE B&B

123 AVE. SW

MIMI'S COTTAGE BY THE SEA

VASHON ISLAND HWY.

ARTIST'S STUDIO LOFT

VASHON ISLAND
RANCH / AYA HOSTEL

COVE RD.

SW 168 ST.

TJOMSLAND HOUSE B&B

BANK RD.

VASHON

SW 176 ST.

CHAMBER OF COMMERCE

SWAN
INN

VASHON
ISLAND

BIKE
SHOP

SBC
COFFEE

SW CEMETERY RD.

BLUE HERON CENTER
FOR THE ARTS

SW 204 ST.

KVI BEACH

111 AVE. SW

SOUND
FOOD

TRAMP HARBOR INN B&B

SW 220 ST.

91 AVE. SW

PARADISE
VALLEY FARM

PEABODY'S B&B

SW 232 ST.

WAX
ORCHARDS

WEE BIT
O'IRELAND B&B

BURTON
ACRES
PARK

MAURY
ISLAND

PT. ROBINSON
LIGHTHOUSE

75 PL. SW

131 AVE. SW

BACK BAY INN B&B

SW 240 ST.

SWALLOW'S NEST

DOCKTON RD.

TAYLORMADE
FARM

ANGELS OF
THE SEA

CASTLE HILL B&B

TAHLEQUAH RD.

131 AVE. SW

TAHLEQUAH

ALL SEASONS'S
WATERFRONT

TACOMA
FERRY

0   1 mi

0   1 km

© MOON PUBLICATIONS, INC.

McDonald's, Burger Kings, or Wendy's here. The residents are a mix of commuting Yupsters, post-hippie artisans, retired folks, and longtime farmers.

Vashon Island was one of the many islands encountered in 1792 by Capt. George Vancouver, who, having named enough things after himself, decided to give this one to his Navy buddy, James Vashon. Maury Island, the piece of land east of Vashon, is connected to it by a natural sandbar and lots of manmade fill (and therefore is not an island at all). Maury was separately named and identified by a member of the Wilkes survey party in 1841. The Vashon piece is 12.5 miles north to south and a maximum four miles wide; Maury is only 5.5 miles long and, at most, two miles wide. Vashon is only 15 minutes by ferry from Tacoma and about the same from West Seattle. In the early years of this century, Vashon was heavily logged over, and fruit orchards and berry crops covered large areas. Today, the trees are slowly returning in many areas, and the main crop seems to be homes.

Farm Products
Gourmet fruits and vegetables are a specialty of Vashon Island. Every Saturday 10 a.m.-3 p.m., from April through December, the **Vashon Market** in downtown Vashon is as much a social gathering as a place to buy food and artwork from islanders. **Wax Orchards**, 22744 Wax Orchard, tel. (206) 463-9735, offers fresh cider and homemade fruit syrups; and **The Country Store and Farm,** on Vashon Hwy. SW at S.W. 204th St., tel. (206) 463-3655, sells island food, natural fiber clothing, herbs, and flowers. Next door is **Maury Island Farm,** tel. (206) 463-5617 or (800) 356-5880, where the gift shop sells locally made preserves, jams, marmalades, and other berry products. Across the highway stands a favorite Vashon restaurant, Sound Food (described below). For a *Ripley's Believe It or Not!* scene, walk 100 feet north of the restaurant and across a tiny creeklet. Here you'll find a child's bike deeply embedded in a two-foot diameter Douglas fir. Nobody knows exactly how the bike got there.

Maury Island's **Taylormade Farm,** tel. (206) 463-9816, raises angora goats and Lincoln sheep—a long-haired English breed—and uses the wool in lamb fleeces and hand-woven rugs.

There are also quite a few llama farms on Vashon; check with the chamber of commerce for places to see them, and also for local U-pick strawberry and raspberry farms.

Other Attractions
The roasting plant for **Seattle's Best Coffee** can be found at Valley Center. The collection of historic coffee-roasting machinery is fun to explore in this funky old building; be sure to check out the "items found in the beans" collection. Half-hour tours of the roasting and tasting facilities are available by calling (206) 463-3932 at least one day ahead. Established in 1968 as Stewart Brothers Coffee, SBC officially changed the company name in 1989 after becoming better known for the SBC initials used on their signs. Fresh whole-bean or ground coffee is available at the plant, in Seattle-area stores, or by calling (800) 962-9659. A block or so north of the SBC building is the **K-2** ski and snowboard manufacturing plant. Tours are not currently available.

The **Blue Heron Center for the Arts,** mid-island at Vashon Island Hwy. and 196th St. SW, tel. (206) 463-5131, has a small gallery with high quality arts and crafts, and a central space for concerts, classes, and plays. The tiny **Vashon Island Harp School,** tel. (206) 567-4768, has classes and harp performances.

Quiet downtown Vashon is the home of **Vashon Hardware Co.,** tel. (206) 463-9551, one of Washington's finest old-time hardware stores. A collection of antique tools lines the walls. Another place worth a look is **Oberton's Wonderful Store,** tel. (206) 463-6621, on S.W. 178th Street. Oberton's bills itself as an antique and curio shop, but is best known for the collection of vintage radios.

There are very few parcels of public land on Vashon Island, meaning that much of the shoreline is posted with "No Trespassing" signs. One exception is **Point Robinson Lighthouse** on the easternmost end of Maury Island. Built in 1893, it is open for tours Sat.-Sun. noon-4 p.m.

A pleasant place for an evening stroll is the pebbly, driftwood-strewn beach and marsh on land owned by radio station KVI. Get to **KVI Beach** by heading east out S.W. Ellisport Rd. and then turning left (north) where it hits the shoreline.

VASHON ISLAND ACCOMMODATIONS

Accommodations are arranged from least to most expensive. Rates may be lower during the winter months. The area code is 206, and Vashon Island is a local call from Seattle.

AYH Ranch & Hostel; 12119 S.W. Cove Rd.; tel. 463-2592; $9-12 pp (summers only) in dorm rooms, $35-60 s or d in private rooms; AYH hostel with full range of facilities, pancake breakfast

Whitaker House; 23016 64th Ave. SW; tel. 463-5934; $45 s or d; room with Seattle view, private entrance

Tjomsland House B&B; 17011 Vashon Hwy. SW; tel. 463-5275; $65 s or d; historic 1890 farmhouse, country breakfast

Paradise Valley Farm; 21831 107th SW; tel. 463-9815; $65 s or d; apartment, food provided

Castle Hill B&B; 26734 94th Ave. SW; tel. 463-5491; $65 s or d; apartment, full breakfast

Wee Bit O'Ireland B&B; 9216 S.W. Harbor Dr.; tel. 463-3881; $65-75 s or d; pool, jacuzzi, fireplace, full Irish breakfast

Angels of the Sea B&B; Dockton Harbor; tel. 463-6980; $65-75 s or d; two guest rooms in small country church (built 1917), full breakfast, live harp music

Artist's Studio Loft; 16529 91st SW; tel. 463-2583; $65-75 s or d; private suite, jacuzzi, woodstove, continental breakfast, no kids

Swan Inn B&B; 18427 Thorsen Rd. SW; tel. 463-3388; $70-90 s or d; replica of 14th century English Inn, fireplace, English antiques, full breakfast

Colvos Passage B&B; 12306 S.W. 144th St.; tel. 567-5102; $75 s or d; waterside duplex with deck, fireplace, full breakfast

The Glen B&B; 8928 S.W. 146th Place; tel. 567-4284; $75 s or d; apartment with private entrance, woodstove, full breakfast, no kids

Tramp Harbor Inn B&B; P.O. Box 741; tel. 463-5794; $75-85 s or d; separate house, fireplace, jacuzzi, full breakfast

Mimi's Cottage by the Sea; 7923 S.W. Hawthorne Lane; tel. 567-4383; $80 s or d, $90 s or d with full breakfast; cottage with deck, beach access, woodstove, mountain bikes, no kids

Peabody's B&B; 23007 64th SW; tel. 463-3506; $80-95 s or d; apartment suite, waterfront views, jacuzzi, breakfast

Betty MacDonald Farm Cottage; 12000 99th Ave. SW; tel. 567-4227; $90-100 s or d; cottage, food provided, woodstove

All Seasons Waterfront; 12817 S.W. Bachelor Rd.; tel. 463-3498; $95 s or d; beautiful shoreside cabin with large deck and views, fireplace, full kitchen, no kids

Back Bay Inn B&B; Burton; tel. 463-5355; $98-113 s or d; four guest rooms, private baths, fireplace, full breakfast, antique furnishings, fine restaurant

The Island Within B&B; P.O. Box 2241; tel. 567-4177; $100-125 s or d; cottage, woodstove, full breakfast

Swallow's Nest Guest Cottages; 6030 S.W. 248th St.; tel. 463-2646 or (800) 269-6378; $60-85 s or d for cottages, $105-180 for houses (sleep 4-8); comfortable cottages, jacuzzi, woodstove

Burton Acres Park faces out onto Quartermaster Harbor and Maury Island and has hiking trails. The local school district has some 500 acres of undeveloped land out on S.W. Bank Road. Although some of it has been logged recently, there are other second-growth forested areas with trails cutting through that are popular with those afoot or on horseback. The school land is at the south end of 115 Ave. SW not far from the hostel.

Accommodations

See the chart for a complete listing of the 20 B&Bs, guest cottages, and other lodging places on Vashon and Maury Islands. If you can't reach any of these, call (206) 463-6737 for a referral. The island has some wonderfully romantic places, making this a great get-away place. You won't go wrong at any of these.

The least expensive place to stay on the island is unique **Vashon Island Ranch and Summer Hostel,** 12119 Cove Rd., tel. (206) 463-2592. The friendly owner, Judy Mulhair, has created an amusing Western-theme hostel with tepees, covered wagons, a log bunkhouse, and a barn. The ranch is situated on 10 acres of meadow land surrounded by second-growth forests. The lodge houses two dorms with 14 bunk beds ($9 per person for AYH members; $12 per person for nonmembers), bathrooms, and a full kitchen. Guests can also stay in the covered wagons and tepees (same rate; very popular with foreign travelers who also enjoy the flags-of-the-world showers), or pitch their own tent for the same price. In addition, couples can stay in a private room with separate bath for $35 d ($45 d for nonmembers).

Guests can borrow the old one-speed bikes for $1.50 per day including helmet and rent sleeping bags or lockers. A free do-it-yourself pancake breakfast, volleyball and horseshoe games, barbecue grill, and the evening campfire provide chances to trade tales with fellow travelers. In the winter months, the ranch becomes a B&B, with rooms going for $25 s, or $35-60 d. This is a very popular place for adventurous travelers from all over the globe, with 50 or so visitors on busy summer nights. The owner picks up folks at the Vashon Thriftway grocery store on weekdays (call from the free phone there) or at the ferry terminal on weekends, but call ahead on Saturday and Sunday so she can meet you.

Food

Several downtown Vashon restaurants pull in both locals and out-of-towners. **Dog Day Cafe,** tel. (206) 463-6404, is a juice-and-java bar with great soups, SBC espressos, delicious sandwiches, and tantalizing desserts. Quite a few vegetarian items too. A few doors away, **Bob's Bakery,** tel. (206) 463-5666, has more sweet-

tooth victuals. **Express Cuisine Restaurant,** tel. (206) 463-6626, is a favorite lunch and dinner spot with moderate prices and a casual order-at-the-counter atmosphere. The menu cuts across the spectrum, from chicken chimichangas to *pad Thai.* For more formal dining, **Cafe Tosca,** 9924 Bank Rd. SW, tel. (206) 463-2125, has a limited but eclectic Northwest cuisine menu that changes daily, with more choices on weekends. The lunchtime salad and pasta specials are reasonable, but dinner entrees start around $13.

Sound Food Restaurant and Bakery, mid-island on the Vashon Island Hwy., has a homey atmosphere and tasty food, along with a fine bakery. There's a good lunch selection and, best of all, a big Sunday brunch.

Back Bay Inn in Burton, tel. (206) 463-5355, is a combination restaurant and inn. The restaurant serves fresh Northwest foods. A full breakfast is offered to guests only; dinner is open to the public, with entrees for $12-18. There are also espresso carts on both ends of the island near the ferry docks: **Second Wind Cafe** at the Heights Dock ferry terminal, and **Cafe Nautica** across from Back Bay Inn.

Events

Vashon's biggest summertime event is the two-day **Strawberry Festival** in mid-July. Parades, music, food, and crafts highlight the event; ferry traffic will be heavy, so it's a good idea to arrive early. **Discovery Days** in May celebrates the island's heritage. The Saturday Market is described above.

Information and Services

The **Vashon-Maury Island Chamber of Commerce,** tel. (206) 463-6217, can be found in the main village of Vashon at 17205 Vashon Hwy. SW. The hours are hit-or-miss much of the year—generally weekdays year-round and some summer weekends. Vashon Island's **area code** is 206.

An outdoor **swimming pool** (open summers only) can be found at the high school on S.W. Ellisport Rd. tel. (206) 463-3787. **Vashon Library,** tel. (206) 463-2069, is at the north end of downtown Vashon, across from the chamber of commerce office.

Getting There

The **Washington State Ferry** has auto and passenger service to both the north and south ends of Vashon Island. The return trip is always free (roundtrip fare is charged on your way to the island), so you can arrive or depart from either end for the same price. There are four departure points for the island. To reach Heights Dock on the north end, you can take the half-hour passenger-only ferry from downtown Seattle's Pier 50 for $3.50 roundtrip. This ferry operates Mon.-Sat., but not on Sunday or holidays, and generally runs from 5:30 a.m. to after midnight.

By car or bus, you can take the daily ferries from West Seattle's Fauntleroy terminal for $9.55 roundtrip. This rate includes the car and driver; passengers and walk-ons $2.30 each roundtrip; winter fares are lower. Ferries also connect Heights Dock with the Southworth ferry terminal on the Kitsap Peninsula, and the Tahlequah dock on the south end of Vashon Island with Tacoma's Point Defiance ferry terminal. Both of these ferry runs have the same rate schedule as from Fauntleroy. Call the ferry system—tel. (206) 464-6400 or (800) 843-3779 statewide—for times, or get a schedule when you buy your ticket.

Getting Around

The main town of Vashon is five miles from the ferry landing. **Metro Transit,** tel. (206) 553-3000 or (800) 542-7876, has Mon.-Sat. bus service around Vashon Island, and direct buses to and from downtown Seattle for $3.20 roundtrip each way, plus the $1.15 roundtrip ferry passenger fare. The bus also connects to the south end of Vashon Island, where you can catch the ferry to Tacoma, and connect to **Pierce Transit** buses, tel. (800) 562-8109. If you're continuing on to Southworth on the Kitsap Peninsula, you can catch **Kitsap Transit** buses, tel. (360) 373-2877.

Cyclists love the quiet roads of Vashon Island. You can carry bikes aboard all state ferries (including the passenger one to Vashon from Seattle) for an extra 50 cents roundtrip. Metro buses all have front bike racks that you can use if your legs poop out while riding around the island, or for getting to the Fauntleroy terminal from Seattle. Surprisingly, bike rentals are not available on Vashon Island, though some lodging places do have bikes that guests can borrow.

PUYALLUP AND SUMNER

Puyallup (pyoo-AL-up; pop. 25,000) sits less than a dozen miles southeast of Tacoma in the scenic, nearly level Puyallup Valley. Spring is a pretty time in the valley, with fields of flowers backdropped by Mt. Rainier. The city of Puyallup grew up on agriculture, and by 1890 it was one of the most important hops producing areas in the country. Unfortunately, an 1891 infestation of hop lice destroyed the crop, forcing farmers to switch to other crops, especially berries and flower bulbs. Agriculture is still a big part of the local economy, but industries have moved in (including a big Matsushita semiconductor plant), along with an all-American suburban sprawl that is rapidly crowding out the farms with shopping malls. Today many folks commute to work in nearby Tacoma or other cities, and the population of Puyallup has grown to 25,000, with another 60,000 in the adjacent suburb called South Hill.

The town of **Sumner** (pop. 7,000)—just three miles east of Puyallup—is a charming settlement with sturdy brick downtown buildings and older homes surrounded by dairies, berry farms, fields of daffodils, tulips, and irises. Hothouse rhubarb is another specialty product from this rich farming land. First called "Stuck Junction," Sumner was settled by whites in the early 1850s. Hops production brought a measure of prosperity that led to the building of stately Victorian-era homes.

Sights

Furnished in 1890s style, the 17-room **Ezra Meeker Mansion** was built by the city's founder and first mayor. The original stained glass pieces, ceiling artwork, six inlaid fireplaces, and a grand staircase offer a taste of life for the elite in this carefully restored Victorian mansion. As a hugely successful hop grower and broker, Meeker earned the moniker "Hop King of the World" and was for a time the richest man in the Pacific Northwest; he once earned more than $500,000 in a single year. The double whammy of the financial panic of 1890 and an infestation of hop lice nearly drove him into bankruptcy. Meeker lived through a fast-changing era: he drove a team of oxen over the Oregon Trail, later rode the route in a train, drove it in an au-

Daffodil Princesses surrounded by Puyallup in bloom

tomobile, and flew over it in an airplane. His fascination with the Oregon Trail led to the erection of markers along the route and the preservation of the historic trail. Located at 312 Spring St., tel (206) 848-1770, Meeker's mansion is today a National Historic Site. It is open for tours Wed.-Sun. 1-4 p.m. March through mid-December; admission $2 for adults, $1.50 for teens and seniors, and $1 for kids.

VanLierop Bulb Farms, 13407 80th St. E (two miles east of Puyallup), tel. (206) 848-7272, was created by Simon VanLierop, a Dutch immigrant from a family with a long history of bulb growing. VanLierop helped establish the bulb industry in the Puyallup area in the 1930s, and the farm is still a family operation, now producing more than 20,000 bulbs each year. Each spring these fields glow with the colors of 150 different varieties of crocus, daffodils, hyacinths, tulips, and other flowers. You can have them shipped or take them with you. The flower shop is open daily 10 a.m.-4:30 p.m. February to June and mid-September through October. Best time to see the flowers in bloom is mid-March to mid-April.

Taste German wines at **Manfred Vierthaler Winery,** tel. (206) 863-1633, a Bavarian-style chalet just east of Sumner on Hwy. 410. The wine tasting room is open daily noon-6 p.m.; be sure to try their port and dessert wines. The adjoining restaurant serves traditional German-Bavarian dishes, and has a dining room overlooking the Puyallup Valley.

The Tacoma Astronomical Society's **Pettinger-Guiley Observatory,** 6103 132nd St. E, tel. (206) 537-2802, contains a 15-inch Swanson Refractor—the largest amateur refracting telescope in the Northwest. The scope is open to the public twice a month (except August), providing a great opportunity to view the moon, planets, and other celestial treats.

Ryan House Museum, 1228 Main St. in Sumner, tel. (206) 863-8936, showcases a Victorian farmhouse from 1875, with tall backyard trees and regional history displays. Named for the first mayor of Sumner—who lived here for many years—the home is on the National Register of Historic Places and is open April-Oct., and December only; hours are Sunday, Wednesday, and Saturday 1-4 p.m.

Accommodations and Campgrounds
See the "Puyallup, Sumner, and Graham Accommodations" chart for a complete listing of lodging options in the Puyallup area.

Local RV parks include **Majestic Mobile Manor,** 7022 River Rd., tel. (206) 845-3144; and **River Road Motor Home Court,** 7824 River Rd. E, tel. (206) 848-7155.

Nearby Graham (10 miles south) has **Camp Benbow's Lake Tanwax Resort,** 32919 Benbow Dr. E, tel. (206) 879-5426; and **Meridan Terrace Mobile Manor,** 9816 193rd E, tel. (206) 847-1443.

Food

Start out your day at **Mr. A's Restaurant,** 816 E. Meridian, tel. (206) 927-5119, for a hearty breakfast. The deck is popular for summertime lunches. Another favorite for American breakfasts and other meals is **Anton's Restaurant,** 3207 E. Main St., tel. (206) 845-7569. Or, start the day with coffee and donuts at **Grandpa's Donuts Bakery,** 1413 E. Main St., tel. (206) 848-7300. At lunch, try **Lonzos,** 109 S. Meridian, tel. (206) 770-0150, which serves specialty sandwiches, soups, and espresso.

Located on a hill east of town, **Vierthaler Winery Restaurant,** tel. (206) 863-1633, offers fine vistas across the valley and traditional Bavarian meals. The small, family run **Balsano's Restaurant,** 127 15th St. SE, tel. (206) 845-4222, features tasty homemade Italian specialties and fresh seafood in a fun atmosphere. For more Italian fare and the best local pizzas, try **Casa Mia,** 505 N. Meridian, tel. (206) 770-0400. **Mazatlan Restaurant,** 215 15th SE, tel. (206) 848-8550, or 13018 Meridian, tel. (206) 770-8702, has Mexican food.

The fanciest place around is **Iron Gate Restaurant,** 1806 River Rd., tel. (206) 845-8854, which features a supper club setting (live country music and a big screen TV in the lounges) and locally famous prime rib.

The popular **Puyallup Farmers Market** features fresh local produce from early May through Labor Day. The market is held downtown next to Pioneer Park on Saturday 9 a.m.-2 p.m. At other times, head out River Rd. to find the produce

---

PUYALLUP, SUMNER, AND GRAHAM ACCOMMODATIONS

Accommodations are arranged from least to most expensive. The area code is 206.

PUYALLUP

Tamarak Motel; 403 W. Meeker, Puyallup; tel. 845-0466; $28 s, $32 d; outdoor pool, kitchenettes available

Brock's Motel; 920 Meridian Ave. N, Puyallup; tel. 843-1193; $29 s, $32 d; kitchenettes

Motel Puyallup; 1412 S. Meridian, Puyallup; tel. 845-8825 or (800) 845-9490; $43 s, $47 d; kitchenettes available

Northwest Motor Inn; 1409 S. Meridian, Puyallup; tel. 841-2600 or (800) 845-9490; $43 s, $47 d; jacuzzi, kitchenettes available, AAA approved

Hart's Tayberry House B&B; 7406 80th St. E, Puyallup; tel. 848-4594; $45-65 s or d; modern Victorian-style home on edge of town, three guest rooms, private or shared bath, full breakfast, no kids under 12

Best Western Park Plaza; 9620 S. Hill Place E, Puyallup; tel. 848-1500 or (800) 528-1234; $63-67 s, $68-73 d; outdoor pool, jacuzzi, kitchenettes available, continental breakfast, AAA approved

SUMNER

Bavarian Chalet Motel; 15007 Main St., Sumner; tel. 863-2243; $29-36 s or d; kitchenettes available

Sumner Motor Inn; 15506 E. Main St., Sumner; tel. 863-3250; $46-49 s, $51-54 d; kitchenettes available, AAA approved

GRAHAM

Country House B&B; 25421 99th Ave., Graham; tel. 846-1889; $55 s or d; contemporary country home, one guest room, private bath, hot tub, full breakfast, kids welcome

stands, or stop by the chamber of commerce for a list of local places.

Taste honey ales at **Kelley Creek Brewing Co.,** 20123 Old Buckley Hwy. in Boney Lake (six miles east of Puyallup), tel. (206) 862-5969. This in-the-country microbrewery opened in 1993, and sells through a number of local taverns. Open for tours Wednesday through Sunday. **Tapps Brewing,** 15625 Main St. in Buckley, tel. (206) 863-8438, is another classy microbrewery with handmade and bottled ales, porters, and seasonal brews.

Events

Puyallup is famous—at least in western Washington—as the home of the **Puyallup Fair,** officially known as the Western Washington Fair. One of the nation's 10 largest, the fair runs for 17 days in September (starting the Friday after Labor Day) and attracts a crowd of more than 1.3 million fairgoers to its top-flight concerts, livestock displays, a PRCA rodeo, carnival rides, and refreshments. Don't miss the justly famous raspberry scones. The fairgrounds are located at the intersection of Meridian St. and 9th Ave. Southwest.

The **Spring Fair and Daffodil Festival** is another of Puyallup's well-known attractions. Sponsored by the region's bulb farms, and in existence since 1934, it's a two-week series of events throughout Pierce County: the Grand Floral Parade (the third-largest parade of flowers in the nation) heads through Puyallup, Tacoma, Sumner, and Orting. For information, call (206) 627-6176. VanLierop Bulb Farm (described above) is one of the festival's sponsors; their spring gardens display a multitude of crocuses, irises, tulips, and, of course, daffodils.

Yet another fair in the Puyallup Valley is the **Pierce County Fair,** held in Graham at 218th and Meridian (Hwy. 161) the second weekend of August. Highlighted by the infamous cow-chip-throwing contest, there are also floral and photo exhibits, livestock displays, and a five-km race. For information call (206) 843-1173 before, or (206) 847-4754 during, the fair. Sumner has a **Sumner Summer Arts Festival** in early Au-

gust, with juried art exhibits, food booths, entertainment, and activities for kids.

Another big summer event is the outdoor production of ***Jesus of Nazareth*** in Puyallup's open-air amphitheater at 14422 Meridian S, performed at 8 p.m. every Friday and Saturday from the third weekend in July through Labor Day. One of seven major passion plays in the country, the cast of more than 600 is assisted by horses, cows, sheep, pigeons, and a donkey. For ticket information call (206) 848-3411 or 474-7328. For something a bit more secular, try the free **Concerts in the Park** on Tuesday and Thursday during July. Call (206) 841-5457 for a schedule of upcoming concerts. Late June brings the **Days of Ezra Meeker Pioneer Festival & Hoedown,** with entertainment, arts and crafts booths, food, and a street dance.

Wrap the season up at the **Victorian Country Christmas,** held at the fairgrounds in late November and early December and featuring more than 450 booths and dozens of stage shows. All vendors are dressed in Victorian period costume, and a living nativity and strolling musicians add to the Christmas spirit. Other popular fairground events include the **Sewing and Stitchery Expo** in early March, and the **Scandinavian Festival** in early October. For a complete listing of upcoming events at the fairground, call (206) 845-1771.

Information and Services

The **Puyallup Area Chamber of Commerce,** 322 2nd St. SW, tel. (206) 845-6755 or (800) 634-2334, is open Mon.-Fri. 9:30 a.m.-4:30 p.m. year-round.

The Puyallup and Sumner telephone **area code** is 206. (The boundary for the 206 area code is just east of here, putting nearby Enumclaw and Buckley in area code 360.)

Transportation

Pierce Transit, tel. (206) 581-8000 or (800) 562-8109, has daily service to Tacoma and other parts of Pierce County, along with Seattle and Olympia. **Capital Aeroporter,** tel. (206) 754-7113, has shuttle service between Puyallup and Sea-Tac Airport.

SOUTHWEST KING COUNTY

The southern end of King County encompasses several rapidly growing suburbs and industrial areas, with Sea-Tac Airport as a central focal point, along with a maze of highways, shopping malls, and the sorts of towns that fill the American dream of escaping from the cities. Unfortunately, this escape has transformed rich farmland into yet more development. This part of Washington has little to offer the traveler, other than cheap lodging and food, though each town has something of interest.

FEDERAL WAY

Just north of Tacoma, over the line into King County, is Federal Way. This recently incorporated city of 128,000 people received its name many years ago when some federal land was sold and the proceeds were used to build a school. The land was next to Highway 99, then known as the Federal highway. The town of Federal Way was incorporated in 1989 as an antidote to the uncontrolled growth that King County was permitting in the area. It is still one of America's fastest growing communities, but the local government tries to keep order to the development.

Amusements

For a commercial form of entertainment, Wild Waves and Enchanted Village, sister enterprises at 36201 Enchanted Parkway, will keep the whole family amused. **Wild Waves** offers 400 feet of whitewater rapids on their Raging River Ride, four giant water slides, a "beach" with artificial five-foot waves for bodysurfing, and scaled-down versions of the adult attractions for the kiddies. All this for the somewhat steep admission price of $18.50 for adults, $16.50 for kids. They're open from late May through Labor Day. All the water is heated so don't worry about the weather. Neighboring **Enchanted Village**, has 16 rides (including a 1906 carousel), bumper boats, a free-flight bird aviary, pony rides, children's museum, petting zoo, and other attractions for $8 per person, free for kids two and

younger. Open early May through Labor Day; hours and days vary by season, so call ahead at (206) 661-8000. Also ask about the periodic discount days.

Gardens and Parks

The Rhododendron Species Foundation Garden on Weyerhaeuser Way has over 2,100 varieties of rhododendrons from around the world in a 24-acre garden. This is the largest such collection on the planet, and something is in bloom March through September. Admission costs $3.50 for adults, students and seniors $2.50, under 12 free. Open Fri.-Wed. 10 a.m.-4 p.m. March-May, and Sat.-Wed. 11 a.m.-4 p.m. the rest of the year. Call (206) 661-9377 for more information. The garden is operated by the nonprofit Rhododendron Species Foundation, which also offers workshops, classes, and tours for members.

Just south of the Rhododendron Garden is **Pacific Rim Bonsai Collection,** tel. (206) 924-5206, operated by the Weyerhaeuser Corporation as a symbol of the importance of trading with Pacific Rim countries; corporate headquarters is just up the way. The collection contains more than 50 bonsai trees from Canada, the U.S., Japan, Korea, China, and Taiwan. Some trees are more than 500 years old. Go three quarters of a mile east from exit 142A, then a half-mile north on Weyerhaeuser Way. By the way, the correct pronunciation for bonsai—Japanese for "a tree in a pot"—is "bone-sigh." Admission is free, and the garden is open Fri.-Wed. 10 a.m.-4 p.m. March-May, and Sat.-Wed. 11 a.m.-4 p.m. the rest of the year. Classes on growing bonsai trees are taught throughout the year.

Saltwater State Park, two miles south of Des Moines on Marine View Drive S, is one of the most popular summer spots around; get here early on summer weekends, or you may have to wait at the gate to enter. The sandy beach is very popular for swimming, scuba diving, and sea kayaking, and a two mile path loops through the forest. Also here are picnic tables, a refreshment stand, and campsites ($10

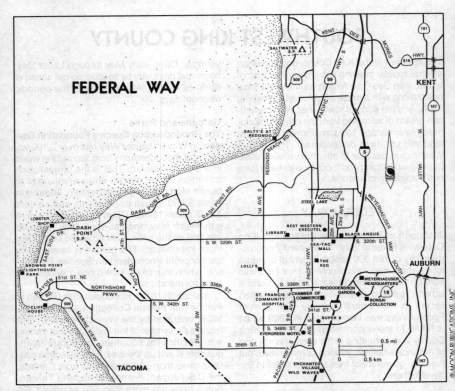

FEDERAL WAY

for tents, no RV hookups). The park is open year-round for day use, and late April to early September for camping. Coin-operated showers are available. Call (206) 764-4128 for information, and (800) 452-5687 for campsite reservations ($6 extra fee), available up to 11 months ahead of time.

Dash Point State Park is located five miles northeast of downtown Tacoma on Puget Sound, on Hwy. 509, a.k.a. Dash Point Road. The wooded camping area on the east side of the road has tent sites ($10) and trailer hookups ($15) on 397 acres. Open year-round. On the west, or Sound, side of the park, are a beach (the water here is warm enough for swimming—or at least wading—in summer), picnic tables, and trails that lead to the water. Call (206) 593-2206 for more info, or (800) 452-5687 for camp-

site reservations ($6 extra fee), available up to 11 months ahead of time.

On the northern edge of Federal Way, also on the Sound, is the community of **Des Moines,** which has one of the larger marinas in the area. The City of Des Moines Marina has 838 moorage slip, and on the marina's north end is a 670-foot fishing pier that has great views of the mountains for fishermen and strollers. To the north of the pier is the **Des Moines Beach Park,** a 20-acre park with Des Moines Creek, to which salmon return each year.

Lodging
See the "Auburn, Kent, and Federal Way Accommodations" chart for local places to stay. Camp at Dash Point State Park and Saltwater State Park, described above.

Food

Federal Way has many restaurants, including such dependable Northwest restaurant chains as **Black Angus** at 2400 S. 320th, where you'll get a decent steak time after time, and **The Keg**, 32724 Pacific Hwy. S, specializing in prime-rib dinners but also featuring a long list of appetizers and sandwiches. Lots of other chain restaurants are in town, from Red Robin to Red Lobster. Order great pizzas by the slice or pie at **Pizzeria Pagliacci,** in the SeaTac Mall, tel. (206) 839-8595.

Redondo, just west of Federal Way on Puget Sound, has a fishing pier, boat launch, and one of the area's best restaurants: **Salty's at Redondo.** Primarily a seafood restaurant (moderate to expensive), Salty's has one of the best sunset views around, and you can drink or dine outdoors on the pier in the summer months.

A good place for a light meal is **Lolli's Broiler & Pub**, 32925 1st Ave. S (in the Quad), a restaurant/tavern that serves huge burgers and good sandwiches, along with an extensive selection of beers on tap (32 at last count); it might feel like a bar, but kids are legal and welcome. It's a fun place to watch sports on the two large-screen televisions. **Azteca Restaurant,** 31406 Pacific Hwy. S, tel. (206) 839-6693, has the best local south-of-the-border meals, along with happy hour specials. Just south of Federal Way at Dash Point are two popular view restaurants: Lobster Shop and Cliff House; see "Tacoma" for specifics on these.

Recreation

Swim at the **Federal Way Pool**, 30421 16th Ave. S, tel. (206) 839-1000, or the **King County Aquatic Center**, 650 S.W. Campus Dr., tel. (206) 296-4444. A third pool is located in nearby Des Moines: **Mount Rainier Pool**, 22722 19th Ave. S, tel. (206) 296-4278. The elaborate King County Aquatic Center was constructed to host the 1990 Goodwill Games and has been used for other national swimming meets. But you don't have to be a hotshot to swim here, or to try out the diving boards. The **North Shore Golf & Country Club**, 4101 North Shore Blvd. NE, tel. (206) 927-1375, is an 18-hole public course.

Shopping and Entertainment

The **Sea-Tac Mall** (on the south side of south 320th St., about two lights into Federal Way from I-5) has a Sears, Mervyn's, Lamonts, and The Bon Marché, plus 100 smaller specialty stores. Other shopping centers and drug, and grocery stores line S. 320th on both sides. Federal Way has an **REI** store with camping and backpacking supplies at 2565 S. Gateway Center Plaza (I-5 at 320th St.), tel. (206) 941-4994.

The **Federal Way Philharmonic,** tel. (206) 838-0565, performs Sept.-April at St. Theresa's Church at S.W. 331st St. and Hoyt Road.

Information and Services

The **Greater Federal Way Chamber of Commerce,** 34004 16th Ave., tel. (206) 838-2605, can help you out with maps and other area information. Open Mon.-Fri. 9 a.m.-5 p.m. year-round. The **Federal Way Public Library** is at 848 S. 320th, tel. (206) 839-0257. **St. Francis Community Hospital** has 24-hour emergency care at 34515 9th Ave. S, tel. (206) 927-9700 or 838-9700; from Pacific Hwy. S, go west on 348th and follow the signs. The **area code** for Federal Way is 206.

Transportation

Metro Transit, tel. (206) 447-4800 or (800) 542-7876, provides bus service to Seattle and other parts of King County. **Pierce Transit,** tel. (206) 581-8000 or (800) 562-8109, has service to Tacoma and other parts of Pierce County, along with Seattle and Olympia.

KENT AND AUBURN

The city of Auburn (pop. 35,000) began as an agricultural settlement in the White River Valley and was originally named Slaughter, for an Army lieutenant who was killed in an Indian battle nearby. Later settlers decided Slaughter wasn't a particularly appealing name for the town, and so they renamed it Auburn. Because of periodic flooding, settlers rerouted the White River southward from its original course into the Stuck River, thus removing the river from the valley it had created. Today Auburn and neighboring Kent (pop. 40,000) are small cities that are rapidly becoming links in the chain of urban growth that continues almost without a break from Seattle to Olympia.

AUBURN, KENT, AND FEDERAL WAY ACCOMMODATIONS

Accommodations are arranged from least to most expensive within each city. Rates may be lower during the winter months. The area code is 206.

AUBURN

Auburn Motel; 1202 Auburn Way S.; tel. 833-7470; $33 s, $40 d; local calls 25 cents

Nendel's Valu Inn; 102 15th St. NE; tel. 833-8007 or (800) 547-0106; $46 s or d; continental breakfast, AAA approved

Valu-U Inn; 9 14th Ave. NW; tel. 735-9600 or (800) 443-7777; $56 s, $66 d; jacuzzi, continental breakfast, free airport shuttle, AAA approved

Best Western Pony Soldier Motor Inn; 1521 D St. NE; tel. 939-5950 or (800) 634-7669; $66-71 s, $69-74 d; outdoor pool, jacuzzi, sauna, AAA approved

Blomeen House B&B; 324 B St. NE; tel. 939-3088; $70-75 s or d; 1912 Queen Anne Victorian home, wraparound veranda, two antique-filled guest rooms, shared baths, light breakfast, no kids under 12

KENT

New Best Inn; 23408 30th Ave. S; tel. 870-1280; $42 s, $50 d; kitchenettes available, AAA approved

Val-U Inn; 22420 84th Ave.; tel. 872-5525 or (800) 443-7777; $51 s or d; jacuzzi, continental breakfast, free airport shuttle, AAA approved

Days Inn; 1711 W. Meeker St.; tel. 854-1950 or (800) 325-2525; $55 s, $60 d; outdoor pool, free airport shuttle, AAA approved

Best Western Pony Soldier Motor Inn; 1233 N. Central; tel. 852-7224 or (800) 528-1234; $66-71 s, $69-74 d; outdoor pool, jacuzzi, sauna, exercise room, free airport shuttle, AAA approved

Cypress Inn; 22218 84th Ave. S; tel. 395-0219 or (800) 752-9991; $67-69 s, $74-77 d; outdoor pool, jacuzzi, free airport shuttle, kitchenettes available, AAA approved

Best Western Choice Lodge; 24415 Russell Rd.; tel. 854-8767 or (800) 528-1234; $72-82 s, $82-92 d; sauna, jacuzzi, exercise room, free airport shuttle, AAA approved

Homecourt All Suite Hotel; 6329 S. 212th; tel. 395-3800; $79 s or d; two-bedroom suites with kitchens, outdoor pool, jacuzzi, exercise room, tennis court, free airport shuttle, AAA approved

FEDERAL WAY

Stevenson Motel; 33330 Pacific Hwy. S; tel. 927-2500; $26 s, $29 d; see rooms first

Siesta Motel; 35620 Pacific Hwy. S; tel. 927-2157; $27 s, $29 d

New Horizon Motel; 33002 Pacific Hwy. S; tel. 927-2337; $30-41 s or d; kitchenettes available

Ridge Crest Motel; 1812 S. 336th; tel. 874-9161; $33-40 s, $35-40 d; older place, quiet location, kitchenettes available

Super 8 Motel; 1688 S. 348th; tel. 838-8808 or (800) 800-8000; $44 s, $48 d

Best Western Federal Way Execute!; 31611 20th Ave. S; tel. 941-6000 or (800) 528-1234; $93 s, $99 d; outdoor pool, jacuzzi, free airport shuttle, AAA approved

Sights and Attractions

Auburn's **White River Valley Historical Museum,** 918 H St. SE, tel. (206) 833-2496, has artifacts from the early days in the valley, including old photos, a one-room schoolhouse, country store, and farm machinery. The museum is open Thurs.-Sun. 1:30-4:30 p.m. year-round. No charge.

The **Auburn's Avenue Theater** at 10 Auburn Ave, tel. (206) 833-5678, has fun musical productions and plays. Gamblers can try their luck at blackjack, craps, roulette, or poker at **Muckleshoot Indian Casino**, 2402 Auburn Way S, tel. (206) 939-7484.

In 1996, the **Emerald Downs Thoroughbred Race Track** opened on the north side of Auburn, replacing the Longacres site that closed in 1992 after being sold to Boeing. Call (206) 939-9515 for details. Another recent addition is the enormous **SuperMall**, with 100 outlet and "rack" stores located just off Hwy. 167 at 15th St. Southwest.

Lodging and Campgrounds

See the "Auburn, Kent, and Federal Way Accommodations" chart for local places to stay. **Blomeen House B&B**, tel. (206) 939-3088, is a classic Victorian home that once served as Auburn's hospital. It has two guest rooms and a wraparound front veranda.

Park RVs or pitch a tent at **KOA Seattle South Campground**, 5801 S. 212th, tel. (206) 872-8652.

Food

Nothing stellar on the local restaurant scene, but several places are worth a visit. For breakfast, head to **Sun Break Cafe**, 309 C St. SW in Auburn, tel. (206) 939-5225, or **Trotter's Restaurant**, 825 Harvey Rd. in Auburn, tel. (206) 833-2323. **China Palace**, 2402 N. Auburn Way in Auburn, tel. (206) 939-9420, has an all-you-can-eat lunch buffet, and **Mazatlan Restaurant**, 110 Cross St. SE in Auburn, tel. (206) 833-7133, has Mexican meals. Get Indian cuisine, including a Tues.-Sat. lunch buffet, at **India Bazaar**, 20936 108th SE, tel. (206) 850-8906.

For fresh produce, visit the **Auburn Farmers Market**, held on Wednesday, June-Sept., in the parking lot at 118 Cross Street.

Events

Auburn events include the **Fourth of July Parade**, and **Good Ol' Days Community Celebration**, held the last weekend of August.

Information and Services

Get local info from the **Auburn Chamber of Commerce**, 228 1st St. NE, tel. (206) 833-0700,

or the **Kent Area Chamber of Commerce**, 841 Central Ave. N, tel. (206) 854-1770. The local **area code** is 206.

Auburn's **swimming pool** is located next to the high school at 516 4th NE, tel. (206) 939-8825, while Kent has pools at 25316 101st Ave. SE, tel. (206) 296-4275, and 18230 S.E. 240th, tel. (206) 296-4276.

Transportation

Metro Transit, tel. (206) 553-3000 or (800) 542-7876, has bus service to all of King County, including Auburn, Kent, Seattle, and Sea-Tac airport. **Shuttle Express**, tel. (206) 622-1424 or (800) 487-7433, provides direct service to Sea-Tac Airport, along with door-to-door connections.

TUKWILA, SEATAC, AND BURIEN

This trio of urban and industrial sprawl occupies the southwestern corner of King County, with Seattle to the north, and Tacoma and Federal Way to the south. The main "attractions" are **Sea-Tac International Airport** in Seatac (pop. 23,000), and **Southcenter Mall**, located south of the intersection of I-5 with I-405 in Tukwila (pop. 15,000). Major department stores here include The Bon Marché, Nordstrom, JCPenney, and Sears (the company's "flagship store"), plus 150 other stores. Coming soon to SeaTac is a mammoth Federal Detention Facility. Okay place to visit, but you wouldn't want to live there.

Practicalities

Because of the proximity to Sea-Tac Airport, Tukwila and SeaTac have literally dozens of motels and hotels of all types, especially along motel row (Pacific Hwy. South/Hwy. 99). See the chart "Seattle Accommodations" for a listing of these.

Not surprisingly, you can find all the standard fast and not-so-fast eating places in the cities. Worth a taste are: **Grazie Ristorante Italiano**, 16943 Southcenter Parkway, tel. (206) 575-1606, for dinners; and **Quick Bite**, 6305 S. 180th, tel. (206) 575-1944, for lunches.

Information and Events

For a handful of local brochures, drop by **Southwest King County Chamber of Commerce**, just south of the Southcenter Mall at 16400

Southcenter Parkway, Suite 210, tel. (206) 575-1633. Open Mon.-Fri. 9 a.m.-5 p.m. The **area code** for this area is 206.

Tukwila has a popular **Summer Festival** each July, while nearby Burien (pop. 28,000; just west of the airport) is home to the **Strawberry Festival** each June, along with a fun **Fourth of July Parade.** SeaTac's Angle Lake Park features a **Music in the Park** series in the summer.

RENTON

Renton was born when coal was mined in the area before the turn of this century but is now home to a massive Boeing plant. As you would expect from its ties with Boeing, the city has an excellent airport as well as a large seaplane base, named the **Will Rogers-Wiley Post Seaplane Base** because it was the place from which those two men launched the flight that ended in their deaths outside Nome, Alaska, on August 7, 1935. A monument commemorates their fateful trip.

Today, with a population of 43,000, Renton is fast becoming just another mass of spreading suburban growth, and most visitors are en route to the Southcenter Mall in nearby Tukwila or other centers of rampant consumer spending. But rock music fans will know that Renton is where Jimi Hendrix is interred.

Sights

The simple grave of **James M. "Jimi" Hendrix** can be found in Greenwood Memorial Park, located east of town on N.E. 3rd at Monroe. Find the ground-level grave marker by heading toward the sundial and then turning right. Born in Seattle in 1942, Hendrix died in 1970 from a drug-related suffocation. Hundreds of people of all ages still make the pilgrimage to his grave each year, leaving behind tokens of all sorts, from flowers to pinwheels to McDonald's "valued customer" coupons. Be sure to stop by the office near the cemetery entrance to sign in the guest book, and to read comments from visitors who arrive from around the globe. A new Jimi Hendrix museum is in the works for Seattle; see the Seattle chapter for details.

Most of the town's history is told in the **Renton Historical Museum** at 235 Mill Ave. S, tel. (206) 255-2330. It has a number of exhibits, among them pioneer furniture, antique vehicles, and Indian and coal mining artifacts. Open Tuesday 10 a.m.-4 p.m., Wednesday, Saturday, and Sunday 1-4 p.m.

Dinner Train

The ever-popular **Spirit of Washington Dinner Train** leaves the Renton Depot year-round, pulled by a 1935 diesel engine, and continues along Lake Washington to the Columbia Winery in Woodinville, 45 miles to the north. There you are given a tour of the winery before returning to Renton three and a half hours later. A gourmet meal is served along the way; the cost is $57 for the parlor car, or $69 for the dome car. Lunches and brunches are $47 and $59 respectively. Call (206) 227-7245 or (800) 876-7245 for more information and reservations. Gray Line, tel. (206) 626-5208 or (800) 426-7532, offers packages ($75-87) that include roundtrip transportation between Seattle and the train station in Renton.

Accommodations

See the "Renton Accommodations" chart for a complete listing of local places to stay. Also nearby are dozens more motels around Sea-Tac Airport; see "Seattle Lodging" for these. The most luxurious place is **Holly Hedge House,** tel. (206) 226-2555, where the entire house is reserved for one couple, including a private jacuzzi, outdoor pool, large video library, and English-country-style furnishings. An ample breakfast is served.

Campers and RVers will enjoy the amenities at **Aqua Barn Ranch,** 15227 Renton-Maple Valley Hwy., tel. (206) 255-4618. The RV and tent sites come with an indoor pool, horse rentals, a big-screen TV, and movies. **Riverbend Park,** 17410 Maple Valley, tel. (206) 255-2613, has adults-only tent sites on 12 acres. Both campgrounds are open year-round.

Food

The atmosphere is similar to a slightly upscale Denny's, but the food—especially the steaks and homemade pies—are impressive in **All City Diner,** 423 Airport Way, tel. (206) 228-7281. Quite popular for breakfast. **Andy's Tukwila**

RENTON ACCOMMODATIONS

These accommodations are listed from least to most expensive. See the "Seattle Area Accommodations" chart for lodging in nearby Tukwila. The area code is 206.

Traveler's Inn; 4710 Lake Washington Blvd.; tel. 228-2858; $35 s, $42 d; outdoor pool, AAA approved

Don-a-Lisa Motel; 111 Meadow N; tel. 255-0441; $36 s, $38 d; amusing clown collection

West Wind Motel; 110 Rainier Ave. S; tel. 226-5060; $40 s, $48 d; kitchenettes available

Silver Cloud at Renton; 1850 Maple Valley Hwy.; tel. 226-7600; $54-57 s, $60-63 d; jacuzzi, exercise room, kitchenettes available, AAA approved

Nendel's Inn Renton; 3700 E. Valley Rd.; tel. 251-9591 or (800) 547-0106; $58 s or d; jacuzzi, kitchenettes available, free airport shuttle, AAA approved

Maple Valley B&B; 20020 S.E. 228th, Maple Valley (10 miles southeast of Renton); tel. 432-1409; $60-65 s or d; distinctive contemporary home on five acres, wildlife pond, two guest rooms, shared bath, full breakfast

Best Western at Southcenter; 15901 W. Valley Rd.; tel. 226-1812 or (800) 544-9863; $81 s or d; outdoor pool, jacuzzi, exercise room, free airport shuttle

Renton Holiday Inn; 800 Rainier Ave. S; tel. 226-7700 or (800) 465-4329; $99 s, $109 d; pool, free airport shuttle, AAA approved

Holly Hedge House; 908 Grant Ave. S; tel. 226-2555; $110 d for the entire house; renovated older home, panoramic views, jacuzzi, outdoor pool, full breakfast, no kids, two-night minimum stay

Station has steaks, seafood, chicken, sandwiches, and salads, served in restored railroad cars at 2408 W. Valley Hwy., tel. (206) 235-1212. Get good Italian food at **Armondo's Cafe Italiano,** 919 S. 3rd, tel. (206) 228-0759. Vegetarians will want to squeeze into the **Real Squeeze Juice Co.** a few doors away at 905 S. 3rd, offering all types of fresh juices.

Rainier Ave. is the city's commercial strip, lined with fast- and slow-food restaurants. Mexican food fanciers will appreciate **Torero's,** 431 Rainier Ave. S, tel. (206) 228-6180, or the simple **Rodriguez Taqueria** on 3rd near Wilkens. Tasty and inexpensive Thai food can be found at **Little Bangkok Thai Restaurant,** 304 Wells S, tel. (206) 255-4820.

Shopping

The major shopping center here is **Renton Center,** which has Sears, JCPenney, and other shops; also on Rainier Ave. are Kmart, Pay-Less Drug Store, and grocery stores.

Several smaller shopping plazas and fast-food restaurants surround Renton Center, in-

cluding **The Pavilion,** an off-price mall one mile south of Southcenter. For a more authentic shopping experience—including a surprisingly complete selection of Western garb—be sure to tie up at the spacious **Renton Western Wear,** 724 S. 3rd, tel. (206) 255-3922. Antique lovers will have fun wandering through the downtown antique shops along Wells Ave. S near 3rd.

Information and Services

The **Renton Area Chamber of Commerce,** 300 Rainier N, tel. (206) 226-4560, is open Mon.-Fri. 8:30 a.m.-5 p.m. and has hundreds of brochures on the U.S. and Canada, but only one on Renton itself! The local **area code** is 206. Swim at the **Renton Pool,** 16740 128th Ave. SE, tel. (206) 296-4335.

Transportation

Metro Transit, tel. (206) 447-4800 or (800) 542-7876, provides daily bus service to Seattle and other parts of King County. **Shuttle Express,** tel. (206) 622-1424 or (800) 487-7433, has frequent direct service from Renton's Travelers Inn to Sea-Tac Airport for $11, along with door-to-door connections.

ENUMCLAW AREA

Enumclaw (pop. 7,500; pronounced "EE-num-claw") occupies a low plateau surrounded by dairy farms. The views of Mt. Rainier are outstanding from just about anywhere in town. Although housing developments are starting to move in, much of the surrounding country still retains much of its rural charm, and 50 or so dairies still survive. The distinctive "eau de Enumclaw" from these farms hangs in the air on many summer days, and one local entrepreneur even offers cans of "DairyAir" for a whiff of the Enumclaw's best-known aerial export.

History
Enumclaw ("Place of the Evil Spirits") was established in 1885 and named for a nearby mountain where local Indians were once frightened by a severe thunderstorm. The town grew up along the Northern Pacific Railroad, and was platted shortly after the railroad arrived in 1885. Dense forests here provided lumber and shingles for many years, and the logged-over land was transformed into productive dairy farms.

Sights
Enumclaw itself doesn't have a lot to offer in the way of attractions for the traveler, but do stop by **MacRae's Indian Bookstore,** 1605 Cole St., tel. (360) 825-3737, where you'll fined a remarkable collection of books on the original inhabitants of this land. It's said to be the largest bookstore of its kind anywhere; a mail order catalog is available. For a taste of farming life, head to the **Enumclaw Sales Pavilion,** 22712 S.E. 436th St., tel. (360) 825-3151, on Wednesday or Saturday for auctions of cattle, horses, and other animals. The **Rachel-Dee Herb Farm,** 40622 196th Ave. SE, tel. (360) 825-2797, features herb gardens with more than 165 varieties. They also have a gift shop and offer gardening and cooking classes.

For an especially pretty drive, head south from Enumclaw through Buckley and then on to minuscule Kapowsin, where the winding road

takes you past small lakes, old dairy barns, and newer homes on a tree-draped valley floor. Get a taste of the Enumclaw Plateau's rich farming land by heading north from town toward Black Diamond on Hwy. 169. Lots of cows and horses along the way, including Rainier Stables, home to thoroughbred race horses.

Mud Mountain Dam Park, seven miles southeast of Enumclaw off Hwy. 410, tel. (360) 825-3211, contains one of the nation's highest earth and rock flood-control dams, a 430-foot-high structure. The park features hiking trails, wading pool, playground, picnic areas, and overlooks.

Federation Forest State Park
Eighteen miles southeast of Enumclaw on Hwy. 410, Federation Forest State Park, tel. (360) 663-2207, has 619 acres of old-growth forest along the White River. This is one of the only patches of virgin timber left in the area. An interpretive center (open Wed.-Sun. 10 a.m.-5 p.m. in the summer; closed winters) houses displays on plants and animals in the forest. The park contains 11 miles of hiking trails, including two short interpretive paths and remnants of the historic Naches Trail—a pioneer trail that connected eastern Washington with Puget Sound. Federation Forest is also popular for fishing and picnicking. No camping in the park.

Green River Gorge
A dozen miles northeast of Enumclaw on Hwy. 169, **Green River Gorge Conservation Area** is a 14-mile-long protected area that includes narrow gorges, whitewater rapids, wildflowers, fossils, and caves along the Green River. Several state parks have been developed along the river, the most dramatic being the **Hanging Gardens Area,** where a trail leads to the fern-covered cliffs lining the river. Access is via S.E. 386th St. (Franklin-Enumclaw Rd.); ask locally for specific directions.

Flaming Geyser State Park occupies several big bends in the Green River four miles southeast of Black Diamond on Flaming Geyser Road. Old coal-mining test holes produce two geysers, one burning an eight-inch flame and the other sending methane gas bubbling up through a stream. Enjoy hiking, picnicking, fishing, boating, and a playground; no camping. This is a takeout point for kayakers and rafters floating the Green River Gorge, and the quiet waters below here (at least in the summer) are very popular with inner tubers. No camping at Flaming Geyser State Park.

Eleven miles northeast of Enumclaw on Farman Rd., **Kanaskat-Palmer State Park** is a popular play area on the Green River with fishing (especially for steelhead in the winter), camping, and trails through the riverside forests. Several access points in the park are used by river rafters and kayakers heading down the gorge. Because of several Class III-IV stretches, this part of the river is not for beginners; see below for rafting companies able to offer a safer trip. Call the Army Corps of Engineers in Seattle at (206) 764-6702 for a recording of current conditions on the Green River.

Nolte State Park, six miles northeast of Enumclaw, is a favorite hangout for picnicking, swimming, and fishing. The main attraction is Deep Lake, and the 1.4-mile trail that offers a pleasant stroll around this 39-acre lake.

Green River Rafting

The Green River Gorge is a 14-mile stretch of river north of Enumclaw rated Class III-IV, including many well-known rapids with names like Nozzle, Pipeline, and Ledge Drop. The river has a short spring season, generally March and April, since a dam holds the water back for Tacoma's water supply the rest of the year. Expect to pay $55-75 for a half-day excursion. Contact one of the following companies for more info: **Blue Sky Outfitters,** tel. (800) 228-7238; **Cascade Adventures,** tel. (800) 723-8386; **Downstream River Runners,** tel. (800) 234-4644; **North Cascades River Expeditions,** tel. (800) 634-8433; **Northern Wilderness River Riders, Inc.,** tel. (800) 448-7238; **River Recreation,** tel. (800) 464-5899; **Wild & Scenic River Tours,** tel. (206) 323-1220; and **Wildwater River Tours,** tel. (800) 522-9453.

Buckley

The town of Buckley (pop. 3,600; motto: "Below the snow, above the fog") lies just four miles south of Enumclaw, on the south side of the White River. This plateau country was originally densely forested, but loggers took care of that problem, and the rich soil was turned into

agricultural land. A large Weyerhaeuser lumber mill still provides many local jobs.

Buckley is home to the **Buckley Foothills Historical Society Museum,** tel. (360) 829-1533, with memorabilia from the early part of this century spread across both sides of River Avenue. Open Sunday noon-4 p.m., and Thursday 1-4 p.m. in the summer, and Thursday 1-4 p.m. in the winter months. **Main St. Antiques and Collectibles,** 712 Main St., tel. (360) 829-2624, is a small mall housing 20 different antique shops.

Buckley has a little club called **Vi's Place** at 737 Main St., where the mother-daughter Childs team performs stand-up comedy on Friday and Saturday nights. Well worth the drive; you may even meet European travelers who have heard of the act.

Black Diamond

The town of Black Diamond (pop. 1,500), seven miles north of Enumclaw, is named for the coal that is still mined here. The first mines were underground; now the John Henry No. 1 Mine strip-mines 200,000 tons of coal a year just outside town. The small **Black Diamond Museum,** tel. (360) 886-1168, houses various pieces of mining equipment, along with a model of a coal mine, a blacksmith shop, and the old town jail. Out front is a 1920s caboose. The museum is open Thursday 9 a.m.-4 p.m., and Sat.-Sun. noon-3 p.m.

The town's best-known stopping place is the wonderful **Black Diamond Bakery,** tel. (360) 886-2741, where the wood-fired oven still bakes dozens of types of breads and pastries.

Lodging

The White Rose B&B Inn, 1610 Griffin Ave., tel. (360) 825-7194 or (800) 404-7194, is an elegant 1922 colonial mansion with a rose garden and five guest rooms, each with private bath. Gourmet breakfasts are served in the formal dining room. No kids under 12. Lodging rates are $85-95 s or d.

A 1918 farmhouse has been transformed into the **Homestead B&B,** 2510 Griffin, tel. (360) 825-7816, with one guest room (private bath), and antique furnishings. Kids are welcome. Lodging is $55 s, $65 d, including a full breakfast.

King's Motel, 1334 Roosevelt Ave. E, tel. (360) 825-1626, has rooms for $35-50 s or d, including a kitchen and outdoor pool. **Best Western Park Center Motel,** 1000 Griffin, tel. (360) 825-4490 or (800) 528-1234, has rooms for $58-72 s or d, including a jacuzzi, exercise room, and courtyard patio.

Over in Buckley, stay at **West Main Motor Inn,** 466 W. Main St., tel. (360) 829-2400, where rooms go for $35 s, $40 d. Also in Buckley, the **Mountain View Inn,** 29405 Hwy. 410 E, tel. (360) 829-1100 or (800) 582-4111, is a modern facility with an outdoor pool, jacuzzi, and sauna, plus a free continental breakfast. Rates are $55 s, $60 d.

Campgrounds

Eleven miles northeast of Enumclaw on Farman Rd., **Kanaskat-Palmer State Park,** tel. (360) 886-0148, has tent spaces ($10) and RV sites ($15) on the Green River. Showers and boat rentals are also available. Open all year, but with limited winter facilities. Call (800) 452-5687 for campsite reservations ($6 extra fee), available up to 11 months ahead of time. The closest Forest Service campground is **Dalles Campground,** 26 miles east of Enumclaw on Hwy. 410; campsites are $10. Free dispersed camping is allowed throughout the Mt. Baker-Snoqualmie National Forest. Park RVs at **Uncle John's RV Park,** tel. (360) 862-1003, on Hwy. 410 between Bonney Lake and Buckley.

Food

Charlie's Cafe, 1335 Roosevelt, tel. (360) 825-5191, is a very popular breakfast eatery, that serves blueberry pancakes, home fries, and big omelettes. East Coast-style delis are hard to find in the Northwest, but Enumclaw has a fine one at **Baumgartner's Restaurant,** 1008 E. Roosevelt, tel. (360) 825-1067. Pick up a sausage sandwich, croissant, or some wine and cheese for a picnic at Mt. Rainier or a day at the ski slopes. Great pastries and cakes too. In Buckley, be sure to stop by **The Sweet Shoppe, Etc.,** 760 Main, tel. (360) 829-2229, for sandwiches, soups, salads, and wonderful homemade pies.

The best all-round dinner places are: **Loading Dock Restaurant & Lounge,** 1502 Railroad, tel. (360) 825-6565, where marinated steaks

and fresh steamer clams are the house specialties; and **Lee Restaurant,** 1110 Griffin, tel. (360) 825-3761. Try **Mazatlan Restaurant,** 951 Roosevelt E, tel. (360) 825-3544, for Mexican meals, or **Oriental Garden,** 1225 Griffin, tel. (360) 825-6528, for Chinese food.

Over in Buckley, **D'Jon's Restaurant & Steakhouse,** 720 Main St., tel. (360) 829-2127, cranks out the best local steaks, prime rib, and seafood. Also in Buckley is **Wally's White River Drive-In,** 282 Hwy. 410 N, tel. (360) 829-0871, with real old-fashioned burgers and fries.

Head north to Black Diamond for **Black Diamond Bakery,** 32805 Railroad Ave., tel. (360) 886-2741, where over 30 varieties of bread emerge from their wood-fired oven, along with apple-cinnamon wheat rolls, cookies, and other goodies. Be sure to try the Crystal Mountain loaf, made from potato flour. Closed Monday. A deli next door serves tasty breakfasts and lunches.

Events and Entertainment

The **Kaleidoscope of Arts Festival** comes to town in mid-June, with arts and crafts booths, live music, a juried art competition, and the Hat and Flag Parade, featuring kids with hats made from recyclables. The oldest county fair in the state, **King County Fair,** is held the third week of July at Enumclaw's fairgrounds. A rodeo, live music (including top names), 4-H exhibits, food, crafts, racing pigs, and a logger's show highlight this popular event. There's more rodeo action at Enumclaw's **Northwest Junior Rodeo** in late August. Another big summertime activity at the fairgrounds is the **Pacific Northwest Highland Games,** held the last weekend in July. In addition to the tests of brute strength that are the main attraction, the games include bagpipe and dance competitions, animal exhibits, and vendors selling Scottish crafts, clothing, and foods.

See loggers in action at the **Buckley Log Show** on the last full weekend of June. Other Buckley events of note are the **Flashback Antique Rod and Car Show** in August, and **Clarence Hamilton Day** with a horseback parade and Western art show each September. In the little place called Wilkeson (four miles south of Buckley), the **National Handcar Races** are held in mid-June each year. In addition to the railroad handcar races, an Indian powwow, parade, antique show, and arts and crafts festival provide diversions.

True Grit Saloon, 23525 S.E. 436th in Enumclaw, tel. (360) 825-5648, is a fun place with live music and bar stools made from old saddles.

Recreation

Rent mountain bikes from **Ski and Mountain Company,** 414 Roosevelt E, tel. (360) 825-6910, and **swim** at Enumclaw High School's indoor pool, 226 Semanski S, tel. (360) 825-1128.

Information and Services

The **Enumclaw Visitor's Center,** 1421 Cole St., tel. (360) 825-7666, is open Mon.-Fri. 8 a.m.-5 p.m., and Sat.-Sun. 9 a.m.-5 p.m. during the summer; and Mon.-Fri. 9 a.m.-5 p.m., and Saturday 10 a.m.-4 p.m. the rest of the year.

The Mt. Baker-Snoqualmie National Forest's **White River Ranger District,** 857 Roosevelt Ave. E, tel. (360) 825-6585, has information on nearby hiking trails. Summer hours are: Sunday noon-4 p.m., Mon.-Fri. 8 a.m.-4:30 p.m., and Saturday 7:30-11:30 a.m.; in winter, the hours are Mon.-Fri. 8 a.m.-4:30 p.m. Unfortunately, much of the Forest Service and private land in this area has been heavily logged, and a checkerboard ownership pattern makes for difficult access. The two small wilderness areas—Clearwater Wilderness and Norse Wilderness (see "Vicinity of Mt. Rainier")—get very heavy use. The **area code** for Enumclaw is 360.

Transportation

Pierce Transit, tel. (206) 581-8000 or (800) 562-8109, has daily service to Tacoma and other parts of Pierce County, with connections onward to Seattle and Olympia.

OLYMPIA

Washington's state capital, Olympia is surprisingly small and still has the friendly feel of a town that doesn't yet realize it has become a city of 37,000 people. It's a fits-like-a-shoe, comfortable place with tall shade trees, attractive older housing areas, and turn-of-the-century mansions. The location, at the southern end of Puget Sound, offers outstanding views, and the quietly beautiful Capitol Campus gives Olympia a distinctively elegant flavor. But there is more here, including the nearby Olympia Brewery (in Tumwater), an abundance of art galleries and reasonable but creative restaurants, and three colleges.

Much of Olympia's economy runs on government jobs; in fact, 44% of Thurston County workers are employed in the public sector. Things really hum during the legislative session. Being at the southernmost end of Puget Sound would presumably mean an active shipping industry, but Olympia's port is primarily a log-moving convenience, as lumber from the forests of the Olympic Peninsula is shipped to its destination. The Olympia Brewery in nearby Tumwater is among the area's biggest businesses; oysters, berries, and mushrooms round out the county's agricultural business.

HISTORY

Among the oldest of Washington's cities, Olympia was settled in 1846 by Edmund Sylvester and Levi Smith, who filed claims of 320 acres each under the Oregon Land Law. The town was named Smithfield until Smith died, leaving his share to Sylvester, who platted the new town. In 1851 Col. Isaac Ebey (who was later beheaded in a Whidbey Island Indian raid) persuaded the town to change its name to Olympia, which he took from a book, *Life of Olympia.*

When Washington became a territory in 1853, Governor Isaac Stevens named Olympia the capital, and Edmund Sylvester donated land for a town square (now Sylvester Park) and for the new capitol building. He then turned to selling lots from his other holdings. For the next 40 years, Olympia fought Seattle, North Yakima, Vancouver, Port Townsend, Ellensburg, Centralia, and other growing cities to retain the title. Some, such as Ellensburg, even built capital buildings in anticipation of the event. A bill was actually passed in 1861 moving the capital to Vancouver, but because of a minor flaw in word-

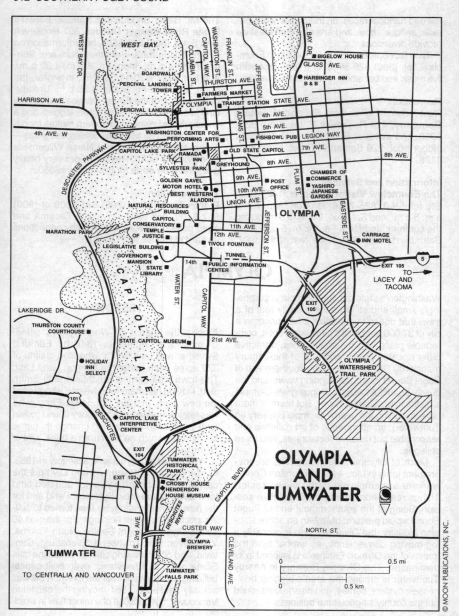

OLYMPIA AND TUMWATER

WEST BAY

WEST BAY DR.

COLUMBIA ST.

CAPITOL WAY

WASHINGTON ST.

FRANKLIN ST.

THURSTON AVE.

JEFFERSON ST.

E. BAY DR.

BIGELOW HOUSE

GLASS AVE.

HARBINGER INN B & B

BOARDWALK

PERCIVAL LANDING TOWER

PERCIVAL LANDING

HARRISON AVE.

FARMERS MARKET

OLYMPIA TRANSIT STATION STATE AVE.

4th AVE.

4th AVE. W

5th AVE.

LEGION WAY

DESCHUTES PARKWAY

WASHINGTON CENTER FOR PERFORMING ARTS

FISHBOWL PUB

7th AVE.

8th AVE.

CAPITOL LAKE PARK

RAMADA INN

OLD STATE CAPITOL

ADAMS ST.

SYLVESTER PARK

GREYHOUND

8th AVE.

CHAMBER OF COMMERCE

GOLDEN GAVEL MOTOR HOTEL

9th AVE.

POST OFFICE

PLUM ST.

YASHIRO JAPANESE GARDEN

BEST WESTERN ALADDIN

10th AVE.

EASTSIDE ST.

OLYMPIA

NATURAL RESOURCES BUILDING

UNION AVE.

CAPITOL CONSERVATORY

11th AVE.

CARRIAGE INN MOTEL

MARATHON PARK

TEMPLE OF JUSTICE

JEFFERSON ST.

12th AVE.

TIVOLI FOUNTAIN

LEGISLATIVE BUILDING

GOVERNOR'S MANSION

14th

TUNNEL

PUBLIC INFORMATION CENTER

EXIT 105

TO LACEY AND TACOMA

STATE LIBRARY

WATER ST.

CAPITOL WAY

HENDERSON BLVD.

EXIT 105

CAPITOL LAKE

LAKERIDGE DR.

21st AVE.

OLYMPIA WATERSHED TRAIL PARK

THURSTON COUNTY COURTHOUSE

STATE CAPITOL MUSEUM

HOLIDAY INN SELECT

101

CAPITOL LAKE INTERPRETIVE CENTER

DESCHUTES

EXIT 104

TUMWATER HISTORICAL PARK

EXIT 103

CROSBY HOUSE

HENDERSON HOUSE MUSEUM

CAPITOL BLVD.

OLYMPIA AND TUMWATER

S. 2nd AVE.

DESCHUTES RIVER

CUSTER WAY

NORTH ST.

TUMWATER

OLYMPIA BREWERY

CLEVELAND AVE.

TO CENTRALIA AND VANCOUVER

TUMWATER FALLS PARK

5

0   0.5 mi

0   0.5 km

© MOON PUBLICATIONS, INC.

ing and the omission of the date, the bill was ruled unconstitutional. (This faulty document is on display at the Washington State Capital Museum.) It wasn't until 1890 that Olympia was finally officially named Washington's state capital.

CAPITOL CAMPUS SIGHTS

Clearly the highlight of the city—and one of the most visited attractions in the state—the landscaped grounds and majestic buildings of Olympia's Capitol Campus make it one of the country's most beautiful state capitals. Located between 11th and 14th Avenues off Capitol Way, the campus consists of 55 acres of greenery, including an arboretum, a sunken rose garden, and an abundance of rhododendrons and cherry blossoms; a replica of Denmark's Tivoli fountain, memorials to veterans from the various wars (WW I, WW II, Korea, and Vietnam); and a number of historical buildings dating back to the early 1900s. Come here in the spring to see the Japanese cherry trees in full bloom.

The best place to start is the **Public Information Center,** tel. (360) 586-3460; open daily 8 a.m.-5 p.m. from Memorial Day to Labor Day, and Mon.-Fri. 8 a.m.-5 p.m. the rest of the year. Here you can get maps of the campus, brochures, post cards, made-in-Washington crafts, and tour information, plus a metered parking space. All of the on-street parking is leased, so either park in one of the visitor lots or follow the signs from I-5 exit 105A to the free shuttle bus.

Legislative Building

The imposing Legislative Building (the Capitol) is hard to miss: its 287-foot dome was completed in 1928, and it is still the fifth-largest masonry domed building in the world. It shows a strong resemblance to the U.S. Capitol. This is the third state capitol building. The first—a simple log structure—stood on this site until 1903, when the Thurston County Courthouse was purchased to replace it. Construction on the present building began in 1921, but it took seven more years to gain adequate funding for completion. The central rotunda is the focal point, with a 25-foot-long Tiffany chandelier suspended overhead (this was the last major piece created by Comfort

the Legislative Building

Tiffany), enormous bronze doors, busts of George Washington and Martin Luther King Jr., Belgian marble steps, and gargoyle-capped draperies. Enter the Senate and House of Representatives gallery chambers from the fourth floor. Come here between early January and early March on even-numbered years, or early January to mid-April on odd-numbered years to see the legislators in session. The capitol is open daily, with free 45-minute tours departing hourly from 10 a.m. to 3 p.m. most of the year.

Governor's Mansion

The Georgian-style red brick Governor's Mansion is the oldest building on the campus, dating back to 1908. Inside is a fine collection of antique furniture, including pieces by Duncan Phyfe. Free tours are given Wednesday 1-2:45 p.m. by appointment only; call (360) 586-8687.

Greenhouse

One of the most popular tourist stops is the **Capitol Conservatory,** open daily 8 a.m.-3 p.m. from Memorial Day to Labor Day, and Mon.-Fri.

A GILBERT AND SULLIVAN PLOT

During Olympia's earliest days as State Capitol, an incident occurred that today sounds like it could have been written by Gilbert and Sullivan. The story's rivals were Territorial Governor Isaac Ingalls Stevens, a bantam-sized military man and the territory's first governor, and territory Chief Justice Edward Lander, a judge every bit as stubborn as Stevens.

The incident occurred during the winter of 1855-56, the so-called "blockhouse winter," when Indian attacks made life dangerous for white Washingtonians. Little is known about Judge Lander and his career, except that a street was named for him in Seattle. Much is known about Governor Stevens, whose strident manner made him a lightning rod for trouble.

A New Englander, Stevens was both brilliant and very small—some speculate that he suffered from a form of dwarfism. He built up an impressive résumé before he arrived in the wilderness. A West Point graduate, he fought in the Mexican War, was assigned to the U.S. Coast Survey, and, because he had served well under General Franklin Pierce in Mexico, was one of several to receive political spoils. He was named governor of the newly created Washington Territory, Superintendent of Indian Affairs, and commander of the Northern Pacific Railroad Survey.

None of his jobs was simple and Stevens wasn't the most patient of men. He wanted everything done immediately, and his methods of rounding up Indian chiefs and getting them to sign treaties were akin to those of a modern aluminum-siding salesman. Though basically honest and free of scandal, Stevens had a tendency to act brashly.

When a series of Indian attacks suspiciously left a number of British settlers unscathed, Stevens ordered them into the blockhouses with the other settlers. When the British settlers refused, Stevens declared martial law in the county and had them arrested.

Lawyers immediately attempted to get them released under writ of habeas corpus. The presiding judge of Pierce County was ill, thus the case fell to Edward Lander, who was also commander of a militia company in Seattle. Without permission from Stevens, his commanding officer, Lander left his post for Steilacoom to free the Englishmen.

Lander opened civil court in defiance of Stevens' martial law proclamation. Stevens reacted quickly, sending a detachment of soldiers to arrest Lander for being AWOL. Once in custody, the judge and his court clerks were taken to Olympia in Thurston County, home to Lander's proper courtroom. Stevens released Lander so he could open his regular court term, but, taking no chances on a legal glitch, he declared Thurston County under martial law, too.

When his court came to order, Lander immediately, perhaps gleefully, ordered the arrest of Governor Stevens for contempt of court, sending a U.S. marshall to arrest him. But when the marshall met Stevens face to face, he looked down at the brilliant and determined man and returned to Olympia empty-handed.

The incident made Stevens even more furious. He sent a force of militia into Olympia after Lander. When Lander heard they were coming he adjourned court and ran for cover. The militia kicked down the door to one of his friends' law offices, found Lander hiding there, and placed him under arrest. He was taken to Fort Montgomery nearby and held in "honorable custody" until Stevens released him to return to the bench.

Angry and stubborn, Lander continued his case against the governor for contempt of court. Tired of the whole affair, Stevens agreed to appear in court with counsel, and Lander fined him $50.

Everyone thought the case was closed. Lander stayed out of the limelight, and Stevens was later killed in the second battle of Chantilly in the Civil War. Just after the turn of the century, however, an astute clerk rummaging through old records in Olympia found a remarkable document signed by Stevens and dated a short time after he was fined. It stated that Isaac I. Stevens, as governor, had pardoned Isaac I. Stevens, convicted of contempt of court.

---

8 a.m.-3 p.m. the rest of the year. Inside are 500 varieties of tropical and desert plants, along with seasonal displays of flowers.

State Library and Supreme Court

In addition to state and federal publications, the **State Library** on the south side of the Capitol, houses a collection of murals, mosaics, paintings, and sculpture by Northwest artists. It's a nice place to sit inside on a rainy day (a common occurrence in Olympia).

The **Temple of Justice** is not a sequel to

Indiana Jones and the Temple of Doom, though it may mean doom for certain individuals. Instead, this is where the State Supreme Court meets. Open Mon.-Fri. 8 a.m.-5 p.m. year-round. Also inside is the Washington State Law Library.

Other State Buildings

A few blocks off the campus at 211 W. 21st Ave., the **Washington State Capital Museum,** tel. (360) 753-2580, houses permanent exhibits that include a marvelous collection of Indian baskets, and a hands-on Indian house with smoked salmon hanging from overhead racks. Lots more on the political and cultural history of Washington, including pioneer settlements and the early history of Northwest publishing, plus rotating exhibits, lectures, and programs. The building itself is historical, built in 1920 as a 32-room California mission-style mansion for banker C.J. Lord. After his death, it was deeded to the state as a museum. Open Tues.-Fri. 10 a.m.-4 p.m., and Sat.-Sun. noon-4 p.m. year-round.

Also off campus, at Legion Way and Franklin St., the **Old State Capitol Building,** tel. (360) 753-6740, was constructed in 1891 as the Thurston County Courthouse and served as the state capitol from 1903 until the completion of the current Legislative Building in 1928. Today the flamboyant turreted building—complete with gargoyles—is on the National Register of Historic Places and houses the State Department of Public Instruction. The Old Capitol is open Mon.-Fri. 8 a.m.-5 p.m. and has historical exhibits in the hallways; group tours are only available by appointment.

OTHER SIGHTS

Historical Tours

Pick up self-guided tour brochures describing Olympia's historic downtown, Bigelow, South Capitol, and Westside neighborhoods from the chamber of commerce office at 1000 Plum St., tel. (360) 357-3362. The gingerbread-decorated **Bigelow House** located on Glass Ave. just off East Bay Dr. overlooks Budd Inlet and is one of the oldest frame buildings in Washington. It was built in 1854 by Daniel and Ann Bigelow and is still owned by their descendants.

Zabel's Rhododendrons

Washington's state flower is displayed in force at this four-acre park, where 1,200 rhodies and azaleas are yours to behold on an hour-long, self-guided tour from early May through Memorial Day. This is private property, so pets and picnicking are not allowed. To get there, go east on San Francisco Ave. from E. Bay Dr., then go north on N. Bethel St. and follow the signs to 2432 N. Bethel Street.

Evergreen State College

Olympia is home to Evergreen State College, a liberal arts institution with a beautiful campus and a reputation for eclecticism. This alternative school was founded in the 1960s; the mascot is the geoduck clam. Even the commencement ceremonies (Super Saturday) are offbeat.

Olympia Oysters

These tiny and sweet-tasting oysters—approximately the size of a silver dollar—were found at one time all the way from San Francisco Bay to Alaska, but overfishing, pollution, and parasites blighted the population. Today, Olympia oysters survive only in the southernmost reaches of Puget Sound in beds within Big Skookum, Little Skookum, Oyster, and Mud bays. In the mid-1920s the average annual harvest peaked at about 48,000 bushels, but it went into a tailspin due to overharvesting and toxic wastewater from a Shelton pulp mill. The oyster population dwindled still further in the 1930s, when the importation of Japanese oysters began. These oysters brought with them two pests: the Japanese oyster drill and the Japanese flatworm, harmful only to smaller oysters like the Olympia. Although the pulp mill closed in 1957, it has taken 40 years for the water quality to improve enough to support the oysters again. Biologists are optimistic now that within a few years the southern Puget Sound population will be approaching their original levels

Olympia oysters are bisexual in the truest sense, performing as males in the spring when they release a large quantity of sperm into the water, then changing into females and producing up to 300,000 eggs, which become fertilized as the oyster takes in the sperm it had previously expelled.

To see how Olympia oysters are raised, visit the largest and oldest producer (in business since 1876), **Olympia Oyster Co.**, .S.E. 1042 Bloomfield Rd., tel. (360) 426-3354. The plant is located halfway between Olympia and Shelton along Totten Inlet. Olympia oysters are available locally from Budd Bay Cafe, Genoas on the Bay, and Falls Terrace Restaurant.

For the Kids
Olympia's **Hands On Children's Museum,** 108 Franklin NE, tel. (360) 956-0818, has kids exhibits and is a fun space for play and exploration. Open Tues.-Sat. 10 a.m.-5 p.m. year-round; $2.50 per person.

PARKS AND RECREATION

Parks
Located at the north end of Capitol Lake at 5th Ave. and Water St., **Capitol Lake Park** offers cherry blossoms in April, the Lakefair festival in July and swimming, sunbathing, sailing, hiking, biking, and picnicking the rest of the year. It also makes a fine reflecting pool for the Legislative Building. Each fall, the Capitol Lake fish ladder is used by thousands of king salmon returning home to spawn in the Deschutes River.

Downtown at 7th Ave. and Capitol Way, **Sylvester Park**—named for city founder Edmund Sylvester—hosts concerts in the gazebo in July and August on Friday at noon, and Wednesday evenings. Directly behind the park is the Old Capitol Building (described above).

The **Yashiro Japanese Garden** is directly behind the chamber of commerce building on Plum St. near Union Ave., tel. (360) 753-8380. Built in cooperation with Olympia's sister city of Yashiro, Japan, this small and peaceful park has a main gate built without nails, a garden lantern of cut granite, a bamboo grove, and an 18-foot pagoda. The central feature is a pond and waterfall. Open daily 10 a.m. to dusk; no charge.

Percival Landing Tower sits at the north end of a 1.5-mile shoreline boardwalk along Budd Inlet. Climb the tower (open daylight hours only) for a panoramic view of the yacht-filled harbor with the Capitol behind, the Olympic Mountains, and freighters loading logs for Asian markets.

Located a mere mile and a half north of downtown Olympia on East Bay Dr., **Priest Point Park** has 253 wooded acres that include pic-

nic areas, a wading pool, and a playground, plus access to Budd Inlet, and excellent trails—including a fine three-mile loop that circles Ellis Cove. No overnight camping. Located on Henderson Blvd., the main attraction of **Olympia Watershed Park** is its two-mile hiking trail through woods, marsh, and streams.

Six miles north of Olympia on Boston Harbor Rd., **Burfoot County Park** has an interpretive trail, hiking trails, a saltwater beach, a playground, and an open, grassy picnic area.

A six-mile cycling and walking trail leads from Martin Way in town north to Woodard Bay along an old railroad track. Eventually this will continue south six more miles to Offutt Lake. At Woodard Bay, the Dept. of Natural Resources has purchased 190 acres of land, managed as the **Woodard Bay Natural Resources Area.**

Recreation
Follow Capitol Blvd. south to the **Trails Arena** at 7824 Trails End Dr. SE (technically in Tumwater), where horse shows of various types are held several times a week, as well as an occasional circus and BMX race. Entry to the lower arena is generally free.

The Horse Ranch in the town of Roy (25 miles east of Olympia), has horseback rides on a 120-acre ranch. Call (360) 458-7074 for details.

Local public pools can be found at the campus recreation center at **Evergreen State College,** tel. (360) 866-6000; **Tanglewilde Pool,** 414 Wildcat SE, tel. (360) 491-3907 (summers only); and the **YMCA,** 510 Franklin St. SE, tel. (360) 357-6609.

Motocross fans and four-wheelers may want to try out the 150-acre **ORV Sports Park,** located 16 miles west of Olympia off Hwy. 8, tel. (360) 495-3243. Camping sites and showers are also available here.

ACCOMMODATIONS AND CAMPING

See "Olympia, Tumwater, and Lacey Accommodations" for a complete listing of local lodging choices. Perched atop the hill on Evergreen Park Dr., the **Holiday Inn Select,** tel. (360) 943-4000 or (800) 551-8500, has the city's best viewpoint, taking in the Capitol Dome, Capitol Lake, and the Cascades.

Bed and Breakfasts

For cozy and reasonably priced accommodations, **Cinnamon Rabbit B&B,** tel. (360) 357-5520, is an older home on the west side of town with a hot tub, piano, and cats. **Puget View Guesthouse,** tel. (360) 459-1676, is a romantic cottage just 500 feet from the entrance to Tolmie State Park, with views across Puget Sound. Guests can borrow a canoe to explore the peaceful Nisqually Reach. Overnight anchorage is available for boaters.

Built in 1910, **Harbinger Inn B&B,** tel. (360) 754-0389, is a classy three-story mansion facing Budd Inlet with wide balconies, a hidden tunnel to the street, an artesian-fed waterfall, and antique furnishings. Guests can borrow a bike to explore the area.

Britt's Place B&B, tel. (360) 264-2764, southwest of Olympia near Wolf Haven, has a hot tub, floating dock, and a canoe to paddle around Offutt Lake.

Campgrounds

The closest public camping can be found at **Millersylvania State Park,** 12 miles south of Olympia, off I-5 (exit 95). Tent ($10) and RV

OLYMPIA, TUMWATER, AND LACEY ACCOMMODATIONS

Accommodations are arranged from least to most expensive. Rates may be lower in the winter months. The area code is 360.

BED AND BREAKFASTS

7C's Guest Ranch; 11123 128th St. SE, Olympia, tel. 446-7957; $35 s, $45 d ($100 d in honeymoon suite); six guest rooms in ranch house, shared or private baths, full breakfast, hot tub in gazebo, kids welcome

Cinnamon Rabbit B&B; 1304 7th Ave. SW, Olympia; tel. 357-5520 $52 s, $57 d; comfortable older home in quiet neighborhood, hot tub, piano, one guest room, private bath, full breakfast, kids welcome

Harbinger Inn B&B; 1136 E. Bay Dr., Olympia; tel. 754-0389; $55-85 s, $60-100 d; 1910 mansion along Budd Inlet, four guest rooms, shared or private baths, antique furnishings, continental breakfast, bikes, no kids under 12, AAA approved

Britt's Place B&B; 4301 Waldrick Rd. SE, Olympia; tel. 264-2764; $75 s or d; contemporary home on Offutt Lake, hot tub, antiques, one unit, private bath, floating dock, canoe, full breakfast

Puget View Guesthouse; 7924 61st Ave. NE, Olympia; tel. 459-1676; $79 s, $89 d; quiet waterside cottage, light breakfast, canoe, kids okay

MOTELS AND HOTELS

Holly Motel; 2816 Martin Way, Olympia; tel. 943-3000; $27 s, $31 d

Ranchotel Motel; 8819 Martin Way E., Olympia; tel. 491-5410; $30 s, $35 d

Motel 6; 400 W. Lee St., Tumwater; tel. 754-7320 or (800) 466-8356; $32 s, $38 d; outdoor pool

Bailey Motor Inn; 333 Martin Way, Olympia; tel. 491-7515; $34 s, $40 d; local calls 25 cents

Shalimar Suites; 5895 Capitol Blvd. S, Tumwater; tel. 943-8391; $36-48 s or d; studios, one- and two-bedroom suites, kitchens, four-night minimum stay, weekly and monthly rates

Golden Gavel Motor Hotel; 909 Capitol Way, Olympia; tel. 352-8533; $41 s, $44 d; AAA approved

Carriage Inn Motel; 1211 S. Quince, Olympia; tel. 943-4710; $46 s, $51 d; outdoor pool, continental breakfast, AAA approved

(continues on next page)

OLYMPIA, TUMWATER, AND LACEY ACCOMMODATIONS

(continued)

Capital Inn Motel; 120 College SE, Lacey; tel. 493-1991 or (800) 282-7028; $48-56 s, $51-66 d; sauna, exercise room, kitchenettes available, free continental breakfast, AAA approved

Super 8 Motel; 4615 Martin Way, Lacey; tel. 459-8888 or (800) 800-8000; $49 s, $53 d; indoor pool

Comfort Inn; 4700 Park Center Ave. NE, Lacey; tel. 456-6300 or (800) 221-2222; $55-75 s, $60-85 d; indoor pool, jacuzzi, exercise room, continental breakfast, AAA approved

Best Western Tumwater Inn; 5188 Capitol Blvd., Tumwater; tel. 956-1235 or (800) 528-1234; $58 s, $62 d; sauna, jacuzzi, exercise room, kitchenettes available, free continental breakfast, local calls 25 cents, AAA approved

Best Western Aladdin Hotel; 900 Capitol Way, Olympia; tel. 352-7200 or (800) 367-7771; $60-70 s, $65-75 d; outdoor pool, AAA approved

Ramada Inn Governor House Hotel; 621 S. Capitol Way; tel. 352-7700 or (800) 228-2828; $67-77 s, $75-88 d; eight-story hotel overlooking Sylvester Park and Capitol Lake, outdoor pool, jacuzzi, sauna, exercise room, kitchenettes available, AAA approved

Tyee Hotel; 500 Tyee Dr., Tumwater; tel. 352-0511 or (800) 386-8933; $71 s, $75 d; outdoor pool, tennis court, AAA approved

Holiday Inn Select; 2300 Evergreen Park Dr., Olympia; tel. 943-4000 or (800) 551-8500; $89 s or d; hilltop hotel with views of the capitol and Cascades, outdoor pool, jacuzzi, volleyball court, AAA approved

---

($15) sites are available year-round. Call (360) 753-1519 for details, or (800) 452-5687 for campsite reservations ($6 extra fee), available up to 11 months ahead of time. **Capitol Forest,** approximately 20 miles southwest of Olympia, has an abundance of primitive campsites (free; no water). Call the Dept. of Natural Resources at (360) 902-1234, or (800) 527-3305 in Washington, for details and a map. Showers are available at East Bay Marina in Olympia.

Olympia has an abundance of RV parks, including several just a few miles from the center of town. These include: **Black Lake RV Park,** 4325 Black Lake-Belmore Rd. SW, tel. (360) 357-6775; **Alderbrook Estates,** 2110 54th Ave., tel. (360) 357-9448; **American Heritage Campground,** 9610 Kimmie St. SW, tel. (360) 943-8778; **The Coach Post,** 3633 7th Ave. SW, tel. (360) 754-7580; **Columbus Park,** 5700 Black Lake Blvd., tel. (360) 786-9460; **Deep Lake Resort,** 12405 Tilley Rd. S, tel. (360) 352-7388; **Lakeside RV Park and Campground,** 7225 14th Ave. SE, Lacey, tel. (360) 491-3660; **Olympia Campground,** 1441 83rd Ave. SW,

tel. (360) 352-2551 or (800) 943-8778; **Riverbend Campground,** 1152 Durgin Rd. SE, tel. (360) 491-2534; and **Salmon Shores Resort,** 5446 Black Lake Blvd., tel. (360) 357-8618.

FOOD AND DRINK

Olympia is an eating-out town, with restaurants, cafes, and coffeehouses filling the downtown core. If you happen to be on the Capitol grounds at lunchtime, head to the basement of the Legislative Building for cheap eats in the cafeteria.

Breakfast and Lunch

For an all-natural breakfast, lunch, or dinner, try the **Urban Onion** at the corner of Legion and Washington, tel. (360) 943-9242. Their wholesome cuisine, which consists of salads, soups, sandwiches, Mexican meals, and vegetarian specials, is served daily 7 a.m.-midnight. No smoking. Try the open-face shrimp and cheese haystacks at lunch, or the *huevos rancheros* for breakfast.

More healthy food at **J-Vee Health Foods & Cafe,** a longtime natural foods store at 3720 Pacific Ave. SE, tel. (360) 491-1930.

Chattery Down, a little downtown eatery at 209 5th Ave. E, tel. (360) 352-9301, is popular for lunch, and their tasty appetizers make a fine light dinner.

Coffeehouses and Bakeries
Olympia has discovered espresso in a big way, and it's hard to find any cafe that doesn't have an espresso machine. **Batdorf and Bronson Roaster,** 513 Capitol Way S, tel. (360) 786-6717, sells teas and freshly roasted-on-the-premises coffee beans. A bit more on the counterculture side is **Asterisk and Cheese Library,** at Westside Center, tel. (360) 357-7573. **Carnagie's Cafe** is located inside the old Carnagie library at 620 Franklin St., tel. (360) 357-5550, and features light lunches, espresso, and books.

Get fresh bagels from **Otto's Bagels,** 111 Washington NE, tel. (360) 352-8640, located just a few doors down from **Dancing Goats Espresso Co.,** 124 4th Ave. E, tel. (360) 754-8187, a relaxed place to meet the hip Olympia set over a tempting dessert. Their shop is a favorite of the college crowd; it's the sort of place where you can read a book for two hours and nobody cares.

Get some of the best pastries in southern Puget Sound at **Wagner's European Bakery & Cafe,** 1013 Capitol Way S, tel. (360) 357-7268, where they also serve soups, salads, and sandwiches for lunch, as well as light breakfasts. Be prepared for a line of state workers on a weekday lunch. **Dakota's Coffeehouse,** 1018 Capitol Way S, tel. (360) 705-4886, also makes good sandwiches using their home-baked breads.

Especially Yogurt, 101 Capitol Way N, tel. (360) 754-6480, is a favorite of kids. In addition to frozen yogurt, they have salads and pizza by the slice.

San Francisco St. Bakery, 1320 San Francisco St. NE, tel. (360) 753-8553, bakes wonderful earthy breads (using organic grains), plus pastries and bagels.

On the Water
Waterfront and view restaurants aren't as common in Olympia as in other Puget Sound cities, but they also exist. **The Whale's Tale,** on Percival Landing dock at 501 N. Columbia St., tel. (360) 956-1928, has light breakfasts and lunches (including soup in a breadbowl), along with espresso, ice cream, and Italian sodas.

Genoas on the Bay, 1525 Washington St. NE, tel. (360) 943-7770, is an elegant steak, chicken, pasta, and seafood restaurant overlooking Budd Bay. They also have a Sunday champagne brunch. Located in a gorgeous Victorian home at 1205 W. Bay Dr., **Seven Gables Restaurant,** looks across Budd Bay to the Olympic Mountains. The food is equally attractive, with an emphasis on fresh seafood with a Northwest twist.

Budd Bay Cafe at Percival Landing, 525 Columbia St. NW, tel. (360) 357-6963, is open for lunch and dinner daily and has a very popular Sunday brunch buffet, with outdoor dining in summer featuring a marina view. This and Genoas are good places to sample the famous Olympia oysters on the half shell.

American and Seafood
Get Olympia oysters, geoduck clams, and other perfectly prepared seafood at **Gardner's Seafood and Pasta,** 111 W. Thurston St., tel. (360) 786-8466.

Spar Cafe & Bar, 114 4th Ave. E, tel. (360) 357-6444, is a family place serving solid all-American breakfasts, lunches, and dinners. In business since the 1930s, the Spar is now on the National Register of Historic Places, and has a decor to match: classic Northwest logging photos line the walls.

Ben Moore's Restaurant, 112 W. 4th Ave., tel. (360) 357-7527, serves reasonably priced Northwest seasonal dishes, along with steaks, oysters, and prawns. Also try **Bristol House,** 2401 B Bristol Court, tel. (360) 352-9494, for great steaks and seafood.

International
Meet legislators and lobbyists on expense accounts at **La Petite Maison,** 2005 Ascension Ave. NW, tel. (360) 943-8812, a France-meets-Northwest restaurant with an emphasis on seafood and game.

Saigon Rendez-Vous, 117 5th Ave. W, tel. (360) 352-1989, is one of the best Asian restaurants, with Vietnamese and Chinese menus, and vegetarian specialties. **China Town Restaurant,** 213 E. 4th Ave., tel. (360) 357-7292, is a very popular Chinese restaurant with happy hour specials Mon.-Fri. 4-6 p.m. Get quick and reasonable meals at either location of **Happy Teriyaki:** downtown at 530 Capitol Way S, tel. (360) 705-8000, and over in West Olympia at 2915 Harrison Ave. NW, tel. (360) 786-8866. Good Thai restaurants include **Thai Garden Restaurant,** 270 Capitol Mall, tel. (360) 786-1959, and **Thai Dish Restaurant,** 2010 Black Lake Blvd., tel. (360) 352-3484.

For Mexican meals, head to **La Palma Restaurant,** 523 S. Sound Center, tel. (360) 459-9805, with a big menu with all the favorites, including fajitas and seafood dishes.

Pizza and Italian

The wood-fired brick oven at **Levity Cafe,** 430 Legion Way SE, tel. (360) 357-7446, bakes the best pizzas in Olympia, hands-down. Also on the menu are pastas, seafood, and sandwiches, and you can take your order next door to Fishbowl Pub, where the beer is as good as Levity's pizza. Thumbs up. Another place with distinctive pizzas is **Jo Mamas,** 120 Pear St. NE, tel. (360) 943-9849, where the atmosphere is funky and the pizzas are thick whole-wheat-crust versions with healthy toppings.

Good Italian restaurants in Olympia include **Pellegrino's Italian Gardens,** 7321 Martin Way SE, tel. (360) 923-2150, and **Casa Mia,** 716 Plum St., tel. (360) 459-0440.

Pubs

Fish Brewing Company, 515 Jefferson St. SE, tel. (360) 943-6480, offers a surprising contrast to Olympia's better known brew. Located downtown and right next door to the Levity Cafe (see above), this small brewery and pub (Fishbowl Pub) produces seven different beers, all with such fishy names as "Trout Stout" and "Fish Tale Ale." Get a pizza or sandwich from the cafe next door and

enjoy it in this friendly lounge-around place. Highly recommended.

Another fun and relaxed place is **Columbia Street Public House,** 200 W. 4th Ave., tel. (360) 943-5575, with a good range of pub grub for late-night dining, plus live music several nights a week.

Markets

Olympia's Farmers Market at 401 N. Capitol Way, tel. (360) 352-9096, is the second largest such market in the state (after Pike Place Market). In addition to the expected fresh fruits and veggies, you'll discover all sorts of handcrafted items, plants, meats and seafood, baked goods, and ethnic foods. The market has festivals throughout the summer, including: Cinco de Mayo in May, Strawberry Festival in June, the "Zucchini 500" in September, and Elfland in December. Open Thurs.-Sun. 10 a.m.-3 p.m. May-Oct., and Sat.-Sun. 10 a.m.-3 p.m. during April and November to mid-December.

For natural foods at other times, visit the **Olympia Food Co-op,** 921 Rogers NW, tel. (360) 754-7666, and 3111 Pacific Ave. SE, tel. (360) 956-3870. Get fresh-squeezed apple cider, U-bake apple pies, eggs, honey, and more at **Lattin's Country Cider Mill,** 9402 Rich Rd. SE, tel. (360) 491-7328. They are located just a short ways south of the Amtrak station in East Olympia.

ENTERTAINMENT AND THE ARTS

Nightlife

The **Columbia St. Public House,** 220 Columbia St., tel. (360) 943-5575, is known for its Saturday night jazz sessions. Also try **Thekla,** 116 E. 5th Ave., tel. (360) 352-1855, and **Studio 321,** 321 Jefferson St. SE, tel. (360) 754-3525.

Hannah's, at 123 5th Ave. SW, tel. (360) 357-9890, has live blues and alternative rock bands on Friday, and **The Slow Ride Pub,** 311 E. 4th Ave., has rock bands on weekends.

FISH BREWING CO.

Performing Arts

Olympia's **Washington Center for the Performing Arts** is a state-of-the-art facility with seating for 987 people, and hundreds of activities throughout the year—from ballet to rock concerts. Located at 512 Washington St. SE, tel. (360) 753-8586, featured performances (Oct.-April) include nationally renowned artists, along with many local groups. Both the **Olympia Symphony Orchestra,** tel. (360) 753-0074, and the **Masterworks Choral Ensemble,** tel. (360) 491-3305, perform at the Washington Center for the Performing Arts. See "Events," below, for other artistic activities.

Capitol Playhouse '24, located in the historic Capitol Theatre at 206 E. 5th Ave., tel. (360) 754-5378, produces plays from December to May as well as a summer Shakespeare Festival, consisting of three plays, from June through August. The Capitol Theater also hosts a film festival in November. The **Olympia Little Theater,** 1925 Miller Ave. NE, tel. (360) 786-9484, is the place for light comedies.

Galleries

Downtown Olympia has a number of art galleries and boutiques on 4th and 5th Avenues. The **Marianne Partlow Gallery** at 5th and Washington, tel. (360) 943-0055, is probably the most impressive, representing artists from the Northwest and beyond. Also of interest are **State of the Arts Gallery,** 500 Washington St., tel. (360) 705-0317; **Site Line Gallery,** at the corner of Jefferson and Legion, tel. (360) 943-9019; and **Artists' Co-Op Gallery,** 610 Columbia St. SW, tel. (360) 357-6920.

EVENTS

Artburst bursts on the scene with a week of downtown activity starting the third Friday in April; tel. (360) 753-8380. Included is **Art Walk** where local galleries are open, and artists take over downtown, painting and performing. A second Art Walk occurs in early October; call (360) 753-8380 for specifics. The **Wooden Boat Festival,** tel. (360) 357-3370, held in mid-May at Percival Landing, includes a regatta and wooden boats open for public viewing. The first Saturday in June, Evergreen State College's **Super Saturday** features hundreds of arts and crafts booths, food, and entertainment for all ages; phone (360) 866-6000, for information.

The city's biggest summer festival is **Lakefair,** held in mid-July, tel. (360) 943-7344. Activities include a twilight parade, carnival, food and craft vendors, and crowning of the Lakefair queen. From mid-July through August, Sylvester Park has **Music in the Park** and **Music in the Dark** events at noon on Wednesday and at 7 p.m. on Friday. Call (360) 943-2375 for details. In August, the **Shakespeare Festival/Renaissance Faire** at Sylvester Park brings out costumed performers of all types, and performances of Shakespeare's classics in the nearby Capitol Theater.

Summer's end brings the **Harbor Days Festival** to Percival Landing over Labor Day weekend, highlighted by a regatta and vintage tugboat races in the Sound; call (360) 754-4567 for information. At the same time, the city comes alive with the **Greater Olympia Dixieland Jazz Festival.** December means the **Parade of Lighted Ships,** put on by the Olympia Yacht Club; tel. (360) 357-6767.

SHOPPING

Given that this is a government/college town, you'd expect to find good bookstores in Olympia. Biggest is **Orca Books,** 509 4th Ave. E, tel. (360) 352-0123, open late most nights for browsers. **Going Places,** 515 Washington SE, tel. (360) 357-6860, has travel books, maps, and outdoor recreation guides. **Bulldog News,** 116 4th Ave. E, tel. (360) 357-6397, has a big choice of foreign magazines and newspapers.

Capital Mall, 9th Ave. SW and Black Lake Blvd., is the area's largest shopping center with nearly 100 shops and restaurants, including The Bon Marché, JCPenney, and Lamonts. Just up Black Lake Blvd. is another shopping plaza, Capital Village, with grocery, drug, and hardware stores plus a sprinkling of fast-food restaurants. **Shipwreck Beads,** 2727 Westmoor Court SW, tel. (360) 754-2323, claims to have the world's largest selection of beads for sale, numbering in the billions.

INFORMATION AND SERVICES

Information

For maps and general information stop by the **Olympia/Thurston County Chamber of Commerce,** 1000 Plum St., tel. (360) 357-3362 or (800) 753-8474. Open Mon.-Fri. 8:30 a.m.-5 p.m. all year. At the Capitol Campus, head to the **Public Information Center,** tel. (360) 586-3460; open daily 8 a.m.-5 p.m. from Memorial Day to Labor Day, and Mon.-Fri. 8 a.m.-5 p.m. the rest of the year. The headquarters office for **Olympic National Forest** is in Olympia at 1835 Black Lake Blvd. SW, tel. (360) 956-2300, or 956-2400 for recreation information.

The **area code** in and around Olympia is 360. (It becomes 206 just north of here in Fort Lewis.)

Hospitals

For medical emergencies, **St. Peter Hospital** has 24-hour emergency room service at 413 N. Lilly Rd., tel. (360) 456-7289. To get there, take exit 107 from I-5 northbound, exit 109 from I-5 southbound. **Black Hills Community Hospital** is near Capital Mall on Olympia's west side, tel. (360) 754-5858. For non-life-threatening emergencies, try **Westcare Clinic,** on the west side at 3000 Limited Lane NW, tel. (360) 357-9392.

TRANSPORTATION

Trains and Planes

Amtrak serves Olympia along its north-south **Coast Starlight** route from Seattle to Los Angeles and via its **Pioneer** route from Seattle to Salt Lake City. The Amtrak station is in east Olympia at 83rd and Rich Rd. Southeast. For schedule and fare information call (800) 872-7245. Amtrak offers great rates Mon.-Thurs.—a quick run down from Seattle is just $16 roundtrip.

There are no scheduled passenger flights to Olympia. To reach the capital city by air, you'll have to fly into Sea-Tac Airport and get ground transportation into the city. **Capital Aeroporter,** tel. (360) 754-7113, serves Olympia from Sea-Tac.

Getting Around by Bus

Intercity Transit serves Olympia, Tumwater, and most of Thurston County with daily service. The regular adult and youth fare is 50 cents, and day passes are $1. They operate two **free shuttles** that serve downtown and the Capitol Campus area weekdays 11 a.m.-2 p.m. For route and schedule information, call (360) 786-1881 or (800) 287-6348, or stop by the Olympia Transit Center on State St. between Franklin and Washington Streets.

Pierce Transit, tel. (206) 581-8000 or (800) 562-8109, offers an "Olympia Express" route from the Lakewood Park and Ride (south of Tacoma at I-5 exit 127) to the Capitol Campus. The one-way fare is $1.25. In Tacoma you can catch a Pierce Transit express bus to downtown Seattle.

Greyhound, tel. (800) 231-2222, and **Northwestern Trailways,** tel. (800) 366-3830, connect Olympia to Seattle, Tacoma, Portland, and other cities along its north-south I-5 corridor, with access to virtually anywhere in the country. The bus station is located at Capitol and 7th.

VICINITY OF OLYMPIA

LACEY AREA

A few miles northeast of Olympia right off I-5, the fast-growing city of Lacey (pop. 23,000) is primarily a suburban shopping area and retirement village. The area has been settled for well over a century, but Lacey was not incorporated until 1966. Just east and slightly north of Lacey proper is the Nisqually Delta, preserved wetlands geographically identical to Tacoma's industrial tideflat area.

Sights

The small **Lacey Historical Museum** is located at 827 Lacey St., tel. (360) 491-0857. The town is also home to **St. Martin's College,** founded in 1895 by Catholic Benedictine monks. Today the school has 1,000 students, and strong programs in education and engineering. Its basketball team is called—fittingly enough—the St. Martin's Saints.

Parks

Just off I-5 at exit 114, **Nisqually National Wildlife Refuge,** tel. (360) 753-9467, is a protected home for 300 species of wildlife, including great blue herons, bald eagles, and red-tailed hawks, as well as a resting area for over 20,000 migrating ducks and geese each spring and fall. This is one of the largest surviving estuaries in the state of Washington. Several trails, ranging from a half-mile interpretive trail to a six-mile hiking loop trail provide a chance to stretch your legs on portions of the 3,870-acre refuge, and photo blinds assist you in your birdwatching. Be sure to bring binoculars and a field guide! A boat-launch ramp is available at Luhr Beach, along with an environmental education center. Visitors are welcome at the refuge seven days a week during daylight hours; $2 per carload. No jogging, bicycling, motorbikes, pets, fires, or camping.

Managed by the Audubon Society, the **Nisqually Reach Nature Center,** 4949 D'Milluhr Rd. NE at Luhr Beach, tel. (360) 459-0387, has marine animals and birds, a museum, fishing dock, boat launch, picnic area, guided tours, and raft trips. Open Wed.-Sat. noon-4 p.m.; no charge.

Tolmie State Park, five miles from exit 111, has 1,800 feet of waterfront on Nisqually Reach with swimming, fishing, 3.5 miles of hiking trails, and an underwater park with an artificial reef created by the intentional sinking of three wooden barges. Open for day use only (no camping), the park also provides an outdoor shower for swimmers and divers near the lower restroom. The park was named for Dr. William Frazer Tolmie, who spent 16 years at Fort Nisqually as physician, surgeon, botanist, and fur trader for Hudson's Bay Company. Tolmie also studied the languages of the Northwest people—his communication skills proved invaluable during negotiations during the Indian Wars of 1855-56.

Accommodations and Food

See the chart "Olympia, Tumwater, and Lacey Accommodations" for a complete listing of local lodging choices.

Meconi's Italian Subs, 5225 Lacey Blvd. SE, tel. (360) 459-0213, is the best and most authentic sub shop in the Olympia area—very popular with state workers. Good pizzas at **Brewery City Pizza,** 4354 Martin Way, tel. (360) 491-6630. Next door, **O'Blarney's Pub,** 4411 Martin Way, has Irish music on Tuesday. **La Palma II** has Mexican food and a lounge at 523 South Sound Center, tel. (360) 459-9805.

Fairs and Festivals

Lacey's **Music, Arts, and Dance Festival** (MADFEST) is held in late June or early July. The **Thurston County Fair,** held the first full weekend in August at the County Fairgrounds in Lacey, is a five-day festival with entertainment, food, and booths. Call (360) 786-5453 for hours and information. Lacey also features the **Northwest Hot Rod & Custom Car National** at the fairgrounds in late August, and the **Capital Food & Wine Festival** in late October, with food from local restaurants and wine from Washington wineries.

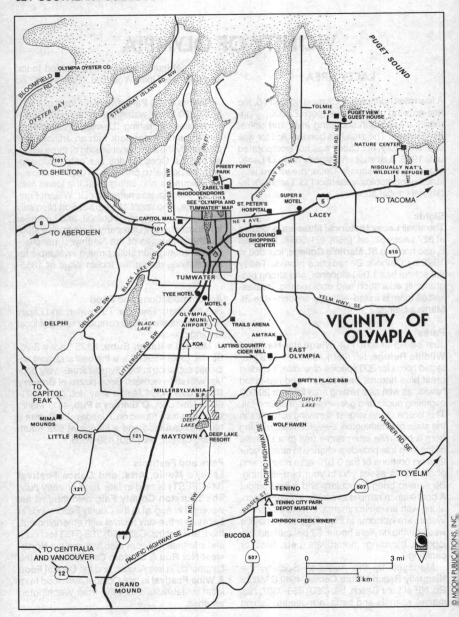

VICINITY OF OLYMPIA

TO SHELTON

TO ABERDEEN

TO TACOMA

PUGET SOUND

OLYMPIA OYSTER CO.

BLOOMFIELD RD. NW

OYSTER BAY

STEAMBOAT ISLAND RD. NW

BUDD INLET

COOPER RD. NW

PRIEST POINT PARK

ZABEL'S RHODODENDRONS

SEE "OLYMPIA AND TUMWATER" MAP

CAPITOL MALL

CAPITOL PEAK

SOUTH BAY RD. NE

MARVIN RD. NE

TOLMIE S.P.

PUGET VIEW GUEST HOUSE

NATURE CENTER

NISQUALLY NAT'L WILDLIFE REFUGE

ST. PETER'S HOSPITAL

SUPER 8 MOTEL

LACEY

NE 4 AVE.

SOUTH SOUND SHOPPING CENTER

YELM HWY. SE

TUMWATER

TYEE HOTEL

MOTEL 6

OLYMPIA MUNI. AIRPORT

KOA

TRAILS ARENA

LATTINS COUNTRY CIDER MILL

AMTRAK

EAST OLYMPIA

BRITT'S PLACE B&B

OFFUTT LAKE

WOLF HAVEN

DELPHI

BLACK LAKE BLVD. SW

DELPHI RD. SW

BLACK LAKE

LITTLEROCK RD. SW

MILLERSYLVANIA S.P.

DEEP LAKE

DEEP LAKE RESORT

MAYTOWN

MIMA MOUNDS

LITTLE ROCK

RAINIER RD. SE

PACIFIC HIGHWAY SE

TENINO

TO YELM

TENINO CITY PARK

DEPOT MUSEUM

JOHNSON CREEK WINERY

SUSSEX ST.

BUCODA

TILLY RD. SW

PACIFIC HIGHWAY SE

TO CENTRALIA AND VANCOUVER

GRAND MOUND

0   3 mi

0   3 km

© MOON PUBLICATIONS, INC.

Shopping

Just off I-5 at exit 108 is **South Sound Center,** an enclosed mall with over 100 shops and restaurants, including Sears, Mervyn's, and Nordstrom Place Two. **Olympia Square,** just off I-5 on both sides of Pacific Ave., has a Ross Dress for Less, Food Pavilion, and Sizzler's Restaurant. Enjoy one-stop shopping for warehouse-priced groceries, clothes, jewelry, and more at **Fred Meyer,** just off Sleater-Kinney Rd. across from South Sound Center.

Information and Services

The **Lacey Chamber of Commerce,** 7 South Sound Center, tel. (360) 491-4141. Lacey's telephone **area code** is 360.

Swim at **North Thurston High School,** 600 Sleater-Kinney Rd. NE, or **Timberline High School,** 6120 Mullen Rd. SE, tel. (360) 491-0857.

Transportation

Intercity Transit, tel. (360) 786-1881 or (800) 287-6348, has daily bus service in Olympia, Tumwater, and most of Thurston County. **Centralia-SeaTac Airport Express,** tel. (800) 773-9490, has direct shuttle service between Lacey and Sea-Tac Airport for $20 one-way. **Capital Aeroporter,** tel. (360) 754-7113, has a similar service.

FISH BREWING CO

FISH BREWING COMPANY
OLYMPIA, WASHINGTON

TUMWATER

The home of Olympia beer was Washington's first community—then named New Market—settled in 1845 along the Deschutes River at the end of one branch of the Oregon Trail. Starting at Independence, Missouri, the families in the Wagon Train of 1844 endured 19 months of cold, rain, and wearying travel through what's now Kansas, Nebraska, Wyoming, Idaho, and Oregon, en route to their final destination above Tumwater Falls. Members of Hudson's Bay Co., who had been stationed at Fort Nisqually since 1833, provided the settlers with the makings for

the first sawmill north of the Columbia and traded Army supplies for wood shingles. Tumwater is now home to 11,000 people and acts as both a suburb of Olympia and a small city in its own right.

Olympia Brewery

Heading down I-5 toward Tumwater, you can't miss the Olympia Brewery immediately adjacent to Tumwater Falls Park (see below) at exit 103. Olympia began as Capital Brewing Co., established in 1895 by a beer maker from Montana, Leopold F. Schmidt. Over the years, the company acquired Hamm's and Lone Star, before being taken over itself by Pabst Brewing Co. in 1982. The mergers continued, and Pabst was bought out by General Brewing Company. The sign out front still says Olympia Brewing Company, but they also make Pabst, Buckhorn, Hamm's, and Olde English malt liquor here.

This is the one of the most popular tourist attractions in Washington, especially in the summer when you need to arrive early to be assured of a place. Smaller crowds in the winter mean a more personalized (and often longer) visit. The fascinating and informative 45-minute free tours run daily (except Thanksgiving, Christmas, and New Year's) starting at 8 a.m., with the last tour departing around 4:15 p.m. They end at a bar where you can sample three Oly brews, and learn why room-temperature beer is preferable to cold beer and how to pour beers to get the most flavor. The real treat at Oly is their incredible collection of more than 250 antique beer steins, including one that holds 32 quarts, and a tankard made from elephant ivory that once belonged to President Theodore Roosevelt. A gift shop sells Oly paraphernalia.

Tumwater Historical Park

This city park is the site of the first American settlement in the Puget Sound region, founded in 1845. The neatly landscaped grounds include picnic areas, a boat launch into the Deschutes River, an exercise trail, and lots of hungry ducks. The **Henderson House Museum,** 602 Deschutes Way, tel. (360) 753-8583, has photographic exhibits depicting life along the Deschutes River during the late 1800s and recent photos of Tumwater's people and events; open Thurs.-Sun. noon-4 p.m. year-round.

The **Crosby House,** adjacent to Tumwater Historical Park at Deschutes Way and Grant St., tel. (360) 753-8583, is Tumwater's oldest home; it was built in 1860 by Bing Crosby's grandfather, Capt. Nathaniel Crosby III, who came around the Horn to the Oregon Territory in 1847 and inspired the whole Crosby clan to follow him out West. Open for tours Thursday 2-4 p.m., or by appointment.

Accommodations and Campgrounds
See the "Olympia, Tumwater, and Lacey Accommodations" chart for a complete listing of local lodging choices. See "Accommodations and Camping" in the Olympia chapter above for a listing of campgrounds and RV parks in the Tumwater area.

Food
In front of the Olympia Brewery and overlooking Tumwater Falls, **Falls Terrace Restaurant** has moderately priced dinners feature chicken, steak, seafood, veal, and traditional meals like pot roast and turkey dinners; a lower-priced early-bird menu is offered before the dinner crowds show up. They also offer a Sunday brunch. The lounge features an outside deck, a favorite place to drop by for a drink. Reservations are highly recommended.

The **Mason Jar,** 478 Cleveland Ave. SE, tel. (360) 754-7776, is a favorite Tumwater lunch spot with homemade soups, freshly baked breads, and sandwiches. Or have a **Brewery City Pizza** delivered free from 5150 Capitol Blvd., tel. (360) 754-6767. The best burgers in the Olympia area come from **Big Tom Drive Inn** at 303 Cleveland Ave. SE, tel. (360) 352-7711. Big Tom and his son Little Tom both work here.

Recreation
Swim at **Tumwater Valley Pool,** 4801 Tumwater Valley Dr. SE, tel. (360) 943-1040. Open to the public, the 18-hole **Tumwater Valley Golf Course,** 4611 Tumwater Valley Dr. SE, tel. (360) 943-9500, has a driving range, pro shop, and lessons.

On Deschutes Way, butting up against the brewery, you'll find **Tumwater Falls Park,** where you may see king salmon heading up the fish ladders late August through October. They spawn in nearby pens. Paths lead to the falls.

Events
The third weekend in May, the **Tumwater Bluegrass Festival** brings fiddlers and banjo-pickers to Tumwater High School on Israel Road. Bluegrass concerts run Fri.-Sun. with contests, booths, and Sunday morning gospel music. Call (360) 357-5153 for information. The **Fourth of July** means a fun parade at Southgate Shopping Center, followed by family events and evening fireworks.

Information and Services
Find the **Tumwater Area Chamber of Commerce** at 488 Tyee Dr. (next to the Tyee Hotel), tel. (360) 357-5153. Tumwater's telephone **area code** is 360.

Transportation
Intercity Transit, tel. (360) 786-1881 or (800) 287-6348, has daily bus service in Olympia, Tumwater, and most of Thurston County.

Centralia-SeaTac Airport Express, tel. (800) 773-9490, has direct shuttle service between Tumwater's Tyee Hotel and Sea-Tac Airport for $20 one-way. **Capital Aeroporter,** tel. (360) 754-7113, has a similar service.

TENINO AND YELM AREA

From downtown Olympia, follow Capitol Blvd. S onto Old Hwy. 99 to Tenino, a quiet old town with stone-fronted buildings lining the main street. These stones came from Tenino's sandstone quarry, now a popular swimming hole. The name Tenino (ten-NINE-oh) has a handful of possible origins, from the Indian name for a fork or junction, to the more colorful Engine Number 1090 (ten-nine-oh) that ran on the Kalama-Tacoma railroad line in the 1870s. Yelm is located 14 miles east of Tenino on Hwy. 507 and is perhaps best known as the place where "psychic channeler" J.Z. Knight considers herself the reincarnation of a 35,000-year-old warrior named Ramtha. You can't miss her ranch; the fence is topped with a string of copper pyramids.

LOUISE FOOTE

Wolf Haven

This 65-acre wolf refuge is home to wolves that were taken in for a variety of reasons; some were no longer needed by researchers, some were mistreated or unwanted by zoos and refuges, and others were family "pets" who grew predictably wild. These former misfits are now loved and wanted—even introduced to visitors by name. The sanctuary offers hourly guided tours and summertime "howl-ins," featuring a marshmallow roast, reciting of Eskimo and Indian folk legends, singing, and howling with the wolves, on Friday and Saturday 7-10 p.m. during the summer. Wolf Haven is at 3111 Offutt Lake Rd., north of Tenino just off Old Hwy. 99, tel. (360) 264-4695 or (800) 448-9563; open daily 10 a.m.-5 p.m. May-Sept., and Wed.-Sun. 10 a.m.-4 p.m. the rest of the year. Tours are $5 for adults, $2.50 for ages five to 12; howl-ins $6 for adults, $3 for ages five to 12.

Parks and Museums

One block off Sussex St., **Tenino City Park,** tel. (360) 264-4620, has overnight camping and picnic areas, plus the **Tenino Depot Museum,** 399 W. Park St., tel. (360) 264-4620, an original sandstone train station housing a collection of historical Tenino and southern Thurston County artifacts. Open Thurs.-Sun. 1-4 p.m.

Tenino's swimming pool is an abandoned sandstone quarry; open mid-June to early September; tel. (360) 264-2368.

Millersylvania State Park, 842-acres of forested land on the north shore of Deep Lake, is less than four miles off I-5 at exit 95. The park has impressive stone picnic shelters and bathhouses constructed between 1933 and 1939 by the Civilian Conservation Corps. Other facilities include two swimming beaches and an environmental learning center for school groups. Enjoy fishing for rainbow trout and boating (five mph speed limit) on Deep Lake. Campsites ($10) and RV sites ($15) are available, along with coin-operated showers. The campground is open year-round. Call (360) 753-1519 for details, or (800) 452-5687 for campsite reservations ($6 extra fee), available up to 11 months ahead of time.

Just south of the entrance to Millersylvania, **Deep Lake Resort,** 12405 Tilley Rd. S, tel. (360) 352-7388, has lakeside cabin rentals, camping, lake swimming, a playground, showers, laundry facilities, boating, and bike rentals on Deep Lake. Open late April-September.

Rochester and Oakville

Heading west from I-5, Hwy. 12 follows the winding Chehalis River through Christmas tree farms, second- and third-growth forests, and dairy farms. You'll meet a constant parade of logging trucks. The don't-blink-or-you'll-miss-it town of Rochester has a few businesses, and Oakville is home to antique shops in old frame buildings and a popular soda fountain. Just west of here is the entrance to Capitol Forest, managed by the Dept. of Natural Resources. Highway 12 joins Hwy. 8 at Elma (see under "Grays Harbor and Vicinity") and continues westward to Aberdeen and Grays Harbor. A big casino is planned on the **Chehalis Indian Reservation,** between Rochester and Oakville. The main summer event here is the **Black Hills Wranglers Rodeo.**

Mima Mounds

Eight miles south of Tumwater is the **Mima Mounds Interpretive Area,** tel.(360) 753-2449, a registered national landmark with nature walks, an interpretive center, and picnic area. These grass-covered mounds, ranging in height up to eight feet, are also scattered throughout southern Thurston County, parts of China, and Alaska. They're often referred to as "mysterious" because no one really knows how they got there; theoretical origins range from glaciers to giant gophers, although the latter is mainly from the same folks who brought you the "jackalope." Indians burned these areas to keep them open and productive, but today Douglas fir trees are gradually spreading across the hilly mounds.

Capitol Forest

From Mima Mounds continue north on Waddell Creek Rd. to Capitol Forest, a multiuse "working" forest (look out for logging trucks) in the Black Hills. The hills received their name when early Anglo settlers found the entire area had been charred by a forest fire. Free primitive campsites are available for tents and RVs at nine locations within the forest; many miles of hiking and horseback riding trails are clustered at the south end of the forest, while trailbikes may use those in the north end. The **McLane Creek Nature Trail** is a mile-long route that circles a beaver pond and meadow; call the Dept. of Natural Resources at (360) 902-1234, or (800) 527-3305 in Washington, for directions. To get a panoramic view of the area, follow the marked dirt road from Waddell Creek Rd. to 2,658-foot Capitol Peak, the highest point in the Black Hills.

Accommodations and Food

Stay at **Kay's Country Inn,** 20333 Old Hwy. 99 SW, in Rochester (west of I-5), tel. (360) 273-6361, where rooms go for $28-35 s or d. Kitchenettes are available. Also in Rochester is **Maharaja Cuisine of India,** 19712 Old Hwy. 99, tel. (360) 273-2442, with northern Indian dishes, including tandoor oven and vegetarian specialties.

Out in the country five miles south of Tenino is **Alice's Restaurant** and **Johnson Creek Winery.** The restaurant—located in a turn-of-the-century farmhouse—serves five-course country-style meals, with the vineyard just outside the door for wine tastings. Call (360) 264-2887 for reservations.

Out in Yelm, 14 miles east of Tenino on Hwy. 507, **Arnold's Country Inn,** tel. (360) 458-3977, is another noteworthy restaurant with American and Continental cuisine.

Events

The fourth weekend in July brings all kinds of commotion to quiet Tenino with the **Oregon Trail Days.** A parade, muzzle-loading camp, and kids' carnival highlight the fair. Then comes the **Blackberry Festival** in September, followed by **Winterfest in Historic Tenino** in early December, with wagon rides, living history demonstrations, a gingerbread house competition, a quilt contest, and 1880s arts and crafts.

Yelm Prairie Days in late July has food and craft booths, carnival rides, and games. And in October, return for the **Yelm Octoberfest** with German food, a beer garden, and kiddie rides.

Information and Transportation

The **Tenino Chamber of Commerce** is located at 208 Sussex Ave., tel. (360) 264-5075. The **area code** for this region is 360.

Intercity Transit, tel. (360) 287-6348 or (800) 287-6348, has Mon.-Sat. bus service to Tenino, Yelm, Rochester, Olympia, and most of Thurston County. Rent canoes ($35 all day) to float the peaceful Black River from **Black River Canoe Trips,** in Littlerock (west of I-5), tel. (360) 754-6190.

THE TWIN CITIES

Washington's "Twin Cities" of Centralia and Chehalis lie halfway between Seattle and Portland (about 85 miles each way) and are accessible from five different I-5 exits. The two small cities are four miles apart, but the route connecting them is lined with retail businesses as Centralia and Chehalis gradually grow together.

Because it is considerably larger, and because it has a more dramatic history, Centralia gets quite a bit more attention than Chehalis, even though the latter is the Lewis County seat. Centralia's population of more than 12,000 makes it nearly twice as big as Chehalis.

The economy of the Twin Cities depends primarily upon a mix of dairy farms, Christmas tree farms, logging, coal mining, power generation, and food processing, but it also has a strong retail focus with its antique malls and discount outlet shops.

CENTRALIA

Centralia is approximately 25 miles south of Olympia, and just east from busy I-5. The town has a rich and interesting history and is becoming a center for antiques in the region. Unfortunately, downtown is suffering somewhat, and many of the old buildings are boarded up.

History

Centralia is the only city in Washington founded by an African-American man. George Washington—born of a mulatto slave father and a white mother—was the slave of James C. Cochran, a Missourian who, in 1850, filed a claim on the land where Centralia now sits. Cochran set him free and adopted Washington as his son. It was illegal then for a black person to own property, so the claim rested in Cochran's name until the Washington Territory was created. (Its laws forbade slavery and placed no restrictions on ownership.)

Cochran returned the land to Washington, who insisted that Cochran take $3,200 for it. Then he platted a town, sold lots, built a home, and donated a parcel of land for the development of George Washington Park. Within 15 years, Washington had sold 2,000 lots, throwing in an extra one to anyone who built a house. He named the thriving town "Centerville." It wasn't long before the Post Office Department discovered there were two towns of the same name in the territory, so the name was changed to Centralia.

During the depression that followed the crash of 1893, Washington hauled supplies up from Portland for his neighbors, offered interest-free loans, found work for Centerville's residents, and saved the town from economic disaster. Though a respected businessman, not everyone liked him: someone once tried to kill him by putting carbolic acid in his wine. But Washington lived to be 88, when he died from being thrown from a buggy.

The "Wobbly War"

Centralia is the site of one of the state's most notorious lynchings. Others occurred from time to time, but none was so immortalized as that of Wesley Everest. The Marxist-oriented Industrial Workers of the World (IWW) strongly urged its members not to enlist when the U.S. declared war on Germany in WW I. Their stance drew fire from the L.A. Times and others, who claimed that IWW stood for "I won't work" and "I want whiskey." The IWW, or "Wobblies," wanted to abolish the wage structure and sometimes resorted to violent means. In September 1918, 100 Wobbly leaders were convicted of obstructing the war effort, and the Wobblies were finished as a major labor force.

American Legionnaires began attacking the IWW hiring halls throughout the West, and rumors had circulated for weeks that the Legionnaires planned an attack in Centralia; both sides were armed. On Armistice Day, 1919, the worst of the fighting began. An American Legion-led parade went past the union hall once, and those inside thought they had escaped. But then the parade turned around and started back. At this point, the stories clash. Supporters of the Legionnaires claimed they were fired upon from inside as they marched past peacefully. IWW members said they were simply defending them-

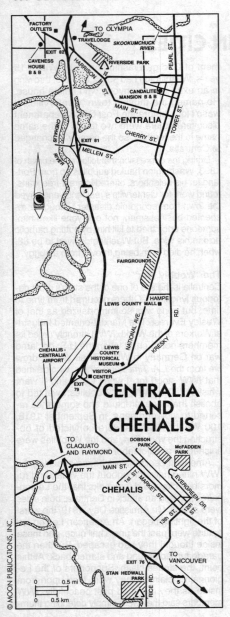

selves from an attack. In the melee that followed, four Legionnaires were shot and killed.

Wesley Everest, an IWW member, emptied his rifle magazine into the attacking Legionnaires and then ran out the back with the mob following. He had a pistol to keep them far enough behind, then ran to the river. He reached waist-deep water, then turned and fired to keep them from rushing him. He offered to surrender to a policeman, but none stepped forward. The mob attacked, dragged him from the river, and deposited him in the jail. That night, during a blackout, a mob rushed the jail, and the guard simply stood aside while they hauled Everest out. They took him to the Chehalis River bridge. After brutally castrating him, the mob hanged him from the bridge.

The coroner reported that Everest had broken out of jail and run to the Chehalis bridge, tied a rope around his neck, and jumped off. The rope was too short, the coroner said, so Everest used it to climb back up to the bridge to get a longer one. Then he jumped off again and broke his neck while shooting himself full of holes.

Only Wobblies were tried for the massacre that left four Legionnaires dead; no one was tried for Everest's lynching. Three witnesses who claimed the Legionnaires stormed the hall were arrested for perjury. A statue in Centralia's town square memorializes the four legionnaires slain, and the town still has an American Legion post, but you won't find a monument to Wesley Everest or the IWW. The case was not discussed by the community for decades, and nobody would give interviews about it. Even today it remains a source of bitterness, and only in the 1990s has the incident even been mentioned in the local historical museum.

Sights

Take exit 81 off I-5, then follow Mellen St. west for one-quarter mile to the Chehalis River bridge. On the streets that Mrs. George Washington named—Iron, Maple, Pearl, Silver, and First—you can still find elegant turn-of-the-century Victorian homes, though often not restored to their earlier splendor. Pick up a brochure that describes them at the museum in Chehalis. The Mellen St. Bridge was where Wesley Everest was hung in 1919. It's pretty hard to miss the **5 or Less Spot;** a bizarre and amusing collec-

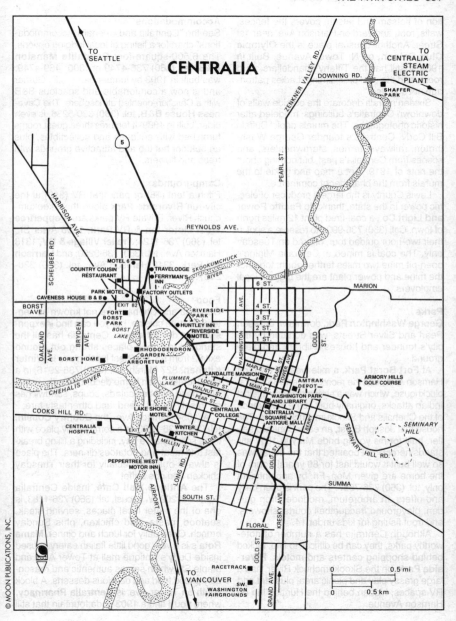

tion of flotsam and jetsam covers the fences, walls, roof, and yard on Harrison Ave. near 1st Street. Another unusual place is the **Olympic Club Saloon,** on N. Tower Avenue. Built in 1908, it still has the Tiffany chandeliers, card room, and the sign proclaiming "Ladies patronage not solicited."

Sixteen murals decorate the outside walls of downtown Centralia's buildings, modeled after historic photographs. The murals depict Buffalo Bill Cody, Centralia's founder George Washington, railways, ferries, sternwheelers, and scenes from Centralia's past, but nothing about the riots of 1919. Get a map and guide to the murals from the chamber of commerce.

Lewis County is the largest producer of electric power in the state, thanks to **Pacific Power and Light Co.,** a coal-fired plant 12 miles north of town. Call (360) 736-9901 to reserve a spot in their two-hour guided tour, offered on Tuesday only. The coal is mined at Centralia Mining's open-pit mine two miles farther north; together the mine and power plant are the biggest local employers.

Parks
George Washington Park, downtown between Pearl and Silver Streets, was donated by the city's founder and houses a library and playground.

At **Fort Borst Park,** a mile west of town off Harrison Ave., visit the reconstructed 1852 Borst blockhouse, which was a strong defense against Indian attacks, originally built at the confluence of the Chehalis and Skookumchuck Rivers. The house that Joseph Borst, an early Centralia settler, built for his young bride Mary in 1857 still stands here; Borst boasted that the house was so well built it would last for 80 years! Tours of the home are given Mon.-Fri. by appointment only, tel. (360) 736-7687. The park is open daily and offers an arboretum, rhododendron garden, playground, racquetball courts, showers, and trout fishing for kids under 14.

Although Centralia has a number of noteworthy parks, they can be difficult to find, tucked behind shopping centers and motels. **Riverside Park,** on the Skookumchuck River, has a large grassy play and picnic area, plus tent and RV spaces, hidden behind the Huntley Inn on Harrison Avenue.

Accommodations
See the "Centralia and Chehalis Accommodations" chart for a listing of local lodging options. The 6,500-square-foot **Candalite Mansion B&B,** tel. (360) 736-4749 or (800) 489-4749, was built in 1903 by lumber baron J.P. Gurrier and is now a comfortable and spacious B&B with a Christian-oriented atmosphere. The **Caveness House B&B,** tel. (360) 330-5236, is even older, built in 1889. It features three guest rooms furnished with antiques and collectibles, plus an outdoor hot tub and attractive grounds with trees and flowers.

Campgrounds
Pitch a tent ($8) or park that RV ($10) at the city-run **Riverside Park** along the Skookumchuck River. Private RV parks are: **Peppertree West Motor Inn & RV Park,** 1208 Alder St., tel. (360) 736-1124; **Trailer Village & RV,** 1313 Harrison Ave., tel. (360) 736-9260; and **Harrison RV Park,** 3312 Harrison Ave., tel. (360) 330-2167.

Food
Centralia and Chehalis are not known as centers of haute cuisine, but you can find inexpensive and decent meals. Centralia has all the standard fast food places strung out around exit 82 from I-5. The best lunch place is **Winter Kitchen,** 827 Marsh, tel. (360) 736-2916, in a small forest-green home decorated with icicles. The menu includes salads, soups, sandwiches on freshly baked bread, and other tasty fare.

At 1054 Harrison Ave., the **Country Cousin,** tel. (360) 736-2200, is a corny family place with three solid meals a day, including a filling breakfast and meat-and-potatoes dinners. The place is always busy, especially for their Tuesday chicken and ribs buffet.

The **Antique Mall Cafe,** inside Centralia Square at 202 W. Locust, tel. (360) 736-1183, is one of the better local places, serving steak, seafood, pasta, and chicken, plus Sunday brunch. Open daily for lunch and dinner. **Mama Rota's** is a very good little Italian eatery housed inside Duffy's Antique mall at Tower Ave. and Maple St., which serves authentic and reasonably priced food and delicious desserts. A block south on Tower Ave. is **Centralia Pharmacy,** where you'll find a 1903 soda fountain that still

CENTRALIA AND CHEHALIS ACCOMMODATIONS

Accommodations are arranged from least to most expensive. Rates may be lower during the winter months. The area code is 360.

Riverside Motel; 614 Harrison, Centralia; tel. 736-4632; $27 s, $30 d; kitchenettes available

Cascade Motel; 550 S.W. Parkland Dr., Chehalis; tel. 748-8608; $28-40 s, $35-40 d; AAA approved

Park Motel; 1011 Belmont, Centralia; tel. 736-9333; $30 s, $35 d; kitchenettes available

Motel 6; 1310 Belmont Ave., Centralia; tel. 330-2057 or (800) 466-8356; $30 s, $36 d; outdoor pool

Peppertree West Motor Inn & RV Park; 1208 Alder St., Centralia; tel. 736-1124; $30-33 s, $32-35 d; kitchenettes available, AAA approved

Lake Shore Motel; 1325 Lake Shore Dr., Centralia; tel. 736-9344; $37 s, $41 d; on Plummer Lake

Ferryman's Inn Motel; 1003 Eckerson Rd., Centralia; tel. 330-2094; $40 s, $43 d; outdoor pool, jacuzzi, exercise facility, kitchenettes available, continental breakfast, AAA approved

Huntley Inn; 702 W. Harrison Ave., Centralia; tel. 736-2875 or (800) 448-5544; $41 s, $48 d; outdoor pool, free continental breakfast, AAA approved

Candalite Mansion B&B; 402 N. Rock, Centralia; tel. 736-4749 or (800) 489-4749; $50-65 s or d; large 1903 mansion, six guest rooms, shared or private baths, ping-pong, pool table, fireplace, full breakfast, no kids

Nendel's Inn; 122 Interstate Ave., Chehalis; tel. 748-0101 or (800) 547-0106; $50-75 s or d; outdoor pool, jacuzzi, free continental breakfast, AAA approved

Travelodge 1049 Eckerson Rd., Centralia; tel. 736-1661 or (800) 578-7878; $60 s or d; new motel, outdoor pool, jacuzzi, kitchenettes available, continental breakfast

Caveness House B&B; 1011 Caveness Dr., Centralia; tel. 330-5236; $65-85 s or d; 1889 home with veranda and decks, three guest rooms with antiques, shared bath, hot tub, continental breakfast

---

serves shakes, malts, and banana splits.

For hot and spicy barbecued ribs, and other down-home meals, drop by **Hickory House BBQ,** 1502 Lum Rd., tel. (360) 330-5494.

The **Centralia Farmers Market** has local fruits, vegetables, dried flowers, baked goods, and crafts. Find it on Friday 9:30 a.m.-1 p.m. May-Oct., next to the Amtrak station on Pine St. and Tower Avenue.

Events and Entertainment

Since 1909, the **Southwest Washington Fair** has been one of the largest summer festivals in the state, attracting crowds of over 125,000 on the third weekend in August. The fairgrounds are at the south end of town on Gold Street. **Evergreen Playhouse,** 226 W. Center St., tel. (360) 736-8628, has live community theater.

Recreation

For a taste of the old days, head to the **Rollerdrome** at 216 W. Maple, tel. (360) 736-7376, to rent skates and circle the ancient wooden floors. Swim at **Centralia Community Pool,** 910 Johnson Ave., tel. (360) 736-0143, where you'll also find an exercise room, sauna, and jacuzzi.

Three golf courses serve the area: **Armory Hills,** 1012 Duffy, tel. (360) 736-5312, has nine holes; **Newaukum Valley,** 3024 Jackson Hwy., in Chehalis, tel. (360) 748-0461, and **Riverside Golf Course,** near Centralia's airport at 1451 N.W. Airport Rd., tel. (360) 748-8182, are 18-hole courses.

Shopping

Downtown's **Centralia Square Antique Mall,** 201 S. Pearl St., tel. (360) 736-6406, is an antique collector's paradise, with more than 80 dealers displaying estate jewelry, furniture, and other collectibles; open daily till 5 p.m. Other large antique places include **Duffy's Antique Decorators Mall,** 310 N. Tower Ave, tel. (360) 736-7572, **Antique Market,** 120 S. Tower, tel. (360) 736-4079, and at least nine other shops.

The Original Mt. St. Helens Volcanic Ash Glass Factory at 520 N. Gold St., tel. (360) 736-3590, produces blown-glass products using ash from the 1980 eruption. Stop by to watch the glassblowers making Christmas tree ornaments and other colorful pieces. An interesting and educational place. To learn more about yourself, visit **The Guiding Star,** a "metaphysical source store" at 448 N. Market Blvd. with crystals, channeling, psychic fairs, and aura readings by Ackbar and Alyeesia. (At least it isn't Akbar and Jeff from *Life in Hell*.)

Centralia's newest designation is **Factory Outlet** Capital of the Northwest. Just off I-5, almost 50 factory owned and operated stores include London Fog, Corning Glass, Guess, Oneida, Levis, and Hanes. Best of the lot is **Northwest Factory Co-Op,** with clothing, jewelry, art, foods, and other items handcrafted in the Northwest.

Information and Services
Get local info from a small **visitor information center** next to the Avia factory outlet store off Lum Rd., tel. (360) 736-7132. Open daily 10 a.m.-5 p.m. in the summer, and daily 10 a.m.-4 p.m. winters. The Centralia **public library** is located at 110 S. Silver, tel. (360) 736-0183. Centralia's **area code** is 360.

Transportation
Amtrak, tel. (360) 736-8653 or (800) 872-7245, serves Centralia from Union Depot, located (appropriately enough) on Railroad Avenue. Amtrak offers great rates Mon.-Thurs.—a quick "shopper's special" trip from Seattle is just $16 roundtrip. Call (800) 831-5334 for details. A free **trolley** operates on Wednesday and Saturday connecting downtown Centralia (including the Amtrak station and the antique malls) with the factory outlet center.

Twin Transit, tel. (360) 330-2072, has daily bus service connecting Centralia and Chehalis for 30 cents and all-day passes for 60 cents.

Grays Harbor Transportation Authority, tel. (800) 562-9730, comes as far as Centralia and Chehalis, and **Trailways,** tel. (360) 736-9811, runs scheduled buses through.

Long distance bus service is provided by **Greyhound,** tel. (360) 736-9811 or (800) 231-2222, with service both north and south on I-5 from the Texaco station at exit 81 (1232 Mellen St).

Centralia-SeaTac Airport Express, tel. (800) 773-9490, and **Capital Aeroporter,** tel. (360) 754-7113, offer direct shuttle service between Centralia and Sea-Tac Airport.

CHEHALIS

Chehalis (pop. 6,700) is just four miles south of Centralia and features a downtown of attractive brick buildings. Nothing fancy or pretentious here. It's a blue-collar place where folks make a living mining coal or processing food. The Darigold plant in Chehalis is the world's second largest producer of powdered milk.

History
When Northern Pacific Railroad built a line north to Puget Sound from Kalama on the Columbia River in 1873, it built a warehouse on the bank of the Chehalis River, and gradually a settlement grew up around this warehouse. The warehouse was called Saundersville in honor of S.S. Saunders, on whose land the town was founded. Later the name was changed to Chehalis, a Native American word meaning "Shifting Sands." It became the Lewis County seat in 1872. Logging quickly became the major industry, and the area was settled by Scandinavians and British. As the valleys were cleared, dairy-farming became a major industry, along with fruit and vegetable packing and coal mining. It is this rich deposit of coal that made the Pacific Power and Light steam plant possible.

Sights
The **Lewis County Historical Museum,** 599 N.W. Front St., tel. (360) 748-0831, is in a former railroad depot, with freight trains rolling past at all hours. The museum has several fine native baskets, a diorama of a native longhouse, and a big collection of pioneer goods, logging equip-

ment, and farm tools. Also here are displays on the Armistice Day Riot of 1919 (but no artifacts). Out front is a surprisingly small WW I tank. Pick up walking tour brochures here describing historic sites in Chehalis. Open Sunday 1-5 p.m., and Tues.-Sat. 9 a.m.-5 p.m. Entrance is $2 for adults, $1.50 for seniors, $1 for ages six to 18, free for kids under six, or $5 for the whole family.

The **McFadden Log Home,** 475 W. Chehalis Ave., built in 1859, is the oldest continuously lived-in home in the state, (though a home in Port Gamble also claims the title). Another historic footnote is the **McKinley Stump,** located at Recreation Park on 13th Street. This was where President McKinley gave what was literally a stump speech in 1903. (The stump originally stood next to the Chehalis Depot.)

The **Claquato Church** is all that remains from the town of Claquato. Built in 1857, it is the oldest Protestant church still at its original location in the Pacific Northwest, and is also noteworthy for its crown-of-thorns octagonal steeple. Get here by heading west on Hwy. 6 (exit 77 off I-5) for two miles, then right on Chilvers Rd., left on Stearns Rd., and another left onto Water Street.

John R. Jackson House State Historic Site (see "Marys Corner to Toledo" under "Mossyrock and Vicinity") is four miles south on Jackson Highway. This is one of the oldest pioneer structures north of the Columbia River, and a meeting place for those organizing the Washington Territory.

For a bit of whimsy, head to **Winlock,** a little place off I-5 exit 63 (southwest of Chehalis). The town was once famous for its egg hatcheries that produced 2.5 million chicks a year in the 1960s. Commemorating this momentous piece of history is a big concrete egg, located three miles west of town.

Parks

Chehalis has several small city parks, the most interesting being **Stan Hedwall Park,** located on Rice Rd. just west of I-5 (take exit 76). The park borders the Newaukum River and has camping spaces, a swimming area, hiking trails, ornamental gardens, and the usual picnic spaces and athletic fields.

Sixteen miles west from Chehalis on Hwy. 6, you come upon the 125-acre **Rainbow Falls**

Rainbow Falls State Park

DIANNE BOUERICE LYONS

State Park, where the mist from a minor waterfall creates sunny day rainbows. Pitch a tent in the tall Douglas fir and hemlock trees, hike the seven miles of forest trails, and try your luck at fishing in the river. A fun stone-and-log supported suspension footbridge built by the CCC in the 1930s crosses the Chehalis River. Call (360) 291-3767 for more info on the park. Open for day-use April-Sept. and on weekends and holidays the rest of the year.

Steam Railroad

Take a ride on the **Centralia/Chehalis Steam Railroad** from Chehalis out to a railroad junction called "Ruth" in the Boistfort Valley. The train—pulled by a 1917 Boldwin locomotive—operates on weekends Memorial Day through Labor Day; phone (360) 748-9593 for details. Fares are $10.50 for adults, $8.50 for ages four to 16, and free for kids under three. A special dinner train is also available on selected weekends.

Accommodations and Campgrounds

See the "Centralia and Chehalis Accommodations" chart for a listing of local motels. Campsites ($10 for tents or RVs) are available at **Hedwall Park** on Rice Rd. just off I-5 at exit 76, tel. (360) 748-0271 for reservations. More camping at **Rainbow Falls State Park,** 16 miles to the west on Hwy. 6, tel. (360) 291-3767. The campground ($10; no RV hookups) is open April-Sept. and has coin-operated showers. Call (800) 452-5687 for campsite reservations ($6 extra fee), available up to 11 months ahead of time. Park RVs at **Scott's KOA,** 118 Hwy. 12, tel. (360) 262-9220.

Food and Shopping

Mary McCrank's Restaurant, four miles south of Chehalis at 2923 Jackson Hwy., tel. (360) 748-3662, is one of the oldest dinner houses in the state, in business since 1935. The food is dependably good, featuring such faves as chicken fried steak, meat loaf with gravy, and pork chops.

Sweet Inspirations, 514 N. Market Blvd., tel. (360) 748-7102, the best place for lunch in Chehalis, offers burgers, sandwiches, vegetarian specials, espresso, and desserts. **Rumors Bar & Grill,** 575 N. Main St., tel. (360) 748-3967, has good prime rib and steaks, microbrews on tap, plus a lighter lunch menu of soups, French dip, burgers, and salads.

Get authentic Mexican food at **Plaza Jalisco,** 1340 N.W. Maryland, tel. (360) 748-4298, and fresh sushi and teriyaki at **Paradise Teriyaki,** 337 N.W. Chehalis Ave., tel. (360) 748-7513.

The **Chehalis Farmers Market** is held on Saturday 9:30 a.m.-1 p.m. May-October next to Colony House at National and Market Street and offers handicrafts, plants, flowers, and baked goods in addition to fresh fruits and veggies.

Most of the shopping attractions are in Centralia, but Chehalis has its share, including the

Lewis County Mall halfway between the two at 151 N.E. Hampe Way.

Recreation

Swim at the summer-only outdoor pool in **Recreation Park** on the east side of Chehalis at 13th St. and William Avenue. Call (360) 748-0271 for details. Also here are picnic tables, a community kitchen, and shady grounds. **Dobson** and **McFadden** parks provide almost 50 acres of undeveloped hillside country with hiking trails and fine views of Mt. Rainier.

Information and Services

For local info, head to the **Twin Cities Chamber of Commerce Visitor Center,** 500 N.W. Chamber of Commerce Way (just west of exit 79 from I-5), tel. (360) 748-8885 or (800) 525-3323. Open summers Mon.-Fri. 8 a.m.-5 p.m., and Sat.-Sun. 10 a.m.-3 p.m., and Mon.-Fri. 8 a.m.-5 p.m. the rest of the year. The Chehalis **public library** is located at 76 N.E. Park St., tel. (360) 748-3301. The **area code** for Chehalis is 360.

For medical emergencies, **Providence Centralia Hospital,** 1820 Cooks Hill Rd., tel. (360) 736-2803, has 24-hour emergency service.

Transportation

Chehalis is about five miles south of Centralia. Driving south from Seattle, you'll know you're near Chehalis when you see the Hamilton Farms billboard, proclaiming a bombastic right wing Rush Limbaugh-style political message. You gotta wonder about these folks.

Twin Transit, tel. (360) 330-2072, has daily bus service connecting Centralia and Chehalis for 30 cents; 60 cents for an all-day pass. **Capital Aeroporter,** tel. (360) 754-7113, goes a bit farther, with transportation between Chehalis and Sea-Tac Airport.

BOB RACE

OLYMPIC PENINSULA

Washington's Olympic Peninsula juts up like a thumb hitchhiking a ride from Canada. The 6,500-square-mile peninsula covers an extraordinary diversity of terrain, from remote rocky beaches to glacier-faced mountains. It is one of the most beautiful parts of Washington and seems to capture the spirit of the Evergreen State. At the core of the peninsula is Olympic National Park, one of the nation's crown jewels, recognized as a Man and the Biosphere Reserve by UNESCO. Much of the Olympic Peninsula is in private and tribal hands, where the emphasis is on logging rather than preservation. Virtually all land outside the park and Olympic National Forest has been cut at one time or another, and much of it is managed as tree farms with perpetual rotations of trees in varying stages of growth. Get ready for some of the most massive clearcuts you've ever seen.

Highway 101 follows three sides of the peninsula and joins Highways 8 and 12 to provide a fine circular route that accesses all the sights. Excellent public transit service means that you can also catch buses to many points along the way, and complete the entire loop for just a few bucks.

Rainforests

Precipitation varies greatly on the peninsula: from Sequim, where only 17 inches fall in a typical year, to the eastern slopes of the Olympic Mountains, where more than 160 inches (that's over 13 feet!) of rain drop to earth. They don't call this the rainforest for nothing. These temperate rainforests are the best-known vegetation on the peninsula. Not much remains of the original old-growth stands, but parts of the Queets, Hoh, and Quinault river drainages still have examples of these forests. The distinguishing features are (in addition to the rain): the presence of Sitka spruce, abundant mosses, clubmosses, and lichens, nurse logs (fallen trees where seedlings grow), colonnades of trees that got their start on nurse logs, trees growing on stilts (they began as seedlings on stumps that later decayed away), and the presence of big leaf or vine maples. Other common trees are Douglas fir, western red cedar, and western hemlock. You aren't likely to remember all these features, but you'll know when you are in an old-growth rainforest. The lush profusion of moss-carpeted trees and dense understory of salal, rhododen-

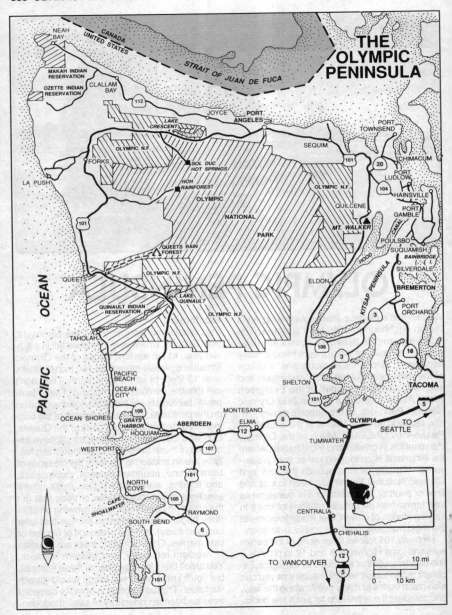

dron, huckleberry, and other plants give it an unforgettably verdant feeling.

The peninsula has its own cadre of animals, including black-tailed deer, black bear, cottontail rabbits, snowshoe hares, cougars, beavers, coyotes, marmots, raccoons, skunks, more than 200 species of birds, and everybody's favorite, the regal Roosevelt elk. The elk now number upwards of 7,000 on the peninsula and are commonly seen in parts of Olympic National Park.

KITSAP PENINSULA

The Kitsap Peninsula is an appendage to the Olympic Peninsula; in fact, visitors and locals alike sometimes confuse the two, thinking that anything west of Seattle must be the Olympic Peninsula. Not true: The Kitsap is separated from the Olympic Peninsula by Hood Canal. This separation has helped prevent the peninsula from being developed as rapidly as the Seattle side of Puget Sound. For those living on the eastern side, the peninsula retains an air of remoteness, similar to that of Whidbey Island, a short ferry ride across Admiralty Inlet from Port Townsend. There are Christmas tree farms, second-growth stands of timber, and boat-filled marinas, but things are changing fast. Rapid growth in some parts of the Kitsap has brought the predictable housing subdivisions, chain restaurants, megamart shopping centers, and traffic congestion that people moving here are fleeing. The Kitsap has a number of places that are particularly notable, including the towns of Port Gamble, Port Orchard, and Poulsbo, the marvelous Naval Undersea Museum in Keyport, and the naval ships in Bremerton.

The Kitsap is readily accessible by ferry from Seattle and Edmonds, and its many back roads are favorite cycling destinations. Bainbridge Island is especially popular because of the easy access, diverse country, lack of traffic, and abundance of fine cafes and B&Bs.

KITSAP PENINSULA

© MOON PUBLICATIONS, INC.

BREMERTON

The blue collar city of Bremerton (pop. 37,000)—the largest settlement on Kitsap Peninsula—offers sweeping views of both the Cascades and the Olympics, and a waterfront crowded with mothballed Navy ships. Bremerton has long suffered in the glare of attention paid to its across-the-sound neighbor, Seattle, so it came as some surprise in 1990 when *Money* magazine selected Bremerton the most livable city in America. A visit to Bremerton will probably leave you asking yourself how they ever came up with that designation. The run-down city center is anything but attractive, and one could easily imagine that it had been hit by an errant missile from one of the destroyers anchored offshore. Many of the businesses have fled to suburban strip malls or to the booming patches of real estate around Belfair and Silverdale. This isn't to say that Bremerton is without its positive attributes. The city has several interesting historical sights, including famous battleships and a naval

KITSAP MALL

SILVERDALE
POPLARS MOTEL

SILVERDALE
ON THE BAY

KITSAP HISTORICAL MUSEUM

CHICO

TO WILCOX
HOUSE B&B

CLEAR CR RD.
SILVERDALE WAY
WAAGA WAY
BUCKLIN HILL RD.

KITSAP CO.
FAIRGROUNDS
FAIRGROUNDS RD.

DYES INLET

CHICO WAY
CHICO WAY

TRACYTON BLVD.

RIDDELL RD.

WHEATON WAY

303

ILLAHEE RD.

ILLAHEE
S.P.

SYLVAN WAY

MIDWAY INN
EAST
BREMERTON

HARRISON
MEMORIAL
HOSPITAL

OSTRICH BAY
PHINNEY BAY
OYSTER
BAY

BEST WESTERN BAYVIEW INN

SUPER 8 MOTEL   DUNES MOTEL

CHIEFTAIN MOTEL

QUALITY INN

KITSAP WAY

11th ST.

6th ST.

BREMERTON

NAVAL MUSEUM
VISITOR INFORMATION

TURNER JOY

3

BREMERTON-SEATTLE FERRY

TO
MANCHESTER
STATE PARK

REFLECTIONS
B&B INN

BEACH DR.

**VICINITY OF
BREMERTON**

PUGET SOUND
NAVAL SHIPYARD

304

SINCLAIR INLET

FERRY

TWETEN'S
LIGHTHOUSE

OLDE CENTRAL
ANTIQUE MALL
SIDNEY GALLERY
LOG CABIN MUSEUM

VISTA MOTEL

MANCHESTER HWY.

160

PORT
ORCHARD

SIDNEY ST.

LUNDBERG
PARK

160

SOUTH KITSAP
COMMUNITY PARK

GORST

CLIFTON RD.

16

BETHEL RD.

LUND AVE.

JACKSON AVE.

TO
SOUTHWORTH

3

SEDGWICK RD.

160

0   1 mi

0   1 km

© MOON PUBLICATIONS, INC.

museum, as well as good restaurants and inexpensive housing.

With all the water around it and the deep harbor at its doorstep, Bremerton is an ideal location for the **Puget Sound Naval Shipyard**, the city's economic mainstay since 1891. Today the facility is where nuclear ships and subs are overhauled and deactivated. It is the second largest industrial employer in Washington (after Boeing). Other nearby military facilities include the Naval Hospital and Naval Supply Center in Bremerton, the Naval Undersea Warfare Center in Keyport, and the Naval Submarine Base in Bangor. Both the USS *Nimitz* and the USS *Midway* aircraft carriers are home-ported in Bremerton. Recent moves to downsize the Navy have hit Bremerton hard and will continue to affect the local economy in the future.

Sights

The famous battleship **USS *Missouri,*** where the surrender documents were signed to end Japan's role in WW II, was last used during the Gulf War and now sits mothballed with other vessels, including the USS *New Jersey* and the USS *Oriskany.* These ships—in varying states of disrepair—are not open to the public, but **Kitsap Harbor Tours,** tel. (360) 377-8924, offers 45-minute boat tours around the ships on a daily basis from mid-May through September, and on weekends in October. The narrated tours are $6 for adults, $5 for seniors, and $4 for kids ages five to 12. Get tickets on the boardwalk at Ship's Store.

Another ship, a much smaller one without such the illustrious career of the *Missouri,* has recently opened as a museum. The destroyer ***Turner Joy*** was one of the ships involved in the Gulf of Tonkin Incident in 1964 that led to the escalation of the Vietnam War. During the shelling of Chu Lai later that year, one of her guns jammed and an ensuing explosion killed three men. The destroyer was decommissioned in 1982 and opened to the public in 1988 for self-guided tours. If you haven't been aboard a Navy ship before, a tour of the *Turner Joy* will be an education, with its tight sleeping quarters and an impressive array of weaponry. The 418-foot ship is open daily 11 a.m.-4 p.m. mid-May through September, and Thurs.-Sun. 11 a.m.-4 p.m. the rest of the year. Admission (good all day

long) is $5 for adults, $4 for seniors, and $3 for kids ages five to 12. For information call (360) 792-2457. Tickets are sold in the **Ship's Store,** tel. (360) 792-1008, an interesting nautical gift shop on the boardwalk.

The **Bremerton Naval Museum,** 130 Washington Ave., tel. (360) 479-7447, has American and Japanese naval artifacts, highly detailed models of the USS *Midway* and other Navy ships, and naval memorabilia of all types. Open Sunday 1-5 p.m., and Tues.-Sat. 10 a.m.-5 p.m.; donations welcome.

Parks and Recreation

Illahee State Park, three miles northeast of Bremerton on Hwy. 306, has campsites on 75 acres close to the urban area, with swimming beaches, a short but steep hiking trail, a boat launch, and a pier for fishing and lolling in the sun.

Hikers will enjoy the two-mile trek to the summit of 1,700-foot **Green Mountain** for spectacular views of Kitsap Peninsula, Puget Sound, and the Seattle skyline. Take Seabeck Hwy. NW for two miles, turn left (west) on Holly Rd., then take a left onto Tahuyeh Rd. for 1.25 miles to Gold Creek Rd.; turn left onto Gold Creek and follow it for 1.5 miles to the trailhead on the left, before Gold Creek Bridge. Be sure to wear proper footwear since the trail is rocky and often wet.

Swim at **Wildcat Lake,** approximately five miles west of Bremerton, where a seasonal lifeguard is on duty. Also here are bathhouses, picnic areas, and a playground.

Accommodations and Campgrounds

See the "Bremerton Area Accommodations" chart for a listing of lodging options in the Bremerton area. **Illahee State Park** has camping ($10, no RV hookups) and coin-operated showers year-round. Call (360) 478-6460 for information, or (800) 452-5687 for campsite reservations ($6 extra fee), available up to 11 months ahead of time. Showers are also available at the Bremerton marina.

Food

Christophe's Waterfront Cafe, 112 Washington Ave. (upstairs from Waterfront Books), tel. (360) 792-1603, is a very popular lunch spot with delicious homemade soups, salads, sandwiches, and espresso.

BREMERTON AREA ACCOMMODATIONS

Accommodations are arranged from least to most expensive. The area code is 360.

Chieftain Motel; 600 National Ave. N; tel. 479-3111; $32 s, $37-42 d; outdoor pool, kitchenettes available

Dunes Motel; 3400 11th St.; tel. 377-0093 or (800) 828-8238; $40 s or d; jacuzzi, kitchenettes available, AAA approved

Super 8 Motel; 5068 Kitsap Way; tel. 377-8881 or (800) 800-8000; $45 s, $49 d

Midway Inn; 2909 Wheaton Way; tel. 479-2909 or (800) 231-0575; $50 s or d; kitchenettes available, free continental breakfast, AAA approved

Flagship Inn; 4320 Kitsap Way; tel. 479-6566 or (800) 447-9396; $50 s, $55 d; bay views, outdoor pool, local calls 35 cents, free continental breakfast, AAA approved

Quality Inn at Oyster Bay; 4303 Kitsap Way; tel. 377-4402 or (800) 776-2291; $55-85 s, $60-90 d; outdoor pool, jacuzzi, exercise room, large rooms, kitchenettes available, free continental breakfast, AAA approved

Best Western Bayview Inn; 5640 Kitsap Way; tel. 373-9900 or (800) 422-5017 or (800) 528-1234; $62-67 s, $67-73 d; overlooks Oyster Bay, indoor pool, jacuzzi, AAA approved

Highland Cottage B&B; 622-A Highland Ave.; tel. 479-2295; $65 s, $75 d in turn-of-the-century home, $85 s, $95 d in cottage; deck with water views, hot tub, antique furnishings, private baths, full breakfast, kids okay

Willcox House; 2390 Tekiu Rd. NW, Seabeck; tel. 830-4492; $95-155 s, $115-175 d; classic 1936 waterfront mansion, outdoor pool, marble and copper fireplaces, antique furniture, water and Olympic views, six guest rooms, private baths, gourmet breakfast, two-night minimum stay on weekends, no kids under 15, AAA approved

Have nachos, fresh seafood, steaks, pasta, sandwiches, or salads over the water at the **Boat Shed,** a mile from the ferry dock at 101 Shore Dr., tel. (360) 377-2600. **Alfredo's at Oyster Bay Inn,** 4412 Kitsap Way, tel. (360) 377-5510, offers traditional Mediterranean lunches and dinners with an emphasis on fresh vegetables and fruits. Get tempura, teriyaki, and sushi at **Hattori Japanese Restaurant,** 3249 Perry Ave. NE (East Bremerton), tel. (360) 479-7150.

The **Camp Union Cookhouse,** 141 N.W. Holly Rd., tel. (360) 830-5298, has home-style cooking in a museum of sorts. The **Bremerton Farmers Market** takes place every Sunday on the waterfront.

Events

The third weekend of May brings the **Armed Forces Festival & Parade,** the largest celebration of its type in the nation. Call (360) 479-3579 for details. In late August the **Kitsap Coun-**ty Fair and Rodeo, tel. (360) 692-3655, comes to the Kitsap County Fairgrounds five miles north of Bremerton off Hwy. 303. Highlighted by a PRCA rodeo, the fair also includes a carnival, circus, and other entertainment. Younger cowboys and cowgirls display their talents at the annual **Little Britches Rodeo,** tel. (360) 876-2040, held at the Fairgrounds in mid-June. In late August, the **Bremerton Air Fair** attracts thousands of spectators for military and civilian aircraft displays and aerobatics.

The Arts

The **Bremerton Symphony Orchestra,** tel. (360) 373-1722, performs concerts throughout the winter season at the high school. **Bremerton Community Theatre,** 599 Lebo Blvd., tel. (360) 373-5152, has comedy, drama, and musical theatrical events.

The **Amy Burnett Gallery,** on Pacific Ave. and 4th St., tel. (360) 373-3187, one of the largest art galleries in the Northwest, has four separate galleries and a wine tasting room.

Information and Services

The people at the **Bremerton/Kitsap Peninsula Visitor and Convention Bureau,** 120 Washington Ave., tel. (360) 479-3588, can answer most of your questions and provide you with maps and brochures to the southern end of the peninsula. Open Mon.-Fri. 9 a.m.-5 p.m. year-round, with additional weekend hours in the summer. Right next door, **Waterfront Books & Maps,** 112 Washington Ave., tel. (360) 373-2343, has an eclectic selection of books. The **area code** for the Kitsap Peninsula is 360.

Bremerton's major medical center is **Harrison Memorial Hospital,** 2520 Cherry Ave., tel. (360) 377-3911.

Ferries and Tours

From the Seattle waterfront you can take a 60-minute trip to Bremerton on the **Washington State Ferries.** Ferries depart about every 70 minutes for Bremerton. Fares are $7.10 one-way for car and driver ($5.90 in winter), $3.50 roundtrip for passengers, and $4 roundtrip for bicycle riders. A passenger-only ferry (same rates) sails from Seattle five times a day and makes the run in 50 minutes. Call (360) 842-2345 or (800) 843-3779 for more information. You'll probably end up paying $3 if you want to park anywhere near downtown because so many folks from the Kitsap park here and ride the ferry to Seattle.

Horluck Transportation Co. Inc., tel. (360) 876-2300, is the oldest operating ferry in the state, providing service across the Sinclair Inlet between Bremerton and Port Orchard for foot traffic and bikes only. The company has five small vessels, including the *Carlisle II,* the last of the working "Mosquito Fleet" that once plied the waters of Puget Sound. The 10-minute crossing costs 85 cents one-way; available daily from 6 a.m. to midnight.

Kitsap Harbor Tours, tel. (360) 377-8924, offers tours of the mothball fleet (see "Sights," above), and daily passenger ferry service to Keyport ($7 roundtrip) and Poulsbo ($9 roundtrip). They also offer tours to Blake Island. Get tickets at the Ship's Store Gift Shop on the boardwalk. The ferry operates mid-May through September only.

Other Transportation

Kitsap Transit, tel. (360) 373-2877 or 697-2877, provides daily bus service to Bremerton, Silverdale, Bangor, Poulsbo, and Bainbridge Island, and meets all state ferries. Fares are 50-75 cents. All Kitsap Transit buses have bike racks.

Bremerton-Kitsap Airporter, tel. (360) 876-1737 or (800) 562-7948, and **Port Angeles-Seattle Bus Lines,** tel. (800) 764-2287, both offer shuttle buses to Sea-Tac Airport.

Lack of traffic and congestion make Kitsap County an excellent place for cyclists. A map of recommended bike routes throughout the county is available for $2 from the visitor and convention bureau. This map shows bike routes, other good roads, circular bike tours, uphill sections, difficult intersections, bike shops, campgrounds, and other points of interest.

PORT ORCHARD

Across the Sinclair Inlet from Bremerton, Port Orchard—the Kitsap County seat—shows a split personality. The prosperous waterfront section faces the marina with covered walkways, colorful murals, antique shops, and cozy cafes. This contrasts sharply with the standard Kmart-and-fast-food section that sprawls outward on the south end. Port Orchard still keeps a small fishing fleet, and boat sheds fill the harbor, but it is primarily a bedroom community for Seattle and Tacoma, and for Bremerton military workers.

Port Orchard was named for H.M. Orchard, the clerk on Captain Vancouver's 1792 expedition who first discovered this bay. The town was founded in 1886 and became the county seat seven years later. Today it is home to 5,600 people.

Sights

Head two blocks uphill on Sidney Ave. to the **Sidney Gallery,** tel. (360) 876-3693. The lower floor contains an excellent gallery with imaginative paintings and ceramic pieces; upstairs is a small, but well-presented collection of historical displays representing various turn-of-the-century shops and industries. ("Sidney" was the original name for Port Orchard.) Housed in a 1913 pioneer log home, the **Log Cabin Museum,** a few doors farther at 416 Sidney, has rotating exhibits of Kitsap Peninsula history. Open Sunday 1-5 p.m. and Monday 11 a.m.-4 p.m.; free.

Parks and Recreation

Follow Beach Dr. from Port Orchard for a scenic approach to **Manchester State Park,** tel. (360) 871-4065, six miles away at the entrance to the Sinclair Inlet. The park's 111 acres include campsites, hiking and interpretive trails, plus swimming, fishing, and scuba diving in Rich Passage. The main attractions here are the various turn-of-the-century military structures, built to protect the Bremerton Naval Shipyard from attack. These include a brick warehouse once used to store underwater mines (now it's an oversized picnic shelter), and a control center where the mines could be set off remotely if enemy warships intruded. Fortunately, the mines were never deployed, and the fort was abandoned and turned into a state park. The park is open from late April to early September.

The 200-acre **South Kitsap Community Park** at the intersection of Jackson and Lund Roads, two miles southwest of downtown, has hiking trails and a picnic area, plus kiddie steam trains (free) daily 11 a.m.-4 p.m. from June to mid-September. Swim or boat at **Long Lake,** approximately four miles south of Port Orchard. For indoor swimming, head to the high school on Mitchell St., tel. (360) 876-7385. Two 18-hole golf courses in the vicinity are **Horseshoe Lake Golf Course,** 15932 Sidney Rd. SW, tel. (360) 857-3326, and **McCormick Woods Golf Course,** 5155 McCormick Woods Dr. SW, tel. (360) 895-0130. The latter is considered one of the finest in the Northwest and is a good place to spot Seattle Seahawks players.

Accommodations

Vista Motel, 1090 Bethel Ave., tel. (360) 876-8046, has rooms for $33 s, and $37 d, with kitchenettes available. Two local B&Bs are approximately three miles north of Port Orchard off Beach Drive. **Reflections B&B Inn,** 3878 Reflection Lane E, tel. (360) 871-5582, is a large two-story home with four guest rooms (shared or private baths), antiques, a hot tub, and full breakfast. The rooms offer views of Port Orchard Passage. Rates are $55-90 s or d. No kids under 15. **Northwest Interlude B&B,** 3377 Sarann Ave.

E, tel. (360) 871-4676, has three guest rooms (shared or private baths), for $55-75 which includes a full breakfast. Ask the B&Bs about ferry pick-up services if you're arriving downtown by foot.

Campgrounds

Pitch a tent at **Manchester State Park** (see above) for $10; no RV hookups. Open late April to early September. Call (800) 452-5687 for campsite reservations ($6 extra fee), available up to 11 months ahead of time. Free camping at the city-owned **Lundberg Park** (a.k.a. Pt. Orchard RV Park, even though it has no RV hookups) southwest of town on Bethel Rd. at Lund Ave., a quarter mile south of the Safeway. This is a pretty five-acre spot in the forest, with a dozen sites, but it's easy to miss the turnoff.

Food

Port Orchard has the usual steak and seafood restaurants one expects, plus a number of other fine establishments. A personal favorite is **Hadi's Restaurant,** downtown at 818 Bay St., tel. (360) 895-0347, with authentic Middle Eastern cooking that includes shish kabobs and a great selection of appetizers. Other places with ethnic eats include **Green Valley Chinese Restaurant,** 691 Bethel Rd., tel. (360) 895-4109, which has a popular lunch buffet; **El Sombrero,** in Kmart Plaza, tel. (360) 895-1315 (one of four local Mexican restaurants); **Happy Teriyaki Restaurant,** 2065 Bay St., tel. (360) 876-1000, and **Little Tokyo Sushi,** 920 Bay St., tel. (360) 895-3115, for quick meals; and **Italia 642,** 642 Bay St., tel. (360) 895-2326, for fresh pasta and unusual pizzas.

For outside dining with a semi-scenic view of the Bremerton shipyards, try **Tweten's Lighthouse,** on the water at the intersection of Bay St. and Port Orchard Blvd., tel. (360) 876-8464. Enormous cinnamon rolls show up at breakfast, and the Monday night seafood buffet and Sunday brunch are especially popular with locals.

Myhre's Terrace Room, 739 Bay St., tel. (360) 876-9916, offers marina views while you taste the reasonably priced steaks, prime rib, and fresh seafood.

A very good breakfast, lunch, and espresso place is **Pot Belly Deli and Baking Co.,** 724 Bay St., tel. (360) 895-1396. Great breads. They also have live acoustical music on Sunday afternoons. For rock, DJ tunes, and a big dance floor, head to **J.A. Michael's** 715 Bay St., tel. (360) 876-8124.

The **Port Orchard Farmers Market** takes place at the marina on Saturday 9 a.m.-3 p.m. from late April through October. This is one of the largest markets in the state and features more than 100 vendors offering homegrown fruits and veggies, homemade crafts, and ethnic foods. A winter market takes place at the community center Nov.-January.

Shopping
Port Orchard's many craft and gift shops generally cater to an audience that appreciates lots of lace and sickly sweet smells. Cute is the operative term, although revolting also comes to mind. Try the **Victorian Rose Tea Room,** 1130 Bethel Ave., tel. (360) 876-5695, to see for yourself. A favorite of the doll and teddy bear crowd. A similar shop is **Little Habitats,** 3238 Locker Rd. SE, tel. (360) 871-1100, which has dollhouses and miniatures. Two big antique malls are filled with pieces of the past: **Olde Central Antique Mall,** 801 Bay St., tel. (360) 895-1902; and **Side Door Mall,** 701 Bay St., tel. (360) 876-8631. The real gem for shoppers in Port Orchard is the excellent **Sidney Gallery,** described under "Sights" above.

Events and the Arts
Port Orchard's most peculiar event is the **Seagull Calling Contest,** held on the Saturday before Easter. Contestants (many in goofy costumes) attempt to see who can call in the most gulls. The **Fathoms O' Fun Festival**—Port Orchard's premier summer festival and one of the state's oldest—is held from the last Saturday in June through the Fourth of July. Highlights include a big parade, carnival, a fun run, fireworks, and various contests. Then comes the **Chris Craft Rendezvous** that attracts more than a hundred vintage boats in mid-July. The **Peninsula Jazz Festival** is a two-day event at the end of July; call (360) 846-1979 for details. The **Cruz-N-Country Street Fair** comes to Port Orchard on the first Sunday of August, and Bay St. is closed off to display more than 1,000 custom cars and hot rods, plus juried arts and crafts, food booths, live music, dancing, and games.

The **Bay Street Playhouse,** 820 Bay St., tel. (360) 876-6610, is home to the Performing Arts Guild of South Kitsap, a group that puts on plays, musicals, and kid's shows throughout the year.

Information and Services
Get information at **Port Orchard Chamber of Commerce,** 839 Bay St., tel. (360) 876-3505 or (800) 982-8139. Open Mon.-Fri. 10 a.m.-5 p.m., and Saturday 10 a.m.-2 p.m. year-round. Be sure to stop here to check out the beautifully crafted seven-foot-long wooden model of the *Virginia V.* The **area code** for Port Orchard is 360.

Ferry Service
Catch the **Washington State Ferry** from the Fauntleroy dock in West Seattle for the 35-minute ride to Southworth on the southeast side of the Kitsap Peninsula near Port Orchard. Fares are $7.10 one-way for car and driver, $3.50 roundtrip for passengers and walk-ons, and $4 roundtrip for bicycle riders. You can also catch a ferry from Southworth to Vashon Island (or vice versa) every hour and a half for $2.30 roundtrip for passengers, $9.55 roundtrip for vehicle and driver ($7.95 in the winter), and $2.80 roundtrip for bikes and riders. Call (360) 842-2345 or (800) 843-3779 for more information.

Horluck Transportation Co. Inc., tel. (360) 876-2300, has the oldest operating ferry in the state, providing ferry service across the Sinclair Inlet between Bremerton and Port Orchard for foot traffic and bikes only. The company has five small vessels, including the *Carlisle II,* the last of the working "Mosquito Fleet" that once plied the waters of Puget Sound. The 10-minute crossing costs 85 cents one-way and is available daily from 6 a.m. to midnight. (It's a seven mile drive around the head of Sinclair Inlet to Bremerton if you drive there instead.)

Other Transportation
Kitsap Transit, tel. (360) 377-2877, provides daily bus service to Bremerton, Silverdale, Bangor, Poulsbo, and Bainbridge Island, and meets all Southworth ferries. Fares are 50-75 cents. All Kitsap Transit buses have bike racks.

Bremerton-Kitsap Airporter, tel. (360) 876-1737 or (800) 562-7948, and **Port Angeles-Seattle Bus Lines,** tel. (800) 764-2287, both offer shuttle buses to Sea-Tac Airport.

BLAKE ISLAND

Accessible only by boat, Blake Island has 476 acres of state park land with year-round camping ($10); sandy beaches for swimming, sunbathing, and clamming; fishing and scuba diving; a three-quarter-mile loop nature trail; and 12 miles of other hiking trails. Call (800) 452-5687 for campsite reservations ($6 extra fee), available up to 11 months ahead of time. The main attraction is Tillicum Village, where Indian dances, a salmon bake, and crafts are offered daily (see below).

To reach the island from the Kitsap, rent a boat from Manchester Boatworks in Port Orchard, or check with local chambers of commerce for charter operators.

Tillicum Village

This native-style village can be visited as part of a full-day trip offered by Argosy Cruises that includes a salmon bake in the cedar longhouse, traditional dances, nature trails, Indian artifacts, and a gift shop. Departing from the Seattle waterfront, the four-hour tour is available daily from May through mid-October, with reduced tours the rest of the year; fares are $47 for adults, $43 for seniors, $30 for ages 13-19, $19 for ages six to 12, $9 for ages four to five, and free for infants. Reservations are required; call (206) 443-1244 in Seattle. For those who want more time to explore the hiking paths around the island, the company offers six-hour trips on Saturday from mid-June to early September, plus Sunday in July and August. **Kitsap Harbor Tours,** tel. (360) 377-8924, offers tours to Blake Island from Bremerton on Friday and Saturday evenings May-October.

SILVERDALE

The unincorporated town of Silverdale has a beautiful setting with some of the best views across Dyes Inlet, but much of what you see today is far less attractive. The Navy's Trident Nuclear Submarine Base has brought prosperity, turning Silverdale into the prime shopping area for the whole peninsula. A busy four-lane road leads through the new parts of town, bordered by a jumble of new homes and condos, shopping plazas, restaurants, and the Kitsap Mall.

Sights

The **Kitsap County Historical Society Museum,** 3343 N.W. Byron St. in "Old Towne," tel. (360) 692-1949, has musical instruments, historical photographs, toys, clocks, nautical artifacts, and even a wood-rimmed bicycle; open Tues.-Sat. 10 a.m.-5 p.m., year-round. Entrance is $1 each, or $2 for families. After visiting the museum, have a picnic lunch at the adjacent **Waterfront Park,** where a pier heads into Dyes Inlet.

Accommodations

Cimarron Motel, 9734 N.W. Silverdale Way, tel. (360) 692-7777, charges $41-50 s or d, including kitchenettes. The **Poplars Motel,** 9800 Silverdale Way, tel. (360) 692-6126 or (800) 824-7517, has rooms for $48 s, $57 d, and a heated pool. A step up in price, **Silverdale on the Bay Resort Hotel,** 3073 N.W. Bucklin Hill Rd., tel. (360) 698-1000 or (800) 426-0670, has two- and three-bedroom units for $75-105 s, or $85-105 d. Amenities include glassed-in pool, sauna, jacuzzi, exercise room, private balconies, putting green, and tennis courts.

Food

Down East Restaurant, 3299 Randall Way, tel. (360) 698-2306, has old-fashioned fish and chips. For more substantial seafood and pasta, served on the outdoor deck in good weather, head to **Yacht Club Broiler,** 9226 Bayshore Dr., tel. (360) 698-1601. The **Mariner Restaurant,** 3073 N.W. Bucklin Hill Rd., tel. (360) 698-1000, features excellent Northwest seafood; open for breakfast, lunch, and dinner.

Waterfront Park Bakery & Cafe, next to the park on N.W. Byron, tel. (360) 698-2991, has fresh baked goods and espresso. **Elsie's Restaurant,** 10424 Silverdale Way NW, tel. (360) 692-2649, has greasy spoon breakfasts and burgers 24 hours a day.

The **Silverdale Farmers Market** takes place Saturday 9 a.m.-1 p.m. at Waterfront Park in Olde Towne from mid-May to mid-October. A good place to pick up produce, herbs, baked goods, flowers, and crafts.

Shopping and Events

The first major shopping mall on the Kitsap Peninsula, **Kitsap Mall,** just south of the junction of Highways 305 and 3, has over 115 stores, including Sears, Lamonts, Barnes & Noble

Books, and Bon Marché. The mall is surrounded by smaller shopping centers, fast-food restaurants, and **Silverdale Cinemas,** a four-theater complex at 9923 Clear Creek Rd. NW, tel. (360) 698-1510. **Silver Bay Herb Farm,** south of Silverdale at 9151 Tracyton Blvd., tel. (360) 692-1340, is a tranquil place with herb gardens, classes, plants, seeds, and a gift shop.

Silverdale's **Whaling Days** festival, held the last weekend of July, is the town's biggest event, with a parade, live music, arts-and-crafts displays, hydroplane races, a carnival, and fireworks.

Information and Transportation

For more information, contact the **Central Kitsap Chamber of Commerce,** 9191 Bay Shore Dr. NW, tel. (360) 692-6800. The telephone **area code** is 360.

Kitsap Transit, tel. (360) 377-2877, provides daily bus service to Bremerton, Bangor, Poulsbo, and Bainbridge Island, and meets all Southworth ferries. All Kitsap Transit buses have bike racks. **Bremerton-Kitsap Airporter,** tel. (360) 876-1737 or (800) 562-7948, and **Port Angeles-Seattle Bus Lines,** tel. (800) 764-2287, both offer shuttle buses to Sea-Tac Airport.

SEABECK

The small town of Seabeck occupies a point of land west of Silverdale on the east shore of Hood Canal, with dramatic panoramic views of the Olympic Mountains. It has a marina and a few restaurants and grocers, and is a favorite of anglers. The oldest outdoor theater in the Northwest, **Mountaineers' Forest Theater** holds productions near Seabeck late May through June. The amphitheater's terraced log seats are beautifully backdropped by rhododendrons, Douglas firs, and hemlocks; be prepared for a one-third-mile hike from your car to the theater. For tickets and information call (360) 284-6310.

Scenic Beach State Park

Scenic Beach State Park has forested campsites ($10; no RV hookups), salmon fishing, oyster gathering in season, and Olympic Mountain views on Hood Canal. The 88-acre park is particularly pleasant when the spring rhododendrons are in bloom. The park is open for day-use year-round, but the campground is only

open from late April to late September. Call (360) 830-5079 for more info, or (800) 452-5687 for campsite reservations ($6 extra fee), available up to 11 months ahead of time.

Accommodations

Once the private residence of Colonel Julian Willcox and built in 1936, the 10,000-square-foot waterfront **Willcox House,** on the Hood Canal south of Seabeck, was described as "the grand entertainment capitol of the Canal region." Five marble and copper fireplaces and the original oak parquet floors are accented by antique and period furniture, and every room is angled to capture a water and Olympic view. Outdoors, a 300-foot pier can accommodate guests' boats. Clark Gable once stayed in the room that now bears his name. Five rooms are available with private baths, a pool, boat dock, and full gourmet breakfast.

Just south of the Bangor Submarine Base, **Seabreeze Beach Cottage,** 16609 Olympic View Rd. NW, tel. (360) 692-4648, features a private cottage with two loft bedrooms, a fully equipped kitchen, jacuzzi, continental breakfast, and Olympic views from the sundeck. Rates are $129-149 d, with a two-night minimum stay.

Summer Song B&B, tel. (360) 830-5089, has a cozy beachfront cottage with a kitchen, fireplace, decks, and a full breakfast for just $69 s or d.

KEYPORT

Keyport is home to the top-secret **Naval Undersea Warfare Center,** a place that sounds like something out of a James Bond film. This is where much of America's torpedo research is conducted, gaining it the moniker "Torpedo Town." Just west of Keyport in Bangor is the **Naval Submarine Base,** where the fleet of eight Trident nuclear submarines is headquartered, and where nuclear warheads are stored. More than 5,000 military personnel live at the base. For visitors, a marvelous museum in Keyport offers a less-secretive look at the world of undersea warfare.

Naval Undersea Museum

This is one of the newest and certainly one of the most unique museums in Washington. The $10 million building features a wealth of fascinating displays, including interactive exhibits about the ocean. Items on display include mines, torpedoes, salvage and rescue equipment, underwater archaeology, and a periscope. There are scale models of Navy ships and subs, plus displays on the history of human underwater, from the Greek divers of 332 B.C., to the old-fashioned dive suits used for deep sea work, to the high-tech equipment of today. A large globe details the mountainous floor of the oceans. Some of the most interesting items are the torpedoes—including such oddities as a 19th century wind-up torpedo and a WW II Japanese version with space for a kamikaze human driver—and a half-scale model of an undersea rescue vehicle that appeared in the movie *Hunt for Red October*. The museum is open daily 10 a.m.-4 p.m. June-Sept., and Wed.-Sun. 10 a.m.-4 p.m. the rest of the year; tel. (360) 396-4148. Entrance is free. Out front is the blimp-like Trieste II, which reached the bottom of the Marianas Trench—the deepest point on earth—in 1960. The bulk of this cumbersome, 88-ton sub was filled with aviation fuel; the two men were suspended below it in a tiny chamber.

Practicalities

Continental Inn, on Hwy. 308 in Keyport, tel. (360) 779-5575 or (800) 537-5766, has motel rooms for $39 s or $44-59 d. Kitchenettes and suites are also available.

Island Lake, halfway between Keyport and Silverdale, has a swimming beach and bathhouse.

Kitsap Harbor Tours, tel. (360) 377-8924, offers daily passenger ferry service to Bremerton ($7 roundtrip) and Poulsbo ($5 roundtrip) from Keyport. The ferry operates mid-May through September only. **Kitsap Transit,** tel. (360) 377-2877, provides daily bus service throughout the peninsula and on Bainbridge Island.

POULSBO

The quaint town of Poulsbo (pop. 5,000) occupies the head of Liberty Bay (originally called Dogfish Bay for the small sharks that are so common here), and could pass for a tourist village on the coast of Maine. The main street is crowded with antique shops—11 at last count—along with cafes, galleries, high quality craft boutiques, a chocolate shop, and a wonderful quilt shop. Sailboats bob in the busy marina just a few feet away, and old-fashioned lamps brighten the evening sky. Locals jokingly call the town "Viking Junction," and it doesn't take much to see that Poulsbo loves to play up its Norwegian heritage.

History

Credit for the establishment of Poulsbo goes to Jorgen Eliason, a Norwegian who rowed across the Sound from Seattle in 1883 and was reminded of the mountains, fjords, and valleys of his homeland. His relatives quickly followed, scratching out a farm at the head of Dogfish Bay. Other Norwegians arrived, and for many years more than half the residents were from Norway; anyone speaking English was likely an outsider. In 1886, Ivar Moe named the town Paulsbo—Norwegian for Paul's Place—but the postmaster general couldn't read his handwriting and listed it instead as Poulsbo. Over the years, Poulsbo survived on logging, farming, and fishing. A fleet of Bering Sea schooners sailed north to Alaska each summer and back home in the fall with cargo holds filled with salted cod. The town's insularity was broken by the arrival of WW II as military personnel moved in to protect the vital naval base at Bremerton. (A long anti-submarine net was stretched across Port Orchard Bay.)

In the early 1960s, Poulsbo was a complacent community in need of an attraction, so they went to the University of Washington for ideas. A survey showed strong support for a "Little Norway" theme, and the concept quickly took hold, just in time for the 1962 World's Fair in Seattle. (The university did a similar makeover for Leavenworth, now a "Bavarian" town.) Scandinavian architecture and festivals perpetuate the culture of "Little Norway's" first immigrants; many of the downtown buildings have Scandinavian decor and sell some Scandinavian products. And yes, there is a Sons of Norway Hall in Poulsbo.

Sights

You can get friendly with sea cucumbers, starfish, sea anemones, and barnacles in the saltwater touch-tank, watch a jellyfish flotilla, and learn about other Puget Sound sea crea-

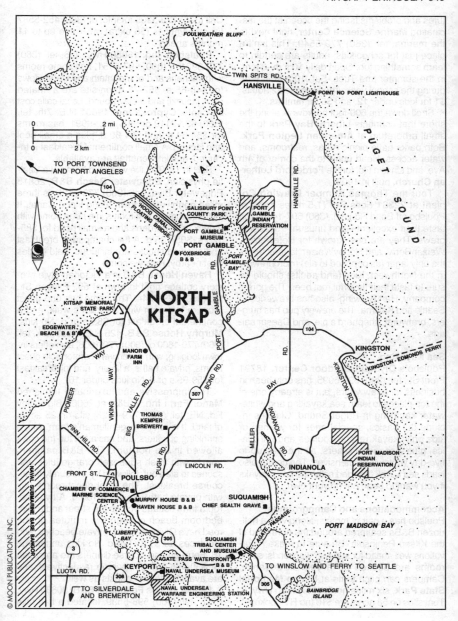

© MOON PUBLICATIONS, INC.

tures and problems facing the ocean at the fascinating **Marine Science Center,** right next to the marina, tel. (360) 779-5549. This isn't a place just for schoolkids; adults are certain to learn something too. Open daily 10 a.m.-6 p.m. in the summer and Tues.-Sat. 10 a.m.-4 p.m. during the school year. Admission is $2 adults, $1 for kids under 12, and $5 for families.

Stroll down the 600-foot boardwalk along the shore that connects **Liberty Bay Park** to the small arboretum at **American Legion Park.** Both parks have picnic areas, restrooms, and water access. Head uphill to the corner of 4th Ave. and Lincoln Rd. for the **Fordefjord Lutheran Church,** built in 1908.

Tour the **Thomas Kemper Brewing Co.** plant at 22381 Foss Rd. (1.5 miles north of Poulsbo off Bond Rd.), tel. (360) 697-1446, and taste their excellent—and unusual—seasonal brews. They are best known for Hefeweizen, WeizenBerry, and HoneyWeizen lagers; this is the only lager (as opposed to ale) microbrewery in the Northwest. Kids (and adults) should be sure to taste their flavorful root beer. The parent company, Hart Brewing, also has breweries in Seattle and Kalama. The brewery pub has burgers, bratwurst, shepherd's pie, and Caesar salads.

Sea Kayaking

Poulsbo's **Olympic Outdoor Center,** 18791 Front St., tel. (360) 697-6095, has only been in business for a few years, but is already one of the top places to learn sea kayaking and whitewater kayaking in Puget Sound. Classes include the basics, special ones for women or kids only, kayak rescue courses and roll clinics, plus a range of others, all the way up to five-day whitewater intensives. The center also leads sea kayak trips and sells and rents kayaks if you want to head out on your own.

Accommodations and Campgrounds

Poulsbo has a pair of motels, along with a half-dozen B&Bs scattered around the north end of the Kitsap Peninsula. Be sure to make reservations well ahead for summer weekends; some rooms are booked up a year in advance. Campers can pitch tents at **Kitsap Memorial State Park,** six miles north of town on Hwy. 3. Tent sites on 58 acres are $10 (no RV hookups).

Call (360) 779-3205 for info, or (800) 452-5587 for reservations ($6 extra), available up to 11 months ahead.

Poulsbo's Inn, 18680 Hwy. 305, tel. (360) 779-3921 or (800) 597-5151, has some rooms with kitchens and/or mountain and water views for $48-65 s, $52-75 d; on-site are a heated pool, jacuzzi, and a playground. Local calls cost 25 cents. **Cypress Inn,** 19801 N.E. 7th, tel. (360) 697-2119 or (800) 752-9991, has rooms for $54-64 s, and $64-69 d, plus a small pool and jacuzzi. A small continental breakfast is included, and kitchenettes are available.

Built in 1929 as the weekend home of a Seattle physician, **Edgewater Beach B&B,** 26818 Edgewater Blvd., tel. (360) 779-2525, is three miles northwest of town along Hood Canal. It includes three guest rooms in a large home with a deck, plus gardens and a small pond for $85-125 s, $95-135 d. A full champagne breakfast and evening snacks are included; bald eagles nest nearby. Kids welcome.

Haven House B&B is a Victorian-style two-story cottage right in town at 592 Eliason St., tel. (360) 779-9544. The home has one guest room, a sunroom with a widow's walk, and a continental breakfast for $89 s or d. No kids. **Murphy House B&B,** 425 N.E. Hostmark, tel. (360) 779-1600 or (800) 779-1606, also offers in-town lodging, with seven very comfortable guest rooms, private baths, a library, and full breakfast for $59-95 s or d. No kids under 16.

The impressive and luxuriously furnished **Manor Farm Inn,** a B&B at 26069 Big Valley Rd. NE, tel. (360) 779-4628, sits on 25 acres of land. It is run as a "gentleman's farm" with a sprinkling of critters, and has a hot tub (no cows allowed in the hot tub). The B&B pampers guests with fresh-squeezed orange juice and scones to start out, followed by a leisurely three-course breakfast. The eight guest rooms (six with private bath) are $100-150 d. A two-bedroom farm cottage across the street and a two-bedroom beach cottage two minutes up the road have Olympic views, private beaches, and fireplaces for $170-190 d. No kids under age 16. Four- and six-course dinners are an option for $30 and $50 per person respectively, and are available for nonguests as well.

Farther away is **Foxbridge B&B,** 30680 Hwy. 3 NE, tel. (360) 598-5599, located a half mile from the Hood Canal floating bridge. The two-story home sits on five heavily wooded acres. The three guest rooms have private baths, and a full breakfast is served. Rates are $75 s or d; no kids under age 16.

Agate Pass Waterfront B&B is on the other end of north Kitsap, next to the Agate Pass bridge southeast of Poulsbo. The grounds—once part of a nursery—front Port Orchard Narrows and the beach. One guest room is available for $70 s or d, including a make-your-own breakfast in the kitchen. No kids.

Food

Despite its small size, Poulsbo has one of the best collections of eating places on the Kitsap Peninsula. Start out for a breakfast inside **Henry's Family Restaurant**, 18887 Hwy. 305, tel. (360) 779-4685, complete with a Norwegian decor. **Poulsbohemian Coffeehouse**, 19003 Front St., tel. (360) 779-9199, is a friendly daytime gathering place, with espresso, giant chocolate chip cookies, cozy couches and chairs, art on the walls, a big rack of local brochures, and ongoing arts events of all sorts—from chess games, to writer's workshops, to haiku poetry sessions. Great water views too.

Get delicious homemade soups (especially the Black Forest) and other lunches, plus a spot of tea at **Judith's Tearooms & Rose Cafe**, on Front St., tel. (360) 697-3449. This is also the place to get pickled herring and other Scandinavian offerings. Another recommended lunchtime place is **Poulsbo Country Deli**, 18937 Front St., tel. (360) 779-2763.

The New Day Seafood Eatery, 325 N.E. Hostmark St., tel. (360) 697-3183, overlooks Liberty Bay and serves tasty fish and chips made from fresh fish caught by their own boat. Head to **Mudflat Willie's**, 225 Lindvig Way, tel. (360) 697-7700, for the finest local seafood and steaks. And yes, there really is a Mudflat Willie. **Viking House Restaurant** on the wharf, tel. (360) 779-9882, is notable for its large outside deck where you can enjoy the seafood, and the lounge with live music and dancing. For the smoked variety, **Poulsbo Smokehouse**, 18881 Front St. NE, tel. (360) 779-1099, has smoked salmon and sausages.

Perhaps the best known food coming from Poulsbo is Poulsbo Bread, originally baked at

Sluys Poulsbo Bakery, 18924 Front St. NE, tel. (360) 779-2798. The Poulsbo bread sold in grocery stores is now made elsewhere, but Sluys still bakes excellent pastries, Norwegian lefse, and coarse-grained breads such as pumpernickel, Swedish limpa, Irish raisin, German sourdough, and rye.

That's a Some Italian Ristorante, 18881 Front St. NE, tel. (360) 779-2266, has the traditional red checked tablecloths, but the Italian food and pizzas have West Coast influences, including an Anaheim chili penne. Get huge thick-crust pizzas and pizza by the slice at **Poulsbo Pizzaria**, 19559 Viking Way, tel. (360) 779-9812.

Jose's Flamingo Cafe, 18830 Front St. NE, tel. (360) 779-7676, is one of the more distinctive Mexican-inspired restaurants in the Puget Sound area. The menu isn't the same old mashed beans and colored rice. Everything is made to order in the open kitchen and packed with flavor. Even the salsa is notable. Recommended.

Head to a different corner of the globe at **Old Copper Kettle** for real English fare, including a traditional ploughman's lunch, Welsh rarebit, and high tea with cucumber finger-sandwiches or fresh scones and cream. The **Blarney Stone**, 20530 Viking Ave. NW, tel. (360) 697-2662, has good burgers and Irish food.

For Chinese food, visit the Vietnamese-run **Golden Lion Restaurant**, 19438 7th Ave. NE, tel. (360) 697-5066.

Festivals

Poulsbo's summer season is packed with ethnic events. The **Viking Fest** in mid-May celebrates Poulsbo's Norwegian heritage with a parade, arts and crafts show, pancake breakfast, food booths, and fun run. The **Scandia Midsommarfest** in June brings Scandinavian food, music, and Norwegian folk dancers, and pole dancing for a solstice celebration at Frank Raab Park. **Thomas Kemper Oktoberfest,** held the last two weekends in September, includes oompah music, folk dancing, a sausage-tossing contest, kids events, German food, and barrels of Thomas Kemper beers, including a specially brewed Oktoberfest Lager. On the third Saturday of October, the First Lutheran Church puts on a **Traditional Lutefisk Dinner** with Swedish meatballs for the wimps. The holiday season brings the **Yule Log Ceremony,** held in early December, featuring Norwegian folk dancers, lighting of the Yule log, and a guest appearance by Santa Claus by boat. A **Lighted Boat Parade** follows in mid-December.

Information and Services

For information, visit the **Greater Poulsbo Chamber of Commerce,** 19131 8th Ave. NE, tel. (360) 779-4848. Open Mon.-Fri. 9 a.m.-5 p.m. If you're downtown, drop by the small visitor center inside Poulsbohemian Coffeehouse, open daily. Pick up a walking tour of Poulsbo's historic buildings at either place. The **area code** for Poulsbo is 360.

Poulsbo is the home of the **Northwest College of Art,** located in an old brick mansion south of town on Hwy. 305, tel. (360) 779-9993.

The **North Kitsap Community Swimming Pool,** 1881 N.E. Hostmark St., tel. (360) 779-3790, has lap swimming and open swim hours.

Two local bookshops are **Shotwell's Book Store,** 18882 Front St. NE, tel. (360) 779-5909, for new titles, and **Book Stop,** 18954-A Front St. NE, tel. (360) 779-9773, with a big choice of used books, including many offbeat titles.

Transportation and Tours

Kitsap Transit, tel. (360) 377-2877, provides daily bus service to Bremerton, Silverdale, Bangor, and Bainbridge Island and meets all Southworth ferries. All Kitsap Transit buses have bike racks. **Bremerton-Kitsap Airporter,** tel. (360) 876-1737 or (800) 562-7948, and **Port Angeles-Seattle Bus Lines,** tel. (800) 764-2287, both offer shuttle buses to Sea-Tac Airport.

New Horizon Tours, tel. (360) 779-9288, has guided historical walking tours of downtown Poulsbo. **Kitsap Harbor Tours,** tel. (360) 377-8924, offers daily passenger ferry service to Bremerton ($9 roundtrip) and Poulsbo ($5 roundtrip) from Poulsbo. The ferry operates mid-May through September only.

BAINBRIDGE ISLAND

Just a 35-minute ferry ride from downtown Seattle, Bainbridge Island offers a comfortable escape from the hordes, a place where yupster commuters retreat to rural waterside homes and retirees enjoy a peaceful escape from the workaday world. Over 17,000 folks call Bainbridge home today.

History

When Vancouver sailed through Puget Sound in 1792, he didn't realize that Bainbridge Island was an island. Then in 1841 Charles N. Wilkes found Agate Pass, the waterway separating the island from the Kitsap Peninsula. Wilkes named the island for Capt. William Bainbridge, a Naval hero from the USS *Constitution.* Within 15 years of its charting, Bainbridge Island was home to one of Puget Sound's greatest lumber mills, and soon thereafter its ports were world renowned. Port Blakely had the biggest sawmill in the world, employing more than 1,000 men, and the shipyard there built the largest sternwheeler at that time in the Pacific Northwest, the *Julia.*

Today the four- by 12-mile island is almost entirely privately owned by politicians, doctors, artists, many stockbrokers, a few fishermen, and a lot of ordinary folks, 70% of whom commute by ferry to Seattle-area jobs. Although the entire island is officially incorporated, there is only one real town: **Winslow,** located along Eagle Harbor where the ferry docks. Winslow is a genuine, albeit gentrified, town with Volvos crawling the streets, yachts in the marina, and classical music in the cafes. Several other small settlements are scattered around Bainbridge, including Lynwood Center and Island Center.

If you're arriving by ferry from Seattle, you'll find Winslow an easy place to explore by foot. Start on the shoreline footpath that heads west from the ferry to **Eagle Harbor Waterfront Park,** a fine place for a sunny-day picnic.

Bainbridge Island Historical Museum

The history of former mill towns Port Madison and Port Blakely (once the largest lumber mill in the world) is preserved in exhibits and displays at the Bainbridge Island Historical Museum in Strawberry Hill Park. The building itself offers a blast from the past; it's a charming little red schoolhouse. Open Saturday 11 a.m.-4 p.m. in the summer, closed winters; admission is free.

Fay-Bainbridge State Park

This park covers a mere 17 acres but has campsites in the trees and along the beach ($10 for

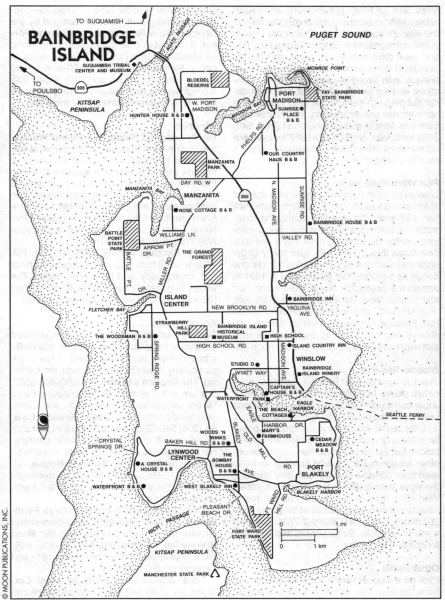

BAINBRIDGE ISLAND

TO SUQUAMISH

PUGET SOUND

SUQUAMISH TRIBAL
CENTER AND MUSEUM

TO
POULSBO

305

KITSAP
PENINSULA

BLOEDEL
RESERVE

MONROE POINT

PORT
MADISON

FAY - BAINBRIDGE
STATE PARK

W. PORT
MADISON

MADISON BAY

SUNRISE
PLACE
B & B

PHELPS RD.

HUNTER HOUSE B & B

OUR COUNTRY
HAUS B & B

MANZANITA
PARK

N MADISON AVE.

SUNRISE RD.

DAY RD. W

MANZANITA BAY

MANZANITA

305

ROSE COTTAGE B & B

BAINBRIDGE HOUSE B & B

VALLEY RD.

BATTLE
POINT
STATE
PARK

WILLIAMS LN.

ARROW PT.
DR.

THE GRAND
FOREST

BATTLE PT. DR.

MILLER RD.

FLETCHER BAY

ISLAND
CENTER

NEW BROOKLYN RD.

BAINBRIDGE INN

YAQUINA
AVE.

SPRING RIDGE RD.

STRAWBERRY
HILL PARK

THE WOODSMAN B & B

BAINBRIDGE
ISLAND
HISTORICAL
MUSEUM

HIGH SCHOOL RD.

HIGH SCHOOL

ISLAND COUNTRY INN

MADISON AVE.

WINSLOW

STUDIO D

WYATT WAY

BAINBRIDGE
ISLAND WINERY

WATERFRONT
PARK

CAPTAIN'S
HOUSE B & B

*EAGLE
HARBOR*

THE BEACH
COTTAGES

SEATTLE FERRY

EAGLE

OLD

BLAKELY

HARBOR
MARY'S
FARMHOUSE

DR.

CEDAR
MEADOW
B & B

WOODS 'N
WINKS
B & B

BAKER HILL RD.

CRYSTAL
SPRINGS DR.

A CRYSTAL
HOUSE B & B

LYNWOOD
CENTER

THE BOMBAY
HOUSE
B & B

MILL

RD.

PORT
BLAKELY

WATERFRONT B & B

WEST BLAKELY INN

AVE.

FT WARD

PLEASANT
BEACH DR.

BLAKELY HARBOR

HILL RD.

0   1 mi
0   1 km

RICH PASSAGE

FORT WARD STATE PARK

KITSAP PENINSULA

MANCHESTER STATE PARK

© MOON PUBLICATIONS, INC.

tents; $15 for RVs), hot showers, and beach access with scuba diving and boating facilities at the island's northeast end. This is the closest public campground to Seattle—just a ferry ride and short drive or bus ride away—so it is very popular in the summer months. The views are fine too, with over-the-water vistas of the Cascades and the twinkling lights of Seattle. A delightful place to escape the city. The park is open for day-use year-round, and for camping from late April to mid-October. Call (360) 842-3931 for details, or (800) 452-5687 for campsite reservations ($6 extra fee), available up to 11 months ahead of time.

Fort Ward State Park

Located six miles from the Winslow ferry terminal at the island's south end, Fort Ward State Park has 137 acres for day-use picnicking, bird-watching, boating, and scuba diving on a mile-long beach. No camping here, but a one-mile path loops through the park. Like many of the state parks surrounding Puget Sound, this one began as a military fort. Established in 1891 to protect the Bremerton Naval Yard, it and Fort Manchester (now Manchester State Park; see "Port Orchard," above) faced each other across Rich Passage. Underwater nets were placed offshore during WW II to snag any Japanese subs that might stray into these waters, but none did.

Bloedel Reserve

The 150-acre Bloedel Reserve contains many native plants from Washington, a bog, pond, Japanese garden, moss garden, and spacious lawns, plus the old Bloedel home, now used as a visitor center. The reserve is especially popular in the spring when the rhododendrons are in bloom, but the 15,000 cyclamen plants are another attraction. Get here by heading six miles west from Winslow on Hwy. 305, and following the signs another mile to the entrance. It's open Wed.-Sun. 10 a.m.-4 p.m. all year, but reservations are necessary because they only let in 200 people a day; call (360) 842-7631. Entrance costs $4 for adults, $2 for seniors and kids, free for children under five.

Other Parks

Pick up a map of hiking trails on Bainbridge from the chamber of commerce office. The largest parcel of public land—280 acres—contains second-growth forests managed by the Dept. of Natural Resources. Called **Grand Forest,** it is located near the center of the island off Mandus Oldon Rd. and has two miles of paths. **Manzanita Park** is a 120-acre parcel with a two-mile hiking and equestrian trail through woods and wetlands. The park is on Day Rd. on the northwest side of the island.

Wineries

Family-operated **Bainbridge Island Winery,** one-quarter mile from the ferry terminal at 682 Hwy. 305 in Winslow, tel. (206) 842-9463, is the only place (outside of a restaurant) to buy their limited-run wines made from grapes and strawberries grown on Bainbridge Island. The outdoor picnic area is a refreshing spot for a lunch break, and the antique wine glass collection is worth a gander. Tours and tastings are held Wed.-Sun. noon-5 p.m.

Rich Passage Winery, 7869 N.E. Day Rd. W, is a small family operation producing pinot noir, chardonnay, and fumé blanc wines. The winery is generally open for tastings, but call (360) 842-8199 to be sure someone is there.

Accommodations

See the "Bainbridge Island Accommodations" chart for a complete listing of the 18 fine B&Bs and one new motel on the island. A few of the particularly notable places include the following. **The Captain's House,** tel. (206) 842-3557, is a turn-of-the-century B&B overlooking Eagle Harbor with rowboats, tennis courts, and an old-fashioned porch swing. **Cedar Meadow B&B,** tel. (206) 842-5291, is a beautiful older home on six acres with grazing sheep, flower gardens, two grand pianos, and friendly hosts. The charming turn-of-the-century **Bombay House,** tel. (206) 842-3926 or (800) 598-3926, overlooks Rich Passage and has country antiques, flowers, and a widow's walk.

Other historic B&Bs include: **Marys Farmhouse,** tel. (206) 842-4952, a 1904 restored country home on five acres, and the **West Blakely Inn,** tel. (206) 842-1427 or (800) 835-1427, built as an Odd Fellows Hall in 1912 and transformed into a B&B.

For a vacation from the kids, try **Beach Cottages,** tel. (206) 842-6081, four waterside cottages on Eagle Harbor with Olympic and Cascade views. The kitchen has ingredients for a cook-it-yourself breakfast.

Food

Streamliner Diner, Winslow Way and Bjune, tel. (360) 842-8595, is famous for its hearty breakfasts that include wonderful home fries and omelettes. Justifiably popular with both locals and tourists; be ready for a long line most mornings. For something lighter, get fresh baked goods and espresso coffees at **Bainbridge Bakers,** 140 Winslow Way W, tel. (360) 842-1822.

Harbour Public House, 231 Parfitt Way SW, tel. (360) 842-9037, has tasty on-the-water eats, including fish and chips and burgers, plus microbrewed beers. On the waterfront at the Winslow Wharf Marina, **Madrona Cafe,** 403 Madison Ave. S, tel. (360) 842-8339, features seafood, pasta, steaks, and salads.

Four Swallows, 4569 Lynwood Center Rd., tel. (360) 842-3397, features a menu that changes frequently, with perfectly prepared pasta, fish, and pizzas. Very good. **Pleasant Beach Grill,** 4738 Lynwood Center Rd., tel. (360) 842-4347, is in a Tudor house with several intimate rooms and a Northwest and international menu.

Noted for serving some of the best Mexican food in the Northwest is the **San Carlos Restaurant,** two blocks from the Winslow ferry terminal at 279 Madison N, tel. (360) 842-1999. Open for lunch Tues.-Fri. and dinner daily.

Two places offer good Thai cooking on the island: **Sawatdy Thai Cuisine,** 8780 Fletcher Bay Rd., Island Center, tel. (360) 780-2429, and **Bainbridge Thai Cuisine,** 330 Madison Ave. S, tel. (360) 780-2403, with waterfront dining. For Chinese food, visit **Golden Turtle Restaurant,** 190 Madison Ave. N, tel. (360) 842-4472.

The **Bainbridge Farmers Market** comes to Winslow Green on Saturday 9 a.m.-2 p.m. May-Sept. and includes flowers, organic fruits and vegetables, handicrafts, and ethnic foods.

BAINBRIDGE ISLAND ACCOMMODATIONS

Accommodations are arranged from least to most expensive. Rates may be lower during the winter months. The area code is 206.

Mary's Farmhouse B&B; 5129 McDonald Rd. NE; tel. 842-4952; $45 s, $50-60 d; 1904 country farmhouse on five acres, two guest rooms, shared bath, grand piano, continental breakfast, kids welcome

Captain's House B&B; 234 Parfitt Way NE; tel. 842-3557; $45-70 s or d; turn-of-the-century home overlooking Eagle Harbor, porch swing, two guest rooms, private baths, full breakfast

Cedar Meadow B&B; 10411 Old Creosote Hill Rd.; tel. 842-5291; $50-80 s or d; large home on six wooded acres, four guest rooms, private or shared bath, full breakfast, kids welcome

Bombay House B&B; 8490 Beck Rd. NE; tel. 842-3926 or (800) 598-3926; $50-80 s, $55-125 s or d; 1907 Victorian home overlooking Rich Passage, gardens, widow's walk, gazebo, four guest rooms with antiques, private or shared baths, full breakfast, no kids under six

Woods 'n Winks B&B; 8190 Baker Hill Rd. NE; tel. 842-4639; $63 s or d; tiny rustic cabin, kitchenette, deck with hot tub, rose garden, continental breakfast

The Woodsman B&B; 7700 Spring Ridge Rd. NE; tel. 842-7386; $65 s or d; Dutch Colonial home on five acres, hot tub, fireplace, library, one guest room, private bath, full breakfast, kids welcome

Sunrise Place B&B; 10245 N.E. Sunrise Place; tel. 842-9537 or (800) 390-9595; $65-85 s or d; Victorian-style home on 2.5 acres, one guest room, one suite with jacuzzi tub, private baths, continental breakfast, no kids

Island Country Inn; 920 Hildebrand Lane NE; tel. 842-6861 or (800) 842-8429; $55-115 s, $65-125 d; new motel, outdoor pool, jacuzzi, kitchenettes available, continental breakfast, AAA approved

(continues on next page)

BAINBRIDGE ISLAND ACCOMMODATIONS
(continued)

Waterfront B&B; 3314 Crystal Spring Dr. NE; tel. 842-2431; $70 s or d; waterside cottage, one guest room, private bath and entrance, honeymoon place, continental breakfast

Bainbridge Inn B&B; 9200 Hemlock St.; tel. 842-7564; $70-85 s or d; hot tub, two bedroom suite, kitchen, private bath, continental breakfast, kids welcome

A Crystal House B&B; 4062 Crystal Springs Dr.; tel. 842-5070; $75 s or d; three-room suite, private bath, woodstove, deck, continental breakfast

Studio D B&B; 1028 Grow Ave. NW; tel. 842-9513; $75 s or d; Winslow carriage house, kitchenette, continental breakfast

Rose Cottage B&B; 11744 Olympic Terrace; tel. 842-6248 or (800) 842-6255; $75 s or d; cottage with private bath, deck, rose garden, continental breakfast, AAA approved

Bainbridge House B&B; 11301 Logg Rd. NE; tel. 842-1599; $75-85 s or d; two large guest rooms in cottage, private baths, full breakfast, kids welcome, hot tub, AAA approved

Harp House B&B; 6490 Ada's Will Lane; tel. 842-2326; $80 s or d; two guest rooms, shared baths, continental breakfast, kids okay

West Blakely Inn B&B; 8494 Odd Fellows Rd.; tel. 842-1427 or (800) 835-1427; $80 s or d; restored 1912 Odd Fellows Hall, hot tub, three large rooms, private baths, full breakfast

Our Country Haus B&B; 13718 Ellingsen Rd. NE; tel. 842-8425; $80 s or d; private carriage house on two acres, gardens and pond, private bath and kitchen, continental breakfast

Beach Cottages B&B; 5831 Ward Ave. NE; tel. 842-6081; $95 s or d; four shore-side cottages, two-night minimum on weekends, Olympic and Cascade views, waterfall, fireplace, robes, cook-it-yourself breakfast, no kids

Hunter House B&B; 6740 Seabold Rd. NE; tel. 842-7777; $95-110 s or d; two guest rooms, king-size beds, private baths, deck with water views, full breakfasts

Events

In February, Puget Sound's cycling season kicks off with the popular **Chilly Hilly** bicycle marathon. More than 4,000 riders pedal around Bainbridge. The island's most unique event is one you're likely to miss, the **Scotch Broom Parade,** held on the spur of the moment sometime in June, whenever local folks decide to put it on. The **Fourth of July** brings a two-day street fair and parade to Winslow. No fireworks, but Bainbridge offers a fine view of Seattle's fireworks show. **Concerts in the Park** take place at Waterfront Park in Winslow on Wednesday evenings in July and August, and an **Outdoor Music Festival** brings more performers to Battle Point Park in August. The **Holiday Faire** features local arts and crafts at Winslow Green on Saturday from Thanksgiving to Christmas.

Shopping

Downtown Winslow is jammed with gift and import shops, including several inside Winslow Green, the little strip mall in town. **The Landing** on Madison Ave. has more than 100 artist's booths and other displays. Two fine bookshops are in the same building at 155 Winslow Way: **Eagle Harbor Books** upstairs has new titles; head downstairs for a great choice of used and out-of-print books at **Fortner Books,** tel. (360) 780-2030.

Information and Services

The **Bainbridge Island Chamber of Commerce Visitor Center,** 590 Winslow Way E, tel. (360) 842-3700, is open Mon.-Fri. 9 a.m.-5 p.m. year-round. It's at the top of the hill as you exit the ferry. Stop by to pick up a map of Winslow's historic buildings. The **area code** for

Bainbridge Island is 206, the same as Seattle's. Swim at **Ray Williamson Memorial Pool,** an indoor pool at the high school.

Transportation

The **Washington State Ferry,** tel. (360) 842-2345 or (800) 843-3779, provides service between downtown Seattle and Winslow on Bainbridge Island every 50 minutes throughout the day. The crossing takes 35 minutes and costs $7.10 one-way for car and driver ($5.90 in winter), $3.50 roundtrip for passengers, and $4 roundtrip for bicycle riders. The Seattle-Bainbridge route is the busiest ferry run in Washington—over six million riders each year. Be ready for long delays—especially in the summer—if you're traveling on Friday evenings from Seattle to Bainbridge, and on Sunday evenings back to Seattle. Avoid the waits by leaving your car behind and taking the bus.

Kitsap Transit, tel. (360) 373-2877 or 697-2877, provides daily service to Bremerton, Silverdale, Bangor, and Poulsbo and meets all state ferries in Winslow. Fares are 50-75 cents. All Kitsap Transit buses have bike racks.

Tours of Bainbridge and surrounding areas are offered by **WeatherVane Tours,** tel. (360) 780-5003. Half-day tours of the island are $45; full-day trips include Port Townsend, Hood Canal, and a short visit to Olympic National Park for $75.

SUQUAMISH

The name "Suquamish" came from the Indian word D'suq'wub (apparently after much mispronunciation), meaning "Place of Clear Salt Water." The Suquamish were a peaceful people, and as the white man took over they were forced to surrender their own culture: children were sent to Tacoma schools, where boys learned trades and girls provided cheap kitchen labor, while the Suquamish men went to work at Port Madison lumber mills.

Historical Sights

The **Suquamish Museum,** tel. (360) 598-3311, off Hwy. 305 just beyond the Bainbridge Island bridge, is a good place to start a tour of Suquamish and the Port Madison Indian Reservation. Chief Seattle, his Suquamish descendants, and Pacific Northwest history come to life in this shoreline museum with exhibits on the history of the people and commercial fishing, plus historical photos and a slide presentation narrated by Suquamish elders. Open daily 10 a.m.-5 p.m. May-Sept., and Fri.-Sun. 11 a.m.-4 p.m. the rest of the year; admission is $2.50 for adults, $2 for seniors, and $1 for kids under 13. The gift shop has a few handmade baskets and books for sale.

Chief Sealth's Grave overlooks Puget Sound with a glimpse of Seattle's skyscrapers in a small, peaceful cemetery on the Port Madison Indian Reservation. It's not hard to tell which grave is his; painted canoes are positioned high above the headstone to honor this leader of the Suquamish Nation and friend to the early settlers. Follow the signs to find the graveyard.

A cedar longhouse 500 feet long and 60 feet wide—the communal home of eight Suquamish chiefs (including Chief Sealth) and their families—stood at the waterfront site now called "Ole-Man-House" until 1870, when federal agents torched it in a subtle effort to discourage this form of accommodation. Today a Washington State Heritage site, a small historical display marks the location of the original longhouse on a lot surrounded by housing developments at the west end of Agate Passage. After seeing the slide show and displays at the Suquamish Museum depicting the peaceful, everyday Suquamish life, this minuscule historical remembrance will break your heart.

Practicalities

Eat at **Karsten's Fine Dining** in Suquamish Village Square, tel. (360) 598-3080, where they offer a Friday prime rib and seafood buffet and a Sunday brunch, plus music several nights a week.

Chief Seattle Days, an annual weekend affair held the third week in August at the downtown Suquamish waterfront park, has been going strong since 1911 with canoe racing, arts and crafts, a powwow with traditional Native American dancing, and a salmon bake.

KINGSTON

Kingston is a pleasant little town toward the northern tip of the Kitsap Peninsula that is best known as the ferry landing directly across the sound from Edmonds. It is mostly a residential community with a cluster of shops near the ferry landing.

Accommodations and Food
Smiley's Colonial Motel, 11057 Hwy. 104, tel. (360) 297-3622, has rooms for $30-40 s or d.

One of the favorite places to eat is **Dickinson's Fish and Ale House,** at the Kingston Cove Marina at the ferry dock, tel. (360) 297-8566. It serves all three meals and has a wide selection of seafood. Also popular is **Kingston Hotel Cafe,** tel. (360) 297-8100, at 1st and Washington, with a deck overlooking the water and good breakfasts and lunches. **Schooner Tavern** occasionally has live music.

The **Kingston Farmers Market** takes place next to the ferry dock Saturday 9 a.m.-2 p.m., May to mid-October. This is a good place to look for handmade clothing and crafts, along with fresh produce.

Events
Kingston's **Sea Fest** takes place on July 4th weekend and includes a parade, music, food booths, dancing in the streets, logging competitions, fireworks, and the speedy slug races.

Transportation
The **Washington State Ferry** system has service between Edmonds and Kingston approximately every 40 minutes during the day, and the crossing takes 30 minutes. Fares are $7.10 one-way for car and driver ($5.90 in winter), $3.50 roundtrip for passengers, and $4 roundtrip for bicycle riders. Call (360) 842-2345 or (800) 843-3779 for details. A word to the wise: If you're returning late from the Olympic Peninsula on the Edmonds ferry, be sure to check the ferry schedules because the Edmonds-Kingston ferry shuts down a couple of hours earlier than the Bainbridge-Seattle ferries. Also note that you can expect delays if you're heading to Kingston on a Friday evening or east to Edmonds on a Sunday evening in the summer.

Kitsap Transit, tel. (360) 373-2877 or 697-2877, provides daily bus service to Bremerton, Silverdale, Bangor, Poulsbo, and Bainbridge Island and meets all Kingston ferries. Fares are 50-75 cents. All Kitsap Transit buses have bike racks.

Olympic Bus Lines, tel. (360) 452-3858, has daily connections to Port Angeles, Sequim, Kingston, Seattle, and Sea-Tac.

HANSVILLE

The **Hansville Recreation Area** occupies the northernmost tip of the Kitsap Peninsula, northeast of Port Gamble and the Hood Canal Bridge. This is the place to catch salmon in Puget Sound—most fishing is done quite close to shore, rarely more than a half mile out. The facilities here are all geared toward fishermen: the accommodations are sparse and the lone restaurant isn't fancy.

The squat **Point No Point Lighthouse** occupies a parcel of land just west of Hansville. It was named by the Wilkes expedition of 1841 because the point that was visible from one approach disappeared from the other. The light station—established in 1879—is open Sat.-Sun. noon-4 p.m. May-Sept., or by appointment only in winter; call (360) 286-5420. The beach here provides good views of Hood Canal, Admiralty Inlet, and Whidbey Island and is a favorite place to dig for clams. Just south of Hansville is tiny **Buck Lake,** which has picnic areas, bathhouses for swimmers, a boat launch, fishing, and a playground.

For something a bit more out of the ordinary, you aren't likely to miss the ship-shape home located on the road to Point No Point; it's one of the most distinctive in the state. For more weirdness, check out the "world's largest rocking chair" at the turnoff to Hansville on Hwy. 104 (west of Kingston).

Captain's Landing, tel. (360) 638-2257, has rustic and modern cabins with kitchenettes ($65-80 for up to four people), an RV park, and a waterfront restaurant and pub. The cabins are open year-round, but the restaurant and pub are seasonal.

PORT GAMBLE AREA

A native of East Machias, Maine, Capt. William Talbot founded a sawmill at Port Gamble in 1853 and modeled the settlement after his hometown, complete with traditional New England-style homes and imported trees from back East. The Pope and Talbot sawmill survived until 1995 when it closed for good and everything was sold off in an auction. It had been the oldest continuously operating sawmill in North America, and the town was entirely owned by the company; all the homes were rented from Pope and Talbot. The homes—restored in the 1960s—are all on the National Register of Historic Places, and the town is preserved as an historic district. Walking down these quiet streets past the neat and recently painted houses and the steeply steepled church while shuffling through the fallen leaves, you'd swear you were in Maine. Many other Washington towns have put on false fronts that turn them into European or wild-west towns, but Port Gamble is the real thing, a place that simply never changed. Unfortunately, changes are bound to happen now that the mill has shut its doors and the blue collar workers are leaving. As of this writing Port Gamble's future was unknown, but another sawmill property owned by the company—Port Ludlow—was recently transformed into a lavish resort. It will be a sad day if Port Gamble becomes yet another hangout of nouveau-riche Seattle commuters.

Historical Sights

Port Gamble's two museums are housed in the charming three-story **General Store** (built in 1914), where you can purchase groceries, sandwiches, and ice cream cones. Head upstairs to discover two levels of seashells in the **Of Sea and Shore Museum.** The collection, assembled by Tom Rice over a period of more than 40 years, is one of the largest shell collections in the country and includes more than 25,000 species (only a fraction of which are on display), plus a variety of other oddities such as gargantuan beetles and other insects from hell. Books and shells of various kinds are offered for sale to help support the museum. Open Tues.-Sun. 11 a.m.-4 p.m. from mid-May to mid-September, and Sat.-Sun. 11 a.m.-4 p.m. the rest of the year; free.

The **Port Gamble Historic Museum,** on the back side of the General Store, tel. (360) 297-3341, houses exhibits from the timber company, original rooms from hotels and houses, sailing ship interiors, and a "Forest of the Future" display. Open daily 10 a.m.-4 p.m. from Memorial Day to Labor Day; $1 for adults, 50 cents for seniors and students, free for kids under age six. Closed during the winter months.

The rest of Port Gamble consists of more than two dozen 19th-century homes, including the **Thompson House,** said to be the oldest continuously lived-in home in Washington (the McFadden home in Chehalis also lays claim to this title). The cemetery has the grave of Gustav Englebrecht, the first U.S. Navy man to die in action in the Pacific. He was killed in 1856 during an Indian raid. Pick up a walking tour of Port Gamble's historic sites at the museum.

Parks

Located four miles south of Port Gamble on Hwy. 3, Kitsap Memorial State Park has saltwater swimming, hiking, fishing, oyster- and clam-gathering, boating, picnicking, scuba diving, and campsites ($10 for tents; no RV hookups) on 58 acres. Call (360) 779-3205 for information, or (800) 452-5687 for campsite reservations ($6 extra fee), available up to 11 months ahead of time. The park's sturdy log hall and kitchen shelters were built by the Work Progress Administration in the 1930s. Open year-round. Additional campsites can be found at **Salisbury Point County Park,** right next to the Hood Canal Floating Bridge.

Hood Canal Nursery

The Hood Canal Nursery, on the edge of town off Hwy. 3 (follow the signs), tel. (360) 297-7555, was established in 1976 to grow more than three million trees annually on Pope and Talbot lands. Tours of the facility include a look at four greenhouses, a water reservoir, pump house, tree shade house, and a film about tree growing; free.

HOOD CANAL AND VICINITY

The Kitsap Peninsula is separated from the Olympic Peninsula by a 1.5-mile-wide channel of saltwater, the 65-mile-long Hood Canal. Highway 101 follows the west side of the "Canal Zone," providing a delicious tidewater drive through second-growth forests with countless vistas of the waterway from every possible angle. The road hugs the canal, tucking in and out of various inlets along the way. Much of the route between Quilcene and Union is only minimally developed, though a few towns provide the essentials, and scattered resort estates dot the shoreline. Several places sell freshly shucked oysters along the way. At the southwest corner of Hood Canal, the waterway makes a sharp bend, angling northward and nearly turning the Kitsap Peninsula into an island. South from this elbow is the largest town in the area,

Hood Canal

Shelton, and at the head of the canal is the fast-growing region around Belfair.

In addition to the fine vistas along Hood Canal, you'll discover camping and hiking at two state parks and on nearby Olympic National Forest and Olympic National Park lands, and outstanding scuba diving and fishing. Lake Cushman is a popular fishing and summer recreation spot, just east of the Staircase entrance to Olympic National Park, and the dam at the lake's southeast end produces some of Tacoma's electricity.

History

Like many other features in Washington, Hood Canal received its name from Capt. George Vancouver during his 1792 exploration of Puget Sound. He called it "Hood's Channel," after a British naval hero, Lord Hood, but a printer's error in Vancouver's report changed the word channel to canal. Hood Canal is *not* a canal, but actually a long, glacially carved fjord. The waters of Hood Canal are more susceptible to pollution than other parts of Puget Sound because of limited tidal flushing. At the head of the canal in Belfair, it takes upwards of six years for a complete change of water. Rapid development around the southern end of Hood Canal has led to increasing concerns over water pollution, and several beaches have been closed to shellfish gathering in recent years.

Hood Canal Bridge

Hood Canal is spanned at only one point along its entire length, the 6,471-foot-long **Hood Canal Floating Bridge** that connects the Kitsap and Olympic peninsulas near Port Gamble. The world's third-longest floating bridge (the longest over tidewater) was opened in 1961 and served the peninsulas well until February 13, 1979, when a violent storm with 100-mph gales broke off and sank nearly a mile of the western portion of the bridge. In a remarkable feat of driving, a trucker in his 18-wheeler backed the semi at almost full throttle off the bridge when it began to sink. Ferry service took over the job of connecting the two peninsulas for the more than

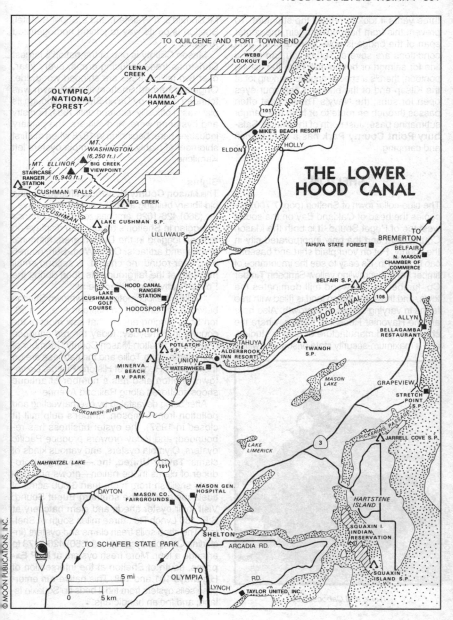

TO QUILCENE AND PORT TOWNSEND

WEBB
LOOKOUT

LENA
CREEK

OLYMPIC
NATIONAL
FOREST

HAMMA
HAMMA

101

MIKE'S BEACH RESORT

MT. WASHINGTON
(6,250 ft.)
BIG CREEK
VIEWPOINT

ELDON

HOLLY

MT. ELLINOR
(5,940 ft.)

STAIRCASE
RANGER
STATION

CUSHMAN FALLS

BIG CREEK

THE LOWER
HOOD CANAL

LAKE CUSHMAN S.P.

LILLIWAUP

TAHUYA STATE FOREST

TO
BREMERTON

BELFAIR

N. MASON
CHAMBER OF
COMMERCE

LAKE
CUSHMAN
GOLF COURSE

HOOD CANAL
RANGER
STATION

BELFAIR S.P.

HOODSPORT

106

HOOD CANAL

ALLYN

POTLATCH

POTLATCH
S.P.

TAHUYA

ALDERBROOK
INN RESORT

TWANOH
S.P.

BELLAGAMBA
RESTAURANT

MINERVA
BEACH
RV PARK

UNION

WATERWHEEL

GRAPEVIEW

MASON
LAKE

STRETCH
POINT S.P.

SKOKOMISH RIVER

LAKE
LIMERICK

3

PICKERING PASSAGE

JARRELL COVE S.P.

NAHWATZEL LAKE

101

DAYTON

MASON CO
FAIRGROUNDS

MASON GEN.
HOSPITAL

HARTSTENE
ISLAND

SHELTON

SQUAXIN I.
INDIAN
RESERVATION

TO SCHAFER STATE PARK

ARCADIA RD.

0   5 mi

0   5 km

TO
OLYMPIA

TO
OLYMPIA

RD.

LYNCH

TAYLOR UNITED, INC.

SQUAXIN
ISLAND S.P.

© MOON PUBLICATIONS, INC.

three years it took to rebuild the structure. To prevent this from happening again, the center span of the bridge is now opened when wind conditions are severe. Today you can cast a line for salmon or bottom fish from the fishing pontoon; there's a special anglers' parking lot at the Kitsap end of the bridge. Keep your eyes open for subs; the Navy's Trident fleet often passes through en route to or from the Bangor submarine base. Just north of the bridge, **Salsbury Point County Park** has a boat launch and camping.

SHELTON

The blue-collar town of Shelton (pop. 7,700) occupies the head of Oakland Bay on the southwest toe of Puget Sound. It is both the Mason County seat and the only incorporated city in the county. Put on your plaid shirt and baseball cap to blend in. It's easy to see the importance of timber here: a sprawling yellow Simpson Timber Co. lumber and plywood mill dominates the town, and the surrounding land is filled with tree farms in varying stages of regrowth. Also here are the Rayonier Research Center, where the chemistry and manufacture of pulp is studied, and a maximum-security state prison. But with a

McDonald's, a WalMart, and a Super 8 Motel, Shelton is on its way to joining homogenized America.

Mason County is one of the nation's largest Christmas tree-producing areas; every year, over two million trees are shipped worldwide. Originally named Sheltonville, the town was founded in 1855 by David Shelton, although its plat wasn't officially recorded until 1884. Forestry and oystering were, and still are, the primary industries here, beginning in 1878 when the first shipment of highly prized Olympia oysters left Kamilche.

Sights

The **Mason County Historical Museum** in the old library building at 5th St. and Railroad Ave., tel. (360) 426-1020, emphasizes the importance of logging in Shelton's history with displays on railroad logging in the Dayton area, historical photos, and artifacts. Open Wed.-Sun. noon-5 p.m. year-round; no charge. A second small museum at the fairgrounds is open during the Forest Festival and other events.

"Tollie," the locomotive in downtown Shelton between 2nd and 3rd on Railroad Ave., is a 90-ton Shay logging engine that saw most of the country in its heyday; today the red caboose houses the Shelton-Mason County Chamber of Commerce. Both Tollie and the caboose are on the National Register of Historic Places. Downtown Shelton also has a number of antique shops scattered along Railroad Avenue.

After being devastated by overharvesting and pollution from Simpson Timber's pulp mill (it closed in 1957), the oyster business has rebounded, and today growers produce Pacific oysters, Olympia oysters, and various kinds of clams. **Taylor United, Inc.**—the largest producer of clams in the nation—grows and harvests shellfish from more than 3,000 acres of tidelands around the southern Puget Sound. Visit their oyster sheds and clam hatchery at S.E. 130 Lynch Rd., three miles south of Shelton. The shop sells fresh clams and oysters (including Olympia oysters); call (360) 426-6178 to arrange a tour. More fresh oysters at **KTP Express,** south of Shelton at the intersection of Highways 101 and 108. This native-run enterprise sells oysters from tribal beds on Squaxin Island, and Indian handicrafts.

DIANNE BOUERICE LYONS

Tollie and Caboose 700

Tour the Dept. of Wildlife's **Shelton Trout Hatchery** on Eells Hill Rd., approximately eight miles north of Shelton, tel. (360) 426-3669; open daily 8 a.m.-5 p.m. Continue up the road, turning right at the sign marking Denny Ahl Seed Orchard, and cross over the 440-foot-high **Steel Arch Bridge** that spans the Skokomish Gorge.

Accommodations

At Shelton's north exit, the **Super 8 Motel,** 6 Northview Circle, tel. (360) 426-1654 or (800) 843-1991, has rooms for $43 s, $47 d. **Shelton Inn Motel,** 628 Railroad Ave., tel. (360) 426-4468 or (800) 451-4560, has rooms for $38-43 s, and $43-48 d, including an outdoor pool and kitchenettes. **City Center Motel,** 128 E. Alder, tel. (360) 426-3397, charges $32-36 s, $36-40 d. **Twin River Ranch B&B,** E. 5730 Hwy. 3, tel. (360) 426-1023, is in a 1918 farmhouse six miles north of Shelton along Hood Canal, with two guest rooms. The B&B features antiques, shared baths, a big stone fireplace, beam ceilings, and full ranch breakfasts. Rates are $55 s, $60 d. The ranch raises black Angus cattle, quail, and pheasants.

Parks and Campgrounds

Jarrell Cove State Park, on a small cove on the north end of Hartstene Island, has campsites ($10; no RV hookups) and is open April-October. Call (360) 426-9226 for information, or (800) 452-5687 for campsite reservations ($6 extra fee), available up to 11 months ahead of time. Get here by heading seven miles northeast of Shelton on Hwy. 3, crossing the bridge to Hartstene Island, and then following the signs another five miles to the park. The 43-acre park is primarily used by boaters and is a fun place to explore in a kayak. The privately run **Jarrell Cove Marina,** E. 220 Wilson Rd., tel. (360) 426-8823, has RV spaces, a marina, groceries, and gas.

You'll need a boat to get to tiny **Stretch Point State Park** (12 miles north of Shelton next to the town of Grapeview), which has no camping, showers, toilets, or drinking water, but has one of the best sandy beaches around Puget Sound. Grapeview itself has vineyards, a country store, marina, and a sometimes-open museum.

Lake Nahwatzel Resort, 10 miles west of Shelton, tel. (360) 426-8323, features cabins ($50 s or d), RV spaces, a couple of tent sites, and a restaurant on the shores of this 280-acre spring-fed lake in the foothills of the Olympics. More RV parking at **We & You RV Park,** S.E. 261 Craig Rd., tel. (360) 426-3169, and **Spencer Lake RV Resort** on Pickering Rd. off Hwy. 3, tel. (360) 426-2505.

Food

A good place to start is **Pine Tree Restaurant,** 102 S. 1st, tel. (360) 426-2604, a family place with reasonable breakfasts, plus seafood and steak for dinner. For traditional American favorites such as steak, roast beef, and turkey, head to **Timbers Restaurant,** 7th and Railroad, tel. (360) 426-9171. They also have a salad bar. **Nita's,** 325 W. Railroad, tel. (360) 426-6143, makes homemade soups, tacos, sandwiches, and wonderful fresh-from-the-oven pies. **Mor's,** 2503 Olympic Hwy. N, tel. (360) 427-6677, is the seafood and steak place in town. Don't miss **Cafe Luna,** 221 W. Railroad Ave., tel. (360) 427-8709. They have outstanding homemade pastas; open Thurs.-Sat. for dinners only.

Orient Express, 2517 Olympic Hwy. N, tel. (360) 427-0560, serves very popular Chinese and American lunch and dinner buffets and is one of the best restaurants in town. **El Sarape,** 318 W. Railroad, tel. (360) 426-4294, is the place for authentic Mexican food.

Get produce at the **farmers market,** on Front and Cota Streets, tel. (360) 427-5163, open daily in the summer.

Events

Early June's **Mason County Forest Festival** in Shelton began as an effort to prevent forest fires; today the event includes two Paul Bunyan parades (one for kids), a carnival, musical entertainment, an arts-and-crafts show, and logging competition in such events as skidder driving, speed climbing, ax throwing, and birling (better known as log-rolling). The **Sahewamish Indian Pow-wow** at the fairgrounds, one-half mile north of downtown Shelton off Hwy. 101, includes dancing and drumming, a salmon bake, and Indian handicrafts. The **Skokomish Canoe Festival** at the end of July attracts teams from around the Northwest for traditional Indian canoe races at Potlatch State Park.

Mason County Fair is held the last weekend in July at the fairgrounds. Highlights include the Olympic Peninsula Draft Horse Show, live entertainment, and traditional county fair favorites such as 4-H exhibits and cake and preserve competitions. Return to the fairgrounds in mid-August for a **Polynesian Luau and Heritage Fair,** which features traditional dancing, food, and crafts from the South Pacific.

The **West Coast Oyster Shucking Championship and Seafood Festival,** a.k.a. "Oyster-Fest," is held annually on the first full weekend of October at the fairgrounds. The main event, high-speed oyster shucking, lasts less than three minutes; the national record, set here in 1984, is held by Diz Schimke, who shucked 24 oysters in 2:41.31 minutes. Surrounding the competition are two days of wine tasting, an oyster cook-off, food booths, art and boating exhibits, dancers, bands, and magicians.

The holiday season brings Santa to Shelton during the annual **Christmas Parade and Bazaar,** held the first weekend in December with a parade by land and by sea. Santa lights the Christmas tree, then he visits the kids at the bazaar.

Entertainment and Recreation
Mill Creek Inn, S.E. 843 Hwy. 3, tel. (360) 427-8755, has music nightly. Both **Cottage Cafe,** 11880 Hwy. 101, tel. (360) 426-3073, and **Dragon Palace,** 2503 Olympic Hwy. N, tel. (360) 426-7975, have live entertainment on Friday and Saturday nights.

Swim at the **Shelton High School pool** on Shelton Springs Rd., tel. (360) 426-4240.

Information and Services
For maps and festival information, contact the **Shelton-Mason County Chamber of Commerce,** located in the caboose on Railroad Ave., tel. (360) 426-2021 or (800) 576-2021. Open Mon.-Fri. 9 a.m.-4 p.m., and Saturday 10 a.m.-2 p.m. in the summer, and Mon.-Fri. 9 a.m.-4 p.m. the rest of the year.

Shelton's spacious **public library** is on 7th and Alder Streets, tel. (360) 426-1362. Find the **post office** at N. 2nd and Railroad Ave., tel. (360) 426-3463. The local **area code** is 360. **Mason General Hospital,** 2100 Sherwood Lane in Shelton, tel. (360) 426-1611, has 24-hour emergency-room service.

Transportation
Mason County Transit, tel. (360) 427-5033 or (800) 374-3747, has free bus service around town, throughout the county, and onward to Olympia and other bus systems in surrounding counties. Bike racks are available on most buses, and they even offer free dial-a-ride service.

Olympic Air, tel. (360) 426-1477, offers scenic airplane flights over the area; $36 for a 20-minute version for up to three folks.

UNION

The disperse settlement of Union occupies land near the "elbow" where Hood Inlet angles abruptly to the northeast. Summer and weekend homes crowd the highway, providing a contrast to the from-another-era waterwheel, built by Edwin J. Dalby in 1923 and still operational (albeit unused). A few miles to the west is the **Skokomish Indian Reservation,** near the intersection of Highways 101 and 106. You can tell you're on the reservation by all the fireworks stands that clutter the highway. The tribal center houses a small museum with arts and crafts.

Twanoh State Park
Seven miles east of Union on Hwy. 106, Twanoh State Park is a very popular spot for picnicking beneath tall trees, and swimming and waterskiing on Hood Canal. The 182-acre park also has several miles of hiking trails along scenic Twanoh Creek, sturdy CCC-constructed structures from the 1930s, a tennis court, a concession stand with snacks and groceries, bathhouses, and camping in tent ($10) and RV ($15) sites with coin-operated showers. Open late April to early September. Call 275-222 for more information, or (800) 452-5687 for campsite reservations ($6 extra fee), available up to 11 months ahead of time.

Accommodations and Food
On Hwy. 106 in Union, the elaborate **Alderbrook Resort on Hood Canal,** E. 7101 Hwy. 106, is a full-service resort with motel rooms, cottages, a restaurant, lounge, heated indoor pool, jacuzzi, saunas, 18-hole golf course, boat rentals, tennis courts, and moorage on the Hood

Canal. Rooms are $75-95 s, or $85-99 d, and cottages are $99-189 for up to four adults. For reservations, call (360) 898-2200 or (800) 622-9370. The restaurant at **Alderbrook Inn Resort** in Union, tel. (360) 898-2200, serves three meals daily from a varied menu that includes steak, seafood, chicken, and veal dishes. They also have a Sunday brunch and live music on weekends. A better bet may be **Victoria's,** E. 6791 Hwy. 106, tel. (360) 898-4400, with well-prepared prime rib, pasta, and seafood specialties.

Robin Hood Village, tel. (360) 898-2163, has four cottages with hot tubs and kitchenettes. Couples can stay in the smaller and older ones for $75-85 d; the larger ones are $120-155 and can sleep up to six. RV hookups are also available.

Transportation

Mason County Transit, tel. (360) 427-5033 or (800) 374-3747, has free bus service throughout the county, with connections to bus systems in surrounding counties. Bike racks are available on most buses.

BELFAIR

Located at the end of Hood Canal, the sprawling town of Belfair (pop. 18,000 at last count, but higher by the time you read this) is one of the fastest growing places in Washington. The waterside location and proximity to Tacoma, Bremerton, and Seattle make it a favorite of folks fleeing crime and looking for a suburban setting to raise kids or retire. In the summer months, Belfair triples in size as tourists roll in. Unfortunately, all this growth has taken place in the ugliest possible way, with the predictable traffic jams and strip mall developments along Hwy. 3 through the "center" (if there is such a thing) of Belfair. History is not the strong suit here.

Parks

Sixty-three-acre **Belfair State Park,** on Hwy. 3, has year-round camping ($10 for tents, $15 for RVs), swimming in a protected lagoon, and fishing on Hood Canal. Call (360) 275-0668 for information, or (800) 452-5687 for campsite reservations ($6 extra fee), available up to 11 months ahead of time.

The **Thieler Wetlands** cover 135 acres of open space behind the Mary E. Thieler Memorial Community Center off Hwy. 3. Nearly four miles of level nature trails take you through the saltwater and freshwater marshes with natural history exhibits and a rich diversity of wildlife.

North of Belfair is **Tahuya State Forest,** covering 23,100 acres of relatively flat multiple-use land. The emphasis here is on logging, but hikers and mountain bikers will find a number of trails and campsites. For a map, contact the Dept. of Natural Resources, tel. (360) 825-1631, or (800) 527-3305 in Washington.

In the tiny waterside village of Allyn, three miles south of Belfair, you'll find a pleasant park with a covered gazebo, boat dock, and boat launching ramp. It is a center for oyster growers and Christmas tree suppliers.

Accommodations and Campgrounds

Belfair Motel, 23322 Hwy. 3, tel. (360) 275-4485, is a clean and modern place with rooms for $45 s, and $50 d, and kitchenettes for $10 extra. **Country Garden Inn,** N.E. 2790 Old Belfair Hwy., tel. (360) 275-3683, has B&B accommodations in a contemporary inn with a hot tub. Rates are $70 s or d, including a full breakfast.

On the north side of Hood Canal and west of Belfair, the little dot of a place called Tahuya is home to **Summertide Resort & Marina,** tel. (206) 925-9277. Also here is a store, restaurant, and RV park.

See above for camping in nearby state parks. Park RVs at **Snooze Junction RV Park,** N.E. 621, Gladwin Beach, tel. (360) 275-2381, or **Sherwood Hills RV Park,** in Allyn, tel. (360) 275-6767.

Food

Clifton Town Deli & Bakery, N.E. 23690 Hwy. 3, tel. (360) 275-4986, has homemade soups, baked goods, salads, sandwiches, and good breakfasts.

Michael G's in Allyn, tel. (360) 275-2871, serves moderately priced steak, seafood, veal, and pasta for lunch and dinner Tues.-Sunday. Also in Allyn is **Leonard Kay's,** tel. (360) 275-2954, a restaurant and tavern with good pizzas, steaks, and burgers. Both Allyn and Belfair have weekend **farmers markets** throughout the summer.

Events and Entertainment

Belfair's **Midsummer Festival** on the last Saturday in June includes food, games and competitions, craft booths, and entertainment, along with walks and educational activities at the Thieler Wetlands. **Allyn Days** in late July features food booths, a big salmon bake, and boat races. For live weekend music, drop by **Allyn Inn** in Allyn (pun intended), tel. (360) 275-5422.

Information and Services

Get info on Belfair and northern Mason County at the **North Mason Visitor Info Center** located in Mary E. Thieler Memorial Community Center/Hood Canal Wetlands, E. 22871 Hwy. 3, tel. (360) 275-5548. Open daily 7:30 a.m.-5 p.m. in the summer, and Mon.-Fri. 7:30 a.m.-3 p.m. the rest of the year. The **public library** is at N.E. 23081 Hwy. 3, tel. (360) 275-3232. The **area code** for Belfair and points westward is 360.

Transportation

Mason County Transit, tel. (360) 427-5033 or (800) 374-3747, has free bus service around town, throughout the county, and onward to other bus systems in surrounding counties. Bike racks are available on most buses.

HOODSPORT AREA

The town of Hoodsport is the largest along the west side of Hood Canal and can provide most of your travel needs. This is the place to get Forest Service and Park Service information and to stock up on food before heading north. Hoodsport's lodging places cater to scuba divers, particularly small groups who come to explore the deep, clear waters just offshore where the creatures are amazingly diverse. The lack of strong currents and only minor tidal fluctuations help make this a good place for beginning divers. Visibility is best in the winter—to 50 feet—when fewer plankton are in the water. Others come to water-ski, sail, windsurf, or to catch shrimp, fish, and crabs.

Five miles north from Hoodsport is the village of Lilliwaup, with a general store and motel, an RV park, and a pair of restaurants. The little burg of Potlatch is two miles south of Hoodsport on Hwy. 101.

Potlatch State Park

Enjoy camping, diving, clamming, crabbing, and fishing in Hood Canal at Potlatch State Park, three miles south of Hoodsport on Hwy. 101. Have a picnic on the water, or explore the underwater park with scuba gear. The campground ($10 for tents, $15 for RVs) is open April-Oct. and year-round for day-use. Call (360) 877-5361 for information, or (800) 452-5687 for campsite reservations ($6 extra fee), available up to 11 months ahead of time.

Lake Cushman Area

Lake Cushman was a popular resort area at the turn of the century, offering fishing, hiking, and hunting. By the 1920s, the two lakeside resorts had shut down and the city of Tacoma built a dam on the Skokomish River. When completed, the dam increased the lake's size tenfold to 4,000 acres. Though private summer homes are springing up around the lake, the area still has a decidedly remote feel, thanks in part to its protected neighbor, Olympic National Park, about 10 miles up the road.

Lake Cushman State Park, seven miles west of Hoodsport, is a popular spot with anglers: cutthroat, Kokanee, and rainbow trout inhabit the lake, the home of the only known entirely freshwater king salmon run. Hikers will enjoy the four miles of hiking trails at the park, leading from lake's edge to deep woods; swimming, waterskiing, and, in winter, cross-country skiing, are also popular. Camp in one of the two campgrounds ($10 for tents; $15 for RVs). Open early March through September. Call (360) 877-5491 for information, or (800) 452-5687 for campsite reservations ($6 extra fee), available up to 11 months ahead of time. Call (360) 383-2471 to arrange a tour of the Tacoma City Light dam and power plant.

Follow Lake Cushman Rd. to a "T" at road's end; go left and follow the lake's edge to 70-foot **Cushman Falls,** near the lake's northwest end, about 11 miles from Hoodsport. Or, turn right at the "T," then turn left in another 1.5 miles onto Big Creek Rd. 2419 for six miles to **Big Creek Viewpoint** for a sweeping view to the east. Continue on for another mile for a waterfall off Mt. Washington. The **Mt. Ellinor Trail** leaves Rd. 2419 at the five-mile point; the trail heads up one mile for a view of Lake Cushman.

The Forest Service's **Big Creek Campground** ($6; open May-Sept.) is nine miles up Lake Cushman Road. The gravel road ends after a total of 16 miles at **Staircase Campground,** just west of the lake along the Staircase Rapids of the North Fork of the Skokomish River. This Olympic National Park site has year-round camping for $10. A $5 entrance fee is collected for access to the park May-September.

Hiking trails lead into Olympic National Park from Staircase Trailhead at the head of Lake Cushman, providing a range of hiking options. The **Flapjacks Lake** area is accessed by hiking up the North Fork Skokomish Trail, and then turning up the 5.6-mile side route to the lake. For longer hikes, you can continue up the North Fork Trail, which connects to others, providing a number of lengthy loop-trip options. A steep and challenging three-mile trail switchbacks from the campground to **Wagonwheel Lake** gaining over 3,200 feet en route.

Wonder Mountain Wilderness

The tiny **Wonder Mountain Wilderness** covers just 2,349 acres that abut the southern edge of Olympic National Park. It has no developed trails, and is not readily accessible. Call (360) 877-5254 for more information.

Hoodsport Winery

If you don't mind your wine served in a plastic cup, stop by Hoodsport Winery, N. 23501 Hwy. 101 in Hoodsport, tel. (360) 877-9894, for a sip of wine produced from Puget Sound fruits and berries, such as their loganberry, rhubarb, and raspberry wines, or their gewürztraminer, riesling, merlot, or chardonnay, made from eastern Washington grapes. The tasting room of this family-run operation is open daily 10 a.m.-6 p.m.

Accommodations

Glen-Ayr Canal Resort, 1.5 miles north of Hoodsport, tel. (360) 877-9522 or (800) 367-9522, is the most elaborate and largest local place, with modern rooms for $55-68 s or d, and suites with kitchenettes for $85 s or d. Two-night minimum stay on summer weekends, and three nights during shrimping season and holidays. Also here are a jacuzzi, recreation room, and marina. Glen-Ayr primarily attracts retirees—especially the RV crowd—and does not allow kids.

Sunrise Motel and Resort, 24520 Hwy. 100 on the north side of Hoodsport, tel. (360) 877-5301, is a favorite of scuba divers and has rooms for $50 s or d ($60 s or d with kitchenettes) and dorm spaces for $50 per person for two nights and three days, plus free air tank refills.

Lilliwaup Motel in the village of Lilliwaup, tel. (360) 877-5375, has rooms with fireplaces for $35 s or d and rooms with kitchenettes for $50. In-room phones, but no televisions. **Canal Side Resort** in Potlatch, tel. (360) 877-9422, has rooms with kitchenettes for $37-49 s or d.

Ask at the Hood Canal Ranger Station on Lake Cushman Dr. in Hoodsport about renting the rustic **Interrorem Cabin,** built in 1907 and available for $25. It sleeps four people. Two short trails—the Interrorem Nature Trail and Ranger Hole Trail—provide access to the densely forested country near the cabin. Call (360) 877-5254 for more information.

Campgrounds

See "Potlatch State Park" and "Lake Cushman Area," above, for public campgrounds near Hoodsport, or stop by the Forest Service office for a complete listing. Several private RV parks are also in the area: **Glen-Ayr RV Park,** 25381 N. Hwy. 101 in Hoodsport, tel. (360) 877-9522; **Sunrise Resort,** 24520 Hwy. 100 in Hoodsport, tel. (360) 877-5301; **Canal Side Resort** in Potlatch, tel. (360) 877-9422; **Minerva Beach RV Park,** four miles south of Hoodsport on Hwy. 101, tel. (360) 877-5145; and **Rest-A-While RV Park,** three miles north of Hoodsport on Hwy. 101, tel. (360) 877-9474. Rest-A-While also rents dive gear and has a marina.

Events and Entertainment

The main summer event is **Celebrate Hoodsport Days,** with a street fair, food, kids' parade, and fireworks on the first full weekend of July. The **Hoodsport Inn,** tel. (360) 877-5526, has live music Thurs.-Sun. nights.

Recreation

The **Hoodsport Dive Center,** N. 21110 Hwy. 101, tel. (360) 877-6818, has rental gear, instruction, and air fills. Golfers can enjoy the summer sunshine at the 18-hole courses at the **Alderbrook Inn,** tel. (360) 898-2200, or the

Lake Cushman Golf Course, four miles west of Hoodsport on Lake Cushman Rd., tel. (360) 877-5505.

Information and Services
Stop at the **Hood Canal Ranger Station** on Lake Cushman Dr. in Hoodsport for a map of trails and forest roads in the Olympic National Forest and current campground and hiking trail information. They also have extensive information on Olympic National Park. Hours are Mon.-Fri. 7 a.m.-4:30 p.m. and Sat.-Sun. 8 a.m.-4:30 p.m. from mid-May to mid-September, and Mon.-Fri. 7 a.m.-4:30 p.m. the remainder of the year. Call (360) 877-5254 for more information.

Hoodsport's **public library** is at N. 64 Lake Cushman Rd., tel. (360) 877-9339.

Transportation
Mason County Transit, tel. (360) 427-5033 or (800) 374-3747, has free bus service throughout the county, with connections north to Port Townsend and south to bus systems in surrounding counties. Bike racks are available on most buses.

ELDON TO BRINNON

Not much to Eldon—just a cafe, gas station, shellfish farms, and a diver's resort. The Hamma Hamma River enters Hood Canal here, and a paved road leads to two Forest Service campgrounds on the edge of Olympic National Park. In the winter, bald eagles gather along the banks of the Hamma Hamma to feed on spawning salmon. Brinnon isn't much bigger than Eldon, but this stretch of Hood Canal has a number of interesting attractions.

Sights
In Brinnon, **Whitney Gardens & Nursery,** tel. (360) 796-4411, has seven acres of display gardens that include more than 3,000 rhododendrons, azaleas, and other flowering plants. The best time to visit is mid-May to mid-June, but you'll find something in bloom from March through October. Entrance is $1; half-hour guided tours are $2.

Learn how oysters, mussels, and clams are raised at Brinnon's **Shellfish Interpretive Cen-**

ter, tel. (360) 796-4601, run by the Washington Dept. of Fisheries. Also in Brinnon, the **Hamma Hamma Oyster Farm Seafood Store,** tel. (360) 877-5811, sells fresh oysters.

Dosewallips State Park
A half-mile south of Brinnon on Hwy. 101, Dosewallips State Park covers 425 acres at the base of the Olympic Mountains, offering both fresh- and saltwater activities at the confluence of Hood Canal and the Dosewallips River. Enjoy camping ($10 for tents, $15 for RVs; open year-round) and fishing for salmon and steelhead in the river, but avoid the clams and oysters—seal poop has contaminated the beaches. Six miles of hiking trails provide access to the forested west end of Dosewallips. Call (360) 796-4415 for information, or (800) 452-5687 for campsite reservations ($6 extra fee), available up to 11 months ahead of time.

Two miles south of Brinnon, **Pleasant Harbor State Park** has a protected dock adjacent to a private marina; but no camping, boat launch, or swimming facilities.

Hamma Hamma Recreation Area
Hamma Hamma Rd. begins two miles north of Eldon and continues to the edge of the Mt. Skokomish Wilderness (see below). **Hamma Hamma Campground** ($5; open May to mid-November) is seven miles up the road; continue another two miles to **Lena Creek Campground** ($5; open mid-May through September). **Lena Lake Campground** is a free walk-in campground at this pretty lake, a 2.5 mile hike from the Lena Creek Campground. Built by the CCC in the 1930s, the historic **Hamma Hamma Cabin** can be rented for $25. It sleeps six; call the Forest Service at (360) 877-5254 for details.

Webb Lookout is a popular high spot, although it offers no Olympic views, just a broad shot of the canal. Take Hamma Hamma Rd. and turn right on a logging road at about 2.5 miles and follow the signs. Park along the road and hike the half-mile trail to the lookout.

Mount Skokomish Wilderness
Covering a little more than 13,000 acres, the Mt. Skokomish Wilderness occupies steep terrain bordering the western edge of Olympic National Park. The **Putvin Trail** starts from For-

est Rd. 25, approximately four miles beyond Lena Creek Campground on Hamma Hamma Rd., and climbs steeply, rising more than 3,700 feet in less than four miles. The trail ends at rock-rimmed Lake of the Angels, just inside the park boundary. The Mt. Skokomish Wilderness is managed by Olympic National Forest, tel. (360) 877-5254.

Dosewallips Recreation Area

The scenic Dosewallips Rd. (Forest Rd. 2610) heads west along the Dosewallips River from Brinnon into the heart of the Olympics, ending 15 miles later at Dosewallips Campground within Olympic National Park. Approximately three miles up is **Rocky Brook Falls**. The turnoff isn't marked, but look for the bridge and small hydro plant on the right side. It's a short walk to the 80-foot falls, but use care since the water levels can change quickly.

The Forest Service's **Elkhorn Campground** ($4; open mid-May through September) is 10 miles up Dosewallips Rd. and has sites right along the river. Continue up the road to milepost 11 to see **Dosewallips Falls** as it cascades over enormous boulders. The road enters Olympic National Park a mile beyond this.

Camping is also available at the Park Service's **Dosewallips Campground** ($8; open June-Sept.) at the end of the road, 15 miles from Hwy. 101. A trailhead at the campground provides access to the park.

Brothers Wilderness

This 16,682-acre wilderness lies within Olympic National Forest and occupies a blip of land on the eastern flank of Olympic National Park. Only a few developed trails exist in the wilderness, the primary one being the **Duckabrush Trail,** which begins a mile up from the Collins Campground on Duckabrush Road. The trail climbs to the park boundary (six miles away), with a fine view from Big Hump rock. Once inside the park, you can connect to a maze of other routes through the high country. From Lena Lake Campground on Hamma Hamma Rd., a hiking trail leads uphill to Lena Lake on the edge of the wilderness, and then on to **Upper Lena Lake** inside Olympic National Park. This is a fine overnight backcountry trip. For more information on the wilderness, call (360) 877-5254.

Accommodations

Mike's Beach Resort, 38470 Hwy. 101 (two miles north of Eldon), tel. (360) 877-5324 or (800) 231-5324, is a fun and friendly place with a variety of accommodations, including dorm beds in a hostel (no kitchen) for $10 per person ($7.50 for American Youth Hostel members). Cabins (with kitchens) and motel units are $35 s, or $55 d. Tent and RV hookups are also available, and divers can fill tanks at the air station. Great scuba diving at an artificial reef just offshore; ask about the eight-foot octopus.

Bayshore Motel at Brinnon, 31503 Hwy. 101, tel. (360) 796-4220 or (800) 488-4230, has large and comfortable rooms for $37 s, $40 d; no phones in rooms.

Campgrounds

Public campgrounds are described above. In addition to these, the Forest Service's **Seal Rock Campground,** tel. (800) 260-2267, ($6; open mid-April through September), is just north of Brinnon and is reserveable for an extra $7.50. **Collins Campground** ($5; open mid-May through September) is five miles up Duckabrush Rd. (Rd. 2519), which meets Hwy. 101 approximately four miles south of Brinnon.

Food

Brinnon's **Half Way House Restaurant,** tel. (360) 796-4715, has a gourmet chef and very reasonable prices on seafood, steak, burgers, and lighter fare. Their Tuesday night five-course dinners are legendary, but be sure to make advance reservations. Call about other nightly specials. This is also the place to go for a homemade breakfast.

The **Geoduck Tavern** in Brinnon, tel. (360) 796-4430, serves meals, and sometimes has live music on weekends.

Events

Brinnon's **Hood Canal ShrimpFest** in late May—the peak of the shrimping season—includes an art fair, street dance, boat show, farmers market, and shrimp cooking contests; call (360) 796-4886 for details.

Transportation

Mason County Transit, tel. (360) 427-5033 or (800) 374-3747, has free bus service throughout the county, with connections north to Port Townsend and south and east to bus systems in surrounding counties. Bike racks are available on most buses.

QUILCENE AREA

Tiny Quilcene has a rough-at-the-edges country feeling reminiscent of places in Northern California. It's a place with simple homes and trailers, piles of split wood in the yards, smoke curling from the chimneys, and where chainsaw carving is considered high art. The surrounding cutover landscape looks like a bad haircut. Two miles south is the **Quilcene National Fish Hatchery**, tel. (360) 765-3334, open daily.

Buckhorn Wilderness
Covering 44,258 acres, the Buckhorn Wilderness occupies barren ridges and peaks topping 7,000 feet within Olympic National Forest and bordering on the extensive wilderness within Olympic National Park. The **Mt. Townsend Trail** begins from Forest Rd. 2760 off Rd. 27, northwest of Quilcene. This six-mile route climbs to the top of 6,280-foot Mt. Townsend, providing incredible vistas in all directions. **Big Quilcene Trail** starts at the three-sided shelter 10 miles up Forest Rd. 2750 from Quilcene, and follows the Big Quilcene River into the high country before switchbacking to the summit of Marmot Pass at 6,000 feet. From here, you can continue into Olympic National Park via the Constance Pass Trail. The Big Quilcene is famous for the multitudes of rhododendrons that bloom here in early summer. Call (360) 765-3368 for more information on the Buckhorn Wilderness.

Mount Walker
The most popular viewpoint along Hood Canal is 2,804-foot **Mt. Walker**, five miles south of Quilcene. A road leads to the summit, and you can hike up via a two-mile path through tall Douglas fir forests and a lush understory of huckleberry and rhododendron. The trail (or road) emerges onto a ridge with panoramic views of Seattle, Mt. Rainier, and the Cascades to the east, and the Olympics to the northwest. Bring a lunch to enjoy at the summit picnic area.

Campgrounds
Quilcene County Park has in-the-trees tent spaces (no RV hookups) on the south side of Quilcene for $8; open year-round. Additional campsites can be found at Lake Leland Recreation Area six miles north of Quilcene. The Forest Service has two campgrounds near Quilcene. Spaces at the very popular **Falls View Campground** ($5; open May-Sept.), 3.5 miles south of Quilcene, can be reserved by calling (800) 280-2267 (extra fee of $7.50). The half-mile **Falls View Canyon Trail** heads down to the Big Quilcene River from the campground. **Rainbow Campground** (free; open May-Sept.), a more primitive site, is another 1.5 miles farther south.

Prime rib and seafood (including ultra-fresh local oysters) distinguish the **Timber House,** a restaurant on Hwy. 101 one-half mile south of Quilcene, tel. (360) 765-3339. Open for lunch and dinner daily except Tuesday.

Quilcene's **Maple Grove Motel,** tel. (360) 765-3410, charges $40-50 s or d and offers kitchenettes on some rooms. Built in 1917 as a railroad workers' place, the **Quilcene Hotel,** tel. (360) 765-3447, has rooms with a bath down the hall for $37-43 s or d. No TVs or phones in the rooms, and the decor is "early Salvation Army." A nice taste of the past.

Events
The **Olympic Music Festival** is an annual summertime concert series held weekends from late June to early September in a turn-of-the-century barn located 10 miles west of Hood Canal Bridge, off Hwy. 104. The concerts feature chamber music in a unique setting: patrons sit on hay bales in the barn or enjoy picnics outside with mountain (and cow) vistas. The Philadelphia String Quartet and guest artists perform these "Concerts in the Barn" one-quarter mile south of Hwy. 104 on Center Road. For tickets and more information, call (360) 527-8839.

Information
The Olympic National Forest **Quilcene Ranger District,** 20482 Hwy. 101, tel. (360) 765-3368, has maps and information on local camping and hiking options on both Forest Service and National Park lands. Open Mon.-Fri. 8 a.m.-4:30 p.m. year-round.

PORT TOWNSEND AND VICINITY

Standing on the northern tip of Quimper Peninsula—a point off the northeast corner of the Olympic Peninsula—Port Townsend (pop. 7,700) is best known for its generous helping of Victorian architecture. It has more authentic remnants of this period than any other town north of San Francisco, including some 70 buildings on the National Register of Historic Places. Wealthy merchants of the late 1800s built these beauties, many of which have been restored and are located in one of the town's two national historic districts. Behind town rise the perpetually snow-covered Olympic Mountains; out front lies the ship-filled Strait of Juan de Fuca.

Given its Victorian opulence, one might expect Port Townsend to be solely focused on tourism, but this is still a genuine town filled with history, and with much to see and explore. Many folks consider it one of the most interesting and beautiful towns in Washington.

HISTORY

As the main port of entry to Puget Sound and the first townsite on the Olympic Peninsula, Port Townsend started off with a bang. Platted in 1852, by the late 1880s the town prospered as a busy seaport; more than a few men made their fortunes here. As the official port of entry for the Pacific Northwest, Port Townsend hosted consulates and agencies from Chile, Sweden, Norway, Germany, France, Great Britain, and Hawaii during its prime. It was supposed to become the New York City of the Pacific Northwest, and elaborate, ostentatious Victorian mansions sprouted atop the hills. Considerably less grandiose accommodations and businesses lined the waterfront, including more than a few saloons and bordellos.

The cornerstone of this speculative boom was the anticipation that Port Townsend would be the end point for the Union Pacific's transcontinental railroad; its location was far better than the Seattle area for sailing ships—the wind seems to be always blowing. The dream went bust when the advent of steamships made travel in Puget Sound easier, allowing the railroad to opt for a shorter Tacoma terminus. History seemed to pass Port Townsend by, as Seattle and Tacoma siphoned off most of the town's shipping, and a financial depression gripped the nation, causing many of the beautiful mansions to be abandoned. Eventually they were converted into rooming houses and apartments, and only later rescued.

Over the years, military bases and a pulp and paper mill restored Port Townsend's economic stability; the largest employer is still the Port Townsend Paper Company Mill at Glen Cove. The away-from-it-all location attracted a hippie crowd in the 1970s, and today tourism accounts for much of Port Townsend's prosperity. This tourism is fed by a gorgeous setting that features commanding views over Admiralty Inlet and the nearby Olympic Mountains, by the abundance of Victorian mansions that have been transformed into lavish B&Bs, and by the plentiful galleries, shops, and gourmet restaurants. Today the citizens of Port Townsend are a blend of blue-collar millworkers, post-hippie new agers, and wealthy newcomers and retirees. Visitors will be pleased to discover a fascinating real town, not a Victorian-era Disneyland.

SIGHTS

Port Townsend's main attractions are its historic late 19th-century homes and businesses, along with impressive Fort Worden State Park. Downtown's main boulevard, Water St., consists of stout brick buildings filled with galleries, restaurants, and shops selling antiques, books, and gifts.

One of the more distinctive town sights is the **Haller Fountain,** which features a bronze, scantily clad maiden emerging from a shell that is supported by water-spraying cherubs and fish. Created for the Mexican exhibit at the 1893 Chicago Exhibition, the fountain was later donated to the city by Theodore N. Haller "in memory of early pioneers."

Port Townsend is still very much a seafaring

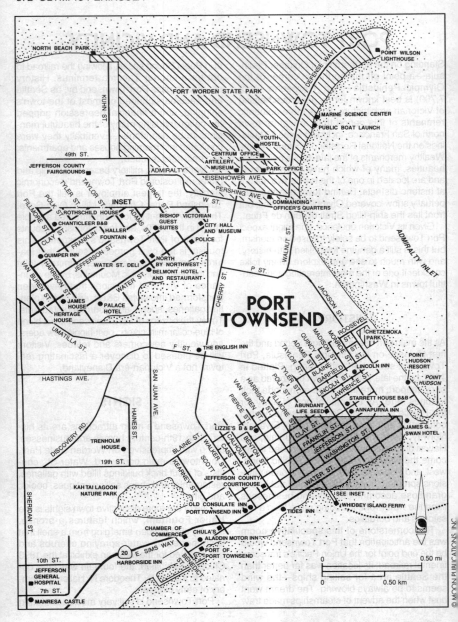

NORTH BEACH PARK

POINT WILSON LIGHTHOUSE

KUHN ST.

DEFENSE WAY

FORT WORDEN STATE PARK

MARINE SCIENCE CENTER

PUBLIC BOAT LAUNCH

49TH ST.

YOUTH HOSTEL

CENTRUM OFFICE

ARTILLERY MUSEUM

PARK OFFICE

ADMIRALTY

EISENHOWER AVE.

JEFFERSON COUNTY FAIRGROUNDS

QUINCY ST.

PERSHING AVE.

W ST.

COMMANDING OFFICER'S QUARTERS

ADMIRALTY INLET

INSET

TYLER ST.
TAYLOR ST.
POLK ST.
FILLMORE ST.

ROTHSCHILD HOUSE
ADAMS ST.
BISHOP VICTORIAN GUEST SUITES

CHANTICLEER B&B
HALLER FOUNTAIN
CITY HALL AND MUSEUM

CLAY ST.
FRANKLIN ST.
JEFFERSON ST.
POLICE

QUIMPER INN
WATER ST. DELI
NORTH BY NORTHWEST

HARRISON ST.
WATER ST.
BELMONT HOTEL AND RESTAURANT

JAMES HOUSE
PALACE HOTEL

VAN BUREN ST.
HERITAGE HOUSE

CHERRY ST.

PORT TOWNSEND

UMATILLA ST.

WALNUT ST.

P ST.

JACKSON ST.

ROOSEVELT ST.

CHETZEMOKA PARK

F ST.
THE ENGLISH INN

MADISON ST.
MONROE ST.
QUINCY ST.
ADAMS ST.

POINT HUDSON RESORT

TAYLOR ST.

BLAINE ST.
GARFIELD ST.

LINCOLN INN

POINT HUDSON

HASTINGS AVE.

SAN JUAN AVE.

TYLER ST.
POLK ST.
FILLMORE ST.
LAWRENCE ST.

STARRETT HOUSE B&B

VAN BUREN ST.
HARRISON ST.
PIERCE ST.

ABUNDANT LIFE SEED

ANNAPURNA INN

DISCOVERY RD.

HAINES ST.

TRENHOLM HOUSE

19TH ST.

BLAINE ST.
CLAY ST.
FRANKLIN ST.
JEFFERSON ST.
WASHINGTON ST.

JAMES G. SWAN HOTEL

LIZZIE'S B & B

CALHOUN ST.
CASS ST.
BENTON ST.

WATER ST.

KEARNEY ST.

WALKER ST.
SCOTT ST.

JEFFERSON COUNTY COURTHOUSE

KAH TAI LAGOON NATURE PARK

OLD CONSULATE INN
PORT TOWNSEND INN

WHIDBEY ISLAND FERRY

SEE INSET

SHERIDAN ST.

CHAMBER OF COMMERCE

TIDES INN

CHULA'S

ALADDIN MOTOR INN

20   E. SIMS WAY

PORT OF PORT TOWNSEND

10TH ST.

HARBORSIDE INN

JEFFERSON GENERAL HOSPITAL

7TH ST.

MANRESA CASTLE

0   0.50 mi

0   0.50 km

MOON PUBLICATIONS INC.

town. Its Port Hudson Harbor is jammed with yachts, and quite a few boatbuilding businesses are based nearby. Of particular note is the **Northwest School of Wooden Boatbuilding,** 251 Otto St., tel. (360) 385-4948, where a six-month program develops skills through intensive classes and hands-on projects.

Historic Tours

For a tour of historic downtown and other parts of Port Townsend, stop by the chamber of commerce (2437 E. Sims Way) and pick up their *Port Townsend Seagull Tour* For a verbal version, guided tours ($5-7) of the waterfront, saloons, and historic homes are also available from **Sidewalk Tours,** 820 Tyler St., tel. (360) 385-1967. You'll learn all sorts of local historical tidbits. **Peninsula Tours,** tel. (360) 385-2422, has van tours of the area.

Historic Home Tours are held the first weekend in May and the third weekend in September; owners of private Victorian residences open

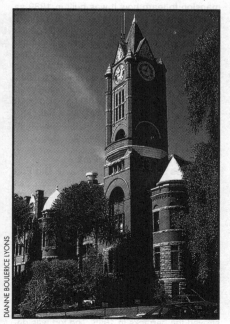

Jefferson County Courthouse, built in 1892

DIANNE BOULERICE LYONS

their doors to the public. Tickets ($12 adults, $7 kids under 12) may be purchased up to a month in advance at the visitor information center, 2437 Sims Way, tel. (360) 385-2722.

Uptown

A second section of historic Port Townsend, "Uptown," covers a block or so of Lawrence St. near Taylor St. and is where you're more likely to meet people who actually live in town. It was originally created as a turn-of-the-century shopping district for the genteel ladies living in the hilltop mansions, a place to avoid the bawdy waterfront shopping district ("the most wicked city north of San Francisco" in the 1880s). Today, uptown contains a delightful collection of offbeat stores catering to the Birkenstock-and-tie-dyed generation: Abundant Life Seed Foundation, Whole Foods Grocery Coop, and the Women & Children's Center, along with a pub, restaurant, upscale grocery store, and espresso shop.

Museums

Housed in the city's 1891 City Hall Complex, **Jefferson County Historical Society Museum,** 210 Madison St., tel. (360) 385-1003, this excellent museum has three floors of boat exhibits and models, intricate Indian baskets, button and bottle collections, a Victorian bedroom, and even two buffalo-horn and bearskin chairs from an old photo studio. Downstairs is the old (and cold) city jail, used until the 1940s. The museum is open daily 11 a.m.-4 p.m. and Sunday 1-4 p.m. in the summer; weekends only in January. Entrance costs $2 for adults, $5 for families.

There's also a small museum inside the lobby of the **post office** at 1322 Washington Street. During the 1880s, this imposing stone building served as the Customs House, the port of entry for all international traffic into Puget Sound.

Another building of interest is the **Jefferson County Courthouse** standing high on a hill at Jefferson and Walker Streets. Built in 1892, this red brick building is one of Washington's oldest courthouses and is notable for the 100-foot-tall clocktower that serves as a beacon to mariners. **Bergstrom's Antique and Classic Automobiles,** 809 Washington St., tel. (360) 385-5061, has a showroom filled with classic cars.

Rothschild House State Park

The Rothschild House on Franklin and Taylor Streets was built in 1868 by D.C.H. Rothschild, a Port Townsend merchant and a distant relative of Germany's famous Rothschild banking family. Notable for its simplicity of style—in contrast to Port Townsend's many flamboyant Victorian-era homes—the house belonged to the family for nearly 90 years. The last remaining son, Eugene, donated it to the state in 1959. Now restored, with much of the original furniture, wallpaper, and carpeting, the house is on the National Register of Historic Places. It is surrounded by herb and flower gardens and is open to the public daily 10 a.m.-5 p.m. April-Oct., and weekends 10 a.m.-5 p.m. in November (closed Dec.-March). Entry is $1; call (360) 385-2722 for more information on this, Washington's smallest state park.

Manresa Castle

The Manresa Castle is an 1892 mansion at 7th and Sheridan that began its life as a home to Port Townsend's first mayor, Charles Eisenbeis. A native of Prussia, Eisenbeis made a fortune supplying crackers and bread for sailing ships and spent a small fortune building this sumptuous hilltop home in the style of a medieval European castle. After his death in 1902, his wife remarried and moved away. In 1925, the Jesuits purchased the castle, added a new wing, and used it as a training college called Manresa Hall (the name came from Manresa, Spain, where the Jesuit order originated). The Jesuits departed in 1968, and the building was turned into a hotel. It is now on the National Register of Historic Places.

Originally Manresa had only one bathroom per floor, but when the film *An Officer and a Gentleman* was being shot, the Hollywood crew ran out of rooms at other hotels and motels. Their contracts called for a bathroom for each room, so the studio made a deal with Manresa's owner: they advanced him money against the rent, and it was used to build the 43 bathrooms of today. Tours of the castle are free. A restaurant and lounge are on the premises, and an attractive rose and rhododendron garden provides a quiet place to enjoy the vista of Port Townsend and Admiralty Inlet.

City Parks

Chetzemoka Park on Admiralty Inlet at Jackson and Roosevelt Streets remembers Chief Chetzemoka, friend to the town's earliest settlers (he was also known, inexplicably, by the name "Duke of York"). Today the small, shady park offers eight flower gardens, picnicking, a bandstand (often used for weddings), and beach access. The wooden rose arbor is covered with some 25 varieties of roses. Birdwatchers may be interested in **Kah Tai Lagoon Nature Park** at 12th St. near Sims Way. It encompasses 85 acres of wetlands, grasslands, and woodlands, plus 2.5 miles of trails.

Ann Starrett Mansion

The Ann Starrett Mansion, easily the most opulent Victorian structure in Port Townsend is a National Historic Landmark and a favorite B&B. Take a tour ($2 adults, $1 kids), available daily noon-3 p.m., or stay here to enjoy the luxury up close. Step inside this stunning 12-room mansion to learn how it was built in 1889 as George Starrett's wedding present for his new wife, Ann. The rooms are furnished with period antiques and offer outstanding views, but the real treat is the three-story circular staircase capped by a domed ceiling. Dormer windows in the dome admit light that illuminates a different red ruby stone for each season of the year. Behind is a carriage house that has also been converted into B&B accommodations. Call (360) 385-3205 or (800) 321-0644 for information on the mansion or B&B reservations.

Old Fort Townsend State Park

Four miles south of town, 377-acre Old Fort Townsend State Park, tel. (360) 385-3595, has campsites and seven miles of hiking trails through tall firs, sloping down to a 150-foot cliff along Port Townsend Bay. The park is open mid-April to mid-September only. A fort was established here in 1856 to guard against possible Indian attacks, and in 1859 troops were sent from the fort to assist England in the San Juan Island boundary dispute commonly known as "The Pig War" (see the special topic for details). Fort Townsend saw sporadic activity throughout the 1800s until a fire—started by an exploding kerosene lamp—destroyed the barracks in 1895. The fort was decommissioned but was used during WW II as an enemy munitions defusing station. In 1958 it was turned over to the State Parks Commission. A short self-guided historical walk starts at the display board near the park entrance.

FORT WORDEN STATE PARK

History
Capping Point Wilson—the peninsula separating the Strait of Juan de Fuca from Admiralty Inlet—Fort Worden State Park served as one of the "Iron Triangle" of forts protecting the entrance to Puget Sound. All three forts (the others were Fort Flagler on Marrowstone Island, and Fort Casey on Whidbey Island) were built at the turn of the century as a first line of defense for the vital Bremerton Naval Ship Yard and the cities of Puget Sound. Fort Worden is named after John L. Worden, the Union commander during the Monitor-Merrimac battle on March 9, 1862; it's the only Army fort named for a Navy man.

Fort Worden's guns were never fired in battle, and advances in military technology made them obsolete almost as soon as they were in place. Many of the guns were pulled out and shipped to Europe during WW I, and in WW II the fort served as the command center to monitor any Japanese submarine activity in Puget Sound and to coordinate coastal defenses. After the army left in 1953, Fort Worden served as a state detention center before becoming a state park in 1973.

Fort Worden Today
Fort Worden is on the National Register of Historic Places and houses a collection of turn-of-the-century homes, historical Army barracks, a dozen massive gun emplacements (the big guns are long gone), and hidden bunkers. Its modern facilities include a campground, boat launch, tennis courts, underwater scuba-diving park, rhododendron garden, hiking trails, refurbished officers' homes, and a hostel. If the place seems familiar, it may be because much of the movie *An Officer and a Gentleman* was filmed here.

The fort's old barracks and command buildings line the north side of a central parade ground, and the more comfortable officer's row

homes form a picket fence to the south. The **Commanding Officer's House** is nearest the shoreline and contains Victorian furnishings representing the way its inhabitants lived. It's open daily 10 a.m.-5 p.m. April to mid-October, and by special appointment the rest of the year.

Fort Worden has a large conference center and an outstanding restaurant (Blackberries; see below), but its most popular civilian role is as home for the **Centrum Foundation,** a nonprofit center for the arts housed in one of the old barracks.

Coast Artillery Museum
One of the old barracks buildings now houses the Coast Artillery Museum, tel. (360) 385-0373, where you'll learn how the enormous gun batteries out on the coastal bluffs worked. Displays include a scale model of one of the batteries, photos of the big guns in action, mannequins in old military uniforms, and various WW I and WW II artifacts. The museum is open daily 11:30 a.m.-4:30 p.m. from Memorial day to Labor Day, and weekends only noon-4 p.m. from early September to mid-November and mid-February to late May (closed December and January). No charge.

Marine Science Center
Also at the park is the Port Townsend Marine Science Center, tel. (360) 385-5582, located on the dock. "Wet tables" offer intimate, hands-on relationships with local sea creatures; beach walks, evening slide shows and lectures, seaweed workshops, and fish-printing classes are also offered. Hours are Tues.-Sun. noon-6 p.m. from mid-June to early September, and weekends only noon-4 p.m. early Sept.-Oct. and April to mid-June (closed Nov.-March).

Lighthouse and Gun Batteries
Built in 1917, the **Point Wilson Lighthouse** (closed to the public) stands on a sandy spit of land jutting into the Strait of Juan de Fuca. The beach here makes for wonderful sunup or sundown strolls, with dramatic Mt. Baker seeming to rise directly across the water, and a constant parade of ship traffic. Several old gun emplacements and a watchtower are near the lighthouse, but the most interesting are atop **Artillery Hill.** Get here by walking up the gated road that begins behind the noncommissioned

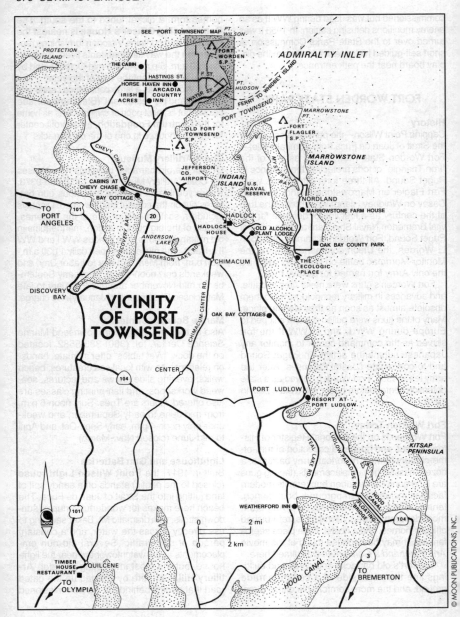

SEE "PORT TOWNSEND" MAP

PT. WILSON

PROTECTION ISLAND

THE CABIN

HASTINGS ST.

HORSE HAVEN INN

IRISH ACRES

ARCADIA COUNTRY INN

FORT WORDEN S.P.

F ST.

WATER ST.

PT. HUDSON

ADMIRALTY INLET

FERRY TO WHIDBEY ISLAND

PORT TOWNSEND

MARROWSTONE PT.

OLD FORT TOWNSEND S.P.

FORT FLAGLER S.P.

MARROWSTONE ISLAND

CHEVY CHASE RD.

CABINS AT CHEVY CHASE

DISCOVERY RD.

BAY COTTAGE

TO PORT ANGELES

101

20

DISCOVERY BAY

JEFFERSON CO. AIRPORT

INDIAN ISLAND

U.S. NAVAL RESERVE

MYSTERY BAY

NORDLAND

MARROWSTONE FARM HOUSE

HADLOCK

HADLOCK HOUSE

OLD ALCOHOL PLANT LODGE

OAK BAY COUNTY PARK

THE ECOLOGIC PLACE

ANDERSON LAKE

ANDERSON LAKE RD.

CHIMACUM

DISCOVERY BAY

VICINITY OF PORT TOWNSEND

CHIMACUM-CENTER RD.

OAK BAY COTTAGES

CENTER

104

PORT LUDLOW

RESORT AT PORT LUDLOW

LUDLOW-PARADISE BAY RD.

KITSAP PENINSULA

TEAL LAKE RD.

HOOD CANAL FLOATING BRIDGE

104

101

MOON

WEATHERFORD INN

0   2 mi

0   2 km

HOOD CANAL

3

TO BREMERTON

TIMBER HOUSE RESTAURANT

QUILCENE

TO OLYMPIA

© MOON PUBLICATIONS, INC.

officers homes, or by walking uphill behind the beachside campground. A series of roads lead through the fascinating old gun emplacements and bunkers; get a walking tour brochure at the park office before heading uphill.

ACCOMMODATIONS AND CAMPING

Port Townsend has some of the finest (and most expensive) lodging choices in the state, most notably the plethora of old Victorian homes that have been turned into luxurious bed and breakfasts. There are at least 17 such B&Bs, along with a dozen or so motels and hotels, and an equal number of cabins and guest houses. See the chamber of commerce office for a complete listing of the cabins; most of the other options are in the lodging chart. See "Port Hadlock" and "Marrowstone Island" for nearby lodging places. Port Townsend is an extremely popular place to visit, and reservations are advised, especially in the summer and on weekends. The most popular B&Bs may book up months ahead during festival weekends. The chamber of commerce, tel. (360) 385-2722, keeps track of local accommodations, and can tell you who has rooms available.

See "Sights" (above) for information on the must-see **Manresa Castle,** tel. (360) 385-5750, or (800) 732-1281 in Washington. For a piece of Hollywood trivia, stay at **Tides Inn,** tel. (360) 385-0595 or (800) 822-8696, where parts of *An Officer and a Gentleman* were filmed. Room 10 is the luxury suite where you can pretend your partner is (take your pick) Richard Gere or Debra Winger. Of considerably less appeal may be room 12, where the shower hanging scene was filmed. **Point Hudson Resort,** tel. (360) 385-2828 or (800) 826-3854, is another unusual place, with shoreside lodging in an old U.S. Coast Gaurd Station. The spartan accommodations aren't to everybody's standards, and some rooms have shared bath, so you may want to check things out first. This is a relatively inexpensive place for families.

Hostel
The **Port Townsend AYH Hostel,** tel. (360) 385-0655, is located in a former barracks building at beautiful Fort Worden. In addition to the dorm facilities, the 28-bed hostel has kitchen facilities, a common room, and five rooms for couples. It's located right in the midst of the summer festival action at Fort Worden and has all-you-can-eat pancake breakfasts. Reservations are strongly advised in summer months, especially for the couples' rooms on summer weekends. The hostel is open year-round, but guests must be out 9:30 a.m.-5 p.m.

Bed and Breakfasts
While some towns have a few old homes turned into B&Bs, Port Townsend seems to burst at the seems with wonderful homes from its late 19th-century glory days. Many of these have been lovingly restored and filled with antiques. (One of the most impressive of these, **Ann Starrett Mansion,** is described in "Sights" above.)

James House, tel. (360) 385-1238 or (800) 385-1238, a Victorian mansion built in 1889, was the first B&B in the Northwest (opened in 1973) and is still going strong. Several of the

James House (1881) was the Northwest's first bed and breakfast.

DIANNE BOUERICE LYONS

PORT TOWNSEND ACCOMMODATIONS

Accommodations are arranged from least to most expensive. Rates may be lower during the winter months. The Port Townsend area code is 360.

HOSTEL

Port Townsend AYH-Hostel; No. 272 Battery Way ; tel. 385-0655; $9 pp for AYH member, or $12 pp for non-members in dorms, $30 d for AYH members, or $36 d for non-members in couples rooms; at Fort Worden, all-you-can-eat pancake breakfasts

HOTELS AND MOTELS

James Swan Hotel; Water and Monroe Streets; tel. 385-1718 or (800) 776-1718; $45-55 s or d in cabins (very plain), $95-105 s or d in hotel; unusual place—see rooms before staying here

Point Hudson Resort; Pt. Hudson; tel. 385-2828 or (800) 826-3854; $46-55 s or d; beachside location, exercise club, no phones, few TVs, local calls 25 cents

The Water Street Hotel; 635 Water St.; tel. 385-5467 or (800) 735-9810; $50-125 s or d; renovated 1889 hotel, continental breakfast, AAA approved

Tides Inn; 1807 Water St.; tel. 385-0595 or (800) 822-8696; $58-124 s or d; used in scenes from *An Officer and a Gentleman,* private decks, some jacuzzis and kitchenettes, AAA approved

Palace Hotel; 1004 Water St.; tel. 385-0773 or (800) 962-0741 (Washington only); $59-119 s or d (some rooms with shared bath); 1889 inn with antiques, continental breakfast, kitchenettes available, AAA approved

Belmont Hotel and Restaurant; 925 Water St.; tel. 385-3007; $59-79 s or d; Victorian inn

Harborside Inn; 330 Benedict St.; tel. 385-7909 or (800) 942-5960; $64-84 s or d; outdoor pool, jacuzzi, continental breakfast, harbor views, kitchenettes available, AAA approved

Port Townsend Inn & Spa; 2020 Washington St.; tel. 385-2211 or (800) 822-8696; $68-94 s or d; dockside location, jacuzzi, continental breakfast, kitchenettes available, AAA approved

Manresa Castle; 7th and Sheridan; tel. 385-5750 or (800) 732-1281 (Washington); $70-175 s or d; unique 1892 castle-hotel, antique furnishings, bay views, continental breakfast, AAA approved

Bishop Victorian Guest Suites; 714 Washington St.; tel. 385-6122 or (800) 824-4738; $72 s, $83-93 d; kitchens, continental breakfast, AAA approved

The Cabins at Chevy Chase; 3710 S. Discovery Rd.; tel. 385-0704; $75-130 s or d; cabins near golf course, swimming pool, fireplaces, kitchens

Aladdin Motor Inn; 2333 Washington St.; tel. 385-3747 or (800) 281-3747; $80 s or d; continental breakfast, microwave and fridge

Bay Cottage; 4346 S. Discovery Rd.; tel. 385-2035; $85 s or d; small oceanside cottages, private beach, kitchens, children welcome

BED AND BREAKFASTS

James House; 1238 Washington St.; tel. 385-1238 or (800) 385-1238; $52-75 s, $65-145 d; 1891 mansion, full breakfast, no kids under 12, AAA approved

Lincoln Inn B&B; 538 Lincoln; tel. 385-6677; $55-65 s or $65-75 d; 1888 brick antique-furnished mansion, full breakfast, bicycles

Lizzie's B&B; 731 Pierce St.; tel. 385-4168 or (800) 700-4168; $58-205 s or d; Victorian house, fireplaces, grand piano, full breakfast

Baker House B&B; 905 Franklin St.; tel. 385-6673; $60-75 s or d; restored 1898 home, two verandas with town views, huge breakfast, no children

Annapurna Inn; 538 Adams; tel. 385-2909 or (800) 868-2662; $60-105 s or d; 1881 house, sauna/steam bath, full vegetarian breakfasts (retreat packages: $225 pp for two nights, including massage, yoga, and reflexology)

Trenholm House B&B; 2037 Haines St.; tel. 385-6059; $62-85 s or d; 1890 farmhouse inn, antique-furnished, full breakfast, children over eight okay

Ft. Worden Recreation Housing; Ft. Worden State Park; tel. 385-4730; $62-200 for historic Officer's Row homes (one to six bedrooms)

Ravenscroft Inn; 533 Quincy St.; tel. 385-2784 or (800) 782-2691; $67-165 s or d; gourmet breakfast, fireplace, Sound and mountain views, eight guest rooms, private baths, no kids under 12, AAA approved

Horse Haven Inn; 2823 Hastings Ave.; tel. 385-7784; $70 s or d; country location, jacuzzi, continental breakfast, fruit and wine basket

Quimper Inn; 1306 Franklin; tel. 385-1060; $70-130 s or d; 1888 home, elaborately furnished rooms, no children, full breakfast

Heritage House; 305 Pierce Street; tel. 385-6800 or (800) 385-6867; $70-140 s or d; 1870 Victorian home, water views, antique furnishings, full breakfast, no kids under eight

Holly Hill House; 611 Polk St.; tel. 385-5619 or (800) 435-1454; $72-160 s or d; luxurious 1872 home, delicious full breakfast, five guest rooms, no kids under 12, AAA approved

SalmonBerry Farm; 2404 35th St.; tel. 385-1517; $75 s or d; country location, make-your-own breakfast

Hunt Manor Guest House; 1110 Jackman St.; tel. 385-9241; $75 s or d; two guest rooms, buffet continental breakfast, no children

English Inn; 718 F St.; tel. 385-5302; $75-95 s or d; jacuzzi, gazebo, garden, no kids under 12

A Rose Cottage B&B; 1310 Clay St.; tel. 385-6944; $75-99 s or d; four guest rooms, continental breakfast, AAA approved

Ann Starrett Mansion B&B; 744 Clay St.; tel. 385-3205 or (800) 321-0644; $75-160 s or d in the home, $145-185 s or d in the cottage; antique-filled 1889 Victorian mansion, AAA approved

Old Consulate Inn/F.W. Hastings House; 313 Walker St.; tel. 385-6753 or (800) 300-6753; $79-175 s or d; 1889 Queen Anne Victorian home with mountain views, fireplaces, eight guest rooms, billiard and game room, gourmet breakfast, AAA approved (four diamond)

Discovery Gardens Cottage; 2607 Haines; tel. 385-4313; $80 s or d; cottage in pastoral location, bicycles, make-your-own breakfast

Chanticleer B&B; 1208 Franklin St.; tel. 385-6239 or (800) 858-9421; $80-105 s or d; 1876 Victorian, antiques in rooms, full breakfast

The Cabin B&B 839 N. Jacob Miller Rd.; tel. 385-7636; $90 s or d; small cabin in woods with private beach, kitchen, make-it-yourself breakfast, no children

Victorian Suite at the Club; 229 Monroe St.; tel. 385-6560; $100 s or d; full breakfast, full health club, no kids

---

11 antique-furnished guest rooms offer commanding views of the town. There's also a secluded cottage with two beds and private bath.

Quimper Inn B&B, tel. (360) 385-1060, is a distinctive three-story home with a two-level porch and five elaborately furnished guest rooms. Built in 1888 and considerably modified over the years, it served as a home, boardinghouse, nurses' home, and furniture warehouse before being restored to its original glory.

Holly Hill House, tel. (360) 385-5619 or (800) 435-1454, built in 1872, has been beautifully renovated to provide three guest rooms, each with queen-sized bed and private bath. Two more rooms with private bath are available in the carriage house, and the home is surrounded by tall holly and elm trees.

Another lovely Victorian B&B, **The Old Consulate Inn,** tel. (360) 385-6753 or (800) 300-6753, overlooks Port Townsend from atop a high bluff, providing panoramic mountain and water views in comfortably elegant surroundings. The inn was built in 1889 by F.W. Hastings, son of Port Townsend's founding father Loren B. Hastings, and served as the office of the German Consul (hence the "Old Consulate" name) in the early part of this century. Enjoy the fireplaces in two parlors, hone your skills in the large billiard and game room, or play the grand piano and antique organ. Eight guest rooms all have private bath.

The English Inn, tel. (360) 385-5302, is a large, boxy, edge-of-town Victorian home built in 1885. This very nice B&B stands on a hill, with a garden, gazebo, and outdoor hot tub on the patio. All five guest rooms have small private baths.

Baker House B&B, tel. (360) 385-6673, is a restored 1898 Victorian home with two wrap-around verandas providing over-the-town views. There are four rooms available (two with private bath).

Three short blocks from downtown, the elegant **Ravenscroft Inn,** tel. (360) 385-2784, features a gourmet breakfast, a great room with an always-lit fireplace, columned piazza with Sound and mountain views, and five guest rooms, all with private bath.

Annapurna Inn, tel. (360) 385-2909 or (800) 868-2662, is a combination B&B and retreat center close to the far-more-elaborate Ann Starrett Mansion. The house and cozy rooms are not fancy, but services (extra charge) include foot reflexology, cranio/sacral massage, yoga, and a steam bath. Organically grown vegan (vegetarian with no eggs or milk products) breakfasts are served.

A Victorian B&B, **Lizzie's,** tel. (360) 385-4168 or (800) 700-4168, has eight guest rooms, some with private bath. Enjoy the two parlors with fireplaces, leather sofas, library, and grand piano.

Breakfast is served around an 11-foot oak table.

Lincoln Inn B&B, tel. (360) 385-6677, is perhaps the most unusual historic home in Port Townsend. Built in 1888 for Elias DeVoe, owner of a local brick company, it mixes the standard Victorian flourishes with an all-brick facade. There are three gracious guest rooms with private baths.

Constructed by a shipbuilder, **Trenholm House B&B,** tel. (360) 385-6059, is a 19th-century farmhouse with original woodwork and antique furnishings. It is in a quiet part of town. **Horse Haven Inn,** tel. (360) 385-7784, has a single suite in a newer home located in the country. There's a hot tub and a basket of fruit, wine, and cheese to welcome your visit. Built in 1868 by shipbuilder John Fuge, **Heritage House,** tel. (360) 385-6800 or (800) 385-6867, offers views of the surrounding waters and mountains. The six guest rooms are filled with antiques.

Officers' Quarters

An interesting alternative lodging—especially for families and groups—is to rent one of the former homes of officers and noncommissioned officers in Fort Worden. Most of the 23 houses have been completely refurbished with reproductions of Victorian furniture, brass headboards, Tiffany lamps, and new carpeting. Those that have not been refurbished are simple but comfortable places with spacious bedrooms. All of these have full kitchens and a wonderful in-the-park location, but no TVs. Meals are available at the cafeteria by prior arrangement. Rates begin at $62 per night for a one-bedroom apartment unit and go up to $200 for a six-bedroom house. Because of their popularity, especially during summer festivals, reservations for these houses should be made far in advance; call (360) 385-4730 for more info.

Campgrounds

Fort Worden State Park, tel. (360) 385-4730, has 50 year-round beachside campsites and another 30 near the conference area. All sites have electricity and water hookups, so even folks in tents get charged $16 per night; coin-operated showers are available. Four miles south of town, **Old Fort Townsend State Park,** tel. (360) 385-3595, has shady campsites ($10 for tents, $15 for RVs) under tall firs along Port

Townsend Bay. It also has coin-operated showers. The campground is open mid-April to mid-September only. Call (800) 452-5687 for campsite reservations at both of these state parks ($6 extra fee), available up to 11 months ahead of time. (See "Fort Flagler State Park," below, for another camping option.)

RVers can park at the private **Point Hudson Resort** on the beach, tel. (360) 385-2828 or (800) 826-3854, for $18. Also check the **Jefferson Country Fairgrounds,** tel. (360) 385-1013, for RV spaces and showers.

FOOD

It's hard *not* to find a good meal in Port Townsend; just walk along Water St. till something strikes your fancy. It's all there, from pizza-by-the-slice to gourmet Northwest cuisine.

Light Meals, Coffees, and Sweets
Salal Cafe, 634 Water St., tel. (360) 385-6532, is a simple down-home eatery with a post-hippie flavor. Come here for the outstanding omelettes and blintzes, as well as earthy lunches. Design your own sandwich at the **Water Street Deli,** 926 Water St., tel. (360) 385-2422, or try their unique clam bisque. Also here are salads, homemade desserts, and a dinner theater. Stop by **Sea J's Cafe,** 2501 Washington St., tel. (360) 385-6312, for the best fish and chips in town.

The **Oasis,** uptown at 720 Tyler, tel. (360) 385-2130, is a shoebox-sized coffee shop with a few stools where you'll encounter locals on espresso-and-pastry missions. They also make healthy and delicious fruit smoothies. **Bread & Roses Bakery,** 230 Quincy, tel. (360) 385-1044, also cranks out delicious pastries, along with from-scratch breads, soups, salads, and espresso. **Elevated Ice Cream,** 627 Water St., tel. (360) 385-1156, has more espresso, along with Italian ices, chocolates, and fresh, homemade ice-cream treats. Chocoholics will love their "Blind Love."

Northwest Cuisine
Fountain Cafe, 920 Washington St., tel. (360) 385-1364, serves excellent natural foods, pastas, and oysters in a tiny backstreet location.

It's a very popular place, so be ready to wait for a table on summer weekends; open for lunch and dinner daily. **Silverwater Cafe** on the corner of Washington and Taylor Streets, tel. (360) 385-6448, is well known for fresh and reasonably priced oysters, calamari, and salmon cooked to perfection, but the killer white chocolate cheesecake is a treat you won't forget.

Manresa Castle, 7th and Sheridan Streets, tel. (360) 385-5750, is a take-the-relatives-out sort of place with fine dining, most notably the Chateaubriand dinner for two ($50). **Blackberries** at Fort Worden, tel. (360) 385-1461, offers outstanding seafood and lamb specials along with other Northwest cuisine, but be prepared to wait since the service can be slow. The Sunday brunch is a favorite.

International Eats
If you're a fan of spicy Thai food (and I do mean spicy), beat tracks to **Khu Larb Thai,** 225 Adams St., tel. (360) 385-5023. Prices are reasonable, and the food—including a dozen vegetarian dishes—is delicious and authentic.

For a diverse variety of Italian pastas and unusual pizzas—all cooked with fresh ingredients and flair—head just south of town to **Cafe Piccolo,** 3040 Hwy. 20, tel. (360) 385-1403. The Sicilian fisherman's stew—with prawns, mussels, clams, scallops, and fresh fish—is especially distinctive.

Lanza's Ristorante/Pizzaria, uptown at 1020 Lawrence St., tel. (360) 385-6221, has several kinds of excellent pizzas, plus outstanding home-cookin' in the form of antipastas and pastas. A simpler—but surprisingly good—choice is to get a slice and a Coke at **Waterfront Pizza,** 951 Water St., tel. (360) 385-6629, and talk grunge rock with the local high school kids. For a fast and massive south-of-the-border fix (made by Asian owners!) hop over to **Burrito Depot,** 609 Washington St., tel. (360) 385-5856. For a more diverse menu, **El Sarape,** 628 Water St., tel. (360) 379-9343, offers typical Mexican food, along with seafood specialties.

Markets and Bakeries
Whole Foods Grocery Coop, on Lawrence St. in "Uptown," is a throwback to the '60s with quality organic and natural foods. On the opposite side of the street, but just a short distance away,

is **Aldrich's Grocery,** 940 Lawrence St., tel. (360) 385-0500. There's a small-town country store feel here, but the food includes gourmet specialties, a big wine selection, and fantastic baked goods. Get a coffee next door at the Oasis, and a pastry here.

For the freshest baked goods, eggs, organic produce, herbs, and flowers head to the **Port Townsend Farmers Market,** held every Saturday morning May-Sept. from 9 a.m. to noon on Water and Madison Streets (next to the police station).

ENTERTAINMENT AND EVENTS

Centrum Foundation

Port Townsend's calendar is jam-packed with activities, many of which are sponsored by the nonprofit Centrum Foundation, located at Fort Worden State Park. Founded in 1976, Centrum organizes major festivals and events each year both downtown and as at the performing arts pavilion (an old balloon hanger) at the fort. These events permit you and thousands of other guests to see and hear performances by some of the country's finest jazz, bluegrass, and classical musicians, along with folk dance festivals, plays, seminars, and readings by well-known authors. For a schedule of upcoming events, contact Centrum Foundation at (360) 385-3102 or (800) 733-3608.

Events

The **Rhododendron Festival** (third week in May) features a big Saturday parade, dances, antique and art shows, a carnival, rhododendron displays, and the crowning of the Rhododendron Queen, whose handprint and signature are captured in the cement sidewalk downtown. July is a particularly busy month, with the **Festival of American Fiddle Tunes** (second weekend in July), the **Port Townsend Writers' Conference** (mid-July), and the **Jazz Port Townsend** gathering (last weekend in July). The jazz festival is a Centrum event that attracts nationally acclaimed performers.

The second weekend in August is reserved for the **Jefferson County Fair,** the old-fashioned kind with livestock shows, 4-H displays, and a mud race. Then comes the **Marrowstone Music Festival** (last three weekends in Au-

gust), and the **Wooden Boat Festival** (second weekend in September), an educational affair with displays, lectures, and classes to promote interest in the dying art of wooden boat building and restoration. The month ends with the **Port Townsend Feature Film Conference** (last weekend in September).

Early October brings the **Kinetic Sculpture Race** to Port Townsend; human-powered mechanical sculptures race over land *and water* to the finish. If you're in town on the first Saturday in December, you'll be able to join the fun as Santa arrives by ferry, and people gather to sing carols on Water St. and watch the **tree lighting ceremony.**

Music and Theater

Both the **Back Alley Tavern,** 923 Washington St., tel. (360) 385-2914, and **The Public House Grill & Ales,** 1038 Water St., tel. (360) 385-9708, have live music on weekends. The latter has seven microbrews on tap and good pub food, especially for lunch. If you're looking for C&W or rock tunes, try the **Hilltop Tavern,** 2510 Sims Way, tel. (360) 385-0101. **Ajax Cafe,** nine miles south of town in Port Hadlock, tel. (360) 385-3450, also has nightly live music.

Water Street Theatre has dinner theater productions throughout the summer inside the Water Front Deli at 926 Water St., tel. (360) 385-2422. The **Port Townsend Orchestra** gives four performances between October and May.

RECREATION

On the Water

Kayak Port Townsend, tel. (360) 385-6240, operates no-experience-needed sea-kayaking tours of the area, with rates beginning at $38 for half-day trips or $70 for all-day treks (including lunch). They also offer a full range of two to six-day paddle trips ($145-225) around Protection Island, Bird Island, Hood Canal, and Lake Ozette, as well as trips to British Columbian and Baja waters.

Anderson Lake State Park, south of Port Townsend on Anderson Lake Rd. off Hwy. 20, is an isolated lake surrounded by trees. No camping or swimming, but it's a popular place to fish for cutthroat and rainbow trout. The public **swim-**

PAUL BOYER

wooden boats at Port Townsend

ming pool is in Port Townsend Intermediate School on Walker and Blaine Streets, tel. (360) 385-7665.

Other Recreation

Rent mountain, touring, and tandem bikes from **P.T. Cyclery,** 100 Tyler St., tel. (360) 385-6470. You can also rent bikes, sea kayaks, and camping gear from **Sport Townsend,** 1044 Water St., tel. (360) 379-9711. Ask them about the Outdoor Connection, a local club offering free camping trips.

SHOPPING

Galleries

Water St. houses numerous art galleries, antique shops, cafes, trendy gift shops, and an import toy store. **North By Northwest,** 918 Water St., tel. (360) 385-0995, features Indian and Eskimo art, masks, and jewelry. Another gallery emphasizing native arts—especially baskets and masks—is **Northwest Native Expressions,** 637 Water St., tel. (360) 385-4770. **Earthenworks Gallery,** 1002 Water St., tel. (360) 385-0328, is a bit glitzy, but sells high quality, creative works, especially ceramics. Other galleries offer a mix of the original and the trendy. **Gallery Walks** are held the first Saturday of each month, 5:30-8 p.m. March-Dec., during which galleries hang new works, serve refreshments, and often have artists on hand.

Other Stores

A number of bookstores can be found on Water St., including the funky and cluttered **Melville & Co.,** 914 Water St., tel. (360) 385-7127, selling used books. Another noteworthy shop is **Jupiter Blues,** 1839 Water St., tel. (360) 379-8039, selling beautiful batik clothing and futon covers, and offering batik classes.

Abundant Life Seed Foundation

Located in Uptown, this cooperatively managed nonprofit organization collects, preserves, and propagates native seeds, especially from rare and endangered species. They run the World Seed Fund, which sends free seeds all over the world to relieve hunger, and have an extraordinary catalog offering thousands of types of seeds—from artichokes to Xeranthemum—along with books about alternative agriculture, medicinal herbs, and seed collecting. You can join this remarkable organization for $20 a year, or call them with any plant or seed questions at (360) 385-7192.

INFORMATION AND SERVICES

For local info and a ton of brochures, head to the **Port Townsend Chamber of Commerce Tourist Information Center,** 2437 E. Sims Way, tel. (360) 385-2722. They are open daily 9 a.m.-5 p.m. all year. The **Jefferson County Info Hotline,** tel. (800) 499-0047, is a 24-hour recorded arts and theater line.

The recently expanded **Port Townsend Public Library,** 1220 Lawrence St., tel. (360) 385-3181, is one of the many Carnagie Libraries built early in this century. For medical emergencies, contact **Jefferson General Hospital** at 9th and Sheridan, tel. (360) 385-2200.

TRANSPORTATION

Bus Service

Jefferson Transit, tel. (360) 385-4777 or (800) 773-7788, serves Port Townsend and Jefferson County and offers connections to Port Angeles via Clallam Transit or Poulsbo, Bainbridge Island, and Bremerton via Kitsap Transit. Bike racks are available on most Jefferson Transit routes. Unfortunately, there is no service to Marrowstone Island. Bus fare is just 50 cents around town, or 75 cents for anywhere in the service area.

Ferry Service

Port Townsend is served directly by the **Washington State Ferry** from Keystone on the southwest side of Whidbey Island. The ferries depart from downtown about every 50 minutes and cost $3.30 roundtrip passenger, $6.65 one-way car and driver ($5.55 in winter), $1.90 one-way cyclist. Call (206) 842-2345 (in Seattle) or (800) 843-3779 for more information.

P.S. Express, tel. (360) 385-5288, provides excellent passenger-only service between Port Townsend and Friday Harbor on San Juan Island. The boat leaves Port Townsend daily, May-Oct., and takes you through Admiralty Inlet and the Strait of Juan de Fuca where you're likely to see seals, sea otters, and orcas. They stay in Friday Harbor long enough for a quick three-hour visit, or you can overnight there and return to Port Townsend later. The charge is $28 one-way, or $40 roundtrip, bikes and kayaks $10 extra.

Tours

The ***Inverness Queen,*** tel. (360) 379-0553, is a classic 1929 wooden motor yacht that offers two hour tours for $25. They sail from the Northwest Native Expressions Gallery at 637 Water St., at 10 a.m., 1 p.m., and 5 p.m. most summer and fall days.

Air Service

Port Townsend Airways, tel. (360) 385-6554 or (800) 385-6554, has direct service to Sea-Tac Airport ($59 one-way) and the San Juan Islands ($39 one-way), and scenic half-hour flights around Port Townsend.

PORT HADLOCK

The tiny towns of Port Hadlock, Irondale, and Chimacum make up the so-called "Tri-Area" (not to be confused with the Tri-Cities!). Each of these has a cluster of businesses; of note in Port Hadlock are **Ferino's Pizzeria,** tel. (360) 385-0840, with gourmet pizzas and pizzas by the slice, and **Ajax Cafe,** tel. (360) 385-3450, with nightly live music. **Chimacum Cafe,** in Chimacum, tel. (360) 732-4631, another locals' favorite, makes all-American steaks, chicken, burgers, pies, and justly famous chocolate malts. The Hadlock area has a number of fascinating historic homes, including **Hadlock Manor** on Curtiss St., built in the 1890s by a Swedish sea captain. For local info, head to **Port Hadlock Chamber of Commerce,** 23 Colwell St., tel. (360) 385-1469, open Mon.-Fri. 9 a.m.-5 p.m.

Accommodations

The Old Alcohol Plant Lodge, tel. (360) 385-6955, stands just east of town on the way to Indian and Marrowstone Islands. Built in 1911 by the Classen Chemical Co., this large brick and concrete building produced alcohol from sawdust and sugar for just two years before the company went bankrupt. It stood abandoned for the next 65 years, but a $4 million revamping has turned it into a most unusual lodge and restaurant. Hotel rooms here go for $49-85 d; townhouses and the penthouse suite for $100-250 d. The reasonable steak and seafood restaurant provides fine harbor views.

Windridge Cottage, 2804 W. Valley Rd., tel. (360) 732-4575, has a modern cedar cottage out in the country along Beausite Lake. There's a full kitchen, fireplace, and bath, and it sleeps up to four for $90.

Oak Bay Cottages, tel. (360) 437-0380, has two furnished houses located between Port Hadlock and Port Ludlow on Oak Bay Road. The beach is just across the road. There's a two night minimum stay, and the cost is $75 d.

MARROWSTONE ISLAND

Quiet Marrowstone Island is off the beaten path but offers wooded country, attractive summer homes, and a fascinating historic fort. The only real business on the island is **Nordland General Store,** which pretty much makes up the entire town of Nordland. The store was completely remodeled in 1994 but maintains a wonderful charm and friendliness. It's a great place to get a cup of coffee and sit in the back by the woodstove while reading the paper.

Upper Oak Bay Jefferson County Park, on the southwest corner of Marrowstone Island, has fine views east across Puget Sound. Summer-only camping is available for $8, or $10 for RVs (no hookups or showers).

Tiny **Mystery Bay State Park,** just north of Nordland, has a picnic area, beach, pier, boat moorage, and protected waters for small boaters, along with striking Olympic views, but no camping. The park's name came from the seemingly mysterious disappearance of boats belonging to Prohibition-era booze-smugglers who brought liquor here from Canada. (The smugglers used the tall overhanging trees here to hide their skiffs.)

Fort Flagler State Park

Marrowstone Island's biggest attraction is Fort Flagler State Park, at the northern tip of Marrowstone Island and surrounded by water on three sides. Boating, picnicking, crabbing, salmon and bottom fishing, wooded hiking trails, and camping at beach sites are available in this 783-acre park. Since it is in the Olympic rain shadow, the park gets lots of sun and only 17 inches of rain per year.

With Fort Worden and Whidbey's Fort Casey, Fort Flagler formed what old-timers called the Iron Triangle, the trio of forts—the others were Fort Worden and Fort Casey—guarding the narrow Admiralty Inlet between Port Townsend and Whidbey Island against attack of Puget Sound. They were equipped with 10-inch "disappearing rifles," the cannons you can see today at Fort Casey. When these cannons were fired, the recoil would cause them to swing down out of sight behind the cement walls for reloading, giving the gun sighter a wild ride, and usually a shiner from being repeatedly struck by the eyepiece. As an aside, Battery Russell at Fort Stevens south of the Columbia River estuary was equipped with these "rifles" when a Japanese submarine fired several rounds at it in 1942. The battery commander knew his artillery was too weak to hope to hit the sub, so he wisely held fire and didn't give away the exact position.

The Iron Triangle forts also had enormous mortars that were proven impractical at the first test: the concussion was so great that windows were broken, pictures fell off walls, and foundations cracked. Fort Flagler was built in the late 1890s and served as a training center during the two world wars, but its guns were never fired in anger. The fort was closed in 1955 and later became a state park. Nine gun batteries remain, and two three-inch guns (obtained from the Philippines) have been installed at Battery Wansboro facing out onto Admiralty Inlet. From here you can watch the ships, barges, sailing boats, and fishing vessels cruise past; pretty easy to see why a fort was built on this strategic bottleneck.

Today, Fort Flagler is on the National Register of Historic Places. The spacious green parade grounds are bordered by barracks and gracious old officers quarters. Several trails cut through wooded sections of the park, including the "Roots of the Forest" interpretive trail. Other activities here include camping, digging for clams on the beaches, scuba diving in an adjacent underwater park, and boating. The **Marrowstone Point Lighthouse** stands on the northeast edge of the fort, with massive Mt. Baker creating an attractive photographic backdrop. It is not open to the public. There's also a small U.S. Fish and Wildlife Service **Fishery Research Center** here, open for tours by advance request; call (360) 385-1007. Several of the fort's old buildings are now used for a state Environmental Learning Center, tel. (360) 385-3701, used primarily by school groups.

The campground (actually two separate areas) is open late February through October only and costs $11 for tents or $16 for RVs; coin-operated showers are available. Call (360) 385-1259 for information, or (800) 452-5687 for campsite reservations ($6 extra fee), available up to 11 months ahead of time.

Accommodations

The **Fort Flagler AYH Hostel,** tel. (360) 385-1288, is in one of the barracks of the old fort and is open April-Sept. only. The cost is $10 for AYH members, $13 for nonmembers; there's also one couples' room for $26 d for members, $32 for nonmembers. The hostel is closed 9:30 a.m.-5 p.m., but the common room may be available during that time.

The Ecologic Place, 10 Beach Dr. in Nordland, tel. (360) 385-3077, has 11 rustic cabins with Oak Bay and Olympic views for $35-85 d (the $85 cabins sleep six). Each comes with complete kitchen and bath facilities, plus a woodstove; minimum stay is two nights. **Marrowstone Farm House,** tel. (360) 385-5425, is just south of the tiny settlement of Nordland and has a two-bedroom country house overlooking Mystery Bay. It goes for $125 per night; two-night minimum.

PORT LUDLOW

The Resort at Port Ludlow makes up just about all of Port Ludlow. Once a major sawmill and shipping town, the sawmill closed and shipping went with it, and the town diminished until the resort arrived. Port Ludlow offers the utmost in luxury: heated outdoor and indoor pools, jacuzzi, saunas, squash and tennis courts, paved bike paths, a 27-hole championship golf course, a 300-slip marina on Port Ludlow Bay complete with rental sailboats, and the **Harbormaster Restaurant,** serving breakfast, lunch, and dinner with entertainment most nights in the lounge. The outside deck is a favorite

place for a romantic evening meal. Rooms range from $85 d for economy rooms, $95 d for a view room, $135 for suites, all the way up to four-bedroom suites for $350 d. Call (360) 437-2222 or (800) 732-1239 for reservations.

On Sunday from late July to early September, the resort puts on free **Music on the Green** concerts featuring a wide range of styles, from jazz to country.

The newly built **Weatherford Inn,** tel. (360) 437-0332 or (800) 481-0332, has five luxurious guest rooms in an elegant home, a large common room with fireplace, and a full breakfast. Rates are $135 s or d. Outside is a sandy beach and views of Hood Canal and the Olympics.

Another new place, **The Inn at Ludlow Bay,** tel. (360) 437-0411, charges a whopping $165-200 s or d, with facilities that include in-room jacuzzis and mountain views. There's a two-night minimum stay on weekends.

Information

The **Olympic Peninsula Gateway Visitor Information Center,** on the corner of Hwy. 104 and Beaver Valley Rd. (four miles north of the Hood Canal Bridge), tel. (360) 437-0120, is open daily 9 a.m.-4 p.m. in the summer. Stop here for local information and brochures. The **area code** is 360.

Transportation

Jefferson Transit, tel. (360) 385-4777 or (800) 773-7788, serves Port Ludlow, Port Townsend, and Jefferson County, with connections to Port Angeles via Clallam Transit or Poulsbo, Bainbridge Island, and Bremerton via Kitsap Transit.

Port Angeles-Seattle Bus Lines, tel. (360) 457-4580 or (800) 764-2287, has daily service on the Kitsap Peninsula, connecting Bremerton, Port Orchard, Port Ludlow, Poulsbo, Silverdale, and Gig Harbor with Seattle, Sea-Tac Airport, Tacoma, Sequim, and Port Angeles. **Olympic Bus Lines,** tel. (360) 452-3858, has daily connections to Port Angeles, Sequim, Kingston, Seattle, and Sea-Tac.

SEQUIM

The weather in Sequim (pronounced "skwim") is odd for the soggy Olympic Peninsula: 17 inches of annual rainfall and habitually clear skies are caused by the town's location in the "blue hole," a locally famous weather pattern. Locals note that Sequim gets less rain than Los Angeles (but the temperatures are not nearly as warm). As storms pass over the peninsula, they split in two; one part clings to the Olympics and the other is blown along by the strait's air currents,

bypassing Sequim and the surrounding Dungeness Valley like an island in the stream. The pleasant temperate climate has transformed this town of 3,800 into a booming retirement community, with more than 20,000 people spread across the Dungeness Valley. Although there are a number of enjoyable spots in the area, the town itself is not especially attractive, consisting of a line of businesses strewn haphazardly along the heavily trafficked Hwy. 101.

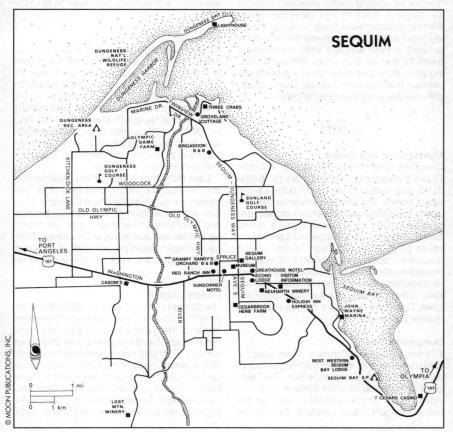

History

The first Anglo settlers in the Dungeness Valley found an arid landscape of grasses and cacti bisected by the mountain-fed waters of the Dungeness River. The first irrigation ditches were dug by hand in 1886, allowing water from the river to transform the prairies into highly productive dairies and farms. Produce from the valley supplied food for the booming city of Victoria, British Columbia, across the Strait of Juan de Fuca. Today, ditches reach for almost 100 miles and irrigate some 12,000 acres.

The village of Sequim grew up as a farm center and mill town and was originally called "Seguin" (till a postal service employee changed it to Sequim). The term was somehow derived from the S'Klallam word "Such-e-kwi-ing," meaning "quiet water." The town was officially incorporated in 1913 and has been a retirement haven for the past thirty years. With each passing year, more and more farms are being developed into suburban homes, paved roads, golf courses, and other developments.

SIGHTS

Museum and Arts Center

One block north of Hwy. 101 at 175 W. Cedar St., the Museum and Arts Center, tel. (360) 683-8110, was built to store the 12,000-year-old tusks, bones, and artifacts unearthed at Sequim's world-famous Manis Mastodon Site, discovered in 1977 by Emanuel Manis, a retired farmer. Archaeologists discovered a prehistoric spear point in the rib cage of one of the mastodons, some of the earliest evidence that humans hunted these elephantine beasts. Other displays include several fine old cedar bark baskets, pioneer farming displays, and timber exhibits. Open daily 9 a.m.-4 p.m. year-round; donations accepted.

Dungeness Spit

The word "Dungeness" means "sandy cape," a fitting description for this 5.5-mile long stretch of sand that creates Dungeness Bay. The **Dungeness National Wildlife Refuge** here provides habitat for 250 species of birds on the nation's longest natural sandspit. As many as 30,000 birds rest at this saltwater lagoon during their migratory journeys. Admission to the refuge is $2 per party; call (360) 457-8451 for further info. Built in 1857, the **New Dungeness Lighthouse** at the tip of the spit is managed by volunteers and has tours, but you'll have to hike a total of 11 miles out and back to see it. It's a good idea to check the tide charts before starting out. For an overview of the area, hike the half-mile trail from the parking lot to a bluff overlooking Dungeness Bay. Clamming, fishing, and canoeing are permitted in this protected wildlife refuge, but no camping, dogs, firearms, or fires. The spit is closed to horses on weekends and holidays from April 15 to October 15.

Wineries

Although Sequim's arid climate would seem to make it a natural place for wineries, the majority of the grapes used here are grown east of the Cascades. Maria and Eugene Neuharth have been producing fine dinner wines (chardonnay, riesling, cabernet, and merlot) since 1978 at **Neuharth Winery,** 148 Still Rd., tel. (360) 683-9652. Their tasting and sales cellar is open daily 9:30 a.m.-5:30 p.m. from mid-May through October, and Wed.-Sun. 9:30 a.m.-5:30 p.m. the rest of the year.

Lost Mountain Winery, 730 Lost Mountain Rd., tel. (360) 683-5229, produces robust red wines such as "Dago Red" from California, Oregon, and Washington grapes; open for tastings and tours most of the time, but no set hours. No sulfides are used in any of their wines. They have an open house the last week of June and the first week of July when the new wines are released.

Cuddly Critters

The **Olympic Game Farm,** tel. (360) 683-4295 or (800) 778-4295, a vacation and retirement home for Hollywood stars, is a 90-acre preserve where Gentle Ben and over 200 other animals of TV and movie fame can be visited. This is where many of the Walt Disney nature specials were filmed, along with parts of many feature movies, including *Never Cry Wolf,* and *The Incredible Journey.* Hour-long guided walking tours are available daily mid-May to early

September for $6 adults, $5 seniors and kids ages five to 12, free for children under five; the park is open all year for driving tours for the same prices. Combined walking and driving tour tickets are $8 adults, $6 kids and seniors. Follow the signs from Sequim five miles northwest to Ward Road.

Other Attractions

John Wayne loved the Northwest because he could visit the area and not be hounded by autograph seekers, and he especially loved the Strait of Juan de Fuca; he often explored the waters with his refurbished Navy minesweeper, the *Wild Goose.* The Duke liked it so much he bought land on Sequim Bay and donated it for a marina. The **John Wayne Marina** has 422 slips, a landscaped park and picnic area, and a bronze statue of the Duke as he appeared in the 1949 flick *She Wore A Yellow Ribbon.*

Gourmet cooks will enjoy a visit to **Cedarbrook Herb Farm,** 986 Sequim Ave. S, tel. (360) 683-7733, where over 200 varieties of herbs, teas, and flowers are organically grown. The gift shop here sells herbal plants, books, herb vinegars, potpourri, dried flowers, decorative straw hats, catnip mice, and even herbal moth repellents. Open daily March to September, weekends October to Christmas.

The Dungeness Fish Hatchery, four miles up Taylor Cutoff Rd. along the Dungeness River, raises 350,000 coho and 300,000 Chinook salmon each year. Open for tours daily 8 a.m.-4:30 p.m.

The enormous **7 Cedars Casino,** tel. (360) 683-7777 or (800) 458-2597, at the minuscule settlement of Blyn near the head of Sequim Bay (seven miles east of Sequim) has bingo, blackjack, craps, keno, poker, roulette, and pulltabs. The casino is run by the Jamestown S'Klallam Tribe, and a gamblers' shuttle bus service is available from Port Townsend and Port Angeles. Inside, the Salish Room Restaurant serves buffet dinners and regional specialties. An adjacent longhouse contains the **Northwest Native Art Expressions Gallery,** tel. (360) 681-4640, with masks, paintings, jewelry, and weaving. Open daily 10 a.m.-6 p.m.

A couple more miles east from Sequim on Hwy. 101 is **Wild Birds Unlimited,** a fun place to visit if you are a birder, or just like to feed birds. You'll find everything from bird tapes to birdhouses, along with all sorts of squirrel-proof feeders.

Olympic Peninsula artists are represented at **Sequim Gallery,** 130 N. Sequim Ave., tel. (360) 683-6503. Drawing and watercolor classes are taught by resident artist Judy Priest. A different kind of art can be found at **Bandy's Troll Haven,** a private residence crowded with all sorts of fairy-tale creatures. Get here by heading east from Sequim on Hwy. 101 to Gardiner, and turning onto Gardiner Beach Road.

ACCOMMODATIONS

Motels and B&Bs

See the "Sequim Accommodations" chart for a complete listing of local accommodations, or call the **Sequim-Dungeness Valley Lodging Association,** tel. (800) 343-5898, for reservations.

Campgrounds

Dungeness Recreation Area, tel. (360) 683-5847, a 216-acre Clallam County park at the base of the refuge, has camping Feb.-Oct. ($10) with showers and a dump station, but no RV hookups. **Sequim Bay State Park,** just east of Sequim on Hwy. 101, has wooded tent sites ($10), hookup sites ($15), a boat launch, scuba diving, hiking, tennis courts, and superb views of Sequim Bay. Open year-round. Call (800) 452-5687 for campsite reservations ($6 extra fee), available up to 11 months ahead of time. More campsites can be found at **South Sequim Bay Recreation Area** east of town along the bay and just off Hwy. 101.

The Forest Service has two primitive campgrounds ($4; open late May to early September) in the mountains south of Sequim. **Dungeness Forks Campground** is 11 miles south via Forest Roads 2909 and 2958; **East Crossing Campground** is 13 miles south via Forest Roads 28 and 2860. Contact the Quilcene Ranger Station, tel. (360) 765-3368, for details.

Sequim's two private RV parks are **Sunshine RV Park,** 259790 Hwy. 101, tel. (360) 683-4769, and **Rainbow's End RV Park,** 261831 Hwy. 101, tel. (360) 683-3863.

SEQUIM ACCOMMODATIONS

Accommodations are arranged from least to most expensive. Rates may be lower during the winter months. The Sequim area code is 360.

MOTELS

Sequim Bay Resort; 2634 W. Sequim Bay Rd. (three miles east of Sequim); tel. 681-3853; $27-40 s or d; cabins with kitchenettes

Greathouse Motel; 740 E. Washington (Hwy. 101 E); tel. 683-7272 or (800) 475-7272; $48 s or d; continental breakfast

Econo Lodge; 801 E. Washington; tel. 683-7113 or (800) 488-7113; $59 s, $65 d; continental breakfast, kitchenettes available, AAA approved

Holiday Inn Express; 1095 E. Washington St.; tel. 683-1775 or (800) 683-1775; $59-135 s, $69-135 d; indoor pool, jacuzzi

Sundowner Motel; 364 W. Washington; tel. 683-5532 or (800) 325-6966; $60 s or d; kitchenettes available, AAA approved

Red Ranch Inn; 830 W. Washington St.; tel. 683-4195 or (800) 777-4195; $60 s or d; kitchenettes available, AAA approved

Best Western Sequim Bay Lodge; 1788 Hwy. 101 E; tel. 683-0691 or (800) 622-0691; $60-140 s, $70-140 d; outdoor pool, jacuzzi, kitchenettes available, AAA approved

Sequim West Inn; 740 W. Washington St.; tel. 683-4144 or (800) 528-4527; $64-71 s or d; AAA approved

Dungeness Bay Motel; 569 Marine Dr.; tel. 683-3013; $75-90 s or d; bayside cabins with kitchens

Juan de Fuca Cottages; 182 Marine Dr. (seven miles north of Sequim); tel. 683-4433; $98-185 d; beachside location, six fully equipped housekeeping cottages overlooking Dungeness Spit, jacuzzi, two-night minimum stay on weekends, AAA approved

BED AND BREAKFASTS

Granny Sandy's Orchard B&B; 405 W. Spruce; tel. 683-5748 or (800) 841-3347; $45-65 s or d; 1920s farmhouse, five guest rooms, simple furnishings, shared or private baths, full breakfasts, children welcome

Groveland Cottage; 4861 Sequim-Dungeness Way (five miles north of Sequim); tel. 683-3565; $58-80 s, $70-95 d; historic turn-of-the-century house, large lawn with pond, four guest rooms (two with private bath), full breakfast, two night minimum stay, AAA approved

Brigadoon B&B; 62 Balmoral Ct. (four miles north of Sequim); tel. 683-2255 or (800) 397-2256; $65-75 d; 1920 farmhouse with English antiques, jacuzzi, full breakfast, no kids

Greywolf Inn; 395 Keeler Rd.; tel. 683-5889; $65-110 s or d; country estate, dramatic vistas, six guest rooms, private baths, jacuzzi, trails, full breakfast, no kids under 12, AAA approved

Margie's Inn on the Bay B&B; 120 Forrest Rd. (five miles east of Sequim); tel. 683-7011 or (800) 730-7011; $69-114 s or d; contemporary home, waterside location, five guest rooms, private bath, full breakfast, AAA approved

Hidden Meadow Inn B&B; 901 W. Sequim Bay Rd. (east end of town); tel. 681-2577; $79-135 d; six-course breakfast, open summers only

FOOD

Start out the day at **Oak Table Cafe,** 292 W. Bell, tel. (360) 683-2179, where the breakfasts are filling and delicious (try the wonderful soufflé-style baked apple pancakes). Fine lunches and dinners featuring pasta and chicken fill out the day.

The Three Crabs, tel. (360) 683-4264, has served Dungeness crab and other local seafood specialties for over 25 years at their waterfront location on Three Crabs Rd.; they also have a retail seafood market. The crabs are well prepared, but the rest of the rather pricey menu isn't especially noteworthy. Reservations recommended.

For fast seafood—including fresh fish and chips—stop by **Vern's Seafood and Chowder Drive-In,** 707 E. Washington, tel. (360) 683-1055. **Jean's Mini Mart & Deli,** 20 Carlsborg Rd., tel. (360) 683-6727, is a surprise, with all sorts of homemade soups, pastries, and sandwiches. Another place for fast and well-prepared lunches is **Hi-way 101 Diner,** 392 W. Washington, tel. (360) 683-3388, a "fabulous fifties" family diner with the biggest local burgers.

The **Dungeness Inn,** tel. (360) 683-3331, overlooking the Dungeness Golf Course at 491A Woodcock Rd., specializes in prime rib, steak, and seafood.

A favorite locals' place is **Casoni's,** 261290 Hwy. 101 (two miles west of Sequim), tel. (360) 683-2415, where the pastas are dependably good. **Tarcisio's,** 609 W. Washington, tel. (360) 683-5809, is the place to go for from-scratch pizzas.

Fans of Mexican food will enjoy two local eateries: **Las Palomas,** 1085 E. Washington, tel. (360) 681-3842, and **El Cazador,** 537 W. Washington, tel. (360) 683-4788.

EVENTS AND ENTERTAINMENT

Established a century ago and still going strong—it's the state's oldest festival—the **Sequim Irrigation Festival** celebrates the beginning of Dungeness Valley agriculture thanks to the hand-dug ditch that first brought water from

the Dungeness River in 1896. The first festival (May 1, 1896) was a picnic in a shady grove; today parades, art and flower shows, a carnival, fireworks, and the crowning of a May Queen commemorate the annual event. Other Sequim events include the **Great American Clam Fest** in mid-July, and a **Salmon Bake** in mid-August.

Red Ranch Restaurant, 830 W. Washington St., tel. (360) 683-6622, has a lounge with live music on Friday and Saturday nights. **Town Tavern,** 735 W. Washington, tel. (360) 683-1013, has pool tables, darts, shuffleboard, pub grub, and "the biggest beer can collection on the peninsula."

RECREATION

Recreation in the Sequim area focuses on the protected waters inside the inner harbor of Dungeness Bay, a favorite place for windsurfers and sea kayakers. The six-mile path to the lighthouse on Dungeness Spit is a very popular place for a seaside walk or horseback ride.

Mountain bike rentals and tours of the nearby foothills are available from **D&G Cyclery,** 551 W. Washington, tel. (360) 681-3868. The **Sequim Aquatic Center,** 610 N. 5th, tel. (360) 683-3344, has two swimming pools, a gym, racquetball courts, exercise equipment, and a sauna. They also have a canoe and other outdoor items for rent here.

Two 18-hole public golf courses in the area are the **SunLand Golf Course,** tel. (360) 683-6800, just north of Sequim at 109 Hilltop Dr., and the **Dungeness Golf Course,** tel. (360) 683-6344, adjacent to the Dungeness Inn Restaurant, north of Carlsborg on Woodcock Road.

INFORMATION

For maps, brochures, and lots of local information drop by the **Sequim-Dungeness Valley Chamber of Commerce Visitor Information Center,** 1192 E. Washington, tel. (360) 683-6197 or (800) 737-8462. The office is open Sunday 10 a.m.-4 p.m. and Mon.-Sat. 9 a.m.-6 p.m. in the summer; and Sunday 10 a.m.-4 p.m. and

Mon.-Sat. 9 a.m.-5 p.m. the rest of the year. The **area code** in Sequim and all of the Olympic Peninsula is 360.

TRANSPORTATION

Clallam Transit, tel. (360) 452-4511 or (800) 858-3747, operates a daily commuter route between Sequim and Port Angeles, including a stop at Fairchild International Airport, and regular routes as far west as Forks and Neah Bay. **Jefferson Transit,** tel. (360) 385-4777, has transportation east to the Port Townsend area, with connections to Kitsap Transit buses.

Both **Port Angeles-Seattle Bus Lines,** tel. (360) 683-9160 or (800) 764-2287, and **Olympic Bus Lines,** tel. (360) 452-3858, offer daily connections to Seattle, and Sea-Tac Airport.

Coastal Airways, tel. (360) 683-4444, has daily flights between Sequim Valley Airport and Sea-Tac Airport.

PORT ANGELES

Port Angeles is the largest city on the northern Olympic Peninsula and the gateway to many of its pleasures. Its busy harbor, protected by the strong sandy arm of Ediz Hook, is visited daily by logging ships, fishing boats, and the Victoria ferry MV *Coho.* The view from the Port Angeles city pier is breathtaking: rocky Hurricane Ridge, made more ominous by a wispy cloud cover, seems to rise straight out of the turbulent waters of the Strait of Juan de Fuca, creating an overwhelming contrast of land and water, height and depth. The city is sandwiched between a pair of large pulp mills: Daishowa makes paper for phone books, and Rayonier makes cellulose pulp. In addition, the large K-Ply mill produces plywood, completing the triumvirate of local timber businesses. Because of its location as an entry point to both Vancouver Island (via the ferry) and to nearby Olympic National Park, Port Angeles is a very busy place during the summer. Parking downtown can be a nightmare on a July weekend.

HISTORY

The original inhabitants along the northern shore of the Olympic Peninsula—members of the S'Klallam, Hoh, Quinault, Quileute, and Makah tribes—lived off the bounty of the land and waters. Their culture emphasized the sharing of these resources rather than their exploitation, but clashes between the tribes were frequent and often violent.

In 1610 the strait that now separates the U.S. and Canada was discovered by Greek pilot Apostolos Valerianus, sailing under the Mexi-can flag and using the Spanish name of Juan de Fuca. The strait would later be named for him. In 1791, the Spanish explorer Juan Francisco de Eliza mapped the harbor and named it Puerto de Nuestra Señora de Los Angeles, "Port of Our Lady of the Angels," but a year later George Vancouver came through and Anglicized it to Port Angeles. The town's first white settler, Angus Johnson, traded with Hudson's Bay Company in Victoria across the strait in 1857.

Shady Dealings

Port Angeles' rise to prominence was aided and abetted by a dark deed or two involving the town's true founder, a duplicitous customs inspector named Victor Smith. In the West's infancy, stealing county seats and post offices was on an entertainment par with daytime television. It happened all the time, and something similar happened when Smith—with help from President Lincoln's Secretary of the Treasury Salmon P. Chase—stole the U.S. custom house from Port Townsend and moved it to Port Angeles in 1862. This was no mean feat, since Port Townsend had no intentions of giving up the records; it was only when Smith sailed into the harbor aboard a warship and pointed the guns at the city that the citizens relented. He later added insult to injury by returning to force the hospital patients and staff out of Port Townsend and onto his ship, which became a floating hospital till a new one could be completed in Port Angeles. These deeds brought no happiness to either Smith or Chase. Chase had to resign from the Cabinet in disgrace and Smith was lost at sea. But Port Angeles is still the county seat.

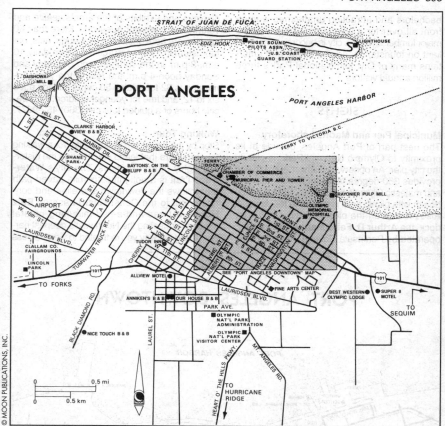

The same year that Smith stole the court-house, he also persuaded President Lincoln to name Port Angeles and Ediz Hook as military reservations. Port Angeles was the second townsite (after Washington, D.C.) to be planned by the federal government; President Lincoln called it the "second National City," in case Washington, D.C. fell to the Confederate Army, even though the town's population at the time was only 10. The real reason for creating a national city was to provide money from land sales to support the war effort, but that effort was a decided failure. With all the free land in surrounding areas, the government finally gave up in 1891, opening the town for settlement.

Later Years

Port Angeles—like Seattle—both benefited from and suffered from its seaside location, and in both cases the downtown had to be built up to raise it above the tideline. In 1914, Peabody Creek was diverted away from town, fill dirt was washed down from nearby hillsides, and the streets were raised a level using walls and pilings, turning two-story buildings into one-story structures. The resulting "underground" is still visible in places around town.

A strong military influence held on for decades here, as parts of the Pacific Fleet anchored in Port Angeles every summer in the 1920s and '30s, providing the town with 30,000 eligible bachelors and attracting unattached women from all over for a little summer fun. Long a major lumber town, the city is becoming more reliant on tourists; it feeds, shelters, and entertains many of Olympic National Park's three million annual visitors.

SIGHTS

Municipal Pier and Marine Laboratory

The best part of Port Angeles, outside of its proximity to Olympic National Park, is clearly the city pier. An observation tower at pier's end provides 360-degree views of the city, harbor, and majestic Olympic mountains, while a sandy beach with picnic area is available for day use. Also located on the pier near the *Coho* ferry dock, the **Arthur D. Feiro Marine Laboratory,** operated by Peninsula College, has hands-on displays and exhibits of the area's sealife and volunteers to answer questions. More than 80 species are here, including sea slugs, eels, octupi, starfish, and sea urchins. Open daily 10 a.m.-8 p.m. in the summer, and Saturday and Sunday noon-4 p.m. the rest of the year. Admission is $2 for adults, 50 cents for kids ages six to 12, and free for younger children. For specific hours or a guided tour call (360) 452-9277.

Walking Tour

Stop by the downtown visitor center for a walking tour brochure that leads you through the historical sights of Port Angeles. The city's **Waterfront Trail** is a delightful six-mile paved path that follows the downtown shoreline and continues out to the Coast Guard base on **Ediz Hook**—a three-and-a-half-mile-long natural sandspit protecting the Northwest's deepest harbor. Along the way you're treated to views across

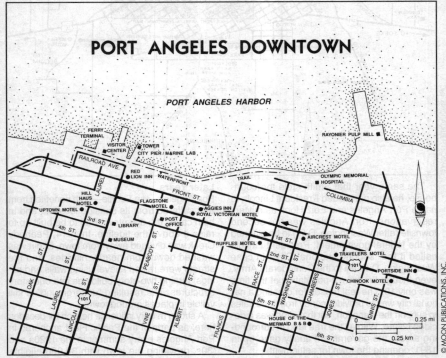

Municipal Pier and observation tower

to Vancouver Island and back toward town with the snowcapped Olympics in the background. Watch as freighters are guided in, or take out your own boat for fishing or sightseeing. Picnicking and beachcombing are also popular activities. The U.S. Coast Guard Air Station occupies the far end of the spit and has the cutter *Active* docked at the city pier when she isn't out on rescue missions or drug searches. Located a short distance from the Coast Guard base, the Puget Sound Pilots Association assigns a pilot to each commercial ship passing this point to steer it on its way through Puget Sound. Another place offering fine vistas across to Vancouver Island is from the top of the Laurel St. stairs, two blocks uphill from the *Coho* ferry dock.

Museums
A state historic site (built in 1914), the old county courthouse contains the **Clallam County Museum**'s displays of Olympic Peninsula history, including local genealogy and a completely stocked old country store. Nothing to write home about here, just the standard collection of local memorabilia. Located at Lincoln and 4th Streets, the museum is open Mon.-Sat. 10 a.m.-4 p.m.; donations accepted.

The **Port Angeles Fine Arts Center,** 1203 E. 8th St., tel. (360) 457-3532, is a bit out of the way, but well worth the side trip. Located on a hill, the building's enormous picture windows face

north to Vancouver Island, offering panoramic vistas that pull your eyes away from the art on the walls. Walk outside to discover a small forest with gardens and a path leading to additional viewpoints. The Fine Arts Center features changing exhibits by prominent Northwest artists and is open Thurs.-Sun. 11 a.m.-5 p.m.; free.

Olympic National Park Visitor Center
Located a mile out of town at 3002 Mt. Angeles Rd., this is often the first stopping place for visitors to Olympic National Park, and the very popular **Hurricane Ridge,** 17 miles south of town (see "Interior Sights" under "Olympic National Park" below). The center includes a large panoramic map, exhibits about the park, a Discovery Room for kids, and a 12-minute slide show that introduces visitors to the Olympics. Behind the visitor center is the historic Beaumont log cabin, built in 1887 and moved here in 1962. Nature trails lead through the forest to park headquarters, a block away. The visitor center is open daily 8:30 a.m.-6 p.m. between Memorial Day and Labor Day, daily 8:30 a.m.-5 p.m. in September, and daily 9 a.m.-4 p.m. the rest of the year. Call (360) 452-0330 for more information.

ACCOMMODATIONS

Motels and B&Bs
See the "Port Angeles Accommodations" chart for a list of local motels and B&Bs. Of particular note is **Tudor Inn,** tel. (360) 452-3138, a lovingly restored B&B built in 1910 with beautifully appointed rooms. Other nearby lodging places are listed under "Olympic National Park" and "Sequim." Because of the popularity of Port Angeles in the summer months, it's a good idea to make reservations ahead of your visit. Unfortunately, Port Angeles no longer has youth hostel accommodations.

Campgrounds
The Park Service's **Heart O' the Hills Campground** ($10; open year-round) is five miles south of Port Angeles on Hurricane Ridge Road. Near the William R. Fairchild International Airport at W. Lauridsen Blvd. and Bean Rd., **Lincoln Park**'s authentic pioneer cabins and an Indian

PORT ANGELES ACCOMMODATIONS

Accommodations are arranged from least to most expensive. Rates may be lower during the winter months. The Port Angeles area code is 360.

BED AND BREAKFASTS

Anniken's B&B; 214 E. Whidby; tel. 457-6177; $60 s or d; 1930s home, fine water views, two guest rooms, shared bath, full breakfast, no kids under 12

Clarks' Harbor View B&B; 1426 W. 4th St.; tel. 457-9891; $60 s or d; new home, harbor views, one guest room, private bath, pool table, free ferry and airport shuttle, full breakfast, no kids

Glimberg House; 2652 Black Diamond (three miles south); tel. 457-6579; $60 s or d; country setting, two guest rooms, continental breakfast, free ferry shuttle

Baytons' On-The-Bluff B&B; 824 W. 4th St.; tel. 457-5569; $60 s, $65 d; panoramic water views, 1920s home, full breakfast, free airport and ferry shuttle

House of the Mermaid B&B; 1128 E. 5th St.; tel. 457-4890; $60-85 s or d; 1920s home, four guest rooms, private or shared bath, jacuzzi, full breakfast, free ferry and airport shuttle, no kids under 12, closed Nov.-April

Blue Mountain Lodge; 380 Lewis Rd.; tel. 457-8540; $65 s or d; outdoor pool, trout pond, one guest unit, continental breakfast, kitchen

Country Cottage; 624 Billy Smith Rd. (two miles east of Port Angeles); tel. 452-7974; $65 s or d; mountain views, new country home, two guest rooms, private bath, free airport and ferry shuttle, no kids, patio, full breakfast, open summers only

A Nice Touch B&B; 1665 Black Diamond Rd. (two miles south of Port Angeles); tel. 457-1938 or (800) 605-6296; $69-120 s or d; contemporary home, country location with water view, pond, patio, four guest rooms (one with jacuzzi), private or shared bath, gourmet breakfast

Freshwater Bay Inn B&B; 2294 Freshwater Bay Rd. (12 miles west of Port Angeles off Hwy. 101); tel. 928-2181; $75 s or d; mountain views, two large guest rooms, shared bath, full breakfast, children welcome

Our House B&B; 218 Whidby Ave.; tel. 452-6338 or (800) 882-9051; $75 s or d; sweeping views, private bath, full breakfast

Glen Mar by the Sea; 318 N. Eunice; tel. 457-6110; $75-85 s or d; three guest rooms with mountain or water views, private baths, patio, grand piano, once owned by John Wayne's sister, full breakfast

Bavarian Inn B&B; 1126 E. 7th; tel. 457-4098; $80 s, $85-95 d; fine home, harbor view, three guest rooms, private bath, gourmet breakfast, no kids, two night minimum stay, AAA approved

Maple Rose Inn B&B; 112 Reservoir Rd. (south of town); tel. 457-7673 or (800) 457-4661; $80-120 s or d; colonial style farmhouse, country location with mountain views, five very nice rooms, private baths, jacuzzi, large decks, pond, free ferry and airport shuttle, children welcome, full breakfast

Elwha Ranch B&B; 7250 Herrick Rd. (10 miles west of Port Angeles); tel. 457-6540; $85-95 s or d; country log home, mountain views, two guest suites, private bath, deck, full breakfast, children welcome

Tudor Inn B&B; 1108 S. Oak; tel. 452-3138; $85-125 s or d; 1910 English Tudor home, five antique-filled guest rooms with mountain and water views, private baths, library, lounge, full breakfast, no kids under 12, AAA approved

Domaine Madeleine; 146 Wildflower Ln. (midway between Sequim and Port Angeles); tel. 457-4174; $125-165 s or d; elegant waterfront estate overlooking gardens, four large rooms with antiques, private bath, fireplaces, multicourse epicurean breakfasts, two-night minimum stay on summer weekends, AAA approved

MOTELS

All-View Motel; 214 E. Lauridsen Blvd.; tel. 457-7779; $37-42 s or d; kitchenettes, free airport and ferry shuttle

Chinook Motel; 1414 E. 1st St.; tel. 452-2336; $38 s, $43 d; outdoor pool, kitchenettes, free airport and ferry shuttle

Sportsmen Motel; 3009 E. Hwy. 101 (one mile east of town); tel. 457-6196; $40 s, $45 d; kitchenettes available

Fairmont Motel; 1137 Hwy. 101 W (one mile west of Port Angeles); tel. 457-6113; $40 s, $45 d

The Pond Motel; 196 Hwy. 101 W (two miles west of Port Angeles); tel. 452-8422; $42 s, $47 d; rural location with pond, kitchenettes available, AAA approved

Ruffles Motel; 812 E. 1st St.; tel. 457-7788; $42 s, $47 d; local calls 25 cents, kitchenettes available

Aircrest Motel; 1006 E. Front St.; tel. 452-9255 or (800) 825-9255; $42 s, $48-52 d; jacuzzi, free ferry shuttle, AAA approved

Travelers Motel; 1133 E. 1st St.; tel. 452-2303; $45 s, $55 d; free airport and ferry shuttle, kitchenettes available, very reasonable off-season rates

Flagstone Motel; 415 E. 1st St.; tel. 457-9494; $46 s, $52 d; indoor pool, sauna, continental breakfast, AAA approved

Aggie's Inn; 602 E. Front St.; tel. 457-0471; $48 s or d; indoor pool, sauna, free airport and ferry shuttle, older place, see rooms first, AAA approved

Royal Victorian Motel; 521 E. 1st St.; tel. 452-2316; $52 s, $65-70 d; kitchenettes available, free airport and ferry shuttle, AAA approved

Portside Inn; 1510 E. Front St.; tel. 452-4015 or (800) 633-8300; $53 s, $59 d; outdoor pool, jacuzzi, AAA approved

Super 8 Motel; 2104 E. 1st St.; tel. 452-8401 or (800) 800-8000; $57 s, $64 d

Uptown Motel; 101 E. 2nd St.; tel. 457-9434; $60-85 s or d; harbor or mountain views, jacuzzi, kitchenettes available, AAA approved

Hill Haus Motel; 111 E. 2nd St.; tel. 452-9285 or (800) 421-0706; $69-110 s or d; AAA approved

Best Western Olympic Lodge; 140 Del Guzzi Dr.; tel. 452-2993 or (800) 528-1234; $100-130 s, $100-140 d; outdoor pool, large rooms, mountain views, jacuzzi, exercise room, free airport and ferry shuttle, AAA approved

Red Lion Bayshore Inn; 221 N. Lincoln; tel. 452-9215 or (800) 547-8010; $95-125 s or d; outdoor pool, jacuzzi, waterfront location, AAA approved

longhouse accompany tennis courts, baseball diamond, campsites (no hookups), nature trails, picnic area, and children's fishing pond at this 144-acre park. Campers can use the showers in Lincoln Park or at the local swimming pool (225 E. 5th St.) or the boat harbor.

Campsites ($10), a marinelife sanctuary, hiking trails, beach, and picnic areas occupy 196-acre **Salt Creek Recreation Area** off Hwy. 112, 20 miles west of Port Angeles, tel. (360) 417-2291; open year-round. Showers are available, but no hookups.

Nearby private RV parks include **Al's RV Park,** 521 N. Lee's Creek Rd. (three miles east of Port Angeles), tel. (360) 457-9844; **Conestoga Quarters RV Park,** Hwy. 101 E at Siebert Rd. (seven miles east of Port Angeles), tel. (360) 452-4637; **Port Angeles/Sequim KOA,** 2065 Hwy. 101 E (seven miles east of Port Angeles), tel. (360) 457-5916; **Log Cabin Resort,** 3183 E. Beach Rd. (on Lake Crescent), tel. (360) 928-3325; **Lyre River Park,** W. Lyre River Rd., tel. (360) 928-3436; **Peabody Creek RV Park,** 127 S. Lincoln, tel. (360) 457-7092;

Shadow Mt. Campground, 232951 Hwy. 101 W (16 miles west of Port Angeles), tel. (360) 928-3043; **Shady Tree RV Park,** 435 Lower Dam Rd. (five miles west of Port Angeles), tel. (360) 452-7054; **View Vista Park,** 1400 View Vista Park (two miles east of Port Angeles), tel. (360) 457-0950; and **Welcome Inn RV Park,** 1215 Hwy. 101 W, tel. (360) 457-1553.

FOOD

Because of its location as a jumping off point for Olympic National Park and Vancouver Island, Port Angeles is packed with high quality eateries of all persuasions. It is difficult to *not* find a good meal here. (Okay, there is a McDonald's in town.)

Breakfast and Lunch

The acclaimed **First Street Haven,** 1st and Laurel, tel. (360) 457-0352, serves hearty breakfasts, along with reasonable sandwiches, quiche, pastas, and salads for lunch. The location is tiny, but the food is hard to beat. Save room for dessert. Another fine place for breakfast or lunch (same owners) is **Cafe Garden,** 1506 E. 1st St., tel. (360) 457-4611, where the menu covers the spectrum from Belgium waffles for breakfast to Asian stir-fries and deli sandwiches for lunch.

For a well-prepared traditional American breakfast—including 64 different omelettes—head to **Pete's Pancake House,** 110 E. Railroad Ave., tel. (360) 452-1948. Good breakfasts, along with the best local fish and chips, can be found just across the street at **Landing Restaurant,** 115 E. Railroad Ave., tel. (360) 457-6768.

The Greenery Restaurant, in the midst of the downtown shopping area at 117-B E. 1st St., tel. (360) 457-4112, serves three meals a day every day but Sunday, specializing in northern Italian sautés, fresh-baked French bread, and fresh homemade pasta in a plants-and-wood decor catering to the city's business crowd.

American

Get the best burgers and fries anywhere around at **Frugals,** 1520 E. Front St., tel. (360) 452-4320. No seating; just drive up or walk up to order. **Rosewood's Family Buffet,** 1936 E.

1st, tel. (360) 457-1400, has one-price dining for lunch ($5) and dinner ($7). A good deal for families.

Seafood and Steak

Part of the Red Lion Bayshore Inn, **Haguewood's,** 221 N. Lincoln St., tel. (360) 457-0424, has an extensive menu with over 75 salads, sandwiches, and entrees, plus a water view and lounge. Local seafood—especially salmon, halibut, and Dungeness crab—are house specialties. Another popular steak and seafood restaurant overlooking the water is **Downriggers Restaurant,** 115 E. Railroad, tel. (360) 452-2700. **The Bushwacker Restaurant,** 1527 E. 1st, tel. (360) 457-4113, specializes in fresh seafood (including a chowder bar) and prime rib, but also has a great salad bar. Open for dinners only.

International

For delicious, reasonably priced, and authentic south-of-the-border meals, be sure to visit **Chihuahua Mexican Restaurant,** 408 S. Lincoln St., tel. (360) 452-8344. The best local place for Asian meals—particularly seafood specials—is **China First Restaurant,** 633 E. 1st St., tel. (360) 457-1647. Offerings include both Cantonese and Mandarin styles. They also have a second restaurant next to the ferry terminal at 222 N. Lincoln, with a popular Mongolian barbecue where you can watch them prepare your meal.

Locals head to **Gordy's Pizza & Pasta,** 1123 E. 1st St., tel. (360) 457-5056, for big Italian sandwiches, homemade pizzas, and fresh pasta dishes. Very popular.

If you're a fan of hearty Bavarian fare, try **Tannhäuser German-American Restaurant,** 1135 E. Front St., tel. (360) 452-5977.

Four miles east of Port Angeles at 2300 Hwy. 101 E, tel. (360) 452-8888, **C'est Si Bon** prepares delicious local seafood with a French accent. The Olympics and rose garden views add to the luxurious ambience; open for dinner Tues.-Sunday.

Coffeehouses and Bakeries

If you're waiting for the ferry to come in, a good hangout spot is **Coffee House Gallery,** 118 E. 1st St., tel. (360) 452-1459. They have light vegetarian meals and espresso, plus live acoustic music most nights. **Incredible Edibles,** 222 N. Lincoln, tel. (360) 457-0542, lives up to its name with the best local espresso, along with fresh baked goods and homemade soups. **Montana Coffee House** on Lincoln St., tel. (360) 452-9769, has fresh bagels, espresso coffees, and pastries.

Bonny's Bakery, 502 E. 1st St., tel. (360) 457-3585, bakes traditional French pastries, Danish rolls, all-American pies, and wonderful cookies. Everything is made from scratch. Housed in an old church, **Gina's Bakery,** 710 S. Lincoln St., tel. (360) 457-3279, has many more sweets, including "sinful cinnamon rolls" and other favorites. Good lunches too.

Produce and Grocers

Get the freshest local fare at **Port Angeles Farmers Market,** held year-round near the corner of 8th and Chase Streets. The market is open Saturday 9 a.m.-4:30 p.m. **Nashi's** on the corner of Chambers and Front Streets, sells home-grown organic produce. **Sunny Farms Country Store,** tel. (360) 683-8003, has a large produce stand located halfway between Port Angeles and Sequim. Also sold here are everything from hanging plants to homemade pizzas.

Port Angeles has the usual grocery chains (including Albertson's and Safeway), but for a big selection of natural and organic foods in a pleasant shop, head to **The Country Aire,** 117 E. 1st St., tel. (360) 452-7175. For the freshest local seafood—along with canned and smoked specialties—stop by **Hegg & Hegg** at 801 Marine Dr., tel. (360) 457-3344, or on Hwy. 101 E, tel. (360) 457-1551. They also have a small gift shop in the Landing Mall (where the ferry docks), tel. (360) 457-3733.

Beer and Wine

Newly opened in 1995, the **Port Angeles Brewing Co.** is housed in the old city hall at 140 W. Front St., tel. (360) 452-6013. For a big selection of bottled beers (150 brands), head to **Parkway Grocery,** 8th and Race, tel. (360) 457-4333. The deli here has sandwiches and other to-go meals.

Camaraderie Cellars, tel. (360) 452-4964, just west of Port Angeles at 165 Benson Rd., specializes in cabernet sauvignon and sauvignon blanc and is open by appointment only.

RECREATION

Playing Around

Rent mountain and road bikes along with kayaks from **Pedal 'n Paddle,** 120 E. Front St., tel. (360) 457-1240. They also rent racing strollers, rain gear, and roof racks, and offer bike and sea kayak tours of surrounding areas. Bike rentals are also available from **Sorenson's Sports,** 222 N. Lincoln, tel. (360) 457-5559.

Two local companies feature sea kayaking tours around Port Angeles, from wildlife watching to lighthouses: **Strait & Narrow Kayak Tripping,** 1306 E. 3rd St., tel. (360) 452-3487, and **Kayaks & More,** in the town of Carlsborg (eight miles east of Port Angeles), tel. (360) 683-3805.

Swim at the **William Shore Memorial Pool,** 225 E. 5th St., tel. (360) 457-0241. For lake swimming, head a dozen miles west of town to **Lake Sutherland,** where the water gets quite warm by late summer.

Hurricane Ridge, 17 miles south of Port Angeles within Olympic National Park, is very popular with cross-country and downhill skiers and snowboarders. See "Interior Sights" under "Olympic National Park" below for details. **Clallam Transit,** tel. (360) 452-4511 or (800) 858-3747, offers bus service on winter weekends to the ski area for $8 roundtrip. Rent skis from **Olympic Mountaineering,** 221 S. Peabody St., tel. (360) 452-0240, or at Hurricane Ridge.

Charter Fishing

Most charter boats provide everything you need for fishing—tackle and bait—and will clean and bag your catch. Some provide lunches, but most do not. Local restaurants and cafes know all about box lunches. Most boats have a coffeepot going, which necessitates some kind of bathroom facilities aboard. Ask about seasickness prevention before heading out. Check with the visitor center for an up-to-date listing of local charter boat operators. Other towns with fishing charters on the northern Olympic Peninsula are Sekiu/Clallam Bay and Neah Bay.

Auto Racing

From mid-April to mid-October, **Port Angeles Speedway,** tel. (360) 452-4666, six miles east of

Port Angeles on Hwy. 101, has stock- and hobby-car races on Saturday nights, plus go-kart rentals at other times.

ENTERTAINMENT AND EVENTS

Nightlife
Quite a few local venues offer dance or listening tunes. Dance to rock and roll at **Smitty's**, 536 Marine Dr., tel. (360) 457-1952, or **Zaks**, 125 W. Front, tel. (360) 452-7575. Country and western fans head to **Cornerhouse Restaurant**, 101 E. Front, tel. (360) 452-9692, while **Aggie's**, 602 E. Front, tel. (360) 457-0471, has a piano bar and sometimes features a small band. For relaxed listening, the **Coffee House Gallery**, 118 E. 1st St., tel. (360) 452-1459, has live jazz, classical, or other acoustic tunes most nights.

Check out the big screen at **Lincoln Theater**, 132 E. 1st St., tel. (360) 457-7997, for the latest flicks.

Performing Arts
The **Port Angeles Symphony Orchestra** performs six concerts during the winter months; for tickets and other information, call (360) 457-5579. The **Port Angeles Light Opera Association** produces a musical each July; call (360) 457-6626 for tickets and information. The **Port Angeles Community Concert Association**, tel. (360) 457-5052, offers a series of concerts throughout the year. Live theater performances are given by **Port Angeles Community Players** year-round at the playhouse on Lauridsen Blvd. and Liberty Street. Call (360) 452-6651 for a schedule of upcoming productions.

The **Juan de Fuca Festival of the Arts** features a wide range of music, dance, theater, art exhibits, and more by well-known visual and performing artists. You might hear Ladysmith Black Mambazo, a Russian dance troupe, the London Ballet, or a rousing light opera. Productions are monthly Sept.-April. Call (360) 457-5411 for more information. For something a bit less formal, free **Concerts on the Pier**, tel. (360) 452-2363, take place every Thursday evening between mid-June and mid-September.

Events
The **Clallam County Fair** comes to Port Angeles in mid-August, with a carnival, rodeo, horse shows, farming exhibits, and a crowd-pleasing smash-'em-up demolition derby. End the year in style with a visit to the **Christmas Fair** at the community center, where local artisans display their works.

SHOPPING

Arts and Crafts
Port Angeles's downtown shopping district is centered on 1st St., where you'll find shops, restaurants, galleries, and movie theaters. Pick up locally made gifts and crafts at **Washington Only**, 122 W. Lauridsen Blvd., tel. (360) 452-6844. **Northwest Native Art Gallery**, 115 E. Railroad, tel. (360) 452-5839, has quality Native American arts and crafts. Also of note is **Michael's**, 126 W. 1st, tel. (360) 452-5250, where you'll find handmade jewelry and bronze sculptures. Other galleries and craft shops worth a look include **Clallam Art Gallery**, 118 W. 1st, tel. (360) 452-8165; **Olympic Stained Glass**, 112 N. Laurel, tel. (360) 457-1090, **North Light Gallery**, 120 N. Laurel, tel. (360) 452-4262, **Golden Crafts Shop**, 105 E. Front, tel. (360) 457-0509. For something completely different, head to **Pacific Rim Hobby**, 124-A W. 1st St., tel. (360) 457-0794, for a voyage back to model railroad heaven. The big HO-scale railroad village makes for fun gawking; look for such details as the giant insect attacking villagers.

Books
Port Angeles also has three good bookstores: **Odyssey Bookshop**, 114 W. Front St., tel. (360) 457-1045; **Port Book and News**, 104 E. 1st, tel. (360) 452-6367 (an expansive choice of magazines here too); and **Olympic Stationers**, 122 E. Front St., tel. (360) 457-6111.

Outdoor Gear
Olympic Mountaineering, 221 S. Peabody St., tel. (360) 452-0240, has a big selection of outdoor gear for sale, along with all sorts of rental gear, including backpacks, tents, stoves, skis, and more.

INFORMATION AND SERVICES

For maps, brochures, and more local information contact the **Port Angeles Chamber of Commerce Visitor Center,** 121 E. Railroad Ave., tel. (360) 452-2363. Open daily 8 a.m.-9 p.m. May-Sept.; and Sunday noon-4 p.m., and Mon.-Sat. 10 a.m.-4 p.m., the rest of the year. Stop by to check the board for space availability at local motels, B&Bs, and RV parks, or to use their phone to make reservations.

Just a few steps away is the **Port Angeles-Victoria Tourist Bureau,** tel. (360) 452-1223, open daily 7 a.m.-9 p.m. July-Sept., and daily 7 a.m.-5 p.m. the rest of the year. Here the focus is on travel and motel reservations for southwest British Columbia—particularly nearby Vancouver Island—but they can also make motel reservations for Port Angeles. Tons of B.C. maps and brochures are free for the taking. Both the chamber of commerce and the tourist bureau are exceptionally helpful. Another source

stained-glass art displayed at the chamber of commerce

of information is the **North Olympic Peninsula Visitor and Convention Bureau,** tel. (800) 942-4042.

Olympic National Park Visitor Center, 3002 Mt. Angeles Rd., tel. (360) 452-0330, can give you hiking, camping, and other park info. The center is described above under "Sights."

Campers and backpackers will appreciate **Peabody Street Coin Laundry** after getting back to nature in Olympic National Park; open seven days a week, 24 hours a day, at 212 S. Peabody.

The Spa, 511 E. 1st St., tel. (360) 452-3257, has been around since 1928, with Finnish style steam rooms, massage, herbal body wraps, and a juice bar and tea room.

For medical emergencies, contact **Olympic Memorial Hospital,** 939 Caroline St., tel. (360) 457-8513.

TRANSPORTATION AND TOURS

Ferry Connections
The Port Townsend, Kingston, Winslow, and Bremerton **Washington State Ferries** deposit you at various points on the west side of Puget Sound; from each of these destinations you can connect, after varying amounts of driving, with Hwy. 101 to Port Angeles. From Seattle, the most direct route is via the Kingston ferry, over the Hood Canal Bridge, and onto Hwy. 104, connecting to Hwy. 101 near Discovery Bay. For specific info on departure times and fares, call the ferry system at (206) 842-2345 (in Seattle) or (800) 843-3779 throughout Washington.

Ferries to Victoria
Port Angeles is a major transit point for travelers heading to or from Victoria, B.C., just 18 miles away across the Strait of Juan de Fuca. The MV *Coho* leaves Port Angeles for Victoria four times daily in summer (mid-May through September), and twice daily the rest of the year. One-way fares for the one-and-a-half-hour crossing are $26 for car and driver, $6.50 for passengers, $3.25 for kids five to 11, free under age five, and $9.60 for bicycle and rider. For specific departure times, contact the Black Ball ferry terminal at the foot of Laurel St. in Port Angeles, tel. (360) 457-4491. No reservations

are accepted for the ferry, and it is out of service for maintenance during late January and early February.

The *Victoria Express,* a passenger-only ferry, makes the same run in an hour, four times a day between mid-June and Labor Day weekend, and twice daily during mid-May to mid-June and after Labor Day weekend until mid-October. Fares are $20 roundtrip for adults, $10 kids five to 11, free for children under age five. Bicycles are welcome on board. The ferry runs between Landing Mall terminal at Port Angeles and Regency Hotel terminal in Victoria, tel. (360) 452-8088 or (800) 633-1589 in Washington, or (604) 361-9144 in Canada. Advance reservations are accepted.

By Air
Horizon Airlines, tel. (800) 547-9308, provides daily commuter service to Victoria, B.C., and Seattle's Sea-Tac Airport from Fairchild International Airport on the city's west side.

Bus Service
Public bus service now extends throughout the Olympic Peninsula, making it possible to reach all the towns for a minimal fare on any of the four statewide public transit systems. **Clallam Transit,** tel. (360) 452-4511 or (800) 858-3747, provides Mon.-Sat. service throughout Port Angeles, east to Diamond Point, and around the Olympic Peninsula to Forks, Neah Bay, La Push, and Olympic National Park's Sol Duc Hot Springs and Lake Crescent. The cost is just 50

cents for adults, or 35 cents for kids. Connect with **Jefferson Transit,** tel. (360) 385-4777 or (800) 773-7788, in Sequim for Port Townsend, Port Ludlow, Quilcene, and other Jefferson County points, and with **Grays Harbor Transit** in Queets for points to the south.

Both **Port Angeles-Seattle Bus Lines,** (360) 457-4580 or (800) 764-2287, and **Olympic Bus Lines,** tel. (360) 452-3858, offer daily service connecting Port Angeles with Seattle and Sea-Tac Airport.

Tours
Clallam Transit operates a 50-minute trolley tour of town that includes a stop at the Olympic National Park Visitor's Center. Tours leave at 1 and 3 p.m. from late June to early September, departing the visitor center on Railroad Avenue. Fares are $6 for adults, $3 for kids ages seven to 12, free for kids under 12. Or pay $12 for the whole family. For more information call Clallam Transit, tel. (360) 452-4511 or (800) 858-3747.

Olympic Van Tours, tel. (360) 452-3858, offers trips to Hurricane Ridge for $13. These guided tours last approximately three hours and depart twice daily during the summer. Olympic also has a full range of other trips available by reservation—including the Hoh Rain Forest—plus backpacker shuttles to Olympic National Park trailheads.

Rite Bros. Aviation, tel. (360) 452-6226, has flightseeing and charter flights over the Olympics from Port Angeles.

OLYMPIC NATIONAL PARK

The diversity of climate and geography in Olympic National Park's 908,720 acres of wilderness is one reason it was among the 100 parks in the world named a "World Heritage Park" by the United Nations in 1981. The park has a central core covering the heart of the Olympic Mountains, and a separate narrow strip that follows the western coast for 57 miles. These disconnected units offer an extraordinary range of habitats, from sea level beaches to mossy rainforests to rugged glaciated peaks. There's something for everyone here, and together these disparate elements provide some of Washington's most spectacular (and most photographed) scenery. The beauty contrasts sharply with surrounding timber-company lands where economics rule and the trees fall, leaving behind a bleak landscape of stumps and tree farms.

Paved roads only skirt the park, with spurs leading a short ways into the mountains, allowing the largest coniferous forest in the Lower 48 to remain the undisturbed home of 180 species of birds and 50 species of animals, including Roosevelt elk (named for Theodore Roosevelt), black bear, deer, bald eagles, and Olympic marmots. Noticeably absent are the grizzly bear, red fox, pika, porcupine, and other species common to the Cascade Range. The reason for this difference between the ranges dates back to the Pleistocene Ice Age, when a Canadian glacier isolated the Olympics from the rest of Washington. It's taken 11,000 years for the red fox and porcupine to advance to the park's southern boundary. Mountain goats native to the Cascades were artificially introduced to the Olympics in the 1920s and now thrive in the park's interior. They thrive so well, in fact, that the National Park Service has been capturing them and removing them from the park because they are causing so much damage to the plantlife. The park service has also talked about shooting many of the goats, which has fed the flames of this controversial issue.

Olympic National Park is famous for the lush rainforests that carpet the western flanks of the mountains. The best known and most visited is Hoh Rainforest, but the others—Quinault and Queets—are equally interesting, and visitors are more likely to have a more personal experience. Visitor centers have pamphlets describing the locations of "record trees" in and around Olympic National Park, including the largest western hemlock, western red cedar, Sitka spruce, subalpine fir, and Alaska cedar remaining in the nation. There's a reason so many of the record trees are here: the rest have all been felled. Only 15% of old-growth stands remain in the Pacific Northwest, and nearly half of these are within Olympic and Mount Rainier National Parks. Nearly all private lands are operated as managed forests; the trees viewed as an agricultural crop to be planted, thinned, and harvested. These tree farms are usually planted with a monoculture of Douglas fir trees and lack the heterogeneity and species richness of a natural forest. On Forest Service lands within Olympic National Forest, logging of old-growth stands has been essentially halted for the last several years because of environmental concerns, most notably the preservation of spotted owl habitat. This has caused immense controversy, especially in timber-dependent communities around the Olympic Peninsula, where jobs are at stake.

History

When English sea captain John Meares first sighted **Mt. Olympus** from aboard ship in 1788, he reputedly said, "If that be not the home where dwell the gods, it is certainly beautiful enough to be, and I therefore will call it Mt. Olympus." He seemed to have forgotten (or never knew) that Juan Perez already named the four peaks "Sierra Nevada de Santa Rosalia" in 1774. George Vancouver used Meares's name for the mountain, following a trend of waning Spanish influence in the Northwest.

The central portion of the Olympics remained unexplored until late in the 19th century. The first substantiated exploration of the area came in 1885 when a small group of soldiers from the Vancouver Barracks got as far as Mt. Anderson on the eastern flank of the mountains. (It took them a month to work their way through the dense forests and fallen trees to Hurricane Ridge, a quick half-hour drive today.)

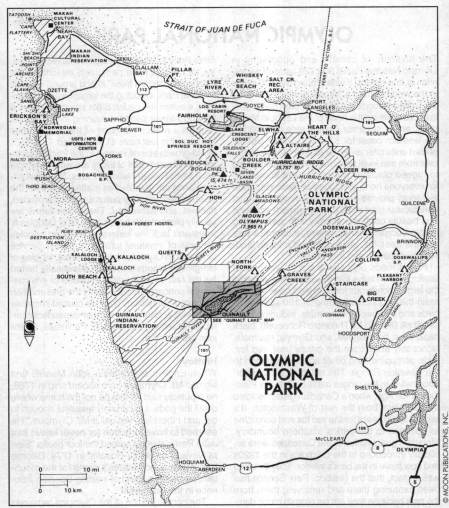

The most famous exploration came in the winter of 1889-90, when a group of six men headed into the mountains, funded by the *Seattle Press* newspaper. Led by James Christie, the "Press Expedition" picked a bad time to start: December of 1889, one of the snowiest winters ever recorded. They ended up spend-

ing the winter exploring the Elwha River valley, and finally headed across the mountains in early May, reaching the coast almost six months after they began. One result of their trip is that many peaks in the Olympics are named for newspaper publishers and editors of that era.

The following summer, Mt. Olympus was climbed by members of a group of military men and scientists who cut a mule trail across the range. The leader, Lieutenant Joseph O'Neil, noted in his report: "In closing I would state that while the country on the outer slope of these mountains is valuable, the interior is useless for all practicable purposes. It would however, serve admirably for a national park. There are numerous elk—that noble animal so fast disappearing from this country—that should be protected." (John Muir and Judge James Wickersham both pushed for creating a national park here earlier.)

Seven years later, Congress created the Olympic Forest Reserve (later called Olympic National Forest), including much of the Olympic Peninsula. In 1909 President Theodore Roosevelt, in one of his last acts, issued a proclamation that created Mount Olympus National Monument to protect elk habitat. Washington congressman Monrad C. Wallgren and another President Roosevelt—FDR this time—were instrumental in making the monument a national park in 1938. The 50-mile coastal strip was added to the park in 1953.

Today Olympic National Park ranks 10th in attendance among U.S. national parks, with over three million visitors a year; because of its enormous size and preserved interior, it's not hard to find peaceful solitude on its lakes and trails.

Climate

Weather in Olympic National Park is as varied and unpredictable as its geography. Rain is an ever-present threat, particularly on the western "wet" side, although three-quarters of the park's precipitation falls Oct.-March. In summer, park temperatures may be in the 80s—or the 60s; at sea level mild temperatures prevail, summer 70s to winter 40s.

Practicalities

A $5 park entrance fee, good for seven days, is charged for vehicles, or $3 for those on foot or bikes. Annual passes cost $15, and seniors can get a Golden Age Passport to all the parks for a one-time charge of just $10. Entrance fees are collected May-Sept. at Elwha, Hurricane

Ridge/Heart O' the Hills, Hoh, Soleduck, and Staircase entrance stations. See "Information and Services" below for visitors centers and ranger stations in the park.

INTERIOR SIGHTS

The main portion of Olympic National Park occupies the mountainous interior of the Olympic Peninsula. Highway 101 circles the park, with paved or dirt roads leading to attractions around the park's periphery. The park is open year-round, although some roads may be closed in winter. The eastern side of Olympic National Park along Hood Canal is accessible from various points between Quilcene and Hoodsport; for details, see "Hood Canal and Vicinity" earlier in this chapter.

Hurricane Ridge

One of the park's most scenic areas and by far the most visited, Hurricane Ridge rises over 5,200 feet seemingly straight up from the Strait of Juan de Fuca, providing an awesome contrast from sea level and breathtaking 360-degree views from the summit. The paved road starts at Race St. in Port Angeles, becoming Hurricane Ridge Rd. as it snakes up mountainsides for 17 miles at an easy seven percent grade; frequent turnouts allow for photo breaks. At the top, the **Hurricane Ridge Visitor Center** provides a must-stop location to peer across a meadow-and-mountain landscape that might have been imported straight from the Swiss Alps. This is one of the park's best areas for spotting wildlife; black-tailed deer often bound across the parking lot, marmots crowd nearby slopes, and black bears are occasionally visible from a distance. The ridge's name isn't without basis in fact: the first lodge at the summit lost its roof in a strong winter blast. The weather can change quickly up here; tune in to AM 530 in Port Angeles for weather and other park information.

Hurricane Ridge Lodge provides food service, a gift shop, winter ski rentals, and ski-tow service. Open daily May-Sept., and on weekends only during October and mid-December through April. Park naturalists offer summertime walks and talks plus wintertime snowshoe

Hurricane Ridge, Olympic National Park

ARCHIE SATTERFIELD

treks. Clallam Transit, tel. (360) 452-4511 or (800) 858-3747, has direct bus service between Port Angeles and Hurricane Ridge.

If the drop-offs and absence of guardrails on Hurricane Ridge Rd. made your palms sweat, you're in for a real treat on **Obstruction Point Road.** Starting from the Hurricane Ridge parking lot, this narrow gravel road (no RVs) follows the ridge for eight miles without a rail or fence, providing spectacular views for the strong-hearted. The road, constructed in the 1930s by the Civilian Conservation Corps, went as far as it could until a steep talus slope prohibited any further roadmaking.

Campgrounds: No camping or overnight lodging at Hurricane Ridge, but **Heart O' the Hills Campground,** five miles south of Port Angeles on Hurricane Ridge Rd., has year-round camping for $10. Campfire programs are offered July through Labor Day.

Deer Park Campground sits at the end of an 18-mile gravel road on the eastern edge of the park (no RVs, and not accessible from the Hurricane Ridge area). Located at an elevation of 5,400 feet, the campground is free and open mid-June to late September.

Hiking: A number of trails begin at Hurricane Ridge, including 1.5-mile **Hurricane Hill Trail,** a paved walk to the top of 5,757-foot Hurricane Hill that passes picnic areas, marmot colonies, and spectacular vistas. A longer hike, the **Klahanee Ridge Trail,** follows the ridge's summit for four miles after leaving the paved trail near the marmot colonies. It continues downhill to Heart O' the Hills Campground, or you can return back to Hurricane Ridge.

In addition to these, visitors to Hurricane Ridge will find three other short paved trails through the flower-filled meadows with views of the Olympics. Longer paths lead downhill to the Elwha Valley and along the Little River. From Obstruction Peak, additional trails provide access into the heart of the Olympics.

Winter Activities: Between late December and late March, Hurricane Ridge is a popular winter destination for cross-country and downhill skiers, snowboarders, and tubers. A small ski area, tel. (360) 457-5559, has two rope tows and a Poma lift. It's open on weekends and during the Christmas-New Year's holiday for $15. Ski rentals, including cross-country and Telemark packages, are also available, along with ski lessons. Clallam Transit, tel. (360) 452-4511 or (800) 858-3747, provides a ski bus between Port Angeles and Hurricane Ridge for $8 roundtrip. Backcountry skiers will discover a wealth of open country at Hurricane Ridge—check avalanche conditions before heading out.

Park Service naturalists offer guided snowshoe walks on weekends and other times in the winter; call (360) 452-0330 for information and reservations. Snowshoes are provided. The visitor center—where you can warm up—and cafeteria are open winter weekends. The road to the top is open Sat.-Mon. from 9 a.m. to dusk, and is closed overnight or during storms. Entrance fees of $5 are charged on weekends. Call (360) 452-0329 for current road and weather conditions, and always come prepared for the worst. No overnight parking at the summit.

Elwha Area

Take Olympic Hot Springs Rd. south from Hwy. 101 just west of Port Angeles into the Elwha River watershed, an area that has been the focus of controversy. The river is dammed by the Elwha and Glines Canyon dams, providing power for the Daishowa paper mill in Port Angeles. The dams—built early in this century before the park was created—devastated salmon runs in the river by lowering the water level, raising water temperatures, blocking upstream migration (neither has a fishpass), and damaging or inundating spawning habitat. The high water temperatures have contributed to salmon kills, and many environmentalists have pushed to have the dams removed. Supporters of the dams point to their economic value in powering the paper mill. A Park Service study proposed that the dams be demolished to restore the Elwha, but given the current national political climate that seems highly unlikely in the near future, if ever.

Pitch your tent at two campgrounds along the road north of Lake Mills (created by Glines Canyon Dam): **Elwha** ($10; open year-round), and **Altaire** ($10; open June-Sept.). Summertime campfire programs and nature walks may be offered at Elwha; see the ranger station for details.

Nearly everyone in Washington knows of Sol Duc Hot Springs (see below), but less well known are **Olympic Hot Springs**, located at the end of Boulder Creek Rd., off Elwha River Road. The springs were once the site of a large resort, but today the springs are essentially undeveloped. Short trails lead to shallow rock-lined pools where the water varies from lukewarm to 138 °F. The Park Service allows but doesn't encourage bathing, and prohibits nudity.

The Elwha River is a popular destination for river-runners, with Class II whitewater conditions. Check with the Park Service for current flow conditions and precautions if you decide to run it yourself. **Olympic Raft and Guide Service,** tel. (360) 452-1443, has scenic two-hour trips down the Elwha River for $35. These are offered daily April to mid-September.

Take the Elwha River Trail for two miles to **Humes Ranch,** built in 1889 by Grant Humes, who made his living leading wilderness expeditions and by hunting and trapping game. Today his cabin is on the National Register of Historic Places.

A number of hiking trails head into the backcountry from the Elwha area, and a variety of short and long hikes are available, including an across-the-park route that follows the Elwha Trail to Low Divide and then drops down to Quinault Lake on the North Quinault Trail, a distance of 44 miles.

Lake Crescent

According to Native American legend, Mount Storm King once became so fed up with the bickering between the Clallams and Quileutes that he broke a rock off his head and threw it down at the warring tribes, damming a river and thereby creating Lake Crescent. The scientific view of the lake's origin isn't much different; it's attributed to an ancient landslide blocking the Lyre River. Today, freshwater Lake Crescent, 624 feet deep and 8.5 miles long, is famous for its Beardslee trout, a subspecies that is large (some are in the 12-14 pound range) and a hard fighter when hooked. Swimming, boating, camping, picnicking, and, of course, fishing are popular lake activities. The lake has an impressive mountain-rimmed setting. The Park Service's **Storm King Ranger Station,** tel. (360) 928-3380, is staffed during the summer months.

Fairholm Campground ($10; open year-round), on the west end of Lake Crescent, has summertime naturalist programs in the evenings. The Forest Service's **Klahowya Campground,** nine miles west of Lake Crescent on Hwy. 101, has sites for $7 that can be reserved ($7.50 extra fee) by calling (800) 280-2267. Open May to mid-October.

One-and-a-quarter-hour tours of the lake are offered on the *Storm King,* a new 65-foot paddlewheel boat, late May to October. The cost is $15 for adults, $14 for seniors, $10 for ages six to 17, and free for kids under six; call (206) 252-6800 (in Everett) or (800) 325-6722 for reservations. You can take your bike along and disembark for several hours of biking on the old Spruce Railroad Trail, returning on a later sailing, for no extra charge. The trip starts from the

Shadow Mountain General Store, with a bus transporting you to the boat dock.

The lake has two concession-operated lodges around its perimeter. Built in 1916, **Lake Crescent Lodge,** tel. (360) 928-3211, is a cozy place with a comfortable feeling from decades of guests, including President Franklin D. Roosevelt, who stayed here in 1937. Sit on the porch for fine views of the mountains and Lake Crescent, or lounge in front of the big fireplace on a cool evening. The lodge has all sorts of accommodations, including lodge rooms (bath down the hall), cottages (some with fireplaces), and modern motel rooms. Rates are $65-117 s or d. Open late April to October. The lodge has a restaurant and gift shop and rents rowboats.

Log Cabin Resort, tel. (360) 928-3325, at the northeast end of the lake, is three miles from Hwy. 101 on E. Beach Road. Lodging rates are $50-87 s or d for very rustic cabins, motel rooms, and waterfront A-frame chalets. Many of the buildings have stood here since the 1920s. In addition to accommodations, the resort also has meals, rowboat, paddleboat, canoe, and kayak rentals, a gift shop, grocery store, RV and tent sites. Open May to September.

Fairholm General Store, tel. (360) 928-3020, on the west end of Lake Crescent, is open April to mid-October and has motorboats, rowboats, and canoes for rent. They also serve meals in the cafe; eat al fresco on a deck overlooking the lake.

Hiking: From the ranger station, follow the **Marymere Falls Trail** three-quarters of a mile for a spectacular view of this 90-foot falls. Not a lot of water, but quite impressive nevertheless. Return via the Crescent Lake Lodge Trail for a two-mile loop hike.

The **Mt. Storm King Trail** splits off from the Marymere Trail and climbs more than 3,000 feet in a bit over a mile with fine views across the lake. The path ends before the summit, and the Park Service recommends against continuing to the top due to hazardous conditions.

A four-mile hike starting at Lyre River Rd. or North Shore Rd. at opposite ends of Lake Crescent, the **Spruce Railroad Trail** follows the tracks of the 1918 Spruce Railroad, built to supply spruce for WW I aircraft. The war was over before the railroad was completed, however, and the spruce was no longer needed. Two tun-

nels and depressions from the never-used railroad ties remain. Besides a taste of local history, the almost-level hike provides a view of Lake Crescent.

The nonprofit **Olympic Park Institute** offers hands-on field seminars covering such diverse topics as Makah cedar bark basketry, butterflies of the Olympic Peninsula, and alpine landscape photography. Seminars last two to five days, cost $70-260, and may be taken for college credit. They also have an Elderhostel with educational programs for seniors. Headquarters for the institute is the historic Rosemary Inn, near Lake Crescent Lodge. Students stay in nearby cabins, and meals are served family style at the inn. For information and registration, contact Olympic Park Institute, tel. (360) 928-3720 or (800) 775-3720.

Sol Duc Hot Springs
About 30 miles west of Port Angeles and 12 miles south of Hwy. 101, Sol Duc (pronounced "sole DUCK") hot springs are a reminder of the area's volcanic ancestry. Bask in the 99-105° F mineral water piped into three large outdoor pools. A fourth freshwater pool is also on the site. The springs ($5.50 for adults, $4.50 for seniors) are open daily 9 a.m.-9 p.m. mid-May through September; weekends 9 a.m.-5 p.m. April to mid-May, and in October. Massage is also available.

In addition to the springs, **Sol Duc Hot Springs Resort,** tel. (360) 327-3583, has a restaurant, grocery store, and gift shop, plus cabins (some with kitchenettes) for $75-85 s or d. Two-night minimum stays on holidays. Open mid-May through September. A campground with RV hookups is also available.

The springs were long known to the native peoples who first lived here, and white settlers were attracted to the area as a place of healing. By 1912, the area had an elegant hotel, theater, bowling alley, a 100-bed sanitorium, plus immaculately landscaped grounds with a golf course, tennis courts, and croquet grounds. A fire, begun by a defective flue, brought this to a crashing halt four years later. As the hotel burned to the ground, a short circuit caused the player organ to begin playing Beethoven's "Funeral March." Today's resort is considerably more modest.

Pitch a tent at the Park Service's **Sol Duc Campground** ($10); open all year, but sometimes closed because of snow in the winter months. Between July and Labor Day, park naturalists lead walks and offer evening programs in the amphitheater.

Hiking: Several trails head up the Soleduck Valley. A favorite is the one-mile **Soleduck River Trail,** which passes through enormous western hemlocks and Douglas firs to Soleduck Falls, one of the state's best-known waterfalls. A footbridge crosses the deep gorge cut by the river. From here, you can climb another three miles (one-way) to **Deer Lake,** bordered by trees. For variety, return to the campground from Soleduck Falls on the **Lovers Lane Trail,** a three-mile path along the south side of the river.

A fine loop trip for backpackers (backcountry permit required) is to head up the Soleduck River Trail to Seven Lakes Basin, then uphill to the summit of Bogachiel Peak and back out for a roundtrip of 22 miles.

Hoh Rain Forest
One of the park's most famous sights is also one of its most remote. The Hoh (pronounced "hoe") Rain Forest sits at the end of a paved 19 mile road that heads east from Hwy. 101 14 miles south of Forks. The **Hoh Rain Forest Visitor Center,** tel. (360) 374-6925, offers interpretive exhibits and summertime guided walks and campfire programs. Open daily 9 a.m.-7 p.m. in July and August, and daily 9 a.m.-4 p.m. the rest of the year. Stop here for brochures, information, books, and educational exhibits on the life of the forest and the climate. It rains a *lot* here; 135 inches of rain per year keep this forest perpetually green and damp under towering conifers over 200 feet tall and up to 10 feet wide. The driest months are July and August. Not far away from the visitor center, the **Hoh Rain Forest Campground** has forested campsites for $10; open year-round. Be sure to bring food with you; there are no stores or restaurants here.

Three short interpretive trails lead through the lush clubmoss-draped forests behind the visitor center. Lacy ferns carpet the forest floor, and some even survive in the tops of the bigleaf and vine maples. A paved wheelchair-accessible mini-trail is directly behind the center, and the **Hall of Mosses Trail** offers an easy three-quar-

ter-mile loop. **Spruce Nature Trail** covers a 1.3-mile loop that crosses a crystalline spring-fed creek and then touches on the muddy glacially fed Hoh River. More adventurous folks can head out the **Hoh River Trail,** an 18-mile path that ends at Blue Glacier and is used to climb Mt. Olympus (see "Hiking and Mountaineering" below for details). Hikers heading into the backcountry need to pick up backcountry permits at the visitor center.

Quinault Valley and the Eastside
Beautiful Lake Quinault on the southwest corner of Olympic National Park features a diversity of trails, accommodations, and other attractions. For details on this fascinating and very popular area, see "Lake Quinault Area" later in this chapter.

See "Lake Cushman Area" under "Hoodsport Area" earlier in this chapter for details on the **Staircase** area on the southeast corner of the park, where trails and a popular campground are located at the upper end of Lake Cushman. Also see "Eldon to Brinnon" earlier in this chapter for access from the Dosewallips River area, and "Quilcene Area" earlier in this chapter for access via the Buckhorn Wilderness.

OLYMPIC COAST SIGHTS

Washington's rocky and essentially undeveloped Olympic coast is truly a national gem, and in 1994 it was declared the **Olympic Coast National Marine Sanctuary,** a designation that helps protect the shore and ocean from development. The coast contains rich fishing grounds, more species of whales, dolphins, and porpoises than anywhere else on earth, some of the largest seabird colonies in the Lower 48, and an unparalleled beauty that attracts painters, photographers, and anyone with a sense of wonder. The shore is dotted with seastacks, cliff-rimmed beaches, and forested hills.

To preserve the natural habitat, automobile access to the park's Pacific Ocean beaches is severely limited, but the picturesque cliffs and sea stacks are worth the effort to get there. Be prepared for soggy, windy weather; 100 inches of annual rainfall combine with sometimes violent winds for less-than-pleasant hiking weather, although thanks to the warming effect of the Japanese Current that flows past the Olympic coast, the temperatures are mild year-round. Only rarely does the thermometer drop below 40° F.

For more details on the park's rugged coastline, get the excellent *Exploring Washington's Wild Olympic Coast,* by David Hooper (Seattle: The Mountaineers). Park Service offices have a helpful *Olympic Coastal Strip* handout with a map and dos and don'ts for backcountry users. Note that The Hoh and Quillayute Rivers are too deep to ford at any time, and that other creeks and rivers may be difficult to cross, particularly at high tide or when runoff is strong. Always take a tide chart and use caution. This is, after all, the wilderness.

Point of Arches and Shi Shi Beach

Near the north park boundary, **Point of Arches** is a testimony to the relentless pounding of the Pacific where, with a force of two tons per square inch, the ocean carves giant arches out of ancient rock. The Arches, legendary children of Destruction Island and Tatoosh Island, were pushed from Mother Tatoosh's canoe when she deserted her husband because, she said, "You'd probably grow up just like your father!" The bluffs above neighboring Shi Shi (pronounced "shy-shy") Beach provide a vantage point for watching the spring and fall gray whale migrations; the best viewing season is March through May.

Both Shi Shi Beach and Point of Arches are accessible—at least for now—through Neah Bay on the northwest tip of the Olympic Peninsula. A long-simmering conflict over access and rights of way led to closures in the early 1990s, and the problem remains unresolved. As of this writing, however, the very muddy trail was unofficially open to public use. This mile-long path begins next to the sign marking the turnoff to the fish hatchery, a bit over a mile south of the bridge over Sooes River. Don't leave a vehicle at the trailhead (there have been thefts); instead, pay to park in a neighbor's yard nearby. The 15 miles of coastline from here to the Ozette Ranger Station feature some of the finest beaches and tidepools anywhere on the Washington coast. You might even find remains from a shipwreck still visible. Call the Park Service, tel. (360) 452-0330, for the latest on access to Shi Shi Beach from the north end.

Ozette Lake Area

Located in the northwest corner of the coastal strip, eight-mile-long Lake Ozette is the third largest natural lake in Washington. In the 19th century this area was crowded with 130 homesteaders scratching out a living, but they gradually gave up and moved away. A 21-mile paved road heads southwest from Sekiu, ending at the **Ozette Ranger Station,** tel. (360) 963-2725, on the north end of the lake. The ranger station is open daily in the summer, but in the winter there are no set hours. This area has one of the most popular overnight hikes along the Olympic coast, and summer weekends attract crowds of outdoor enthusiasts. The small **Ozette Campground** has free camping year-round, but get here early to be sure of a space (no reservations). The lake is a popular place for boats, canoes, and kayaks, but take care since winds can create treacherous wave action at times. The free **Erickson's Bay** boat-in campground is halfway down the lake on the west side. Good fishing for largemouth bass, cutthroat trout, kokanee, and other fish.

Two trails head to the coast from the ranger station. One leads southwest to **Sand Point,** three miles away; the other 3.3 miles northwest to **Cape Alva**—the westernmost point in the Lower 48. By hiking the beach connecting the two, you can create a triangular loop trip of 9.3 miles. You can also continue south on the beach for 2.3 miles to the **Norwegian Memorial,** a tribute to the victims of a 1903 shipwreck. There is much to explore in this area: fascinating tidepools, cannonball shaped rocks, an anchor from one of the ships that ran aground here, and even an occasional Japanese glass ball. This is probably the best place to see wildlife in Olympic National Park, with bald eagles in the air, deer along the beach, sea lions and seals in the water, and migrating gray whales in fall and spring. This area contains the largest population of sea otters in the Lower 48; look for them in the kelp beds off Sand Point. The Wedding Rocks area between Cape Alva and Sand Point is well known for its petroglyphs, which were carved by the original inhabitants of this land at an unknown time. Pick up a handout describing them from the ranger station.

The famous Makah village site is just a short distance from where the Cape Alva trail meets the beach. During the 1970s, archaeologists from Washington State University uncovered a wealth of ancient artifacts. The dig is now closed and buried, but many of the items found are displayed in the Makah Cultural Center at Neah Bay. Although the mudslide caused much damage, the people continued to live in the area for many centuries. It was only early in this century that the last Makah peoples moved away—not because they wanted to, but because the state insisted that their children attend schools, and the closest one was at Neah Bay.

Because of overcrowding, the Park Service has instituted a quota system for overnight hiking in the Ozette area (but no restrictions on day-use). They allow up to 300 people per day between July 15 and Labor Day; get free permits by calling (360) 452-0300. If you don't have a permit, you might try arriving early to grab one of the 18 campsites accessible by car, but if those are gone, you'll have to drive all the way back to a private campground in Sekiu. The busiest times are on weekends in July and August.

If you're planning a one-way coastal hike from the Lake Ozette area, call (360) 374-2501 in Forks to find out about a shuttle service (fee charged) to pick up your car and deliver it to your destination point.

Rialto Beach Area

This is one of the most popular entry points for the coastal strip of Olympic National Park. Rialto Beach is on the north side of the Quillayute River, just west of the Mora campground and ranger station. The one-and-a-half-mile beach is popular with folks out for a stroll or day hike, but continue northward and the crowds thin out as the country becomes a jumble of sea stacks— remnants of the ancient coast. Hole in the Wall is one of the most interesting of these. This treacherous stretch of shore has claimed many lives, as memorials to Chilean and Norwegian sailors attest. The 21 long and remote miles between Rialto Beach and the Ozette Ranger Station feature abundant wildlife—including bald eagles, harbor seals, shorebirds, and migrating whales at different times of the year. The resident raccoons are here year-round, so hang your food!

On the south side of the Quillayute River is the village of La Push (later in this chapter), with access to many more miles of Olympic shore-

enjoying the sun and sand at Olympic National Park

line. A very popular day hike from the La Push area is **Second Beach,** an easy one-mile trail that starts just south of La Push, followed by a mile and a half of beach, tidepools, and sea stacks, including a pointed one called Quillayute Needle. You can camp at a couple of points in the trees, making this some of the most accessible beach camping in the state.

Park at Third Beach, just south of the Second Beach trailhead, for a challenging hike all the way down to **Oil City,** 17 miles away on the north side of the Hoh River. Be sure to carry a tide chart. Oil City has neither oil nor is it a city. Three different exploration parties came here in search of oil—attracted by crude seeping from the ground just north of here. During the 1930s, 11 exploratory wells were drilled and a town was platted, but there simply wasn't enough oil to justify development. A part-paved, part-gravel road leads 11 miles from Hwy. 101 to the Oil City trailhead.

DIANNE BOULERICE LYONS

Pitch a tent at **Mora Campground** ($10; open year-round), where summertime naturalist programs and nature walks are also offered. RVers can park at nearby Ocean Park Resort and Three Rivers Resort (see "La Push" later in this chapter).

Clallam Transit, tel. (360) 452-4511 or (800) 858-3747, provides twice-daily bus service to La Push from Port Angeles and Forks for only 50 cents. Hikers can catch the bus as far as the turnoff to Rialto Beach, and walk or hitch the final three miles.

Hoh River to Queets River
The southern end of Olympic National Park's coastal strip is the most accessible, with Hwy. 101 running right along the bluff for more than a dozen miles. Short trails lead down to the water at half a dozen points, and at the southern end one finds the town (of sorts) called Kalaloch, with a comfortable lodge, two Park Service campgrounds, and other facilities. See "The Coastal Strip" later in this chapter for a description of this area. Beach camping is not allowed along this stretch of the coast.

HIKING AND MOUNTAINEERING

Backcountry Hikes
The only way to cross the central portion of Olympic National Park is on foot; auto roads barely penetrate it. More than 600 miles of hiking trails can be found within the park, covering the park's virgin forest core, its matchless beaches, and its alpine peaks. Shorter day hikes and loop trips are described in appropriate parts of this chapter (e.g., see "Lake Quinault Area" for hiking trails in that area). For complete information on backcountry hiking in the park, see the excellent *Olympic Mountains Trail Guide* by Robert L. Wood (Seattle: The Mountaineers).

Backcountry use permits are required for trail or beach camping; pick one up at the ranger station nearest your point of departure. Because of overuse, reservations are required for Flapjack Lakes and Lake Constance trails; call the Staircase Ranger Station at (360) 877-5569. It's always a good idea to hang your food—raccoons can be a real problem, especially along the coast. Because of excellent public bus systems on roads surrounding the park, long one-way hikes are possible; simply catch the bus back to your starting point.

For a south-to-north (or vice-versa) 44-mile hike, start at the North Fork Ranger Station near Lake Quinault. The **North Fork Trail** follows the North Fork Quinault River for 16.5 miles to Low Divide, then it joins the **Elwha River Trail** terminating at Lake Mills near Elwha (just west of Port Angeles). You'll be hiking in reverse the route of James Halbold Christie, leader of the Seattle Press expedition across the then-unexplored Olympic Peninsula. It took Christie and his party six months and one black bear to complete the route in 1890; it should take you only four days and a packful of gorp. Bring binoculars for a closer look at the mountain goats near Elwha.

For a 24-mile one-way, relatively level hike, start at the end of South Shore Rd. on the south side of the park, follow the east fork of the Quinault River for 13 miles, passing Enchanted Valley Ranger Station and Anderson Pass, then travel alongside the Dosewallips River to the Dosewallips Ranger Station and campground.

Climbing
Climbing the glacier-clad 7,965-foot **Mt. Olympus** is a 44-mile roundtrip. From the Hoh Ranger Station—the closest and most popular departure point—hike 12 flat miles along the Hoh River Trail, then another four steep ones to the Olympus base camp, Glacier Meadows. Crossing Blue Glacier and the Snow Dome requires rope, ice axe, crampons, and mountaineering skills; a hard hat is advised because of rock falls near the summit. Inexperienced climbers should go with a professional guide service. The eight-mile climb from Glacier Meadows to the summit takes about 10 hours. The best months for climbing are late June through early September, the driest months in the park; prior to that time mud and washouts may slow you down. *A Climber's Guide to the Olympic Mountains,* published by The Mountaineers, gives detailed information on this and other climbs in the park. This book, other trail guides, and quadrangle maps can be obtained from The Pacific Northwest National Parks and Forests Association in Port Angeles, tel. (360) 452-4501.

OTHER OUTDOOR ACTIVITIES

Naturalist Programs

Guided walks and campfire programs are held frequently throughout the summer at Fairholm, Heart O' the Hills, Hoh, Kalaloch, Mora, and Sol Duc campgrounds July 4th through Labor Day. Check the campground bulletin board for times and topics.

Olympic Park Institute, tel. (360) 928-3720 or (800) 775-3720, a nonprofit educational organization, offers field seminars for naturalists, photographers, and anyone interested in the ecology or geography of the park. See "Lake Crescent" under "Interior Sights" above for details.

Fishing, Boating, and Rafting

The clear turquoise waters of Lake Crescent are open to fishing and boating; boats and canoes can be rented from Lake Crescent Lodge, Fairholm General Store, and Log Cabin Resort. Bottom fishing is popular in the Strait of Juan de Fuca and along the coast; no license is necessary within park limits, though salmon and steelhead catch record cards are required, available from sporting goods stores. See "Lake Crescent" under "Interior Sights" above for tours of Lake Cresent aboard the paddlewheeler *Storm King*.

Olympic Outdoor Adventures, tel. (800) 659-6095, offers summer raft trips on the Elwha, Dosewallips, Soleduck, and Hoh Rivers, plus surf kayaking and sea kayaking trips. **Olympic Raft and Guide Service,** tel. (360) 452-1443, has a similar operation, with scenic float trips down the Elwha, Hoh, and Queets Rivers. **Chinook Expeditions,** tel. (800) 241-3451, has relaxing rain forest float trips on the Queets River every March and April. Two-day trips cost $210 per person including meals and river shuttle.

Winter Sports

Ski rentals, two rope tows, Poma lift, and crosscountry ski trails provide Nordic and Alpine skiing at Hurricane Ridge ski area, tel. (360) 452-9235; nonskiers can enjoy the sights via a naturalist-led snowshoe walk (snowshoes provided). Snow-tubing is another popular winter activity at the Ridge. The road is plowed and the lodge and ski facilities are open for holiday and weekend day-use only from mid-December to late March.

ACCOMMODATIONS AND FOOD

Within Olympic National Park are a number of concessionaire-operated lodging places: Lake Crescent Lodge and Log Cabin Resort at Lake Crescent, Sol Duc Hot Springs Resort at the springs, and Kalaloch Lodge on the southwestern edge of the park. Kalaloch Lodge is open year-round, but the others are only open during the summer months. All of these, plus Fairholm General Store, also serve three meals a day. See above for descriptions and rates for each of these. In addition, dozens of other places are available in surrounding towns such as Port Angeles, Sequim, Forks, La Push, Quinault, Quilcene, Brinnon, and Hoodsport.

CAMPING

Park Service Sites

Seventeen park campgrounds offer camping on a first-come, first-served basis for $10 a night (free in primitive campgrounds). No showers or laundry facilities are available at any campground; if you really miss bathing, Sequim Bay State Park, Bogachiel State Park, and Dosewallips State Park have showers you can use, or head to one of the nearby RV parks. Although lacking trailer hookups, some campgrounds do have trailer dumping stations. The camping limit is 14 days. Specific campground information is described for each part of the park.

Other Campgrounds

Other campgrounds around the park borders include 24 on Olympic National Forest land, a dozen Dept. of Natural Resources campgrounds, and five state parks. Fees range from free to $12 a night. See appropriate sections for descriptions of these campgrounds. Full RV hookups are available at **Log Cabin Resort** on Lake Crescent, tel. (360) 928-3325, and **Sol Duc Hot Springs Resort,** tel. (360) 327-3583. For additional private RV parks, see the towns surrounding the park.

INFORMATION AND SERVICES

For detailed information on camping, hiking, and accommodations within the park, contact park headquarters at 600 E. Park Ave. in Port Angeles, tel. (360) 452-4501, or stop by the **Olympic National Park Visitor Center,** about one mile from Hwy. 101 on Race St. in Port Angeles, tel. (360) 452-0330. The visitor center is open daily 8:30 a.m.-6 p.m. between Memorial Day and Labor Day, daily 8:30 a.m.-5 p.m. in September, and daily 9 a.m.-4 p.m. the rest of the year.

Other places for information are: **Hoh Rain Forest Visitor Center,** on the east side, tel. (360) 374-6925; **Hurricane Ridge Visitor Center,** tel. (360) 452-2713; **Storm King Ranger Station** on Lake Crescent, tel. (360) 928-3380; plus ranger stations at Quinault Lake, Fairholm, Elwha, Kalaloch, Ozette, Staircase, Sol Duc, and Mora. Forest Service offices in Hoodsport, Quilcene, Quinault, and Forks also have detailed information on the park.

The most up-to-date topographic maps of the Olympic Peninsula are produced by **Custom Correct Maps** produced by Little River Enterprises. They are available in park visitor centers or by calling (360) 457-5667.

TRANSPORTATION

Public buses operate throughout the Olympic Peninsula, making it easy to reach towns surrounding the park for a minimal fare. **Clallam Transit,** tel. (360) 452-4511 or (800) 858-3747, covers the northern end, including Port Angeles, Forks, Neah Bay, La Push, and Olympic National Park's Sol Duc Hot Springs and Lake Crescent. Connect with **Jefferson Transit,** tel. (360) 385-4777 or (800) 773-7788, in Sequim for Port Townsend, Port Ludlow, Quilcene, and other east Jefferson County points; or with **West Jefferson Transit,** tel. (800) 436-3950, in Forks for free transportation south to Kalaloch, Queets, and Lake Quinault. At Lake Quinault, catch **Grays Harbor Transit,** tel. (800) 562-9730, in Quinault for points to the south and east.

WEST END AND PACIFIC COAST

JOYCE

Joyce is the easternmost in a series of small towns on the Strait of Juan de Fuca that cater primarily to commercial and recreational fishermen. Accommodations and restaurants here and in neighboring fishing towns are no-frills enterprises. The town's centerpiece is the **Joyce General Store,** with everything you might need, along with some things you probably don't need. In business since 1911 and owned by the same family for more than four decades, it started out with the same false front, oiled wood floors, beaded ceiling, and fixtures. Added, though, is much of the interior that came from the Markhum House Hotel in the long-gone town of Port Crescent. This is said to be the oldest continuously operated store in the state. Also in Joyce are a cafe, a tavern, and a couple of other small businesses.

The local bash is **Joyce Daze** in early August, with a parade, salmon bake, arts and crafts

show, and the main event, a wild blackberry pie contest. Call (360) 928-3821 for details.

Joyce Museum

Housed in a former railroad station on Hwy. 112, the Joyce Museum, tel. (360) 928-3568, has relics from the town's early days, logging and railroad equipment, photos, and driftwood carvings. Open weekends only June to August.

Accommodations

Crescent Bay Inn, 3424 Crescent Bay Rd., has three rooms with queen-sized beds and shared baths, starting at $65, including a full breakfast. Nearby is **Carol's Crescent Beach,** 3456 Crescent Beach Rd., tel. (360) 928-3454, which has full hookup sites, the use of half a mile of beach, and all RV amenities.

Campgrounds

The county-run **Salt Creek Recreation Area** three miles east of Joyce off Hwy. 112, tel. (360)

928-3441, has camping ($10), a beach, hiking trails, showers, and a marine sanctuary. The Dept. of Natural Resources maintains the free but primitive **Lyre River Campground** five miles west of Joyce; open year-round. Right on the river and only a few steps from the Strait of Juan de Fuca. RVers can stay at **Lyre River Park,** five miles west of Joyce, tel. (360) 928-3436, or **Whiskey Creek Beach,** three miles west of Joyce, tel. (360) 928-3489. Cabins are available at the latter.

CLALLAM BAY AND SEKIU

The twin towns of Clallam Bay and Sekiu (SEE-kyoo) are just a mile apart on the Strait of Juan de Fuca approximately 50 miles west of Port Angeles, and offer the basic services but not much else. The bay has been the site of a salmon cannery, a sawmill town, and a leather-tanning factory, but of late the bay and Sekiu are best known for fishing, both commercial and charters. With the decline of salmon in recent years, the fishing has focused more on bottom-fish, particularly halibut. The area is also popular with scuba divers, and a prison in Clallam Bay provides guaranteed jobs. The land near here is privately owned and managed for timber production. Enormous clearcuts stare down the rugged slopes and logging trucks roll past every few minutes, hauling more former trees to the mill. Learn about private forestry practices in a visit to the 26,000-acre **Pysht Tree Farm,** tel. (360) 963-2382 or (800) 998-2382. The tree farm is east of Clallam Bay near milepost 29 on Hwy. 112.

Motels

Many motels that once thrived around Sekiu have gone out of business with the decline in salmon fishing. All the local lodging places are in Sekiu. **Curley's Resort,** tel. (360) 963-2281, has motel units ($45-80 s or d) and cabins with kitchenettes ($45 for up to five), as well as RV hookups, boat rentals, and a dive shop. **Herb's Motel and Charters,** tel. (360) 963-2346, has motel rooms for $33-70 s or d. Curley's and Herb's are both open year-round. **Bay Motel,** tel. (360) 963-2444, charges $45 s, $50 d for its rooms with kitchenettes. **Van Riper's**

Resort, tel. (360) 963-2334, also has shore-side lodging seasonally.

Parks and Campgrounds

The beaches beyond Slip Point Lighthouse, on the east end of the bay, are great for beach-combing and exploring the tidepools, and the area east of here is famous for its marine fossils. County parks in the Clallam Bay area are **Clallam Bay Spit,** a 33-acre waterfront park for day-use only, and **Pillar Point Park,** just east of Clallam Bay. The latter is a four-acre park with a boat launch and campsites for $8; open mid-May to mid-September.

RVers can park at Curley's Resort in Sekiu (see above); **Coho RV Park,** tel. (360) 963-2333; and **Tretteviks RV Park,** eight miles west of Sekiu, tel. (360) 963-2688, which has the standard RV hookups and tent spaces, plus an attractive sandy beach.

Other Practicalities

Groceries and cheap gas can be found in Clallam Bay, and you can eat at **Breakwater Inn,** tel. (360) 963-2428.

The local festival is **Clallam Bay-Sekiu Fun Days,** held the second weekend in July. Get info from the **Clallam Bay/Sekiu Chamber of Commerce,** in Clallam Bay, tel. (360) 963-2339. The **area code** is 360.

NEAH BAY

Heading west from Sekiu on Hwy. 112, you begin to realize that you really are reaching the end of the line. This is one of the most dramatic shoreline drives in Washington—the narrow road winds along cliff faces and past extraordinary views. The ocean is up-close and personal the entire time. At the end of the road, 72 miles from Port Angeles, Neah Bay sits on the 44-square-mile **Makah Indian Reservation** in virtual isolation, at the northwesternmost point of the contiguous United States.

For many years, the town was a center for salmon fishing, attracting both commercial fishermen and vacationing anglers. As with other settlements on the Olympic Peninsula, the decline of salmon stocks and the resulting lack of a sport-fishing season has had a devastating ef-

STRAIT OF JUAN DE FUCA

TATOOSH ISLAND

CAPE FLATTERY
OVERLOOK

KOITLAH POINT

WADDAH ISLAND

COAST GUARD BASE

NEAH BAY

MAKAH MUSEUM

112

PACIFIC OCEAN

WAATCH

RIVER

HOBUCK BEACH

MAKAH INDIAN RESERVATION

MUKKAW BAY

ANDERSON POINT

MAKAH FISH HATCHERY

0   1 mi

0   1 km

MOON

TO SHI SHI BEACH AND POINT OF ARCHES

© MOON PUBLICATIONS, INC.

fect. Once-thriving motels now stand abandoned, and the village has a gritty down-in-the-dumps feeling. But the fishing is still good for bottom fish, and a few charter boats now target halibut, ling cod, red snapper, and black sea bass. The town also has a small U.S. Coast Guard base.

Makah Cultural Center

In 1970 tidal erosion unearthed old Ozette Indian homes that had been destroyed by a mudslide some 500 years earlier. The slide entombed and preserved the material, and 11 years of excavations by archaeologists from Washington State University unearthed one of the richest finds in North America. Many of the thousands of artifacts discovered are now on display in the $2 million Makah Cultural and Research Center, tel. (360) 645-2711, at Neah Bay. This is the finest collection of Northwest Coast Indian artifacts from pre-contact times, with an extraordinary range of material, including beautifully carved seal clubs, spears, bentwood boxes, combs, paddles, bows and arrows,

clothing, woven baskets, whale bones, and much more. Not on display—it is too fragile—but visible in photos, is an intricate plaid blanket woven from woodpecker feathers, dog hair, cattail fluff, and cedar bark. A re-created 15th-century longhouse is the museum's centerpiece, showing how the people lived in the abundance of the land. Outside, a modern longhouse is sometimes used for basketry and carving demonstrations.

The museum is open daily 10 a.m.-5 p.m. from June to mid-September, and Wed.-Sun. 10 a.m.-5 p.m. the rest of the year. An hour-long video about Neah Bay and the archaeological dig is shown daily at 11 a.m. and 2 p.m. The small gift shop sells local baskets and beadwork. You can also obtain local information here. Admission costs $4 for adults, $3 for seniors and students, free for kids under six.

Other Sights

The setting for Neah Bay is simply spectacular, with rocky Waadah Island just offshore, connected to land by a two-mile-long breakwater. A totem pole stands in the little grassy park across from the BP station, and one often sees bald eagles around town, especially in the spring.

The **Cape Loop Rd.** provides an interesting circle drive or mountain bike ride around the tip of Cape Flattery. The narrow dirt road is very badly rutted in places and definitely not for low-slung vehicles. Follow the Cape Flattery Center signs west from town, and then turn right to the cape (left will take you to Hobuck Beach and a fish hatchery). About 10 miles from town, you will find a trail leading down to the beach at the only place that hasn't been recently (and heavily) logged. For a view across to Tatoosh Island and **Cape Flattery Lighthouse** (built in 1858), turn right at the sign that points to the cove, and continue steeply uphill, turning right at the next two intersections to the overlook. You can return downhill and continue around the cape back to Neah Bay, passing a small waterfall with sculpted pools large enough to sit in on a warm summer day, and several miles later a dump that has to be one of the worst in the state of Washington (but a good place to look for ravens and eagles) Total length of this loop is approximately 16 miles.

On the southwest side of the Makah Indian Reservation are two attractive day-use beaches facing Mukkaw Bay: Hobuck Beach and Sooes Beach. Just south of here is Shi Shi Beach within Olympic National Park, a favorite place for hikers. See "Olympic Coast Sights" earlier in this chapter for details on this fascinating area.

Motels
Tyee Motel and RV Park, in the center of Neah Bay, tel. (360) 645-2223, has units (some with kitchenettes) for $35-42 s or d and RV spaces. The nicest local motel is **The Cape Motel,** tel. (360) 645-2250, with rooms for $35-50 s, $40-60 d; RV and tent spaces are available. **Bay Manor,** tel. (360) 645-2110, is a fully furnished three-bedroom contemporary home with a full kitchen available for $75 d.

If you want to get away from town, **Hilden's Motel,** five miles east on Bowman Beach, has five units for $40-45 s, $50-60 d. The units have full kitchens and sit right on the water with rocky islets just offshore. A fine place to watch the surfbirds or scan the horizon for seals.

Campgrounds
The local motels also have RV parks (of a sort) and allow tents for a fee. More RV parking at **Silver Salmon Resort,** tel. (360) 963-2688. **Hobuck Beach,** three miles southwest of town also has a private campground.

Food and Crafts
Get burgers and similar fare at **Makah Bay Cafe,** tel. (360) 645-2508, or **Rosies II Cafe,** tel. (360) 645-2789. **Washburn's General Store,** tel. (360) 645-2211, has groceries, a deli with fresh sandwiches and espresso (this is Washington after all), and a small gift shop selling Indian jewelry, baskets, carvings, and knitted items. Also check **Ravens Corner** for more locally made baskets and carvings.

Fishing Charters
For information on fishing charters out of Neah Bay, call **Big Salmon Fishing Resort,** tel. (360) 645-2375, or **Far West Fishing Resort,** tel. (360) 645-2270.

Charley Swan dressed to impress for Neah Bay's Makah Days

TACOMA PUBLIC LIBRARY

Events

Makah Days is the town's big annual festival, celebrating the day the reservation first raised the American flag in 1913. Held on the weekend closest to August 26, the three-day festival is highlighted by dances, a parade, fireworks show, salmon bake, canoe races, and bone games (Indian gambling).

Information and Transportation

The Makah Museum has local information. **Clallam Transit,** tel. (360) 452-4511 or (800) 858-3747, provides twice-daily bus service throughout the northern Olympic Peninsula for only 50 cents. You can connect with other public bus systems to take you all the way to Seattle and beyond. For guided tours of the Neah Bay area, contact **Cape Tours,** tel. (360) 645-2378.

FORKS AND VICINITY

The westernmost incorporated city in the Lower 48, Forks is the economic center and logging capital of the western Olympic Peninsula—a big handle for this town of 3,300 with one main drag. Since the spotted-owl controversy began, logging in this area has been severely curtailed on Forest Service lands, and Forks went into something of a depression as loggers searched for alternate means of earning a living. In recent years the town has diversified, emphasizing the clean air, remote location, and abundance of recreational possibilities within a few miles in any direction. For travelers, the town's big selling point is its proximity to the west side of Olympic National Park and Pacific coast beaches.

Sights

The **Forks Timber Museum,** tel. (360) 374-9666, has historical exhibits that include a steam donkey, a logging camp bunkhouse, old logging equipment, an Indian canoe, and various pioneer implements. Out front is a memorial to loggers killed in the woods and a replica of a fire lookout tower. Open Sunday 1-5 p.m., and Tues.-Sat. 10 a.m.-6 p.m. in the summer only; no charge.

The tiny crossroads settlement called **Sappho,** 13 miles north of Forks, is where you'll find the **Solduc Salmon Hatchery.** An interpretive center describes how hatcheries work.

Bogachiel State Park

Six miles south of Forks on Hwy. 101, Bogachiel (Indian for "Muddy Waters") State Park encompasses 123 acres on the usually clear Bogachiel River. Enjoy the short nature trail through a rain forest, or swim, paddle, or fish in the river—famous for its summer and winter steelhead, salmon, and trout. The park has campsites ($10 for tents, $15 for RV hookups) and is open year-round; tel. (360) 374-6356. Call (800) 452-5687 for campsite reservations ($6 extra fee), available up to 11 months ahead of time.

Accommodations

The "Forks Area Accommodations" chart lists lodging places around Forks. See also "La Push Area" and "Hoh River Area" below for more nearby lodging. Budget travelers will certainly want to check out the **Rain Forest Hostel,** tel. (360) 374-2270, run by two of the friendliest hosts in the business, Jim Conomos and Kay Ritchie. The hostel is out in the sticks 23 miles south of Forks (between mileposts 170 and 169) and has 16 bunk beds, a family room, and an old camper outside for couples. Closed 9:30 a.m.-5 p.m., lights out at 11, and no booze allowed. As with most hostels, guest do a small chore. Rates are $10 per person, and $5 for kids. Those without vehicles can catch the twice-a-day bus service from Forks (see below).

Several local B&Bs offer comfortable accommodations in Forks. **River Inn B&B,** tel. (360) 374-6526, is three miles south of town on the Bogachiel River, with two guest rooms, a deck, jacuzzi, and full breakfasts. **Miller Tree Inn,** tel. (360) 374-6806, has six guest rooms in a beautiful old homestead set on a large shady lot on the edge of town. The back deck has a hot tub. **Brightwater House B&B,** tel. (360) 374-5453 is three miles west of town near the Soliduc River; a good place for the fly-fishing crowd. **Eagle Point Inn,** tel. (360) 327-3236, north of town in Beaver, is a modern log home on a bend of the Sol Duc River with a hot tub, comfortable rooms, and a full breakfast.

Campgrounds

Camp at **Bogachiel State Park,** four miles south on Hwy. 101 (see above); at the Park Service's **Mora Campground** ($10; open year-round)14 miles west of Forks, which offers summertime

FORKS AREA ACCOMMODATIONS

Accommodations are arranged from least to most expensive. Rates may be lower during the winter months. The area code is 360.

Rain Forest Hostel; 169312 Hwy. 101 (23 miles south of Forks); tel. 374-2270; $10 per person; friendly AYH hostel, dorm accommodations

Town Motel; 1080 S. Forks Ave.; tel. 374-6231 or (800) 742-2429; $29 s, $35 d; friendly and clean, kitchenettes available, no phones

Bear Creek Motel; Beaver (15 miles northeast of Forks); tel. 327-3660; $30-55 s or d; one kitchenette, RV hookups

Miller Tree Inn B&B; 654 E. Division; tel. 374-6806; $35 s, $55 d; three-story homestead on three acres, six guest rooms, private or shared baths, jacuzzi, full breakfast, no kids under eight, AAA approved

Forks Motel; 432 Forks Ave.; tel. 374-6243 or (800) 544-3416; $38-65 s, $42-65 d; outdoor pool, kitchenettes available, AAA approved

Fisherman's Widow B&B; 31 Huckleberry Lane; tel. 374-5693; $40 s, $50 d; light breakfast

Pacific Inn Motel; 352 S. Forks Ave.; tel. 374-9400 or (800) 235-7344; $43 s, $48 d; AAA approved

Olympic Suites; 800 Olympic Dr. (1.5 miles north of Forks); tel. 374-5400 or (800) 262-3433; $45 s, $55 d; one- and two-bedroom suites with kitchens, AAA approved

Shady Nook Guest House B&B; 41 Ash Ave.; tel. 374-5497; $45-55 s or d in house, $65 for up to four in cabin; private baths, continental breakfast, no kids under 12

River Inn B&B; 2596 Bogachiel Way (three miles southwest of Forks); tel. 374-6526; $50 s, $60 d; along Bogachiel River, two guest rooms, private baths, jacuzzi, full breakfast, no kids

Mill Creek Inn B&B; 1061 S. Forks Ave.; tel. 374-5873; $55 s or d; comfortable older home, two guest rooms, private baths, full breakfast

Brightwater House B&B; 440 Brightwater Dr. (three miles west of Forks); tel. 374-5453; $65 s or d; newer home along Sol Duc River, decks, two guest rooms, shared bath, full breakfast, no kids under 10, popular with fly-fishermen

Eagle Point Inn B&B; 384 Stormin' Norman Rd., Beaver (10 miles north of Forks); tel. 327-3236; $75 s or d; new log home on Sol Duc River, hot tub, fireplace, three guest rooms, private baths, full breakfast, no kids under 12

---

naturalist programs and nature walks; or the Forest Service's free **Klahanie Campground,** approximately five miles east of Forks on Calawah Way. Dispersed camping (pullouts off the road) is also allowed on Forest Service lands throughout Olympic National Forest.

Private campgrounds include: **Forks 101 RV Park,** 901 S. Forks Ave., tel. (360) 374-5073 or (800) 962-9964; **Mile Post 200 RV Park,** in Beaver (15 miles north of Forks), tel. (360) 327-3555; **R&R Sports Center and RV Park,** Rain Forest Rd., tel. (360) 374-9288. Camp for free at Rayonier's **Tumbling Rapids Park,** 11 miles northeast of Forks along Hwy. 101, tel. (360)

374-6565. See also "La Push" and "Hoh River Area" for nearby private campgrounds.

Food
Pay & Save Coffee Shop, 314 Forks Ave. S, tel. (360) 374-6769, has friendly waitresses and dependably good food three meals a day. They also have deli sandwiches and a salad bar. Meet the cops over coffee and donuts here.

Aggie's Place, 80 A St. SW, tel. (360) 374-9777, is *the* place for lunch in Forks, with salads, sandwiches, homemade soups, espresso, and sweets. Also popular is **Rain Drop Cafe,** 111 Forks Ave. S, tel. (360) 374-6612.

Get good Chinese food at **South North Gardens,** 219 Sol Duc Way, tel. (360) 374-9779. For pizza, lasagna, spaghetti, and deli sandwiches try **Pacific Pizza** at Forks Ave. and C Street.

Fifteen miles northeast of Forks on Hwy. 101 in Sappho, the **Hungry Bear Cafe** has good highway food, including a hamburger that weighs a pound. Open daily; call (360) 374-2626 for takeout. A mile north of Forks at the La Push road junction on Hwy. 101, the **Smoke House Restaurant,** tel. (360) 374-6258, is open daily for lunch and dinner with a full menu specializing in seafood.

The **Forks Farmers Market** takes place in the Thriftway Store parking lot on Friday and Saturday 10 a.m.-2 p.m. May through October.

Recreation
Rent bikes from **Olympic Mt. Bike Shop,** 80 A St. SW, tel. (360) 374-9777. Ken Schostak, tel. (360) 374-2501, offers a shuttle and pickup service (fee charged) for hikers, rafters, and anglers heading to remote areas on the Olympic Peninsula. This is very helpful for one-way hikes or river floats. Contact the Forks chamber of commerce for local fishing outfitters.

Events
Fork's **Fourth of July** is actually a four-day festival of fun that includes an art show, pancake breakfast, parades, a loggers show, demolition derby, and fireworks.

Information and Services
Get local info on the south end of town at the **Forks Chamber of Commerce Visitor Center,** 1411 S. Forks Ave., tel. (360) 374-2531 or (800) 443-6757. Open daily 9 a.m.-5 p.m. Memorial Day to Labor Day, and Fri.-Mon. 10 a.m.-3 p.m. the rest of the year. The museum is right next door.

The Olympic National Forest's **Soleduc Ranger Station,** five miles north of Forks on Hwy. 101, has maps, books, and handouts describing recreational opportunities on both Forest Service and Olympic National Park lands, plus an interesting 3-D model of the Olympic Peninsula. Open daily 8:30 a.m.-5 p.m. Memorial Day to Labor Day, and Mon.-Fri. 8:30 a.m.-5 p.m. the rest of the year.

Transportation
Clallam Transit, tel. (360) 452-4511 or (800) 858-3747, provides twice-daily bus service on the Olympic Peninsula for only 50 cents, transporting you north to Port Angeles and Neah Bay, and west to La Push. Catch the free **West Jefferson Transit** bus, tel. (800) 436-3950, south from Forks to Kalaloch, Queets, and Lake Quinault. At Lake Quinault, join the Grays Harbor Transit system for points south and east.

LA PUSH AREA

A 14 mile road heads west from Forks through the Bogachiel/Quillayute River Valley. Nearly all this land has been logged at least once, so be prepared for typical Olympic Peninsula clearcut vistas. The road ends at La Push, a small village bordering the Pacific Ocean on the south side of the Quillayute River, and the center of the **Quileute Indian Reservation.** The name La Push was derived from the French "la bouche," meaning "mouth," a reference to the river mouth here. It is an attractive little town with a fantastic beach for surfing and kayaking in the summer or watching storm waves in the winter. Locals have a small fleet of fishing and crabbing boats, a seafood plant, a fish hatchery, and a resort offering simple shoreside accommodations and camping.

Sights
The main attraction at La Push is simply the setting: James Island and other rocky points sit just offshore, and waves break against the First Beach. The small **Quileute Tribe Museum,** housed in the Tribal Center office, has a few artifacts and is open Mon.-Thurs. 8 a.m.-3 p.m., and Friday 2-4 p.m. Ask here for local folks who sell beadwork and other handicrafts, and about ocean and river tours in traditional cedar canoes ($30).

Mora Rd. branches off from La Push Rd. three miles east of La Push and provides access to **Rialto Beach** within Olympic National Park. It's pretty easy to tell you've entered public land; instead of clearcuts, you'll find tall old-growth trees. The Mora Campground is here, and the beach is a favorite picnicking area and starting point for hikers heading north along the wild Olympic coast. The town of La Push is just across the wide river mouth to the south.

Accommodations

Ocean Park Resort, right on the beach, has rather plain cabins (some with kitchens), two motels, tent sites, and RV hookups. Cabins are $65-125 and can sleep four to six people; motel rooms are $50-57 s or d. Simple "camper cabins" are $36 for up to six, but bring your own bedding. The same folks run **Shoreline Resort,** with older cabins for $42-55 s or d. No phones, maid service, or TVs in any of the rooms or cabins, but you don't come here to watch *Star Trek* reruns. Two-night minimum stay on weekends, and three-night minimums on holiday weekends. The water is very hard; bring in your own for drinking purposes. Make reservations up to a year in advance if you plan to visit in mid-summer. For details about either resort, call (360) 374-5267 or (800) 487-1267.

Three Rivers Resort, tel. (360) 374-5300, at the intersection of La Push and Mora roads (halfway between Forks and La Push), has cabins for $30-40 s or d, and offers guided fishing trips, horseback rides, and float trips.

Manitou Lodge, tel. (360) 374-6295, is a modern country lodge on 10 acres of forested land (surrounded by clearcuts) off Mora Road. Five luxurious guest rooms with private baths are $65-70 s or d each. A full breakfast is included, and they provide a free shuttle to the airport or Forks. Kids accepted. Book up to six months ahead for summer weekends. A gift shop here sells high quality Indian baskets, woodcarvings, and beadwork.

Olson's Cabin, 3243 Mora Rd., tel. (360) 374-3142, has space for up to five in a cozy and quiet cabin just 2.5 miles from Rialto Beach. Facilities include a full kitchen, TV, and phone; rates are $50 s or d, and $5 per person for extra folks.

Campgrounds

Olympic National Park's **Mora Campground** ($10; open year-round) is a pretty in-the-trees place to pitch a tent. Check the ranger station here for summertime naturalist programs and nature walks. Both Ocean Park Resort, tel. (360) 374-5267 or (800) 487-1267, and Three Rivers Resort, tel. (360) 374-5300, have tent camping and RV parks with coin-operated showers.

Food

There are no restaurants in La Push, but you can get locally famous burgers and other fast food east of town at Three Rivers Resort, tel. (360) 374-5300.

Events

The **Surf Frolic Festival** in January attracts surfers and kayakers, but the big event is **Quileute Days** in mid-July, with an Indian tug-of-war, bone games, a fish bake, dancing, and fireworks.

Information and Transportation

The Olympic National Park's **Mora Ranger Station,** tel. (360) 962-2283, next to the Mora Campground, is staffed daily June-Aug., but the rest of the year it's catch-as-catch-can. Stop by for a tide chart and information on hiking along the coast. They offer daily beach walks and short guided hikes, and campfire programs on Fri.-Sun. nights at the amphitheater. The **area code** for the Olympic Peninsula is 360.

Clallam Transit, tel. (360) 452-4511 or (800) 858-3747, provides twice-daily bus service to La Push and other parts of the Olympic Peninsula for only 50 cents, transporting you south as far as Lake Quinault, and north to Port Angeles and Neah Bay.

HOH RIVER AREA

Heading south from Forks on Hwy. 101, you pass through the heart of the Olympics and get a taste of the economic importance of logging and how it has changed the landscape. Despite reductions in the amount of timber cut in recent years on Forest Service lands, you're bound to meet a constant parade of trucks laden with heavy loads of logs from private land and Indian reservations.

Fourteen miles south of Forks is the turnoff to the world-famous **Hoh River Rain Forest,** located at the end of the paved 19 mile Upper Hoh Road. The road follows the river through a beautiful valley with a mix of second-growth stands and DNR clearcuts. Once you enter the park, old-growth stands dominate. Several trails, a campground, and visitor center are located here (see under "Interior Sights" in the Olympic

National Park section for details on this not-to-be-missed Olympic National Park attraction).

The world's largest western red cedar—19 feet wide and 170 feet tall—grows in the middle of a clearcut. To see the tree, go east on Nolan Creek Rd., about six miles south of the Hoh River Bridge on Hwy. 101. Stay on Nolan Creek Rd. for about 1.25 miles, then go right for 1.5 miles on forest road N-1100. Turn right for one-half mile, then take another right for another half mile—it's hard to miss.

Accommodations

Hoh River Resort, 15 miles south of Forks on Hwy. 101, tel. (360) 374-5566, has roadside rustic cabins (bring your own bedding) with kitchenettes for $40 s or d, along with tent and RV spaces. **Ho Humm Ranch,** 20 miles south of Forks on Hwy. 101, tel. (360) 374-5337, is certainly one of the more unique lodging places, with five guest rooms in mobile homes (shared bath) for $30 each, including a full breakfast. The ranch raises a zoo's worth of critters: llamas, strange breeds of cattle, goats, sheep, ducks, geese, rhea birds, and Asian Sika deer. In the same area, **Hoh Chalet,** tel. (360) 374-3338, consists of three separate vacation homes: a two-bedroom home ($80 s or d), a two-story chalet ($75 s or d), and a studio cabin ($55 s or d), all with kitchenettes and access to a wood-fired sauna. For inexpensive lodging check out the **Rain Forest Hostel,** tel. (360) 374-2270, described in "Forks and Vicinity" above.

Campgrounds

The Park Service's **Hoh Rain Forest Campground,** 19 miles east from Hwy. 101 at the end of the road, is open year-round with in-the-trees camping for $10. The visitor center has evening naturalist programs in the summer. The Dept. of Natural Resources has five free, year-round campgrounds near the Hoh River: **Hoh Oxbow,** located directly across from a horrific clearcut near milepost 176; **Cottonwood Campground,** two miles west on Oil City Rd.; **Willoughby Creek,** 3.5 miles east on Hoh Rain Forest Rd.; **Minnie Peterson,** 4.5 miles east on Hoh Rain Forest Rd.; and **South Fork Hoh,** 6.5 miles east on Hoh Mainline Rd. (on the way to the correction center).

THE COASTAL STRIP

Commercialization is minimal from Neah Bay to Grays Harbor because the coast itself is protected nearly all the way down, first by the coastal strip of Olympic National Park, and then by the Quinault Indian Reservation, which was closed to non-Indians in the early 1960s. Not many Washingtonians complain about this lack of development; it suits most just fine and they are proud of the wild coast, a place where you can hike and camp without seeing or hearing any kind of motor vehicle.

When the highway emerges on the coastline south of Forks, you will quickly become aware that the northern half of Washington's coastline—from the state's northwest corner at Neah Bay to the Quinault Indian Reservation—is a picture of how the Pacific coast looks in brochures and calendar photos: pristine beaches, pounding waves, trees sculpted by relentless sea breezes.

West Jefferson Transit, tel. (800) 436-3950, provides free daily bus service to Kalaloch and Queets, and makes flag stops elsewhere on Hwy. 101. Service continues south as far as Lake Quinault, and north to Forks where you can transfer to Clallam Transit buses.

Ruby Beach Area

Highway 101 rejoins the coast at Ruby Beach, just south of the mouth of the Hoh River. A very popular trail leads down to beautiful sandy shoreline dotted with red pebbles (garnets, not rubies), with piles of driftwood and the flat top of **Destruction Island** several miles offshore. The island was named for the many vessels that were wrecked along this deadly coast and is capped by a 94-foot lighthouse.

The tiny, 400-acre **Hoh Indian Reservation** is a couple miles north of Ruby Beach at the mouth of the Hoh River. A three-mile road leads to the tribal center building. Stop here to ask about locally made cedar bark baskets, but be ready to pay upwards of $200. The village is a trashed, badly littered place, but the ocean views are impressive. On the north side of the river is the area called Oil City, accessible via a partly gravel 11 mile road off Hwy. 101.

South of Ruby Beach, the highway cruises

along the bluff, with five more trails dropping to shoreline beaches, creatively named Beach 1, Beach 2, Beach 3, and etceteras. A massive western red cedar tree stands just off the highway near Beach 6.

Kalaloch

The place called Kalaloch (CLAY-lock) has a campground, gas station/country store, and the **Kalaloch Lodge,** tel. (360) 962-2271, operated as a park concessionaire. The lodge consists of three different types of facilities: the main lodge (built in 1953), cabins of various types, and the Seacrest House Motel. No TVs in the rooms, but the sitting room has one for those who can't miss their soaps. Some of the cabins have kitchens and offer waterside views. Summer rates are $51-145, and there's a two-night minimum stay on weekends. Make reservations far ahead for the nicest rooms or the bluff cabins; some places are reserved 11 months ahead of time for July and August. The lodge also has a cafe, gift shop, and lounge.

Across from the lodge is the Park Service's **Kalaloch Visitor Information Center,** tel. (360) 962-2283, where you'll find natural history books, maps, pamphlets, and tide charts for beach walking. Open daily 9 a.m.-6 p.m. June-Sept., and variable hours the rest of the year.

The Park Service's **Kalaloch Campground** ($10; open year-round) sits on a bluff overlooking the beach. During the summer, attend campfire programs, or join a tide pool walk at Beach 4. The primitive **South Beach Campground** is actually just parking spaces in an old gravel pit on the southern edge of the park three miles south of Kalaloch. No fee; open summers only. These are the only two campgrounds on the dozen miles of Pacific shoreline between Queets and the Hoh Indian Reservation. Others wanting to camp should head up the Queets River (see below), or to campgrounds on the Hoh River (see above).

Queets River Area

South of Kalaloch, Hwy. 101 crosses the **Quinault Indian Reservation** where you get to see what clearcuts really look like. A narrow corridor of Olympic National Park extends along the Queets River, protecting a strip of old-growth timber bordered by cutover DNR and private lands. The gravel Queets River Rd. (well marked) follows the river eastward from Hwy. 101, ending 14 miles later at **Queets Campground.** This free, primitive campground has no running water, but it is open year-round. A seasonal ranger station is also here. The **Queets Loop Trail** departs the campground for an easy three-mile walk through second-growth forests and fields where elk are often seen. Another route, the **Queets Trail,** is more challenging. It requires the fording of Queets River near the campground—wait till late summer or fall for this hike, and use caution—and then continues along the river for 15 miles, passing through magnificent old-growth stands of Sitka spruce. Not for beginners, but an impressive hike.

The Department of Natural Resources has additional free campsites approximately 14 miles up Hoh-Clearwater Mainline Road. The turnoff is at milepost 147 on Hwy. 101 (three miles west of the Queets River Rd. turnoff).

Chinook Expeditions, tel. (800) 241-3451, has float trips on the Queets River in the spring. Two-day trips are $210, including meals and river shuttle.

The **Quinault Indian Reservation** beaches, from just south of Queets almost to Moclips, have been closed to the public since 1969 in an effort to forestall further destruction of the natural landscape. However, you can arrange for an escorted tour of Point Grenville or Cape Elizabeth, two good birding spots, by calling (360) 276-8211.

LAKE QUINAULT AREA

Surrounded by steep mountains and dense rain forest, Lake Quinault is bordered on the northwest by Olympic National Park and on the southeast by Olympic National Forest; the lake and land to the southeast are part of the Quinault Indian Reservation and subject to Quinault regulations. Located at the southwestern edge of Olympic National Park, Lake Quinault is a hub of outdoor activity during the summer months. This very scenic tree-rimmed lake is surrounded by cozy lodges, and hiking trails provide a chance for even total couch potatoes to get a taste of the rain forest that once covered vast stretches of the Olympic Peninsula.

QUINAULT LAKE

OLYMPIC NATIONAL PARK

TO LOW DIVIDE

SKYLINE TRAIL

NORTH FORK TRAIL

ELIP CREEK TRAIL

NORTH FORK QUINAULT RIVER

TO ENCHANTED VALLEY

PONY BRIDGE

THREE LAKES TRAIL

THREE LAKES

ENCHANTED VALLEY TRAIL

NORTH FORK

GRAVES CREEK

IRELY LAKE

EAST FORK QUINAULT RIVER

NORTH SHORE RD.

SOUTH SHORE RD.

MAPLE GLADE TRAIL

FLETCHER CANYON TRAIL

TO KALALOCH

NPS QUINAULT RANGER STATION

COLONEL BOB WILDERNESS

LOCHAERIE RESORT

JULY CREEK

RAIN FOREST RESORT

COLONEL BOB (4,492 ft.)

OLYMPIC NATIONAL FOREST

LAKE QUINAULT RESORT

GATTEN CREEK

FALLS CREEK

COLONEL BOB TRAIL

QUINAULT LAKE

101

WILLABY

QUINAULT LODGE / USFS RANGER STATION

QUINAULT INDIAN RESERVATION

QUINAULT LOOP TRAIL

RAIN FOREST NATURE TRAIL

101

TO HOQUIAM

0   3 mi

0   3 km

© MOON PUBLICATIONS, INC.

MOON

The Quinault Rain Forest is one of three major rainforests that survive on the Peninsula; here the annual average rainfall is 140 inches, resulting in enormous trees, lush vegetation, and moss-carpeted buildings. If you arrive in the rainy winter months, bring your heavy rain gear and rubber boots, not just a nylon poncho and running shoes. If you're prepared, a hike in the rain provides a great chance to see this soggy and verdant place at its truest. July and August are the driest months, but even then it rains an average of three inches. Typical Decembers see 22 inches of precipitation.

Day Hikes

The Quinault area is a hiker's paradise. Trails for all abilities snake through a diversity of terrain. The five-mile **Quinault Loop Trail**, accessible from Willaby and Falls Creek campgrounds and Lake Quinault Lodge, provides an easy two-hour trek along the shore and into the rainforest. Easier still is the half-mile **Quinault Rain Forest Nature Trail,** where informative signs explain the natural features. A good hike for those traveling with small children begins at North Fork Campground, following the Three Lakes Trail for the first mile to **Irely Lake.** The half-mile **Maple Glade Rain Forest Trail** begins at the Park Service's Quinault Visitor Center on North Fork Road.

Another easy jaunt is the **Graves Creek Nature Trail,** a one-mile loop that begins at the Graves Creek Campground on the South Shore Road. From the same starting point, the **Enchanted Valley Trail** takes you through a wonderful rainforest along the South Fork of the

Quinault River. Day hikers often go as far as Pony Bridge, 2.5 miles each way, but more ambitious folks can continue to Dosewallips, a one-way distance of 24 miles.

Backcountry Hikes

You'll find two across-the-park hikes that begin or end in the Quinault area, one heading northeast over to Dosewallips (see "Day Hikes" above), and the other heading north over Low Divide to the Lake Elwha area. (See "Elwha Area" under "Interior Sights" in the Olympic National Park section earlier in this chapter.)

The 11,961-acre **Colonel Bob Wilderness** borders the South Shore Rd. just east of Quinault Lake and has a couple of popular backcountry paths. For an overnight hike, the 14-mile **Colonel Bob Trail** provides views of Mt. Olympus, Quinault Valley, and the Pacific Ocean from its 4,492-foot summit, and passes through impressive rainforests. Drive past Lake Quinault on South Shore Rd. till you see the trailhead on the right. The two-mile **Fletcher Canyon Trail** doesn't get a lot of use, but it's a fine chance to see virgin timber and a pretty waterfall. The trail starts from South Shore Rd. just before it enters the park. Access to the wilderness from the south side is via Forest Rd. 2204, northeast from the town of Humptulips. If you enter from this remote area, be sure to visit the beautiful Campbell Tree Campground and to check out the Humptulips Trail that departs from the campground.

A 21-mile loop begins near the North Fork Campground, heads up the **Three Lakes Trail** for seven miles to three shallow alpine lakes, and then turns down the **Elip Creek Trail** for four miles before catching the **North Fork Trail** back through dense rainforests to your starting point. An added advantage of this loop is the chance to see the world's largest Alaska cedar, located just off the trail approximately a mile east of Three Lakes.

Accommodations

Built in 1926 over a period of just 10 weeks, the rambling **Lake Quinault Lodge** occupies a magnificent setting of grassy lawns bordering Lake Quinault. This is how a lodge should look, with a darkly regal interior, and a big central fireplace surrounded by comfortable couches

and tables for writing letters home. Accommodations include a variety of rooms in the main lodge or in newer buildings nearby for $90-220 s or d, including an indoor pool, sauna, and jacuzzi. Some of the rooms have kitchenettes. Call (360) 288-2900 or (800) 562-6672 for reservations. Call two months ahead to be sure of space in mid-summer. The lodge offers two-hour tours of the Quinault area for $5, plus seasonal canoe and boat rentals.

Rain Forest Resort Village, just a short way up South Shore Rd., tel. (360) 288-2535 or (800) 255-6936, has cabins with fireplaces (some with kitchens) for $100-145 s or d, and motel rooms for $75-80 s or d. The resort also has a good restaurant and lounge, a small general store, laundry, RV hookups, and canoe rentals. The **world's largest Sitka spruce**—is on the resort grounds. This thousand-year-old behemoth is more than 13 feet in diameter and 191 feet tall.

On the north side of Lake Quinault is a pair of small resorts. **Lake Quinault Resort Motel,** 314 N. Shore Rd., tel. (360) 288-2362, has newly renovated townhouses (some with kitchenettes), suites, and motel rooms for $79-99 s or d that feature decks and beach access. **Lochaerie Resort,** 638 N. Shore Rd., tel. (360) 288-2215, has six rustically simple cottages, most built in the 1920s and '30s. Each has a complete kitchen and showers, and a woodstove, and the Christie cabin has a spectacular lake view. Borrow a canoe to paddle the lake, or just relax on the shore. Rates are $50-65 s or d, and there's a two-night minimum stay on weekends. In the winter you should call ahead to make sure they are open.

Amanda Park Motel, on the west end of the lake just off Hwy. 101, tel. (360) 288-2237, has rooms for $35 s, $40 d.

Campgrounds

Choose from seven different public campgrounds in the Quinault Lake area. The Forest Service maintains three campgrounds on the south shore of Lake Quinault: **Falls Creek** ($7; open late May to mid-September); **Gatton Creek** ($7; no water; open late May to mid-September); and **Willaby** ($7 for walk-in sites, $12.50 for RVs and cars; open mid-April to mid-November). Willaby is the nicest of these and has a boat ramp. Olympic National Park campgrounds are more scattered, and all three are open year-round. **July Creek** ($10) is a walk-in campground on the north shore of the lake. **Graves Creek** ($10) is near the end of the South Shore Rd., 15 miles from the Hwy. 101 turnoff. The free **North Fork Campground** is at the end of the North Shore Rd. and does not have running water. Not recommended for RVs.

Park RVs at the private **Rain Forest Resort** on the South Shore Rd., tel. (360) 288-2535 or (800) 255-6936, the only campground with showers. More RV parking at **Amanda Park Motel,** tel. (360) 288-2237, on the west end of the lake.

Food

Get groceries at the **Mercantile,** just up the road from Quinault Lodge. Their snack bar sells pizzas, burgers, and sandwiches. Quite good meals are available at **Quinault Lodge,** tel. (360) 288-2571, and just up the road at **Rain Forest Resort,** tel. (360) 288-2535. The tiny village of Amanda Park on the west end of the lake along Hwy. 101 has a fine old country store with narrow aisles and sloping wooden floors.

Information and Services

The Forest Service's **Quinault Ranger District Office,** tel. (360) 288-2525, next door to Quinault Lodge on the south side of the lake, is open daily 8 a.m.-4:30 p.m. from Labor Day to Memorial Day, and Mon.-Fri. 8 a.m.-4:30 p.m. the rest of the year. They have a plethora of informative handouts, and offer guided nature walks and talks at the lodge April to September.

The Olympic National Park **Quinault River Ranger Station** is 5.5 miles up North Fork Rd. and open daily 9 a.m.-5 p.m. June to Labor Day, and intermittently the rest of the year. Stop by for

brochures, maps, and information on the park. The area around the station is a good place to see elk, especially in early summer and after September.

In Amanda Park along Hwy. 101, the small **Quinault Rain Forest Visitor Information Center** is open summers only. Not far away, you'll find the essentials: a motel, library, church, school, general store, gas station, post office, cafe, and liquor store.

Transportation

A paved road circles Lake Quinault, with side routes up both the East and North Fork of the Quinault River for a total of 31 scenic miles. This makes a great bike ride. One of the nicest sections is up the South Shore Rd., which passes scenic **Merriman Falls** and continues through towering old growth forests to the Graves Creek Campground.

West Jefferson Transit, tel. (800) 436-3950, provides free daily bus service between Forks and the Amanda Park. Continue southward from Lake Quinault on **Grays Harbor Transit,** tel. (360) 532-2770 or (800) 562-9730, to Moclips, Ocean Shores, and Aberdeen.

Quinault to Grays Harbor

After Lake Quinault Hwy. 101 continues through the forest that has been clear-cut in many places and passes through the minuscule settlements of **Nielton** and **Humptulips** before finally arriving at Hoquiam. Nielton has old-fashioned country stores and lots of "we support the timber industry" yard signs. Camping is available just west of here at **Humptulips Recreation Area** and Rayonier's **Promised Land Park,** just north of town on Stevens Creek. Take a good country road (paved) off Hwy. 101 for the beach at Humptulips, or continue to Hoquiam and turn back west of Hwy. 109.

NORTH BEACH

Grays Harbor—one of just three deepwater ports on the West Coast—forms the southern border to the Olympic Peninsula. The north-western part of the bay and the Pacific Coast north to the Quinault Indian Reservation is commonly called North Beach. Towns included in this 22-mile long stretch of beachfront are Moclips, Pacific Beach, Copalis Beach, Ocean City, and Ocean Shores.

The drive from Moclips south to Ocean Shores marks the transition from the timber-dominated lands of the Olympic Peninsula to beachside resorts. Between Moclips and Copalis Beach, Hwy. 109 winds along the crest of a steep bluff, with dramatic views of the coastline (and more than a few recent clearcuts in the

other direction). From Copalis Beach southward to Ocean Shores, the country is far less interesting and the highway straightens out on the nearly level land. The broad sandy beaches are backed by grassy dunes and fronted by summer and retirement homes. The entire 22 miles of beach between Moclips and Ocean Shores is open to the public, with various vehicle entry points along the way. Check with the Ocean Shores Chamber of Commerce for a map of access points, seasons of use, and driving rules. (Forty percent of the beach is closed to vehicles between April 15 and Labor Day, when access is restricted to pedestrians only.)

Some commercial development has occurred along this stretch, but the only significant development is Ocean Shores. This resort/residential complex was developed as a summer resort area in the '60s and '70s and has never become as popular as its developers expected, in part because of the overcast, damp, windy weather, and in part because it lacks the offshore rugged beauty of, say, a Cannon Beach, Oregon. Still, it is one of the most popular resort areas on the Washington coast.

MOCLIPS, PACIFIC BEACH, AND TAHOLAH

Two small settlements, Moclips and Pacific Beach, occupy the northern end of the North Beach region, with a handful of stores, lodging places, and cafes. Moclips is connected to Hwy. 101 by the 20-mile-long Moclips-Quinalt Road. Ten of these miles are on a sometimes-rutted gravel road; nearly all of this time you'll be heading through clearcuts, logging slash, and scrubby trees. Early in this century, Moclips was home to a major destination resort, with a 285-room hotel and an end-of-the-line railway station for excursions trains from Seattle. The building was destroyed one violently stormy winter day in 1904 when ocean waves eroded away the cliff sending the hotel to the rocks below. It was never rebuilt.

NORTH BEACH ACCOMMODATIONS

Accommodations are arranged from least to most expensive within each town. Many places in Ocean Shores have a two-night minimum stay on weekends and during July and August. Rates may be lower during the winter months and on weekdays in the summer. The area code is 360.

OCEAN SHORES

Oceanside Motel; 773 Ocean Shores Blvd. NW; tel. 289-2040 or (800) 562-6373; $20 s or d without TV, $30 s or d with TV; ocean front location, jacuzzi, game room

Ebb Tide Motel; 839 Ocean Shores Blvd. NW; tel. 289-3700; $35-79 s or d; ocean views, fireplaces, kitchens

Vagabond House; 686 Ocean Shores Blvd. NW; tel. 289-2350; $36-130 s or d; kitchenettes available

Ocean Sands Motel; Ocean Shores Blvd.; tel. 289-3585 or (800) 404-3585; $45 s or d; kitchenettes available

Silver King Motel; 1070 Discovery Ave. SE (five miles south of town); tel. 289-3386 or (800) 562-6001; $45-75 s or d; next to marina, condo motel, kitchenettes available

Gitche Gumee Motel; 648 Ocean Shores Blvd. NW; tel. 289-3323 or (800) 448-2433; $45-85 s or d in condo motel, $130 s or d for one-bedroom townhouse; indoor and outdoor pools, saunas, kitchenettes, fireplaces, AAA approved

Offshore Motel; 165 N.W. Barnacle St.; tel. 289-2249 or (800) 562-9748; $49-59 s or d; kitchenettes available

Sands Resort; 801 Ocean Shores Blvd. NW; tel. 289-2444 or (800) 841-4001; $49-85 s or d; ocean views, indoor pool, game room, hot tub, sauna, kitchenettes available

Royal Pacific Motel; 781 Ocean Shores Blvd. NW; tel. 289-3306 or (800) 562-9748; $49-89 s or d; ocean views, outdoor pool, kitchenettes available

Discovery Inn; 1031 Discovery Ave. SE (five miles south); tel. 289-3371 or (800) 882-8821; $52-78 s or d; condo motel on marina, outdoor pool, jacuzzi, playground, AAA approved

Westerly Motel; 870 Ocean Shores Blvd. NW; tel. 289-3711; $54-64 s or d; kitchenettes available

Chris' by the Sea Motel; 17 Chickiman Rd., tel. 289-3066 or (800) 446-5747; $55 s or d; kitchenettes available

Ocean Shores Motel; 681 Ocean Shores Blvd. NW; tel. 289-3351 or (800) 464-2526; $58-85 s or d; ocean front location, kitchenettes available, jacuzzi rooms available

Weatherly Inn Condos; 201 Ocean Shores Blvd. SW; tel. 289-3088 or (800) 562-8612; $60-150 s or d; ocean front location, indoor pool, hot tub, sauna, fitness room, game room, kitchenettes

Polynesian Condominium Resort; 615 Ocean Shores Blvd. NW; tel. 289-3361 or (800) 562-4836; $69-92 s or d for motel rooms or suites; indoor pool, sauna, jacuzzi, fireplaces, balconies, kitchenettes available, AAA approved

Chalet Village; 659 Ocean Shores Blvd. NW.; tel. 289-4297 or (800) 303-4297; $75-85 s or d; cabins with kitchenettes and fireplaces

Canterbury Inn; 643 Ocean Shores Blvd. NW; tel. 289-3317 or (800) 562-6678; $78-118 s or d; on the beach, indoor pool, hot tub, private balconies, two-bedroom suites with full kitchen and fireplace, two-night minimum stay on weekends, AAA approved

Casa Del Oro; 665 Point Brown Ave. NW; tel. 289-2281 or (800) 291-2281; $85 s or d; kitchenettes available

Nautilus Motel; 835 Ocean Shores Blvd. NW; tel. 289-2722 or (800) 221-4541; $90-120 s or d; condo motel, kitchenettes available

Best Western Lighthouse Suites Inn; 491 Damon Rd.; tel. 289-2311 or (800) 757-7873; $97-157 s or d; new motel, ocean views, indoor pool, jacuzzi, sauna, exercise room, AAA approved

Grey Gull Motel; 651 Ocean Shores Blvd. SW; tel. 289-3381 or (800) 562-9712; $98-129 s or d; efficiencies, one- and two-bedroom suites, or penthouses, ocean vistas, kitchens, fireplaces, outdoor pool, sauna, two-night minimum stay on weekends, AAA approved

Shilo Inn; 707 Ocean Shores Blvd. NW; tel. 289-4600 or (800) 222-2244; $99-179 s or d; new motel, indoor pool, sauna, jacuzzi, steam room, exercise facility, continental breakfast, AAA approved

Caroline Inn; 1341 Ocean Shores Blvd. SW; tel. 289-0450; $140 s or d; ocean view, one-bedroom suites, kitchens, heart-shaped jacuzzis

OCEAN CITY

North Beach Motel; tel. 289-4116 or (800) 640-8053; $30-35 s or d; kitchenettes available

West Winds Resort Motel; tel. 289-3448; $32-60 s or d; cabins and motel rooms, kitchenettes available

Blue Pacific Motel; tel. 289-2262; $37 s, $40 d; kitchenettes available

Pacific Sands Resort; tel. 289-3588; $40-55 s or d; outdoor pool, kitchenettes available

COPALIS BEACH

Linda's Low Tide Motel; tel. 289-3450; $30-60 s or d; open March-Nov. only

Shades by the Sea Motel; tel. 289-3358; $40-80 s or d; kitchenettes available

Dunes RV Resort & Motel; tel. 289-3873; $50 s or d; kitchenettes

Beachwood Resort; tel. 289-2177; $50-75 s or d; outdoor pool, hot tub, sauna, mini-golf, kitchenettes

Iron Springs Resort; tel. 276-4230; $55-120 s or d; family cottages with ocean views, indoor pool, kitchens, three-night minimum stay in summer

PACIFIC BEACH

Shoreline Motel; 12 1st St. S; tel. 276-4433; $45 s or d; ocean views, kitchenettes available

Sand Dollar Motel; 2nd and Central; tel. 276-4525; $43-53 s or d in motel rooms; $70-100 in cabins with ocean views, kitchenettes

Sandpiper Resort; 1.5 miles south; tel. 276-4580; $55-160 s or d; ocean views, family resort, kitchenettes, fireplaces, no TVs or phones, book far ahead, two-night minimum stay on weekends

MOCLIPS

Moclips Motel; 4852 Pacific Ave.; tel. 276-4228; $35-60 s or d; kitchenettes available

Moonstone Beach Motel; 4849 Pacific Ave.; tel. 276-4346; $43-57 s or d in motel rooms, $60-65 s or d in cabins; along beach, kitchenettes

Barnacle Motel; 4816 Pacific Ave.; tel. 276-4318; $45-60 s or d; two units with kitchenettes, fireplace

Ocean Crest Resort; Sunset Beach; tel. 276-4465; $54-108 s or d; fine beachside resort, indoor pool, sauna, jacuzzi, exercise room, fireplaces, kitchens, AAA approved

O'Brien's; tel. 276-4676; $65-75 s or d; two-bedroom house (sleeps six), kitchen, woodstove

Hi Tide Ocean Beach Resort; 4890 Railroad Ave.; tel. 276-4142 or (800) 662-5477; $79-89 s or d; next to ocean, one- and two-bedroom suites, kitchens, decks, AAA approved

The shabby and badly littered village of Taholah is situated on the south bank of the Quinault River mouth, nine miles north of Moclips. This is the main settlement on the **Quinault Indian Reservation.** Come here in the fall to watch the fishermen netting salmon in the river, and stop by the tribal headquarters if you want to head out on the reservation or to request beach access. Taholah has no tourist facilities of any kind, though you might visit **Quinault Pride,** tel. (360) 276-4431 or (800) 821-8650, where smoked salmon and other seafood are processed. A spiderweb of logging roads covers the entire reservation, and the once grand forests here are long gone.

Practicalities

See the "North Beach Accommodations" chart for a list of local places to stay.

Pacific Beach State Park, tel. (360) 289-3553, in Pacific Beach offers surf fishing, clamming, and beachcombing with beachfront campsites. The nine-acre park is really little more than a parking area for RVs and has no protection from the wind. Open for day-use and camping late February to October, and on weekends and holidays the rest of the year. Call (800) 452-5687 for campsite reservations ($6 extra fee), available up to 11 months ahead of time.

For ocean-view dining at the north end, try the excellent **Ocean Crest Restaurant** at the resort in Moclips, tel. (360) 276-4465. Open for three meals, the varied dinner menu features Northwest specialties such as Willapa Bay oysters, trout, quail, steak, and seafood, with weekend entertainment in the lounge.

Grays Harbor Transit, tel. (360) 532-2770 or (800) 562-9730, has daily service throughout the entire county, including North Beach from Ocean Shores to Taholah, for 25 cents.

Events

The **Chief Taholah Day Celebration** in early July features Indian arts and crafts, a powwow, salmon bake, canoe races, a parade, and games on the reservation. The **Kelper's Parade & Celebration** is Pacific Beach's festival, which features two parades on Labor Day weekend. It's followed in mid-September by a **Sandcastle Sculpture Contest** that is open to everyone.

COPALIS BEACH AND OCEAN CITY

The dinky town of Copalis Beach has a cluster of older buildings on the Copalis River, along with RV parks, motels, and gift shops. Ocean City, three miles farther south, is a bit larger and has simple homes set in the trees. This decidedly unpretentious town contrasts sharply with its bigger and newer neighbor to the south, Ocean Shores; there's probably more character in a few of the buildings here than in all of Ocean Shores. The **Anderson Cabin,** on the east side of the highway, tel. (360) 289-3842, is open in the summer. Built of beach logs in the 1920s, the cabin contains period furnishings and a display on local author Norah Berg.

Copalis Beach and Ocean City are "Home of the Razor Clam." The State Dept. of Fisheries sponsors clam-digging clinics and beach walks throughout the summer at Ocean City State Park to better prepare you for the short, intense razor clam season; call (360) 249-4628.

State Parks

Just west of Copalis Beach, **Griffiths-Priday State Park** is a day-use facility for picnicking, kite flying, beachcombing, surf fishing, and bird-watching at the mouth of the Copalis River. The Copalis Spit is one of three snowy plover breeding grounds on the Washington coast. These birds—an endangered species—are very sensitive to human intrusion. To protect them, large areas of the beach north of the park entrance are closed to the public—from the high-tide mark to the dunes—between mid-March and late August. The restricted areas are marked on the map at the park entrance. A boardwalk leads to the beach where you can dig for razor clams below the tide line.

Accommodations and Campgrounds

See the "North Beach Accommodations" chart for a listing of local motels.

Ocean City State Park ($10 tent, $15 RV; year-round) is 14 miles to the south and features coin-operated showers. Call (800) 452-5687 for campsite reservations ($6 extra fee), available up to 11 months ahead of time.

Private RV parks in Copalis Beach include:

Copalis Beach RV Park, tel. (360) 289-2707; **Driftwood Acres,** tel. (360) 289-3484; **Dunes RV Resort,** tel. (360) 289-3873; **Riverside RV Park,** tel. (360) 289-2111; **Rod's Beach Resort,** tel. (360) 289-2222; **Shade's by the Sea Motel & RV Park,** tel. (360) 289-3358. In Ocean City: **Lookout RV Park,** tel. (360) 289-2220; **Ocean Mist Resort,** tel. (360) 289-3656; **Silver Maple Trailer Park,** tel. (360) 289-0166; **Sturgeon Trailer Harbor,** tel. (360) 289-2101; and **Blue Pacific Motel and Trailer Park,** tel. (360) 289-2262.

Other Practicalities

Ocean City's **Fine Art Bakery & Cafe** serves a big country breakfast all day, plus lunch and dinner specials, including great clam chowder. The bakery cranks out delicious fresh breads and sweet rolls. In Copalis Beach, try **Copalis Beach Restaurant and Lounge,** tel. (360) 289-2240, for three meals a day.

Ocean City sponsors the area's **Fourth of July** fireworks and picnic, with live music, arts and crafts, and helicopter rides. In early August, Copalis Beach comes alive with **Copalis Days,** featuring a car parade, street dancing, and food booths. Head to Copalis Beach on Labor Day weekend in September for a popular **Sand-sculpture Contest** with contestants of all levels of ability.

Grays Harbor Transit, tel. (360) 532-2770 or (800) 562-9730, has daily service throughout the entire county, including North Beach from Ocean Shores to Taholah, for 25 cents.

OCEAN SHORES

The summer-home/retirement community of Ocean Shores (pop. 2,800) occupies the six-mile dune-covered peninsula at the north side of the entrance to Grays Harbor. It's an odd place out here so far from other developments, with a big gate that welcomes visitors, businesses strewn along a wide main drag, and homes on a network of 23 miles of canals. Some of these homes are elaborate contemporary structures, other lots simply have a concrete pad to park an RV, and many more feature for-sale signs. Many of the working folks live in trailer parks in nearby

Ocean City. Two main roads head down the peninsula: the four-lane Ocean Shores Blvd. near the shore, and the bumpy Point Brown Ave. in the center. The latter follows the canals to the marina area. There are no trees on the east side of the peninsula, just low sand dunes.

History

Built on a 6,000-acre, six-mile-long peninsula, Ocean Shores was Indian clam-digging grounds until May 7, 1792, when Robert Gray's ship *Columbia Rediviva* found the harbor entrance. Gray's discovery led to a slow settlement of the area, started in 1860 by the peninsula's original homesteader, Matthew McGee, and followed shortly thereafter by A.O. Damon, who bought the southern tip of the peninsula from McGee. It wasn't until 1970 that Ocean Shores became an incorporated city, after investors bought the 6,000 acres from Damon's grandchildren and began selling lots for $595 and up. They dredged freshwater canals into the center of the peninsula, along with a four-mile-long lake with islands. An airport was built, four-lane highways constructed, and hotels and restaurants soon lined the beach. The development still has many empty lots and there's a lot of beachfront property available, but the town is growing as a destination and is now one of the most popular in Washington. More than three million visitors come to Ocean Shores annually.

Sights

The **Ocean Shores Environmental Interpretative Center,** 1013 Catala Ave. SE (five miles south of town center, at the marina), tel. (360) 289-4617, features saltwater and freshwater aquariums and displays on the history of the area, how the peninsula was formed, and how it continues to grow as sand is added each year. Other exhibits detail the birds, fish, shellfish, and other animals of the area, and you can also watch the natural history slide shows. The center is open Wed.-Sun. 11 a.m.-6 p.m. Memorial Day to Labor Day, and closed the rest of the year.

A pair of wildlife reserves on the southern end of the peninsula offers outstanding bird-watching—more than 200 species have been recorded. **Damon Point** (a.k.a. Protection Is-

DAMON RD.

POST OFFICE

NAUTILUS MOTEL

OCEAN SANDS MOTEL

VISITOR INFORMATION CENTER

OCEAN SHORES BLVD.

SANDS RESORT

ROYAL PACIFIC MOTEL

OCEAN SHORES MOTEL

CONVENTION CENTER

SHORES MALL

LIBRARY

CHANCE A LA MER

POINT BROWN AVE.

CHALET VILLAGE

VAGABOND HOUSE

GREY GULL MOTEL

GITCHE GUMEE MOTEL

CANTERBURY INN

POLYNESIAN CONDOMINIUM RESORT

OCEAN SHORES

SEE DETAIL

DAMON RD.

115

TO OCEAN CITY STATE PARK, OCEAN CITY, AND ABERDEEN

BEACH ACCESS

POINT BROWN AVE.

CHANCE A LA MER

NORTH BAY AVE.

MINARD

ALBATROSS ST.

OCEAN SHORES GOLF COURSE

PARKWAY

OCEAN LAKE WAY

BEACH ACCESS

OCEAN SHORES BLVD.

PT. BROWN DR.

CANAL DR.

DUCK LAKE DR.

DUCK LAKE

TAURUS ST.

MT. OLYMPUS AVE.

DISCOVERY AVE.

MARINE VIEW DR.

PT. BROWN AVE.

ENVIRONMENTAL INTERPRETIVE CENTER

MARINA

DAMON POINT

OYHUT WILDLIFE RECREATION AREA

SPORTSMEN WAY

OCEAN SHORES BLVD.

OCEAN SHORES BLVD. E

GRAYS HARBOR

POINT BROWN

NORTH JETTY

OCEAN

PACIFIC

0   1 mi

0   1 km

land) is an important breeding area for the rare snowy plover (their northernmost nesting area) and semipalmated plovers (their southernmost nesting area). This is the only place in the world where both species coexist as breeding birds. Parts of the 300-acre preserve are closed March-Sept. to protect the plovers, but the wet sands in the tidal zone are open to fishing and walking. The 682-acre **Oyhut Wildlife Recreation Area** (sometimes spelled "Oyehut")at the south end of the peninsula is another good place for birdwatching, with trails through the marshy landscape.

Also on the south end of the peninsula, **North Jetty** reaches a mile out into the Pacific and is a great place to fish, watch storm waves, or enjoy the sunset.

Two miles north of Ocean Shores on Hwy. 115, **Ocean City State Park,** tel. (360) 289-3553, has campsites close to the town's restaurants and shops. Open year-round, the park has camping in the trees, picnicking, two little ponds for birdwatching, and a path leading through the dunes to the beach. No vehicle access here, but there are six access points in Ocean Shores—just head south along Ocean Shores Blvd. and look for the turnoffs. Signs are posted with beach driving regulations and safety warnings.

With all that ocean out there, it's easy to overlook Ocean Shores' six-mile-long **Duck Lake,** but it's a haven for small boats, canoes, anglers (trout, bass, and crappie are all here), swimmers, and water-skiers. You can launch your boat from City Park, at Albatross and Chance à la Mer, or Chinook Park Boat Launch on Duck Lake Drive. At the south end, the lake connects with a maze of canals that lead past housing developments. Pick up a map before heading out, since these channels can be confusing.

Recreation
Beachcombing is a favorite activity on the six miles of sandy beach along Ocean Shores, as is digging for razor clams in season (generally in March and October). Check with the chamber of commerce for the regulations and where to buy a license. Rent boats and canoes from **Summer Sails,** tel. (360) 289-2884, located on the canal at the south end of Pt. Brown Avenue. Several local companies offer horseback rides along the shore: **Nan-Sea Stable,** tel. (360)

289-0194, **Seahorse Ranch,** tel. (360) 532-6791, and **Chenois Creek Horse Rentals,** tel. (360) 533-5591.

Ocean Shores is a great place for kite flying, with strong offshore winds much of the year. If you didn't bring your own, head to one of the three local kite shops: **Cutting Edge Kites,** 676 Ocean Shores Blvd. NW, tel. (360) 289-0667; **Winds Northwest,** 420 Damon Rd., tel. (360) 289-4578; and **Ocean Shores Kites,** Ocean Shore Mall, tel. (360) 289-4103.

At Canal and Albatross in Ocean Shores, **Ocean Shores Golf Course,** tel. (360) 289-3357, is an 18-hole championship course open to the public.

Olympic Outdoor, 773 Pt. Brown Ave. NW, tel. (360) 289-3736, rents mountain bikes and mopeds. You can also rent mopeds from **O.W.W. Inc.,** at the Shores Mall on Chance à la Mer, tel. (360) 289-3830.

Few charter fishing boats operate from the Ocean Shores side of Grays Harbor; head to Westport (later in this chapter) instead. A summertime passenger ferry (see "Transportation," below) connects Ocean Shores with Westport, but it does not arrive in time for the early morning departures of most Westport charter boats.

Accommodations
Ocean Shores has more than two dozen motels, along with dozens more private home rentals. See the "North Beach Accommodations" chart for a listing of these. **Ocean Shores Reservations Bureau,** tel. (360) 289-2430 or (800) 562-8612, is very helpful and can make reservations at many of these motels. They also rent houses and condos in the $100-200 range. **Ocean Front Beach Rentals,** tel. (360) 289-3568 or (800) 544-8887, has many more condo and home rentals in the same price range. Other reservation services are: **Chris' by the Sea,** tel. (360) 289-3066 or (800) 446-5747, **Destination Ocean Shores,** tel. (360) 289-8795, and **Ocean View Resort Homes,** tel. (360) 289-4416 or (800) 927-6394. Note that many places have a two-night minimum stay on weekends and during July and August, and a three-night minimum on holidays. On holidays, the chamber of commerce keeps track of room availability; call them at (360) 289-0226 or (800) 762-3224.

Campgrounds

Camp year-round at **Ocean City State Park,** two miles north of Ocean Shores. Both tent ($10) and RV sites ($15) are available, along with coin-operated showers. Find more campsites at **Pacific Beach State Park,** 14 miles north in the town of Pacific Beach (see above). Call (800) 452-5687 for state park campsite reservations ($6 extra fee), available up to 11 months ahead of time. The nearest private RV park—**Yesterday's RV Park**—is in Oyehut, just north of Ocean Shores, tel. (360) 289-8657 or (800) 242-8795.

Food

Our Place, 676 Ocean Shores Blvd. NW, tel. (360) 289-8763, is a tiny eatery with inexpensive but filling breakfasts and all-American lunches. Get good breakfasts and lunches along with excellent seafood chowder at **Barnacle Bill's,** 880 Point Brown Ave. NE, tel. (360) 289-0218. **The Home Port Restaurant,** 857 Pt. Brown Ave., tel. (360) 289-2600, serves three meals including good breakfasts and specialties such as salmon, Dungeness crab, and steak and lobster dinners.

Very good south-of-the-border meals at **Las Marachas Mexican Restaurant,** 729 Point Brown Ave. NW, tel. (360) 289-2054. For pizza, head to **Dugan's,** 690 Ocean Shores Blvd. NW, tel. (360) 289-2330.

Mariah's tel. (360) 289-3315, at the Polynesian Resort, is the most upscale local restaurant, with good seafood, steak, and pasta, along with a weekend breakfast buffet. The lounge has live music Friday and Saturday evenings.

Mike's Seafood, 830 Point Brown Ave. NE, tel. (360) 289-0532, has a stand selling fresh-cooked crab. Several places have fish and chips in town; a good one is **Flipper's Fish Bar,** 185 W. Chance à la Mer NW, tel. (360) 289-4676. And if you just want something quick, Ocean Shores has a McDonald's.

Events

Ocean Shores hosts an annual **Beachcombers Fun Fair** at the convention center in early March. See displays of glass floats and driftwood art, and sample the fresh seafood. Ocean Shores' annual **Festival of Colors,** held each May, is family fun with a sandcastle contest, arts and crafts bazaar, and kite festival. In late July, the leather-jacket crowd rolls into Ocean Shores for the **Harley Owners Group Sun & Surf Run,** an event that attracts 2,000 bikes and riders. It's followed in mid-August by the **Pacific Northwest Kite Festival,** with displays at the convention center and colorful kites filling the air on the shore. The **Dixieland Jazz Festival** in early November features acts from all over the Northwest at the convention center and around town.

Shopping

Ocean Shores' **Shores Mall** has bike and moped rentals, a kite shop, bank, clothing store, and state liquor store on Chance à la Mer, just before the beach. In Homeport Plaza on Pt. Brown Ave., Ocean Shores' **Gallery Marjuli,** tel. (360) 289-2858, is open daily with art and gifts created by Northwest artists. **Tide Creations Gift Shop,** tel. (360) 289-2550, near the marina on Pt. Brown Ave., has thousands of items, from kites and windsocks to fudge.

Information and Services

Get information from the helpful folks at **Ocean Shores Chamber of Commerce Visitor Information Center,** 899 Pt. Brown Ave., just inside the entry archway on the right, tel. (360) 289-0226 or (800) 762-3224. Open daily 9 a.m.-4 p.m. year-round.

The **Washington Coast Chamber of Commerce,** has a small information center three miles north of town on Hwy. 109, tel. (360) 289-4552 or (800) 286-4552. Open Thurs.-Mon. 11 a.m.-5 p.m. summers, and Fri.-Sat. 11 a.m.-5 p.m. the rest of the year.

The new **Ocean Shores Library** is at 573 Pt. Brown Ave. NW, tel. (360) 289-3919. The telephone **area code** is 360.

Transportation

Grays Harbor Transit, tel. (360) 532-2770 or (800) 562-9730, has daily bus service throughout the entire county, including North Beach from Ocean Shores to Taholah, along with Aberdeen, Hoquiam, Lake Quinault, and even Olympia. Fares are a mere 25 cents. Ocean Shores has an airport, but no commercial service.

The **Westport-Ocean Shores Passenger Ferry,** El Matador, is a 74-foot passenger boat with service to Westport for $8 roundtrip ($4.50 one-way), and free for kids under five. Gray whales are often seen along the way. The ferry leaves six times a day and takes 20-40 minutes, with daily service mid-June to Labor Day, and weekend-only service early May to mid-June and in September. No service the rest of the year. The boat leaves from the marina; get tickets at Silver King Motel, 1070 Discovery Ave. SE, tel. (360) 289-3386.

Scoot around town on a moped rented from **O.W.W. Inc.** on Chance à la Mer, tel. (360) 289-

3830. Mopeds and bicycles can also be rented at the Shores Mall in Ocean Shores.

To get to any of the central or southern Washington beaches, just follow the green or brown "Beach" signs pointing seaward from the beachfront highway, in this case Hwy. 109. The advantages of state parks are restrooms, camping facilities (usually), and sometimes no vehicle access to the beach—a plus or a minus depending on your perspective.

GRAYS HARBOR AND VICINITY

Grays Harbor has long been a major center for the timber industry, and the surrounding country bears witness to this. Heading toward Aberdeen and Hoquiam from any direction leads you through mile after mile of tree farms, with second- or third-growth forests interspersed with newly logged hillsides. Logging and fishing have long been the primary focus of workers here, and remain so.

ABERDEEN AND HOQUIAM

Aberdeen and Hoquiam (HO-qwee-um) are twin cities on the easterly tip of Grays Harbor; Aberdeen is the larger of the two, with a population of 17,000, almost doubling the 9,000 of Hoquiam. The population is clustered along the eastern end of Grays Harbor where the rivers come into the harbor. The Hoquiam River separates Hoquiam from Aberdeen. The area could easily be called another Tri-Cities because a third town, Cosmopolis (pop. 1,400), is just across the Chehalis River from Aberdeen. These are not tourist towns, but a number of attractions are worth a visit.

With the recent drastic reduction in timber harvesting and the poor salmon runs of late, the towns have fallen on hard times as timber industry workers are forced to retrain and go into other lines of work. The hard times show on these struggling, working-class milltowns, but folks aren't giving up. Aberdeen has a downtown core of long-established businesses in solid brick buildings, the ubiquitous mega-marts on the outskirts, and a bevy of tidy but plain working-class homes. Downtown Hoquiam is smaller,

with the Hoquiam River winding through. An observation tower at 8th St. Landing provides a view up the river (and a fine pigeon roosting place as evidenced by the thick layer of droppings).

History
Grays Harbor was discovered by, and named for, Capt. Robert Gray, an American en route to China to trade sea otter pelts for tea. On May 7, 1792, Gray sailed his ship, *Columbia Rediviva,* across the bar and into the harbor, had a look around, calling it a "safe harbor, well sheltered from the sea," and continued on his way. A few days later he discovered the mouth of the Columbia River, another major feature missed by Capt. James Vancouver, who had passed by a few weeks earlier.

The first European to settle in the area is believed to be William O'Leary in 1843, but the first real settlement began in 1859 when James Karr and his family arrived just ahead of a family of four brothers named Campbell. They used the local Chehalis Indians' name for the area; Hoquiam meant "hungry for wood" because they collected driftwood there for their fires. In another 10 years the site had grown enough to deserve a post office, and in 1873 the first school opened.

A plat for a city named Wishkah was filed on December 18, 1883, but few liked the name, so on February, 16, 1884, the plat was re-filed as Aberdeen in honor of the Aberdeen Packing Company of Ilwaco that had a plant on the Wishkah River near its junction with the Chehalis River. (The Scottish name means, fittingly enough, "where two rivers merge.") After a dev-

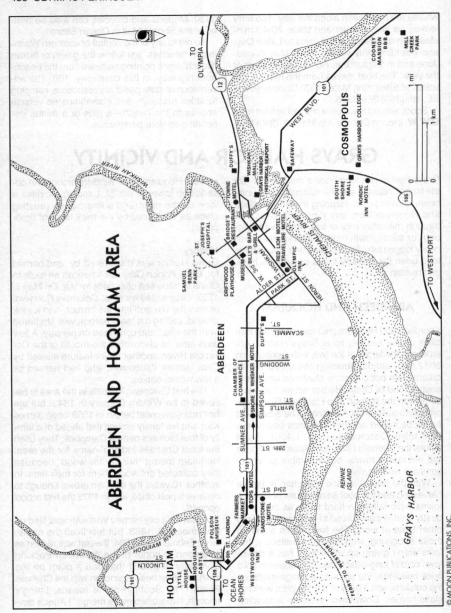

ABERDEEN AND HOQUIAM AREA

HOQUIAM

WISHKAH RIVER

TO OLYMPIA

COSMOPOLIS

COONEY MANSION B&B

MILL CREEK PARK

WEST BLVD.

GRAYS HARBOR COLLEGE

SAFEWAY

DUFFY'S

WISHKAH MALL

TODAY'S GRAYS HARBOR HISTORICAL SEAPORT

TOWNE MOTEL

SOUTH SHORE MALL

NORDIC INN MOTEL

CHEHALIS RIVER

TO WESTPORT

BRIDGE'S RESTAURANT

ST. JOSEPH'S HOSPITAL

SAMUEL BENN PARK

DRIFTWOOD PLAYHOUSE

BILLY'S BAR & GRILL

MUSEUM

RED LION MOTEL

TRAVELURE MOTEL

OLYMPIC INN

ABERDEEN

ALDER ST.

3rd ST. WISHKAH

PARK ST.

HERON ST.

SCAMMEL ST.

DUFFY'S

CHAMBER OF COMMERCE

WOODING MOTEL

SNORE & WHISKER MOTEL

SUMNER AVE.

SIMPSON AVE.

MYRTLE ST.

28TH ST.

23RD ST.

RENNIE ISLAND

GRAYS HARBOR

FARMERS MARKET

TOPS MOTEL

SANDSTONE MOTEL

6th ST. LANDING

WESTWOOD INN

TO OCEAN SHORES

FERRY TO WESTPORT

POLSON MUSEUM

HOQUIAM RIVER

HOQUIAM'S CASTLE

LYTLE HOUSE

LINCOLN ST.

TO OLYMPIA

101

109

© MOON PUBLICATIONS, INC.

0   1 mi

0   1 km

astating fire destroyed Aberdeen's business district in 1903, the downtown was rebuilt using brick, and many of these buildings still stand.

From the beginning it was wood that kept the towns going. The area is rich with Douglas fir, cedar, hemlock, and spruce, and several of the major timber companies—notably Weyerhaeuser and Rayonier—own thousands of acres of tree farms nearby. Grays Harbor is a major shipping port for logs and lumber headed to Asian markets. The enormous Weyerhaeuser pulp mill in Cosmopolis stretches along Hwy. 101 for almost a mile, and Grays Harbor Paper still belches smoke into the sky. Befitting the logging heritage, the Grays Harbor College teams call themselves the "Chokers."

Grays Harbor Historical Seaport

Early in 1788, two ships—the *Lady Washington* and *Columbia Rediviva*—sailed around South America and north to the west coast of the new world. Commanded by Capt. Robert Gray, the vessels were the first American ships to land on these shores and were instrumental in later claims to this land. Shipbuilding was later an important industry in Aberdeen; some 130 ships were built in the shipyards here between 1887 and 1920.

To celebrate Washington's centennial in 1989, a magnificent full-scale replica of the 107-ton *Lady Washington* was constructed to serve as the central part of Aberdeen's Grays Harbor Historical Seaport. (You may recognize her from the 1994 film, *Star Trek Generations*.) The *Lady Washington* sails to various seaports all over America and even as far away as Japan, sometimes with her two 26-foot longboats. The ship is in port at Aberdeen only one or two months a year, but if it happens to be here, be sure to take a free tour (a fee is charged in other ports). The ship is used as a living-history vessel for school groups, and older volunteers can join the crew for two weeks of first-hand shipboard life. This is not for everyone—simple food, cramped quarters, limited water, and lots of hard work—but at least you aren't subjected to floggings or surgery without anesthetics. No grog either. You'll need to pay $250 for food and other necessities (including the Coast Guard's required drug test), and be willing to help with guided tours and other activities along with traditional seamanship. This is an incredible chance to learn about sailing the old-fashioned way. For details on volunteering, along with an itinerary schedule of this year's voyages, call (360) 532-8611. The ship docks at Grays Harbor Historical Seaport, on Heron St. at the mouth of the Wishram River. The smaller *Sylvia*, a privately owned vessel from the 1880s, also docks here.

Mansions and Museums

In 1897, lumber baron Robert Lytle built **Hoquiam's Castle,** a 20-room Victorian beauty at 515 Chenault Ave. in Hoquiam. The stunning three-story mansion has been restored to its original luster, with the original oak woodwork, and completely furnished in turn-of-the-century antiques, Tiffany-style lamps, and cut-crystal chandeliers. Open daily 10 a.m.-5 p.m. in the summer, and Sat.-Sun. 11 a.m.-5 p.m. the rest of the year, closed in December. Entrance is $4 for adults, $1 for kids, tel. (360) 533-2005. Half-hour tours are offered throughout the day. For tours, ring the doorbell and be ready to wait up to 15 minutes. The hillside mansion overlooks town and has a distinctive monkey-puzzle tree outside. Right next door is the equally elegant Lytle House B&B, built for Robert Lytle's brother (see below).

Another wealthy lumber magnate, Alex Polson, once owned the largest logging operation in the world, Polson Logging Company (now a

LOUISE FOOTE

part of Rayonier). In 1923 he funded the building of a home for his son and daughter-in-law on property adjoining his own house. This 26-room mansion at 1611 Riverside Ave. in Hoquiam is now the **Polson Museum.** Alex Polson's own home was razed after his death in 1939; his widow didn't want anyone else to live in it. The site of their home is now a small park with a rose garden, historic logging equipment, and a blacksmith shop. The museum, tel. (360) 533-5862, houses all sorts of memorabilia: a magnificent old grandfather clock, a fun model railroad, a model of an old logging camp, a two-man chainsaw, and even an old boxing bag. Open Wed.-Sun. 11 a.m.-4 p.m. June to Labor Day, and Sat.-Sun. noon-4 p.m. the rest of the year; $2 for adults, 50 cents for children.

In the old National Guard Armory at 117 E. 3rd St., the **Aberdeen Museum of History,** tel. (360) 533-1976, has exhibits of local history including a turn-of-the-century kitchen and bedroom, pioneer church, blacksmith shop, four antique fire trucks, a dugout canoe, thousands of pro-union buttons, and a 20-minute slide show on local history. A short video shows the great fire of 1903 that destroyed 140 buildings. Lots of offbeat what-was-that-used-for stuff here. Open Wed.-Sun. 11 a.m.-4 p.m. in summer, and Mon.-Fri. 8 a.m.-5 p.m. and Sat.-Sun. noon-4 p.m. the rest of the year; donation.

Wildlife Refuge

Due west of Hoquiam off Hwy. 109, **Grays Harbor National Wildlife Refuge,** tel. (360) 533-5228, is a 500-acre wetland in the northeast corner of Grays Harbor Estuary. This is one of the most important staging areas for shorebirds in North America, attracting up to a million birds each spring. The two dozen shorebird species that visit the basin include the western sandpiper, dunlin, short- and long-billed dowitcher, and red knot; other birds seen here are the peregrine falcon, northern harrier, and red-tailed hawk. A one-mile path leads to the viewing areas, but bring your boots since it's often muddy. The best viewing time is one hour before and one hour after high tide.

Accommodations

See the "Aberdeen, Hoquiam, and Cosmopolis Accommodations" chart for a listing of local lodging options. In addition to these, Aberdeen has

a number of marginal motels downtown that might do in a pinch, but see the rooms first.

Built in 1900, **Lytle House B&B** is a gorgeous Queen Ann Victorian mansion next door to Hoquiam's Castle. Seven guest rooms share baths down the hall with clawfoot tubs and heated towel racks. The **Aberdeen Mansion Inn B&B** is another lumber-baron mansion from the turn of the century. The inn features a magnificent entry hall, five guest rooms, and attractively landscaped grounds covering an acre.

Cooney Mansion B&B, in Cosmopolis, was built in 1908 by lumber baron Neil Cooney, and sits adjacent to woods and a golf course on a dead-end street. Now on the National Register of Historic Places, the B&B has nine antique-decorated guest rooms, a jacuzzi, sauna, and fireplace.

Campgrounds and RV Parks

Campsites ($11 for tents, $16 for RVs) are available at **Lake Sylvia State Park** near Montesano (see below), approximately 12 miles east of Aberdeen. Open late March through September. Call (360) 249-3621 for information, or (800) 452-5687 for campsite reservations ($6 extra fee), available up to 11 months ahead of time. Park RVs at **Arctic Park,** 893 Hwy. 101, tel. (360) 533-4470.

Food

Duffy's is the local family restaurant, featuring a varied, inexpensive-to-moderate seafood and steak menu and great pies. There are three Duffy's in an incredibly small area: 1605 Simpson Ave., tel. (360) 532-3842, in Aberdeen; 1212 E. Wishkah St., tel. (360) 538-0606, in Aberdeen; and 825 Simpson Ave., tel. (360) 532-1519 in Hoquiam.

Aberdeen's **Nordic Inn,** 1700 S. Boone St., serves moderately priced steak and seafood and has a popular Sunday brunch. Open 24 hours. In Hoquiam, the **Levee Street Restaurant,** 709 Levee St., tel. (360) 532-1959, serves fine sautés, fettuccine, prime rib, and steaks with a European flair and a river view.

At 112 N. G St. in Aberdeen, **Bridge's,** tel. (360) 532-6563, has prime rib, steak, and seafood dinners, including razor clams. The atmosphere is elegant but not stuffy, and there's a wide selection of nonalcoholic drinks in addition to a full bar; open for lunch and dinner daily

ABERDEEN, HOQUIAM, AND COSMOPOLIS ACCOMMODATIONS

Accommodations are arranged from least to most expensive within each town. Rates may be lower during the winter months. The area code is 360.

ABERDEEN

Central Park Motel; 6504 Olympic Hwy. (five miles east of Aberdeen); tel. 533-1210 or (800) 927-1210; $30 s, $45 d; rural location, kitchenettes available

Travelure Motel; 623 W. Wishkah St.; tel. 532-3280; $33-37 s, $40-45 d; AAA approved

Towne Motel; 712 E. Wishkah St.; tel. 533-2340; $35 s, $38 d

Thunderbird Motel; 410 W. Wishkah St.; tel. 532-3153; $38, $47 d; jacuzzi

Olympic Inn; 616 W. Heron St.; tel. 533-4200 or (800) 562-8618; $40-65 s, $50-70 d; large rooms, kitchenettes available, AAA approved

Nordic Inn; 1700 S. Boone St.; tel. 533-0100 or (800) 442-0101; $52-72 s, $62-77 d; indoor pool, jacuzzi, exercise room, AAA approved

Red Lion Inn; 521 W. Wishkah St.; tel. 532-5210 or (800) 547-8010; $52-72 s, $62-77 d; free continental breakfast on weekdays, AAA approved

Aberdeen Mansion Inn B&B; 807 N. M St.; tel. 533-7079; $75-95 s or d; 1905 Victorian mansion, five guest rooms, private baths, full breakfast, AAA approved

HOQUIAM

Tops Motel; 2403 Simpson Ave.; tel. 532-7373; $30 s, $32 d

Sandstone Motel; 2424 Aberdeen Ave.; tel. 563-6383; $34 s, $39 d

Snore & Whisker Motel; 3031 Simpson Ave.; tel. 532-5060; $35 s, $40 d; kitchenettes available, AAA approved

Westwood Inn; 910 Simpson Ave.; tel. 532-8161 or (800) 562-0994; $40-90 s or d; spacious rooms, two-bedroom suites and kitchens available, AAA approved

Timberline Inn; 415 Perry Ave.; tel. 533-8048; $49 s, $55 d (lower on weekdays); kitchenettes available

Lytle House B&B; 509 Chenault; tel. 533-2320 or (800) 677-2320; $60 s, $75-105 d; beautiful three-story Victorian home, four parlors, seven guest rooms with antiques, shared or private baths, full breakfast, no kids under 10, AAA approved

COSMOPOLIS

Cooney Mansion B&B; 1705 5th St.; tel. 533-0602; $65-115 s or d; 1908 mansion, jacuzzi, sauna, exercise room, sundeck, rose garden, nine guest rooms, private or shared baths, antiques, AAA approved

---

plus Sunday brunch. **Billy's Bar & Grill,** a restored saloon at 322 E. Heron, tel. (360) 533-7144, serves delicious and reasonably priced steaks, seafood, and burgers; with that gold and bright green paint job, you can't miss it.

Parma in Aberdeen at 116 W. Heron St., tel. (360) 532-3166, is open for dinner with fresh homemade pasta, veal cordon bleu, delicious breads, and homemade desserts. Very good. More Italian food and the best local pizzas are at **Casa Mia Pizza,** 2936 Simpson Ave. in Hoquiam, tel. (360) 533-2010. Get Mexican meals at **Louise's Authentic Mexican & Seafood Restaurant,** 1915 Simpson Ave. in Aberdeen, tel. (360) 533-3104, or **Mazatlan Restaurant,** 202 E. Wishkah St. in Aberdeen, tel. (360) 532-0940. The best local Chinese eatery is **Kun Chi Restaurant,** 501 W. Wishkah in Aberdeen, tel. (360) 532-6341.

If you're in the hunt for fast food, avoid the big chains and head to **Happy Teriyaki,** at the Wishkah Mall in Aberdeen, tel. (360) 533-1500. And, for a stuff-yourself cafeteria-style meal, roll in to **Granny's Buffet,** 2701 Sumner in Aberdeen, tel. (360) 533-0282. Oh, and just for the record, if you stop by the Nutrisystems Weight Loss Center on the east end of Aberdeen, you can walk next door to Baskin-Robbins 31 Flavors for an after-meeting treat.

The **Aberdeen-Grays Harbor Farmers Market and Crafts Fair** takes place at Hoquiam's Levee Park, on the river on Hwy. 101 N. Open Tuesday 9 a.m.-4 p.m. July to Christmas, and Fri.-Sat. 9 a.m.-4 p.m. year-round.

Recreation
At E. 9th and N. I Streets, Aberdeen's **Samuel Benn Park** has rose and rhododendron gardens, tennis courts, playground, and picnic facilities. **Lake Aberdeen** at the east entrance to town has swimming and nonmotorized boating and play equipment. For an indoor pool, head to the **Hoquiam Aquatic Center,** 717 K St., tel. (360) 533-3474.

The **Grays Harbor Gulls** play independent professional baseball May-Aug. at Hoquiam's Olympic Stadium, one of the few surviving wooden stadiums in the country. Call (360) 532-4488 for ticket info.

Events and Entertainment
Kick the year off with a fun time at Aberdeen's **Dixieland Jazz Festival** held on Presidents Day weekend in mid-February. In early May the city's **Discovery Days Celebration** attracts longboats from throughout the Northwest for rowing and sailing races. This is a often good time to see the *Lady Washington* in port; call (360) 532-8611 for details. The **Family Fun Festival** in late July is a tri-city event with parades, concerts, a carnival, and other events.

Hoquiam's **Loggers Playday,** held the second weekend in September, is an opportunity for sedentary executives to see what real work is all about. After kicking off the event with a parade

and salmon barbecue, loggers compete in ax-throwing, log-chopping, tree-climbing, and more. Evening brings a big fireworks show.

The **Driftwood Players,** a community theatrical company, puts on several plays a year at Driftwood Playhouse, 120 E. 3rd in Aberdeen, tel. (360) 538-1213.

Shopping
In Aberdeen, follow Hwy. 105 over the bridge and around the corner to the **South Shore Mall,** featuring Sears, JCPenney, Kmart, plus 60 other stores and a cinema. The smaller **Wishkah Mall,** on Hwy. 12 at the east end of Aberdeen, has 30 stores including Ernst, Pay 'N' Save, and Lamonts. For something different, visit the **Fandrich Piano Company,** 3001 Murphy in Hoquiam, where they build upright pianos with a grand piano sound. Call (360) 533-8053 for tour information.

Information and Services
The **Grays Harbor Chamber of Commerce and Visitor Center,** 2704 Sumner Ave. in Ab-

---

BEACH DRIVING

Part of Washington's Pacific shoreline south of the Quinault Indian Reservation is open to vehicular traffic. This causes considerable debate among the residents, many of who don't like looking both ways before going for a swim, or don't want to see their kids flattened by RVs. Here are a few rules, regulations, and driving tips:

Check with local chambers of commerce for restrictions on vehicle access to the beaches since approximately 40% of the beaches are closed for all or part of the year.

The shoreline is considered a state highway; therefore, only registered vehicles driven by licensed drivers are allowed.

Pedestrians have the right of way; cars and horses must yield.

Drive only on the higher hard sand, not in the water, on the clam beds, or in the dunes, and observe a 25 mph speed limit.

If you get stuck, put boards or other hard, flat material under your tires and pull out slowly.

Be sure to hose down your car after driving on the beach, since salt spray can lead to rust.

erdeen, tel. (360) 532-1924 or (800) 321-1924, is open Mon.-Fri. 9 a.m.-5 p.m. The **area code** is 360. For emergencies, head for **St. Joseph's Hospital,** 1006 N. H St. (near Samuel Benn Park), tel. (360) 533-0450 or (800) 634-0030, for 24-hour service.

Transportation
Aberdeen and Hoquiam are well served by **Grays Harbor Transit,** tel. (360) 532-2770 or (800) 562-9730. Buses take you throughout the county seven days a week, including Lake Quinault, Westport, Ocean Shores, and even east to Olympia. Connecting buses will transport you all over the Olympic Peninsula. The fare is hard to beat: 25 cents ($1 to Olympia).

MONTESANO

The cozy town of Montesano (pop. 3,500) occupies the juncture of the Chehalis, Satsop, and Wynoochee Rivers. The town has tidy brick buildings and the hilltop Grays Harbor County Courthouse, built in 1910 of marble and granite. Not far away is the nation's first tree farm, established by Weyerhaeuser in 1941. **Chehalis Valley Historical Museum,** 703 W. Pioneer Ave., tel. (360) 249-5800, houses historical displays in what was originally a Scandinavian Lutheran church built in 1906. Open Wed.-Sun. noon-4 p.m. June through Labor Day, and Sat.-Sun. noon-4 p.m. the rest of the year; no charge.

Lake Sylvia State Park
About a mile north of Montesano off Hwy. 12, Lake Sylvia State Park encompasses 233 acres around this narrow but scenic reservoir. The lake was created by a dam built in 1909 to supply water and power and is a popular place to swim, canoe, or fish. Two miles of trails circle the lake and connect with two more miles of trail in adjacent Chapin Collins Memorial Forest. Be sure to check out the four-foot wooden ball, carved by loggers from a spruce log and used for log rolling until it became waterlogged and sank. The ball was rediscovered in 1974 when the lake level was lowered and is now on display. The park is open late March through September; tel. (360) 249-3621.

Accommodations
Local motels are: **Monte Square Motel,** 528 1/2 S. 1st St., tel. (360) 249-4424, with rooms for $30 s or d; and **Palm Tree Inn,** 822 Pioneer E, tel. (360) 249-3931, charging $35 s or d.

Abel House B&B, 117 Fleet St. S, tel. (360) 249-6002 or (800) 235-2235, is an historic 1908 home with five guest rooms (shared or private bath), Tiffany chandeliers, and attractive grounds. A full breakfast is served. Rates start at $60-80 s or d; no kids. **Sylvan Haus B&B,** 417 Wilder Hill Lane, tel. (360) 249-3453, is a contemporary home located near Lake Sylvia with five guest rooms (private or shared bath), and a hot tub for relaxation. Rates are $65-110 s or d, including a gourmet breakfast; no kids under 12.

Campgrounds
Lake Sylvia State Park (see above) has wooded campsites along the shore for $11 and RV hookups for $16; open late March to September. Call (800) 452-5687 for campsite reservations ($6 extra fee), available up to 11 months ahead of time.

Food
Several places provide surprisingly good meals in town. For breakfasts and lunches, the small **Savory Faire,** 135 S. Main St., tel. (360) 249-3701, is hard to beat, with a menu that includes omelettes, from-scratch soups, fresh salads, sandwiches, plus fresh-baked breads, pastries, and espresso to go. Another good lunch place is **Columbine Cafe,** in the old red Montesano Mercantile Building at 728 E. Pioneer, tel. (360) 249-5555. The cafe features salads, sandwiches, and vegetarian burritos. Also try **Bee Hive Restaurant,** on the corner of Main and Pioneer, tel. (360) 249-4131, for all-American meals.

Events
The **Festival of People** in late July includes a parade, arts and crafts, live music, and other activities.

Information and Transportation
Get local info from the **Montesano Chamber of Commerce,** tel. (360) 249-5522. **Grays Harbor Transit** provides daily bus service throughout the county, including Lake Quinault, Westport, Ocean Shores, and east to Olympia. Connecting

buses will transport you all over the Olympic Peninsula. The fare is just 25 cents ($1 to Olympia); tel. (360) 532-2770 or (800) 562-9730.

ELMA AND McCLEARY

The small town of Elma (pop. 3,000) has a wide main street, several old-timey murals, and the now-required espresso shops. Just west of here is the **Satsop Nuclear Power Plant,** with tours on Friday at 10 a.m. or at other times by advance appointment. Call (360) 482-4428, ext. 5052, for details. Be sure to ask what they plan to do with the spent fuel rods for the next several thousand years. The **Satsop Methodist Church,** built in 1872, is visible three miles west of Elma along Hwy. 410.

McCleary (pop. 1,500) has a Simpson Co. door manufacturing plant, a small museum, several eating places, and a fascinating old hotel. **Vance Creek County Park,** just west of Elma, has nature trails, jogging paths, and swimming in two small lakes. McCleary's **Carnal House Museum,** 314 2nd St., is open Sat.-Sun. noon-4 p.m., Memorial Day through Labor Day only. Inside are historic photos and a collection of farming, logging, and household equipment from the past.

Lodging and Food

The **Grays Harbor Hostel,** 6 Jenny Lane (near the fairgrounds) in Elma, tel. (360) 482-3119, is located in a sprawling ranch house situated on eight acres of land. Facilities include an outdoor jacuzzi, two common rooms, a kitchen, a back patio, and storage rooms. Blankets and pillows are available. Shared rooms go for $10 per person; open all year, but closed during the day. Check-in time is 5-9 p.m., with check out at 9 a.m.

Parkhurst Motel, 208 E. Main St., Elma, tel. (360) 482-2541, has rooms with kitchenettes for $45 s, $55 d.

Built in 1912, the **Old McCleary Hotel** was originally the home of Henry McCleary, for whom the town is named. Today it is owned by Penny Challstedt, who has kept the place as something of a museum, with the original furniture, brass beds, unusual toilets, dark paneling, and Victorian wallpaper. Don't expect a TV or fax machine here. The hotel is located at 42 Summit Rd., tel. (360) 495-3678; rooms are $35-45 s

or d. The owner also serves family-style meals, but these are mainly for groups. Otherwise, try **The Rose Garden,** a mom-and-pop restaurant. **Links Restaurant,** near the Oaksridge Golf Course, 1050 Monte-Elma Rd., tel. (360) 482-5755, is the on-the-town place in the Elma/Montesano area with quality steak and seafood.

Campgrounds

Follow the signs for 12 miles north of Elma to **Schafer State Park** on the Satsop River. Originally a park for Schafer Logging Company employees, today it has public campsites ($10 for tents, $15 for RVs), riverside picnic areas, and a fine collection of mossy trees. Good fishing for steelhead (late winter) and sea-run cutthroat (summers) in the East Fork of the Satsop River. The park is open April-September. Call (800) 452-5687 for campsite reservations ($6 extra fee), available up to 11 months ahead of time.

Weyerhaeuser's **Swinging Bridge Park** is about 10 miles from Elma in the middle of nowhere, forking left off the road to Schafer; here you'll find free camping with a five-day limit, free firewood, and secluded picnic and play areas. Park RVs in Elma at **Elma RV Park,** Hwy. 12 and 30 S, tel. (360) 482-4053, or **Travel Inn Resort & Campground,** 801 E. Main, tel. (360) 482-3877.

Events

Elma is home to the county fairgrounds, where you can take in an indoor pro rodeo in late March, horse racing in late July, the old-fashioned **Grays Harbor County Fair** in mid-August, and Saturday night auto racing April-September. The **McCleary Bear Festival** in mid-July offers two parades, entertainment, arts and crafts, and food booths. Not to mention bear stew. In mid-September, Elma has a **Wild Blackberry Festival** with a pie contest, car show, arts and crafts, and parade. Local information sources are the **Elma Chamber of Commerce,** tel. (360) 482-2411, and the **McCleary Community Chamber of Commerce,** tel. (360) 495-4659.

Transportation

Grays Harbor Transit provides daily bus service throughout the county, including Lake Quinault, Westport, Ocean Shores, and east to Olympia for just 25 cents ($1 to Olympia). For info, call (360) 532-2770 or (800) 562-9730.

SOUTH BEACH

The section of coastline between Westport and North Cove is known as both "South Beach" and the "Cranberry Coast"; the former because it is the southern entrance to Grays Harber, the latter because of the bogs east near Grayland that produce much of the state's cranberry crop. The area is especially popular for sportfishing but also offers long beaches, good surfing, and reasonably priced lodging. The beaches are popular with post-storm beachcombers who still turn up an occasional glass ball from old Japanese fishing floats.

WESTPORT AND GRAYLAND

Westport (pop. 2,000), the principal South Beach city, once called itself "The Salmon Capital of the World," and charter services and commercial fishing and crabbing boats still line the waterfront. This is one of the most active ports in Washington. The town also has a crab cannery and several seafood markets, plus the expected waterfront shops offering kitschy gifts, saltwater taffy and fudge, and kites.

Grayland is a frumpy, old fashioned little place with simple accommodations and a ragged appearance. It's the sort of place where the local gallery sells sea shells, pottery, and paintings from the school of sawblade art. Locals complain of the influx of wealthy Californians buying up the land, punching taxes to the sky, and pinching struggling local businesses.

Sights

At 2201 Westhaven Dr. in Westport, the **Westport Maritime Museum,** tel. (360) 268-0078, is housed in a magnificent old Coast Guard station built in 1939. Capped by six gables and a watchtower with a widow's walk, the building was used until 1974, when newer quarters were completed just down the road. Inside are photographs of the early Aberdeen-Westport plank road, cranberry and logging industry exhibits, and Coast Guard memorabilia. Out front in glass cases are gray whale, sea lion, and porpoise skeletons. On weekends March-May, the mu-

seum offers talks about whales and whale-watching. Open daily 10 a.m.-5 p.m. June-Sept.; Wed.-Fri. noon-4 p.m., and Sat.-Sun. 10 a.m.-5 p.m. the rest of the year. Suggested donation $1 for adults, 50 cents for kids.

Housed inside a tacky gift shop, the private **Westport Aquarium,** 321 Harbor St., tel. (360) 268-0471, open daily April-Dec., offers large display tanks holding octopus, sharks, bottom fish, and anemones, plus a chance to feed the performing seals. Entrance is $2.50 for adults, $1.50 for ages five to 16, and free for kids under four.

On the south end of Grayland along Hwy. 105 is the privately run **Furford Picker Co. Cranberry Museum,** tel. (360) 267-7314, an old cranberry warehouse displaying all sorts of cranberry rakes and planting and harvesting tools and equipment, plus junk of all sorts for sale. Funky and worth a stop. Open Fri.-Sun. 10 a.m.-5 p.m. The cranberry bogs are a short ways east of here off Cranberry and Larkin Roads. The **Ocean Spray Cranberry** processing plant is east of Westport in Markham, tel. (360) 267-4922. Stop by to watch them making the juice. Elk are often see across the highway from the Ocean Spray plant at the **Johns River Wildlife Area** in the winter and spring.

Head to the three-quarter-mile **South Jetty** at the end of State Park Access Rd. for a chance to fish, look for birds and marine mammals, or watch the winter storms roll in. Use care on the slippery rocks. The road passes Half Moon Bay, popular with scuba divers. A tall **observation tower** on the east end of Nettie Rose Dr. in town provides a fine vantage point to view freighter activity, scenery, sunsets, or an occasional whale, and a lower **ramp tower** on the east end of Nettie Rose looks into the marina. In front of this is a small memorial to fishermen lost at sea.

Parks and Viewpoints

Open for day-use only, **Westhaven State Park,** on Hwy. 105 just north of Westport, is popular with rockhounds, beachcombers, and divers. Surfers and sea kayakers find some of the most consistent waves in Washington. The jetty was built here to increase the velocity of the seago-

WESTPORT AND GRAYLAND

GRAYS HARBOR

SEE DETAIL
CHARTER BOATS
MARITIME MUSEUM
U.S. COAST GUARD STATION
SOUTH JETTY
HALF MOON BAY
WESTHAVEN STATE PARK
STATE PARK ACCESS RD.
WESTPORT
WESTPORT LIGHT STATE PARK
WESTPORT LIGHTHOUSE BEACH ACCESS
OCEAN AVE.
WINDJAMMER MOTEL
FRANK L. MOTEL
SURF SPRAY MOTEL
SILVER SANDS MOTEL
CRANBERRY MOTEL
SANDS MOTEL
SPORTSMEN'S MOTEL
NEWELL AVE.
CHEHALIS AVE.
TO ABERDEEN
CHAMBER OF COMMERCE / VISITORS CENTER
TWIN HARBORS STATE PARK

DETAIL

OBSERVATION RAMP
OBSERVATION TOWER
HARBOR RESORT
ISLANDER MOTEL
SHIPWRECK MOTEL
COHO MOTEL
MARINA MOTEL
ALBATROSS MOTEL
DOCK
HARBOR
WESTHAVEN DR.
WESTPORT INN MOTEL
HARMS ST.
NYHUS ST.
COAST GUARD STATION
MONTESANO ST.
WILSON AVE.
105
POST OFFICE
LIBRARY
PACIFIC AVE.
FORREST ST.
OCEAN AVE.
GLENACRES INN B & B
OCEAN AVE. INN
ERIN MOTEL
MARINERS COVE INN
PACIFIC MOTEL

GRAYLAND

SAND DUNES

0   2 mi
0   2 km

CRANBERRY BOGS
CRANBERRY RD.

GRAYLAND BEACH STATE PARK
FURFORD CRANBERRY MUSEUM

TO TOKELAND AND RAYMOND
COUNTY LINE RD.

© MOON PUBLICATIONS, INC.

ing water, collected from six rivers flowing into Grays Harbor. Prior to the construction of the jetty, deposits of sediment mandated annual channel dredging. The jetty worked—the channel hasn't required dredging since 1942.

Westport Light State Park, about a mile south of Westhaven off Hwy. 105 (continue straight when 105 goes left), is another day-use park (no camping) good for kite flying, rockhounding, and fishing for ocean perch. A paved, mile-long nature trail wanders through the dunes, providing several observation platforms that overlook the water. There's vehicular beach access here, but the sand is considerably softer than at other driveable beaches; be careful if you don't have 4WD. Check with the park for regulations on beach driving, since some sections are closed part or all of the year. The classic lighthouse inside the park—tallest on the West Coast—was built in 1898 and is visible from an observation platform on Ocean Avenue. Take the short trail to the lighthouse from here, but the building is not open to the public. The lighthouse originally stood closer to the water, but the accretion of sand has pushed the beachfront seaward.

On Hwy. 105, two miles south of Westport, **Twin Harbors State Park** has campsites, a three-quarter-mile sand dune nature trail, picnic areas, and a playground. This is one of the most popular ocean-side campgrounds, especially when razor clam harvesting is allowed (usually March and October). Twin Harbors is open for day-use all year.

A mile south of Grayland on Hwy. 105, **Grayland Beach State Park** has 7,450 feet of ocean frontage, a self-guided nature trail through huckleberry, Sitka spruce, and lodgepole pine, and 200 acres for picnicking and camping. This is another popular place to dig for clams.

Fishing

Even the casual visitor to Westport will see that this is a major sport and commercial fishing port. The harbor is packed with vessels of all dimensions, and charter operators line the marina. You don't have to charter a boat to go fishing; the whole stretch from Westport to North Cove is popular for surf fishing. The rock jetty near Westhaven State Park (see above) is a good spot for catching salmon, rockfish, ling cod, surf perch, and crabs. In September and October, a coho

salmon run returns to the marina area (the young are raised in pens here, so this is "home"). Clamming is seasonal and requires a license; see the chamber of commerce for a copy of the regulations. The 1,000-foot-long **Westport Fishing Pier,** off the end of Float 20 at the Westport Marina, is another landlubber fishing option.

Offshore rocks and reefs are feeding grounds for salmon, bottom fish, even halibut; take a charter boat to find the best spots, not to mention having your fish cleaned and ready to cook by the time you get back to shore. The charter services all charge about the same amount, so when you call for reservations be sure to check whether the price includes bait and tackle, cleaning, sales tax, etc., to see if your "bargain" is really a good deal. Note, however, that most departures are at the frightfully early hour of 6 a.m., with a return around 3:30 p.m. Be sure to take along your seasickness pills. Some companies also offer overnight trips that head far offshore in search of tuna. Wander along Westhaven Dr. to check out the various charter companies, or call one of the following: **Bran Lee Charters,** 2467 Westhaven Dr., tel. (360) 268-9177 or (800) 562-0163; **Cachalot Charters,** 2511 Westhaven Dr., tel. (360) 268-0323 or (800) 356-0323; **Coho Charters,** 2501 Nyhus St., tel. (360) 268-0111 or (800) 572-0177; **Deep Sea Charters,** across from Float 6, tel. (360) 268-9300 or (800) 562-0151; **Islander Motel Charters,** 421 E. Neddie Rose Dr., tel. (360) 268-9166 or (800) 322-1740; **Neptune Charters,** 2601 Westhaven Dr., tel. (360) 268-0124 or (800) 422-0425; **Ocean Charters,** 2315 Westhaven Dr., tel. (360) 268-9144; **Olympic Sportfishing,** 2309 N. Nyhus St., tel. (360) 268-9593; **Rainbow Charters,** 2647 Westhaven Dr., tel. (360) 268-9182; **Travis Charters,** 321 Dock St., tel. (360) 268-9140 or (800) 648-1520; **Washington Charters,** 2411 Westhaven Dr., tel. (360) 268-0900; and **Westport Charters** 2401 Westhaven Dr., tel. (360) 268-9120 or (800) 562-0157.

Whalewatching

Many of the charter operators listed above provide whalewatching trips March through May, when the gray whales are heading north from their winter quarters off Baja California. Expect to pay around $32 for a three-hour trip. You may also spot whales from the jetty or from the

WESTPORT AND GRAYLAND ACCOMMODATIONS

Accommodations are arranged from least to most expensive within each town. Rates may be considerably lower during the winter months. The area code is 360.

WESTPORT

Cranberry Motel; 920 S. Montsano St.; tel. 268-0807; $30-48 s or d; see rooms first

Marina Motel; 2339 Nyhus St.; tel. 268-9633; $31 s or d; very plain, see rooms first

Erin Motel; 613 Ocean Ave.; tel. 268-0572; $35 s or d; kitchenettes available

Shipwreck Motel; 2653 Nyhus St., tel. 268-9151; $35 s, $45 d; kitchenettes $65 s or d; distinctive '60s-era round motel with piece-of-pie shaped rooms

Silver Sands Motel; 1001 S. Montesano St.; tel. 268-9029; $38 s, $48 d

Walsh Motel; 1593 Hwy. 105; tel. 267-2191; $36-96 s or d; kitchenettes available

Windjammer Motel; 461 E. Pacific Ave.; tel. 268-9351; $40-45 s, $45-50 d; kitchenettes available, AAA approved

Sands Motel; 1416 S. Montesano St.; tel. 268-0091; $40-55 s or d; kitchenettes available

Surf Spray Motel; 949 S. Montesano St.; tel. 268-9149; $42-55 s, $48-55 d; kitchenettes available

Albatross Motel; 200 E. Dock St.; tel. 268-9233; $44 s or d; kitchenettes available

Ocean Avenue Inn; 275 W. Ocean Ave.; tel. 268-9278; $45 s or d; kitchenettes available, clean and friendly

Ocean Spray Motel; 1757 Hwy. 105 S; tel. 267-2205; $45 s or d; kitchenettes available

Frank L. Motel; 725 S. Montesano St.; tel. 268-9200; $45 s or d, two-room apartments $65 d; kitchenettes available, jacuzzi

Harbor Resort Motel; 871 Neddie Rose Dr.; tel. 268-0169; $45-55 s or d; kitchenettes available; $90 for up to five in cottage

Westport viewing towers. The passenger ferry to Ocean Shores (see "Transportation" below) is an inexpensive way to watch for the whales that periodically wander into Grays Harbor. The Maritime Museum offers weekend whalewatching seminars, films, and workshops in season.

Other Recreation

Surfers can check out the waves at Westhaven State Park, one of the most popular surfing beaches in the state. Rent boogie boards from **Harbor Diving Service,** 200 S. Montesano, tel. (360) 268-0080; they also have scuba equipment rentals, tank fills, and instruction. Protected Half Moon Bay at Westport is a favorite diving area. In Grayland, stop by the **Beach Shop,** 2191 Hwy. 105, tel. (360) 267-7691, for boogie board and mountain bike rentals.

Both **Cachalot Kites,** 2511 Westhaven Dr., tel. (360) 268-0323 or (800) 356-0323, and **Pic a Patch Kite Shop,** 2549 Westhaven Dr., tel. (360) 268-0877, have kites of every description, windsocks, and toys.

Accommodations

See the "Westport and Grayland Accommodations" chart for a listing of local lodging places. Accommodations here are fairly simple. Many have kitchenettes, but only a few offer jacuzzis or pools. As one owner told me in her broken English, "no pool; big giant ocean out there!"

Campgrounds

Camp two miles south of town at the very popular **Twin Harbors State Park** for $10 ($15 for

Sportsmen's Resort; 1500 S. Montesano St.; tel. 268-0055; $45-65 s or d; kitchenettes available

Mariners Cove Inn; 303 Ocean Ave.; tel. 268-0531; $48-65 s or d; newer motel, kitchenettes available, AAA approved

Pacific Motel; 330 S. Forrest Ave.; tel. 268-9325; $49-59 s or d; outdoor pool, kitchenettes available

Coho Motel; 2501 N. Nyhus; tel. 268-0111 or (800) 572-0177; $54 s, $56 d; AAA approved

Islander Motel; Westhaven and Nettie Rose; tel. 268-9166; $65 s, $70 d; outdoor pool, kitchenettes available

Chateau Westport Motel; 710 Hancock; tel. 268-9101 or (800) 255-9101; $65-70 s or d; ocean views, indoor pool, jacuzzi, continental breakfast, balconies, fireplaces, kitchenettes available, AAA approved

Glenacres Inn B&B; 222 N. Montesano St.; tel. 268-9391; $65-80 s or d; 1898 Victorian, eight guest rooms, private baths, hot tub, fireplace, full breakfast, no kids under 12; $150 for cottages (up to eight people)

GRAYLAND

North Coast Motel; 1738 Hwy. 105; tel. 267-5051; $30-45 s or d; older place

Western Shores Motel and RV Park; 2193 Hwy. 105; tel. 267-6115; $30-50 s or d

Walsh Motel; 1593 Hwy. 105; tel. 267-2191; $32-78 s or d; modern on-the-beach motel, some jacuzzi tubs, nicest in town, kitchenettes available

Surf Motel & Cottages; 2029 Hwy. 105; tel. 267-2244; $35 s or d in motel; $50 for up to four in cottages with kitchenettes; jacuzzi

Ocean Gate Resort; 1939 Hwy. 105 S; tel. 267-1956 or (800) 473-1956; $35-45 s or d; plain older cottages near beach, kitchenettes

Ocean Spray Motel; 1757 Hwy. 105; tel. 267-2205; $40 s or d; cabins with kitchenettes

Grayland Motel & Cottages; 2013 Hwy. 105; tel. 267-2395 or (800) 292-0845; $40 s or d; kitchenettes available

RV hookups). Some campsites are just steps away from the beach. The campground is open late February through October. A mile south of Grayland on Hwy. 105, **Grayland Beach State Park** has camping for $11 and RV hookups for $16; open year-round. For campsite reservations ($6 extra fee) at both parks, call (800) 452-5687. Reservations are available up to 11 months ahead of time. Both parks also have coin-operated showers.

RV Parks
Westport is jam-packed with RV parks catering to the fishing crowd. They include: **Coho Charters RV Park,** 2501 N. Nyhus St., tel. (360) 268-0111 or (800) 572-0177; **Connie Lee's RV Park,** 743 Neddie Rose Dr., tel. (360) 368-5555; **Cranberry Motel & RV Park,** 920 S. Montesano St., tel. (360) 268-0807; **Harbor Resort & RV Park,** 871 E. Neddie Rose Dr., tel. (360)

268-0169; **Holiday Motel & RV Park,** 871 Neddie Rose Dr., tel. (360) 268-9356; **Islander Motel & RV Park,** Westhaven and Nettie Rose, tel. (360) 268-9166 or (800) 322-1740; **Kila Hana Camperland,** 931 S. Forrest Ave., tel. (360) 268-9528 or (800) 262-9528; **Pacific Aire RV Park,** tel. (360) 268-0207; **Pacific Motel & RV Park,** 330 S. Forrest Ave., tel. (360) 268-9325; **Surf Spray Motel & RV Park,** 949 S. Montesano St., tel. (360) 268-9149; and **Totem RV Park,** 2421 Nyhus St., tel. (360) 268-0025.

There are three private campgrounds in Grayland: **Kenanna RV Park,** 2959 S. Hwy. 105, tel. (360) 267-3515; **Ocean Gate Resort,** 1939 Hwy. 105 S, tel. (360) 267-1956 or (800) 473-1956; **Twin Spruce RV Park,** 1658 Schmid Rd., tel. (360) 267-1275 or (800) 438-1474; and **Western Shores Motel & RV Park,** 2193 Hwy. 105, tel. (360) 267-6115. The last of these also rents crab pots and clam "guns."

Food

Because of the early morning departure of fishing charters, several local cafes are already open when the clock strikes five in the morning. **Rich's Family Diner,** 203 S. Montesano, tel. (360) 268-0545, is the local greasy spoon; the sort of place where you meet the local furnace repair man and the early-morning fishing crowd. Nothing fancy, but dependable breakfasts and lunches. **The Bakery Cottage,** 389 W. Ocean Ave., tel. (360) 268-1100, has lighter breakfasts and lunches that are quite good.

Pelican Point Restaurant, 2681 N. Westhaven Dr., tel. (360) 268-1333, is a bit more expensive, but has fine seafood, prime rib, and big salads. You'll find a similar "surf and turf" menu at **Sourdough Lil's,** 301 E. Dock St., tel. (360) 268-9700, and at **King's LeDomaine,** 105 Wilson St., tel. (360) 268-0312. Get freshly shucked oysters to go from **Brady's Oysters,** 3714 Oyster Place E, tel. (360) 268-0077. They were the first to grow oysters on suspended lines, a method that many claim produces a more delicately flavored oyster. You can often buy ultra-fresh fish from commercial fishermen at the marina.

Sea Star Restaurant, 1800 S. Hwy. 105 in Grayland, tel. (360) 267-1011, has very good seafood and the best clam chowder and pies around. They also have a big salad bar. Also in Grayland, **The Dunes Restaurant,** 783 Dunes Rd. in Grayland, tel. (360) 267-1441, is a longtime favorite with fresh seafood in a relaxed atmosphere. Nice seaside location, too.

Constantin's Restaurant, 320 E. Dock St., tel. (360) 268-0550, has authentic Greek specials, along with tasty fish, pastas, and steaks. Very good, and surprisingly reasonable. You won't go wrong here.

The Original House of Pizza, 623 N. Montesano, tel. (360) 268-0901, has the best local pizzas.

Events and Entertainment

The third weekend of March, Grayland-area artists display their driftwood and shell creations at the town's **Driftwood Show.** Westport's **Annual Crab Races** in mid-April are not a good time to be a crab; the races are followed by a big crab feed. Live music too, but they don't make the crabs play the instruments. The **Blessing of the Fleet,** held annually in May, includes a memorial service for people lost at sea and demonstrations of Coast Guard sea-air rescues. Held in late June or early July, the two-day **Festival of the Wind** has contests for the youngest and oldest kite flyers, best crash event, longest train of kites, and more. The **Fourth of July** means a big fireworks display over Booming Bay, and a fun run, arts and crafts, and food booths in Grayland. In August, an **International Nautical Chain Saw Carving Contest** (no it is not done underwater), and the **Brady's Oyster Feed** come early in the month. Mid-August has the **Longboard Classic Surf Festival,** attracting top longboard surfers from throughout the Northwest.

A very popular event—it's been going on for more than 50 years—is the **Westport Seafood Festival** on Labor Day weekend. Taste fresh salmon, oysters, crab, and all sorts of other fresh-from-the-sea foods, with musical accompaniment.

For live music, head to: **Fisherman's Inn,** 604 S. Montesano, tel. (360) 268-0368, **Cowboy Bob's,** 2581 Westhaven Dr., tel. (360) 268-9228, or **Kings LeDomaine,** 105 E. Wilson St., tel. (360) 268-0312.

Information and Services

At 2985 N. Montesano St. in Westport, the **Westport-Grayland Chamber of Commerce Visitors Center,** tel. (360) 268-9422 or (800) 345-6223, is open Sunday 10 a.m.-4 p.m., Mon.-Sat. 9 a.m.-5 p.m. in the summer, and Mon.-Sat. 9 a.m.-5 p.m. the rest of the year. Stop by for maps, brochures, and festival and tour information. The small **Grayland Beach Information Center,** next to Grandma's Treasure Chest store, has local flyers; tel. (800) 473-6018.

Transportation

Grays Harbor Transit provides daily bus service from Westport throughout the county, including Grayland, Aberdeen, Lake Quinault, and Ocean Shores for just 25 cents ($1 to Olympia). Call (360) 532-2770 or (800) 562-9730, for details.

The **Westport-Ocean Shores Passenger Ferry,** *El Matador* is a 74-passenger foot ferry that runs between Ocean Shores and Westport for $8 ($4.50 one-way) roundtrip, and free for kids under five. The ferry leaves six times a day; daily service mid-June to Labor Day, and weekend-only service early May to mid-June and in September. No service the rest of the year. The ferry departs from Float 10 at the Westport marina, tel. (360) 268-0047.

The **Westport-Hoquiam Passenger Ferry,** tel. (800) 562-9730, operates in summer only, providing service to Hoquiam and Ocean Shores with three trips each way daily.

NORTH COVE AND TOKELAND

The town of North Cove occupies the northern edge of the entrance to Willapa Harbor and was once considerably larger. Over the years the sea has been winning the war with the land, pulling a lighthouse, life-saving station, canneries, homes, hotels, and schools over the retreating cliff. The shore is now more than two miles back from its position a century ago. Although the rate of erosion has slowed, there's often something ready to go over the edge at the aptly named Washaway Beach in North Cove.

Protruding into the north end of Willapa Bay off Hwy. 105, tiny Tokeland (pop. 200) is the site of a number of turn-of-the-century homes and commercial buildings and a marina and public dock (a favorite place for recreational crabbing). The waterfront community—protected by a long rock wall fronting the ocean—attracts retirees, summer visitors, and anglers.

Practicalities

A focal point for Tokeland is the wonderfully old fashioned **Tokeland Hotel,** Kindred Rd. and Hotel Rd., tel. (360) 267-7006. Built as a home in 1885, it became an inn in 1899 and is now on the National Register. The hotel and town are named for Chief Toke, whose daughter married a worker at the lifesaving station here. Together they built a home that was later turned into the Tokeland Hotel. Now on the National Register of Historic Places, it's said to be the oldest resort hotel in Washington, and the spacious front lawn, brick fireplace, and jigsaw puzzles provide an air of relaxation. The restored hotel has upstairs rooms with bath down the hall for $55 s, $65 d; reserve several weeks ahead for summer weekend stays. A full breakfast is included—served downstairs in the open dining room overlooking Willapa Bay. The restaurant also serves lunch and dinner, specializing in very reasonably priced seafood. Next door is the Tokeland Arts Gallery. More lodging at **Tradewinds on the Bay Motel,** 4305 Pomeroy Ave., tel. (360) 267-7500, with an outdoor pool, and rooms for $45-65 s or d. Get fresh-cooked crab and other seafood at **Nelson Crab, Inc.,** tel. (360) 267-2911. The Shoalwater Bay Tribe has a small reservation and tribal offices at Tokeland (Willapa Bay was originally called Shoalwater Bay).

Park RVs at **Bayshore RV Park,** 2941 Kindred Ave., tel. (360) 267-2625; or **Willapa RV Park,** 3230 Front St., tel. (360) 267-7710.

Tokeland has a small but fun **Fourth of July Parade** that winds through town.

BOB RACE

SOUTHWESTERN WASHINGTON AND COLUMBIA GORGE

WILLAPA BAY

East and south from Tokeland, Washington's coastline wraps around Willapa Bay, a 25-mile-long inlet protected by the Long Beach Peninsula. It is believed to be the cleanest and least developed estuary on the West Coast of the Lower 48 states. Locals posit that these waters produce the best-tasting oysters in the nation (a claim disputed by folks in Grays Harbor and Shelton). Highways 105 and 101 skirt Willapa's scenic marshy shoreline, and tree farms carpet the surrounding hills. This is timber country. A handful of small settlements—notably Raymond and South Bend—offer accommodations, meals, and a few attractions.

RAYMOND

Raymond (pop. 2,900), on the Willapa River just east of the bay, began as a booming milltown, with 20 lumber mills processing Pacific

Coast trees. Today foresters are still harvesting the same hills, thanks to years of tree farming, with just two mills, including a state-of-the-art Weyerhaeuser plant.

Highway 101 continues north from Raymond to Aberdeen, past a patchwork of Weyerhaeuser tree farms and clearcuts. The winding road can be a traffic nightmare of speeding logging trucks, poking RVs, and too-few passing lanes. Take it easy, and you'll make it in one piece.

Sights

Not a lot to see in Raymond, but do stop by the **Dennis Company,** a big, old fashioned dry goods store at 146 5th St., tel. (360) 942-2427. In addition to hardware, clothing, and sporting goods, the store has many historic photos. A big mural—said to be the largest in Washington—covers one wall of the building and depicts the early days of logging. Across the street is a display of antique logging and farm equipment. You may also want to visit the **Edwards Flower Garden and Tree Farm,** 1736 Ocean, tel. (360) 942-3622, covering 150 acres of hill country between Raymond and South Bend. The attractively landscaped area includes five trout ponds with ducks and geese and 10 acres of flowering shrubs and trees.

Accommodations

Maunu's Mountcastle Motel, 524 3rd St., tel. (360) 942-5571, has rooms for $36 s, $44 d. Kitchenettes are available. **Riverview Inn B&B,** 544 Ballentine St., tel. (360) 942-5271, was originally the home of Elmer Case, a turn-of-the-century lumber baron and the founder of four shingle mills—he was called the "shingle king of America." Built in 1908, this grand home has a wraparound porch, a fireplace, and two guest rooms with antiques and private baths. A full breakfast is served. Rates are $65 s or d; no kids under 12. Newer accommodations are at **Brackett's B&B** on Hunt Club Rd., tel. (360) 942-6111 or (800) 942-6113, which features a cottage in the trees four miles east of town. The fridge is stocked for a make-your-own breakfast. Rates are $60 s or d.

Timberland RV Park at Park and Crescent, tel. (360) 942-3325, has RV hookups.

Food

For screaming hot fast food, stop by **Willapa Willy's Chili,** 524 N. 3rd St., tel. (360) 942-3438, where the owner, Everett "Tiny" McVey uses five different types of peppers. The chili is so hot that even he won't eat it; gives him the hiccups he claims. The chili/hot dog/burger stand is also home to the **Raymond Chamber of Commerce,** tel. (360) 942-5419, open whenever the chili stand is open, meaning daily 10 a.m.-10 p.m. or so.

For sit-down meals and pizza, head to **The Barge,** 160 Laurel St., tel. (360) 942-5100, or **Raymond Cafe,** 216 N. 3rd St., tel. (360) 942-3408.

The **Willapa Harbor Farmers Market** takes place at 2nd and Duryea on Saturday 10 a.m.-2 p.m. from early July through September.

Other Practicalities

Raymond's main event is the **Willapa Harbor Festival,** held the first weekend of August, where you'll find a parade, car show, crafts fair, music, pancake breakfast, and food booths.

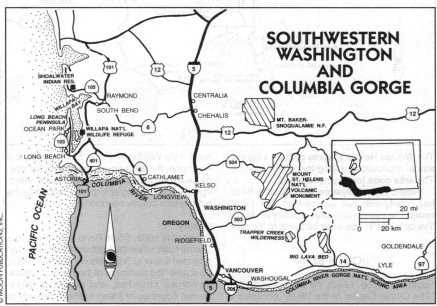

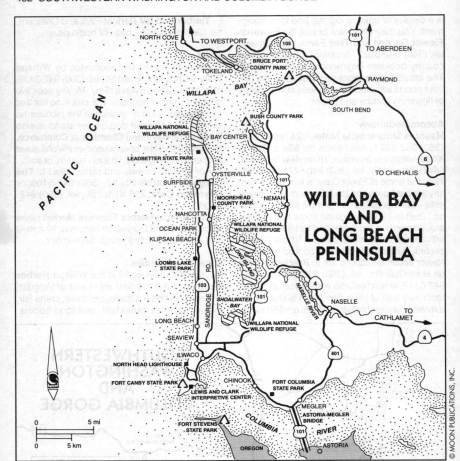

WILLAPA BAY AND LONG BEACH PENINSULA

(Map labels:)
NORTH COVE
TO WESTPORT
TO ABERDEEN
TOKELAND
BRUCE PORT COUNTY PARK
RAYMOND
WILLAPA BAY
SOUTH BEND
BUSH COUNTY PARK
WILLAPA NATIONAL WILDLIFE REFUGE
BAY CENTER
TO CHEHALIS
LEADBETTER STATE PARK
OYSTERVILLE
SURFSIDE
NEMAH
MOOREHEAD COUNTY PARK
NAHCOTTA
OCEAN PARK
WILLAPA NATIONAL WILDLIFE REFUGE
KLIPSAN BEACH
LONG ISLAND
LOOMIS LAKE STATE PARK
NASELLE
SANDRIDGE RD.
103
SHOALWATER BAY
TO CATHLAMET
LONG BEACH
WILLAPA NATIONAL WILDLIFE REFUGE
SEAVIEW
ILWACO
NORTH HEAD LIGHTHOUSE
NASELLE RIVER
FORT CANBY STATE PARK
CHINOOK
FORT COLUMBIA STATE PARK
LEWIS AND CLARK INTERPRETIVE CENTER
MEGLER
ASTORIA-MEGLER BRIDGE
FORT STEVENS STATE PARK
COLUMBIA RIVER
OREGON
ASTORIA
PACIFIC OCEAN
WILLAPA

0   5 mi
0   5 km

© MOON PUBLICATIONS, INC.

The **Willapa Harbor Players** perform local theatrical productions during the winter months. The **area code** for Raymond is 360.

Pacific Transit System, tel. (360) 875-9418, has county-wide bus service Mon.-Sat. for 50 cents. The system connects with Grays Harbor Transit buses in Aberdeen for points to the east.

SOUTH BEND

South Bend (pop. 1,600), the city that calls itself "The Oyster Capital of the West," occupies a bend in the Willapa River just four miles west of Raymond. It's a rough-edged blue-collar seaport with a mix of abandoned downtown storefronts and flourishing enterprises capped by the out-of-place county courthouse.

History
Founded in 1869, South Bend started out as a sawmill town; when the Northern Pacific Railroad extended a spur to South Bend in the late 1880s, it became "the Baltimore of the Pacific." Victorian homes, churches, and an ornate glass-domed courthouse attest to the prosperity of

the times. The Panic of 1893 put an end to South Bend's grandiose logging plans, while the Willapa Bay oysters that had brought great sums of wealth to a few shrewd businessmen were just about farmed out.

Aquaculture had its start in the early 1900s, when 95 carloads of Chesapeake oysters were "planted" in the bay. Oyster-processing plants flourished until 1919, when a mysterious pestilence wiped out the crop. In 1924, the Japanese oyster was introduced; they began spawning faster than they could be harvested. When the Great Depression finished off South Bend's lumber business, the oyster plants were still going strong—as they are today. The largest oyster processing plant in the nation—Coast Oyster Company—is located here. South Bend's other contribution to the state is Helen Davis; she composed the state song, "Washington, My Home."

Sights

Follow the signs up the hill to the **Pacific County Courthouse,** built in 1910 and covered by an immense, multicolored stained-glass dome over mosaic-tile flooring. This "gilded palace of reckless extravagance" as it has long been called, was built at a cost of $132,000, but not everything is as it appears: the marble columns are actually concrete painted to look like marble. A county jail inmate painted the columns and created the decorative panels inside. The courthouse's parklike grounds—complete with a stocked duck pond—offer views of Weyerhaeuser-shaved hills and the town below. South Bend's raucous battle for the county seat led local citizens to ransack the Oysterville courthouse in 1893, thus "liberating" the county records. (See "Oysterville," below, for this odd tale.)

Also in South Bend, the **Pacific County Museum,** tel. (360) 875-5224, has an impressive collection of Indian and pioneer artifacts and historic photos at 1008 W. Robert Bush Drive. Open daily 11 a.m.-4 p.m. in the summer. Pick up the brochure describing South Bend's many historic buildings at the museum. A mural on the side of the museum depicts the harbor at the turn of the century.

Coast Seafoods, 1200 E. Robert Bush Dr., tel. (360) 875-5557, sells fresh oysters on weekdays.

Willie Keil's Grave

Three miles east of Raymond along Hwy. 6 is Willie Keil's Grave, a testimony to a father's devotion to his son. The elder Keil was founder and titular head of a Christian communal organization called the Bethelites, in honor of the town they founded in northern Missouri. They became very wealthy on the community-owned farms and town, and when the great migration over the Oregon Trail occurred, the Bethelites decided to establish a branch of their belief and business empire at the opposite end of the Oregon Trail. Nineteen-year-old Willie Keil was excited about the trip, but as the departure date neared, he fell ill with malaria. In his final delirium he imagined himself at the head of the wagon train going across the continent.

Willie's brokenhearted dad promised the boy he *would* lead a wagon train west; when Willie died in Bethel, in 1855, his father put the body in a lead-lined, whiskey-filled casket and carried his remains to Washington in honor of his pledge. Willie was buried on the little knoll where the park stands today. After a short time in the area, the Bethelites gave up on the Willapa Bay site and moved south of Portland to found Aurora.

Accommodations

H & H Motel on E. Water at Pennsylvania, tel. (360) 875-5523, has rooms for $34-44 s or d, some with kitchenettes. **Sequest Motel,** 801 W. 1st St., tel. (360) 875-5349, has rooms for $34-48 s or d, including a hot tub. The nicest place is **Maring's Courthouse Hill B&B,** W. 2nd St., tel. (360) 875-6519 or (800) 875-6519. Built in 1892, this hillside home was originally a church. It has three guest rooms for $55 s, $60 d, with a shared bath, full breakfast, and friendly hosts.

Campgrounds

Camp at **Bruceport County Park,** six miles south of town on Hwy. 101, tel. (360) 875-5261. Rates are $10 for tents, $14 for full hookups; open year-round. Park RVs at **Gypsy RV Park,** 524 Central, tel. (360) 875-5165, or H & H Motel.

Food

The Boondocks Restaurant, 1015 W. Robert Bush Dr., tel. (360) 875-5155, is *the* place to eat in South Bend. The specialty, not surprisingly, is oysters, and for breakfast (served anytime) you'll get "hangtown fry," fresh Willapa oysters pan-fried. Also featured are seafood quiche, pastas, veal, and fresh fish.

Gardiner's Restaurant, 702 W. Robert Bush Dr., tel. (360) 875-5154, emphasizes fresh pasta and seafood and homemade desserts. **H & H Cafe** on E. Water at Pennsylvania, tel. (360) 875-5523, is a good place to meet the locals over homemade pie and coffee.

Get fresh oysters in South Bend at **Coast Oyster,** tel. (360) 875-5557, **E.H. Bendiksen Co.,** tel. (360) 875-6632, and **East Point Seafood Co.,** tel. (360) 875-5507.

Festivals

South Bend's Memorial Day weekend **Oyster Stampede** includes oyster shucking and eating contests, oyster plant tours, and country music and dancing. Menlo, six miles east of Raymond on Hwy. 6, sponsors the annual **Pacific County Fair,** a four-day event in late August with all the usual 4-H contests, carnival rides, and sweet treats. Summer ends with the **Come and Play on Labor Day** festival that includes a big parade, food and crafts fair, dances, and fireworks.

Fifteen miles east of Raymond, the ghost town of Frances comes to life twice each year for Swiss festivals: **Schwingfest** in July, a tribute to Switzerland's national sport, wrestling, and autumn's **Oktoberfest,** with beer, polka music, and lots of bratwurst.

Information and Services

The **South Bend Visitor Information Center,** across from Coast Seafoods on Robert Bush Dr., tel. (360) 875-5939, has maps and other current information on the Willapa Bay area. Open daily 10 a.m.-5 p.m. in the summer.

For medical emergencies, South Bend has **Willapa Harbor Hospital** at Alder and Cedar, tel. (360) 875-5526. The **area code** is 360.

Transportation

The **Pacific Transit System,** tel. (360) 875-9418, has county-wide bus service (50 cents) from the South Bend/Raymond area to Long Beach Peninsula, Aberdeen, and other points. You can connect with Grays Harbor Transit buses in Aberdeen for points north and east.

SOUTH TO LONG BEACH

Highway 101 curves along scenic Willapa Bay from South Bend en route to the Long Beach Peninsula in the southwest corner of Washington. The country is a ragged mix of forest and farms—similar to Maine—with tree farm signs proclaiming the date the forest was last harvested and planted. It's a place for trailer homes, pickup trucks, and woodstoves.

Bay Center

This historic fishing town has a New England feel, with simple frame homes and a wonderful Willapa Bay setting. It is still home to productive oyster beds, as evidenced by the enormous piles of shells and the cluster of shoreside oyster plants, several of which offer fresh oysters for sale. Camping and great views across the bay are available at nearby **Bush Pioneer Park,** open summers only. Park RVs at **Bay Center KOA,** tel. (360) 875-6344.

Willapa National Wildlife Refuge

The 12,000-acre Willapa National Wildlife Refuge encompasses all of Long Island, plus the northern tip of the Long Beach Peninsula, and freshwater marshes on the south end of Willapa Bay, which provide important feeding grounds for migrating geese, ducks, and shorebirds.

Long Island

Part of Willapa National Wildlife Refuge, 5,000-acre Long Island can be reached only by boat from launch areas at refuge headquarters (nine miles west of Naselle and 12 miles north of Ilwaco on Hwy. 101, tel. 360-484-3482), Nahcotta, or points on the Long Beach Peninsula. Before heading to the island, get a map and more information from refuge headquarters. The island has five primitive campgrounds that often fill up on summer weekends (bring your own water; no reservations), but getting there can be tough due to tidal fluctuations—during low tide, you can practically walk out to it. No motorized travel is permitted. Like the rest of this cutover corner of the state, much of Long Island has been repeatedly logged and is still being cut. Because of its remote location, a small 247-acre stand of cedars managed to avoid Weyerhaeuser's chainsaws long enough to be purchased by the refuge. This is one of the few old-growth forests remaining in southwest Washington. A three-quarter mile trail passes through part of this wonderful old grove, with enormous cedars and a lush rainforest floor; some of the trees are over a thousand years old. The muddy tide flats and rich salt grass marshes around Long Island are important resting and feeding areas for migratory waterfowl. You don't have to get out to the island to enjoy the wildlife; there are numerous turnouts along Highways 105 and 101 where you can pull off and watch herds of elk or black-tailed deer.

LONG BEACH PENINSULA

The Long Beach Peninsula is a 28-mile-long strip of sand and fun off the southwesternmost corner of Washington. Locals call it the "World's Longest Beach," though you're bound to hear disagreement from folks in Australia and New Zealand. Be that as it may, this is one *very* long stretch of sand, and a favorite getaway for folks from Seattle and Portland.

Ask most Puget Sounders who frequent the Long Beach Peninsula what they think about it, and you'll probably get the same protective response Washingtonians have about their state when talking to Californians and North Dakotans: they love it and don't want it to change. The towns on this peninsula have a lived-in look to them, and many of the houses are so sand-peppered and rain-washed that they look as though a designer talked everyone into the weathered-home look. The peninsula is the kind of place where you'll find rubber boots and heavy raingear on almost every porch—it rains over 70 inches a year here, so be ready to get wet even in the summer—and somewhere in every house is a glass float from a Japanese fishing net and a piece of driftwood.

This is one place in the state where you can find decent art by local artists. Artwork isn't limited to studios; the towns of Long Beach and Ilwaco have joined the public mural parade in a big way, and it is hard to fault any town for putting something on the side of their buildings other than shingles or aluminum siding.

The peninsula begins at the Astoria-Megler bridge, and the first town is Chinook, although technically it isn't on the peninsula. Ilwaco is next, then comes Seaview, the town of Long Beach, Klipsan Beach, and Ocean Park on the Pacific Ocean side. On the Willapa Bay side are Nahcotta and Oysterville.

The town of Long Beach has the only walkable downtown area on the coast, with little shops and the typical souvenir joints—like a *real* beach

ARCHIE SATTERFIELD

Long Beach

town. At the north end of the peninsula, things are drastically different, with beautifully restored turn-of-the-century homes in Oysterville, and an isolated natural area at Leadbetter Point. In recent years, a controversy has brewed over development on the sand dunes that line Long Beach. Real estate interests, speculators, and conservative politicians are pushing to open them to wholesale development; environmentalists have attempted to block this encroachment. So far, things are at a stalemate, but look for massive changes if the developers get their way.

FORT CANBY STATE PARK

Located 2.5 miles southwest of Ilwaco, Fort Canby State Park is the peninsula's most scenic state park, and a place packed with history. In this 1,882-acre facility you'll find a museum dedicated to Lewis and Clark, historic lighthouses, dramatic vistas across the mouth of the Columbia River, old-growth forests, white beaches, famous fishing, campsites (see "Campgrounds," under "Peninsula Accommodations," below), and turn-of-the-century military fortifications.

The park is located on Cape Disappointment—Washington's southernmost point. The name originated in 1788, when British fur trader John Meares was searching for the fabled Northwest Passage. He had heard tales of an enormous river near here from a Spaniard, Bruno Heceta, who had noted it in 1775. Meares failed to find the river, hence the cape's disappointing name. The mighty river is apparently easy to miss from the sea; Capt. George Vancouver also sailed past. The river wasn't officially "discovered" until 1792 when an American, Capt. Robert Gray, sailed his *Columbia Rediviva* into the treacherous river mouth.

More than 230 ships were wrecked or sunk on the Columbia bar before jetties were constructed to control the sand. The longest of these—North Jetty—reaches a half-mile out from the end of the cape and is a very popular place to fish for salmon, rock cod, perch, and sea bass. Although the jetties succeeded in stabilizing the shifting Columbia bar, they also caused sand dunes to accumulate north of here and worsened an undertow that makes for dangerous swimming conditions.

History

Fort Canby holds an important place in history, for on this hill Meriwether Lewis and William Clark stood in November of 1806; they had finally "reached the great Pacific Ocean which we been so long anxious to See." Because game proved scarce and this side of the Columbia lacked protection from winter storms, they crossed the river to build a winter camp called Fort Clatsop near present-day Astoria, Oregon.

The commanding presence and strategic location of Cape Disappointment made it a vital fort location for the new Oregon Territory. The initial cannons arrived in 1862, and the fort itself was later named for Major General Edward Canby, killed in California's Modoc Indian War. During the two world wars, the fort served as a command post for underwater mines placed at the mouth of the Columbia. The fort never fired its guns at enemy ships, but in 1942, a Japanese submarine fired on—and missed—Fort Stevens, across the river in Oregon. After WW II Fort Canby was decommissioned, becoming a state park in 1957. Many of the old bunkers and gun emplacements remain, making for interesting explorations.

Lewis and Clark Interpretive Center

This fascinating museum is one of the must-see places on Long Beach Peninsula. Open daily 10 a.m.-5 p.m. year-round, the interpretive center (tel. 360-642-3029) is an excellent introduction to the 1804-06 expedition led by William Clark and Meriwether Lewis. A ramp leads you to a lower level where you can watch a 20-minute slide show (shown every half-hour), and then back up to the second floor again. Along the way you pass fascinating exhibits detailing their trip up the Missouri River, over the Rockies, and then down the Columbia River. You'll learn about the various participants, the unusual air gun they used to impress the Indians, how they constructed dugout canoes, and the everyday experiences in their winter camp at Fort Clatsop.

The ramp emerges in a large room with expansive windows fronting on Cape Disappointment Lighthouse, the Columbia River, and the mighty Pacific. You're certain to see ships plying the waters offshore or moving upriver. Turn around to find displays detailing the "Graveyard of the Pacific" on the bar at the mouth of the Columbia; more than 230 ships (along with hundreds more smaller boats) have gone down in these treacherous waters, killing over 700 people. You'll learn about early rescue methods, and how they have advanced to the sophisticated helicopter rescues of today. The Coast Guard still operates a major rescue station at Point Disappointment, as well as a **Motor Lifeboat School** that trains seafarers to handle boats under extreme weather conditions and in dangerous seas. This is the only such school in the United States.

Lighthouses and Trails

You can see the mouth of the Columbia by turning right at the concession area and driving to the road's end; park here and walk through the sand to the lookout atop North Jetty. **Cape Disappointment Lighthouse** is the Northwest's oldest, built in 1856; follow the quarter-mile trail

ARCHIE SATTERFIELD

North Head Lighthouse

from the interpretive center or a steep quarter-mile path from the Coast Guard Station. (This was intended to be the first lighthouse on the Pacific Coast, but a storm wrecked the ship loaded with lighthouse materials just as it was coming in to the Columbia River, so construction was delayed three years.) Great vistas from here across the mouth of the Columbia; look for an old wrecked ship along the south jetty. Deer are common sights near the lighthouse, especially around dusk.

North Head Lighthouse was built in 1898 and stands above Dead Man's Hollow, which commemorates the sailors of the ill-fated *Vandelia,* which sank here in 1853; it's a short walk through the trees from the upper parking lot, or a two-mile hike from McKenzie Head (just west of the campground). The dunes and driftwood piles of **Benson Beach** spread out to the south (no vehicles allowed), with Long Beach pointing its finger northward. This lighthouse signals to ships coming from the north, out of sight of Cape Disappointment Lighthouse.

North Head is a favorite place to watch for migrating **gray whales** heading north March-May or south late December to early February. It's also an awe-inspiring place during winter storms when waves pound hard against the rocks below.

Tiny **Waikiki Beach** is a favorite local spot for picnics and swimming in the summer (but no lifeguard). The beach received its name when a Hawaiian sailor's body washed ashore here after his ship was wrecked in a failed attempt to cross the Columbia River bar in 1811. You can follow a trail uphill from Waikiki to the Lewis and Clark Interpetive Center, and then on to Cape Disappointment Lighthouse.

For a taste of old-growth forests, take the 1.5-mile **Coastal Forest Trail** that begins at the boat ramp along Baker Bay. This is a very enjoyable loop hike.

ILWACO

Historic Ilwaco (ill-WOK-o; pop. 900) is a charter, sports, and commercial fishing town on the south end of the Long Beach Peninsula, with docks on protected Baker Bay. The town was named for a Chinook leader, Chief Elowahka Jim. Walk

a good day's catch at Ilwaco

STATE OF WASHINGTON TOURISM DIVISION

around town to find five murals on the sides of local businesses, and some wonderful old buildings. Ilwaco's old Fire Station No. 1 on Lake St. contains the "Mankiller," an 1846 hand pumper that was the first fire-fighting apparatus of its kind in Washington Territory. You can view the Mankiller through a window when the building isn't open.

Visit the excellent and spacious **Ilwaco Heritage Museum** at 115 S.E. Lake St., tel. (360) 642-3446, for a look into Pacific Coast history via models, exhibits, and photographs of early settlers' fishing, oystering, and logging methods, and Cape Disappointment shipwrecks and rescues. Of particular interest is a detailed scale model of the Columbia River estuary, and a display on the *Sector,* a 26-foot boat that Gérard D'Aboville rowed from Japan to Ilwaco in 1991. The museum is open Mon.-Sat. 9 a.m.-5 p.m., Sunday 10 a.m.-2 p.m. in the summer; and Mon.-Sat. 9 a.m.-4 p.m., Sunday 10 a.m.-2 p.m. in the winter. Entrance costs $2 for adults, $1.75 for seniors, 75 cents for children under 12, and $5 for families.

SEAVIEW

Seaview grew up around a small beach resort established in 1881 by Jonathon L. Stout. Today, it is home to a number of restaurants, motels, and B&Bs, as well as the Long Beach Peninsula Visitors Bureau at the junction of Highways 101 and 103 (Pacific Highway).

Although the same sort of developments are creeping into Seaview as in its rowdy make-a-buck neighbor to the north, Long Beach, the settlement is best known as home to the historic Shelbourne Inn (see "Peninsula Accommodations," below). A number of antique shops line the highway, and not far away is the **Charles Mulvey Gallery,** 46th Pl. at L St., tel. (360) 642-2189, open weekends, and selling works by this well-known but formulaic watercolorist.

LONG BEACH

Long Beach (pop. 1,400) comprises the commercial core of the peninsula, with all the typical beachfront services, including kitschy gift shops, fish and chips takeouts, real estate offices, kite stores, taffy shops, mini-strip malls, RV parks, motels, and bumper boat, go-kart, and mini-golf amusement parks. Not everything is tacky, but don't come here expecting a classy, romantic experience; this is a family fun-for-all place. In the summer this town hums with traffic and the ringing of cash registers; in winter it slows to a quieter pace but is still popular as a weekend getaway.

History

The first whites to arrive in Long Beach were the Lewis and Clark party who traveled through this area of sand dunes and pine trees in late 1805, stopping long enough for William Clark to carve his name on a tree; it's the western-most point reached by the expedition. A life-sized bronze statue of the explorers can be found in downtown Long Beach. The town did not come into existence until 1880, when Henry Harrison Tinker—an adventurer from Maine—settled here and gradually attracted summer visitors from Portland, Oregon, and other cities.

Kite Museum

Befitting its beachside location, Long Beach is home to the **World Kite Museum and Hall of Fame.** Inside, you'll learn the history of kites and how they were used during wartime and in developing airplanes. Also here are kites from around the globe, a re-created Japanese kite artist workshop, videos of local kite festivals, and a gift shop with books about kite making and kite history. Located near the corner of 3rd St. NW and Pacific Hwy., tel. (360) 642-4020, the museum is open daily 11 a.m.-5 p.m. during June, July, and August; Fri.-Mon. 11 a.m.-5 p.m. in September and October; and Sat.-Sun. 11 a.m.-5 p.m. the rest of the year. Admission is $1 for adults, 50 cents for children or seniors, and $3 for families. The museum offers kite-making workshops the first Saturday of the month May-August.

Marsh's Free Museum

It may be campy, but you definitely don't want to miss Marsh's Free Museum, a huge souvenir shop in downtown Long Beach, tel. (360) 642-2188. Inside is a delightful collection of the tacky and bizarre, much of it from old amusement parks, traveling shows, and attics. You'll find an impressive collection of glass fishing balls, the world's largest frying pan, a vampire bat skeleton, an old bottle with a human tapeworm, a gruesome photo of a 1920 triple hanging, and a two-headed calf. Drop a nickel for a flapper-era peep show, pay a dime to test your passion factor on the "throne of love," or search the jam-packed shelves for a tasteless postcard, goofy T-shirt, cheap trinket, or bright seashell. Oh, and you won't want to miss "Jake the Alligator Man," stuck in a back corner inside a glass aquarium; he once starred in that arbiter of tabloid discernment, the *Weekly World News*. If you like tasteless junk, you'll rate this as Washington's finest gift shop!

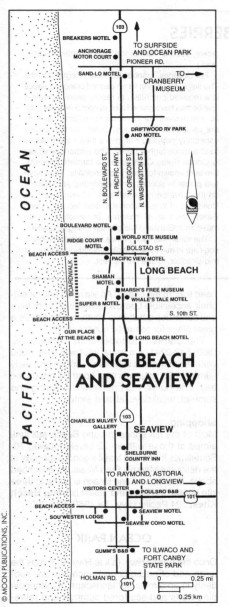

© MOON PUBLICATIONS, INC.

CRANBERRIES

Cranberries are one of two native American fruits (the other being the blueberry) grown in wetlands. The berries originated on the East Coast, and Massachusetts still leads in cranberry production, but they now are also raised in New Jersey, Wisconsin, Oregon, and Washington, as well as Canada. They were introduced to Washington in the 1930s, and the state now produces 7,500 tons of cranberries annually, four percent of the nation's total output. Nearly all of the 130 cranberry farms in the state are small family-run operations with an average of just 11 acres each.

Cranberries grow on perennial vines in acidic peat bogs and are named for the flowers that resemble the head and bill of a crane. The traditional way to harvest cranberries has been to flood the fields, causing the berries to float to the surface for harvesting. This is still done on some bogs, but most in Washington use dry-harvesting equipment that combs the vines to pull the berries. (The Furford picker, used for harvesting, was invented in Grayland.)

For decades, cranberries were relegated to the Thanksgiving season when canned cranberry sauce is a required purchase. In recent years, however, cranberries have gained a bit of caché with the public, and demand for them has risen rapidly as they are used in various foods. Dried cranberries are especially popular, with more flavor than raisins (and a much higher price). The primary producer is Ocean Spray Cranberries, a farmers cooperative best known for their juice cocktails. They have two plants in southeast Washington: at Grayland on the "Cranberry Coast" and in Long Beach. A University of Washington research facility at Long Beach has a small museum, and another private museum in Grayland has old harvesting equipment.

The most interesting times to visit the cranberry bogs are in mid-June, the peak blooming season, or mid-October, to see the harvest.

Cranberries

On Pioneer Rd. about a mile northeast of Long Beach, is the **Cranberry Museum & Gift Shop,** open Fri.-Sun. 10 a.m.-3 p.m. Sponsored by the University of Washington but privately funded, this is home to a cranberry research staff that studies the private lives of cranberries; take a tour to see the bogs, picking equipment, and a slide show. Try to time your visit for June, the peak bloom season, or October, to see the harvest. Around 550 acres of cranberries are grown in the Long Beach Peninsula area, and you're bound to see them growing along Hwy. 101 as you approach the peninsula. Cranberries were originally called "crane berries" by early settlers who thought the blossoms resembled cranes' heads. Ocean Spray Cranberries, Inc. has a processing plant on Sandridge Rd. in Long Beach, and a second one in Westport. **Gray Whale Gallery & Gifts,** 105 Pacific Ave., sells cranberry products made from the local crop.

Other Sights

Several fine murals grace the sides of buildings in Long Beach. One of the peninsula's most photographed local spots is the "World's Longest Beach" arch that rises over Bolsted St. as you head toward the ocean. An elevated and wheel-chair-accessible boardwalk takes off from here and continues a half-mile south to 10th St.; it's a great place for romantic sunset strolls.

The **Clarke Rhododendron Nursery,** tel. (360) 642-2241, is a visual treat with over 1,000 varieties of rhodies in bloom in spring and early summer, 6.5 miles north of Long Beach on the bay. The nursery is open daily in spring and summer, weekdays fall and winter.

Shopping

Most of the gift shops in Long Beach sell junk aimed at those with an IQ barely topping 70. Sometimes it's so bad that it's good, especially at the delightful Marsh's Free Museum, described above. Downtown Long Beach is home to three kite shops; the best and oldest is **Long Beach Kites,** 104 Pacific Hwy., tel. (360) 642-2202.

OCEAN PARK

Once the Pacific Hwy. (a.k.a. Hwy. 103) exits the north end of hectic Long Beach you are suddenly in an almost flat landscape of lodgepole pine trees and scattered summer and retirement homes. You can't see the ocean or Willapa Bay from here, but there are access points all along the way. After 11 miles of this, the highway widens into Ocean Park (pop. 1,400), a place that is considerably more sedate than Long Beach, but nevertheless a popular summer retreat.

Established in 1883 as a Methodist church camp and revival center—and a place to escape the booze and wildness of nearby Oysterville—Ocean Park was transformed into a summer refuge after construction of the narrow-gauge "Clamshell Railroad" in the late 1880s. The church camp remains, but gone are the laws prohibiting saloons. Today, Ocean Park consists of a cluster of shops and businesses lining the highway, surrounded by a spread of summer homes.

The **Wreckage,** on the south side of 256th just west of Hwy. 103, is a unique house constructed in 1912 from logs salvaged after a storm broke apart a raft of logs being towed off the coast. It's on the National Register of Historic Places. **Wiegardt Studio Gallery,** 2607 Bay Ave., tel. (360) 665-5976, contains the watercolor works of Eric Wiegardt, one of several respected local artists. **Shoalwater Cove Gallery,** 25712 Sandridge Rd., tel. (360) 665-4382, has beautifully detailed pastels by Marie Powell.

Nearby **Surfside** is a residential area with a couple of businesses, a golf course, and lots of retired folks.

Loomis Lake State Park, south of Klipsan Beach, has picnic tables and restrooms on the ocean, not the lake; the real Loomis Lake is about a quarter mile north. No camping here.

NAHCOTTA

Named for Chinook Indian leader, Chief Nahcati, tiny Nahcotta (nah-COT-ah) consists of a smattering of businesses—mainly oyster farms and canneries—along quiet Willapa Bay. Established in 1889, the town was the northern terminus of the narrow-gauge Ilwaco Railroad and Navigation Co. (alias the "Clamshell Railroad") that ran up Long Beach Peninsula. Its dock was used to ship oysters south to San Francisco. In 1915 a fire destroyed much of the business district, and it was never entirely rebuilt. The railroad

ran until 1930, when cars and ferries ushered in a new era. Nahcotta is the center for the oyster industry on the peninsula, an industry that contributes more than $20 million to the economy and leaves enormous piles of whitened shells along the shore.

Tour the **Willapa Bay Shellfish Laboratory** weekdays 8:30 a.m.-noon and 1-4 p.m., and hear a tape about oyster biology. The actual oyster beds are closed to the public, but you can purchase fresh oysters and other seafood at **Wiegart Brothers Oyster Co., Bendiksen's East Point,** or the smaller **Nahcotta Oyster Farm.** Also in Nahcotta is the famous **Ark Restaurant** (see "Peninsula Food," below).

Across from Bendiksen's is the small **Willapa Bay Interpretive Center,** tel. (360) 665-4547, open Fri.-Sun. 10 a.m.-3 p.m., May-Oct. only, with exhibits on the oyster industry and the natural history of Willapa Bay (also known as Shoalwater Bay).

Nahcotta Natural Store and Cafe, tel. (360) 665-4449, has become something of a local center for ecotourism. The market sells natural foods, and the cafe delivers soups, salads, and tasty sandwiches made with fresh-baked breads for lunch, plus full dinners. Be sure to check out the handmade paper sold here; it's fabricated from local Spartina grass. Upstairs is Nahcotta B&B (see "Peninsula Accommodations," below), plus kayak and bike rentals and boat tours of Willapa Bay.

OYSTERVILLE

Approximately 16 miles north of Long Beach and just off Hwy. 103 is the small, somnambulant settlement of Oysterville. It was not always thus; for many years this was one of the busiest places in southwestern Washington.

History
Following the discovery of gold in California, San Franciscans had both gold and a yen to spend it on good food, especially fresh oysters. With oysters selling for up to $50 a plate, the demand led men to search far and wide for new sources. In 1854, Chief Nahcati (the source of the name Nahcotta) showed R.H. Espy and I.A. Clark the rich oyster beds of Willapa Bay. Sens-

ing a profit, they quickly built the new town of Oysterville on the site, and within a scant few months another 500 boomers had arrived.

The rowdy town grew to become the county seat within two years, and even had a college for a period, before overharvesting and winter freezes made the oysters scarce in the late 1880s. With the loss of oysters and the money and jobs they attracted, the Oysterville's economy collapsed, and county voters decided to move the Pacific County seat to the logging town of South Bend. Oysterville charged ballot box stuffing by railroad workers in South Bend and sued to overturn the vote.

A bitter legal battle ensued that threatened to keep the matter tied up in the courts for years, so a group of South Bend men decided to force the issue. On a Sunday morning in February of 1893, some 85 men crossed to Oysterville abroad two steamships. They first stopped for liquid reinforcement at a local saloon. Then, finding most everyone in church, the mob proceeded to plunder the county courthouse, stealing (or legally removing, depending upon who is telling the story) all the records and furniture. After returning to South Bend with the booty, they sent a bill to Oysterville for services rendered in the process of moving the county records! The county seat has been in South Bend ever since, but the bill was never paid.

Oysterville Today

The loss of the county courthouse sounded the death knell for Oysterville, and over the decades that followed, many homes and three entire streets were swallowed by the bay as storms eroded the shoreline. It wasn't until the 1930s with the introduction of a new species of oyster—this time from Japan—that the beds again became productive. Today, you can stop at **Oysterville Sea Farms,** tel. (360) 665-6585, for fresh or smoked oysters and clams.

A number of homes constructed during the town's heyday have been restored and are now part of the Oysterville National Historic District. For a self-guided walking tour map, visit the beautiful white and red **Oysterville Baptist Church,** built in 1892 but no longer used for regular church services. Not far away is the old **Oysterville School,** constructed in 1908. The historic Espy House is especially notable. Built

in 1854 by the cofounder of Oysterville, this big white house with gingerbread ornamentation has a classic country feel. The cemetery contains the grave of **Chief Nahcati,** who first brought the oyster beds to the attention of the whites.

Leadbetter Point State Park

The northern tip of Long Beach Peninsula is capped by two publicly owned natural areas, Leadbetter Point State Park, and a portion of the Willapa National Wildlife Refuge (see above). Leadbetter has a 1.5 mile trail through the evergreen forest, connecting both parking lots. From the north lot, you can enter Willapa and walk through stunted lodgepole pine forests to beachgrass-covered sand dunes along the Pacific Ocean, or head down to the shore of Willapa Bay for a beach walk. The northern end of Willapa National Wildlife Refuge is closed to all entry April-Aug. to protect the threatened snowy plover that nests on the dunes here. This area is also a very important sanctuary for waterfowl, particularly during spring and fall migrations. Birdwatchers will see thousands (and sometimes hundreds of thousands) of black brant, Canada geese, dunlin, plovers, sandpipers, and other birds in the marshes and beaches during these times. No fires or camping allowed.

PENINSULA ACCOMMODATIONS

See the "Long Beach Area Accommodations" chart for a complete listing of the Long Beach Peninsula's lodging choices. Accommodations can be hard to come by on summer weekends, especially during the main festivals. Many rooms are booked a year ahead for the Memorial Day weekend, the International Kite Festival in August, and Labor Day weekend. It's a good idea to reserve two to four weeks ahead for other summer weekends. The visitors bureau, tel. (360) 642-2400 or (800) 451-2542, doesn't make reservations but tries to keep track of who has space. They also have a listing of local guesthouses and cabins available for longer periods of time. The **Bed & Breakfast Association of Long Beach Peninsula,** tel. (360) 642-8484, publishes a brochure that lists local B&Bs.

LONG BEACH AREA ACCOMMODATIONS

Accommodations are arranged from least to most expensive. Winter rates at many motels and B&Bs are often 20-40% cheaper. The area code is 360.

HOSTEL

Fort Columbia AYH Hostel; Chinook; tel. 777-8755; $10 pp AYH members or $13 pp nonmembers in dorms; at historic Fort Columbia, full kitchen, reservations advised, open March-Oct. only

MOTELS

Sands Motel; Long Beach; tel. 642-2100; $32-65 s or d; cabins with kitchens

Sand-Lo Motel; Long Beach; tel. 642-2600 or (800) 676-2601; $35-60 s or d; kitchens available

Sou'wester Lodge; 38th Place, Seaview; tel. 642-2542; $35-84 d in trailers (sleep up to six), $54-58 d in the lodge, $70-73 d in cottages with kitchens; funky love-it-or-hate-it lodge

Heidi's Inn; 126 Spruce St., Ilwaco; tel. 642-2387 or (800) 576-1032; $36 s or d; jacuzzi, kitchenettes available

Driftwood Motel; Long Beach; tel. 642-2711; $40 s or d; kitchens available

Harbor View Motel; Nahcotta; tel. 642-4959; $40 s or d; kitchenettes available

Seaview Coho Motel; 3701 Pacific Hwy., Seaview; tel. 642-2531; $40 s or d; kitchenettes $50-75 s or d

101 Haciendas; Spruce at Brumbach, Ilwaco; tel. 642-8459; $40 s, $43 d

Arcadia Motel; Long Beach; tel. 642-2613; $40-49 s or d; kitchens available

Westgate Motel; Ocean Park; tel. 642-4211; $40-53 s or d; kitchenettes available, game room, ocean view

Ocean Park Resort; 259th and R St., Ocean Park; tel. 642-4585 or (800) 835-4634; $40-70 s or d in cabins, $50-55 s or d in motel; kitchens available, outdoor pool, rec room, jacuzzi, Saturday pancake breakfast, AAA approved

Ocean Lodge; 101 Boulevard St. N, Long Beach; tel. 642-2777; $45 s or d in motel, $75 for cabin (sleeps six); spa, sauna, outdoor pool, ocean view, kitchens available

Pacific View Motel; Long Beach; tel. 642-2415; $45 s or d in motel, $56-85 s or d in cabins with kitchens; ocean view

Lighthouse Motel; Long Beach; tel. 642-3622; $45-55 s or d; cabins with kitchens, ocean view

Ridge Court Motel; Long Beach; tel. 642-2412; $45-55 s or d; kitchenettes available, outdoor pool

Boulevard Motel; Long Beach; tel. 642-2434; $45-60 s or d in motel, $65-70 s or d in cabins; indoor pool, kitchens available

Seaview Motel; Seaview; tel. 642-2450; $50 s or d in motel rooms; $60 for up to four in cabins with kitchenettes

Long Beach Motel; 1200 Pacific Hwy. S in Long Beach; tel. 642-3500; $52 s or d motel rooms, $59-102 s or d cottages with kitchens

Our Place at the Beach; Long Beach; tel. 642-3793 or (800) 538-5107; $54-100 s or d; kitchenettes available, jacuzzi, sauna, ocean view, AAA approved

Col-Pacific Motel; Ilwaco; tel. 642-3177; $55 s or d weekends, $48 s or d Mon.-Fri.; kitchenettes available, river view

(continues on next page)

LONG BEACH AREA ACCOMMODATIONS
(continued)

Chautauqua Lodge Resort Motel; Long Beach; tel. 642-4401 or (800) 869-8401; $55-100 s or d; indoor pool, jacuzzi, sauna, kitchenettes available, ocean view

Sunset View Resort; 25517 Park Ave., Ocean Park; tel. 642-4494 or (800) 272-9199; $59 s or d in motel rooms, $84-119 s or d in suites with kitchens; hot tubs, sauna, tennis, volleyball, basketball, continental breakfast

Whale's Tale Motel; Long Beach; tel. 642-3455 or (800) 559-4253; $60-85 s or d; suites with kitchens, sauna, jacuzzi, fitness center

Boardwalk Cottages; 800 Boulevard S., Long Beach; tel. 642-2305; $63-68 s or d; cabins with kitchens

Super 8 Motel; Long Beach; tel. 642-8988 or (800) 800-8000; $64 s, $69 d; AAA approved

The Breakers Motel; Long Beach; tel. 642-4414 or (800) 288-8890; $65 motel rooms, $127-171 s or d suites; indoor pool, spa, kitchens, ocean view

Anchorage Motor Court; Long Beach; tel. 642-2351; $65-84 s, $73-98 d; apartments with kitchens, ocean view, AAA approved

Harbor Lights Motel; Ilwaco; tel. 642-3196; $69 s or d

Shaman Motel; 115 3rd St. SW, Long Beach; tel. 642-3714 or (800) 642-3714; $74-89 s or d; outdoor pool, kitchens available, two-night minimum stay on weekends, AAA approved

Klipsan Beach Cottages; Ocean Park; tel. 642-4888; $80-100 s or d; comfortable older cottages with kitchens, ocean views, very nice place

BED AND BREAKFASTS

Shakti Cove Cottages; 1204 253rd Place, Ocean Park; tel. 665-4000; $49 s or d; 10 cottages (built in 1939) with kitchenettes

Coastal Cottages; 1511 264th Place, Ocean Park; tel. 665-4658; $55-65 s or d; kitchenettes available

The Inn at Ilwaco B&B; 120 Williams St. NE, Ilwaco; tel. 642-8686; $55-80 d; nine guest rooms in a beautifully restored 1928 church, river view

Boreas B&B; 607 N. Boulevard, Long Beach; tel. 642-8069; $55-85 s, $65-95 d; 1920s beach home, ocean view, jacuzzi, stone fireplace, sundeck

Kola House B&B; 211 Pearl, Ilwaco; tel. 642-2819; $60-70 s, $65-75 d; 1919 boardinghouse, sauna

Moby Dick Hotel B&B; Nahcotta; tel. 665-4543; $60-75 s, $70-85 d; restored 1930s hotel with bay view, organic garden, oyster farm, full country breakfast, dinners by reservation

Poulsbo B&B; 3911 N. Place, Seaview; tel. 642-4393; $65 s or d; restored 1887 home with antiques

Gumm's B&B Inn; 3310 Hwy. 101, Seaview; tel. 642-8887; $65-80 s or d; beautiful 1911 home with hot tub, stone fireplace, sunporch, full breakfast

Our House in Nahcotta B&B; Nahcotta; tel. 665-6667; $75-100 s or d; Victorian home

Scandinavian Gardens Inn B&B; 1610 California St., Long Beach; tel. 642-8877 or (800) 988-9277; $75-125 s or d; hot tub and sauna, gourmet Scandinavian breakfast

Land's End B&B; Long Beach; tel. 642-8268; $80-95 s or d; elegant ocean-view home with antiques and grand piano, three miles north of Long Beach

Coast Watch B&B; Ocean Park; tel. 665-6774; $85 d and up; ocean-view suites, full breakfast

---

Caswell's on the Bay; 25204 Sandridge Rd., Ocean Park; tel. 665-6535; $85-150; elaborate new Victorian-style B&B on Willapa Bay, furnished with antiques, no kids, full breakfast

Shelburne Country Inn; 4415 Pacific Way, Seaview; tel. 642-2442; $89-159 s, $105-165 d; luxurious world-class inn, antique furnishings, gourmet breakfasts, no TVs, AAA approved

Nahcotta B&B; Nahcotta; tel. 665-4449; $90 s or d; historic train depot, bay views, private baths, full breakfast

---

Budget travelers will want to check out the excellent **youth hostel** located at Fort Columbia in Chinook (11 miles east), tel. (360) 777-8755. It's open March-Oct. only; a year-round hostel (tel. 503-738-7911) is in Seaside, Oregon, 25 miles south of here.

Special Places

If you're looking for standard motel accommodations, but there are plenty of places along the peninsula, but if you want a friendly place with a sense of nostalgia, character, and charm, look no farther than Seaview's **Sou'wester Lodge,** 38th Place, tel (360) 642-2542. Here, literary owners Leonard and Miriam Atkins have created a rustic haven for those who appreciate a place with simple comfort rather than ostentatiousness. The accommodations include "Bed and Make Your Own Damn Breakfast" rooms in the stately three-story lodge built in 1892 as a summer estate by Henry Winslow Corbett, a wealthy timber baron, banker, and U.S. Senator from Oregon. Outside are weathered beach cottages furnished in "early Salvation Army" decor, and even a hodgepodge of 1950s-era trailers. Artists and writers often "book in" for months at a time, relaxing in this cozy and informal lodge. On many Saturday nights, the sitting room comes to life with lectures, concerts, or poetry. You're likely to find everything from chamber music to kelp basketry weaving workshops!

A 1926 Presbyterian church has been restored and converted into **The Inn at Ilwaco,** 120 Williams St. N.E., tel (360) 642-8686. The inn's guest quarters occupy the old Sunday school rooms, and the sanctuary is now a playhouse and performance center.

Seaview's acclaimed **Shelburne Inn**—*Condé Nast Traveler* proclaimed it one of the "Top 25 inns worldwide"—is in an elegant 1896 Victorian

at 4415 Pacific Way, tel. (360) 642-2442. The oldest continuously used lodging place in Washington, the inn is packed with tasteful antiques, stained glass windows (from an old English church), and original artwork. A full country breakfast (including omelettes, smoked salmon, razor clam fritters, homemade breads, and fresh fruit) is included; for many, it's the highlight of their stay. It is, however, located right along busy Pacific Hwy., so the roadside rooms may be a bit noisy. Also beware of the ghost who is rumored to wander the third floor some nights. In the same building is the equally famous **Shoalwater Restaurant,** definitely worth at least a mealtime visit, if you can't swing an overnight stay at the inn.

Other noteworthy B&Bs include: **Moby Dick Hotel B&B** in Nahcotta, tel. (360) 665-4543, located in a 1930s hotel; **Our House in Nahcotta,** tel. (360) 665-6667, a three-story Victorian home; **Scandinavian Gardens Inn,** 1610 California St., Long Beach, tel. (360) 642-8807 or (800) 988-9277, a quiet hideaway featuring a Scandinavian breakfast buffet plus a sauna and spa; **Poulsbo B&B,** 3911 N. Place, Seaview, tel. (360) 642-4393, in a pretty antique-filled 1887 home right behind the visitors center; **Kola House B&B,** 211 Pearl, Ilwaco, tel. (360) 642-2819, located in a 1919 boardinghouse with sauna; and **Gumm's B&B Inn,** 3310 Hwy. 101, Seaview, tel. (360) 642-8887, a beautifully restored 1911 home that features a stone fireplace, sunporch, and hot tub. The spacious Victorian-style **Caswell's on the Bay B&B,** 25204 Sandridge Rd., Ocean Park, tel. (360) 665-6535, was completed in 1995, and offers friendly, spacious, and comfortable accommodations facing onto Willapa Bay. This is a very quiet and relaxing place, and the weather is usually warmer here than on the ocean side.

Campgrounds

One of the most popular places to camp in Washington, **Fort Canby State Park** (described above) has tent sites ($11) and RV sites ($16), plus coin-operated showers. The campground—within a few yards of beautiful Benson Beach—is open all year. Call (800) 452-5687 for campsite reservations ($6 extra fee), available up to 11 months ahead of time. It is illegal to camp on the sand along Long Beach, but a small campground is available at **Moorehead County Park** in Nahcotta, and additional county parks with camping can be found in Chinook (11 miles east), Naselle (22 miles east), Bay Center (30 miles northeast), and Bruceport (32 miles northeast). Rates are $10 for tents (only Bruceport has RV hookups), $5 for bike camping.

RVers will find two dozen different parking lots along the Long Beach Peninsula. Get a complete listing at the visitor center, or just drive along Pacific Hwy. till one looks acceptable.

PENINSULA FOOD

The Long Beach Peninsula is blessed with restaurants of all types, including some of the most innovative purveyors of Northwest cuisine in Washington.

Two good breakfast spots are **Chucks Restaurant,** N. 19th at Pacific Hwy. in Long Beach, tel. (360) 642-2721, with all-American meals; and **Lightship Restaurant,** above the ugly Nendel's Inn, off S. 10th St. in Long Beach, tel. (360) 642-3252. The Lightship is better known for gourmet dinners—pan-fried oysters, pastas, and prime rib—and also as one of the few local places with an ocean view. (Note, however, that their location right in the otherwise-undeveloped dunes is controversial; this is the sort of development environmentalists are trying to prevent.)

B.J. Squidley's in Ocean Park, tel. (360) 665-5262, features inexpensive fresh seafood and home-baked goods, along with big home-style breakfasts.

If you're in search of traditional American food, look no further than **42nd St. Cafe,** 42nd and Pacific Hwy. in Seaview, tel. (360) 642-2323. The restaurant features iron-skillet fried chicken, pot roast, steaks, and seafood, with homemade bread and jam, all served in heaping helpings. For Italian food, visit **Alphonds** in Surfside, tel. (360) 665-5148.

Light Meals

Get sandwiches, bagels, and good pizzas too, at **And Pizza Too,** 101 N. 2nd St. in Long Beach, tel. (360) 642-8133. Another popular pizza place is **Ilwaco Waterfront Pizzeria,** on the dock in Ilwaco, tel. (360) 642-8750.

Don't miss **Pastimes,** a collectibles shop, espresso bar, and restaurant at S. 5th and Pacific Hwy., tel. (360) 642-8303. Clocks, china, and glassware for antique hounds; cappuccino, hot chocolate, iced egg creams, and baked goods for the rest.

Dos Amigos Cafe, 2nd and Pacific Hwy. in Long Beach, tel. (360) 642-8365, makes fast and cheap Mexican burritos and Indian tacos. Other fast food—in the form of fish and chips—is available all over the peninsula; of note are **Sea Breeze Cafe,** 30th and Hwy. 101 in Seaview, tel. (360) 642-3033; and **Kopa Wecoma** near the beach in Ocean Park.

If you want to cook your own fish, stop at the best local fish and crab shop, **P&K Seafood Market,** in Ocean Park, tel. (360) 665-6800.

Bakeries and Espresso

Cottage Bakery, in downtown Long Beach, tel. (360) 642-4441, has cabinets filled with sticky-sweet old-fashioned American pastries. It's a favorite place to get a coffee and dessert while watching the people stroll by.

My Mom's Pie Kitchen, 12th and Pacific Hwy. in Long Beach, tel. (360) 642-2342, will cut you a big slice of one of their delicious homemade pies, or try the fresh crab quiche or creamy clam chowder. My Mom's trailer house location is vintage Long Beach kitsch.

Plain Jane's, 811 Pacific Hwy. S in Long Beach, tel. (360) 642-4933, bakes off-the-meter chocoholic cookies, including one with almonds, chocolate chips, and coconut.

Gourmet Meals

Some of the best food on the peninsula—if not in Washington—can be found at the **Shoalwater Restaurant,** 4415 Pacific Hwy., tel. (360) 642-

4142, at the Shelburne Inn. Dinners include Northwest seafood and game enhanced by in-season vegetables and berries, Northwest wines, and homemade breads, pastries, and desserts. Open in summer for Sunday brunch, and daily for lunch and dinner; reservations are required. Across the hall is **Heron and Beaver Pub** with microbrewed beers and light meals from the same kitchen.

The Ark Restaurant, tel. (360) 665-4133, is another local legend, located in Nahcotta, 12 miles north of Long Beach. The rustic building overlooks Willapa Bay, the source of oysters for which the restaurant is justly famous.

PENINSULA EVENTS AND ENTERTAINMENT

Events

In April, come to Long Beach for the **Ragtime Rhodie Dixieland Jazz Festival.** Then comes Ocean Park's **Garlic Festival,** held the third weekend of June, which features garlic shucking and garlic eating contests, plus all sorts of garlicky meals. Bring a couple of bottles of Listerine along. Long Beach hosts the annual Fourth of July **Fireworks on the Beach,** and Ocean Park has a popular **Street Fair** the same weekend. Then comes **Sandsations Sand Sculptures** at the end of the month.

The first weekend of August is time for the **Long Beach Rodeo,** an event that is more than 50 years old and features bareback and saddle bronc riding, barrel racing, and bull riding. The year's biggest event, the **Washington State International Kite Festival,** lasts the entire third week of August and draws well over 150,000 spectators and participants. This is the largest kite festival in the western hemisphere, and every day brings a different contest, ending with Sunday's grand finale in which the sky teems with thousands of kites of all sorts. The world record for keeping a kite aloft (over 180 hours) was set here.

Ocean Park hosts an enormously popular classic car show, the **Rod Run to the End of the World,** on Labor Day weekend that ends with a 15-mile long parade. The annual **Cranberry Festival,** held in Ilwaco in mid-October,

celebrates more than a century of coastal cranberry farming. Bog tours give you the chance to see the flooded fields with thousands of floating berries awaiting harvest. It's followed the third weekend of October by **Water Music Festival** with chamber music concerts all over the peninsula.

Nightlife

Every Saturday all summer long, you'll find free concerts in Long Beach's downtown gazebo. Seaview's **Sou'wester Lodge,** tel. (360) 642-2542, often has concerts, lectures, or poetry on Saturday nights. During the summer and fall, the **Bent Rudder** has country or rock bands on the weekends.

PENINSULA RECREATION

Fishing and Boating

Ilwaco is home to the peninsula's fishing fleet, with charter boats leaving daily for deep-sea rockfish, flounder, sole, and ling cod, migrating albacore tuna, sturgeon, and salmon. Recent years have seen curtailment of the salmon season due to poor returns. Salmon punch cards are available on the boats themselves or in the charter offices. Stop by the visitors center for a complete listing of local charter operators. They also have info on clam seasons and harvesting.

The *Seven Sons* is a custom-built flat-bottom boat used for half-day excursions around Long Island; it leaves from the Nahcotta dock. These excellent natural history trips provide a chance to drift among waterfowl and watch wildlife along the shore. Trips cost $40 per person; call (360) 665-4449 for details.

Rent sea kayaks in Nahcotta from **Willapa Bay Kayak Rentals,** tel. (360) 642-4892, to explore Willapa Bay on your own. They go for $25 per day; lessons cost $12 for a two-hour session.

Other Recreation

Contrary to expectations, the 28 miles of sandy beach on Long Beach Peninsula are not safe for swimming. Not only are there dangerous undertows and riptides, but rogue waves can occur, and there are no lifeguards. Every year waders or swimmers get trapped in these bitterly cold waters; sometimes the accidents end in tragedy. Locals and visitors looking for a chance to swim generally head to Waikiki Beach in Fort Canby State Park, or to local motel swimming pools.

Horse enthusiasts can rent horses for beach rides from **Skipper's Horse Rental,** behind the Long Beach go-kart track, tel. (360) 642-3676; or **Double D Horse Rentals,** on 10th St. in Long Beach, tel. (360) 642-2576. **Jim's Biplane Rides,** tel. (800) 359-1929, has unique flightseeing trips in a 1929 TravelAir biplane. Prices start at $90 for a 20-minute trip for two people. Two local golf courses are open to the public: **Peninsula Golf Course,** tel. (360) 642-2828, and **Surfside Golf Course,** tel. (360) 665-4148.

PENINSULA INFORMATION AND SERVICES

Long Beach is the place to go to do your laundry, buy groceries, or get your car washed. Get information at the **Long Beach Peninsula Visitors Bureau** at the junction of Highways 101 and 103, tel. (360) 642-2400 or (800) 451-2542, open daily 9 a.m.-5 p.m. all year. While here, be sure to pick up a copy of the free *Chinook Observer Visitor's Guide,* which often has two-for-one coupons for local motels. The **area code** for Long Beach is 360.

The two local **public libraries** are in Ilwaco at 158 1st Ave. N, tel. (360) 642-3908, and in Ocean Park at 1308 256th Pl., tel. (360) 665-4184.

You can't miss Ilwaco's **Ocean Beach Hospital,** just off the main drag; tel. (360) 642-3181.

PENINSULA TRANSPORTATION

Getting Around
The Long Beach Peninsula is divided by two parallel main roads: Highway 103, going through the commercial centers on the ocean side, and Sandridge Road, passing the largely residential sections on the bay side. The roads intersect at Oysterville, where only one road continues to Leadbetter Point.

Surprisingly, the only places to rent bikes are the **Mini Mart** in the Surfside Mall, tel. (360) 665-6880, and **Nahcotta Natural,** tel. (360) 665-4449, in Nahcotta.

Pacific Transit, tel. (360) 642-9418, has county-wide bus service Mon.-Sat., and dial-a-ride service in certain areas. Fares are 50 cents. The system connects with Grays Harbor Transit buses in Aberdeen, and also crosses the bridge to Astoria, Oregon. There is no Greyhound or Trailways service, and the nearest airport with commercial service is Astoria, Oregon.

Beach Driving
Approximately 15 miles of Long Beach are open to driving during the summer, but stay on the hard-packed sand, away from the car-eating soft sand and rich clam beds along the water's edge. The sand dunes are off limits to all vehicles. The maximum speed is 25 mph, and it *is* enforced. If you decide to drive the beach, be sure to wash the salt spray off your car immediately to prevent later rust problems. Check at the visitors center for a current description of areas open and closed to beach driving.

LOWER COLUMBIA RIVER

The stretch of river from the ocean to Bonneville Dam is the only part of the river still subject to the ebb and flow of the tides. The tidal force is so strong in the river that tugs pulling log booms upstream must tie up when the current and the tide are flowing in the same direction. From the mouth of the Willamette River on down, the Columbia has a distinct saltwater ambience to it. Seagoing ships steam back and forth in the 40-foot-deep channel, loading and unloading in Portland, Kalama, Longview, and Astoria. Seagulls wheel overhead with their rusty-hinge cries, and fishing boats share the waterway with the ships and tugs.

Chinook

Although it's hard to believe this today, the tiny fishing settlement of Chinook was once one of the richest towns per capita anywhere in America. Built on an old Indian village site, Chinook prospered in the 1880s from fish traps that crowded Baker Bay. In a single day, one man is said to have hauled in some 12,000 pounds of salmon, netting a then-unheard-of $500 profit. After the fish traps were outlawed early in this century, the town went into decline, but many of the wealthy fishermen's regal old homes still stand. The port in Chinook is still home to a small fleet of commercial fishing boats. Just east of town are the carved wooden statues of Lewis and Clark; the explorers camped here in late November 1805 on their way to the Pacific Ocean.

Chinook's claim to gastronomic fame is the **Sanctuary Restaurant,** tel. (360) 777-8380. Housed in a turn-of-the-century church, the dinner restaurant features fresh seafood and Scandinavian specialties prepared in unusual ways. The desserts are a special treat. Also in Chinook is the private **Sea Resources Hatchery,** where you can watch high school students raising salmon at the state's oldest hatchery, opened in 1893.

Camp at **Chinook County Park** along the river in Chinook, $5 for tents, $10 for RVs. Open May to mid-October, tel. (360) 777-8442. Local RV parks are **Chris' RV Park,** tel. (360) 777-8475, **Mulch's Sundown RV Park,** tel. (360) 777-8713, and **Rivers End RV Park,** tel. (360) 777-8317.

Fort Columbia State Park

Two miles southeast of Chinook on Hwy. 101, Fort Columbia State Park is a National Historic Site built in the late 1890s. It, along with Fort Canby and Fort Stephens (in Oregon) formed a triad of military bases guarding the mouth of the Columbia. Fort Columbia remained in use through WW II, but never engaged in battle. It still has 30 of the original buildings, along with various concrete batteries and two rapid firing six-inch guns (inoperable) that face out over the mouth of the Columbia. (The original guns were removed after WW II, and these were moved here from an old fort in Newfoundland, Canada, in 1994.)

An **interpretive center** in the enlisted men's barracks features two floors' worth of history, with displays on the Indian inhabitants, exploration, commercial fishing, and the military presence here. Upstairs are the bunks of enlisted men. The lives of military families are revealed in a second museum—furnished with period pieces—located in the old **Commander's House.** Hike up Scarborough Hill behind the fort for a view of the Columbia River or walk down to the riverside cliffs to see why this made such an easily defended spot. The fort is open daily 10 a.m.-5 p.m. from late April to early September; call (360) 642-3028 for more information.

On the grounds is the **Hostel International Fort Columbia,** tel. (360) 777-8755. Located in the old post hospital, this is a friendly and very popular place for budget travelers. If you don't want to camp out and can't afford to pay the high lodging rates on Long Beach Peninsula, this is an outstanding option. Besides the enjoyable historic structure, you get a big warm kitchen and the chance to watch dramatic sunsets from the cliffs along the Columbia River. Try the delicious blackberry pancakes for breakfast. Dorm spaces go for $10 per person for AYH members or $13 per person nonmembers. There is one private room that rents for $26 d for AYH members or $32 d for nonmembers. Reservations are advised during mid-summer, especially on weekends; they are imperative if you want the "couples" room. The hostel is open March-Oct. only.

Astoria-Megler Bridge

Completed in 1966, this 4.4-mile bridge is—according to the *Guiness Book of Records*—the longest continuous-truss span bridge in North America. If you don't know what a continuous-truss span is, take a look at the bridge. It looks like one to me, but they could have just as well called it a discontinuous truss and I'd believe it. Anyway, it's a long, tall bridge with a corkscrew approach into Astoria on the Oregon side. The toll that was collected here for almost three decades was discontinued at the end of 1993, so you won't be charged for a sidetrip into Oregon. By the way, the pilings visible on sandbars near the middle of the river once housed horse stalls. The horses were used to drag fishing nets to catch salmon; the process was known as "horse-seining."

Astoria, Oregon, has all sorts of interesting sights and a number of motels; for specifics, see *Oregon Handbook* by Stuart Warren and Ted Long Ishikawa. One place is well worth the drive: **Ship Inn,** on 2nd St. a half-mile east of the bridge, tel. (541) 325-0033. The halibut fish and chips are some the best in the Northwest, and the lounge has a big choice of microbrews on tap, including room-temperature Guinness. Historical enthusiasts shouldn't miss **Fort Clatsop,** the winter encampment site of the Lewis and Clark expedition, where a reconstructed fort features buckskin-clad park rangers and demonstrations all summer long. Nearby is **Fort Stevens,** one of a trio of forts built to guard the mouth of the Columbia River; the others—Fort Columbia and Fort Canby—are on the Washington side of the river. Camping is available at Fort Stevens. Also in Astoria is the **Columbia River Maritime Museum.**

Back on the Washington side you'll find the small **Megler Visitor Information Center,** tel. (360) 777-8388, a mile east of the Astoria Bridge on Hwy. 401. Open daily 9 a.m.-5 p.m. May-Sept., and Friday 11 a.m.-5 p.m., Saturday 9 a.m.-5 p.m., and Sunday 10 a.m.-4 p.m. in fall and spring; closed Dec.-February.

Naselle Area

East of the Astoria-Megler bridge, Hwy. 401 continues along the river for another three miles, passing the old **St. Mary McGowan Church**—built in 1904 and still in use—and the pilings that once supported a U.S. Customs and Detention Center. Early in this century, thousands of Chinese immigrants entered the country here and were forced to remain 30 days in quarantine before being allowed to look for work. Immediately after this, the highway turns inland and north to connect with Hwy. 4 at the weather-beaten little town of **Naselle.** This is lumbering country, and an abundance of "We support the timber industry" lawn signs and cutover forests all around are evidence of this support. The town's Finnish heritage comes to the fore in the **Finnish-American Folk Festival,** in mid-July. It features folk art, a children's choir, crafts, music, and of course, Finnish food. Lodging is available at **Hunter's Inn,** tel. (360) 484-9215; **Naselle Village Inn Motel,** tel. (360) 484-3111; and **Sleepy Hollow Motel,** tel. (360) 484-3232.

Ask locally for directions to **Radar Ridge,** seven miles out of town, which offers impressive vistas of the entire region. Approximately two miles east of Naselle along Hwy. 4 is the pocket-sized **Salmon Creek Park,** a clump of old-growth forest surrounded by clearcuts and waiting-to-be-logged second-growth land. Camp here for free under the big trees along Salmon Creek.

Grays River Area

East of Salmon Creek Park, the sinuous Grays River (no, it doesn't flow into Grays Harbor) cuts a wide swath, with bucolic farms and fields on both sides, and timber country climbing the hillsides. A few miles east on Hwy. 4 brings you to the country store-post office town of **Rosburg.** Here you can turn south on Hwy. 403 and follow Grays River down to the broad Grays Bay. Out on the open river are the remains of three cannery towns; Cottardi, Altoona, and, farther up-river on a dirt road, Pillar Rock. The dormitories housed workers, often Chinese brought in and treated as indentured servants.

Follow the signs from Rosburg to the only covered bridge in Washington still in use. The 158-foot-long **Grays River Covered Bridge,** on the National Register, was built in 1905 and covered five years later. The bridge was carefully restored in 1989 and is now a National Historic Landmark. A **Grays River Covered Bridge Festival** is held at the local Grange each August, and includes a parade, crafts booths, music, and a logging contest.

From here on east to Skamokawa you pass through timber company land. This corner of the state has almost no public timber holdings, and it's easy to see what happens when pure economics rules how the land is managed. Money and jobs always yell louder than preserving the environment.

Skamokawa

After a detour away from the Columbia at Grays River, Hwy. 4 rejoins the river at Skamokawa (ska-MOCK-away), and then follows it all the way to Longview. The quiet little town of Skamokawa has no lodging, and dining is limited to the local tavern, but it is as picturesque as it is small. The word comes from a Wahkiakum tribal chief whose name meant "Smoke on the water," a reference to the dense fog that frequently drapes the Columbia River mouth. The town's most notable building is **Redmen Hall,** located on a steep bluff overlooking the creek and river. The 1894 schoolhouse was taken over by the Redmen, a fraternal organization that died out in the 1950s. The restored hall is now the **River Life Interpretive Center,** tel. (360) 795-3007, open Tues.-Sat. noon-4 p.m., Sunday 1-4 p.m. in the summer, and Wed.-Sat. noon-4 p.m., Sunday 1-4 p.m. the rest of the year. The center features historical photos and regional displays. Be sure to stop here and climb the belfry for extraordinary views over the Columbia River estuary.

Skamokawa Vista Park, tel. (360) 795-8605, has tent and RV sites and solar-heated showers. Besides camping, the park also has a boat ramp and a sandy beach for swimmers, but no lifeguard. This park is a good place to watch ships crossing the treacherous Columbia River Bar; the busiest time is an hour before or an hour after low tide. When conditions are rough, you'll see enormous swells and waves breaking over these sandbars. Skamokawa is also home to the Wahkiakum County Fairgrounds.

Columbian White-Tailed Deer Refuge

Just downstream from Cathlamet is the 4,400-acre **Julia Butler Hansen National Wildlife Refuge,** established in 1972 to protect the few remaining members of the Columbian white-tailed deer. The subspecies became endangered by the sort of habitat loss readily visible all around here—logging and agricultural development. From a low of just 230 animals, the population has rebounded to 900, and there are hopes that the deer can be eventually removed from the Endangered Species list. Brooks Slough Rd. and Steamboat Slough Rd. circle the refuge, offering a chance to see the small deer sharing grazing rights with dairy cattle and numerous birds, including bald eagles. To protect the deer from disturbance, hiking is prohibited. As an aside, the refuge is named for the first woman to chair a congressional appropriations subcommittee. For information on the refuge, call (360) 795-3915.

Cathlamet

Cathlamet (cath-LAM-et), with a population of about 600, is the largest town between Longview-Kelso and the Pacific Ocean. It was built on the side of a steep hill overlooking Puget Island, and was a favorite haunt of Ulysses S. Grant when he was a lieutenant stationed at Fort Vancouver before the Civil War.

Before WW II this area was one of the most remote in America; many emigrants never bothered to learn English because they had little use for it, and their children born along the Columbia still speak with Scandinavian and Finnish accents. Today, Cathlamet is a quiet burg with a cluster of businesses along the mighty Columbia.

The small **Wahkiakum Museum,** tel. (360) 795-3954, contains photos and exhibits on early logging practices and is open Tues.-Sun. 11 a.m.-4 p.m. June-Sept., and Thurs.-Sun. 1-4 p.m. the rest of the year. Admission is $1 for adults, 50 cents for kids. Next door is Strong Park and Waterfront Trail. In the park is an unusual geared steam locomotive that hauled logs up steep grades from 1923 to 1958. There's a "fine" view of the local sewage treatment plant from here. Also in town is Pioneer Church and an old cemetery with the graves of early settlers and Chief Wahkiakum. Meals are available at **Ranch House Restaurant** and **Birnie's Retreat.** Two salmon hatcheries—Beaver Creek Hatchery and Elokomin Hatchery are up Schoonover Rd. north of Cathlamet.

The Cathlamet area has several good places to stay. **Nassa Point Motel,** three miles east of town on Hwy. 4, tel. (360) 795-3941, charges $30-35 s or d with kitchenettes. **Country Keep-**

er B&B, 61 Main St., tel. (360) 795-3030 or (800) 551-1691, is a two-story 1907 mansion and later town library that is now an elegant small inn. It has four rooms, two of which have private baths. Rates are $60-75 s or $70-85 d, full breakfast included; children over age eight okay. **Little Cape Horn Gallery B&B,** six miles east of Cathlamet, tel. (360) 425-7395, is a contemporary house with five guest rooms right along the Columbia River. There's a private beach (popular with windsurfers), full breakfasts, and a hot tub. Rates are $40-55 s, or $80-135 d. If you're fond of beautiful calligraphy, be sure to ask the owner for a sample of her flawless script. Also check out the refurbished **Cathlamet Hotel,** tel. (360) 795-3122, in downtown Cathlamet.

Puget Island

As you drive east along the Columbia on Hwy. 4, the lower river is marked by a series of islands, many little more than sandbars with a fringe of willows and grass. Most are named, but only one is inhabited: **Puget Island,** which is between Cathlamet and the Oregon side. It is connected to the Washington side by a bridge across the narrow channel, and to Oregon by the small ferry, the *Wahkiakum.* The ferry runs daily 5 a.m.-10 p.m. and costs $2 for cars, 50 cents for passengers.

Puget Island was settled by dairy farmers from Switzerland who built high levees to protect their rich farmland, and by fishermen from the Scandinavian countries. Some of the best commercial fishing boats used on the Columbia River were built on Puget Island. Over the years many of the boats were taken to Bristol Bay, Alaska, where they can still be found. The 27 miles of almost-level roads make for great bike riding. Stay at **Redfern Farm B&B,** 277 Cross Dike Rd., tel. (360) 849-4108, where the accommodations include a private bath and jacuzzi.

East to Longview

East of Cathlamet, Hwy. 4 hugs the Columbia River for 20 scenic miles, passing through undeveloped land. Tall cottonwood trees line the riverbanks; high rocky cliffs and Douglas fir trees line the slopes above the highway. For an interesting side trip, follow the signs to **Abernathy National Fish Hatchery.** Cheap lodging is available at **Traveller's Rest B&B,** tel. (360) 423-6515, near milepost 44 at the Cowlitz County line. Stay at a trailer home here overlooking the river for $45 s, $55 d, including a continental breakfast.

There's a small historical museum in **Stella** with local artifacts and photos. A turn-of-the-century blacksmith shop is open by appointment; call (360) 423-8663 or 423-4981. Not much else to Stella, and nothing in the way of businesses.

LONGVIEW AND KELSO VICINITY

LONGVIEW

Longview (pop. 33,000) and Kelso (pop. 12,000) are twin cities sandwiched between I-5 and the Columbia River, approximately 40 miles north of Portland. The Cowlitz River separates the two, with the older town of Kelso on the east side, and Longview right across two busy bridges. Longview was a planned city; the main streets head out like wheel spokes from the civic center. The main drag through both cities is Hwy. 4, a heavily trafficked route that seems to be always jammed with vehicles.

History

The Lewis and Clark expedition camped at the mouth of the Cowlitz River in 1805 near the site of present-day Longview, and the first white settlers arrived in 1849 to establish a place they called "Monticello." On November 25, 1852, a group of settlers met in the "Monticello Convention" to petition the formation of a new territory north of the Columbia River. Within weeks the U.S. Congress had approved the creation of Washington Territory. In 1854 the Territorial government established Cowlitz County and made Monticello its seat. Unfortunately, Monticello sat on a peninsula surrounded by the Columbia and Cowlitz Rivers, and it flooded seasonally. In the winter of 1866-67 it was almost washed away, so the townsite was abandoned and the county seat moved across the Cowlitz River onto higher ground upriver in Kalama.

It wasn't until the 1920s that the city experienced its first growth spurt. Engineers from the

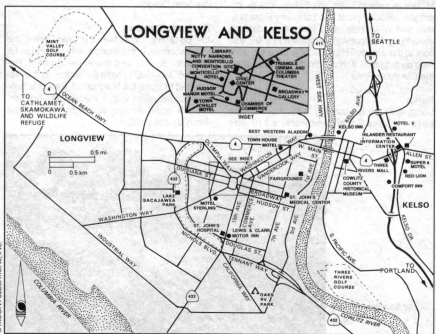

LONGVIEW AND KELSO

© MOON PUBLICATIONS, INC.

Long-Bell Lumber Company sought a new supply for timber as their resources were running out in Texas and Louisiana. Southwest Washington had an abundant supply of old-growth timber and, from a logging viewpoint, Longview's location on a major river with deep-water frontage and rail lines was ideal. They bought 70,000 acres of timber and started cutting.

Lumber baron and multimillionaire R.A. Long founded the city in 1923, and Longview became the first planned city in the Pacific Northwest, designed by nationally known planners working with stringent zoning requirements and an eye toward the aesthetic. Unfortunately, the planners also created a traffic nightmare, with a rabbit warren of confusing streets that meet at odd angles. Be prepared to get lost sometime in your visit to Longview. The twin cities of Longview and Kelso represent one of southwestern Washington's largest retail shopping centers. Longview's original mill is gone, but the city is home to several big plants, including a Reynolds Metals aluminum plant, the Solvay Interox hydrogen peroxide plant, the Longview Fibre pulp mill, and Weyerhaeuser's $40 million state-of-the-art pulp mill that was completed in 1995. Visitors to the area will immediately notice the acrid "eau de pulp mill" stench from these plants along the Columbia River.

Parks

Longview's early planning is revealed by the beautiful **Lake Sacajawea Park,** a 110-acre greenbelt that bisects the city along Nichols Blvd. with a string of serene lakes surrounded by grassy hillsides, shady trees, and a gravel jogging/cycling path.

R.A. Long Park (a.k.a. Civic Center) is a grassy green in the city's core, at the intersection of Olympia and Washington Ways. Surrounding the green are many of the city's oldest buildings, including the wonderful red brick **Public Library** donated by the town's founder and finished in 1926. It is now on the National Register of Historic Places. Featured attractions on the library grounds are the Nutty Narrows bridge and giant squirrel statue, an old logging locomotive, and a rose garden. The **Monticello Hotel,** built in 1923 and still the town's most elegant building, faces R.A. Long Park from 17th Avenue.

A small park at 18th, Maple, and Olympia in Longview marks the **Monticello Convention Site,** where Washington residents met to petition the government to separate Washington Territory from Oregon.

The Nutty Narrows

Just up Olympia Way from the Civic Center, the Nutty Narrows is the world's only skybridge for squirrels. Builder and developer Amos J. Peters built it in 1963 to save the critters as they attempted to cross the busy street. Peters is honored for his effort with a many-times-greater-than-life-sized squirrel sculpture between the library and skybridge.

Lake Sacajawea Park

DIANNE BOULERICE LYONS

LONGVIEW AND KELSO ACCOMMODATIONS

Accommodations are arranged from least to most expensive within each city. Rates may be lower during the winter months. The area code is 360.

LONGVIEW

Hudson Manor Motel; 1616 Hudson; tel. 425-1100; $26-30 s, $32-36 d; kitchenettes available, AAA approved

Town House Motel; 744 Washington Way; tel. 423-7200; $28 s, $34 d; outdoor pool, AAA approved

Town Chalet Motel; 1822 Washington Way; tel. 423-2020; $29-33 s, $33-37 d; kitchenettes available, AAA approved

Motel Sterling; 1808 Hemlock; tel. 423-6980; $34 s, $44 d; outdoor pool

Lewis & Clark Motor Inn; 838 15th Ave.; tel. 423-6460; $36-39 s, $39-44 d; kitchenettes available, AAA approved

Monticello Motel; 17th and Larch; tel. 425-9900; $39 s, $43 d; jacuzzi, kitchenettes available, AAA approved

Rutherglen Mansion B&B; 420 Rutherglen Rd.; tel. 425-5816; $80 s or d; full breakfast

KELSO

Kelso Inn Motel; 505 N. Pacific; tel. 636-4610; $33 s, $38 d; kitchenettes available, AAA approved

Motel 6; 106 Minor Rd.; tel. 425-3229 or (800) 466-8356; $34 s, $40 d; outdoor pool

Super 8 Motel; 250 Kelso Dr.; tel. 423-8880 or (800) 800-8000; $42 s, $46 d; indoor pool

Comfort Inn; 440 Three Rivers Dr.; tel. 425-4600 or (800) 221-2222; $55 s, $60 d; outdoor pool, kitchenettes available, continental breakfast, AAA approved

Red Lion Inn; 510 Kelso Dr.; tel. 636-4400 or (800) 547-8010; $69-87 s, $79-99 d; outdoor pool, jacuzzi, AAA approved

Best Western Aladdin; 310 Long Ave.; tel. 425-9660 or (800) 528-1234; $60 s, $65 d; indoor pool, jacuzzi, exercise facility, AAA approved

Accommodations and Campgrounds

See the "Longview and Kelso Accommodations" chart for a listing of local lodging options. The closest public camping spaces are at Lewis and Clark State Park, 10 miles north on I-5 and six miles east on Hwy. 504. Camp for $10 (no hookups) April-September. Call (800) 452-5687 for campsite reservations ($6 extra fee), available up to 11 months ahead of time. Nearby RV parks include **Deluxe Trailer Court,** 1112 Tennant Way, tel. (360) 425-4147, and **Oaks RV Park,** 636 California Way, tel. (360) 425-2708.

Food

Hilander Restaurant, 1509 Allen St., tel. (360) 423-1500, is a real surprise. Located in—of all places—the bowling alley, it has great strawberry waffles and big omelettes for breakfast, a salad bar, homemade soups, and wonderful halibut fish and chips. Also popular for family breakfast and lunch are **Charlie's Restaurant,** 1826 1st Ave., tel. (360) 636-5661, and **Commerce Cafe,** Commerce and Broadway, tel. (360) 577-0115.

Get excellent sandwiches and other lunch fare at **Country Folks Deli,** 1323 Commerce Ave., tel. (360) 425-3837. The enormous sweet rolls here should best be moved with a forklift. A few doors away at the corner of Broadway and Commerce is the Mercantile Building, where you'll find **The Merk Deli,** a good place for an espresso. Pick up a book at Books on Broadway here or Benevolent Bookworm (across the street) and plunk yourself down at a table in the courtyard to read.

Henri's Restaurant, 4545 Ocean Beach Hwy., tel. (360) 425-7970, is a very popular spot for the "power-lunch" business crowd or for an evening out. Specializing in moderately priced salmon or steak dinners and an impressive wine collection, it's open weekdays for lunch, Mon.-Sat. for dinner. **Monticello Restaurant and Lounge,** 17th and Larch in the Monticello Hotel, tel. (360) 425-9900, serves primarily steak and seafood in a 1920s decor; open for lunch and dinner.

La Playa, 1310 Ocean Beach Hwy., tel. (360) 425-1660, has the best Mexican food in the Longview/Kelso area. Decent Chinese eats at **Golden Palace Restaurant,** 1245 14th Ave., tel. (360) 423-4261.

Longview's **Cowlitz Community Farmers Market,** held Tuesday and Saturday 8 a.m.-1 p.m. May-Oct. at the fairgrounds on 7th Ave. and Washington Way, has fruits, flowers, fresh vegetables, honey, bedding plants, berries, and more.

Recreation

Swim in the local YMCA pool at 15th and Douglas, tel. (360) 423-4770, or play a round of golf at **Mint Valley,** 4002 Pennsylvania in Longview, tel. (360) 577-3395. If you have a canoe, the Cowlitz River from Castle Rock to Longview is a fine 16-mile float. The current can be strong and sandbars are visible at low water, but there are no major obstructions along the way.

Windsurfers are starting to flock to the Columbia River west and south of Longview, where wind conditions are often perfect for intermediate-level boarders (in contrast to the advanced-level waters of the Columbia Gorge).

Events

In late June, the **Cowlitz River Canoe Race,** is a fast 14-mile river run that starts in Castle Rock and pulls out at Kelso. The Independence Day **Go 4th Celebration** is said to be one of the largest in the country, with a parade, logging show, concession stands, and a big fireworks show. In mid-July, the **Summer Arts Festival** attracts artisans from throughout the Lower Columbia. Held at the fairgrounds in late July or early August, the **Cowlitz County Fair** has exhibits and entertainment, including the PRCA Thunder Mountain Rodeo; tel. (360) 577-3121.

In late August, the **Unique Tin Weekend** features old cars, street cruising, and dancing at the fairgrounds.

Arts and Entertainment

The **Columbia Theatre for the Performing Arts,** 1231 Vandercook Way, tel. (360) 423-8626, a legacy from the prosperous 1920s, hosts local theater and dance groups as well as national acts. The **Southwest Washington Symphony** gives performances there from November through May; tel. (360) 425-5346. During July and August music lovers head to Lake Sacajawea for free Sunday **concerts in the park** featuring everything from tuba fests to country-western bands.

Hillman's Restaurant, 1125 Commerce Ave., tel. (360) 423-7040, has live music and dancing nightly in the lounge, and the **Triangle Cinema,** 1228 Washington Way, tel. (360) 425-5448, has four screens showing first-run films.

Stop by downtown Longview's **Broadway Gallery,** 1418 Commerce Ave., tel. (360) 577-0544, to see an outstanding collection of southwestern Washington art produced by more than 30 area artists, including jewelry, pottery, watercolors, weaving, baskets, sculpture, and more.

Information and Services

For information on the town, contact the **Longview Chamber of Commerce,** near the Civic Center at 1563 Olympia Way, tel. (360) 423-8400. Their hours are Mon.-Fri. 9 a.m.-5 p.m., but a computer out front features a touch-screen for local info when they're closed. The **area code** for all of southwest Washington including Longview and Kelso is 360. See "Kelso" (below) for local transportation options.

The **St. John's Medical Center,** Broadway and 7th, tel. (360) 636-7253, has a 24-hour physician-staffed emergency room; or try **St. John's Hospital,** 1614 E. Kessler Blvd., tel. (360) 636-4818.

KELSO

Kelso is much older than Longview. It got its start in the 1840s when the Hudson's Bay Co. grazed cattle nearby and used Cowlitz and Columbia River ports to export beef from the wharves here. Settlement began in 1847, when Peter Crawford donated land on the Cowlitz River for the town of Crawford. It was renamed Kelso in 1884 after the founder's Scottish birthplace (now officially a Sister City). Kelso was incorporated in 1889, became county seat in 1923, and has since been an important logging, milling, and fishing town. Kelso is called "The Smelt Capital of the World" in honor of the abundant winter run of these fish up the Cowlitz River. The first Cowlitz County cannery was built in 1886, and the smelt industry is still a dominant force in Kelso's economy as tons of fish are shipped annually to Asia. Also important is the boat-building company, Tollycraft.

Cowlitz County Historical Museum

Visit the Cowlitz County Historical Museum, 405 Allen St. in Kelso, to see well presented Chinook and Cowlitz Indian artifacts, a cabin from 1884, historic photos from the heyday of logging, and changing exhibits. Open Mon.-Sat. 9 a.m.-5 p.m. and Sunday 1-5 p.m. year-round; tel. (360) 577-3119. Entrance is $1.

Accommodations and Food

See the "Longview and Kelso Accommodations" chart for a listing of local lodging options.

Stuffy's Restaurant, 418 Long Ave., tel. (360) 423-6356, *the* place for breakfast in Longview, features an extensive menu, friendly family service, and enormous servings. The food has such creative names as "deep fried gobbs," "weird fries" (topped with chili and cheese or sausage gravy), and "almost a dozen egg omelet."

For pizza, head to **Izzy's Pizza Restaurant,** at Three Rivers Mall, tel. (360) 578-1626. Get good Thai food at **Khu Larb Thai,** 408 N. 23rd, Kelso, tel. (360) 636-5895. Also in Kelso, **Peter's Gay '90s Restaurant,** 310 S. Pacific, tel. (360) 423-9620, specializes in steaks in an 1890s atmosphere highlighted by a solid marble bar, antique lamps, and stained glass.

Recreation and Events

Swim at the Kelso high school pool, 1904 Allen St., tel. (360) 577-2442. Golfers should head to Kelso's **Three Rivers Golf Course,** 2222 S. River Rd., tel. (360) 423-4653.

In late August, the **Three Rivers Air Show** attracts stunt pilots, military aircraft, and private planes of all types. The **Kelso Highlander Festival,** held in mid-September each year, features a parade, Scottish bagpipe music, dancing, and food at Tam O'Shanter Park.

Shopping

For a shopping mall frenzy, the impressive **Three Rivers Mall,** just off I-5 at Longview/Kelso exit 39 has The Bon Marché, JCPenney, Emporium, Sears, Target, and scores of smaller specialty shops.

Information and Services

The **Kelso Tourist Information Center,** just east of the I-5 entrance ramp at 105 Minor Rd., is a small-time exhibit for those who may have missed the *real* Mount St. Helens visitor centers closer to the mountain. This one has a 15-foot model of the volcano and Toutle River valley, plus photos and exhibits of the 1980 eruption. Open daily 8 a.m.-6 p.m. May-Oct., and Wed.-Sun. 9 a.m.-5 p.m. the rest of the year. The **area code** for Kelso and Longview is 360.

Transportation

Community Urban Bus Service (CUBS), 254 Oregon Way, provides local service in the Kelso-Longview area Mon.-Sat.; call (360) 577-3399 for schedule information. **Greyhound,** tel. (360) 423-7380 or (800) 231-2222, and **Northwestern Trailways,** tel. (800) 366-3830, provide cross-country bus connections from the terminal at 1136 Washington in Longview.

Blue Star Airporter, tel. (800) 247-2272, has shuttle van service between Longview/Kelso and Portland International Airport.

Amtrak trains head north from Kelso to Centralia, Olympia, Tacoma, Seattle, and points beyond, and south to Portland, Vancouver, and California. Service is daily; call (800) 872-7245 for details.

CASTLE ROCK

Castle Rock (pop. 2,100) lies just west of I-5 along the Cowlitz River. The town is named for a 150-foot-high rocky knob that can be climbed by an easy-to-find path. The town was hit hard by the eruption of Mt. St. Helens in 1980, when mud flows turned the Cowlitz into a raging torrent that washed out bridges and damaged or destroyed more than 200 homes. In town is a memorial to Harry Truman, the old-timer who died at his Spirit Lake home when the volcano erupted and buried the lake in hundreds of feet of debris.

Sights
The **Castle Rock Exhibit Hall** at 147 Front Ave. NW, tel. (360) 274-6603, contains three rooms that detail the town and its connection to the Cowlitz River, the importance of the timber industry to the economy, and the impact of the 1980 eruption of Mt. St. Helens. The Exhibit Hall is open daily 9 a.m.-6 p.m. from Memorial Day through September, and Wed.-Sat. 10 a.m.-2 p.m. the rest of the year. No charge. The Exhibit Hall also serves as the local information office.

Mount St. Helens Cinedome Theater, 1239 Mount St. Helens Way NE, tel. (360) 274-8000, has continuous showings of the eruption on an impressive screen that stands three stories tall.

Accommodations and Food
Motel 7 West, 864 Walsh Ave. NE, tel. (360) 274-7526, has the cheapest rooms in Castle Rock: $30 s, $40 d. **Timberland Motor Inn,** 206 Spirit Lake Hwy., tel. (360) 274-6002, has rooms for $38-50 s, $45-60 d, which includes use of their jacuzzi and exercise facility. The **Mount St. Helens Motel,** 227 Spirit Lake Hwy., tel. (360) 274-7721, has rooms for $38 s, $42 d.

At 3201 Spirit Lake Hwy. in Silver Lake, **Silver Lake Motel and Resort,** tel. (360) 274-6141, has motel rooms, rustic two-bedroom cabins with full kitchens, and RV and tent sites, and offers boat rentals for fishing. Rooms are $55-70 d, with a porch over the water. **The Rock Hideaway,** 1579 Huntington Ave. S, tel. (360) 274-3101 or (800) 684-3101, is south of Castle Rock on 10 acres near the Cowlitz River and has five guest rooms available with private baths and full breakfasts.

Eat at **Waldo's Restaurant,** 51 Cowlitz St., or one of the local fast food joints.

Campgrounds
Camp amid tall trees at **Seaquest State Park,** six miles east of Castle Rock on Silver Lake; $10 for tents, $15 for RVs. Call (800) 452-5687 for campsite reservations ($6 extra fee), available up to 11 months ahead of time. Private RV parks in the Castle Rock area include: **Mount St. Helens RV Park,** 167 Schaffran Rd., tel. (360) 274-8522; **Mermac RV Park,** 112 Burma Rd., tel. (360) 274-6785; and **Toutle Village RV Park,** 5037 Spirit Lake Hwy., Toutle, tel. (360) 274-6208.

Events
The **Castle Rock Festival** in late July is the big local event each year, including a pancake breakfast, antique car show, parade, Mountain Man and Mountain Mama contests, dancing, rubber duck race, and carnival. The Mount St. Helens Motorcycle Club sponsors **Pro-Am TT Motorcycle Races** all summer at Castle Rock racetrack.

LEWIS RIVER VALLEY

The Lewis River and its tributaries drain the southern side of Mt. St. Helens and the eastern slopes of Mt. Adams, cutting through the farm-and-forest country of northern Clark County. A number of towns and parks dot the lowland areas, separated by a confusing grid of roads. This is rural Washington, a great place to enjoy a drive or bike ride on a country route.

KALAMA

Interstate 5 slices through the center of Kalama (pop. 1,200), leaving the main part of town with its abundance of antique shops to the east, while to the west lie enormous piles of logs at a sawmill, industrial buildings, a state-of-the-art grain export facility, and the harbor. Right across the Columbia River on the Oregon side is the now defunct Trojan Nuclear Plant, owned by Portland General Electric. It closed abruptly in 1993 when cracks were discovered in thousands of the vital heat-exchange tubes, and is expected to cost an astounding $1 billion to decommission.

The section of the Columbia River near Kalama has in recent years become a favorite of windsurfers. The wind is generally not as strong here as upriver in the Columbia Gorge, so this area is more popular with intermediate-level boarders.

Sights
Kalama is well known for its many antique shops, the biggest collection in southwest Washington. More than 100 dealers are spread through several large antique malls, the biggest being the **Columbia Antique Mall.** Next to railroad tracks in the industrial part of town is Washington's second largest brewery, **Pyramid Ales,** 110 W. Marine Dr., tel. (360) 673-2121, with tours and tasting Mon.-Fri. 10 a.m.-4 p.m. (and Saturday in the summer, but the production line doesn't run on Saturday). Although it began as a microbrewery, the company now rolls out more than 50,000 barrels a year of their excellent beers. The parent company, Hart Brewing, also

has breweries in Seattle and Poulsbo. Pyramid makes six ales, including their best known brew, Pyramid Pale Ale (called Pyramid Special Bitter on draught), plus several seasonal brews.

A short distance south of the brewery is a 149-foot **totem pole.** Carved by Chief Don Lelooska, it is the world's tallest single-tree totem, and was based upon two poles in the Royal Ontario Museum in Canada.

Practicalities
Stay at **Columbia Inn Motel,** 602 N.E. Frontage Rd., tel. (360) 673-2855, for $35 s, or $45 d; kitchenettes are available.

Pitch a tent at **Louis Rasmussen Park,** tel. (360) 673-2626, just south of the Pyramid Ale plant, for $7, or park RVs for $12. **Camp Kalama RV Park,** 5055 N. Meeker Dr., tel. (360) 673-2456, has camping and RV spots along the Kalama River.

The **Kalama Community Fair** in mid-July includes a parade, barbecue, talent show, FFA exhibits, and beer garden (featuring Pyramid Ale).

WOODLAND AND VICINITY

Woodland (pop. 2,600) acts as the southern gateway to Mt. St. Helens, with Hwy. 503 heading northeast to the volcano. The area was first settled in the 1840s, and the town was incorporated in 1906.

Sights
There isn't a lot to the town of Woodland, but be sure to follow the signs to **Hulda Klager Lilac Gardens,** tel. (360) 225-8996, where you'll find a farmhouse built in 1889 surrounded by three acres of grounds filled with lilacs and other colorful flowers and trees of all descriptions. Hulda Klager began hybridizing lilacs in 1903, and developed more than 250 new varieties, including 10 that can be found in the gardens here. The gardens are open year-round and lilac starts (rooted lilac cuttings) are available weekdays, but the lovely Victorian-era home is open only for Lilac Week (late April through Mothers Day).

LEWIS RIVER VALLEY

© MOON PUBLICATIONS, INC.

Entrance to the gardens is $1. The Lilac Gardens sit near **Horseshoe Lake,** formerly part of the Lewis River. It was created in 1940 when the river was rerouted to construct what is now I-5. The lake is a popular place with trout and largemouth bass anglers.

Another nearby sight is the **Highland Lutheran Church,** built in 1883 and used for years by the Scandinavian community in this part of Washington. Now on the National Register of Historic Places, the beautiful old church sits against a backdrop of pastures and second-growth forests; it's still used for special services. The church is

five miles east of Woodland near the corner of N.E. 389th St. and N.E. 41st Avenue.

La Center

La Center (pop. 500) was established in the 1850s as a supply post for nearby settlers. This was the farthest up the East Fork of the Lewis River that boats could travel, and the remains of one of these boats, the sternwheeler *Leona,* sits just west of the bridge in La Center. The town is the only place in this part of Washington where card room gambling is legal in several small casinos.

The **La Center Farmers Market** comes to downtown La Center between mid-May and early October on Saturday 8 a.m.-1 p.m.

Salishan Vineyards, North Fork Rd. in La Center, tel. (360) 263-2713, is a small family-owned winery that produces award-winning pinot noirs and dry rieslings. Open for tours and tastings Saturday and Sunday 1-5 p.m. May-Dec., or by appointment.

Grist Mill

The **Cedar Creek Grist Mill,** 10 miles east of Woodland off N.E. Cedar Creek Rd., tel. (360) 225-9552, is one of the few 19th century water-powered grist mills remaining in the Northwest. Built in 1876, it has been carefully restored, with water fed in by a 650-foot log flume. Volunteers grind wheat here Saturday 1-4 p.m. and Sunday 2-4 p.m. in the summer. Upstairs is a small museum detailing the reconstruction process. Donation requested.

Lodging

There are half-a-dozen lodging choices in the Woodland area. Cheapest is **Lakeside Motel,** 785 Lakeshore Dr., tel. (360) 225-8240, with rooms for $28-36 s or d. A step up is **Scandia Motel,** 1123 Hoffman St., tel. (360) 225-8006, with rooms for $38 s, $40 d, including an outdoor jacuzzi; $5 extra for kitchenettes. **Hansen's Motel,** 1215 Pacific, tel. (360) 225-7018, charges $34 s, $44 d. Stay at **Lewis River Inn,** 1100 Lewis River Rd., tel. (360) 225-6257 or (800) 543-4344, for $41-56 s, $45-56 d. It's located along the river, with balconies offering a view from the more expensive rooms. **Woodlander Inn,** 1500 Atlantic St., tel. (360) 225-6548 or (800) 444-9667, has quality rooms for $42 s, $46 d, including an indoor pool and jacuzzi. **Grandma's House B&B,** 4551 Old Lewis River Rd., tel. (360) 225-7002, is nine miles east of Woodland on Hwy. 503 in an old farmhouse with views of the Lewis River. The three guest rooms come with a full breakfast for $40 s, $58 d.

Campgrounds

Five miles southeast of Woodland and just off I-5, **Paradise Point State Park,** tel. (360) 263-2350, offers fishing, boating, and swimming in the East Fork Lewis River, a two-mile hiking trail, and camping ($10, no hookups). Open for day-use and camping April-Sept., plus weekends and holidays the rest of the year. Because of its location right along I-5, this isn't a particularly quiet place to spend a night, but at least the highway makes for easy access. Call (800) 452-5687 for campsite reservations ($6 extra fee), available up to 11 months ahead of time.

More camping is available at **Woodland Special Campground** in dense forests three miles east of Woodland on N.W. 389th Street. The latter is run by the Dept. of Natural Resources and is free; open mid-May to mid-October. Call (800) 527-3305 in Washington for details.

Local private RV parks are: **Columbia Riverfront RV Park,** 1881 Dike Rd., tel. (360) 225-8051; **Woodland Shores RV Park,** 109 A St., tel. (360) 225-2222 or (800) 481-2224; and **Lewis River RV Park,** 3125 Lewis River Rd., tel. (360) 225-9556.

Food and Events

Woodland's **The Oak Tree** is a very popular place for steaks.

Planters' Day is billed as the state's oldest continuously running festival. The four-day event celebrates the building of dikes to prevent flooding of Woodland and includes a carnival, fun run, pancake breakfast, firemen's barbecue, frog jumping contest, and car show.

COUGAR

The hamlet of Cougar is a 32-mile scenic climb into the hills east of Woodland on Hwy. 503. The narrow road cuts through second-growth forests, with periodic glimpses of Lake Merwin and Yale Lake—reservoirs that were created by dams on the Lewis River. Anglers may want to stop at the Lewis River and Speelyai hatcheries, while picnickers and swimmers may want to stop at Yale Park Recreation Area on Yale Lake. The highway also passes through the tiny burg of **Ariel,** along the Cowlitz River, believed to be the approximate landing place of the 1971 skyjacker known as D.B. Cooper, who demanded $200,000 before jumping from a Northwest Airlines jet. Some of the money was found many years later along the banks of the Columbia River. A local tavern still celebrates the escapade each November.

Cougar serves as a jumping off point (so to speak) for access to the southern and eastern sides of Mount St. Helens National Volcanic Monument. Climbers register here outside Jack's Store; see "Mount St. Helens National Volcanic Monument" in the Cascade Range chapter for specifics on the climb. The **Mount St. Helens National Volcanic Monument Headquarters,** tel. (360) 750-3900, is out in the boonies on Hwy. 503, three miles north of Amboy and seven miles north of the town of Yacolt. Much of this area was consumed in the 1902 Yacolt Burn that killed 38 people and burned 238,000 acres of timber. The area is still recovering.

Lodging
Stay at the comfortable **Monfort's B&B,** 132 Cougar Rd., tel. (360) 238-5229, for $50 s, $60 d, including a full breakfast; $10 extra for use of the jacuzzi. **Lone Fir Resort,** 16806 Lewis River Rd., tel. (360) 238-5210, has motel rooms and a cabin in a wooded location for $38-60 s or d, including an outdoor pool. **Speelyai Ridge B&B,** 615 Yale Bridge Rd., tel. (360) 231-4334, sits atop Wolverton Mountain with panoramic views of Mt. St. Helens and Yale Lake. This new log home has four guest rooms with private baths and serves a buffet breakfast.

See "Mount St. Helens National Volcanic Monument" in the Cascade Range chapter for camping and other recreational options in the area around Cougar.

Other Practicalities
Get home-cooked dinners at **The Landing** and gourmet burgers at **Jack's Wildwood Inn.**

Blue Bird Helicopters, tel. (360) 238-5326, has scenic half-hour helicopter flights over Mt. St. Helens out of Cougar.

RIDGEFIELD

Ridgefield (pop. 1,400) is just west of I-5 and south of Woodland along the Columbia River. The **Lancaster House** here was built in 1850 and is one of the oldest structures in the state. Also of interest is **Ridgefield Hardware,** one of the few old-time hardware stores remaining in Washington.

The **Ridgefield National Wildlife Refuge,** tel. (360) 887-4106, just off I-5, has 5,150 acres of fields, woodlands, and marshes for the protection of otters, deer, beavers, as many as 180 species of birds, and, in winter, up to 10,000 geese and 40,000 ducks. Hiking and fishing are permitted—the mile-long "Oaks to Wetlands Wildlife Trail" is popular with all ages. The Carty Unit Trail is a two-mile loop hike with descriptive signs.

Campgrounds
The closest public campgrounds are at Paradise Point State Park near La Center (described above) and Battle Ground Lake State Park (described below). The privately run **Big Fir Campground** is a mile east of Ridgefield, with wooded campsites for $10 and RV hookups for $15. Open all year; call (360) 887-8970 or (800) 532-4397.

Food
Victoria Bakery and Restaurant, 807 Pioneer St., tel. (360) 887-8001, is certainly unusual for a small town. The menu changes each day, depending on what the owner/chef/waitress decides to create. Lots of heavy meaty dishes and fresh baked goods. The food is always well prepared, but may not be to your taste.

Events
Ridgefield's **Fourth of July** celebration features an old-fashioned parade, a pet parade, arts and crafts displays, music, and a big community breakfast and salmon bake. The **Clark County Fair** in early August is the fifth largest in the nation, held at the fairgrounds in Ridgefield; call (360) 573-1921 for a schedule of fair events. The fair attracts big name entertainers and always includes agricultural exhibits, a carnival, horse shows, art exhibits, and all the other events you'd expect at a summer fair.

BATTLE GROUND

Battle Ground (pop. 3,900) is a nondescript settlement strewn along a lengthy Main Street with the now-standard strip malls. The town's name came from a battle that never took place. During the conflict between Klickitat Indians and white settlers in 1855, a tribal chief was accidentally killed. Soldiers from nearby Fort Vancouver allowed a traditional burial, but when they returned to the fort without forcing the Indians to come with them, their officers chastised them for not provoking a battle on the "battle ground." The name stuck, even though the battle never actually occurred.

Parks

Battle Ground Lake State Park is a popular summer getaway three miles northeast of Battle Ground on N.E. 244th Street. Covering just 280 acres, the park features a sandy beach that attract swimmers, a snack bar, and a lakeside campground ($11, no RV hookups). Hikers and horseback riders will enjoy the many trails that circle this small, cold spring-fed lake in a caldera. The park is open year-round. Call (360) 687-4621 for details or (800) 452-5687 for campsite reservations ($6 extra fee), available up to 11 months ahead of time.

Lewisville County Park covers 154 forested acres just north of Battle Ground along the East Fork of the Lewis River. This exceptionally pretty place has rustic shelters and other structures built by the Works Progress Administration in the 1930s, and is a great place for a picnic in the trees or a weekend walk. No camping at Lewisville Park. Parking fees are charged in the summer.

Moulton Falls County Park, tel. (360) 699-2467, is 10 miles northwest of Battle Ground on N.E. Lucia Falls Rd. and was an historic meeting place for Indians in the area. A swinging footbridge over Big Tree Creek offers fine views of Moulton Falls, trails lead three miles through the forest, and the Lewis and Clark Railway trains stop here. No camping.

Living History Museum

Several miles northeast of Battle Ground is the **Pomeroy House/Living History Farm,** 20902 N.E. Lucia Falls Rd., tel. (360) 686-3537, where visitors are given a glimpse into Clark County's rural lifestyle of the 1920s. Located in the beautiful Lewis River Valley with its fill of classic farmsteads and second-growth forests, Pomeroy includes a working blacksmith shop, herb garden, and historic log home, all in the same family for five generations. Open the first full weekend of each month, June-Oct.; admission is $2 for adults, $1 for kids ages three to 11. The farm

and house are on the National Register of Historic Places. Also on the grounds in the carriage house is an interesting gift shop (open daily) selling imported British items, from brass door knockers to "true Brit" foods.

Excursion Train

The **Lewis and Clark Railway,** tel. (360) 687-2626, runs two-and-a-half-hour rail journeys the 30 miles from Battle Ground through the Cascade foothills and along the Lewis River to beautiful Moulton Falls County Park. Trains leave the downtown depot Saturday and Sunday at 10 a.m. and 1:30 p.m. from Memorial Day to Labor Day, with a reduced schedule continuing through October. The trips cost $10 for adults, $9 for seniors, and $5 for ages three to 15.

Practicalities

No motels in Battle Ground, but you can stay at two local B&Bs. **Pheasant Run B&B,** 27308 N.E. 182nd Ave., tel. (360) 687-0942, is a Cape Cod style home in a quiet country setting northeast of town near Battle Ground Lake. Two antique-furnished guest rooms are available with shared bath for $40-65 d, including a full breakfast. **Fir 'N Fin B&B,** tel. (360) 686-3064, is located northwest of town on 38 wooded acres; it has a veranda with impressive vistas and serves a full breakfast.

Nothing great on the food scene, but **Rocky's Pizza,** tel. (360) 687-1914, in the big log cabin on Main St. near 112th, is a favorite of locals.

The main local festival is **Harvest Days,** which features a parade, carnival, food booths, street dance, root beer float garden, and other entertainment on the third weekend of July.

If you're in the market for antiques, check out the high quality antique shops around Battle Ground.

Information and Services

Get local information at the **Battle Ground Chamber of Commerce,** 1012 E. Main (next to the train depot), tel. (360) 687-1510. It's open Mon.-Fri. 8 a.m.-4:30 p.m. all year. The Gee Creek Rest Area on I-5 between Richfield and Vancouver has a small **visitor information center** open May-September.

C-TRAN, tel. (360) 695-0123, has local bus connections to Vancouver.

VANCOUVER

A two-time winner of the All-America City Award, Vancouver has a population of over 56,000 supported by wood products, electronics, food processing, and the neighboring Portland economy, where many of Clark County's 270,000 residents are employed. Besides serving as a Portland suburb and Washington's I-5 gateway city, Vancouver enjoys a colorful history, kept alive by the Fort Vancouver National Historic Site and Officers' Row. Vancouver is also a gateway to recreational opportunities at nearby Mt. St. Helens and the Columbia River.

The name, honoring Capt. George Vancouver, who explored the Columbia River in 1792, came from the Hudson's Bay post named Fort Vancouver. While the city was still part of the Oregon Territory, the Oregon Territorial Legislature named it Columbia City. However in 1855 the Legislature changed it back to its original name, creating a situation that will always cause confusion. Locals point out that Vancouver, British Columbia, is a Johnny-come-lately city and if any name should be changed, it should be the Canadian one. That prospect is very doubtful. To help avoid confusion, the city is often referred to as Vancouver, U.S.A.

HISTORY

Fort Vancouver

The United States and Great Britain had been

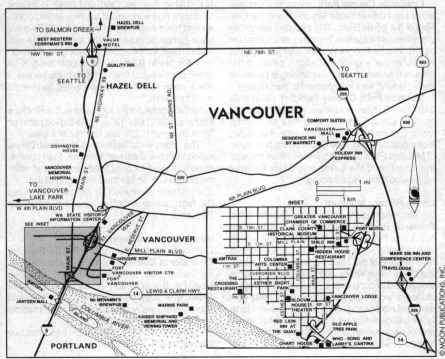

unable to come to terms on the ownership of Oregon Country, a fur- and lumber-rich land that included the Northwest Coast of North America. In 1818, the two powers had agreed to share the land until an agreement could be reached, but seven years later the British-owned Hudson's Bay Company moved its headquarters from Fort George, at the mouth of the Columbia, to Fort Vancouver, 100 miles inland, in hopes of solidifying the British claim to the region.

Fort Vancouver became the Pacific Northwest's commercial and cultural center for fur trading from Utah to Hawaii; shops, fields, pastures, and mills made the fort a self-sufficient, bustling pioneer community. By the 1840s it was the "New York" of the Northwest and was home to a widely diverse set of workers, including many "Kanakas" from the Hawaiian Islands. The blacksmith shop employed eight men full-time to manufacture more than 50,000 beaver traps, plus countless knives, axes, and other tools of the trade. Other important work included maintaining 2,500 acres of farms and orchards outside the fort itself.

The American Years

Droves of pioneering Americans were drawn to Oregon's fertile Willamette Valley farmland in the 1840s, leading to the division of the territory along the 49th parallel in 1846—a boundary that put Britain's Fort Vancouver squarely on American soil. By 1860 all of Fort Vancouver was in the hands of the U.S. Army—which proceeded to carry off anything of value. Decay and fire had destroyed all of the remaining structures by 1866. The Army built new buildings on the slope behind the fort at **Vancouver Barracks,** including grand officers' quarters and not-so-grand barracks and other facilities for those of lower rank. Several of these lesser buildings are still used by the Army.

The city of Vancouver initially served as the Washington state capital, but legislators feared it was too close to Oregon and might come under their sway, so moved the seat of government to Olympia. During WW II, Vancouver's Kaiser Shipyards employed 38,000 people (including activist and musician Woodie Guthrie) in the building of more than 140 ships for the war effort. The shipyard closed after the war.

Fort Vancouver National Historic Site

TACOMA PUBLIC LIBRARY

SIGHTS

Fort Vancouver

Beginning in 1948, archaeologists recovered more than a million artifacts, leading to the accurate reconstruction of six of Fort Vancouver's 27 buildings on the original location as they were in 1845, now preserved as a national historic site. The buildings are surrounded by a tall wooden stockade and guarded by a three-story tower (bastion) that was originally built in 1845 as protection from American settlers and to salute arriving ships with its eight three-pound cannons. The fort was a peaceful place, however, and the occupants never had to hide in fear. Other reconstructed buildings include a blacksmith's shop, bakery, Indian trade shop, storage house, and the elegant residence of Dr. John McLoughlin, the chief factor who looked so fearsome with his hard stare and great head of white hair, but who was one of the most generous men in those pioneer years. Although McLoughlin had been charged with keeping the

American settlers out of the market, he quickly realized that trade was far more practical. When the land was officially declared American soil, he resigned, became an American citizen, and moved to Oregon City where he was hailed as the "Father of Oregon."

Historic Fort Vancouver is open daily 9 a.m.-5 p.m. from Memorial Day to Labor Day, and daily 9 a.m.-4 p.m. the rest of the year (closed Thanksgiving, Christmas, and New Year's). Amazingly detailed guided tours are given by Park Service rangers hourly 9 a.m.-4 p.m. The tour includes a visit to the fully restored home of chief factor John McLoughlin, along with a visit to the working blacksmith shop (open Thurs.-Mon.) where you will learn how the Hudson's Bay Co. produced beaver traps and other goods. Today the shop is used to train apprentices to create iron pieces for National Park Service historic facilities across the nation. Also of interest during the tour are the kitchen (operated daily in the summer), bake house (open summer weekends), and the fur store, housing displays on the fur trade in one section and ongoing archaeological research in the other half. The fort's period gardens are interesting to view, and gardeners will be happy to tell you of the crops that were—and are—grown here. A block north of the fort is the **visitor center,** 1511 E. Evergreen Blvd., where you can watch a 15-minute orientation video, and view displays on the fort along with artifacts found during the excavations.

From downtown, catch the free shuttle bus to Fort Vancouver, or drive east for a half mile on E. Evergreen Boulevard. A $2 entrance fee ($4 for families, kids under 17 free) is charged May-Sept., free the rest of the year; call (360) 696-7655 or (800) 832-3599 for details on the fort. See "Events and Entertainment," below, for several of the fort's seasonal activities.

Officers' Row
The only fully restored row of officers' homes in the nation is at Vancouver's Officers' Row National Historic District. In 1988, the city of Vancouver paid a hefty $10 million price tag to restore these 21 turn-of-the-century homes. They occupy one side of a tree-draped street and are used by local businesses; opposite is spacious **Central Park**—a favorite place for lo-

cals to relax on a sunny day. Less impressive old Army barracks lie just west of the central park in various stages of repair. A free shuttle bus connects Officers' Row with downtown.

The two most famous buildings on Officers' Row are the Marshall House and Grant House, named for their onetime residents Gen. George C. Marshall and President Ulysses S. Grant. Other famous residents included Phillip Sheridan, Benjamin Bonneville, and Omar Bradley; presidents Rutherford B. Hayes and Franklin D. Roosevelt attended receptions here.

The **Marshall House,** 1313 Officers' Row, tel. (360) 693-3103, is open for free tours and has a 20-minute videotape about the fort and Officers' Row. The building is very popular for weddings and other events, so it is often closed to the public on weekends. Open Mon.-Fri. 9 a.m.-5 p.m., and on wedding-less weekends. Named for the man who authored the famous postwar Marshall Plan, it was George C. Marshall's home during his time as commanding officer at Vancouver Barracks from 1936 to 1938.

Built in 1849, the **Grant House Folk Art Center & Cafe,** 1101 Officers' Row, tel. (360) 694-5252, features changing exhibitions of folk art from throughout the Northwest. Also here is a pleasant cafe with reasonably priced lunches and dinners. Grant was stationed at the fort as a quartermaster in the 1850s and visited this building many times, but he did not actually live here, since it was home to the fort's commanding officer at the time.

Museums and Other Historic Buildings
The **Clark County Historical Museum,** 1511 Main St., tel. (360) 695-4681, is open Tues.-Sun. 1-5 p.m. Free exhibits include an 1890 country store, a 1900 doctor's office, Indian artifacts, and a railroad exhibit.

The **Covington House,** 4201 Main St., tel. (360) 693-9571, is one of the state's oldest log cabins. Built in 1848, it housed the area's first school. Open to the public June-Aug. Tuesday and Thursday 10 a.m.-4 p.m.; free. Another interesting building is the **St. James Church** at 12th and Washington Streets. Built in 1885, this was the first Gothic Revival style church in Washington and is home to the state's oldest Catholic congregation.

Exhibits at **Pearson Air Museum,** 1105 E. 5th St. (near Fort Vancouver), include a fully restored Curtiss Jenny, and displays on Lindbergh's 1927 flight that landed here, the 1937 Soviet landing in Vancouver from the world's first transpolar flight, and operating vintage aircraft. Admission is $2 adults, $1 students and kids; tel. (360) 694-7026. Hours are Wed.-Sun. noon-5 p.m. The adjacent Pearson Airfield is one of the oldest operating fields in the nation; its first landing was a dirigible that floated over from Portland in 1905, and the first plane arrived seven years later.

At the **Vancouver Fire Department Museum,** 900 W. Evergreen Blvd., tel. (360) 696-8166, visitors will find a restored 1934 fire engine and a collection of historic photos. Tours are given daily 8 a.m.-5 p.m.

City Parks
Vancouver Lake Park is a local hot spot for both windsurfers and fishermen. The nearly 300-acre strip of land on the south and west shores of 2,800-acre Vancouver Lake offers picnicking, swimming, grassy and shady areas, and you can fish for shad, sturgeon, steelhead, and more. It is also home to one of the largest great blue heron rookeries in the region, and bald eagles can be found roosting in the trees during the winter months. Take Hwy. 501 (a.k.a. 4th Plain Blvd.) west for about three miles; bear right at the giant arrow, just after you see the huge lake on your right, a few hundred feet to the parking lot.

Old Apple Tree Park, along the river just east of I-5, honors what is believed to be the oldest apple tree in the Northwest. The tree was planted in 1826, when Fort Vancouver was a Hudson's Bay Co. trading center, and it still bears small green apples each summer.

Marine Park occupies the site of the Kaiser Shipyards, where more than 140 ships were hurriedly constructed during WW II by "Rosie the Riveter." Today you can climb a three-story riverside tower next to Kaiser Center for dramatic views of Vancouver and Portland. Not far away is a monument to the Soviet transpolar flight of 1937, when three Russian aviators were the first to cross over the pole en route to America.

Shady **Esther Short Park,** at W. 6th and Esther, contains the historic Slocum House (see "The Arts," below), along with a Victorian rose garden, 1917 steam locomotive, playground, and a monument to pioneer women. It is named for the wife of an early settler who jumped another settler's claim and later murdered two of his supporters. Despite this (or perhaps because of it), Short's children gained legal title to the land.

ACCOMMODATIONS

See the chart "Vancouver Accommodations" for a complete listing of local lodging options. Dozens more motels are available just across the river in Portland, Oregon. The closest public campgrounds are **Paradise Point State Park,** 16 miles north on I-5 near Woodland, tel. (360) 263-2350, and **Battle Ground Lake State Park,** 20 miles northeast of town in Battle Ground, tel. (360) 687-4621. **Jantzen Beach RV Park,** 1503 N. Hayden Dr., tel. (503) 289-7626 or (800) 443-7248, is on Hayden Island in the Columbia River, just south of Vancouver on I-5.

FOOD

Ask someone from Vancouver where to eat, and half the time you'll be steered across the bridge to Portland, where the abundance of great restaurants rivals Seattle's. But Vancouver does quite well for itself, with a number of quality restaurants covering the spectrum of tastes.

Breakfast and Lunch
One place wins hands-down on the Vancouver breakfast front: **Dunlin's Village Cafe,** 1905 Main St., tel. (360) 737-9907. They serve breakfast all day—including great home fries and spinach omelettes—and are a popular lunch place for the downtown crowd. Another notable place for light breakfasts and healthy lunches is **Tyrone's Patisserie,** 106 E. Evergreen Blvd., tel. (360) 699-1212.

Travelers can pretend they're in Seattle with an espresso and croissant at **Java House,** 210 W. Evergreen Blvd., tel. (360) 737-2925; or **Starbucks,** 5001 N.E. Thurston Way, tel. (360) 896-0640, and 11054 E. Mill Plain Blvd., tel. (360) 253-5270.

VANCOUVER ACCOMMODATIONS

Accommodations are arranged from least to most expensive. Rates may be lower during the winter months. The area code is 360.

Value Motel; 708 N.E. 78th St.; tel. 574-2345; $20 s, $22 d shared bath, $28 s, $34 d private bath; questionable neighborhood, see rooms first

Riverside Motel; 4400 Lewis & Clark Hwy.; tel. 693-3677; $36 s, $38 d; kitchenettes available

Fort Motel; 500 E. 13th St.; tel. 694-3327; $34 s, $40 d; kitchenettes available

Guest House Motel; 11504 N.E. 2nd St.; tel. 254-4511; $40 s, $42 d

Sunnyside Motel; 12200 N.E. Hwy. 99, Salmon Creek; tel. 573-4141; $40 s, $48 d; kitchenettes available, local calls 25 cents

Salmon Creek Motel; 11901 N.E. Hwy. 99, Salmon Creek; tel. 573-0751; $40-48 s, $45-54 d; kitchenettes available, local calls 25 cents, AAA approved

Vancouver Lodge; 601 Broadway; tel. 693-3668; $40-50 s, $50-55 d; kitchenettes available, AAA approved

Quality Inn; 7001 N.E. Hwy. 99; tel. 696-0516 or (800) 228-5151; $44-48 s, $50-53 d; outdoor pool, jacuzzi, free continental breakfast, kitchenettes available, AAA approved

Mark 205 Inn & Conference Center; 221 N.E. Chkalov Dr.; tel. 256-7044 or (800) 426-5110; $45-55 s, $55-60 d; indoor pool, jacuzzi, continental breakfast, free airport shuttle, AAA approved

Country Heart B&B; 7507 N.E. 51st St.; tel. 896-8316; $50-80 s or d; turn-of-the-century farmhouse on one acre, four guest rooms, full breakfast

Comfort Inn; 13207 N.E. 20th Ave., Salmon Creek; tel. 574-6000 or (800) 221-2222; $53-60 s, $59-70 d; indoor pool, jacuzzi, exercise facility, continental breakfast, free airport shuttle, AAA approved

Travelodge; 11506 N.E. 3rd St.; tel. 254-4000 or (800) 578-7878; $55s, $60 d; indoor pool, jacuzzi, continental breakfast, AAA approved

Holiday Inn Express; 9107 N.E. Vancouver Mall Dr., Orchards; tel. 253-5000 or (800) 465-4329; $55 s, $60 d; indoor pool, jacuzzi, continental breakfast, AAA approved

Best Western Ferryman's Inn; 7901 N.E. 6th Ave.; tel. 574-2151 or (800) 528-1234; $59 s or d; outdoor pool, jacuzzi, kitchenettes available, continental breakfast, AAA approved

Shilo Inn—Hazel Dell; 13206 N.E. Hwy. 99, Salmon Creek; tel. 573-0511 or (800) 222-2244; $62 s or d; indoor pool, jacuzzi, steam room, sauna, continental breakfast, kitchenettes available, airport shuttle, AAA approved

Comfort Suites; 4714 N.E. 94th Ave., Orchards; tel. 253-3100 or (800) 221-2222; $68-78 s, $73-83 d; indoor pool, jacuzzi, continental breakfast, AAA approved

Shilo Inn Downtown; 401 E. 13th St.; tel. 696-0411 or (800) 222-2244; $68-96 s or d; outdoor pool, jacuzzi, sauna, continental breakfast, free airport shuttle, AAA approved

Red Lion Inn at the Quay; 100 Columbia St.; tel. 694-8341 or (800) 733-5466; $89-107 s, $104-122 d; overlooks Columbia River, outdoor pool, free airport shuttle, AAA approved

Residence Inn by Marriott; 8005 N.E. Parkway Dr., Orchards; tel. 253-4800 or (800) 331-3131; $119 s or d; apartment-style rooms, fireplaces, outdoor pool, jacuzzi, continental breakfast, evening dessert, free newspaper, kitchenettes available, free airport shuttle, AAA approved

American

The Holland Restaurant, on the corner of Main and McLoughlin, tel. (360) 694-7842, has been around since the 1930s and still serves rea-

sonable all-American fare. It has a good salad and soup bar. Enjoy entrees of prime rib, seafood, steak, and chicken in a railroad diner car at **The Crossing,** 900 W. 7th St., tel. (360)

695-3374. The best local pizzas are at **Juliano Pizzeria,** 16209 S.E. McGillivray Blvd., tel. (360) 254-1286, and **Izzy's,** 1503 N.E. 78th St., tel. (360) 573-2962, or 7615 E. Mill Plain Blvd., tel. (360) 693-3228. Izzy's features a salad bar stocked with more than 50 items.

Eats with a View
Three waterside restaurants are popular for sunny lunches and sunset dinners on the patio. Enjoy the Columbia River view with your Mexican food at **Who-Song and Larry's Cantina,** 111 E. Columbia Way, tel. (360) 695-1198, where the singing waiters are a local phenomenon; at **The Chart House,** 101 E. Columbia Way, tel. (360) 693-9211, with steak, seafood, prime rib, an oyster bar, and a good wine list; or **The Quay,** 100 Columbia St. (at the Red Lion Inn), tel. (360) 694-8341, specializing in steak and seafood in a nautical decor.

International
For south-of-the border meals served north of the border, head to **Bernabe's Family Cafe,** 9803 N.E. Hwy. 99, tel. (360) 574-5993, or **Salsa Mexican Restaurant,** 5406A E. 4th Plain Blvd., tel. (360) 693-3102. **Phoenicia Restaurant,** 14415 S.E. Mill Plain Blvd., tel. (360) 253-4789, has very good Lebanese meals.

Three local restaurants offer an authentic taste of Asia: **Little India Cuisine,** 316 S.E. 123rd, tel. (360) 944-9883; **Thai Little Home,** 3214 E. 4th Plain Blvd., tel. (360) 693-4061; and **Oriental Fast Bowl,** 905 Main St., tel. (360) 737-2730, for quick Japanese meals.

Cafe Augustino's, 1109 Washington St., tel. (360) 750-1272, has good Italian and continental cuisine, along with an extensive wine list. Also recommended is **DeCicco's Italian Ristorante,** 611 W. 11th St., tel. (360) 693-3252, where the excellent lunch menu includes seafood pasta, foccacia sandwiches, and homemade biscotti. **The Olive Garden,** one of a chain of Italian restaurants, has moderately priced pasta, veal, chicken, and seafood dishes at 8000 N.E. Parkway Dr., Orchards.

Northwest Cuisine and Beyond
Enjoy delicious homemade lunches and dinners (pastas, salads, soups, and seafood) in an elegant historic setting at **Grant House Folk Art Center & Cafe,** 1101 Officers' Row, tel.

(360) 699-1213. The building also houses a folk art museum, so you're surrounded by charming pieces that match the reasonably priced Northwest cuisine. Also open for Sunday brunch.

Hidden House was built in 1885 for a prominent Vancouver citizen, Lowell M. Hidden. **Hidden House Restaurant,** 100 W. 13th St., tel. (360) 696-2847, still retains the original brick exterior, stained glass, shutters, and woodwork—but now it offers an eclectic and rather pricey lunch and dinner menu that changes throughout the year. Next door is another of the Hidden family homes (now a business); the family continues to manufacture the bricks found in many local homes and businesses at Hidden Brick Co. on Kauffman Avenue.

Pinot Ganache, 1004 Washington St., tel. (360) 695-7786, calls its menu "multi-ethnic," which means it has entrees from all over the globe. The sparkling bistro is open for lunch and dinner and is justly famous for its decadent chocolatey desserts. Be sure to save room!

Brewpubs
Hazel Dell Brew Pub, 8513 N.E. Hwy. 99, tel. (360) 576-0996, serves pub meals, including fish and chips, burgers, and pasta in a lively, noisy setting to accompany their 10 different brewed-on-the-premises beers. **McMenamins of the Columbia Brew Pub,** tel. (360) 699-1521, is a new place located next to the river on Hidden Way just east of Marine Park.

Bakeries and Produce
MaMa's Bake Shop, 708 N.E. 78th St. in Hazel Dell, tel. (360) 573-5803, is more than a bakery. The cafe has many kinds of pancakes for breakfast, Italian cuisine for dinner, and wonderful desserts all the time.

The **Vancouver Farmers Market** takes place at 5th and Broadway Streets on Saturday 9 a.m.-3 p.m., early May through October.

EVENTS AND ENTERTAINMENT

Festivals
Summer starts in earnest with the **Vancouver Festival** in mid-June, featuring a children's parade, live music, and arts and crafts. **Fort Van-**

couver Days, the big July 4th weekend celebration, has historic tours of the fort, a chili cook-off, golf tournament, rodeo, jazz concert, food, crafts, and the largest fireworks display west of the Mississippi. Call (360) 693-1313 for details of this year's activities.

In late July, the **Fort Vancouver Brigade Encampment** fills the fort with trappers and traders dressed in 1840 period costumes. There are tepees, baking and cooking demonstrations, tomahawk throwing, and other demonstrations. Call (360) 696-7655 for details.

The big **Clark County Fair** in early August is held at the fairgrounds in the town of Ridgefield; call (360) 573-1921 for details. In early October, don't miss the **Fort Vancouver Candlelight Tours** with interpreters dressed in 1840s period clothing; events include a seven-course meal for the fort's gentlemen followed by dancing. The **Christmas Parade of Boats** is a favorite event, with decorated vessels plying the Columbia and Willamette Rivers on the second and third weeks of December. You'll also find Officers' Row decorated with traditional evergreens for the holidays, plus concerts and carriage rides to get you in the spirit of the holidays.

The Arts
At 400 W. Evergreen Blvd., the **Columbia Arts Center** offers a full, year-round schedule of theatrical productions, art shows, and concerts. For information on current events or a copy of their latest newsletter with calendar, call (360) 693-0350.

Listed on the National Register of Historic Homes, the 60-seat **Slocum House Theater** was built in 1867 and moved to Esther Short Park at W. 6th and Esther in 1966. The theater is now most famous for its August Victorian Festival, though it stages productions year-round. Free **Six to Sunset** summer concerts take place in the Waterworks Park amphitheater on the corner of 4th Plain Blvd. and Ft. Vancouver Way.

Since hopping Portland is just a short drive away, you won't find a lot on Vancouver's live music scene. To see who has something going on in town, take a gander at the Friday entertainment section of the local newspaper.

SHOPPING

The two-level **Vancouver Mall** has over 115 shops, restaurants, and services, including five major department stores—JCPenney, Nordstrom, Mervyn's, Sears, and Meier & Frank—at the junction of I-205 and Hwy. 500, or from downtown, follow 4th Plain Blvd. east. Just outside the mall, Vancouver Mall Cinemas features four first-run films; call (360) 254-0000 for listing. One of the largest malls in the Portland/Vancouver area is the jazzy **Jantzen Beach Center** on Hayden Island in the Columbia River. Included is a big REI store, where you'll find quality outdoors gear and all sorts of special events. And while you're crossing the bridge, keep going to downtown Portland, where you'll find **Powell's,** one of the largest and most interesting bookstores this side of the Mississippi.

INFORMATION AND SERVICES

The **area code** for all of southwest Washington is 360. For maps or other information, visit the **Vancouver/Clark County Visitors and Convention Services** at 404 E. 15th St. (left off the I-5 Mill Plains exit 1D), tel. (360) 694-2588 or (800) 377-7084. Open Monday 9 a.m.-5 p.m., and Tues.-Fri. 8 a.m.-5 p.m. all year. Easier to find is the **State Visitor Center** at exit 1D (4th Plain) off I-5, tel. (360) 696-1155, with brochures from all over Washington. Open daily 8 a.m.-6 p.m. Memorial Day to Labor Day, and daily 8 a.m.-4 p.m. the rest of the year.

The **Gifford Pinchot National Forest Supervisor's Office** is in Vancouver at 6926 E. 4th Plain, tel. (360) 750-5001. Stop by for information on Mt. St. Helens and other nearby outdoor attractions. (By the way, Pinchot is pronounced "PINCH-oh"; Gifford Pinchot was the founder of the U.S. Forest Service.)

Swim at the indoor pool at **Marshall Community Center,** 1009 E. McLoughlin Blvd., tel. (360) 693-7946.

For the full scoop on Vancouver's big sister city of Portland, see *Oregon Handbook* by Stuart Warren and Ted Long Ishikawa (Moon Publications).

For emergency-room services, try **St. Joseph's Hospital**, 600 N.E. 92nd Ave., tel. (360) 256-2064, or **Vancouver Memorial**, 3400 Main St., tel. (360) 696-5232.

TRANSPORTATION

By Car
From Seattle, Vancouver is about 165 miles south on I-5. The city is bypassed by through traffic on I-405, which swings east of town, crosses the Columbia River east of Portland International Airport, and rejoins I-5 south of Portland.

By Bus
The local transit system is **C-TRAN**, tel. (360) 695-0123, which provides daily service throughout Clark County as well as to downtown Portland. Fares are 60 cents to $1.80 depending upon the distance you're traveling. Free shuttle buses operate throughout downtown and to Officers' Row at Fort Vancouver.

For cross-country trips, contact **Greyhound**, 512 Columbia St., tel. (360) 696-0186 or (800) 528-0447.

By Train
Amtrak provides nationwide daily service from its station at the foot of W. 11th St.; call (360) 694-7307 or (800) 872-7245 for information. See "Battle Ground," above, for details on the scenic train that takes you into the Cascade foothills.

By Air
The Vancouver area is served by most major carriers at **Portland International Airport** just across the Columbia River. **Vancouver Aviation**, at Pearson Field in Vancouver, tel. (360) 283-3242, has hour-long scenic flights over Mt. St. Helens for $50 per person (two person minimum).

Tours
Custom Tailored Tours, tel. (360) 256-0536, has customized van tours of the Vancouver area's historic sites, outlet stores, Mt. St. Helens, and more.

THE COLUMBIA GORGE

This stretch of the Columbia River is one of the truly special places for both Washington and Oregon. No matter the season, no matter the weather conditions, the gorge is always beautiful. And you have a choice of highway types. The Oregon side has I-94 roaring along its full length and at river level, and the completely restored Columbia River Highway that was carved from the mountains a la roads in Switzerland. Across on the Washington side (which is where we're supposed to be, anyway) is Hwy. 14, a combination country road and highway that tends to follow the contours of the land rather than burrowing and bulldozing along a surveyor's line. On the western end, the Lewis and Clark Highway (Hwy. 14) winds through maple and Douglas fir forests punctuated by periodic vistas into the river valley far below.

The only sea level route through the Cascades, the Columbia has been an important migration route for centuries. Driving this route

is a geology, meteorology, and botany course combined with a drive through great beauty. The scenery takes a dramatic turn, from the green forested hills of the western section to the dry basaltic and barren hills of the eastern half. In a distance of just 40 miles—from Cascade Locks to The Dalles—average annual rainfall changes by 40 inches! The gorge has its own climate, and temperature extremes on the east side range from zero or less in winter to 110° F of dry heat in summer. This often means the gorge has one set of conditions while over the hill is another kind of weather. It isn't unusual to descend into the gorge and into a gale because this narrow gap is the only place weather systems can get through the mountains rather than over them. Sometimes in the winter a sudden Arctic blast comes down the gorge to create an ice storm, which is locally called a "silver thaw."

The gorge between Hwy. 97 and I-5 is heavily traveled on both sides of the river, but the area from Hwy. 97 at Maryhill Museum east to Paterson is the least traveled stretch of the gorge and signs alert you to its lack of facilities. The description below follows the river up from Vancouver to McNary Dam, where the highway heads away from the river and north to the Tri-Cities area.

For more on the equally interesting Oregon side of the gorge, including such famous sights as Vista House and Multnomah Falls, see *Oregon Handbook* by Stuart Warren and Ted Long Ishikawa (Moon Publications), or contact the **Columbia Gorge Visitors Association,** tel. (541) 386-6262.

HISTORY

When Capt. George Vancouver's 1792 expedition sailed up the Northwest coast, they must have been napping as they passed the Columbia River—George never saw it. That same year, American trading captain Robert Gray discovered this great river on his journey to become the first American to sail around the world. Gray claimed the river and its huge drainage area for the U.S., naming the river after his ship, the *Columbia Rediviva,* "Columbus lives again."

After Gray's discovery, Vancouver sent William Broughton out to explore the upriver territory; Broughton asserted that Gray hadn't found the true channel, and claimed the river for England. Canadian traders searched western Canada for the Columbia's source. Finally, in 1811, David Thompson found it and canoed to the confluence of the Snake and Columbia where he erected a sign, stating, in part, "Know thereby that this country is claimed by Great Britain." The conflicting claims weren't settled until the U.S.-Canada boundary treaty of 1846.

Lewis and Clark Expedition
The most famous Columbia River explorers were Meriwether Lewis and William Clark. Selected by Thomas Jefferson in 1803 to lead an expedition from St. Louis to the Pacific Coast, they were to keep extensive logs of the flora, fauna, and geography of this unknown territory, and to establish friendly relations with the area's Indians. The 28 members of the expedition, accompanied by an Army detachment, set out on May 13, 1804 in several canoes and a 55-foot barge powered by 22 oars and men towing it along the bank. When they ran out of river, the party of 28 got horses from the Indians and headed for the mountains, where they nearly

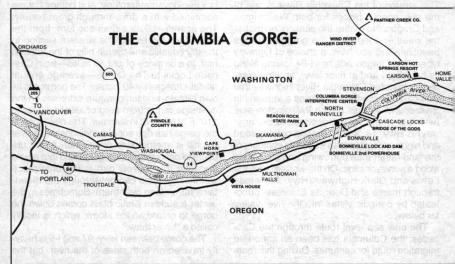

starved to death. The Plateau Indians helped them find the Columbia River, where they built canoes and paddled downstream, arriving at Fort Clatsop on the Pacific Coast in late November 1805. Upon his arrival, Clark wrote in his journal: "I beheld the grandest and most pleasing prospects which my eyes ever surveyed. . . a boundless ocean . . . raging with immense waves and breaking with great force from the rocks."

Northwesterners won't be surprised to hear that Lewis and Clark recorded 31 consecutive days of rain during their visit to the Northwest! In March 1806, the party headed home. After a two-year absence, many had given them up for dead, but only one member of the party died en route, apparently of a ruptured appendix.

The Great Migration
Following the Lewis and Clark expedition, American interest in the "Oregon Country" began to rise, led first by fur trappers, and then by missionaries. The turning point came in 1843, when the Applegate Wagon Train left Independence, Missouri, with 1,000 people, 120 wagons, and 5,000 head of livestock. It was the largest wagon train ever assembled. Under the leadership of Dr. Marcus Whitman—a missionary who had

come west in 1836, and guided by mountain man Bill Sublette, they made it all the way to the Columbia and Willamette Rivers by September. It had taken six long months to travel the 2,000 miles, but they had shown that the "Oregon Trail" route was feasible. The gates of history had been cracked open, and they could never be closed again. Soon, the trickle westward turned into a flood tide.

Americans emigrated west for a number of reasons: for the free and productive lands in Oregon and California, to escape a severe economic depression in the East, to get out of the crowded and polluted cities, to find religious freedom in Utah, to search for gold in the mountains of California, or simply to join in a great adventure in a new and undiscovered land. Most travelers tried to depart Independence or St. Joseph, Missouri, in the spring, leaving as soon as the grass would support their stock. Typically, each evening found the emigrant just 15 miles farther down the trail, and it generally took five or six months to travel from Missouri to Oregon or California. They had to be over the mountains before the first snows of winter struck, and those who erred—such as the infamous Donner Party of 1846—paid a high price.

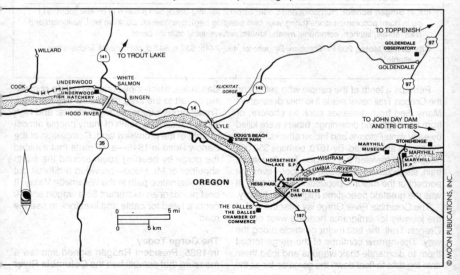

COLUMBIA GORGE ACCOMMODATIONS

Accommodations are arranged from least to most expensive within each area. Many other lodging places are just across the river in Oregon towns. The area code is 509 unless otherwise noted.

WASHOUGAL

Econo Lodge; 544 6th St., Washougal; tel. (360) 835-8591 or (800) 446-6900; $40 s, $45 d; outdoor pool, kitchenettes available, AAA approved

STEVENSON AND CARSON AREA

Carson Hot Springs Resort; Carson; tel. 427-8292; $35 d in hotel (bath down the hall), $38-43 d in cabins, $120 d in hot tub suite; historic hotel, mineral baths, massages

Econo Lodge; Frank-John Rd., Stevenson; tel. 427-5628 or (800) 424-4777; $40-45 s, $45-50 d; kitchenettes available, AAA approved

Columbia Gorge Motel; Wind River Rd., Carson; tel. 427-7777; $40-50 s, $50-60 d; cottages with kitchens

Evergreen Inn B&B; Stevenson; tel. 427-4303; $45 s, $50 d; 1910 home, two guest rooms, shared bath, full breakfast

Sojourner Inn B&B; Home Valley (five miles east of Stevenson); tel. 427-7070; $60-115 s or d; newer Japanese-style home, five guest rooms, private baths, gourmet breakfast, dinners by reservation

Skamania Lodge; Stevenson; tel. 427-7700 or (800) 221-7117; $100-155 s or d; elaborate modern lodge, indoor pool, saunas, jacuzzis, tennis courts, exercise room, panoramic vistas, AAA approved

WHITE SALMON AND BINGEN AREA

Inn at Bingen School; Humboldt and Cedar Streets; tel. 493-3363; $29 s $39 d in private room, $11 pp in dorm accommodations (bring your own sleeping bag); gymnasium, climbing wall, sailboard and bike rentals, kitchen, communal meals, shuttle service, local calls 25 cents

City Center Motel; 208 W. Steuben, Bingen; tel. 493-2445; $32 s, $43 d; plain motel, kitchenettes available

Perhaps a tenth of the people who set out on the Oregon Trail never made it to their destination. Many died from diseases such as cholera, or from accidents and drownings; others were killed by early winter storms and Indian attacks. Few of the graves are marked. By 1870, perhaps 350,000 people had traveled the Oregon Trail by wagon train, stagecoach, horseback, and foot—over one percent of the nation's population at that time. It was the greatest peacetime migration in history.

The Columbia River Gorge lay near the end of the journey for emigrants heading west on the Oregon Trail, the last major obstacle along the way. The narrow confines of the gorge forced them to dismantle their wagons and load them onto log rafts to float down the gorge as far as the

Cascades, which they portaged before continuing by raft to the area of present-day Portland. Treacherous rapids, strong currents, and high winds caused the death of many people almost in sight of the promised land. Completion of the Barlow Road in 1846—a toll route that avoided the gorge by heading south around the south shoulder of Mt. Hood—provided a difficult but safer alternative path to the Willamette Valley. It cost pioneers an exorbitant $5 a wagon and 10 cents a head for cattle and livestock to use the road.

The Gorge Today

In 1986, President Reagan signed into law a measure that established the **Columbia River**

Bingen Haus B&B; ¾ mile east of Hood River Bridge, Bingen; tel. 493-4888; $35-70 s, $50-85 d; historic 1860 home, jacuzzi, full breakfast

Lyle Hotel; Lyle (nine miles east of White Salmon); tel. 365-3010; $38 s, $48 d; 1905 hotel, small rooms, river views, continental breakfast, open May-Sept. only

Orchard Hill Inn; 199 Oak Ridge Rd., 11 miles north of White Salmon; tel. 493-3024; $48 s, $58 d; secluded location, four guest rooms (one with private bath), full breakfast, children okay

Ya' At' Eeh; three miles east of Bingen; tel. 493-3750; $55 s, $65-85 d; country location, fantastic views, outdoor pool, jacuzzi, private or shared bath, full breakfast

Inn of the White Salmon; 172 W. Jewett, White Salmon; tel. 493-2335 or (800) 972-5226; $75-115 s, $89-115 d; European-style hotel, jacuzzi, antique-furnished rooms, fireplace, gourmet breakfast, AAA approved

GOLDENDALE AREA

Barchris Motel; 128 N. Academy, Goldendale; tel. 773-4325; $29 s, $35 d; older place

Ponderosa Motel; 775 E. Broadway St., Goldendale; tel. 773-5842; $36 s, $42 d; kitchenettes available, AAA approved

Far Vue Motel; 808 E. Simcoe Dr., Goldendale; tel. 773-5881 or (800) 358-5881; $43 s, $49 d; outdoor pool, kitchenettes available, AAA approved

The Sleeper House B&B; 203 W. Broadway, Goldendale; tel. 773-4749; $50 s or d; 1889 home, two antique-furnished guest rooms, full breakfast

Victorian House B&B; 415 E. Broadway, Goldendale; tel. 773-5338; $55 s, $60 d full breakfast, $40 s, $45 d no breakfast; 1910 Victorian home, two guest rooms, shared bath, nicely furnished second floor bedrooms, children okay

Highland Creeks Resort; eight miles north of Goldendale; tel. 773-4026 or (800) 458-0174; $99-119 d Fri.-Sat., $89-109 Sun.-Thurs. in luxury condos and chalets; private decks and jacuzzis, kitchenettes available, tennis courts, hiking trails

Gorge National Scenic Area, encompassing 292,000 acres on both sides of the river from Washougal to Maryhill. The national scenic area is managed jointly by the U.S. Forest Service, the states of Washington and Oregon, and the six local counties involved in an attempt to protect the rich scenic and recreational values of the gorge.

WINDSURFING

Because the Columbia is the only major break in the Cascade Range, it acts as an 80-mile-long wind tunnel. The wind blowing through the Columbia Gorge provides some of the best windsurfing conditions in the nation. In 1991, a windsurfer set the national speed record, 47.4 miles per hour. This place isn't for beginners. Gusty winds, large waves, a strong current, and frigid

water make the Gorge challenging for even experienced sailors, and the constant parade of tugs and barges adds more hazards. Winds average 16 mph between March and mid-October, but most windsurfers prefer to come in July and August when the water is warmer.

The most protected waters in the Gorge are at **Drano Lake** near the town of Underwood, and at **Horsethief Lake,** but here strong winds may make it difficult for the beginner to return to the upwind launch area. A good place to learn windsurfing is The Dalles Riverfront Park, just across the river in Oregon, where you can take lessons and rent equipment in a relatively protected location. Board rentals are also available in Stevenson and Bingen, Washington, and Hood River, Oregon. If you just want to watch, the best place is near the Hood River Bridge just west of Bingen, where you may see upwards of 300 boarders on a windy August day.

Columbia Gorge

DIANNE BOULERICE LYONS

Several good places for intermediate level boarders are in Stevenson, Home Valley, Bingen, Hood Vista Sailpark (just west of the Hood River toll bridge), and Avery Park (east of Horsethief Lake). The last of these is especially good because it has a long straight stretch of river that gets nicely formed waves.

Expert-level conditions can be found at Swell City, four miles west of the Bingen Marina; the Fish Hatchery, 3.5 miles west of Hood River; Doug's Beach, 2.5 miles east of Lyle; Maryhill State Park, where the river is less than a half mile wide; and the east end of the river near Roosevelt Park. For information on the sport, contact the **Columbia Gorge Boardsailors Association,** P.O. Box 887, Hood River, OR 97031.

TRANSPORTATION

By Car
While the trip along Highway 14 does offer some beautiful Gorge scenery, by the time you arrive at Maryhill Museum you'll realize this Columbia River trek is a lot longer than it looks on the map—especially if your destination is Tri-Cities, more than 200 miles from Camas. The crowds at Maryhill probably have less to do with art appreciation than with sore fannies. This is truly a remote part of the state, so stock up on Cokes, chips, or whatever gets you through the drive.

Scenic Cruises
Take a cruise on the Columbia, with views of steep basalt cliffs and stops at Cascade Locks, Bonneville Dam, and Stevenson, aboard the sternwheeler **Columbia Gorge,** tel. (541) 374-8427. The boat can accommodate 599 people and has full food and beverage services. The standard two-hour summertime cruises start at Oregon's Cascade Locks, just across the river on the Bridge of the Gods, and are available daily from mid-June to mid-October. You can also board in Stevenson or Bonneville Dam. These summer tours generally focus on a specific historical aspect of the river, such as the Oregon Trail or the Lewis and Clark Expedition, and cost $12 for adults, or $6 for kids. In the off-season, the *Columbia Gorge* operates out of Portland, offering a wide variety of cruises, from an hour or two for special occasions, to two-day cruises through the Columbia River Gorge and downriver to Astoria.

Alaska Sightseeing Cruise West, tel. (800) 888-9378, takes you up the river on two small cruise ships: *Spirit of Columbia* and *Spirit of '98.* The 1,000-mile trips leave from Portland and head upriver through locks all the way to the Idaho border and back. Along the way are stops at Fort Clatsop, Bonneville Dam, Hood River, Maryhill Museum, the Whitman Mission, Hells Canyon, and other places. These week-long trips cost $1400-4000 per person, all inclusive.

Board **YachtShip CruiseLine's** four-deck

Executive Explorer for a six-day cruise following Lewis and Clark's route through the Columbia and Snake Rivers. Starting in Portland, the cruise takes you to Astoria, Tri-Cities, Whitman Mission, Lewiston and Hell's Canyon, Maryhill Museum, and the Columbia Gorge. Call (360) 623-4245 for more information.

Special Expeditions' twin ships *Sea Bird* and *Sea Lion* make weeklong cruises on the river, usually in the fall. For information call (800) 762-0003.

Train Service
Amtrak has service up the Columbia Gorge, departing from Portland or Vancouver and stopping at Bingen/White Salmon and Wishram before continuing on to Pasco, Spokane, and points east. Call (800) 872-7245 for details. From July to Labor Day the Forest Service has onboard interpreters who provide information on the natural and historical sights as the train chugs up the Gorge.

By Bus
Bus service to these parts is close to nonexistent: Vancouver's **C-TRAN,** tel. (360) 695-0123, will get you as far east as Camas and Washougal. **Columbia River Gorge Tours,** tel. (800) 886-4416, has half- and full-day tours of the Columbia River Gorge by van and helicopter.

CAMAS AND WASHOUGAL AREA

It's pretty easy to see—and smell—what makes Camas (pop. 6,900) tick; the enormous James River Corporation paper mill dominates the center of town. Established in 1883 to provide paper for the Portland newspaper, *The Oregonian,* the mill was the first to operate in Washington Territory. Camas itself is an attractive town right along the Columbia, with big trees lining the main route.

The town of Washougal (pop. 4,800), just a couple miles east of Camas on Hwy. 14, was the first place settled by American pioneers in what would become Washington. David C. Parker and his family settled here in 1844, building a small dock on the river. Not far away, the Lewis and Clark Expedition paused to camp on their return trip up the Columbia River in 1806.

Washougal's claim to fame is the **Pendleton Woolen Mill,** in operation since 1912 and still producing acclaimed woolen products. The mill at 217th St. is open for hour-long guided tours Mon.-Fri.; call (360) 835-2131 for more information. An outlet store sells seconds and overstocked items.

Sights
The **Camas/Washougal Historical Society Museum,** 421 N.E. Franklin in Camas, tel. (360) 834-2472, has local historical items and is open Fri.-Sat. noon-4 p.m.

On Hwy. 14 between Washougal and North Bonneville, the **Cape Horn Viewpoint** offers a good spot for photographing the dramatic west entrance to the Gorge and for viewing massive Beacon Rock. For a short and scenic side trip, take Cape Horn Dr. downhill to the river, through overhanging maples and Douglas fir trees.

Practicalities
Stay at the Econo Lodge (see the "Columbia Gorge Accommodations" chart) in Washougal. Campsites are available at **Prindle County Park** along the Washougal River approximately four miles north of town.

The Camas/Washougal area features a number of small restaurants and pizza places, including a **Dairy Queen** in Camas. Mexican food aficionados will enjoy **Juanita's,** 231 3rd in Camas, tel. (360) 834-5856.

Camas Days in late July includes a parade, street dance, live entertainment, craft and food booths, and beer garden.

Find the **Camas-Washougal Chamber of Commerce** at 422 N.E. 4th Ave., tel. (360) 834-2472. Open Mon.-Fri. 9 a.m.-5 p.m. all year.

Camas also has a summer-only outdoor **swimming pool** at 120 N.E. 17th, tel. (360) 834-2382. The **area code** for Camas and Washougal is 360, but it is 509 just east of here in Skamania, North Bonneville, Stevenson, and Carson.

BEACON ROCK STATE PARK

Beacon Rock State Park is 35 miles east of Vancouver on Hwy. 14, and just west of the little town of North Bonneville. The core of an ancient volcano, 848-foot-high Beacon Rock is the largest such monolith in North America and the second largest in the world (after Gibraltar). The rock was named by Lewis and Clark in 1805. It was a "beacon" informing river travelers that there were no further obstructions in the river from here to the Pacific Ocean, 150 miles away! Henry J. Biddle bought the rock in 1915 to preserve it and spent two years blazing the 4,500-foot trail to the summit; his heirs donated the rock to the state in 1935.

Hike Biddle's steep one-mile trail for spectacular views of the Gorge; the trail boasts a 15% grade, but handrails make the hiking both easier and safer. This and other trails provide 14 miles of hiking in the park. Advanced climbers only may attempt to climb on the south side of the rock; register at the trailhead. The main part of the park is north of the highway, and old roads are perfect for mountain biking and horseback riding. A four-mile trail switchbacks to the 1,200-foot summit of **Hamilton Mountain,** passing the very scenic Rodney Falls inside a cavern. Fishermen can launch their boats from the boat ramp to catch Columbia River white sturgeon, and campers can stay in the densely forested sites (no RV hookups) for $10. The campground is open April-October. Call (800) 452-5687 for campsite reservations ($6 extra fee), available up to 11 months ahead of time. A smaller state park campground below the noisy railroad tracks along the river is open all year, but you'll need to take showers at the nearby private Beacon Rock RV Park, tel. (360) 427-8473.

Reed Island State Park, a 506-acre park near Beacon Rock, is accessible only by boat. Primitive campsites are available, and the island has a heron rookery and a half-mile hiking trail.

BONNEVILLE DAM AREA

Bonneville Dam snakes across the Columbia in three sections, connecting dot-to-dot between the shorelines and Bradford and Cascades Islands. This was the site of the famous Columbia River Cascades that made travel down the river so treacherous for Oregon Trail emigrants. An Army base, **Fort Cascades,** was constructed on the Washington side of the Cascades in the

early 1850s, and remained in use until 1861, when the Indians of the region had been forcibly moved onto reservations. A small settlement grew up around the Cascades, providing a railroad portage until the opening of the Cascades Canal and Locks in 1896 made it possible for ships to pass freely around the falls. Today the old Fort Cascades site has an interesting 1.5 mile loop path with interpretive signs describing the area's rich history.

Bonneville Dam
The original Bonneville dam and power plant were built here between 1933 and 1937; a second plant was added on the Washington shore that opened in 1981. Together they produce over 1,000 kilowatts of power that feeds into a grid for the Northwest and California.

Visit the **Bonneville Second Powerhouse** visitor center, on the Washington side of the Bonneville Dam, to see the inner workings of the powerhouse (including a peek inside a spinning turbine), and informative displays. You'll feel dwarfed by the enormity of the river, dam, and surrounding hills. Windows offer a chance to watch coho, sockeye, and king salmon, along with steelhead, shad, lamprey, and other fish as they head upstream each summer and fall. Only a quarter of the salmon that historically negotiated the Columbia River to spawn still do so. Massive dams such as these, upstream developments, changing ocean currents, and overfishing have all contributed to their decline. The visitor center is open daily 8 a.m.-6 p.m. from Labor Day to Memorial Day, and daily 9 a.m.-5 p.m. the rest of the year.

Cross "The Bridge of the Gods" (75 cents toll each way) into Oregon and visit the original **Bonneville Lock and Dam,** a popular tourist spot with continuous presentations, exhibits, and another fish-eye view of the Columbia's inhabitants as they head up the fishpass. The **Bradford Island Visitor Center** here has hourly movies and dam tours in the summer; in the winter they offer movies on request but no tours. You can also watch migrating fish at the fish ladder on Bradford Island. Open daily 8 a.m.-8 p.m. in the summer, and daily 9 a.m.-5 p.m. the rest of the year. Call (541) 374-8820 for details. The adjacent **Bonneville Fish Hatchery** has informative displays and ponds filled with fat rainbow trout and a half-dozen massive white sturgeon looking quite unhappy in their small pool. Just across I-84 is the trail to scenic Wahclella Falls, one of many waterfalls that line the Oregon side of the Columbia River. Stop by the locks to watch ships and barges heading through or to watch Indian fishermen dipnetting salmon from rickety wooden platforms in the summer.

Bridge of the Gods

According to Indian legend, a stone arch once spanned the river at the Cascades, allowing people to move freely across the river. There are different versions of the tale, but each of them involves two brothers feuding over a beautiful young woman. The Great Spirit had built the bridge to promote peace in the land, and when he saw the fighting, he shook the ground and caused the stone bridge to collapse. An old woman tried in vain to stop the fighting, and the Great Spirit rewarded her by making her young again. The various participants became the still-feuding volcanic peaks that dot this region and periodically hurl rocks at one another—Mt. Adams and Mt. Hood are the brothers, Squaw Mountain is the young woman they fought over, and Mt. St. Helens is the old woman turned young maiden.

Interestingly, geologists believe that the Cascades were indeed a crossing point at one time. Approximately 750 years ago a great earthquake triggered the collapse of a mountain on the Washington side of the river, blocking the Columbia River and creating a 270-foot high dam that held the water back for several years. Eventually, water topped the dam and washed most of the landslide away, but leaving behind the rocky islands that created the Cascades. The turbulent water that resulted made for treacherous river travel until the creation of the Cascade Locks in 1896. You can see these locks, no longer in use, at **Cascade Locks Marine Park,** on the Oregon side of the river. A small museum here relates Columbia River history and includes the Northwest's first steam locomotive, the Oregon Pony.

In 1926, the modern version of the legendary rock span was constructed at the site of the former Cascade Rapids. The "Bridge of the Gods" had to be raised 44 feet following construction of

the Bonneville Dam in 1938. Today it provides a link across the Columbia to the Oregon side of Bonneville Dam (described above) and to the town of Cascade Locks, where you can catch the sternwheeler *Columbia Gorge* for a two-hour cruise up the river (see "Scenic Cruises" under "Transportation," above). The **Pacific Crest National Scenic Trail** crosses the Columbia River along the Bridge of the Gods, heading north from here through Indian Heaven, Mt. Adams, and Goat Rocks wilderness areas—some of Washington's most scenic and middle-of-nowhere real estate—on its way to the Canadian border.

STEVENSON

The small town of Stevenson (pop. 1,150) has been the governmental seat for Skamania County since 1893—when the county records were stolen from nearby Cascades, transforming Stevenson overnight into the new county seat—but is only now starting to come into its own, with a sparkling new museum, one of the finest new lodges in Washington, and hordes of summertime windsurfers.

Sights

The **Skamania County Historical Museum,** tel. (509) 427-5141, has displays of pioneer life, Native American artifacts, and historical photos in the Courthouse Annex basement on Vancouver Avenue. Open Mon.-Sat. noon-5 p.m., Sunday 1-6 p.m.; free. Over in **Rock Creek Park,** on the west side of town, you'll find a Corliss steam engine and an old Spokane, Portland, and Seattle Railway caboose.

Columbia Gorge Interpretive Center

Located a mile west of Stevenson, this extraordinary multimillion-dollar museum opened with much fanfare in 1995. As you enter the building, a 40-foot floor-to-ceiling window offers a wide vista across a meadow to the mighty Columbia River. The interior of the main room is built around a tall simulated basalt cliff, with its crevices filled with Indian and pioneer artifacts. Wander through the museum to discover the area's rich human and natural history, which includes a waterfall, a 37-foot high replica of a fishwheel, and a restored Corliss steam engine that once powered a sawmill. The theater has stunning visual programs, and another section introduces you to the spiritual side of the Columbia Gorge. A Russian refugee and member of the Imperial family, Baron Eugene Fersen, claimed that the Gorge was a spiritual vortex. His objets d'art and furniture are housed here, along with the world's largest collection of rosaries—nearly 4,000—gathered from around the world and fashioned from a variety of materials. A museum store features the works of local artisans. The museum is open daily 10 a.m.-7 p.m. in the summer, and daily 10 a.m.-5 p.m. the rest of the year. Admission is $5 for adults, $4 for seniors, $3 for ages six to 12, and free for kids under six. Call (509) 427-8211 for more information.

Lodging
The **Skamania Lodge,** 1131 S.W. Skamania Lodge Dr., tel. (509) 427-7700, the finest luxury resort in the gorge, has an indoor pool, saunas, jacuzzis, tennis courts, convention facilities, and an exercise room. Nearby is the 18-hole **Bridge of the Gods Golf Course.** The lodge has a classic feeling, with wood flooring recycled from a 200-year-old building, petroglyph rubbings, Pendleton fabrics, and mission-style wood furnishings. The Forest Service has a small information center, tel. (509) 427-2528, at the lodge. The center is open daily 9 a.m.-7 p.m. June to Labor Day, with interpretive programs every afternoon and several evenings a week. See the "Columbia Gorge Accommodations" chart for other places to stay in the Stevenson area.

Campgrounds
Camp at **Beacon Rock State Park,** tel. (509) 427-8265, for $10 (described above, no RV hookups). Call (800) 452-5687 for campsite reservations ($6 extra fee), available up to 11 months ahead of time.

Park RVs at **Lewis & Clark RV Park** in North Bonneville, tel. (509) 427-5982; **NW Guide Service** in Skamania, tel. (509) 427-4625; **Beacon Rock RV Park** in Skamania, tel. (509) 427-8473; **Big Foot RV Park** in Carson, tel. (509) 427-4441; or **Valley RV Park** in Home Valley, tel. (509) 427-5300.

Food
The Crossing, tel. (509) 427-8097, has homemade soups, deli sandwiches, and various lunch specials. Get very good brewpub fare and microbrews on tap at the friendly **Big River Grill,** tel. (509) 427-4888. Be forewarned that portions are huge; go with the half-orders or you'll roll away. They also brew their own beer on the premises. **El Rio,** tel. (509) 427-4479, has authentic Mexican cuisine to eat in or carry out. **Skamania Lodge,** just west of town, tel. (509) 427-7700, serves three Northwest meals a day in an elaborate setting.

Recreation
Rent sailboards, kayaks, canoes, and bikes from **Waterwalker,** 371 S.W. Hwy. 14, tel. (509) 427-2727. They also offer sailboard lessons most summer afternoons. Skamania Lodge has downhill half-day mountain bike rides for $35; call (509) 427-7700 for details.

Events
July 4th brings the usual fireworks, picnics, and concessions to Skamania County; the best way to see the fireworks is aboard the sternwheeler *Columbia Gorge,* which offers a special tour (see below). The **Full Sail Gorge Cup Race Series** features a series of windsurfing contests culminating in the "Blowout" in early July. Later that month, the **Columbia Gorge Bluegrass Festival** brings foot-stompin' music and plenty of food all day long at the Rock Creek Fairgrounds.

The annual **Skamania County Fair and Timber Carnival,** held the fourth weekend in August, offers entertainment, a parade, timber contests, exhibits, and food. Then comes the **Columbia Gorge Blues Festival** on Labor Day weekend.

Information and Transportation
The **Stevenson Chamber of Commerce and Visitor Information Center,** tel. (509) 427-8911, is the place to go for the scoop on Stevenson. Hours are daily 8 a.m.-5 p.m. in the summer, and Mon.-Fri. 8 a.m.-5 p.m. in the winter. The **area code** for Stevenson, North Bonneville, and other towns on the east end of the Columbia Gorge is 509; west of here in Washougal and Camas it becomes 360.

The sternwheeler *Columbia Gorge* stops in Stevenson on its summertime cruises up the river; call (503) 374-8427 for details.

CARSON AREA

Just a few miles east of Stevenson is minuscule Carson, known for its hot springs and as an entry point into Gifford Pinchot National Forest. The drive north from Carson to the east side of Mt. St. Helens provides ample photographic and recreational opportunities. **Home Valley** has the Sojourner Inn—and not much else—with B&B accommodations (see the "Columbia Gorge Accommodations" chart), and delicious gourmet meals by reservation only. Call (509) 427-7070 for details.

Carson Hot Springs

The historic Carson Hot Springs Resort, tel. (509) 427-8292, has been drawing visitors to its 126° F natural mineral baths since the springs were discovered in 1876. At that time, the baths were seen as a cure for everything from arthritis to kidney disorders. The St. Martin Hotel was built here in 1897 to replace the tents that had accommodated the droves of guests; cabins were added in the 1920s. Today you can stay in the same aging and rather funky lodgings—and enjoy the same relaxing bath plus a massage—with no TVs or radios to distract. The resort attracts visitors from all over the globe. Hot mineral baths are $8 for an hour that includes 20 minutes in the tub and 30 minutes in a hot wrap, $32 for an hour-long massage, facials $36 an hour; rooms are also available (see the "Columbia Gorge Accommodations" chart), as are RV spaces ($13), and tent spaces ($5). The restaurant serves three home-style meals daily. Reserve early if you plan to stay at Carson Hot Springs on a weekend.

Hiking

Several day hikes are possible nearby, including the Bob Kuse Memorial Trail to the 1,000-foot summit of **Wind Mountain,** a three mile hike that offers dramatic views over the Columbia Gorge. The trailhead is a mile up Wind Mountain Rd. on the east side.

For a good view of the area's peaks, take a short hike to the top of **Little Huckleberry Mountain,** best hiked mid-July to October. Take Forest Service Rd. 66 (along the east edge of the lava bed) to the 49 trailhead; climb the steep grade for 2.5 miles to the summit and a refreshing berry break.

Lava Beds

The **Big Lava Bed Geologic Area** encompasses 12,500 acres of lava beds (remains of an ancient volcano). In the north section of the beds the crater, now covered by trees, rises 800 feet; inside the walls slope down almost to lava-bed level; a small meadow covers the bottom of the bowl. Another visually interesting feature is the 100-foot-deep trough or sink of unknown geologic origin, northeast of the crater. When exploring the lava beds, be sure to bring your own water; by mid-June all the creeks are dry. Be careful in your wanderings since there are no trails or landmarks to follow. Get here by heading north up Cook-Underwood Rd. from the town of Cook, eight miles east of Carson on Hwy. 14. It turns into South Prairie Rd. (Forest Rd. 66) after several miles and continues to the lava beds, approximately 14 miles up. The road follows the east side of the lava for the next 10 miles or so.

Campgrounds

Several Forest Service campgrounds are north of Carson off Wind River Road. Closest is **Panther Creek,** nine miles up Wind River Rd., and 1.5 miles up Forest Service Rd. 6517. The campground is open mid-May to mid-November. **Beaver Campground** is 12 miles up Wind River Rd.; open mid-April through October. **Paradise Creek Campground** is 20 miles up Wind River Rd., and another six miles on Forest Rd. 30; it's open mid-May to mid-November. All three of these charge $9; make reservations for them ($7.50 extra) by calling (800) 280-2267.

More camping is available at **Big Cedars County Park** north of Willard on Oklahoma Rd. and **Home Valley County Park,** tel. (509) 427-9478, for $11. RVers can park at **Carson Hot Springs Resort,** tel. (509) 427-8292, or **Bigfoot Park,** tel. (509) 427-4441.

Events

Late July brings the **Chiliympiad** to Carson, with prizes for the best chili, best vegetarian chili, and most creative entry. **Bigfoot Daze** in late August features live entertainment and other activities.

Information

Gifford Pinchot National Forest has the **Wind River Ranger Station** office in Carson, tel. (509) 427-5645, with information on local hikes, including the nearby Pacific Crest Trail. Open Mon.-Fri. 8 a.m.-4:30 p.m. all year. The **area code** for Carson and other towns in the eastern part of the Columbia River Gorge is 509.

WHITE SALMON AND BINGEN AREA

Continuing eastward from Carson and Home Valley, the highway passes the trailhead for **Dog Mountain Trail,** a rugged, switchback-filled 3.5 mile climb to the summit of this 2,900-foot peak. This is a good chance to stretch your legs and enjoy wildflower-filled meadows in spring. Beyond here Hwy. 14 parallels an old log flume. For decades the Broughton Lumber Co. logged in the mountains north of here, sending their logs to the riverside mill on this nine-mile flume. The mill has been closed for several years, and the old flume is slowly rotting away. Between the don't-blink-or-you'll-miss-them places called Cook and Underwood, the Lewis and Clark Highway cuts through five short tunnels and the landscape begins to open up, with fewer trees. Often, you'll find the weather changing simultaneously, as the wet west side of the Cascades gives way to the drier east. After awhile you pass the **Little White Salmon National Fish Hatchery** (13 miles east of Stevenson) and the **Spring Creek National Fish Hatchery** (two miles west of the Hood River Bridge); both are open Mon.-Fri. 7:30 a.m.-4 p.m., plus weekends in the winter months. A tiny visitor information center stands near the toll bridge (50 cents) that crosses the Columbia to Hood River Oregon just before you reach Bingen.

The attractive little town of Bingen (pop. 700) straddles Hwy. 14; its twin, White Salmon (pop. 1,900), is just a mile and a half up the hill. The latter has several Bavarian-style buildings, a glockenspiel, and the **Klitchat Pottery** shop for local crafts. East of these two, the road continues past barren cliffs along the river's edge and through the flyspeck called **Lyle.**

Klickitat River Rafting

The Klickitat Gorge, just north of Lyle, is a strikingly scenic area accented by rope bridges, where you can often see local Indians fishing with dip nets. The Klickitat River is one of the more remote rivers in Washington, quite unlike many of the Cascade rivers that are paralleled by roads the entire way. Rated class III-IV, the river drops through a narrow, pine-forested canyon with high rock walls on either side. Most rafting takes place in May and June, with runs covering 15 river miles. Expect to pay $55-75 for a half-day excursion, depending upon the number in your group and the company. Contact one of the following companies for more info: **All Rivers Adventures,** tel. (800) 743-5628; **Blue Sky Outfitters,** tel. (800) 228-7238; **Downstream River Runners,** tel. (800) 234-4644; **North Cascades River Expeditions,** tel. (800) 634-8433; **Northern Wilderness River Riders, Inc.,** tel. (800) 448-7238; **River Recreation,** tel. (800) 464-5899; **Rivers Incorporated,** tel. (206) 822-5296; **White Water Adventure,** tel. (800) 366-2004; and **Wildwater River Tours,** tel. (800) 522-9453. Downstream River Runners and Rivers Incorporated also offer overnight trips down the Klickitat for $175 with meals included. White Salmon-based White Water Adventure is the only one of these that is a local company.

White Salmon River Rafting

The White Salmon River—a National Wild and Scenic River—offers a fairly short but intense and exciting eight-mile whitewater trip. The river cuts through a 150-foot-deep gorge, requiring rafts to be dropped into the river by a cable system. This class III-IV river is generally run May through August, with the highest water in May. (The class-V rated Husum Falls is always portaged, except by experts.) Expect to pay $45-75 for a half-day excursion. Contact one of the following companies for more information: **All Rivers Adventures,** tel. (800) 743-5628; **Blue Sky Outfitters,** tel. (800) 228-7238; **North Cas-**

cades River Expeditions, tel. (800) 634-8433; Northern Wilderness River Riders, Inc., tel. (800) 448-7238; River Recreation, tel. (800) 464-5899; White Water Adventure, tel. (800) 366-2004; and Wildwater River Tours, tel. (800) 522-9453. White Salmon-based White Water Adventure is the local company.

Gorge Heritage Museum

The Gorge Heritage Museum, 202 E. Humbolt in Bingen, tel. (509) 493-2444, has local historical items, Indian artifacts, historic photos, and even an old permanent wave machine that could pass for an electric chair, all housed in a building that was built as a Congregational church in 1911. Open Sat.-Sun. 1-4 p.m. from late May to late September.

Accommodations

See the "Columbia Gorge Accommodations" chart for a complete list of White Salmon and Bingen lodging options, including the historic Bingen Haus B&B, tel. (509) 493-4888, the cozy Orchard Hill Inn, tel. (509) 493-3024, and the historic Inn of the White Salmon, tel. (509) 493-2335 or (800) 972-5226. The Inn at Bingen School, tel. (509) 493-3363, is certainly the most unusual place to stay. Located in a rambling wooden grade school built in 1938, this is a very popular place for young windsurfers and mountain climbers. Run something like a hostel (bring your own linen), it attracts travelers from all over the globe. Both dorm beds and private rooms are available, along with a gymnasium (including a climbing wall), kitchen area, and communal meals in the summer ($4.50 extra). You can rent mountain bikes ($15) or sailboards ($25-40) here. They also offer shuttle services for windsurfing. Reservations are recommended.

For up-to-date windsurfing conditions, check with the windsurfing shop across the bridge in Hood River, or listen to radio station 104 FM for daily wind reports.

Food

The Inn of the White Salmon, tel. (509) 493-2335, has locally famous country breakfasts, but be sure to phone ahead for reservations. More very good breakfasts and lunches are served in a beautifully restored historic home, at Bingen Haus, tel. (509) 493-4888.

Guido's, tel. (509) 493-3880, in Bingen looks like a little burger joint but has authentic and inexpensive Italian dinners and a pleasant patio. Very popular with locals who call it the best Italian food in the Gorge. Fidel's, tel. (509) 493-1017, serves very good Mexican food and big margaritas in Bingen. Large helpings, so arrive hungry.

Lyle Hotel, in the town of Lyle, nine miles east of White Salmon, tel. (509) 365-3010, has fresh grilled entrees, pasta, and other Northwest cuisine, plus delicious desserts in a turn-of-the-century hotel.

Get fresh fruits and vegetables (especially sweet corn, green onions, eggplant, spinach, and lettuce) at Dickey Farms in Bingen.

Other Practicalities

Local events include the White Salmon's Mayfest on the third weekend of May, Lyle Pioneer Days on Memorial Day weekend, and Bingen's Huckleberry Festival on the second weekend of September.

The area code for the White Salmon/Bingen area is 509.

The Bingen Amtrak station is located at 800 N.W. 6th, tel. (509) 248-1146 or (800) 872-7245. Service is four times a week, heading west to Vancouver and Portland, and east to Wishram, Pasco, Spokane, and all the way east to Chicago.

THE DALLES AREA

East of the Bingen area, the country opens up dramatically into rolling dry hills of grass and rock. In this desolate place the rumble of long freight trains and the sounds of tugs pushing barges upriver are never too far away. Look across the river to Oregon's busy I-84 and be glad you're on the less-hurried side of the river.

The Dalles Dam

"The Dalles" is from the French "La Grand Dalle de la Columbia," meaning "The Trough." This was the most dangerous point in the river for early navigators because it was a virtual staircase of rapids called Celiclo Falls. Most Oregon Trail travelers opted to portage around the rapids at The Dalles. For centuries the falls were a major fishing spot for Indians who caught salmon as they headed upstream to spawn. When Lewis and Clark visited this area in 1805, they reported a village of 21 large wooden houses and called the place a "great emporium . . . where all the neighboring nations assemble." The dam at The Dalles was completed in 1957, covering forever this famous old falls, along with countless cultural sites, and ending forever a way of life.

The **North Shore Visitor Center** has displays on the 1.5-mile-long dam, along with a fishpass, but the main center of activity is on the other side. Cross over into Oregon via Hwy. 197 to see The Dalles Dam and the adjacent city of the same name. Take the free train from the **Dalles Dam Visitors Center** tel. (541) 396-1181 for a guided tour of the dam, displays on Lewis and Clark, petroglyphs recovered before the dam was completed, and fish ladders; open daily 9 a.m.-5 p.m., June to Labor Day. Just east of The Dalles on Oregon's I-84, the **Fort Dalles Museum,** tel. (541) 296-4547, boasts a number of intact 1850s structures, including the 1856 Surgeon's Quarters that now houses the museum, and the original 1859 Wasco County Courthouse, now housing the visitor center. Stop here for a free walking-tour map. The 48,000-square-foot **Columbia Gorge Discovery Center** opens on the Oregon side in 1997 with exhibits on the area's rich natural and cultural history.

Camp for free at **Hess Park** or **Spearfish Park** on the Washington side of the Dalles Bridge. No developed facilities at these Army Corps of Engineers areas.

Doug's Beach State Park

This tiny park is basically a staging area for the throngs of windsurfers who come here all summer long to play on the Columbia River. This is not a place for beginners since the swells can reach six to eight feet at times. No water or camping, but it does have outhouses. The park is located 2.5 miles east of the town of Lyle along Hwy. 14, and seven miles west of Horsethief Lake State Park.

Horsethief Lake State Park

Located two miles east of Hwy. 197 on Hwy. 14, Horsethief Lake State Park has good trout and bass fishing from your boat or one of the park's rentals, with two boat launches—one on the lake, one on the river. Nearby is 500-foot-high Horsethief Butte, a favorite of rock climbers. The park is surrounded by Indian petroglyphs on natural rock formations, including the famous *Tsagaglalal* ("She who Watches") petroglyph. Legend has it that this carved rock represents a woman who was once a tribal chief, and who still sees all that goes on through her stone eyes. Because of vandalism, the rock art site is only open for guided tours Friday and Saturday at 10 a.m. April-October. Make reservations by calling (509) 767-1159. The tours last approximately an hour. A small campground at Horsethief has out-in-the-open sites for $11 (no RV hookups); open April-October. Call (800) 452-5687 for campsite reservations ($6 extra fee), available up to 11 months ahead of time.

Wineries

Founded in 1975, **Mont Elise Vineyards,** 315 W. Steuben in Bingen, tel. (509) 493-3001, is one of the oldest family-run wineries in the state. This is a friendly and funky operation located in a 19th-century building with wines not available outside the area. They produce gewürztraminer, pinot noir blanc, gamay beaujolais, and pinot noir, along with a champagne. Open for tastings daily noon-5 p.m. The vineyards are just three miles north of here.

Eleven miles north of White Salmon on the road to Trout Lake, the family-run **Hooper Family Winery** produces white riesling, chardonnay, gewürztraminer, and pinot noir blanc. All are pure varietals, not blends. The winery is open daily 11 a.m.-5 p.m. in the summer, and weekends 11 a.m.-5 p.m. in the winter; call (509) 493-2324 for information.

Transportation

Amtrak trains stop at the little settlement of Wishram, nine miles east of the Dalles dam. Service is four times a week, heading west to Bingen, Vancouver, and Portland, and east to Pasco, Spokane, and all the way east to Chicago. Call (800) 872-7245 for more information.

GOLDENDALE AREA

Highway 97 heads north from the Columbia to the rather plain little town of Goldendale (pop. 3,300), 10 miles away, passing cattle ranches and fields of dryland wheat along the way. The horizon is dominated by the snowcapped summits of Mt. Hood to the south and Mt. Adams, Mt. St. Helens, and Mt. Rainier to the west. North of Goldendale, Hwy. 97 climbs through ponderosa pine forests as it reaches 3,107-foot **Satus Pass,** before descending into the scenic and lonely Yakama Indian Reservation, and the town of Toppenish in Yakima Valley, 50 miles away. Goldendale began when the first farmers and loggers settled here in 1879 and has grown slowly over the decades since.

Presby Mansion
Goldendale's 20-room Presby Mansion, 127 W. Broadway, tel. (509) 773-4303, is the home of the **Klickitat County Historical Museum.** Built in 1903, this beautifully restored white-clapboard mansion is filled with pioneer furniture, a collection of coffee mills, and other exhibits; it's open daily 9 a.m.-5 p.m. May-Oct., the rest of the year by appointment. Admission is $3 for adults, $1 for ages 12-18, free for children under 12.

Goldendale Observatory State Park
Head a mile north of town and uphill through open ponderosa pine forests to Goldendale Observatory State Park, tel. (509) 773-3141, which has one of the nation's largest telescopes open to public viewing, a 24.5-inch reflecting Cassegrain. Also here are several smaller portable telescopes. Take a tour and enjoy free audiovisual programs, displays, and demonstrations Wed.-Sun. 2-5 p.m. and 8 p.m.-midnight April-Sept.; winter hours are Sunday 1-5 p.m. and Saturday 1-5 p.m. and 7-9 p.m. The observatory is a gathering place for amateur astronomers, and facilities include a kitchenette, restroom, and all-purpose room. Group camping only here. Come here for great views of Mt. Adams during the day.

Brooks Memorial State Park
Camp at Brooks Memorial State Park, tel. (509) 773-4611, 15 miles north of Goldendale on Hwy. 97. Tent sites ($10) and RV hookups ($15) on 700 forested acres are available year-round. Enjoy the nine miles of hiking trails through the cool ponderosa pine forests and good trout fishing in the Klickitat River, and cross-country skiing in winter. An environmental learning center

here is used mainly by school groups. Call (800) 452-5687 for campsite reservations ($6 extra fee), available up to 11 months ahead of time.

Lodging
See the "Columbia Gorge Accommodations" chart for a listing of places to stay in the area. The most elaborate is **Highland Creeks Resort,** tel. (509) 773-4026 or (800) 458-0174, located in the forested Simcoe Mountains north of town with all the amenities you'd expect in a luxury resort, including gourmet meals. In town, both **Victorian House B&B,** tel. (509) 773-5338, and **The Sleeper House,** tel. (509) 773-4749, offer B&B accommodations in historic homes.

Food
Highland Creeks Resort, tel. (509) 773-4026 or (800) 458-0174, eight miles north of Goldendale on Hwy. 97, is one of the better restaurants in the area, with seafood, steak, and other fare, including a Sunday champagne brunch. Try **The Homestead Restaurant** for standard family meals.

Events
Goldendale Community Days in early July features arts and crafts, ethnic food, a flea market, antique auction, beer garden, and parade. The **Klickitat County Fair and Rodeo** is held annually in Goldendale over Labor Day weekend.

Information and Services
For local information, contact the **Goldendale Chamber of Commerce,** on Columbus and Main, tel. (509) 773-3400 or (800) 648-5462. Swim in the outdoor pool at the Community Park during the summer months. The **area code** for the Goldendale area and the rest of eastern Washington is 509.

MARYHILL AND VICINITY

There isn't much left of the settlement known as Maryhill, near the intersection of Highways 14 and 97, but several sights make this remote area well worth a visit, particularly the famous Maryhill Museum.

The **Columbia Cliffs Winery,** just west of the town of Wishram, tel. (509) 767-1100, is a small family winery that produces red wines, including merlot, petite sirah, and nebbiolo. Open Tues.-Sun. 11 a.m.-5 p.m. April-Nov., and weekends in the winter.

Just down the hill from Stonehenge are fruit orchards surrounding the small settlement of Maryhill with its New England-style white church and old steam engine. Not much remains of Sam Hill's grandiose dreams of a Quaker community. The **Maryhill Fruit Stand** and **Gunkel Orchards** sell some of the finest fresh peaches, apricots, cherries, and other fresh fruits that you'll ever taste.

Maryhill Museum

The eccentric collection exhibited here veers all over the spectrum with everything from Indian rock art to neon sculptures. On the entry level, you'll find a gift shop, a room describing the life of Sam Hill, and items donated by Queen Marie of Romania: collections of Russ-

ian Orthodox icons and her intricately carved throne and elaborate coronation gown. Also on this floor are miniature French fashion mannequins outfitted by the finest couturiers of post-WW II Paris, and donated by Alma Spreckels. (Postwar Europe had such severe shortages of fabric that designers were forced to display their creations on dolls.) Upstairs are special exhibitions, works by American painters, and other pieces. The lower level is the largest space, with a wing devoted to the sculptures and drawings of Auguste Rodin, two small rooms filled with intricate chess sets from all over the world, and a separate wing with Native American works—basketry, beaded dresses, Inuit carvings, and rock art. The lower level also has a collection of pieces by contemporary artists, and a small cafe with a pleasant patio where you can watch the peacocks roaming the spacious grounds and enjoy the Columbia River vistas that brought Sam Hill here. (See the special topic "Castle Nowhere" for more on the life and times of Sam Hill, the

CASTLE NOWHERE

The Northwest has no Hearst Castles or Winchester Mystery Houses, no Death Valley Scotties. In that favorite tourist catagory of eccentric mansions, the Northwest offers only the **Maryhill Museum of Art,** a place whose evolution from barren hillside to empty palatial home to museum took 26 years.

The museum—jokingly called "Castle Nowhere"—stands in isolated splendor on a bleak, sagebrush-strewn section of desert along the Columbia River, 100 miles east of Portland-Vancouver and 60 miles south of Yakima. This was just the setting that the Seattle attorney and entrepreneur Sam Hill wanted when he was searching for a homesite early in this century. Forced to be the primary breadwinner for his family at age 10, Hill grew up fast. He later went on to the finest schools before becoming an attorney and gaining a strong reputation for his lawsuits against the Great Northern Railway, run by James J. Hill (no relation). James Hill was so impressed that he decided to put Sam Hill on his payroll to have him as an ally rather than an adversary. Sam would later marry the railway magnate's daughter, Mary Hill. Although many of his later ventures failed, he went on to form the "Good Roads" program and

was a major force behind the creation of the Columbia River Highway, the coastal highway (101), and what would become today's I-5.

Maryhill

Hill's most extravagent venture was an attempt to establish a utopian Quaker town "where the rain of the west and the sunshine of the east meet." He purchased 7,000 acres of treeless terrain on the north side of the Columbia River south of Goldendale, and in 1914, began building his concrete palace, which was to be the farm's centerpiece. He named the spread Maryhill, after his wife, daughter, and mother-in-law, all three named Mary Hill. Hill attempted to interest Quakers—who shared his pacifist philosophy—to invest in his community. He built them a meeting hall and a few other facilities as enticement, but the Quakers declined; they wanted no part of that sun- and wind-blasted countryside. His wife refused to live in this God-forsaken place, taking the children and returning to Minnesota, and all the buildings he constructed for the utopian town were destroyed in a fire in 1958. The mansion was built with two garages big enough for 48 automobiles, along with a sweeping ramp entrance that al-founder of this remote but extraordinary museum overlooking the Columbia River.)

Maryhill Museum is open daily 9 a.m.-5 p.m. March 15 to November 15, and closed the rest of the year. Admission is $5 for adults, $4.50 for seniors, $1.50 for kids ages six to 16, and free for kids under six. Call (509) 773-3733 for more information.

Stonehenge

Three miles east of Maryhill is another oddity. On a hilltop surrounded by open grass and sage sits a poured concrete replica of England's Stonehenge, but with all the rocks neatly in place rather than scattered around. This is another of Sam Hill's monumental creations, this time in memory of the 13 Skamania County men who died in WW I. It was built between 1918 and 1930 in the mistaken belief that the original Stonehenge had been used for human sacrifice and is believed to be the nation's first WW I memorial. The ashes of Sam Hill himself are in an urn just down the slope from Stonehenge. The monument is open 7 a.m.-10 p.m.

Maryhill State Park

This popular park is five miles east of the Maryhill Museum and right along the Columbia River near the intersection of Highways 14 and 97. Maryhill State Park offers Columbia River access for boating, windsurfing, and fishing, plus full-hookup campsites ($15) and coin-operated showers. Open year-round. Call (509) 773-5007 for details, or (800) 452-5687 for campsite reservations ($6 extra fee), available up to 11 months ahead of time. A **Travel Information Center** here has Columbia Gorge info.

EAST TO TRI-CITIES

The stretch of Hwy. 14 between Maryhill and McNary Dam is some of the most desolate country to be found in Washington. Dry grassy hills provide grazing land for cattle, and a few scattered old farmsteads are slowly returning to the land. The land is bisected by tall power lines marching like misshapen insects over the landscape. Not much traffic here, so tune in to the Spanish-language radio station, KDNA (FM 92) for music.

---

lowed vehicles to drive right into the mansion to drop off passengers.

About three miles upriver from the museum, just east of Hwy 97, Hill built a concrete replica of England's Stonehenge, as it might have looked when intact, and dedicated it to the Klickitat County soldiers who died in WW I. Hill also built the Peace Arch that marks the U.S.-Canadian border at Blaine, Washington.

The WW I years saw the mansion incomplete and bereft of inhabitants. After the war, President Herbert Hoover appointed Hill to a commission to help with Europe's reconstruction. There he met the three women who were responsible for Maryhill becoming a museum: Loie Fuller, a modern-dance pioneer at the Folies Bergere; Alma Spreckles of a prominant California sugar family; and Queen Marie of Romania, whose country Hill aided during the recovery period.

Fuller was particularly enthusiastic about the project and introduced Hill to members of the Parisian artistic community. Hill soon bought the large Auguste Rodin collection of sculptures and drawings.

When the 1926 dedication of the still-unfinished museum neared, Queen Marie agreed to come to

New York and cross America by train to attend the ceremonies—the first visit of any European royalty to this country. She brought along a large collection of furniture, jewelry, clothing, and religious objects to be donated to the museum. Today her collection is one of the museum's largest.

Hill died in 1931. He was buried in a crypt just below the Stonehenge monument, overlooking the river. At the time of Hill's death, the museum still wasn't complete. Alma Spreckles took over the project, donating many pieces from her extensive art collection and seeing to it that the museum was finished and opened in 1940. On that occasion *Time* magazine called it "the loneliest museum in the world."

Sam Hill's original 7,000 acre spread remains intact. Most of the land is leased to ranchers and farmers. Adjoining the Stonehenge monument is the Maryhill State Park, featuring a swimming area, boat launch onto the Columbia, picnic areas, and 50 overnight campsites with restrooms and hot showers.

Only in the past decade or so has the museum enjoyed much popularity or prominance; weekend travelers have begun driving farther to the remote site, and the curators have lined up respected exhibits.

STATE OF WASHINGTON TOURISM DIVISION

Stonehenge replica, near Maryhill

Two podunk settlements—**Roosevelt** and **Paterson**—are the only places on this side of the river. Roosevelt's controversial claim to fame (or infamy) is its regional landfill—said to be the nation's most technologically advanced—where Regional Disposal Company brings trash from Everett and other Snohomish County cities by railcar. They dump 75,000 carloads of garbage here each year. Paterson is known for its expansive vineyards and several wineries.

John Day Lock and Dam

The John Day Lock and Dam, 24 miles upriver from The Dalles and a half-dozen miles east of Stonehenge, gave birth to Lake Umatilla and produces enough electricity for two cities the size of Seattle. Here you'll find one of the largest single-lift locks in the world, hefting vessels 113 feet. At the dam on Oregon's I-84, enjoy the fish-viewing room, visitor's gallery, and Giles French Park, which has a boat launch, a picnic area, and fishing.

A good portion of this power is used in the enormous Columbia Aluminum Corporation plant that stretches for two-thirds of a mile next to the dam. Camp for free at undeveloped **Cliffs Park** approximately three miles off the highway on John Day Road.

Bickleton

For a pleasant side trip, drive north from Roosevelt to the tiny town of Bickleton, with a friendly cafe on one side of the street and a tavern on the other. The town has something of a Clint Eastwood western look to it with a few Victorian homes, some no longer occupied. But it does have another kind of home, hundreds of them, that are seasonally occupied: Bickleton is the **bluebird capital of the world.** It has blue and white houses for bluebirds on fence posts, on mailboxes, on trees, and virtually everywhere you look. There's even one in front of the community church, a mirror-image (although considerably smaller) of the church. The bluebird housing project started in the 1960s when Jess and Elva Brinkerhoff built one, then another and another, and soon it was a community project. When the birds leave for the winter, the 700 houses are taken down, cleaned, and painted if they need it, and everyone has the pleasure of watching for the first arrivals each spring. Spring is the best time to view the bluebirds, but you're likely to see them all summer long.

In Cleveland Park, four miles west of town, is a delightful old **carousel** with 24 wooden horses and a musical calliope. Built at the turn of the century, the carousel has been here since 1928 and is a rare type that moves around a track. It only operates for a two-day period each summer: during the Alder Creek Pioneer Picnic and Rodeo in June. For another piece of history, visit **Bluebird Inn,** one of the state's oldest taverns. Built in 1892, it has a classic turn-of-the-century Brunswick pool table with leather pockets, along with other local artifacts.

The **Alder Creek Pioneer Picnic and Rodeo** comes to Cleveland Park in mid-June. This is the oldest rodeo in the state of Washington.

The **Whoop-N-Holler Ranch Museum** on East Rd. between Bickleton and Roosevelt, tel. (509) 896-2344, contains a lifetime of collecting by Lawrence and Ada Whitmore. Two large buildings are filled with Model T Fords and other antique cars, a horse-drawn hearse on sled runners, local historical items, and family heirlooms (including an electrified lunch box to heat your food). This is one of the largest collections of antique and classic cars in the state and is open daily 10 a.m.-4 p.m. April-September. Admission is $3.

Winery
The big **Columbia Crest Winery,** tel. (509) 875-2061, is just north of Paterson, with tours and tasting daily 10 a.m.-4:30 p.m. Nearly 90% of the winery is below ground, making it easier to maintain cool temperatures throughout the year. The winery is situated on a high hill with stunning vistas across the Columbia River and across a thousand acres of adjacent vineyards. The winery has a courtyard with picnic tables and a luxurious lobby and tasting room. Columbia Crest is owned by American Tobacco Company.

Crow Butte State Park
Located at the site of a camping place for the Lewis and Clark Expedition, this 1,312-acre park sits along a virtually unpopulated stretch of highway halfway between the nowhere towns of Roosevelt and Paterson. It offers boating, swimming, fishing, and waterskiing, with tent ($10) and RV sites ($15) and coin-operated showers. The campground is open daily late March to late October, plus winter weekends. Call (800) 452-5687 for campsite reservations ($6 extra fee), available up to 11 months ahead of time. Crow Butte State Park covers half of an island created when the John Day Dam backed up the river to form Lake Umatilla; the other half is within **Umatilla National Wildlife Refuge,** which straddles both sides of the Columbia. A three-quarter-mile trail leads to the top of Crow Butte (671 feet), with views across the Columbia to Mt. Hood when the weather permits; keep your eyes open for rattlesnakes.

The Umatilla National Wildlife Refuge has an overlook a few miles east of Crow Butte where you can peer across the river below and pick up a brochure describing the refuge and its abundant waterfowl. For more on the refuge, call their office in Umatilla, Oregon, at (541) 922-3232.

McNary Dam
By the time you reach the McNary Dam area, the land has opened into an almost-level desert of sage and grass, broken only by center-pivot irrigation systems. The Columbia River's McNary Lock and Dam, 30 miles south of Pasco in Umatilla, Oregon, creates 61-mile-long Lake Wallula, which reaches up past the Tri-Cities to Ice Harbor Dam. The McNary Dam, tel. (509) 922-3211, completed in 1953, is open daily 8 a.m.-5 p.m. April-Sept. and offers hourly guided tours of the facility and fishpass.

The **McNary National Wildlife Refuge,** next to McNary Dam, has a mile-long hiking trail popular with birdwatchers. Area species include hawks, golden and bald eagles, and prairie falcons.

BOB RACE

THE CASCADE RANGE

INTRODUCTION

The Cascade Range is Washington's great divide. In addition to creating almost opposite climates on either side of the state, the Cascades also serve as a political and psychological barrier between east and west, resulting in what seems like two states within one. Many historians have said the founding fathers erred in creating the state, and that they should have drawn the state border along the crest of the Cascades. Perhaps—but that would have robbed the state of much of its cultural and geographical richness.

The two halves of the state are different not only in appearance but also in other less-obvious ways. Speaking very generally, western Washington is urban-oriented, with an emphasis on commerce and manufacturing, while eastern Washington is mainly rural and agricultural.

Crossing the Cascade passes in winter—an adventure many Washingtonians prefer to forgo—is an experience that thousands of avid skiers tolerate to reach the slopes. They simply learn to live with the snow-tire and chain requirements, snow-packed and icy roads, and occasional pass closures.

In summer, the Cascades take on a more benign image and become a popular destination for all manner of travelers, who have a wide variety of places and experiences from which to choose. Millions of acres have been set aside for recreation. The North Cascades and Mt. Rainier National Parks, Mt. St. Helens National Volcanic Monument, the areas around Mt. Baker and Mt. Adams, along with numerous wilderness areas and wildlife refuges—all constitute the backbone of Washington's outdoor recreation.

This lengthy chapter roughly follows the Cascade Range from Mt. Baker at the north all the way to the Mt. Adams area near the state's southern border, following the main highways over the passes, and visiting the sights, backcountry trails, and settlements en route.

Geology and Climate

The Cascade Range is about 25 million years old, but the range's volcanoes in Washington—Adams, St. Helens, Rainier, Glacier Peak, and Baker—plus another 15 or so in Oregon and California, are less than a million years old. Although none can be declared totally dead, only two have erupted in this century: Northern California's Mt. Lassen in 1914, and Mt. St. Helens in 1980. Not long before Mt. St. Helens came to life in such a violent manner, Mt. Baker began heating up and sent out clouds of steam and melted some of its glaciers, but Mt. St. Helens stole the show in 1980.

The only break in the Cascade Range is the Columbia Gorge (see previous chapter), which lets the Columbia River flow through and also permits an exchange of air between east and west that is impossible elsewhere along the range. Because it is the only such corridor for hundreds of miles, the resulting winds are strong and almost constant and provide some of the country's best windsurfing conditions.

The rest of the range continues uninterrupted, shielding the interior from storms coming off the ocean and resulting in two vastly different climates: wet on the west side, dry on the east. This weather variation is caused by what is commonly called the rain-shadow effect: incoming storms dump most of their rain and snow on the western side of the ridge as the air is forced up and over the mountain range, leaving the back side drier.

MOUNT BAKER AND VICINITY

Mount Baker, the northernmost of the Cascade volcanoes, towers dramatically over the surrounding hills. At 10,778 feet, it is bathed in glaciers and snowfields and serves as a scenic backdrop for Bellingham and Vancouver, B.C. Besides improving the scenery, the Mt. Baker area offers up a wealth of recreational activities, from skiing to hiking to whitewater rafting. Much of this land lies within the Mt. Baker Wilderness and National Recreation Area. Bordering them to the east is North Cascades National Park, another favorite of those who love the outdoors.

The Natural World

The four "life zones" on the mountain, from sea-level forest to alpine meadows, have a wide variety of wildlife, including coyotes, black bear, black-tailed deer, porcupines, elk, marmots, and mountain goats. Forest birds include grouse, gray jays (the black-and-white equivalent of the eastern blue jay), ptarmigan, and a large winter population of bald eagles on the Skagit (rhymes with "gadget") and Nooksack Rivers. All five species of Pacific salmon spawn in the rivers, and the insect population is well represented by three of its least popular members, the mosquito, black fly, and "no-see-um."

HISTORY

Discovered in 1792 by Captain Vancouver's first mate, Joseph Baker, Mt. Baker had been known for centuries to local Indians as "Koma Kulshan," meaning "Broken One," a reference to an early eruption that blew out part of its summit. Like other Cascade volcanoes, Baker is asleep, but not dead. In 1843 it awoke from its slumber, spewing vast amounts of smoke and ash for the next 16 years, and causing a major forest fire on the east shore of Baker Lake. The mountain lay dormant from 1884 to 1975, when it again began to release steam, leading seismologists to believe it would erupt, but it was upstaged in a grand manner in 1980 by Mt. St. Helens. Since that time the mountain continues to vent steam periodically, with small clouds frequently visible over the summit. There is little evidence of a return to life—but this could change at any time.

Mount Baker has been a source for year-round recreation since 1868, when librarian-turned-mountaineer Edmund Coleman and his party climbed to the summit after two failed attempts. Either poor planners or extremely conscious of pack weight, the entire climbing party shared one plate and spoon and ate only bacon, bread, and tea during the 10-day ascent. By 1911, the mountain had become an integral part

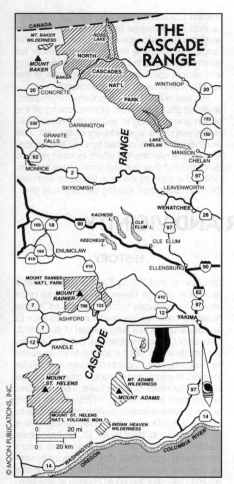

THE CASCADE RANGE

© MOON PUBLICATIONS, INC.

of the Mt. Baker marathon, a 118-mile roundtrip between Bellingham and the summit using any mode of transportation in addition to at least 24 miles on foot. The marathons were discontinued two years later after one competitor fell into a crevasse, though he lived to tell about it. More recently the race has been revived as the 85-mile long **Ski to Sea Marathon,** where teams begin by skiing down Mt. Baker, and relays of bike riders, paddlers in canoes, and runners complete the course to Puget Sound.

SIGHTS

Mt. Baker Highway

Highway 542 is the primary access road to Mt. Baker, a 62-mile drive from Bellingham, through the little towns of **Nugents Corner, Deming, Kendall, Maple Falls,** and **Glacier,** and then all the way to the end of the road at Heather Meadows. Not much to these settlements, but you may want to stop by for the **Deming Logging Show** in mid-June, the **Everson-Nooksack Summer Festival** on the second weekend in July, or the **Bigfoot Festival** in Maple Falls each September.

The Nooksack Indian Tribe runs **Nooksack River Casino,** 5048 Mt. Baker Hwy. (near the town of Deming), tel. (360) 592-5472, where you can try your hand at blackjack, craps, roulette, poker, and pull-tabs. They also have a cocktail lounge and all-you-can-eat buffet. Open daily.

Mount Baker Vineyards, between Deming and Nugents Corner on Hwy. 542, tel. (360) 592-2300, has tours and tastings daily 11 a.m.-5 p.m. April-December. The vineyard grows several unusual varieties of grapes, including Madeline Angevine and Müller-Thurgau, and has a popular **Grape Stomp** in mid-September.

Cloudy Mountain Pottery, five miles north of Kendall, tel. (360) 988-8645, is a cooperative gallery with pottery by several local artisans.

Stop by **Twin Sisters Mushroom Farm,** 5410 Saxon Rd. in Acme, tel. (360) 595-2979, for free tours on Sunday afternoons. The retail shop sells fresh mushrooms and mushroom-growing kits.

Nooksack Valley

The highway climbs along the beautiful Nooksack River Valley, gently at first, then in a series of steep switchbacks as you approach the terminus near the mountain. The road enters Mt. Baker-Snoqualmie National Forest just east of Glacier, where you'll find the **Glacier Public Service Center** (see "Information and Transportation," below), along with a handful of businesses. East from here to the end, the road is officially a National Forest Scenic Byway. Enjoy the finest views of Mt. Baker at the end of paved Glacier Creek Rd. (Forest Rd. 39), which begins just east of Glacier and heads south for seven miles to a parking lot and trailhead at an elevation of almost 2,900 feet.

East of Glacier, the highway cruises through a wonderful stand of 700-year-old Douglas firs. Seven miles east of Glacier is the turnoff to impressive **Nooksack Falls,** one mile away along a gravel side road. As you wend your way eastward from here, you'll find periodic views down the valley. The road passes columnar volcanic rock just below the **Mt. Baker Ski Area** (see "Skiing," below), where you can purchase snacks on summer weekends or full meals in the winter, and then circles around famous **Picture Lake.** Join the crowd for a photo of Mt. Shuksan rising behind the mirrored waters of this small lake. It's one of Kodak's favorite places in America.

Heather Meadows Area

The highway ends at 5,200-foot **Artist Point** in Austin Pass, 23 miles east of Glacier—the only alpine area in the North Cascades accessible by car. The surrounding area—Heather Meadows—delivers up incredible vistas, more than 40 picnic sites, and a multitude of hiking trails to explore in late summer. The stone-walled **Heather Meadows Visitor Center,** built by the CCC in 1940, offers up local information and is open daily 10 a.m.-4:30 p.m. July-September.

Heather Meadows, stuck between Mounts Baker and Shuksan, has been drawing tourists since the first lodge was built here in 1927 (it burned to the ground four years later). The lakes, meadows, and rock formations surrounded by snowcapped peaks were the setting for Clark Gable's *Call of the Wild* and Robert DeNiro's *The Deer Hunter.*

The road to Picture Lake is kept plowed all winter, but the last five miles from here to Artist Point close with the first snows—generally mid to late October—and usually don't open till late July. Because of the short season, the months of August and September are busy beyond belief, especially on weekends. Try to visit on a weekday instead.

RECREATION

River Rafting

The Nooksack River emerges from Nooksack

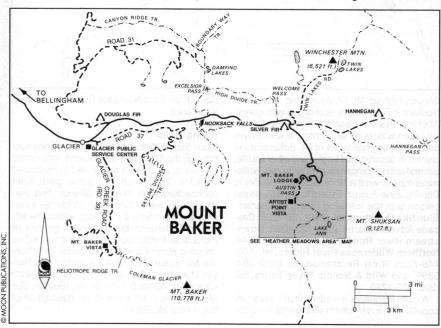

HEATHER MEADOWS AREA

TO GLACIER AND BELLINGHAM

BAKER SCENIC BYWAY

542

PICTURE LAKE

MT. BAKER SKI AREA

LAKES

CHAIN

CHAIN LAKES

BAGLEY LAKES

TRAIL

FIRE AND ICE TRAIL

TABLE

MOUNTAIN

TRAIL

ARTIST POINT

ARTIST RIDGE TRAIL

RIDGE

PTARMIGAN

VISITOR CENTER / AUSTIN PASS

PANORAMA DOME TRAIL

LAKE

ANN

TRAIL

LAKE ANN

0 1 mi
0 1 km

© MOON PUBLICATIONS, INC.

Glacier, high up Mt. Shuksan, and drops over Nooksack Falls before entering a wild gorge. After four miles of class II to III whitewater, the silt-laden waters emerge into the lower river delta, providing fine views of Mt. Baker and the chance to observe bald eagles and other wildlife. Several rafting companies offer eight-mile whitewater trips down the Nooksack from Glacier to Deming June-August. Expect to pay $55-65 per person with the following rafting companies: **Blue Sky Outfitters,** tel. (800) 228-7238; **Cascade Adventures,** tel. (800) 723-8386; **Downstream River Runners,** tel. (800) 234-4644; **Northern Wilderness River Riders,** tel. (800) 448-7238; **River Recreation,** tel. (800) 464-5899; and **Wild & Scenic River Tours,** tel. (206) 323-1220.

A more leisurely summertime float—extremely popular with inner tubers and families—is the South Fork of the Nooksack River from Acme to Van Zandt.

Hiking Trails

More than 200 miles of hiking trails meander through the Mt. Baker district, and, fortunately for hikers, all of them are closed to motorized vehicles. The variety of trails is great: both backpackers and one-milers alike can find striking scenery within their reach. Wilderness permits are not needed for hiking within the Mt. Baker Wilderness, but be sure to get one at the Glacier Public Service Center if you will be entering North Cascades National Park from the Mt. Baker area. See Ira Spring and Harvey Manning's *100 Hikes in Washington's North Cascades: National Park Region* (Seattle: The Mountaineers) for a complete description of hikes near Mt. Baker.

One of the most popular—and overused—hikes is the 3.5-mile roundtrip **Heliotrope Ridge Trail** to the edge of **Coleman Glacier,** the starting point for Mt. Baker summit climbs. (Don't attempt to climb Mt. Baker without previous climbing experience; accidents and even deaths are not uncommon.) The trail begins from Rd. 39 off Mt. Baker Hwy. and gains 1,500 feet along the way.

An easy four-mile roundtrip hike leaves from the end of Twin Lakes Rd. off Mt. Baker Hwy. to a lookout atop **Winchester Mountain,** with excellent views of Mt. Baker, Mt. Shuksan, and the North Cascades.

Popular with equestrians and hikers alike is the six-mile roundtrip **Skyline Divide** trail, beginning 13 miles up Rd. 37 and providing ample Baker views and wildflower meadows.

Loop Trips

Only a few loop trails are suitable for overnight trips; most Mt. Baker trails are in-and-out propositions. Still, the scenery here is good enough to see twice. One loop trip, perhaps too short for the more robust, starts across from Nooksack Falls, seven miles east of Glacier, for a 4.5-mile hike to **Excelsior Pass,** gaining a tortuous 3,800 feet en route. It then follows the **High Divide Trail** for four miles, with spectacular views of Baker and Shuksan, and returns to Rd. 3060 via **Welcome Pass** for 1.8 miles. The descent is via 67 demented switchbacks. Sections of this loop make popular, albeit difficult, day hikes. To stretch it out, travel north for three miles past the Excelsior Pass/High Divide junction to **Damfino Lakes** and Forest Rd. 31.

The **Copper Ridge-Chilliwack Loop Trail** is an extremely popular 35-mile trek into Mount Baker Wilderness and North Cascades National Park that begins from the Hannegan Campground at the east end of Forest Rd. 32. The first four miles are gentle, but after that the trail climbs abruptly to **Hannegan Pass,** then back down to a fork at the entrance to North Cascades National Park. The right fork continues east over Whatcom Pass and eventually to Ross Lake. Take the left fork instead, and climb along the spine of **Copper Ridge** with vistas across the top of the Cascades. From here, the trail drops into Indian Creek, where you join the Chilliwack Trail for the return trip along Chilli-wack River. A cable car provides a crossing over the river. This trail is best hiked from late July through September. Wilderness permits are required for this hike; get them at the Glacier Public Service Center.

Heather Meadows Hikes

The Heather Meadows area is an immensely popular late-summer hiking area. Access is easy, since the Mt. Baker Hwy. (Hwy. 542) ends at 4,700-foot Austin Pass, with trails branching out in all directions for all levels of ability. Easiest is the **Artist Ridge Trail,** a mile-long loop with interpretive signs and views all the way to Mt. Rainier on clear days. The first 200 feet are wheelchair-accessible. Another easy path, **Fire and Ice Trail,** is paved to an overlook above Bagley Lakes.

Starting at Austin Pass near the end of Mt. Baker Hwy., the four-mile one-way hike to **Lake Ann,** one of the Cascades' most beautiful backcountry lakes, is a very popular route with day-hikers and the major approach trail to 9,127-foot Mt. Shuksan. Lake Ann Trail is often covered by snow till late summer.

From the end of Hwy. 542 at Artist Point, follow the steep 2.5-mile trail up lava cliffs to the appropriately named, flat-topped **Table Mountain.** Incredible views of Mt. Baker and Mt. Shuksan from here.

The 5.5-mile **Chain Lakes Trail** begins at the end of the road, traverses Table Mountain, and passes a series of alpine lakes. Beyond this, the trail climbs over Herrmann Saddle, enters the Bagley Lakes basin, and ends near the Mt. Baker Ski Area. For a return loop, take the **Wild Goose Trail** back to Artist Point.

Skiing

Downhill skiing at **Mt. Baker Ski Resort** lasts from early November through April, the longest ski and snowboarding season in the state. The snow here is considered the best in Washington. Eight chair lifts (two of these are quads) put 1,500 vertical feet of slope underfoot, from machine-groomed intermediate runs to open powder bowls. Other facilities include a 17,000-square-foot day lodge, child care, ski school, rentals, restaurant, and bar; but no night skiing. Lift tickets are $28 adults, $20 youth (ages seven to 15) or seniors; lower rates on weekdays. For a ski report, call (360) 671-0211 from Bellingham or (206) 634-0200 from Seattle; the business office number is (360) 734-6771.

ACCOMMODATIONS

See "Bellingham" and "North to Canada" (both in the Northern Puget Sound chapter) for a wide selection of B&Bs, motels, hotels, and campgrounds within an hour of Mt. Baker. Accommodations near the mountain are quite limited; the closest are in the town of Glacier, 15 miles below Mt. Baker Ski Area. The **Mt. Baker Lodging Hotline,** tel. (800) 258-2405, can make cabin and B&B reservations for you. A smaller lodging service, Mt. Baker Lodging, tel. (360) 599-2453, also has vacation cabins. Note that many places require a two-night minimum stay on weekends. Call well ahead for weekend reservations during the ski season. Outdoor equipment, clothing, maps, and cross-country ski rentals are available in Bellingham at **Base Camp, Inc.,** 901 W. Holly, tel. (360) 733-5461.

Bed and Breakfasts
Three places in Maple Falls offer B&B accommodations. **The Yodeler Inn,** 7485 Mt. Baker Hwy., tel. (360) 599-2156 or (800) 642-9033, is a countrified B&B, built by an early settler in 1917. The inn's five guest rooms and a cottage have private or shared baths and a hot tub; rates are $65 s or d. **Country Hill B&B,** 9512 Silver Lake Rd. in Maple Falls, tel. (360) 599-1049, has lakeside accommodations that include a three-room suite and a cabin with a kitchen and fireplace. Rates are $65 s or d, including a full breakfast and jacuzzi. **Thurston House B&B,** tel. (360) 599-2261, also features a lakefront location with rowboat and jacuzzi. Their suite sleeps four, and the cabin sleeps up to eight and has a kitchen. Rates for either are $65 d with breakfast or $50 d without breakfast.

Three miles north of the little town of Everson, **Wilkins Farm B&B,** 4165 S. Pass Rd., tel. (360) 966-7616, may have the least expensive B&B accommodations in the state: just $22 s or $35 d in a 120-year-old farmhouse surrounded by cattle pastures. Three guest rooms share a bath, and a full breakfast is served. Kids are okay, too.

Cabins and Inns
Glacier Creek Motel, in Glacier, tel. (360) 599-2991, has nine motel rooms and a number of small creekside cabins accommodating up to six people. They also have an outdoor jacuzzi. Rates are $40 s, $42-54 d for the motel rooms, $55 d and up for cabins. **Mount Baker Chalet,** 9857 Mt. Baker Hwy. at Mile 33, tel. (360) 599-2405, has a wide range of private cabins, chalets, and condos starting at $50.

Snowline Inn, 10433 Mt. Baker Hwy., tel. (360) 599-2788 or (800) 228-0119, is the closest lodging to Mt. Baker—one mile east of Glacier—with condos containing kitchenettes for $55-75 s or d in the summer, $65-75 s or d in the winter. **The Logs,** 9002 Mt. Baker Hwy., tel. (360) 599-2711, has five cabins with fireplaces and kitchens along the Nooksack River for $64 s or d.

Campgrounds
Camp at one of three Forest Service campgrounds ($10) in the Mt. Baker area. **Douglas Fir Campground,** two miles east of Glacier on Mt. Baker Hwy., is situated in a beautiful old-growth forest along the Nooksack River, and is open all winter (no water and no fee during the winter). **Silver Fir Campground,** 13 miles east of Glacier, is open mid-May to mid-September. Make reservations for Douglas Fir and Silver Fir Campgrounds ($7.50 fee charged) by calling (800) 365-2267. **Hannegan Campground,** 17 miles east of Glacier and right next to the Mount Baker Wilderness on Forest Rd. 32, is a primitive campground with no running water and no fees; open mid-May to mid-September.

The 411-acre **Silver Lake County Park,** three miles north of Maple Falls, has year-round camping along with RV hookups, showers, swimming, plus cabin and boat rentals; call (360) 599-2776 for reservations. **Hutchinson Creek Campground,** on Mosquito Creek Rd. near Acme, has free camping, but no water. More free camping at **Nooksack City Park.**

Dispersed camping (free) is fine on Forest Service land below milepost 52; just find a good off-the-road place to camp. Check at the Glacier Public Service Center for any restrictions.

Campers and hikers can take showers (25 cents) at the Texaco minimart near the intersection of Highways 9 and 542.

FOOD

If you love fresh homemade pastas and raviolis, don't miss **Milano's** in Glacier, tel. (360) 599-2863. The prices are reasonable, the atmosphere is friendly and light-hearted, and the food is simply wonderful. Try the Pasta Puttanesca, a spicy mix of fresh tomatoes, capers, Greek olives, garlic, and hot chilies. Milano's also has a deli for lunchtime sandwiches.

For fine dining after a tiring romp in the woods, the **Innisfree Restaurant,** tel. (360) 599-2373, serves Northwest regional foods in an elegant setting. The emphasis is on organic produce, Washington-grown lamb and chicken, and a fresh menu that changes with the seasons. On the pricey side, but outstanding quality.

The **Chandelier Restaurant** in Glacier, tel. (360) 599-2233, is popular for family dining, pizzas, and noteworthy desserts. The bar features rock, country, or blues bands on winter weekends. Stop by to watch games on the big-screen TV.

The **Deming Tavern,** in Deming, tel. (360) 592-5282, has locally famous steaks and a big choice of brews. Also in Deming is **Carol's Coffee Cup,** tel. (360) 592-5641, a favorite place to treat your sweet tooth.

INFORMATION AND TRANSPORTATION

The **Glacier Public Service Center** in the town of Glacier is the place to go for information on Mt. Baker and surrounding areas, and to obtain backcountry permits. Ask about summertime interpretive talks and walks here. Located in a stone building built by the CCC in 1938, the center is open daily 8:30 a.m.-4:30 p.m. from mid-June to mid-September; Thurs.-Mon. 8:30 a.m.-4:30 p.m. mid-May to mid-June and mid-September through December; and Fri.-Sun. 8:30 a.m.-4:30 p.m. from January to mid-May. Call (360) 599-2714 for more information.

Heather Meadows Visitor Center, at the end of Mt. Baker Hwy., is open daily 10 a.m.-4:30 p.m. July-Sept. and has a variety of interpretive activities on late summer weekends. The **Mt. Baker Ranger District** office is in Sedro-Woolley at 2105 Hwy. 20, tel. (360) 856-5700 and is open daily 8 a.m.-4:30 p.m. (Friday till 6) in the summer.

Mt. Baker Shuttle & Limo, tel. (360) 599-1180 or (800) 845-1180, has service between Glacier and the end of Mt. Baker Hwy. year-round.

THE MOUNTAIN LOOP: GRANITE FALLS TO DARRINGTON

The scenic Mountain Loop Highway, one of the state's most popular weekend drives, connects Granite Falls to Darrington via a 55 mile long, partly gravel road. From Granite Falls, the road is paved for the first 22 miles as it follows the South Fork of the Stillaguamish River to its headwaters at Barlow Pass, entering the Mt. Baker-Snoqualmie National Forest near Verlot. Numerous campgrounds and hiking trails offer diversions along the way, and access to three fabulous swaths of wild mountain country: Boulder River Wilderness, Henry M. Jackson Wilderness, and Glacier Peak Wilderness. North of Barlow Pass, the road turns to gravel and becomes narrow and winding as it drops along the Sauk River. It remains gravel for 14 miles; the last seven miles to Darrington are paved. West of Darrington, the Mountain Loop Road passes through a wide valley bisected by the North Fork of the Stillaguamish River and filled with hay piles, beehives, horses, sheep, chickens, hogs, big red barns, cut-your-own Christmas tree farms, lumber mills, clearcuts, and regenerating stands of trees. Openings provide glimpses of the snowy peaks that cap the Cascade Range.

History

Parts of today's Mountain Loop Hwy. overlay trails were used for centuries by the Indians who first inhabited these lands. The 1889 discovery of gold and silver in the Monte Cristo area (see below) led to a mad rush of miners and others attempting to get rich quick. To transport the (assumed) mineral wealth, a railroad was constructed from Monte Cristo over Barlow Pass, down the canyon created by the South Fork of the Stillaguamish River, through the new town of Granite Falls, and on to Everett, where the ore would be refined. Funded by an East-Coast syndicate with financial backing from John D. Rockefeller, the railroad was poorly designed and subject to repeated flooding. These floods, combined with a financial depression in the 1890s, forced the mine owners to sell out to Rockefeller in 1899, and even he was compelled to give up when the ore petered out a few years later.

With cessation of mining, the Monte Cristo area began attracting tourists, and the trains turned to offering weekend excursions into the mountains. Business flourished in the 1920s, and hotels were added in Silverton and near Big Four Mountain to cater to the wealthy—the latter even featured a nine-hole golf course. All this came to a screeching halt following the stock market crash of 1929. The railroad shut down in 1936, and the old railroad grade became an automobile road. Two years later, the CCC began construction of a narrow mountain route north from Barlow Pass to Darrington, completing the final link in today's Mountain Loop Highway.

Weather

The Darrington area is an anomaly in the Cascades. Whereas the Seattle area receives 30-40 inches of rain per year, Darrington gets an average of 80 inches, while Monte Cristo gets over 140 inches, creating a dense rainforest much like those of the Olympics. The low elevation here means questionable snowfall, though cross-country skiing and snowmobiling are popular area activities.

It is imperative to carry adequate clothing while hiking in this part of the Cascades, even if you're out on a short hike. The weather changes rapidly sometimes, and nearly every summer someone dies of hypothermia a short distance from their car.

The highway and logging roads are popular snowmobile routes in winter, but that portion of the road over 2,361-foot Barlow Pass is blocked by snow beyond Elliot Creek on the north side and Deer Creek on the south side from mid-November to mid-April.

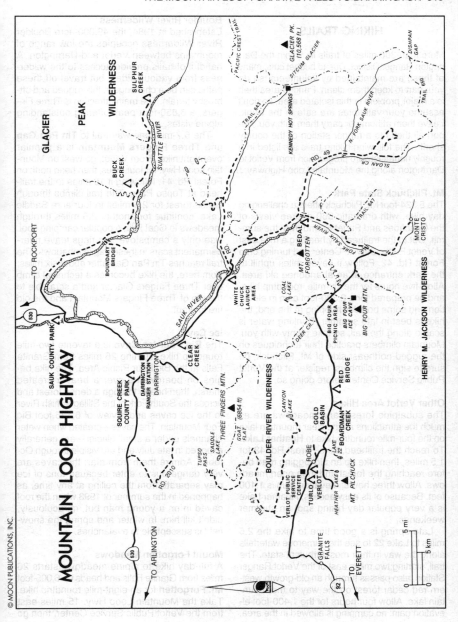

MOUNTAIN LOOP HIGHWAY

© MOON PUBLICATIONS, INC.

TO ROCKPORT

TO ARLINGTON

TO EVERETT

GLACIER PEAK WILDERNESS

HENRY M. JACKSON WILDERNESS

BOULDER RIVER WILDERNESS

GLACIER PK. (10,568 ft.)

SITCUM GLACIER

PACIFIC CREST TRAIL

DISHPAN GAP

TRAIL 650

KENNEDY HOT SPRINGS

N. FORK SAUK RIVER

SLOAN CR.

TRAIL 643

RD. 49

MONTE CRISTO

SULPHUR CREEK

BUCK CREEK

SUIATTLE RIVER

BOUNDARY BRIDGE

SAUK RIVER

RD. 23

MT. BEDAL

S. FORK SAUK RIVER

MT. FORGOTTEN

COAL LAKE

WHITE CHUCK LAUNCH AREA

TRAIL 647

DEER CR.

BIG FOUR ICE CAVE

BIG FOUR PICNIC AREA

BIG FOUR MTN.

RED BRIDGE

CLEAR CREEK

DARRINGTON RANGER STATION

DARRINGTON

SQUIRE CREEK COUNTY PARK

THREE FINGERS MTN. (6854 ft)

GOAT FLAT

SADDLE LAKE

TUPSO PASS

CANYON LAKE

GOLD BASIN

BOARDMAN CREEK

RD. 2010

ROBE

LAKE 22

MT. PILCHUCK

HEATHER LAKE

VERLOT PUBLIC SERVICE CENTER

VERLOT

TURLO

GRANITE FALLS

5 mi

5 km

HIKING TRAILS

More than 300 miles of trails lie within the Darrington Ranger District. Due to budget cuts, many of these are maintained by volunteers, so do your part to keep them clean. Parking-area theft is a major problem in this isolated area, so don't assume your valuables are safe in the trunk. Leave them at home or carry them with you. Report all thefts to a ranger station or the county sheriff. The following hiking trails are listed in a roughly northeastward progression from Verlot to Darrington along the Mountain Loop Highway.

Mt. Pilchuck State Park

The 5,324-foot Mt. Pilchuck offers a challenging day hike, with dramatic 360-degree views of the Cascades and Puget Sound from the summit. Get to the trailhead by heading a mile east of Verlot Public Service Center and turning onto Forest Rd. 42. Follow it seven miles uphill to the park entrance at an abandoned ski area. Allow five hours for the six-mile, roundtrip hike, and be prepared for a 2,300-foot gain in elevation and some boulder-hopping at the end; the hike is best in late summer. Drinking water is scarce along the trail, so take plenty with you. Mountain climbers practice their techniques on the rugged northeast side of Mt. Pilchuck; be sure to sign the climbers' register at the Verlot Public Service Center before doing so.

Other Verlot Area Hikes

The subalpine forests and meadows are as much the attractions as the clear mountain lake on the four-mile roundtrip hike to **Heather Lake.** To reach the trailhead, take Forest Rd. 42 for 1.5 miles, then hike up an old logging road before reaching the forest and then open meadows. Allow three hours; elevation gain is 1,100 feet. Because of its easy access, Heather Lake is a very popular day-hiking spot on summer weekends.

Late spring is a good time to hike the 2.5 miles to **Lake 22** to see the numerous waterfalls along the way in their most turbulent state. The trail, starting two miles east of the Verlot Ranger Station, also passes through an old-growth western red cedar forest on the way to the mountain lake. Allow four hours for the 1,400-foot elevation gain; no camping is allowed in the area.

Boulder River Wilderness

Established in 1984, the 49,000-acre Boulder River Wilderness occupies the low range of mountains between Verlot and Darrington. A handful of trails provide access to the wilderness from various sides, but travel off these paths can be a challenge in this rugged and oft-brushy terrain. The main attraction is Three Fingers, a 6,850-foot peak offering outstanding alpine vistas.

The 6.7-mile one-way trail to **Tin Pan Gap** and **Three Fingers Mountain** is a popular overnight hike. From Verlot, go west on Mountain Loop Hwy. for four miles, then head north on Forest Rd. 41, following it 18 miles to the trailhead at Tupso Pass. The trail climbs through dense forest for 2.5 miles to four-acre Saddle Lake; continue for another 2.5 miles through meadows to Goat Flat, a popular camping spot. Use only a campstove; fire rings leave near-permanent scars in this fragile meadows. The trail reaches Tin Pan Gap after about six miles; from here, the hike becomes a technical climb over Three Fingers Glacier and a scramble to the top of Three Fingers Mountain and the old fire lookout.

Ice Cave

The **Big Four Ice Cave** is a favorite two-mile roundtrip hike, starting 26 miles from Granite Falls at the Big Four Picnic Area. The hike begins on boardwalks over a beaver-created marsh, then heads through a dense forest and across the South Fork of the Stillaguamish River to the ice caves and a view of 6,135-foot Big Four Mountain. The caves—created when water channels under a small glacier—are generally exposed in late July and are visible through October. Admire them from afar; the caves are very dangerous to enter because tons of ice may separate from the ceiling at any time, as happened in the summer of 1993 when the roof caved in on a young man but, miraculously, didn't kill him. In winter and spring the snowfield is susceptible to avalanches.

Mount Forgotten Meadows

A full-day hike to alpine meadows starts 26 miles from Granite Falls and heads up 6,005-foot **Mt. Forgotten** for an eight-mile roundtrip hike. Take the Mountain Loop Hwy. 15 miles east from the Verlot Public Service Center, then go north on Perry Creek Rd. (No. 4063) for a mile to the Perry Creek trailhead. The trail climbs past waterfalls at about two miles, heading through an old-growth forest for another 1.7 miles to the first meadow. Allow seven hours to reach the meadows at 5,200 feet, an elevation gain of 3,100 feet. The trail continues through meadows to Mt. Forgotten's climbing route (for experienced alpine climbers only).

Monte Cristo Area

See "Recreation" in the Stevens Pass and Skykomish Valley section for details on the magnificent alpine-topped 103,591-acre **Henry M. Jackson Wilderness Area,** accessible from several trailheads on the eastern end of the Mountain Loop. The most popular hiking paths here center around the fascinating old mining town of Monte Cristo. In the 1890s, gold and silver strikes lured 2,000 people to this boomtown, but the ore turned out to be of poor quality, and within 20 years Monte Cristo had become a ghost town. The fireplace and foundation of the Big Four Inn—a luxurious turn-of-the-century resort that burned to the ground in 1949—stand as mute reminders of the town's earlier glory. During the Depression, the railroad to Monte Cristo was replaced by the Mountain Loop Highway. Today, the townsite and abandoned mines around Monte Cristo remain privately owned.

Get here by driving 20 miles east from Verlot to Barlow Pass, where the four-mile side road to Monte Cristo begins. Floods in 1980 and 1990 left it impassable to cars, but it remains a popular place for mountain bikers and hikers in the summer, and cross-country skiers and snowmobilers in the winter. Check at the Forest Service offices in Darrington or Verlot for current road and bridge conditions. The Forest Service's free **Monte Cristo Campground** offers a pleasant overnighting spot near the ghost town.

Glacier Basin Trail is a popular two-mile hiking route from Monte Cristo into nearby high country. The trail follows an old railroad grade for the first half-mile, then climbs steeply past Glacier Falls, around Mystery Hill, and into gorgeous Glacier Basin, gaining 1,300 feet in elevation. The route passes all sorts of rusting mining equipment, pieces of the cable tramway, and old mine shafts on the way. Bring your stove, since no campfires are allowed in the

high country, and avoid camping on the fragile meadow areas. Good campsites can be found at Ray's Knoll and Mystery Ridge.

Another very steep hike (4.4 miles each way) climbs over **Poodle Dog Pass** from Monte Cristo. This trail leaves from the townsite, ascends to Silver Lake, and then on to an open ridge offering panoramic views of the surrounding mountains.

Glacier Peak Wilderness

Covering 576,865 acres—35 miles long by 20 miles wide—massive Glacier Peak Wilderness is one of Washington's largest stretches of wilderness landscape. Its dominant geologic feature, Glacier Peak, is the fourth highest mountain in the state, reaching 10,541 feet. A dormant volcano, Glacier Peak last erupted some 12,000 years ago; today its summit is almost encircled by glaciers. In the Glacier Peak Wilderness, you're likely to see deer, blue grouse, and marmots, plus an occasional lynx, mountain goat, and cougar. Deep snow buries much of the wilderness high country till late July, and some trails are not free of snow until mid-August.

More than 450 miles of backcountry trails provide diverse hiking opportunities in the wilderness, with access from all sides, including the Marblemount (under "North Cascades Highway," above), Lake Chelan (see "Sports and Recreation" under "Chelan and Vicinity," below), and Entiat River areas (see "Entiat Area" under "Chelan and Vicinity," below). The western side of the wilderness reaches almost to the Mountain Loop Hwy., with access via several Forest Service spur roads. The ultimate hiking experience, the **Pacific Crest Trail,** cuts right through the heart of Glacier Peak Wilderness, following the ridges for 60 miles of ascending and descending paths. For a complete description of hiking trails in the wilderness, see *100 Hikes in Washington's North Cascades: Glacier Peak Region,* by Ira Spring and Harvey Manning (Seattle: The Mountaineers).

The most popular path in the wilderness is the seven-mile-long **White Chuck Trail** (No. 643). This trail begins at the end of Forest Rd. 23, near the Sulphur Creek Campground, and follows the White Chuck River along a fairly gentle route for the first five miles, passing ancient groves of trees along the way. A short detour

4.2 miles in takes hikers to **Kennedy Hot Springs,** where the warm (not hot) natural pool is a favorite soaking spot for day-hikers. More adventurous folks continue up White Chuck Trail to its junction with the Pacific Crest Trail, or follow side trails into other parts of the wilderness. Mountaineers heading up the glaciers of Glacier Peak often use White Chuck Trail to reach the base of the mountain, scrambling to the timberline and following the Sitkum Glacier to the summit. Consult a North Cascades climbing guide for a detailed description of the route. In spring, call (360) 527-6677 for avalanche information.

The Pacific Crest Trail is accessible from the west side at various points off the Mountain Loop Highway. One of the best of these is the **North Fork Sauk Trail** (No. 649), an 8.4-mile path offering a gentle riverside route through a magnificent old-growth cedar forest, before relentlessly switchbacking upwards to the Pacific Crest Trail, gaining 3,900 feet en route. An excellent loop hike (26 miles roundtrip) is to continue south on the PCT to its junction with the **Pilot Ridge Trail** (No. 652), and then follow that trail back downhill past alpine lakes to its junction with the North Fork Sauk Trail. The Pilot Ridge Trail offers hikers vistas of Glacier Peak and Mt. Rainier, but be sure to carry plenty of water, since portions of this loop hike lack water sources. Get to the North Fork Sauk trailhead by driving east from the Verlot Public Service Center for 27 miles (or south from Darrington for 20 miles), and turning east onto Sloan Creek Rd. 49 near the Bedal Campground. The trailhead is located 6.6 miles up, where the road crosses Sloan Creek.

Darrington Area Trails

Several short paths provide fun dayhikes in the Darrington area. **Old Sauk Trail** (No. 728) is an easy three-mile stroll that departs from Clear Creek Campground, four miles south of Darrington. The trail parallels the Sauk River, passing riverside alder stands and moss-covered cedar stumps. Salmon and steelhead spawn in Murphy Creek at the southern end of the Old Sauk Trail.

An almost-level three-mile path, **Beaver Lake Trail** (No. 629), starts across from White Chuck Campground, 10 miles south of Darrington. The trail sits atop an old railroad grade and crosses beaver ponds where you're likely to see ducks

The Darrington area is popular with hikers and backpackers.

and herons. It continues through a beautiful stand of old-growth cedar trees at the upper end before looping back to the Mountain Loop Highway. Both of these are also good for mountain bikes.

Another hike through virgin timber is the **Boulder River Trail** (No. 734). Get here by heading 8.2 miles west from Darrington, turn south onto French Creek Rd. 2010, branch right after a mile, and then follow it another 2.8 miles to the trailhead. In addition to thick old-growth forests, this four-mile trail passes a delightful series of Boulder River waterfalls and cascades.

OTHER RECREATION

Whitewater Trips

The **Sauk River,** a National Wild and Scenic River that rises in the Henry M. Jackson Wilderness and joins the Skagit River near Rockport, offers a combination of fast and complex rapids, fantastic mountain scenery, and plenty of wildlife.

Trips generally start 10 miles upriver and end in Darrington, with lots of class III-IV whitewater along the way. The primary season is May to mid-August; expect to pay $55-65 per person for a half-day trip. Companies offering this whitewater trip are: **Downstream River Runners,** tel. (800) 234-4644; **North Cascades River Expeditions,** tel. (800) 634-8433; **Orion Expeditions,** tel. (800) 553-7466; and **Wild & Scenic River Tours,** tel. (206) 323-1220.

The **Suiattle River** (soo-AT-ul) starts in the Glacier Peak Wilderness and meets the Sauk River north of Darrington. This is a good whitewater river for families and folks starting out, with great mountain scenery and lots of small rapids along the 13 miles of river. Because of its glacial origins, the Suiattle has a milky, silt-laden appearance and braided channels. The main season for river-running is June to early September; expect to pay $55-65 per person for a half-day trip. Companies offering whitewater floats down the Suiattle are: **All Rivers Adventures,** tel. (800) 743-5628; **Blue Sky Outfitters,** tel. (800) 228-7238; **Cascade Adventures,** tel. (800) 723-8386; **Downstream River Runners,** tel. (800) 234-4644; **North Cascades River Expeditions,** tel. (800) 634-8433; **Northern Wilderness River Riders,** tel. (800) 448-7238; **Rivers Incorporated,** tel. (206) 822-5296; **Wild & Scenic River Tours,** tel. (206) 323-1220; and **Wildwater River Tours,** tel. (800) 522-9453.

On Your Own

Experienced, do-it-yourself river runners will enjoy the challenges of the Sauk and Suiattle Rivers. The Suiattle is the tamer of the two, rated class II to III from Boundary Bridge to the Sauk River; it's not navigable within the national forest due to logjams, hidden stumps, and debris. Put in at Boundary bridge. The Sauk River ranges from class I to V; from the White Chuck launch area to Clear Creek it's a IV or V, with difficult rapids through narrow passages. From Bedal to White Chuck, the river is classified as a class III-IV, and below Clear Creek it ranges from class I to III. North of Darrington, the river is considerably calmer and is popular for canoeing.

Canoeing and Fishing

The Darrington District boasts a large number of small lakes, some of which provide excellent fishing. Check at the ranger station or public service center for a list of lakes and suggestions on the best ones for boating, fishing, or paddling.

Paddlers and rafters will enjoy exploring six-acre **Coal Lake,** a subalpine lake at 3,600 feet elevation. Go east on the Mountain Loop Hwy. for 15 miles from the Verlot Public Service Center, then go north on Coal Lake Rd. 4060 for 4.5 miles to the trailhead. Carry your boat for about 50 feet to the lake, where you'll find a limited number of campsites that fill up very quickly.

Another lake with easy canoe and raft access is five-acre **Canyon Lake.** From the Verlot Public Service Center, drive four miles on the Mountain Loop Hwy. to Rd. 41; turn right, continuing for two miles to Green Mt. Rd. 4110. Turn right again (heading east now), driving almost 1.4 miles to Rd. 4111; follow this road for 10.75 miles to the trailhead on the left side of the road. Carry your boat along the 50-foot trail to Canyon Lake, surrounded by trees and a few campsites; fair fishing.

Cross-Country Skiing

Skiers and snowshoers can count on solitude when exploring the Darrington District; most roads aren't plowed and snowfall is unpredictable at this low elevation. Any existing snow here is often wet and difficult to ski through. Still determined? Take these routes as suggestions; if the roads themselves aren't snow-covered, keep driving along the route until you come to some that are.

From Hwy. 530 on the way to Darrington, go south on **French Creek Rd. 2010** to the snowline, and then ski uphill from there. The road takes you through dense forest and switchbacks for great views and a fast, downhill trip back. Or, from the Darrington Ranger Station, drive north on Hwy. 530 for 6.5 miles to **Suiattle River Rd. 26;** follow it till you hit snow, and then ski up the road and along the river. Fine views of Glacier Peak along the way.

On the Granite Falls side, the **Big Four** area is very popular with skiers, snowshoers, snowmobilers, and winter hikers; take the Mountain Loop Hwy. 23 miles from Granite Falls to the end of the maintained road at Deer Creek Rd. 4052. Ski two miles from the parking area to Big Four Picnic Area, following the South Fork of the Stillaguamish River; continue another mile to the snowfield near the Big Four Ice Cave. The avalanche danger here is severe; don't travel beyond the edge of the clearing—it's the force of avalanches that created and maintains that clearing! Allow three to five hours roundtrip; suitable for beginning skiers.

A more challenging route is the **Deer Creek/Kelcema Lake Ski Route** that follows Deer Creek Road uphill to Kelcema Lake, a distance of 4.6 miles, with an elevation gain of 1,600 feet. Allow five to seven hours for the roundtrip, and avoid during periods of high avalanche danger. Get here by heading 12 miles east from the Verlot Public Service Center to the end of snow plowing and the start of the ski route. No snowmobiles are allowed here.

Another popular cross-country ski route (for advanced skiers only) begins at the Deer Creek parking area and continues 11 miles to the old mining town of Monte Cristo, gaining 1,275 feet in elevation en route. This is best done as an overnight trip due to its length; be sure to check on avalanche conditions before heading out.

CAMPING

The Forest Service operates 16 campgrounds in the Darrington Ranger District, most on a first-come, first-served basis; no electrical hookups, showers, or dump stations. Campgrounds are generally open from Memorial Day to mid-September (or longer), and campers are limited to a 14-day stay. Free dispersed camping is allowed on Forest Service lands away from the campgrounds.

From Granite Falls, neighboring **Turlo** and **Verlot** Campgrounds are near the Verlot Public Service Center, while **Gold Basin Campground** is 2.4 miles east of the service center. All three have piped well water, trailer space, flush or vault toilets, and garbage service, and charge a $10 fee. Make reservations ($7.50 extra) by calling (800) 280-2267. Gold Basin also features an amphitheater where Saturday night campfire programs are presented in the summer. Across the road is a short wheelchair-accessible interpretive trail.

All the other Forest Service campgrounds (with the exception of group sites) are free, but they also do not have potable water or garbage

collection. From the Verlot Service Center these include: **Boardman Creek Campground** (open all year), six miles east; and **Red Bridge Campground,** seven miles east. From Darrington, they include: **Clear Creek Campground,** four miles south; **White Chuck Campground,** 10 miles south; and **Bedal Campground,** 18 miles south. All three of these are open year-round. A mile east of Bedal Campground on Forest Rd. 49, a quarter-mile path leads to the base of spectacular **North Fork Sauk Falls,** where the river plunges 45 feet.

From Darrington via Suiattle River Rd. No. 26, **Buck Creek Campground,** 22 miles northeast of town, features a quiet riverside setting in an old-growth forest. **Sulphur Creek Campground,** 28 miles from Darrington (near the end of Suiattle River Rd.), has additional campsites. This campground is just a mile away from the Glacier Peak Wilderness and is open year-round. A short trail leads from the campground along Sulphur Creek to colorful pools containing rather odoriferous hydrogen sulfide gas.

In addition to the places listed above, five Forest Service group campgrounds are available only by reservation. Contact the Darrington Ranger Station, tel. (360) 436-1155, for specifics.

Squire Creek County Park, tel. (360) 435-3441, offers year-round camping ($10) and picnicking amid old-growth Douglas fir and cedar trees four miles west of Darrington on Hwy. 530.

Sauk River County Park, seven miles north of Darrington on Sauk Valley Rd., has more campsites. No charge and no drinking water.

INFORMATION

Get detailed camping, hiking, and historical information at the Mt. Baker-Snoqualmie National Forest's **Verlot Public Service Center,** tel. (360) 691-7791, located 11 miles east of Granite Falls; open daily 8 a.m.-5 p.m. May-Sept. and Sat.-Sun. 9 a.m.-1 p.m. the rest of the year (budget cuts may result in its closure during the winter months). The buildings at Verlot were built by the CCC between 1933 and 1942. The **Darrington Ranger District,** 1405 Emmens St. in Darrington, tel. (360) 436-1155, has year-round information and is open daily 8 a.m.-5 p.m. Memorial Day to Labor Day, and Mon.-Fri. 8 a.m.-4:30 p.m. the rest of the year.

GRANITE FALLS

Granite Falls (pop. just over 1,100) sits at the southwest end of the Mountain Loop Hwy. with Pilchuck Mountain offering a dramatic backdrop. The town began in 1889 as construction headquarters for the railroad route to the mines at Monte Cristo, and grew up as a waystation and center for logging and farming in the area. Because of its location at the base of the Cascades, the town provides a jumping-off point for hikers, campers, cross-country skiers, and snowmobilers exploring the Mt. Baker-Snoqualmie National Forest. Granite Falls is a tobacco-chewing, pickup truck, beergut, ballcap-and-jeans sort of place, where you'll find live music at the Corner Tavern on summer weekends, and a rough-at-the-edges feel every day of the week. The older houses are accentuated by mossy roofs, while the false-fronted buildings of downtown show their heritage with pride. This conservative, country feel is in the process of changing, as the first wave of new housing development rolls in, and as the first neon "Espresso" signs are turned on.

Sights
The **Granite Falls Museum** (open Sunday 1-4 p.m. during the summer; closed winters) houses local memorabilia; check out the cross-section from an enormous 1,200-year-old Douglas-fir tree in the front.

Just east of town is the **Granite Falls Fish Ladder,** the world's longest vertical baffle fish ladder when it was built in 1954. Stop here to marvel at the raging South Fork of the Stillaguamish River as it roils over the falls (actually more of a giant rapids) for which the town was named. Salmon swim up a 240-foot tunnel dug through the granite.

Practicalities
Good Mexican eats at **Los Flamingos,** 101 S. Granite Ave., tel. (360) 691-7575. Walk down the main drag to find several places with standard American fare.

Mountain View Inn, 32005 Mt. Loop Hwy. (approximately 10 miles east of town in the rustic Robe Valley), tel. (360) 691-6668, has rooms for $40 s or d.

Local events include the **Show 'N Shine Festival** on the first weekend of August, and **Railroad Reunion Days** on the first weekend of October.

The **area code** for Granite Falls is 360. Pick up a handful of local brochures at **Granite Falls Town Hall,** tel. (360) 691-6441.

Community Transit, tel. (360) 778-2185 or (800) 562-1375, connects Granite Falls with Everett and other cities and towns throughout Snohomish County for $1. Buses run seven days a week.

DARRINGTON

Darrington (pop. 1,100), in the foothills of the Cascades northeast of Everett, was home to the Sauk and Suiattle Indians until white miners in search of gold and silver arrived in the late 1800s and early 1900s. Though some deposits were found, the real money in this area was in logging. Swedish, Irish, Welsh, and Norwegian loggers, plus a very large group from North Carolina, Georgia, and Tennessee, founded a community that still reflects its ethnic origins, especially the North Carolinians, who take great pride in their Tarheel heritage and mountain music.

Darrington, backdropped to the southwest by the 6,563-foot summit of Whitehorse Mountain, is located in a low pass separating the Sauk River from the North Fork of the Stillaguamish River. A collection of old buildings occupies the streets. Prominent among these is the **Trafton School,** a two-story white clapboard structure built in 1907. The town has a run-down feel, as if it were just waiting to be discovered by the next wave of outmigrating Seattleites in search of a peaceful place to escape the city life. With a setting like this, that shouldn't take long.

Accommodations
Darrington's **Stagecoach Inn,** 1100 Seaman St., tel. (360) 436-1776 or (800) 428-1776, is an attractive, small motel with rooms offering mountain views for $55 s or d, including a continental breakfast. Kitchenettes are $5 extra. **Hemlock Hills B&B,** 612 Stillaguamish, tel. (360) 436-1274, has two guest rooms at $50 s or d, including a full breakfast. **Sauk River Farm B&B,** 3.5 miles east of Darrington, tel. (360) 436-1794, has two guest rooms for $40-50 s or d, including a jacuzzi and full breakfast.

Food

Most of Darrington's eateries offer pretty standard American fare, but **Country Coffee and Deli,** 1015 Sauk Ave., tel. (360) 436-0213, cranks out tasty homemade soups and sandwiches. **Backwoods Cafe,** 45700 Hwy. 530, tel. (360) 436-1845, is the only real "sit-down" place in Darrington. For pizzas and salads, try **Pizza Plus,** 1180 Cascade, tel. (360) 436-1712. Stop at the **Whitehorse Store,** five miles west of Darrington, for old fashioned ice cream cones.

Campgrounds

The closest Forest Service campground is the free **Clear Creek Campground,** four miles south of town on Forest Rd. 20. **Squire Creek County Park,** tel. (360) 435-3441, offers camping and picnicking amid old growth fir and cedar trees four miles west of Darrington on Hwy. 530. Camping ($10) is available year-round; no RV hookups. The park is also home to the largest cottonwood tree in Washington.

Sauk River County Park, seven miles north of Darrington on Sauk Valley Rd., has more campsites. No charge, and no drinking water.

Hikers and campers can stock up on supplies at **Forrister's Sport Shop** on Hwy. 530 in Darrington; for groceries, visit the **IGA** across the street.

Events

The last weekend in June brings the **Timber Bowl Rodeo** to the rodeo grounds four miles west of town. Darrington's three-day **Bluegrass Festival and Street Fair** in mid-July is one of the most popular musical events in the Puget Sound Basin, in part because the area has developed some of the best bluegrass musicians outside Kentucky and Tennessee. Darrington also hosts the **National Archery Tournament** every third year; upcoming dates are the years 1997 and 2000.

Information and Services

Darrington's **area code** is 360. For up-to-date information on trail conditions, campgrounds, fishing, and other outdoor activities contact the **Darrington Ranger Station,** a half-mile north of town, tel. (360) 436-1155.

Across the street from the Darrington Ranger Station is **Nels Bruseth Memorial Garden,** with several Sauk cedar canoes on display.

Transportation

Community Transit, tel. (360) 778-2185 or (800) 562-1375, connects Darrington with Everett and other cities and towns throughout Snohomish County for $1. Buses run seven days a week.

NORTH CASCADES HIGHWAY

The North Cascades Highway—State Highway 20—begins in the Skagit River Valley, and follows this drainage to 5,477-foot Washington Pass, before descending into Methow Valley on the east side of the Cascade Range. Along the way, the road passes several small towns—Sedro-Woolley, Concrete, Rockport, and Marblemount—but after this you enter North Cascades National Park and Okanogan National Forest lands. This is magnificent mountain country, with numerous pullouts for viewing the striking scenery and a multitude of recreation options—campgrounds, visitors centers, and access to many other hiking paths, including the Pacific Crest Trail. Because of this, Hwy. 20 is one of the most popular and scenic drives in Washington. But don't plan on just driving through; bring your hiking boots, map, and a flexible schedule to really experience the North Cascades. Highway 20 is also a popular cycling route in the summer months, providing an official Bikecentennial route across rural America from Anacortes, Washington, to Bangor, Maine. This description of the North Cascades Highway starts on the eastern end at Sedro-Woolley and follows the road over the mountains into the Methow Valley.

History

The earliest white men to explore the North Cascades were Alexander Ross and his party, who crossed today's southern park boundary at Cascade Pass in 1814. In 1859, Henry Custer, working as an assistant of reconnaissances for the International Boundary Commission, traversed the region and commented: "Nowhere do the mountain masses and peaks present such strange, fantastic, dauntless and startling outlines as here. . . . [It] must be seen, it cannot be described." From 1880 to 1910, prospectors struck gold, platinum, lead, and zinc, but mountain travel was too difficult to justify the modest return.

On the west side of the mountains, the potential of the Skagit River wasn't harnessed until 1924, when the first of three dams was built by Seattle City Light. This rugged area was preserved as the North Cascades National Park

Service Complex in 1968, incorporating Ross Lake and Lake Chelan National Recreation Areas that were created as buffers to the park.

The North Cascades Scenic Highway (Highway 20) was originally commissioned in 1893, when state legislators set aside $20,000 for the completion of the Cascade Wagon Route. Over the decades that followed, sections of the road were gradually completed, and by 1968—the year the national park was established—a rough dirt road crossed the summit. The highway finally opened in 1972, some 79 years after the first shovel of dirt had been dug.

Climate

Summer weather on the west side of the North Cascades is cooler and wetter than the eastern portion, which is protected by the rain-shadow effect. The east side of the range gets quite hot in the summer and is almost always dry. One of the major attractions of the Methow Valley for Puget Sounders is the usually sunny weather, the cold Colorado-style winters and the hot, dry summers that make a perfect antidote to the damp, often overcast Puget Sound weather.

Driving Highway 20

No gas stations, restaurants, or other facilities (except restrooms at Washington Pass) are found along the 75 miles of Hwy. 20 between Ross Dam and Mazama, so fill up when you leave I-5 (Sedro-Woolley is cheapest if you get lots of miles per tank). No bus service goes along this route either; the closest you'll get is Mount Vernon on the west and Pateros and Okanogan on the east.

The middle section of Hwy. 20 closes for the winter after the first major snowfall because of avalanche danger. It is usually gated in late November and doesn't open again until late April, sometimes nearly June, depending on the amount of snow. In mid-winter, snow depths can exceed 15 feet at the summit. Parts of the highway remain open to snowmobile traffic from Colonial Creek Campground on the west side to Early Winters Campground near Mazama.

Lower-elevation hiking trails, such as those along Ross Lake, are generally accessible from April through mid-October; at higher elevations, trails are open from mid-July through September.

Cascade Loop Trips

Highway 20 joins Hwy. 153 at Twisp, Hwy. 97 near Pateros, and Hwy. 2 near Wenatchee to form the northwest portion of the "Cascade Loop." This 400-mile scenic drive winds through the North Cascades, past Lake Chelan, through Leavenworth on its approach to Stevens Pass, and returns to western Washington and Whidbey Island. You'll find free *Cascade Loop* booklets at visitors centers along the way, or call the Cascade Loop Association in Wenatchee, tel. (509) 662-3888, for a copy.

A similar promotional highway route has been organized and is called the "North Cascades Loop." It follows the same route over Hwy. 20, continues on to the twin towns of Omak and Okanogan, turns north on Hwy. 97 and goes across into British Columbia's Okanagan (note that Canada and the U.S. spell the word differently), then heads west on the Trans-Canada Highway to the Vancouver area. Look for free *International Loop* booklets at visitors centers, or call Osprey Press in Sedro-Woolley, tel. (360) 855-1641, for a copy.

North Cascades Institute

The nonprofit North Cascades Institute offers a wide spectrum of classes, lectures, kayak trips, whalewatching cruises, birdwatching safaris, photography training, and even poetry workshops. Also offered are youth camps and elder hostel programs. You'll find something going almost all the time between April and December: be it a drum-making workshop near Anacortes, a weeklong backpacking adventure in Pasayten Wilderness, or a discussion of frogs and toads in Methow Valley. For more information, contact the North Cascades Institute, 2105 Hwy. 20, Sedro-Woolley, WA 98284, tel. (360) 856-5700, ext. 209.

SEDRO-WOOLLEY

The riverside town of Sedro-Woolley (pop. 6,700) is a place in transition. The decline of the logging industry in recent years has hit hard,

forcing the town to look elsewhere for an economic base. It remains a commercial center for the farmlands that surround it, while becoming an outfitting town for adventurers on their way east into North Cascades National Park.

History

Settlement of land at the mouth of the Skagit River began as early as 1863, but a huge natural logjam prevented any upriver development until it was dynamited apart in 1879. After this, sternwheelers could move up and down the river, opening the country to mining and logging. Five years later, Mortimer Cook opened a general store in a riverside town he named "Bug"—for the mosquitoes that tormented him in the summer. Cook later succumbed to local pressure and changed the name to Sedro, a corruption of "cedra," the Spanish word for the cedar trees that once covered this area. About the same time, P.A. Woolley built a sawmill a few miles away that became the economic basis of a small but thriving community. The towns were so close together it was difficult to determine their borders, so in 1898 they agreed to join forces while retaining both names. Hence the only hyphenated town name in Washington, and one of just two in America. After a pair of devastating turn-of-the-century fires, the town was rebuilt using bricks.

As a major logging settlement, Sedro-Woolley attracted many of its residents from North Carolina, a heritage that is still evident today. By early in this century, the town was home to 17 lumber mills, a steel foundry, and a big state hospital. Very little of these remain. An effort is now underway to re-create Sedro-Woolley's 1920s-era downtown with old-style lamps and restored brick buildings.

Sights

Sedro-Woolley Museum, 727 Murdock St., tel. (360) 855-2390, contains local memorabilia and old logging and farming equipment. It is open on weekends only, year-round. Seven of the historic logging pictures by Darius Kinsey—a world-famous turn-of-the-century documentary photographer—have been turned into large murals that decorate the sides of downtown buildings. Stop by the information caboose at W. Ferry St. and Hwy. 20 for a walking tour of other historic sights, including stately old homes, a steam donkey from 1913, and other old logging equipment.

Though dwarfed by the nearby mountain lakes in the national park, **Clear Lake** has swimming beaches, boating, and fishing just three miles south of town.

North from Sedro-Woolley
Highway 9 north from Sedro-Woolley leads through quiet Nooksack Valley with its aging dairy barns, big bales of hay, and comfortable homesteads. A series of podunk towns form wide spots in the road: **Wickersham, Acme, Clipper, Van Zandt, Deming, Nugents Corner,** and **Nooksack.** A favorite tubing float trip is down the warm South Fork of the Nooksack River from Saxon to Van Zandt. On hot August weekends several thousand folks join in the fun, creating traffic congestion and conflicts with spawning salmon.

The **Lake Whatcom Railway,** tel. (360) 595-2218, has classic steam engines that pull antique passengers on hour-long trips from Wickersham, near Bellingham. Trains depart on Saturday and Tuesday mid-June through August, with special tours on holidays (Valentine's Day, Easter, Fathers Day, Independence Day) and during the autumn color season, plus special Santa trains in early December. Fares are $10 adults; $5 ages 17 and under.

Everybody stops at the turn-of-the-century **Everybody's Store** in Van Zandt, where the shelves are filled with all manner of supplies: delicious baked goods, wool caps, 40 kinds of cheese, Chinese medicinal herbs, organic produce from the backyard garden, and even pickles for a nickel. The deli here makes great sandwiches.

Woolly Prairie Buffalo Co., tel. (360) 856-0310, just north of Sedro-Woolley, offers summertime hay rides where you can watch bison grazing and learn about the lives of bison.

Accommodations and Food
Three Rivers Inn, 210 Ball St., tel. (360) 855-2626 or (800) 221-5122, has comfortable lodging for $55 s, $61 d, including an outdoor pool, jacuzzi, and free breakfast. **Skagit Motel,** 1977 Hwy. 20, tel. (360) 856-6001, has rooms for $32 s, $35 d. Next door to the motel, **Timbers Restaurant,** tel. (360) 856-4460, serves prime rib, pasta, and seafood in a cheerful interior. Housed in the old Bingham Bank building at

210 Ferry St., the **Gateway Restaurant,** tel. (360) 855-0060, serves dinners in two lounges, several dining rooms, a coffee shop, and bakery.

Annie's Cafe/Anna's Italian Cuisine, 818 Metcalf St., tel. (360) 855-0044, has a schizophrenic personality, creating delicious homestyle country food during the day, and mutating into a fine Italian restaurant at night.

Riverfront Park on McDonald Ave., tel (360) 855-1661, has tent camping and RV places on the banks of the Skagit River.

Events
The Fourth of July brings the weeklong **Loggerodeo** to Sedro-Woolley—an annual event for more than 60 years—with logging contests, parades, a rodeo, a street dance, bed race, carnival, vintage car show, crafts fair, and big fireworks display.

Information and Services
On Hwy. 20, just east of the Sedro-Woolley town line, you'll find the **Mt. Baker Ranger Station/North Cascades National Park Service Complex,** with a North Cascades relief map, books and brochures for sale, and information on road closures and conditions. It's open daily 8 a.m.-4:30 p.m. in the summer (till 6 p.m. on Friday), and Mon.-Fri. 8 a.m.-4:30 p.m. in winter.

The **Sedro-Woolley Chamber of Commerce,** 116 Woodward, tel. (360) 855-1841, is open weekdays. The city also has an **Information Caboose** in Harry Osborne Park at the junction of Hwy. 20 and W. Ferry St., tel. (360) 855-0974. The **area code** for Sedro-Woolley is 360.

BAKER LAKE

Nine-mile-long Baker Lake was created by the Upper Dam on the Baker River; the Lower Baker Dam created Lake Shannon, just off Hwy. 20 near Concrete. Baker Lake is very popular with campers, swimmers, motor boaters, and waterskiers, despite the enormous stumps that lurk just below the water's surface. To get there, take Baker Lake-Grandy Lake Rd. north from Hwy. 20. Get to 100-foot-high **Rainbow Falls** by driving 20 miles out Baker Lake Rd., and then another five miles up Forest Rd. 1130. The name comes from the rainbow that appears at the base on sunny days.

BRIAN BARDWELL

Campgrounds

Puget Power maintains the free **Kulshan Campground** near Upper Baker Dam; no running water. More free camping (no running water) at **Grandy Lake County Park,** four miles northeast of Hwy. 20 on Baker Lake Highway. Farther up Baker Lake Rd. are five Forest Service campgrounds; **Horseshoe Cove** and **Panorama Point** campgrounds charge $8, **Boulder Creek** and **Park Creek** campgrounds are $6.50, and **Shannon Creek,** is $10 per night. All five of these can be reserved ($7.50 extra) by calling (800) 280-2267. A boat-in only campground at Maple Grove is also available. The campgrounds are usually open mid-May to mid-September; call the Forest Service at (360) 856-5700 for specifics.

Baker Lake Resort

Six miles past the Forest Service's Koma Kulshan Guard Station on the west shore, Baker Lake Resort has a dozen rustic cabins with full kitchens ($40-85 d), camping and RV sites ($15-20), boat rentals ($25-80 for eight hours), a store, and a restaurant. There's a two night minimum stay on weekends (three nights on holidays), and the resort is open only from mid-April through October. Call (360) 853-8325 or 424-0943 for reservations.

Hiking Trails

The easiest hike around is the half-mile wheelchair-accessible **Shadow of the Sentinels Trail** that winds through an old-growth Douglas fir stand. It begins a mile beyond the Koma Kulshan guard station.

An excellent, gentle rainforest hike is up the **Baker River.** To reach the trailhead for this six-mile roundtrip hike, drive north on Baker Lake-Grandy Lake Rd. for 14 miles to the Komo Kulshan Guard Station. Follow the Forest Service road for 11.5 miles, then left a mile, then right on the first side road for half a mile to the start of Trail 606. This level, low-elevation trail affords views of glaciers and beaver ponds on the way to Sulphur Creek, the turnaround point. Because of its low elevation, the trail is snow-free from early spring to late fall.

Another Baker Lake hike takes you to **Park Butte,** a 5,450-foot summit with incredible views of Mt. Baker glaciers. This summer-only trek is seven miles roundtrip, but with an elevation gain of over 2,200 feet it'll take a good part of the day to complete. Go north for 12.5 miles on Baker Lake-Grandy Lake Rd., then turn left on Loomis-Nooksack Rd. 13 for nine miles to the road's end. The trail is west of the road, crossing Sulphur Creek before the switchbacks begin.

CONCRETE

East from Sedro-Woolley, Hwy. 20 skirts the Skagit River, climbing easily toward the first Cascade foothills. The landscape is farms, fields, and forests, with the serrated summit of Sauk Mountain to the east. Clearcut hillsides, second (or third) growth forests, and closed lumber mills offer contrasting versions of the logging heritage.

The quiet town of Concrete (pop. 700) was home for many years to the largest cement plant in the state, and the source for cement used in building Grand Coulee Dam, as well as the Ross and Diablo dams. Although environmental regulations closed the outdated, dusty plant in 1968, the prosaic town name remains. (It could have been worse; the town's original name was Cement City.) The town burned several times in the early part of this century, and was finally rebuilt, using concrete, of course. Concrete block restrooms welcome you to Concrete, and the 5,537-foot summit of Sauk Mountain rises straight behind Main St. (see "Rockport State Park" under "Rockport," below, for access to the top). Today, the town depends on a mix of tourism and timber for its survival. All that remains of the cement industry are the big silos on the west end of town, a scattering of other buildings, and the quarry near Lake Shannon.

Sights

There aren't a lot of in-town attractions; your best bet is to pick a Main St. bench and sit with the locals a spell. Of minor interest is Superior St., with its unique under-the-high-school access to the airport. Eagles are visible along the Skagit River Dec.-Feb. (see "Bald Eagle Viewing and Whitewater Rafting," below), and elk herds can be seen just west of town in winter and spring.

Camp 7 Logger's Museum is a small private collection of logging-era flotsam and jetsam on Railroad Avenue. Open weekends in the summer. Just east of town is the **Henry Thompson Bridge** over the Baker River. When completed in 1918, it was the longest single-span cement bridge in the world. A quarter mile east of this is the **Puget Power Visitors Center.** Check out the unusual fish elevator nearby, used to help get returning salmon around the Baker

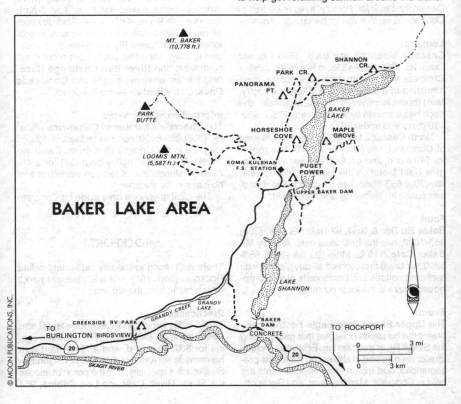

BAKER LAKE AREA

MT. BAKER (10,778 ft.)

PARK BUTTE

LOOMIS MTN. (5,587 ft.)

KOMA KULSHAN F.S. STATION

SHANNON CR.

PARK CR.

PANORAMA PT.

HORSESHOE COVE

BAKER LAKE

MAPLE GROVE

PUGET POWER

UPPER BAKER DAM

LAKE SHANNON

BAKER DAM

CONCRETE

TO ROCKPORT

CREEKSIDE RV PARK
BIRDSVIEW

GRANDY CREEK
GRANDY LAKE

TO BURLINGTON

SKAGIT RIVER

20

0   3 mi
0   3 km

© MOON PUBLICATIONS, INC.

Diablo Dam

DIANNE BOULERICE LYONS

Dam; see the salmon here between June and December. **Sauk Mt. Pottery,** three miles east of Concrete, is worth a visit for handmade ceramics.

Lodging

Cascade Mountain Inn B&B, 3840 Pioneer Lane, tel. (360) 826-4333, is five miles west of Concrete, with six very nice guest rooms, each furnished in the theme of a different country. Most rooms have views of Sauk Mountain, and each has a private bath. Rates are $75 s, $89-110 d; no kids under 10.

North Cascade Inn, 4284 Hwy. 20 (just west of Concrete), tel. (360) 853-8870, has rooms for $40 s or d, and a full service restaurant. **Eagles Nest Motel** on the east end of Concrete, tel. (360) 853-8662, has rooms for $35 s or d, and space for tents ($9) and RVs ($15).

Food

Baker St. Bar & Grill, 92 Baker St., tel. (360) 853-7002, has the best local eats. Also try **Mt. Baker Cafe,** 119 E. Main St., tel. (360) 853-8200, for breakfast (served all day), along with espresso coffees and homemade pies. **Pumphouse Pizza** is the local pizzeria.

Events

The **Upper Skagit Bald Eagle Festival** celebrates the hundreds of eagles that gather along the Skagit River each spring. Festivities include music, an arts and crafts show, naturalist presentations, and Indian storytelling. Events are held in Concrete, Marblemount, and Rockport.

Visit Concrete's **Saturday Market,** where produce, crafts, baked goods, and art are offered for sale 9 a.m.-4 p.m. every Saturday from Memorial Day to Labor Day. Other local events include the **Concrete Fly-Inn** on the third weekend in May, attracting pilots from around the Northwest, the **River Raft Challenge Race,** held the last weekend in July, and **Good Olde Days,** on the third weekend in August.

Information and Services

The **Concrete Chamber of Commerce** office, tel. (360) 853-8400, open weekdays, is right off Hwy. 20 in the Community Center. Catch the "Sockeye Express" trolley here ($2) for a 45-minute historical tour of town on weekends and holidays in the summer.

The local telephone **area code** for Concrete is 360.

ROCKPORT

There isn't much to the tiny settlement called Rockport (pop. 150), but two pleasant parks offer a break from the highway.

Practicalities

The friendly, family run **Riverhouse Hotel and Restaurant,** tel. (360) 853-8557, has three cabins for $37-40 s or d, and a restaurant with homemade all-American cooking Fri.-Sunday. Steaks are a specialty, and the porch overlooks the Skagit River. **Cascade Log Cabins,** 954

Alaythia Dr., tel. (360) 873-4106, has cabins with full kitchens for $50 s or d.

Rockport Country Store has something you don't see every day, a "self-kicking machine." Great for masochists. **Cascadian Farm Roadside Stand,** tel. (360) 853-8629, sells organic strawberries, blueberries, and raspberries, along with sweet corn and other produce from the cooperative's gardens. They also offer homemade ice cream, espresso, and wonderful fresh berry shortcakes. Open May-October.

Howard Miller Steelhead Park is a small county park that has big grassy lawns right along the river and coin-operated showers. Tent sites are $8, Adirondack shelters and RV hookups cost $12. In the park you'll find Chief Campbell's old dugout canoe and a log cabin built in the early 1880s. The old Rockport Ferry, last used in 1961, sits along the river. Right across the street is **Pleasant View Inn Tavern,** which has live music on summer weekends.

The **area code** for Rockport is 360.

Rockport State Park

As you drive east from Concrete on Hwy. 20, the clearcuts are recent and hideous in places. There are very few old growth trees remaining on private land anywhere in the area, and it isn't till you reach Rockport State Park, about 10 miles east of Baker Lake, that you realize what has been lost. Covering 457 acres, the park has five miles of wooded hiking trails, Skagit River steelhead fishing, and camping at tent sites with Adirondack shelters ($10) and RV sites ($15) beneath incredible 250-foot high old-growth Douglas fir trees. The campground is open mid-April through October and has coin-operated showers. Call (800) 452-5687 for campsite reservations ($6 extra fee), available up to 11 months ahead of time. The paved and wheelchair-accessible **Skagit View Trail** leads right down to the riverbank, providing a great place to look for bald eagles in the winter.

Immediately west of the park is the start of **Sauk Mountain Rd.,** a 7.5 mile gravel road that takes you to a trailhead most of the way up this 5,537-foot peak. A steep, switchback-filled trail begins at the parking lot, climbing another 1.5 miles to the summit, where you're treated to views of the northern Cascades and the Skagit and Sauk River valleys.

BALD EAGLE VIEWING AND WHITEWATER RAFTING

The Skagit River is one of the best places in the Lower 48 to watch wintering bald eagles, with over 300 birds stopping by for a salmon feast on their journey south from Alaska and Canada. Just east of Rockport, the Nature Conservancy's 1,500-acre **Skagit River Bald Eagle Natural Area** is a haven for these birds; they arrive in October and feast on Skagit River salmon through March. Eagles are visible from Hwy. 20 pullouts all along the Skagit River Valley, but the best way to see them is on a scenic float trip down the river. You're likely to see at least 50 of these majestic birds perched in trees along the nine-mile float from Marblemount to Rockport.

Float Trips

A number of companies offer essentially the same scenic bald eagle float trip; prices and amenities vary. Float trips run December through February, when the population is at a peak. The river is so gentle that wetsuits are not necessary; just wear warm winter clothing. Expect to pay $45-80 for the three and a half hour float. One of the oldest and best companies offering eagle float trips is **Chinook Expeditions,** tel. (800) 241-3451. Other companies with similar raft trips are: **Alpine Adventures,** tel. (800) 926-7238; **Blue Sky Outfitters,** tel. (800) 228-7238; **Cascade Adventures,** tel. (800) 723-8386; **Downstream River Runners,** tel. (800) 234-4644; **North Cascades River Expeditions,** tel. (800) 634-8433; **Northern Wilderness River Riders,** tel. (800) 448-7238; **Orion Expeditions,** tel. (800) 553-7466; **Osprey Rafting,** tel. (800) 743-6269, **Rivers Incorporated,** tel. (206) 822-5296; **River Recreation,** tel. (800) 464-5899; **Wild & Scenic River Tours,** tel. (206) 323-1220; and **Wildwater River Tours,** tel. (800) 522-9453.

Whitewater Trips

In the summer, you can float eight miles of the upper Skagit River through North Cascades National Park, where the water is a bit rougher, but nothing over class III. A good beginning river for whitewater enthusiasts. The following companies have upper Skagit trips: Alpine Adventures, Cascade Adventures, Downstream River Runners, Orion Expeditions, Osprey Rafting, Rivers Incorporated, and Wildwater River Tours (see above for telephone numbers).

If you have the skills and are really daring, **Downstream River Runners,** tel. (800) 234-4644, for details.has wild eight-mile trips down the **Cascade River**—a tributary of the Skagit—in July and August. This class IV to V river is considered the most challenging in Washington, and the company requires paddlers to have previous river experience and pass a paddling test.

MARBLEMOUNT

Entering Marblemount from the west, signs warn "Last Gas for 69 Miles" and, more importantly, "Last Tavern for 89 Miles." The little town is a good place to stock up on these—and other—essentials, and to get information and backcountry permits for North Cascades National Park. A small museum features displays on the area's logging history. This pretty country settlement is surrounded by open fields and big-leaf maple trees (brilliant yellow in the fall), and is split by two rivers: the Skagit and the Cascade.

The **Marblemount Fish Hatchery,** a mile southeast of town on Fish Hatchery Rd., rears and releases thousands of king, silver, and chum salmon each year.

Accommodations and Food

Halfway between Rockport and Marblemount is **Totem Trail Motel,** tel. (360) 873-4535, with rooms for $40-50 s or d. Right across the road is **Wilderness Village RV Park,** tel. (360) 873-2571, offering tent sites ($9), bike spaces ($5), and RV spaces ($14). The public laundromat here has coin-operated showers.

Cascade Log Cabins, three miles west of Marblemount, tel. (360) 873-4106, has modern cabins with full kitchens for $50 s or d. Friendly folks, too.

Clark's Skagit River Cabins, three miles west of Marblemount, tel. (360) 873-2250, has cute rustic cabins for $47-78 s or d, space for tents ($10) and RVs ($15), and showers for 25 cents (available also to folks who aren't staying here). Also here is **The Eatery Museum**

with burgers and fresh fruit milk shakes; be sure to check out the curious handsewn flag made in 1890 by an ancestor of the present owners. Rabbit lovers will have a hopping time here; dozens of bunnies are all over the big green grounds. Some will eat out of your hand.

Across the road among the big-leaf maples is quaint **Wildwood Chapel,** covering barely enough space for a minister and the couple to be married. The chapel was built here in 1977 and has been used for weddings and countless I-was-there photos. **Log House Inn,** tel. (360) 873-4311, has more lodging and food; it was built in 1890 as a roadhouse for workers who were attempting a road over the mountains. The road they began was not completed until the 1972 opening of Hwy. 20.

Mountain Song Restaurant, tel. (360) 873-2461, easily takes the prize for the best—and most reasonable—meals in the area. Stop by for a big and healthy buffet breakfast, lunch, or dinner, or to order fish, fowl, pastas, or tempeh burgers from the menu. The home-baked breads, berry pies, hearty soups, and fresh-from-the-garden organic greens are special treats.

Backcountry Permits

Follow the signs to the National Park Service's **Marblemount Wilderness Office;** open daily 7 a.m.-8 p.m. from July to mid-September, with reduced weekend hours from mid-May through June and mid-September through October. In the winter months, it's catch as catch can. Get backcountry permits here for the park. Because there are no advance reservations, weekend campers arrive early to get permits for the most popular sites, especially Cascade Pass, Hidden Lake, Monagram Lake, and Thornton Lakes. If you're willing to accept alternate destinations, you should be able to get into the backcountry under most circumstances. Call (360) 873-4500 for recorded information on backcountry use in the park. The office also has information on Glacier Peak Wilderness (see "Hiking Trails" under "The Mountain Loop: Granite Falls to Darrington," above), accessible from the end of the Cascade River Rd., southeast of Marblemount. Behind the Wilderness Office is a greenhouse used to grow plants to revegetate damaged backcountry areas.

NEWHALEM AND EASTWARD

Heading east from Marblemount, Hwy. 20 enters North Cascades National Park after five miles, then passes Goodell Creek and Newhalem Campgrounds (see "Campgrounds," below), the turnoff to North Cascades Visitor Center (see "Information and a View," below), and **Skagit General Store** in Newhalem.

The little settlement of Newhalem is a quiet company town with only one focus, producing electricity for Seattle at nearby Gorge, Diablo, and Ross Dams. The parklike grounds are surrounded by trim clapboard homes occupied by employees of Seattle City Light. In the town park find **Old Number Six,** a 1928 Baldwin steam locomotive that hauled passengers and supplies to the Skagit River dams; today it's a favorite of kids. The small **Seattle City Light Visitor Center** here makes a good bathroom stop.

Over the Top

East of Newhalem, Hwy. 20 begins a serious climb into the forested Cascades, and quickly passes a chain of three dams and reservoirs—Gorge, Diablo, and Ross—that constitute the centerpiece of Ross Lake National Recreation Area (a part of North Cascades National Park). Tours of Diablo Dam and Lake are a popular attraction here. Be sure to stop at the Forge Creek Falls overlook near milepost 123 for views of the creek plunging into the gorge below. Colonial Creek Campground (see "Campgrounds," below) is along the highway near Diablo Lake, and a mile east is an overlook where you can peer down on the emerald green lake waters and across to the jagged summits of Pyramid Peak and Colonial Peak.

Continuing eastward, the highway climbs along Granite Creek before topping two passes—4,855-foot Rainy Pass and 5,447-foot Washington Pass. A short paved trail leads from Washington Pass to over-the-highway viewpoints of 7,720-foot Liberty Bell—the symbol of the North Cascades Highway—and Early Winters Spires. Beyond this, the highway spirals downward to Methow Valley and the town of Winthrop, 30 miles to the east and 3,600 feet lower.

NORTH CASCADES NATIONAL PARK

The half-million-acre North Cascades National Park is one of the wildest in the Lower 48, and an outdoor lover's paradise. It has a total of 318 glaciers—more than half of the total number outside Alaska. Few roads spoil this pristine wilderness, where rugged peaks, mountain lakes, and waterfalls greet the determined backcountry hiker. Nearly all the park lies within the **Stephen Mather Wilderness,** and it is surrounded by additional wilderness buffers covering well over a million acres: Liberty Bell Primitive Area, Noisy-Diobsud Wilderness Area, Glacier Peak Wilderness Area, Pasaytan Wilderness Area, and Mt. Baker Wilderness Area.

North Cascades National Park is actually a complex of three distinct units: the park itself is split into northern and southern units by Ross Lake National Recreation Area (Hwy. 20 passes along this corridor), while the south end includes Lake Chelan National Recreation Area. All three sections are managed by the National Park Service, but Ross Lake National Recreation Area contains dams and power plants that are operated by Seattle City Light; these three plants supply nearly all of Seattle's electrical needs. If this isn't confusing enough, look at the maps to find that east-side portions of Mt. Baker-Snoqualmie National Forest are administered by Okanogan National Forest. Actually, to most visitors these distinctions are of little meaning; this is all public land, and although the dams and reservoirs are certainly not natural, almost everything else is wild and undeveloped, providing fantastic opportunities for explorations afoot and afloat.

Gorge and Diablo Lakes

Two small reservoirs created by Seattle City Light dams on the upper Skagit River are Gorge Lake, covering 210 acres, and Diablo Lake, covering 910 acres; both are accessible from Hwy. 20. Diablo and Gorge Lakes get their emerald-green color from fine sediments in the glacial runoff. Motorboat and rowboat rentals are available at both lakes, but the water is too cold for swimming.

The **Gorge Powerhouse** observation lobby is open daily 8 a.m.-4 p.m. May-Sept., and is ac-

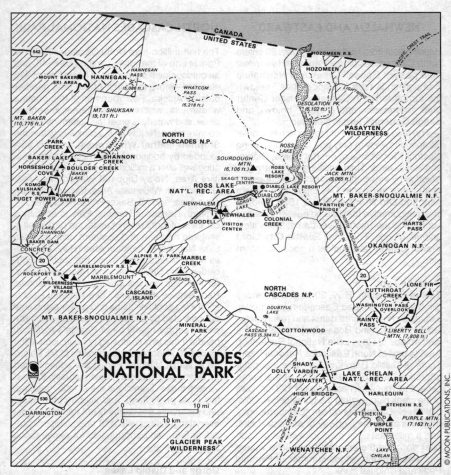

cessed by a cable suspension footbridge. Continue beyond the power plant to **Ladder Creek Falls and Rock Gardens.** The colorful flower gardens were first planted here in the 1920s and form a delightful setting for the adjacent falls. At night both are lit up.

A mile off Hwy. 20 is the tiny company town of **Diablo,** the home of Diablo Powerplant and the Skagit Tour Center. A half-dozen free campsites (no potable water) are available at nearby **Gorge Lake Campground,** and a popular (but

very steep) five-mile trail leads from here to the 5,985-foot summit of **Sourdough Mountain.** Hikers are treated to lush alpine meadows and panoramic views.

Seattle City Light Tours

Seattle City Light has been offering regularly scheduled tours of their Skagit facilities since 1928. Today, a four-and-a-half-hour guided tour begins with a slide presentation at the Skagit Tour Center in Diablo, followed by a 558-foot ride up Sourdough Mountain on an antique incline railway that was used to haul supplies during the construction of the Diablo Dam. Then, enjoy a cruise across deep-green Diablo Lake and back to an all-you-can-eat baked chicken or vegetarian spaghetti dinner.

Tours leave three times a day Thurs.-Mon. from mid-June to early September, and once a day on weekends only from early September to early October. The total cost of the tour and dinner is $25 adults, $22 seniors, $13 kids six to 11, children under five free. For reservations (strongly recommended), contact the **Seattle City Light Tour Desk,** 1015 3rd Ave. in Seattle, tel. (206) 684-3030, or, from late June to Labor Day, stop by the Skagit Tour Center in Newhalem.

A quicker 90-minute tour is also given twice a day Thurs.-Mon. from mid-June to early September. This 90-minute version includes a slide show, ride on the incline lift, and tour of the Diablo Powerhouse (sorry, no boat ride); $5 adults, free for kids under age 12. No reservations are needed.

Ross Lake

The second-largest lake in the North Cascades after Lake Chelan, Ross Lake is 24 miles long and up to two miles wide, covering 12,000 acres from the Skagit River up to and beyond the Canadian border. It was created by a 540-foot high hydroelectric dam completed in 1949 by Seattle City Light. Fortunately, efforts to enlarge the dam were thwarted in the 1980s by environmentalists and the government of British Columbia. You can see the reservoir from the Ross Lake overlook at milepost 135 on Hwy. 20 or area hiking trails (see below), but the only vehicle access and motorboat launch is at the lake's north end, via a 39-mile gravel road from Canada. This means that Ross Lake is more of a canoeing and kayaking lake than other reservoirs in the Cascades. The glacier-fed waters of Ross Lake are too cold for swimming.

Although you can't drive to **Ross Lake Resort,** tel. (360) 386-4437, you can catch the **Seattle City Light tugboat taxi** ($2.50 each way) that leaves the parking lot across Diablo Dam daily at 8:30 a.m. and 3 p.m. The tug takes you to the end of Diablo Lake, where a truck carries you on to Ross Lake. This is one of the most unique lodging places in Washington; everything here is literally on the water, with cabins and bunkhouses built on log floats. Visitors can stay in modern cabins for $77 d ($10 per person extra for up to six people), rustic 1950s-era cabins for $51 d ($6 per person extra for up to four people), and bunkhouses for $99 (up to six people). Enjoy fantastic views up the lake to 8,300-foot Mt. Hozomeen at the Canadian border. You can rent a small motorboat, kayak, or canoe here, but there are no telephones, groceries, food service, and they don't take credit cards. The lodge is open June-October.

Ross Lake has water-side campsites and half-a-dozen trailheads that provide access into adjacent North Cascades National Park. Ross Lake Resort runs a **water taxi** service to these, along with boat tours and portages from Diablo Lake for small boats and canoes. The water taxi fares are by the boat load (it can hold six), not per person, so it's best if you can coordinate your travel with other folks to save money. Call (360) 386-4437 for specifics. These water taxi trips are a fun way to reach the backcountry, but be sure to pick up backcountry permits from the Marblemount Ranger Station before heading out to camp along Ross Lake or hike in the backcountry.

Campgrounds

Park Service campgrounds accessible by car on the North Cascades Hwy. include **Goodell Creek** ($7; open year-round), **Newhalem Creek** ($10; open Memorial Day to mid-October), and **Colonial Creek** ($10; open Memorial Day to mid-October). Brave the 39-mile gravel road from Canada and camp at the free **Hozomeen Campground** at the north end of Ross Lake, from mid-May through October. A handful of free campsites (no potable water) are available at **Gorge Lake Campground** near Diablo Dam. Enjoy summer naturalist activities including nature walks and evening programs at Colonial Creek, with less frequent productions at Newhalem and Hozomeen Campgrounds.

Along Cascade River Rd. southwest of Marblemount, stay at campgrounds in **Cascade Island State Park** (free and open all year), **Marble Creek** (free; open mid-May to mid-September), or **Mineral Park** (free; open mid-May to mid-

September). On the east side of Washington Pass, you can camp at the very popular **Lone Fir, Klipchuck,** and **Early Winters** Campgrounds managed by the Forest Service. They are open June-Sept. and cost $6.

Day Hikes

More than 300 miles of maintained trails provide ample opportunities to explore North Cascades National Park. Short hikes—some are wheelchair accessible—abound around Colonial Campground and Newhalem; pick up flyers describing these and others at the visitor centers. Trails below 3,000 feet are generally open by mid-April or May; higher up, you may meet snow in July, so be prepared.

Some of the park's most spectacular scenery can be seen at **Cascade Pass.** This is a day-use-only area; no camping is allowed between the end of Cascade River Rd. and Cottonwood Camp on the south side of the pass. Drive to the trailhead at the end of Cascade River Rd., a 25-mile trip from Marblemount. The first two miles of the seven-mile roundtrip hike climb steadily through forest and meadows to the 5,400-foot pass at 3.5 miles. Allow about five hours for this summer-only hike.

Backcountry Treks

A free **backcountry permit** is required for all overnight trips into the park, a policy meant to reduce overcrowding and preserve the fragile alpine environment. Pick one up at the information or ranger stations in Marblemount, Hozomeen, Stehekin, Early Winters, or Concrete (summer only). The North Cascades are among the most rugged mountains in the Lower 48, so plan accordingly: lots of wool clothing, extra food, a waterproof tarp, and a flexible schedule for waiting out storms or resting feet and muscles sore from all the ups and downs.

From June to November, enjoy the 31-mile trip from Panther Creek to Hozomeen along Ross Lake's **East Bank Trail.** The trailhead is on Hwy. 20, eight miles east of the Colonial Creek Campground at the Panther Creek bridge. The trail leads through low forest and along the lakeshore for 18 miles, at which point you have the option of continuing to Hozomeen or taking a side trip up 6,085-foot **Desolation Peak.** The roundtrip up the peak is nine miles, almost

straight up, with an elevation gain of 4,400 feet; you'll be rewarded with views of Mt. Baker, Shuksan, Jack Mountain, and The Pickets. To get right to the peak, skip the first 18 miles of hiking by taking the water taxi to the Desolation Peak trailhead; stay overnight at Lightning Creek Campground, since you probably won't return in time to catch the boat. Beat Generation fans will want to make this pilgrimage to spend time with one of their own; Jack Kerouac spent the summer of 1955 as a fire lookout here.

The **Pacific Crest Trail** enters the park from the south from Glacier Peak Wilderness Area (see "Hiking Trails" under "The Mountain Loop: Granite Falls to Darrington," above), crossing Hwy. 20 at Rainy Pass and heading north through the Liberty Bell Roadless Area (see below) and the Pasaytan Wilderness Area (see below) to the Canadian border.

If you can set up a vehicle shuttle or are willing to hitchhike, an excellent long hike begins at the Colonial Creek Campground (24 miles east of Marblemount), climbs over 6,063-foot **Park Pass** via Thunder Creek and Park Creek trails, and ends at Park Creek Campground. From here, you can catch the shuttle bus to Stehekin, and then ride the *Lady of the Lake II* down Lake Chelan to the town of Chelan. An alternative ending would be to hike (or catch the shuttle bus) four miles up the Stehekin Valley Rd., and follow **Cascade Pass Trail** over this 5,423-foot pass to the end of Cascade River Rd. (25 miles south of Marblemount).

If you don't mind a long uphill slog, **Easy Pass** makes a fine overnight hike. The trailhead is six miles west of Rainy Pass on Hwy. 20 (46 miles east of Marblemount), and the misnamed Easy Pass Trail climbs steadily for 3.7 miles to this 6,500-foot summit, where you enter North Cascades National Park. The magnificent vista includes knife-edged mountains and active glaciers. From here, you can continue deeper into the wilderness on **Fisher Creek Trail.** Easy Pass Trail is usually open from late July to late September.

See "Hiking Trails" under "Mount Baker and Vicinity" (above), "Baker Lake" (above), "Liberty Bell Roadless Area" (below), "Harts Pass Area," under "Methow Valley" (below), and "Stehekin," under "Chelan and Vicinity" (below), for trails leading into the park from these surrounding areas. For more detailed descriptions of these and many other North Cascade hikes, see Ira Spring and Harvey Manning's *100 Hikes in Washington's North Cascades: National Park Region,* published by The Mountaineers in Seattle.

Pack Trips
Early Winters Outfitters, tel. (509) 996-2659 or (800) 843-7951, has horse pack trips of all types throughout the northern Cascades. If you're traveling with young children, your best bet may be **Back Country Burro Treks,** tel. (509) 779-4421. The outfitters will supply you with a burro for the child, packing all of your camping equipment and meeting you at a designated campsite. Rates are $50 per person per day if you bring your own food, or $100 per person per day with meals prepared by the outfitters. **Deli Llama Wilderness Adventures,** tel. (509) 757-4212, is another good way to go trekking in the Cascades.

Information and a View
The newly opened—and elaborate—**North Cascades Visitor Center,** tel. (360) 856-5700, is 14 miles east of Marblemount and a half-mile south of Hwy. 20 in Newhalem. Inside are natural history exhibits (including a kid-sized banana slug), a large relief model of the region, a theater with slide shows, movies, and other presentations, and a gift shop. The visitor center is open daily 9 a.m.-5 p.m. from April through mid-November, and weekends only 9 a.m.-4:30 p.m.

the rest of the year. (You may find longer hours in mid-summer.) Ask at the center about borrowing one of the free audiotapes that describe the region's rich natural and human history. Daily naturalist walks are offered during the summer, with weekend talks in the winter months.

Immediately behind the center is a guaranteed-to-please 330-foot saunter to a view of the precipitous **Picket Range.** This is a great place to take in the view and to enjoy the sounds of bird calls. The path is wheelchair accessible.

See "Backcountry Permits" under "Marblemount," above, for another park service information center, the **Marblemount Wilderness Office.** In addition to these two, a **Forest Service and Park Service Information Center** can be found near the Early Winters Campground, 16 miles northwest of Winthrop on Hwy. 20. It's open Fri.-Sun. from late May to mid-June, and daily 8 a.m.-7 p.m. from mid-June to Labor Day weekend. Closed the rest of the year. This historic structure was built by the Civilian Conservation Corps in 1936 as a ranger station.

LIBERTY BELL ROADLESS AREA
The 141,000-acre Liberty Bell Roadless Area adjoins Hwy. 20 at Washington Pass and includes a long stretch of the Pacific Crest Trail, as well as some of the finest rock climbing in the Cascades. An outstanding day hike takes

DIANNE BOUERICE LYONS

Liberty Bell at Washington Pass in the North Cascades

you past two forest-rimmed lakes and over **Maple Pass.** The trail begins right along Hwy. 20, from the south parking lot at Rainy Pass (30 miles west of Winthrop). A level, paved trail (wheelchair accessible) leads a mile to **Rainy Lake,** with interpretive signs along the way. The cirque lake is backed by high cliffs with plummeting waterfalls. From here, you can continue up a steep trail to Maple Pass, and then loop back past **Lake Ann** (good fishing for cutthroat trout) before returning to the parking area, a total distance of approximately six miles. No camping is allowed anywhere along this very popular route.

Also popular is an easy two-mile trail to **Blue Lake** that leads through subalpine meadows to the emerald waters of this mountain lake. Surrounding it are a trio of spectacular summits: Liberty Bell Mountain, Whistler Mountain, and Cutthroat Peak. The Blue Lake trailhead is a half-mile west of Washington Pass.

PASAYTEN WILDERNESS

One of the largest wilderness areas in Washington, the Pasayten (pa-SAY-tin) Wilderness covers 530,000 acres of mountain country. Its northern edge is the U.S.-Canadian border, while to the south it extends almost to Methow Valley. The country contains deep canyons, mountains topping 7,500 feet, and an abundance of wildlife that includes a few gray wolves and grizzly bears.

Hiking

The Pasayten Wilderness contains more than 600 miles of trails; see *100 Hikes in Washing-* *ton's North Cascades: National Park Region* by Ira Spring and Harvey Manning (Seattle: The Mountaineers) for details. An enjoyable short hike is the 12-mile long **Billy Goat Loop Trail.** To get here, drive nine miles north from Winthrop on West Chewuch Rd., and turn left onto Eightmile Creek Road. Continue another 17 miles to the trailhead at the end of the road. The trail climbs through evergreen forests and then over Billy Goat Pass before dropping into the narrow Drake Creek Valley. From here, it circles back around the other side of Billy Goat Mountain, and over Eightmile Pass, before returning you to the starting point.

The trailhead for a longer loop hike (approximately 30 miles) is 20 miles west of Mazama at the second switchback above Harts Pass on the way to Slate Peak (see "Harts Pass Area," below). Follow the **Buckskin Ridge Trail** (No. 498) from here through high meadows and past Silver Lake to Silver Pass and Buckskin Ridge (7,300 feet), before descending to the Pasayten River. Here you catch trail No. 478 and follow it upriver through old-growth forests to trail No. 498, which takes you back to your starting point. See the Green Trails maps or talk with folks at the Winthorp Forest Service office before heading up this interesting but challenging route.

Horseback Treks

Several companies provide horse pack trips into the Pasayten, with rates generally around $125 per day, or $95 if you hike and they carry the gear. The companies include: **Early Winters Outfitters,** tel. (509) 996-2659 or (800) 843-7951; **North Cascade Safari,** tel. (509) 996-2350; and **Claude Miller Pack Trips,** tel. (509) 996-2350.

METHOW VALLEY

Scenic Methow Valley is a land of contrasts. To the west are the massive, glacially carved summits of the Cascades, with dense Douglas fir forests carpeting their lower flanks, but as you enter the valley, the forests are replaced by irrigated pastures surrounded by rounded hills covered with sage, grass, and scattered pines. Highway 20 follows the Methow River, with tall bankside cottonwoods providing a shady screen from the hot summer sun. In recent years the Methow (pronounced "MET-how") has become a haven for mountain bikers, river-rafters, and cross-country skiers. There are excellent lodges and restaurants, and a comfortably relaxed country atmosphere. Unfortunately, there's an alarming amount of new development taking place as ranchettes replace real ranches and fancy inns sprout up along the riverbanks. Some places are downright ugly, and as they spread across the valley, its quiet country flavor is being replaced by a Disneylandish version of the West. These same schleppy developments threaten other much-loved places in the West: Jackson Hole, Sedona, and Park City.

The bustling town of Winthrop is the center of activity in Methow Valley, with its made-over Western theme. Thirteen miles northwest of here is minuscule Mazama (the name means "mountain goat" in Greek); 11 miles south is the ranching town called Twisp. The valley is accessible from all sides during the summer, but Hwy. 20 closes from late November through April (or longer).

Harts Pass Area

After the discovery of gold and silver near Harts Pass in 1893, prospectors hurriedly built a road from Methow Valley to the mines. The precious metals petered out, but in the 1940s, fear of a Japanese invasion led the military to flatten the top of the Slate Peak and erect an early warning station, supplied in winter via dogsled. The site was later used for a Cold War radar station.

Today, a gravel road leads 19 miles from Mazama past the 2,000-foot slopes of glacially carved **Goat Wall,** and on to Harts Pass (6,197 feet), where it crosses the Pacific Crest Trail

(PCT). The road splits at the pass. Turn left (south) for nine downhill miles to the ghost towns of Barron and Chancellor—once home to 2,000 miners. Turn right (north) for three steep miles to **Slate Peak Lookout.** When you park here, you're at the highest point you can drive to in Washington: 7,440 feet. A short walk leads to the lookout tower; be ready for spectacular 360-degree views of the entire Cascade Range. Beware that Harts Pass Rd. is steep and narrow; RVs and trailers are prohibited. It's a great, but tiring, mountain bike ride. The road is not plowed beyond Lost River in the winter.

Near Harts Pass, you can camp at two free Forest Service campgrounds with gorgeous alpine settings: **Meadows** and **Harts Pass.** They are usually open mid-July to late September; no potable water.

This high alpine country offers some of the most popular day-hiking in this part of the state. **Windy Pass Trail** begins 1.5 miles up Slate Peak Rd. from Harts Pass and follows the PCT for 3.5 miles to Windy Pass. The hike begins at 6,800 feet with little additional elevation gain but offers striking views of peaks and meadows all along the route. A second fun hike with little change in elevation begins at Harts Pass and proceeds along the PCT south to **Grasshopper Pass.** The roundtrip distance is 11 miles, and the route follows the crest of the mountains to beautiful meadows at Grasshopper Pass. Because of the high elevation, these trails are often covered with snow until late July.

WINTHROP

Winthrop's Main Street buildings have been remodeled with an Old West theme to reflect the town's 1890s mining boom—and to encourage hungry, tired Hwy. 20 drivers to stop for a meal, gas, and souvenirs. Winthrop also hosts annual festivals and rodeos that reflect the Western mood. Located near the junction of the Methow and Chewuch (CHEE-wuk) Rivers, Winthrop began as a mining settlement, settled into middle age as a ranching town, and has reemerged

METHOW VALLEY ACCOMMODATIONS

Accommodations are arranged from least to most expensive within each town. Rates may be lower during the winter months. The telephone area code is 509.

WINTHROP

The Farmhouse Inn; three-quarter mile southeast of Winthrop on Hwy. 20; tel. 996-2191 or (800) 996-2193; $37-66 s or d; outdoor jacuzzi

Winthrop Inn; one mile southeast of Winthrop; tel. 996-2217 or (800) 444-1972; $49-60 s, $56-65 d; jacuzzi, outdoor pool, riverside location

Dammann's B&B; half-mile southeast of Winthrop on Hwy. 20; tel. 996-2484 or (800) 423-0040; $50 s or d; three antique-filled guest rooms (one with private bath) along Methow River, piano and pool table, full breakfast, no kids

Westar Lodge; four miles north of Winthrop; tel. 996-2697; $50 s or d in lodge, $150 s or d in cottages; along Chewuch River, jacuzzi, kitchen, group use only in winter

Virginian Resort; three-quarter mile southeast of Winthrop on Hwy. 20; tel. 996-2535 or (800) 854-2834; $52-75 s or d; outdoor pool, jacuzzi, cabins with kitchenettes, AAA approved

Chewack River Guest Ranch; north of Winthrop; tel. 996-2497; $55 s or d; jacuzzi, country setting

Mountain View B&B; 224 Castle Ave., Winthrop; tel. 996-3234; $55 s or d and up; no kids

Winthrop Inn; one mile southeast of Winthrop on Hwy. 20; tel. 996-2217 or (800) 444-1972; $55 s, $60 d Fri.-Sat.; $49 s, $56 d Sun.-Thurs.; Methow River location, jacuzzi, AAA approved

Trail's End Motel; downtown Winthrop; tel. 996-2303; $55-65 s or d; sauna

WolfRidge Resort; five miles west of Winthrop on Twin Lakes Rd.; tel. 996-2828 or (800) 237-2388; $55-65 s or d in hotel, $89-139 s or d in suites; modern log townhouses along river, outdoor pool, jacuzzi, rec room

River Run Inn & Resort; 27 Rader Rd.; tel. 996-2173; $55-75 s or d; indoor pool, riverside location, shared bath, continental breakfast

Duck Brand Hotel; downtown Winthrop; tel. 996-2192 or (800) 996-2192; $56-66 s or d; private baths

Winthrop Mt. View Chalets; two miles southeast of Winthrop on Hwy. 20; tel. 996-3113 or (800) 527-3113; $59 s or d; little boxes called "chalets," kitchenettes, AAA approved

Brown's Farm; three miles west of Winthrop on Wolf Creek Rd.; tel. 996-2571; $60 s or d; country location, cabins with kitchens, friendly owner

Sunny Meadows Inn; three miles north of Winthrop on W. Chewuch Rd.; tel. 996-3103 or (800) 433-3121; $60-80 s or d; apartments in a country location along Chewuch River, free golf course access, ice rink in winter

Chewuch Inn; 223 White Ave., Winthrop; tel. 996-3107; $70-90 s or d; apartment building, continental breakfast

Marigot Motel; 960 Hwy. 20; tel. 996-3100 or (800) 468-6754; $73 s, $80 d; jacuzzi, continental breakfast, AAA approved

Lost River Bess' B&B; 98 Lost River Rd.; tel. 996-2457; $75 s or d; full breakfast, nice views, decks

Hotel Rio Vista; 285 Riverside (half-mile south of Winthrop); tel. 996-3535; $80 s or d; jacuzzi, decks overlooking Methow River, nice rooms, AAA approved

Spring Creek Ranch; 491 Twin Lakes Rd.; tel. 996-2495; $120 s or d, $10 pp for additional people; large 1929 refurbished country house

Sun Mountain Lodge; nine miles southwest of Winthrop; tel. 996-2211 or (800) 572-0493; $130-230 s or d; mountaintop location, lodge or cabin rooms with view, swimming pool, exercise room, jacuzzis, two-night minimum stay on weekends, AAA four diamond resort

TWISP

Blue Spruce Motel; Twisp; tel. 997-8852; $30 s, $35 d; kitchenettes for $35 s, $45 d

Sportsmen Motel; three miles east of Twisp on Hwy. 20; tel. 997-2911; $31 s, $36 d; kitchens, local calls 25 cents, very friendly

Wagon Wheel Motel; three miles east of Twisp on Hwy. 20; tel. 997-4671; $35 s or d; country setting

Idle-A-While Motel; Twisp; tel. 997-3222; $41-57 s or d; jacuzzi, sauna, kitchenettes available, AAA approved

Methow Valley Inn B&B; 234 2nd E. Ave., Twisp; tel. 997-3014 or (800) 261-4619; $50-65 s or d; historic 1923 home, seven upstairs guest rooms (three with private bath), full country breakfast

MAZAMA AREA

North Cascades Base Camp; 255 Lost River Rd., Mazama; tel. 996-2334; $40 s, $60 d with breakfast, $105 s or d with three meals, jacuzzi, shared bath

Lost River Resort; 672 Lost River Rd., Mazama; tel. 996-2537 or (800) 996-2537; $65 s, $75 d; rustic cabins, full breakfast, woodstoves, kitchens, families welcome

Chokecherry Inn; Mazama; tel. 996-2049; $68 s or d; jacuzzi, on Methow River

Mazama Country Inn; Mazama; tel. 996-2681 or (800) 843-7951; $80 s or d in summer (no meals), $165-175 d in winter with three meals, $95-120 in cabins (no meals); jacuzzi, sauna, children welcome in summer, no kids under 13 in winter

Aspen Loft; three miles east of Mazama; tel. 996-2110; $80-90 s or d, sleeps six, $10 for additional people; popular X-C ski lodging, kitchen

Early Winters Cabins; Mazama; tel. 996-2355 or (800) 422-3048; $100 s or d; small cabins with kitchens

---

as a tourist Mecca. Home to just 340 year-round residents, Winthrop greets over 600,000 visitors annually.

History

The Methow Valley was originally part of the Moses Indian Reservation, but when members of the Moses-Columbia tribe refused to be placed on land away from their home along the Columbia River, the government opened the valley to homesteaders. The first white settlers reached the site of present-day Winthrop in the 1880s, lured by gold fever. The town itself goes back to 1891, when an easterner named Guy Waring opened Methow Trading Company. A devastating fire two years later nearly destroyed the new town and forced Waring to return East to recoup his losses and get East Coast financing. After returning, Waring incorporated the

town in 1897 and named it in honor of John Winthrop, the colonial governor of Massachusetts (another version says it was for Theodore Winthrop, an early Washington settler killed in the Civil War). Waring stayed in business for almost half a century, and at one time owned every building on the main street except town hall. One of Waring's Harvard classmates, Owen Wister, came to visit and used some of his friend's experiences in his famous novel, *The Virginian*—considered the first Western novel. (This is the Washington version; folks in Medicine Bow, Wyoming, say it was inspired by their townfolks, and they seem to have a stronger point. A hero has many fathers.)

After the collapse of mining in the area, Winthrop headed toward oblivion; even the founder went bankrupt and moved back East. But then, as the North Cascades Highway was

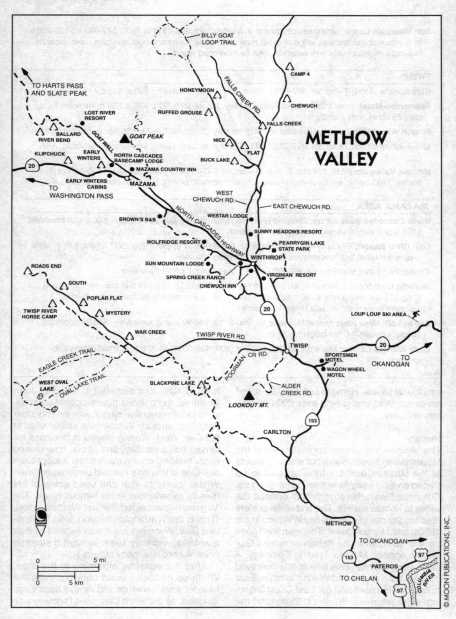

BILLY GOAT
LOOP TRAIL

CAMP 4

HONEYMOON

FALLS CREEK RD.

CHEWUCH

RUFFED GROUSE

FALLS CREEK

TO HARTS PASS
AND SLATE PEAK

LOST RIVER RESORT

BALLARD
RIVER BEND

GOAT WALL

GOAT PEAK

NICE

FLAT

METHOW
VALLEY

EARLY WINTERS

NORTH CASCADES
BASECAMP LODGE

BUCK LAKE

KLIPCHUCK

20

MAZAMA COUNTRY INN

EARLY WINTERS CABINS

MAZAMA

WEST CHEWUCH RD.

TO
WASHINGTON PASS

EAST CHEWUCH RD.

BROWN'S B&B

NORTH CASCADES HIGHWAY

WESTAR LODGE

SUNNY MEADOWS RESORT

WOLFRIDGE RESORT

PEARRYGIN LAKE
STATE PARK

SUN MOUNTAIN LODGE

WINTHROP

ROADS END

SOUTH

SPRING CREEK RANCH

CHEWUCH INN

VIRGINIAN RESORT

POPLAR FLAT

20

TWISP RIVER
HORSE CAMP

MYSTERY

LOUP LOUP SKI AREA

WAR CREEK

TWISP RIVER RD.

TWISP

20

TO
OKANOGAN

EAGLE CREEK TRAIL

SPORTSMEN
MOTEL

WAGON WHEEL
MOTEL

WEST OVAL
LAKE

OVAL LAKE TRAIL

BLACKPINE LAKE

POORMAN CR RD.

ALDER
CREEK RD.

LOOKOUT MT.

CARLTON

153

0   5 mi

0   5 km

METHOW

TO OKANOGAN

153

TO CHELAN

COLUMBIA
RIVER

PATEROS

97

97

© MOON PUBLICATIONS, INC.

being completed in the late 1960s, the citizens of Winthrop began looking for a way to pull themselves out of the doldrums. The successful transformation of nearby Leavenworth into a Bavarian theme town inspired locals to do their own makeover into a Hollywoodesque Old West town. A local benefactor, Kathryn Wagner, widow of a sawmill owner, put up matching funds, and Leavenworth architects brought in their design expertise. By the time the first carloads of tourists crossed Washington Pass in 1972, Winthrop had covered its concrete buildings with false fronts, laid down wooden sidewalks, and added Old West signs and hitching posts. Today the shops are crowded with trendy gear, trinkets, upscale foods, books, and, of course, espresso. Warning: Gas prices here are some of the highest in the state of Washington. Tank-up elsewhere!

Shafer Museum

Winthrop's Shafer Museum on Castle Ave., tel. (509) 996-2817, is housed in an 1897 log home (alias "The Castle") built by the town's founder, Guy Waring. Displays include pioneer farming and mining tools, bicycles, furniture, an impressive rifle collection, and other relics from the early days in the Methow Valley. Outside, you'll find a town's worth of buildings, including a general store, print shop, homestead cabin, schoolhouse, and assay office, plus old wagons, mining equipment, and aging farm implements. The 1923 Rickenbacker automobile here is one of just 80 still in existence. Shafer Museum is open daily 10 a.m.-5 p.m. late May to September, closed the rest of the year; donations appreciated.

Other Sights

Walk down Riverside ("Main Street") to find all sorts of Western shops, some with authentic items, most with junk. **White Buck Trading Co.,** tel. (509) 996-3500, is named for a big white buck displayed inside. It was shot in 1953. Also here are more stuffed critters and a collection of trivial items from the past, including—of all things—the first dial phone in Chicago. **Last Trading Post,** tel. (509) 996-2103, is packed with Old West Americana, from antiques to painted cattle skulls. Downstairs is a museum of sorts, with historic flotsam and jetsam, plus various Indian artifacts.

The Forest Service's **North Cascade Smokejumper Base,** tel. (509) 997-2031, halfway between Winthrop and Twisp along Hwy. 20, is open for tours daily 8 a.m.-5 p.m. during the fire season (June-Sept.). It was here in the fall of 1939 that the first experimental parachute jumps were held to determine the safety and effectiveness of reaching remote mountain forest fires from the air. The first fires were successfully attacked by smoke jumpers from this base the following summer. Today, the "birthplace of smoke jumping" has historical photos, but it is also a very active center during the peak of fire season and home to an elite group of firefighters. Other smoke jump bases are in Alaska, California, Idaho, and Oregon.

The **Winthrop National Fish Hatchery,** a mile south of town, raises 1.5 million spring chinook salmon and 750,000 trout annually in large, covered raceways. Open daily 7:30 a.m.-4:30 p.m.

Lodging

The "Methow Valley Lodging" chart shows Winthrop, Twisp, Mazama, and other Methow Valley accommodations. Visitors should reserve well ahead for summer weekends. Many of these lodging places are just southeast of Winthrop along the Methow River, and most of these are recently completed, sterile structures with little charm. If you plan to stay at one of the cross-country ski lodges over the hectic Christmas-New Year's holiday, you'll find some places full six months in advance. Contact **Methow Valley Central Reservations,** tel. (509) 996-2148 or (800) 422-3048, for reservations at most of the places on the chart or other vacation rental cabins, guesthouses, and apartments. They are open Mon.-Fri. 9 a.m.-5 p.m. **Central Reservations,** tel. (800) 445-1822, also makes local lodging reservations.

Mazama Country Inn, tel. (509) 996-2681 or (800) 843-7941, has comfortable guest rooms in a delightful country setting. Mountain bike or cross-country ski trails are accessible from the door of the inn, and they rent skis and offer ski lessons to get you started. During the winter, lodging includes three excellent meals.

Spring Creek Ranch, tel. (509) 996-2495, is another refurbished historic place with a picturesque setting. The antique-filled house is located in the middle of a big pasture with an old dairy barn and a mountain backdrop.

Atop a 5,000-foot peak with 360-degree views into the North Cascades and the Methow Valley is **Sun Mountain Lodge,** tel. (509) 996-2211 or (800) 572-0493, one of the premier destination resorts in Washington. Owned by the Haub family of Germany—who also own the A&P grocery chain—Sun Mountain has almost every amenity (for an extra charge): fly-fishing lessons, boat rentals, guided hikes, a big swimming pool, two jacuzzis, mountain bike rentals, tennis courts, cross-country ski trails, and the largest string of saddle horses in the region.

Campgrounds
Pearrygin Lake State Park, five miles north of Winthrop, has lakeside campsites that are open mid-April through October for $11 tents, $16 RVs. Call (509) 996-2370 for information, or (800) 452-5687 for campsite reservations ($6 extra fee), available up to 11 months ahead of time.

The Forest Service maintains a dozen campgrounds ($8) within 25 miles of Winthrop, and most other areas are open to free dispersed camping (with the exception of the Hwy. 20 corridor). Closest are the campgrounds up West Chewuch Rd.: **Falls Creek, Nice, Flat,** and **Buck Lake.** Falls Creek has the added attraction of a beautiful falls just a quarter mile hike away, while quiet Buck Lake has ducks and cattails. Three other often-full Forest Service campgrounds are west of Winthrop along Hwy. 20: **Early Winters, Klipchuck** (very quiet spot), and **Lone Fir.** Most of these campgrounds are open June-September. Get more information from the Winthrop Ranger District office.

Private RV parks include: **Big Twin Lake Campground,** tel. (509) 996-2650; **5-Y Resort,** tel. (509) 996-2448; **Derry's Resort,** tel. (509) 996-2322; **Methow KOA,** tel. (509) 996-2258; **Lost River Resort,** tel. (509) 996-2537; and **Pine Near RV Park,** tel. (509) 996-2391.

Food
For casual dining in a cluttered and funky atmosphere, downtown's **Duck Brand Hotel & Cantina,** tel. (509) 996-2192, serves outstanding, artfully presented, and moderately priced Mexican and American food. There's an outside deck for sunny days; be sure to ask about

lunch specials. Breakfasts are a real treat: huge piles of potatoes come with the meals, and monstrous cinnamon rolls sit temptingly on the bakery counter. Highly recommended.

Riverside Rib Company, downtown, tel. (509) 996-2444, is a casual bistro-style eatery with delicious barbecue chicken and ribs, burgers, and smoked sausages. Great desserts too. **The Virginian,** at the motel of the same name just south of Winthrop on Hwy. 20, tel. (509) 996-2536, serves steak, chicken, pasta, and other dinners. **Bombers Restaurant** in the bowling alley, has standard American fare and serves breakfast all day.

Coffee fiends will be pleased to note the presence of at least nine espresso spots in town (that's one for every 38 permanent residents!). One of the best of these is **Trail's End,** tel. (509) 996-2303. The shop is half-filled with books and VCR tapes (including some rather esoteric titles), while the other half features a deli offering sandwiches, salads, and espresso, along with great homemade soups, breads, and pies. **Mazama Store** in Mazama, tel. (509) 996-2855, another very good place for lunch, serves sandwiches, salads, pastas, and espresso.

The small **Winthrop Brewing Company,** tel. (509) 996-3174, has a riverside deck and beer garden. They usually have at least four freshly brewed ales on tap and a creative dinner menu, along with an outdoor barbecue in the summer.

For pizza, snacks, sandwiches, and ribs, the over-21 crowd will enjoy **3 Fingered Jack's Saloon,** also downtown. They serve an anytime breakfast, all-you-can-eat spaghetti feeds on Monday nights, and prime rib specials on Friday nights.

Sun Mountain Dining Room, in Sun Mountain Resort, tel. (509) 996-2211 or (800) 572-0493, is the most famous local restaurant and one of the few in the state to receive AAA's four-diamond rating. The menu leans toward Northwest cuisine and continental dishes, with stellar prices to match.

Events
If you're in town on summer Saturdays around 4 p.m., be ready for a **Wild West Medicine Show** and "gunfight" on the main street. The second weekend of May marks the start of Winthrop's festival season with **49ers Days,** featuring a

parade, dance, and baseball tournament. This is followed by Memorial Day weekend's popular **Winthrop Rodeo Days.** The **Methow Arts Festival** in early July includes a street fair and live music at the Winthrop Barn.

The **River Rat Race** begins in Winthrop on the Fourth of July weekend and includes a 12-mile race on the Methow River on rafts, inner tubes, and canoes. The four-day long **Winthrop Rhythm and Blues Festival** in mid-July is fast becoming a major event, with past performances by such stars as Bo Diddley, John Hammond, and J.J. Kale. (And if you like the blues, be sure to tune in to the unique "Methow Community Radio," KVLR at 106.3 FM.)

Summer ends the way it begins, with a big rodeo for **Labor Day Weekend.** The **Antique Auto Rally** in mid-September features more than 60 old vehicles and is followed in early October by the **Methow Valley Mountain Bike Festival,** which brings over 500 participants for races, hill climbs, and group rides.

Entertainment
Both **The Winthrop Palace** and **3-Fingered Jack's Saloon** usually have rock or R&B bands on summer weekends. **Winthrop Brewing Company,** tel. (509) 996-3174, has Friday night jam sessions.

Mountain Biking
Winthrop is fast becoming a summer Mecca for cyclists—an incredible range of trails and country roads spreads through the valley and into the surrounding mountains. There are routes for every ability level. Pick up maps and descriptions of local routes at the Forest Service visitor center. Mountain bikes can be rented at the **Mazama Store,** tel. (509) 996-2855, for $25 per day. Call the nonprofit **Methow Valley Sports Trail Association** at (800) 682-5787 for information on more than a hundred miles of mountain biking and hiking trails in the area; these become cross-country ski paths when winter rolls around.

River Rafting
The Methow River is a favorite of whitewater enthusiasts, with many access points and a wide range of conditions, from easy float trips to class III-IV whitewater. Rafters generally float the river from early May till early July, when the river is running hard from spring runoff but the air is warm and dry. The sections below Winthrop grow progressively more difficult as you follow the Methow to the Columbia, 17 miles down river. Black Canyon is the pinnacle, with rollercoaster waves and wild action as the river plunges through dozens of rapids.

Expect to pay $45-75 for day trips, more for the overnight adventures offered by several companies. Wetsuits can be rented from most companies. **Osprey Rafting** in Twisp, tel. (509) 997-4116 or (800) 743-6269, is the only local company doing river trips on the Methow. Other companies offering float and whitewater trips down the Methow River are: **All Rivers Adventures,** tel. (800) 743-5628; **Alpine Adventures,** tel. (800) 926-7238; **Blue Sky Outfitters,** tel. (800) 228-7238; **Cascade Adventures,** tel. (800) 723-8386; **Downstream River Runners,** tel. (800) 234-4644; **Four Seasons Outfitters,** tel. (800) 642-7334; **North Cascades River Expeditions,** tel. (800) 634-8433; **Northern Wilderness River Riders,** tel. (800) 448-7238; **Orion Expeditions,** tel. (800) 553-7466; **River Recreation,** tel. (800) 464-5899; **Rivers Incorporated,** tel. (206) 822-5296; **Wild & Scenic River Tours,** tel. (206) 323-1220; and **Wildwater River Tours,** tel. (800) 522-9453.

Other Summer Activities
A multitude of hiking trails surround the Methow Valley; see above for "Liberty Bell Roadless Area," "Harts Pass Area," and "Pasayten Wilderness Area" for a small sampling of these. **Early Winters Outfitters** in Mazama, tel. (509) 996-2659 or (800) 843-7951, has horseback rides ($15 for one hour, $45 for half-day) as well as longer pack trips into the nearby Pasayten Wilderness. **Chewack River Riding Stables,** six miles north of town, tel. (509) 996-2497, also offers horseback rides ($18 for a half-day) and overnight campouts ($110 with dinner and breakfast).

The 578-acre **Pearrygin Lake State Park,** five miles north of Winthrop, offers a sandy beach for swimming, plus fishing, camping, a boat launch, store, and boat rentals. This small spring-fed, glacially carved lake is a delightful break from the dry summer hills of sage and pine that surround it.

Winthrop's **Bear Creek Golf Course,** tel. (509) 996-2284, is a nine-hole course.

Cross-Country Skiing

In winter, the valley often has two or three feet of snow on the ground, and the major outdoor recreation changes from hiking, biking, and river-running to cross-country skiing. The nonprofit **Methow Valley Sports Trail Association** (MVSTA) maintains three sets of interconnected cross-country ski trails throughout the valley. They groom more than 175 km of trails—second longest in America—setting tracks for both classical and skate skis. Fees are $10 for one day or $25 for three days. Call MVSTA at (800) 682-5787 for info on current ski conditions, or get trail maps and ski passes from Winthrop Mountain Sports, tel. (509) 996-2886 or (800) 719-3826.

The MVSTA's ski trail systems connect to several local lodges, making it possible to walk outside and ski right from your door. These places include Sun Mountain Resort, Mazama Country Inn, The Virginian Resort, Winthrop Mountain View Chalets, WolfRidge Resort, Browns Farm Resort, Early Winters Cabins, and North Cascade Base Camp. A public warming hut is located at WolfRidge Resort, and several of the lodges welcome skiers with hot drinks.

Backcountry skiers will be very interested in the hut-to-hut skiing opportunities on the MVSTA-maintained Rendezvous Trail system. A series of five fully equipped cabins (each sleeps eight; $25 per person per night) are located six to eight km apart in the mountains north of Winthrop. Call **Rendezvous Outfitters,** tel. (509) 996-2148 or (800) 422-3048, for details. Also available is a wonderful remote cabin in 6,500-foot Panther Basin (generally accessed by helicopter) where you can really get away from it all.

Ski shops are located at Sun Mountain Re-sort, tel. (509) 996-2211 or (800) 572-0493; **Mazama Country Inn,** tel. (509) 996-2681 or (800) 843-7951; and **Winthrop Mountain Sports,** tel. (509) 996-2886 or (800) 719-3826.

Downhill Skiing

The nearest place for alpine skiers and snowboarders is **Loup Loup Ski Bowl,** tel. (509) 826-2720, a small family place 12 miles east of Twisp on Hwy. 20. Loup Loup has two Poma lifts, a rope tow, and a vertical drop of 1,240 feet. Shredders will have fun on the half-pipe. Ski lessons, rentals, and groomed cross-country tracks are here, along with a snack bar. Lift rates are $16 on Sunday, Wednesday, and Saturday, and just $10 on Friday.

For those with the bucks ($420 per day), **North Cascade Heli-Skiing,** tel. (509) 996-3272 or (800) 494-4354, will take downhillers into untracked powder, or provide drop-offs for backcountry telemark skiers.

Other Winter Sports

Malamute Express, tel. (509) 997-6402, has drive-your-own-team dogsled rides in the Twisp River area. Public **ice skating** ponds are available at Sun Mountain Resort and North Cascade Base Camp. Mazama Country Inn offers hour-long sleigh rides for $10; for details, call (509) 996-2681 or (800) 843-7951.

Information and Services

Local information is available at several Winthrop locales. The downtown **Chamber of Commerce Information Station,** tel. (509) 996-2125, is open daily 10 a.m.-5 p.m. from mid-April through October, and weekends 11 a.m.-4 p.m. in the winter.

The **Methow Valley Visitors Center** is just west of town along Hwy. 20, tel. (509) 996-3194. It's open daily 9 a.m.-5 p.m. from mid-April to mid-October, and Fri.-Sun. 9 a.m.-5 p.m. the rest of the year, and is staffed by locals and Forest Service employees. Purchase booklets on mountain biking, scenic drives, and day hikes here. You can also stop by the **Winthrop Ranger Station** on W. Chewuch Rd., tel. (509) 996-2266 for detailed recreation info, including a list of outfitters that provide horse trips into the backcountry. It's open Mon.-Fri. 7:45 a.m.-5 p.m., and summers-only Saturday 8:30 a.m.-5 p.m.

The telephone **area code** for Winthrop—and all of eastern Washington—is 509.

Transportation

The Methow Valley has no bus service of any kind, and there is no scheduled air service; the nearest commercial airport with service is in Wenatchee. **Winthrop Flight Service,** tel. (509) 997-6962, has charter flights and flightseeing trips.

TWISP

Twisp (pop. 900) offers quite a contrast to nearby Winthrop. Although espresso is available at several shops (including a drive-through), the town doesn't pretend to be anything other than a minor ranching and logging center. The name Twisp is believed to have originated from an Indian word, "Twasp-tsp," an onomatopoetic sound based upon the noise made by yellow jacket wasps.

History

Established in 1898, Twisp grew up on a diet of precious metals from the now-defunct Alder Mine, but then suffered through a string of disasters. A devastating 1924 fire destroyed all but a few of the town's buildings, and a 1948 flood rampaged through, carrying more buildings downstream. This was followed in 1968 by a bitter freeze (temperatures dropped to -48° F!) that wiped out local apple orchards.

Accommodations

See the "Methow Valley Lodging" chart for a list of Twisp accommodations. The attractively restored old **Methow Valley Inn B&B**, tel. (509) 997-3014 or (800) 261-4619, in Twisp is one of the few structures to survive the fire of 1924. It's a friendly and homey place, and guests are served a full country breakfast.

Campgrounds

A half-dozen Forest Service campgrounds are west of town out Twisp River Road. Closest is **War Creek Campground**, 15 miles out, $7; open late May to early September. RV parking is available at **River Bend RV Park**, two miles north of Twisp on Hwy. 20, tel. (509) 997-3500.

Hiking

To visit a working fire tower with mountain vistas in all directions, take the Alder Creek Rd. southwest from Twisp to Lookout Mountain. At the end of the road a trail leads 1.3 miles to **Lookout Mountain Lookout.**

Twisp River Rd., west of town, provides access to the north side of the 145,667-acre **Lake Chelan-Sawtooth Wilderness**, with a dozen different paths taking off from the valley. A fine loop trip of approximately 15 miles begins just southwest of War Creek Campground on Forest Rd. 4420. The **Eagle Creek Trail** starts at an elevation of 3,000 feet and climbs steadily through Douglas fir forests and meadows, reaching 7,280-foot Eagle Pass after seven miles. Here it meets the **Summit Trail,** with connections to the Stehekin end of Lake Chelan (see "Chelan and Vicinity," below), or to other points in the wilderness. To continue the loop hike, follow it south a mile to **Oval Creek Trail.** This path leads back down to the trailhead, passing beautiful West Oval Lake on the way; a two-mile detour climbs to two additional cirque lakes.

Food

Queen of Tarts Cafe, tel. (509) 997-1335, makes the finest local breakfasts and lunches. Come here to taste the sandwiches, salads, and made-from-scratch soups. Next door is the **Confluence Art Gallery,** which displays changing exhibits of local artists. Two best-in-the-valley eateries are **Wagon Wheel,** three miles west of Twisp, with outstanding burgers and shakes, and **Hometown Pizza,** tel. (509) 997-2100.

Cinnamon Twisp Bakery has fresh breads and healthy foods. Get organic produce at **Glover Street Market,** or come to town on Saturday mornings between May and October for Twisp's **Farmers Market.**

Events

The annual **Freeze Yer Buns Run** takes place in late January and features a 10-km run with a Hawaiian vacation to the winner. The **Lou Tice Ranch** in Twisp attracts big name country music acts for concerts each September.

Information and Services

The **visitor information center,** downtown in the library building, is open Mon.-Fri. 8 a.m.-noon and 1-5 p.m. Behind here is a pseudo-totem pole. The Forest Service's **Twisp Ranger District** office is at 502 Glover St., tel. (509) 997-2131. It is open Mon.-Fri. 7:45 a.m.-5 p.m. all year, plus Saturday 8 a.m.-5 p.m. in the summer.

Twisp has an outdoor **swimming pool** on the northeast edge of town; open mid-June to Labor Day. The **area code** for Twisp—and all of eastern Washington—is 509.

METHOW AND PATEROS

Scenic Drives

East of Twisp the highway splits; Hwy. 20 continues east to Okanogan and Omak, and Hwy. 153 turns south along the Methow River. Highway 20 offers a chance to cruise past old farms and ranches with aging wooden barns, horses grazing in the pastures, and hay piles draped with sky-blue tarps. The road then climbs into Ponderosa pine forests with openings of sage, before topping out in the western larch forests of Okanogan National Forest. These larch trees are especially pretty in the fall when the needles turn a vivid yellow. Near the summit of Loup Loup Pass is Loup Loup Ski Bowl (described above under "Downhill Skiing").

Highway 153 is another gorgeous drive, with the cottonwood-lined Methow River bottom surrounded by ranches, and rolling hills covered with sage and Ponderosa and lodgepole pines. It leads to the small towns of Methow and Pateros.

Methow

There isn't much to the settlement of Methow, 21 miles south of Twisp on Hwy. 153. The exception is **Cafe Bienville,** tel. (509) 923-2228, where the food is a huge surprise: outstanding New Orleans-inspired dishes, along with traditional French meals at this country cafe.

Pateros

Five miles south of Methow, at the junction of Highways 97 and 153, is Pateros (pop. 600). The town has more to it, including popular Alta Lake State Park, and access to the Lake Pateros (the dammed up Columbia River). Pateros was moved here during construction of Wells Dam, just a few miles downstream on the Columbia. The landscape near here is crowded with fruit orchards and apple processing plants. For a taste, stop at **Rest Awhile Fruit Stand,** along Hwy. 153 just north of town. Pateros itself consists of a few stores and a pretty waterfront park; it's a popular place to stop and fish or play in the reservoir. Be sure to look up into the hills above town to one of the state's more unusual art installations—15,000 circular reflectors covering two old water towers.

Accommodations

Stay at **Amy's Manor B&B,** five miles north of Pateros on Hwy. 153, tel. (509) 923-2334, a charming 170-acre estate overlooking the Methow River and featuring four guest rooms, a fireplace, basketball and tennis courts, and a small farm with goats, chickens, rabbits, and cows. Rooms are $45 s, $55 d, with a light breakfast. No kids under 12.

Lodging is also available at modern **Los Pateros Motor Inn,** tel. (509) 923-2203 or (800) 444-1985, for $52 s, $56 d. The motel has an outdoor pool and dock on Lake Pateros. **Alta Lake Resort,** two miles from Pateros, tel. (509) 923-2359, has rooms with kitchenettes, an outdoor pool, and more, adjacent to an 18-hole golf course. Rooms are $45-65 s or d.

Whistlin' Pine Resort, off Hwy. 153 on the south end of Alta Lake, tel. (509) 923-2548, has summer-only accommodations ranging from tent spaces to deluxe cabins, and entertainment from boating to windsurfing to pack trips. Camp for $13 a night in a tent space, stay in rustic small cabins for $30, or in tent cabins for $40 s or d.

Recreation and Campgrounds

Right in the town of Pateros is Peninsula Park, a verdant green stretch along Lake Pateros. Here are picnic areas, swimming, water skiing, RV parking ($5), and coin-operated showers. Sprinklers keep tenters away.

Popular with the summer crowd is **Alta Lake State Park,** two miles southwest of Pateros off Hwy. 153. Fish for rainbow trout, swim in the clear waters, or just enjoy the east-of-the-mountains sunshine. A mile-long trail takes you 900 feet higher to a scenic plateau overlooking the Columbia River Valley. The campground has both tent sites ($10) and RV hookups ($15) and is open April-Oct., and on weekends and holidays the rest of the year. In winter, the park is a favorite of cross-country skiers and snowmobilers. Call (800) 452-5687 for campsite reservations ($6 extra fee), available up to 11 months ahead of time.

Events

The popular and tasty **Apple Pie Jamboree**

hits Pateros the third weekend of July and includes outboard hydroplane races, a parade, street dance, arts and crafts fair, and fireworks. But people really come for the big pie feed, featuring over 500 volunteer-baked apple pies and homemade ice cream.

The seven-liter **Hydroplane Races** in mid-August are a big Pateros attraction, with boats topping 150 mph.

South to Chelan

Highway 97 south from Pateros is a busy thoroughfare paralleling the reservoir all the way to Chelan, 17 miles away. **Wells Dam,** seven miles south of Pateros, has a vista viewpoint where you can look across the blue lake to the surrounding rocky, arid landscape of grass and sage. The visitors center here is open daily 8 a.m.-6 p.m. and includes a fish-viewing area and salmon hatchery.

CHELAN AND VICINITY

Lake Chelan (sha-LAN) occupies a long, glacially carved valley on the eastern edge of the Cascades. The town of Chelan (pop. 3,200) sits on the southeast shore of the lake; Manson is seven miles northwest, and tiny Stehekin 55 miles away on the north shore. Stehekin is the only town on the Washington mainland that cannot be reached by road.

Lake Chelan is one of Washington's favorite summer playgrounds, offering resort accommodations, fine restaurants, waterskiing, swimming, and boating, but also delivering magnificent wilderness country just a boat ride away. Over the years the Chelan area has developed into a resort community that has—so far—managed to retain its small-town charm. It's still a genuine town with real orchardists, farmers, wilderness outfitters, and forest and park rangers standing in line with you in the grocery checkout line. Your children can meet and play with the children of residents and visitors from all over the world. Few other small towns in Washington have such a wide cross-section of people.

The summer of 1994 will long be remembered by the residents of Chelan. Many were forced to evacuate when the massive Tyee Creek Fire headed north toward town. Fortunately, it was halted before reaching Chelan; see the special topic "Firestorm in the Cascades" for more on this blaze.

The vast majority of the Lake Chelan watershed is in public ownership and not open to major development (unless Newt Gingrich gets elected president), but such is not the case on the privately held portions. Here, the lake's popularity may prove its undoing. Tacky developments of all sorts are packing the shoreline between Chelan and Manson, as timeshare condos, elaborate resorts, ranch-style homes, retirement villas, and summer cottages crowd up the hillsides and through the apple orchards. The first orchard in the area—at Wapato Point—is now the site of the elaborate Wapato Point Resort. The area is still magnificent, but one wonders how long till all the orchards are replaced by urban sprawl, and the pristine lakeshore becomes just another housing development.

Climate

These statistics will tell you why Chelan is so popular in Puget Sound: an average of only 24 days per year register temperatures below 32°, and 33 days are above 90°. Rainfall occurs less than nine days in an average year, and snow, sleet, or hail in excess of 1 inch falls on 31 days per year. The lake never freezes. The most telling statistic is this: although no official records are kept on the number of sunny days, it is roughly 300 days per year.

The Lake

Ice Age glaciers carved the deep trough that forms Lake Chelan. At its deepest point, the glacier- and stream-fed lake dips down 1,486 feet, or 450 feet below sea level. The only two deeper lakes in America are Oregon's Crater Lake (1,962 feet) and California and Nevada's Lake Tahoe (1,645 feet). Lake Chelan is 55 miles long, but seldom more than two miles wide. A dam built here in 1927 to increase electrical production raised the lake's level by 24 feet and increased its length by a mile. Water flows from the dam through a tunnel to a power plant at Chelan Falls, four miles away and 390 feet lower. Because of this hydroelectric proj-

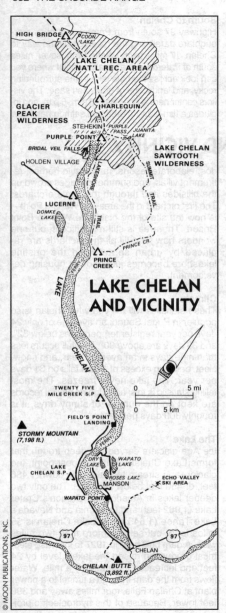

LAKE CHELAN AND VICINITY

HIGH BRIDGE
RACOON 'LAKE'
LAKE CHELAN NAT'L REC. AREA
HARLEQUIN
GLACIER PEAK WILDERNESS
STEHEKIN
PURPLE PASS
JUANITA LAKE
PURPLE POINT
BRIDAL VEIL FALLS
HOLDEN VILLAGE
LAKE CHELAN SAWTOOTH WILDERNESS
SUMMIT TRAIL
LAKESHORE TRAIL
LUCERNE
DOMKE LAKE
PRINCE CR.
PRINCE CREEK
LAKE CHELAN
TWENTY FIVE MILE CREEK S.P.
FIELD'S POINT LANDING
STORMY MOUNTAIN (7,198 ft.)
LAKE CHELAN S.P.
FERRY
DRY LAKE
WAPATO LAKE
ROSES LAKE
MANSON
ECHO VALLEY SKI AREA
WAPATO POINT
STORMY MOUNTAIN
CHELAN BUTTE (3,892 ft.)
CHELAN
97
0   5 mi
0   5 km

© MOON PUBLICATIONS, INC.

ect, the gorge cut by the Chelan River is now dry much of the year, and the lake level fluctuates 10-18 feet through the season.

Apple Land

Most visitors to Lake Chelan tend to think of it in terms of recreational opportunities, but in agricultural circles, the shores of the lake are much better known for something else: the finest apples in the world. This isn't a slogan created by the local community; Chelan apples are known all over the world for their excellent taste, long shelf life, and vivid colors.

Gross income from the apple industry is in the $100 million-per-year range, and upwards of 10,000 acres are devoted to apple orchards. Most of these are relatively small, averaging 30 acres or less. Annual production is in the range of 8 million boxes. The most popular apples are red delicious and golden delicious, followed by the reddish-yellow galas and the pinkish-red fujis, an apple developed in Japan.

Nobody is quite sure why Chelan apples are so much better than those grown only a few miles away. Some believe it is due to the soil, which was created by the retreating glaciers that carved the valley. Also, the lake helps moderate the air temperature, keeping the valley above freezing during most of the winter, and cooling things down in the summer. This keeps the apples from being damaged by the heat, helping create a crisper and juicier apple that remains fresh longer in storage. Some also believe that the lake water used to irrigate the orchards contributes to the quality because it is colder than irrigation water used elsewhere.

Although apples are the major crop grown around the lake, some soft fruits are also grown. Scattered among the apple orchards are smaller plots of cherries, pears, apricots, and peaches.

SIGHTS

In Town

Visit the **Lake Chelan Museum** at Woodin Ave. and Emerson St. in Chelan, tel. (509) 687-3470, to see displays of pioneer and Native American relics, and a big collection of colorful applebox labels. Open Mon.-Sat. 1-4 p.m. June-Sept., and by appointment the rest of the year; no charge.

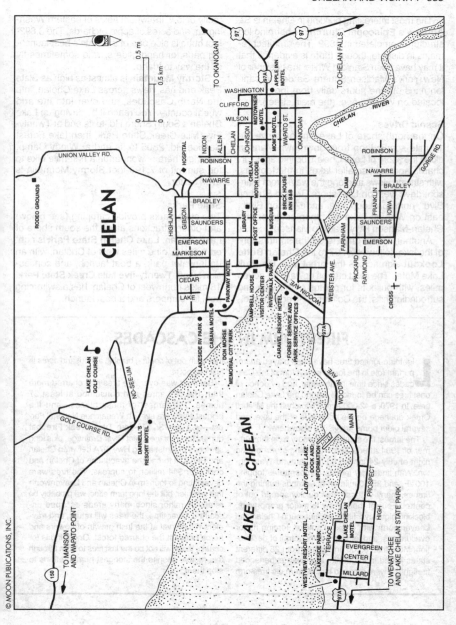

© MOON PUBLICATIONS, INC.

CHELAN

LAKE CHELAN

TO OKANOGAN

TO CHELAN FALLS

CHELAN RIVER

UNION VALLEY RD.

RODEO GROUNDS

HOSPITAL

HIGHLAND

GIBSON

NAVARRE

BRADLEY

SAUNDERS

EMERSON

MARKESON

CEDAR

LAKE

NIXON

ALLEN

CHELAN

ROBINSON

JOHNSON

CLIFFORD

WILSON

WASHINGTON

WAPATO ST.

OKANOGAN

DAM

ROBINSON

NAVARRE

BRADLEY

FRANKLIN

IOWA

SAUNDERS

EMERSON

FARNHAM

PACKARD

RAYMOND

CROSS

GORGE RD.

WEBSTER AVE.

WOODIN AVE.

LAKE CHELAN GOLF COURSE

NO-SEE-UM

GOLF COURSE RD.

DARNELL'S RESORT MOTEL

LAKESIDE RV PARK

CABANA MOTEL

DON MORSE MEMORIAL CITY PARK

PARKWAY MOTEL

CAMPBELL HOUSE

VISITOR CENTER

RIVERWALK PARK

CARAVEL RESORT MOTEL

FOREST SERVICE AND PARK SERVICE OFFICES

Lady of the Lake DOCK AND INFORMATION

LIBRARY

POST OFFICE

MUSEUM

CHELAN MOTOR LODGE

MON'S MOTEL

MIDTOWNER MOTEL

APPLE INN MOTEL

BRICK HOUSE INN B&B

WOODIN AVE.

MAIN

PROSPECT

HIGH

EVERGREEN

CENTER

MILLARD

WESTVIEW RESORT MOTEL

LAKESIDE PARK

TERRACE

LAKE CHELAN MOTEL

TO MANSON AND WAPATO POINT

TO WENATCHEE AND LAKE CHELAN STATE PARK

0   0.5 mi

0   0.5 km

The most interesting building in Chelan is **St. Andrew's Episcopal Church,** a charming log structure completed in 1899. The architect remains in dispute, though there is evidence that it may have been Stanford White, the designer of New York's Madison Square Garden. A carillon rings out the hours daily from the church, located on Woodin Ave. (the main street).

Scenic Drives

On the north shore of Lake Chelan, drive the 12-mile scenic loop from downtown Manson along the shore of Lake Chelan, up into apple orchards and past smaller lakes in the foothills, with striking views all along the way. From Manson, drive west on Lakeshore Dr. and Summit Blvd., north on Loop Ave. and Manson Blvd., east on Wapato Lake Rd., then south on the Chelan-Manson Hwy. back to Manson.

Another scenic drive is on the south shore of the lake; follow Hwy. 97 to the **Chelan Butte Lookout** sign across the street from the Park Lake Motel. The road curves upward for seven miles, with pullouts for photos of the lake and surrounding hills, the Columbia River almost directly below, the wheat fields of eastern Washington, and acres of apple orchards. The 3,892-foot butte is also one of the state's best launching pads for hang gliders, who sometimes fly all the way to Idaho.

Stormy Mountain is almost as high as Slate Peak and has views across Lake Chelan, into the North Cascades, and over into the arid wheat country. You reach it by driving up Lake Chelan's South Shore Rd. to its end at Twenty-Five Mile Creek State Park, then take Forest Service Rd. 2805 to its end at Windy Camp. The view here is wonderful; a half-mile hike to the summit of 7,198-foot Stormy Mountain is even better.

State Parks

Two state parks provide camping (see below) and other attractions along the south shore of Lake Chelan. **Lake Chelan State Park** is right on the lake, nine miles west of Chelan, with an underwater park, a boat launch, and concession stand. **Twenty-five Mile Creek State Park,** 18 miles northwest of Chelan, has a swimming pool for campers and a boat launch.

FIRESTORM IN THE CASCADES

Lightning-ignited fires have been played an important role in the forest ecosystem of the Cascades since time immemorial, and evidence of past fires can be found all around the Lake Chelan area. In 1970, a 42,000-acre fire torched the Mitchell Creek drainage on the north side of the lake, and several older burns are visible elsewhere.

The largest fire season in memory hit in the summer of 1994 after a fierce lightning storm on the night of July 24 ignited 99 fires around Washington. With tinder-dry forests, temperatures topping 100° F, and 35-50 mile-an-hour winds fanning the flames, many of these fires quickly spread out of control. Four of them grew to major proportions, blocking highways, filling the air around Chelan and Leavenworth with choking smoke, forcing major evacuations, and leaving behind a trail of destruction. More than 8,000 firefighters from 25 different states joined in the battle, and even experienced firefighters were amazed by the dramatic firestorm that spun out of control, burning a thousand acres in just two hours.

Before it was over, the fires had charred more than 180,000 acres and consumed at least 37 homes. The largest of these blazes—and the biggest single fire ever on Wenatchee National Forest—was the 135,170-acre **Tyee Creek Fire** that burned much of the Entiat River Drainage, plus long stretches of forest along Hwy. 97A between Chelan and Entiat. It forced the evacuation of Chelan and cost over $44 million to supress. The fires were devastating to tourism in Chelan and Leavenworth that summer, but the long term effect will probably be relatively minor since many areas escaped unscathed. Over time, the trees will return, and travelers will marvel at the lush growth of flowers and herbs beneath the charred forest. One thing is for certain, these will not be the last fires to burn through this region, despite the stongest human efforts to stop them.

Apple Tours

Chelan's apple warehouses offer free guided tours. Scheduled tours are offered by **Trout/ Blue Chelan,** tel. (509) 682-4541, on Wednesday at 1:15 and 2:15 p.m., March-August. Tours of the warehouse and fruit packing shed are available Nov.-July. Also try **Beebe Orchard Company,** tel. (509) 682-2526, for tours. Their huge apple processing facilities are just southeast of town on the road to Chelan Falls. **Sunshine Fruit Market,** just west of town at the junction of Hwy. 97A and South Lakeshore, tel. (509) 682-5695, has a roadside fruit stand open daily in the summer.

ACCOMMODATIONS

See the "Lake Chelan Area Accommodations" chart for a complete listing of places to stay in the area. Make mid-summer reservations as early as possible; many of the rooms book up six months ahead of time for weekends in July and August. Winter rates are often 30% lower than the listed summer rates. In addition to the places listed, the Chelan area has many private vacation homes available; see the Lake Chelan Chamber of Commerce for a complete list. Stehekin lodging places are described separately below.

Bed and Breakfasts

The **Brick House Inn,** tel. (509) 682-4791, is a turn-of-the-century home with four bedrooms and two baths, a porch, kitchen, and a TV in the lounge. Relax in Victorian splendor at the romantic **Mary Kay's Whaley Mansion,** tel. (509) 682-5735 or (800) 729-2408, a 1911 frame house that has been restored with French wallpaper, custom carpeting, and elegant draperies, plus modern conveniences such as private baths. **Highland Guest House,** tel. (509) 682-2892 or (800) 681-2892, is one of Chelan's oldest homes, with a distinctively Victorian design, a wraparound porch, and commanding views of the town and valley. Out in Manson, **Proctor House Inn,** tel. (509) 687-6361 or (800) 441-1233, is a modern three-level home in a country setting. Another modern place with lakeshore views, hospitable owners, and an outside hot tub is **Captain's Quarters,** tel (509) 682-5886.

Holden Village B&B, tel. (509) 687-9695, is a newer home surrounded by eight acres of land with mountain and lake vistas. It's on S. Lakeshore Dr. 25 miles west of Chelan near Twenty-Five Mile State Park, and is associated with the Lutheran Church retreat at the old copper mining town of Holden (accessible only by boat). Holden Village itself is a beautiful and comfortable out-of-the-way place with an ecumenical atmosphere; call (509) 687-3644 for more information.

Resorts

The oldest and best-established resort on the lake, **Campbell's Resort,** tel. (509) 682-2561 or (800) 553-8225, is right in town and offers 150 rooms, plus heated pools, hot tubs, boat moorage, and a 1,200-foot sandy beach. Campbell's is also a popular convention facility for groups up to 250. **Darnell's Resort Motel,** tel. (509) 682-2015 or (800) 967-8149, features luxury family accommodations with a heated pool, hot tub, sauna, exercise room, lighted tennis courts, putting greens, rowboats, bicycles, moorage, kids' play area—you name it. The **Westview Resort Hotel,** tel. (509) 682-4396 or (800) 468-2781, is around the bend from the main part of town and features views back across the lake to Chelan and the Cascades. **Kelly's Resort,** tel. (509) 687-3220, is a friendly family resort 13 miles from Chelan with shoreside cottages, kitchens, fireplaces, boat moorage, and lake swimming.

Condos

The Chelan and Manson areas have many condo units for rent by the day or week. Some of these, such as Peterson's, are massive shoreside developments with dozens of units. For specifics, contact one of the following companies: **B.J. Enterprise,** tel. (509) 682-4011 or (800) 356-9756; **Chelan Land Vacation Rentals,** tel. (509) 682-4134; **Lake Chelan Shores Resort,** tel. (509) 682-4575; **Peterson's Waterfront,** tel. (509) 682-4002; and **Wapato Point Development Corp.,** tel. (509) 687-9511.

Campgrounds

Right in town, the **City of Chelan Lakeside RV Park,** tel. (509) 682-5031, has both tent sites ($18) and RV spaces ($20), along with showers,

LAKE CHELAN AREA ACCOMMODATIONS

Accommodations are arranged from least to most expensive. See the text for Stehekin area lodges. Rates may be lower during the winter months and on summer weekdays. The area code is 509.

BED AND BREAKFASTS

Holden Village B&B; 25 miles west of Chelan; tel. 687-9695; $33 s, $45 d in private room, $19 pp in dorm accommodations; quiet setting, mountain and lake views, full breakfast

Brick House Inn; Wapato and Saunders Streets; tel. 682-4791; $55-65 s, $65-85 d; turn-of-the-century home, four guest rooms, shared baths, wraparound porch, continental breakfast

Apple Country B&B; 5220 Manson Blvd., Manson; tel. 687-3982; $60 s, $65 d; country home, full breakfast, two guest rooms, shared bath, no kids, open May-September

Captain's Quarters; 283 Minneapolis Beach Rd. (five miles west of Chelan); tel. 682-5886; $80-90 s, $85-95 d; three guest rooms, shared or private bath, hot tub, deck with lake views, full breakfast

Highland Guest House; 121 E. Highland; tel. 682-2892 or (800) 681-2892; $75-95 s or d; classic 1902 Victorian home, antiques, wraparound porch, great views, three guest rooms, one with private bath

Hubbard House B&B; 911 Wapato Way, Manson; tel. 687-3058; $75-95 s or d; three guest rooms, shared bath, private lake access, big continental breakfast, open Memorial Day-October

Silver Bay Inn at Stehekin; Stehekin; tel. 682-2212; $75-120 in lakeside cabins; open year-round, full breakfast, beautiful views, five night minimum stay in summer, no kids under eight

Proctor House Inn B&B; 495 Lloyd Rd., Manson; tel. 687-6361 or (800) 441-1233; $85-115 s or d; six guest rooms, some with private baths, decks, full breakfast, impressive vistas, no kids

Mary Kay's Whaley Mansion Inn; 415 3rd St.; tel. 682-5735 or (800) 729-2408; $115-125 s or d; 1911 Victorian mansion, 11 guest rooms, private baths, gourmet breakfast, AAA approved

MOTELS, RESORTS, AND LODGES

Lake Chelan Motel; 2044 W. Woodin Ave.; tel. 682-2742; $50 s or d; outdoor pool

Parkway Motel; 402 N. Manson Rd.; tel. 682-2822; $35 s, $40 d; kitchenettes available $60 d, quiet, attractive, and clean

Mom's Montlake Motel; 823 Wapato St.; tel. 682-5715; $48-58 s or d; friendly and clean, kitchenettes available, quiet location

Apple Inn Motel; 1002 E. Woodin Ave.; tel. 682-4044; $49-59 s or d; jacuzzi, outdoor pool, indoor jacuzzi, kitchenettes available, AAA approved

Chelan Country Lodge; 531 E. Woodin Ave.; tel. 682-8474 or (800) 373-8474; $49 s, $75 d; beautifully restored century-old home

Midtowner Motel; 721 E. Woodin Ave.; tel. 682-4051; $50 s, $55 d; outdoor pool, sauna, jacuzzi, kitchenettes available

Stehekin Valley Ranch; Stehekin; tel. 682-4677; $55 pp with three meals in rustic tent-cabins; shared bath, no TV or phones

North Cascades Lodge; Stehekin; tel. 682-4494; $69-95 s or d; open year-round, bicycles, boats, and snowshoes for rent, kitchenettes available, no TV or phones

Cabana Motel; 420 Manson Rd.; tel. 682-2233; $63-78 s or d; outdoor pool, kitchenettes available

Traveler's Motel; 204 E. Wapato; tel. 682-4215; $69 s or d; shared baths

Mountain View Lodge; 25 Wapato Point Parkway, Manson; tel. 687-9505 or (800) 967-8105; $75 s or d; outdoor pool, jacuzzi, good view, free airport shuttle, AAA approved

Kelly's Resort; 13 miles west of Chelan on South Shore Rd.; tel. 687-3220; $75 s or d for cottages in the woods, $110-120 s or d for lakeside units; kitchenettes available, fireplaces, private beach, comfortable family place

Darnell's Resort Motel; 901 Spader Bay Rd.; tel. 682-2015 or (800) 967-8149; $75-145 s or d; outdoor pool, jacuzzi, sauna, exercise room, tennis courts, bicycles, putting green, canoes, private beach, kitchenettes available

Caravel Resort Motel; 322 W. Woodin Ave.; tel. 682-2582 or (800) 962-8723; $92-125 s or d; outdoor pool, jacuzzi, fireplaces, impersonal place, AAA approved

Westview Resort Hotel; 2312 W. Woodin Ave.; tel. 682-4396 or (800) 468-2781; $98 s or d, outdoor pool, jacuzzi, kitchenettes available, decks with lake views, AAA approved

Campbell's Resort; 104 W. Woodin Ave.; tel. 682-2561 or (800) 553-8225; $98 s, $114 d; two outdoor pools, two jacuzzis, private beach, kitchenettes available, AAA approved

Watson's Harverene Resort; 10 miles west near Lake Chelan State Park; tel. 687-3720 or (800) 687-3720; $130 for beachfront cottages (sleep four); family resort, outdoor pool, jacuzzi, kitchenettes available, yacht rides, no TV or phones

---

public swimming, and picnic areas. Rates are lower in the off-season; open all year.

Lake Chelan State Park, tel. (509) 687-3710, is 12 miles up-lake from Chelan along the south shore and offers swimming, tent sites ($11), and RV sites ($16). Call (509) 687-3710 for information, or (800) 452-5687 for campsite reservations ($6 extra fee), available up to 11 months ahead of time. The park is open daily April-Oct., and on weekends and holidays the rest of the year. This is the largest and most popular park in the area, with a swimming beach, boat ramp, docks, and summertime campfire programs.

Twenty-Five Mile Creek State Park, tel. (509) 687-3710, open May-Sept., has tent sites for $11 and RV hookups for $16. Call (800) 452-5687 for campsite reservations ($6 extra fee), available up to 11 months ahead of time. This pleasant, wooded park is 22 miles west of Chelan at the end of S. Lakeshore Dr., and 10 miles beyond Lake Chelan State Park. It's a favorite place for boaters who use the launch ramp here and purchase supplies at the marina store.

Tiny **Daroga State Park,** tel. (509) 664-6380, is 22 miles southeast of Chelan on the east bank of the Columbia River and just off Hwy. 97. Be ready for towering high-voltage power lines right next to the campground. Tent and RV sites here are $15 ($7 for the bike sites); open late March to late October. Call (800) 452-5687 for campsite reservations ($6 extra fee), available up to 11 months ahead of time.

The shore of Lake Chelan is dotted with 14 boat-in campgrounds, accessible by private boat or from the *Lady of the Lake II;* see the Forest Service office for specifics. Several other campgrounds are on the road system, including Antilon Lake Campground, north of Manson.

Beebe Bridge Park sits along the Columbia River across from the town of Chelan Falls, and has tent and RV sites for $15, along with coin-operated showers, a swimming area, and play fields.

FOOD AND ENTERTAINMENT

Chelan has a large number of restaurants from which to choose. They tend to change quite frequently, and new owners or chefs can dramatically improve (or worsen) the reputation, so ask around to see who's hot, or simply take a look inside to see what looks interesting.

Breakfast

Apple Cup Cafe is a family-type place with very good breakfasts (great cheese blintzes) in a Denny's-like setting. Another popular breakfast place with home cooking is **Calico Cow,** 2220 W. Woodin, tel. (509) 682-4064; relax on the front patio on summer mornings.

Dinner

Chelan House, 502 E. Woodin, tel. (509) 682-2013, has some of the cheapest eats in town and is a good place for light meals and coffees, along with prime rib, chicken, and pasta. **Coyote Cafe** at Mill Bay Casino near Manson, tel. (509) 687-2102, also has surprisingly good—and reasonable—meals, including steaks, prime rib, and delicious Indian tacos.

Goochi's, 104 E. Woodin Ave., tel. (509) 682-2436, is a noisy, happening place with an old cherry wood back bar that delivers lots of microbrews on tap. The trendy but tasty menu features gourmet burgers, fresh seafood, chicken, pastas, and homemade soups. Goochi's has comedy acts on Wednesday, blues on Thursday, and more live music on weekends.

El Vaquero in Manson, tel. (509) 687-3179, has authentic Mexican meals, big portions, and fast service. For a more Americanized version and great views over the lake from the outdoor seats, try **Cosina del Lago** on the Manson Hwy. next to Chelan Shores; tel. (509) 682-4071. Get south-of-the-border fast food at one of the taco trucks parked around town.

The **Campbell House,** 104 W. Woodin Ave., tel. (509) 682-2561, is the old standby, offering elegant dining and a continental menu specializing in Angus steaks and fresh seafood; prices are moderate to expensive. Reservations highly recommended in the summer. Built in 1930, this classic house is now part of the expansive Campbell's Resort.

Grocers, Bakeries, and Espresso

Chelan has both a Safeway and a Red Apple Market. **Golden Florins General Store,** 125 E. Woodin Ave. tel. (509) 682-5535, doesn't appear like much outside, but is actually a very spacious natural foods store with a big selection of organic produce and other goods.

Get a cup of java at **The Espresso Depot,** 137 E. Woodin Ave., tel. (509) 682-8822. For the finest local pastries and breads, monster cinnamon rolls, and good deli sandwiches and espresso, head to **Village Bake Shop** in Manson, tel. (509) 687-3774. A few doors away is **Laura's Kaffee House,** tel. (509) 687-6105, where the homemade pies are famous hereabouts.

EVENTS

The year begins with **Lake Chelan Winterfest,** featuring fireworks, a cross-country ski race, snow sculpting contest, snowmobile events,

Christmas tree bonfire, chili cookoff, and splash in the lake for the really bold. The nine-day **Lake Chelan Bach Feste** comes to town each July with concerts in the new Performing Arts Center, and in local churches and parks. The **Apple Blossom Festival** is held the second weekend in May in Manson, with a parade, car shows, and a chicken-noodle dinner (!) at the American Legion Hall. It's been happening here for over 75 years. Manson's **Fourth of July** brings fireworks, an arts and crafts fair, a sparerib barbecue, and a watermelon-seed-spitting contest. See a popular PRCA rodeo and watch the crowning of the rodeo queen at **Lake Chelan Western Days** the third weekend in July, or visit the **Manson Carnival** with rides, food, and games in early August.

SPORTS AND RECREATION

Hiking

The entire Chelan Valley is user-friendly for walkers and runners because the heaviest vehicle traffic is limited to the main routes—Hwy. 97A, the Chelan-Manson Hwy., and the south shore route. Several day hikes are available in the 25-Mile Creek area; for a complete description of hiking trails around the lake, stop by the Chelan District office at 428 W. Woodin Avenue. Trails out of Stehekin are described below.

If you're just out for a walk and want to enjoy the scenery, one of the nicest is **Riverwalk Park.** It runs a mile along the Chelan River from the Woodin Avenue bridge to the next bridge downstream and just above the dam. The park has restrooms, a picnic area, and boat launch.

A steep but brief climb is up the cross-topped hill overlooking town, nearby apple orchards, and the lake. The path begins at the intersection of S. Saunders St. and E. Iowa Avenue.

Hang Gliding

Chelan has an international reputation as an excellent place to hang glide or paraglide. The best place for launching (or watching hang gliders) is the summit of 3,892-foot Chelan Butte where the hot winds blowing in from the Columbia River Basin give enormous lift. The flying is so good, in fact, that it isn't unusual for a hang glider to launch there and go nonstop to Spokane or into Idaho. They can also be launched to the west over the town and lake with a choice of several landing sites along the lake shore.

Golf

The **Chelan Municipal Golf Course,** tel. (509) 682-5421, has one of the most beautiful settings of any course in the region, overlooking the lake. A small "executive" course, **Ma-8 Golf Course,** tel. (509) 687-6338, is southeast of Manson near Mill Bay Casino, and the acclaimed **Desert Canyon Resort** is halfway between Lake Chelan and Wenatchee, tel. (509) 682-2697 or (800) 258-4173.

Swimming

The lower end of Lake Chelan is lined with sandy beaches just right for swimming in the clean, cool waters. By late summer the water at the lower end of the lake is a bearable 70° F. Most public parks have popular swimming beaches, including Lake Chelan State Park, Chelan City Park, and the newer parks built by Chelan County—Manson Bay Park, Old Mill Park, Chelan Riverwalk Park, Chelan Falls Park, and Beebe Bridge Park. Up-lake beyond Manson and Lake Chelan State Park, the beaches become fewer due to the steep terrain. Swimming is possible in the Stehekin area, but with the water seldom above 50°, few people are found in the lake by choice. The lake never freezes.

Fishing

Like fishermen everywhere, anglers in the Lake Chelan valley are certain that record-sized fish reside in the lake. Two decades ago the lake was stocked with landlocked kokanee salmon to join the lake trout, rainbow trout, and burbot cod. Tiny mysid shrimp were recently planted in the lake to feed the salmon and trout. The largest salmon caught to date weighed in at 19.9 pounds. A 24-pound lake trout has been caught in the lake, and with 30 pounds as the state record, many believe the new record will eventually be set with a trout from Lake Chelan. Nearby, on the Columbia River and in mountain lakes, you will find smallmouth bass, rainbow, cutthroat, brown and eastern brook trout, and other game fish.

Boating

Whatever kind of boating activity you like, you'll find it at Lake Chelan; sightseeing by boat, sailboarding, waterskiing, jet-skiing, kayaking, canoeing, rowing, and paddleboating are all popular along the lake. You will also see sailboards and sailboats of all sizes. You can bring your own craft or rent jet-skis, sailboats, canoes, and water-ski boats from **Chelan Boat Rentals,** 1210 W. Woodin, tel. (509) 682-4444, or **Ship 'n Shore Boat Rentals,** 1230 W. Woodin, tel. (509) 682-5125. **Chelan Parasailing,** tel. (509) 682-7245, brings this resort sport to Lake Chelan each summer.

Play Parks

Slidewaters at Lake Chelan, 102 Waterslide Dr., tel. (509) 682-5751, one of Chelan's most popular places for children, is a short walk from the downtown area. Nine water slides overlook the town and lake, in addition to kiddie slides, a 60-person hot tub, swimming, inner tube ride, picnic area, video arcade, gift shop, and concession stand. The newest attraction is a 400-foot "Tube Blaster" with two 360-degree turns. Open daily Memorial Day through Labor Day; $11 for adults, $8 for ages four to seven, free to kids under four.

Lakeshore Bumper Boats in Don Morse Memorial City Park, tel. (509) 793-2126, open daily 10 a.m.-10 p.m. Memorial Day to Labor Day, is the floating equivalent of bumper cars; very popular with kids. Paddle boats, miniature golf, and go-carts can also be found in Don Morse Park.

Bicycling

The popularity of mountain biking has made the Lake Chelan area a particular favorite with bike riders. All sorts of scenic loop trips are possible, covering a wide diversity of terrain. Both highways that go uplake from Chelan are popular, as are several roads with lighter traffic such as the Manson Loop, the Echo Ridge cross-country ski trails, and numerous Forest Service roads and trails that are open to mountain bikes. Check with the Chelan Ranger District for information and maps on roads and trails.

Winter Sports

The Lake Chelan Valley is a heavily skied area. Unfortunately, the premier cross-country skiing resort here, Bear Mountain Ranch, was destroyed in the Tyee Complex Fire of 1994 and will probably not be rebuilt since much of the surrounding area is now a thicket of blackened trees. In Echo Valley, 12 miles northwest of Chelan, **Echo Valley Ski Area** has day and night downhill skiing on 3,000-foot Echo Mountain, served by three rope tows and a Poma lift; open Saturday and Sunday. Lift tickets cost $15. Other facilities here include ice-skating and snowmobile trails. Rent skis (downhill and Nordic) and snowboards from **Lakeland Ski,** tel. (509) 687-3204, in Manson. Get to Echo Valley aboard the free Link buses connecting Chelan with Manson; ski racks are on all the buses.

The Echo Valley and Echo Ridge areas contain 27 km of groomed cross-country ski trails (including both traditional and skate tracks) for every level of ability. Vistas from the summit are extraordinary, encompassing Lake Chelan, the Cascades, and the Columbia River Valley. These are maintained by the **Lake Chelan Nordic Ski Club** and are used as mountain bike paths in the summer. Use is by donation ($5 suggested), and a Sno-Park permit is needed for vehicles. Get permits ($20 per year or $10 for three days) from the Forest Service or chamber of commerce offices in Chelan. Other Chelan-area Nordic ski trails include five km of groomed runs at **Lake Chelan Golf Course** ($3 donation suggested), and another 30 km of groomed trails plus plenty of backcountry touring at Stehekin (described below). For maps of ski trails around Chelan, stop by the chamber of commerce office.

Popular ski areas near Lake Chelan are in Methow Valley (see "Cross-Country Skiing" under "Winthrop," above) for cross-country skiing, and Mission Ridge (see "Sports and Recreation" under "Wenatchee") for downhill skiing or snowboarding. Rent cross-country and downhill equipment at **Lake Chelan Sports,** 137 E. Woodin Ave., tel. (509) 682-2629; **Lakeland Ski** in Manson, tel. (509) 687-2629; or **LeProv Ski & Cycle,** 106 S. Emerson, tel. (509) 682-5377.

Snowmobilers will enjoy the 150 miles of trails on both sides of Lake Chelan, accessible from three Sno-Parks. For information contact the Lake Chelan Ranger Station, tel. (509) 682-2576.

Ice-skaters will find outdoor rinks at Don Morse Memorial Park in Chelan, Echo Valley Ski Area, and Roses, Wapato, and Dry Lakes in Manson.

Gambling
For a bit of mini-Vegas, head to **Mill Bay Casino,** tel. (509) 687-2102 or (800) 648-2946, a mile southeast of Manson and open 24 hours a day. The prefab buildings (supposedly, a fancier casino will come later) house smoke-filled rooms with folks playing blackjack, craps, keno, roulette, poker, or yanking the handles on the 400 slot machines. Located on land owned by the Colville Tribe and staffed in part by workers who commute all the way from the reservation, this controversial casino opened despite the lack of an agreement with the state. Lawyers should keep things tentative for quite a while. Most local motels have discount vouchers, and direct bus service is available from Seattle and Spokane. Next door is **Coyote Cafe** with decent meals from 7 a.m. to midnight (till 2 a.m. Fri.-Sunday).

SHOPPING

In addition to the restaurants and markets, Chelan and Manson have some specialty gift shops of interest. Not surprisingly, some of the shops specialize in shipping apples. **The Harvest Tree,** 109 E. Woodin, tel. (800) 568-6062, offers baskets of apples, some with additional foods such as trail mix, Aplets, Cotlets, and honey.

Three local galleries are well worth a visit: **Manson Bay Art Gallery** in Manson, tel. (509) 687-3908; **The Gallery at Allisons** also in Manson, tel. (509) 687-3534; and **Wapato Studio and Fine Art,** 108 E. Woodin Ave. in Chelan, tel. (509) 682-2423. Wapato has works by the famed sculptor Rich Beyer and oils by Rod Weagant.

INFORMATION AND SERVICES

For maps or other information, contact the **Lake Chelan Chamber of Commerce,** tel. (509) 682-3503 or (800) 424-3526; open Sunday 11 a.m.-

1 p.m., Mon.-Fri. 9 a.m.-5 p.m., and Saturday 10 a.m.-3 p.m. in the summer, or Mon.-Fri. 9 a.m.-5 p.m. in the winter.

The combined Forest Service/National Park Service, **Chelan Ranger District office,** 428 W. Woodin, tel. (509) 682-2576, dispenses information on all forms of outdoor recreation, including many places to camp, picnic, or just have a look around. The office is open Mon.-Fri. 7:45 a.m.-4:30 p.m. all year, plus Sat.-Sun. 7:45 a.m.-4:30 p.m. from late June to early September.

Local **public libraries** are in Chelan at 317 E. Johnson, tel. (509) 682-5131, and in Manson above the fire station, tel. (509) 687-3420. **Lake Chelan Community Hospital,** 503 E. Highland, tel. (509) 682-2531, is a modern facility with all the basic services. The **area code** for the Chelan area and all points east is 509.

TRANSPORTATION AND TOURS

See "Stehekin," below, for info on the ever-popular scenic boat and plane trips up Lake Chelan.

Bus Service
Link, tel. (509) 662-1155 or (800) 851-5465, is one of the more remarkable public-transportation services in America. And it's free! The buses cover the entire county, from Chelan and Manson to Wenatchee and up Hwy. 2 as far as Lake Wenatchee. You can put your skis on the bus in Chelan and ride to Wenatchee, then change to Route 40 and ski at Mission Ridge. Or you can go from Chelan to Wenatchee and on to Leavenworth or Waterville. Or put your bicycle on the special racks and ride anywhere one-way and pedal back. Buses run Mon.-Fri. 5 a.m.-8 p.m., and Saturday 8 a.m.-8 p.m.; no Sunday service.

Intercity bus service is provided by **Empire Bus Line,** tel. (509) 689-3183, with daily connections to Wenatchee, Seattle, Spokane, and British Columbia. The bus stops at 115 S. Emerson Street.

Air Service
Chelan Airways, tel. (509) 682-5555, offers daily seaplane service to Stehekin, Domke Lake, and other up-lake destinations aboard four- and six-passenger planes. Fares to Stehekin are $50 one-way, $80 roundtrip, two-passenger minimum. Sightseeing flights over the Stehekin Valley cost $50, and a 110-mile tour of all of Lake Chelan with a short stopover at Stehekin is $100. Advance reservations recommended. The nearest airport with scheduled air service is at Wenatchee.

Tours
In addition to the boat and plane trips up the lake, **Lake Chelan & North Cascades Tours,** tel. (509) 682-8287, offers personalized tours of the lake from a 25-foot boat, along with chartered floatplane trips into the Cascades. Their office is at the Lake Chelan Marina, 1228 Woodin Avenue. **Ads Up Aviation,** tel. (509) 682-8618, offers scenic flights in a 1941 open-cockpit biplane. Pretend to be an old war ace in the helmet, goggles, scarf, and leather flight jacket.

STEHEKIN

Stehekin (ste-HEE-kin) sits at the northwest end of Lake Chelan and can be reached only by boat, plane, or foot; thousands of visitors take the boat trip from Chelan for lunch or an overnight stay at one of Stehekin's resorts. Or they use this as a launching point for treks into the heart of North Cascades National Park, or beyond into Lake Chelan-Sawtooth Wilderness or Glacier Peak Wilderness.

The word "Stehekin," an Indian term meaning "the way through," seems to fit this mountain gateway well. The town began in the late 1880s when prospectors came here in search of gold and silver. They found the minerals, but not in sufficient quantity to establish a large mine, and Stehekin has never been connected to the outside world by road. Today it is home to less than 100 permanent residents, but has all the basics, including a post office, grocery store, restaurant, and grade school. A summer-only outdoor supply shop and bakery are also in town.

Hiking
The Stehekin area is a favorite of hikers—trails wander in all directions and for all levels of ability. The shuttle buses (described below) make it

easy to get to the trailheads or back to Stehekin. Keep your eyes open when you walk since the area has a fair number of rattlesnakes.

A short three-quarter-mile-long loop hike—the **Imus Creek Nature Trail**—begins behind the visitor center and climbs a nearby hill overlooking the lake. Take the shuttle for a couple of other easy jaunts. Spectacular **Rainbow Falls**—a towering cataract of water plummeting 312 feet—is surrounded by tall western red cedar trees three and a half miles northwest of town. Take the shuttle to High Bridge for a beautiful day hike to **Coon Lake.** The 1.2-mile trail leads uphill to this scenic lake, with excellent views of Agnes Mountain and good birdwatching. Those with more energy can continue another seven miles to the 8,122-foot summit of **McGregor Mountain,** a tortuous climb up countless switchbacks.

An easy, albeit not especially challenging hike is the **Lakeshore Trail** that connects Stehekin with Prince Creek Campground, 17 miles to the southeast. At Prince Creek you can flag down the *Lady of the Lake II* (described below) for a return to Chelan.

Use the *Lady of the Lake II* to make a 38-mile loop trip from Prince Creek Campground up the Prince Creek Trail, then along the **Summit Trail** over 6,770-foot War Creek Pass and past tiny Lake Juanita, to Stehekin. This hike features lots of ups and downs through forests and alpine meadows, and striking views of mountain peaks, including 8,690-foot Star Peak. Much of the Summit Trail passes through the **Lake Chelan-Sawtooth Wilderness** with side trails leading north into the Twisp River drainage (see "North Cascades National Park," earlier in this chapter for details on longer hikes over Cascade Pass and Park Pass).

Accommodations
Stehekin is a wonderful place to relax and enjoy the wilderness splendor without interference from TVs or phones. As with all places in the Lake Chelan area, advance reservations are a must in the summer. The newly remodeled **North Cascades Stehekin Lodge,** tel. (509) 682-4494, offers lodge rooms and housekeeping units for $69-95 s or d. Amenities include a restaurant, bar, bike and boat rentals, gas, and groceries. During the winter, the Park Service

and Stehekin Lodge jointly maintain 10 miles of free **cross-country ski trails** (both track and skate lanes); roundtrip transportation to the trails is $7.50 adults, $4.50 kids. Rent skis in Chelan or bring your own, but the lodge does have snowshoes for rent.

At **Stehekin Valley Ranch,** tel. (509) 682-4677, nine miles up from Stehekin, your lodging, three hearty meals, and local transportation are included in the price of your cabin: $55 per person, $45 per person for ages six to 11, $30 per person for kids ages four to six, and $15 for those three or younger. These are primitive tent cabins with no running water or electricity, and kerosene lamps for light. Showers are nearby. The ranch is open early June to early October and offers a variety of activities: two-and-a-half-hour horseback rides, raft trips down the Stehekin River, mountain bike rentals, and mountain hiking and horseback trips.

Silver Bay Inn at Stehekin, tel. (509) 682-2212, has cabins (open all year) and a B&B at the house (open May-Sept.). The fully furnished cabins with kitchens hold four to six people and cost $135 d, plus $20 per person for additional guests. There's a five-night minimum stay for these cabins mid-June through September, and two nights the rest of the year. Guests can also stay at three rooms in the house for $65-120 d, including a light breakfast. There's a two-night minimum stay in these rooms. No kids under eight in the house, but families are welcome in the cabins. The inn also has an outdoor hot tub, and free transportation to and from the boat landing, is provided.

Flick Creek House, tel. (509) 884-1730, is a modern cedar house two and a half miles downlake from Stehekin along the Lakeshore Trail. Access is by foot from Stehekin, or by boat; the *Lady II* will drop you off. Rates are $95 d; open all year.

Campgrounds
Campers can ride the shuttle bus from Stehekin to **Harlequin, High Bridge, Tumwater, Dolly Varden, Shady,** and **Cottonwood** Campgrounds along the Stehekin River. **Weaver Campground,** is a very popular boat-access campground at the north end of the lake across from Stehekin. The old Weaver homestead here was the site where *The Courage of Lassie* was

filmed in 1944, starring none other than Elizabeth Taylor (and Lassie, of course). All of these campgrounds are free.

Food

Stehekin Valley Ranch Restaurant, tel. (509) 682-4677, is open June-Sept. with a menu that includes steaks, burgers, salad bar, and homemade desserts—all of which will taste pretty good after a week of backcountry travel or a long day in the saddle. Reservations are required. The restaurant is nine miles up the valley from Stehekin, but free transportation is provided by Stehekin Valley Ranch. Two miles up from the boat dock is **Stehekin Pastry Company,** which offers delicious baked goods, ice cream, and espresso; open summers only. Another restaurant—open all year—is inside **Stehekin Lodge,** tel. (509) 682-4494, just a short walk from the dock.

Information and Services

The National Park Service-run **Golden Next door to the Golden West Visitor Center,** tel. (509) 856-5703, ext. 14, in Stehekin is the place to go for information on hiking and camping in the area with books and exhibits, and various programs during the summer. Golden West is open daily 7:30-4:30 between mid-May and mid-September, and daily 12:30-2 p.m. in the spring and fall. Next door are **The House That Jack Built,** selling locally made crafts, and **McGregor Mt. Outdoor Supply.**

Stop by the Stehekin Valley Ranch or the **Courtney Log Office** (just north of the post office) for information on rafting trips down the Stehekin River. The cost for these relatively easy rolling rides is $40 for adults, $30 for kids. Rent mountain bikes at **Discovery Bikes** in the Courtney Log Office or from North Cascades Lodge.

Boat Access

A longtime favorite of visitors to Lake Chelan is the 55-mile voyage from Chelan or Manson to Stehekin. Lake Chelan Boat Company has been operating boats along this route for more than 65 years and now runs two vessels: the massive 350-passenger *Lady of the Lake II,* which takes fours hours to reach Stehekin, and the 65-foot-long *Lady Express,* which gets there twice as fast. Food is available on both boats, and onboard Forest Service interpreters give talks on the human and natural history of the area. Service is year-round, but only the *Lady Express* operates Nov.-April, and only the *Lady of the Lake II,* operates May and October. (No winter boat service on Tuesday and Thursday.) In addition to Chelan and Manson, the boats stop at Field's Point (accessible by car along the south shore), Lucerne, and Stehekin, and the *Lady II* also makes flag stops at any Forest Service campsite upon request during the summer season. Service changes through the year, and the rules get a bit complex; pick up a copy of the schedule with all the gory details at the visitors center or from Lake Chelan Boat Company, tel. (509) 682-2224. Their dock and office are located across the bridge at 1319 W. Woodin Ave. on the southwest end of Chelan. A separate service provides weekly barge trips up the lake carrying vehicles, fuel, groceries, and supplies to Stehekin.

The *Lady of the Lake II,* tel. (509) 682-2224, departs daily May-Oct., leaving at 8:30 a.m., arriving in Stehekin at 12:30 p.m. After a 90-minute layover for lunch and exploring, the boat heads back for a 6 p.m. return to Chelan. No reservations are needed for the *Lady II.* Fares are $14 one-way, or $21 roundtrip.

The *Lady Express* has a similar service, but returns to Chelan earlier in the afternoon and operates all year (except the months of May and October when just the *Lady of the Lake II* is in service). Fares are $25 one-way, $39 roundtrip (cheaper rates in the winter). Reservations are recommended for the *Lady Express* during the summer, particularly on weekends. Travelers looking for more time in Stehekin often take the speedier *Lady Express* up in the morning, returning on the *Lady II* in the afternoon, giving them a bit over three hours to wander around (but you're better off spending more time around Stehekin!). This combination costs $39 roundtrip. You can also carry bikes, canoes, or kayaks aboard either boat for an extra charge.

Air Access

Chelan Airways, tel. (509) 682-5555, offers daily seaplane service to Stehekin ($50 one-way, $80 roundtrip) and sightseeing flights over the Stehekin Valley for $50. Or, fly one-way and take a boat in the other direction.

Shuttle Buses

Take the boat up Lake Chelan, and the summer shuttle bus from Stehekin to campgrounds and hiking trails along Stehekin Valley Rd. for an extensive, no-car journey into the Cascades backcountry. The **Park Service shuttle bus** ($5-10) runs 23 miles to the end of the road at Cottonwood Campground, with twice-daily service from mid-May through September (till mid-October if the budget allows). Reservations are recommended; call (509) 856-5703, ext. 14, for specifics, or stop by the visitor centers in Stehekin or Chelan. The NPS bus carries backpacks, but not bikes.

Stehekin Adventures has a 36-passenger bus ($4) with service four times a day between Stehekin and High Bridge, 11 miles up, and can carry both backpacks and bikes. This bus operates from early June to mid-September only, and reservations are not needed. Be sure to pick up a schedule for both shuttle services at the Chelan or Stehekin Ranger Station before setting out. Passengers on both services are given a narrated tour along the way, and you can get on or off at any point along the route.

Tours

Stehekin Discovery, tel. (509) 682-4558, has bike tours, horseback riding, river rafting, and other tours in the area. **Stehekin Lodge** (tel. 509-682-4494) offers daily trips to Rainbow Falls. Their bus meets the *Lady Express* and *Lady of the Lake II* boats when they arrive in Stehekin and provides a narrated 45-minute tour for $4.25. They also offer bus tours that include lunch at Stehekin Valley Ranch and bus/bike tours through Buckner Orchard (said to be the largest common red delicious orchard surviving in the U.S.) and Rainbow falls.

ENTIAT AREA

Heading south from Chelan on Hwy. 97A, you pass through the center of the large Tyee Complex Fire of 1994, with extensive areas of charred timber. After several miles of this, the highway enters a tunnel and then descends to the Columbia (or the dammed version thereof) through hills draped in sage and grass.

Entiat

The town of Entiat (ANN-ee-at; pop. 500) sits along Lake Entiat, that portion of the Columbia River that backs up behind massive Rocky Reach Dam 10 miles downriver. This is orchard country; stop at a local fruit stand for fresh apples, cherries, apricots, peaches, or pears in season.

For information on the area, head to the Wenatchee National Forest **Entiat Ranger Station,** tel. (509) 784-1511. Camping ($10) and RV places ($12) are available along the lake at **Entiat City Park;** call the **Entiat Valley Chamber of Commerce,** tel. (509) 784-1500 or (800) 736-8428, for reservations; open April to mid-September. Near the city park, the **Entiat Historical Museum,** tel. (509) 784-1832, contains local memorabilia in an 1895 farmhouse.

Rent boats and jet-skis from **RSI Sports,** tel. (509) 784-2399 or (800) 786-2637.

Link, tel. (509) 662-1155 or (800) 851-5465, has daily bus service (free) between Entiat and other parts of Chelan and Douglas Counties.

Entiat River Valley

South of Entiat, Hwy. 97A hugs the shore of the lake, passing rugged rocky slopes. Orchards edge the east shoreline. A mile south of Entiat is the turnoff to **Entiat River Rd.** (Forest Rd. 51), which leads to **Entiat National Fish Hatchery,** and eventually to the Entiat trailhead for the Glacier Peak Wilderness. Along the way are seven Forest Service campgrounds; closest is the free **Pine Flat Campground,** 10 miles up, open mid-April through October. This small cluster of campsites is located along the Mad River; hiking trails leading up to mountain lakes. Most of the other campgrounds charge a $7 fee and are open May-October. Get supplies at the small store in the tiny settlement of **Ardenvoir,** nine miles up. The wildfires of 1994 burned much of this country; check with the Forest Service office in Entiat for current trail and campground conditions.

CASHMERE

Tucked between strip-mall Wenatchee and Bavarian-mall Leavenworth, tiny Cashmere (pop. 2,300) has long featured a Colonial American theme on its buildings. Highway 2 between Leavenworth and Cashmere is lined with fruit orchards, and the dry climate helps produce the finest D'Anjou pears in America. A half-dozen fruit stands sell fresh apples, pears, cherries, apricots, peaches, plums, and berries in season. Because of this fruit production, Cashmere was a logical place to establish a business that produces a confection made from fruit juices, walnuts, and powdered sugar—the treats known as Aplets and Cotlets.

SIGHTS

Candy Town

If you have a sweet tooth, be certain to stop at **Liberty Orchards,** 117 Mission St., tel. (509) 782-2191, the home of Aplets and Cotlets. These all-natural confections are made of fruit juices (apple, grape, and apricot) and walnuts, and are coated with powdered sugar and corn starch. Tours take 15 minutes or so and end back in the gift shop where you can sample a number of different candies and purchase gift boxes and various knickknacks. The original sweets were developed by two Armenian immigrants, Mark Balaban and Armen Tertsagian, who had established fruit orchards in the Cashmere area. Unable to sell all the fruit they produced, they decided to mix apple juice and walnuts to make a Middle Eastern confection called locum. More than 75 years have passed, but the candy is still made in Cashmere (two million pounds a year), and the company president is a grandson of the original owners. Old standbys such as Aplets and Cotlets are still around, along with several dozen other varieties, from chocolate passion fruit to sugar-free, nut-free versions. Tour hours are Mon.-Fri. 8 a.m.-5:30 p.m., Sat.-Sun. 10 a.m.-4 p.m., April-Dec.; Mon.-Fri. 8:30 a.m.-4:30 p.m. Jan.-March. On weekends you aren't likely to see a lot of activity in the plant during a tour, but the free samples make any stop worthwhile. Call (800) 888-5696 for a mail-order catalog of gift boxes.

Süsswaren Chocolatiers, 114 Cottage Ave., tel. (509) 782-4218, makes Bavarian chocolates in the back of their shop. Tours are available weekdays. **Rosemary's Kitchen,** 603 Cottage Ave., tel. (509) 782-2498, produces preserves, jams, and pie fillings. Visitors can watch production through large windows.

Chelan County Historical Museum

Considered one of the top pioneer villages in the country, the Chelan County Historical Museum, 600 Cottage Ave., tel. (509) 782-3230, has restored and furnished more than 20 of the oldest buildings in Chelan County to create an authentic Old West atmosphere. A blacksmith shop, railroad passenger car, school, gold mine, mission building, hotel, and assay office are part of the Pioneer Village; there's also a large waterwheel that lifted water out of the Wenatchee River to irrigate the orchards. The main museum building houses an extraordinary collection of Native American artifacts—baskets, prehistoric antler carvings, beaded clothing, medicines, pipes, and more—along with natural history and pioneer exhibits. Hours are Mon.-Sat. 10 a.m.-4:30 p.m., and Sunday 1-4:30 p.m.; closed Nov.-March. Admission is adults $3, children $1, and families $5.

PRACTICALITIES

Accommodations

The "Leavenworth Area Accommodations" chart includes descriptions of Cashmere's two comfortable motels, Cashmere Country Inn, and Village Inn Motel. Camping ($12) and RV spaces ($17) with coin-operated showers are available at **Wenatchee River County Park,** just west of town, tel. (509) 662-2525. Open April to late October. No reservations accepted.

Food

Among Cashmere's more elegant eateries is **The Pewter Pot,** 124 Cottage Ave., tel. (509) 782-2036, a colonial-style restaurant featuring fresh-baked bread, locally grown produce, and from-scratch cooking. Open for lunch and dinner only, with traditional English dinners such as beef Wellington, Cornish game hen, and Plymouth turkey. Or just stop by for an afternoon spot of tea with scones. Be sure to save space for their wonderful desserts. More tasty baked goods across the street at **Sure to Rise Bakery,** tel. (509) 782-2424. **Cashmere Coffee and Confectionery Company,** a few doors up from Pewter Pot, is a relaxing place to drink an espresso while reading the paper.

For pasta, steak, fish, and Greek specialties, head to the attractive **Siraco's Restaurant,** 106 Cottage Ave., tel. (509) 782-3444. This is also the place to go for breakfast in Cashmere.

Events
Celebrated the first week in July, the highlight of **Founder's Days** is the "Stillman Miller Hill Climb," inspired by an early resident who claimed he could pour himself a beer in the local tavern, run up Numbers Hill, and be back before the head settled. Whether or not he actually made it is anybody's guess, but the concept was so appealing that runners are still trying it today. Other events include a parade, barbecue, arts and crafts show, and street dance.

Cashmere is also home to the **Chelan County Fair,** held the second week in September, highlighted by rodeos, musical entertainment, a carnival, and exhibits. The first weekend in October brings **Cashmere Apple Days;** apple bin races, an apple-pie-baking contest, music, dancing, and staged shoot-outs are all part of the fun.

LEAVENWORTH

One of the most distinctive towns in the Pacific Northwest, Leavenworth has a scant 2,000 residents but manages to attract more than a million visitors per year. They aren't coming to see the Leavenworth Fruit Co. warehouse, but to step into a fanciful Bavarian village, complete with authentic architecture, hand-carved benches, flower-bedecked streets, and a gorgeous mountain setting. Add in the female clerks in Bavarian dirndl dresses and waiters in lederhosen, and the town gets a bit hokey at times, but is certainly unique in America. With over 60 lodging places and almost as many restaurants and shops, it's pretty clear that people love this place.

HISTORY

Although developed by prospectors and Hudson's Bay fur traders, the first Anglo settlers in the Leavenworth area didn't arrive until the late 1880s, with the news that the Great Northern Railway planned to lay tracks through the valley. The resulting population "boom" brought Leavenworth (originally called Icicle) about 300 people by the turn of the century. They were mostly railroad men or lumberjacks employed by the Lamb-Davis Lumber Co., operators of one of the state's largest sawmills. The after-hours rowdiness of these laborers gave little Leavenworth a rather unrefined reputation that took years to live down. Even so, by the early 1920s a wave of families bought tracts of land to grow "Wenatchee Big Red" apples.

When the railroad moved its switching yard from Leavenworth to Wenatchee, and the sawmill closed its doors after logging all its waterfront land, these family-based fruit farms provided much of the town's income. But by the 1960s, it was clear that Leavenworth needed more than apples to survive. With help from the University of Washington, a committee on tourism was formed to brainstorm, and it suggested a fall festival and a major remodeling job.

Suggestions for the town's new motif ranged from a Gay '90s theme to a Western town, but with the impressive mountain backdrop, an alpine village seemed the best answer. One of the first proponents was Ted Price, owner of a Swiss Bavarian-style cafe in Coles Corner. (The building, now Squirrel Tree Inn, still stands 14 miles northwest of Leavenworth.) The town's renovation was financed with private funds and backed by local bankers. It quickly earned national recognition for the attention to detail, aggressive promotion, and bootstraps efforts. Many of the buildings were designed by Karl Heinz Ulbricht, who had fled his native East

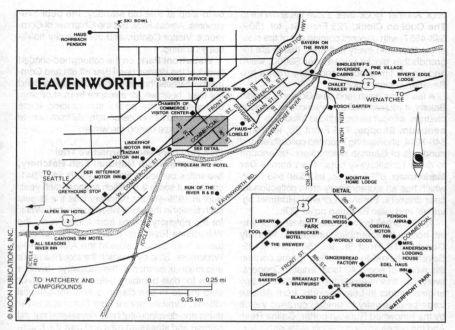

Germany in the 1950s and who insisted upon close attention to detail and quality construction. By the late '60s, the Bavarian theme had taken hold; it now covers almost every commercial building in town. Tourism has transformed a going-nowhere place into one of the premier success stories in community improvement.

The summer of 1994 brought devastating forest fires to the hills around Leavenworth, scaring away tourists for a while and forcing the rescue of backcountry hikers, but the town itself escaped almost unscathed. The burned areas—varying from conspicuously blackened swatches to patchy ground fires—are visible for miles along Hwy. 2 as you head over the Cascades from Leavenworth, up the Icicle Canyon drainage, and along Hwy. 97 north of Blewett Pass. They are part of the Hatchery Creek and Rat Creek complex of fires that consumed more than 85,000 acres of forest and brushland. See the special topic "Firestorm in the Cascades" for more on these blazes.

SIGHTS

The Bavarian Village

Start your tour of the Bavarian Village in the heart of town—on Front Street, where there's plenty of on-street parking. Shops, restaurants, taverns, and hotels are squeezed side by side, all beautifully decorated with carved wood, flower boxes, and murals—even the automated teller machine is surrounded by a painted alpine scene.

Trinket and gewgaw places are spread throughout town—shops with plastic Santas, inane T-shirts, and made-in-Taiwan Bavarian figurines—but fortunately, Leavenworth also has more than its share of distinctive, great-for-browsing places. **A Matter of Taste,** 647 Front St., tel. (509) 548-6949 or (800) 497-3995, lets you savor all sorts of unusual treats, from "Ass Kickin' Chicken Wing Sauce" to coffee jelly. One story above their entrance is the town **glockenspiel** with carved dancers who clog on the hour. Another "glock" lives above the entrance to **The Cuckoo Clock,** 725 Front St., tel. (509) 548-4857, with dancers coming out of the closet (so to speak) every half-hour. Inside are tall grandfather clocks priced over $3000, weird and wacky timepieces, and more than a few Bavarian cuckoo clocks.

A few doors down (and past Gorden's Danish Bakery, if you can make it beyond their luscious pastries without being enticed inside) is **Tannenbaum Shoppe,** 735 Front St., tel. (509) 548-7014, showcasing imported collectibles and hundreds of German nutcrackers. Its enough to drive Tchaikovsky nuts. Then comes **Der Marketplatz,** 801 Front St., tel. (509) 548-7422, which has an extraordinary stein collection for beer drinkers, European crystal, Hummel figurines, and even Bavarian polka CDs.

Take a break from the mega-dose of Bavarian hoopla by scrambling upstairs to **Worldly Goods,** 819 Front St., tel. (509) 548-6499. Several packed-to-the-ceiling rooms contain the works of some 40 local artists. Cooperatively run, this is easily the best place to buy original works in Leavenworth, from African trade-bead jewelry to unique ceramic vases by the renowned Russian potter, Galina Rein. And the prices are surprisingly reasonable (except for Rein's works, which run upwards of $4,500). Continue down the block and down the basement stairs to **Die Musik Box,** 837 Front St., tel. (509) 548-6152 or (800) 288-5883, where 5,000 intricate music boxes from around the globe create a chorus of whimsical sounds.

Work your way back through the side streets and onto Commercial Street for more shops. Be sure to visit the basement shops of Alpenhof Mall at 217 9th St., including **The Train Store,** tel. (509) 546-5018, and **Seba Gallery,** tel. (509) 548-4150. Inside the Train Store you're likely to meet nationally known railroad artist H.L. "Scotty" Scott, III whose intricate pen and ink drawings and prints line the walls. Seba Gallery features imported Russian handicrafts, including nesting eggs and painted icons.

Front St. Park, sandwiched between Hwy. 2 and the shops of Front St., is a relaxing, sunny spot for a picnic lunch or noontime break in the central gazebo. It's also the place to see street dances, art exhibits, and other public events,

or to stop at that old standby, the public restrooms. Across Hwy. 2 is the Chamber of Commerce Visitor Center, and the new city hall/library building.

Waterfront Park, on the cottonwood-shaded banks of the Wenatchee River off 8th and Commercial Streets, has walkways over and around the river, benches for a respite from shopping, and views of the peaks surrounding Icicle Canyon. You can cross-country ski from here to the golf course during the winter.

Fish Hatchery and Interpretive Trail
The **Leavenworth National Fish Hatchery,** two miles out Icicle Rd., tel. (509) 548-7641, cranks out some 2.5 million salmon each year. Built in 1939-40, the hatchery was the largest such facility in the world when completed. Water for the hatchery comes from Icicle Creek, the Wenatchee River, deep wells, and a half-mile tunnel from Snow Lakes in the Alpine Lakes Wilderness. Stop by to watch the steelhead trout and chinook salmon in the raceways (favorite spots for dive-bombing belted kingfishers), or step inside to see displays and educational videos. Exhibits reveal how Columbia River dams and development have devastated natural salmon and steelhead runs and how the hatchery attempts to mitigate some of the damage. The real attraction here is an "outdoor aquarium" where you can watch rainbow trout in the eye-level concrete "stream." The hatchery is open daily 7:30 a.m.-4 p.m. all year.

Icicle Creek Interpretive Trail provides a mile-long circular path from the hatchery. Pick up one of the informative trail brochures before heading out to see various sites along the creek, including a wildlife viewing blind. Keep your eyes open for the resident ospreys.

Nearby State Parks
Twenty-three miles north of Leavenworth on Hwy. 207, **Lake Wenatchee State Park** is a popular year-round recreation area, with cross-country skiing in winter, plus swimming, fishing, and canoeing on over 12,000 feet of spectacular Lake Wenatchee waterfront, set against a backdrop of majestic snow-covered peaks. Other facilities include boat rentals, weekend-evening interpretive programs, and wooded campsites (no hookups). Summer camping is $6

per site; a number of sites are plowed for winter camping at $4.50 a night. Rent a horse from **Icicle Outfitters and Guides,** tel. (509) 784-1145 or (800) 497-3912, for a guided one- or two-hour ride from their barn at the park for $8 an hour. Rides are available Memorial Day through Labor Day; no reservations necessary.

Eight miles east of Leavenworth on Hwy. 2 is **Peshastin Pinnacles State Park.** This 35-acre park is a recent addition to the state system, created in 1991 to provide public access to what had long been a popular rock-climbing Mecca. There are routes for all ranges of ability here, and nonclimbers can stop to photograph the dramatic pinnacles, walk the short trails, or watch more daring folks. No camping, but the park does have picnic tables and pit toilets.

Blewett Pass

Highway 97 heads south from the Leavenworth area, connecting Hwy. 2 with I-90. The road climbs 21 miles to 4,102-foot Blewett Pass, a popular area for hiking, skiing, and snowmobiling. **Blewett Pass Interpretive Trail** offers a three-mile loop through high-country forests. Several nearby Forest Service campgrounds (Bonanza, Tronsen, Swauk, and Mineral Springs) have campsites for $5 or less. For more adventure, take the slightly shorter, but significantly steeper, sinuous, and serpentine old highway over Blewett Pass.

The **Swauk Forest Discovery Trail** is an easy 2.6-mile path at the summit of Swauk/Blewett Pass. The trail passes through both old-growth forests and clearcuts, and educational signs are scattered along the way.

Blue Creek Rd. (Forest Rd. 9738) leads to the Mineral Springs area west approximately seven miles to an old fire lookout on Red Top Mountain, providing vistas in all directions. This is a popular area to search for blue agates and geodes (a.k.a "thunder eggs"). Also in the Mineral Springs area is **Mineral Springs Resort,** tel. (509) 857-2361, which has lodging, RV spaces, and good lunches and pies. Come winter, this area is very popular with snowmobilers and cross-country skiers. Sno-Parks at Swauk Campground and Pipe Creek provide skier-only access to many miles of cross-country trails. For details, contact the Forest Service's Cle Elum Ranger District, tel. (509) 674-4411.

SUMMER RECREATION

River Runnin'

The rivers of the central Cascades support many rafting outfitters, but the Wenatchee is easily the most popular river in the state. Above Leavenworth, the Wenatchee drops through rugged Tumwater Canyon, with several class VI stretches before calming down to more manageable class III rapids below town. Leavenworth is the most common put-in point, and whitewater trips cover 16-24 miles, depending upon the takeout spot. Conditions change through the year; high spring runoff creates excellent whitewater conditions from April to mid-July (and often longer). Gentler float trips begin at Lake Wenatchee and cover the stretch of easy water before the river enters Tumwater Canyon near Tumwater Campground (the take-out point). These are especially popular when flow levels drop during August and September. Inner tubers often float down slower parts of the Icicle and Wenatchee Rivers to Blackbird Island near Leavenworth's Waterfront Park. Rent inner tubes at **Leavenworth Sports Center,** Hwy. 2 at Icicle Rd., tel. (509) 548-7864, or rent kayaks ($30 per day) and canoes ($45 per day) at Lake Wenatchee from **Leavenworth Outfitters,** tel. (509) 763-3733 or (800) 347-7934.

LAKE WENATCHEE

© MOON PUBLICATIONS, INC.

For half-day rafting excursions, expect to pay $65-80 for whitewater trips, $50-65 for scenic float trips. Most companies include guides, wetsuits, booties, meals, and shuttle bus service. Contact one of the following companies for more info, or look for their brochures in the visitor center: **All Rivers Adventures,** tel. (800) 743-5628; **Alpine Whitewater** (this is the only company actually based in Leavenworth), tel. (800) 926-7238; **Chinook Expeditions,** tel. (800) 241-3451; **Leavenworth Outfitters,** tel. (800) 347-7934; **Northern Wilderness River Riders, Inc.,** tel. (800) 448-7238; **Olympic Outdoor Adventures,** tel. (800) 659-6095; **Orion Expeditions,** tel. (800) 553-7466; **Osprey Rafting,** tel. (800) 743-6269; **River Recreation,** tel. (800) 464-5899; and **High Mountain Recreation, Inc.,** tel. (800) 423-9381. **Das Photo Haus,** 9th and Front Streets, tel. (509) 548-6767 or (800) 788-3767, has "floatographers" who shoot pics as you rock and roll through the rapids, and have prints ready by the time you're back in town.

Mountain Biking

Cyclists will love the back roads around Leavenworth, including an almost-level seven-mile loop through Icicle Valley. A more adventurous ride climbs the dirt road up Tumwater Mountain, just north of town, and offers vistas into Tumwater Canyon and the Wenatchee Valley far below. Stop by the local Forest Service offices for descriptions of other mountain biking trails. **Gator's Gravity,** Hwy. 2 at Icicle Creek Rd., tel. (509) 548-5102, runs half-day downhill mountain bike tours along Icicle Creek Rd. for $51, including transportation, bikes, helmets, and lunch. Over the 17-mile roll, you drop fully 2,000 feet in elevation. A similar service is run by **Leavenworth Outfitters,** tel. (509) 763-3733 or (800) 347-7934. Rent mountain bikes from **Leavenworth Sports Center,** Hwy. 2 at Icicle Rd., tel. (509) 548-7864. Other places with mountain bikes rentals are **Der Sportsman,** 837 Front St., tel. (509) 548-5623, and **Surrey Cycles,** 1117 Front St. (Evergreen Inn), tel. (509) 548-5515.

Hiking

The Alpine Lakes Wilderness Area, one of the most popular and scenic hiking destinations in Washington, lies just a few miles west of Leavenworth (see "Sports and Recreation" under "Stevens Pass and Skykomish Valley," below, for details). Stop by the Wenatchee National Forest's **Leavenworth Ranger District,** 600 Sherbourne, tel. (509) 782-1413, for a brochure on nearby day hikes and a detailed trail guide to longer treks. Although several local trails were burned over during the dramatic 1994 fires, they have since been reopened, and most areas (especially in the high country) escaped or only experienced ground fires.

Lake Wenatchee Ranger District, centered around Lake Wenatchee and Fish Lake at the north end of Hwy. 207, has an extensive system of hiking trails. Popular with hikers and photographers is the **Dirtyface Trail,** a steep 4.5-mile one-way hike from the Lake Wenatchee Ranger Station to the Dirtyface Lookout at 6,000 feet with views of the lake and surrounding scenery. Backpackers may want to try the **Nason Ridge Trail,** a 22-mile one-way scenic trail along the length of the Nason Ridge, starting at South Shore Rd. off Hwy. 207. A number of other one-day or longer hikes start from various points along a complicated network of numbered forest roads; your best bet is to check at the ranger station for detailed maps and printed trail descriptions. This is black bear country; hikers and campers should use standard bear precautions (see "Land Animals" in the general Introduction).

Equine Expeditions and Excursions

During the summer months, **Eagle Creek Ranch** (a 580-acre ranch surrounded by Wenatchee National Forest) offers a number of pack trips to the Alpine Lakes, Glacier Lakes, and Henry M. Jackson Wilderness Areas. Deluxe pack trips (including wrangler, cook, food, and horses) costs $135 per person per day, while their you-hike, we-pack trips are $100 per person per day. Drop-camp packages, in which the wrangler takes you to a favorite spot for as long as you like and then comes back to carry you out, include pack and saddle horses and cost $270 per person. They also offer six-hour horseback rides along mountain trails for $75 per person, and shorter two-hour jaunts for $30 per person. For a brochure or additional information, call (509) 548-7798 or (800) 221-

7433. Wagon rides ($12) and barbecue dinner rides are also available. For hay rides, contact **Red-Tail Canyon Farm,** 11780 Freund Canyon Rd., tel. (509) 548-4512 or (800) 678-4512. For something even easier, hop on one of the **horse-drawn carriages** that roll through Leavenworth all summer long. A 20-minute ride for up to four people costs $25; call (509) 548-6825 or (800) 200-3354 for info.

Icicle Outfitters and Guides provides guided all-day rides into the Cascades for $80 per person, and an assortment of pack trips, including drop-camps for $325 per person, hike and pack trips (you hike, the horses carry the gear) for $100 per person per day, and deluxe pack trips that include horses, wrangler, cook, food, and tent for $130 per person per day. For a detailed brochure describing these trips and more, call (509) 784-1145 or (800) 497-3912. Icicle's day trips leave from riding stables at both Lake Wenatchee State Park and near the fish hatchery just outside Leavenworth.

Swimming and More

The city's outdoor **swimming pool,** 500 Hwy. 2, tel. (509) 548-4142, is open mid-June through August. Other options are the Wenatchee River at Waterfront Park or Lake Wenatchee State Park. **Club West,** 10421 Titus Rd., tel. (509) 548-4028, has saunas, a jacuzzi, racquetball courts, a weight room, and other facilities open to the public for a fee. The two local golf courses are **Leavenworth Golf Club,** out Icicle Rd. along the Wenatchee River, tel. (509) 548-7267, and **Kahler Glen Golf Course,** near Lake Wenatchee, tel. (509) 763-3785.

WINTER RECREATION

Cross-Country Skiing

Leavenworth, a popular spot with cross-country ski enthusiasts, offers 25 km of groomed trails within minutes of downtown. Three ski areas are maintained by the Leavenworth Winter Sports Club with both classical and skate-skiing lanes. The most accessible of these—**Leavenworth Golf Course Trail**—begins at Waterfront Park right in town and covers 12 km of rolling terrain along the Wenatchee River. **Icicle River Trail,** one mile from Leavenworth on Icicle Rd.,

has eight km of level tracks at the mouth of Icicle Canyon, through meadows and forests above the fish hatchery. Skiers can stop at the warming hut for a hot chocolate. **Ski Hill Trail** has a five-km track, with two km lighted for night skiing (till 9 p.m.) that roll over the hills adjacent to the downhill ski area. Here you get the added benefit of a lodge and weekend food service. The club also often grooms trails up the last several miles of Icicle River Rd., on an unplowed stretch. Trail fees are $6 per day for adults, kids under five free. For more information, contact the **Leavenworth Winter Sports Club,** tel. (509) 548-5115. Rent cross-country and skate skis at **Der Sportsman,** 837 Front St., tel. (509) 548-5623, or **Leavenworth Sports Center,** Hwy. 2 at Icicle Rd., tel. (509) 548-7864.

Lake Wenatchee State Park, 23 miles northwest of Leavenworth, has 10 km of maintained free trails in the park and on surrounding land, but you'll need a Sno-Park permit to park here ($7 per day, $10 for three days, or $20 for a season pass). Cross-country ski lessons and rentals are available nearby at **Leavenworth Outfitters,** tel. (509) 763-3733 or (800) 347-7934, next to Parkside Grocery; or rent skis from another Lake Wenatchee place, **Cougar Inn,** tel. (509) 763-3354.

The privately owned **Rose Ridge,** tel. (509) 548-6721, has a few kilometers of groomed cross-country trails and a popular toboggan and sledding hill located a few miles south of town on Hwy. 97. Contact the Leavenworth Ranger District office, tel. (509) 782-1413, for more skiing options (ungroomed wilderness trails and logging roads) around Blewett Pass in Wenatchee National Forest. Skiers need a Sno-Park permit to park here. (See "Sports and Recreation" under "Stevens Pass and Skykomish Valley," below, for more on the Stevens Pass Nordic Center, located 32 miles west of Leavenworth along Hwy. 2.)

Backcountry Skiing

For overnight cross-country skiing (16 miles of maintained ski trails) and some of the finest Telemark skiing in the high Cascades, stay in semi-luxury at **Scottish Lakes Backcountry Cabins,** tel. (509) 884-2000 or (800) 909-9916. Seven rustic but newly refurbished cabins come equipped with woodstoves, mattresses, propane stoves, kerosene lamps, and cooking utensils. The cabins cost $20-30 per person per day. From the parking area near Coles Corner (16 miles northwest of Leavenworth), the cabins are eight and a half miles and 3,000 feet higher in elevation. Most folks choose to ride up and back aboard their 12-passenger Sno-Cat for $50 per person, but they will haul your gear for $15 per person if you have the energy to ski up and back yourself. The cabins are on private timber company land near 5,000-foot McCue Ridge in the Alpine Lakes Wilderness and are generally open Thanksgiving to mid-May. Recommended.

Downhill Skiing

Leavenworth has its own tiny ski area, **Leavenworth Ski Bowl,** with two rope tows providing uphill transportation for the handful of runs. There's also a snowboard half-pipe. The ski season here is generally shorter than at the bigger areas because of the lower elevation; call (509) 548-5115 for conditions.

Two larger ski areas are close by: **Stevens Pass,** 35 miles to the west on Hwy. 2 (see "Sports and Recreation" under "Stevens Pass and Skykomish Valley," below), and **Mission Ridge,** 35 miles in the other direction near Wenatchee (see "Sports and Recreation" under Wenatchee). Mission Ridge is a favorite of locals because of the dry snow and less crowded slopes.

Sleigh Rides

Sleigh rides are available from three local places in winter for $10-15 adults, $5-10 children. **Red-Tail Canyon Farm,** 11780 Freund Canyon Rd., tel. (509) 548-4512 or (800) 678-4512, has champion Belgian draft horses that pull you through scenic Red-Tail Canyon. **Eagle Creek Ranch,** tel. (509) 548-7798 or (800) 221-7433, offers sleigh rides over the meadows and through the woods surrounding the ranch, two miles north of town off Hwy. 209. **Mountain Springs Lodge,** 14 miles north of Leavenworth, tel. (509) 763-2713 or (800) 858-2276, has a similar service.

Dogsled and Snowmobile Tours

See the Cascades and the Leavenworth valley from a unique perspective aboard a dogsled

from **Enchanted Mountain Tours,** 18555 Hazel Lane, tel. (509) 763-2975; one-hour tours for $55, half-day trips for $110. **Mountain Spring Lodge** runs snowmobile tours out of Plain; call (509) 763-3483 or (800) 858-2276 for reservations and prices.

ACCOMMODATIONS

As a favorite vacation spot in both winter and summer, Leavenworth is jam-packed with accommodations options. Because of their popularity, prices are high, and you'll have a tough time finding anything under $55 d a night. Leavenworth has no hostel, so travelers on a tight budget should consider staying in nearby Wenatchee or camping out. Prices at many motels and B&Bs rise on Friday and Saturday nights, and many places require a two-night minimum stay for weekends (especially festival weekends). If you're arriving on a weekend or in the peak summer or winter holiday seasons, try to book your lodging as soon as possible, since rooms fill up early. Many folks reserve several months ahead for festival weekends (Friday and Saturday nights). Those who don't may find themselves looking for a manger. Crowding is not nearly as much of a problem on weekdays, especially in the winter.

See the "Leavenworth Area Accommodations" chart for a complete listing of local motels, B&Bs, lodges, cabins, and houses. At the low end, you won't go wrong at **Mrs. Anderson's Lodging House,** tel. (509) 548-6984 or (800) 253-8990, where two small but comfortable rooms (one has a balcony) are available for less than $50 d apiece, including a light breakfast.

Bavarian Bedfinders, tel. (509) 548-4410 or (800) 323-2920, provides free reservation assistance 24 hours a day. Call them for B&B's, cabins, condos, and vacation homes. Other lodging reservation companies are: **Destination Leavenworth,** tel. (509) 548-5802 or (800) 962-7359, and **Leavenworth Vacation Getaways,** tel. (509) 548-4171 or (800) 548-4808.

Campgrounds

Wenatchee National Forest campgrounds near Leavenworth are generally open May to late October and charge $6-8. The closest of these

LEAVENWORTH AREA ACCOMMODATIONS

Included below are lodging places in Leavenworth, Peshastin, Cashmere, and Lake Wenatchee, arranged from least to most expensive. Many of these require a two-night minimum stay on festival weekends. Rates may be lower during the winter months. The area code is 509.

MOTELS AND LODGES

Edelweiss Hotel; 843 Front St.; tel. 548-7015; $30 s or d with shared bath, $40 s or d with private bath; plain rooms

Trading Post; 3057 Hwy. 97 (13 miles south of Leavenworth at Blewett Pass); tel. 548-5142; $30 s or d with bath down the hall, $45 s or d with private bath

Mrs. Anderson's Lodging House; 917 Commercial St.; tel. 548-6984 or (800) 253-8990; $44-70 s or d; historic lodging house, light breakfast

Valley Cottage Motel; 8912 Motel Rd., Dryden (five miles east of Leavenworth); tel. 548-5731; $45 d without kitchens, $55 d with kitchens; cute older cottages

Squirrel Tree Motel; Coles Corner (16 miles northwest of Leavenworth); tel. 763-3157; $50 s or d; no TV, phones, or alarm clocks

Tyrolean Ritz Hotel; 633 Front St.; tel. 548-5455 or (800) 854-6365; $50-60 s or d; European-style hotel, AAA approved

Village Inn Motel; 229 Cottage Ave., Cashmere (11 miles east of Leavenworth); tel. 782-3522 or (800) 793-3522; $51 s or d Fri.-Sat.; $45 s or d Sun.-Thurs.; AAA approved

The Alpen Inn Hotel; 405 Hwy. 2; tel. 548-4326 or (800) 423-9380; $55 s, $63 d; pool, hot tub, continental breakfast, AAA approved

River's Edge Lodge; 8401 Hwy. 2 (four miles east of town); tel. 548-7612 or (800) 451-5285; $55-75 s or d; along Wenatchee River, outdoor pool, hot tub, kitchenettes, two night minimum stay, AAA approved

Haus Rohrbach Pension; 12882 Ranger Rd.; tel. 548-7074 or (800) 548-4477; $55-150 s, $65-160 d; outdoor pool, jacuzzi, full breakfast, AAA approved

Wedge Mountain Inn; 7335 Hwy. 2, Peshastin (five miles east of Leavenworth); tel. 548-6694 or (800) 666-9664; $58 s or d Fri.-Sat.; $49 s or d Sun.-Thurs.; outdoor pool, two night minimum stay, AAA approved

Pine River Ranch; 19668 Hwy. 207, Lake Wenatchee; tel. 763-3959 or (800) 669-3877; $59-125 s or d; jacuzzis, fireplaces, mountain views, AAA approved

Evergreen Inn; 1117 Front St.; tel. 548-5515 or (800) 327-7212; $60-125 s or d; hot tub, continental breakfast, kitchenettes available, AAA approved

Canyons Inn Motel; 185 Hwy. 2; tel. 548-7992 or (800) 537-9382; $61 s or d; indoor pool, jacuzzi, AAA approved

Obertal Village Motor Inn; 922 Commercial St.; tel. 548-5204 or (800) 537-9382; $61-99 s or d; jacuzzi, AAA approved

Innsbrucker Motel; 703 Hwy. 2; tel. 548-5401; $62 s

Bayern on the River; 1505 Alpensee Strausse; tel. 548-5875 or (800) 873-3960 (U.S.) or (800) 255-3151 (Canada); $62 s, $69-95 d; outdoor pool, jacuzzi, AAA approved

Der Ritterhof Motor Inn; 190 Hwy. 2; tel. 548-5845 or (800) 255-5845; $63 s, $69 d; outdoor pool, jacuzzis, putting green, kitchenettes available, AAA approved *(continues on next page)*

LEAVENWORTH AREA ACCOMMODATIONS

(continued)

Hotel-Pension Anna; 926 Commercial St.; tel. 548-6273 or (800) 509-2662; $65-150 s, $75-165 d; continental breakfast, jacuzzi, Austrian decor

Edel Haus Inn; 320 9th St.; tel. 548-4412 or (800) 487-3335; $70-95 Fri.-Sat.; $50-75 s or d Sun.-Thurs.; jacuzzi

Abendblume Inn; 12570 Ranger Rd.; tel. 548-4059 or (800) 669-7634; $70-145 s or d; jacuzzi, fireplace, Austrian breakfast

Leavenworth Village Inn; 1016 Commercial; tel. 548-6620 or (800) 343-8198; $70-175 s or d; continental breakfast

The Alpine; 12728 Wilson; tel. 548-5352; $75 s or d; two-bedroom apartment with kitchen, fireplace, jacuzzi

Enzian Motor Inn; 590 Hwy. 2; tel. 548-5269 or (800) 223-8511; $78-165 s, $88-165 d; indoor and outdoor pools, jacuzzis, buffet breakfast, European furnishings, AAA approved

Mountain Home Lodge; Mt. Home Rd. (three miles E of Leavenworth); tel. 548-7077; $78-168 d; outdoor pool, jacuzzi, tennis, winter rates: $168-258 d includes all meals, toboggan, and skis, two night minimum stay

Blackbird Lodge; 309 8th St.; tel. 548-5800 or (800) 446-0240; $79-99 s or d Fri.-Sat.; $59-79 s or d Sun.-Thurs.; jacuzzi, AAA approved

Linderhof Motor Inn; 690 Hwy. 2; tel. 548-5283 or (800) 828-5680; $80-125 s or d; outdoor pool, jacuzzi, free breakfast buffet, kitchenettes available, AAA approved

Alpen Rose Inn; 500 Alpine Place; tel. 548-3000 or (800) 582-2474; $80-150 s or d Sun.-Thurs., $85-150 s or d Fri.-Sat.; $68-125 s or d Sun.-Thurs.; jacuzzis, exercise room, full breakfast, fireplaces, AAA approved

Best Western Icicle Inn; 505 W. Hwy. 2; tel. 548-7000 or (800) 528-1234; $89 s, $94 d Fri.-Sat.; $79 s, $84 d Sun.-Thurs.; outdoor pool, jacuzzi, exercise room, continental breakfast, AAA approved

Pension Einer; 167 W. Whitman St.; tel. 548-6674; $100 s or d; one-bedroom apartment, hot tub, fireplace

Mountain Springs Lodge; 19115 Chiwawa Loop Rd. (18 miles northwest of Leavenworth); tel. 763-2713 or (800) 858-2276; $125 d for guest cabins, jacuzzi, sun deck, kitchens, pool table, two night minimum stay on weekends, horseback or sleigh rides available

Dirty Face Lodge; 16705 Brown Rd., Lake Wenatchee; tel. 763-3538; $160 d, $20 each additional person; guest lodge sleeps 10, outdoor pool, jacuzzi, kitchen, fireplaces

BED AND BREAKFASTS

Das Wisenhaus; 8089 Icicle Rd.; tel. 548-6746; $55 s, $70-80 d; mountain view, Bavarian breakfast, no kids

Mt. Valley Vista; 8695 Larson Rd., Peshastin (four miles east of Leavenworth); tel. 548-5301; $55-65 s or d; panoramic view, full breakfast

Tabak B&B; 8309 Riverview Rd., Peshastin (three miles east of Leavenworth); tel. 548-4390; $60 s or d; antique-filled home, full breakfast

Leirvangen B&B; 7586 Icicle Rd.; tel. 548-5165; $60-85 s or d, full breakfast, Norwegian owner

Old Blewett Pass B&B; 3470 Hwy. 97; tel. 548-4475; $60-85 s, $75-85 d; 1908 homestead, outdoor pool, full breakfast, sundeck, 12 miles south of Leavenworth

Phippen's B&B; 10285 Ski Hill Dr.; tel. 548-7755 or (800) 666-9806; $60-85 s, $65-90 d; outdoor pool, hot tub, full breakfast, adults only

Creekside B&B; 15966 Chumstick Hwy., (eight miles north of Leavenworth); tel. 548-8102 or (800) 860-1322; $65 s or d; full breakfast, evening dessert, antique decor, no kids

Autumn Pond B&B; 10388 Titus Rd.; tel. 548-4482 or (800) 222-9661; $65 d; hot tub, full breakfast

Cashmere Country Inn; 5801 Pioneer, Cashmere (ten miles E of Leavenworth); tel. 782-4212 or (800) 291-9144; $75-80 d; 1907 farmhouse; outdoor pool, hot tub, full country breakfast, two night minimum stay on weekends, no kids

Haus Lorelei; 347 Division St.; tel. 548-5726; $79-89 s or d; gorgeous 1903 guest house along Wenatchee River, hot tub, full breakfast, children welcome, two night minimum stay on weekends

Bosch Garten; 9846 Dye Rd.; tel. 548-6900 or (800) 535-0069; $95-105 Fri.-Sat.; $85-95 s or d Sun.-Thurs.; hot tub, full breakfast, king-size beds, children accepted, AAA approved

All Seasons River Inn; 8751 Icicle Rd.; tel. 548-1425; $85-115 s, $95-125 d Fri.-Sat.; $75-105 s, $85-115 d Sun.-Thurs.; fireplaces, jacuzzis, riverfront decks, antique decor, gourmet breakfast, adults only, two-night minimum stay on weekends

Run of the River; 9308 E. Leavenworth Rd.; tel. 548-7171 or (800) 288-6491; $90-140 s or d; luxurious log home along Icicle Creek with flower-filled yard, full breakfast, adults only, two-night minimum stay on weekends, AAA approved

Featherwind's Farm; 17033 River Rd.; tel. 763-2011; $95-110 s or d; beautiful old farmhouse, outdoor pool, jacuzzi, full breakfast

Enchantment Haus B&B; 8158 E. Leavenworth Rd.; tel. 548-1421; $100-125 d, three-bedroom home, fireplace, continental breakfast, adults only

CABINS, HOUSES, AND CONDOS

The Cougar Inn; 23379 Hwy. 207, Lake Wenatchee; tel. 763-3354; $45-55 s or d for rooms, $75-85 for cabins (sleep four); lakeside location

Bindlestiff's Riverside Cabins; 11798 Hwy. 2; tel. 548-5015; $50 s or d in cabins; continental breakfast, wooded setting along Wenatchee River

The Cabin; 8835 Icicle Rd.; tel. 548-7359; $85 s or d; cabin with kitchen, wooded setting, two-night minimum on weekends

Wolfe's Place on the River; 9764 E. Leavenworth Rd.; tel. 548-4684 or (800) 424-3445; $85-125 d; three-bedroom house , and cottage along Wenatchee River, hot tub, fireplace

Lake Wenatchee Hide-A-Ways; 2611 Kinnikinick Dr., Lake Wenatchee; tel. 763-2611; $85-125 d; comfortable lakeside cabins

Saimons Hide-A-Ways; 16408 River Rd. (18 miles northwest of Leavenworth); tel. 763-3213 or (800) 845-8638; $85-125 d; cabins with jacuzzis

The Farmhouse; 12751 Ranger Rd.; tel. 548-4212 or (800) 548-4808; $100 d; old two-bedroom farmhouse with kitchen, sleeps six

White River Lodging; 23809 White River Rd., Lake Wenatchee; tel. 763-3503; $105 d; two-bedroom house (sleeps eight), fireplace, hot tub, kitchen

Riggs on the River; 8330 Main St., Peshastin (five miles E of Leavenworth); tel. 548-6101; $110 d; two-bedroom condo, sleeps six

Beaver Valley Lodge; Plain Valley (14 miles north of Leavenworth); tel. 763-3072; $125 d ($10 pp after two); turn-of-the-century four-bedroom farmhouse, sleeps eight, kitchen

The River House; 18632 Hwy. 209 (14 miles northwest of Leavenworth); tel. 763-3462; $125 for up to six; two-bedroom house, kitchen, fireplace, overlooks Wenatchee River *(continues on next page)*

LEAVENWORTH AREA ACCOMMODATIONS

(continued)

Natapoc Lodging; 12338 Bretz Rd. (18 miles northwest of Leavenworth); tel. 763-3313; $130-225 d; six Wenatchee River homes in Plain Valley

Cranberry Cottage Cabin; 15947 River Rd.; tel. (206) 883-1307 (call collect); $135 d; riverfront chalet, kitchen, fireplace, view, sleeps ten

Gustav's House on the Golf Course; Icicle Rd.; tel. 548-5141; $150 for up to four; two-bedroom house, jacuzzi

Chiwawa River Retreat; 2633 Kinnikinick Dr.; tel. 763-3543; $165 s or d; lodge sleeps 12, kitchen, fireplaces

can be found at the appropriately named **Eight-mile Campground,** eight miles up Icicle Road. Six more Forest Service campgrounds are spread within 20 miles of Leavenworth along this road. Note that the 1994 Rat Creek Fire burned through much of this country, so be ready for blackened trees in some campgrounds. Another very popular Forest Service tenting spot, **Tumwater Campground,** is 10 miles northwest from Leavenworth along Hwy. 2. Farther afield (16 miles northwest) is Lake Wenatchee; camp at the Forest Service's **Nason Creek** and **Glacier View** Campgrounds. Four more Forest Service campgrounds lie northwest of the lake.

Lake Wenatchee State Park at the east end of the lake has 197 oft-filled campsites for $10 ($15 for RVs) including coin-operated showers. It's open from early April to late October. Call (509) 763-3101 for information, or (800) 452-5687 for campsite reservations ($6 extra fee), available up to 11 months ahead of time. Showers are also available at **Oxbow Trading Post** in Cole Corner (16 miles northwest of Leavenworth). No reservations are accepted at **Wenatchee River County Park,** tel. (509) 662-2525, 11 miles east in Cashmere. Camping ($12) and RV spaces ($17) with coin-operated showers are available April to late October.

Eighteen miles southeast of Leavenworth along Hwy. 97 is the Forest Service's free but tiny **Bonanza Campground.** No potable water here.

Hikers and campers will find **Die Wascherei** at 1317 Front St. (behind Food Giant) a relief: laundry facilities and hot showers in the same place! Open daily 7 a.m.-10 p.m.

RV Parks

Several RV parks (summer only) can be found around Leavenworth: **Pine Village KOA,** 11401 River Bend Dr., tel. (509) 548-7709; **Chalet Trailer Park,** 9825 Duncan Rd., tel. (509) 548-4578 or (800) 477-2697; **Icicle River RV Park,** 7305 Icicle Rd., tel. (509) 548-5420; and **Blu Shastin RV Park,** 3300 Hwy. 97 (11 miles southeast of Leavenworth), tel. (509) 548-4184.

FOOD

Leavenworth village has a number of restaurants, all very Bavarian from the outside, but often more diverse on the inside; even the local McDonald's features pseudo-German architecture (but no bratwurst or *leberkäse*).

Bavarian Eats

Several eateries dish out the dense, meaty German fare one expects to find. You'll get the real thing at **Reiner's Gasthaus,** 829 Front St., tel. (509) 548-5111, serving authentic and moderately priced Austrian, Bavarian, and Hungarian cuisine with live accordion music on Saturday nights. Meals are served on long, shared tables. Another popular (but less noteworthy) German restaurant with live polka tunes on weekends is **Andreas Keller,** 829 Front St., tel. (509) 548-6000. Be sure to order the big Bavarian-style pretzels with homemade mustard—quite unlike the standard shopping-mall variety—with your brew. **Gustav's,** 617 Hwy. 2, tel. (509) 548-4509, has additional Germanic fare but is best known for the great hamburgers, including an Ortega Mexican burger.

Breakfast and Lunch Places

For the best local breakfast, start your day with the hometown folks at **Breakfast and Bratwurst,** 217 8th St., tel. (509) 548-6121. There are many lunchtime choices, from simple wiener stands to delectable soup, sandwich, salad, and sausage places like **Rumpelstilzchen's,** 1133 Hwy. 2, tel. (509) 548-4663, or the earth-bound deli at **The Gingerbread Factory,** 828 Commercial St., tel. (509) 548-6592. **Cafe Crista,** 801 Front St. (upstairs), tel. (509) 548-5074, lists Bavarian food for lunch or dinner but is equally known for its lighter Euro-American specialties. Come here Friday evening for a Mexican buffet, plus live music some nights.

What's for Dinner?

Ask the locals their favorite dinner place, and you're likely to hear the **Edel Haus Inn,** 320 9th St., tel. (509) 548-4412. Their menu changes every month or so, but always includes a good choice of flavorful Northwest cuisine and luscious desserts served in an elegant setting. Vegetarians will find at least a few dishes here as well, and the pizza is guaranteed to please. Another good spot for pizzas is **Leavenworth Pizza Co.** at 894 Hwy. 2, tel. (509) 548-7766.

Two favorite places owned by the same folks are **Walter's Other Place,** 820 Commercial St., tel. (509) 548-6125, and **Terrace Bistro,** 200 8th St. (upstairs), tel. (509) 548-4193. Walter's serves delicious, moderately priced Greek food

and pasta in a modest setting, while the Terrace has international cuisine for the linen-and-fine-crystal crowd. The latter is a bit intimidating if you're just looking for a simple lunch spot but has a pleasant outdoor terrace for leisurely summer evenings. **Katzenjammer's,** 221 8th St., tel. (509) 548-5826, is the place for a romantic evening with a dinner of Alaskan king crab or prime rib, but don't come here if you're on a tight budget.

Tumwater Inn, 219 9th St., tel. (509) 548-4232, has good breakfasts but an otherwise middle-brow menu. The real exception to this is their to-die-for chocolate cake. Tumwater also has a big selection of European beers and live music on weekends. The local brewpub, **Leavenworth Brewery Restaurant & Pub,** 636 Front St., tel. (509) 548-4545, gets mixed reviews for their suds—they aren't always allowed to age sufficiently—but the pub grub is decent. Tours are available daily at 2 p.m. Next door is **Casa Mia,** tel. (509) 548-5621, which serves surprisingly good Mexican food.

If you're headed up to Lake Wenatchee, try **Cougar Inn Resort,** 23379 Hwy. 207, tel. (509) 763-3353, for a scrumptious Friday night prime rib and seafood buffet or a Sunday champagne brunch with stunning lake and mountain views to boot; call (509) 763-3354 for reservations. The food is worth the drive. On the way to Cougar Inn is **Beaver Hill Cafe,** 18630 Hwy. 209, tel. (509) 763-3072, with excellent homemade breads and delicious breakfasts.

Leavenworth's streets have a Bavarian flair.

ARCHIE SATTERFIELD

the festival capital
of the state,
Leavenworth

ARCHIE SATTERFIELD

Bakeries, Delis, and Espresso

Hansel & Gretel Deli, 819 Front St., tel. (509) 548-7721, has German sausages, sandwiches, homemade pies, ice cream, and picnics-to-go. Or just hang out with the locals over coffee and a donut. Four different bakeshops provide something for all tastes. **The Gingerbread Factory,** 828 Commercial St., tel. (509) 548-6592 or (800) 296-7097, is famous for its wonderful soft gingerbread cookies and houses; try the amusingly decorated cookies even if you aren't generally a gingerbread fanatic. They even offer a mail-order service for gingerbread houses and other treats. The lunchtime deli here is a locals' favorite for earthy salads, sandwiches, and espresso. Also recommended for espresso is—surprisingly—the kitschy teddy bear shop called **Alpen Bear** at 827 Front St., tel. (509) 548-6695. **Hoelgaard's Danish Bakery,** 731 Front St., tel. (509) 548-7514, sells fresh soft pretzels and outstanding Danish pastries and cookies. **Oberland Bakery & Cafe,** 703 Front St., tel. (509) 548-7216, offers sweets, healthy sandwiches, and espresso coffees. Out of the way and near the fish hatchery is **Homefires Bakery,** 13013 Bayne Rd., tel. (509) 548-7362, where delicious sourdough breads, pies, and cinnamon rolls emerge from a German brick oven. Homefires is a popular stopping place for hikers and cyclists. Closed Tuesday and Wednesday.

EVENTS AND ENTERTAINMENT

Festivals

The people in Leavenworth always find something to celebrate—festivals and fairs circle the calendar. January brings **The Great Bavarian Ice Fest** and its snowshoe and cross-country ski races, dogsled pulls, a tug of war, and fireworks in mid-month. Smaller festivals fill the months until the big **Maifest,** held on Mother's Day weekend, when costumed Bavarian dancers circle the Maypole, and concerts, a parade, and Saturday night street dance are accompanied by oompa music from the bandstand and the chiming of bells from the Marlin Handbell Ringers. This weekend also marks the start of **Art in the Park,** during which area artists display their talents every weekend May-Oct. in Front St. Park.

Other summer festivals are **Craftfair** in early June, and **The International Folk Dance Festival** in mid-June. The **Washington State Autumn Leaf Festival,** spread over two weekends at the end of September, starts with a grand parade featuring dozens of marching bands, and includes daily polka music in the gazebo, Saturday night street dances, a pancake feed, flea market, and casino night.

Christmas is Leavenworth's most festive holiday: the **Christmas Lighting Festival** is held the first and second Saturday in December when all the Christmas lights go on simultaneously at dusk and Mr. and Mrs. Claus appear in their house in the park while Scrooge wanders curmudgeonly around. Caroling, sleigh rides, concerts, and food booths add to the holiday festivities. (Cynics call this one a nonevent, since they switch on the lights the first weekend, then turn them off in time to do it again the following Friday. Besides, the lights stay lit till February, so no need to hurry up to see them.)

Live Music

Accordion-playing musicians and polka-dancin' fools can be found at several local restaurants throughout the year, including: **Adler Bier Garten,** 633 Front St. (downstairs), tel. (509) 548-7733; **Andreas Keller,** 829 Front St. (downstairs), tel. (509) 548-6000; and **Reiner's Gasthaus,** 829 Front St. (upstairs), tel. (509) 548-5111. Other places with live music (and not always Bavarian oompa bands) are: **Leavenworth Brewery,** 636 Front St., tel. (509) 548-4545, and **Burgermeister Bier Garten,** 921 Front St., tel. (509) 548-6625. The **Community Coffeehouse** at the Adler, 633 Front St., has live music and poetry most Friday nights in a no-smoking, non-alcohol setting.

Theater

Every Thursday through Sunday from mid-July to Labor Day, the **Leavenworth Summer Theatre** puts on an all-ages musical production of Hansel & Gretel. Tickets are $12 for adults, $10 for children and seniors; call (509) 548-4607 for details.

INFORMATION AND SERVICES

For maps, brochures, and additional information, stop by the **Leavenworth Chamber of Commerce Visitor Center,** 894 Hwy. 2 (the Clocktower Building), tel. (509) 548-5807. They're open Sunday 10 a.m.-4 p.m., Mon.-Fri. 9 a.m.-6 p.m., and Saturday 8 a.m.-6 p.m. year-round.

Two Wenatchee National Forest offices are located near town: **Leavenworth Ranger District,** 600 Sherbourne St., tel. (509) 548-4067, is open summers every day 7:45 a.m.-4:30 p.m.,

and winters Mon.-Fri. 7:45 a.m.-4:30 p.m., while **Lake Wenatchee Ranger District,** 22976 Hwy. 207, tel. (509) 763-3103, is open Mon.-Sat. 8 a.m.-4:30 p.m. in summer, and Mon.-Fri. 8 a.m.-4:30 p.m. in winter.

The sparkling new **public library,** tel. (509) 548-7923, sits right across from Front St. Park and features a periodicals room with a fireplace and stunning mountain vistas. For medical emergencies, head to **Cascade Hospital,** 817 Commercial St., tel. (509) 548-5815.

The **area code** for Leavenworth and all of eastern Washington is 509.

TRANSPORTATION AND TOURS

By Car

Driving to Leavenworth in the winter over Stevens Pass has been described as "driving through a Christmas card." Rocky, snow-covered peaks surround the highway as you approach the 4,061-foot pass; then, closer to Leavenworth, the Wenatchee River rushes alongside the road through high, rocky walls and areas burned in the 1994 forest fires. The trip from Seattle is about 125 miles. From late fall to early spring, be sure to call (509) 976-7623 for pass conditions before setting out—and have your chains ready! As an alternate route, take I-90 over Snoqualmie Pass to Hwy. 97 north over Sauk Pass; these passes are generally drier and snow-free earlier than Stevens.

Bus Transport

Free (!) local buses connect Leavenworth with other parts of Chelan and Douglas counties, including Cashmere, Wenatchee, and the popular tourist destinations of Lake Chelan and the Mission Ridge Ski Area. Buses run hourly 8 a.m.-8 p.m. Mon.-Sat. all year, and can carry bikes in the summer or skis in the winter; contact the **LINK,** tel. (800) 851-5465, for details. **Greyhound Bus Lines,** tel. (509) 662-2183, serves Leavenworth from their Kountry Kitchen Drive-In "station" at the east end of town. **High Mountain Recreation,** tel. (509) 548-4326 or (800) 423-9380, runs shuttle vans from Leavenworth to Lake Wenatchee ($40 roundtrip) or other destinations throughout the state. Call them for raft or ski shuttles, too. The nearest commercial airport and Amtrak station is in Wenatchee, 30 miles east of Leavenworth.

Tours

Gray Line of Seattle offers tours ($34 roundtrip) from Seattle to Leavenworth for Maifest in early May as well as the Christmas Tree Lighting Ceremony on the first two Saturdays of December. Prices for both one-day trips include a snack on the bus. For more information call Gray Line at (206) 624-5813 or (800) 524-1134. Also operating out of Seattle, **Don & Diane FunTours** has one-day bus tours ($50 roundtrip) for Maifest, the Autumn Leaf Festival, and the Christmas Lighting Festival. For reservations or information call (206) 282-3508.

Cascade Helitours, five miles east of Leavenworth, tel. (509) 548-4759, provides scenic helicopter flights over the Cascades.

STEVENS PASS AND SKYKOMISH VALLEY

US Highway 2 is one of the state's most beautiful drives, and the western end of a transcontinental two-lane route that runs eastward all the way to Maine. Heading west from Leavenworth, the highway enters spectacular Tumwater Canyon, with the roiling Wenatchee River—a popular rafting and kayaking waterway—as a guide into the mountains. The road eventually tops out at 4,061-foot **Stevens Pass,** named for John F. Stevens, the chief locating engineer for the Great Northern Railway that was pushed through here in 1892. (Stevens is perhaps better known as the builder of the Panama Canal.)

At Stevens Pass you'll find popular downhill and cross-country ski areas, and a jumping off point for the **Pacific Crest Trail.** Serious backpackers can hook up with the PCT and hike clear up to Canada or down to Mexico if they like—or, more likely, just hike a short chunk of the trail. Two wilderness areas on either side of the pass—Henry M. Jackson Wilderness and Alpine Lakes Wilderness—contain striking natural features, from glaciers and alpine meadows, to dense forests intersected by clear, clean rivers. Much of the area's beauty can be seen through your car windows and from short roadside paths, but hundreds of miles of hiking trails let you experience its splendor at close range.

On the western side of the pass, Hwy. 2 drops quickly—2,000 feet in 14 miles to the little town of Skykomish. As you switchback down from the summit, the Burlington Northern railroad tracks emerge from seven-mile-long **Cascade Railroad Tunnel,** one of the longest in the western hemisphere. The drive downhill takes you past rugged snow-covered peaks, plunging waterfalls, popular campgrounds, fishing holes in the Skykomish River, and nature trails to explore along the way. Finally, the grade lessens in the wide Skykomish Valley (alias "Sky Valley"), as the highway slips through a chain of small towns before emerging into the flat farmland (and spreading suburbia) near Monroe.

RECREATION

Alpine Lakes Wilderness Area

The spectacular Alpine Lakes Wilderness covers 393,000 acres of high Cascades country. This diverse landscape ranges in elevation from 1,000-foot valleys to towering 9,000-foot mountain spires. Much of the area—hence the name—is high alpine country filled with some 700 crystalline lakes, ponds, and tarns.

Because of its proximity to Seattle, an abundance of short and long hiking possibilities, and the dramatic alpine-and-lake scenery, this is one of the most heavily used wild places in Washington. In some ways, Alpine Lakes Wilderness is being loved to death by those who come to escape city life, but find instead crowded backcountry sites and abused trails. To alleviate some of these problems, the Forest Service has instituted a somewhat confusing wilderness permit system that limits use in the three most popular sections—Enchantment area near Leavenworth, West Fork Foss near Skykomish, and Snoqualmie Pass near I-90. There is a $5 charge for these permit reservations, and reservations can be made at ranger stations. Permits (these are free, and available at all trailheads) are also required for all other parts of the Alpine Lakes Wilderness, but the number of visitors at these places is not yet limited. The policy is still evolving, so check at a local ranger station for the latest details before heading out. Along Hwy. 2, the ranger stations are found in Skykomish (tel. 360-677-2414) and Leavenworth (tel. 509-763-3103). Along I-90, they are in North Bend (tel. 206-888-1421), Cle Elum (tel. 509-674-4411), and the Snoqualmie Pass Visitor Center (tel. 206-434-6111). The following hikes are a tiny sample of those available. For a more complete description, pick up a copy of *100 Hikes in Washington's Alpine Lakes,* by Vicky Spring, Ira Spring, and Harvey Manning (Seattle: The Mountaineers). Forest Service offices also have detailed information on individual trails within the wilderness.

Heading south from Hwy. 2, the **Pacific Crest Trail** climbs past the downhill ski area and Lake Susan June, before reaching Josephine Lake on the wilderness boundary (four and a half miles from the highway). From here, you enter a web of trails that covers the high alpine land, opening up many loop-trip possibilities. Two fun and very popular trails (wilderness permits required) begin from the Foss River Rd. (Forest Rd. 68; two miles east of Skykomish). One of these, the **Necklace Valley Trail,** starts up an old narrow-gauge railroad bed before entering a tight canyon and ascending quickly to a cluster of lakes in upper Necklace Valley. The one-way length is seven and a half miles, with a gain of 3,140 feet in elevation. A second excellent short hike is to follow **West Fork Foss River Trail** to Trout Lake, and then on to a chain of half-a-dozen jewel-like lakes. The one-way distance is seven miles, with an elevation gain of 2,900 feet. Deception Creek Trail, another access path off Hwy. 2, is described below under "Waterfalls." Many popular trails lead into the wilderness from the Icicle Rd. out of Leavenworth, but the 1994 fires burned through much of this area. Check with the Leavenworth Ranger Station for the latest on trail conditions and recommended routes there.

Henry M. Jackson Wilderness Area

This 103,591-acre mountain wilderness is accessible from the Stevens Pass, Skykomish, Lake Wenatchee, and Darrington areas; see Forest Service maps for specifics. It was named for a longtime U.S. Senator from Washington,

Henry M. Jackson, who was instrumental in helping establish wilderness areas throughout the West. The glacier-carved landscape has a Swiss-Alps quality: numerous alpine lakes, prominent knife-edged ridges, and deep U-shaped valleys. Dozens of backcountry hikes are possible, and ambitious backpackers could continue on into the adjacent Glacier Peak Wilderness Area. The Pacific Crest Trail passes through the center of Henry M. Jackson Wilderness before crossing Hwy. 2 and continuing on southward into the Alpine Lakes Wilderness.

An interesting and very scenic 18-mile loop trek can be made by following the Beckler River Rd. (Forest Rd. 65) from the town of Skykomish to Jack Pass, and continuing another mile to Forest Rd. 63. Turn right here, and proceed to the trailhead at the end of the road. The **North Fork Trail** climbs into high mountain country from here, through masses of hillside wildflowers in mid-summer, eventually emerging into the alpine after five miles or so. It meets the Pacific Crest Trail at Dishpan Gap. Turn right and follow the PCT past Lake Sally and then back around 6,368-foot Skykomish Peak to the Pass Creek Trail, which will take you back to your starting point. Another option is to turn left at Dishpan Gap and follow **Bald Eagle Mt. Trail** back to trail No. 1050, which leads back to the road.

See *100 Hikes in Washington's North Cascades: Glacier Peak Region,* by Ira Spring and Harvey Manning (Seattle: The Mountaineers) for detailed descriptions of these and other interesting hikes, or stop by the **Skykomish Ranger Station** for current conditions and trail descriptions.

Downhill Skiing

About halfway between Skykomish and Lake Wenatchee is **Stevens Pass Ski Area,** a major downhill area that is popular with Seattleites. With a base elevation of 3,821 feet, and a summit elevation of 5,845 feet, its 10 lifts serve 1,125 acres of beginner through expert terrain. Call (206) 634-1645 in Seattle or (206) 973-2441 in Skykomish for the latest snow conditions. Stevens Pass is generally open mid-November through late April, offering ski and snowboard rentals and lessons, a ski shop, restaurant, cafeteria, and cocktail lounges. More than 25 different ski and snowboard schools operate out of

Stevens Pass, and many of these include transportation from the Seattle area in the cost. Contact the ski area for a complete listing. A tubing and sledding area is adjacent to the ski hill.

Weekend lift tickets cost $31 for adults, $24 for kids, and $26 for seniors; ages six and under or 70 and older ski free. Weekday rates (excluding holidays) are $15 Monday and Tuesday, $20 for Wed.-Friday. The lifts are open 9 a.m. to 10 p.m. every day, with lighted night skiing on 12 major runs. Night skiers pay just $10 Sun.-Thurs., $25 on Friday and Saturday.

Lodging is not available at Stevens Pass, although RVs can park in the lot (no hookups). The nearest overnight accommodations are in Skykomish (16 miles west), and the Lake Wenatchee/Leavenworth area (21-37 miles east).

Cross-Country Skiing

Stevens Pass Nordic Center, tel. (360) 973-2441, is five miles east of the Stevens Pass downhill area and costs $7.50 for adults, $6.50 for children or seniors. Classical and skating skis can be rented here, and a small snack bar has hot food. Stevens Pass is open 9 a.m.-4 p.m. Friday, Saturday, and Sunday, and on winter holidays. There are 30 km of groomed trails, most of which follow closely along the very noisy overhead power lines. The main route climbs uphill for 7.5 km, gaining over 700 feet along the way.

Raft Trips

The Skykomish River is an extremely popular rafting place during the peak snowmelt period from mid-March to mid-July. The upper portion of the "Sky" from Skykomish to Baring and the South Fork from Skykomish to Index are *not* for beginners. The famous "Boulder Drop" section is class IV+ water, and there are many other deep plunges and vertical drops of class IV. The various commercial rafting companies recommend that anyone running the upper Skykomish have previous rafting experience and be in good physical condition. Rates for these four-hour, eight-mile-long float trips range from $55 to $75 depending upon the company, the number of people in the group, how far ahead you book your trip, and whether it's the weekend or not. Trips are available on most early summer weekends, with fewer weekday runs. Note that some com-

panies restrict Skykomish rafting to those at least 16 years old.

Based in Index, **Chinook Expeditions** runs excellent float and whitewater trips around Washington, and even as far away as Maui. Call (800) 241-3451 for current river conditions and reservations. Chinook also offers Skykomish trips in the winter months when conditions are fast and wild, but when the weather can be wet. Two other recommended professional companies that offer rafting trips all over the state are **Downstream River Runners,** tel. (800) 234-4644, and **Wild & Scenic River Tours,** tel. (206) 323-1220. Wild & Scenic also offers trips down the "kick-ass" Upper North Fork Skykomish for $89, taking you through 10 miles of hairy class IV rapids. Not for the faint of heart, or for inexperienced rafters. **Wave Trek,** tel. (206) 793-1705 or (800) 543-7971, is an Index-based rafting company with trips down both the main fork of the Sky, and the wild North Fork ($75). They also teach three-, four-, and five-day kayaking classes for those who want to take a bigger step into river running. Other rafting outfitters waiting to take you down the Sky are: **Alpine Adventures,** tel. (800) 926-7238; **Blue Sky Outfitters,** tel. (800) 228-7238; **Cascade Adventures,** tel. (360) 323-5488 or (800) 723-8386; **North Cascades River Expeditions,** tel. (800) 634-8433; **Orion River Expeditions,** tel. (800) 553-7466; **River Recreation,** tel. (360) 339-9133 or (800) 464-5899; and **Wildwater River Tours,** tel. (800) 522-9453.

For a do-it-yourself trip, the lower Skykomish is a peaceful river to raft or kayak, with a few small, generally avoidable rapids above Sultan. It's rated class II+ from Big Eddy State Park (a.k.a. Sky River State Scenic Park; two miles east of Gold Bar where Hwy. 2 cross the river) to Sultan, and class I from Sultan to Monroe.

Waterfalls

The Highway 2 planners must have loved waterfalls: several raging falls are right along the roadside. Easternmost of these is **Deception Falls,** right along the highway approximately seven miles west of Stevens Pass. A short paved path crosses the Tye River and continues to a cascading torrent of water, but much more interesting is the half-mile nature trail that drops down along the river. Educational plaques describe the forest and river, and lead to two more-impressive cataracts, both backdropped by the deep green rainforest. Some of this is second growth timber, while other parts were never logged. The lowest falls is the biggest surprise, but I'll let you discover it for yourself. **Deception Creek Trail** starts on the south side of Hwy. 2, and provides a delicious old-growth forest hike. The trail climbs 10 miles (gaining almost 2,500 feet along the way) to Deception Pass in the Alpine Lakes Wilderness Area, where you can join up with the Pacific Crest Trail.

About one and a half miles farther west, **Alpine Falls** drops 50 feet into the Tye River below; park on the south side of the highway and follow the can't-miss path. **Bridal Veil Falls,** a quarter mile east of the Index junction, vary with the season; summer brings two distinctive "veils," while winter freezes the falls into a glistening sheet of ice. The highest falls of all—265-foot Wallace Falls—is described below under the town of Index. Scenic **Eagle Falls** on the South Fork Skykomish River is a favorite place for summertime swimmers who play in the big jade-green plunge pool. Be careful if you join in the fun since there are more falls just downstream. The falls are 11 miles west of Skykomish and right along Hwy. 2.

PRACTICALITIES

Campgrounds

Four Forest Service campgrounds provide in-the-woods lodging options in the Skykomish vicinity. Three of these—**Beckler River, Miller River,** and **Money Creek**—have running water and can be reserved ($7.50 extra) by calling (800) 280-2267. Both campgrounds are generally open late May through September and cost $10 per site. Beckler River Campground is two miles north of Skykomish on Forest Rd. 65. Money Creek Campground is four miles west of Skykomish and right along Hwy. 2. The more primitive places—Troublesome Creek and San Juan Campgrounds—are described below under "Over Jack Pass."

Transportation

Stevens Pass is often a challenge to traverse and is sometimes closed by winter storms. If you're heading up to ski at Stevens Pass or continuing east to Leavenworth or Wenatchee, be sure to call the State Patrol's recorded message at (206) 455-7700 (in Seattle) for road conditions before you set out; you don't want to have to buy chains at the only gas station in Skykomish. Another number for mountain pass reports is the Dept. of Transportation's (900) 407-7277, but the cost is 35 cents per minute (two minute maximum). For avalanche and mountain weather information in the winter, call (206) 526-6677.

SKY VALLEY

As you head down from the Cascades into Skykomish ("Sky") Valley, several towns pop up along Hwy. 2, each a little larger than the last, till you reach the edge of Seattle's sprawl at fast-growing Monroe.

Community Transit, tel. (360) 778-2185 or (800) 562-1375, has daily bus service throughout the Skykomish Valley, along with all of Snohomish County. The **area code** for eastern Snohomish County, including all of Sky Valley, is 360.

Skykomish

The historic railroad town of Skykomish (pop. 250; pronounced "sky-KOH-mish") is primarily a resting point on the way into or out of the mountains. There's a cafe with respectable food, a motel and hotel, gas station, Forest Service office, and not much else. **Sky River Inn,** tel. (360) 677-2261, has comfortable rooms for $55-60 s or d, $5 extra for kitchenettes. This is a popular stopping point for weekend skiers in the winter, so it's a good idea to reserve ahead at those times. Cheaper and simpler lodging can be found at the historic **Skykomish Hotel and Restaurant,** tel. (360) 677-2477, where bath-down-the-hall rooms go for $25-45 s or d. The hotel was constructed in 1905, and the back room was very popular with card-playing railroad crews. The old **depot** still stands next to the tracks, and Amtrak's Empire Builder rolls through town four days a week, connecting Chicago with Seattle. (No stops here, alas.)

Skykomish Ranger Station, tel. (360) 677-2414, has recreation and topographic maps, books, and current information on trails and

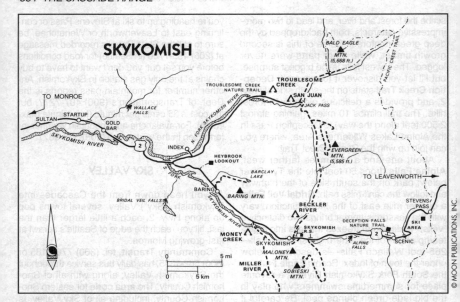

SKYKOMISH

TO MONROE

SULTAN STARTUP GOLD BAR

WALLACE FALLS

SKYKOMISH RIVER

INDEX

HEYBROOK LOOKOUT

BRIDAL VEIL FALLS

BARING

N. FORK SKYKOMISH RIVER

TROUBLESOME CREEK NATURE TRAIL

TROUBLESOME CREEK

SAN JUAN

JACK PASS

BALD EAGLE MTN. (5,668 ft.)

PACIFIC CREST TRAIL

EVERGREEN MTN. (5,585 ft.)

BARCLAY LAKE

BARING MTN.

BECKLER RIVER

S. FORK SKYKOMISH RIVER

SKYKOMISH R.S.

MONEY CREEK

SKYKOMISH

MALONEY MTN.

MILLER RIVER

SOBIESKI MTN.

DECEPTION FALLS NATURE TRAIL

ALPINE FALLS

SCENIC

STEVENS PASS

SKI AREA

TO LEAVENWORTH

0   5 mi

0   5 km

© MOON PUBLICATIONS, INC.

---

campgrounds. The ranger station is open daily 8 a.m.-4:30 p.m. Memorial Day to Labor Day, and Mon.-Fri. 8 a.m.-4:30 p.m. the rest of the year.

The **Maloney-Sobieski Mountain Road** provides views of Glacier Peak and deep valleys. To get there, head east from the ranger station for a half mile, then turn left onto Foss River Rd. 68. Drive about 5.5 miles to the intersection of Roads 68 and 6840; go right onto 6840. When you reach the next fork, stay to the right onto 6846 until the next fork; then go left to Sobieski Mountain or right to Maloney Mountain, with spectacular views on either route.

Community Transit, tel. (360) 778-2185 or (800) 562-1375, has daily bus service to Skykomish and the rest of Snohomish County.

Over Jack Pass
For a fascinating 26-mile side trip away from busy Hwy. 2, head up Beckler River Rd., which starts a half-mile east of Skykomish. The road (Forest Rd. 65) climbs 13 miles up—the last five are dusty gravel—along the river into Mt. Baker-Snoqualmie National Forest before switchbacking over Jack Pass and down the Galena Road. A forest lookout tower atop **Evergreen Mountain** can be reached via a 1.5-mile

one-way hike from the end of Evergreen Mountain Rd. 6554. The road takes off to the right (east) from the Beckler River Rd. just before you reach Jack Pass. The trail gains 1,300 feet in elevation, but on a clear day the 360-degree view includes Glacier Peak and Mt. Rainier. Regrettably, this trail is open to off-road vehicles.

Privately owned Garland Hot Springs (near Jack Pass) has a few old buildings and a caretaker who shoos away stray tourists. A mile down Galena Rd. is the free **San Juan Campground,** followed by **Troublesome Creek Campground,** two miles farther downhill. A fee is charged at Troublesome Creek, and reservations ($7.50 extra) can be made by calling (800) 280-2267. Both of these Forest Service campgrounds are open late May to September; neither has running water. The latter is home to **Troublesome Creek Nature Trail,** a delightful half-mile path through rainforest and canyon. Beyond the campgrounds, Galena Rd. parallels the North Fork Skykomish River for 10 miles—paved the entire way—ending at Hwy. 2 near the town of Index. You can also camp for free anywhere on Forest Service land in what is termed "dispersed recreation." Just look for the side roads heading into the woods.

Index

Tiny Index (pop. 150) lies a mile off Hwy. 2 and just across the clear waters of the Skykomish River. This quaint old mining, logging, and quarrying camp has tidy homes, a delightful old lodge, a Cascade Range backdrop that features Mt. Index, and plenty of hiking, rock climbing, steelhead fishing, and mountain biking options. The granite quarry (closed in the 1930s) was the source of stones for the steps to the state capitol in Olympia.

Sights: Directly behind town rises **Index Town Wall,** a 400-foot granite cliff that's a favorite of Seattle-area rock climbers. It was recently purchased by the state to be run as a small state park, and trails and restrooms are planned. A steep path leads much of the way up the slope for those who aren't climbers; ask at the Bush House for directions. **Wave Trek,** tel. (360) 793-1705 or (800) 543-7971, is an Index-based company that teaches beginner-level climbing classes at the Index Wall.

Pickett Historical Museum, tel. (360) 793-1534, is housed in one of the little clapboard structures that dot Index. Entrance is $1 for adults or 50 cents for kids. Open Sunday noon-3 p.m., Memorial Day to Labor Day only; pick up a brochure here that indexes Index's historic buildings. Lee Pickett's extraordinary collection of photographs from the early part of this century make up the centerpiece of the museum. (He was the official photographer for the Great Northern Railway.)

Index General Store, tel. (360) 793-0693, is one of the finest old-time general stores left in the state, selling everything from gardening supplies to espresso coffees. Their home-baked goods are especially noteworthy, and the friendliness is legendary. **Index Tavern,** tel. (360) 793-0584, has live music throughout the year, dart boards and a pool table inside, and a beer garden overlooking the Skykomish River.

Lodging and Food: A don't-miss-it place is the beautifully restored **Bush House Country Inn,** 300 5th St., tel. (360) 793-2312 or (800) 428-2874. Several U.S. presidents stayed at Bush House in the early days, including Teddy Roosevelt (but not George Bush). Built in 1898, the hotel has nine guest rooms with shared baths ($59-70 s or d), and two with private half-baths ($80 s or d). Rates include a $10 credit to one of their scrumptious breakfasts, served in

the garden-side dining room with a stone fireplace. The restaurant makes a romantic back-from-the-slopes stopping place. Great food from a diverse menu, including famous blackberry cobbler with ice cream for dessert. Outside is a fragrant rose garden. Reserve ahead for weekends (especially in ski season), or come on a weekday to avoid the crowds.

Another very nice historic place to stay is **A Stone's Throw B&B,** tel. (360) 793-0100. Only one room is available ($65 s, $75 d) in this 1912 home, but you get the entire upper floor to yourself, including a private bath, stereo, TV, and VCR with video tapes. Outside is a private jacuzzi. The full breakfast comes complete with fresh-squeezed OJ.

The Cabin at Index, tel. (360) 827-2102 , is a modern cabin along the Skykomish River, complete with decks offering great views of the mountains, a woodstove, and kitchen, but no phone or TV (and they aren't needed). The cabin costs $80 d, and there's a two-night minimum stay.

Events: Index has a popular **Easter Sunday Pancake Breakfast,** but the town's big shindig comes on **Memorial Day Weekend** with ballgames, a goofy relay fun run, and a popular spaghetti feed. Of course, the town's **Fourth of July** has the all-American standards: a parade, crafts fair, live music, a rubber duck derby, and fireworks echoing off the surrounding mountains.

Nearby Trails: For a short day hike near Index, try the one-mile one-way hike from Hwy. 2 just east of town to **Heybrook Lookout.** This Forest Service fire tower provides views of Mt. Index, Baring Mountain, and the Skykomish Valley. Slightly longer (2.2 miles one-way) but with little elevation gain is the **Barclay Lake Trail,** which follows the course of Barclay Creek to the lake with a nice view of Baring Mountain. To get to the trailhead, take Barclay Creek Rd. 6024 for four miles.

Transportation: Community Transit, tel. (360) 778-2185 or (800) 562-1375, has daily bus service ($1) to Index and other parts of Snohomish County.

Wallace Falls State Park

Located two miles northeast of Gold Bar, this 678-acre park is famous for its towering 265-foot cataract (visible from Hwy. 2). The park is open daily in the summer, and Wed.-Sun. from

October to mid-April. A half-dozen gorgeously situated walk-in tent sites are available ($10; no showers), but the main attraction is the falls. Two routes lead to Wallace Falls, an easy path along an old railroad grade that's open to mountain bikes, and a steeper route (Woody Trail) that follows closer to the river. The two trails join together for the last mile and a half, with several viewpoints along the way, including one atop the falls. The hike to the falls is six miles roundtrip via Woody Trail and eight miles roundtrip via the old railroad grade. Along the way, you gain almost 1,400 feet in elevation. Call (360) 793-0420 for park information.

Startup and Gold Bar

Located in an old church, the **Parallax Gallery,** tel. (360) 793-9588, in minuscule Startup has an interesting collection of fine art, ceramics, and jewelry by local artists. They also serve espresso coffees. The **Clock Museum** has over 75 unusual clocks on display and is open Thurs.-Mon. 10 a.m.-4 p.m. (closed Tuesday and Wednesday). Admission is $2 for adults, kids free.

For an interesting drive or mountain bike ride, head up Kellogg Lake Rd. out of Startup and follow it four miles to Sultan Basin Road. Turn right and continue uphill along Olney Creek to Spada Lake (Everett's water source; no swimming or motorboating). The last part of the road is gravel, and can be dusty in the summer, but the fine mountain and river vistas make this a pleasant trip.

Just west of Gold Bar (pop. 1,200) is the turnoff to **Skykomish State Salmon Hatchery,** a small operation of interest to anglers.

Community Transit, tel. (360) 778-2185 or (800) 562-1375, has daily bus service ($1) to Gold Bar and Startup, along with other parts of Snohomish County.

Sultan

Sultan (pop. 2,400) is home to the **Sultan Summer Shindig and Logging Show** the second weekend of July, with a parade, games, food booths, as well as arts and crafts displays. You'll also find live music at Sultan River Park on Sunday in the summer. The town itself doesn't have much to offer, though you may want to take a look at the **Sultan Museum,** located atop the post office. The clean and friendly **Dutch Cup**

Motel, tel. (360) 793-2215 or (800) 844-0488, charges $44 s and $52 d, and has kitchenettes in some rooms. This is the Sultan's de facto chamber of commerce.

Community Transit, tel. (360) 778-2185 or (800) 562-1375, has daily bus service ($1) to Sultan and other parts of Snohomish County.

MONROE

Located just 30 commuter-miles away from Seattle and 50 weekend-miles from downhill skiing at Stevens Pass, the town of Monroe (pop. 5,300) is a booming bedroom community of condos, tract houses, and more-established residences. A local promotional brochure brags about Monroe's "thoughtful planning" that makes it such a great place to live. But first impressions—especially if you're coming from the relatively undeveloped Cascades—are a bit different. Highway 2 through Monroe is a long and ugly chain of new strip malls, fast food joints, and neon signs. If this is planning, one wonders what it would look like without planning! Despite this, there are several redeeming qualities that attract visitors, especially the state fair.

The small **Monroe Historical Society Museum,** 207 E. Main St., tel. (360) 794-7056, is open Saturday 2:30-4:30 p.m. and houses local memorabilia and videos from old-timers. Also of interest is the open farmland that surrounds Monroe (at least till the "thoughtful planning" spreads out more), and pleasant backcountry roads that are great for bike riding. To the south are **U-pick farms** for strawberries, raspberries, and blueberries, and farm stands offering fresh produce. Horse owners especially like the mild climate here, making Monroe a regional center for horse training and breeding.

Evergreen State Fairgrounds

On the west end of Monroe sits the enormous Evergreen State Fair complex, which features a raceway, outdoor arena, exhibit halls, and a 3,000-seat indoor Equestrian Park—one of the finest on the West Coast. The fairgrounds are the site of major equestrian shows all year long, including the **Washington Hunter/Jumper Spring Nationals** in April, the **Lipizzaner Horse Show** in June, and the **Washington Draft**

Horse & Mule Extravaganza in September, along with a diversity of other events: medieval tournaments in January, a big craft show in April, an antique car show in May, and a Christmas crafts fair in December.

The biggest month is August, when the calendar is packed with activities: **Art in the Park** (held at Triangle Park), an **Old Time Threshing Bee,** and the ever-popular **Evergreen State Fair,** the largest fair in Washington. Besides all the usual fair activities—agricultural displays, live entertainment, food and craft booths, and carnival rides—there's a fun run, parade, and all sorts of other activities. The fair lasts for 11 days, from the last full week in August through Labor Day weekend. For details on upcoming events, call the fairgrounds at (360) 794-7832 for a recording of upcoming events, or (360) 794-4344 to speak to a real person.

Also at the fairgrounds is the **Evergreen Speedway,** where you can watch Nascar auto racing, demolition derbies, and other contests of bravado every Friday and Saturday night from March to mid-September. There are banked ovals along with a figure-eight flat track; call (360) 794-5917 for speedway events.

Food

Although the scent of deep-fry cookers often pervades Monroe's air, several local places go beyond this greasy menu. Start the day at **Monroe Cafe,** 19837 Hwy. 2, tel. (360) 794-6940, where breakfast is served all day. For lunch, head to **Bear Cave Cafe & Deli,** 116 W. Main St., tel. (360) 794-3354, or stop by the old-fashioned soda fountain at **Main St. Cafe,** 107 W. Main St., tel. (360) 794-8181. You'll find very good Mexican food at **Ixtapa,** 19303 Hwy. 2, tel. (360) 794-8484; and tasty seafood at **Sailfish Bar & Grill,** 104 N. Lewis, tel. (360) 794-4056. And, of course, there's always McDonald's, Burger King, Domino's, Skippers, or Taco Time if you just want to eat and run.

Lodging

The best local place to stay is the charming old Dutch Colonial home of Nora and Ed Phillips. **Nora & Ed's Bed & Breakfast,** 215 S. Blakely, tel. (360) 794-8875, has two guest rooms with a shared bath and light breakfast for $45 s, $55 d ($5 less without breakfast). The nicest local motel is **Best Western Baron Inn,** 19233 Hwy. 2, tel. (360) 794-3111 or (800) 528-1234, where rooms are $56-64 s, $60-64 d, including an outdoor pool and jacuzzi. Kitchenettes are available.

Fairground Inn Motel, 18950 Hwy. 2, tel. (360) 794-5401, charges $48 s or d, including an indoor hot tub, and comfortable rooms. **Monroe Motel,** 20310 Old Owen Rd., tel. (360) 794-6751, has older motel rooms for $32 s, $36 d (kitchenettes cost $4 extra). Rooms at **Brookside Motel,** 19930 Hwy. 2, tel. (360) 794-8832, are $39-42 s or d.

Campgrounds

The closest public campsites are two county parks: **Flowing Lake Park,** 10 miles north of Monroe, tel. (360) 568-2274, open year-round (no water in the winter months); and **Lake Roesiger Park,** 12 miles north of Monroe, tel. (360) 568-5836, open mid-May through September. Tent camping costs $10 at both places; RV spaces are available at Flowing Lake Park for $14. Both of these parks have popular swimming beaches, and Flowing Lake has ranger-led nature hikes, along with Saturday-night amphitheater programs, in the summer. RVs (no tents) can also hook up at the **Evergreen State Fairgrounds** during events for $10 per night. Call (360) 794-4344 for reservations during the state fair. Other nearby public camping can be found eight miles east in Snohomish (see below), and at Forest Service sites near Skykomish (see "Campgrounds" under "Practicalities," above).

Information and Services

The **Monroe Chamber of Commerce,** 211 E. Main St., tel. (360) 794-5488, is open Mon.-Fri. 9:30-5 and Saturday 9 a.m.-3 p.m. May-Sept., and Mon.-Fri. 9:30-4 the rest of the year. The **public library** is at 201 Hill, tel. (360) 794-7851, and the local **post office,** tel. (360) 794-7729, is on N. Blakeley near Main Street. The **area code** for eastern Snohomish County, including Monroe, is 360.

Transportation

Community Transit, tel. (360) 778-2185 or (800) 562-1375, has daily bus service ($1) from Monroe to other parts of Snohomish County.

SNOHOMISH

If you're arriving in the town of Snohomish (pop. 6,500) after stopping in Monroe, you're in for a delightful surprise. Snohomish has charm, character, and a classic small-town feel—quite unlike damn-the-torpedoes Monroe. Early Indians called Snohomish something like "Sdob-dwahlb-bluh," meaning "Indian Moon," because that's where they believed their tribe came from. The town was settled in 1859 along the banks of the Snohomish and Pilchuck Rivers, making it one of Washington's oldest communities. The first settler was a merchant named E.C. Ferguson, who set up shop with some goods to sell, believing a military road between Fort Steilacoom and Fort Bellingham would soon come through. The road never arrived, but other people did because the Snohomish River was the natural transportation corridor for boats and log rafts. There's still an active and noisy sawmill right downtown, but the past has become the focal point for most visitors in the form of old homes and antique shops.

Sights

The **Blackman Historic Museum,** 118 Ave. B, tel. (360) 568-5235, is an 1878 mansion built by a lumberman as a proud display of his cedar shingles; today it's filled with area artifacts and Victorian furniture. Open Wed.-Sun. noon-4 p.m.; $1 for adults or 50 cents for seniors or children. The **Snohomish Chamber of Commerce,** tel. (360) 568-2526, is right next door to the museum and is open daily noon-4 p.m. in the summer, and Mon.-Fri. 9:30 a.m.-4 p.m. in the winter. Pick up a self-guided tour brochure for the town's elegant Victorian-era homes (part of the Snohomish National Historic District), particularly in the area north of Second St., or see the inside during the annual **Historic Homes Tour & Vintage Car Show** in late September. For more history, head to the **Pioneer Village Museum** at 2nd and Pine Streets, tel. (360) 568-5235. Open summers only; $1 adults, children or seniors 50 cents.

Antiques

Snohomish calls itself "Antique Capital of the Pacific Northwest." Antique shops of all sorts line Main St., including ones specializing in old toys, unrealistically realistic models of sailing ships, Persian rugs, Victorian furnishings, and clocks. The biggest of all is **Star Center Antique Mall** at 829 2nd St., where 150 dealers have small booths inside.

Lodging Places

The comfortable **Inn at Snohomish,** 323 2nd St., tel. (360) 568-2208 or (800) 548-9993, has rooms for $51 s, $57 d. **CountryMan B&B,** 119 Cedar, tel. (360) 568-9622 or (800) 700-9622, has three rooms with private baths on the second floor of an historic Queen Anne Victorian home. Rates are $55 s, $65 d, with a full breakfast; $10 less without breakfast. **Cabbage Patch Inn,** 111 Ave. A, tel. (360) 568-9091, has three rooms for $40-50 s, $45-55 d, including a full breakfast in an early 1900s home.

Snohomish Grand Hotel, 902½ 1st St., tel. (360) 568-8854, has six antique-filled rooms, most with private bath, for $50-70 s or d, including a light breakfast. The hotel is above a downtown antique store, and has a hot tub. **The Country Manner,** 1120 1st St., tel. (360) 568-3284, is located downtown above the antique shop of the same name. There are four rooms (two with private bath) for $49-59 s or d, including a light breakfast.

Eddy's B&B, 425 9th St., tel. (360) 568-7081, is in a carefully restored 1884 Victorian estate with an outdoor pool and gourmet breakfasts. The rooms offer comfortable, homey accommodations and panoramic mountain vistas. Rates are $60-70 s, 70-80 d.

Campgrounds

Ferguson Park, on Blackman Lake in Snohomish, tel. (360) 568-3115, is a city park with a picnic area, lake access, camping ($10 for tents, $15 for RVs), and showers. Open mid-May to mid-September, this is a fun place to feed the ducks and geese. See "Monroe" (above) for info on two nearby county parks where you can camp: Flowing Lake Park and Lake Roesiger Park.

Food and Wine

Silver King Cafe, 1101 1st St., tel. (360) 568-4589, specializes in steak and seafood, including Hood Canal oysters and the hard-to-find fried geoduck clams. For coffee or a light snack, the **Rivers Edge Cafe**, tel. (360) 568-5835, on 1st St. has a comfortable, historic feeling and tasty breakfasts. Get down-to-earth meals in a relaxed atmosphere at **Sweet Life Cafe,** 1024 1st St., tel. (360) 568-3554. They have delicious sandwiches and soups for lunch, along with a more substantial dinner menu.

Cafe Cheyenne Bakery & Deli, 920 1st St., tel. (360) 568-2020, has light lunch fare. Also of note is **Oxford Tavern**, 913 1st St., tel. (360) 568-3845, with pub grub and live music. For inexpensive Chinese food, try **Peking Duck**, 1208 2nd St., tel. (360) 568-7634. Open for breakfast, lunch, and dinner daily, the **Cabbage Patch Restaurant,** tel. (360) 568-9091, offers sandwiches, salads, pasta, beef, and seafood plus homemade desserts in an old home at 111 Ave. A. **Mardini's,** 1001 1st St., tel. (360) 568-8080, has pasta, quiche, steaks, seafood, stir-fry, and sauté dinners with a pink-and-antique-lace decor.

For ultra-fresh fruits and veggies, head to the **Snohomish Farmers Market**, held downtown June-Sept. on Thursday 5-9 p.m.

Quilceda Creek Vintners, 5226 Old Machias Rd., tel. (360) 568-2389, is a small family-run operation producing just a thousand cases per year of highly regarded cabernet sauvignon. The winery is open only by appointment.

Sports and Recreation
The town's indoor **swimming pool** is on the corner of Pine Ave. and 3rd Street. Two Snohomish companies offer hot air balloon rides: **The Aerial Balloon Co.,** tel. (360) 485-3658, and **Northwest Adventure,** tel. (360) 367-9090. Scenic airplane flights are also available at **Harvey Airfield,** tel. (360) 568-1541.

Information and Transportation
Community Transit, tel. (360) 778-2185 or (800) 562-1375, has daily bus service ($1) between Snohomish and other parts of Snohomish County.

The **area code** for Snohomish is 360. Snohomish's **public library** can be found at 1st and Cedar, tel. (360) 568-2898.

SNOQUALMIE VALLEY AND SNOQUALMIE PASS

When most Washington residents hear "Snoqualmie," they think first of Snoqualmie Pass and its ski areas, then Snoqualmie Falls, which looked so ominous in the credits to the 1980s TV show, *Twin Peaks.* The small town of Snoqualmie is usually an afterthought, unless you live there or have come to appreciate the great restaurants and beautiful scenery of the area. Snoqualmie Pass is the easiest way through the Cascades in winter, and it has both the widest highway (I-5) and lowest elevation of any of the mountain passes; the four ski areas at the summit bring a lot of vehicular traffic through the region.

The **area code** in the Snoqualmie/Snoqualmie Pass area is 206—the same as for Seattle.

SNOQUALMIE

The sleepy little town of Snoqualmie (pop. 1,500), with about two blocks of civilization on either side of the tracks, has a number of attractions worth a look, including nearby Snoqualmie Falls. As you approach the town, dozens of aging train engines and railcars in varying states of repair crowd the railroad tracks.

The **Snoqualmie Depot,** built in 1890, contains a small museum and ticket office (open Thurs.-Sun. 11 a.m.-3 p.m. April-Oct.) for the **Puget Sound & Snoqualmie Valley Railroad,** which operates diesel trains through the Snoqualmie Valley to North Bend (a 40-minute ride to cover seven miles roundtrip). Trains depart the Snoqualmie and North Bend depots on weekends April-October. The fare is $6 for adults, $5 for seniors, $4 for kids ages three to 12, and free for kids under three. Call (206) 746-4025 for details. You can depart from either town, and layover before catching a later train. Reservations are not needed. They also have special Halloween and Santa trains.

Winery

The **Snoqualmie Winery,** 1000 Winery Rd. in Snoqualmie (take a right off the Snoqualmie Falls exit from I-90), tel. (206) 888-4000, produces several varieties of wine, including Johannesburg riesling, merlot, and muscat canelli. Besides the usual gift shop, this one has a big picnic area with panoramic views of the Cascades and Snoqualmie Valley. Open for tours and tastings daily 10 a.m.-4:30 p.m.

Snoqualmie Falls

Located a mile north of the town of Snoqualmie, the 270-foot tall Snoqualmie Falls—a hundred feet higher than Niagara—has been awe-inspiring since the last ice age. As Washington's most famous waterfall, Snoqualmie attracts 1.5 million visitors annually. Unfortunately, the falls also attracted the attention of civil engineers in the 1890s as a potential source of electricity. Puget Power excavated a 1,215-foot tunnel through the rock to divert water into the world's first totally underground generating facility, with an above-ground plant added later. Visitors don't come to see the power plant, and in fact, most may not even know it exists since the only obvious evidence from below is water pouring from a hole at the base of the falls. The falls still run, but because of this diversion they do so at a vastly reduced level from the natural flow. Compared to the historical falls, these are but a trickle.

Stop at Snoqualmie Falls for a picnic lunch, or to stand in awe on the viewing platform as the noisy river plummets to the rocks far below. A steep half-mile **River Trail** leads downhill to the second power plant where you can view the falls from below. While you're standing here, think how much more powerful these falls were before over 90% of the water was siphoned off into power plants. You can check today's water flow in cubic feet per second inside the nearby Salish Lodge. The Snoqualmie Falls Preservation Project, 4759 15th Ave. NE, Seattle, tel. (206) 528-2421, is an environmental group attempting to restore Snoqualmie Falls to its original majesty, and to prevent Puget Power from expanding its power plants even more.

A mile north of the falls, Hwy. 202 passes **Tokul Creek State Fish Hatchery,** tel. (206) 222-5464, where trout and steelhead are raised. Open for public visits daily.

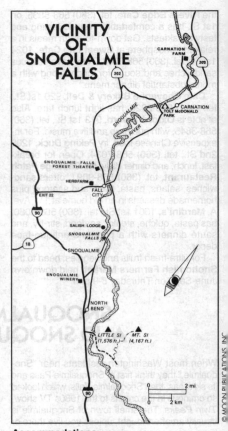

Accommodations

The **Salish Lodge,** tel. (206) 888-2556 or (800) 826-6124, atop Snoqualmie Falls, is the most luxurious hotel in the area, featuring a fireplace, jacuzzi, and honor bar in every room, plus a balcony in most. Also here is a fully equipped exercise room, sauna and steam room, hydrotherapy pools, tanning booths, massage rooms, library, and one of the finest restaurants in the area. A great place for a honeymoon or a getaway weekend; rooms are budget priced (if your name is Rockefeller) at $165-500 d Sun.-Thurs., and $180-575 on Fri.-Sat. and holidays.

For more homey accommodations in a country setting, stay at **The Old Honey Farm Coun-**

try Inn, 8910 384th Ave. SE, tel. (206) 888-9399, where guest rooms go for $75-125 s or d.

Food
The **Salish Lodge Restaurant,** tel. (206) 888-2556, atop Snoqualmie Falls has been in operation (under various names) since 1916. Today's dinner menu features six entrees (especially seafood and game) in the $25-30 range, and the farm-style four-course Sunday brunch remains a regional favorite. The homey lodge atmosphere, with overstuffed chairs surrounding a warm fire in the lounge, is worth the price of admission. Reservations are virtually required, especially if you want a window seat.

Theater
Set amongst towering evergreens at the foot of the falls, the **Snoqualmie Falls Forest Theater** has stage performances and dinners every weekend from late June to September. This is the only outdoor dinner theater in Washington, with food catered by Colonial Inn. Adult prices are $12 for entrance, plus $10 for dinner. For current productions and ticket information call (206) 222-7044.

Transportation and Tours
Seattle's **Metro** buses serve Fall City (right to the falls), Snoqualmie, and North Bend; call (206) 447-4800 for a schedule. The telephone **area code** for Snoqualmie is 206.

Customized Tours, tel. (206) 878-3965, offers three-hour van tours from Seattle to Snoqualmie Falls, Carnation Farm, and the Herbfarm for $25.

FALL CITY, CARNATION, AND DUVALL

The attractive little riverside town of Fall City is situated three miles northwest of Snoqualmie Falls, and six miles south of the even smaller settlement of Carnation. Highway 202 ties the towns together. The road is narrow, with tight corners, and is posted at 30 miles an hour all the way through Carnation. Exceed this at your own risk; the cops are always out in force here! Continue another nine miles north from Carnation on Hwy. 203 through dairy farming land (rich with

eau de manure) to the quaint small town of Duvall, where older places survive next to trendy espresso and book shops.

Tolt McDonald Park, just west of Carnation at the confluence of the Tolt and Snoqualmie Rivers, is a pleasant place to relax or pitch a tent. Riverside campsites are $10; no RV hookups or showers. Open late March to October.

Carnation Farm
Carnation Farm is owned and operated by the Carnation milk-and-ice-cream, dog- and cat-food people. The farm was purchased in 1910 by E.A. Stuart, the founder of Carnation Company, as a place to improve milk production. Many champion cows (defined by their ability to produce milk, not their speed on the track), have been raised here, and one—Segis Pietertje Prospect—even merited a statue on the grounds. The farm still raises 360 holstein cows that are milked twice a day. Free, self-guided tours include "The Birth of a Calf" video, the milking carousel, maternity barn and recovery room, and the petting area in "Frisky Acres" with Labrador retrievers and cats. Bring your picnic lunch to enjoy in the flower gardens. Carnation Farm, tel. (206) 788-1511, is open April-Oct. Mon.-Sat. 10 a.m.-3 p.m. (closed Sunday and holidays).

Herbfarm
More than a 20 years ago, Lola Zimmerman put out a few pots of her home-grown herbs at a roadside stand. Today, The Herbfarm boasts over 600 kinds of live herb plants (including 27 varieties of thyme!), 120 species of succulents, and 300 classes in everything from folk herbalism to herbal soapmaking. Pick up an herbal flea collar, beer bread mix, live plants, books, herbal deodorant, or gourmet coffees at the farm's country store. Tours of the 17 herb gardens are given on summer weekends at 1 p.m. The Herbfarm is open daily April-Sept. 9 a.m.-6 p.m., and daily 10 a.m.-5 p.m. the rest of the year. It's located at 32804 Issaquah-Fall City Rd., Fall City, tel. (206) 784-2222 or (800) 866-4372 (outside Washington).

If you have the cash (or are willing to mortgage your house), and are lucky enough to get reservations, the Herbfarm's immensely popular luncheons are served on various weekends (and some Thursdays) throughout the year.

The schedule is confusing, so call the restaurant for details. Luncheons ($60 per person) are a six-course feast featuring fresh local game and fish, accompanied by vegetables from The Herbfarm's gardens. Dinners ($119 per person) are even more elaborate: nine-course meals with five matched wines and a thematic menu that follows the seasons. This is Northwest cuisine at its finest. Set aside three or four leisurely hours for the meals, including a guided tour of the farm's herb gardens. Reservations are absolutely required; some seats are booked six months ahead, while a few are left till the Friday before.

Food
See the Herbfarm, above, for the area's most famous restaurant. **The Original Brown Bag Restaurant & Bakery**, 4366 Tolt Ave., tel. (206) 333-6100, is well worth a stop for fresh baked goods and deli sandwiches. Stop at the historic Falls City's **Colonial Inn**, built in 1920, for a cup of coffee and a slice of pie. North of town, the road follows the river past a mix of old farmsteads, timbered lands, and rural homes. In the middle of this is **Reminger Farms**, 32610 N.E. 32nd in Carnation, tel. (206) 333-4135, with pick-your-own berries, pumpkins, and other produce in season.

Accommodations and Campgrounds
Stay at **Idyl Inn on the River**, 4548 Tolt River Rd. in Carnation, tel. (206) 881-5606, where rooms go for $65-155 d Sun.-Fri., and $85-185 Saturday and holidays. These luxurious accommodations include an indoor pool, sauna, steam room, and soaking tub, plus a beach along the Tolt River, and an abundance of wild birds.

The privately run **Snoqualmie River Campground**, 34807 S.E. 44th Place in Fall City, tel. (206) 222-5545, has RV and tent spaces.

Events
The Herbfarm, tel. (206) 784-2222, has a number of popular annual events, including the **Garlic Frolic and World Slug Games** on Labor Day weekend, and the big **Northwest Microbrewery Festival** on Father's Day weekend in mid-June. The Herbfarm also puts on "Signature Dishes" programs periodically, where noted chefs demonstrate their craft.

Information and Transportation
Seattle's **Metro** buses serve Fall City (right to the falls), Snoqualmie, and North Bend; call (206) 447-4800 for a schedule. The local **area code** is 206.

NORTH BEND

Located at the foot of Mt. Si, the settlement of North Bend (pop. 2,600) is the last Snoqualmie River town before I-90 climbs into the Cascade Range. Nothing special here, although a few buildings carry a Swiss theme, and several others are recognizable from the old *Twin Peaks* television series. North Bend is fast becoming yet another in a string of bedroom communities, with new condos being added all the time. Nintendo Corporation has a big plant here, and a collection of some 35 factory outlet stores can be found just off I-90's exit 31.

Sights
The **Snoqualmie Valley Historical Museum**, 320 North Bend Blvd. S, tel. (206) 888-3200, has permanent displays of Indian artifacts and pioneer and logging history, and a small gift shop. Open Thurs.-Sun. 1-5 p.m. April-Nov.; $1.

Puget Sound & Snoqualmie Valley Railroad operates steam trains through the Snoqualmie Valley to the nearby town of Snoqualmie (40 minutes roundtrip). Trains depart from the North Bend and Snoqualmie depots on weekends April-Oct. for $6 adults, $5 seniors, and $4 kids ages three to 12. Call (206) 746-4025 for details.

Mount Si Bonsai, 43321 S.E. Mt. Si Rd., tel. (206) 888-0350, features a collection of these miniature trees.

Mount Si and Little Si
The 4,167-foot-tall Mt. Si is one of the most climbed mountains in the state; 10,000 people a year take the eight-hour roundtrip hike. It's not just the length of the hike that's tough, but the elevation gain of 3,100 feet that keeps you puffing. Be prepared for lots of switchbacks! The views west to Mt. Rainier, Puget Sound, Seattle, and the Olympics, however, are worth the effort. To reach the trailhead, turn left on 432nd SE (Mt. Si Rd.) about a mile from the east edge of North

Bend. After you cross the Middle Fork of the Snoqualmie River, go right at the first intersection then drive two and a half miles to the parking lot, trailhead, and picnic area. The trail is generally snow-free April to November. Avoid the crowds by getting an early morning start.

An easier alternative to Mt. Si is Little Si, offering views across Snoqualmie Valley. The trail is two and half miles each way. Get to the trailhead by following North Bend Way a half mile southeast from the Forest Service Ranger Station to Mt. Si Rd.; then turn left and go a half mile to a bridge. Park at the gravel lot here across the bridge, and walk downhill to the signed trailhead just past the fifth house on the right.

Twin Falls

Just a short distance from busy I-90, at **Olallie State Park** the South Fork of the Snoqualmie River drops 300 feet over a stunning series of cataracts. The park is accessible from exit 34 (five miles east of North Bend); after exiting, turn right on Edgewick Rd., and then left onto S.E. 159th St.; continue a half mile to the park. A 1.3-mile path leads to Twin Falls, and from there, you can cross a footbridge and continue uphill another 1.6 miles to a second trailhead near exit 38. Day-use only, and no mountain bikes or horses allowed on the trails. Olallie State Park continues eastward along the river above Twin Falls, with several good fishing holes.

Accommodations

North Bend Motel, 322 E. North Bend Way, tel. (206) 888-1121, has rooms for $36 s, $40 d, including a jacuzzi. Three miles east of town, the **Edgewick Inn,** 14600 468th Ave. SE, tel. (206) 888-9000, has modern rooms for $38 s, $40 d, with access to a jacuzzi. Rooms cost $36 s, $38-42 d, at **Sunset Motel,** 227 W. North Bend Way, tel. (206) 888-0381, and kitchenettes are available. **Nor'West Motel & RV Park,** 45810 S.E. North Bend Way, tel. (206) 888-1939, has rooms for $40 s, $46-50 d, with kitchenettes available.

The Roaring River at North Bend B&B, 46715 S.E. 129th St., tel. (206) 888-4834, offers views of the Middle Fork of the Snoqualmie River, along with surrounding forests. The four rooms all have private entrances, baths, and decks; a breakfast basket is delivered each morning. Rates are $85 d; no kids.

Campgrounds

The closest public camping is the Forest Service's **Tinkham Campground,** 10 miles east on I-90 at exit 42. Sites are $9; open May-September. Another seven miles east on I-90 is **Denny Creek Campground,** which has the same rates and season. Park RVs in town at **Nor'West Motel & RV Park,** 45810 S.E. North Bend Way, tel. (206) 888-1939.

Food

George's Bakery, 127 W. North Bend Way, tel. (206) 888-0632, is a favorite local gathering place that serves sweets, fresh-baked breads, sandwiches, and salads. Get pizzas at **Anthony's New York Pizza,** 480 E. North Bend Way, tel. (206) 831-6836, and Italian faves at **Mama Lucia's Pasta and Steak House,** 101 W. North Bend Way, tel. (206) 831-5460.

Information and Services

The **North Bend Ranger Station,** 42404 S.E. North Bend Way (a half mile east of town), tel. (206) 888-1421, has Forest Service information on local trails, mountain bike routes, and campgrounds. Open Mon.-Fri. 8 a.m.-4:30 p.m., plus Saturday during the summer. The **Upper Snoqualmie Valley Chamber of Commerce,** tel. (206) 888-4440, has a small visitor center on the west end of town that dispenses maps, brochures, and other information.

The **area code** for North Bend and other parts of the Snoqualmie Valley is 206.

Transportation

Seattle's **Metro** buses serve North Bend and surrounding communities; call (206) 447-4800 for a schedule. **Greyhound Bus Lines,** tel. (800) 231-2222, stops in North Bend at the corner of North Bend Way and Main Ave. N, with connections throughout the nation.

SNOQUALMIE PASS

Skiing

Located 53 miles from downtown Seattle, and right along I-90, Snoqualmie Pass is Washington's oldest and largest downhill ski area. Webb Moffett opened a rope tow here in 1937, and things are still run by the Moffett family. Today they own a complex of four major ski areas in a

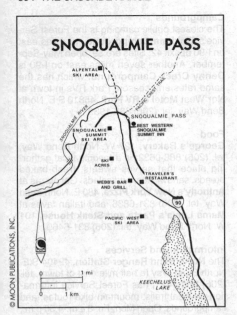

SNOQUALMIE PASS

ALPENTAL
SKI AREA

SNOQUALMIE PASS

BEST WESTERN
SNOQUALMIE
SUMMIT INN

SNOQUALMIE
SUMMIT
SKI AREA

SKI
ACRES

TRAVELER'S
RESTAURANT

WEBB'S BAR
AND GRILL

PACIFIC WEST
SKI AREA

90

KEECHELUS
LAKE

0   1 mi

0   1 km

© MOON PUBLICATIONS, INC.

space of two miles at the pass: **Alpental, Ski Acres, Snoqualmie Summit,** and **Hyak.** The four are operated jointly, with 23 chair lifts and 11 rope tows among them. On weekends, skiers can ride the free shuttle among the various areas. All told, Snoqualmie Pass's ski areas cover more than 1,900 skiable acres and constitute the largest night skiing area in the world. The summit elevation is 3,675-5,400 feet, with a base of 3,000 feet, for a vertical drop reaching up to 2,200 feet.

Snowboarders are welcome at all four areas, and two cross-country ski areas (at Ski Acres and Hyak; $5-9 for adults) provide 55 km of groomed and tracked trails. You can ski at all four hills on the same lift ticket, but ski lift prices vary considerably, depending upon the day of the week, the time of the day, your age, and the second letter of your middle name (okay, not the last of these). Typical adult weekend rates are $27, with adult weekday rates of $14-18. There are all sorts of bargains for old or young skiers, for Telemarkers who ski at night, and military personnel, but none for left-handed skiers. The Snowflake Tubing and Snowplay area rents inner tubes and offers rope tows and lights for kids of all ages.

Services at Snoqualmie Pass include ski shops, equipment rentals, ski schools, day lodges, food service, child care, and bus service to the area. For rates, operating hours, snow conditions, and general info on all four, call (206) 236-1600.

Come summer, the **Ski Acres Mountain Bike & Hiking Center,** tel. (206) 434-6646, offers chairlift service, mountain bike rentals, lessons, and a deli-cafe.

Accommodations
The **Best Western Snoqualmie Summit Inn,** tel. (206) 434-6300 (at the pass), (206) 624-4040 (in Seattle), or (800) 528-1234, has an indoor pool, jacuzzi, sauna, and a restaurant. Rates are $79 s or d. Lodging is also available at **Wardholm West B&B,** tel. (206) 434-6540, where rooms are $45-75 s or d with a shared or private bath.

Ski groups of 25 people or more need to book far ahead for **Kachess Lodge,** tel. (206) 656-2465, where the rate is $600 per night, including a large kitchen, pool table, fireplace, hot tub, and sauna. **Valley High Mountain Lodge,** right on the slopes, tel. (206) 432-1409, has space for groups of up to 16 people in a large home with a kitchen and two fireplaces. Rates are $250 per night on weekends, $300 on holiday weekends.

Campgrounds
RV parking is permitted at the summit parking lots, but no hookups are available. The Forest Service has two popular summertime campgrounds west of I-90 on the west side of Snoqualmie Pass. **Tinkham Campground** is on Forest Rd. 55, approximately 12 miles east of the town of North Bend, while **Denny Creek Campground** is another six miles east, and just two miles west of Snoqualmie Pass. Both are open mid-May to mid-September and cost $9. Reservations are possible ($7.50 extra) by calling (800) 280-2267.

Food
Atop Snoqualmie Pass, **Webb's Bar and Grill,** tel. (206) 434-6343, specializes in fondues; open daily for lunch and dinner, breakfast on weekends. Also at the pass, **Traveler's Restaurant** has inexpensive sandwiches, burgers, light meals, and take-out food.

Transportation and Information

Although Snoqualmie Pass is generally the easiest way to traverse the Cascades, it does get snowy and sometimes closes during heavy storms; call (206) 455-7900 or (900) 407-7277 (35-cent charge) for current road conditions and information on snow tire or chain requirements.

The **I-90 Ski Bus**, tel. (206) 232-8210, provides service from Seattle, Bellevue, and Issaquah between January and early March.

The telephone **area code** for Snoqualmie Pass is 206, the same as Seattle's.

CLE ELUM AND VICINITY

The towns of Cle Elum and Roslyn provide interesting side trips or starting points for hiking or horseback treks into the magnificent Cascade mountain country just to the north and west. Access is easy, with I-90 cutting down from Snoqualmie Pass along the upper Yakima River Valley, passing fields, farms, and stream-laced valleys as you descend.

CLE ELUM

Cle Elum (KLEE-elum), an Indian name meaning "Swift Water," was settled in 1870 by Thomas L. Gamble, but growth was slow until geologists working for the Northern Pacific Railroad discovered coal in 1884. A forest fire in the late 1880s wiped out a large part of the mining town, but additional coal veins discovered in 1889 gave Cle Elum four quite prosperous years. Today the town is a jumping-off point for hiking, fishing, and other recreational activities in the Wenatchee National Forest.

Museums

Cle Elum was the last place in America to use a manually operated switchboard, and the last to institute the touch-tone dial system. The old phone building was transformed into the **Cle Elum Historical Telephone Museum** at 1st and Wright, tel. (509) 674-5702. Inside this surprisingly well-done little museum are switchboard exhibits, photographs of early Cle Elum, and other memorabilia. Open Tues.-Fri. 9 a.m.-4 p.m., Sat.-Sun. noon-4 p.m., from Memorial Day to Labor Day, and Tues.-Fri. 9 a.m.-4 p.m. the rest of the year; no charge. For something different, try the "coal" candy sold here.

The spacious **Carpenter Museum**, 302 W. 3rd St., tel. (509) 674-5702, was built in 1914 by a prosperous local banker, Frank Carpenter. His granddaughter donated it, along with much of the original furnishings (including Tiffany lamps, an oak dining table with 11 leaves, and a beautifully carved rosewood chair), to the local historical society in 1989, and they have been hard at work restoring the sumptuous old home ever since. The museum is open Sat.-Sun. noon-4 p.m. between Memorial Day and Labor Day. Entrance is $2 for adults, $1.50 for seniors, and $1 for kids.

Iron Horse State Park

East of Cle Elum off I-90, Iron Horse State Park is the start of the 25-mile-long **John Wayne Pioneer Trail** that extends to the Yakima-Teanaway River Canyon on property once belonging to the Milwaukee Railroad. (The railroad ran electric trains across the Cascades from 1909 until their bankruptcy in 1980.) Open to hikers, skiers, mountain bikers, and horseback riders, but closed to motorized vehicles, the trail begins in a Douglas fir and pine forest and follows the Yakima River through canyons and farmland. No overnight camping. Day-hikers can reach the trail at either Easton or South Cle Elum. In Easton, take I-90 exit 71 and follow the signs; park at the trailhead gate; in South Cle Elum, park at the end of 7th St. to reach the trailhead east of the old depot. There are no restrooms or facilities of any kind here yet, just a gentle, graveled trail, so plan ahead. Call (509) 656-2230 for details. Iron Horse State Park actually extends from Rattlesnake Lake on the west side of the Cascades all the way to the Columbia River, but access to other sections requires a special permit (fee charged); call (206) 455-7010 for the western section, or (509) 856-2700 for the eastern section to the Columbia.

Lake Easton State Park

About 15 miles west of Cle Elum just off I-90, Lake Easton State Park encompasses 247 forested acres on the west and north sides of Lake Easton and is a popular camping spot (if you can ignore the traffic noise). The mile-long reservoir is good for swimming, boating, trout fishing, and waterskiing; hiking, cross-country skiing, and snowmobiling are popular dry-land sports. Kids enjoy the big-toy playground. The water level changes through the year in this reservoir, and it is drained each winter to provide irrigation water for eastern Washington farms.

Hiking and Cross-Country Skiing

The **Cle Elum Ranger District** office of the Wenatchee National Forest has information on more than 750 miles of hiking trails. Stop by their office at the west end of 2nd St., tel. (509) 674-4411, for maps, a detailed trail guidebook, and camping, cross-country skiing, and snowmobiling information. The office is open daily 7:45 a.m.-4:30 p.m. in the summer, and Mon.-Fri. 7:45 a.m.-4:30 p.m. in the winter months.

Take Hwy. 903 from Cle Elum northwest to Cle Elum Lake; a number of forest roads leave it for backcountry hiking trails, including access to the south end of Alpine Lakes Wilderness Area (see "Recreation" under "Stevens Pass and Skykomish Valley," above). From the north end of the lake, take forest roads 4308 and 4312 to the Thorp Creek trailhead for a 3.1-mile hike to tiny **Thorp Lake** and **Kachess Ridge.**

A 6.2-mile one-way hike on Trail 1307 leaves Salmon la Sac Campground and follows a ridge to an excellent view atop **Jolly Mountain.**

For horseback trips into the backcountry, contact **Three Queens Outfitter/Guide Service,** tel. (509) 674-5647, and **High Country Outfitters,** tel. (509) 392-0111. See "Sights" under "Leavenworth," above, for information on Blewett Pass, a popular hiking and cross-country skiing destination halfway between Cle Elum and Leavenworth. More cross-country skiing at **Cabin Creek Nordic Ski Area,** at exit 63 off I-90, and west of Lake Easton State Park.

CLE ELUM AREA HIKING TRAILS

© MOON PUBLICATIONS, INC.

CLE ELUM AND ROSLYN ACCOMMODATIONS

Accommodations are arranged from least to most expensive within each town. Rates may be lower during the winter months. The area code is 509.

CLE ELUM

Bonita Motel; 906 E. 1st St.; tel. 674-2380; $27 s, $34 d; kitchenette

Mus Motel; 521 E. 1st St.; tel. 674-2551; $30 s, $35 d; kitchenettes

Cedars Motel; 1001 E. 1st St.; tel. 674-5535; $32 s, $42 d; AAA approved

Wind Blew Inn Motel; Hwy. 97 at I-90 exit 85; tel. 674-2294; $36 s, $38 d; kitchenettes

Timber Lodge Motel; 301 W. 1st St.; tel. 674-5966; $42 s, $47 d; jacuzzi, AAA approved

Stewart Lodge; 805 W. 1st St.; tel. 674-4548; $43 s, $48 d; outdoor pool, jacuzzi, AAA approved

Moore House B&B; 526 Marie Ave.; tel. 674-5939 or (800) 228-9246; $58-115 s or d in lodge, $105-115 in caboose (sleeps five); historic railroad lodge, jacuzzi, full breakfast, two night minimum stay on winter weekends

ROSLYN

The Last Resort; Lake Cle Elum; tel. 649-2222; $45 s or d

Little Roslyn Inn; tel. 649-2936; $48 s or d; kitchen, piano, sundeck

Coal Country Inn; 46 N. 2nd St.; tel. 649-3222 or (800) 543-2566; $57 s, $62 d; 19th-century rooming house, three rooms, shared bath, full breakfast

Roslyn Inn; tel. 649-2936; $180 for seven bedrooms, kitchen, bathroom, piano, sundeck, balcony, 1880s home

Roslyn B&B; 109 Arizona Ave. W; tel. 649-2463; $75 s or d; 1889 home, three guest rooms, private baths, antique furnished, full breakfast and wake-up tray

The Inn Between; tel. 649-2936; $260 for 10 bedrooms and loft, full kitchen, two bathrooms, 1880s home

Accommodations

Now a B&B on the National Historic Register, the **Moore House,** tel. (509) 674-5939 or (800) 228-9246, was built in 1909 by the Chicago, Milwaukee, Pacific, and St. Paul Railroads to serve the men who worked on some of the most treacherous mountain tracks in the country. The 10 restored inn rooms are named after some of the railroad men who lived there; photographs and antique toy trains complete the decor, and a jacuzzi on the deck makes a nice place to relax. One minor problem is that the beds are on the short side in these small rooms, so tall folks may feel cramped. Iron Horse State Park Trail is just a few feet from here, making this a great place for cross-country skiers or cyclists. Outside, the railroad theme continues with two cabooses that have been transformed into cozy quarters for up to five people. These are a good option for folks with kids or couples looking for something different. Highly recommended.

Hidden Valley Guest Ranch, off Hwy. 97, is the state's oldest dude ranch. Here you can indulge your cowboy fantasies while still enjoying heated cabins, hot showers, a heated pool, and someone else's cooking. Horseback rides leave twice daily, last one and a half hours, and cost $25; you don't have to be an overnight guest to join the rides. In winter, the ranch is generally open on January and February weekends for cross-country skiing; call ahead to check on conditions. Cabins begin at $190 per person for two nights, including delicious ranch-style meals. Call (509) 857-2344 for more information.

Campgrounds

The Forest Service maintains 20 campgrounds in the Cle Elum area. The most popular places charge $5-9 a night (extra fee for additional vehicles), while several campgrounds with more primitive facilities are free. Get a complete listing from the Cle Elum Ranger Station, tel. (509) 674-4411. Closest is **Wish Poosh Campground,** eight miles northwest of town on the eastern shore of Cle Elum Lake, where sites cost $9 a night. Continue up Salmon la Sac Rd. to three more campgrounds: **Cle Elum River** ($6), **Red Mountain** (free), and **Salmon la Sac** ($9). Make reservations ($7.50 extra) for Salmon la Sac by calling (800) 280-2267. More camping is available at **Kachess Lake** (pronounced "ka-CHEES"), approximately 27 miles east of Cle Elum. This beautiful blue-green lake offers swimming, boating, picnicking, a nature trail through old-growth forests, and campsites for $9. Make reservations for Kachess Lake ($7.50 extra) by calling (800) 280-2267. More campgrounds are northeast of town on Hwy. 97 over Blewett Pass en route to Leavenworth.

About 15 miles west of Cle Elum and just off I-90, **Lake Easton State Park** has additional camping ($10 for tents, $15 for RVs), along with hot showers. Open late April to mid-October. Call (509) 656-2230 for details, or (800) 452-5687 for campsite reservations ($6 extra fee), available up to 11 months ahead of time.

Sun Country Golf Resort, six miles west of Cle Elum, tel. (509) 674-2226, has an RV park and a nine-hole golf course.

Food
MaMa Vallone's Steak House and Inn, 302 W. 1st St., tel. (509) 674-5174, serves a large selection of steaks as well as Italian dishes made with homemade pasta. A country buffet is offered on Sunday. **Cottage Cafe** is a truck stop that is popular for breakfast. **El Caporal,** 107 W. 1st St., tel. (509) 674-4284, has quite good Mexican meals and margaritas.

Get cinnamon rolls and espresso for the road, or a crusty loaf of Dutch crunch bread fresh from the brick oven (in use since 1906) of **Cle Elum Bakery,** 501 E. 1st St., tel. (509) 674-2233.

Event
Cle Elum's big event is **Pioneer Days** in late June, which features a street fair, parade, softball and bocci ball tournaments, and races.

Information and Services
For local information, stop by the **Cle Elum Chamber of Commerce** office inside the Cle Elum Historical Telephone Museum at 1st and Wright, tel. (509) 674-5702; open Tues.-Fri. 9 a.m.-4 p.m.

The **area code** for Cle Elum and all of eastern Washington is 509.

ROSLYN

Located almost at road's end on Hwy. 903, the little town of Roslyn (pop. 900) has always been a favorite of Washingtonians. Roslyn contains the largest collection of cemeteries in the state, but is best known as the site where the CBS television series *Northern Exposure* was filmed.

Coal Mining
When large coal deposits were discovered in this area, the Northern Pacific Railroad bought up all the land and opened a mine in 1886. The town that grew up around the mine (and other nearby coal mines) was named by Logan M. Bullitt, general manager of the Northern Pacific Coal Co., in honor of Roslyn, New York, the hometown of his sweetheart. The coal mines attracted many European immigrants—Slavs, Italians, Austrians, Croats, Germans, Italians, Scots, Swedes, Hungarians—who brought interesting customs with them, including the Central European method of proposing marriage. The man wishing to propose gathered his friends to accompany him to his beloved's house, where on bended knee he proposed. If she rejected him, he bought a keg of beer in which to drown his sorrow in their company. If she accepted, his friends had to pay the wedding expenses. This variety of nationalities and religions, plus various fraternal lodges in Roslyn, led to each group having its own cemetery along 5th St. on the edge of town. Today there are 26 different small cemeteries spread over 15 acres here.

At its peak in 1910, some 4,000 people lived in Roslyn. The mines that produced more than a million tons of coal were deadly; an 1892 explosion killed 45 men, and another in 1909 killed another 10 men. Eventually, competition from cheaper coal, and the conversion of train engines from coal to diesel fuel, led to the closing of Roslyn's mines.

Northern Exposure

The last coal mine shut its doors in 1963, and it wasn't till the arrival of the *Northern Exposure* crew that things really started to change in this sleepy burg. Today, Roslyn is best known as the outdoor set for the television series, which supposedly took place in Cicely, Alaska. The Emmy-award-winning program was a major hit for several years, but the departure of its central character led to its cancellation in 1995. Filming brought new businesses, increased tourism, and even a new fire truck (purchased by the production company).

Sights and Tours

Roslyn's main attractions are its old-West false-fronted buildings, many of which appeared in *Northern Exposure,* including the famous Roslyn's Cafe sign. Fans of the TV show will recognize at least a dozen different locations where the program was filmed, from the doctor's office to the dump. For the complete rundown of set locations, pick up a copy of *The Roslyn Guide,* an entertaining introduction to the rich history of this small town. It's available at **Central Sundries,** tel. (509) 649-2210, the de facto chamber of commerce, and the location of "Ruth-Anne's General Store" when the program was in production. The **Brick Tavern,** across the street, is the oldest licensed tavern in Washington. It opened in 1889 and is famous for the 23-foot long running water spittoon that still washes away tobacco juice from patrons.

The **Roslyn Museum,** next to the Roslyn Cafe, houses an interesting collection of historic photos, coal mining equipment, and other items from Roslyn's past.

Customized Tours, tel. (206) 878-3965, offers three-hour van tours from Seattle to Snoqualmie Pass and Roslyn for $45.

Accommodations

See the "Cle Elum and Roslyn Accommodations" chart for a complete listing of local lodging options.

Food and Drink

For such a small town, Roslyn has remarkably good food. **Roslyn Cafe,** 28 Pennsylvania Ave., tel. (509) 649-2763, is best known for its colorful mural (altered to say "Roslyn's" for the television show), but the food here is also noteworthy. It's easily the best breakfast place around, but the burgers, sandwiches, and homemade soups for lunch are fine, as are the more substantial dinners. The old juke box still plays 78s for a measly nickel.

If you've got a penchant for perfectly prepared pizzas, don't miss **Village Pizza,** 6 Pennsylvania Ave., tel. (509) 649-2992, where the staff is friendly and the topping choices range all over the map. **Pioneer Restaurant and Sody-Licious Lounge** has steaks, fresh seafood, and desserts, along with a big screen TV and live music on weekends.

Roslyn Bakery, 30 N. 1st St., tel. (509) 649-2521, is a friendly place with excellent fresh European-style breads, pastries, and bagels. Get espressos and Hawaiian shaved ice, along with a dose of Native American enlightenment at **Illuminated Myst Bookstore** on 2nd Street.

For more than 80 years, folks have been coming to **Carek's Meat Market** to purchase fresh and smoked meats. Today, folks make the pilgrimage all the way from Seattle for their Polish sausages, beef jerky, and pepperoni.

The Brick Tavern, tel. (509) 649-2643, features live music and dancing on weekends and is famous for its running water spittoon. The **Roslyn Brewing Company,** 33 Pennsylvania Ave., tel. (509) 649-2232, is a new microbrewery open for tours on weekends noon-5 p.m. all year.

Events

The annual **Wing Ding Parade** is Roslyn's biggest event. Held in early September, it always includes a fun mix of performers, plus a street fair in the park.

STATE OF WASHINGTON TOURISM DIVISION

MOUNT RAINIER NATIONAL PARK

Washington's tallest and best-known peak, the perennially snowcapped Mt. Rainier towers over surrounding Cascade summits. To the residents of Puget Sound, it is simply "The Mountain," and its presence is so dominant that even the state's best-known beer is named Rainier. (Beer connoisseurs may view this as an insult to the mountain, however.) With 300 miles of hiking trails covering terrain from the lowland forests all the way to the ice-topped summit at 14,411 feet, Mt. Rainier is a recreational paradise. More than two million people visit Mount Rainier National Park annually, viewing towering waterfalls from the winding mountain roads, strolling through flower-filled mountain meadows at Paradise, camping beneath old-growth Douglas fir forests, climbing the mountain's glacier-clad slopes, listening to the bugling of elk on a fall evening, and skiing backcountry trails in the winter.

HISTORY

Although various tribes of Indians made seasonal fishing, hunting, and berry-picking forays into the foothills around Mt. Rainier, they ap-

parently avoided the mountain itself, either in reverence for the great mountain, or because of its severe weather. The Klickitat Indians who lived near present-day Ashford called the peak "Ta-ho-ma," a word that probably simply means "The Mountain," or "Snowiest Peak." The city of Tacoma gained its name from the mountain that rises so tall behind it. Unfortunately, the Indian name for the peak itself was supplanted by an English name. In 1792, Capt. George Vancouver named it after his friend, Rear Admiral Peter Rainier. Thus Rainier—a minor character in British naval history—lives on in an American mountain that he never even saw. It would be almost like naming the nation's tallest peak after a minor president who had nothing to do with it. (Oops, they already did that with a mountain called Denali and a president named McKinley.)

First to the Top

It is said that the Native American inhabitants of the mountain viewed "Tahoma" as a sacred ground, inhabited by a vengeful deity who didn't welcome visitors. Although there are stories that an Indian guide led two white men to the summit as early as 1855, the men's names are long forgotten. Hazard Stevens, the Union's youngest Civil War general, was determined to be the first to (officially) reach Rainier's summit. So in 1870 he began assembling his climbing party. An unemployed miner, Philomon Beecher Van Trump, and landscape artist Edward T. Coleman would accompany him to the summit; James Longmire, a local farmer, would guide them as far as Bear Prairie, at 2,630 feet. But the group needed someone with expertise. They found it in Sluiskin, a nomad Indian who had taken up residence at Bear Prairie, and whose grandfather, going against Indian tradition, had once attempted a summit climb—without success.

The first day out after Bear Prairie, Coleman turned back. He'd found himself in a precarious position on a precipice where he could go neither forward nor back with his 40-pound pack; so he chucked it, along with most of the party's food. Stevens, Van Trump, and Sluiskin continued.

As the climbers progressed, Sluiskin began losing his nerve. Stevens wrote about him in an article for *Atlantic Monthly* in 1876:

Takhoma, he said, was an enchanted mountain, inhabited by an evil spirit who dwelt in a fiery lake on its summit. No human being could ascend it or even attempt its ascent and survive . . . at first, indeed, the way was easy . . . but above [the broad snow fields] the rash adventurer would be compelled to climb up steeps of loose, rolling rocks, which would turn beneath his feet and cast him headlong into the deep abyss below. . . . Moreover, a furious tempest continually swept the crown of the mountain, and the luckless adventurer, even if he wonderfully escaped the perils below, would be torn from the mountain and whirled through the air by this fearful blast.

Begging off, Sluiskin promised to wait three days for the climbers to return; then he'd go to Olympia to tell their friends they were dead.

Sluiskin's description of the mountain wasn't far from the truth. Stevens wrote,

Our course . . . brought us first to the southwest peak. This is a long, exceedingly sharp, narrow ridge springing out from the main dome for a mile into mid-air. The ridge affords not over ten or twelve feet of foothold on top, and the sides descend almost vertically. . . . The wind blew so violently that we were obliged to brace ourselves with our Alpine staffs and use great caution to guard against being swept off the ridge.

After reaching the true summit of the mountain, Stevens and Van Trump found a volcanic steam cave where they huddled for warmth. In spite of the rotten-egg stench of the sulfuric steam, they spent the night. The next day the two men returned to Sluiskin, who was *really* surprised to see them, and expressed his deep admiration for the men who had conquered Takhoma: "Strong men," he said; "stout hearts." The first woman to top the summit was a schoolteacher named Fay Fuller, who climbed the mountain in 1890.

Creating a Park

In 1883, James Longmire—who had guided climbers to the base of Mt. Rainier for many years—discovered a mineral springs near the Nisqually River and staked a mining claim on the site. Longmire recognized the land for its true value—as a place to enjoy the wild beauty and grand mountain views. His Longmire Springs Resort was built in 1906 on what is now national park land in the park's oldest developed area: Longmire.

Mount Rainier became the nation's fifth national park in 1899, due in large part to pressure from a prominent group of Northern Pacific Railroad stockholders who not only appreciated the beauty of the mountain, but also saw money to be made in the proposition. The railroad had earlier been given alternating square-mile chunks of land in a checkerboard pattern as part of the federal government's incentive to promote building a transcontinental railroad. To allow the park to be created, the company exchanged land around Mt. Rainier—most of which happened to lack trees—for federal government parcels—that just happened to contain commercially valuable timber. The Northern Pacific Railroad then proceeded to log their new land while simultaneously hauling visitors to the new park that they helped create. Not a bad business deal! The awesome beauty of this sleeping volcano has been drawing visitors ever since. Some 228,400 acres (97%) of the park was declared the Mount Rainier Wilderness Area in 1988.

GEOLOGY AND CLIMATE

Building a Mountain
The volcanic summit of Mt. Rainier—fourth highest in the Lower 48 states—was created over a period of many millennia. Around a million years ago, lava began flowing through a weak spot in the earth's crust. A series of massive lava flows and sometimes-explosive eruptions created the volcanic cone of Mt. Rainier, scraping the clouds at more than 16,000 feet high. Around 5,700 years ago, something happened—perhaps an earthquake—that triggered an enormous collapse of one side of the mountain. More than a half cubic mile of debris (the Osceola Mudflow) roared down the White River valley in a mudflow that reached almost to Puget Sound. The collapse knocked nearly 2,000 feet off the summit of Mt. Rainier, and the mud and debris inundated areas where the cities of Enumclaw, Buckley, Puyallup, and Kent are now located. Additional large mudflows have continued to occur every 500 to 1,000 years, and geologists say that they may well return without warning, engulfing cities in their path. Smaller mudflows have occurred in this century, including one in 1947 that created a "ghost forest" of trees along Kautz Creek.

Today's Mt. Rainier actually consists of three primary summits, with the highest, Columbia Crest, forming the rim of a relatively recent lava cone. The other two, Liberty Cap and Point Success, remain from the older cone that once reached to 16,000 feet. The volcano has been relatively quiet for the past 2,500 years, but an eruption approximately 150 years ago released a plume of pumice, and steam explosions in the 1960s and '70s show that the mountain is still very much alive. The danger of a catastrophic eruption is not out of the question, but geologists warn that devastating mudflows are a more obvious danger to the mountain's neighbors.

Glaciation
While forces from within the earth have created massive Mt. Rainier, the forces from above have worked to wear it down. Glaciers—created when more snow falls than melts off—have proven one of the most important of these erosional processes. After a period of several years and under the weight of additional snow, the accumulated snow crystals change into ice. Gravity pulls this ice slowly downhill, creating what is essentially a frozen river that grinds against whatever lies in the way, plucking loose rocks and soil and polishing hard bedrock. This debris moves slowly down the glacier as if on a conveyer belt, eventually reaching its terminus.

During the last ice age, which ended around 10,000 years ago, the glaciers flowing out from Rainier stretched for up to 40 miles into lowland valleys, while smaller glaciers filled the mountain cirques. Since that time, several thousand years of warming was followed by a period of cooling—the Little Ice Age—that caused the glaciers to expand. Geologists say that we are still in that cooler period, although a long warming trend (accentuated by human activities in this century) has caused Mt. Rainier's glaciers to retreat considerably since the 1930s.

Spreading out from Mt. Rainier are some 75 glaciers, 26 that have names. Together, they represent the largest single-peak glacial system in the U.S. outside Alaska. (They probably wouldn't even rank in Alaska's top 50, however.) The largest of these, **Emmons Glacier,** heads down the northeast side and is visible from Sunrise, while Paradise Visitor Center showcases the **Nisqually Glacier.**

Climate
Because of its incredible height, Rainier creates its own weather by interrupting the air flow around it and causing wet air blowing off the Pacific Ocean to release its moisture. This produces massive amounts of snowfall on the western slopes of the mountain; a world-record 1,122 inches (more than 93 feet!) fell at Paradise in 1971-72. The mountain's height also accounts for its lenticular clouds—the upside-down, saucer-shaped clouds that obscure or hover just above the summit on otherwise clear days.

Although it can rain or snow any month of the year on Rainier, most of the precipitation arrives between October and early May, and nearly all of this falls as snow at the higher elevations. July and August are the driest and sunniest months. At Paradise (5,400 feet in elevation), the snowpack often tops 15 feet by late March, remaining on the ground until early July. Down the mountain at Longmire (2,761 feet in elevation), snow depths average four feet in midwinter, and it is generally gone after early May.

Throughout most of the park, temperatures are not much different from those around Puget Sound; the nasty summer heat will sometimes follow you right up to Paradise, although generally the higher elevations enjoy cooler temperatures. The average summer day at Longmire is in the 70s, with nights dipping into the high 40s. Temperatures at Paradise are commonly around 10° cooler than this during the summer. Spring and fall are the times to be careful; rain at Longmire

can very often translate to snow at Paradise. But fall weather also means fewer people and the brilliant yellow and red leaves of cottonwoods, vine maples, bigleaf maples, Sitka mountain-ash, and blueberry bushes.

SIGHTS

Driving through Mount Rainier National Park provides numerous sightseeing and photographic opportunities; the surrounding mountains, waterfalls, forests, and canyons alone justify the trip. Several easily accessible places are especially noteworthy and are highlights of many travelers' journeys in Washington. The following descriptive tour begins in the southwest corner of the park and follows the main roads to the northeast corner.

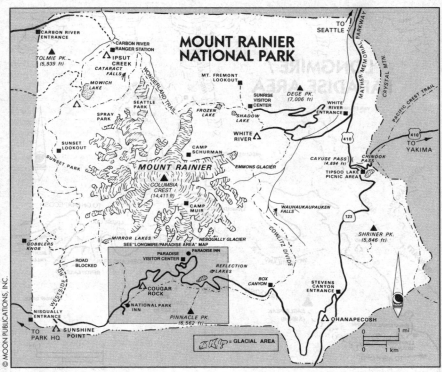

MOUNT RAINIER NATIONAL PARK

Longmire Area

Longmire is seven miles from the Nisqually entrance in the southwest corner of the park. Named for James Longmire, whose Longmire Springs Resort first attracted large numbers of travelers to the park, Longmire is home to the National Park Inn (housed in and old Longmire Mineral Springs Resort building; see "Accommodations," below), and the **Longmire Museum,** one of the oldest national park museums in existence. The small museum—located in the original park headquarters—contains displays on the park's natural history, along with exhibits of Indian basketry, a small totem pole, and photos from the early days of the park. It is open daily year-round 9 a.m.-4:30 p.m., with additional summertime hours.

Day Hikes: Several nearby hiking trails cover the gamut, from easy strolls through the woods to steep mountain climbs. The **Hiker Information Center** at Longmire, tel. (360) 569-2211, ext. 3317, can provide you with all the options. It's open daily early June through September. Less than a mile in length, the **Trail of the Shadows** takes you on a stroll around the meadow where Longmire's resort stood, with views of the mountain. A longer loop hike continues on from here up Ramparts Ridge to a majestic view over the Nisqually River far below, and then joins the Wonderland Trail. Follow this back to Longmire for a total distance of five miles.

More adventurous hikers can climb the many switchbacks to the summit of 5,958-foot **Eagle Peak,** a distance of three and a half miles one-way. The route passes through a wide range of vegetation, from dense old-growth stands along the Nisqually River to flowery alpine meadows offering extraordinary vistas across to Mt.

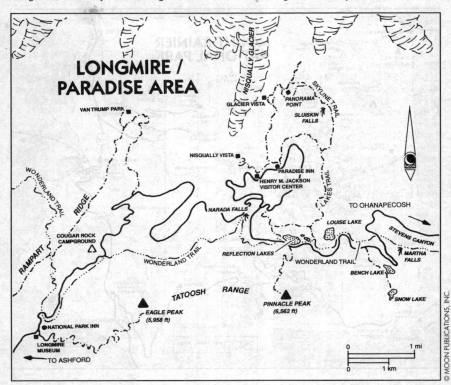

LONGMIRE / PARADISE AREA

© MOON PUBLICATIONS, INC.

Longmire's mineral springs resort

Rainier. The mountain-encircling Wonderland Trail (see below) also passes through Longmire, making this is a favorite starting point for backcountry hikes of varying lengths.

Paradise Area

The 11-mile drive from Longmire to Paradise is a delightful climb through tall evergreen forests where periodic openings provide down-valley and up-mountain vistas. Three miles before you reach Paradise is a pullout overlooking **Narada Falls,** where a steep trail leads to the plunge pool at its base. At an elevation of 5,400 feet, and with views across to the nearby mountain, Paradise Valley is appropriately named. When Virinda Longmire first visited this gorgeous area in the summer of 1885, the abundant wildflowers created a colorful contrast to the snowy summit of Mt. Rainier. "This must be what paradise is like!" she exclaimed, and thousands of tourists have concurred ever since. Get here in late July and August to see the peak of the floral display (and to join the throngs of fellow visitors who jam the parking lots and mountain trails on weekends.) Paradise is easily the most popular place in the park, with an abundance of short and long hiking trails, grand scenery, and ample winter recreation opportunities.

The flying saucer-shaped **Henry M. Jackson Visitor Center** at Paradise offers 360-degree views of the park from its circular glass walls. During the summer, naturalists lead walks and give talks on a daily basis, and a 20-minute video is shown every half-hour 10 a.m.-6 p.m. daily. Check the information desk for upcoming activities. The visitor center is open daily 9 a.m.-7 p.m. in the summer, with reduced daily hours in the spring and fall. It is open weekends and holidays only October 15 through April 30. Call (360) 569-2211, ext. 2328, for specifics. Built in 1917, Paradise Inn offers mountain-vista accommodations and meals mid-May through September only.

Day Hikes: A spider web of trails spin out over the subalpine forests and high-country meadows at Paradise; see the visitor center for a detailed map. Easiest is the **Nisqually Vista Trail,** a 1.2-mile loop hike that leads through flamboyantly floral high country meadows west of the visitor center. Almost everyone in decent physical condition takes the oft-crowded **Skyline Trail,** a five-mile romp above the timberline to Glacier Vista and Panorama Point. Needless to say, the views are extraordinary. Be sure to carry water along and to stay on the path. Far too many folks wander off, creating damage to the meadows that takes years to restore.

Heading east from Paradise toward Stevens Canyon, the road passes **Reflection Lakes,** where on a calm and clear day the mirror-like surface reflects Mt. Rainier and a rim of forest. The **Pinnacle Peak Trail** starts at the Reflection Lakes parking lot; hike this one-and-a-half-mile trail to the saddle between Pinnacle and Plummer Peaks for Mt. Rainier vistas. You'll gain 1,100 feet in elevation along the way.

An easier trail takes you uphill to **Bench and Snow Lakes.** The trailhead is a mile east of Reflection Lakes on Stevens Canyon Rd., and the path goes 1.25 miles each way, through late-summer meadows filled with bear grass and flowers.

Stevens Canyon/Ohanapecosh Area

East of Paradise, the road passes 100-foot-high **Martha Falls** and cuts across the slopes of Stevens Canyon as it follows Stevens Creek downhill. At **Box Canyon** a short trail leads to a footbridge spanning the deep but narrow gorge created by the Muddy Fork of the Cowlitz River. By the time you reach the junction with Hwy. 123, the road is deep within old-growth forests of Douglas fir and western hemlock at an elevation of just 2,200 feet.

The **Ohanapecosh Visitor Center** is open daily 9 a.m.-6 p.m. from mid-June through September, and weekends 9 a.m.-5 p.m. late May to mid-June and in early October. It is closed mid-October to late May. Call (360) 569-2211, ext. 2352, for specifics. Rangers lead two-hour walks several times a week during the summer months; see the information desk for specifics.

The **Grove of the Patriarchs Trail** starts just west of the Stevens Canyon entrance station and covers 1.5 miles of virgin forest terrain. This easy loop trail circles an island in the crystalline Ohanapecosh (oh-HAH-na-pee-kahsh) River, passing thousand-year-old Douglas firs, western hemlocks, and western red cedars that tower over a verdant fern-filled understory.

A longer hike, the **Silver Falls Trail,** follows the river in a three-mile loop that takes you to the 75-foot cataract of Silver Falls, passing a side-trail to the site of Ohanapecosh Hot Springs Resort along the way. The resort was a popular Roaring-'20s vacation place, but it closed in the 1960s and was torn down by the Park Service. It's illegal to enter the shallow springs here, and there are no pools anyway. The trail begins at the Ohanapecosh Campground.

The **Shriner Peak Trail** starts from Hwy. 123, three and a half miles north of the Stevens Canyon entrance; park on the west side of the road about a half mile from the Panther Creek bridge. This eight-mile hike—about five hours roundtrip—is almost completely devoid of shade and ends up at a lookout/ranger station at Shriner Peak (5,846 feet).

Cayuse Pass

North from Ohanapecosh, Hwy. 123 climbs into the headwaters of the Ohanapecosh River, reaching 4,694 feet at Cayuse Pass, 11 miles from the Stevens Canyon entrance station. Here the road meets Hwy. 410, which continues north past the White River entrance and east over Chinook Pass (see under "Vicinity of Mount Rainier," below), where Tipsoo Lake creates a picture-postcard image. Yakima is another 64 miles to the east.

Sunrise Area

The Sunrise area occupies a high subalpine plateau showcasing the northeast side of Mt. Rainier. Getting here is half the fun; a long series of switchbacks takes you 11 miles up from Hwy. 410, past the White River entrance station, and through tall evergreen forests along the river, before finally emerging into subalpine meadows offering all-encompassing vistas. Because of the rain-shadow effect, this side of Mt. Rainier gets far less precipitation than the western side, and the vegetation reflects this: grasses, sedges, and even whitebark pine are common here. The Sunrise area is also home to large numbers of elk during the summer and fall. Elk are not native to the park but were brought here from Yellowstone and other parts of the West between 1903 and 1933; around 1,500 of them now inhabit the park.

Located at 6,400 feet, the log cabin **Sunrise Visitor Center,** tel. (360) 569-2211, ext. 2357, is open daily 9 a.m.-6 p.m. from late June to mid-September; closed the rest of the year. It houses natural history displays and has viewing telescopes where you can check out Mt. Rainier's glaciers, including massive Emmons Glacier, largest in the Lower 48. The interpretive staff leads nature walks on a daily basis; stop by the information desk for times and destinations. Not far away is **Sunrise Lodge** with food and gifts, but no lodging. Open July-Sept. only.

Day Hikes: Many trails head out from the Sunrise area, including sections of the Wonderland Trail and shorter hikes to nearby lakes and mountains. The **White River Hiker Information Center** at the entrance station has backcountry and climbing permits, along with maps and other information. The center is open daily late May through September. **Shadow Lake Trail** is one of the most popular of these, a three-mile jaunt that departs from Sunrise parking lot, drops to a rim overlooking the White River Valley, and then follows that ridge to Shadow Lake. Return via Frozen Lake and Sourdough Ridge.

To get to **Mt. Fremont Lookout** from the Sunrise parking lot, follow the trails to Sourdough Ridge and Frozen Lake, then branch off to the north. The mountain is 7,181 feet high, a gain of 1,200 feet. This well-marked six-mile path takes about three hours roundtrip.

For **Dege Peak**, start between Sunshine Point and the Sunrise parking area; this one-mile trail climbs 7,006-foot Dege Peak in the Sourdough Mountains.

Carbon River Area

Because of its location in the far northwest corner of the park, this part of Mount Rainier National Park sees considerably less visitation than others. The region is named for the coal deposits that once attracted miners, but it is best known today for its magnificent temperate rainforest. Access is via Hwy. 165 south from Buckley; a gravel road continues past the Carbon River Ranger Station to Ipsut Creek Campground, six miles inside the park. A second gravel road enters the park south of here and climbs to Mowich Lake, located in a high glacial cirque. Get information at the **Carbon River Ranger Station,** open daily 9 a.m.-5 p.m. during the summer and until mid-November.

Day Hikes: Take the quarter-mile **Carbon River Rain Forest Trail** for a quick taste of Mt. Rainier's only true rainforest. The **Carbon Glacier** extends northwest from Mt. Rainier, reaching just 1,100 feet in elevation at its terminus, the lowest of any glacier in the U.S. outside Alaska. A section of the Wonderland Trail leads from Ipsut Creek Campground to the snout of the glacier, three and a half miles each way. Watch out for rocks falling off the glacier.

From Mowich Lake, hike the three-mile trail past pretty Eunice Lake and on to the **Tolmie Peak** fire lookout at 5,939 feet in elevation.

BACKCOUNTRY HIKING

Rainier's hiking season is quite short: most trails are snow-free only from mid-July to mid-October, though trails at the lower elevations may open earlier and remain snow-free later in the year. It's always advisable to dress for *all* seasons when hiking in the Cascades, carrying cotton, wool, and rain gear. About 300 miles of hiking trails crisscross the park, many miles of which are suitable for day hikes. More than a dozen of the most popular of these are described above under "Sights"; drop by one of the hiking or visitor centers upon your arrival for up-to-date trail info. The park has a helpful *Wilderness Trip Planner* available by mail; get a copy, along with other information, by calling the park's backcountry desk at (360) 569-2211, ext. 3317. *50 Hikes in Mount Rainier National Park,* by Ira Spring and Harvey Manning (Seattle: The Mountaineers), is a detailed guide to the park's many backcountry trails.

Backcountry Regulations

Backcountry permits are required for all overnight trips in the park throughout the year and are available free from the Hiker Information Centers in Longmire and White River, or from the various entrance stations and visitor centers. Permits are available up to 24 hours before you depart. If you're heading into a popular area on a busy weekend, your first choice may be full. Sunday through Thursday nights are far less crowded, so head out on these days if possible. Fires are not allowed in the backcountry, so bring a stove along. Be sure to filter or otherwise treat any drinking water, since the protozoan *Giardia* (causes "beaver fever") and other harmful micro-organisms may be present. Always practice no-trace camping and haul out any garbage. Hikers in backcountry meadows should stay on the trails at all times; plants here have only a brief growing season, and damaged areas take a long time to recover. Pets are not allowed on any park trails.

There are three types of backcountry camps within the park. "Trailside camps" are located every three to seven miles along backcountry trails, including the mountain-circling Wonderland Trail. Each of these has space for up to 10 tenting parties, along with a nearby water source and pit toilet. The vast majority of hikers use these established campsites. If you choose to camp away from these, you'll need to stay at "cross-country camps," sites located a quarter-mile away from the trail and other camps and at least 100 feet from water sources. "Alpine camps" are in areas above 6,000 feet, and have their own rules; see the hiker information centers for details.

Wonderland Trail

The Wonderland Trail is a backpacker's dream: 93 miles of mountain passes, forests, streams, and alpine meadows that completely encircle the mountain. The trail has lots of ups and downs, including 3,500-foot changes in elevation in several stretches of the route. Allow 10 days to two weeks for the entire trip. Food (but not fuel) can be cached at ranger stations along the way by mailing packages to yourself; contact the Park Service at (360) 569-2211 for addresses and other specifics.

You can start your Wonderland hike almost anywhere—Mowich Lake, Longmire, White River, Box Canyon—but Ipsut Creek may be the best choice, since you'd be hitting the only showers in the park at Paradise about halfway through. A wide range of shorter one-way and loop hikes are also possible along the Wonderland Trail.

Also for marathon packers, the **Pacific Crest Trail** touches the east edge of the park at Tipsoo Lake on Hwy. 410, continuing north to British Columbia and south to Mexico. (See "William O. Douglas Wilderness Area" under "Wilderness Areas" in the Vicinity of Mount Rainier section, below.)

Other Trails

For a rewarding one- or two-night trip in the northwest section of the park, begin at the Ipsut Creek Campground, follow the Wonderland Trail along the Carbon River, and then turn onto the **Seattle Park Trail.** The trail approaches Cataract Falls (a quick side trip), and crosses Marmot Creek. Camping is permitted about one mile below Seattle Park in Cataract Valley. Hike across a permanent snowfield into Spray Park (where avalanche lilies carpet the meadows late in the summer), and continue on to Mowich Lake, turning northeast to follow the Wonderland Trail down Ipsut Creek and back to your starting point. It's about 16 miles roundtrip.

Another good overnighter, though not a circular route, is **Indian Bar.** This hike starts at Box Canyon on Stevens Canyon Rd., crosses Nickel Creek, then turns left to follow the Cowlitz Divide. At Indian Bar, the Ohanapecosh River divides a meadow; the shelter is on the west side, just above Wauhaukaupauken Falls. Return by the same route for a total of 15 miles.

Gobbler's Knob is a fire lookout (5,500 feet) that can be reached from Round Pass on Westside Rd., near the Nisqually entrance. This two-and-a-half-mile trail passes Lake George. Westside Rd. is closed at Fish Creek, three miles up, due to recurring floods that have washed out the bridge, so you will need to wade across (sometimes this is not safe). Bikes are allowed on the road beyond here, but be sure to get current conditions from the Park Service before heading up. The lookout is also accessible from outside the park via the tiny Glacier View Wilderness (see "Wilderness Areas" under "Vicinity of Mount Rainier," below).

CLIMBING

Because of its many glaciers and rocky faces, Mt. Rainier has long been one of the premier training peaks for American climbers. More than 4,500 people reach Mt. Rainier's summit every year—of some 9,000 who attempt it. Two days are usually required for the trek: the first day involves a four- to five-hour hike over trails and snowfields to Camp Muir, the south-side base camp at 10,000 feet, or Camp Schurman, on the northeast side at 9,500 feet. The second day starts early (about 2 a.m.) for the summit climb and the return to the Paradise starting point. Reservations are not accepted for the high camps, so be prepared to camp outside: Muir's 25-person capacity is frequently filled, and Schurman has no public shelter—your only luxury is a pit toilet.

All climbers must be in top physical condition before heading out, and experience in glacier travel is highly recommended. Rainier is a difficult climb, and before heading up, you need to undertake a rigorous conditioning program. Above the high camps climbers are roped, using ice axes and crampons to inch their way over glaciers to the summit. All climbers must register and get a **climbing card** (a backcountry permit is not needed) at a hiker information center, visitor center, or ranger station before their climb; solo climbers need the park superintendent's approval. To offset increasing costs (and decreasing support from a Republican Congress), the Park Service has instituted a $15 per person fee for all climbers heading above 10,000 feet on the mountain, and $25 per person for an annual pass to climb.

Guided Climbs

Even inexperienced climbers can conquer the mountain if they are in excellent physical condition. **Rainier Mountaineering, Inc.**—founded in part by famed mountain climber Louis Whittaker in 1968—offers guided treks up Mt. Rainier, along with snow- and ice-climbing seminars for climbers of all skill levels. The guides—including some of the most experienced in America—operate from the Guide House at Paradise (open daily in the summer). Rates are $80 for their one-day snow- and ice-climbing school (no reservations necessary), $420 for a three-day summit climb package (one day of instruction plus the two-day climb), and $510 for a four-day Emmons Glacier package (one day of instruction plus a three-day roundtrip). RMI also offers seminars in crevasse rescue, advanced seminars, private lessons, and six-day winter mountaineering seminars ($785). Some of the required equipment—including boots, crampons, ice axe, and pack—is available for rent at the Guide House in Paradise. RMI recommends that persons under 15 not attempt the summit climb, and that climbers be in top physical condition. RMI's climbing programs operate from late May to late September. For a brochure, call RMI in Paradise at (360) 569-2227 during the summer, or in Tacoma at (206) 627-6242 during the winter (October to mid-May).

OTHER SUMMER RECREATION

Fishing is generally disappointing at Rainier; the fish, if you get any, are small. Or, as the Park Service notes, "angler's success is often less than anticipated." Park waters are not stocked—the trout and char are native, so restrictions are plentiful, and barbless hooks are recommended. No fishing license is required. Stop at any ranger station for current info on limits, fishing season, and closures. The park's lakes and ponds are ice-free from July to October; rivers, streams, and beaver ponds from late-May through late-October.

Nonmotorized **boating** is allowed on all park lakes except Frozen Lake, Reflection Lakes, Ghost Lake, and Tipsoo Lake; canoes are a great way to view the wildlife.

Horses are allowed on 100 miles of park trails; contact the Park Service for a horse trail map.

Cyclists find Mt. Rainier's roads to be steep, winding, and narrow—a prescription for trouble due to the heavy automobile traffic. Use extreme caution when cycling in the park since RVers have a reputation for not always knowing the width of their vehicles. None of the backcountry trails in the park are open to mountain bikes, although nearby Forest Service land has hundreds of miles of such trails.

WINTER RECREATION

Cross-Country Skiing

Mount Rainier is famous for its abundant backcountry, where the snow seems to reach out forever, and the Telemark skiing is unmatched in Washington. Many beginners head to the Paradise parking lot to ski up the unplowed road, or out the trails to Nisqually Vista, Narada Falls, or Reflection Lake. None of these are groomed, but it generally doesn't take long for other folks to set down tracks in the new snow. The area gets an incredible 630 inches of snow in a typical year, and often much more than this.

Half-a-dozen ski trails of varying difficulty can be found in the Longmire/Nisqually area; check with the visitor center for specifics. The eastside roads provide other skiing options, including, of course, the groomed slopes at Crystal Mountain Ski Area, just a few miles outside the park's northeast corner (see "Crystal Mountain and Greenwater" under "Vicinity of Mount Rainier" for details). For a quieter experience, the Ohanapecosh area is a good bet. Park near the ranger station and ski up the roads toward Cayuse Pass or Box Canyon if you are ambitious, but be sure to check about avalanche dangers before heading up. Easier skiing can be found in the unplowed Ohanapecosh Campground loops.

Rent cross-country skis, Telemark skis, or snowshoes at the **Longmire Ski Touring Center,** open daily in the winter. They also provide ski lessons and tours for a fee. Ski rentals are not available at Paradise. If you plan to overnight in the backcountry, be sure to get a permit before heading out; they are required year-round. Call (206) 526-6677 for current avalanche conditions, or talk with Park Service folks in Longmire before heading up the hill.

Other Snow Play

Facilities are open for winter sports at Paradise from December to April. The area is very popular with sliders, but "soft" sleds only; wooden toboggans and sleds with metal runners are verboten. Bring your own sleds since they are not available for rent at Mt. Rainier. The park usually constructs a sledding, snowboarding, and skiing area at Paradise in early December; no snow sliding is allowed here before that time to protect the vegetation.

Ranger-led **Snowshoe walks** are offered at the Paradise Visitor Center on weekends and holidays late December to March. Rent snowshoes for just $1. Soft platters and inner tubes may be used in designated play areas only.

Winter camping is allowed at Paradise once the snow depth tops five feet; get permits and details on locating your camp from the visitor center.

ACCOMMODATIONS AND CAMPING

Inns

There are two inns within the park itself; both are run by the park concessionaire, Mount Rainier Guest Services. The **National Park Inn** at Longmire is open daily year-round. This inn has rooms for $58-80 s or d. Built in 1917, **Paradise Inn** is an imposing wooden lodge with high ceilings, stone fireplaces, and unsurpassed mountain views from its elevation of 5,400 feet. The lodge is open daily from late May through September; rooms are $62-88 s or d. Call (360) 569-2275 for reservations at either of these.

For a broad spectrum of accommodations both inside and outside the park, see the "Accommodations near Mount Rainier" chart.

Campgrounds

Mount Rainier National Park has 577 drive-in campsites available on a first-come, first-served basis only. (Group sites are reservable; for details call 360-569-2211, ext. 3301.) All of these campsites have running water and flush or pit toilets, but no RV hookups. Public showers (25 cents) are available at the Paradise Visitor Center when it is open, but you'll need to head to Ashford or other towns for laundry facilities. Gathering firewood is prohibited in the park, but it can be purchased at the Cougar Rock and Ohanapecosh Campgrounds, as well as the Longmire General Store.

The park's five campgrounds are: **Sunshine Point Campground,** located just inside the southwest entrance at Nisqually ($6; open year-round); **Cougar Rock Campground,** two and a half miles northeast of Longmire ($8; open late May to mid-October); **Ohanapecosh Campground,** near the southeast entrance on Hwy. 123 ($10; open late May to mid-October); **White River Campground,** on the east side in the Sunrise area ($8; open late June to late September); and **Ipsut Creek Campground,** at the end of the Carbon River Rd. in the northwest corner ($6; open late May to late September; free walk-in use only in the winter, but no water). Camping is not permitted in the Paradise area or along park roads.

FOOD

Longmire has a sit-down restaurant inside the **National Park Inn,** tel. (360) 569-2411, which is open year-round. The dining room at **Paradise Inn,** tel. (360) 569-2413, serves three meals a day and a big Sunday brunch during its season of operation from late May through September. For something less formal, the **Henry M. Jackson Visitor Center** at Paradise contains a snack bar with typical fast food; open daily May to early October, and on weekends and holidays the rest of the year.

The cafeteria at **Sunrise Lodge** operates only between late June and early September. Limited groceries are available year-round at Longmire General Store and during the summer at Sunrise. For food outside park limits, see the towns of Greenwater, Ashford, Elbe, Eatonville, Packwood, Randle, Morton, and Mossyrock (all listed in the Vicinity of Mount Rainier section, below).

INFORMATION AND SERVICES

Getting In

Entrance to Mount Rainier National Park is $5 per vehicle, and $3 per person for folks arriving by foot and on bikes, motorcycles, buses, or horses (they don't say anything about skateboards). Your entrance fee is good for seven

MT. RAINIER AREA ACCOMMODATIONS

Accommodations are arranged from least to most expensive in each area. See also the towns of Enumclaw, Eatonville, Elbe, and Morton for lodging options within 30 miles of the park entrances. Reserve at least two weeks ahead for summer weekends. Rates may be lower during the winter months and on weekdays. The area code is 360.

NATIONAL PARK LODGES

National Park Inn; Longmire; tel. 569-2275; $60-109 s or d; stone fireplace in lodge, shared or private baths, open year-round

Paradise Inn; Paradise; tel. 569-2275; $64-117 s or d; classic 1920s lodge, rustic furnishings, shared or private baths, open late May to early October

ASHFORD AREA (SOUTHWEST ENTRANCE)

Whittaker's Bunkhouse; 30205 Hwy. 706 E; tel. 569-2439; $19 per person in bunkhouse rooms with shared bath; $56 s or d with private bath; historic logger's bunkhouse

Gateway Inn Motel; 38820 Hwy. 706 E; tel. 569-2506; $30 s, $35 d in motel; $50-60 s or d in log cabins with fireplaces; near park entrance

Mounthaven at Cedar Park; 38210 Hwy. 706 E; tel. 569-2594; $44-86 s or d; cabins with kitchens, fireplaces, two-night minimum stay on weekends

The Lodge Near Mt. Rainier; 38608 Hwy. 706 E; tel. 569-2312; $45-65 s or d; cottages with kitchens, fireplaces, two-night minimum stay on weekends and holidays

Jasmer's Guest House and Cabins; 30005 Hwy. 706 E; tel. 569-2682; $45-95 s or d for guesthouse with continental breakfast; $70-150 for cabins (sleep six) with jacuzzi and kitchens available, two-night minimum stay in cabins

Mt. Rainier Country Cabins; 38624 Hwy. 706 E; tel. 569-2355; $55-60 s or d; near park entrance, cabins with kitchenettes and fireplaces

Growly Bear B&B; 37311 Hwy. 706 E; tel. 569-2339; $60-80 s or d; 1890 home, two guest rooms, full breakfast

Rainier Overland Lodge; 31811 Hwy. 706 E; tel. 569-0851; $65 s or d; cabins or motel

Nisqually Lodge; 31609 Hwy. 706 E; tel. 569-8804; $67 s, $67-77 d; large rooms, jacuzzi, free continental breakfast, AAA approved

Hershey Homestead B&B; 33514 Mt. Tahoma Canyon Rd.; tel. 569-2897; $68 s or d in a contemporary two-story home with continental breakfast; $99 for up to three in a small cottage with kitchen and fireplace; $175 for up to five in larger cottage (sleeps 11; $13 pp for additional folks) with kitchen and fireplace; quiet off-highway location with mountain views and century-old apple orchard

Alexander's Country Inn; 37515 Hwy. 706 E (a mile west of the park entrance); tel. 569-2300 or (800) 654-7615; $75 s or d with shared bath, $89-125 s or d with private bath; classic country inn, jacuzzi, antiques and handmade quilts, fireplaces, stained-glass windows, full breakfast included, AAA approved

Mountain Meadows Inn B&B; 28912 Hwy. 706 E; tel. 569-2788; $75 s, $95 d; 1910 home, five guest rooms with railroad items, private baths, sauna, pond, nature trails, full breakfast, AAA approved

Wellspring; two miles east of Ashford; tel. 569-2514; $85 s or d; log cabins in quiet off-highway location, private baths, jacuzzi, wood-fired saunas (for two rooms), continental breakfast

The Cabinette; Ashford; tel. 569-2954; $90 d; small luxurious cabins, hot tub, kitchens, some fireplaces, couples only, no kids

(continues on next page)

MT. RAINIER AREA ACCOMMODATIONS

(continued)

Nisqually Park Chalet; Ashford; tel. (206) 854-2222; $120 d ($250 d on holiday weekends), $10 pp for additional people; large home, sleeps 10 people, large cedar hot tub, outside decks, newly remodeled and redecorated, woodstove, full kitchen, two-night minimum stay

PACKWOOD AND RANDLE AREA (SOUTHEAST ENTRANCE)

Hotel Packwood; 104 Main St., Packwood; tel. 494-5431; $20 s, $25 d with bath down the hall, $30-35 s or d with private bath; renovated 1912 hotel, cozy and friendly

Woodland Motel; 11890 Hwy. 12 (five miles west of Packwood); tel. 494-6766; $25-35 s, $38-42 d; simple country accommodations, kitchenettes available, AAA approved

Silver Brook Motel; 10111 Hwy. 12, Randle; tel. 497-5647; $30 s or d

Mountain View Lodge & Motel; 13163 Hwy. 12, Packwood; tel. 494-5555; $31-67 s, $34-49 d; outdoor pool, jacuzzi, kitchenettes available, AAA approved

Medici Motel; 661 Cispus Rd. (three miles south of Randle); tel. 497-7700; $35 s or d; country setting with trout pond

Randle Motel; 9780 Hwy. 12, Randle; tel. 497-5346; $30-35 s, $35-45 d

Peter's Inn; 13059 Hwy. 12, Packwood; tel. 494-4000; $40 s or d

Tall Timber Motel; one mile east of Randle on Hwy. 12; tel. 497-2991; $40 s, $45 d; kitchenette

Mt. Adams Inn; 9514 Hwy. 12, Randle; tel. 497-7007; $43-48 s or d; jacuzzi, exercise facility, continental breakfast, kitchenettes

Inn of Packwood; 12032 Hwy. 12, Packwood; tel. 494-5500; $45 s, $53 d; outdoor pool, jacuzzi, AAA approved

Tatoosh Motel; 12880 Hwy. 12, Packwood; tel. 494-5321; $45-75 s or d; homey rooms, kitchenettes available, jacuzzi, AAA approved

Cowlitz River Lodge; 13069 Hwy. 12, Packwood; tel. 494-4444; $50 s or d; fine views, outdoor jacuzzi, continental breakfast, AAA approved

Timberline Village Resort; 13807 Hwy. 12 (four miles east of Packwood); tel. 494-9224; $50-70 s or d

CRYSTAL MOUNTAIN AREA (NORTHEAST ENTRANCE)

Alpine Inn; Crystal Mt.; tel. 663-2262; $40-72 s or d; shared or private bath; outdoor pool, jacuzzi, open early November-April only

Crystal Mountain Resort; Crystal Mt.; tel. 663-2265; weekend rates: $77-95 s or d in hotel rooms (Village Inn Hotel and Quicksilver Lodge), $110-145 for up to four in one-bedroom apartments with heated outdoor pool (Crystal Chalet Condos and Silver Skis Chalet Condos); tennis courts, open year-round with lower weekday rates

Alta Crystal Resort; 68317 Hwy. 410 E (two miles north of the entrance to Mt. Rainier); tel. 663-2500 or (800) 277-6475; summer weekend rates: $89-129 d; winter weekend rates: $99-159 d in cabins, lodge rooms, or loft chalets; outdoor pool, jacuzzi, kitchens, fireplaces

days. If you plan to return several times, purchase an annual Mount Rainier Park pass for $15, or pay $25 to get a Golden Eagle Pass that lets you in all of the nation's national parks for a year. Seniors over age 62 can pay a one-time fee of $10 for a Golden Age Passport that lets them in all national parks. No charge for disabled visitors to Mount Rainier. Park headquarters are located nine miles outside the park in Ashford's Tahoma Woods area.

Publications

Information and assorted publications are available at visitor centers in Longmire, Paradise, Ohanapecosh, and Sunrise, and from the various entrance stations. (See "Sights," above, for hours and seasons of the various visitor centers.) Mount Rainier National Park's official newspaper, the *Tahoma,* is published quarterly and is packed with up-to-date details on park activities, camping, hiking, climbing, and facilities. Get a copy in advance of your visit, along with a park map and other brochures, by calling the Park Service at (360) 569-2211. The **Northwest Interpretive Association** has a mail-order catalog of publications and topographic maps; for a copy, call (360) 569-2211, ext. 3320.

Park headquarters are located nine miles outside the park in Ashford's Tahoma Woods area.

Services

Gift shops are found at Sunrise, Paradise, and Longmire. Camping supplies are limited in the park; better to bring yours in from the outside. Climbing supplies—including boots, crampons, ice axes, and packs—can be rented from the Guide House at Paradise.

Park **post offices** are in Paradise Inn (summers) and Longmire's National Park Inn (all year). Short on cash? The closest ATM is located in Ashford at Ashford Valley Grocery.

The **area code** for Mount Rainier National Park area and all of southwest Washington is 360.

Interpretive Programs

The National Park Service schedules nature walks, campfire programs, and children's activities from late May to late September. Program schedules are posted at visitor centers and campgrounds, as well as in the park newspaper, *Tahoma.* During the winter, naturalists also offer snowshoe walks from the Paradise visitor center.

Field Seminars

The Pacific Northwest National Parks and Forests Association offers one- to three-day seminars in glaciology, alpine ecology, photography, geology, and more at Mt. Rainier, plus similar courses at Mt. St. Helens. Seminars fill up fast; to get on the mailing list, call Pacific Northwest Field Seminars in Seattle at (206) 442-2636.

TRANSPORTATION AND TOURS

In 1911, the first automobile to reach Mount Rainier National Park carried president William H. Taft aboard. Since then, the car has become the primary means of transportation to the park, with many visitors following the roads along the park's southern and eastern margins. (See "Sights," above, for a tour of the most popular at-

Snowdrifts permit skiing on the roof of Paradise Lodge.

TACOMA PUBLIC LIBRARY

tractions along the way.) Gasoline is not available inside the park, so be sure to fill your tank in surrounding towns.

Winter Roads

Winter snow closes most of Mt. Rainier's roads, with the exception of the section between the Nisqually entrance and Paradise. This road closes each night and reopens in the morning after the plows have cleared any new-fallen snow. Chains are frequently required and should always be carried. The road between Paradise and Ohanapecosh is generally open Memorial Day to early November, while Hwy. 123 and 410 over Cayuse Pass usually opens in late April and remains open till the first heavy snowfall (November). Chinook Pass is open from early June to sometime in November, and the road to Sunrise generally opens by the first of July and closes once the snow gets too deep, frequently in early October. Early snows can close any of these, so be sure to call ahead at (360) 569-2211 to see which roads are open.

Bus Tours

Mount Rainier National Park has no public transportation, but two companies offer summertime trips from Seattle to the park. **Scenic Bound Tours,** tel. (206) 433-6907, offers summertime day trips from Seattle that take you to Mt. Rainier for $47, or that combine Mt. Rainier and Mt. St. Helens for $55. These trips always include at least one hike.

Adventure Outdoors, tel. (206) 842-3189, provides guided day trips from Seattle to Mt. Rainier and Mt. St. Helens for $99. Their two-day tours of Mt. Rainier cost $459 per person for two people, or $299 per person for four people, including all meals and overnight accommodations. Three-day tours include an additional scenic trip to Mt. St. Helens, plus meals and a second night's accommodations for $696 per person for two, or $435 per person for four people.

VICINITY OF MOUNT RAINIER

WILDERNESS AREAS

Half-a-dozen wilderness areas cover more than 356,000 acres of mountainous Forest Service terrain in the Mt. Rainier Area. The largest of these—Norse Peak, William O. Douglas, and Goat Rocks Wilderness Areas—form an almost continuous reach of wild country along the crest of the southern Cascades, broken only by Hwy. 410 near Chinook Pass and Hwy. 12 at White Pass.

Norse Peak Wilderness

This 50,923-acre wilderness reaches north from Hwy. 410 and just west of the Crystal Mountain Ski Area and covers rocky ridges, steep valleys, and forests of Douglas fir, western red cedar, and western hemlock. The **Pacific Crest Trail** climbs across the backbone of these ridges for approximately 27 miles from Government Meadow (accessible via Forest Rd. 70) on the north end, to Hwy. 410 near Chinook Pass on the south end. Along the way it cruises over high ridges, including two that top 6,400 feet; a popular side path leads to the summit of 6,856-foot Norse Peak for extraordinary views across to Mt. Rainier. The **Fifes Peaks** area on the east side of the wilderness is popular with rock climbers, but the rock can be weak in places. Some of the easiest access to the Pacific Crest Trail comes from near the Crystal Mountain Ski Area. Several paths leave from this area, including the **Silver Creek Trail** (No. 1192) and **Bullion Basin Trail** (No. 1156), both of which reach the PCT in a bit over two miles of hiking.

For a short hike with excellent views of Mt. Rainier, head 32 miles east from Enumclaw on Hwy. 410 to Corral Pass Rd. (No. 7174), and follow it seven miles to a parking area just before the Corral Pass Campground. From here, the appropriately named **Rainier View Trail** climbs for a mile to a 6,080-foot ridge overlooking the mountain. This is a popular camping place, but carry water since none is available at the ridge. The trail continues beyond this, connecting with the Castle Mountain Trail, 2.2 miles from your starting point. An additional five miles of hiking brings you to the Pacific Crest Trail near Martinson Gap. Check with the Forest Service for the condition of Castle Mountain Trail; at last check it was difficult to follow.

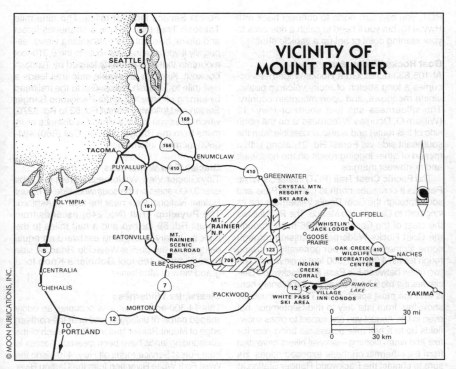

VICINITY OF MOUNT RAINIER

William O. Douglas Wilderness

Covering 167,195 acres, the William O. Douglas Wilderness is a delightful slice of wild mountain country that includes hundreds of small lakes, more than 250 miles of trails, and grand ridges that offer panoramic views. The wilderness is named for the Supreme Court Justice whose environmental stands helped create areas such as this, and who spent considerable time hiking in these mountains.

William O. Douglas Wilderness is accessible via Hwy. 410 on the north side, Hwy. 12 on the south, and the Bumping River Rd. in the center, along with various Forest Service roads on the east side. Bumping Lake Rd. leads past eight Forest Service campgrounds, the little settlement of Goose Prairie, and Bumping Lake. Boats can be rented and RV spaces are available at **Bumping Lake Marina,** tel. (509) 575-0417.

The **Pacific Crest Trail** heads through the southwest side of the wilderness for 14 miles;

access it from Highways 12 and 410 on either end. Within the wilderness, the PCT passes many small lakes, marshes, tarns, and meadows, topping out on a 5,740-foot ridge where you can enjoy the mountain spectacle.

For an interesting loop trip that includes a section of the PCT, take Bumping River Rd. past Bumping Lake, and turn onto Rd. 18 to its end where the **Bumping Lake Trail** (No. 971) climbs the headwaters of the Bumping River to Fish Lake. Here you turn north on the PCT, follow it to the **American Ridge Trail** (No. 958), and then two miles to the **Swamp Lake Trail** (No. 970), where you turn again to reach your starting point. The roundtrip distance is approximately 27 miles for this loop hike.

A long one-way trek is the **American Ridge Trail** (No. 958), which starts just off Hwy. 410 and eventually meets the PCT after coursing over 27 miles of forests, ridges, and mountaintops, including 7,473-foot Goat Peak. At the

PCT, you can turn north to connect back with Hwy. 410, but you'll need to catch a ride back to your starting point or set up a vehicle shuttle.

Goat Rocks Wilderness

At 105,633 acres, Goat Rocks Wilderness occupies a long stretch of rocky volcanic peaks, alpine meadows, and open mountain country. The wilderness sits just south of Hwy. 12 (William O. Douglas Wilderness is on the north side of this route) and is also accessible from the southeast side via Forest Rd. 21, along with a myriad of other logging roads on the northeast and northwest margins.

The **Pacific Crest Trail** (PCT) intersects White Pass as it continues north to Chinook Pass and south through the Goat Rocks Wilderness, on its long path to Canada and Mexico. The PCT follows the crest of the Cascades for 36 miles through the Goat Rocks Wilderness, passing through some alpine meadows but generally following rough terrain 4,200 to 7,500 feet in elevation. The two miles between Elk Pass and Packwood Glacier are the most hazardous, but the scenery here is also the most spectacular. The trail is usually snow-free from late July to mid-September, but even in late August you can expect to cross snowfields up to a half mile across, so bring your ice axe and warm clothing—several hikers have died from hypothermia on these exposed ridges. Be sure to contact the Packwood Ranger Station at (360) 494-5515 when planning your trip for updated information on snow levels and trail conditions. **Susee's Skyline Packers,** tel. (206) 472-5558 (in Tacoma), has horseback trail rides and drop-camp trips from the Naches area.

For a fine, but oft-crowded 13-mile loop trip, begin at the Berry Patch trailhead near Chambers Lake Campground at the end of Forest Rd. 2150 on the southwest side of the wilderness. The **Snowgrass Trail** (No. 96) climbs past high meadows near Snowgrass Flat, well known for its summertime wildflowers; no camping here. From here, you can connect in with the PCT, or follow **Lily Basin Trail** (No. 86) along the ridge, and then return via exposed **Goat Ridge Trail** (No. 95) to your starting point.

Tatoosh Wilderness

This 15,800-acre wilderness abuts the southeast flank of Mount Rainier National Park and is one of the few remaining parcels of unlogged Forest Service land for miles. The nine-mile **Tatoosh Trail** (No. 161) is a strenuous forest and alpine hike but has outstanding views, especially if you take the side route to the 6,310-foot mountain that was formerly topped by Tatoosh Lookout. Another enjoyable side trail leads a half-mile to Tatoosh Lakes. Get to the trailhead by turning off Hwy. 12 at the Packwood Ranger Station and following Forest Rd. 52 to Rd. 5270, which takes you to the trailhead, a distance of 11 miles from the Ranger Station. Call (360) 494-0600 for more information.

Glacier View Wilderness

Tiny Glacier View Wilderness covers just a bit over 3,000 acres on the southwest side of Mount Rainier National Park near the town of Ashford. The **Puyallup Trail** (No. 248) ascends from Forest Rd. 59 for two and a half miles to the park boundary, continuing eastward an equal distance to the park's Westside Road. A side route climbs 5,485-foot **Gobbler's Knob** for a grand view of Mt. Rainier.

Clearwater Wilderness

This 14,300-acre wilderness occupies an oddly shaped parcel of unlogged land near the northern edge of Mount Rainier National Park. Much of the surrounding lands have been clearcut. Access is from Forest Service roads off Hwy. 410 along the West Fork White River and from the Carbon River Rd. area. The **Carbon Trail** (No. 1179) cuts across this small wilderness for 9.4 miles, with a mile-long spur to the summit of 6,089-foot Bearhead Mountain, which provides views across the alpine meadows to still-wild Mt. Rainier and the heavily logged slopes of adjacent private and Forest Service lands. Get to the eastern end of Carbon Trail by following Forest Rd. 74 from Hwy. 410, and turning up Rd. 7450 to its end at the trailhead. From the west, take the Carbon River Rd. from Wilkenson, and turn up Rd. 7810 to its end beyond Copley Lake at the trailhead.

CHINOOK PASS

The highest of the Cascade mountain passes, Chinook Pass rises more than a mile above sea level (5,440 feet) on Hwy. 410. This is a fair-weather route, closed in winter and often dusted with snow as late as June. Just west of the pass, the highway enters Mount Rainier National Park, passing **Tipsoo Lake,** one of the most beautiful and easily accessed Cascade alpine lakes. Enjoy a picnic lunch here against a striking Mt. Rainier backdrop. More adventurous folks will enjoy the **Naches Peak Loop,** a three-and-a-half-mile hike that skirts the lakeshore and then circles this mountain. Part of this loop follows the Pacific Crest Trail.

Boulder Cave is up a forest road just west of the little settlement of Cliffdell on Hwy. 410. Take a flashlight to explore this tunnel-like cavern.

The **area code** for Chinook Pass—and points east all the way to Idaho—is 509.

Cliffdell to Naches

Whistlin' Jack Lodge, 25 miles northwest of Naches on Hwy. 410, tel. (509) 658-2433 or (800) 827-2299, borders on the sunny side of the mountains, with just 15 inches of precipitation annually and over 300 days of sunshine. Open year-round, the lodge includes a motel, cottages, restaurant, lounge, gas, and groceries. Rooms cost $89 s or d for motel units, $129-189 s or d for cabins (the more expensive ones have hot tubs). The food is fine: fresh blueberry pancakes for breakfast, a buffet lunch, and prime rib, mountain trout, or tenderloin for dinner.

Squaw Rock Resort, 20 miles northwest of Naches on Hwy. 410, tel. (509) 658-2926, has cabins for $59-69 s or d with fireplaces and kitchens, and motel units for $49-54 s or d; amenities include a heated pool, hot tub, restaurant, store, and public showers.

Elkridge Lodge, 18 miles northwest of Naches on Hwy. 410, tel. (509) 658-2258, has cabins that sleep four with kitchens, woodstoves, and a shared bathhouse for $45 s or d. Recreational vehicle hookups are also available.

The Cozy Cat B&B, 17 miles west of Naches on Hwy. 410, tel. (509) 658-2953, has two guest rooms with private baths for $55-80 s or d, including a light breakfast. The location is close to a small pond and offers fine mountain vistas.

In Naches, stay at **Van's Naches Motel,** tel. (509) 653-2445, for $25 s, $35 d.

Campgrounds

The Forest Service has many popular campgrounds along Hwy. 410 between Enumclaw and Naches, including **The Dalles Campground,** located 26 miles southeast of Enum-

claw and five miles from the northern edge of Mount Rainier National Park. The short and easy **Dalles River Trail** leaves from the campground and follows the White River. The main attraction here is a Douglas fir tree that reaches almost 10 feet in diameter. **Silver Springs Campground** is even closer to Enumclaw, near the turnoff to Crystal Mountain Resort on Hwy. 410. Both of these are open mid-May to late September, cost $8, and can be reserved ($7.50 extra) by calling (800) 280-2267. More than a dozen other Forest Service campgrounds can be found just off Hwy. 410 between the park and the town of Naches; some are free, others charge $5-7. These are only available on a first-come, first-camp basis.

WHITE PASS

Highway 12 between Yakima and Mt. Rainier traverses 4,500-foot White Pass. The route climbs westward along the Tieton River through heavily forested areas with a few clear views of Rainier along the way.

White Pass Ski Area

Located off Hwy. 12 about 55 miles west of Yakima, and 12 miles southeast of Mount Rainier National Park, White Pass Ski Area offers a 1,500-foot vertical drop and 650 acres of skiing, served by five chairlifts (including a high-speed quad chair), a Poma, and rope tow. The base elevation is 4,500 feet. Amenities include a ski school, ski rentals, child care, cafeteria, bar, and privately owned condos. Rates are $29 for adults, $18 for kids and seniors on weekends, with lower weekday rates, including a Wed.-Thurs. special that costs just $13 for adults. Call (509) 453-8731 for more information, or (509) 672-3100 for the snow report. This is where Olympic champion skiers Phil and Steve Mahre can sometimes be found skiing.

Practicalities

Near the ski area, **White Pass Village Inn,** tel. (509) 672-3131, has condos of various sizes for rent ($48-98 in the summer, $85-140 in the winter), including a winter-only heated outdoor pool, and showers for Pacific Crest Trail hikers. Nearby, find a store, gas station, and the **Summit House Restaurant,** tel. (509) 672-3111.

Eight miles east of White Pass Ski Area on Hwy. 12, **Indian Creek Corral** offers one-hour to three-day horseback rides in the summer. Hikers can take advantage of their drop-camp service; for a fee they'll drop up to 75 pounds of gear at a selected site and pick it up whenever you like. Call (509) 925-2062 for more info.

The **Parnassus Chamber Music Festival** brings Bach and Beethoven to White Pass in late June, with concerts at White Pass Day Lodge. Call (509) 453-8731 for ticket information.

The **area code** for White Pass and points east from here is 509.

Rimrock Lake Area

Traveling along Hwy. 12, you can't miss **Rimrock Lake,** just a few miles east of White Pass. This massive blue-green lake was created in 1927 by what was then one of the largest earthfilled dams in the country. Today Rimrock is popular with anglers in search of good-sized silvers mid-May to late June, and with boaters, swimmers, and campers.

On the lake, **Twelve West,** tel. (509) 672-2460, has RV hookups, a marina, and a fine restaurant serving three meals daily. Open yearround. **The Cove Resort,** tel. (509) 672-2470, two miles to the east, also has an RV park, marina, and a restaurant on Rimrock Lake.

Silver Beach Resort, 40350 Hwy. 12, tel. (509) 672-2500, has rustic cabins with kitchenettes for $60 (sleeps four), RV hookups, and a boat dock. **Silver Beach Motel,** 40380 Hwy. 12, tel. (509) 672-2499, has modern motel units for $35 s, $42 d, while **Trout Lodge,** 27090 Hwy. 12 , tel. (509) 672-2211, has a four-unit motel ($28 s, $40 d), store, and restaurant. **Game Ridge Motel & Lodge,** tel. (509) 672-2212, has additional motel rooms with kitchenettes for $37-52 s, $47-62 d, and a small cabin with private hot tub for $85 s or d. The motel is right along the Tieton River, with a striking mountain backdrop. An outdoor pool and jacuzzi are also on the premises.

Tieton River Rafting

The Tieton River is one of the more challenging rivers in Washington, dropping 50 feet per mile from Rimrock Dam to the confluence of the Tieton and Naches River, 20 miles downriver. The river is rated class III (intermediate), and the terrain begins high in the mountains and descends through basalt canyons into the dry valley on the east side of the Cascades. It is best late in the season; most rafting companies run it in September, though you'll find folks out there August through October. Trip lengths vary between the companies. Expect to pay $55-75 for a half-day excursion, depending upon the number in your group and the company. Contact one of the following for more info: **All Rivers Adventures,** tel. (800) 743-5628; **Alpine Adventures,** (800) 926-7238; **Alpine Whitewater,** tel. (800) 926-7238; **Blue Sky Outfitters,** tel. (800) 228-7238; **Downstream River Runners,** tel. (800) 234-4644; **North Cascades River Expeditions,** tel. (800) 634-8433; **Northern Wilderness River Riders, Inc.,** tel. (800) 448-7238; **Olympic Outdoor Adventures,** tel. (800) 659-6095; **Orion Expeditions,** tel. (800) 553-7466; **River Recreation,** tel. (800) 464-5899; **Rivers Incorporated,** tel. (206) 822-5296; **Wild & Scenic River Tours,** tel. (206) 323-1220; and **Wildwater River Tours,** tel. (800) 522-9453.

Elk and Bighorn Sheep

During most winters, the large White Pass elk population and a small herd of bighorn sheep are fed at the **Oak Creek Wildlife Recreation Area,** two miles west of the intersection of Highways 410 and 12, and 17 miles west of Yakima. Best times to see them are early morning or late afternoon when the animals are most active.

CRYSTAL MOUNTAIN AND GREENWATER

Crystal Mountain Ski Area

This year-round resort on Hwy. 410, just outside the north Mount Rainier National Park boundary, has winter Nordic and alpine skiing, plus hiking, fishing, swimming, tennis, horseback riding, and chairlift sightseeing rides from July to early September. Many folks consider this Washington's finest skiing and snowboarding, with a wide diversity of runs and state-of-the-art snow grooming. It is also unique in being run as a not-for-profit operation. The ski resort boasts 3,100 vertical feet, 10 lifts (including a high-speed quad chair) serving 2,300 acres, plus 34 expert backcountry trails and night skiing. With a top elevation of 7,002 feet—highest in the state—you'll have a fantastic view of nearby Mt. Rainier on clear days.

Adult lift rates are $32 on weekends, and $16-20 on weekdays. Other services at Crystal Mountain include rentals, ski and snowboard schools, day care, and lots of food and lodging options. A $3 charge provides access to a hot tub, fitness room, sauna, and showers. For more info on the resort, contact Crystal Mountain at (360) 663-2265 or (800) 852-1444. Get snow conditions by calling (206) 634-3771 in Seattle, or (206) 922-1832 in Tacoma.

Crystal Mountain is 76 miles from Seattle. The **Crystal Mountain Express,** tel. (206) 626-5208, provides bus service to the ski area from Seattle, Bellevue, Renton, Auburn, and Enumclaw for $22 roundtrip. The buses run Fri.-Mon. during the ski season.

During the summer months, visitors ride the chairlift to the Summit Restaurant (see below) for $7, but check local tourist papers for discounts.

Hiking Trails

Several popular hiking trails lead from the Crystal Mountain area to the **Pacific Crest Trail** in the nearby Norse Peak Wilderness Area. Another favorite is the **Crystal Mountain Trail** (No. 1163), a 12-mile loop hike (or mountain bike ride) that follows the ridge along Crystal Mountain. The lazy way to do this is to ride the chairlift to Summit House and hike down. During the summer months, **Crystal Mountain Corral,** tel. (360) 663-2589, has group trail rides, overnight barbecues, fishing, hunting, and photography trips.

River Running

White River Outpost, located inside Wapiti Woolies, 58414 Hwy. 410 E, tel. (360) 663-2268, has whitewater rafting trips down the White River and rents inflatable kayaks.

Practicalities

See "Accommodations near Mount Rainier" for a listing of lodging options in the Crystal Mountain area. RV hookups are available year-round at the resort.

Food of all types is available at on-the-mountain and base eateries. The **Summit House,** tel.

(360) 663-2300, accessible only by chairlift, is the highest restaurant in the state and offers a phenomenal view of Mt. Rainier; watch for climbers approaching the summit. Open for lunch and dinner, the Summit House is a favorite place to watch the sunset over Mt. Rainier. Reservations are strongly recommended on weekends.

In Greenwater, the **Naches Tavern,** tel. (360) 663-2267, is a cozy country place with a friendly atmosphere and good food served in large quantities.

The **area code** for the Crystal Mountain and Greenwater vicinity is 360.

ASHFORD

Ashford is your last chance for food, lodging, and gas before you enter the Mount Rainier National Park. Rather than being a "last resort," some of the hotels, cabins, and restaurants here are as good or better than park facilities. Established in 1891, Ashford began as an end-of-the-line town where tourists stepped off the Tacoma Eastern Railroad cars to enter the park.

For incredible views of Mt. Rainier, head north from Ashford on Copper Creek Rd. (Forest Rd. 59). The road also provides access to the Glacier View Wilderness (see "Wilderness Areas," above). Unfortunately, there's also a lot of deforested land around here, including an enormous gouge cut from the hills just south of Ashford and right next to the national park.

Accommodations

Lodging abounds in Ashford, see the "Accommodations near Mount Rainier" chart for a complete list. At the budget end, **Whittaker's Bunkhouse** is a well-maintained facility popular with the climbing and hiking crowd. Built in 1912 as a logger's bunkhouse, it was renovated in 1990, but the floors are still pockmarked by the corked boots from loggers who once stayed here. Another unique place is **Wellspring,** which offers log cabin lodging, including two rooms that have their own wood-fired saunas.

Alexander's Country Inn occupies the top end of the lodging spectrum. Constructed in 1912 (with more recent additions), the inn was visited by presidents Theodore Roosevelt and William Howard Taft early in this century, was closed for many years, and has been lovingly restored to its original beauty.

Campgrounds

The closest public campsites ($6; open year-round) are just inside the southwest entrance to Mount Rainier National Park at **Sunshine Point Campground.**

Park RVs at **Mounthaven at Cedar Park,** 38210 Hwy. 706 E, tel. (360) 569-2594; **Ashford Valley Store,** tel. (360) 569-2560; **Gateway Inn,** 38820 Hwy. 706, tel. (360) 569-2506. **Highlander Tavern and Laundry,** tel. 569-2953, offers an unusual mix: suds on tap, suds in the laundromat, and coin-operated showers to soap up with more suds after a backcountry trip.

Food

The finest food (priced accordingly) in the Mt. Rainier area is served at **Alexander's Country Inn,** tel. (360) 569-2300, where specialties include salmon, fresh trout (catch your own from the backyard pond), home-baked bread, and famous wild blackberry pie. They also offer a large wine list.

Rainier Overland Lodge, 31811 Hwy. 706, tel. (360) 569-0851, serves big family style breakfasts, tasty fish and chips, and a choice of all-American faves. Reasonably priced too.

Get espresso coffees and sweets at **Whittaker's Bunkhouse,** 30205 Hwy. 706 E, tel. (360) 569-2439.

For pizza, sandwiches, nachos, and over 60 beers and wines, head to **Wild Berry Restaurant,** 37720 Hwy. 706 E, tel. (360) 569-2628. It is open every day and has an imaginative menu of chicken crepes, pizzas, and, of course, blackberry pie.

Information and Services

Several local places offer gifts and crafts for sale in the Ashford area. After a weekend of hiking in the park, head to **Wellspring,** two miles east of town, tel. (360) 569-2514, for a relaxing massage and jacuzzi.

Llama Wilderness Pack Trips runs day trips ($35 for four hours) and longer hikes during the summer, operating out of the Wild Berry Restaurant. Call (360) 491-5262 for details.

The telephone **area code** for Ashford and the Mt. Rainier region is 360.

ELBE

Fourteen miles from Mount Rainier National Park, Elbe is a wide spot in the road and a pleasant place to enjoy the foothill sights with a dose of railroad memorabilia. Visitors can eat dinner aboard the Cascadian Dinner Train, spend a night in a caboose at Hobo Inn, or peek inside Elbe's **Evangelische Lutherische Kirche,** a tiny white clapboard church measuring just 18 by 24 feet.

Mount Rainier Scenic Railroad

One way to view the area west of Mt. Rainier, with an occasional glimpse of it through the timber, is from the Mt. Rainier Scenic Railroad, tel. (360) 569-2588. The vintage steam train leaves Elbe Station for a 14-mile, 90-minute ride over bridges and through forests, with live music accompanying the impressive views. The train runs weekends Memorial Day through September, and daily from June 15 through Labor Day. Fares are $8.50 for adults, $7.50 for seniors, $6.50 for ages 12-17, and $5.50 for kids under 12.

A more luxurious option is the **Cascadian Dinner Train** that leaves the Elbe station and cruises over 40 miles of country. The prime rib dinner is served to you by waiters in tuxedos, and you can enjoy the view from the observation car. Dinner trains run April-Nov. on either Saturday or Sunday; call (360) 569-2588 for reservations and more information. Fare is $55 per person for this four-hour journey into the past.

Mount Tahoma Trails

Halfway between Elbe and Ashford is Mt. Tahoma Trails, featuring 88 miles of groomed cross-country skiing in the winter, and mountain biking, horseback riding, and hiking on the trails in the summer. A series of huts, shelters, and a yurt provide overnight accommodations for six people (up to 12 in some of these), making it possible to ski or hike from hut to hut. No charge to stay in the huts, but a $25 damage deposit is required in advance, and you'll need a Sno-Park permit ($10 for three days) to park your vehicle. Call (360) 569-2451 for details and a map of the trails.

Accommodations and Campgrounds

Stay at the quiet **Eagles Nest Motel,** 52120 Hwy. 7 East (two miles west of Elbe near Alder Lake), tel. (360) 569-2533, where rooms are $43 s or d. Kitchenettes are available, along with RV hookups. For something more unique, stay right in town at **Hobo Inn,** tel. (360) 569-2500, Elbe's train going nowhere. Stay in one of the eight cabooses—some date back to 1916—that have been completely reconditioned, with beds and bathrooms added, for $70-85; one even features a jacuzzi. Make reservations a month ahead in the summer to be assured of your own caboose.

The local Lions Club manages campsites at **Mineral Lake,** three miles south of Elbe. The lake is famous for its exceptional trout fishing, including rainbows and German brown trout (some to 10 pounds). Cabins and RV spaces are available at **Mineral Lake Resort,** tel. (360) 492-5367.

Food

In addition to caboose lodging, **Hobo Inn,** tel. (360) 569-2500, has a restaurant and lounge where you can enjoy dinner in dining cars from a bygone era. Be sure to try the enormous and tasty scaleburgers and fries. See above for another train-dining option, the Cascadian Dinner Train.

EATONVILLE

Rural Eatonville (pop. 1,400) is located in farming and logging country in the foothills west of Mt. Rainier and boasts of its many horses—Pierce County is said to have more horses per capita than anywhere else in America. Mount Rainier is just 25 miles away. In recent years, Eatonville has gained a number of artists and craftspeople, and several small galleries dot downtown.

Northwest Trek Wildlife Park

One of the region's biggest attractions is Northwest Trek Wildlife Park. Located on Hwy. 161 near Eatonville, this 600-acre wildlife park is a refuge for grizzly and black bears, bighorn sheep, great blue herons, wild turkeys, elk, moose, and even a herd of bison. A tram transports visitors on a six-mile, hour-long tour of the park; also available are five miles of nature trails. Join in a park-sponsored weekend festival, salmon bake, or photo tour. The park opens daily Feb.-Oct. at 9:30 a.m. (closing times vary); open weekends only the rest of the year. The trams leave hourly beginning at 10 a.m. Admission costs $8 adults, $7 seniors, $5.50 five to 17 years, $3.50 three to four years, free for ages two and under. For details, call (360) 832-6116 or (800) 433-8735.

Pioneer Farm Museum and Ohop Indian Village

Three miles north of Eatonville, between Highways 7 and 161, is the Pioneer Farm Museum and Ohop Indian Village. Here you can experience what pioneer life was really like as you grind grain, churn butter, and milk a cow. Ninety-minute guided tours are available daily 11 a.m.-4 p.m. in the summer, with reduced hours in the spring and fall. Closed Thanksgiving through February. Admission is $5 for adults, $4 for seniors and kids. The farm is also home to a replica Indian village where you can learn about traditional hunting and fishing, tool making, and native foods. Hour-long tours of the Indian village are available only on summer weekends at 1 and 2:30 p.m. and cost an additional $5 for adults and $4 for kids (a buck off if you take both tours). A trading post sells old-fashioned candy, trinkets, books, and rabbit skins. Call (360) 832-6300 for details on the farm and Indian village.

Pack Experimental Forest

Pack Experimental Forest is on University of Washington land just west of Eatonville. The roads across Pack Forest are open weekdays only, but hiking trails are open daily. Call (360) 832-6534 for more information. Short hiking trails crisscross the forest, taking you through stands of trees of varying ages, including a 42-acre preserve of old-growth Douglas fir, cedar, and hemlock—one of the few unlogged patches of trees remaining in this part of Washington. (Clearcuts on private land line the roads throughout the Cascade foothills; only small bits of the public land have been saved from this onslaught. It doesn't take much to see that the whole spotted owl controversy comes down to arguing over the few parcels of old-growth forest that have somehow escaped.)

Accommodations and Campgrounds

Stay at the spacious and modern **Mill Village Motel,** 210 Center St., tel. (360) 832-3200, for $53-59 s or d. Kitchenettes and RV parking are also available here.

Camp at **Alder Lake Park,** seven miles south of Eatonville, tel. (360) 569-2928, where both tent sites ($10) and RV spaces ($14) are available, along with coin-operated showers. The seven-mile-long lake was created by a dam that produces hydroelectric power for Tacoma City Light. Reservations are advised for summer weekends; call (360) 569-2778 for the applications. The lake also has a very popular sandy beach for sunbathing and swimming.

Nearby private RV parks include: **Clear Lake Resort,** 35805 Meridian E, tel. (360) 832-4477; **La Grande RV Park,** 46719 Hwy. 7 E, tel. (360) 832-6643; **Mill Village RV Park,** 220 Center St. E, tel. (360) 832-4279; and **Silver Lake Resort,** 40718 Silver Lake Rd. E, tel. (360) 832-3580.

Food

Eat very good Mexican food at **Puerto Vallerta,** tel. (360) 832-4033. The **Eatonville Farmers Market** is held at the corner of Washington and Center Streets from May through the first week of October on Saturday 10 a.m.-4 p.m., and features fresh produce, flowers, and local crafts.

Events

Local events of note include the **Fourth of July** with all the fun of a small-town festival, and **Eatonville Arts Festival** held the first weekend of August. For something out of the ordinary, head to Eatonville for **Robin Hood Days,** with its English village fair and medieval tournament camp, held on Father's Day weekend in mid-June.

Information

The **Eatonville Visitor Information Center,** 220 Center St., tel. (360) 832-4000, is open daily year-round. Eatonville's **area code** is 360.

PACKWOOD

There isn't a lot to Packwood, just a stretch of businesses scattered along the highway, but be sure to stop at the old library, set in a grove of Douglas fir trees—some of the few big ones remaining in these parts. The town runs on the Packwood Lumber Co. mill west of town, and you're likely to meet loaded logging trucks rolling in from all directions. It also gets by with a dose of Mt. Rainier tourism for good measure; Packwood motels offer fairly reasonable accommodations near the southern edge of the national park.

The small and virtually unknown **Packwood State Park** lies just northwest of town along Skate Creek. This park has tall trees and decent fishing, but no facilities. Access is via Forest Rd. 52 across the Cowlitz River.

Accommodations and Campgrounds

See "Accommodations near Mount Rainier" for a list of lodging places in Packwood. Built in 1911, the **Packwood Hotel** includes the Roosevelt Suite, where President Theodore Roosevelt once slept. The closest Forest Service camping can be found at **La Wis Wis Campground,** seven miles northeast of town on Hwy. 12, where campsites are $8-10. Also fairly close is the free **Summit Creek Campground,** 12 miles north of town, and just east of the Hwy. 12 and Hwy. 123 junction on Forest Rd. 2160. No trailers here. Park RVs at **Packwood RV Park,** tel. (360) 494-5145.

Food

Eat at **Club Cafe,** where the food can be inconsistent, but when it's good, it's stellar. **Peters Inn** has good breakfasts, seafood in season, steaks and prime rib, and homemade pies; or try **Chateau Inn,** five miles east of Packwood, for a night out. **Packwood Pizza Parlor** bakes tasty pizzas.

Other Practicalities

Little Cayuse Ranch, 121 Baker Rd., tel. (360) 494-7126, has guided hour-long horseback rides for $15 during the summer.

Get information on nearby Gifford Pinchot National Forest at **Packwood Ranger Station,** open Mon.-Sat. 7:45-11:45 a.m. and 12:30-4:30 p.m. in the summer, and Mon.-Fri. winters. Call (360) 494-5515 for information. Packwood's telephone **area code** is 360.

RANDLE

Randle is another in a string of logging towns along Hwy. 12, with scalped nearby hills as a reminder of what makes the economy tick. The town acts as a northern access point to the east side of Mount St. Helens National Volcanic Monument, with Forest Rd. 25 cutting south to the Spirit Lake/Windy Ridge area. It's also an entry point for travelers continuing north to Mount Rainier National Park.

Accommodations and Campgrounds

See the chart "Accommodations near Mount Rainier" for a list of Randle's lodging places. Public campsites can be found south of town on the Gifford Pinchot National Forest, along the east side of Mt. St. Helens. Nearest is **Iron Creek Campground,** 12 miles south on Forest Rd. 25, which has sites mid-May to late October for $9. Make reservations ($7.50 extra) by calling (800) 280-2267. Campfire programs are given at Iron Creek Saturday evenings in the summer. **Tower Rock Campground,** six miles east of Iron Creek on Rd. 76, is open mid-May to late September and offers sites for $9. Randle's private RV parks are: **Maple Grove RV Park,** tel. (360) 497-7680; **Shady Firs Campground,** 107 Young Rd., tel. (360) 497-6108; and **Tower Rock U-Fish RV Park,** 137 Cispus Rd., tel. (360) 497-7680.

Other Practicalities

Big Bottom Bar & Grill, tel. 497-9982, is a fun place for lunch or dinner with great service and dependably good all-American steaks and burgers. Open till 2 a.m. most nights.

The **Randle Ranger Station,** three miles east of town, tel. (360) 497-1100, is open daily 8 a.m.-4:30 p.m. from late May through September, and Mon.-Fri. 8 a.m.-4:30 p.m. the rest of the year. The office has detailed information on local hiking and mountain biking trails.

MORTON

Morton (pop. 1,100) is a redneck timber town in the Cascade foothills. It grew up as a center for the production of railroad ties and other wood products. the **Old Settlers Museum** has local exibits; stop by city hall for access to the museum. Not much else of note here, but you may want to stop at **Mains Gift Shop,** four miles west of Morton on Hwy. 12 at the foot of the Hopkins Hill viewpoint, for Mt. St. Helens glass ornaments, plus the usual T-shirts and other trinkets. Three miles west of Morton on Short Rd. is a fine binocular-view of the crater opening and lava dome.

Practicalities

See the "Morton Accommodations" chart for a complete listing of local lodging options. For something quite out of the ordinary, the historic **St. Helens Manor House B&B,** tel. (360) 498-5243 or (800) 551-3290, is said to be haunted by two female ghosts that slam doors, appear in hallways, and toy with the security system. The home and its ghostly apparitions were even featured on the *Evening Magazine* television show. Camp or park RVs at **Backstrom Park** on the Tilton River, tel. (360) 496-3361.

MORTON ACCOMMODATIONS

Accommodations are arranged from least to most expensive. Rates may be lower during the winter months. The area code is 360.

Evergreen Motel; Main and Front; tel. 496-5407; $25 s, $35 d; kitchenettes

Stiltner Motel; just north of town on Hwy. 7; $30 s, $35 d; kitchenettes

Roy's Motel & RV Park; 161 N. 2nd St.; tel. 496-5000; $35 s, $42 d

The Seasons Motel; 200 Westlake; tel. 496-6835; $50 s or d; continental breakfast; AAA approved

Resort of the Mountains; 1130 Morton Rd. (five miles north of Morton); tel. 496-5885; $55 s, $70 d; condo-style apartments, fireplaces, full kitchens

St. Helens Manor House B&B; six miles east of Morton on Hwy. 12; tel. 498-5243 or (800) 551-3290, $59-69 s or d; beautiful 1910 three-story home along Riffe Lake, four guest rooms (two with private baths), full gourmet breakfast, no kids under 12, AAA approved

The **Wheel Cafe,** tel. (360) 496-3240, has steaks, seafood, a salad bar, and chicken and sandwiches to go, plus a lounge. It is almost always open (7 a.m.-2 a.m.). Also in Morton, the **Roadhouse Inn,** tel. (360) 496-5029, is strictly sit-down, serving steak and seafood dinners plus breakfast and lunch.

The **Morton Loggers Jubilee,** held the second weekend in August, is one of the largest timber carnivals in Washington. In addition to the standard axe throwing, log rolling, and other contests, you'll discover a riding lawnmower race, parades, barbeques, and dancing, along with an arts and crafts fair. For additional local information, contact the **Morton Chamber of Commerce,** tel. (360) 496-6086.

MOSSYROCK AND VICINITY

Mossyrock (pop. 450) occupies farming country along the Cowlitz River northwest of Mt. St. Helens and east of Chehalis. The primary crops raised here are tulips, blueberries, and Christmas trees. Two dams have created nearby Riffe and Mayfield Lakes, ironically named for the towns they inundated.

Sights
A pullout four miles east of Mossyrock leads to a viewpoint offering a glimpse—on clear days—of Mt. St. Helens, 24 miles to the south. The **Cowlitz Salmon Hatchery** is on the Cowlitz River just below the Mayfield Lake dam, providing a good chance to watch salmon returning up a fish ladder in the spring and fall. Get there by following the signs from the Hwy. 12 turnoff, nine miles west of Mossyrock.

Mayfield Lake County Park, off Hwy. 12 just west of Mossyrock, has a campground (open May-Sept. only), swimming beach, boat launch, small picnic area, and playground. Follow Hwy. 12 east to Mossyrock and the **Mayfield Dam;** there's a nice roadside viewpoint about three miles east of Mossyrock.

Marys Corner to Toledo
Twenty miles west of Mossyrock on Hwy. 12, and just three miles east from I-5 is the crossroads called Marys Corner. Just south of the intersection on Jackson Hwy. is the **John R.**

Jackson House, a log cabin built in 1845 that was a popular stopping place for Oregon Trail travelers. Jackson was one of the first American settlers north of the Columbia River, and this building served as the first U.S. District Court in what would become the state of Washington. Just north of Marys Center on Jackson Rd. is a monument to John Jackson's wife, Matilda. (Technically, this five-acre plot of land is **Matilda N. Jackson State Park.**)

Two miles south of Marys Corner, the road passes **Lewis and Clark State Park.** This wonderful 528-acre parcel represents one of the few remaining stands of old-growth forest in this part of Washington. Several short trails provide loop hikes through the tall Douglas fir, western hemlock, grand fir, and western red cedar trees. The west side of Lewis and Clark State Park emphasizes horseback use. Camp beneath the forest for $10 (no hookups) April-September. Call (800) 452-5687 for campsite reservations ($6 extra fee), available up to 11 months ahead of time.

Four miles beyond the park is **St. Francis Xavier Mission,** founded in 1838 by French Catholic missionaries from the Winnipeg area. The first priest here, Father Francis Blanchet, was so intent upon converting the Indians that he devised a system of lines, dots, and other designs to explain the intricacies of Catholicism. The end result was a six-foot-long parchment called the "Catholic Ladder," a replica of which stands outside the church. The red brick church was built in 1932; the first three versions of this church were destroyed by fire.

Accommodations
Lake Mayfield Motel, 350A Hadaller Rd. in Mossyrock, tel. (360) 985-2484, has motel room for $35 s or d, and cabins with kitchens for $50-60 d. **Botzer House B&B,** 323 Court St. in Mossyrock, tel. (360) 983-3792, has a basement apartment with a private entrance for $45-55 s or d, including a full breakfast.

Over in Salkum (eight miles west of Mossyrock), **Shepherds Inn B&B,** 168 Autumn Heights Dr., tel. (360) 985-2434, is a country home with five guest rooms (shared or private baths) for $55-65 s, $60-70 d, including a jacuzzi and full breakfast. Cozy and clean rooms are also available at Salkum's **White Spot Motel,** tel. (360) 985-2737, for just $28 s or d.

Campgrounds

To reach **Mossyrock Park,** turn south at the Mossyrock flashing light and follow the signs three miles east. Here you'll find hundreds of campsites, picnic tables, and boat launches on the green-blue Riffe Lake. The 24-mile-long lake was dam-created in 1968; it was named Riffe Lake to honor the settlers of Riffe, founded in 1898 and now covered by about 225 feet of water.

If you turn north at the Mossyrock light you'll eventually get to **Ike Kinswa State Park,** about three miles off the highway. This 454-acre park is open year-round for trout fishing on Mayfield Lake, with swimming, picnicking, and lakeside campsites ($11) and RV sites ($16). In the winter, look for bald eagles on the trees along the shore. Call (360) 983-3402 for more info, or (800) 452-5687 for campsite reservations ($6 extra fee), available up to 11 months ahead of time.

Private RV parks in the area include **Harmony RV Park,** 563 Harmony Rd., Silver Creek, tel. (360) 983-3804; **Lake Mayfield Resort,** 350-A Hadlaller Rd., Silver Creek, tel. (360) 985-2357; **Barrier Dam Campground and RV Park,** 273 Fuller Rd., Salkum, tel. (360) 985-2495; and **Mountain Road RV Park,** 262 Mossyrock Rd. W, tel. (360) 983-3094.

MOUNT ST. HELENS NATIONAL VOLCANIC MONUMENT

The 1980 explosion of Mt. St. Helens transformed a quiet and beautiful landscape into a moonscape of devastation. Today plants and animals are returning to the land as it recovers, but the immensity of the eruption continues to overwhelm and astound visitors. Mount St. Helens has become one of Washington's must-see sights, and a fine set of visitor facilities, access roads, and trails now offer ample opportunities to learn about the power of this active volcano.

THE SLEEPING DRAGON AWAKES

Prior to May 18, 1980, Mt. St. Helens had the most perfectly shaped cone in the Pacific Northwest volcanic chain. The mountain was named by Capt. George Vancouver in 1792 for Baron St. Helens, the British Ambassador to Spain. Often called "the ice-cream cone in the sky," and compared constantly with Japan's Mt. Fujiyama, 9,677-foot Mt. St. Helens was viewed as a sleeping beauty, popular with hikers, climbers, and other outdoor adventurers. It was silent for as long as any of them could remember—the volcano had been dormant for 123 years.

The Eruption

On March 20, 1980, Mt. St. Helens began to rumble. By March 30, steam was rising from two brand-new craters, which had merged by April 4 into one huge crater measuring 1,700 feet across. Seven weeks of minor earthquakes followed.

At 8:32 a.m. on May 18, 1980, Mt. St. Helens blew her top in an eruption that had the explosive power of several atomic bombs. The eruption was triggered by an earthquake measuring 5.1 on the Richter scale that sent a massive avalanche of rock, snow, and ice down the mountain's north slope at 200 mph, filling Spirit Lake—whose surface was instantly raised by 200 feet—and cresting over a 1,200-foot ridge. A second debris avalanche blasted down the North Fork of the Toutle River, and additional flows sent muddy water, rocks, and logs down the river, destroying bridges and homes along the way.

The landslide allowed pressure inside the volcano to escape explosively in an eruption that blew 1,312 feet (8.8 *billion* cubic yards) off the volcano's summit. A lateral blast shot northeast at 670 miles an hour, searing surrounding forests and flattening them up to 15 miles away. Temperatures 15 miles away reached an incredible 572° F, and the blast was followed by a plume of ash that rose 16 miles into the atmosphere. This explosion, along with the intense heat, landslides, and falling trees, killed 57 people within the blast zone, and destroyed more than 220 homes and 17 miles of railroad. The wildlife death toll was upward of 5,000 black-tailed deer, 1,500 Roosevelt elk, 200 black bear, and millions of birds and fish; the economic loss included 4.5 billion board feet of usable timber on 96,000 acres.

The damage wasn't limited to the area of the blast itself; 60,000 acres not destroyed by the blast were covered with more than eight inches of ash. Six hours after the eruption, river water at Castle Rock, 40 miles downstream, was over 100° F, and towns in eastern Washington—150 miles away—were coated with up to three inches of ash, clogging carburetors and shrouding the towns in thick darkness at noon. Traces of ash were detected as far away as mid-Montana, Vancouver, B.C., and Denver.

After the Explosion

In the next six years, Mt. St. Helens experienced 21 additional eruptions, mostly dome-building eruptions and irregular spurts of activity. The steaming lava dome inside the crater grew 1,000 feet but has been fairly quiet of late, with occasional bursts of steam as water comes into con-

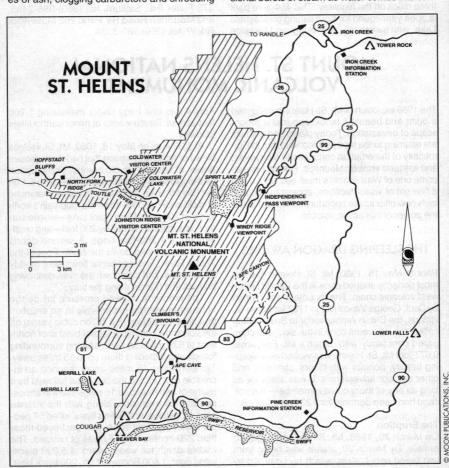

MOUNT ST. HELENS

tact with the superheated rock. Because of this, the crater itself remains off limits, and even scientists don't venture in for long, fearful that boulders may start flying in their direction.

In 1982, the 110,000-acre **Mount St. Helens National Volcanic Monument** was created, and the area has been gradually opened to visitors as roads, bridges, visitors centers, and trails are built. The government still keeps parts of it off-limits to serve as a natural laboratory for scientists. They have learned one basic fact so far: nature heals itself more quickly than anyone expected. Plant and animal life is returning quite rapidly considering the extent of the destruction.

The Forest Service has imposed stringent regulations on activity within the National Monument, both to protect visitors from potential hazards and to protect the area as a natural laboratory of ecological change. These rules include that visitors stay away from certain areas and not venture off trails; they are stringently enforced. A minimum $100 fine awaits those who travel off-trail. See the various visitor centers for specific rules.

VISITING MOUNT ST. HELENS

Until 1987, the area immediately surrounding Mt. St. Helens' crater was closed to the public because of sporadic volcanic activity, logging, and construction, but now the "forbidden zone" is open, and the newly completed Spirit Lake Memorial Highway provides access to the heart of the national monument. Roads approach the volcano from both the east and west sides, offering dramatic views into its center, while more adventurous visitors can climb to the summit from the south side. Be sure to fill your gas tank before you start your final approach to the visitor center or any of the Mt. St. Helens access roads; gas stations are few and far between, especially on the east side. Specific access routes are described below from the east, south, and west. From the north side you are limited to distant views from a roadside pullout near Mossyrock Dam.

Campgrounds

Specific campgrounds are described below for each side of Mt. St. Helens. Dispersed camping is allowed only outside the restricted areas around the volcano. No camping is permitted within the upper North Fork of the Toutle River drainage, around Coldwater Lake and Spirit Lake, or around the volcano itself; check with the Forest Service for specifics.

Information

Call (360) 274-4038 for recorded road and other visitor information. For more general area information, visit the small travel information building just west of I-5 at exit 49 in Castle Rock, or stop at any of the visitor centers on the Spirit Lake Highway. Closest to I-5 is **Spirit Lake Visitor Center,** just five miles east of the interstate on Hwy. 504. The **ranger stations** can also help; they're located in Packwood, tel. (360) 494-5515, Randle, tel. (360) 497-1100; and Wind River, tel. (360) 427-5645.

The **Mount St. Helens Volcanic Headquarters,** tel. (360) 750-3900, is three miles north of Amboy on Hwy. 503. Call them for brochures and the latest on conditions at Mt. St. Helens, including the status of volcanic activity and any trail closures.

All Mt. St. Helens and southwest Washington phone numbers are in the 360 **area code.**

Seminars

If you're clever enough to plan ahead, you can get in on one of the field seminars at Mt. St. Helens offered by the **Pacific Northwest National Parks and Forests Association.** Scheduled in late summer, these three-day weekend seminars include such topics as Mt. St. Helens photography, geology, and elk recolonization. For a descriptive brochure, call Pacific Northwest Field Seminars, tel. (360) 274-2100.

Bus and Van Tours

Mount St. Helens Adventure Tours, tel. (360) 274-6542, has four-hour van tours from Castle Rock to the various sights along the Spirit Lake Memorial Highway. The company is run by the owners of Spirit Lake Lodge, which was destroyed in the eruption, and offers a personalized version of the events of 1980 that goes beyond the canned bus tours.

Scenic Bound Tours, tel. (360) 433-6907, offers summertime day trips from Seattle that combine Mt. Rainier and Mt. St. Helens for $55. These trips always include at least one hike.

Gray Line of Seattle offers a few summertime day trips to Mt. St. Helens for $45 per person. Call (206) 626-5208 in Seattle or (800) 426-7532 for info and reservations.

Scenic Flights

Several aviation companies offer scenic flights over Mt. St. Helens, affording passengers a view of the crater and lava dome that you just can't get otherwise. Departing from just across the Oregon border at Portland International Airport, **Aero West Aviation**, tel. (503) 661-4940, has hour-and-a-half fixed-wing flights at $150 for up to three people.

Thirty-minute helicopter overflights of the volcano are provided by **Bluebird Helicopters** from Cougar year-round, tel. (360) 238-5326, or from Touttle during the summer, tel. (360) 274-6789. These cost $69 per person. From Hoffstadt Bluffs along the Spirit Lake Memorial Hwy., **Hillsboro Helicopters**, tel. (360) 274-7750, has 25-minute summertime flights for $69 per person.

WEST SIDE ACCESS

The west side of Mt. St. Helens offers the quickest access and has some of the finest views and the most developed facilities for the average visitor to the volcano. More than 700,000 visitors take this route each year. With not just one, but four elaborate visitor centers, and a wide new paved road reaching the center of the monument, this is the place most folks view the volcano. The main access route to the west side is Hwy. 504, the **Spirit Lake Memorial Highway.** Starting from the town of Castle Rock (exit 49 from I-5; see under "Longview and Kelso Vicinity" for more on this town), Hwy. 504 offers a 52-mile scenic climb right to the heart of the volcanic destruction that resulted from the 1980 eruption. A secondary access is Hwy. 505, which cuts east from I-5 at the tiny town of **Toledo** (exit 60) and joins Hwy. 504 after 16 miles near the town of Toutle (TOOT-ul). The description below follows Spirit Lake Memorial Hwy. from I-5 to its terminus inside the national monument.

Silver Lake

Your first stop will be the impressive **Silver Lake Visitor Center,** tel. (360) 274-2100, just five miles from I-5 on Hwy. 504. The focus here is on the eruption and it's impacts. The centerpiece is a walk-in volcano that reveals the geological forces at work, but the other exhibits are equally well-done, including models comparing the 1980 eruption with other volcanic eruptions (this was puny compared to the eruption that created Crater Lake), descriptions of the buildup to the eruption and images of the volcano in action, descriptions of ongoing research, a working seismograph to see the latest shakers, and newspaper front pages from 1980. The mountain is 30 miles from here, but can be seen—on a clear day—through the spotting scopes outside. An extraordinary 10-minute slide show (using 15 projectors) and a 22-minute movie alternate every half-hour throughout the day. Silver Lake Visitor Center is open daily 9 a.m.-6 p.m. April-Sept., and daily 9 a.m.-5 p.m. the rest of the year. In addition to maps, books, and current trail and road information, the center offers interpretive programs on a daily basis throughout the year.

Seaquest State Park is right next to the visitor center, within a beautiful stand of gigantic old-growth Douglas firs and hemlocks. Camping is available here year-round (see below). Silver Lake is one of the best bass fishing lakes in the state, and a public boat ramp is a mile east of the park.

As you continue east on Hwy. 504 from Silver Lake, the road slips past the ugly collection of trailers and homes called **Toutle** at the juncture of the South and North Fork of the Toutle River, and then up along the North Fork into the mountains. Much of the route is on private timberland, with Weyerhaeuser tree plantations lining both sides of the road. You may want to stop at the Army Corps of Engineers 184-foot-high **sediment retention dam,** built in 1989, to see the muddy water spewing out and to pick up tourist trinkets and T-shirts at a nearby gift shop. A few miles west, signs to the famous **Buried A-Frame,** another place to purchase souvenirs and to check out the corny "Big Foot" statue. The structure was one of the casualties of the mudflows created by the eruption.

Hoffstadt Bluffs and Creek

Continue east through the Weyerhaeuser tree farms to **Hoffstadt Bluffs Visitor Center,** tel. (360) 274-7750, at milepost 27. In 1995, Cowlitz County and private concessionaires opened an

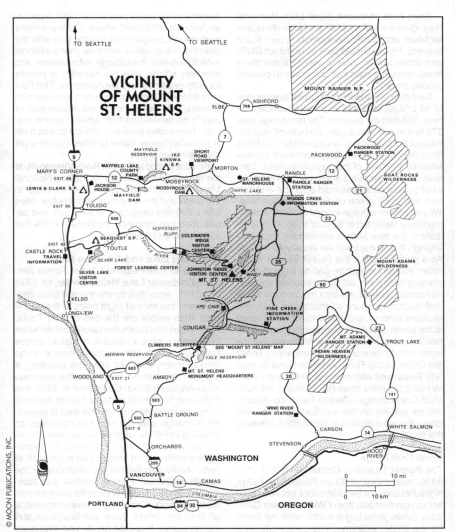

VICINITY OF MOUNT ST. HELENS

TO SEATTLE

TO SEATTLE

MOUNT RAINIER N.P.

ASHFORD

ELBE 706

7

SHORT ROAD VIEWPOINT

MORTON

MAYFIELD RESERVOIR

IKE KINSWA S.P.

MARY'S CORNER

EXIT 68

LEWIS & CLARK S.P.

12

MAYFIELD LAKE COUNTY PARK

JACKSON HOUSE

MOSSYROCK

MOSSYROCK DAM

ST. HELENS MANORHOUSE

RIFFE LAKE

PACKWOOD

PACKWOOD RANGER STATION

RANDLE

RANDLE RANGER STATION

GOAT ROCKS WILDERNESS

EXIT 60

TOLEDO

MAYFIELD DAM

21

WOODS CREEK INFORMATION STATION

505

SEAQUEST S.P.

EXIT 49

CASTLE ROCK TRAVEL INFORMATION

TOUTLE

SILVER LAKE

HOFFSTADT BLUFF

TOUTLE RIVER

COLDWATER RIDGE VISITOR CENTER

23

MOUNT ADAMS WILDERNESS

SILVER LAKE VISITOR CENTER

FOREST LEARNING CENTER

JOHNSTON RIDGE VISITOR CENTER

MT. ST. HELENS

WINDY RIDGE

26

KELSO

APE CAVE

PINE CREEK INFORMATION STATION

90

LONGVIEW

COUGAR

SEE "MOUNT ST. HELENS" MAP

MT. ADAMS RANGER STATION

TROUT LAKE

23

CLIMBERS REGISTER

MERWIN RESERVOIR

YALE RESERVOIR

INDIAN HEAVEN WILDERNESS

141

MT. ST. HELENS MONUMENT HEADQUARTERS

WOODLAND

EXIT 21

503

AMBOY

30

503

BATTLE GROUND

WIND RIVER RANGER STATION

502

EXIT 9

ORCHARDS

CARSON

WHITE SALMON

205

WASHINGTON

STEVENSON

HOOD RIVER

14

VANCOUVER

CAMAS

COLUMBIA RIVER

5

14

PORTLAND

84

30

OREGON

0 10 mi

0 10 km

© MOON PUBLICATIONS, INC.

impressive building housing two gift shops and an attractive restaurant that serves three meals a day (including five-course dinner specials for just $11; make reservations for dinner). Eat inside and enjoy the picture-window panorama, or outside on the patio overlooking the North Toutle Valley and Mt. St. Helens. A picnic area is

also available, along with telescopes to watch the elk below and the mountain above. Despite the name, this really isn't a visitor center, so head elsewhere for information on the volcano. The center is open daily 9 a.m.-9 p.m. year-round. Scenic helicopter flights are also available here during the summer months.

From here eastward, Spirit Lake Memorial Hwy. climbs steadily uphill, with wide shoulders for bikes, and numerous turnouts to take in the scenery. RVers should park at Hoffstadt Bluffs and those towing trailers should leave them there, since the road has some seven percent grades ahead.

Next stop is the **Hoffstadt Creek Bridge,** one of 14 bridges that had to be reconstructed on Hwy. 504 after the eruption. The new bridge rises 370 feet above the canyon, and stands near the edge of the blast zone—an incredible 14.8 miles from the crater. Everything from here on was killed by the heat of the explosion. Also, from here on you can see a sharp contrast between what private companies did after the eruption and what took place on Forest Service land. Weyerhaeuser salvage-logged its lands and immediately replanted millions of trees. With fertilization, the new stands are coming back surprisingly fast; some trees are already 40 feet tall! As a public agency, the Forest Service had a rather different mandate, and no logging or replanting took place within the national volcanic monument. Instead, the area has become a natural laboratory where scientists can study the recovery process, and where visitors can marvel at the power of nature. (Salvage logging and replanting were, however, done on Forest Service lands outside the monument boundaries.) Today the upper Toutle River Valley is home to over 500 **Roosevelt elk,** many of which are visible by hiking two miles down Rd. 3100 near the Hoffstadt Creek Bridge. Despite harsh conditions, the elk survive on the nutritious grasses and clover that were planted in the mudflow following the eruption.

North Fork Ridge

The **Forest Learning Center,** tel. (360) 414-3439, near milepost 33 on North Fork Ridge highlights some of the differences between public management and that of Weyerhaeuser Company (while providing a public relations boost for the timber industry). The center sits on a 2,700-foot high bluff over the North Fork of the Toutle River and is open daily 10 a.m.-6 p.m. from May to mid-October (closed winters); no charge. The emphasis here is on Weyerhaeuser's salvage and recovery efforts after the eruption. Elaborate exhibits take you through a diorama of the forest prior to the 1980 eruption, an "eruption chamber" where a you-are-there multi-media program surrounds you with the power of the eruption, and then past additional exhibits extolling the salvage, reforestation, and recovery efforts, plus the benefits of private forestry practices and conservation. The Forest Learning Center is especially popular with families; kids can climb aboard a helicopter or play in the seven-foot-high rubber volcano outside. Telescopes provide a chance to watch elk in the valley below. Other facilities include a gift shop and picnic area.

Be sure to stop at the **Elk Rock Viewpoint,** at the entrance to the Mount St. Helens National Monument, for magnificent views of the crater to the south and the deep river valley below, filled with a 700-foot-deep layer of rock, ash, and debris. Also look below for the Roosevelt elk that have returned to this valley.

Coldwater Lake and Johnston Ridge

Located 45 miles east of I-5, the Forest Service's **Coldwater Lake Visitor Center,** tel. (360) 274-2131, peers directly into the volcano's gaping crater mouth, just eight miles to the southeast. Also visible are the debris-filled Toutle River Valley and Coldwater Lake—formed when the eruption sent a massive landslide across Coldwater Creek. The emphasis here is on the long recovery process after the eruption, a process that can be seen from the spacious glass-enclosed foyer. Completed in 1993, this high-tech multi-million-dollar facility features computer-animation of how the area is expected to change over the next two centuries, an amusing exhibit in which a ranger mannequin explains the recovery to mannequins representing visitors, and educational exhibits of all sorts. Audio translations are available for the exhibits in Spanish, French, German, and Japanese. A seven-minute multimedia program provides an introduction to the recovery process, a gift shop sells books, maps, and brochures, and the restaurant has light meals and espresso. Coldwater Lake Visitor Center is open daily 9 a.m.-6 p.m. April-Sept., and daily 9 a.m.-5 p.m. the rest of the year. Interpretive walks and talks are given on a daily basis throughout the year; check the bulletin board for today's activities around Coldwater Lake.

One unfortunate side effect of the razzle-dazzle show at Coldwater is that it may give visitors the sense of having visited Mt. St. Helens without having actually experienced the land. You really need to get away from the computer animations and out onto the trails to appreciate the immense power of this volcano. An easy way to begin is the quarter-mile **Winds of Change Interpretive Trail,** just outside the visitor center. For another short hike, head two miles downhill to five-mile-long Coldwater Lake, where the quarter-mile **Birth of a Lake Trail** takes you by boardwalk past the debris avalanche left behind by the eruption. The lake is well-known for excellent rainbow and cutthroat trout fishing, with a minimum size of 16 inches for keepers. Rafts or float tubes are recommended to lessen the damage from bankside anglers, and gasoline-powered motorboats are prohibited. No camping, and be sure to stay on the trails (or risk a $100 fine).

The Spirit Lake Memorial Hwy. ends eight miles uphill from Coldwater Lake at the 4,220-foot level and the **Johnston Ridge Visitor Center** that opened in late 1996. This facility emphasizes the geology of Mt. St. Helens and ongoing scientific research work, and is named for David Johnston, the geologist who was working here in 1980 when the volcano erupted. His last radio transmission, sent out as the mountain gave way, still haunts anyone who hears it: "Vancouver, Vancouver, this is it!" This new visitor facility peers directly into the lava dome formed after the eruption and is open year-round.

West Side Hiking

The five-and-a-half-mile **Lakes Trail** (No. 211) extends from Coldwater Lake to Boundary Trail No. 1, which heads southwest to the Johnston Ridge area, or east to the Norway Pass Trailhead on Forest Rd. 26. For a mostly downhill trek (if you can set up a vehicle shuttle), start near Johnston Ridge and hike to Coldwater Lake. Note that hikers need to stick very closely to the trails. This is a research area, and scientists are attempting to keep human impacts to a minimum.

West Side Campgrounds

There are no developed campsites within Mount St. Helens National Volcanic Monument, but camping is available across from the Silver Lake

Visitor Center at **Seaquest State Park,** with both tent sites ($10) and RV hookup sites ($15) available year-round. Call (800) 452-5687 for campsite reservations ($6 extra fee), available up to 11 months ahead of time. Camping is prohibited along the Spirit Lake Memorial Hwy. inside the monument boundaries.

EAST SIDE ACCESS

Unlike the west side, where a wide, new highway passes four visitor centers that seem to compete with each other to see which one can offer the most wows per minute, visitors to Mt. St. Helens' eastern flanks will discover narrow, winding one-lane routes, simple information stations, and more basic facilities. This is the wild side of the mountain, where the crowds are less and you're allowed to draw your own conclusions without being inundated with flashy multimedia shows and elaborate computer animations. Information and maps are available at the **Woods Creek Information Station,** approximately seven miles south of Randle, and the **Pine Creek Information Station,** on the east end of Swift Reservoir (20 miles east of Cougar).

The east side of Mt. St. Helens is accessed by Forest Rd. 25, which heads south from the town of Randle. This paved, but steep one-lane road (with turnouts) continues all the way to Pine Creek Ranger Station on Swift Creek Reservoir, south of the mountain. It is closed due to snow from late October to Memorial Day weekend and is not recommended for trailers or RVs. For easier driving, drop off your trailer at the Woods Creek Information Station or Iron Creek Picnic Site on Forest Service Rd. 25 if traveling from the north, or at the Pine Creek Information Station if you're coming from the south.

To Windy Ridge

Forest Roads 26 and 99 provide access to the east side of Mt. St. Helens from Forest Rd. 25. The primary destination on the east side is Windy Ridge, where you can see Spirit Lake and a magnificent up-close view of the volcano. Forest Rd. 26 passes several interesting places to stop on the way to Windy Ridge, including a half-mile path at **Quartz Creek Big Trees** where you can see old-growth Douglas firs that escaped the eruption, and—just a mile away—the edge of the zone where trees were flattened in the blast (trees in this area were salvaged after the eruption). From here on, everything was destroyed by the force of the eruption.

At **Ryan Lake** another short trail provides views of the lake filled with downed trees. This area is usually accessible year-round, with open, flat areas for cross-country skiing. **Meta Lake**—at the junction of Forest Roads 26 and 99—has a paved trail and the famous **Miner's Car,** destroyed in the blast. Three people had driven here the night before the volcano gave way on May 18, 1980, and were killed in a nearby cabin by the superheated explosion. Meta Lake is coming back surprisingly fast from the destruction, in part because ice and snow protected fish and other animals from the heat. Nature walks are offered here daily during the summer months. The Norway Pass Trailhead (see "East Side Hiking Trails," below) is just a mile north of Meta Lake; a water pump is also here.

Windy Ridge stands at the end of Rd. 99, 4,000 feet above sea level and 34 miles southwest of Randle. It is just five miles from the crater itself. Climb the 361 steps for an incredible view into the volcano, across the devastated pumice plain, and over the log-choked Spirit Lake. Forest Service interpretive personnel are here daily May-Oct., providing frequent talks about the volcano from the amphitheater.

East Side Campgrounds
Iron Creek Campground is located in a stand of old-growth trees along the Cispus River 12 miles south of Randle on Forest Rd. 25 and is open mid-May to late October. The charge is $9 for this popular campground, and reservations can be made ($7.50 extra) by calling (800) 280-2267. Saturday evening campfire programs are provided at Iron Creek in the summer. **Tower Rock Campground,** six miles east of Iron Creek on Rd. 76, is open mid-May to late September and has sites for $9.

East Side Hiking Trails
The **Woods Creek Watchable Wildlife Trail,** an easy one-and-a-half-mile path through mixed

forests, a meadow, and past several beaver ponds, leaves from the Woods Creek Information Station. Two other easy walks are the quarter-mile **Iron Creek Old-Growth Trail** and the one-and-a-half-mile **Iron Creek Campground Trail,** both of which depart from Iron Creek Campground and offer treks though tall stands of cedar and Douglas fir. Also nearby—at the end of a quarter-mile path—is beautiful 60-foot **Iron Creek Falls.**

For something more strenuous, follow the two-and-a-half-mile **Norway Pass Trail** (No. 1) through blown-down forests to the 4,500-foot pass, gaining 900 feet in elevation along the way. You can continue beyond to the Coldwater Lake area, return the same way you came, or return to Independence Pass along Rd. 99 via **Independence Pass Trail** (No. 227), with extraordinary views over Spirit Lake. The roundtrip distance for this is six miles.

Harmony Trail drops 600 feet in just a mile, offering the only legal access to the shore of Spirit Lake. Most living things were killed when pyroclastic flows filled it in 1980, causing water temperatures to reach almost 100° F. The trailhead is halfway between the Independence Pass trailhead and Windy Ridge.

At Windy Ridge you can hike the **Truman Trail** (No. 207) for up-close-and-personal views of the lava dome inside the crater, and to connect with the round-the-mountain **Loowit Trail** (No. 216). A spur of this (216 E) leads to the Loowit Falls, where 100° F water pours out of the crater (no swimming).

East Side Information
Get information on Mt. St. Helens at the Forest Service's **Woods Creek Information Station,** six miles south of Randle on Forest Rd. 25. Open daily 9 a.m.-4 p.m., late May through September, they even offer drive-through service! **Randle Ranger Station,** three miles east of Randle on Hwy. 12, tel. (360) 497-1100, is open daily 8 a.m.-4:30 p.m. from Memorial Day to Labor Day, and weekdays the rest of the year. **Pine Creek Information Station,** 17 miles east of Cougar on Forest Rd. 90 (and 45 miles south of Randle) has information for the southeast side of St. Helens. Open daily 9 a.m.-6 p.m. from late May through September.

SOUTH SIDE ACCESS

The south side of Mt. St. Helens was not impacted nearly as much by the 1980 eruption and is best known as the access route to climb the summit, for Ape Cave, and for various hiking trails, including the Loowit System that circles the mountain.

Ape Cave

This 12,810-foot lava tube is one of the longest such caves in the nation, and one of the most popular visitor attractions at Mt. St. Helens. The cave is 10 miles northeast of Cougar at the junction of Forest Roads 83 and 90, and is open all the time. From the entrance a staircase leads down to a chamber where the route splits. The downhill arm ends after an easy three-quarter-mile walk, while the uphill route is more difficult and rocky, continuing one and a half miles to an exit where an above-ground trail leads back to the starting point. Forest Service interpreters lead half-hour tours of Ape Cave several times a day from late June to Labor Day. Be sure to bring drinking water and two flashlights and extra batteries (or rent a lantern). Wear hiking boots, gloves, and warm clothes (the air is a steady 42° F all year). A small visitor center at Ape Cave can provide assistance, publications, and lantern rentals ($3) daily 10 a.m.-5:30 p.m., Memorial Day through September. The road is plowed to the Trail of Two Forests, a half mile away, in the winter.

Climbing Mount St. Helens

Mount St. Helens is said to be the second most climbed peak on the planet, exceeded only by Japan's Mt. Fujiyama. With 16,000 people making the pilgrimage each year up Mt. St. Helens, you're bound to have company on your trip to the top. While there is still a small risk that steam explosions could cause injury or death to climbers, the reduced activity in recent years has made this unlikely. You're probably in more danger driving to the mountain in your car. Nevertheless, be sure to check with the Forest Service on current conditions before heading up.

All climbing routes up Mt. St. Helens are from the south side of the peak, and a permit is required for travel above the 4,800-foot level during the summer. From mid-May through October, 110 permits are issued per day on a first-come basis, with up to 70 of these available by advance reservation. Permits are not required the rest of the year. Make reservations as early as possible after February 1, since most summer weekends are reserved by late March. Call (360) 247-5800 to get an application form. The other 40 permits are issued on a first-come basis at Jack's Store, located at the intersection of Hwy. 503 and Lewis River Rd., 23 miles east of Woodland. You can start signing up at 11 a.m. for the following day, and the 40 permits are given out at 6 p.m. Conditions change frequently, so always check with the monument before planning a climb; call (360) 750-3961 for a recorded message or (360) 247-5800 for a real person. You need to sign in both before and after the climb at Jack's Store.

The climb begins past the entrance to Ape Cave. Follow Forest Rd. 83 a mile beyond the cave, then turn left on Rd. 8100 for another mile, and finally right on Rd. 830 for the final three miles to Climbers Bivouac at an elevation of 3,750 feet. Even though the climb is not technically difficult, don't underestimate the steep slopes and severe weather. The first stretch ascends through the forest at a gradual pace, but above the 4,800-foot level the pole-marked route is a scramble over boulderfields, volcanic pumice, ash, and snowfields (often present till mid-July). The crater itself is off limits to the general public because steam explosions can create extremely dangerous conditions. Avoid the edge of the crater when snow tops the peak, since you may be stepping on a cornice that could give way.

Watch the weather reports before heading up the mountain; it can snow at any time of year, and low clouds can drastically reduce visibility. Call (503) 243-7575 for the latest weather forecast. Climbing boots, sunscreen, and plenty of water are requirements (no water is available on the route or at Climbers Bivouac), and you need to start early—say 7 a.m.—to have enough time to get up and back before nightfall. Most folks take eight to 10 hours for the nine-mile (roundtrip) trek. Take an ice axe when snow is present, along with plenty of warm clothes and rain gear. Goggles are helpful in the blowing dust, and gaiters may help keep the ash out of your boots. Don't wear contact lenses on this climb! Primitive camping is available in the woods at the trailhead. Some climbers prefer to get a head start the night before, camping three miles up at the 4,800-foot level where you'll find a composting toilet. Camping is not allowed above this point.

Other South Side Hiking Trails

A very easy path is the **Trail of Two Forests,** a brief boardwalk that takes you past the molds left when trees were immersed in lava flows 2,000 years ago. You can even crawl through two of these ancient impressions. The trail is right across from Ape Cave on Rd. 8303.

One of the most interesting hikes on the south end of Mt. St. Helens is the two-and-a-half-mile **Lava Canyon Trail** that drops 1,400 feet along the Muddy River. This canyon was scoured out by a mudflow during the 1980 eruption, revealing sharp cliffs and tall waterfalls. Although the upper end is wheelchair-accessible, the lower part crosses a long suspension bridge and then descends a cliff face by a steel ladder. Great for the adventurous, not fun if you have a case of acrophobia. Get to the trail by following Forest Rd. 83 nine miles (paved the entire way) beyond Ape Cave to the trailhead.

The **Loowit System** (No. 216) is a difficult 29-mile trail that circles Mt. St. Helens and is accessible from trailheads on all sides of the mountain. Plan on three days to get all the way around, and be prepared for lots of up-and-down hiking and faint trails in places. Camping is available at various points along the way, but contact the Forest Service for specifics since some areas are off limits.

For an enjoyable loop hike, head to the end of Forest Rd. 8123 on the southwest side of the mountain and the start of **Sheep Canyon Trail** (No. 240). This path climbs through old-growth forests and drainages that were ravaged by volcanic mudflows and into a flower-filled alpine meadow along the Loowit Trail before returning downhill on the Toutle Trail (No. 238), which connects to the Sheep Canyon Trail and your starting point. Total distance is approximately seven miles.

The **Lewis River Trail** (No. 31) follows along this beautiful river from the Curly Creek Falls to Lower Falls (a fun swimming hole), a dis-

tance of more than 10 miles. Between Curly Creek Falls and Lower Falls on Rd. 99 is Big Creek Falls, plummeting 125 feet into a pool that makes a popular place for a summer dip. Above Lower Falls, you can follow the road to a series of roadside falls, including the very scenic Middle Falls and Upper Falls.

South Side Campgrounds

The Forest Service's **Lower Falls Campground** is a fine camping place, with views of three large falls along the Lewis River and a hiking trail that heads downriver for 10 miles. The campground is 15 miles east of the Pine Creek Information Station on Forest Rd. 90 and is open mid-May to mid-October. The charge is $9, and reservations can be made ($7.50 extra) by calling (800) 280-2267.

Several other non-Forest Service public campgrounds provide camping on the south side of Mt. St. Helens. Near the town of Cougar (see under "Lewis River Valley"), **Cougar Campground** and **Beaver Bay Campground** offer tent camping and showers, for $8 a night on the Yale Reservoir along Forest Rd. 90. Go north on Rd. 8100 to **Merrill Lake Campground,** a free Department of Natural Resources camping area, or head east on Rd. 90 to **Swift Campground** for $8 campsites just south of the Pine Creek Information Station; reserve a spot by calling Pacific Power and Light, tel. (503) 464-5035. They also have very popular summer-only campgrounds (fee charged; showers available) at **Cresap Bay Park,** seven miles north of Amboy on Hwy. 503, and **Saddle Dam Park,** near the Yale Lake dam on Frasier Road. Cresap Bay and Swift Campgrounds have campfire programs on Friday and Saturday nights June-August. **Volcano View Campground,** just south of Yale on Hwy. 503, tel. (360) 231-4329, is a private RV park.

Winter Sports

Forest Service Rd. 83's two Sno-Parks offer a wide area for winter activities, including cross-country skiing, snowshoeing, and snowmobiling. Most popular is the **Marble Mountain Sno-Park,** located seven miles east of Cougar on Forest Rd. 90, and another six miles up Rd. 83. Get a Sno-Park permit and ski trail maps at Cougar area stores.

South Side Information
The **Mount St. Helens Volcanic Headquarters** is located at 42218 N.E. Yale Bridge Rd. (three miles north of Amboy on Hwy. 503) and is open Mon.-Fri. 7:30 a.m.-5 p.m. year-round; call (360) 750-3900 for information. The Forest Service's **Pine Creek Information Station,** 17 miles east of Cougar on Forest Rd. 90, also has information. Open daily 9 a.m.-6 p.m. from mid-June through September.

MOUNT ADAMS AND VICINITY

If it stood alone, 12,276-foot Mt. Adams would be a prime recreation site, silhouetted on license plates and key chains. But from a Seattle viewpoint, Adams is geographically behind and below its attention-getting neighbors: Mt. Rainier, a heavily used national park, and Mt. St. Helens, a rumbling national volcanic monument. The lack of good access roads (you've got to drive behind Mt. St. Helens along gravel Forest Service roads), and the remote Yakama Indian Reservation bordering on the east, make Mt. Adams an isolated, relatively unpopulated mountain. Those willing to venture out onto remote forest roads will find trails, unusual geologic formations, and scenic areas; if your goal is to escape civilization, this is the place to do it.

Geology
Like its more active neighbors, Mt. Adams is of volcanic origins, but unlike its neighbors, the mountain is believed to have been formed by a congregation of volcanic cones instead of a single large one. The mountain has been relatively quiescent for probably 10,000 years, and large glaciers crown its summit, including the Klickitat Glacier, second biggest of all Cascadian glaciers.

SIGHTS

Viewpoints
Approaching Trout Lake from the south on Hwy. 141, the **Indian Sacred Viewpoint** provides a spectacular view of Mt. Adams. For a closer look, take Forest Service Rd. 23—the main Mt. Adams access road—about eight miles north from Trout Lake. Just before the pavement gives way to gravel, you'll have a fine view of the mountain to the east.

Ice Cave
Ancient volcanic activity formed this 650-foot-long, four-section lava tube cave, which during pioneer times supplied ice for the towns of The Dalles and Hood River. Accessible from Ice Caves Campground, 10 miles west of Trout

Mount Adams is popular among novice mountaineers.

DIANNE BOUERICE LYONS

MOUNT ADAMS AND VICINITY

© MOON PUBLICATIONS, INC.

Lake, the cave entrance is a collapsed sink, 15 feet across and 14 feet deep, connected to three other collapsed sinks by passageways. Wear warm clothing and boots, and bring at least two dependable light sources. A helmet is also a good idea.

PRACTICALITIES

Campgrounds
The Mount Adams Ranger District has 17 developed campgrounds on the south side of Mt. Adams. Most are free, but there is a $6-10 fee at the larger campgrounds, including **Cultus Creek, Moss Creek, Oklahoma,** and **Peterson Prairie.** The **Peterson Prairie Cabin,** west of Trout Lake, can be rented during the winter months by skiers, snowshoers, and snowmobilers. See the Mount Adams Ranger Station in Trout Lake, tel. (509) 395-2501, for a complete list of campground locations and other facilities.

Other Forest Service campgrounds line Forest Rd. 23, the route that connects the town of Randle with the northwest side of Mt. Adams. These are managed by the Randle Ranger District, tel. (360) 497-1100, and range from free to $9 a night. Closest to the Mount Adams Wilderness Area are Council Lake, Olallie Lake, Takhalakh Lake, and Horseshoe Lake campgrounds. All of these are free, except for Takha-

lakh Lake, which charges $5 a night, and has affords a fine view of Mt. Adams.

Getting There
There are two ways to approach Mt. Adams: from Seattle, take I-5 south to I-205 near Vancouver, then follow I-205 to Hwy. 14 and head east. At Underwood, take Hwy. 141 north to Trout Lake. An alternative is to take I-5 south past Chehalis, then east on Hwy. 12 to Randle and take the **Randle Road** (Forest Service Rd. 23) south for 56 miles to Trout Lake. This isolated road is definitely the scenic route, and the entire length was recently paved. Approaching from the east, you can drive down Hwy. 97 to Goldendale and west on Hwy. 142 to Klickitat and take the Glenwood-Trout Lake Rd., or follow Hwy. 14 from Maryhill to Underwood and drive north. The roads into the Mt. Adams area are closed each winter due to heavy snowfall.

MOUNT ADAMS WILDERNESS

This 42,280-acre wilderness covers the summit of Mt. Adams, along with the entire eastern and northern flanks. The east side of the peak lies within the Yakama Indian Reservation, and is termed "Tract D." Trails—including the Pacific Crest Trail—provide a semicircular path through the heart of the wilderness.

MT. ADAMS AREA ACCOMMODATIONS

Accommodations are listed from least to most expensive. The area code is 509.

Llama Ranch B&B; Hwy. 141, Trout Lake; tel. 395-2786 or (800) 800-5262; $55-75 s or d; llama walks, seven guest rooms (two with private baths), full breakfast

Trout Lake Country Inn; 15 Guler Rd., Trout Lake; tel. 395-2894; $60 s or d; historic inn, two guest rooms, full breakfast

Huckleberry Ridge B&B; 2473 Hwy. 141, Trout Lake; tel. 395-2965; $60 s, $65 d; rural ranch-style home, two guest rooms, shared bath, continental breakfast

The Farm—A B&B; 490 Sunnyside Rd., Trout Lake; tel. 395-2488; $60-75 s or d; two guest rooms, shared bath, full breakfast

Mio Amore Pensione; Little Mt. Rd., Trout Lake; tel. 395-2264; $60-135 s or d; jacuzzi, four guest rooms, gourmet breakfast, no kids under 15, epicurean Northern Italian dinners available

Flying L Ranch; 25 Flying L Lane, Glenwood; tel. 364-3488; $65-90 d in lodge or guesthouse, $95-100 d in cabins; 160-acre ranch, jacuzzi, full breakfast, bikes

Hiking

The most heavily used trail in the Mount Adams Wilderness is **South Climb,** a 2.2-mile trail from Cold Springs Campground to timberline, from where climbers depart for routes to the summit. Those who prefer to stay low, can follow the **Around the Mountain Trail** (No. 9) northwest for about six miles to the **Pacific Crest Trail** (PCT).

The 21 miles of the PCT that pass through Mt. Adams Wilderness are accessible from Forest Service Rd. 23, near its intersection with Forest Service Rd. 8810, on the south; on the north, the PCT crosses Forest Service Rd. 5603 near Potato Hill. Subalpine meadows, glacial streams, dense forest, wildflowers, and scenic viewpoints reward the adventurous hiker.

Beginning at Morrison Creek Horse Camp on the south side of Mt. Adams, 2.7-mile **Crofton Butte Trail** (No. 73) follows the mountain's lower slopes for scenic views of the butte. Take Forest Service Roads 80 and 8040 for about 10 miles from Trout Lake.

Climbing Mount Adams

Mount Adams is one of the easiest Northwest volcanic peaks to climb; in fact, it's often used as a first climb by area mountaineering clubs. Before you begin, be sure to register with the Mt. Adams Ranger Station in Trout Lake, tel. (509) 395-2501. The south slope route is least difficult: it begins at the end of Forest Roads 8040 and 500 at Cold Springs Camp, 13 miles north at an elevation of 6,000 feet; follow the old road for two miles to Timberline Camp. From here the **South Climb Trail** (No. 183) leads to a large snowfield. Bear right across the snowfield to the ridge, following the ridge to the false summit at 11,500 feet. A zigzag trail leads through pumice to the summit, for a six-hour one-way trip. Climbers should carry an ice axe, rope, crampons, warm clothing, sunglasses, and other basic supplies. Other, more difficult routes are described in the American Alpine Club's Climber's Guide.

TRAPPER CREEK WILDERNESS

Located halfway between Mt. St. Helens and the Columbia River and covering just 6,050 acres, this is one of the smaller wilderness areas in Washington. It is also one of the few places where the forests have been spared from logging in this part of the state. Several trails provide access; longest is the **Observation Trail** (No. 132), which takes you through dense old-growth stands of timber, across a ridge, and to a spur trail that edges up 4,207-foot Observation Peak for panoramic views. From here, you can continue down to the junction with **Trapper Creek Trail** (No. 192), which takes you back along this pretty creek to your starting point. This loop hike is approximately 12 miles long.

INDIAN HEAVEN WILDERNESS

The 20,960-acres Indian Heaven Wilderness offers miles of little-used hiking trails; you won't find Mt. Rainier's crowds here because the average day-hiker isn't willing to drive this far into the woods on beat-up forest roads. So if it's seclusion you want, check at the Trout Lake Ranger Station for a map and rudimentary—but free—trail guide. The wilderness covers a high plateau that is split through by the Pacific Crest Trail and pockmarked with small ponds, evergreen forests, meadows, and mosquitoes. It is located due west of Trout Lake and north of Carson.

Hiking Trails

Thomas Lake Trail is a well-used 3.3-mile path that starts on the west side of the wilderness from Forest Rd. 65, and passes Dee, Thomas, Naha, Umtux, and Sahalee Tyee lakes before intersecting with the Pacific Crest Trail near Blue Lake. Head north on the main road from Carson, then turn right onto Forest Service Rd. 65 for about 17 miles to the trailhead.

The Pacific Crest Trail traverses Indian Heaven Wilderness from south to north: start at Crest Horse Camp, just south of the wilderness boundary on Forest Rd. 60 (right off Forest Service Rd. 65); the trail passes lakes, meadows, and forest for 17 miles through the wilderness area, then connects with Forest Service Rd. 24 near Surprise Lakes on the north side.

Forest Service's **Mt. Adams District Ranger District** office, tel. (509) 395-2501, where you can get maps, camping information, and current trail conditions. Open Mon.-Fri. 7:45 a.m.-4:30 p.m. all year. Just east of Trout Lake is a magnificent view of Mt. Adams, with a foreground of ripening huckleberry bushes in late August.

The equally small town of Glenwood is approximately 10 miles east of Trout Lake and six miles north of **Conboy Lake National Wildlife Refuge.** This 5,800-acre refuge provides a feeding and resting area for thousands of geese, ducks, swans, and sandhill cranes during their spring and fall migrations. A two-mile loop hike makes for a nice shoreline and forest hike, with the chance to view the waterfowl. Call (509) 364-3410 for more information.

Practicalities

Mio Amore Pensione, tel. (509) 395-2264, on the southern edge of Trout Lake, is one of the better places to stay and eat in the Mt. Adams-Columbia Gorge area. This converted farmhouse has three rooms in the main house and room for four in the former icehouse outside. Guests get a mountainous breakfast and access to the jacuzzi. No kids under age 15. The owners of Mio Amore also operate an excellent restaurant, serving epicurean Northern Italian dinners.

Glenwood's 160-acre **Flying L Ranch,** tel. (509) 364-3488, sits in a secluded valley on the eastern slope of the Cascades, with a spectacular skyline dominated by Mt. Adams. The inn ($65-90 d) and two adjacent cabins ($90-100 d) provide comfortably rustic accommodations, and guests can relax in the jacuzzi. Breakfasts are provided; otherwise, you can eat in Glenwood or cook your own in the kitchens. Kids of all ages can swim or raft in their small lake, or take a hike or mountain bike ride on nearby trails. A special hiking package combines guided hikes, lodging, meals, transportation, and permits.

Several other places offer country lodging around Trout Lake. **Llama Ranch B&B,** on Hwy. 141, tel. (509) 395-2786 or (800) 800-5262, has seven guest rooms (two with private baths) for $55-75 s or d. Guests can take the llamas for a walk after enjoying the full country

FLORENCE BOULERICE

TROUT LAKE AND GLENWOOD

Trout Lake is a tiny agricultural settlement with dairy and horse farms (along with a llama ranch), found approximately 30 miles north of the Columbia Gorge town of White Salmon. The world's largest D'Anjou pear orchard (Mt. Adams Orchards) is just a few miles south of here on the way to White Salmon. Trout Lake is the main access point for the Mt. Adams area, but has minimal services—a restaurant, grocery store, and gas station. For more dining variety and other services, head south to the Columbia River or east to Goldendale. The town does have the

breakfast. **Trout Lake Country Inn,** 15 Guler Rd., tel. (509) 395-2894, has two guest rooms in an historic turn-of-the-century inn with antiques. Rates are $60 s or d, including a full breakfast. No kids under 12.

Huckleberry Ridge B&B, 2473 Hwy. 141, tel. (509) 395-2965, is a rural ranch-style home with two guest rooms sharing a bath. They charge $60 s, $65 d, including a continental breakfast. And last, but not least, **The Farm—a**

Bed & Breakfast, 490 Sunnyside Rd., tel. (509) 395-2488, has two guest rooms with a shared bath in a farmhouse. Rates are $60-75 s or d, including a full breakfast.

Events

The main local events are Glenwood's **Ketchum Kalf Rodeo** on the third weekend of July, and **Trout Lake Community Fair and Dairy Show** on the first weekend of August.

BOB RACE

SOUTHCENTRAL WASHINGTON

WENATCHEE

Driving east on Highway 2 from the damp Puget Sound area, the transition to the "dry side of the mountains" is abrupt. The heavily forested, snowcapped Cascades give way to bone-dry hills, blanketed by snow in winter and covered only by dry brown grass in summer. You'll experience few of Puget Sound's mostly cloudy days here: Wenatchee gets over 300 sunny days and only 10-15 inches of rain per year. The warm, sunny days, cool nights, and volcanic ash soil combine to provide ideal apple-growing conditions. The area also grows pears, cherries, peaches, and other fruits.

The city of Wenatchee (pop. 22,000) faces it's twin, East Wenatchee (pop. 4,000), across the Columbia River, teaming up to form a major population center smack-dab in the middle of Washington's apple orchards. Although the historic center of Wenatchee has a certain degree of charm, the main thoroughfare—Wenatchee Ave.—has little, if any, appeal. It's the standard mix of shopping and cars, with all the big mega-

marts strewn along both sides as you exit town. It's sad to see the rich agricultural land around the twin Wenatchees being swallowed up by shopping malls, roads, and housing developments. In 1994 alone, 160 acres of orchards were lost to development.

Despite initial appearances, Wenatchee actually has several places that would stand out anywhere: Ohme Gardens, the North Central Washington Museum, and Rocky Reach Dam. Don't miss these!

HISTORY

The name Wenatchee comes from Wa-Nat-hee, an Indian word describing the area in poetic terms; it means "Robe of the Rainbow." Philip Miller was Wenatchee's pioneer apple grower and one of the first white settlers. In 1872, Miller took squatter's rights on a parcel of land in the Wenatchee Valley and planted a handful of

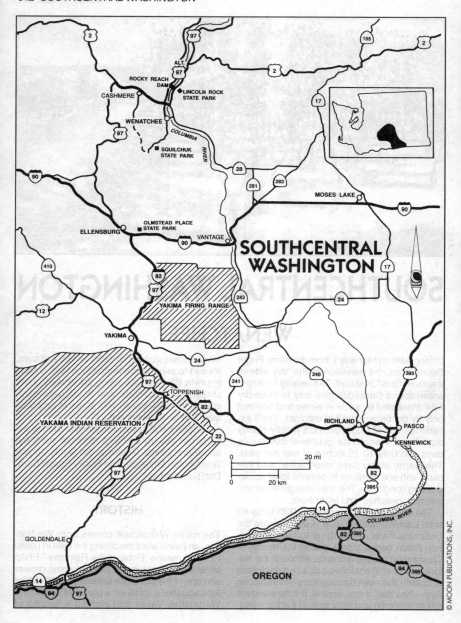

SOUTHCENTRAL WASHINGTON

© MOON PUBLICATIONS, INC.

apple seedlings. The trees flourished, and when the railroad came to Wenatchee in 1892, Miller drove in the silver pike to link the last rails—and to help determine Wenatchee's economic future. Miller's ranch shipped its first full carload of apples to Seattle in 1901. Irrigation projects, beginning with the Highline Canal in 1904, brought much-needed water to this arid region and helped the apple industry blossom. Today, an average of 30,000 carloads of apples are shipped from the Wenatchee Valley every year. The local economy of Wenatchee is still heavily based in agriculture and food processing, but a huge Alcoa aluminum plant, an underground gold mine, and the many retail businesses are also major employers.

SIGHTS

Ohme Gardens

Located just north of Wenatchee on a bluff overlooking the Wenatchee Valley, Ohme Gardens is a testimony to over 50 years of watering and weed-pulling by the Ohme family. Their hard work transformed a barren hillside of sagebrush into one of America's most highly acclaimed gardens. Originally created for the Ohmes' personal use, the patch of green on the otherwise desolate hillside attracted visitors' attention, and was eventually purchased by the state to be managed by Chelan County. Now covering nine acres, the gardens resemble natural alpine scenery: evergreens, grass, ponds, and waterfalls blend with the existing rock—a cool reprieve from the scorching Wenatchee sunshine. A lookout from the gardens' highest point provides broad views of the valley, Cascades, and Columbia River. The gardens are near the junction of Highways 2 and 97, three miles north of Wenatchee, at 3327 Ohme Rd., tel. (509) 662-5785; open April 15 to October 15, daily 9 a.m.-7 p.m. in the summer, or daily 9 a.m.-6 p.m. in spring and fall. Admission is $5 for adults, $3 for ages seven to 18, free for kids under seven. Steep drop-offs in some sections make this a hazardous place for uncontrollable toddlers.

Rocky Reach Dam

Although this looks like just another large Columbia River dam, Rocky Reach is actually one of the most unusual and interesting visitor attractions in Washington. The 4,800-foot-long dam, seven miles north of Wenatchee on Hwy. 97A, was built across the Columbia between 1956 and 1962, with additions completed in 1971. Picnic tables and elaborately landscaped areas cover 18 acres of grounds (including a floral U.S. flag composed of red, white, and blue petunias), while a visitor center sells snacks and gifts, and offers summertime guided tours. A variety of films and videos are shown upon request in the theater, including the interesting 18-minute "Tale of the Salmon." The visitor center and exhibit galleries are open daily 8 a.m.-8 p.m. from late June to Labor Day, with earlier closing hours in the spring and fall; closed entirely January to mid-February.

Be sure to visit the fish-viewing room where you can watch salmon and steelhead heading upriver from mid-April to mid-November. They are also visible in the fish ladder outside. Enter the powerhouse where you can view the enormous gantry crane and row of 11 generators producing 1.3 million kilowatts, enough to supply power for all of Seattle. Nearly a quarter of this energy goes to power an enormous Alcoa aluminum plant in Wenatchee. But the real treat is a long—and I do mean long—gallery filled with an astounding collection of educational exhibits.

In the **Gallery of the Columbia** you will learn about the channeled scablands, see the pilothouse of the late 1800s steamer *Bridgeport,* explore Indian artifacts (including a unique steatite pipe enclosed in a carved wood case), learn about early explorers and settlers, and follow the development of the region. Be sure to check out the Waterville Tramway exhibit; this ingenious device was used early in this century to transport wheat to steamers on the Columbia River and simultaneously haul coal and other supplies 9,200-feet uphill to the settlement. An extensive **Gallery of Electricity** relates the history of electricity in displays and photos, and allows visitors to generate their own power. All told, these exhibits are enough to keep history and science buffs occupied for several hours.

North Central Washington Museum

Wenatchee's North Central Washington Museum, 127 S. Mission St., tel. (509) 664-3340,

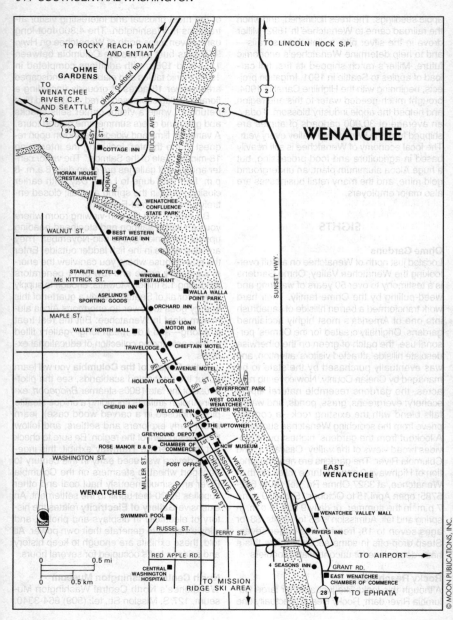

is one of the finest museums in the state, a surprisingly large collection spread over two floors and two connected buildings. The main level takes you on a tour of Wenatchee at the turn of the century, past a beautifully restored 1917 Oldsmobile sedan and the Liberty Theater pipe organ (1919), used for occasional performances with silent films in the performance center, and an exhibit on Clyde Edward Pangborn, who made the first nonstop trans-Pacific flight. He left Japan on October 3, 1931, and landed in Wenatchee 41 hours later, at an airfield that now bears his name. Upstairs, you'll discover an impressive model railroad that chugs through a Cascades mountain setting, many historic photos, a pithouse where you sit inside to learn Native American creation tales, and Indian petroglyphs from the site of Rock Island Dam (the others are under water). Across the skybridge is an art gallery with changing exhibits from contemporary artists, a delightful collection of miniatures (including the world's smallest belt), and even a 1916 bathroom. Head down the stairs to apple industry exhibits and videos, displays of colorful applebox labels, and an ingenious 1920s-era apple sorter (be sure to ask the docents to run this machine for you).

The museum is open Mon.-Fri. 10 a.m.-4 p.m., Sat.-Sun. 1-4 p.m. (closed January weekends and holidays). Admission is $3 for adults, $2 for ages six to 12, free for kids under five, $5 for families. While here, pick up a walking tour brochure describing Wenatchee's historic downtown buildings.

Apples

At 2900 Euclid Ave., the **Washington State Apple Commission Visitor Center,** tel. (509) 663-9600, has an 18-minute video and displays about the apple industry, along with apples and apple juice samples. Open Sunday 11 a.m.-5 p.m., Mon.-Fri. 8 a.m.-5 p.m., and Saturday 9 a.m.-5 p.m. April-Dec.; Mon.-Fri. 8 a.m.-5 p.m. the rest of the year. While here, you'll learn that Washington produces 10 billion apples each year, fully 60% of the nation's apples, and three times as many apples as its nearest competitor, New York. Ask here about tours of local apple warehouses. Generally, your best bet is **Skookum Inc.,** tel. (509) 662-3602, with good

weekday tours at their facility just north of town. Near the town of Chelan, Beebe Orchard Co., Blue Chelan, and Trout, Inc. offer tours (see "Apple Tours" in the Sights section of "Chelan and Vicinity"). Most apples are picked mid-September to mid-October, so get here before this to see the heavily laden fruit trees.

ACCOMMODATIONS

Motels and B&Bs

See the lodging chart for a full listing of local hotels, motels, and B&Bs. The Wenatchee Area Chamber of Commerce, tel. (800) 572-7753, keeps track of room availability and can transfer you directly to local motels and B&Bs that are chamber members.

Campgrounds

Wenatchee Confluence State Park, tel. (509) 664-6373, sits at the confluence of the Wenatchee and Columbia Rivers, just north of town, and has a bike and footbridge across the Wenatchee to marshes on the south side. Camp at the park in an open grassy field (hot in the summer). Tent sites are $11, RV hookups $16, including coin-operated showers; open yearround. Call (800) 452-5687 for campsite reservations ($6 extra fee), available up to 11 months ahead of time.

Wenatchee River County Park, six miles west of Wenatchee on Hwy. 2, has playgrounds, picnic areas, and camping for tents ($12) and RVs ($17). The park is open April-Oct., and all camping is on a first-come, first-served basis.

Lincoln Rock State Park—named for a geologic feature across the river that some say resembles President Lincoln's profile—is seven miles north of E. Wenatchee on Hwy. 2. The day-use area has a swimming beach on the Columbia River, boat moorage, and tennis courts. The park has tent sites ($11) and RV spaces ($16), and is open mid-March through October. Interpretive programs are offered at the amphitheater here on summer evenings. Call (509) 884-8702 for more information, or (800) 452-5687 for campsite reservations ($6 extra fee), available up to 11 months ahead of time.

WENATCHEE AREA ACCOMMODATIONS

Accommodations are arranged from least to most expensive. Rates may be lower during the winter months. The area code is 509.

Welcome Inn; 232 N. Wenatchee Ave.; tel. 663-7121; $30 s, $35 d Sun.-Thurs.; $35 s, $40 d Fri.-Sat.; outdoor pool

Starlite Motel; 1640 N. Wenatchee Ave.; tel. 663-8115; $36 s, $40 d; outdoor pool, kitchenettes available

Lyle's Motel; 924 N. Wenatchee Ave.; tel. 663-5155 or (800) 582-3788; $38 s, $44 d; outdoor pool, jacuzzi, kitchenettes available, AAA approved

Hill Crest Motel; 2921 School St.; tel. 663-5157 or (800) 245-5157; $40 s, $45 d; outdoor pool, kitchenettes available

Holiday Lodge; 610 N. Wenatchee Ave.; tel. 663-8167 or (800) 722-0852; $44-55 s, $48-60 d; outdoor pool, jacuzzi, sauna, AAA approved

The Uptowner; 101 N. Mission; tel. 663-8516 or (800) 288-5279; $44 s, $50 d; outdoor pool, sauna, kitchenettes available

Four Seasons Inn; 11 W. Grant Rd. in E. Wenatchee; tel. 884-6611 or (800) 223-6611; $44-52 s, $52-58 d; overlooking the Columbia River, outdoor pool, sauna, jacuzzi, kitchenettes available, AAA approved

Avenue Motel; 720 N. Wenatchee Ave.; tel. 663-7161 or (800) 733-8981; $45 s or d; outdoor pool, jacuzzi, kitchenettes available, AAA approved

Wenatchee Travelodge; 1004 N. Wenatchee Ave.; tel. 662-8165 or (800) 578-7878; $45 s, $49 d; outdoor pool, jacuzzi, sauna, kitchenettes available

Chieftain Motel; 1005 N. Wenatchee Ave.; tel. 663-8141 or (800) 572-4456; $45 s, $55 d; outdoor pool, jacuzzi

Rivers Inn; 580 Valley Mall Parkway in E. Wenatchee; tel. 884-1474 or (800) 922-3199; $47 s, $52-57 d; outdoor pool, jacuzzi, AAA approved

Coventry Inn B&B; 519 King St.; tel. 662-6771; $55 s or d; 1915 home, two guest rooms, shared bath, antique furnishings, full breakfast, no kids

Bruce's Place B&B; 504 Kittitas; tel. 664-2420 or (800) 858-7917; $55-75 s, $64-84 d; outdoor pool, two guest rooms, shared bath, full breakfast, no kids

Orchard Inn; 1401 N. Miller; tel. 662-3443 or (800) 368-4571; $48 s, $53 d; outdoor pool, jacuzzi, AAA approved

Rose Manor B&B; 156 S. Emerson; tel. 662-1093; $50-80 s or d; spacious 1904 home, mountain views, five guest rooms, private or shared bath, full breakfast

Warm Springs Inn; 1611 Love Lane; tel. 662-8365 or (800) 543-3645; $65-85 s or d; 1914 plantation-style mansion, four guest rooms, private baths, full breakfast

Best Western Heritage Inn; 1905 N. Wenatchee Ave.; tel. 664-6565 or (800) 528-1234; $70-100 s, $80-125 d; outdoor pool, jacuzzi, sauna, kitchenettes available, AAA approved

Cherub Inn B&B; 410 N. Miller; tel. 662-6011; $75 s or d Sun.-Thurs., $85 s or d Fri.-Sat.; 1930 English Tudor home, four guest rooms, outdoor pool, jacuzzi, grand piano, full breakfast

Red Lion Inn; 1225 N. Wenatchee Ave.; tel. 663-0711 or (800) 547-8010; $85-95 s, $95-105 d; indoor pool, jacuzzi, AAA approved

WestCoast Wenatchee Center Hotel; 201 N. Wenatchee Ave.; tel. 662-1234 or (800) 426-0670; $85-95 s, $95-105 d; indoor and outdoor pools, jacuzzi, exercise room, free airport shuttle, AAA approved

FOOD

Breakfast and Bakeries
Two popular places to start the day are **Smitty's Pancake & Steak House,** 1621 N. Wenatchee Ave., tel. (509) 662-2784, and E. Wenatchee's **Pizza N,** 340 Valley Mall Parkway, tel. (509) 884-1531. If you're just looking for a good cup of java, the ubiquitous **Starbucks,** 10 Grant Rd. in E. Wenatchee, tel. (509) 884-1924, will certainly fill the cup. Great Mexican pastries at **La Espiga Panaderia,** 818 S. Wenatchee Ave., tel. (509) 664-7254. **Edible Art Bakery,** 104 11th St. NE in E. Wenatchee, tel. (509) 884-0542, creates tasty caramel pecan nut rolls, cookies, scones, and other treats. The **Roaster & Ale House** at WestCoast Wenatchee Center, 201 N. Wenatchee Ave., tel. (509) 662-1234, has delicious breakfasts, great Caesar salads for lunch, and excellent dinners. A bit pricey.

Lunches and Delis
Located in an old brick-walled pub, **McGlinn's Ale House & Espresso Bar,** 111 Orondo, tel. (509) 663-9073, makes some of the best lunches and espresso in Wenatchee. They also have lots of microbrews on tap, good pub-grub for a light dinner, and jazz on weekends. Excellent lunches and dinners at **Lemolo Cafe & Deli,** 114 N. Wenatchee Ave., tel. (509) 664-6576. They offer deli sandwiches, soups, salads, and distinctive stone-oven pizzas. Another good sandwich spot is E. Wenatchee's **Yogurt Connection,** 210 Valley Mall Parkway, tel. (509) 884-7103.

Bonzetti's Fresh Pasta, 406 N. Mission, tel. (509) 663-5460, is an Italian take-out deli with gourmet pastas and salads, along with a good selection of wines.

All-American
The Cottage Inn, tel. (509) 663-4435, has been serving chicken, steak, and seafood at the 134 Easy St. location since 1940. Open for dinner only Tues.-Saturday. If you're a lover of red meat, **The Windmill,** 1501 N. Wenatchee Ave., tel. (509) 663-3478, is *the* place for absolutely perfect steaks in Wenatchee, along with fresh seafood and great pies.

Chieftain Restaurant, next to the motel of the same name at 1005 N. Wenatchee Ave., tel. (509) 663-8141, specializes in moderately priced seafood and prime rib; they also feature live entertainment Tues.-Sat. nights.

For the best local pizzas, made with a distinctively spicy sauce, head to **Abby's Legendary Pizza,** 5th and Western, tel. (509) 662-2226, or 702 Grant Rd. in E. Wenatchee, tel. (509) 884-7211.

Goochi's, 29 N. Columbia, tel. (509) 664-3200, is the Wenatchee version of this popular Chelan restaurant with 30 beers on tap and a big range of steaks, pastas, burgers, and other well-prepared meals. The 10-foot-wide TV is popular for sporting events.

Fine Dining
The **John Horan House Restaurant,** 2 Horan Rd., tel. (509) 663-0018, serves steak, seafood, and other fine meals in an elegant farmhouse built in 1899 by John Horan, one of the valley's "Apple Kings." Open daily for dinner only, and lunch on Sunday; reservations are suggested.

Steven's at Mission Square, 218 N. Mission, tel. (509) 663-6573, is a bit on the pricey side, but the Northwest cuisine dinners, the freshest seafood in town, delicious desserts, and exquisite setting are worth the price.

International Restaurants
Viscounti's Italian Restaurant, 1737 N. Wenatchee, tel. (509) 662-5013, serves quite good Northern Italian food in a white-linen setting. Prices are fairly reasonable. Another good Italian place over in E. Wenatchee is **Garlini's Italian Restaurant,** 810 Valley Mall Parkway E, tel. (509) 884-1707. Get very good Mexican meals at **Tequila's,** 800 N. Wenatchee Ave., tel. (509) 662-7239, or stop by one of the vans scattered around town for cheap and meaty tacos.

Get authentic Thai cookery at **The Thai Restaurant,** 1211 N. Mission, tel. (509) 662-8077. For Chinese food, try **Golden East Restaurant,** 230 Grant Rd. in E. Wenatchee, tel. (509) 884-1510, or **Mandarin Restaurant,** 1300 N. Miller, tel. (509) 663-5801. The Golden East has more authentic fare (including Sichuan), while Mandarin is a bit more Americanized.

Fresh Produce

The Wenatchee area is filled with fruit stands offering fresh apples, apricots, cherries, peaches, and pears in season. The **Wenatchee Valley Farmers Market** takes place mid-June through October at Riverfront Park on Wednesday and Saturday 8 a.m.-noon.

EVENTS

Ridge to River Relay consists of six different competitions, with teams competing over a 35-mile course that includes cross-country and downhill skiing, running, cycling, and canoeing. It attracts over 2,000 participants each year and is held in early April.

The self-proclaimed "Apple Capital of the World" is the only proper place to hold the annual **Apple Blossom Festival,** tel. (509) 662-3616, going strong since 1919. This 10-day event starts the last weekend of April and is highlighted by a youth parade and the Apple Blossom Parade on the first Saturday in May; other festivities include carnivals, a "Classy Chassis" auto parade, pancake breakfast, arts and crafts fair, gem and mineral exhibits, and a play staged by local talent. **Gray Line of Seattle,** tel. (206) 624-5813, has two-day bus tours from downtown Seattle to Wenatchee for the Apple Blossom Festival.

The **Wenatchee Youth Circus,** tel. (509) 662-0722, perhaps the best amateur youth circus in America, opens in July in Wenatchee then travels throughout the Pacific Northwest all summer.

ENTERTAINMENT

The **Roaster & Ale House** at WestCoast Wenatchee Center, 201 N. Wenatchee Ave., tel. (509) 662-1234, has live music most nights. **McGlinn's Ale House & Espresso Bar,** 111 Orondo, tel. (509) 663-9073, features live jazz on weekends in a friendly and convivial atmosphere. The downtown Convention Center fountain has live music or theatrical performances on Wednesday at noon all summer long.

SPORTS AND RECREATION

Parks

Several local parks provide enjoyable places to walk, ride bikes, rollerblade, or enjoy a riverside picnic. **Riverfront Park** stretches north along the shore from downtown, with miles of trails and a steam train for the kids that runs at odd hours in the summer. Paths connect it to **Walla Walla Point Park,** where you'll find all sorts of sports fields and a swimming area. North of here is Wenatchee Confluence State Park (see "Campgrounds" above) with more trails and good birdwatching.

A footbridge/bike path crosses the river just north of the Hwy. 2 bridge, providing access to E. Wenatchee, and additional paved riverfront paths. A mile south on the paved path is tiny **View Point Park,** a great place to watch sunsets. Two miles farther south is **Rock Island Hydro Park,** another riverside park with paths, a boat ramp, a swimming area, and other recreation.

Rent mountain bikes at **The Second Wind,** 85 N.E. 9th St. in E. Wenatchee, tel. (509) 884-0821.

Swimming

Swim at the roped-off area in **Wenatchee Confluence State Park,** the **Wenatchee swimming pool,** 220 Fuller, tel. (509) 664-3397, the **YMCA,** 217 Orondo, tel. (509) 662-2109, or at the covered pool at **Eastmont County Park** in E. Wenatchee, tel. (509) 884-3113.

Skiing

Just 12 miles from Wenatchee, **Mission Ridge Ski Area** is the area's largest and Washington's east-side secret, with drier snow and more sun than other Cascade ski areas. It has 33 runs spread across 2,200 acres, and a base elevation of 4,570 feet. At the base, you'll find a restaurant, lounge, ski and snowboard rental shop, ski school, and child care facility. Midway Cafe is halfway up the mountain. The ski area is generally open from Thanksgiving to early April, and weekend tickets cost $28 for adults, $20 for students and seniors, and $15 for kids ages seven to 15. Kids under seven ski free. Midweek rates drop to $15 for adults. Night skiing is also available Thurs.-Sat. in midwinter. Mission Ridge does not publicize its snow depth because it is often considerably lower than elsewhere in the Cascades, but the snow is often of better quality than in places where the base is deeper. To check on conditions, call (509) 626-5208 or (800) 426-7532. A SkiLink bus (tel. 800-851-5465) means that you can reach Mission Ridge from Wenatchee, Leavenworth, or Chelan absolutely free. Ski racks are attached to the side of the bus.

Squilchuck State Park, tel. (509) 664-6373, has winter cross-country skiing amidst a forested mountain setting, plus a small downhill ski area with two rope tows, ski school, and coffee shop operated by Wenatchee Valley College. The park is seven miles southwest of Wenatchee on Squilchuck Road. Camping here is limited to large groups with advance reservations.

Auto Racing
Wenatchee Valley Raceway on Fancher Heights above E. Wenatchee has auto racing on Sunday nights all summer long.

Golf
Golfers will enjoy playing at three local courses: **Kahler Glen Golf Course,** three and a half miles north off Hwy. 2, tel. (509) 763-4025; **Three Lakes Golf Course,** on W. Malaga Rd. off the Wenatchee-Malaga Hwy., tel. (509) 663-5448; and **Rock Island Golf Course,** in Rock Island, tel. (509) 884-2806.

SHOPPING

The **Wenatchee Valley Mall** is the area's largest, with 48 stores, including Sears, Lamonts, and Ernst, across the bridge in E. Wenatchee. The **Valley North Mall,** Miller St. in N. Wenatchee, is a smaller version with 38 stores, highlighted by JCPenney. At 2nd and Mission, **Mission Square** has an assortment of boutiques, including a kitchen shop, fine art and custom-framing shop, craft supply store, deli, and restaurant. Skiers and other outdoors enthusiasts will want to visit **Asplund's,** a sporting goods store at 1544 N.

Wenatchee Ave., tel. (509) 662-6539. Here you'll find everything from swimsuits to bicycles to backpacking supplies, plus cross-country ski equipment, rentals, and lessons. The **Victorian Village,** at 611 S. Mission, is a collection of small shops and restaurants. And if you just want something cheap, head up Wenatchee Ave. to find all the major discount chains, from Fred Meyers to WalMart.

INFORMATION AND SERVICES

For maps, brochures, or specific information on the Wenatchee area, contact the **Wenatchee Area Chamber of Commerce,** 2 S. Chelan Ave., tel. (509) 662-4774 or (800) 572-7753. Open Mon.-Fri. 9 a.m.-5 p.m. year-round. The **East Wenatchee Chamber of Commerce** is located at 44 Rock Island Rd., tel. (509) 884-2514 or (800) 245-3922.

The **public library** is located at 310 Douglas, tel. (509) 662-5021. All phone numbers from Wenatchee eastward are preceded by **area code** 509. For medical emergencies or problems, contact **Central Washington Hospital,** 1300 Fuller, tel. (509) 662-1511.

TRANSPORTATION

Arriving by Air
Wenatchee's airport, **Pangborn Field,** was named in honor of Clyde Pangborn, a pilot who piled up aviation record after record in the '20s and '30s. Pangborn's most notable feat was accomplished on October 6, 1931, when he and Hugh Herndon completed the first nonstop flight over the Pacific Ocean, landing at the Wenatchee airport—minus the landing gear they had intentionally dropped when excess weight threatened to shorten their flight. The trip was an eventful one—the pair was charged with spying and held in Tokyo for several weeks before being released with a hefty fine; then, while crossing the Pacific, icy wings and an empty gas tank nearly ended the flight prematurely.

Today Pangborn Field connects Wenatchee with Seattle via **Horizon Air,** tel. (509) 884-1502 or (800) 547-9308.

Link Buses

Wenatchee, and all of Chelan County for that matter, have one of the best public bus systems in the state, if not the country, because the whole thing is free (paid for with local sales tax dollars). You can ride all over Wenatchee, to Chelan and Manson, to Cashmere and Leavenworth, to Lake Wenatchee, to Mission Ridge Ski Area, and across the Columbia River to East Wenatchee, Orondo, and Waterville in Douglas County. All for free, and in most cases, service is offered several times daily. The buses are outfitted with special racks for bicycles and the Link system carries more bicycle riders than any other public bus system in the state, in-

cluding King County. For information call (509) 662-1155 or (800) 851-5465.

Longhaul Buses

Greyhound, tel. (509) 662-2183 or (800) 231-2222, and **Empire Lines,** tel. (509) 662-2183, provide daily service to the Northwest from the bus depot at 301 1st Street.

Arriving by Train

Amtrak's Empire Builder serves Wenatchee, with service four days a week east to Ephrata, Spokane, Minneapolis, and Chicago, and west to Everett, Edmonds, and Seattle. For reservations and information call (800) 872-7245.

ELLENSBURG

One of Washington's best-known Western towns, Ellensburg is famous for its Labor Day weekend rodeo that attracts thousands of spectators and top rodeo talent from across the country. It is also home to the Western Art Association, which has an annual show and convention of the top Western artists, and to the Clymer Museum, devoted to the Western art of John Clymer. Yet the town isn't particularly Western in appearance; the Western clothing stores, tack shops, and country-western bars that you might expect in a rodeo town just aren't there. Instead you'll find an old, quiet college

town of fewer than 13,000 with progress squeezing in on an historic city center. Ellensburg sits near the geographic center of the state, serving as commercial center for the small mining towns and cattle ranches surrounding it. Besides the rodeo, Ellensburg has something found nowhere else in the world: the beautiful "Ellensburg Blue" agate, fashioned at local jewelry stores into earrings, necklaces, and rings.

Driving toward Ellensburg from Puget Sound, the change in weather and geography is dramatic. From Seattle to Snoqualmie Pass, you'll pass forested hills and snow-covered peaks, often under a thick cloud cover. By the time you're 20 miles west of Ellensburg, the clouds have thinned out, the temperature rises in the summer and falls in the winter, and the landscape flattens to low, rolling hills dotted with bushes and an occasional tree. Out here the summers are sunnier and hotter—nearly every motel has a pool—but the winters are harsh, with snow and bitter cold that the Puget Sound region rarely sees. You'll also note that in the Ellensburg area most trees have a permanent eastward tilt from the almost constant wind that blows down from the Cascades.

HISTORY

From the beginning, the Kittitas Valley has been blessed with an abundance of fish and wildlife. Indians from the otherwise hostile Nez Percé,

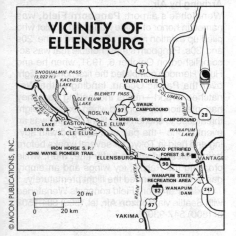

VICINITY OF ELLENSBURG

SNOQUALMIE PASS (3,022 ft.)
KACHESS LAKE
BLEWETT PASS
CLE ELUM LAKE
KEECHELUS LAKE
ROSLYN
WENATCHEE
COLUMBIA RIVER
SWAUK CAMPGROUND
MINERAL SPRINGS CAMPGROUND
28
LAKE EASTON
EASTON S.P.
EASTON
CLE ELUM
S. CLE ELUM
WANAPUM LAKE
IRON HORSE S.P. /
JOHN WAYNE PIONEER TRAIL
ELLENSBURG
GINGKO PETRIFIED FOREST S.P.
VANTAGE
90
YAKIMA RIVER
WANAPUM STATE RECREATION AREA
82
WANAPUM DAM
243
97
YAKIMA

0   20 mi
0   20 km

© MOON PUBLICATIONS, INC.

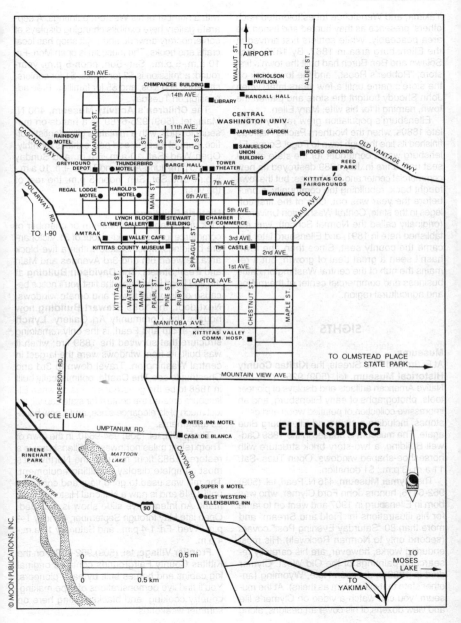

TO AIRPORT

WALNUT ST.

ALDER ST.

15th AVE.

CHIMPANZEE BUILDING

NICHOLSON PAVILION

14th AVE.

LIBRARY

RANDALL HALL

CENTRAL WASHINGTON UNIV.

OKANOGAN ST.

11th AVE.

JAPANESE GARDEN

A ST.

B ST.

C ST.

D ST.

CASCADE WAY

RAINBOW MOTEL

OLD VANTAGE HWY.

SAMUELSON UNION BUILDING

RODEO GROUNDS

REED PARK

GREYHOUND DEPOT

THUNDERBIRD MOTEL

BARGE HALL

TOWER THEATER

KITTITAS CO. FAIRGROUNDS

TO I-90

REGAL LODGE MOTEL

HAROLD'S MOTEL

MAIN ST.

8th AVE.

7th AVE.

6th AVE.

SWIMMING POOL

CRAIG AVE.

DOLARWAY RD.

5th AVE.

LYNCH BLOCK

STEWART BUILDING

CHAMBER OF COMMERCE

AMTRAK

CLYMER GALLERY

SPRAGUE ST.

3rd AVE.

VALLEY CAFE

KITTITAS COUNTY MUSEUM

THE CASTLE

2nd AVE.

KITTITAS ST.

WATER ST.

MAIN ST.

PEARL ST.

PINE ST.

RUBY ST.

CAPITOL AVE.

1st AVE.

CHESTNUT ST.

MAPLE ST.

ANDERSON RD.

MANITOBA AVE.

KITTITAS VALLEY COMM. HOSP.

TO OLMSTEAD PLACE STATE PARK

MOUNTAIN VIEW AVE.

TO CLE ELUM

UMPTANUM RD.

NITES INN MOTEL

CANYON RD.

CASA DE BLANCA

ELLENSBURG

IRENE RINEHART PARK

MATTOON LAKE

YAKIMA RIVER

90

SUPER 8 MOTEL

BEST WESTERN ELLENSBURG INN

TO MOSES LAKE

© MOON PUBLICATIONS, INC.

0   0.5 mi

0   0.5 km

TO YAKIMA

Yakima, and Wenatchee tribes tolerated each others' presence as they hunted and fished the area peaceably. White settlers first arrived in the Ellensburg area in 1867. By 1870, Jack Splawn and Ben Burch had built the town's first store, "Robber's Roost," and the town took on the store's name until a few years later, when John Shoudy bought the store and platted the town, naming it for his wife, Mary Ellen.

Ellensburg's population grew rapidly in the late 1880s, when the Northern Pacific Railroad finished its line through town to Puget Sound. Ellensburg was a contender for the state capitol seat until a fire in July 1889 destroyed its new commercial center and 200 homes; but the town fought back, rebuilding the community in brick before the year was out. One of the first colleges in the state, Central Washington University (originally called the Normal School), was established here in 1891, and Ellensburg later became the county seat. Since then, the town hasn't seen a great deal of growth, but it remains the hub of the central Washington cattle business and commercial center of the mining and agricultural region.

SIGHTS

Museums

At E. 3rd and Pine Streets, the **Kittitas County Historical Museum,** tel. (509) 925-3778, has Native American artifacts and displays of pioneer tools, photographs of early Ellensburg, and an impressive collection of petrified wood and gemstones, including a six-pound Ellensburg Blue agate. The museum is housed in the 1889 Cadwell Building, a two-story brick structure with horseshoe-shaped windows. Open Tues.-Sat. 11 a.m.-3 p.m.; $1 donation.

The **Clymer Museum,** 416 N. Pearl, tel. (509) 962-6416, honors John Ford Clymer, who was born in Ellensburg in 1907 and went on to fame for his illustrations in "Field and Stream" and more than 80 "Saturday Evening Post" covers (second only to Norman Rockwell). His most enduring works, however, are his carefully researched paintings of the Old West. Clymer died in 1989 in Jackson Hole, Wyoming (another state that claims him as theirs). At the museum, you can watch a video on Clymer's life and view dozens of his cover art designs, along with a number of his Western paintings. A separate gallery here exhibits changing displays of contemporary artwork, and a gift shop has local crafts and books. The museum is open Mon.-Fri. 10 a.m.-5 p.m., Sat.-Sun. noon-5 p.m. year-round; admission is $2 for adults, $1 for seniors, students, and kids, and $5 for families. Free admission on Tuesday.

The **Children's Activity Museum,** 400 N. Main, tel. (509) 925-6789, is a hands-on museum for kids, with a miniature city, dentist's office, puppet theater, and new exhibits monthly. Open Wed.-Sat. 10 a.m.-5 p.m. and Sunday noon-5 p.m. June-Aug., and Thurs.-Fri. 10 a.m.-5 p.m. and Sat.-Sun. noon-5 p.m. the rest of the year.

Historic Buildings

Pick up a map at the museum or chamber of commerce for a self-guided tour of 31 Victorian-era buildings, most located within a five-block area between 6th and 3rd Avenues and Main and Pearl Streets. The **Davidson Building** at 4th and Pearl is probably the first you'll notice because of its proud tower and ornate windows. Next door, the 1889 **Stewart Building** now houses the Community Art Gallery. **Lynch Block,** at 5th and Pearl, is the only remaining structure that survived the 1889 fire; when it was built, its front windows were the largest in central Washington. Travel down to 3rd and Chestnut to see **The Castle,** optimistically built in 1888 to be the governor's mansion when Ellensburg entered the contest for state capital; it's lost much of its elegance since, and it now houses apartments.

Thorp Mill, tel. (509) 964-9640, in the town of Thorp (eight miles northwest of Ellensburg) is a restored 1883 flour mill with the Northwest's most complete display of milling equipment. The mill was used to grind flour and cornmeal until 1946 and is now a National Historic Landmark. An interpretive slide show is provided. Open late May through September, Sunday 1-4 p.m., Wed.-Fri. 1-4 p.m., and Saturday 10 a.m.-4 p.m.

Frontier Village, tel. (509) 962-7639, on the Kittitas County Fairgrounds contains original log cabins and homes built by early pioneers. You'll find live demonstrations of rope making, country cooking, and blacksmithing here on summer weekends.

Offbeat Sights

The park bench on 4th and Pearl has a friendly *Ellensburg Bull,* complete with strategically placed hat and blue balls. It was created by noted sculptor Richard Beyer. An amusing gunslinger sculpture by Dan Klennerd guards the corner of 5th and Pearl. Also in town is **Dick & Jane's Spot,** at 101 N. Pearl, an odd collection of cast-off items that never cease to bring a smile.

Central Washington University

In existence since 1891, the 350-acre Central Washington University campus makes a fine place for a stroll. For tours of the campus, call the Admissions Office at (509) 963-3001. The university runs popular Elderhostel and Senior Ventures programs in the summer. A **Japanese Garden** near the center of campus is open year-round and contains interesting Japanese lanterns and grounds landscaped with dozens of types of plants, including cherry trees donated by the Japanese Consulate General. No charge.

Central Washington University's **Sarah Spurgeon Art Gallery,** tel. (509) 963-2665, has regional artists' and students' work displayed in Randall Hall; open Mon.-Fri. 7:30 a.m.-4:30 p.m. in the summer, longer in the school year.

Built in 1893-94, four-story **Barge Hall,** 8th and D at Central Washington University, is the oldest building on campus. The center of student life is the **Samuelson Union Building** (SUB), where visitors can shop for books at the largest bookstore in the area and eat at the cafeteria for the cheapest meals in town. Another building worth a visit is **Lind Hall,** which contains a huge relief map of the state of Washington and a two-story pendulum. The **CWU Library** contains more than 350,000 volumes. **Nicholson Pavilion** contains a gymnasium, fieldhouse, and other facilities beneath a unique cable-supported roof built to withstand earthquakes.

The CWU's **Chimpanzee & Human Communication Institute,** tel. (509) 963-2244, is where the world famous sign language chimps live. Begun in 1966, this research project now has five chimpanzees that use American Sign Language to communicate with humans and each other. It is a training center for students, a research center for scientists studying primate communication, and a visitor education facility. Visitors can attend hour-long **Chimposiums**

on Saturday mornings and Sunday afternoons for $10 adults, $7.50 students. Reservations are recommended; the center is not open to the public at other times.

Art Galleries

At 408½ N. Pearl (upstairs), the **Gallery One,** tel. (509) 925-2670, is open Mon.-Sat., with eight large exhibit and sales rooms surrounding a central atrium in the 1889 G.R. Stewart Building. It features works by some of the best regional artists. **Fairchild's,** 109 E. 6th Ave., tel. (509) 925-2326, is a print and gift shop located in an attractive Victorian home built in 1885. Other galleries (described above) are the Sarah Spurgeon Art Gallery on the EWU campus and the Clymer Museum and Gallery.

Parks

Four miles southeast of Ellensburg on Ferguson Rd., see one of the first Kittitas Valley farms at **Olmstead Place State Park,** tel. (509) 925-1943. The log cabin dates back to 1875; you can tour the eight buildings filled with old farming equipment, including a granary, dairy barn, and wagon shed, open Sat.-Sun. noon-4 p.m. between Memorial Day and Labor Day, or the rest of the year by appointment. The three-quarter mile **Altapes Creek Trail** leads from the red barn to the Seaton Cabin Schoolhouse, originally located farther away in a meadow; the kids didn't trudge miles through blizzards—they rode horseback.

Irene Rinehart Park, on the Yakima River off Umptanum Rd., is a welcome relief from the relentless summer sunshine. You can cool your toes in the swift green river, take a walk along shaded paths, or enjoy a riverside picnic. **Reed Park** at the end of Craig Ave. has a small shaded green for reading and relaxing, plus superb views of the county below and the snow-covered Stuart Range to the northwest.

ACCOMMODATIONS

Motels

See the lodging chart for a complete listing of local motels and B&Bs. Lodging can be very hard to come by during the Ellensburg Rodeo in early September, the Western Art show in May, and the Gorge Concerts on summer weekends.

ELLENSBURG ACCOMMODATIONS

Accommodations are arranged from least to most expensive. Rates may be lower during the winter months. The area code is 509.

MOTELS

Rainbow Motel; 1025 Cascade Way; tel. 925-3544; $35 s, $38 d; kitchenettes, AAA approved

I-90 Inn Motel; 1390 Dolarway Rd. (Exit 106 off I-90); tel. 925-9844; $36 s, $40 d; lake view, AAA approved

Thunderbird Motel; 403 W. 8th; tel. 962-9856 or (800) 843-3492; $38 s, $42 d; outdoor pool

Harold's Motel; 601 N. Water; tel. 925-4141; $39-45 s, $45-50 d; outdoor pool, kitchenettes, AAA approved

Nites Inn Motel; 1200 S. Ruby; tel. 962-9600; $40 s, $44 d; park-like grounds, AAA approved

Super 8 Motel; 1500 Canyon Rd.; tel. 962-6888 or (800) 800-8000; $49 s, $54 d; indoor pool, jacuzzi

Ellensburg Regal Lodge; 300 W. 6th Ave.; tel. 925-3116 or (800) 523-4972; $50 s, $60 d; indoor pool, kitchenettes, complimentary breakfast Mon.-Thurs., AAA approved

Best Western Ellensburg Inn; 1700 Canyon Rd., tel. 925-9801 or (800) 321-8791; $59 s, $64 d, indoor pool, sauna, jacuzzis, AAA approved

BED AND BREAKFASTS AND RANCHES

Surrey House Guest Rooms; 715 E. Capitol; tel. 962-9853; $48 s, $53 d; birthplace of artist John Clymer, continental breakfast

Murphy's Country B&B; 2830 Thorp Hwy. S; tel. 925-7986; $55 s, $60 d; 1915 country home, two guest rooms, shared bath, full breakfast, sweeping views, AAA approved

Circle H Holiday Ranch; 15 miles west; tel. 964-2000; $130-150 d in cabins with three meals in the summer, $110 d in cabins with breakfast in the winter, two night minimum, horseback rides $12.50/hour

Carriage House Cottage; 140 Rosebriar Lane; tel. 925-2108; $125 sleeps four; two-bedroom cottage, jacuzzi, sauna, garage, full kitchen, breakfast supplies

The Chamber of Commerce, tel. (509) 925-3137, keeps track of who has lodging space. Reservations should be made far in advance for these times, and before mid-January for the rodeo. Also be forewarned that rates may be considerably higher than those listed during this time. Central Washington University opens its residence halls and other facilities for lodging ($40-140 d) during the rodeo; call (800) 752-4379 for more information and reservations.

Campgrounds
The nearest public campground is 27 miles east at **Wanapum State Recreation Area** (see under "Wanapum Lake Area" in the Columbia Basin section). RV spaces are available at the **Kittitas County Fairgrounds** for $10 during the summer months; call (800) 637-2444 for details. More camping and RV spaces at **KOA Kampground,** in west Ellensburg, tel. (509) 925-9319.

FOOD

The Valley Cafe, 103 W. 3rd Ave., tel. (509) 925-3050, is a European-style bistro where you won't go wrong any meal of the day. Their breakfasts include all the standards, exceptionally well prepared. Stop for lunch at **Valley Take-Out** next door for wonderful sandwiches, distinctive salads, espresso, and tempting cheesecakes.

Then come back to the cafe for an evening dinner of Ellensburg lamb, seafood, steaks, chicken, or pasta. The attractive brick building was built in the 1930s.

Frazzini's Pizza Place, 716 E. 8th Ave., tel. (509) 925-9855, has quick food: pizzas, nachos, chicken hot wings, and a salad bar. Don't confuse it with **Frazz's Sports Emporium & Eatery,** a sports bar with family fare of steak, seafood, and a salad bar. More all-American food—notably prime rib on Friday and Saturday—at **The Blue Grouse,** 1401 N. Dolarway, tel. (509) 925-4808. Locals say **Main St. Steak House,** 207 N. Main St., tel. (509) 925-3180, grills the finest steaks in the Kittitas Valley.

International

For an elegant night out on the town, **Giovanni's on Pearl,** 1889 Davidson Bldg., 402 N. Pearl St., tel. (509) 962-2260, features Italian pastas, fresh fish, the famous Ellensburg lamb (the lamb kabobs are especially good), and great desserts. Open for lunch and dinner; closed Sunday.

Casa de Blanca, Canyon and Ruby Roads, tel. (509) 925-1693, has Mexican specialties and moderately priced American-style steak and prime rib. For Americanized Chinese food, including inexpensive lunch specials, try **China Inn,** 116 W. 3rd Ave., tel. (509) 925-4140.

Baked Goods, Espresso, and Produce

Get fresh baked breads, soups, salads, and unusual sweets at **Sweet Memories,** 319 N. Pearl, tel. (509) 925-4783. For an authentic Wild West cup of cowboy espresso, hop along to **Jaguar's,** 423 N. Pearl, tel. (509) 962-6081, where the seats are old saddles.

The **Kittitas County Farmers Market** comes to the corner of 6th and Anderson Wednesday 3-6 p.m., and Saturday 9 a.m.-noon from mid-June to early September.

SPORTS AND RECREATION

On the Water

Swim at the **Ellensburg City Pool,** 815 E. 6th Ave., tel. (509) 962-7211, where you'll also find a sauna, fitness center, and jacuzzi.

The Yakima River is a favorite place for floaters during the summer, and a great place to cool off when temperatures top 100° F. Much of the 40-mile stretch between Cle Elum and Roza Dam is a relaxing float, but you need to watch for dangerous sweepers and logs in the water. For specific put-in points and hazardous areas, check with the chamber of commerce visitor center. The most popular run is the 15 miles from Teanaway Bridge (below Cle Elum) to the diversion dam; it generally takes five to six hours. Rent rafts ($35-50) and kayaks ($15) for a do-it-yourself float from **River Raft Rentals,** tel. (509) 964-2145. They can also provide a equipment delivery service. The river is a popular fly-fishing place, as there are many large rainbow trout.

On Wheels

The Ellensburg area has an abundance of enjoyable backcountry roads for bike riding, along with more strenuous trips into the Cascades to the west. Rent bikes from **The Recycle Bicycle Shop,** 307 N. Main, tel. (509) 925-3326. **Mountain High Sports,** 105 E. 4th Ave., tel. (509) 925-2626, also rents mountain bikes, along with rollerblades, tents, climbing shoes, skis, backpacks, and other outdoor gear.

Ellensburg Equine Trolley, tel. (509) 962-1889, has stagecoach trips into the countryside, hay rides, sleigh rides, and other activities all year. For horseback rides, wagon train trips, and other old-West adventures, contact **Happy Trails Horseback Riding Ranch,** tel. (509) 925-9428.

Rockhounding

Kittitas County is the only place on Earth that you'll find the "Ellensburg Blue" agate. Most finds are made on private or leased land northwest of Ellensburg (you'll need permission to hunt there), but you can check Dry Creek, on Hwy. 97, or Horse Canyon Road. Here are the rules: no digging—surface hunting only; respect property lines and fences; and don't bother the cows. If you come up empty handed, Ellensburg stores sell the uncut stones as well as jewelry.

Elk Watching

Winter visitors to the Ellensburg area can watch around 750 elk at the feeding station in Joe Watt Canyon, 15 miles west of town. The elk are fed hay by the Washington Dept. of Wildlife.

Get here by heading west on I-90 to exit 102, then across the freeway and uphill a quarter mile. Turn right on Old Thorp Cemetery Rd. and follow it to Joe Watt Canyon Rd. where you turn left and continue a mile to the elk feeding site.

EVENTS AND ENTERTAINMENT

Events

Visit the **National Western Art Show and Auction,** tel. (509) 962-2934, the third weekend in May, for Western paintings. More than 200 artists display their works, and the Western Art Association reserves the entire Best Western Ellensburg Inn for the event, renting out rooms to various artists to display their work. Three auctions give you a chance to purchase your favorites, but the highlight for many is the "Quick Draw," when about a dozen artists each create a work of art in 45 minutes.

The **Whisky Dick Triathlon,** held annually in July, consists of a one-mile swim, 26-mile bicycle ride, and eight-mile run—not impossible, even though the swim is in the 60° F Columbia River and the bike leg climbs 1,900 feet in the first 12 miles. At least the running leg is on level ground! Contact the chamber of commerce, tel. (509) 925-3137, for specifics.

Labor Day weekend's **Ellensburg Rodeo** is one of the top rodeos in the nation, attracting cowboys from all over with a $100,000 purse. The rodeo has been around since 1923 and features calf roping, wild horse races, cliff races, Brahma bull riding, and wild cow milking during this four-day event. It's held in conjunction with the carnival, parade, exhibits, and top-notch country entertainment of the **Kittitas County Fair** at the fairgrounds at the east end of 6th Avenue. Rodeo tickets ($9-18) include admission to the fair; you should order far in advance by calling the Ellensburg Rodeo Ticket Office, tel. (509) 962-7831 or (800) 637-2444. Nearly all the tickets are gone for the weekend events by early August, and some folks reserve a year in advance.

Held in mid-September at Olmstead Place State Park, the **Threshing Bee** gives city slickers an opportunity to see blacksmithing, plowing, and steam and gas threshing. A big country breakfast is served in the morning, and an antique tractor pull contest is a highlight. Call (509) 925-3137 for details.

Theater

Central Washington University's **Laughing Horse Summer Theatre** presents four professional productions during July and August, in Tower Theatre at 8th Ave. and Anderson St. on the campus. For schedule information, call the box office at (509) 963-3400.

Nightlife

In addition to lounges at the **Thunderbird Motel,** 403 W. 8th, tel. (509) 962-9856, and the **Best Western Ellensburg Inn,** 1700 Canyon Rd. tel. (509) 925-9801, you can hear live music weekends at **The Buckboard,** 1302 S. Ruby, tel. (509) 925-9921.

INFORMATION AND SERVICES

All of Eastern Washington's **area code** is 509. The **Ellensburg Chamber of Commerce** is located at 436 N. Sprague, tel. (509) 925-3137. Hours are Mon.-Fri. 8 a.m.-5 p.m. year-round. **Kittitas Valley Community Hospital** is located at 603 S. Chestnut, tel. (509) 962-9841.

TRANSPORTATION

Ellensburg sits at the junction of I-90 and I-82. **Greyhound Bus Lines,** tel. (509) 925-1177 or (800) 231-2222, can get you out of town from their 801 Okanogan depot. **Northwestern Trailways,** tel. (800) 366-3830, stops at the Thunderbird Motel, with connections throughout the Northwest. The nearest commercial airport is in Yakima, 36 miles to the south.

YAKIMA

Yakima (pop. 58,000; pronounced "YA-ka-ma") is among the largest cities in Central Washington and the commercial hub of the Yakima Valley. The population includes a rapidly growing Hispanic community; by the end of the decade they are expected to represent more than half of the Yakima County population. Immediately north of Yakima is the Biblically named town of **Selah,** home to 5,100 people. Like neighboring Yakima, Selah is an agricultural center with fruit warehouses and strips of shopping malls and fast food joints. Seven miles north is the Army's **Yakima Training Center,** the premier training and weapons firing area in the Northwest (though some Seattle neighborhoods run a close second on the weapons firing claim). It covers more than 261,000 acres. **Union Gap** (pop. 3,100) is home to the biggest local shopping center, Valley Mall. **Wapato** (pop. 3,800) is a dozen miles southeast of Yakima in the middle of apple and other orchards and filled with huge fruit processing warehouses.

Yakima, a far cry weatherwise from its neighbors to the west, averages 300 sunny days per year with just eight inches of precipitation. The "wet" season—November through January—accounts for almost half of the annual rain or snowfall. Summer temperatures on the dry side of the mountains generally run 10 or more degrees higher than in Puget Sound cities, explaining why virtually every motel, no matter how cheap, has a pool. Despite the dry, brown hills surrounding the city, Yakima's suburbs are green, due to the constant chit-chit-chit of lawn sprinklers.

The Yakima Valley's volcanic soil is twice as productive as ordinary soil—teamed with irrigation and a 200-day growing season, it's hard to beat. The county ranks first in the nation in apples, winter pears, fruit trees, hops, and mint, with pears, grapes, cherries, peaches, and apricots as major crops. The largest local employers include many of the major fruit companies, including Tree Top, Del Monte, and Snokist.

HISTORY

Yakima-area Indians defended their ground, preventing any permanent white settlement here until the end of the 1855-57 Indian War. With the Indians' acceptance of the Yakama Reservation in 1858, pioneer cattlemen settled in the valley—farmers weren't interested in this arid region. In 1861, Fielding M. Thorpe and his wife Margaret became Yakima's first homesteaders. Dry soil was the area's biggest drawback, so in the 1860s Sebastian Lauber and Joseph and Charles Schamo built an irrigation ditch to shift some of the Yakima River's water into town, paving the way for agriculture.

In 1870, John W. Beck planted 50 apple trees and 50 peach trees in the region's first orchards, marking the end of the cattle era and the start of a major fruit industry.

Moving Yakima

With a population of 400, "Yakima City" was incorporated in 1883. The Northern Pacific Railroad had a problem acquiring land from some of the property owners, so they built their Yakima Valley station four miles north of town, offering to move the buildings at the railroad's expense, plus free land. Since the railroad couldn't come to the city, most townspeople put their houses on skids and rollers and moved the city to the railroad—in time to meet the first train pulling into town on December 14, 1884. The new town was officially called "North Yakima," but in 1919, representatives from North Yakima persuaded the state to amend the charter of Yakima City, forcing it to adopt the new name of Union Gap. Thus the original Yakima City lost its name to the upstart.

SIGHTS

Historical Sights

The North Front St. Historical District boasts some of Yakima's oldest buildings, including the 1898 Lund Building, which once housed a

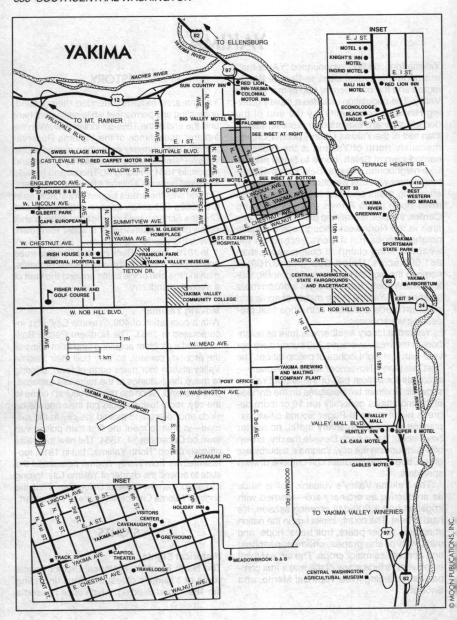

YAKIMA

TO ELLENSBURG

NACHES RIVER

YAKIMA RIVER

82

97

TO MT. RAINIER

12

FRUITVALE BLVD.

SUN COUNTRY INN

RED LION INN-YAKIMA
COLONIAL MOTOR INN

BIG VALLEY MOTEL

PALOMINO MOTEL

SEE INSET AT RIGHT

SWISS VILLAGE MOTEL

CASTLEVALE RD. RED CARPET MOTOR INN

N. 40th AVE.

ENGLEWOOD AVE.

'37 HOUSE B & B

W. LINCOLN AVE.

GILBERT PARK

CAFE EUROPEAN

SUMMITVIEW AVE.

H. M. Gilbert
HOMEPLACE

W. YAKIMA AVE.

W. CHESTNUT AVE.

IRISH HOUSE B & B

MEMORIAL HOSPITAL

FRANKLIN PARK

YAKIMA VALLEY MUSEUM

TIETON DR.

FISHER PARK AND
GOLF COURSE

YAKIMA VALLEY
COMMUNITY COLLEGE

W. NOB HILL BLVD.

40th AVE.

0   1 mi

0   1 km

W. MEAD AVE.

YAKIMA MUNICIPAL AIRPORT

POST OFFICE

W. WASHINGTON AVE.

S. 16th AVE.

AHTANUM RD.

WILLOW ST.

E. I ST.

FRUITVALE BLVD.

N. 5th AVE.

N. 16th AVE.

N. 6th AVE.

N. 1st ST.

N. 2nd ST.

N. 3rd ST.

SEE INSET AT BOTTOM

RED APPLE MOTEL

CHERRY AVE.

PIERCE AVE.

N. 18th AVE.

N. 26th AVE.

N. 33rd AVE.

E. LINCOLN AVE.

E. A ST.

E. YAKIMA AVE.

E. CHESTNUT AVE.

E. WALNUT AVE.

ST. ELIZABETH
HOSPITAL

FRONT ST.

S. 10th ST.

EXIT 33

TERRACE HEIGHTS DR.

410

BEST
WESTERN
RIO MIRADA

YAKIMA
RIVER
GREENWAY

YAKIMA
SPORTSMAN
STATE PARK

PACIFIC AVE.

82

YAKIMA
ARBORETUM

EXIT 34

24

CENTRAL WASHINGTON
STATE FAIRGROUNDS
AND RACETRACK

E. NOB HILL BLVD.

S. 1st ST.

S. 18th ST.

YAKIMA BREWING AND
MALTING
COMPANY PLANT

S. 3rd AVE.

VALLEY MALL BLVD.

VALLEY
MALL

HUNTLEY INN   SUPER 8 MOTEL

LA CASA MOTEL

GABLES MOTEL

GOODMAN RD.

TO YAKIMA VALLEY WINERIES

97

MEADOWBROOK B & B

CENTRAL WASHINGTON
AGRICULTURAL MUSEUM

82

INSET (top right)

INSET

E. J ST.

MOTEL 6

KNIGHT'S INN
MOTEL

INGRID MOTEL

E. I ST.

BALI HAI
MOTEL

RED LION INN

ECONOLODGE
BLACK
ANGUS

E. H ST.

N. 1st ST.

N. 2nd ST.

INSET (bottom)

INSET

E. LINCOLN AVE.

E. B ST.

E. A ST.

N. 6th ST.

N. 9th ST.

HOLIDAY INN

VISITORS
CENTER

CAVENAUGH'S

GREYHOUND

N. 1st ST.

N. 2nd ST.

N. 3rd ST.

YAKIMA MALL

TRACK 29

CAPITOL
THEATER

TRAVELODGE

FRONT ST.

E. CHESTNUT AVE.

E. WALNUT AVE.

MOON

© MOON PUBLICATIONS, INC.

saloon and brothel (now the Greystone Restaurant) directly across from the Northern Pacific Railroad depot.

Three miles northwest of Yakima on Hwy. 12 you'll find the mysterious **Indian Painted Rocks,** a state historical site. Although the pictographs were partially destroyed by an early irrigation flume, some remain at Naches Highway and Powerhouse Road.

The **Ahtanum Mission,** east of Yakima along Ahtanum Creek, was built in 1852 by Oblate priests. Though it burned down during the Yakama Indian wars of the 1850s, the church was rebuilt in 1869 and is still used. You can visit the mission and surrounding park for a small fee.

Museums

Start your visit to Yakima at the unusually spacious (50,000 square feet) and complete **Yakima Valley Museum,** 2105 Tieton Dr., tel. (509) 248-0747. This is one of the finest large museums in Washington, with an extraordinary collection of Yakama Indian clothing, beadwork, basketry, and artifacts, a replica of Chief Justice William O. Douglas's office (Douglas was a Yakima native son), and one of the finest collections of horse-drawn vehicles west of the Mississippi, from buckboard and carts to elaborate carriages. The display on Conestoga wagons and the Oregon Trail is particularly notable, as are the exhibits in the Yakima Valley's fruit tree industry and a hands-on exploratorium for kids. Local boys made good Phil and Steve Mahre have their Olympic gold and silver medals here; you might catch them skiing at White Pass, west of Yakima. The museum is open Mon.-Fri. 10 a.m.-5 p.m. and Sat.-Sun. noon-5 p.m. year-round; admission is $2.50 adults, $1.25 students and seniors, $5 families, free under age 10. They also have a gift shop with a fine collection of history books.

A block away from the museum is the **H. M. Gilbert Homeplace,** 2109 W. Yakima Ave., tel. (509) 248-0747, built in 1898 amidst 20 acres of sagebrush. Horace M. Gilbert was a farmer, land developer, and one of the pioneers in the irrigation of the Yakima Valley. You can tour his early Yakima Valley farm home on Friday 10 a.m.-3 p.m. March-Dec., and noon-4 p.m. on the first Sunday of each month. Entrance is $2.50 (includes access to the Yakima Valley Museum).

The **Yakima Electric Railway Museum,** 306 W. Pine St., tel. (509) 575-1700, was built in 1910 and is home to the local trolleys (see "Transportation," below) that connect Yakima and Selah. Inside are interpretive displays on the history of the trolleys. Open when the trolleys are running: weekends May-October.

The **World Famous Fantastic Museum,** 15 W. Yakima Ave., tel. (509) 575-0100, is a private collection of antique toys, Elvis Presley's 1957 pink Cadillac, Hollywood movie artifacts, 1962 Seattle World's Fair exhibits, and a miniature golf course. Open daily 10 a.m.-6 p.m.; fee charged.

Union Gap's **Central Washington Agricultural Museum,** tel. (509) 457-8735, displays tractors, pea pickers, threshers, wagons, balers, and other early Yakima Valley farm equipment on 15 acres in Fulbright Park. The collection is spread over more than a dozen buildings arranged in a semi-circle around a working windmill. A Burlington-Northern boxcar houses railroad memorabilia, and the Magness Room is a special treat, packed with more than 3,000 antique hand tools. The same building houses a small Grange museum and library. Most folks view this as a drive-through museum, taking their vehicles past the many open-sided buildings and stopping at those of interest. The main collection is open at any time, and the Magness Room is open daily 9 a.m.-5 p.m. An old WW I Army tank sits just outside the museum in Fulbright Park. A popular threshing bee is held here each August.

Wine and Beer

If you're a wine lover, visit **The Wine Cellar,** 15 W. Yakima Ave., tel. (509) 248-3590, for a good selection of Yakima Valley and other wines; staffed by a friendly, knowledgeable staff, the shop always has a few bottles open for you to taste. The small, family-run **Thurston Wolfe Winery** has a tasting room just a few doors away at 27 N. Front St., tel. (509) 452-0335. (See "Yakima Valley Wineries" under "Yakima Valley," below, for a visit to the many other wineries in Yakima Valley.)

In a region known for its wineries, it's easy for beer drinkers to feel left out—but there's a place here for you too! The **Yakima Brewing and Malting Co.,** 1803 Presson Place, tel. (509) 575-1900, became the nation's first microbrew-

DIANNE BOULERICE LYONS

view from Umtanum Ridge midway between Yakima and Ellensburg

ery when investors got a taste of Bert Grant's home brew in 1981. Grant's Scottish Ale launched the brewery and remains the flagship product, but they now also produce half-a-dozen others, including Grant's Imperial Stout (a Russian-style stout), India Pale Ale, and others from locally grown Cascade hops. Grant's even makes a surprisingly tasty hard cider. They continue to maintain a reputation for brewing some of the finest beers anywhere, in large part due to the personal control by Bert Grant and his refusal to let the business grow too large. Make reservations for their excellent, detailed brewery tours as far ahead as possible. Or stop by Grant's Brewery Pub, at 32 N. Front St. in the historic train depot, for a taste of their best.

Scenic Drives

Driving on I-82 between Ellensburg and Yakima, you'll realize that Central Washington isn't the flat desert wasteland that it's sometimes made out

to be—a desert wasteland, maybe, but not flat. As the road snakes up treeless ridges over 2,000 feet high, the brown hills in the distance look as if they're covered with velvet; up close, sagebrush dots the brown grass (in an imitation of a scruffy three-day beard). Pull in at the Viewpoint sign for broad vistas of green valley farmland below and the snowcapped Stuart Range to the north. Along the way, you'll cross the largest single concrete span bridge in North America. The **Fred Redmon Memorial Bridge** twin spans are 1,336 feet long and 330 feet high. Pull into the rest stop at the south end of the bridge for a striking view of the summits of Mt. Adams and Mt. Rainier.

The **Jacob Durr Wagon Road** (a.k.a. Wenas Rd.) was the only route linking Yakima and Ellensburg in the 1880s; today it's surely the most scenic, climbing over Umtanum Ridge for a 360-degree view of the Cascades and Yakima Valley. Drive north from Selah on N. Wenas Ave., which becomes Wenas Rd., the old Durr Wagon Road. The more standard route northward—I-90—also offers excellent vistas from the **Manatash Ridge Viewpoint** into the lush Kittitas Valley, with the Wenatchee Mountains rising behind the town of Ellensburg.

City Parks

The **Yakima River Greenway** encompasses 3,600 acres east of the city, connecting Selah, Yakima, and Union Gap along a 10-mile biking and walking path; almost half of this is paved.

The **Yakima Area Arboretum,** I-90 and Nob Hill Blvd., tel. (509) 248-7337, is a 70-acre park with a Japanese garden and bird sanctuary, and a small interpretive center, gift shop, and library. Open Sunday noon-4 p.m., Saturday 9 a.m.-4 p.m.

At **Eschbach Park,** five miles past the fish hatchery on the Old Naches Hwy., rent a tube ($1) and take a lazy float down the Yakima River. The day-use, 175-acre county park offers boating, swimming, picnicking, and play areas.

Randall Park, south of Nob Hill Blvd. on S. 48th Ave., has a picnic area, nature trails, duck pond, and creek on 38 grassy acres. **Franklin Park,** behind the museum at Tieton Dr. and 20th Ave., has tennis courts, a swimming pool, and grassy hills for romping or winter sledding.

Across the Yakima River from Union Gap, **Moxee Bog,** a spring-fed preserve, is home to a rare breed of monarch butterfly that feeds on the violets that grow here. Birders will want to visit the **Boise Cascade Bird Sanctuary** in the Wenas Valley, five miles west of Selah on Wean Road. The corporation donated 40 acres for the sanctuary where over 100 species of birds have been sighted.

Cowiche Canyon is a scenic and remote rocky canyon just a few minutes west of Naches. An almost-level trail follows the old railroad route along and across Cowiche Creek as it winds past distinctive rock formations, some that resemble the Easter Island faces. The canyon is managed by Cowiche Canyon Conservancy,

tel. (509) 966-8608, which produces a brochure on the three-mile trail.

ACCOMMODATIONS

Most of Yakima's motels can be found along the Hwy. 97 corridor through town (1st Street). See the chart for a list of these and other lodging places in Yakima. Several cheaper places on the south end of Union Gap are not listed, but may be acceptable if you're desperate enough.

Bed and Breakfasts
Birchfield Manor, tel. (509) 452-1960, is out in the country two miles east of town with five

---

YAKIMA AREA ACCOMMODATIONS

Accommodations are arranged from least to most expensive. Rates may be lower during the winter months. The area code is 509.

BED AND BREAKFASTS

Irish House B&B; 210 S. 28th Ave.; tel. 453-5474; $55 s, $60 d Fri.-Sat., $50 s, $55 d Sun.-Thurs.; 1903 Victorian farmhouse, three antique-furnished guest rooms, shared baths, light breakfast, no kids under 12

'37 House B&B; 4002 Englewood Ave.; tel. 965-5537; $59-108 s, $65-120 d; elegant 1937 home, six guest rooms, shared baths, stone fireplaces, garden, tennis court, full breakfast, AAA approved

Meadowbrook B&B; 1010 Meadowbrook Rd.; tel. 248-2387; $69 s, $79 d; country location, panoramic views, four guest rooms, private or shared baths, full breakfast, no children

Birchfield Manor; 2018 Birchfield Rd.; tel. 452-1960; $70-100 s or d; 1910 Victorian farmhouse, outdoor pool, indoor jacuzzi, five antique-filled guest rooms, private baths, gourmet breakfast

MOTELS

Gables Motel; 3107 Main St., Union Gap; tel. 453-0218; $25-30 s or d

Bali Hai Motel; 710 N. 1st St.; tel. 452-7178; $25-30 s, $30-35 d; outdoor pool, AAA approved

La Casa Motel; 2703 S. 1st St., Union Gap; tel. 457-6147; $32 s, $40 d; outdoor pool

Palomino Motel; 1223 N. 1st St.; tel. 452-6551; $33 s, $37 d; kitchenettes available

Motel 6; 1104 N. 1st St.; tel. 891-6161 or (800) 466-8356; $34 s, $40 d; outdoor pool

Red Carpet Motor Inn; 1608 Fruitvale Blvd.; tel. 457-1131; $34-37 s, $38-41 d; outdoor pool, sauna, kitchenettes available, AAA approved

Red Apple Motel; 416 N. 1st St.; tel. 298-7150; $35 s, $43 d Sun.-Thurs., $38 s, $48 d Fri.-Sat.; outdoor pool

Knight's Inn Motel; 1022 N. 1st St.; tel. 453-5615; $36 s, $38 d Sun.-Thurs., or $48 s, $50 d Fri.-Sat.

Ingrid Motel; 803 N. 1st St.; tel. 248-9120; $38 s, $45 d; kitchenettes $7 extra

(continues on next page)

YAKIMA AREA ACCOMMODATIONS

(continued)

Econo Lodge; 510 N. 1st St.; tel. 457-6155 or (800) 446-6900; $40 s, $45 d; outdoor pool, AAA approved

Colonial Motor Inn; 1405 N. 1st St.; tel. 453-8981; $41 s, $47 d; indoor pool, two jacuzzis, continental breakfast, AAA approved

Big Valley Motel; 1504 N. 1st St.; tel. 248-3393 or (800) 248-3360; $46 s, $51 d Sun.-Thurs., $62 s or d Fri.-Sat.; outdoor pool

Super 8 Motel; 2605 Rudkin Rd.; Union Gap; tel. 248-8880 or (800) 800-8000; $46 s, $52 d; indoor pool

Huntley Inn; 12 Valley Mall Blvd., Union Gap; tel. 248-6924 or (800) 448-5544; $48-53 s, $56-64 d; outdoor pool, free continental breakfast, free airport shuttle, AAA approved

Days Inn Motor Inn; 2408 Rudkin Rd., Union Gap; tel. 248-9700 or (800) 329-7466; $50 s or d; outdoor pool, free airport shuttle

Travelodge; 110 S. Naches Ave.; tel. 453-7151 or (800) 255-3050; $50 s or d; outdoor pool

Best Western Rio Mirada Motor Inn; 1603 Terrace Heights Dr.; tel. 457-4444 or (800) 521-3050; $51 s, $56 d; on the river, jacuzzi, outdoor pool, exercise facilities, kitchenettes available, free airport shuttle, all rooms have river views, AAA approved

Sun Country Inn; 1700 N. 1st St.; tel. 248-5650; $52-66 s, $57-67 d; outdoor pool, sauna, kitchenettes available, free continental breakfast, AAA approved

Red Lion Inn; 818 N. 1st St.; tel. 453-0391 or (800) 733-5466; $59-69 s, $69-79 d; outdoor pool, AAA approved

Holiday Inn; 9 N. 9th St.; tel. 452-6511 or (800) 465-4329; $61-78 s or d; outdoor pool, jacuzzi, kitchenettes available, free airport shuttle, AAA approved

Cavanaugh's at Yakima Center; 607 E. Yakima Ave.; tel. 248-5900 or (800) 843-4667; $57-90 s, $67-90 d; two pools, free airport shuttle, AAA approved

Red Lion Inn/Yakima Valley; 1507 N. 1st St.; tel. 248-7850 or (800) 547-8010; $77-84 s, $87-94 d; two pools, jacuzzi, free airport shuttle, AAA approved

comfortable rooms with chandeliers and antiques, private baths, a pool, and an indoor jacuzzi. This Victorian home was built in 1910 and is surrounded by parklike grounds. Meals are scrumptious, and dinners are some of the finest around.

Irish House B&B, tel. (509) 453-5474, located at a 1903 Victorian farmhouse in one of Yakima's finest neighborhoods, has three antique-furnished guest rooms. Out back is the second largest black walnut tree in Washington.

The **'37 House,** tel. (509) 965-5537, is an attractive three-story Dutch Colonial home that is now a B&B. Built in 1937, it contains a curved stairway, six guest rooms with shared baths, English garden, tennis court, stone fireplaces, and a knotty-pine library.

Meadowbrook B&B, tel. (509) 248-2387, is a newer Dutch Colonial style ridgetop home. The spacious grounds provide fine views across the cherry and apple orchards of Yakima Valley. It has four guest rooms, two with private baths.

Campgrounds

About a mile east of town off I-82, **Yakima Sportsman State Park** has a stocked pond for kids to fish—adults can try their luck in the nearby Yakima River—plus tent sites ($11) and RV hookup sites ($16) along the greenbelt; a great spot to escape the summer heat. Coin-operated showers are available; open year-round. Call (800) 452-5687 for campsite reservations ($6 extra fee), available up to 11 months ahead of time. The **Boise Cascade Bird Sanctuary** in the Wenas Valley, five miles west of Selah on Wean Rd., also has a campground.

Yakima area RV parks include: **Circle H Ranch RV Park,** 1107 S. 18th St., tel. (509) 457-3683; **KOA Kampground,** 1500 Keyes Rd., tel. (509) 248-5882; **Stagecoach RV Park,** northwest of Yakima at Wenas Lake, tel. (509) 697-5431; **Trailer Inns,** 1610 N. 1st St., tel. (509) 452-9561. The most elaborate local RV park is **Yakima Nation RV Park,** tel. (509) 865-2000, in Toppenish.

FOOD AND DRINK

Breakfast and Lunch
Start your day out in suburbia at **Cafe European,** 3105 Summitview, tel. (509) 248-5844, with eggs Florentine, waffles with strawberries, or fresh-baked pastries and espresso. The adjacent bakery has tables where you can relax with a fresh scone or croissant and coffee. The carrot cake is heavenly, but decidedly not fat free. Great lunches here too. Another popular coffee shop (meet the cops and lawyers here) is **City Espresso/Country Charm,** 25 N. Front St., tel. (509) 248-2483.

Mel's Diner, 314 N. 1st St., tel. (509) 248-5382, is the local greasy spoon popular for breakfast and lunch. Another good place for lunch is **'37 House,** 4002 Englewood Ave., tel. (509) 965-5537, with sandwiches, salads, soups, stir fry, and pasta served in an historic inn. Also of note is **Jack-Son's Sports Bar,** 432 S. 48th Ave., tel. (509) 966-4340, a fun place with burgers, sandwiches, and a big screen TV.

Pulse Foods, 4315 Main St. in Union Gap, tel. (509) 452-5386, has earthy fresh breads, vitamins, and health foods.

American
Marti's Cafe, 1601 Terrace Heights Rd., tel. (509) 248-2062, overlooking the Yakima River, serves everything from steak to seafood to pizza. They also have a fine bakery. More all-American steak and seafood at **Restaurant at the Airport,** tel. (509) 248-4710, located—where else—but the airport. They also have a popular Sunday brunch. Another fine steak house is **Black Angus,** 501 N. Front St., tel. (509) 248-4540, where you'll find a free happy hour spread weeknights.

Two very good burger joints are: **Miner's Drive-In,** 2415 S. 1st St., tel. (509) 457-8194, and **Lariat Bar-B-Q,** 621 W. Yakima Ave., tel. (509) 248-0888, and 1205 N. 1st St., tel. (509) 453-2733. **Settler's Inn,** 1406 N. 1st St., tel. (509) 453-9060, is a family place with good breakfasts and outstanding pies.

One of Yakima's finest eating places is **Birchfield Manor,** tel. (509) 452-1960, a restored 1910 farmhouse two miles east of the city on Birchfield Rd. that also serves as a luxurious B&B. Dinners ($25) are served Thurs.-Sat., complemented by a vast selection of Yakima Valley wines. This is a formal restaurant with innovative cuisine that changes seasonally.

In the historic district, **The Greystone Restaurant,** 5 N. Front St., tel. (509) 248-9801, has moderately priced Northwest cuisine, fresh seafood, and homemade pasta in an elegant atmosphere; open for dinner only Tues.-Saturday.

The best local pizzas are at **Mr. C's Pizza & Spaghetti House,** 12 S. 3rd Ave., tel. (509) 453-2765.

International Food
For delicious (but pricey) Italian food and Northwest specialties, try **Gasparetti's,** 1013 N. 1st St., tel. (509) 248-0628; open for dinner only Tues.-Saturday. The pastas are all freshly made, and desserts are a real treat.

Despite the name, **Deli de Pasta,** 7 N. Front St., tel. (509) 453-0571, isn't a deli but does offer excellent fresh pastas and other Italian specialties such as Chicken Parmesan and Shrimp Primavera. It has a good Yakima Valley wine list too.

Santiago's, 111 E. Yakima Ave., tel. (509) 453-1644, is a lively and very popular Mexican restaurant with all the standards and excellent daily specials. **Tequilla's,** Yakima Ave. and N. 1st St., serves Mexican dishes for lunch and dinner daily in two restored 1920s railroad cars; enjoy a beer and appetizers on their sunny patio.

For Cantonese and American cuisine, try the **Golden Wheel,** 9 S. 1st St., tel. (509) 457-8400, or **Golden Moon Restaurant,** 1527 Summitview Ave., tel. (509) 575-7563. Get authentic Japanese food, including fresh sushi, at **Ichiban,** 1107 Tieton Dr., tel. (509) 248-2585. **Mustard Seed Cafe,** 402 E. Yakima Ave., tel. (509) 576-

8013, has a blend of menu items from all over Asia. **Siam House Restaurant,** 110 S. 4th St., tel. (509) 248-5565, serves authentic Thai cuisine.

Brewpub

Visit **Grant's Brewery Pub** in the historic train depot at 32 N. Front St., tel. (509) 575-2922, where you'll find at least five different brews on tap at all times, plus British bangers, Scotch eggs, fish and chips, burgers, and other tasty pub grub. No smoking. (See "Wine and Beer" under "Sights," above, for tours of the Yakima Brewing and Malting Co. brewery where these great beers are produced.)

Produce

There are fresh fruit and vegetable stands and U-pick places throughout the Yakima Valley that offer seasonal produce; get a complete listing from the Yakima Valley Visitors and Convention Bureau, or just head down Highways 97 and 22 till something looks interesting. Right on the west edge of town is **Johnson Orchards,** 4906 Summitview Ave., tel. (509) 966-7479. **Donald Fruit & Mercantile,** in Wapato, tel. (509) 877-3115, is a working orchard with produce (12 kinds of peaches at various times of the summer) and gourmet foods and gifts. At **Spring Creek Ranch,** 3213 Tacoma St. in Union Gap, tel. (509) 248-6621, you can wander among the 800 acres of vegetables and flowers to harvest your own tomatoes, strawberries, peppers, pumpkins, and other vegetables and fruits in season. They also have a petting zoo where kids can meet farm animals and a duck pond with mallards. Many other places offer fresh fruits and veggies throughout the summer months.

SPORTS AND RECREATION

Cycling and Swimming

The Yakima Valley farming country makes for great back-roads cycling, with a multitude of possible loop trips. Rent mountain and tandem bikes, and rafts, kayaks, and canoes from **Richies River Rentals,** tel. (509) 453-2112. They also offer a river shuttle service for folks floating the Yakima River. (See "Sports and

Recreation" under Ellensburg, below, for raft trips down the Upper Yakima.) **Sagebrush Cycles,** 14061/2 Fruitvale Blvd., tel. (509) 248-5393, also rents mountain and road bikes.

Yakima contains five public pools; four are outdoors and open only in the summer, and one indoor pool at **Lions Park** is open all year (the **Franklin Park** pool has a spiral water slide). Call (509) 575-6020 for details. The **YMCA,** 5 N. Naches Ave., tel. (509) 248-1202, has a complete sports facility with gyms, handball courts, an indoor jogging track, exercise equipment, and indoor pool. The nearby town of Wapato also has a fine Olympic-sized outdoor pool in the city park.

Golf

Yakima has four public golf courses: **Sun Tides,** 2215 Pence, tel. (509) 966-9065, eight miles west of town on Hwy. 12; **Fisher Golf Course,** S. 40th Ave. and W. Arlington, tel. (509) 575-6075; **Apple Tree Golf Course,** 8804 Occidental Rd., tel. (509) 966-5877; and **Westwood Golf Course,** 6408 Tieton Dr., tel. (509) 966-0890.

Spectator Sports

The **Yakima Valley SunDome,** a concrete-covered facility that opened in 1990, is home to the Yakima SunKings basketball team, along with various sporting and concert events all year. It is located at the fairgrounds. **Yakima County Stadium** is nearby and is home to the Yakima Bears professional baseball team (a class A affiliate of the L.A. Dodgers).

ENTERTAINMENT

Music

Every Tuesday evening during July and August, you'll find free **Something for Everyone Concerts** at Robertson Amphitheater in Sarg Hubbard Park, with country, folk, Mexican, blues, and jazz music. The **Yakima Community Band** has free concerts on Wednesday evenings from mid-July to mid-August in Randall Park.

The smoke-free **Grant's Pub Brewery,** 32 N. Front St., tel. (509) 575-2922, has live jazz and blues on weekends and occasional folk groups. Great brews, too. For live pop and rock music try **Colours Nightclub,** 216 W. Yakima Ave., tel. (509) 575-7892; **Johnny's Lounge** in the Cavanaugh's Inn at 607 E. Yakima, tel. (509) 248-5900; and **Premier Pub,** 5625 Summitview Ave., tel. (509) 965-9757. Hear country and western tunes at **Colby's,** 7200 W. Nob Hill Blvd., tel. (509) 965-9659; and **Country Connection,** 115 E. Naches Ave., Selah, tel. (509) 697-5533.

Theater and Cinema

The historic **Capitol Theater** at 19 S. 3rd St., tel. (509) 575-6267, first opened its doors in 1920 featuring vaudeville and feature films. Today the beautifully restored and elegant theater hosts a full schedule of theatrical productions nearly year-round.

Yakima is one of few cities where you can still find drive-ins; in fact, they have two: **Country Drive-In,** 4309 W. Nob Hill, tel. (509) 966-5340, and **Fruitvale Triple Drive-In,** 1819 Fruitvale, tel. (509) 248-3650. Indoor theaters include **Uptown Plaza** at 202 E. Chestnut, tel. (509) 248-0245; **Mercy 6-Plex** at the Valley Mall, tel. (509) 248-0242; and **Yakima Cinema,** 1305 N. 16th Ave., tel. (509) 248-0243.

EVENTS

Selah's **Community Days** starts the summer off with a festival that's been going on for three quarters of a century. Held the third weekend of May, it includes a parade, beauty pageant, pancake feed, dancing, bingo, golf tournament, and local entertainment. The **Yakima Air Fair** in late May is one of the larger air shows in this part of Washington—all sorts of aircraft converge on the Yakima airport.

The **Tinowit International Pow Wow** comes to Yakima in mid-June and brings Indian dancing and other events. Held in mid-June at the Central Washington State Fairgrounds on Fair Ave., the **Washington State Open Horse Show** is one of the largest in the country. Another mid-June event is the **Union Gap Kite and Flight Festival,** which attracts kite enthusiasts from all over the region.

The most popular fairgrounds event is the **Central Washington State Fair,** held in late September, which features a PRCA champi-

onship rodeo, carnival, country music, and all sorts of agricultural displays. It attracts well over 300,000 visitors each year. The **Washington State Pioneer Power Show** on the third weekend of August attracts thousands of folks to the Central Washington Agricultural Museum for an old-time threshing bee and working displays of farm equipment.

For quarter-horse and thoroughbred racing, check out **Yakima Meadows Racetrack** at the fairgrounds on Fair Avenue. With the closing of Renton's Longacres Park, this is the only one-mile race track remaining in Washington (a new park in Auburn is under construction). The horses run all year; call (509) 248-3920 for details.

The **Yakima Speedway,** tel. (509) 248-0647, 1600 Pacific Ave., has Nascar racing every Saturday night April 9 to October 2. More cars at the **Yakima Northwest Nationals** car show and rod run held the first weekend in August. It's the largest gathering of vintage cars in the Northwest.

Labor Day weekend means the **Wapato Harvest Festival** with a small-town parade, carnival rides, food and concession booths, and musical entertainment.

The **Great Yakima Duck Race** is a popular raffle event where hundreds of rubber duckies float down the Yakima River in early October. Top prize is $20,000, so it pays to plunk down $5 for a duck.

SHOPPING

Usually the giant covered shopping malls are found in suburbia, but Yakima's biggest shopping center is in the heart of downtown: the **Yakima Mall** has over 75 shops including The Bon Marché, Nordstrom, JCPenney, and Mervyn's, plus 1,200 covered parking spaces to keep your car cool. At Yakima Ave. and N. 1st, a trainfull of 22 old railroad cars house the **Track 29 Shopping Mall** where you'll find gift shops and eateries. Many more places—including the largest collection of antique pedal cars on the West Coast—can be found in antique shops inside the adjacent **Yesterday's Village.** Just over the line into Union Gap, **Valley Mall** on S. 1st St. has 44 stores including Sears, Lamonts, and PayLess.

Art galleries abound in Yakima. Visit **Gallery Gage,** 1007 N. 1st St., **Warehouse Gallery** and **The Attic** at 5000 W. Lincoln, and **House of Art,** 3509 Summitview.

INFORMATION AND SERVICES

For maps, brochures, and current festival information, contact the **Yakima Valley Visitors and Convention Bureau,** 10 N. 8th St., tel. (509) 575-1300 or (800) 221-0751. Hours are Mon.-Fri. 8:30 a.m.-5 p.m. and Sat.-Sun. 9 a.m.-5 p.m. April-Oct.; and Mon.-Fri. 8:30 a.m.-5 p.m. and Saturday 9 a.m.-3 p.m. Nov.-March. If they are closed, stop next door at Cavanaugh's for brochures.

The **area code** from Chinook Pass to the eastern border of Washington is 509. Post offices are located at 205 W. Washington and 112 S. 3rd Avenue. For medical emergencies, contact **Yakima Valley Memorial Hospital,** 2811 Tieton Dr., tel. (509) 575-8000, or **St. Elizabeth Hospital,** 110 S. 9th Ave., tel. (509) 575-5060.

TRANSPORTATION

By Car

Coming from Seattle, the fastest and best winter or bad-weather route to Yakima is on I-90 over Snoqualmie Pass, turning south onto I-82 in Ellensburg. If you have time to spare, the routes through or near Mount Rainier National Park are more scenic. In the best weather, pick up Hwy. 410 in Enumclaw and follow it through the park and over two mountain passes; or continue south from Cayuse Pass onto Hwy. 123, then go east on Hwy. 12 over White Pass (see "Vicinity of Mount Rainier"). Before you try these routes in winter, phone (509) 976-7623 for pass conditions Nov.-March.

Getting oriented after you've arrived in Yakima can be difficult until you figure out the system. North Front St., along the railroad tracks, di-

vides the downtown area; from here, street numbers ascend, starting with "1," in both directions, leading to a confusing situation in which 6th St. and 6th Ave. are 12 blocks apart.

Here's the key: "streets" are on the east side; "avenues" are on the west. East Yakima Ave. runs perpendicular to N. Front St. and divides the numbered streets into north and south sections, e.g., S. 2nd Street. Simple?

By Air

The **Yakima Municipal Airport** off Washington Ave. is the largest in the area, served by **Horizon Airlines,** tel. (800) 547-9308, and **United Express,** tel. (509) 457-3368 or (800) 241-6522.

By Trolley

Ride the Yakima Trolley Line's restored trolley cars on the two-hour ride through orchards, over the Naches River to the town of Selah and back. The trolley cars were first brought to Yakima in 1930 and operated till 1947. Service returned in 1989 when the original cars were leased from a railroad museum in Snoqualmie. The two trolley cars depart several times a day on weekends from the Yakima Electric Railway Museum at 306 W. Pine St., late April to Labor Day. Fares are $4 adults, $3 for seniors, $2.50 for kids, or $12 for the whole brood; call (509) 575-1700 for recorded information.

By Bus

Yakima Transit, tel. (509) 575-6175, has 10 routes serving the Yakima area, including the municipal airport. Fares are just 35 cents for adults and 20 cents for kids, and the buses run Mon.-Fri. 5:30 a.m. to 6:30 p.m. and Saturday 7 a.m. to 6:30 p.m.

To get out of town or across the country, hop aboard **Greyhound** from their station at 602 E. Yakima Ave., tel. (509) 457-5131 or (800) 231-2222. **Northwestern Trailways,** tel. (800) 366-3830, also has bus connections throughout the Northwest.

TOPPENISH

Located 18 miles southeast of Yakima, Toppenish (TOP-pen-ish; pop. 7,500) has a comfortable Western flavor and an unusual mix of cultures that is approximately 65% Hispanic and 20% Indian. The prosperous center of town is made even more attractive by an outdoor mural program that has resulted in more than 35 wall murals of superior quality. At least another dozen are in the planning stages.

The town name comes from the Indian word "Thappahn-ish," which means, more or less, "People of the trail that comes from the foot of the hills." Its name was committed to maps, again more or less, by Capt. George McClellan when he wandered through in 1853. He spelled it "Sahpenis," which was written on maps as "Toppenish."

Yakama Indian Reservation

Toppenish is the home of the Yakama Indian Agency and the commercial center for the 1.37 million-acre Yakama Indian Reservation. (Note: The tribal council decided in 1994 that the correct spelling for their tribe is "Yakama," rather than "Yakima," hence the spelling differences. And no, Dan Quayle had nothing to do with the change.) The reservation reaches from Grandview on the east to the slopes of 12,276-foot

Mt. Adams and is home to approximately 5,000 native people from 14 different tribes and bands, along with another 20,000 non-Indians. It was established by the 1855 Walla Walla Treaty and originally covered much of central Washington before other sections were ceded to the U.S. government. Employment on the reservation comes mainly in farming, lumber, and cattle ranching.

As you're driving near the reservation, keep an eye out for UFOs! The Yakama Indian Reservation made the ever-reliable *National Enquirer* in late 1986 because of their alleged high frequency of UFO sightings, reportedly "an everyday part" of their culture. (And as an historical aside, the very first UFO sighting reported to officials was in the Mt. Rainier area.)

SIGHTS

Yakama Nation Cultural Center

The Yakama Nation Cultural Center, tel. (509) 865-2800, features a museum that tells the story of the Yakama Nation from its beginnings to the present; a library specializing in Indian books; a theater that presents first-run movies and stage productions; a restaurant; and an RV park. The

Rosalie Harry and Annie May of the Yakima tribe

McCLELLAN SUCCEEDS AT FAILURE

Anyone who thinks military blundering began this century would be well advised to study the careers of several Union Army generals just before and during the Civil War. A good place to start would be with the career of George Brinton McClellan.

The Secretary of War at that time was Jefferson Davis, who would soon become President of the Confederacy. But for the time being he was in a responsible job in Franklin Pierce's cabinet. When Millard Fillmore was leaving the presidency, one of his last acts was to create the Washington Territory, and when Pierce came into office, one of his first official acts was to appoint Major Isaac Ingalls Stevens the governor of the territory. He instructed Stevens to go overland to his new post all the while surveying a railroad route from the Great Lakes to Puget Sound. Stevens left with 240 soldiers, engineers, and naturalists. He and his crew explored a wide swath of the countryside, some 400 miles wide, and more than 2,000 miles long.

Jefferson Davis didn't like this activity because he didn't want a railroad built across the northern part of the country for fear it would interfere with his plan for a confederacy of southern slave states. Davis tried to stop Stevens, but the little soldier and statesman would have none of it. He wanted the railroad, and he opposed slavery.

Davis came up with an alternate plan: he would prove there was no practical route for a railroad through the Cascades. Davis didn't dare try to disprove the routes through the Rockies because this range was too familiar to too many people. But the Cascades were *terra incognito* to most Americans. Davis sent McClellan out to explore the Cascades while Stevens was occupied with the Rockies. McClellan was told to report directly to Davis, in spite of his being under Stevens' jurisdiction. McClellan proved to be good at not finding things, and in his report wrote, "There is nothing to be seen but mountain piled upon mountain, rugged and impassable."

He reached Fort Vancouver on June 27, 1853, where he found Captain Ulysses S. Grant busy working in his potato patch. McClellan was disgusted to see an officer doing such menial labor, and he took an instant dislike to Grant. (The dislike lasted into the Civil War, when McClellan arrested Grant after his victory at Fort Donelson, a battle that had turned the direction of the war.) It took McClellan three weeks to assemble 66 men, 73 saddle horses, 100 pack horses, and 46 mules. On July 18 he finally left Fort Vancouver on his quest not to find the passes. They traveled 1.75 miles, set up camp, and sat there for three days before moving on.

When they struck out again, they went six miles this time before setting up camp, and this hectic

---

museum is centered around a 76-foot-tall tepee-shaped building and contains fine dioramas on the sad history of the Yakama peoples. History is presented from a Yakama perspective, emphasizing how their land was stolen and divided up, how Indian children were sent off to boarding schools to destroy their heritage, and how their Celilo Falls fishing grounds near the present-day Dalles Dam were destroyed by the damming of the Columbia River. Especially interesting are the time ball—used to record events and to recount stories—and the huge winter lodge and sweathouse in the center. A visit to this outstanding museum is an eye-opening experience, revealing what happens when a people's culture is ripped away from them and they are dumped into a new system.

The museum's library contains the collection of 10,000 books from **Nipo Stongheart,** who

began his show-business career with Buffalo Bill's Wild West Show at the age of 11 and went on to star in many Hollywood Westerns. Born in White Swan, Nipo was the grandson of a Hudson's Bay Company trader and was given an honorary Yakama tribal membership in 1950. He died in 1966 and is buried on the reservation.

The museum is open daily 9 a.m.-5 p.m. all year; admission costs $4 adults, $2 seniors and kids ages seven to 10, 75 cents for children under seven, or $10 for the family.

Murals
The dozens of murals covering Toppenish walls are a very popular attraction, and the chamber of commerce produces a free guide describing the various scenes. **Old Timers Plaza** downtown is bordered by two long murals and has an old wagon, along with a bronze sculpture of an In-

pace took them 25 miles in seven days. For the rest of July and into August McClellan averaged a little more than three miles a day when normal travelers would have averaged around 25 miles a day. The historian Robert Cantwell estimated that if the people crossing the plains on the Oregon Trail had traveled at that pace, it would have taken them six years, instead of five months, to get to the Oregon Country.

McClellan was just doing his job, and it took careful planning to avoid all the 11 passes the Indians used to cross the mountains. It was well known that the Hudson's Bay Company routinely drove cattle through Snoqualmie Pass. When it appeared they might stumble onto a route, Mcclellan would swing wide to avoid it. Thus, rather than going along the west side of Mt. Adams, he led his party east so they could go around the southern side, and swing down south so that they ended up at Goose Lake, out on the plains. McClellan took his party farther east, and by the time they reached about where the town of Yakima would later be built, they were out of food, in part because McClellan had only three hunters to supply 66 men. They were in luck because a Catholic mission had been there several years and McClellan and his men almost swept the priests' cupboards bare. They also bought some cattle from the Indians who lived around the mission, and the next several days were spent butchering the cattle and jerking the meat to preserve it for the rest of the trip.

It took them 11 days to get ready, and by now it was almost September. McClellan divided his force and instructed one group to head north toward Canada in search of a route up there, while two other groups were sent back to the Columbia River. He sent still another group over Naches Pass, which McClellan knew existed but also knew it was too dangerous for a railroad. After dividing his party into so many pieces, that left him and his personal escort to explore the Cascades for a pass, and that apparently was what the exercise was all about: he wanted to not find the passes without too many witnesses. He passed by every route across the Cascades, and went as far north as Stevens Pass. He went by Chinook Pass, Stampede Pass, White Pass, Cowlitz Pass, Carleton Pass, Hart's Pass, Cascade Pass, Cispus Pass, and Twisp Pass. He thus determined that only two routes went through the mountains: the Thompson River far up in Canada, and the Columbia.

Governor Stevens was infuriated at McClellan's report and sent Abiel Tinkham over Snoqualmie Pass in the dead of winter. Tinkham snowshoed across the pass, then turned around and snowshoed back home.

McClellan went on to become a total failure as a general in the Civil War. Stevens was killed in the war, and Grant, of course, came into his own late in the war and won it for the Union. It wasn't long before several railroads went through the Cascades at several places, and trails were followed by wagon roads, then highways. None of these routes bear the name of McClellan.

dian woman gathering hops. For a rolling visit past the murals, take one of the wagon tours ($7.50-12.50) offered by **Conestoga Tours,** tel. (509) 865-2898, that leave the Cultural Center. **Double JJ Ranch,** tel. (509) 697-3385, offers carriage rides and horse-drawn trolley tours of the murals.

Toppenish Museum

This small but impressive museum is upstairs in the library building at 1 S. Elm St., tel. (509) 865-4510. Inside is the surprising Estelle Reel Meyer collection of Native American basketry and beadwork, including a war bonnet of eagle feathers found on the battlefield of Custer's last stand. (One of the first women to hold a federal job, she collected these pieces during her travels as Superintendent of Indian Affairs from 1898 to 1910.) Also here are exhibits on the cattle industry in the valley, a gorgeous quilt filled with local brands, and such oddities as an egg sorter, a curtain stretcher, and gold pans. Open Tues.-Thurs. 1:30-4:30 p.m., and Fri.-Sat. 2-4:30 p.m. (closed Sunday, Monday, and holidays). Admission is $1.50 adults, 50 cents for children.

American Hop Museum

Hops—a vital bittering ingredient in the production of beer and ale—have been grown in America for almost 400 years and in the Northwest since the 1860s. Today, Yakima Valley is one of the major hop-growing regions in the world, accounting for 75% of the total U.S. production. Despite its importance to beer drinkers, few people know what hops are, let alone have ever seen hop vines. (By the way, did you know that hops and marijuana come from the same plant family?)

THE RAWHIDE RAILROAD

Pioneers used rawhide for a variety of things, but Dr. Dorsey Syng Baker was probably the only one to use it instead of metal on railroad rails. Dr. Baker was born in Iowa in 1823, and, after becoming a doctor, followed the overland migration to Oregon in 1848. The following year he headed south to the California gold rush, and made some money on it, although he never explained how to historians. A few years later he was back in the Northwest with a hardware store in Portland and a flour mill in Oakland, Oregon. In 1861 the gold rush in Idaho got him interested in that part of the country and he went into the outfitting business in Walla Walla.

But his true genius came into its own when he got interested in the transportation business. He joined forces with two other men and built the steamboat *Spray* and ran it on the Columbia River between Lewiston and Celilo Falls, which until then had been the end of the line for river traffic. So the good doctor did something about it: He built a mile-long tramway around the falls, and before long he was meeting a schedule between Portland and Lewiston and towns between.

As he became better acquainted in the area, he saw that a railroad was needed to connect the Columbia River to the rich farmlands around Walla Walla. At that time, there wasn't a railroad anywhere in the Northwest. In the spring of 1871 Dr. Baker made up his mind to build that railroad, and placed an order for two small, narrow-gauge locomotives along with 100 pairs of car wheels and 1,000 plug hats.

He laid out 32 miles of roadbed between Wallula and Walla Walla and signed a contract with a logger for timber to make the track. The logging contractor took his men up the Yakima River for the logs and was going to float them down the river to Wallula, but the season was dry and the log drive failed. Dr. Baker pressed ahead with his plans as though nothing had happened. He built a sawmill, and then following spring another logger showed up claiming he could deliver the logs. This one did, and when spring thaw came, Dr. Baker's men began laying square ties to support the six-by-six timbers that would be the rails.

Soon the locomotives, wheels, and plug hats arrived on the river, and it was at Celilo Falls that the plug hats came into their own: Dr. Baker knew the Indians loved hats, and he used them as pay for the Indians whose help he needed to unload the locomotives and muscle them onto the tramway and onto the *Spray* for the rest of the trip. When they reached Wallula, the locomotives were dragged onto the rails built for them, and Dr. Baker had a railroad. Cars to go on the sets of wheels were built from lumber milled at his sawmill, and the railroad inched its way eastward across the prairies.

Then it became obvious, after several split and worn-out rails, that some kind of protection was needed for them. And it is here that the story of the rawhide-covered rails enters history. How much was used, and how long it was used, is not known, but it couldn't have been long because Dr. Baker placed an order for strap iron, an inch and a half wide with pre-drilled holes for nails. The rawhide strips worked reasonably well, according to the folklore that grew up around the railroad, but some said Dr. Baker was plagued by wolves eating the rawhide.

One passenger in the 1870s, John M. Murphy, wrote of the railroad in his book, *Rambles in North-Western America From the Pacific Ocean to the Rocky Mountains.* Murphy saw the whole operation—the tiny train, the rails that looked like they had been gnawed, the rattle-trap cars and the man who collected his $2 and was "the president, secretary, conductor, and brakeman of the road." He was a little nervous about the journey from Wallula to Walla Walla and decided he would be safer on a flatcar than in the coach. He was "placed on some iron in an open truck and told to cling to the sides, and to be careful not to stand on the wooden floor if I cared anything about my limbs." So he stood in the hot sun waiting for the train to depart the station. To his astonishment, the conductor told the engineer to go ahead without him, that he had a few things to do and he would catch up with them. The engineer nodded and put the train into motion "The miserable little engine gave a grunt or two, several wheezy puffs, a cat-like scream, and finally the car attached to it got under way" until it reached its top speed of about two miles an hour. Soon the conductor came strolling along the track, passed all the cars and slowed to chat with the engineer. He walked the whole six miles.

"Before I had proceeded half a mile, I saw why I was not permitted to stand on the floor of the truck," Murphy wrote. "For a piece of hoop-iron, which covered the wooden rails in some places, curled into what is called a 'snake head' and pushed through the wood with such force that it nearly stopped the train." The 15-mile trip took Murphy seven hours. At the station, which was a "rude board shanty," Murphy found a ride into town on a farmer's wagon and agreed to drive the team while sitting beside the owner, who slept all the way into town. He wrote that he came to regret his decision to drive the wagon because every driver he met had something to say about his attire.

"The badinage was, as a rule, so original and witty that I had several good laughs at my own expense; and I found after awhile that the chaff was richly merited, as my black broadcloth coat was one mass of burnt holes in the back, and my silk hat looked like a sieve."

Another story, perhaps a bit of exaggeration, involved the day a train jumped the track. A man walking along the road that paralleled the railroad stopped to help. When the train was back to normal on the track, the engineer offered the man a ride.

"No, thank you," he replied. "I'm in a hurry."

One of the continuing problems for the Bonanza Line was cattle wandering onto the track and being killed or injured by the train. Dr. Baker came up with a novel solution. He built a small platform on the front of the engine, and then trained a dog to ride on the platform. When the engineer blasted the whistle, the dog would leap off and run ahead and clear the track of cattle. When his duty was done, the dog would lie down on the track and wait for the second locomotive so he could ride on it. One day the dog fell asleep and was run over. Dr. Baker decided then that a mechanical cowcatcher used by trains throughout the world was in order.

Passengers became accustomed to the unusual while riding Dr. Baker's train. Engineers and firemen stopped at bridges and creeks to refill the boiler, and since oil for the bearings was expensive and sometimes hard to find, the crewmen carried buckets of hog lard to use instead, which added an olfactory treat to riders. It was unique in at least one other aspect: Dr. Baker always paid dividends to its stockholders, and the railroad was never in debt. It ran until 1877, when Dr. Baker sold six-sevenths interest to the Oregon Railway & Navigation Company, and two years later the railroad was converted to standard gauge so it could be absorbed into the whole system.

This small museum is the only one of its kind, offering a glimpse into the unique, traditional, and sometimes gossipy stories rising from the annual harvests, a family affair for many ethnic cultures. The museum is located at 22 S. B St., tel. (509) 865-4677, and is open Wed.-Sun. 10 a.m.-3 p.m. (closed Monday and Tuesday). Admission costs $2 for adults, $1 for seniors and kids, $5 for families.

Yakima Valley Rail and Steam Museum
The newly restored Toppenish railroad depot houses this museum located at 1 A Street. Inside are rail and steam artifacts, a restored telegraph office, and gift shop. Picnic in Railroad Park adjacent to the depot. A steam locomotive in the rail yard is in the initial stages of restoration. The museum is open Sunday 1-5 p.m. and Mon.-Sat. 10 a.m.-5 p.m. May-Oct., with more limited hours the rest of the year. Admission costs $2 for adults, $1 for kids and seniors, and $5 for families.

The **Toppenish, Simcoe and Western Railroad** now operates a diesel locomotive and two passenger cars from Harrah (10 miles west of Toppenish) to White Swan, providing a panoramic view of the orchards, hop fields, and farms of Yakima Valley, with Mt. Adams as a backdrop. Fares for this three-hour ride are $8 for adults, $5 for kids under 12; the trains depart Saturday at 11 a.m. and Sunday at 2 p.m. March-September. They also offer special dinner trains and charter excursions. Call (509) 865-1911 for details.

Toppenish National Wildlife Refuge
More than 250 species of birds have been sighted on this refuge located five miles south on Hwy. 97, then south a half mile on Pump House Road. It has an interpretive center and nature trail. For information call (509) 865-2405.

Fort Simcoe State Park
Head 27 miles west from Toppenish through the heart of the Yakama Indian Reservation to Fort Simcoe State Park, tel. (509) 874-2372. The drive takes you through fields of grapes and hops, and past Indian burial grounds with

decorated gravesites to the forested fort site. Fort Simcoe was erected by the Army in 1856 as a base for military operations against nearby Indians but was abandoned just three years later. It then served as a Bureau of Indian Affairs school and Indian Agency headquarters until becoming a state park in 1953. (The land is under a 99-year lease from the Yakama Nation.) Two blockhouses and a barracks have been reconstructed, and five of the original buildings have been restored and furnished, including the New England-style commanding officer's house, three captain's quarters, and a log blockhouse. Tour the buildings and the brick interpretive center/museum, then enjoy a picnic lunch on the landscaped grounds. The grounds are open Wed.-Sun. 9 a.m.-4 p.m. April-Sept., and weekends and holidays 9 a.m.-4 p.m. the rest of the year; the museum and interpretive center are open Wed.-Sun. April-October. No camping at Fort Simcoe.

PRACTICALITIES

Accommodations and Campgrounds

See the "Yakima Valley Lodging" chart for Toppenish motels. The nicest and newest is **Toppenish Inn Motel,** tel. (509) 865-7444 or (800) 222-3161, which features an indoor pool, jacuzzi, exercise room, and continental breakfast. The **Yakama Nation Resort RV Park,** next to the Cultural Center, tel. (509) 865-2000 or (800) 874-3087, has parking spaces for RVs ($16), plus 14 very popular tepees ($38 for up to five people), a tent-camping area ($10), outdoor pool, hot tub, and other facilities.

Food

Toppenish's strong Hispanic culture is evidenced in the plethora of Mexican restaurants, clothing stores, and bilingual signs. Favorite eateries are **Villaseñors,** 225 S. Toppenish Ave., tel. (509) 865-4707, with traditional Mexican favorites, and the new **Los Murales,** 202 W. 1st, tel. (509) 865-7555, specializing in lighter and less spicy Mexican lunches and dinners, along with steaks and seafood. For authentic Mexican pastries, stop by **El Porvenir Panaderia,** 209 S. Toppenish, tel. (509) 865-7900. For a rather different taste of ethnic food, **Lotus Restaurant,** 901 W. 1st Ave., tel. (509) 865-4552, is the place to go for the best Chinese food in the area.

The **Yakama Nation Cultural Center** (see "Sights," above) has a popular restaurant with a large salad bar, salmon, buffalo, and Indian fry bread. Not open Sunday after 2 p.m. More Indian foods, including buffalo burgers, salmon, and fry bread at **Huba Huba Cafe,** 206 S. Toppenish Ave., tel. (509) 865-3299. They also have a fine Sunday brunch.

For a homemade breakfast with the locals, head to **Sue's Pioneer Kitchen,** 227 S. Toppenish Ave., tel. (509) 865-3201. You'll discover the best burgers around, along with floats, shakes, and cold drinks, at the old-fashioned soda fountain in **Gibbon's Pharmacy,** 117 S. Toppenish Ave., tel. (509) 865-2722. Enjoy a root beer float and chili dog at **A&W,** 433 S. Elm St., tel. (509) 865-4349, or a hearty barbecue ribs dinner at the **Cattlemen's Restaurant,** 2 S. Division St., tel. (509) 865-1800. **New West Family Restaurant,** 419 E. Toppenish Ave., tel. (509) 865-6737, has down-home all-American mashed potatoes and gravy-doused fare. More American food at **The Branding Iron,** at Highways 22 and 97, where the cinnamon rolls are said to be the biggest in the civilized world (we're talking buns big enough to feed a small nation).

Events

The **Speely-Mi Arts & Craft Trade Fair** in mid-March brings exhibitions of native artisans to the Cultural Center in Toppenish. Each year on the first Saturday in June, Toppenish sponsors a **Mural-in-a-Day** program in which more than two dozen artists complete a wall-sized mural in a day's work. The chamber of commerce simultaneously sponsors an arts and crafts and food fair.

Treaty Days in early June celebrates the signing of the Treaty of 1855 between the U.S. government and the Yakama Indian Nation and features a pow wow, salmon feed, parade, and storytelling at the Yakama Nation Cultural Center.

The Fourth of July weekend brings a frenzy of activity to Toppenish: the **Pow Wow Rodeo, Pioneer Fair, and Indian Village.** This event has something for everyone—a carnival, nightly rodeos, Indian stick games, dancing, an Indian village, fireworks, a Wild West Parade featuring cowboys, cowgirls, and Indians dressed in full regalia, an antique power show, and arts and crafts booths. Various Mexican rodeos are held in Toppenish most summer weekends, and the second weekend of June brings the **All-Indian Rodeo and Pow Wow** to nearby White Swan.

The last weekend in August attracts some 100 artists who display their art at the **Toppenish Western Art Show,** held at the Yakama Indian Nation Cultural Center. This event features an auction Friday and Saturday nights and attracts top Northwest artists.

One of the more surprising local events is the **Heritage Cup Polo Tournament,** held in mid-September at the Kent Polo Field near White Swan. This event attracts some of the finest players in the nation and has even brought the British royalty.

Shopping

For authentic arts and crafts from the Yakima Indian Reservation, visit the gift shop at Yakama

Nation Cultural Center, or stop by **Wind Flower Indian Trading Co.,** 7A S. Toppenish Ave., tel. (509) 865-1888. You'll find quality silver jewelry, pottery, clothing, baskets, pipes, and beadwork. Next door to Wind Flower is **The Amish Connection,** tel. (509) 865-5300, with handcrafted Amish furniture, dolls, quilts, and other items.

Kraff's, 111 S. Toppenish, tel. (509) 865-3000, is an interesting clothing store and the largest retailer of Pendleton blankets in the United States. **Inter Tribal,** 2 Buena Way, tel. (509) 865-7775, creates beautiful coats and clothing, including ones made from Pendleton blankets. For Mexican clothing, including ponchos, leather jackets, skirts, hats, and more, visit **Reflexion de Mexico,** on the corner of Hwy. 97 and Fort Rd., tel. (509) 865-7888.

Information and Services

For information, head to the very helpful **Toppenish Chamber of Commerce,** 11 S. Toppenish Ave., tel. (509) 865-3262. The **area code** for all of eastern Washington is 509. Catch **Greyhound** buses at 602 W. 1st, tel. (509) 865-3773 or (800) 231-2222.

YAKIMA VALLEY

While Toppenish is virtually a world—or a nation—apart, the rest of the Yakima Valley blends together to form a single conceptual region, basing its reputation, if not its economy, on the wineries that line the Yakima River. Interstate 82 cuts across the north side of the valley, with the older Hwy. 22 following a parallel route on the south side. Other than Toppenish (described above), several small towns dot the route between Yakima and the Tri-Cities; largest are Zillah, Granger, Sunnyside, Grandview, and Prosser. The many wineries spread across the valley are described below under "Yakima Valley Wineries."

ZILLAH

Zillah (pop. 1,900) was named for Zillah Oakes, the 17-year-old daughter of the president of the Northern Pacific Railroad, by one of the first settlers in the area; apparently he was infatuat-

ed with her. Or maybe he just wanted to curry favor with the owner of the railroad.

Sights

Certainly the strangest local sight is the **Teapot Dome** gas station located just south of I-82. This tiny station consists of a one-room teapot-shaped structure with a concrete handle on one side and a long spout on the other. Built in 1922 as a protest over the Teapot Dome scandal that sent President Harding's interior secretary to prison, the station is now a National Historic Site. Fill up at the nation's oldest working gas station and chat with the owner about his golf game or about local politics. Zillah's **First Christian Church** at 202 5th St. was built in 1910 and has intricate stained glass windows and unusual twin steeples.

Food

For Mexican food, antiques, gifts, or tortillas to take home (made on the premises), steer your steers toward **El Ranchito,** just off the Zillah exit,

YAKIMA VALLEY ACCOMMODATIONS

Accommodations are arranged from least to most expensive within each town. Rates may be lower during the winter months. The area code is 509.

TOPPENISH

Oxbow Motor Inn; 511 S. Elm; tel. 865-5800; $33 s, $36 d; kitchenettes available, AAA approved

El Corral Motel; 61731 Hwy. 97; tel. 865-2365; $34 s, $39 d

Toppenish Inn Motel; 515 S. Elm St.; tel. 865-7444 or (800) 222-3161; $39-46 s or d; indoor pool, jacuzzi, exercise room, continental breakfast, indoor corridors, kitchenettes available, AAA approved

GRANGER

An English B&B; 1420 Nelson Rd.; tel. 854-2272; $52-68 s or d; three guest rooms, private or shared bath, panoramic vistas, full breakfast

SUNNYSIDE

Friendship Inn; 724 Yakima Valley Hwy.; tel. 837-4721; $32 s, $44 d; outdoor pool, continental breakfast

Nendel's Inn; 408 Yakima Valley Hwy.; tel. 837-7878; $37-41 s, $41-50 d; outdoor pool, kitchenettes available, continental breakfast, AAA approved

Town House Motel; 509 Hwy. 12; tel. 837-5500; $38 s or d; kitchenettes available, AAA approved

Von Hellstrum Inn B&B; 51 Branden Rd.; tel. 839-2505; $45-60 s or d; 1908 country home, four antique-furnished guest rooms, private baths, mountain and valley views, porch and gazebos, country breakfast

Sunnyside Inn B&B; 800 E. Edison Ave.; tel. 839-5557; $49-79 s or d; historic 1919 home, eight guest rooms, private baths, jacuzzis, light breakfast

GRANDVIEW

Grandview Motel; 522 E. Wine Country Rd.; tel. 882-1323; $26-28 s, $30-36 d; outdoor pool, AAA approved

Apple Valley Motel; Hwy. 12; tel. 882-3003; $30 s, $38 d; outdoor pool, kitchenettes available

PROSSER

Prosser Motel; 1206 Wine Country Rd.; tel. 786-2855; $25 s, $29 d

The Barn Motel; 490 Wine Country Rd.; tel. 786-2121; $38 s, $44 d; outdoor pool, AAA approved

Best Western Prosser Inn; 225 Merlot Dr.; tel. 786-7977 or (800) 528-1234; $49 s, $52 d; new motel, outdoor pool, jacuzzi, kitchenettes available, continental breakfast, AAA approved

Wine Country Inn B&B; 1106 Wine Country Rd.; tel. 786-2855; $55-65 s or d; four guest rooms (two with private bath), full breakfast

---

tel. (509) 829-5880; sorry, no alcohol. The factory here makes some of the best-selling flour and corn tortillas in the Northwest, and the restaurant is considered one of the finest south-of-the-border eateries in Washington. It's been here since 1950.

Another very popular Zillah restaurant is **Squeeze Inn,** 611 1st Ave., tel. (509) 829-6226, where the breakfasts bring out the coffee klatch crowd, and the dinners of steak, prime rib, and seafood attract folks from all over the Valley.

Shrimp cocktails come with all dinners. Squeeze Inn has been in the same family for more than 60 years.

Doc's Pizza, 505 1st Ave., tel. (509) 829-6259, in Zillah, makes some of the Valley's best pizzas. Their antique bathtub salad bar is unusual, to put it mildly.

Rocky Mountain Chocolate Factory in Zillah, tel. (509) 829-3330 or (800) 454-7623, makes all sorts of chocolate goodies, including fudge, macadamia clusters, truffles, and another 75 or so varieties of candy.

Events and Information
Zillah's **Community Days** in mid-May features a Lions Club breakfast, footraces, parade, fishing derby, and the crowning of Miss Zillah. For local information, head to the **Zillah Chamber of Commerce**, 503 N. 1st St., tel. (509) 829-5055.

GRANGER

The farming town of Granger (pop. 2,000) sits along the north side of the Yakima River and just a few miles east of Zillah. Granger is home to the only nonprofit Spanish-language radio station in Washington, KDNA. An Hispanic Cultural Center is in the works for Granger. Eight dinosaurs welcome you to Granger's "Jurassic Pond" (one Brontosaurus is in the water). Get a good view of the surrounding country from **Cherry Hill,** just east of town (Stewart Vineyards has a wine tasting room here).

Granger's **Cherry Festival** in early May includes a carnival, music, dancing, a fishing derby, and a Mexican fiesta.

SUNNYSIDE

Sunnyside (pop. 11,000) is near the center of Yakima Valley's grape-, hop-, and fruit-producing region. The **Sunnyside Museum,** 704 S. 4th St., tel. (509) 837-6010, has Native American artifacts, pioneer items, and ice age fossils; open Sunday, Tuesday, and Thursday 1:30-4:30 p.m. all year. Entrance is 50 cents for adults, free for kids. Nearby is the **Ben Snipes Cabin,** built in 1859. It was once home to the

man who introduced cattle into Yakima Valley. He raised cattle all over this area for the gold mining camps of British Columbia, Colville, and Idaho, and eventually became known as the "Northwest cattle king."

Lodging
See the "Yakima Valley Accommodations" chart for local lodging options. The nicest places are **Von Hellstrum Inn B&B,** tel. (509) 839-2505, located in a hilltop Sears Catalog home built in 1908, and **Sunnyside Inn B&B,** tel. (509) 839-5557, another historic home with jacuzzis.

Food
The **Tillicum Restaurant,** tel. (509) 837-7222, 410 Hwy. 12, serves only Yakima Valley wines with their steak and prime rib dinners. For Sichuan and Mandarin cooking, try **China Grove,** 325 Hwy. 12, tel. (509) 839-3663. Eat authentic Mexican food for reasonable prices at **Taqueria La Fogata,** 1204 Yakima Valley Hwy., tel. (509) 839-9019.

Yakima Valley Cheese Co., tel. (509) 837-6005, produces gouda cheese; pick up a pound in their shop at Alexander and Midvale Roads.

Events
The Yakima Valley is fast becoming a major center for Hispanic culture in Washington, and **Cinco de Mayo Fiesta Days** bring a major celebration time to Sunnyside in early May with art, music, food, and dancing. The **Taste of Mexico** in July is a weekend event featuring a Mexican cooking contest, food booths, and entertainment. In early December, the **Country Christmas Lighted Farm Implement Parade** features tractors, farm machinery, and horse-drawn carriages and wagons, all lit up with lights.

Information and Services
For local information, visit the **Sunnyside Chamber of Commerce,** 812 E. Edison Ave., tel. (509) 837-5939. Sunnyside has a beautiful 50-meter outdoor **swimming pool** with a water slide in the town park. The **Greyhound** bus depot is at 13th St. and Hwy. 12, tel. (509) 837-5344 or (800) 231-2222. The local telephone **area code** is 509.

GRANDVIEW

Grandview (pop. 7,500) is another in a chain of small Yakima Valley villages that depends on agriculture as its mainstay. The **Ray E. Powell Museum**, tel. (509) 882-9217, is next to the town library at 313 S. Division St. and contains local memorabilia, including Indian artifacts, pioneer items, antique clocks and guns, and a turn-of-the-century Kiblinger car, one of just two in existence. It is open Sunday and Tues.-Fri. 2-4 p.m. March-October.

Practicalities

See the "Yakima Valley Accommodations" chart for local lodging options. **Dykstra House**, 114 Birch Ave., tel. (509) 882-2082, serves lunches on weekdays and Italian cuisine on Friday and Saturday nights; reservations recommended. The menu changes to match what's fresh that day but always includes delicious homemade breads and desserts.

The **Grandview Grape Stomp** is one of the stranger events in Yakima Valley; contestants see who can squeeze out the most juice using traditional foot-power. It attracts competitors from all over the Northwest.

PROSSER

When you enter the small town of Prosser (pop. 4,500), you're greeted by a sign proclaiming it, "A pleasant place with pleasant people." Hard to argue about this, especially after a saunter through Prosser's clean streets and prospering downtown. It's one of the prettiest places in this part of Washington, and it's the center of government for Benton County. Much of this prosperity comes from agriculture, with not only the many Yakima Valley wineries, but also the enormous Twin City Foods plant in town (they process Tater Tots, hash browns, and other frozen potato products here).

Sights

In Prosser City Park, the **Benton County Historical Museum** includes a natural history display, historical photographs, a replica of the Holt combine that was pulled by 26 horses, a 1910

homestead, and an 1867 Chickering Square grand piano. Open Sunday 1-5 p.m., Tues.-Sat. 10 a.m.-4 p.m.; admission is $1 adults, 50 cents for kids. The brick and stone **Benton County Courthouse** on Market St. was built in 1926 and is on the National Register of Historic Places.

Be sure to stop at the **Chukar Cherries** store on the west end of town to taste the dried cherries, chocolate-covered berries, and other delicious sweets. They also have branch stores in Seattle, Issaquah, and Pasco, plus a mail-order business; call (800) 624-9544 for a catalog.

Storyland, tel. (509) 786-6900, is a miniature golf place with an amusing fairy tale collection that includes a castle, dinosaur, sleeping giant, the three bears, Humpty Dumpty, and other storybook creatures. Open daily April-September.

Accommodations and Food

See the "Yakima Valley Accommodations" chart for Prosser's motels and B&B.

The **Barn Restaurant**, on the west end of town, tel. (509) 786-2121, is one of the best local restaurants for steak and seafood; munch the great appetizers while watching sports on the big-screen TV. They also have RV spaces ($18). Another local favorite is **The Blue Goose**, 306 7th St., tel. (509) 786-1774, which features a menu that includes prime rib, pastas, and seafood. Come here for a breakfast omelette.

The **Prosser Farmers Market** takes place Saturday 8 a.m.-1 p.m. June-Oct. in the city park.

Events and Information

The **Prosser Wine and Food Fair** in mid-August is the largest outdoor food show in the state, attracting thousands of people for a chance to sample from more than 20 local wineries, two microbreweries, and many food vendors. The event usually sells out, so order advance tickets ($6) by calling (509) 786-4545. It is only open to people over age 21.

The **Prosser Balloon Rally and Harvest Festival** in late September attracts both visitors and balloon enthusiasts for morning launches, nighttime lighted balloons, and arts and crafts exhibits.

The **Prosser Chamber of Commerce** is located in the old railroad depot at 611 6th St., tel. (509) 786-3177.

YAKIMA VALLEY WINERIES

The Yakima and Columbia valleys comprise the premier wine-growing regions in the state and have helped make Washington the second largest producer of fine wine grapes in America. Yakima Valley is located along the same latitude as France's Burgundy and Bordeaux regions, and the dry climate, sunny weather, and ample irrigation waters make for ideal growing conditions. The wineries along the Yakima River provide more than a day's touring; all of these wineries have tasting rooms, and all but Hinzerling have picnic facilities.

Events

In mid-February, visit the Valley for a **Celebration of Chocolates and Red Wine** during which the various wineries provide chocolate sweets to match their reds. The Biggest annual wine event is the **Yakima Valley Spring Barrel Tasting** in late April. During this festival all the wineries pour samples of their new releases straight from the barrel and offer tours, hors d'oeuvres, and

educational exhibits. All wineries are open 10 a.m.-5 p.m. during this three-day event.

The season winds down with **Thanksgiving in the Wine Country,** featuring food and wine tasting at most local wineries. This is a fine way to taste a variety of foods and get recipe ideas.

Wine Tour

Stop by the Yakima Valley Visitors and Convention Bureau office for a map of 22 Yakima Valley wineries, or send a long, self-addressed, stamped envelope to the Yakima Valley Wine Growers Association, P.O. Box 39, Grandview, WA 98930. The following tour is based upon their brochure.

From Yakima, your first stop is **Staton Hills,** 2290 Gangl Rd. in Wapato, tel. (509) 877-2112, open for tastings every day 11 a.m.-5:30 p.m. in the summer, and noon-5 p.m. Nov.-February. You'll get a fine view of the Yakima Valley from their hilltop location. Next comes **Zillah Oakes Winery,** Vintage Valley Parkway in Zillah, tel. (509) 829-6690; open for tastings Sunday noon-5 p.m. and Mon.-Sat. 10 a.m.-5 p.m. summers, and Sunday noon-4:30 p.m. and Mon.-Sat. 11 a.m.-4:30 p.m. winters. **Bonair Winery,** 500 S. Bonair Rd. in Zillah, tel. (509) 829-6027, is a small, family-run place specializing in chardonnay, riesling, and cabernet sauvi-

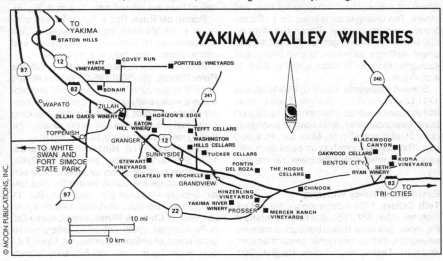

YAKIMA VALLEY WINERIES

gnon and is open daily 10 a.m.-5 p.m. summers, and Sat.-Sun. 10 a.m.-4:30 p.m. winters. They sell most of their production from the winery. Another small family place is **Hyatt Vineyards Winery,** 2020 Gilbert Rd. in Zillah, tel. (509) 829-6333, featuring chardonnay, sauvignon blanc, rieslings, cabernet sauvignon, and merlot, plus the very sweet ice wine; open daily 11 a.m.-5 p.m. April-Oct., daily 11 a.m.-4:30 p.m. winters, and closed January.

West Yakima Valley Wineries

Covey Run, at 1500 Vintage Rd. in Zillah, tel. (509) 829-6235, is one of the area's big-name wineries and was the first major Washington winery to use only Yakima Valley grapes. Most of their production is white wine, primarily riesling. The mezzanine tasting room affords a nice vineyard view; open Sunday noon-5 p.m. and Mon.-Sat. 10 a.m.-5 p.m. summers, Sunday noon-4:30 p.m. and Mon.-Sat. 11 a.m.-4:30 p.m. winters. Call ahead for tours. **Portteus Vineyards,** 5201 Highland Dr. in Zillah, tel. (509) 829-6970, produced Washington's first zinfandel; open daily noon-5 p.m. and by appointment.

Also in Zillah, at 4530 E. Zillah Dr., is **Horizon's Edge Winery,** tel. (509) 829-6401, another of the valley's newer wineries, with dramatic views across the valley. Releases include sparkling wines, chardonnay, pinot noir, and others. The tasting room is open daily 10 a.m.-5 p.m. (except January). **Eaton Hill Winery,** 530 Gurley Rd. in Granger, tel. (509) 854-2508, offers rieslings, semillon, chenin blanc, and sauvignon blanc for tastings; open Fri.-Wed. 10 a.m.-5 p.m.

Stewart Vineyards, tel. (509) 854-1882, is at 1711 Cherry Hill Rd. in Granger. Their production includes rieslings, chardonnay, sauvignon blanc, gewürztraminer, and cabernet sauvignon; open Sunday noon-5 p.m., Mon.-Sat. 10 a.m.-5 p.m. The tasting room has an open deck with panoramic views across the lower Yakima Valley.

East Yakima Valley Wineries

Tefft Cellars, 1320 Independence Rd. in Outlook, tel. (509) 837-7651, the newest winery in the valley, produces limited bottlings of cabernet sauvignon, merlot, grenache, gewürztraminer, and port. Tasting room hours are Sat.-Sun. noon-5 p.m. Closed December 15 to March 1. **Washington Hills Cellars,** 111 E. Lincoln Ave. in Sunnyside, tel. (509) 839-9463, is in the old Carnation Dairy building and has a retail shop and picnic area; open for tours and tasting daily 11 a.m.-5:30 p.m. May-Dec., Thurs.-Mon. 11 a.m.-5 p.m. the rest of the year. They produce a wide variety of wines under the Bridgman, Apex, and Washington Hills labels.

Tucker Cellars, 70 Ray Rd. in Sunnyside, tel. (509) 837-8701, is a family winery established in 1981 that now produces nine varieties. The tasting room is open daily 9 a.m.-5 p.m. summers, and daily 10 a.m.-4:30 p.m. winters.

Chateau Ste. Michelle, W. 5th and Ave. B in Grandview, tel. (509) 882-3928, is Washington's oldest winery and the biggest tourist draw in Yakima Valley. Established in 1934 as the National Wine Company—shortly after the end of Prohibition—and renamed Ste. Michelle Vintners in 1965, it has come to represent the Washington wine industry across the country. It is now owned by U.S. Tobacco Co., a fact they aren't likely to tell you on the tour. Grandview is the site of all Ste. Michelle red wine fermentation; two other facilities are located in Woodinville (see under "North from Seattle") and Paterson (no tours here). Try their award-winning cabernet sauvignon and merlot or other wines. Excellent tours are offered daily 10 a.m.-4:30 p.m.

Pontin del Roza, Rte. 1, Box 1129, in Prosser, tel. (509) 786-4449, was established in 1984 and produces chardonnay, white riesling, and chenin blanc; open daily 10 a.m.-5 p.m.

Also in Prosser at Rte. 1, Box 1657, **Yakima River Winery,** tel. (509) 786-2805, was started in 1978 by the John W. Rauner family and produces a wide variety of wines from dry and semidry whites and reds to dessert wines, including some that are available only at the winery. The tasting room is open daily 10 a.m.-5 p.m.

Founded in 1976, **Hinzerling Vineyards,** 1520 Sheridan in Prosser, tel. (509) 786-2163, specializes in estate-grown cabernet and dessert wines. Tastings are usually held in the wine cellar, Sunday 11 a.m.-4 p.m. and Mon.-Sat. 11 a.m.-5 p.m. April-Dec., Mon.-Sat. 11 a.m.-5 p.m. Jan.-March. **Chinook Wines,** Wine Country Rd. in Prosser, tel. (509) 786-2725, offers sauvignon blanc, chardonnay, or merlot. Open Fri.-Sun. noon-5 p.m. from mid-February to mid-

December, closed the rest of the year.

The Hogue Cellars, Wine Country Rd., tel. (509) 786-4557, is the big-name Prosser winery (and third largest in Washington), with a range of products, from rieslings to merlot to a very nice cabernet blush. Their tasting room, gift shop, and art gallery are open daily 10 a.m.-5 p.m.

Benton City Area Wineries

The quiet small town of Benton City provides a sharp contrast to the bustling Tri-Cities area, just a few miles to the east. Stop here for fresh produce at **Dee's Fruit Stand,** or just enjoy the lush valley with vineyards and fruit trees. **Seth Ryan Winery,** Sunset Rd. in Benton City, tel. (509) 588-6780, produces riesling, gewürztraminer, and chardonnays; open Sat.-Sun. noon-5 p.m. **Oakwood Cellars,** Rte. 2, Box 2321 in Benton City, tel. (509) 588-5332, has

chardonnay, merlot, muscat, and lemberger; open Wed.-Fri. 6-8 p.m. and Sat.-Sun. noon-6 p.m. summers, weekends only Nov.-February. **Kiona Vineyards,** Rte. 2, Box 2169E, in Benton City, tel. (509) 588-6716, sits on Red Mountain with a nice tasting-room view of the vineyards. In business since 1980, Kiona produces a full range of varietal wines; open daily noon-5 p.m.

One of the most interesting and personable wineries is Benton City's **Blackwood Canyon,** Rte. 2, Box 2169H, tel. (509) 588-6249, open daily 10 a.m.-6 p.m. The winery sits at the end of a rough gravel road in the middle of the vineyards, and the tasting room is just a counter in the warehouse. Their chardonnays, cabernets, fumé blanc, semillon, and late-harvest wines are available only at the winery and select restaurants but are quite distinctive.

TRI-CITIES

The Tri-Cities comprise three adjacent cities: Kennewick faces its poorer cousin Pasco across the Columbia River, and the "Atomic City" of Richland is seven miles to the west near the entrance to the massive Hanford Site. Together, these three make up the fourth-largest metropolitan area in the state (over 100,000 people). They have prospered in recent years from the cleanup of the nearby Hanford Site, and by the mid-1990s, the area was positively booming from the billions of federal dollars being dumped into the economy. Besides Hanford, the Tri-Cities are famous for their hydroplane race, held annually in July, and their wineries, at the southeast end of the fruitful Yakima Valley. The area is also becoming something of a retirement destination, in part because of the dry and sunny weather.

The Setting

The Tri-Cities are located near the center of Pasco Basin on the Columbia Plateau, a desert land at the confluence of the Yakima, Snake, and Columbia Rivers. Pasco is in Franklin County, Kennewick and Richland are in Benton County. Columbia and Snake River dams provide water recreation, electrical power, and water for agriculture. Upstream from Richmond is the

last free-flowing segment of the Columbia River in Washington—the "Hanford Reach." It is under study for possible Wild and Scenic River status, but given the current political climate that status seems unlikely any time soon.

Farms cover 1.3 million acres—400,000 of them irrigated—in Benton and Franklin Counties; potatoes, wheat, apples, grapes, alfalfa, strawberries, asparagus, corn, and hops are the big money producers here. Much of this production is shipped from the port facilities in the Tri-Cities to the Pacific Rim.

The Cities

Kennewick, at 45,000 residents, is the largest and fastest growing of the Tri-Cities. With its pleasant downtown surrounded by wide, shady streets with quiet older homes, Kennewick could double for a Midwestern town. Unfortunately, Clearwater Ave.—the main business thoroughfare—is an ugly stretch of fast food joints, car repair shops, and strip malls with the standard jumble of glaring neon signs vying for attention. The giant Columbia Center Mall is the largest in this part of the state.

Richland—with 34,000 people it's the second-most populous of the Tri-Cities—has an attractive older downtown right along the river, and several

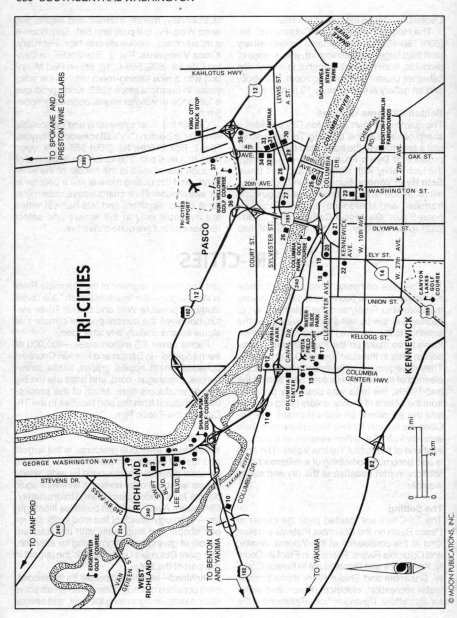

TRI-CITIES

© MOON PUBLICATIONS, INC.

TRI-CITIES

RICHLAND

1. Best Western
2. Bali Hai Motel
3. Kadlec Medical Center
4. Hanford Science Center
5. Red Lion Inn/Hanford House
6. Richland Chamber of Commerce
7. Nendel's Inn

KENNEWICK

8. Econo Lodge
9. Shilo Motel
10. Bookwalter Winery
11. Lloyd's Desert Gold Motel
12. Columbia Center Dunes Motel
13. Silver Cloud Inn
14. Comfort Inn
15. Cavanaugh's at Columbia Center
16. Super 8 Motel
17. Tri-Cities Visitors Center
18. Shaniko Motel
19. Kennewick Chamber of Commerce
20. Tapadera Inn
21. Dogwood Cottage B & B
22. Nendel's Inn
23. East Benton County Museum
24. Kennewick General Hospital
25. Quality Inn
26. Moore Mansion
27. Goal Post Motor Inn
28. Vineyard Inn
29. Hallmark Motel
30. Farmer's Market
31. Greyhound
32. hospital
33. Franklin County Museum
34. Court House
35. Motel 6
36. Red Lion
37. Starlite Motel

fine city parks, but an unsightly sprawl of enormous homes belonging to the elite spreads to the south along Columbia Drive. This is the "Atomic City," and it grew up as a secret settlement during the 1940s, with the nearby Hanford Site as an ominous neighbor. In 1949, *Time* magazine proclaimed Richland "an atomic age utopia." During WW II, only government workers could live here, but the buildings were returned to private hands in 1958. The Richland high school's sports teams are still called "The Bombers."

Pasco has 21,000 residents and contrasts sharply with its prosperous neighbors. It is separated from Kennewick by a pair of bridges across the Columbia: the 10th Ave. bridge is notable for its distinctive girder-span design, the Hwy. 395 bridge is better known as the "Blue Bridge." Pasco—the Franklin County seat—is a working-class town with thrift stores, run-down businesses, and a seedy, hard-times feeling. You won't find the elaborate shopping malls of Kennewick here. Pasco's redeeming attribute is a plethora of fine Mexican bakeries *(panaderias)*, shops *(tiendas)*, taco vans, and close to a dozen Mexican restaurants.

Weather

The Tri-Cities endure weather extremes that western Washingtonians never see. Plenty of below-zero days have been recorded here, as well as summer temperatures soaring over 100 bone-dry degrees; fortunately, a fairly constant breeze makes the heat almost tolerable (of course, the breeze can also stir up dust). The area receives an average annual precipitation of just six inches, scattered between 225 sunny days. Most of the total occurs November through April, and snow is not uncommon in the winter months, though it rarely exceeds six inches on the ground.

HISTORY

The Lewis and Clark expedition arrived at the confluence of the Columbia and Snake Rivers in 1805. The first permanent settlers arrived in 1861 to raise cattle on these wide-open plains. Railroad workers established the town of Ainsworth, now Ainsworth Junction, in 1871 at the terminus of the Northern Pacific Railway. Ainsworth grew rapidly until the workers completed the Snake River railroad bridge; then the railroaders packed their bags, and Ainsworth faded into history.

The Northern Pacific Railway platted the twin towns of Pasco and Kennewick on either side of the Columbia River railroad bridge and advertised for settlers with flyers that proclaimed this stark, dusty place as the "lordly plain of the Columbia." Settlers moved in, and Pasco eventually became the hub of the rail traffic in the region, as well as the county seat. (The name came from Cerro de Pasco in Peru. Apparently a construction engineer for the Northern Pacific Railway had helped build an Andes railroad there and contrasted the beautiful high mountain country with this then-desolate spot as something of a joke.)

Incorporated in 1891, Pasco became a major transportation center. The airport—built in 1910—was the first one west of the Mississippi; the first U.S. airmail service operated out of Tri-Cities Regional Airport by what would later become United Airlines; and Pasco became a significant upriver terminal for Columbia River steamboat and barge traffic.

Franklin County irrigation projects began in the 1890s, when schemes were developed to pump water from the Snake River onto the dry fields. Kennewick grew into a small agricultural center following the opening of the Northern Pacific Irrigation Company Canal in 1903, and then prospered from the massive Columbia Basin Irrigation Project that now irrigates over 500,000 acres. But the big story in Tri-Cities is not agriculture, but nuclear weapons (see the special topic "Nuclear Legacy"). The development of the massive Hanford Site just north of Richmond brought well-paying jobs and a high-tech status to the area. Today it is the site of the nation's largest cleanup, a multi-billion-dollar effort that helped fuel a boom in growth during the early '90s, with more than 16,000 new residents in just three years time.

SIGHTS

Museums
Kennewick's **East Benton County Historical Museum,** 205 Keewaydin Dr., tel. (509) 582-7704, has exhibits from pioneer days in the Tri-Cities area; free. Open daily 1-4 p.m. Memorial Day to Labor Day, and Wed.-Sat. 1-4 p.m. the rest of the year.

At 304 N. 4th Ave. in Pasco, the **Franklin County Historical Museum,** tel. (509) 547-3714, has exhibits depicting early Native Amer-

ican culture, railroad and aviation history, pioneer life, and agriculture. It's open Sunday 1-6 p.m., Wed.-Fri. 1-6 p.m., and Saturday 10 a.m.-6 p.m. May-Aug., and Wed.-Sun. 1-5 p.m. the rest of the year; free.

Three Rivers Children's Museum, 873 Columbia Center Mall in Kennewick, tel. (509) 783-6311, has fun hands-on science exhibits for kids. Open Sunday noon-5 p.m., Tues.-Sat. 10 a.m.-5 p.m.; $2 for adults or kids.

The **Hanford Museums of Science and History,** in the Federal Building next to the Richland post office, tel. (509) 376-6374, is open Mon.-Fri. 8 a.m.-5 p.m., Saturday 9 a.m.-5 p.m. Visitors can walk inside a tank similar to those that contain the 60 *million* gallons of radioactive waste, and check out models of the Hanford reactors and exhibits on the massive cleanup operation. A seismograph shows the latest quakes to shake the waste around, and videos provide an introduction to the cleanup activities. Kids love the computer exhibits and the glove box that lets you manipulate items with a mechanical arm. Just be glad they don't use real nuclear fuel rods here.

City Parks
Columbia Park forms a 609-acre border along the south shore of the Columbia River (Lake Wallula) in Kennewick, with four boat ramps for fishing and waterskiing, an 18-hole golf course, tennis courts, a picnic area, nature trails, and campsites. One of the main attractions is a six-mile paved path that's a favorite of cyclists, rollerbladers, joggers, and lovers out for a riverside stroll.

Volunteer Park in downtown Pasco is an attractive, shady place, perfect for a picnic lunch. An old Northern Pacific Steam engine sits in the park across from the white-domed **County Courthouse** on 4th St., built in 1913. Richland's **General Leslie R. Groves Park** forms a scenic five-mile-long border along the Columbia River.

Nuke Plants
No, you can't visit the decommissioned plutonium facilities on the Hanford Site; though you might find a job walking around in one of those space suits cleaning up 45 years of nuclear waste. Instead, head to the **Plant 2 Visitors Center,** tel. (509) 372-5860 run by Washing-

A NUCLEAR LEGACY

C ruise around the Tri-Cities and you'll find Atomic Auto Sales, Atomic Body Shop, Atomic Bowling Center, Atomic Laundry, Atomic Foods (now that's scary!), and Atomic Health Center (even scarier). There's a reason for this—the 560-square-mile Hanford Site just north of Richland, the source of much of the plutonium in America's nuclear arsenal.

The Buildup

With the start of WW II, the U.S. began a frenzied race to develop an atomic bomb. The first controlled nuclear chain reaction experiments were conducted in late 1942, and within a few months the government had selected the Hanford site for its plutonium production plant. The location seemed perfect: remote enough so that accidents would not immediately kill thousands of people, but still near railroads, an abundant source of water for cooling, and hydroelectric power for energy. The original scattering of residents was evacuated from the towns of Hanford, White Bluffs, and Richland, and a flood of some 51,000 workers took their place. The secret government city of Richmond was open only to Hanford construction workers and scientists; only they could live there, and they were permitted to live nowhere else. The entire "Manhattan Project" was done with such secrecy that few of the construction workers knew what they were building, and even Vice President Harry S. Truman didn't know of the project till after Roosevelt's death. Three plutonium production reactors were quickly constructed along the banks of the Columbia River, providing the concentrated nuclear material for the bomb that destroyed Nagasaki, Japan (the Hiroshima bomb used uranium manufactured in Oak Ridge, Tennessee), just 28 months after construction began.

Cold War

The end of WW II saw a new threat on the horizon, the Soviet Union. Fearful over the rapid expansion of communism into Eastern Europe and China, the U.S. embarked on a massive nuclear warhead buildup based upon Eisenhower's policy of "massive retaliation." Hanford became the center of fuel fabrication, chemical processing, and nuclear waste management and research during the Cold War, and by 1964 had grown to include nine plutonium production reactors. Production began to slow after

this, and by 1971 only one plant was still making plutonium for nuclear weapons. It was finally shut down in 1988; a plutonium-uranium extraction plant was closed two years later. Only the experimental Fast Flux Test Facility remains open today, as the Federal government ponders the prospect of using the $5 billion facility as a source of tritium for medical research. The Hanford Site is also still home to a Washington Public Power Supply System (WPPSS) nuclear plant.

Toxic Soup

After the closing of the last plutonium reactor, the environmental problems that had been hidden in secrecy for more than 45 years began to surface. The worst disasters emerged from the early years of operation, when the hazards were not as well understood, and when the pressure to build nuclear bombs as quickly as possible meant lax safety measures. Military leaders were also fearful of telling workers the truth, lest they refuse to work, so they calmed them with promises that everything was fine. The officer who oversaw the Manhattan Project, Gen. Leslie Groves, noted that: "Leaks are bound to occur; people are bound to talk . . . but the less the better and the less disclosure there will be to unauthorized persons." Secrecy was more important than safety, and it wasn't until the 1980s that documents detailing the radioactive hazards were finally released.

The production of plutonium 239 creates many unwanted byproducts, and in more than four decades of production, Hanford left behind 60 million gallons of radioactive chemical waste. At first, the waste was simply dumped onto the land; when radioactive swamps began to form, it was pumped into the ground, and later it was stored in 177 large underground tanks (at least 66 of which leaked). Not surprisingly, this highly concentrated plume of radioactive contaminants spread underground into the water table, and airborne radioactive iodine collected on plants where they were eaten by people and cattle (and people who drank milk from cows). More than 685,000 curies of radioactive iodine 131 spewed from the separation plants in just the first three years of operation, causing thousands of people to be exposed to potentially lethal doses of radiation. Ongoing studies are trying to determine what happened to these people and others who

(continues on next page)

A NUCLEAR LEGACY

(continued)

were exposed, but there are many stories of entire "downwind" families stricken by mysterious cancers, of a high incidence of multiple sclerosis, stillborn babies, immune-system disorders, and brain tumors.

Another legacy of plutonium production was contamination of the Columbia River. Water from the river was used to cool the nuclear plants, and between 1958 and 1964 so much heat and radioactivity were being dumped into the Columbia that the Grand Coulee Dam had to release massive quantities of water to keep the river from becoming dangerously hot as it flowed past Hanford. Heavily contaminated fish and shellfish began showing up at the Columbia's mouth, and there was concern for public safety since both Pasco and Kennewick drinking water supplies came from the river downstream of the nuclear plants. Fortunately, the radionuclide levels in river water have dropped to background levels since the closure of the plants.

The Cleanup

In 1989, the U.S. Dept. of Energy, the Washington State Dept. of Ecology, and the U.S. Environmental Protection Agency signed a "Tri-Party Agreement" to spend the next 30 years in the largest and most complex waste cleanup ever. Hanford is considered the worst hazardous waste mess anywhere in the nation, the sort of place that makes most other sites pale by comparison. The easiest places at Hanford have been cleaned up in the last few years, but the real problems remain, particularly the toxic stew of radioactive waste that sits in un-

derground tanks or has escaped into the ground (we're talking groundwater contamination covering hundreds of square miles). The tanks were meant to be temporary, but there is little chance that this waste will be removed for decades to come, since no other storage options exist. And then there are the nuclear reactors with their miles of contaminated pipes and other materials, the plutonium/uranium solution sitting in tanks at an old processing plant, other buildings with large quantities of highly carcinogenic PCBs, and boiling pools filled with cesium and strontium capsules. You get the picture, Hanford's an environmental nightmare, and even politicians are starting to suggest that it will never be entirely cleaned up. Critics talk of the potential for explosions that could spew radiation into the air, and leaking storage tanks polluting local water supplies. Supporters of Hanford say the amount of radiation received by Tri-Cities residents from the plant is far less than what Spokane residents receive from natural sources such as radon gas.

One surprising effect of the shutdown of Hanford and subsequent cleanup has been that it actually spawned economic growth in the Tri-Cities. Billions of Federal dollars have flowed into the region, providing employment for more than 19,000 engineers, spill experts, construction workers, and others. With an eventual price tag of at least $30 billion (and possibly $100 billion), the environmental cleanup has proven to be a far bigger project than the reactors ever were. Because of all the research needs, there are more Ph.D.s per capita in Kennewick than any other town in the western U.S.

---

ton Public Power Supply System (WPPSS; commonly called "Whoops," and for good reason) at their plant approximately 10 miles north of Richland on Route 4. The center is open Thurs.-Fri. 11 a.m.-4 p.m., and Sat.-Sun. noon-5 p.m. Inside, you can watch a video about the power plant, learn the wonders of nuclear power, and see how uranium is mined and processed. Great fun for the whole family; be sure to ask what they do with all the radioactive waste the plant produces and how they're going to make sure it's still safe for the next 10,000 years or so.

Ice Harbor Dam and Lake Sacajawea

Nine miles east of Pasco on the Snake River, Ice Harbor Lock and Dam is the first of four dams on the Lower Snake, with one of the highest single-lift locks in the world, rising 103 feet. Take a self-guided tour, watch the fish climb the ladders, or stop by the visitor center, open daily 9 a.m.-5 p.m. April-October. The Ice Harbor Dam creates Lake Sacajawea, accessible for fishing, waterskiing, or swimming at **Levey Park** on the Pasco-Kahlotus Rd. on the lake's west side, **Charbonneau Park,** and **Fishhook Park** off Hwy. 124 on the east side.

Lake Wallula

McNary Dam (see under "East to Tri-Cities" in The Columbia Gorge section), 30 miles south of Pasco, backs up the Columbia River to form the 64-mile-long Lake Wallula. Slack water extends to Richland on the Columbia River and to the Ice Harbor Dam on the Snake River, creating ideal conditions for the popular hydroplane races each July.

Five miles east of Kennewick off Finley Rd., **Two Rivers County Park** is open daily for boating, swimming, and picnicking along the Columbia River/Lake Wallula.

Sacajawea State Park

Two miles east of Pasco off Hwy. 12, Sacajawea State Park sits at the confluence of the Snake and Columbia Rivers at the site where Lewis and Clark camped in 1805 on their way to the Pacific Ocean. You can fish, water-ski, or picnic here Wed.-Sun. April-Sept.; no camping. An **interpretive center** here contains exhibits on Sacajawea—the Shoshoni girl who acted as interpreter for the Lewis and Clark party—plus information about the expedition, videos, and Indian artifacts.

Juniper Dunes Wilderness

This 7,100-acre parcel of BLM wilderness is 16 miles northeast of Pasco on Pasco-Kahlotus Road. It contains the six largest remaining western juniper groves in Washington and sand dunes that top 130 feet high and are up to 1,200 feet long. Access is only through private land, so you'll need to get the permission of local ranchers to reach the dunes, and you may need a 4WD vehicle for the last several miles of road. Call the Spokane District Office of the Bureau of Land Management at (509) 456-2570 for details. There are no trails or drinking water, and summer temperatures often exceed 100° F, so come prepared. The best time to visit is in the spring and fall when temperatures are more moderate. Overnight camping is possible, but permits are recommended from the BLM.

Wineries

Most of the 35 or so wineries in southeast Washington are covered in "Yakima Valley Wineries," above, including four in nearby Benton City: Seth Ryan Winery, Oakwood Cellars, Kiona Vineyards, and Blackwood Canyon Winery. The Tri-Cities area has a handful of its own, including **Preston Wine Cellars,** tel. (509) 545-1990, one of the area's biggest, five miles north of Pasco off Hwy. 395. Established in the early 1970s, Preston is the state's largest family owned and operated winery. They produce a full range of wines but are especially known for their chardonnays and rieslings. The tasting room and gift shop are open daily 10 a.m.-5:30 p.m.; take a self-guided tour or enjoy a picnic on the parklike grounds. Preston has frequent events throughout the year, including a kite festival in late April and a chili cook-off in mid-September.

Bookwalter Winery, 710 S. Windmill Rd., Richland, tel. (509) 627-5000, opened in 1984 and now makes a full range of wines. The winery is open daily 10 a.m.-5 p.m.

Started in 1985, **Gordon Brothers Cellars,** tel. (509) 547-6224, overlooking the Snake River at 531 Levey Rd. in Pasco, primarily grows grapes for other wineries but also produces a number of varieties. Open for tasting and tours Sat.-Sun. 11 a.m.-5 p.m. June-August.

Badger Mountain Winery, 110 Jurupa, Kennewick, tel. (800) 643-9463, is one of the first certified organic vineyards making estate wines. Open for tastings and tours by appointment.

Chateau Gallant, 1355 Gallant Rd. in Pasco, tel. (509) 545-9570, is adjacent to the McNary Game Refuge (a good place to watch ducks and geese) and produces wine that include chardonnay, gewürztraminer, and white riesling. The tasting room is open daily 2-5 p.m.

ACCOMMODATIONS

See the Tri-Cities accommodations chart for a complete listing of hotel and motel accommodations. Because of the recent construction boom, many rooms are taken up by workers who stay on a weekly basis. It's a good idea to book ahead, especially during July when the hydroplane races attract throngs of visitors from across the Northwest.

Campgrounds

Camp at the Army Corps of Engineers' **Hood Park,** on the Snake River near its confluence with the Columbia, four miles southeast of Pasco. Tent sites are $10, RV sites $12; open

TRI-CITIES ACCOMMODATIONS

Accommodations are arranged from least to most expensive within each city. Rates may be lower during the winter months. The area code is 509.

KENNEWICK

Columbia Motor Inn; 1133 W. Columbia Dr.; tel. 586-4739; $31 s, $37 d

Green Gable Motel; 515 W. Columbia Dr.; tel. 582-5811; $35 s or d; kitchenettes

Tapadera Budget Inn; 300 N. Ely; tel. 783-6191; $36-46 s, $44-54 d; outdoor pool, AAA approved

Super 8 Motel; 626 N. Columbia Center Blvd.; tel. 736-6888 or (800) 800-8000; $43 s, $47 d; indoor pool, jacuzzi

Nendel's Inn; 2811 W. 2nd; tel. 735-9511 or (800) 547-0106; $43 s, $51 d; outdoor pool, kitchenettes available, continental breakfast, airport shuttle

Shaniko Motel; 321 N. Johnson; tel. 735-6385; $45 s, $50 d; outdoor pool, kitchenettes, AAA approved

Comfort Inn; 7801 W. Quinault; tel. 783-8396 or (800) 221-2222; $47-59 s, $52-64 d; indoor pool, jacuzzi, AAA approved

Silver Cloud Inn; 7901 W. Quinault Ave.; tel. 735-6100 or (800) 551-7207; $57 s, $63 d; indoor and outdoor pools, jacuzzi, exercise room, continental breakfast, AAA approved

The Dogwood Cottage; 109 N. Yelm; tel. 783-5337; $65 s or d; full breakfast

Ramada Inn on Clover Island; tel. 586-0541 or (800) 272-6232; $68-87 s, $73-92 d; outdoor pool, jacuzzi, sauna, exercise room, riverside location, airport shuttle, AAA approved

Cavanaugh's at Columbia Center; 1101 N. Columbia Center Blvd.; tel. 783-0611 or (800) 843-4667; $73 s, $83 d; outdoor pool, jacuzzi, free airport shuttle, AAA approved

PASCO

Starlite Motel; 2634 N. 4th Ave.; tel. 547-7531; $28 s, $33 d; airport transport, kitchenettes, next to noisy railroad tracks, AAA approved

Motel 6; 1520 N. Oregon St.; tel. 546-2010 or (800) 466-8356; $28 s, $34 d; outdoor pool

Goal Post Motor Inn; 2724 W. Lewis St.; tel. 547-7322; $30 s, $35 d; outdoor pool, kitchenettes

Airport Motel; 2532 N. 4th St.; tel. 545-1460; $32 s, $34 d; kitchenettes

Hallmark Motel; 720 W. Lewis St.; tel. 547-7766; $32 s, $36 d; outdoor pool, continental breakfast, AAA approved

King City Truck Stop; 2100 E. Hillsboro Rd.; tel. 547-3475; $38 s, $43 d; AAA approved

Vineyard Inn; 1800 W. Lewis; tel. 547-0791 or (800) 824-5457; $40-45 s, $45-55 d; indoor pool, jacuzzi, sauna, free continental breakfast, kitchenettes available, free airport shuttle, AAA approved

Red Lion Inn; 2525 N. 20th Ave.; tel. 547-0701 or (800) 733-5466; $80-90 s, $90-100 d; two outdoor pools, jacuzzi, exercise room, AAA approved

RICHLAND

Columbia Center Dunes; 1751 Fowler St.; tel. 783-8181 or (800) 638-6168; $33 s, $35-37 d; outdoor pool, sauna, kitchenettes, AAA approved

Econo Lodge; 515 George Washington Way; tel. 946-6117 or (800) 446-6900; $36 s, $40 d; outdoor pool

Bali Hi Motel; 1201 George Washington Way; tel. 943-3101; $38 s, $42 d; outdoor pool, sun deck, AAA approved

Nendel's Inn; 615 Jadwin Ave.; tel. 943-4611 or (800) 547-0106; $42-47 s, $47-52 d; outdoor pool, continental breakfast, free airport shuttle, AAA approved

Bedford Inn B&B; 706 Taylor St.; tel. 946-5259; $45 s, $60 d; two antique-furnished guest rooms, full breakfast

Shilo Inn; 50 Comstock; tel. 946-4661 or (800) 222-2244; $53-60 s or d; outdoor pool, jacuzzi, kitchenettes, tennis, free airport shuttle, AAA approved

Red Lion Inn Hanford House; 802 George Washington Way; tel. 946-7611 or (800) 733-5466; $69-80 s, $79-89 d; outdoor pool, jacuzzi, boat dock, very nice riverside lodging, airport transport, AAA approved

Best Western Tower Inn; 1515 George Washington Way; tel. 946-4121 or (800) 528-1234; $70 s, $80 d; indoor pool, jacuzzi, saunas, recreation area, airport transportation, AAA approved

April to late October. More camping at **Charbonneau Park,** 14 miles northeast of Pasco on Lake Sacajawea (Snake River). Open year-round, with tent sites for $11, RV places for $15. Farther away is **Fishhook Park,** 23 miles northeast of Pasco on Lake Sacajawea. Tent camping ($10) and RV parking ($12) are available April to late September. **Columbia Park,** tel. (509) 783-3711, two miles west of Kennewick on Hwy. 240, has campsites ($6) and RV spaces ($12). Open mid-April through October.

Private RV parks in the Tri-Cities area include **Columbia Mobile Village,** 4901 W. Clearwater Ave. in Kennewick, tel. (509) 783-3314; **Green Tree RV Park,** 2200 N. 4th in Pasco, tel. (509) 547-6220; **Lloyd's Desert Gold RV Park,** 611 Columbia Dr. SE in Richland, tel. (509) 627-1000; **Maxey's Mobile Home Park,** 3708 W. Clearwater Ave. in Kennewick, tel. (509) 783-6411; **Riviera Trailer Village,** W. Sylvester and Rd. 32 in Pasco, tel. (509) 547-3521; and **Trailer City Park,** 7120 W. Bonnie Ave. in Kennewick, tel. (509) 783-2513.

FOOD

Breakfast, Bakeries, and Coffeehouses

Start your day at **Blackberry's Restaurant,** 329 N. Kellogg in Kennewick, tel. (509) 735-7253, for the best local breakfasts.

Panaderia Colina, 102 N. 10th Ave. in Pasco, tel. (509) 545-3938, makes wonderful and amazingly inexpensive Mexican pastries. If you don't

speak Spanish, you may be the only one here who doesn't. **Jennifer's Bread & Bakery,** 2417 W. Kennewick Ave. in Kennewick, tel. (509) 586-3904 (they also have two shops in Richland), bakes fresh breads, rolls, and sweets and makes good lunchtime sandwiches. Get bagels at **Some Bagels,** 1317 George Washington Way, tel. (509) 946-3185.

The ubiquitous **Starbucks,** 2801 W. Clearwater Ave. in Kennewick, tel. (509) 735-9464, has dependably good espresso coffees, as do a number of other local places, such as **Amore Espresso,** 1257 Guyer Ave. in Richland, tel. (509) 946-4160.

American Food

For seafood, steak, prime rib, and pasta with outside riverside seating, head to **Cedars Pier 1,** 7 Clover Island (next to the Quality Inn), tel. (509) 582-2143. Also good for steaks is **Henry's,** 1435 George Washington Way in Richmond, tel. (509) 946-8706, or 3013 W. Clearwater Ave. in Kennewick, tel. (509) 735-1996.

Bruce's Steak and Lobster House, 131 Vista Way in Kennewick, tel. (509) 783-8213, serves lunch and dinner daily with entertainment in the lounge. **Red Robin,** 924 George Washington Way in Richland, tel. (509) 943-8484, is a very popular family place for burgers, salads, and pastas. Big salad bar too.

Boulevard Bar & Grill, 1250 Columbia Center Blvd. in Richland, tel. (509) 735-6575, is one of the nicer local places and features outside dining along the Columbia River.

Get surprisingly good pizzas at **Gaslight Restaurant and Bar,** 99 Lee Blvd. in Richland, tel. (509) 946-1900.

If you're heading north from Pasco, take a back route 12 miles north from town to visit the only Mennonite restaurant in the area, **Goose & Gander Restaurant & Gift Shop,** 11760 N. Glade Rd., tel. (509) 297-4458. Enjoy wonderful country cooking, homemade pies, and soups.

International Eats

Chez Chaz Bistro, 5011 W. Clearwater Ave. in Kennewick, tel. (509) 735-2138, is a very popular lunch emporium with sandwiches, quiche, and other fare. **Giacci's Italian Specialties,** 94 Lee Blvd., tel. (509) 946-4855, has reasonably priced Italian lunches and dinners with outside tables to relax in the sun. **Mama Vallone's,** 2800 W. Clearwater Ave. in Kennewick, tel. (509) 736-1085, is another notable Italian eatery. **Pasta Mama's** manufactures pasta and sauces that are shipped all over the United States. They're available locally from their retail outlet at 1270 Lee Blvd. in Richland, tel. (509) 946-8282.

Emerald of Siam, 1134 Jadwin Ave. in Richmond, tel. (509) 946-9328, creates authentic and delicious Thai food and has an inexpensive lunch buffet Mon.-Friday. **Bangkok Restaurant,** 8300 Gage Blvd. in Kennewick, tel. (509) 735-7631, is also popular for Thai cooking.

Because of the large number of agricultural workers from Mexico and other points south, the Tri-Cities have an abundance of Mexican restaurants. The finest of these is probably **Casa Chapala,** 107 E. Columbia Dr. in Kennewick, tel. (509) 586-4224, which provides excellent food and ultra-fresh tortillas. They have a second outlet next to Columbia Center Mall, and a third one in Pasco at 508 N. 4th, tel. (509) 546-0673. Also good are two Richmond Mexican restaurants: **Isla Bonita,** 1520 Jadwin Ave., tel. (509) 946-3383, and **Las Margaritas,** 627 Jadwin Ave., tel. (509) 946-7755.

Fine Dining

The Moore Mansion Restaurant, 200 Rd. 34 in Pasco (near the Blue Bridge), tel. (509) 547-8760, is the Tri-Cities's most elegant dining establishment. Located in an enormous antebellum-style home built in 1908 along the Columbia

River levee, the building is worth a visit even if you aren't eating here. The mansion has served many purposes over the years. Tunnels once connected it to the river, allowing for the smuggling of stolen horses, and it was a speakeasy in the Prohibition era and a commune in the 1970s before being restored to its original glory. The food is gourmet Northwest cuisine, a special-occasion sort of place where a dinner for two could easily cost $50. Reservations recommended.

The **Blue Moon,** 21 W. Canal Dr., Kennewick, tel. (509) 582-6598, is one of the best restaurants in the region. The seven-course prix-fixe menu features seafood, lamb, pork, chicken, and more, and the wines are all local; open weekends for dinner only. Reservations required.

Another fine local establishment is **Green Gage Plum Restaurant,** 3892 W. Van Giesen in West Richmond, tel. (509) 967-2424, where the menu specializes in pasta and seafood, and the pastries are homemade.

Produce and Treats

Visit the **Pasco Farmer's Market,** 4th and Lewis Streets, tel. (509) 545-0738 for local produce, sausages, fresh breads, arts, and crafts on Wednesday and Saturday 8 a.m.-1 p.m. May-November. This is the largest open-air farmers market in Washington. The **Kennewick Central Open Air Market,** tel. (509) 586-3101, is held on Flag Plaza at the corner of Kennewick Ave. and Benton St. on Wednesday and Saturday 9 a.m.-noon from June through October.

Adam's Place Gourmet, Route 11 in Pasco, tel. (509) 582-8564, is located in an apple orchard and makes all sorts of sweet confections, even chocolate-covered pizzas.

ENTERTAINMENT

Pubs and Nightclubs

The Pub Tavern, 7001 W. Clearwater Ave. in Kennewick, tel. (509) 735-7868, has a light menu to accompany their 20 beers on tap. **R.F. McDougall's,** 1705 Columbia Dr. SE in Richmond, tel. (509) 735-6418, has hors d'oeuvres, pizzas, pasta, and burgers, along with many imported beers and cocktails. Eat outside on the riverside deck in the summer.

Enjoy live music or comedy on weekends at **Harry's Bar & Grill,** in Richland's Best Western Tower Inn at 1515 George Washington Way, tel. (509) 946-4121. **Cavanaugh's at Columbia Center,** 1101 N. Columbia Center Blvd. in Kennewick, tel. (509) 783-0611, features Top-40 entertainment nightly. **Mustang Sally's Lounge,** 1800 W. Lewis in Pasco, tel. (509) 544-0982, has the hottest rock and blues bands in the area Thurs.-Sat. nights. Also try the **Crow's Nest Lounge,** at Quality Inn on Clover Island in Kennewick, tel. (509) 586-0541; **Bruce's Steak & Lobster,** 131 Vista Way in Kennewick, tel. (509) 783-8213; **Killarney's Irish Pub,** 3330 W. Court St. in Pasco, tel. (509) 547-2595; and **The Steak Out Restaurant & Lounge,** 213 W. Kennewick Ave. in Kennewick, tel. (509) 582-5048.

Events
The festival season begins in late April with a **Kite Festival** at Preston Winery in Pasco, and kicks into high gear for the **Cinco de Mayo** Mexican festivities in Pasco. The **Tri-Cities Wineries Barrel Tasting** in early June is a favorite introduction to local wineries.

Richland's **Sunfest** is a summer-long series of weekend activities that feature international food, music, and dancing. Sunfest events include the **Tri-Cities Children's Festival** in mid-June, **Ye Merrie Greenwood Renaissance Faire** in late June, **Pickin' in the Park Country Music Festival** in mid-July, **Allied Arts Sidewalk Show** in late July (southeast Washington's largest arts and crafts show), and the **Fabulous '50s, '60s, and '70s Festival** in mid-August.

In mid-July, Pasco hosts the **Tri-Cities Air Show** featuring high-flying acrobatics. One of the Tri-Cities' biggest events is the annual **unlimited hydroplane races** on the Columbia River, the highlight of the late-July **Tri-Cities Water Follies and Columbia Cup.** Originally called the "Atomic Cup," the races have been going on for more than three decades. The action centers around Columbia Park in Kennewick, but you can also watch from the Pasco side if you don't mind the sun in your face; get to the park early on Friday or Saturday to take a pit tour before the races. Other Water Follies activities include basketball, volleyball, and tennis tour-

naments, a carnival, dancing, and a talent show.

Kennewick hosts the **County Fair and Rodeo** every August, with top entertainers performing at the fairgrounds at 1500 S. Oak St., off 10th Avenue. More music, arts, food, and dancing at the **Pasco Autumn Festival** on the weekend after Labor Day in September.

November brings the **Tri-Cities Northwest Wine Festival** to Kennewick, featuring 60 different wineries. December's big event is the **Christmas Lights Boat Parade,** when decorated boats cruise down the Columbia.

Art Galleries and Shows
In the Tri-Cities area, Richland comes out ahead in art galleries; perhaps it's a reflection of the highbrow tastes of all the Ph.D.s. Visit the **Allied Arts Association Gallery,** 89 Lee Blvd., tel. (509) 943-9815, and see paintings, pottery, and weavings by local artists. Also here are **Alexander Art Gallery,** 1507 George Washington Way, tel. (509) 946-6802, and **Anvil Studio & Gallery,** 1955 Birch Ave., tel. (509) 946-6735.

In Kennewick, **The Appleseed Gallery and Shops,** 108 Vista Way, tel. (509) 735-2874, has 11 shops filled with local arts and crafts, oil and watercolor paintings, toys, cards, and more. Across the street at 135 Vista Way, **Beaux Art Gallery,** tel. (509) 783-4549, has stained glass, pottery, paintings, and crafts.

Music and Dance
For those of classical taste, call for scheduled events staged by the **Mid-Columbia Symphony Society,** tel. (509) 735-7356, in existence for more than 50 years, or the **Mid-Columbia Regional Ballet,** 1405 Goethals, Richland, tel. (509) 946-1531.

Movies
Escape the heat and reality with a movie at Kennewick's **Clearwater Cinema,** 325 N. Johnson, tel. (509) 735-7511; Richland's **Uptown Cinema,** 1300 Jadwin, tel. (509) 943-6671; **Columbia Center Cinema,** 900 Columbia Center Blvd., tel. (509) 783-1354; or **Metro 4 Cinemas,** 1390 Columbia Center Blvd., tel. (509) 735-0414. For drive-in fun, head to **River-Vue Drive-In,** W. Sylvester and Rd. 28 in Pasco, tel. (509) 547-4361.

SPORTS AND RECREATION

Spectator Sports
The Tri-Cities are home to two professional sports teams that play at Kennewick's Tri-Cities Coliseum. The **Tri-City Chinook** (tel. 509-735-0500 for tickets) play basketball in the Continental Basketball Association, while the **Tri-City Americans** (tel. 509-783-9999 for tickets) play hockey in the Western Hockey League.

Cycling
Riverfront bike paths link Pasco city parks. Kennewick's **Columbia Park** has a popular six-mile paved, nearly level path. Rent bikes from **Kennewick Schwinn**, 3101 W. Clearwater Ave. in Kennewick, tel. (509) 735-8525.

Swimming and Boating
With all this heat and unrelenting sunshine, you'll need a place to cool off. The city of Pasco has two public **swimming pools,** and other public pools can be found in Kennewick and Richland. The **YMCA** is at 19 N. Cascade in Kennewick, tel. (509) 586-0015.

Take your swimsuit to **Oasis Waterworks,** 6321 W. Canal Dr. in Kennewick, tel. (509) 735-8442, and try their 10 water slides, a "rolling rapids river ride," 5,000-square-foot swimming pool, shaded picnic area, AstroTurf sunbathing area, 100-person hot tub, basketball and volleyball courts, and more. Open daily in the summer. Admission is $12.50 for all day, $9.25 for the afternoon.

Rent boats and jet-skis at **Columbia Park Marina,** 1776 Columbia Dr. SE in Richland, tel. (509) 736-1493, or from **Sundown Marine,** 1238 Columbia Dr. SE in Richland, tel. (509) 783-1649.

Racing
The favorite local racing events are the hydroplane races during the Tri-City Water Follies in late July (see "Events," above). Watch auto racing on Saturday nights in the summer at **Tri-City Raceway,** two miles west of West Richmond, tel. (509) 967-3851. At Kennewick's Benton-Franklin Fairgrounds on E. 10th Ave., **Sun Downs Horse Racing Track,** tel. (509) 586-9211, has quarter-horse racing in spring and fall.

Horn Rapids Off-Road Vehicle Park, tel. (509) 967-5814, off Hwy. 240 in Richland, has two motocross tracks, a four-by-four obstacle course, a sand drag strip, a go-cart track, and camping ($5). Open all year.

Golf
Golfers will find seven public courses in the Tri-Cities area, including Pasco's **Sun Willows Golf Course,** 2335 N. 20th, tel. (509) 545-3440; Kennewick's **Columbia Park Golf Course** at Columbia Park, tel. (509) 586-4069; **Canyon Lakes,** 3700 Canyon Lakes Dr., tel. (509) 582-3736; **Tri-Cities Country Club,** 314 N. Underwood, tel. (509) 783-6014; Richland's **Sham-Na-Pum Golf Course,** 72 George Washington Way, tel. (509) 946-1914; West Richland's **Tapteal Community Golf Course,** 4000 Fallon Dr., tel. (509) 967-2165; and Richland's **Horn Rapids,** tel. (509) 375-4714. These are all 18-hole courses.

SHOPPING

Columbia Center in Kennewick is the Tri-Cities's largest shopping mall, with 100 stores including The Bon Marché, Lamonts, Sears, and JCPenney; take the Columbia Center Blvd. exit off Hwy. 12. Not far from here are practically every known mega-store: Kmart, Best, Target, ad nauseam. For something a bit less hectic, head to **Pasco Village Marketplace,** on the corner of 4th and Lewis in Pasco, where various shops sell arts and crafts, clothing, gourmet food, imported textiles, jewelry, and more. In Richland, **The Indian Basket,** 1229 Columbia Dr., tel. (509) 735-2323, has jewelry, sand paintings, glassware, dream catchers, and other Native American crafts.

INFORMATION AND SERVICES

Pick up all the current maps and information you need from the **Tri-Cities Visitor and Convention Bureau,** housed in the Vista Airport building at the end of Grandridge Blvd. in Kennewick, tel. (509) 735-8486 or (800) 666-1929. Open Mon.-Fri. 8:30-5 year-round. You might also want to stop by the **Kennewick Chamber** of Commerce, 3180 W. Clearwater, Suite F, tel. (509) 736-0510 (hidden in a shopping mall behind the Sizzler Restaurant); **Richland Chamber of Commerce,** 515 Lee Blvd., tel. (509) 946-1651; or the not especially helpful **Pasco Chamber of Commerce,** 1600 N. 20th, tel. (509) 547-9755, open Mon.-Fri. 9 a.m.-5 p.m.

The eastern Washington **area code** is 509. For medical attention, contact **Our Lady of Lourdes Hospital,** 520 N. 4th, Pasco, tel. (509) 547-0009; **Kadlec Medical Center,** open 24 hours at 888 Swift Blvd. in Richland, tel. (509) 946-4611; or **Kennewick General,** W. 10th Ave. and Dayton, tel. (509) 586-6111.

TRANSPORTATION AND TOURS

By Train
The Tri-Cities are served by **Amtrak**'s Empire Builder, which provides service four days a week east to Spokane, Minneapolis, and Chicago, and west to Wishram, Bingen, Vancouver, and Portland. The station is at W. Clark and N. Tacoma in Pasco, tel. (509) 545-1554 or (800) 872-7245.

By Bus
Hop aboard **Ben Franklin Transit,** tel. (509) 735-5100, to get around town for 50 cents Mon.-Fri. 6 a.m.-7 p.m. and Saturday 8 a.m.-7 p.m. Ben Franklin provides service to Tri-Cities Air-

port, downtown Kennewick, Richland, and Pasco, and out to West Richland, and has curb-to-curb night service till 11 p.m. (tel. 509-582-5555).

Greyhound serves the Tri-Cities from 115 N. 2nd in Pasco, tel. (509) 547-3151 or (800) 231-2222. **Northwestern Trailways,** tel. (800) 366-3830, stops in Pasco and has connections throughout the Northwest.

By Air
Departing from the Tri-Cities Airport in Pasco—the first airport west of the Mississippi—are **Horizon Air,** tel. (800) 547-9308, **Delta Air Lines,** (800) 221-1212, and **United Express,** tel. (800) 241-6522. The Richland airport is a popular place for skydiving; call **Richland Skysports,** tel. (509) 946-3483 for details.

Tours
King's Fisher Guide Service, tel. (509) 375-7442, offers all-day boat trips up one of the last free-flowing stretches of the Columbia River in Washington, the "Hanford Reach." This tour is led by professional geologist Dave Myers and includes information on the geology, the Hanford nuclear reactors and their cleanup, and the abundant wildlife along the way. The trip continues 60 miles upriver to Priest Rapids Dam.

River City Tours, tel. (509) 735-9578, offers a wide range of tours around the Tri-Cities area, including boat trips, winery tours, and farm visits.

BOB RACE

EASTERN WASHINGTON

When you cross the Columbia River on I-90 headed toward Spokane, you are entering the northernmost reaches of the Great American Desert, which runs through portions of eastern Washington, Oregon, Nevada, and California, and down into Arizona and Mexico. It ends with the trees of the Spokane area and the Okanogan Highlands. The Columbia River, in its huge S-shaped turn across the state, helps define the desert's northern and western boundaries.

Despite open country that alternately freezes in the winter and sears in the summer, scarce rainfall, and precious few year-round streams, this basaltic desert has always had several small, scattered natural lakes. Their numbers increased dramatically when the enormous Columbia Basin Irrigation Project created Lake Roosevelt, Moses Lake, and Banks Lake, and raised the water table to create hundreds of small ponds. Much of the region receives less than 10 inches of rain a year and sees 300-plus days of sunshine. Wind can sometimes be a problem, especially in the spring when blinding dust storms can arise.

Geology
Probably the most exciting event in eastern Washington history was witnessed by no one: the **Spokane Flood,** which occurred 18,000-20,000 years ago. As the last ice age came to an end, the glaciers melted and water backed up behind the ice-dammed Clark Fork River in the great basin where Missoula, Montana, now stands. The ice-and-earthen dam created an enormous lake covering more than 3,000 square miles—larger than Puget Sound—and marks from its shoreline can still be seen along the mountains above the basin.

As the ice dam melted, the great pressure from the backed-up water caused it to suddenly collapse, sending an unimaginable rush of water over all of eastern Washington, flattening the landscape, gouging out coulees, washing away soil, and emptying the great lake in as little as two days. It is said to have been the greatest flood ever recorded on the planet. Evidence of the flood is shown on the landscape between Spokane and the Columbia River around the Tri-Cities area, a region known as the **Channeled Scablands.** Most protruding rocks and mesas are ship-shaped, all pointing in a northeasterly direction, and there's no evidence that the erosion process was caused by streams, the normal source of such erosion. The prevailing geological theory is that there may have been many of these floods (see the special topic "The Catastrophist").

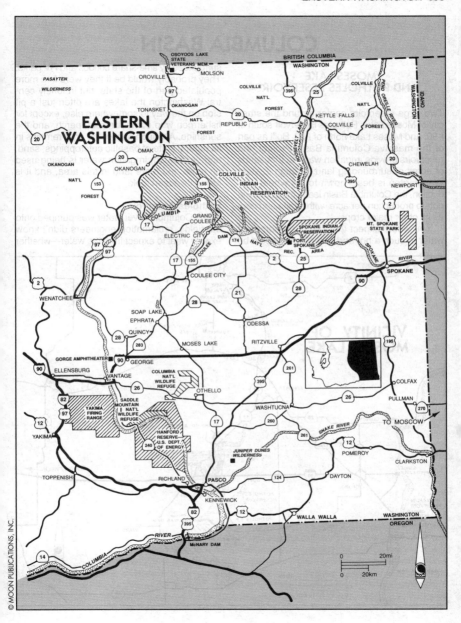

COLUMBIA BASIN

MOSES LAKE AND POTHOLES RESERVOIR

Two large reservoirs center around the small city of Moses Lake: Potholes Reservoir south of I-90, and Moses Lake north of I-90. Built as part of the massive Columbia Basin Project, the reservoirs provide irrigation water to thousands of acres of surrounding land. Though eastern Washington is best known for its wheat production, the Columbia Basin leads the country in potato production per acre, with alfalfa and corn as its other major crops.

You would expect that two large bodies of water in such a hot and arid climate would be surrounded by time-share condos and RV parks. They probably would be if they were in a more populated part of the state, but in lonely central Washington the lakes are often just a pit stop on the way to somewhere else, except for fishermen who come for trout, perch, and the sunshine. Although a lot of the area remains in its natural state of basaltic outcroppings, sand, and sagebrush, irrigation water is being used on more and more land in this area, and it is losing its desert look.

Potholes Reservoir
When Columbia River water was pumped onto the fields, reclamation engineers didn't know exactly what to expect from the water—whether

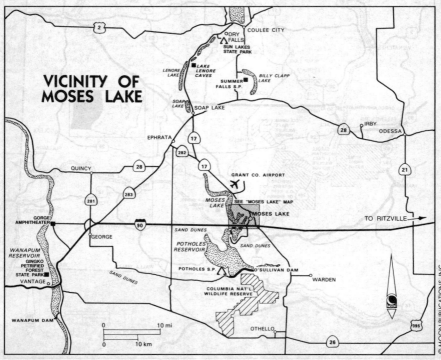

MOSES LAKE AREA ACCOMMODATIONS

Accommodations are arranged from least to most expensive. Rates may be lower during the winter months. The area code is 509.

Maples Motel; 1006 W. 3rd Ave.; tel. 765-5665 or (800) 359-5605; $24 s, $35 d; outdoor pool, kitchenettes

Sunland Motor Inn; 309 E. 3rd Ave.; tel. 765-1170; $28 s, $30 d; outdoor pool

El Rancho Motel; 1214 S. Pioneer Way; tel. 765-9173 or (800) 341-8000; $28 s, $31 d; outdoor pool, kitchenettes

Motel 6; 2822 Wapato Dr.; tel. 766-0250 or (800) 466-8356; $28 s, $34 d; outdoor pool

Imperial Inn; 905 W. Broadway; tel. 765-8626; $32 s or d; outdoor pool, kitchenettes

Mar Don Resort; 8198 Hwy. 262 E; tel. 346-2651; $35 s or d; swimming beach on Potholes Reservoir, kitchenettes, no TV or phones

Oasis Budget Inn; 466 Melva Lane; tel. 765-8636 or (800) 456-2247; $36 s, $38 d; kitchenettes, jacuzzi, sauna, continental breakfast

Interstate Inn; 2801 W. Broadway Ave.; tel. 765-1777 or (800) 777-5889; $39 s, $46 d; swimming pool, jacuzzi, sauna, kitchenettes

Lakeside Motel; 802 W. Broadway Ave.; tel. 765-8651; $40 s, $54 d; kitchenettes

Super 8 Motel; 449 Melva Lane; tel. 765-8886 or (800) 800-8000; $43 s, $47 d; outdoor pool

Travelodge; 316 S. Pioneer Way; tel. 765-8631 or (800) 255-3050; $45 s, $55 d; outdoor pool, jacuzzi, AAA approved

Holiday Inn Express; 1735 E. Kittleson; tel. 766-2000 or (800) 465-4329; $63-75 s, $68-75 d; indoor pool, jacuzzi, kitchenettes, continental breakfast, fitness center, AAA approved

Heritage Suites; 511 S. Division St.; tel. 765-7707 or (800) 457-0271; $64 s or d; townhouse suites with kitchens, two night minimum stay

Best Western Hallmark Inn; 3000 Marina Dr.; tel. 765-9211 or (800) 235-4255; $69-80 s, $73-85 d; outdoor pool, jacuzzi, exercise facility, tennis courts, AAA approved

Shilo Inn; 1819 E. Kittleson Rd.; tel. 765-9317 or (800) 222-2244; $78-83 s or d; indoor pool, jacuzzi, sauna, steam room, exercise facility, free airport shuttle, kitchenettes available, AAA approved

Carriage House B&B; 2801 W. Peninsula Dr.; tel. 766-7466 or (800) 761-7466; $95-130 s or d; new Victorian-style home, four guest rooms, private baths, soaking tubs, antique furnishings, full breakfast, wedding and small conference facilities

it would stand and create lakes, or flow underground. It did both. The irrigation water in the Moses Lake area and farther north toward Grand Coulee generally seeps southward—following the natural slope of the land—and collects in Potholes Reservoir behind O'Sullivan Dam.

The **O'Sullivan Dam,** on Hwy. 17 at the south end of Potholes Lake and Othello (halfway between Moses Lake and Othello) is one of the largest earth-filled dams in the nation. The reservoir collects overflow from irrigated lands to the north, transferring the water into the Potholes East

Canal and feeding farms to the south. South of the dam are more than 50 seep lakes included within Columbia National Wildlife Refuge (see under "Othello," below). In the winter, Potholes Reservoir is a major resting place for waterfowl—thousands of ducks are visible.

Parks

Located at the southwest end of O'Sullivan Dam, **Potholes State Park** is a popular spot for launching a boat to catch the reservoir's trout, walleye, and perch. Waterskiers, picnickers, and swimmers also enjoy the sunny east-of-the-mountains weather at this 2,500-acre park. The park offers summertime slide shows and nature hikes. Tent ($10) and RV hookup sites ($15) are available year-round. Call (509) 765-7271 for information, and (800) 452-5687 for campsite reservations ($6 extra fee), available up to 11 months ahead of time.

The city-run **Cascade Park** on Valley Rd., and Cascade Valley on Moses Lake, offers swimming, boating, waterskiing, showers, camping, and RV hookups. Open mid-April through mid-October. Call (509) 766-9240 for reservations ($5 extra).

Moses Lake State Park, immediately north of I-90 (take exit 175), has swimming, fishing for trout, crappie, and catfish, a grassy picnic area, and a snack bar—but no camping. In the winter, this is a favorite ice-skating spot.

Explore Moses Lake on a motorboat rented from **Cascade Marina,** 2242 Scott Rd., tel. (509) 765-6718; or **Mar Don Resort,** 8198 Hwy. 262 E., tel. (509) 765-5061.

Sand Dunes

Hike, slide, or ride your off-road vehicle on over 3,000 acres of sand dunes south of the city of Moses Lake. Go four miles south on Division St., then follow the signs—and six miles of gravel road—to the ORV park. Camping is permitted here, but there are no facilities.

MOSES LAKE (THE CITY)

The bustling small city of Moses Lake (pop. 11,700) is a growing desert settlement with all the usual trappings of American "progress": Wal-Mart, Kmart, fast-food chains, strip malls, and developments spreading across the landscape. It isn't especially attractive but will do as a stopping point. The main attractions here are nearby Moses Lake and Potholes Reservoir, along with the immensely popular summertime concerts at the Gorge Amphitheater near George on the Columbia River (see under "Quincy and George," below). Like most of eastern Washington, the Moses Lake area gets little rainfall—about eight inches a year—and some of the state's highest summer temperatures.

History

Moses Lake is named for Chief Moses of the Sinkiuse tribe. Early white settlers came on the promises of developers and the Northern Pacific Railroad but found a hard scrabble existence in this desert country. One wrote of it being "100 miles to town, 20 miles to water, six inches to hell!" However, two major government developments changed this. The first was the construction of Grand Coulee Dam in the 1930s, and more important, the completion of the Columbia Basin Irrigation Project in 1952. This brought large quantities of cheap water to the region and transformed it into some of the most productive fields in Washington. During WW II, a major army air base was developed on the flat lands near Moses Lake; eventually this became Larson Air Force Base. It closed in 1966, but the citizens of Moses Lake turned it into a training center for Boeing where the pilots and crews of various international airlines—most notably Japan Air Lines—flight test new planes. Visitors to the area are likely to see jumbo jets circling slowly overhead, practicing maneuvers (look out below!).

Sights

Eighteen-mile-long Moses Lake is two miles west of town and a popular attraction for boaters and anglers. **Adam East Museum and Art Center,** 122 W. 3rd Ave., tel. (509) 766-9395, displays fossils from prehistoric animals, geological specimens, old photos, Indian artifacts, and works of local artists. Open Tues.-Sat. noon-5 p.m. all year; call (509) 766-9240 for free info. **Monty Holm's House of Poverty and Mon Road Railroad,** 228 S. Commerce, tel. (509) 765-6342, contains things Monty has collected over the years, including entire trains, gasoline engines, antique cars, fire engines, and just plain stuff. The yard out front is packed with vehicles of all types, from sheepwagons to a steam engine. Free admission; open Mon.-Fri. 8 a.m.-3:45 p.m. summers only. Armed forces buffs may want to check out the small **Schiffner Military and Police Museum,** 4840 Westshore Dr., tel. (509) 765-6374, with over a hundred uniforms on display. Open by appointment only.

Kids may want to visit the **Petting Zoo** run by the local Humane Society on Randolph Rd. at

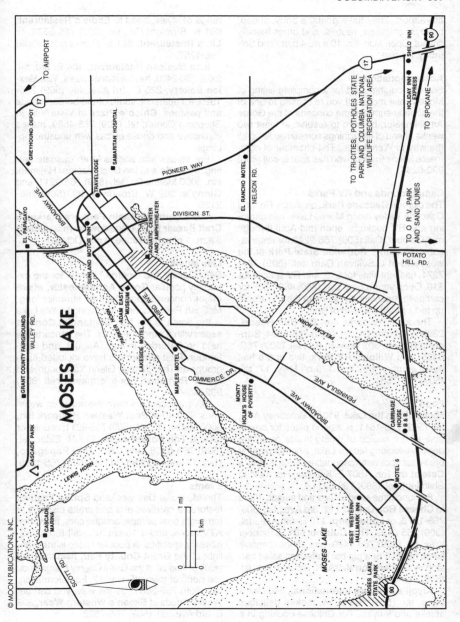

MOSES LAKE

TO AIRPORT

TO SPOKANE

© MOON PUBLICATIONS, INC.

the airport. They have goats, a pony, sheep, turkeys, chickens, rabbits, and other friendly critters. Open Mon.-Fri. 10 a.m.-4 p.m., and Saturday 1-4 p.m.

Accommodations

See the lodging chart for a complete listing of Moses Lake motels. If you're coming to one of the popular summertime concerts at the Gorge Amphitheater, be sure to reserve at least two weeks ahead of time; things sometimes fill up all the way to Wenatchee. The chamber of commerce keeps track of who has space; call (800) 992-6234.

Campgrounds and RV Parks

The city-run **Cascade Park,** on Valley Rd. and Cascade Valley along Moses Lake, has camping and RV hookups; open mid-April through mid-October. Call (509) 766-9240 for reservations ($5 extra). **Potholes State Park** at the west end of O'Sullivan Dam, tel. (509) 765-7271, has tent sites for $10, and RV spaces for $10. Open year-round. Call (800) 452-5687 for campsite reservations ($6 extra fee), available up to 11 months ahead of time.

The local RV parks are: **Big Sun Resort,** 2300 W. Marina Dr., tel. (509) 765-8294; **Suncrest Resort,** 303 Hansen Rd., tel. (509) 765-0355; and **Willows RV Park,** two and a half miles south of I-90 exit 179 off Hwy. 17, tel. (509) 765-7531.

Food

Michael's on the Lake, 910 W. Broadway Ave., tel. (509) 765-1611, is a good place for breakfast, with a choice of dining inside or on the deck overlooking Moses Lake. Another popular breakfast spot with reasonable prices is **Bob's Cafe at the Inn,** 1807 E. Kittleson Rd. (next to Shilo Inn), tel. (509) 765-3211.

For lunchtime sandwiches and salads, head to **Cheese Box Deli,** 121 W. 3rd Ave., tel. (509) 765-1276, or **Little Shop,** 110 E. 5th Ave., tel. (509) 765-9132. **Thai Cuisine,** 601 S. Pioneer Way, tel. (509) 766-1489, has an inexpensive lunch buffet. For a pig-out buffet and salad bar, stop by **Golden Corral,** 930 N. Stratford Rd., tel. (509) 765-0565.

Kiyoji's Sapporo International, 440 Melva Lane, tel. (509) 765-9314, makes delicious steaks and teriyaki. For Chinese cooking in a range of styles, head to **Eddie's Restaurant,** 801 N. Stratford Rd., tel. (509) 765-5334, or **Lin's Restaurant,** 621 S. Pioneer, tel. (509) 766-4257.

Inca Mexican Restaurant, 404 E. 3rd, tel. (509) 766-2426, has traditional meals. Visit **Mexico Bakery,** 225 E. 3rd Ave., tel. (509) 765-1829, for authentic south-of-the-border breads and pastries. **Chico's Pizza** in Vista Village Shopping Center, tel. (509) 765-4589, makes distinctive and dense pizzas with unusual toppings.

For steaks and pastas in an upscale setting, try **Cade's** at the Best Western Hallmark Inn, 3000 Marina Dr., tel. (509) 765-9211, and **Ginny's,** 302 W. Broadway, tel. (509) 766-2125.

The **Columbia Basin Farmers Market & Craft Bazaar** takes place downtown Saturdays 8 a.m.-1 p.m. from June to mid-October.

Live Music

See "Quincy and George," below, for the extremely popular **Gorge Amphitheater,** where major concerts take place all summer long. McCosh Park Amphitheater along Moses Lake is the home to the free **Centennial Concert** series with a range of styles. The concerts are held on Saturday in July, August, and September. Past performers have included such groups as The Platters, Glenn Yarbrough, and Ranch Romance. For information call (800) 992-6234.

Several local bars have live music on weekends: Top-40 at **Best Western Hallmark Inn,** 3000 Marina Dr., tel. (509) 765-9211; country or rock at **The Porterhouse,** 217 N. Elder, tel. (509) 766-0308; and C&W at **El Papagayo,** Hwy. 17 and Stratford Rd., tel. (509) 765-1265.

Events

The Memorial Day weekend **Spring Festival** features a carnival, arts and crafts displays, a torchlight boat parade, antique cars, fireworks, ATV races, and a 10-km run; call (509) 765-8248 for specifics. A popular rodeo is the highlight of the **Grant County Fair,** held the third week of August at the Grant County Fairgrounds just north of town off Hwy. 17. For information, call (509) 765-3581. By the way, you can get Western duds at **Skeen's Western Wear,** 305 E. 3rd Ave., tel. (509) 765-7522.

A HOME FOR VOLGA GERMANS

One of Washington's most interesting migrations was that of the Volga Germans to the wheat country, particularly in the dryland area around Ritzville. The Volga Germans had a history of migration that went back a century when their ancestors were lured to Russia from Germany. Russia's Empress Catherine II, like all of Russia's royalty in the 18th and 19th centuries, was German. She was born and reared in Germany, but when she ascended to the throne, she became fluent in Russian and wanted Russia to mature and develop.

The Volga River valley had some of Russia's richest soil, but it was hardly tilled because few people lived there, partially due to the frequent attacks by Turks only a short distance south. So Catherine II decided to colonize the area with a people she knew from her childhood: the poor, often displaced German farmers. She brought in an estimated 27,000 farmers who proved themselves industrious, perhaps to a fault because their presence was resented by many Russians from the start. Half a century later, the dislike of the immigrants grew into hostility as the Slavophile movement gained momentum. This movement was originated in the Volga area by misguided intellectuals, and stressed the superiority of the Orthodox church over all others, especially the German's Lutheran Church, and the superiority of the Slavic people in general.

Almost coincidental with this unrest was the emergence of an American industrialist named Henry Villard, who began as a journalist and became a major railroad and land entrepreneur with a special interest in the rich farming land of eastern Washington. He was reared in Germany and was educated there before coming to America, so he saw the connection between European immigrants and the building of America more clearly than most railroad men.

Villard at one time had more than 900 agents traveling around Europe handing out pamphlets urging people to come to America and take his trains and his steamships to eastern Washington where they could buy land from Villard for between $5 and $10 an acre at seven percent interest.

An estimated 100,000 Volga Germans sold everything they owned and bought tickets to America. Many of them stopped first in the Great Plains states of Kansas, Nebraska, and the Dakotas, but many of those had to give up and move on to Washington because of blizzards, droughts, locusts, hail, windstorms, and the other weather conditions that have always plagued farmers there. To their pleasant surprise, when they came to Washington they found that Villard's claim of having the "best wheat, farming, and grazing lands in the world" weren't exaggerated.

While some settled in the rich Palouse Country, the largest number went into what is now called the dryland area. One of the first towns established was Ritzville, named for its founder, Philip Ritz, who came up from Walla Walla after amassing a fortune as a farmer and businessman. Ritz hired some Volga Germans to work on his farm and quickly learned to value their industriousness and sense of community. He began encouraging others to come to the area, and today most of the names on mailboxes and in the telephone directory date back to the time when Philip Ritz encouraged and assisted these newcomers.

It wasn't easy at first, because almost none of the Volga Germans had any money. Most arrived in America with little more than their clothing, and had left the Great Plains with not much more than that. Many had to live in dugouts in the Great Plains the first year or two, and many did so again on their arrival in the Ritzville area. But this didn't last long, and today the third and fourth generation of the Volga Germans are among Washington's most successful farmers.

Recreation

The sparkling new **Moses Lake Family Aquatic Center** in McCosh Park at 4th and Dogwood, tel. (509) 766-9246, has an Olympic-size outdoor swimming pool, two 200-foot water slides, a tube slide, sand volleyball courts, concession stands, and lots of fun places for kids to play. It's open May through Labor day and costs $2.50 for adults, $1.50 for kids.

Rent mountain bikes from **Sports Elite,** 108 W. 3rd Ave., tel. (509) 765-6181. Play golf in the sunshine at: **Sage Hills Golf Course,** 12 miles south of Moses Lake on Hwy. 17, tel. (509) 349-7794; **South Campus Golf Course,** 1475 E. Nelson Rd., tel. (509) 766-1228; and **Potholes Golf Course,** 6897 O'Sullivan Dam SE, tel. (509) 346-2447.

Information and Services

For local information, contact the **Moses Lake Chamber of Commerce,** 324 S. Pioneer Way, tel. (509) 765-7888 or (800) 992-6234; open Mon.-Fri. 8 a.m.-4 p.m.

The **area code** in Moses Lake and all of eastern Washington is 509. The **Moses Lake Public Library** is located at 5th and Pioneer Way, tel. (509) 765-3489. **Samaritan Hospital,** 801 E. Wheeler Rd., tel. (509) 765-5606, has 24-hour emergency room service.

Transportation

Both **Greyhound,** tel. (509) 765-6441 or (800) 231-2222, and **Northwestern Trailways,** tel. (800) 366-3830, have bus service throughout the Northwest from the bus station at 630 E. Broadway. **Horizon Air,** tel. (800) 547-9308, offers scheduled passenger service to Seattle from Grant County Airport (one of the longest civilian runways west of the Mississippi), north of town off Randolph Road. The nearest **Amtrak** station is in Ephrata.

QUINCY AND GEORGE

The almost-flat Quincy Valley is a study in contrasts: although receiving just eight inches of rainfall, it contains some of the most productive farms in Washington, producing potatoes, apples, wheat, alfalfa, corn, and many other vegetable crops. This is possible because of the West Canal that feeds water from the Columbia River via Banks Lake to irrigate these fields. The valley was first settled in the late 19th century; it struggled along until 1951 when irrigation waters first reached here. Today the town of Quincy contains 4,000 people and is the primary agricultural center in the area. It has frozen food processing plants, produce facilities, a diatomaceous earth chemical plant, and even a still to extract mint flavoring. Good views across Quincy Valley, from the top of **Monument Hill,** north of town.

Over in George (pop. 300), **White Heron Cellars,** tel. (509) 785-5521, has tours and tastings Wed.-Sun. noon-5 p.m. This isn't your standard hoity-toity winery. Located in an old gas station, they advertise "three different grades of wine guaranteed to increase the mileage of any meal, while providing motor protection &

lubrication." For a look at one of the more unusual geologic features in the area, take exit 143 (six miles southwest of George) from I-90, and follow Old Vantage Rd. west to **The Pinnacles,** a favorite rock-climbing spot.

Gorge Amphitheater

Located 14 miles southwest of Quincy and seven miles northwest of George, the Gorge Amphitheater, tel. (509) 255-3600, is a natural amphitheater in the basaltic bluffs overlooking the Columbia River and a highly successful concert venue operated by MCA Concerts Northwest. The amphitheater is home each summer to Saturday concerts by major musicians (REM, Tom Petty, Janet Jackson, Stone Temple Pilots, James Taylor, Dwight Yoakam, among others) that attract upwards of 15,000 people. These shows mean packed motels as far away as Wenatchee and Moses Lake, so reserve ahead. Camping and RV spaces are available on adjacent grounds, and a full range of food services are offered.

Practicalities

There are three places to stay in Quincy: **Traditional Inns,** tel. (509) 787-3525, where rooms go for $43 s, $51 d ($53 s, $61 d on Gorge concert weekends); **Sundowner Motel,** tel. (509) 787-3587, for $35 s or d ($50 s or d on Gorge concert weekends); or **Villager Inn Motel,** 711 2nd Ave. SW, tel. (509) 787-3515, $48 s or d. All of these have kitchenettes.

Eight miles west of Quincy off Hwy. 28, **Crescent Bar Resort,** tel. (509) 787-1511, on Wanapum Reservoir offers swimming, boating, waterskiing, picnicking, fishing, a playground, condo rentals, tennis courts, a nine-hole golf course, a restaurant, RV spots, and camping.

Get local information from the **Quincy Valley Chamber of Commerce,** 119 F St. SE, tel. (509) 787-2140. The **library** is located at 108 B St. SW. An outdoor **swimming pool** is also in Quincy at Jaycee Municipal Park.

Quincy is served by **Greyhound Bus,** from Kissel's Variety Store on the corner of 1st Ave. and B St. SE, tel. (800) 231-2222.

Events

Other than the amphitheater concerts, the main local event is the catchily named **Farmer Consumer Awareness Day** on the second Saturday of September. It includes a fun run, parade, food booths, exhibits, live music, and free guided tours of local food processing plants.

The tiny town of George is best known for its **George, Washington** celebration on the Fourth of July (pretty obvious where the town name originated). Each year locals bake the "world's largest cherry pie" and have various pie-eating and pit-spitting contests, plus fireworks when evening comes.

WANAPUM LAKE AREA

Gingko Petrified Forest State Park
Fifteen to 20 million years ago, this part of Washington was first covered by lush forests and then by molten lava that poured out of fissures in the earth's crust. Logs that had washed into nearby lakes were preserved intact by the lava cover; water eventually leaked through to the logs, and the silica in the groundwater replaced the natural structure of the wood. The tremendous erosion during the last ice age exposed 259 species of petrified trees in this area, including the prehistoric gingko, a "living fossil" that still grows in Japan and has been planted in city parks throughout America.

An **interpretive center,** tel. (509) 856-2700, just north of the town of Vantage (exit 136 of I-90) houses displays on the geologic history of the area and offers a slide show about gingkoes. Outside are large pieces of petrified wood. The center is open daily 10 a.m.-6 p.m. from mid-May to mid-September.

For a beautiful country drive, head west from the interpretive center along the Vantage Hwy. that connects Vantage to Ellensburg. This is the back way and makes a good bike ride (narrow shoulders, alas). Sagebrush, rugged land, cattle, and ranches give this a Western appeal. Tune in the AM radio for cowboy or Mexican music to fit the mood. Two miles west on Vantage Hwy. are several interpretive trails that lead uphill past more samples of various species (walnut, spruce, Douglas fir, elm, sweetgum, and gingko) beneath wire cages. A two-and-a-half-mile trail leads across the dry, windblown hills past an assortment of scrappy wildflowers, sagebrush, and broad views. Watch for bald eagles, hawks, deer, elk, coyote, and a variety of lizards and snakes, including the poisonous Northern Pacific rattlesnake.

Camping is available at **Wanapum State Recreation Area,** four and a half miles south of the Gingko Visitor Center. All sites have complete hookups and cost $16; open April-Oct., plus weekends and holidays the rest of the year.

Wanapum and Priest Rapids Dams
Wanapum Dam was named for the Wanapum Indians, a peaceful and religious tribe that lived along the river between present-day Pasco and Vantage. The last Indian peoples to live in traditional tule mat long houses, the Wanapum refused to leave their ancestral home along the Columbia. Finally, in the early 1950s, four men—the last full-blooded Wanapum—agreed to allow a dam at the site. They had been forced from their land south of here when Hanford Atomic Works began in the 1930s. (Lewis and Clark found 2,500 Wanapum in the region, but introduced diseases devastated the tribe.) Following this agreement, Grant County built the Wanapum and Priest Rapids dams here and added the **Wanapum Dam Heritage Center,** tel. (509) 754-3541. Open daily 9 a.m.-8 p.m. April-Nov., and Mon.-Fri. in the winter, the center houses a collection of artifacts and other Wanapum materials, a replica of the steamship *Columbia,* and exhibits on the development of the Columbia River Basin and the building of the dams. Watch a 12-minute slide show on the Wanapum people, and check out the 29-foot long dugout canoe they once used. A stone object here is of particular interest; some archaeologists theorize that it served as a calendar, while others say it was used to record songs and dance ceremonies. Tours are available on weekdays.

One of the major attractions at the Wanapum Dam is a fish ladder and fish viewing room where you can watch salmon, steelhead, and other fish heading upstream April through November. An artificial spawning channel and hatchery downstream from Priest Rapids Dam provide a chance for salmon to spawn; their original spawning creeks were nearly all destroyed when the dams were built. Nearby is a dramatic vista point overlooking the Columbia River.

Priest Rapids Dam is 12 miles downriver from Wanapum Dam, at the site of seven now-inundated rapids. It was here in 1811 that fur trappers saw Wanapum Indian spiritual leaders performing ceremonies.

OTHELLO

Othello (pop. 4,700) is about 20 miles south of Moses Lake and 46 miles north of the Tri-Cities area. Named for the Shakespearean play, Othello began as a stop along the Milwaukee Railroad early in this century but did not come into its own until the 1950s, when water from the Columbia River—50 miles to the north—reached the area in irrigation canals. Earlier farming and ranching efforts failed due to the desert conditions, and it took the massive Columbia Basin Project of the New Deal to transform this land by the building of Grand Coulee Dam, Banks Lake, and a series of three canals to send water into the Columbia Basin deserts.

Today, Othello is surrounded by pool-table flat agricultural fields with giant circular irrigation systems fed by water from the Columbia River. These farms grow potatoes and other vegetables, as well as a wide variety of fruits. With two major processing plants (Carnation Company and McCain Foods), Othello lays claims to the potato processing capital of the world. Also in town is a plant that makes Seneca apple juice.

Columbia National Wildlife Refuge

The Columbia National Wildlife Refuge covers 23,000 acres of scenic desert land between Moses Lake and the Othello area. The refuge contains a rugged jumble of cliffs, wide open sagebrush grasslands, eroded canyons, and a scattering of more than 50 lakes and ponds created by rising groundwater due to irrigation. Most impressive of all are the **Drumheller Channels**, just south of Potholes Reservoir. They are visible from a viewpoint along Mc-Manamon Rd., approximately nine miles northwest of Othello. The refuge is home to more than 100,000 birds each fall and is a vital winter resting area for mallards and Canada geese. Although the refuge is closed to public entry during the peak season (to protect the birds from disturbance), it is open for birdwatching, hiking, camping, and fishing in the spring and summer. Several short trails lead through; stop

by the headquarters at 44 S. 8th St. in Othello, tel. (509) 488-2668, for maps and other specifics.

Sights

Browse through local arts and crafts at **The Old Hotel,** a 1912 hotel-boardinghouse at 33 E. Larch St., tel. (509) 488-5936. The local **chamber of commerce** is also inside, tel. (509) 488-2683 or (800) 684-2556; open Mon.-Sat. 9 a.m.-5 p.m. all year.

Othello Community Museum at 3rd and Larch Streets is open June-Oct. on Saturday only 1-5 p.m. Inside this 1908 Presbyterian church—the oldest building in town—are exhibits on the area's irrigation, railroad history, the "day the lights went out" after the eruption of Mt. St. Helens, and the usual pioneer items.

Hunter Hill Vineyards, 2752 W. McManamon Rd., tel. (509) 346-2736, is open for tours and tastings daily 11 a.m.-5:30 p.m. Located nine miles northwest of Othello, the winery overlooks the canyons of Columbia National Wildlife Refuge.

Accommodations

Cabana Motel, 655 E. Windsor, tel. (509) 488-2605 or (800) 442-4581, has an outdoor pool, jacuzzi, and kitchenettes; rooms go for $25-35 s, $30-40 d. **Cimarron Motel,** 1450 Main St., tel. (509) 488-6612, has an outdoor pool, jacuzzi, and rooms for $30 s, $35 d. Both Cabana and Cimarron also have RV parking. The AAA-approved **Aladin Motor Inn,** 1020 E. Cedar St., tel. (509) 488-5671, has an outdoor pool and kitchenettes for $35-39 s, $40-44 d.

Campsites are available in **Scooteney Park,** 11 miles south along Hwy. 17 for $7 (no hookups), and at **Soda Lake Campground,** 20 miles north of town within Columbia National Wildlife Refuge.

Food and Entertainment

Marian's Old Hotel Restaurant, tel. (509) 488-9466, in the Old Hotel, features delicious homemade soups, sandwiches, and desserts for lunch, plus prime rib and seafood selections for dinner. The finest local steaks, along with a big salad bar and hefty sandwiches can be found at **Brunswick Bar & Grill,** 28 E. Main, tel. (509) 488-9861.

Like many other eastern Washington farming centers, Othello has a large number of migrant workers and a growing community of immigrants from Mexico and Central America. Because of this, you'll find a tortilla factory and several authentic Mexican restaurants, including **Benavidez Cafe,** 32 E. Main St., tel. (509) 488-2078, and **El Caporal Restaurant,** 1244 E. Main, tel. (509) 488-0487. Locals particularly recommend **Casa Mexican,** 1224 E. Main, tel. (509) 488-6163. Find live music most weekends at the **Cimarron Restaurant,** 1450 Main St., tel. (509) 488-6612.

Each Saturday 8 a.m.-1 p.m. from mid-May through September, you'll find a **farmers market** in Pioneer Park on Main St. between 3rd and 4th Avenues, with fresh fruits and veggies, honey, baked goods, and local crafts.

Events

Othello's main event is the **Adams County Fair and Rodeo,** held in mid-September at the fairgrounds two miles south of town. Come here for country music, PRCA rodeos, arts and crafts displays, a livestock auction, parade, carnival, food booths, demolition derby, and the crowning of Miss Othello Rodeo. The **Fourth of July** brings a remote-controlled aircraft event, an arts and crafts "Sun Faire," a children's parade, sports tournaments, and evening fireworks.

Recreation

Othello has an outdoor **swimming pool,** as well as the **Othello Golf Club** three miles south of town. Other nearby golf courses are in Royal City (23 miles west) and Warden (10 miles north).

RITZVILLE

Ritzville (pop. 1,700) is a small wheat-farming town about 45 miles northeast of Moses Lake on I-90. It is the main town in an area settled by Volga Germans during the latter part of last century. These folks were descendants of German citizens lured to the Volga River Valley in Russia by Catherine the Great, a German herself. The Volga Germans were harshly discriminated against by the Russians after Catherine died, and all had to flee the country. Many managed to immigrate to America, and most settled across the northern part of the country. (See the special topic "A Home for Volga Germans.")

Museums

The **Dr. Frank R. Burroughs Home,** 408 West Main in Ritzville, was built in 1890 and served for 37 years as the physician's office, containing records of house calls, births, and fees charged. The 1907 **Andrew Carnegie Library,** also in Ritzville at 302 W. Main, houses photos and artifacts from Ritzville's history, as well as the city's public library and a time capsule buried in its front lawn in 1981.

Practicalities

In Ritzville, the **Best Western Heritage Inn,** 1405 Smitty's Blvd., tel. (509) 659-1007 or (800) 528-1234, has rooms for $51-61 s, $58-68 d, including a continental breakfast. **Colwell Motor Inn,** 501 W. 1st Ave., tel. (509) 659-1620 or (800) 341-8000, has rooms for $40-50 s or d, including an outdoor pool and sauna. **Top Hat Motel,** 210 E. 1st, tel. (509) 659-1100, charges $24-30 s or d. The most interesting place to stay is **Portico Victorian B&B,** 502 S. Adams St., tel. (509) 659-0800, where a 1902 mansion has been transformed into an antique-filled lodging place. Rates are $59-74 s or d, including a full breakfast.

The **Ritzville City Park,** just off I-90 at the Washtucna exit, covers almost three acres and has a public swimming pool, playground equipment, an outdoor kitchen, restrooms, and horseshoe pits. No overnight camping.

Both **Greyhound,** tel. (509) 659-1792 or (800) 231-2222, and **Northwestern Trailways,** tel. (800) 366-3830, have service from the bus station at 1176 S. Division. Get local information at the old **Burlington Northern Depot,** tel. (800) 873-8648, open daily in the summer 9 a.m.-6 p.m.

ODESSA

Odessa is a tiny town of fewer than a thousand folks, and a minor agricultural and retirement center. Like neighboring Ritzville, Odessa was settled by Volga Germans in the late 19th century. The wide main street (1st Ave.) passes neat small homes of brick and wood, along with a handful of German-style buildings, including city hall. Odessa gets blazing hot in the summer months.

Sights

The **Odessa Historisches Museum** on the west edge of town has exhibits on the Germans from Russia who settled the area, and a replica of a barn from early Odessa. It is open Sunday 2-5 p.m. from Memorial Day through September. Nine miles west of Odessa off Hwy. 28 is the ghost town of **Irby,** where the 90-year-old Irby Hotel stands surrounded by desolate desert country. Immediately north of here are rich Palouse soils—prime wheat-growing areas— that escaped the massive floods of the ice ages. Southwest of here is the **Marlin Hutterite Colony.** Visitors should call ahead to arrange a tour by contacting Sara Gross, tel. (509) 345-2390, or Empire Tours, tel. (509) 783-0942.

Geology

Much of the land surrounding Odessa is raw, rough-edged desert, the heart of two cataclysmic geologic episodes. The first was a series of 150 volcanic eruptions starting 17 million years ago that covered much of the Northwest in lava up to three miles thick, followed by the ice ages that led to massive Columbia River floods. These floods carved enormous gouges in the basalt, creating the dry coulees prominent in eastern Washington. The Odessa area has dozens of shallow craters of varying sizes; some reach 2,000 feet across. There are as many theories on their origin as there are geologists who have studied these odd features.

To tour the Channeled Scablands around Odessa, stop by the visitor center and pick up the excellent, detailed brochure. The center also has a 12-minute video on the Scablands. The tour takes you west of town along the bizarre formations of Crab Creek, past the ghost town of Irby, and on to the fascinating region around **Lakeview Ranch** on BLM land. Nearby are a series of large craters to explore, a picnic area, a few primitive campsites, and shady trees. Keep your eyes open for rattlesnakes, however.

Practicalities

Lodging is available at **Odessa Motel,** tel. (509) 982-2412, where rooms go for $35 s or d (with kitchenette $40 s or d). The **Odessa Tourist Park** on the corner of 1st Ave. and 2nd St. has free camping, and you can eat with the farmers at **Farmer's Inn,** or shop in one of the German-style stores around town. And yes, you can even get espresso in Odessa.

Odessa Golf Course, tel. (509) 982-0093, is a nine-hole course on the west end of town and has space for RV hookups ($7). Odessa also has an aquatic center with an outdoor **swimming pool** and jacuzzi open mid-June to Labor Day.

The **Odessa Visitor Center,** tel. (509) 982-0049, is at 3 W. 1st Ave. in the Record Square cluster of shops.

Events

Odessa's Germanic heritage comes out in **Deutschesfest,** on the third weekend of September. The festival includes a parade, German food (borscht kuchens from Odessa Baptist Church, krautranzas from St. Joseph Altar Society, apple strudel from Christ Lutheran Church, and cabbage rolls from Heritage United Church of Christ), arts and crafts, a carnival, and fun run, but the main attraction is a *biergarten* with polka music (by the OomPas and Mas), big band tunes, and country western music. Deutschesfest attracts retired folks by the busloads, and more than 650 RVs fill the athletic field.

EPHRATA

Ephrata (ee-FRAY-ta) is a tidy town of 5,600 set amidst a sprinkling of trees and surrounded by miles of flat and desolate desertscape with short grasses and sage, and irrigated fields with verdant crops. The town stretches for over a mile along Basin St. and is headquarters to the Columbia Basin Reclamation Project, the irrigation arm of the Grand Coulee Dam project. Few towns in Washington were more desolate than Ephrata before the irrigation project arrived in the 1950s.

The town's name comes from the Biblical village where Christ was born, Bethlehem Ephrathah, and supposedly originated when a traveler on the Great Northern Railway stopped here and found a prospering orchard irrigated by a spring. It reminded him of the Holy Land, and the name stuck. ("Ephrathah" means "fertile region.")

Grant County Historical Museum and Pioneer Village

Ephrata is home to an outstanding collection of Indian and pioneer artifacts, clothing, tools, diaries, documents, and relics arranged chronologically from prehistoric to modern times, at Grant County Historical Museum and Pioneer Village, 742 N. Basin St., tel. (509) 754-3334. One of the finest historical collections in Washington, the museum covers almost four acres of downtown. The 27-building pioneer village includes a saloon, dress shop, barbershop, watch repair shop, Catholic church, jail, printing office, blacksmith, and even a house built from polished petrified wood. The buildings are both original structures and reproductions.

In the crowded main museum, be sure to find the 1895 Rockaway carriage, a beautifully refurbished glass-enclosed carriage used by the local postmaster who also happened to be a Scottish nobleman, Lord Thomas Blythe. An aimless young man, Blythe was sent to America by his father in an attempt to force him into maturity; it obviously worked, because Thomas Blythe went on to become a highly successful cattle rancher. Also surprising are the live snakes that occupy a back room, including a northern Pacific rattlesnake. Downstairs is an amusing collection of carved wooden creatures.

The museum and pioneer village are open Sunday 1-4 p.m., and Monday, Tuesday, and Thurs.-Sat. 10 a.m.-6 p.m. (closed Wednesday), May to mid-September. Guided tours are available until 4 p.m. Entrance costs $2 for adults, $1.50 for ages six to 15, and free for kids under six.

Demonstrations of pioneer crafts are given during the **Living Museum,** held the second weekend in June, when Pioneer Village comes alive with costumed participants in every building—from apple pressing to wool spinning—and cowboy poetry. Kids get to make their own horseshoes at the blacksmith shop.

Accommodations

The **Travelodge,** 31 Basin St. SW, tel. (509) 754-4651 or (800) 255-3050, has rooms for $45-70 s, $55-70 d, and a heated pool. For something a little cheaper, the **Sharlyn Motel,** 848 Basin St., tel. (509) 754-3575 or (800) 292-

2965, has no-frills accommodations for $35 s, $45 d. **Lariat Motel,** 1639 Basin SW, tel. (509) 754-2437, features an outdoor pool and kitchenettes for $30 s or $32 d. **Columbia Motel,** 1257 Basin SW, tel. (509) 754-5226, charges $43 s or d for rooms with kitchenettes.

Ivy Chapel Inn B&B, 164 D St. SW, tel. (509) 754-0629, was originally a Presbyterian Church, but is now a distinctive and friendly bed and breakfast. The ivy-covered red brick building contains six guest rooms with private baths and queen-size beds. Rates are $55 s or $70 d, including a full breakfast. No children under 14.

No public campsites are nearby, but travelers can pitch tents or park RVs at **Stars and Stripes RV Park,** 5707 Hwy. 28 W, tel. (509) 787-1062; or **Oasis RV Park,** 5103 Hwy. 28, tel. (509) 754-5102.

Food

Downtown Ephrata is no bustling commercial hub, but you can get a pizza at **Pizza Extravaganza,** or authentic Mexican food at **El Charo Restuarante,** 33 Basin St. NW, tel. (509) 754-3920.

Events

Ephrata's annual **Sage and Sun Festival,** held in June, features a parade, arts and crafts, antique cars, and a circus. The popular **Living Museum,** described above, comes around in June.

Information and Services

For maps or other area information, contact the **Ephrata Chamber of Commerce,** 12 Basin St. SW, Ephrata, tel. (509) 754-4656 or (800) 345-4656. Open Mon.-Fri. 9 a.m.-4 p.m. all year. The city has an outdoor **swimming pool** on the south end of town. The **area code** for Ephrata is 509.

Transportation

Amtrak, tel. (800) 872-7245, provides service west to Wenatchee, Everett, Edmonds, and Seattle, and east to Spokane and Chicago. The Amtrak depot is on 1st Street.

Greyhound provides bus connections from its Ephrata station at 741 Basin NW, tel. (509) 754-3322 or (800) 231-2222.

SOAP LAKE

Located five miles northeast of Ephrata, Soap Lake is a small body of salty, highly alkaline water surrounded by the deserts of the Columbia Basin. The town of Soap Lake (pop. 1,300) occupies the south shore of the lake, and has long been a place for "taking the cure" for such ailments as psoriasis and arthritis. Others come to soak in the warm sunshine; it shines 310 days a year over Soap Lake, and only rains eight inches annually.

History

Though you'd never suspect it today, Soap Lake was once a bustling resort area surrounding the Soap Lake Sanitorium, a health retreat that capitalized on the lake's legendary medicinal qualities. The Tsincayuse Indians sent their sick to soak in the *smokiam* or "healing waters"; early white explorers called it Soap Lake because its 17 natural minerals and oils give the water a soft soapy feel and create a suds-like foam on windy days. The only other place on earth with similar water is said to be Baden Baden, Germany.

In the early 1900s, great crowds of people from around the country came here to drink and bathe in the alkaline water to cure joint, skin, digestive, and circulatory ailments. Most of the visitors weren't too sick: they found time for drinking, dancing, and general hell-raising, leading the local newspaper to admonish them to "be more careful" about remembering their swimsuits! The drought and Depression of 1933 brought an end to the revelry, turning Soap Lake into a curiosity in the midst of a desolate region. It has been making a steady comeback, though, and the chamber of commerce actively promotes the curative powers of the lake's water with testimonials from satisfied customers ("After only nine days, the pain has gone, and I feel like a new person. . ."). John's Thrift on Hwy. 17 sells soaps and other products made from the lake waters, and the mineral-rich water is piped into several motels for your convenience.

East Beach has play equipment, lake access, and restrooms; the Soap Lake Chamber of Commerce is also here if you need maps or directions. **West Beach** is on the other side of town. One warning: Swim in loose-fitting suits to avoid chafing that can be aggravated by the highly alkaline water. Also be careful to rinse off at the showers and to put on sunscreen after bathing since the minerals in the water act to increase tanning and burning.

Lodging

In Soap Lake, everyone talks about the spacious log **Notaras Lodge,** 231 Main St., tel. (509) 246-0462. It features imaginative rooms named after the slightly famous and decorated with their belongings, such as the Bonnie Guitar Room, with one of the singer's guitars encased in plastic and used as a coffee table, and the Norma Zimmer room, named for the old Lawrence Welk Show's "Champagne Lady." Rooms cost $38-100 s, $45-125 d; the more expensive units feature in-room whirlpools with Soap Lake water piped in, bathroom phones, skylights, and balconies. Also ask about massages and a one-night pass to the members-only club.

The Inn at Soap Lake, 226 Main Ave. E, tel. (509) 246-1132, built in 1905 from rounded river stones, was recently completely remodeled. The rooms are nicely furnished with antiques and have kitchenettes and mineral water soaking tubs. Rates are $45-90 s or 50-95 d, including a continental breakfast. Canoe and paddleboat rentals are available here.

Several places cost cheaper, if more standard, lodging in Soap Lake. **Lake Motel,** 322 Daisy St., tel. (509) 246-1611, has an outdoor pool, jacuzzi, sauna, mineral water baths, and kitchenettes. Rooms cost $25 s, $32 d. **Royal View Motel,** near East Beach, tel. (509) 246-1831, has rooms with kitchenettes for $37-45 s or d. **Tolo Vista Motel,** 22 Daisy N., tel. (509) 246-1512, rents small cabins with kitchens for $39 s, $44 d. **Tumwata Lodge,** 340 W. Main, tel. (509) 246-1416, has a heated pool, mineral baths, and private beach, but no phones. Cabins go for $35-50 s or d.

Campgrounds

Smokiam Campground, tel. (509) 246-1211, adjacent to the chamber of commerce, has waterfront camping for $10 for all sites; open April-October. This is actually just a gravel lot sandwiched between the lake and the highway. More RV sites at **Soap Lake Trailer Court,** 510 5th St. SE, tel. (509) 246-0211. **Soap Lake Resort,** tel. (509) 246-1103, at the north end of the lake, has RV camping, an outdoor pool, jacuzzi, sauna, and swimming beach.

Food
For a good home-cooked meal, visit **Doc's Home Plate Restaurant,** 332 E. Main Ave., tel. (509) 246-1256; hours can be a bit strange since the owner often heads out fishing on a whim! **Don's Steak House,** 14 Canna St. across from Notaras Lodge, tel. (509) 246-1217, specializes in delicious steak, seafood, and Greek dishes; open daily for dinner.

Events
Several local events attract out-of-towners to Soap Lake. The **Panayiri Greek Festival** on Memorial Day weekend kicks things off with a parade, auction, Greek food, Greek folk dancing, belly dancing, and even country and western music (this is Greek?). The town has a big fireworks show on the **Fourth of July,** and a popular **Great Canoe Race** the second weekend of July. The latter covers almost 18 miles of paddling and portaging, and ends with a sprint across Soap Lake to the finish line. The second weekend of August brings the **Soap Lake Pig Run & Feed,** an odd combination that includes a fun run, pig barbecue, and classic car show.

Information and Services
The summer-only **Soap Lake Chamber of Commerce** is right along the lake in a small building, tel. (509) 246-1821. Next door is East Beach, a favorite swimming, picnic, and camping area. The **public library** is located at 191 Main St., tel. (509) 246-1313.

GRAND COULEE DAM AND VICINITY

If you've been driving through the desert country of central Washington, Grand Coulee Dam comes as quite a surprise. Instead of barren sage, grass, and rock, you're suddenly in a cluster of small towns with lush green lawns and split-level suburban homes. This oasis in the desert is the result of one of the largest construction projects ever undertaken. The Grand Coulee is a 50-mile-long gorge carved by the Columbia River during the ice ages, when glaciers forced the river south of its current path. Much of the carving took place during the cataclysmic Spokane Floods (see "Sun Lakes State Park and Dry Falls" under "Lower Grand Coulee Area," below). By the way, the word "coulee" means dry ravine.

The dam is surrounded by a confusing cluster of towns with similar names. Electric City and Grand Coulee are south of the dam, Coulee Dam and Elmer City are north of the dam. All but Elmer City have services. Coulee City sits adjacent to Dry Falls Dam on Banks Lake, 30 miles south of Grand Coulee Dam. All four towns are described below.

GRAND COULEE DAM

Massive Grand Coulee Dam is a place of superlatives and the main destination for travelers in this part of Washington. The dam and surrounding facilities serve a variety of functions, including irrigation, power production, and flood control. Twice as high as Niagara Falls and nearly a mile long, the dam is one of the world's greatest producers of electricity, generating an incredible 22,000 megawatts of energy annually for cities in several states. Only Guri Dam in Venezuela and Itaipu Dam between Paraguay and Brazil generate more electricity. The dam stands 550 feet above bedrock—taller than the Washington Monument—with a 1,650-foot-wide spillway. The 12 million cubic yards of concrete and steel that it contains are enough to build a six-foot sidewalk around the equator (assuming, of course, that you could build a sidewalk around the equator even if you wanted to do so).

On the slope just west of the dam are gigantic pipes through which water is pumped 280

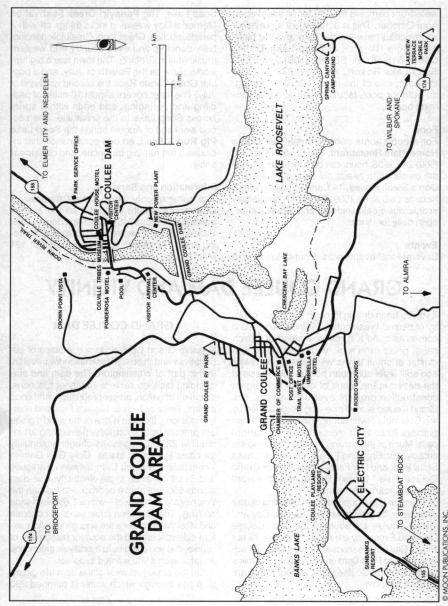

GRAND COULEE DAM AREA

TO BRIDGEPORT

TO ELMER CITY and NESPELEM

PARK SERVICE OFFICE

COULEE DAM

COULEE HOUSE MOTEL

VISITOR CENTER

NEW POWER PLANT

COLVILLE TRIBES MUSEUM

PONDEROSA MOTEL

POOL

CROWN POINT VISTA

VISITOR ARRIVAL CENTER

DOWN RIVER TRAIL

GRAND COULEE DAM

LAKE ROOSEVELT

SPRING CANYON CAMPGROUND

TO WILBUR and SPOKANE

LAKEVIEW TERRACE MOBILE PARK

CRESCENT BAY LAKE

TO ALMIRA

GRAND COULEE RV PARK

GRAND COULEE

CHAMBER OF COMMERCE

POST OFFICE

TRAIL WEST MOTEL

UMBRELLA

RODEO GROUNDS

ELECTRIC CITY

COULEE PLAYLAND RESORT

TO STEAMBOAT ROCK

SUNBANKS RESORT

BANKS LAKE

1 km

1 mi

© MOON PUBLICATIONS, INC.

GRAND COULEE DAM AREA ACCOMMODATIONS

Accommodations are arranged from least to most expensive. Rates may be lower during the winter months. The area code is 509.

NEAR THE DAM

Umbrella Motel; 404 Spokane Way, Grand Coulee; tel. 633-1691; $25 s, $30 d; clean older rooms, kitchenettes available

Trail West Motel; 108 Spokane Way, Grand Coulee; tel. 633-3155; $37 s, $42 d, outdoor pool, kitchenettes available

Sky Deck Motel; Electric City; tel. 633-0290; $47-80 s or d; attractive new motel, outdoor pool, jacuzzi, kitchenettes available, along Banks Lake

Coulee House Motel; 110 Roosevelt Way, Coulee Dam; tel. 633-1101 or (800) 715-7767; $48-94 s or d; outdoor pool, jacuzzi, sauna, exercise room, kitchenettes available, overlooks dam, AAA approved

Ponderosa Motel; 10 Lincoln St., Coulee Dam; tel. 633-2100 or (800) 633-6421; $48-86 s or d; outdoor pool, kitchenettes available, view of dam

Four Winds Guest House B&B; 301 Lincoln St., Coulee Dam; tel. 633-3146 or (800) 786-3146; $55-65 s or d; 10 guest rooms, historic lodging place, shared bath, full breakfast

COULEE CITY AREA

Blue Lake Resort; six miles north of Coulee City at Blue Lake; tel. 632-5634; $27-44 d for cabins; boat rentals, open April-September

Coulee Lodge Resort; six miles north of Coulee City at Blue Lake; tel. 632-5565; $29-39 d for cabins; kitchenettes available, boat rentals, open April-September

Lakeview II Motel; 9811 Fordair Rd. NE, Coulee City; tel. 632-5792; $30 s, $35 d; jacuzzi, sauna, kitchenettes available

Blue Top Motel; 109 N. 6th, Coulee City; tel. 632-5596; $32-35 s or d, kitchenettes available

Main Stay B&B; 110 W. Main, Coulee City; tel. 632-5687; $35 s, $40 d; modern home, continental breakfast, children okay

Ala Cozy Motel; 9988 Hwy. 2 E, Coulee City; tel. 632-5703; $35 s, $40 d; outdoor pool, jacuzzi, sauna, kitchenettes available

Sun Lakes Park Resort; seven miles south of Coulee City; tel. 632-5291; $56-64 d for cabins; outdoor pool, kitchenettes available, boat rentals, open mid-April through September

feet uphill into Banks Lake during periods of high flow. This water then feeds into a series of canals to irrigate a half-million acres of farmland in the Columbia Basin Project. In periods of high energy demand, the pumps become generators as water is released from Banks Lake back down these pipes.

History

For years, the Columbia Basin was recognized as an area of rich soils but low rainfall. Pressure built to harness the Columbia River—sec-

ond largest in America—as a source of irrigation water, and to provide cheap power for the growing Pacific Northwest. Under the urging of President Franklin D. Roosevelt, Congress appropriated $60 million to build this massive project, the linchpin in the Columbia Basin Project. The construction of Grand Coulee Dam, at that time "the biggest thing built by the hand of man," employed thousands of workers during the Great Depression. Work began in 1933, as massive amounts of dirt were removed to get to bedrock. Temporary coffer dams were constructed to

Grand Coulee is one of 14 dams on the Columbia River.

DIANNE BOUERICE LYONS

shift the river while excavation of the riverbed took place, and the first concrete was poured in 1935. Gradually the workers completed a foundation across the riverbed and began pouring the concrete. The dam was finally completed late in 1941, and the Third Power Plant was added in the 1970s. Today, Grand Coulee is one of 11 major dams along the Columbia River within Washington; there are some 200 dams within the entire Columbia River drainage.

Although rumors still abound of men buried alive in the concrete of Grand Coulee Dam, such was not the case. The work was dangerous, however, and 77 men were killed from drownings and blasting or vehicle accidents. Another four men died during completion of the Third Power Plant.

Unfortunately, the "eighth wonder of the world," as it is sometimes still called, inundated rich salmon fishing grounds that had been used by Native Americans for at least 9,000 years. It wasn't until 1994—after 43 years of contentious litigation—that the U.S. Congress finally agreed to pay the Colville Tribe $53 million (plus additional annual payments of $15 million) as compensation for the loss of this way of life.

Tours and Information
Start your visit to the recreation area with a stop at the Bureau of Reclamation's **Visitor Arrival Center,** just north of the dam on Hwy. 155, tel. (509) 633-9265. It's open daily 8:30 a.m. to 9:30 p.m. (or later) from Memorial Day through Sep-

tember, and daily 9 a.m.-5 p.m. the rest of the year (closed Thanksgiving, Christmas, and New Year's). Self-guided tours of the dam are available throughout the year when the center is open, and documentary movies are shown in the auditorium all day. The Visitor Arrival Center also houses one of the world's most advanced computer-controlled laser projection systems, used for spectacular summer shows. A gift shop sells books about the dam and local natural history.

Half-hour guided tours of the third power plant take place every half-hour between 10 a.m. and 6 p.m. in the summer, and four times a day in the winter. A highlight of the dam tour is riding the glass incline elevator to the face of the power plant for a spectacular view of the spillway from an outside balcony. An artifact room displays the Native American tools and arrowheads uncovered during the construction of the dam, along with agate stones.

Laser Light Show
Each summer evening brings a most unusual and immensely popular event to Grand Coulee Dam: an elaborate high-tech laser light show that paints 300-foot figures on the face of the dam and tells the history of the Columbia River, of the Indian people who first lived here, and of the dam and how it transformed the desert land. (You *won't* hear how the dam helped devastate the Columbia's salmon runs.) Created in 1989 and paid for with $785,700 in federal tax dollars, this program packs the house, even

though the "house" can sit on surrounding hillsides or in their vehicles. Best vantage points are from the Visitor Arrival Center, from the parking lot just below here, from the park at the east end of the bridge in Coulee Dam, and from Crown Point Vista (farther away, but overlooking the entire area). If you're planning to park at the visitor center, get there an hour early to be sure of a spot, especially on weekends. Thousands of other folks are looking for the same vista point.

The free 36-minute laser shows are offered from Memorial Day weekend through the end of September, with show time at 10 p.m. from Memorial Day through July, at 9:30 p.m. in August, and at 8:30 p.m. in September. If you're too far away to hear the broadcast sound from the speakers, tune to 98.5 FM or 1490 AM for nightly broadcasts of the music and story. It's all done in an entertaining and patriotic way, ending in a Neil Diamond song. Perfect for a Republican convention.

One of the best views of the dam and the evening spillway light show is from **Crown Point Vista,** 626 feet above the river, and about three miles west of the Grand Coulee four corners on Hwy. 174.

Sports and Recreation
Enormous **Franklin D. Roosevelt Lake**—stretching more than 150 miles from the dam almost to the Canadian border—is popular with boaters, waterskiers, swimmers, anglers, and campers. **Banks Lake** (see below under "Coulee City, Banks Lake, and Wilbur") and the parks to the southwest of the dam—in the coulee formed by the Columbia River during the last ice age—are also scenic summer playgrounds.

The dry, sunny climate is perfect for lake activities; summer temperatures range from the mid-70s to 100° F, with evenings cooling off to the 50s or 60s. The area is a popular winter recreation spot as well, with cross-country skiers, ice fishermen, and snowmobilers enjoying the off-season, along with the many bald eagles that winter here before heading north to British Columbia for the spring. You won't be the only one around if you visit in the summer; more than 1.8 million folks pass through the area each year.

Hiking Trails
Several local paths provide a chance to get away from the dam and explore. The **Candy Point Trail** was first built by the CCC in the 1930s, and their hand-laid stone is still in evidence. The path begins from a trailhead 300 feet down the hill behind the Coulee Dam Credit Union in the town of Coulee Dam and climbs steeply to Crown Point overlook, then over Candy Point, before returning to the river near Coulee Dam City Hall.

The **Down River Trail** is a gentle six-and-a-half-mile path along the river north from the bridge with several tree-lined rest areas. A less developed trail heads south from the dam to the towns of Grand Coulee and Electric City. More hiking can be found at nearby Steamboat Rock State Park, see under "Coulee City, Banks Lake, and Wilbur," below.

LAKE ROOSEVELT

Much of Franklin D. Roosevelt Lake—from Grand Coulee Dam to just below the town of Northport—was designated the sprawling **Coulee Dam National Recreation Area** in 1946 and is a favorite boating, waterskiing, fishing, camping, and swimming destination. The reservoir backs up not just the Columbia River waters, but also parts of the Spokane, Kettle, Colville, and Sanpoil Rivers. At more than 150 miles long, it is said to be the second largest human-created lake in the world.

Campgrounds
Campers can stay at one of 35 campgrounds (10 of these are accessible only by boat) that line both sides of Lake Roosevelt and the Spokane River arm. None of the campgrounds offer hookups; all of them have restrooms (but no showers or RV hookups); and all but the most primitive have running water. A $10 fee is charged at Evans, Fort Spokane, Gifford, Hunters, Keller Ferry, Kettle Falls, Marcus Island, Porcupine Bay, and Spring Canyon; the rest are free. The fee is not charged from October to mid-May. Summer **campfire programs** are offered Saturday evenings at Spring Canyon, Keller Ferry, and Fort Spokane Campgrounds. Most campgrounds are open year-

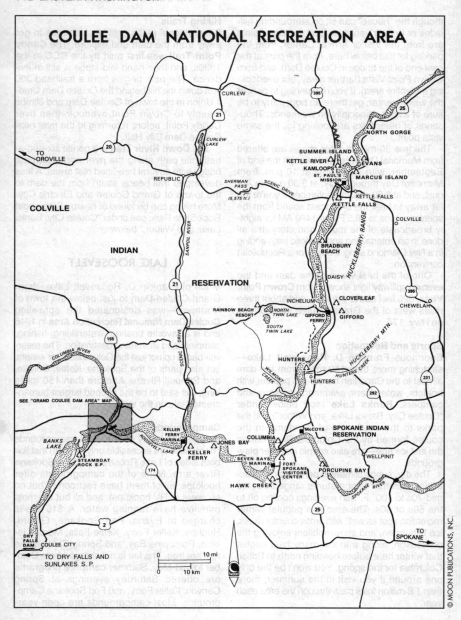

COULEE DAM NATIONAL RECREATION AREA

© MOON PUBLICATIONS, INC.

round; Porcupine Bay, Hunters, and Detillion are open May-October. There is a 14-day camping limit.

Houseboat Rentals

One of the best ways to explore the reaches of Lake Roosevelt is aboard a rented houseboat. Swimming and fishing are just outside your bedroom window; no noisy neighbors to contend with; and you'll see parts of the lake you just can't reach by car. Each houseboat is at least 46 feet long and comes equipped with a kitchen, bath, sleeping areas for up to 13, swim slide and ladder, gas grill, and more. You can also rent 18-foot ski boats or 14-foot fishing boats to take along. Weekend rates in the summer (two nights and three days) are steep, around $1,000; save money by renting in the off-season or for longer periods. For more information, contact **Lake Roosevelt Resorts and Marinas,** tel. (509) 738-6121 or (800) 635-7585; or **Roosevelt Recreational Enterprises,** tel. (800) 648-5253.

Swimming

Swim at four lifeguard-protected beaches from July through Labor Day at **Spring Canyon** and **Keller Ferry** in lower Lake Roosevelt, and at **Fort Spokane** and **Porcupine Bay** on the Spokane River arm. The water in the Spokane River arm tends to be five to eight degrees warmer than the rest of the lake, where they average in the 60s in June, rising to the 70s in August. If you're swimming outside a protected area, keep an eye out for boats!

Boating

Twenty-three free public boat launches line Lake Roosevelt. From April through June only a few of them are usable, because the lake is lowered about 100 feet to accommodate the spring runoff; from late June through October, all boat launches are accessible. The lowest-elevation launches are at Kettle Falls, Hunters, Keller Ferry, and Porcupine Bay, at 1,230-1,240 feet; the highest launches are at approximately 1,280 feet at Hawk Creek, Marcus Island, Evans, and North Gorge. Call the reservoir hotline at (800) 824-4916 for an estimate of current and future water levels. Be sure to steer clear of protected swimming beaches and the waters near the dam.

Fishing

A state fishing license is required to fish in the recreation area; you can pick one up, along with current fishing regulations, at most area hardware or sporting goods stores or marinas. The 30 plus species of fish inhabiting these waters include walleye (more than 90% of the annual catch), rainbow trout, and enormous white sturgeon, averaging 100-300 pounds but growing up to 20 feet long and 1,800 pounds.

Other residents include the kokanee salmon, yellow perch, bass, cutthroat trout, perch, and pike. The best months for fishing are Sept.-Nov. and May-June; in midsummer, the fish retreat to cooler waters in streams or deep in the lake. Popular fishing spots are at the points where rivers and streams meet the lake—the Sanpoil River, Wilmont Creek, Hunters Creek, Kettle River, and others—or the waters near high shoreline cliffs, such as those near Keller Ferry.

Cross-Lake Ferries

Two ferries cross Lake Roosevelt year-round: the **Keller Ferry** connects Hwy. 21 in the south part of the recreation area, and, farther north, the **Gifford Ferry** joins Hwy. 25 near Inchelium. Both ferries are free. They carry passengers and vehicles and take about 15 minutes for the crossing. Keller operates from 6:15 a.m. to 11:45 p.m. daily; Gifford runs 6:30 a.m. to 9:30 p.m.

Information and Services

For information on programs, park brochures, or books on the area's natural history, contact the **Coulee Dam National Recreation Area Headquarters,** 1008 Crest Dr. at Coulee Dam, tel. (509) 633-9441; open Mon.-Fri. 7:30 a.m.-4 p.m. year-round. Information is also available at the ranger stations in Kettle Falls, tel. (509) 738-6266, and Fort Spokane, tel. (509) 725-2715, or from the **Grand Coulee Dam Visitor Arrival Center,** at the dam, tel. (509) 633-9193.

Services in the recreation area are generally open from June to early September. There are small stores with groceries and supplies at Daisy Station, and in the marinas at McCoys, Seven Bays, Keller Ferry, and Kettle Falls. The surrounding towns of Kettle Falls, Coulee Dam, Grand Coulee, Colville, and Northport have food, lodging, and other services. Rent boats at Keller Ferry Marina (tel. 509-647-2253),

Seven Bays Marina (tel. 509-633-0201 or 800-648-5253), or Kettle Falls Marina (tel. 509-738-6121 or 800-635-7585).

ELECTRIC CITY, GRAND COULEE, AND COULEE DAM

The towns of Electric City (pop. 900), Grand Coulee (pop. 1,000), and Coulee Dam (pop. 1,100) surround the Grand Coulee Dam and offer accommodations and food and a chance to explore the dam and nearby Lake Roosevelt and Banks Lake Reservoirs. A fourth settlement, **Elmer City,** has 300 people and sits two miles north of the dam.

Sights

See "Grand Coulee Dam," above, for attractions at the dam itself, including the famous laser light show, and "Lake Roosevelt," also above, for info on this popular recreation area managed by the National Park Service.

The **Colville Confederated Tribes Museum,** 516 Birch St., tel. (509) 633-0751, has two crowded rooms with excellent exhibits relating to the Colville Indians, including a white coyote, old photos, murals, a sweat lodge, tule mat tepee, cedar root and bear grass baskets, fine old cornhusk bags, and a Thomas Jefferson peace medal given to the Nez Percé by the Lewis and Clark expedition in 1804. Placards provide disturbing commentary on how a way of life was destroyed and how the dam ended salmon fishing at Kettle Falls and other places. A gift shop sells locally made moccasins, beaded goods, turquoise jewelry, baskets, and blankets. The museum is open daily 10 a.m.-6 p.m. May-Sept.; Mon.-Sat. 10 a.m.-6 p.m. Oct.-Dec.; and Tues.-Sat. 10 a.m.-6 p.m. Jan.-April. Entrance is $1 for adults, 50 cents for children.

Rainbow Gallery, 215 Main in Grand Coulee, also has Indian beadwork and art.

The famous **Gehrke Windmills** can be found at Bicentennial Park in the town of Grand Coulee. These amusing, brightly colored pieces of folk art were created by the late Emil Gehrke from scraps of iron.

For an extraordinary view of the entire area, head to **Crown Point Vista,** high on the bluff over the river. Get here by heading two miles west up Hwy. 174 from the town of Grand Coulee. Follow the signs to the viewpoint.

Lodging

Lodging is mostly unpretentious in the Coulee area. See the chart "Grand Coulee Area Accommodations" for a complete listing of motels in the Grand Coulee, Electric City, Coulee Dam, and Coulee City area. Many folks make lodging reservations up to a year ahead for busy summer weekends in the better motels. It probably isn't necessary to act this much in advance, but the earlier you make your reservations, the better your chances. One or two months ahead should get you weekend lodging at the better motels. Winter rates can really plummet; places charging $42 d in summer can be had for $28 d in the off season. Call the Grand Coulee Dam Area Chamber of Commerce at (509) 633-3074 or (800) 268-5332 to see who has space.

The finest local lodging places are **Coulee House Motel,** tel. (509) 633-1101 or (800) 715-7767, and **Ponderosa Motel,** tel. (509) 633-2100 or (800) 633-6421, where rooms offer views of the laser light show each summer evening. Another interesting place (great breakfasts) is the historic **Four Winds Guest House B&B,** tel. (509) 633-3146 or (800) 786-3146.

Campgrounds and RV Parks

The Park Service operates campgrounds (no showers or RV hookups) all along Lake Roosevelt (see under "Lake Roosevelt," above, for specifics). Closest to the dam is **Spring Canyon,** three miles east of the town of Grand Coulee; $10 fee, open year-round, no reservations. Saturday evening campfire programs are held here during the summer months, and you can swim at the lifeguarded beach.

Eight miles southwest of the dam on Hwy. 155, **Steamboat Rock State Park** has tent sites for $7-11, and RV hookups for $16; reserveable. It is open all year; see below for more on this interesting place. Call (800) 452-5687 for campsite reservations ($6 extra fee), available up to 11 months ahead of time.

Private RV parks in the area include: **Banks Lake Golf & Country Club,** two miles south of Electric City on Hwy. 155, tel. (509) 633-0163;

Coulee Playland Resort, on Banks Lake in Electric City, tel. (509) 633-2671; **Grand Coulee RV Park,** Hwy. 174 east, tel. (509) 633-0750; **King's Court RV Park,** Hwy. 174 east of Grand Coulee, tel. (509) 633-0103; **Lakeview Terrace Mobile Park,** four miles east of Grand Coulee on Hwy. 174, tel. (509) 633-2169; **Spirit Ridge RV Park,** seven miles north of the dam, tel. (509) 633-1933 or (800) 548-1408; and **Sunbanks Resort,** on Banks Lake just south of Electric City, tel. (509) 633-3786.

Food

The Coulee Dam area is not for gourmands, but you will find good food, generous portions, and friendly service. **Pat & Emily's New Flo's Cafe,** 316 Spokane Way in Grand Coulee, tel. (509) 633-3216, has a strange name and is somewhat smokey, but serves big solid American breakfasts and lunches for a reasonable price. A great place to meet the locals.

Tee Pee Drive In, in Grand Coulee, tel. (509) 633-2111, makes the best local burgers in a straight-from-the'60s setting. Go back a decade more in time for the **Rock 'N Robin,** with its Elvis-era decor and car hop service. In addition to the standard burgers, sandwiches, and shakes, they also serve a very '90s drink, espresso.

R & A Cafe, 514 Birch St. in Coulee Dam, tel. (509) 633-2233, serves generous portions of family-style home cooking. Another good all-American place is **Melody Restaurant,** 512 River, Dr. in Coulee Dam, tel. (509) 633-1151. Come here in the evening for a view of the laser light show while you eat. Try Grand Coulee's **Sage Inn,** 415 Midway Ave., tel. (509) 633-0550, for sandwiches and meals in dark, diner-style surroundings.

For excellent Chinese, Thai, and American food, visit **Siam Palace,** tel. (509) 633-2921, open daily for lunch and dinner at 213 Main St. in Grand Coulee. **That Italian Place,** 515 Grand Coulee E. in Grand Coulee, tel. (509) 633-1818, is a bit on the pricey side but makes very good pasta and pizzas.

Events and Entertainment

The second weekend in May, the **Colorama Festival** brings bull-riding, a parade, cowboy breakfast, and carnival to the Coulee Dam area.

The annual **Memorial Day Festival** features arts and crafts, music, food, a fun run, and the grand opening of the laser light show followed by a big fireworks display off the top of the dam; most events are held at the park below the visitor arrival center. This festival attracts some 75,000 visitors. More fireworks from the dam, along with arts and crafts, food, and entertainment on the **Fourth of July.** The **Junior Rodeo** comes to Grand Coulee the last weekend in June, and mid-August brings the nationally known **Golden Over the Dam Run,** with five-km and 10-km races; contact the Grand Coulee Dam Chamber of Commerce for registration information.

The **Wild Life Restaurant & Lounge,** 113 Midway Ave. in Grand Coulee, tel. (509) 633-1160, has live rock and roll.

Sports and Recreation

The Park Service has free guided canoe trips around **Crescent Bay Lake** behind the town of Grand Coulee. These 90-minute paddles take place June-Aug. and offer a good opportunity to see wildlife; call (509) 633-9188 for specifics. Canoes, paddles, and life jackets are provided.

Swim at the outdoor **swimming pool** in Cole Park at the town of Coulee Dam, at Spring Canyon Campground along Lake Roosevelt (lifeguard is present), or at Steamboat Rock State Park, eight miles south along Banks Lake.

About a mile south of Electric City on Grand Coulee Airport Rd., **Banks Lake Golf and Country Club** is a nine-hole public course, tel. (509) 633-0163.

Information and Services

For information on the surrounding area, contact the **Grand Coulee Dam Area Chamber of Commerce,** 306 Midway in Grand Coulee, tel. (509) 633-3074 or (800) 268-5332. Hours are Mon.-Sat. 8 a.m.-5 p.m. in the summer, and Mon.-Fri. 8 a.m.-1 p.m. and 2-5 p.m. in the winter. A summer-only **visitor center,** tel. (509) 632-5713, is located in Mason City Park (just uphill from the grocery store) in Coulee City. The Bureau of Reclamation's **Visitor Arrival Center** is just north of the dam on Hwy. 155, tel. 633-9265. The **area code** for Electric City, Grand Coulee, and Coulee Dam is 509.

COULEE CITY, BANKS LAKE, AND WILBUR

Coulee City

The little town of Coulee City (pop. 600) sits on the eastern edge of Dry Falls Dam, the dam that creates Banks Lake. See the chart "Grand Coulee Area Accommodations" for a complete listing of motels in the Grand Coulee, Electric City, Coulee Dam, and Coulee City area. Camp at **Coulee City Community Park** for $8 for tent sites, $10 for RVs. **Sun Lakes State Park** is seven miles southwest of Coulee City on Hwy. 17; $11 tents, $16 RVs. Call (800) 452-5687 for campsite reservations at Sun Lakes ($6 extra fee), available up to 11 months ahead of time. Nearby private RV parks include: Blue Top Motel, 109 N. 6th, tel. (509) 632-5596; and **Coulee Lodge Resort,** tel. (509) 632-5565, six miles south along Blue Lake.

Eat dinners at **The Crossing** in Coulee City. **The Branding Iron** has a bar and good pub grub, including the best burgers in town. Get steaks and salads at **Dry Falls Cafe,** tel. (509) 632-5634. **Steamboat Rock Restaurant** has basic fare, but get here early since they close at 8 p.m. Red meat lovers will want to make the 20-mile trek from Coulee City east to Almira, where **Bubba's Steakhouse,** tel. (509) 639-0176 or (800) 400-0176, has the finest and thickest steaks in these parts, along with filet mignon, lobster tails, barbecue pork ribs, and mud pie.

Their ads note that Almira is "located at the exact center of the universe." Pretty hard to argue with that.

Banks Lake

Banks Lake, which lies outside Coulee Dam National Recreation Area on the southwest side of the dam, is a 27-mile-long, clear-blue beauty surrounded by the deep sides of the coulee. In the early '50s, the coulee was dammed on both ends and filled with water from the Columbia. To get here, the water must be pumped 280 feet uphill from Lake Roosevelt through enormous pipes visible on the north side of Grand Coulee Dam. As well as being a popular recreational alternative to Lake Roosevelt for fishermen and waterskiers, water from Banks Lake irrigates over a half-million acres of farmland stretching south to the Oregon border.

Steamboat Rock State Park

Eight miles south of Grand Coulee on Hwy. 155, Steamboat Rock State Park has campsites ($11 tents, $7 primitive sites, $16 RVs), swimming, good fishing, play equipment, and an underwater park on Banks Lake. The park is open all year. Call (509) 633-1304 for more information, or (800) 452-5687 for campsite reservations ($6 extra fee), available up to 11 months ahead of time.

Steamboat Rock, an island in the Columbia River during the last ice age, is now a scenic volcanic butte rising 700 feet above Banks Lake. You can hike a mile to the top of the butte for a

Steamboat Rock State Park

DIANNE BOUERICE LYONS

panoramic view, and then explore the 640 acres on the flat top. The trail starts near the north campground. Bring repellent to combat the vicious mosquitoes. Winter sports are also popular here, from ice fishing to snowmobiling and cross-country skiing.

Wilbur

Wilbur (pop. 900) is 28 miles northeast of Grand Coulee City and 19 miles southwest of the Grand Coulee Dam. The town's **Big Bend Historical Society Museum** contains historic photos, displays of items from the past, and a collection of gems and minerals. Be sure to check out items from Samuel Wilbur Condon, the town founder who died in 1895 after a gun battle over a woman who refused to marry him. The museum is open Saturday 2-4 p.m. in the summers only.

Stay at **Settle Inn Motel,** tel. (509) 647-5812, where rooms with kitchenettes go for $23 s, $28 d. Camping is available in the Park Service campground at Kellers Crossing 14 miles north of Wilbur, or in town at **Crescent Oaks RV Park,** tel. (509) 647-5608, and **Bell's Court Trailer Court,** tel. (509) 647-5888. Wilbur also has an outdoor swimming pool open in the summer. The annual event for Wilbur is **Wild Goose Bill Days** on the third weekend of May, featuring a small-town parade, fun run, craft and food booths, dancing, and a barbecue in the park.

LOWER GRAND COULEE AREA

Sun Lakes State Park and Dry Falls

Sun Lakes State Park, seven miles southwest of Coulee City on Hwy. 17, is a large park famous for its "dry falls." The main part of Sun Lakes Park boasts 3,300 acres with year-round camping ($11 tents, $16 RVs) along Park Lake, horse trails, boating, swimming, and rainbow trout fishing. Call (800) 452-5687 for campsite reservations ($6 extra fee), available up to 11 months ahead of time. Concessions offer snacks, fishing supplies, horse rentals, and groceries. The park also has an Environmental Learning Center for kids.

At least 10 smaller lakes pockmark the park; they are ancient plunge pools from a stupendous waterfall that once raged through here. A road leads east from Park Lake along the basalt cliff walls lining Meadow Creek to Deep Lake,

and hiking trails provide access to other parts of this fascinating park.

Four miles north of the main park entrance along Hwy. 17 is **Dry Falls Interpretive Center,** tel. (509) 632-5583, open Wed.-Sun. 10 a.m.-6 p.m. from mid-May to mid-September. The center describes the incredible geologic history of this area and sells books on geology and natural history; outside, the cliff-edge viewpoints reveal a cluster of lakes bordered by green plants set against stark basalt cliffs. There is a certain strange beauty about this place, especially at dusk. A steep path leads a half mile down from the overlook to Dry Falls Lake. Look around the 400-foot cliff face and you may find the entrance to a small cave.

The Columbia River ran through this ancient volcanic landscape for eons, but during the ice ages that began a million years ago, glaciers forced the river to change course through the now-dry canyons called coulees. The ice also dammed the Columbia River in northern Idaho, creating an enormous body of water, Lake Missoula. When this ice dam burst around 17,000 years ago, a 2,000-foot high wall of water rushed downstream, carving the land in a way that is almost beyond imagination. Today's Dry Falls was once the mightiest waterfall on the planet, reaching 400 feet high and over three miles across! This massive rush of water—at an estimated 386 million cubic feet per second, its volume was 10 times that of the combined flow of all rivers on earth—probably lasted but a few days or weeks but was repeated many times, as glaciers advanced and blocked the river, and as the ice dam broke again. The ripple marks left by the flood are up to 35 feet high and 350 feet apart. Over time, the periodic floods (geologists refer to these as the **Spokane Floods**) eroded the lip of the falls for a distance of almost 20 miles. Below this lip is Lower Grand Coulee, a deep 50-mile-long gorge that held the Columbia River during the Ice Ages. To get an idea of the magnitude of the flood, imagine this 900-foot deep, three-mile wide canyon filled with rushing water! After the glaciers retreated, the river returned to its old channel, leaving behind the dry coulees.

Lake Lenore Caves

Approximately nine miles south of Sun Lakes State Park, Hwy. 17 passes a series of four shallow caves, located high up the coulee cliffs.

A trail leads from an information sign to several of these rock openings, which were created by the erosive action of floods that swept through the canyon during the Ice Ages. The caves were occupied by nomadic prehistoric peoples. Across the highway is a sign describing the Lahontan cutthroat trout that have been planted in the creek here.

Summer Falls State Park

Nine miles south of Coulee City on Pinto Ridge Rd., Summer Falls State Park is an appropriately named park since the falls created by the irrigation project exist only in the summer when irrigation water is needed. (The water reaches here from Banks Lake via an irrigation canal.) This is a cool spot for a picnic or fishing, but no camping, and sirens warn of sudden flow increases that make it very dangerous to swim; a memorial stands to one boy who drowned in the whirlpools here in 1978.

COLVILLE INDIAN RESERVATION

The Colville Indian Reservation covers more than 2,100 square miles of forested mountains, rolling rangeland, and rich farms in the Okanogan Highlands and Valley. They also have hunting, fishing, and mineral rights to an equal area to the north that was originally included in the reservation but was later opened to settlement.

The Indian peoples on the Colville subsist on income from various tribal businesses: a sawmill, grocery stores, wood treatment plant, houseboat rentals, marina, and bingo parlor. The last of these—Colville Tribal Bingo in Okanogan—has proven a major source of income. The reservation has a population of 8,500 people; tribal headquarters are just south of Nespelem. The **Colville Confederated Tribes Museum** is located in Grand Coulee (see "Sights" under "Electric City, Grand Coulee, and Coulee Dam," above, for specifics). Anglers will need to purchase a special reservation fishing permit from stores in nearby towns. Call (509) 634-8845 for specifics.

History

The Colville Reservation is home to 11 different tribes—Okanogan, Lakes, San Poil, Nespelem, Methow, Entiat, Chelan, Wenatchee, Moses-Columbia, Palouse, and Nez Percé—all shoehorned together by President Grant's executive order of 1872. The reservation was greatly reduced in 1886, when the Moses-Columbia tribe refused to be placed on land west of the Okanogan River—away from their home along the Columbia River—and these lands were opened to settlement by non-Indians. The tribes' traditional lands once reached from the Cascades to the Rockies, and from southern British Columbia to Oregon. The tribes have some similarities in language and cultural background, but many people still retain a clear tribal identity.

Scenic Drives

Two very scenic country drives are Hwy. 21 between Keller and Republic, and Bridge Creek/Twin Lakes Rd. connecting Inchelium to Hwy. 21. The latter of these climbs west from Inchelium into remote hills covered with ponderosa pine and other evergreens, and past **Rainbow Beach Resort**, tel. (509) 722-5901, which offers cabins, tent and RV sites, boat rentals, and a store on mile-wide North Twin Lake. West of the lake, the narrow, winding road climbs through rounded mountains dense with trees but sliced by periodic clearcuts. It eventually descends from the trees into rolling hills covered in grass and sage as you reach the Nespelem area.

St. Mary's Mission

This Jesuit mission was founded in 1896 by Father Steven DeRouge to bring Catholicism to the Okanogan and Chelan Indians. DeRouge's presence met stiff resistance until he saved an Indian child who had fallen into the swift waters of Omak Creek. This act of mercy led Indian leaders to change their minds, and Chief Smitkin provided land to construct the mission. It began as a log cabin and gradually grew until two fires destroyed nearly everything early in this century.

A new church was completed in 1915, with local settlers and Indians cooperating in the building of the altar; the side altars were shipped around the Horn from France. Today the mission contains a mix of old and new buildings, including the Paschal Sherman Indian School, now run by the Colville tribe, not the Jesuits. Up the hill behind the church is an old graveyard decorated with a thicket of wooden crosses and even a carved wooden burro. The surrounding rocky, dry hills are covered with grass and sage.

To reach the mission, take Hwy. 155 east of Omak for four miles, then go 1.5 miles south. Open daily; tel. (509) 826-2097.

Inchelium

The free **Gifford Ferry** crosses Lake Roosevelt between Gifford and Inchelium, operating daily between 6:30 a.m. and 9:30 p.m. Hardly anything to the village of Inchelium, other than the Seem-Uss-Spooss Restaurant (the word means "What's in your heart?"), where you can snack on an Indian taco.

Nespelem Area

Chief Joseph, leader of the Nez Percé Indians during the famous retreat of 1877 (see the special topic "The Nez Percé War"), is buried in Nespelem (nes-PEEL-em). He, along with 150 other tribal members, was exiled here in 1884. The cemetery is on the north end of town; follow 10th St. uphill to reach it. The **Chief Joseph grave** is a simple white obelisk with a few offerings and bandannas decorating a nearby tree; the monument notes that Hin-Mah-Too-Yah-Lat-Kekt ("Thunder Rolling in the Mountains") died here September 21, 1904. He was approximately 60 years old. The nearby land is not greatly changed from the day of his passing: wide open spaces of rolling grassy hills.

South of Nespelem is the **Colville Indian Agency,** headquarters for the reservation. Stop here for information on the reservation and the names of local artisans. Local beadwork is sold in the nearby **Trading Post Store.** Out front is the **Skolaskin Church,** built in 1874 at the behest of Chief Skolaskin, renowned for predicting a large earthquake in 1872 that caused a rock slide that briefly halted the flow of the Columbia. The log building was the first church on the Colville Reservation.

Events

Across the highway from the tribal offices is the Nespelem Community Center and a powwow circle that comes to life during the **Nespelem Fourth of July Indian Encampment,** a powwow that features Indian dance competitions—some in full regalia—along with drumming, "stick" gambling, and delicious Indian fry bread. The compound is bordered with dozens of tepees during the festivities. Do not enter the dance cir-

cle or take photos without asking first. An **All-Indian Rodeo** takes place here that same weekend. Another powwow is held at the Nespelem Community Center in mid-November.

CHIEF JOSEPH DAM AREA

Chief Joseph Dam

Though overshadowed by the Grand Coulee to the east, the Chief Joseph Dam boasts a 2,000-foot-long powerhouse—largest in the world—and reaches over a mile across the Columbia River. It is the second biggest producer of hydropower in the nation (after Grand Coulee), supplying the electrical needs of 1.5 million people throughout the West. The dam was built in the 1950s, with a major addition in the 1970s. Water backed up behind the dam forms Rufus Woods Lake. The dam itself was named for Chief Joseph, famous leader of the Nez Percé Indians in the 1870s, who is buried on the nearby Colville Indian Reservation (see above). One has to wonder how he would respond to having a dam named in his "honor." In late summer you may see Indians from the area fishing below the dam; unfortunately, no fish ladder was built around this massive dam, so all salmon runs above this point were wiped out.

You'll find vantage points of the dam from both sides of the river. A **visitor center,** tel. (509) 686-5501, open daily 10 a.m.-6 p.m. all year, is located near the center of the dam and is accessible from the north bank. From here you can peer through windows across the lineup of 27 massive generators and feel the rumble as they spin. A nine-minute slide show describes the dam, and exhibits reveal the history of the region with an emphasis on hydropower. It's a strange and sterile place with no guides, just surveillance cameras watching your every move. A big wall map shows the 200 dams that block the Columbia River at points all along its basin. Outside, be sure to visit the trunnion bridge where you get an up-close view of the massive spillway gates.

Bridgeport

The town of Bridgeport (pop. 1,600) sits just west of Chief Joseph Dam and has a couple of places to stay. **The Y Motel,** tel. (509) 686-2002, has rooms for $35 s or d and up, including an outdoor pool and jacuzzi. They also operate a restaurant and lounge and have RV parking. There's a public **swimming pool** at Berryman Park.

The land east of Bridgeport is not unlike Nevada or Utah, an arid plateau of grass and sage interrupted by scattered volcanic boulders deposited by glaciers during the Ice Age, with the sky dominating the land. As you approach Grand Coulee Dam, the road is accompanied by long sets of electrical towers radiating outward to supply energy for the Northwest.

Bridgeport State Park
Three miles northeast of Bridgeport on Rufus Woods Lake, Bridgeport State Park offers boating, fishing, swimming, campsites ($11 tents, $16 RVs), and showers. Call (800) 452-5687 for campsite reservations ($6 extra fee), available up to 11 months ahead of time. The 750-acre park is an oasis of cottonwood and aspen trees surrounded by dark, beehive-shaped volcanic formations. Keep your eyes open for rattlesnakes. The park is open April-Oct. and includes the nine-hole **Lakewood Golf Course** within the boundaries.

Fort Okanogan State Park
Nine miles north of Bridgeport on Hwy. 17 near the intersection with Hwy. 97, Fort Okanogan State Park is open daily 10 a.m.-6 p.m. from mid-May to mid-September (no camping, alas). Enjoy a picnic lunch on the grassy lawn overlooking Lake Pateros and step inside the **interpretive center,** filled with interesting artifacts, displays, and dioramas of this historic fort.

Beneath the waters of Lake Pateros lies the site of Fort Okanogan, an historic fur-trading post established near the juncture of the Okanogan and Columbia Rivers. Begun in July of 1811 by David Thompson and other trappers working for John Jacob Astor's Pacific Fur Company, this was the first place to hoist the American flag in what would become Washington. The business proved lucrative at first; Okanogan Indians were given trade items worth $160 in exchange for pelts that brought $10,000 in the East! Despite this, supply problems, stiff competition, and the threat of war with England forced Astor to sell his operation to Canadian interests. In 1821, the fort joined the vast Hudson's Bay Company holdings, operating as a major shipping point for buf-

falo hides down the Columbia River. Hudson's Bay continued to operate the fort until 1860, when an influx of settlers and the waning fur trade led them to pull out. The fort sites were excavated by archaeologists in the 1950s and early '60s, prior to completion of Wells Dam. The old fort location—as with many historic and cultural sites—is now buried beneath a Columbia River reservoir. So history becomes a collection of artifacts in a small museum.

Brewster
The town of Brewster (pop. 1,600) sits right on Lake Pateros (Columbia River), a couple miles west from the mouth of Okanogan River. This is a rich agricultural area, with expansive apple, pear, and cherry orchards on the flats near the river mouth, plus additional orchards lining Hwy. 97 southwest of town. The region is also crowded with fruit processing plants. Stay at the appropriately named and modern **Apple Avenue Motel,** tel. (509) 689-3000, for $52 s or $58 d. Cheaper digs (but the same owners) at **Brewster Motel,** 806 Bridge St., tel. (509) 689-2625, where rooms go for $32 s or $38 d.

Columbia Cove RV Park has RV spaces in town. Head to **Rock Gardens Park,** halfway between Brewster and Bridgeport on Hwy. 173, for tent and RV spaces.

Because of an abundance of Spanish-speaking farm workers, Brewster is gaining a distinctly south-of-the-border flavor. **La Milpa Grocery** has fresh corn tortillas and delicious Mexican pastries made in their bakery across the street. **El Zarape,** 25 E. Main St., tel. (509) 689-3078, has a big collection of piñatas, Mexican videos, and more. **Mi Casita Restaurant,** 702 Jay Ave., tel. (509) 689-2071, has excellent Mexican food, including homemade sopapillas, but you're more likely to meet other patrons speaking Spanish at the less pretentious **Alicia's Mexican Food** on Main Street. If this isn't enough, try one of three local taco wagons.

The main local event is **Bonanza Days,** held the third weekend of June. **Hydroplane races** also take place here in the summer. The active Hispanic community comes out in force to celebrate **Fiesta de Septiembre** in early September. In addition to swimming in Lake Pateros, Brewster has an outdoor **swimming pool** in the grassy city park along the lake.

OMAK AND OKANOGAN

Omak and Okanogan (oh-ka-NO-gan), the valley's largest cities, are separated only by name and are strung along the west bank of the Okanogan River. The Colville Indian Reservation comes down to the river on the opposite bank, with Hwy. 97 running along that side of the river.

Nestled between the east and west sections of the Okanogan National Forest, the twin towns serve as the commercial hub for a sparsely populated area dominated by apple orchards along the river valleys, plus logging, cattle grazing, and recreation in the national forest. Okanogan (pop. 2,400), the older of the two towns, serves as the county seat, while thriving Omak (pop. 4,300) is the place for groceries, gas, and other necessities. Omak is home to the state's first WalMart (there are plenty more now). Both Omak and Okanogan are plain-vanilla, conservative, rough-at-the-edges towns, but recent years have seen an influx of migrant workers from south of the border, and a growing permanent Hispanic influence.

HISTORY

The city of Okanogan came about shortly after this region was opened to non-Indian settlers in 1886. Frank Cummings built a trading post at the mouth of Salmon Creek, and the town grew up around him. Omak was established in 1907 when Dr. J.I. Pogue, a disgruntled resident of Okanogan (they refused to name the town after him), moved north to found his own settlement. The two towns have had a low-level feud ever since, and despite their proximity, local voters have steadfastly refused to combine operations. Because of this, Omak and Okanogan have separate schools, city governments, and services.

Omak was chartered in 1910, but was slow to develop until the Biles-Coleman Lumber Company built a sawmill in 1922; it eventually became today's Omak Wood Products. You can't miss the plume of white smoke billowing into the air at the lumber and plywood mill. Recent years have seen less timber harvesting on nearby Okanogan National Forest due to the spotted

owl and salmon controversies, but Omak still runs on timber. The native-owned Colville Precision Pine Mill uses timber from the adjacent Colville Reservation.

Both town names are from native words. Okanogan is derived from the Salish Indian term, *Ocanuckane,* meaning "rendezvous," while Omak comes from the word *Omache,* meaning "good medicine."

SIGHTS

The **Okanogan County Historical Museum,** 1410 2nd N in Okanogan, tel. (509) 422-4272, is open daily 11 a.m.-5 p.m. from mid-May to mid-September; free. Inside are displays depicting pioneer life in the county; outside find a replica of an Old West village, including a log cabin from 1879.

Built in 1915, the **Okanogan County Courthouse** on 3rd and Oak in Okanogan has a Mediterranean-style red-tile roof and a gothic castle-like exterior. A **mural** on the side of Main Street Market features a painting of the Suicide Race. A walking trail—marked by big horseshoes denoting past Suicide Race winners—leads from downtown Omak to East Side Park. Five miles east of Omak is **St. Mary's Mission** (see above under "Colville Indian Reservation" for more on this interesting historical place).

PRACTICALITIES

Accommodations

See the "Omak and Okanogan Accommodations" chart for a listing of Omak and Okanogan motels. There are no nearby B&Bs. Be sure to make reservations far in advance if you plan to attend the Omak Stampede and Suicide Race in August.

Campgrounds and RV Parks

Okanogan's **Legion Park** on the north end of town offers overnight camping and sho~ along the Okanogan River; $10 for tents~

TO CONCONULLY

TO OMAK AIRPORT

ROBINSON CANYON

20
97
TO RIVERSIDE

ROSS CANYON RD.

MOTEL NICOLAS

WALMART

ROYAL MOTEL

RIVERSIDE DR.

OMAK

OKANOGAN RIVER

CONCONULLY RD.

THRIFTLODGE

EASTSIDE PARK

OMAK CHAMBER AND INFO CENTER

MAIN ST.

ASH ST.

BREADLINE CAFE

155

LUMBER MILL

KERMEL RD.

LEISURE VILLAGE MOTEL

STAMPEDE MOTEL

TO ST. MARY'S MISSION

MID-VALLEY HOSPITAL

GOLF COURSE

SALMON CREEK RD.

ELMWAY AVE.

FAIRGROUNDS

OKANOGAN COUNTY HISTORICAL MUSEUM

20
97

LEGION PARK

OKANOGAN RIVER

FAIRGROUNDS ACCESS

U & I MOTEL

COUNTY COURTHOUSE

OKANOGAN

5th ST.

OMAK AND OKANOGAN

OKANOGAN AIRPORT

ALMA PARK SWIMMING POOL

PONDEROSA MOTOR LODGE AND RV PARK

FOREST SERVICE OFFICE

1st ST.

NOT TO SCALE

TO TWISP AND WINTHROP

20

CEDARS INN

97

TO BRIDGEPORT

© MOON PUBLICATIONS, INC.

OMAK AND OKANOGAN ACCOMMODATIONS

Accommodations are arranged from least to most expensive. Rates may be lower during the winter months. The area code is 509.

U & I Motel; 838 2nd N, Okanogan; tel. 422-2920; $26 s, $33 d; kitchenettes available, clean place, along Okanogan River

Stampede Motel; 215 W. 4th, Omak; tel. 826-1161; $28 s, $30 d; very plain, see rooms first

Thriftlodge; 122 N. Main, Omak; tel. 826-0400 or (800) 578-7878; $30 s, $36 d

Royal Motel; 514 E. Riverside Dr., Omak; tel. 826-5715; $31 s, $36 d; clean

Ponderosa Motor Lodge; 1034 S. 2nd Ave., Okanogan; tel. 422-0400; $32-35 s or d; nice place, kitchenettes available, AAA approved

Motel Nicholas; half-mile north of Omak on Hwy. 215; tel. 826-4611; $35 s, $40 d; AAA approved

Leisure Village Motel; 630 Okoma Dr., Omak; tel. 826-4442; $35 s, $40 d; indoor pool, jacuzzi, sauna, AAA approved

Cedars Inn; junction of Highways 97 and 20, Okanogan; tel. 422-6431; $46 s, $51 d; heated pool, free airport shuttle

---

bikes, $12 for RVs. Camping and RV hookups ($10) are also available at **East Side Park,** tel. (509) 826-1170, in Omak (next to the visitors center). Both of these are open all year. Private RV parks include **Log Cabin Trailer Court,** 509 Okoma Dr. in Omak, tel. (509) 826-4462, and **Ponderosa RV Park,** 1034 2nd Ave. S in Okanogan, tel. (509) 422-0400.

Food

Get the finest local breakfasts at **Our Place Cafe,** 19 E. Apple in Omak, tel. (509) 826-4811. Omak's **Breadline Cafe,** 102 S. Ash St., tel. (509) 826-5836, is *the* place for lunch in the area. In addition to soups, sandwiches (made with homemade bread), and espresso, the restaurant often has Asian and vegetarian specials, and live music in the evening. The decor in this old soda pop bottling warehouse is of funky mismatched chairs and tables, aging signs, and painted exposed beams.

For Mexican lunches and dinners (in a former A&W), head to **Tequila's,** 635 Okoma Dr. in Omak, tel. (509) 826-5417. Get good pizzas at **Hometown Pizza,** 2237 Elmway in Okanogan, tel. (509) 422-0744.

Two Okanogan restaurants, **Cedars Inn,** on Appleway and Hwy. 97, tel. (509) 422-6431, and **The Western Restaurant,** 1930 N. 2nd

Ave., tel. (509) 422-3499, have well-prepared steaks and burgers. A full complement of fast food joints can be found in Omak near the junction of Highways 20 and 210: McDonald's, Pizza Hut, Arby's, Dairy Queen, Burger King, etc.

Legion Park in Okanogan has a **farmers market** May-Oct.; open Tuesday 4-6 p.m. and Saturday 9 a.m.-noon.

EVENTS

Omak Stampede and Suicide Race

Omak is world-famous for its annual Stampede and Suicide Race, held the second weekend in August at East Side Park. Tickets for the three-day event cost $5-12 and are available in advance by calling (509) 826-1002 or (800) 933-6625. Festivities include two parades, a big Western art show, carnival, and a major professional rodeo. A shuttle bus provides service (by donation) between Omak and Okanogan during the Stampede. During the week of the Stampede, a major attraction is the **Indian Encampment** in East Side Park. Hundreds of Indians come from all over the West to live in tepees, take part in traditional dance contests, or play the stick games— a form of gambling. (Be sure to request p[...] sion before taking photos at the encam[...]

The main event features four chaotic horse races down a steep slope, across the Okanogan River, and into the crowded arena. Most of the 20 or so participants come from the nearby Colville Indian Reservation, and this is a tradition that has gone on for more than 60 years. The dangerous downhill section often creates pileups that injure both riders and horses, sometimes leading to the death of the horse. This has led to vocal opposition from animal-rights organizations. Locals defend the race as a part of Indian and Western traditions.

Other Events

The weekend before the Stampede, Omak's **Not Quite White Water Race** is a slow float down the lazy Okanogan River. Rafters display their creative talents in their costumes and raft design while spectators bomb the participants with water balloons.

Okanogan Days in late May features a parade, music, and airport fly-in. The **Okanogan County Fair** at the fairgrounds in Omak brings more rodeo action, horse racing, a livestock auction, and musical entertainment in early September. A **Balloon Rendezvous** on Labor Day weekend features at least 20 colorful hot air balloons. Another popular Omak event is the **Cowboy Poetry Jubilee** in mid-March.

ENTERTAINMENT AND RECREATION

The Omak Performing Arts Center is the site of all sorts of events through the year, including concerts by **Okanogan Valley Orchestra and Chorus** from October to mid-April. The **Breadline Cafe,** 102 S. Ash in Omak, tel. (509) 826-5836, has folk, jazz, rock, or R&B most nights. For country music head to **Cariboo Inn,** 233 Queen St. in Okanogan, tel. (509) 422-6109, or **The Western Restaurant,** 1930 N. 2nd Ave. in Okanogan, tel. (509) 422-3499.

Recreation

Swim at the Olympic-sized outdoor **pools** in Omak's East Side Park, or in Okanogan's Alma Park. The Okanogan River is a popular place for tubing in the summer months. For a rather different type of recreation, head to the **Colville Tribal Bingo Parlor** on Hwy. 97 in Okanogan. Play golf at the **Okanogan Valley Golf Club,** just west of town, tel. (509) 826-9902.

Loup Loup Ski Bowl, between Okanogan and Twisp on Hwy. 20, has Alpine skiing on a 1,250-foot vertical drop. (See "Downhill Skiing" under "Winthrop" in the Methow Valley section for specifics.)

INFORMATION, SERVICES, AND TRANSPORTATION

Information

The **Omak Visitor Information Center,** 401 Omak Ave., tel. (509) 826-1880 or (800) 225-6625, is right along the Okanogan River in East Side Park. Stop here to get a ton of local info or to watch a video on the Suicide Race. Open Sunday 1-5 p.m., Mon.-Fri. 9 a.m.-5 p.m., and Saturday 9 a.m.-5 p.m. May-Oct.; Mon.-Fri. 9 a.m.-5 p.m. the rest of the year. Okanogan has a summer-only **visitor information center** in Legion Park on the north end of town, tel. (509) 422-1541. The Okanogan National Forest **Supervisors Office,** 1240 S. 2nd Ave. in Okanogan, tel. (509) 826-3275, has hiking and camping information for the Okanogan highland country. It's open Mon.-Fri. 7:45 a.m.-4:30 p.m. all year. The **area code** for Omak and Okanogan is 509.

Services and Transportation

I can't vouch for their hair-trimming ability, but **Wak N' Yak Beauty Salon** in Okanogan wins first prize in the name-freak category. **Trailways,** tel. (800) 351-1060, has bus service to Omak, Okanogan, and beyond.

OKANOGAN VALLEY

Okanogan Valley is a dry area surrounded by mountains, with 28 inches of annual snowfall and a sizzling hot, dry summer. Major irrigation projects make this an ideal place to grow apples, pears, peaches, and cherries.

The valley served as a major route to British Columbia's Cariboo gold fields in 1857-58, and in later years the 800-mile "Cariboo Trail" was used by cowboys to drive beef from the Yakima Valley to the mining towns. The old trail is now Highway 97, a busy north-south route along the wide Okanogan Valley. The highway cuts through most of the major towns—Okanogan, Omak, Tonasket, and Oroville—before entering Canada at a 24-hour border station. East of the valley are the Okanogan Highlands, a low range of mountains and hills covered with forests and rangeland. The highlands are essentially unpeopled, with a few small towns; only Republic is large enough to have all the services.

CONCONULLY

Tiny Conconully (pop. 170) is 22 miles northwest of Omak on Conconully Road and sits at an elevation of 2,300 feet. This means temperatures are much cooler here in the summer than in the Okanogan Valley. Conconully (derived from the Okanogan Indian word for "money hole," a reference to the valuable beaver pelts found here) has a couple of stores and restaurants, along with several popular lakeside resorts. (Historic Salmon Meadows Lodge, built by the CCC in 1937, was destroyed in a 1994 fire.)

Conconully sits between the natural Conconully Lake and the unnatural Conconully Reservoir. Built in 1910, the latter was the first Bureau of Reclamation irrigation project in America. The **Outhouse Race** in January is one of those wacky events that attracts folks to Conconully from around the region.

Accommodations

There are three comfortable resorts around Conconully: **Conconully Lake Resort,** tel. (509) 826-0813, with cabins for $25-45 d; **Liar's Cove**

Resort, tel. (509) 826-1288, with cabins for $40-50 d; and **Shady Pines Resort,** tel. (509) 826-2287, with cabins for $54-60 d. Other lodging can be found at **Jacks RV Park & Motel,** tel. (509) 826-0132, for $48 d; and **Conconully Motel,** tel. (509) 826-1610, for $40 d.

Hidden Hills Resort, one mile from Fish Lake on Fish Lake Rd., tel. (509) 486-1890 or (800) 468-1890, has fine country lodging in an 1890s-era lodge. Rates are $59 s, $69-79 d, including breakfast.

Campgrounds

Five Forest Service campgrounds are within nine miles of Conconully; closest is **Cottonwood Campground** ($5; open mid-May to mid-September), just two miles out Forest Rd. 38. The others are **Sugarloaf, Oriole, Kerr, and Salmon Meadows;** all except the free Sugarloaf Campground charge $5. See also Conconully State Park, below. RVers will find a half-dozen local places to park and plug in, including the state park.

Conconully State Park

This cozy state park sits along the shore of Conconully Reservoir and contains a log cabin and a sod-roofed replica of the first Okanogan County courthouse; Conconully was the county seat from 1889 to 1914. The reservoir is a popular place for boating, fishing, and swimming. Trees surround spacious grassy lawns that make fine picnicking spots; take the half-mile nature trail for a relaxing stroll. Campsites are $10 (no RV hookups); open mid-April through October, and on weekends and holidays the rest of the year. Call (509) 826-7408 for more information, or (800) 452-5687 for campsite reservations ($6 extra fee), available up to 11 months ahead of time.

RIVERSIDE

Just eight miles north of Omak, the little settlement of Riverside (pop. 250) is a cool and quiet place to relax along the Okanogan River. This was the head of upriver navigation until the railroad rolled through this area in 1914.

The main attraction here is **Detro's Triangle L Western Store,** tel. (509) 826-2200, where you'll find an amazing selection of Western gear: saddles, Indian jewelry (mostly from the Southwest), ranch clothes, fancy belt buckles, cowboy boots, and fashionable Western wear. Up the road is **Rumpelstillzkins,** a spinning and weaving shop filled with handmade goods. Be sure to also keep your eyes open for the collection of whirligigs filling a local yard.

Camp at **Margie's Riverside RV Park,** $10 for tents, $5 for bikes, and $12 for RVs. Open March-November.

North of Riverside, Hwy. 97 heads away from the river through dry sage and grassy hills topped by open stands of ponderosa pine, before dropping back to the Okanogan River near Tonasket. From Tonasket all the way to Oroville both sides of the highway are crowded with irrigated apple orchards, laden with fruit by late summer. Old wooden barns in varying states of repair decorate the back roads.

TONASKET

This town of a thousand folks was named for the Okanogan Chief To-nas-ket, the first successful Indian cattleman in this part of Washington and a strong supporter of peace with whites. The town of Tonasket (TAWN-a-sket) is a minor timber, cattle, and apple orchard center.

Accommodations

The AAA-approved **Red Apple Inn** at Hwy. 97 and 1st, tel. (509) 486-2119, charges $37-43 s, $41-47 d, and has an outdoor pool. Park RVs in the lot next to the visitor information center on the north end of town for $10.

Three resorts lie northwest of Tonasket near the tiny settlement of **Loomis: Spectacle Lake Resort,** 12 miles northwest on Loomis Hwy., tel. (509) 223-3433, has $40 motel rooms, and a three-bedroom house for $100; **Rainbow Resort,** 14 miles northwest on Loomis Hwy., tel. (509) 223-3700, charges $35-40 for cabins with kitchens April-Oct.; and **Spectacle Falls Resort,** another mile northwest on Loomis Hwy., tel. (509) 223-4141, has mobile home units (!) for $40 s or d.

Food

Okanogan River Coop sells natural foods, local organic produce, bulk foods, sandwiches, and coffees. Several picnic tables next to the store make a nice place to munch. This is the center for the counterculture crowd in the area. Beyond this, you can try **Don's Drive-In** for burgers, or **Hometown Pizza** for hometown pizzas. Out in Loomis (12 miles northwest of town), **Palmer Mountain Barbecue,** tel. (509) 223-3311, serves barbecued steak, chicken, brisket, seafood, and ribs.

Be sure to stop for fresh apples and other fruits at one of the several fruit stands between Tonasket and Oroville.

Events

Tonasket Founders Day Rodeo in early June includes a big PRCA-sanctioned rodeo, parade, fun run, and cowboy breakfast, followed later that month by the **Tonasket Bluegrass Festival.** The main event of the summer is the **Sagebrush Logger's Tourney** on the last weekend of August. It includes hand-bucking, choker setting, axe throwing, tree chopping, and even truck driving contests. In late May, a **Friendship Pony Express Ride** takes place between Tonasket and Princeton, B.C.

Skiing

About 12 miles northeast of Tonasket, **Sitzmark,** tel. (509) 488-3323, is a family place with a 680-foot vertical drop served by a chair, Poma, and rope tow, plus six km of groomed cross-country trails; open Wed.-Sun. and holidays. The area generally opens just after Christmas and charges $10 on weekdays, $15 on weekends. Call (509) 486-2700 for information; the snow can be marginal at times. Nearby is the Havillah Lutheran Church, built in 1910 and still in use.

Highland Park Sno-Park, 10 miles northeast of Tonasket, has 12 km of groomed cross-country trails.

Information and Services

Get local facts at the **Tonasket Visitor Information Center,** on the north end of town. Ask here about tours of local apple warehouses. The **Tonasket Ranger Station,** tel. (509) 486-2186, is open Mon.-Fri. 7:45 a.m.-4:30 p.m. all year. Stop here for a detailed free guide to local hiking trails. During the summer, hop in the water at the outdoor **swimming pool** in History Park next to the river. The **area code** for Tonasket is 509.

Highland Stage Company, tel. (509) 486-4699, has two-and four-day stagecoach rides over the Okanogan Highlands.

OROVILLE

Oroville (pop. 1,500) lies four miles south of the Canadian border on Hwy. 97, near the south shore of Lake Osoyoos, in a region of orchards and pine-topped hills. It was first settled in 1858, shortly after gold was discovered in British Columbia's Cariboo region, and its name was based on the Spanish word for gold, "oro." The "Cariboo Trail" passed right through town, and this became the last chance to get American supplies before crossing the border. Today, the town survives on a sawmill, cross-border traffic, and fruit orchards. You'll find several cheap gas station/minimarts right along the border.

Apple trees grew well here, and orchards are still a prominent feature in the valley, as 10,000 acres of farmland are irrigated along the Okanogan River from Oroville to Tonasket. An old irrigation flume follows the highway north from Oroville to the border. (By the way, the Okanogan River is called the Okanagan River once it crosses into Canada, another of the strange spelling quirks that pop up throughout this region.)

Sights

A mile north of Oroville on Hwy. 97, **Osoyoos Lake State Veterans Memorial Park** offers fishing, swimming, waterskiing, and concessions on a natural lake shared with our Canadian neighbors.

The east side of Osoyoos Lake has apple and pear trees planted in the early 1860s by Hiram F. "Okanogan" Smith, the first permanent white resident of the area. Smith brought his trees in from Fort Hope, British Columbia, by backpack. Several of the 135-plus year old trees are still bearing fruit.

Palmer Lake, 18 miles west of Oroville, a popular spot with fishermen, is managed by the Bureau of Land Management; a boat launch and picnic area are at the south end of the lake.

The **Old Depot Museum and Community Hall** documents local history and includes considerable railroad memorabilia. Open Tuesday and Thursday 10 a.m.-4 p.m. in the summer months. For more train fun, be sure to drop by Whistle Stop Restaurant (described below).

Accommodations and Campgrounds

Camaray Motel, tel. (509) 476-3684, has comfortable rooms, an outdoor pool, and kitchenettes for $44 s or d. For AAA-approved motel accommodations, try the **Red Apple Inn,** Hwy. 97 and 18th, tel. (509) 476-3694. Rooms are $36 s, $43 d, and include a heated pool, riverfront picnic area, and laundry facilities.

Visit **Sun Cove Resort** on two-mile-long Wannacut Lake (11 miles southwest of Oroville) for a delightful family retreat with cozy cabins ($53 d), hiking, swimming, and fishing, plus a swimming pool, boat, kayak, and canoe rentals, and guided horse-trail rides. Tent and RV spaces are also available. Open April-Oct.; call (509) 476-2223 for reservations. More RV slots can be found at **Border RV Park,** four miles north of town, the parking lot at **Prince's Center,** and **Eisen's RV Park,** on the north end of town along the river; none of these are particularly notable. Much better is **Osoyoos Lake State Veterans Memorial Park,** tel. (509) 476-3321, a mile north of town, with tent sites for $11 (no RV hookups). Open April-Oct., plus weekends and holidays the rest of the year.

Food

For reasonable and tasty breakfasts—plus the chance to check out several extraordinary handmade wooden trains and paddlewheel boats—one of which is 10 feet long—toot on in to **Whistle Stop Restaurant,** 1918 Main, tel. (509) 476-2515. Even if you aren't hungry, stop here for a cup of coffee.

Cricko's Restaurant, 1321 Main St., tel. (509) 476-2037, has a popular Mexican luncheon buffet. Try **Fishermen's Choice,** 1417 Main St., tel. (509) 476-3098, for fish and chips or fresh seafood, or **Hometown Pizza,** 806 Central, tel. (509) 476-2410, for pizzas.

Peerless Restaurant & Lounge, 1401 Main St., tel. (509) 476-4344, is the nicest place around with an attractive decor and bargain-basement Wednesday night steak and chicken specials.

Oroville is home to the huge **Prince's Center** grocery store, very popular with Canadians in search of lower prices. The town also has a summertime **farmers market** in the city park.

Events
The second weekend of May means **May Day,** a two-day festival featuring a parade, pancake breakfast, dancing around the Maypole, bass tournament, arts and crafts, and basketball tournament.

Information and Services
The **Washington State Information Center,** tel. (509) 476-3321, is along Hwy. 97 on the north end of town and is open daily in the summer, weekends in the winter. The **area code** for Oroville is 509.

OKANOGAN HIGHLANDS

Okanogan National Forest
The 1.7-million acre Okanogan National Forest reaches from the Methow Valley to the Canadian border and offers a plethora of recreational activities from 1,600 miles of hiking trails, dozens of campgrounds, and hundreds of miles of cross-country skiing and mountain biking trails. Included within these boundaries are vast reaches of ponderosa pine, Douglas fir, and western larch forests, plus numerous peaks topping 7,000 feet. Two wilderness areas, Pasayten (see "Pasayten Winderness" under "North Cascades Highway") and Lake Chelan-Sawtooth (see "Hiking" under "Twisp" in the Methow Valley section) are found within the forest boundaries. Forest headquarters is in Okanogan at 1240 S. 2nd Ave., tel. (509) 422-2704; stop here for backcountry permits, maps, or other information. Ranger district offices are located in Tonasket, tel. (509) 486-2186, Twisp, tel. (509) 997-2131, and Winthrop, (509) 996-2266.

Molson
The Oroville-Toroda Creek Rd. cuts east from Oroville to Chesaw, climbing a canyon and emerging into open rolling grass hills with caps of western larch, Douglas fir, and ponderosa pine. Scattered ranch houses dot these hills. After eight miles, a side road leads five miles north to Molson, Washington's best known almost-ghost town, a delightful place in a wildly remote setting. Only a handful of folks still live here, surrounded by pieces of the past and the expansive land.

In the early 1900s, Molson became a major shipping point along the Great Northern Railroad, providing supplies for ranchers and miners, and sending their production to market. A spat over land—a local farmer claimed the town was entirely on his property—forced everyone to move a half-mile north, leaving behind the buildings of Old Molson. New Molson declined when the railroad stopped running in the late '20s.

Old Molson town consists of eight weathered log and clapboard structures from early in this century, including a false-fronted bank, shingle mill, homestead cabin, and assay office. Inside are collections of antiques and historic photos from the area; outside are old wagons, threshers, and fascinating aging farm equipment. The site is open April-December.

The **Molson Museum** is housed in a three-story brick schoolhouse a quarter mile up the road. Inside, find antique hand tools, historic photos, and a collection of artifacts from the area's rich mining history. The museum is open daily 10 a.m.-5 p.m. from Memorial Day to Labor Day.

Chesaw
Tiny Chesaw consists of something like 30 people in a smattering of homes, along with a store, cafe, and abandoned old buildings. The town was named for Joe "Chee-saw," a Chinese settler who, with his Indian wife, constructed a cabin along Meyers Creek in the 1880s. An influx of gold miners and prospectors led to establishment of a town around this cabin. Today Chesaw is in the center of summer homes, recreational cabins, and ranches.

Be sure to stop in the false-fronted **Chesaw Tavern,** where the ceiling is carpeted with dollar bills, the signs are pro-logging, and the beer is al-

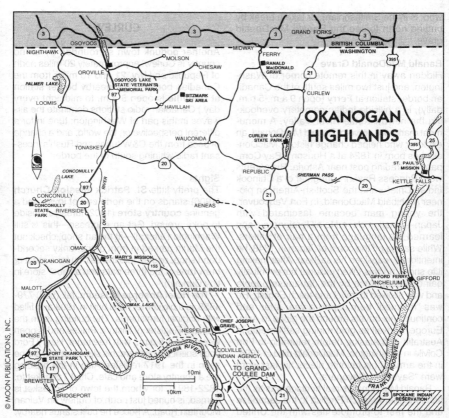

ways cold. Hang around awhile and you're bound to meet "Chesaw Charlie," a former accountant who gave up the city life, grew a long white beard, rides around on a burro, and formed the "Church of the Utterly Indifferent." He'll be happy to perform marriage ceremonies.

Chesaw has a very popular small-town **rodeo** and fireworks on July Fourth weekend.

Chesaw Vicinity

Four Forest Service campgrounds—**Beth Lake, Lost Lake, Bonaparte,** and **Beaver Lake**—are located south of Chesaw on the back way to Wauconda. They are open mid-May to mid-September and cost $6. **Big Tree Botanical Area** is a mile northeast of Lost Lake Campground (seven miles south of Chesaw) and includes enormous western larch (tamarack) trees. A short interpretive trail leads through the forest.

East of Chesaw, quiet country roads take you along bucolic Toroda Creek and Kettle River lined with tall riparian forests and populated by hunters each fall. The land is marked with country homes and farmsteads, irrigated pastures, hilltop pine trees, open meadows, and grazing cattle. It's a fantastic place for bike riding, especially in the fall when leaves turn a brilliant yellow. During Prohibition, this part of Washington was a major center for smuggling Canadian liquor across the border.

Stop at **Kettle River Pottery,** tel. (509) 779-4695, for fine handmade pieces (some of their work is in the Smithsonian), or take a break by cutting north to see the Ranald MacDonald grave.

Ranald MacDonald Grave

Hidden away in this remote corner of Washington, and just two miles south of the Canadian border station at **Ferry** (open 9 a.m.-5 p.m. daily), is a hillside Indian cemetery overlooking the narrow Kettle River Valley. A monument marks the grave of Ranald MacDonald, an explorer who helped change history. MacDonald was born in 1824 at a Hudson's Bay Company fur-trading post near Astoria. His parents were Princess Raven—daughter of a Chinook Indian Chief—and the Scottish-American pioneer Archibald MacDonald. In Fort Vancouver, the young man became fascinated with Japan—a nation closed to all foreigners—and learned the language from a pair of sailors. While sailing off the coast of Japan in 1848, he intentionally capsized his sailboat. After making it to shore, he was taken prisoner but eventually gained acceptance by the Japanese people and was allowed to travel and teach English. He was "rescued" from Japan a year later, and continued his travels around the globe to Asia, Europe, as well as gold mining settlements in Australia and Alaska, before returning to Fort Colvile in Washington. MacDonald died in 1894, in the arms of his favorite niece; his last word were "Sayonara, Sayonara."

Ranald MacDonald's real heritage was as the first foreigner to teach English to the Japanese and the first to promote ties with the United States. One of his students, Monyama Einsouke, served as interpreter for Commander Matthew Perry's vital trip to Japan in 1854. Although Ranald MacDonald is virtually unknown in America, he is revered in Japan, and pilgrims occasionally come to this remote grave site to pay homage. A memorial to him now stands at Rishiri Island, Japan—the place he came ashore.

East of here is the **Danville Port of Entry,** where a single building is occupied by both U.S. and Canadian customs agents. If you're heading north, be sure to check out the **Doukhabor Museum** just a mile or so away. The Doukhabor were a group of Russian pacifists who settled in communal villages here around the turn of the century.

CURLEW

Another podunk town surrounded by grand country is Curlew, approximately 20 miles north of Republic on Hwy. 21 and 10 miles from the Canadian border. (The nearby border station at **Danville** is open 8 a.m. to midnight every day.) Canadian radio stations dominate the airwaves in this part of Washington; tune in for a different perspective on the world, and a change of pace from the C&W tunes and Rush's incessant radio whining south of the border.

Sights

The pretty little **St. Patrick Mission Church** (1906) stands on the north end of town, and a genuine **country store** (1902) lures you inside to poke around. Get an espresso—this *is* still Washington after all—at the art shop, check out the Marlin parked in front of the funky secondhand shop, or step into the saloon for a meal or brew (one of the three bars and a liquor store in tiny Curlew!).

The **Hotel Ansorge Museum,** tel. (509) 779-4955, is a big corner hotel built in 1903 and filled with original furnishings. The building is on the National Register of Historic Places and is open weekends 1-5 p.m., with free tours. Henry Ford once spent a night here; his signature can still be seen in the 1917 register. Also in the building are a country store and cafe. Chief Tonasket (c. 1822-1891), for whom the town of Tonasket is named, is buried just north of Curlew on Vulcan Mountain Road. A house he built stands nearby.

Practicalities

Dine on big steaks, Mexican specialties, and sweet desserts at **Riverside Restaurant,** tel. (509) 779-4813, Curlew's best eatery. Open for dinners only. It's a popular resting place for travelers. Stay at **Blue Cougar Motel and Bar** for $30 s or d, or stop by for live bands on weekends.

A few miles south of Curlew is **Malo General Store,** built in 1903 and packed with everything you might need.

Curlew Lake State Park

Located on the eastern shore of Curlew Lake, and 12 miles south of Curlew (nine miles north of Republic), this pretty little park has attractive shady campsites ($10 tents, $15 RVs) and good fishing and swimming. The park is open April-October. Call (800) 452-5687 for campsite reservations ($6 extra fee), available up to 11 months ahead of time. Private resorts at the lake include: **Black's Beach Resort,** tel. (509) 775-3989, with cabins for $33 and up, motel units for $30-35 d, and tent and RV sites; and **Pine Point Resort,** tel. (509) 775-3643, with cabins for $29-74, plus tent and RV sites. Other places to stay are **Fishermans Cove,** tel. (509) 775-3641, and **Tiffany's Resort,** tel. (509) 775-3152.

Auto and Truck Museum

Four miles south of Curlew is the unique Auto and Truck Museum, tel. (509) 779-4987, open daily 11 a.m.-5 p.m. May-Sept., or by appointment the rest of the year (ask next door at Stotts Pre-Mix). Donation requested. A commodious aluminum building houses dozens of old vehicles, including a beautifully restored 1928 Ford Phaeton owned by Walter Brennen (and used in several movies), a 1925 Howard Cooper (built in Spokane, and one of four in existence), and the smallest legal car ever built—the Orange Peel. All sorts of other oddities add to this wonderful collection—maintained by local car buffs—the only such museum in Washington. Even more amazing is that all the cars still run.

WAUCONDA

There aren't very many single-building towns left in Washington, but Wauconda, about halfway between Tonasket and Republic on Hwy. 20, is one of them. In one moderately sized building you will find a restaurant, general store, video rental shop, gas station, and post office. You get to the post office by walking sideways past the cash register, the groceries and odds and ends to the back wall. To the left of the door, another squeeze past the cash register puts you in a small dining room with booths that overlook the valley below. Here you'll get ample servings of well-prepared food—including homemade breads and soups, plus steaks (Thursday), and prime rib (Friday and Saturday); tel. (509) 486-2322.

Bonaparte Lake Resort, tel. (509) 486-2828, has rustic cabins for $22-37 d. Get to the lake by heading three miles west from Wauconda on Hwy. 20, and then six miles north on Forest Rd. 32. Bring your own linen, towels, and kitchen utensils. The restaurant here has the finest steaks in the area.

REPUBLIC

Although recent years have been hard, Republic (pop. 1,000) is one of the few real mining and logging towns remaining in Washington, with at least one, and maybe two operating gold mines. (Echo Bay Mining is still active, Hecla Mining may or may not be operating.) Gold has been mined in the area almost continuously since John Welty discovered it on Granite Creek on February 20, 1896, attracting an influx of miners. Eureka Gulch and the surrounding countryside proved to contain some of the richest gold ore in the world. The Republic Mine produced $300,000 worth of gold in its first year, and the local paper reported that in May, "Large quantities of whiskey, flour, and other necessities arrived during the week." By the summer of 1898, Republic was one of the largest towns in eastern Washington. Things have calmed down a bit, but it is still the only incorporated town in Ferry County.

Today mining, along with a busy Vaagen Bros. Lumber mill, are the town's largest employers, but tourism is growing because of the hiking, camping, fishing, and hunting opportunities in the Okanogan Highlands. Despite the espresso bar added to a local cafe, Republic remains an unpretentious blue-collar town with a split personality. The majority of folks are of the don't-tread-on-my-logging-rights school, though the community also has a surprising post-hippie greenie crowd.

Stonerose Interpretive Center

A popular place for visitors is the Stonerose Interpretive Center, named for a 50-million-year-old fossil of an extinct rose found at a nearby rockpit. Many other plants, fish, and insects have been found here; they were deposited in an ancient lakebed.

Stonerose Center, tel. (509) 775-2295, is open

Sunday 10 a.m.-4 p.m. and Tues.-Sat. 10 a.m.-5 p.m., mid-June to mid-September; and Tues.-Sat. 10 a.m.-5 p.m. May to mid-June and mid-September through October. It has displays of fossils found at the site, and literature on fossils.

Also in the same building is the **Republic Historical Center** with old photos lining the walls and a fine small gift shop selling local arts and crafts. History buffs will want to purchase the fascinating *North Ferry County Historical Tour* booklet here.

The public is invited to dig fossils at the **Boot Hill Fossil Site** on the northern edge of town ($1 per person, $2 for families), but you must get permission through the Stonerose Center and can only keep three fossils. Hammers and chisels may be rented for $2.50.

Accommodations
Triangle J Ranch, 423 Old Kettle Falls Rd., tel. (509) 775-3933, has a private youth hostel with dorm accommodations for $10 per person, and a hot tub. The **Cottonwood Motel,** 852 S. Clark Ave., tel. (509) 775-3371, has rooms for $24 s, $28 d. **Klondike Motel,** 150 N. Clark Ave., tel. (509) 775-3555, charges $36 s, $38 d, and has kitchenettes available for $2 extra. The **Frontier Motel,** 797 S. Clark Ave., tel. (509) 775-3361, charges $36 s, $39 d, for rooms and has a sauna and jacuzzi.

Campgrounds and RV Parks
Camp at **Ferry County Fairgrounds,** tel. (509) 775-3677, three and a half miles east of town on Hwy. 20 for $6 tents, $8 RVs. Showers are available; open summers only. More RV sites at Cottonwood Motel and **Eastside RV Park,** tel. (509) 486-1316. The nearest Forest Service camping areas ($6) are **Ferry Lake, Swan Lake,** and **Fish Lake** Campgrounds, approximately 15 miles southwest of town off Hwy. 21 along Scatter Creek Rd.; open May-September. There are groomed **cross-country ski trails** here during the winter months. Closer camping can be found at **Curlew Lake State Park,** nine miles north (see above under "Curlew").

Food
Most Republic eateries offer pretty standard fare; walk around till something strikes your fancy. **Wild Rose Cafe,** 644 S. Clark Ave., tel. (509) 775-2096, has the usuals in an historic location—the building was built in 1899. The old-fashioned counter here delivers up milk shakes and banana splits. **The Other Place,** 645 S. Clark Ave., tel. (509) 775-2907, has the best local breakfasts. A few doors away is **Back Alley Pizza,** tel. (509) 775-3500, the local pizza joint. Republic also has a genuine old-fashioned corner drug store.

One place *does* stand out on the eating scene, however: **Ferry County Co-op,** 34 N. Clark Ave., tel. (509) 775-3754, a counterculture store with an earthy bakery and surprisingly good serve-yourself deli. Come here for a filling and tasty lunch, or to stock up on groceries and the latest environmental news. Cool place.

Events
Prospector's Days, held the second weekend of June, is the main local event, with a parade, golf tournament, crafts show, pancake feed, rodeo, stock car races, and even a cattle drive. Republic's **Fourth of July** festivities include a big picnic in the park.

The **Ferry County Fair** is held on the fairgrounds three and a half miles east of Republic on Labor Day weekend. This is one of the oldest fairs in the state, begun in the early 1900s as a chance to race horses. Today it includes 4-H demonstrations, livestock auctions, a parade, live entertainment, and, of course, horse racing.

Entertainment
Several local bars and restaurants have live music off and on through the year: **San Poil Saloon, The Other Place,** and **Hitch-N-Post Restaurant.**

Hiking
For an easy and very scenic walk, take the half-mile hike to **Nine Mile Falls.** The trailhead is southeast of Republic; get here by driving eight miles east on Hwy. 20, turning south onto Hall Creek Rd. and following it two and a half miles to Refrigerator Canyon Road. Turn here and continue five miles to the intersection of Forest Roads 2053 and 2054; the trailhead is just beyond this junction. The path leads to a small ridge overlooking the falls.

Information

Republic's **visitor information center** is located at 61 N. Kean St., tel. (509) 775-3387, and is open April-October. Call ahead for tours of Republic's **Vaagen Bros. Lumber Mill**, tel. (509) 775-3774.

The Colville National Forest **Republic Ranger District** office on Monroe at Delaware is up the hill behind the courthouse, tel. (509) 775-3305. They have detailed brochures on hiking and mountain biking routes in the area, including the popular **Lakes Area Mt. Bike Loop** south of town and Sherman Pass area to the east (see below). Ask here about the "Mystery Man Trees" on North Namankin Creek, images of a man emblazoned on trees. The **area code** for all of eastern Washington is 509.

OVER SHERMAN PASS

From Republic, Hwy. 20 climbs easily into Colville National Forest through mixed forests of western larch (these turn a brilliant yellow each fall), Douglas fir, ponderosa pine, lodgepole pine, and aspen. The ascent tops out at **Sherman Pass,** the state's highest at 5,575 feet. In spite of the elevation, you won't see dramatic snowcapped peaks, just thousands of acres of forested hills. A 10-minute hike leads to fine views of lands to the east. Stop here for a pleasant picnic among the larch trees.

Hiking

At the pass, a side road leads to a trailhead for the **Kettle Crest Trail,** an excellent 30-mile-long hike that cuts north over the summit of the Kettle River Range. The area is popular with backcountry skiers in the winter. You can also choose to head south from Sherman Pass along the Kettle Creek Trail for 13 miles, but portions of this country were burned in the 1988 White Mountain Fire.

Two miles up the Kettle Crest Trail is a spur to the top of 6,782-foot Columbia Mountain. Take this path—**Columbia Mountain Trail**—for a wonderful short (but steep) climb to the summit where you'll find a decrepit CCC lookout cabin and wide-angle vistas. It's a bit over five miles roundtrip from the trailhead to the top of the mountain, making a fine chance to stretch your legs and enjoy the quiet, forested land and the ravens playing in the thermals. Water is available from a spring along the trail. Get additional information on these trails at the Forest Service office in Republic.

THE NORTHEAST CORNER

Washington's northeast corner, north of Spokane and east of Lake Roosevelt, is dominated by Stevens and Pend Oreille (pon-der-RAY) Counties. (Pend Oreille is French for "pendant" or "earring," and is believed to have originated from French trappers who used the term for the earring-wearing Indians of this area.) The region is a paradise of good fishing in lakes and rivers, all-season recreation from swimming to snow-skiing, an abundance of wildlife, and very few people. The largest city in this not-quite-urban sprawl is Colville with about 4,400 residents.

This uninhabited forest land gives wildlife photographers plenty of opportunities: the Pend Oreille River attracts ospreys, ducks, cranes, and geese, plus bighorn sheep, bears, cougars, elk, and an occasional moose or grizzly. For the most part, the area's beauty is understated and its resources must be sought out; it's easy to drive right by and miss trails, lakes, and wildlife. This corner of the state isn't on the way to anywhere else in Washington, so only a determination to escape civilization or a strong exploratory drive brings visitors out here.

Several small towns serve the area: Kettle Falls, Colville, Chewelah, Ione, Metaline Falls, and Newport. They are unpretentious and friendly places and, although all have overnight accommodations and places to eat, most things of interest to visitors are out in the forests and along the rivers and lakes.

Except for a bus that connects Colville with Spokane and Trail, B.C., there are no buses, trains, or planes servicing this part of Washington. The **area code** in the northeast corner (and all of eastern Washington) is 509.

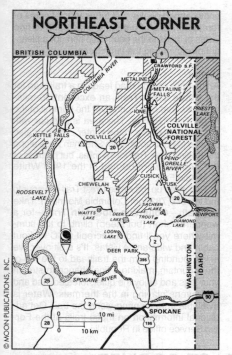

NORTHEAST CORNER

BRITISH COLUMBIA

© MOON PUBLICATIONS, INC.

Rivers and Lakes

Pend Oreille River is one of just two rivers in North America that flow northward; it enters Canada north of Metaline Falls before circling back south to join the Columbia River near the town of Boundary. Small lakes are scattered throughout northeast Washington. Many are encircled by summer cabins, modest year-round homes, or low-budget resorts and RV parks. As is common in eastern Washington, the natural features here aren't played up or exploited to the degree they would be on the more crowded, beach-hungry East Coast or other more populous areas of the country; yours is likely to be the only boat on the lake. With this serenity comes a corresponding lack of services, so keep the fuel tank and ice chest full.

While traveling Hwy. 395, between Spokane and the Canadian border, you can pull off at several lakes—Loon, Deer, and Waitts in particular. On Hwy. 2, between Spokane and New-

port, you'll find Diamond, Eloika, Trout, Sacheen, and Davis Lakes. These and other lakes are generally clearly marked and easily accessible from the highway, though facilities are often limited to a boat ramp and portable toilet. The Pend Oreille River, popular for fishing and boating, follows Highways 31 and 20 from the Canadian border to Newport and on into Idaho's Pend Oreille Lake.

COLVILLE NATIONAL FOREST

Colville National Forest spreads over 1.1 million acres in half-a-dozen scattered puzzle pieces, reaching from Metaline Falls to Wauconda, 67 air-miles away. Abutting it on both sides are additional public lands: Okanogan National Forest to the west and Kaniksu National Forest reaching eastward into Idaho. The eastern portions of the Colville are capped by the Selkirk Mountains, one of the last places in the Lower 48 where grizzlies survive. The forests are a true mixture of evergreen and deciduous species, with grand fir, subalpine fir, lodgepole pine, aspen, Douglas fir, western white pine, western red cedar, western larch, birch, and cottonwood trees.

Hiking and Campgrounds

Contact any Colville National Forest ranger station for a map and detailed, printed descriptions of day hikes and longer treks. This is bear country—even a few grizzlies have been spotted—so make noise, store your food safely, and don't be too proud to choose another route if you encounter bears, bear tracks, or droppings.

Abercrombie Mountain Trail is a three-mile one-way hike to a ridge top with panoramic views of the Pend Oreille and Columbia River valleys from 7,300 feet. From Colville, take Aladdin Hwy. north for 23 miles to Deep Creek Rd., turn north onto Deep Creek Rd. for seven miles, then turn right on Silver Creek Rd. 4720 to the junction with Rd. 7078. Take 7078 north to Rd. 300, then follow it to the road's end where the trail begins. Most of the three miles is wooded, crossing several streams and huckleberry bushes on the way to the ridge. This trail is also popular with hunters because of the abundant deer—so look conspicuous!

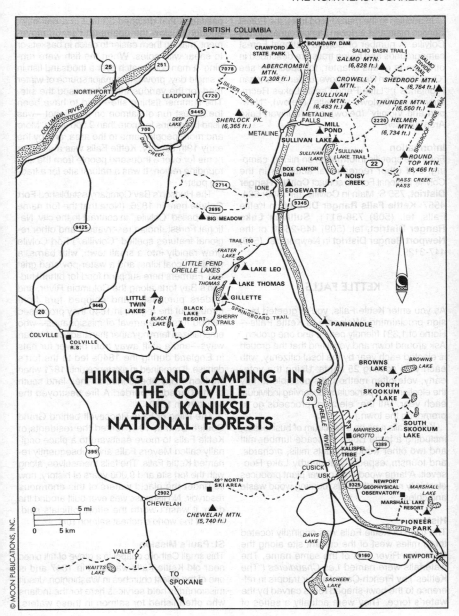

BRITISH COLUMBIA

CRAWFORD STATE PARK

BOUNDARY DAM

SALMO BASIN TRAIL

SALMO MTN. (6,828 ft.)

ABERCROMBIE MTN. (7,308 ft.)

CROWELL MTN.

SHEDROOF MTN. (6,764 ft.)

SALMO DIVIDE TRAIL

SULLIVAN MTN. (6,483 ft.)

THUNDER MTN. (6,560 ft.)

TRAIL 515

METALINE FALLS

SHERLOCK PK. (6,365 ft.)

MILL POND

SULLIVAN LAKE

HELMER MTN. (6,734 ft.)

SHEDROOF DIVIDE TRAIL

METALINE

SULLIVAN LAKE

SULLIVAN LAKE TRAIL

ROUND TOP MTN. (6,466 ft.)

BOX CANYON DAM

NOISY CREEK

PASS CREEK PASS

IONE

EDGEWATER

BIG MEADOW

TRAIL 150

FRATER LAKE

LITTLE PEND OREILLE LAKES

LAKE THOMAS

LAKE LEO

LAKE THOMAS

GILLETTE

LITTLE TWIN LAKES

BLACK LAKE

BLACK LAKE RESORT

SHERRY TRAILS

SPRINGBOARD TRAIL

PANHANDLE

COLVILLE

COLVILLE R.S.

HIKING AND CAMPING IN THE COLVILLE AND KANIKSU NATIONAL FORESTS

BROWNS LAKE

BROWNS LAKE

NORTH SKOOKUM LAKE

SOUTH SKOOKUM LAKE

MANRESA GROTTO

KALISPEL TRIBE

CUSICK

USK

NEWPORT GEOPHYSICAL OBSERVATORY

MARSHALL LAKE

MARSHALL LAKE RESORT

PIONEER PARK

49° NORTH SKI AREA

CHEWELAH

CHEWELAH MTN. (5,740 ft.)

DAVIS LAKE

NEWPORT

VALLEY

WAITTS LAKE

TO SPOKANE

SACHEEN LAKE

0   5 mi

0   5 km

© MOON PUBLICATIONS, INC.

NORTHPORT

LEADPOINT

DEEP LAKE

DEEP CREEK

COLUMBIA RIVER

PEND OREILLE RIVER

In addition to the many hiking trails, the Forest Service maintains a dozen campgrounds on the Colville. A number of Colville National Forest campgrounds and hiking trails are described in other parts of this chapter; for specifics, see "Over Sherman Pass" (above, under "Okanogan Highlands"), "Little Pend Oreille Lakes Recreation Area" (below), "Colville" (below), "Newport and Vicinity" (below), and "Sullivan Lake Area" (below).

Information

For more specific information on hiking, camping, and other recreational activities in the Colville National Forest, contact **Colville Ranger District,** 755 S. Main in Colville, tel. (509) 684-4557; **Kettle Falls Ranger District,** in Kettle Falls, tel. (509) 738-6111; **Sullivan Lake Ranger District,** tel. (509) 446-2681; or the **Newport Ranger District** in Newport, tel. (509) 447-3129.

KETTLE FALLS

As you enter Kettle Falls, you're greeted by a sign proclaiming "Welcome to Kettle Falls—Home of 1,381 friendly people and one grouch." Ask around town and you'll find that the grouch is elected each year by the local citizenry, with each vote costing 25 cents. Using the vote-early, vote-often method, it's possible to buy the election for a particularly deserving individual each year. (All the "election" proceeds go to promoting the town.)

Kettle Falls runs on a spectrum of businesses, including a large Boise Cascade lumber mill and two other wood products mills, orchards, and tourism, especially at nearby Lake Roosevelt. A large wood-fired power plant produces electricity near Kettle Falls, burning wood waste and chips.

History

The town of Kettle Falls was originally located three miles west of the current site along the Columbia River falls of the same name. The waterfalls were named *Les Chaudieres* ("The Kettles") by French-Canadian fur traders in reference to the bowl-shaped rocks carved by the water's force. They were actually a series of cascades that dropped 33 feet in a half mile, enough to slow the upstream salmon movement, making them easier to catch in baskets or to spear with poles. When the fish were running, a man could catch over a thousand fish in a single day, providing a major source of winter food for the various tribes that used the site. The summer fishing site—said to have been the richest run of salmon on the planet—was used by Indians for more than 9,000 years. More and more people came to the area, and by the early 19th century, Kettle Falls was a summer home for over a thousand people from the surrounding region. It was a natural site for a trading post.

The Hudson's Bay Company established **Fort Colvile** here in 1826. (Note that the fort name was spelled "Colvile," in contrast to the city, National Forest, Indian reservation, and other regional features spelled "Colville.") Fort Colvile grew rapidly into a small town, with barns, a windmill, coal kilns, and a water-powered grist mill. Farmers here supplied food for other Hudson's Bay forts along the Columbia River, and traders purchased and shipped furs from throughout the region; in 1840 they processed 18,000 furs. The arrival of missionaries—who emphasized farming rather than traditional Indian ways—and a shift away from beaver fur hats in England during the 1840s led to the fort's demise. It remained in existence until 1871 when Hudson's Bay abandoned all their land south of the Canadian border. A fire destroyed the structure in 1910.

The filling of Lake Roosevelt behind Grand Coulee Dam in 1941 forced the residents of Kettle Falls to move eastward to a place originally called Meyers Falls and subsequently renamed Kettle Falls. The falls themselves, along with the fort site and 9,000 years of history, now lie under the placid waters of this enormous reservoir. No fishpass was ever built around the dam; it wasn't worth the effort, officials said. End of the world's richest salmon run.

St. Paul's Mission

This small Catholic chapel in a grove of tall pines near old Kettle Falls was built in 1847 and is one of the oldest churches in Washington. Jesuit missionaries held services here for the Indians who often fished for salmon in these waters.

The chapel was closed 1858-62 when gold fever brought an influx of white settlers and their booze, but it reopened for the summer salmon runs in the 1870s, after which it fell into disrepair. Reconstructed in 1939 using hand-hewn logs, the structure was turned over to the National Park Service in 1974.

Not far away is the **Kettle Falls Historical Center,** a small building that houses murals, artifacts, and exhibits portraying the old ways of Indian life before Lake Roosevelt flooded the falls and ended salmon fishing here. It is open Wed.-Sun. 11 a.m.-5 p.m. and contains a gift shop selling books and local handicrafts.

Meyers Falls

Meyers Falls—the oldest continually used source of industrial power in the Pacific Northwest—has a small log building that houses the **Meyers Falls Interpretive Center** where historic photos line the walls. Outside is a replica of the 16-foot high water wheel that operated here for many decades, along with the original stone wheels used to grind the grain. The cascades are a few feet distant, dropping 20 feet into a pretty plunge pool below a small dam that has been producing electrical power here since 1903. Prior to its completion, the falls turned three gristmills, the first built in 1826 by the Hudson's Bay Company. It milled wheat, oats, barley, and corn for their trading posts along the upper Columbia River and is said to have produced the first patented flour in the United States. The old mill was destroyed by a fire in 1916. The falls are located a mile south of town on Juniper St.; follow the signs from the highway.

Accommodations

Double H Motel, 205 E. 3rd St., tel. (509) 738-6514, charges $36 s or $41 d, and has kitchenettes available. **Barney's Junction Motel,** at the junction of Highways 395 and 20, tel. (509) 738-6546, has rooms for $25 s, $32 d. **Grandview Inn Motel,** 978 Hwy. 395, tel. (509) 738-6733, has a delightful woodsy location overlooking Lake Roosevelt and comfortable rooms for $32 s, $34 d; some rooms have kitchenettes.

The Lake House, eight miles northeast of Kettle Falls, tel. (509) 684-5132, is a spacious country home with two bedrooms, a full kitchen, hot tub, and woodstove. Rent it for $95 d, or $495 per week. No children under 12.

The most elaborate place to stay is **My Parent's Estate B&B,** tel. (509) 738-6220, a mile east of Kettle Falls on Hwy. 395. It began in 1869 as the St. Regis Mission and convent, was turned into a boys' school, then a Dominican convent, then a home for troubled boys. The present owners, Bev and Al Parent, opened it in 1989 as a country inn on a 49-acre spread. It features three rooms with private baths ($75 d) and a honeymoon suite ($110 d), and a jacuzzi and pool table. No children.

Campgrounds and RV Parks

The Park Service operates **Kettle Falls Campground,** tel. (509) 738-6266, in tall ponderosa pines along Lake Roosevelt. The campground is approximately two miles south of Hwy. 395/20 on Boise Road. Follow the signs. It is open year-round and costs $10 (no RV hookups). Campfire programs take place most summer evenings; check at the Ranger Station for other offerings. No reservations, so get here early for summer holiday weekends.

Private RV parks around Kettle Falls include: **Circle Up RV Park,** on Boise Rd. south of the Park Service office, tel. (509) 738-6617; **Grandview Inn,** 978 Hwy. 395/20, tel. (509) 738-6733; and **Panorama RV Park,** 460 W. 6th St., tel. (509) 738-6831.

Food

Cafe Italiano, 560 Meyers St., tel. (509) 738-6480, is the star of local restaurants with delicious and authentic Italian food in a relaxed atmosphere. Great pizzas too. **Little Gallea,** 270 W. 3rd, tel. (509) 738-6776, is the local breakfast and lunch joint with well-prepared and inexpensive American food in a smoke-filled room. For good steaks and seafood, stop by **Hudson Bay Co.,** three miles west of town on Hwy. 395/20.

More than a dozen local orchards produce cherries, apricots, peaches, pears, apples, and other fruits. Many of these operate fruit stands or have U-pick operations near the site of old Kettle Falls along Lake Roosevelt. Get a brochure from the chamber of commerce, or just head down Peachcrest Rd. till a place looks interesting.

Events and Entertainment

Town & Country Days is the big summer event in Kettle Falls, arriving the first weekend of June and featuring a parade, fun run, and local arts and crafts. This is also when the town grouch is chosen. July brings **Lake Roosevelt Regatta** on the second weekend, and the **Governor's Cup Walleye Tournament** the third weekend.

Freddie's Cafe, downtown, tel. (509) 738-6714, has live music on Friday and Saturday nights.

Recreation

The Park Service maintains a very popular campground, boat ramp, and swimming beach (no lifeguard) along the shore of Lake Roosevelt just south of Hwy. 395/20. There's an outdoor summer-only public **swimming pool** in the city park at the corner of Meyers and 7th Streets.

Fishing is a favorite activity in Lake Roosevelt. A net pen project near Kettle Falls produces 500,000 rainbow trout a year, and the **Sherman Creek Hatchery,** four miles west of Kettle Falls, raises 1.7 million kokanee salmon annually for Lake Roosevelt. For the current lake elevation, call (800) 824-4916.

Lake Roosevelt is a feeding area for more than 200 **bald eagles** during the winter months, particularly the portion from Kettle Falls south to Gifford Ferry. Best time to see these birds is late November to mid-February.

Information and Services

The **Kettle Falls Area Chamber of Commerce** is downtown along Hwy. 395/20, tel. (509) 738-2300. Hours are Mon.-Fri. 11 a.m.-4 p.m. Find the local **library** at Meyers and 6th Streets, tel. (509) 738-6817. The **area code** for Kettle Falls is 509.

The Park Service's **Kettle Falls Ranger Station** is at S. 1230 Boise Rd., tel. (509) 738-6266; stop by to view the displays of Indian artifacts and other items found at old Kettle Falls. Get Colville National Forest information at **Kettle Falls Ranger District,** 255 W. 11th St., tel. (509) 738-6111.

COLVILLE

Like many of its neighbors in this part of Washington, Colville (pop. 4,500) depends on timber, mining, farming, and tourism to survive. There are still three sawmills in Colville fed by timber from Colville National Forest and private lands. The town began as a U.S. Army post called Fort Colville (not to be confused with the older Fort Colvile run by Hudson's Bay Company). The fort was abandoned in the early 1880s, but the settlement survived to become today's Colville, the largest "city" in northeastern Washington. Downtown Colville is a prosperous slice of middle America, and the surrounding area shows even more evidence: a sparkling new high school on the edge of town and the only WalMart in this part of the state.

Sights

Keller Heritage Center, 700 N. Wynne St., tel. (509) 684-5968, contains an extensive collection of items from Fort Colville and Fort Colvile, an impressive set of Indian artifacts (a dugout canoe, headdresses, intricately woven baskets, and more), plus many historic photos. Be sure to ask the docents to play the old music box for you. Outside the museum you'll find spacious grounds containing the three-story **Keller House,** completed in 1912 and essentially unchanged today, with beautiful beveled glass windows on the front door and filled with historical furnishings. Walk down the hill under tall walnut trees to a collection of farm machinery and old buildings moved here from around the region, including a sawmill, farmstead cabin, schoolhouse, fire lookout, and trapper's cabin. The museum is open daily 10 a.m.-4 p.m. May-Sept.; try knocking on the office door if you come by in the winter months.

Accommodations

Downtown Motel, 369 S. Main, tel. (509) 684-2565, has basic rooms for $34 s, $39 d. **Colville Inn,** 915 S. Main, tel. (509) 684-2517 or (800) 680-2517, is the largest place in Colville with lodging for $40 s, $46 d.

For reasonable B&B accommodations, stay at **Maple at Sixth B&B,** 407 E. 6th Ave., tel. (509) 684-5251 or (800) 446-2750. Two rooms are available in this 1928 home for $45 s or $55 d, including a continental breakfast.

Carefree B&B Guest Ranch is seven miles south of town on Arden Butte Rd., tel. (509) 684-4739. You'll find a beautiful modern wood home, outdoor jacuzzi, stone fireplace, and deck. There are three guest rooms, and a big

THE NORTHEAST CORNER 739

country-style breakfast is served. Rates are 45 s or $65-70 d, including horseback rides.

Campgrounds
Tent ($5) and RV spaces ($10) are available at the **Northeast Washington Fairgrounds** on Columbia Street. Four Forest Service campgrounds (described below) are located in the **Little Pend Oreille Lakes Recreation Area,** 25 miles northeast of Colville along Hwy. 20. Several more remote campgrounds are free, including **Big Meadow Lake Campground** 27 miles northeast of Colville on Meadow Creek Road. Here you'll find three miles of hiking trails (partly handicapped-accessible), a replica of a homestead cabin, and a 35-foot wildlife-viewing tower where you may see moose, beavers, ospreys, or even black bears.

Food and Nightlife
For a relaxing lunch or espresso, visit **Cafe al Mundo** in the alleyway behind Main St. at Astor Avenue. More espresso, along with ice cream and sinfully rich desserts, are served at **Barman's Antiques** on Main near Birch Ave.; open till 10 p.m. for late-hour snacking.

North Country Coop, 282 W. Astor Ave., tel. (509) 684-6132, is a real surprise in this meat-and-potatoes town, offering fresh-baked breads, a serve-yourself deli for breakfast and lunch, and reasonably priced organic produce.

Mandarin Garden, 155 S. Main, tel. (509) 684-8989, has Chinese food, and **Rancho Chico** on S. Main between 1st and 2nd serves Mexican meals. Get burgers and a good choice of microbrew beers on tap at **Woody's American Grill,** in Southtown Plaza (S. Main and Hawthorne).

Colville has a **farmers market** on Saturday 8 a.m.-1 p.m. May-Nov. at the corner of Main St. and 3rd Avenue. For live music and dancing, head to **King Cole's** on 1st and Main, tel. (509) 684-2345.

Events
Fort Colvile Rodeo Days comes to town in June. **Rendezvous Days** in August features a rodeo, fair, firemen's competitions, horseshoe tournament, and more. Early September brings the **Northeast Washington State Fair** with a parade, animal judging, carnival, and live music.

Sports and Recreation
Swim at the outdoor **swimming pool** in City Park, or just hang out under the beautiful tall ponderosa pines and Douglas fir trees that cover the grassy lawns. This is a wonderful spot for a picnic lunch on a hot summer day. Golfers can putt around at **Colville Elks Golf Course,** tel. (509) 684-5508, a nine-hole course.

Information, Services, and Transportation
The **Chamber of Commerce Visitor Information Center** is on Astor between Oak and Main St., tel. (509) 684-5973; open Mon.-Fri. 10 a.m.-noon and 1-4 p.m. Ask here for directions to the big "C" on Colville Mountain behind town. The **area code** for Colville is 509.

For Forest Service info, visit **Colville Ranger District,** 755 S. Main (in the Federal Building), tel. (509) 684-4557; open Mon.-Friday. The library and post office are at Oak and Astor.

Borderline Stage, 127 E. Astor, tel. (509) 684-3950, has bus service connecting Colville with Spokane and Trail, British Columbia.

LITTLE PEND OREILLE LAKES RECREATION AREA

Heading east from Colville on Hwy. 20, the road cuts through beautiful mixed forests. Be sure to stop at **Crystal Falls,** 12 miles east of Colville, where the waters of Little Pend Oreille River drop over a 30-foot cascade. It's a fine place for a picnic beneath the trees.

Approximately 25 miles northeast of Colville on Hwy. 20 is a chain of eight glacially formed bodies of water: the Little Pend Oreille Lakes. These are a favorite getaway spot for folks from Spokane, offering more than 75 miles of multi-use trails open to hiking, motorcycles, mountain bikes, and horses. In winter, the Forest Service maintains 15 miles of groomed cross-country ski trails here. The lakes themselves are popular for swimming, sailing, boating, fishing, and canoeing. The country around here is a beautiful mix of open meadows and dense forests with plenty of larch trees (bright yellow in the fall). A couple miles east of Little Pend Oreille Lakes the road switchbacks sharply down into Pend Oreille Valley and the crossroads called **Tiger,** three miles south of Ione. The **Tiger Historical Center** has a small collection of memorabilia, along with local crafts; open summer only.

Resorts

Black Lake Resort, tel. (509) 684-2093, has campsites, RV spaces, a fishing dock, and swimming. **Beaver Lodge Resort** is a fun family or couples place on Lake Gillette, tel. (509) 684-5657, with comfortable cabins at $35 for four people, tent and RV spaces, and boat and canoe rentals. Open all year. There's also a store, deli, and laundromat here.

Campgrounds

You'll find four Forest Service campgrounds in the Little Pend Oreille Lakes area. **Lake Leo, Lake Thomas, Little Gillette,** and **Lake Gillette** Campgrounds are open Memorial Day to Labor Day and have a $6 fee. Make reservations for the Gillette Campground ($7.50 extra) by calling (800) 280-2267.

Hiking and Cross-Country Skiing Trails

A popular 2.4-mile-loop trail, **Springboard Trail** begins at the east end of the Gillette Campground. This is a self-guided interpretive trail relating the history of an early homesteader and leading to a viewing platform at 3,600 feet in elevation.

Sherry Trail is a set of three short loops that total four miles in length and begin at the trailhead just west of Lake Sherry. This hike or ski route passes through lodgepole pine and Douglas fir and provides views of the lake and Little Pend Oreille River.

Frater Lake Trail has two ski/hike loops—one three miles long, the other two—that start at Frater Lake on the east end of the recreation area. The shorter Tiger Loop cuts through Douglas fir close to the lake on gentle terrain and should be traveled in a counterclockwise direction for the easiest skiing. The longer and steeper Coyote Rock Loop crosses a stream and meadow and has a viewpoint from Coyote Rock; it's less difficult in the clockwise direction. Another 2.6-mile loop near here is the **Lake Leo Trail,** popular with beginning cross-country skiers because of its gentle terrain.

IONE

Ione (pop. 600) is a lumber and tourism town along the Pend Oreille River 35 miles north of Usk. Steamboats plied the Pend Oreille River in the 1880s; today nearby Box Canyon Dam backs up the river to create a popular place to waterski and fish. The Vaagen Brothers sawmill is Ione's main employer.

Three miles north of Ione is **Box Canyon Dam,** the source of electrical power for much of the county. Stop at the visitors center for tours, tel. (509) 446-3083, open Monday and Tuesday 7 a.m.-3:30 p.m., Wed.-Sun. 9 a.m.-5:30 p.m. in the summer; and Mon.-Fri. 7 a.m.-3:30 p.m. in the winter. The pond here (complete with float) makes a great swimming hole and picnic area.

Lodging

Plaza Motel, tel. (509) 442-3534, charges $30 s or d. The friendly and clean **Ione Motel,** tel. (509) 442-3213, offers rooms for $32 s or d and up. **Pend Oreille Inn** on the south end of town, tel. (509) 442-3418, has new rooms overlooking the river for $35 s, $40 d.

On Hwy. 20 between Cusick and Ione, **Outpost Resort,** tel. (509) 445-1317, has four cabins for $40 and up and RV parking and tent sites for $10, plus a restaurant, groceries, and boat launch.

Campgrounds

The Forest Service's **Edgewater Campground** sits across the Pend Oreille River and two miles north up Box Canyon-LeClerc Rd. (County Rd. 3669). No charge; open Memorial Day to Labor Day. RV hookup sites are available at Ione Motel.

Food and Drink

Papa's Place, tel. (509) 442-3200, has excellent chicken, pizza, and burgers. **Ione Supermarket,** tel. (509) 442-3710, cooks burgers around back in the summer. Looking for a drink? Ione has four bars and an espresso shop.

Events

The North Pend Oreille Valley Lions Club **Excursion Train** ($4; reservations suggested) chugs between Ione and Metaline Falls two weekends a month between mid-June and early

October, crossing Box Canyon Dam along the way. Trains leave Ione at 11 a.m., 1 p.m., and 3 p.m., with a stop in Metaline Falls before returning. Call (509) 442-3397 for information and reservations.

Ione's **Down River Days** at the end of July features boat races, a parade, fun run, and street dance. In early October, come here for **Octoberfest,** with German food, arts, crafts, and special train rides through the fall colors.

Information and Services
Get local information at **Reed's Shop & Save,** tel. (509) 442-3223, in the old depot; behind here are the restored rail cars used in the weekend excursion trains. **Ione City Park** along the lake has a picnic area, boat launch, and outdoor swimming pool, open in the summer.

SULLIVAN LAKE AREA

Four-mile-long Sullivan Lake anchors a large section of Forest Service land within Colville National Forest, providing outstanding camping and hiking opportunities. A feeding station at the south end of Sullivan Lake is a good place to look for **bighorn sheep** in the winter. Much of this country has been clearcut, but the Salmo-Priest Wilderness is here, along with Grassy Top Roadless Area. The Forest Service's **Sullivan Lake Ranger District** office, tel. (509) 446-7500, is at the north end of the lake and has all sorts of recreation info.

Campgrounds
Three Forest Service campgrounds are along the shore of Sullivan Lake and nearby Mill Pond: **Sullivan Lake, Mill Pond,** and **Noisy Creek.** All are open Memorial Day to Labor Day, and cost $6. Make reservations ($7.50 extra) by calling (800) 280-2267. Find good swimming beaches at Noisy Creek and Sullivan Lake.

Hiking
Sullivan Lake Trail is a four-mile one-way hike along the eastern shore of Sullivan Lake through forested areas, connecting Sullivan Lake Campground with Noisy Creek Campground. The clear blue lake is the main attraction, but watch

for bighorn sheep, black bear, and white-tailed deer. A very nice hike, especially in the fall. For a short historical hike, head to **Mill Pond Historical Site,** where a trail leads past displays on the 1910 hydroelectric project here.

Salmo-Priest Wilderness
One of Washington's least-known wilderness areas, the 39,937-acre Salmo-Priest Wilderness sits in the northeastern-most corner of the state, bordering on Idaho and Canada. Much of the surrounding land has been heavily logged, but this small corner reveals the land as it once was: dense old-growth western red cedar, Douglas fir, grand fir, and western larch forests at the middle elevations, and subalpine openings atop the mountains. A number of trails provide hiking opportunities for the adventurous.

A fine loop trip begins from the east end of Forest Rd. 2220 that leaves Forest Rd. 9345 just north of Sullivan Lake. The **Salmo Basin Trail** climbs up through virgin evergreen forests and crosses into Idaho (and almost into Canada) before joining the **Shedroof Divide Trail** near 7,572-foot Snowy Top (a rough but rewarding side trip). Follow Shedroof Divide Trail back across into Washington and its junction with **Salmo Divide Trail,** which will take you back to your starting point, a total distance of approximately 19 miles. Much of the trail is at 6,000 feet in elevation, so sea-level dwellers should expect to hike a little more slowly than usual.

METALINE AND METALINE FALLS

The twin towns of Metaline and Metaline Falls—jointly home to 500 people—sit across the Pend Oreille River from each other and just 10 miles from Canada. Metaline began as a mining camp around 1865 and was named for the metals the miners found here; Metaline Falls came later as the site of a big cement plant (now closed). There's still lead and zinc mining going on north of Metaline. Metaline Falls is a delightful little burg with quiet streets and small frame homes with neatly trimmed lawns.

Stop at **Metaline City Park** where the spacious lawns provide a place to picnic, toss a Frisbee, or just hang out by the water.

Crawford State Park

You can tour one of the largest limestone caves in the state, **Gardner Cave,** at Crawford State Park, 12 miles northwest of Metaline Falls off Hwy. 31. The cave is open May to mid-September, with guided tours Wed.-Sat. every two hours between 10 a.m. and 4 p.m. Free tours take you almost 500 feet into this 1,055-foot cavern, past fanciful (and fancifully named) stalactites, stalagmites, and columns. Dress warmly, it's always cold inside Gardner Cave. Call (509) 446-4065 for more information. Camping is limited to 10 primitive campsites ($5).

Boundary Dam, just east of Gardner Cave, has a visitor center next to the 340-foot arched concrete dam (completed in 1971) that is jammed between two tall cliffs. Free tours of the dam and tunnels are given daily 11 a.m.-5:30 p.m. in the summer; call (509) 446-3073 for reservations. A viewing deck 500 feet above the river provides impressive vistas.

Accommodations

Built in 1910, the historic **Washington Hotel,** tel. (509) 446-4415, stands on a corner in downtown Metaline Falls and is home to Lee McGowan, the local dynamo. Inside are 18 restored rooms ($25 s or d) with handmade quilts, rugs, book swap shelves, original "workingmans" furnishings, and bath down the hall. A studio and gallery include works in progress. Be sure to ask her about the "Santa's workshop" sculptures, a collection of 50 figures that are displayed around town each Christmas.

Mt. Linton Motel in Metaline Falls, tel. (509) 446-2238, has motel rooms with microwaves and fridges along an interior hallway for $30 s or d. **Mt. Linton RV Park** in Metaline, tel. (509) 446-4553, has RV and tent spaces. Primitive camping is also available at nearby **Crawford State Park** (see above).

Food

Katie's Oven Bakery, tel. (509) 446-4806, at the Washington Hotel, is one of the anchors in this fascinating little town. Great breads, light breakfasts and lunches, and espresso in a cozy sit-back-and-relax atmosphere. Recommended. Get big juicy steaks at **Hoogy's Steak House & Lounge** in Metaline Falls, tel. (509) 446-3901. **Cathy's Cafe,** serves big and hearty meals for lunch and dinner.

Events

All summer long, the historic **Cutter Theatre** in Metaline Falls (an old school named for a famous Spokane architect, Kirtland Cutter) features live—and surprisingly good—summer weekend performances of comedic melodramas ($6) such as *Pirates of Penzance,* or *They Ain't Done Right by Nell.* Call (509) 446-4108 for ticket information. In the winter months you'll find more serious plays and concerts. For surprising first-run films (for a small town), head down the block to the **Clark Fork Theater.**

The North Pend Oreille Valley Lions Club **Excursion Train** ($4; reservations suggested) rolls into Metaline Falls from Ione two weekends a month between mid-June and mid-October. Performances at the Cutter Theatre are often timed so you can see a play during your stop in Metaline Falls. Call (509) 442-3397 for train information and reservations.

Affair on Main Street is the local summer event, with a downtown arts and crafts show. If you're in the region around Christmas, be sure to visit Metaline Falls for a display of 50 amusing Christmas sculptures.

Information

The **Metaline Falls Visitor Center** is open Memorial Day to Labor Day only; stop by the Washington Hotel at other times.

USK, CUSICK, AND KALISPEL LANDS

Thirty-five miles south of Ione is the little settlement of Usk, home to the enormous Ponderay Newsprint factory; call (509) 445-1511 for tours. Usk is named for the town of Usk, England, and you can see "sister-town" photos inside the country store. The pilings visible all along the Pend Oreille River near here were used to corral logs as they floated downstream to local sawmills.

Cusick (pop. 240; pronounced "Q-sick") is just two miles north of here and is home to the county fairgrounds.

The Kalispel Tribe (approximately 200 people) own a small section of land along the east side of the Pend Oreille River; they originally lived on a three-million acre spread. The tribal lands were made official in 1934; this is one of the few non-reservation Indian homelands in the Lower 48.

Sights

Manresa Grotto is a 70-foot-wide cavern on Kalispel Tribal lands, right along LeClerc Creek Rd. and five miles north of the Pend Oreille River bridge at Usk. This spacious rock grotto was used by Father Jean Pierre DeSmet in the 1840s as a combination home and church to preach to local Indians. A stone alter and pews (of a sort) are still inside, and mass is held in mid-September every year. Osprey nest near here along the shore of the lake.

The Kalispel Tribal offices and the **Our Lady of Sorrows** church (built in 1914) are two miles south of here. Stop in to see who is making Indian crafts in the area. Also ask to see the enormous mounted buffalo head (in a back room); the herd of 100 buffalo is immediately south of the office. Behind here is the powwow grounds used for the Salish Fairs.

Practicalities

The **Inn at Usk,** 410 River Rd., tel. (509) 445-1526, is a delightful family-run hotel in tiny Usk, 16 miles north of Newport. Built around 1910, it served as a boardinghouse for many years and has been lovingly restored by Stan and Andrea Davey. The inn has 10 bath-down-the-hall rooms for $22 s or d. They also rent canoes ($25), and offer tent sites ($8).

Blueside Resort, 18 miles north of Cusick, tel. (509) 445-1327, is a nice family-oriented place with a motel ($32 s or d) and cabins ($40 s or d), along with tent camping ($10) and RV spots ($15) on the Pend Oreille River. Facilities include a boat ramp and dock, swimming pool, and store, but no TVs.

Just south of Usk at the junction of Highways 211 and 20 is **Crossroads Restaurant & Lounge,** tel. (509) 445-1515, a large bar and all-American eatery with live music on weekends.

Events

The first weekend of August brings the unusual **Salish Fair** at the Kalispel powwow grounds. It includes a buffalo barbecue, arts and crafts, stick games (gambling), Indian war dancing, and a baseball tournament. Another enjoyable pair of events is the **Salish Barter Fairs** held here in late May and late September. This is a great place to purchase or trade Indian crafts and other works.

The **Pend Oreille County Fair and Rodeo** comes to Cusick in mid-August.

NEWPORT AND VICINITY

The town of Newport (pop. 1,800) is the Pend Oreille County seat and the largest settlement in these parts. It sits along the Pend Oreille River; the smaller Oldtown, Idaho, is on the other side of the bridge. The town was founded in Oldtown in 1889, but most everyone moved across the river when the Great Northern Railway built a depot on the Washington side three years later. Nothing particularly notable about Newport, but it is a pleasant small town with an attractive, bustling main drag (Washington Avenue).

Sights

The **County Historical Society Museum,** tel. (509) 447-5388, sits in Centennial Plaza Park on the corner of Washington Ave. and 4th St., with a Corliss steam engine from 1909 out front. Originally built as a train depot along the Idaho & Washington Northern Railroad, the museum now contains all sorts of obscure flotsam and jetsam, including a pencil collection. Also in the yard are a pair of historic cabins with additional items. The museum (free) is open daily 10 a.m.-4 p.m. mid-May through September. Next door is another old depot, which was used for many years by the competing Great Northern Railway and now houses Plum Creek Timber Company.

Built in 1915, the **Pend Oreille County Courthouse** occupies the block at 4th St. and Warren Avenue. It is on the National Register of Historic Places.

Motels

The lodging choices in Newport are limited and surprisingly pricey. **Golden Spur Motel,** 924 W. Hwy. 2, tel. (509) 447-3823, has rooms for $38 s or $43 d. **Newport City Inn,** 220 N. Washington, tel. (509) 447-3463, charges almost identical rates but is not nearly as nice. **Knotty Pines Motel & Cottages,** 10 miles southwest of Newport at Diamond Lake, tel. (509) 447-5427, has motel rooms for $25-50 s, $30-60 d, and cottages with kitchens for $50 s, $60 d.

Campgrounds

Four Forest Service campgrounds are close to Newport: **Brown's Lake, South Skookum Lake, Pioneer Park,** and **Panhandle.** All of these charge $8 and are open Memorial Day to September (Brown's Lake is kept open all year but may be blocked by snow). Pioneer Park Campground is a quick two miles north of town on LeClerc Rd.; cross the bridge over the Pend Oreille River, and turn left. A short loop hike here is the **Pioneer Park Heritage Trail,** leading past a series of 12 interpretive signs that detail the life of the Kalispel tribe. Of particular interest along the path is an archaeological excavation of a camas oven, once used to cook the roots of the starchy blue camas plant. This trail is wheelchair-accessible.

Old American Campground, 701 N. Newport Ave., tel. (509) 447-3663, has tent and RV spaces. **Marshall Lake Resort,** seven miles north of Newport on Leclerc Rd., tel. (509) 447-4158, has campsites and RV hookups, boat and canoe rentals, and trails to hike. More campsites ($4 tents, $8 RVs) can be found in Usk behind the general store and right along the Pend Oreille River.

Food and Drink

Golden China Restaurant, 924 W. Hwy. 2, tel. (509) 447-3823, has a wide range of Chinese meals, with lunch specials starting at $4. Many folks call this the best Chinese restaurant in northwest Washington. **Big Wheel Pizza,** 201 N. Washington Ave., tel. (509) 447-5531, makes decent pizzas. Try the local bowling alley for lunchtime soups and sandwiches. **Fay's Restaurant** in Oldtown has standard American meals. For a different sort of menu, head east a few miles to Priest River, Idaho, where you'll find the quaint **River Pigs Inn.**

Kelly's Tavern, 324 W. 4th St., tel. (509) 447-3526, is Newport's oldest building (built in 1894) and has a back bar that came here via ship around South America, and by wagon to Newport. In a bygone era the saloon kept a black bear in a cage, ready to wrestle any patron foolish enough to try.

Recreation

The **Pioneer Park Heritage Trail** begins at the Pioneer Park Campground and leads past 12 in-

terpretive signs that detail the life of the Kalispel tribe. An archaeological highlight of the trail is the excavation of a camas oven. This trail is wheelchair-accessible. **Lower Wolf Trail,** a short loop trail beginning from the north edge of town passes through forest and wildflowers, affording views of Ashenfelder Bay. To reach it turn north on Warren Ave. at its junction with Hwy. 20, continuing about a mile to the trailhead. The path is actually a series of short loops totaling 1.5 miles; half of them are wheelchair-accessible (but graveled).

The **Upper Wolf Trail System** consists of two and a half miles of loop trails located just north of Newport off Laurel-Hurst Street. The trail system is popular with mountain bikers in the summer and is groomed for cross-country skiers (both traditional and skate skis) in the winter.

A longer ski/bike/hike trail is the **Geophysical Trail System,** located approximately nine miles northwest of town on Indian Creek Road. In the winter, the Forest Service grooms six miles of trails in a series of seven loops. You'll need a Sno-Park permit to park here for skiing. The **Geophysical Observatory** was originally used for earthquake monitoring but now serves to detect the detonation of nuclear weapons. It is one of three such sites in America.

Events

The **Newport Rodeo** in late June includes a parade, carnival, cowboy breakfast, food and craft booths, and the main attraction, a PRCA-sanctioned rodeo. **Fourth of July** brings all the usual activities, including fireworks at Diamond Lake.

The annual **Poker Paddle,** held the third weekend in July, consists of a 40-mile canoe trip down the Pend Oreille River; participants collect Poker cards at various stops along the two-day route. A crowd congregates at the finish to greet the paddlers and enjoy food and game booths. That same weekend, Newport has a popular **Oldtime Fiddle Contest.**

Information

For local info, head to the museum. The **library** can be found at 116 S. Washington Ave., tel. (509) 447-2111. Stop by the **Newport Ranger District** office at 315 N. Warren Ave. (immediately north of town off Hwy. 20), tel. (509) 447-

7300, for brochures on local trails and campgrounds. Ask here for directions to the **South Baldy Lookout** and the **Roosevelt Grove of Ancient Cedars.**

CHEWELAH

Chewelah (pop. 2,200; pronounced "chew-WEE-lah") is a pretty little town with tidy brick stores lining the main thoroughfare, Park Street. Chewelah received its name from the Indian word for water snake. The region was first settled in 1845 when Jesuit missionaries established St. Regis Mission. It was later destroyed in a fire, but an Indian agency and various stores arrived, followed by an influx of miners. They discovered silver, copper, lead, and magnetite. The magnetite mines proved crucial during WW I, and a tramway was built (pieces are still visible south of town) to haul ore from the mines five miles to the Chewelah reduction plant. **Quartzite Mountain** rises just east of town, with steep cliff faces. Today, mining remains important to Chewelah, but so are logging, ranching, and tourism.

Sights

The small **Chewelah Museum,** N. 501 3rd St. (behind the bowling alley), tel. (509) 935-6091, is open daily 1-4 p.m. in the summer months. The historic **St. Mary of the Rosary** church is a beautiful old chapel topped by a gold-colored dome and cross. An exotic game farm with camels, zebras, emu, and other critters can be found eight miles south of Chewelah on Hwy. 231. Call (509) 937-2971 for specifics.

Accommodations

New 49er Motel, tel. (509) 935-8613, is a clean motel with an indoor pool and jacuzzi; rooms go for $32 s, $37 d. Tent and RV sites are also available here April-Oct., or camp or park that RV for free at **City Park** on Park Street. The AAA-approved **Nordlig Motel,** 101 W. Grant St., tel. (509) 935-6704, is the best place in town with a quiet off-street location and rooms for $33 s, $39 d.

Carpenter Manor House, tel. (509) 935-6503, is a spacious home on an 82-acre spread six miles southwest of Chewelah. The B&B has three guest rooms with private baths ($50-95 s

or d), a jacuzzi, full breakfast, front deck to watch the sunsets, and nearby hiking trails.

Resorts

Ten miles southwest of town off Hwy. 231 is Waitts Lake, a favorite getaway place for folks from Spokane. The largest rainbow trout caught in the state came from this lake; excellent fishing here for trout, perch, and bass. **Silver Beach Resort,** tel. (509) 937-2811, has modern cabins for $42-51, and RV spaces, plus a restaurant, store, and motorboat rentals. **Teal's Resort,** tel. (509) 937-2400, has cabins for $37-53. **Winona Beach Resort,** tel. (509) 937-2231, has cabins for $43-65, along with tent and RV spaces, a swimming beach, fishing dock, boat rentals, and store.

Also nearby are resorts at Deer Lake (**Deer Lake Resort,** tel. 509-233-2081); and Loon Lake (**Granite Point Park,** tel. 509-233-2100, and **Shore Acres,** tel. 509-233-2474). During July and August many of these resorts rent by the week only, so call ahead.

Food

Nothing really noteworthy on the Chewelah food scene, and the locally controversial arrival of McDonald's won't improve the situation, but several places offer better than standard meals. Try the **Parkside Restaurant,** next to the city park on Hwy. 395, for inexpensive sandwiches and light meals. **Park Avenue Square Restaurant,** N. 209 Park St., tel. (509) 935-8120, offers fine dining in Chewelah.

Get Chinese food at the **Shanghai Inn** downtown. **Polanski's Pizza,** just south of downtown on Hwy. 395, tel. (509) 935-4443, is a good family place with tasty pizzas, spaghetti, sandwiches, and chicken.

Sports and Recreation

Nine miles east of Chewelah, **49° North** has day and night skiing on 1,900 vertical feet of slope from four chairlifts. It's about an hour north of Spokane off Hwy. 395. Sixteen runs offer beginner through expert skiing; terrain is set aside for powder skiing on weekends. Weekend lift tickets are $23, $17 midweek; students and seniors pay $18 weekends, $15 on weekdays. Snowboarders and cross-country skiers are also welcome. Call (509) 935-6649 for information.

Be sure to drive to the ski area from Hwy. 395 on the Chewelah (west) side; the road in from Hwy. 20 on the east is a narrow gravel logging road, impassable in winter and no fun the rest of the year.

Play golf at **Chewelah Golf & Country Club,** 2537 Sand Canyon Rd., tel. (509) 935-6807.

Events
The big local event is a celebration of the arts called **Chataqua Days,** held the second weekend of July, with arts and crafts, entertainment, and food.

Information and Services
The **visitors information center,** 110 E. Main, tel. (509) 935-8991, is open Mon.-Sat. 10 a.m.- 4 p.m. The **library** is located in the yellow brick building on Clay Ave., tel. (509) 935-6805.

HUCKLEBERRY MOUNTAIN/ SPOKANE RIVER AREA

For a beautiful country drive, head west from Chewelah along the paved road connecting the one-store towns of Bluecreek and Cedonia. It takes you through lush valleys with big old dairy barns in varying stages of disrepair, and over gentle Huckleberry Mountain, covered with forests of ponderosa pine and western larch.

Highway 25 is another delightful drive, following the shore of Lake Roosevelt from Northport all the way to Fort Spokane, 90 miles to the south. The dark blue lake waters contrast sharply with hills of pine and grass. Numerous campsites line this shore (see "Lake Roosevelt" under "Grand Coulee Dam and Vicinity" for specifics). **Gifford Ferry** crosses the reservoir, taking you to the town of Inchelium on the Colville Indian Reservation (see "Colville Indian Reservation under "Grand Coulee Dam and Vicinity"). This free ferry runs from 6:30 a.m. to 9:45 p.m. every day.

Spokane Indian Reservation
South of the tiny town called Fruitland, Hwy. 25 heads away from Lake Roosevelt and across the Spokane Indian Reservation to Fort Spokane and Davenport. **Wellpinit,** the only settlement on the reservation, has a community store, post

office, and big high school with "Wellpinit Redskins" emblazoned on the front. The essentially undeveloped reservation is scenic hilly land covered in open ponderosa pine, large sections of which have been logged.

Fort Spokane
From 1880 to 1898, the U.S. Army post at Fort Spokane served to keep the peace between the Indians on the Colville Reservation in the forested hills to the north and the white settlers on the grassy plains to the south. The fort was built at the confluence of the Spokane River and the Columbia River and had 45 buildings at its peak in the 1890s. Those were peaceful years, in this area at least, so the soldiers practiced their drills and played a lot of baseball. They also drank more than a little, and many of the soldiers treated in the fort hospital were there because of bad whiskey or drunken brawls. The fort was closed at the outbreak of the Spanish-American War in 1898 and was later used as headquarters for the Colville Indian Agency and as a tuberculosis sanitorium. The grounds were abandoned in 1929 and transferred to the National Park Service in 1960, which has restored the remaining structures.

Take a walking tour through the grounds to see four of the original buildings, including an 1884 stable that housed the dozens of mules needed to haul supplies from the nearest railroad depot in Sprague. Trailside displays relate the fort's history, and the brick guardhouse (1892) has a **visitor center** open daily 9:30 a.m.-5:30 p.m. from mid-May to early September. Rangers in 19th century costumes offer hour-long tours of the fort on Sunday mornings in the summer; call (509) 725-2715 for specifics.

The Park Service maintains a nearby swimming beach, campground ($10; free in winter), and amphitheater for Saturday campfire programs from mid-June to early September. Across the river on reservation land you'll find the **Two Rivers Casino,** tel. (509) 722-4000, with 200 or so one-armed bandits; RV hookups are available. Nearby is a stand selling Indian tacos. Heading south toward Davenport, Hwy. 25 passes through an open landscape of rolling wheatfields with scattered old red barns and two-story white houses. Side roads off the highway provide access to **Seven Bays Marina** and

Porcupine Bay, very popular camping, fishing, swimming, and boating areas within Lake Roosevelt National Recreation Area.

Long Lake Area

The **Long Lake Dam,** spans the Spokane River near the east edge of the Spokane Indian Reservation. The grounds here offer a pleasant picnic spot beneath ponderosa pines; free lakeside summer-only campsites are available at **Long Lake Camp,** five miles east on Long Lake Dam Road.

Approximately five miles east of the junction between Highways 291 and 231 are a couple of large boulders surrounded by a chain link fence. Behind the fence are several red-painted figures of unknown age, the **Long Lake petroglyphs.** Nothing special if you've seen the far more impressive petroglyphs of Utah and Wyoming, but worth a stop, nonetheless. East from here on Hwy. 291 the road follows the beautiful shore of Long Lake for quite a few miles, passing several small resorts and the podunk settlement called **Tumtum.** Forested hills climb up away from the blue lake waters. The road continues past Riverside State Park and then on to Spokane, 35 miles from the junction with Hwy. 231.

DAVENPORT

Located just 35 miles from bustling Spokane, Davenport (pop. 1,500) is the seat for Lincoln County and a minor farming and ranching center in this open land of cattle ranches and wheatfields. The brick county courthouse overlooks town, and a wide main street divides the business district. For a taste of ranch life, visit the **Davenport Livestock Exchange,** the home of frequent livestock auctions.

Sights

Stop by the **Lincoln County Historical Museum,** at Park and 7th Streets, open Mon.-Sat. 9 a.m.-5 p.m. May-Sept., for local memorabilia, and a fine collection of agricultural equipment in the back building. The strangest sight here is the death mask of the outlaw Harry Tracy, a member of the Hole-in-the-Wall gang who committed suicide after being cornered by lawmen nearby. The museum also houses a visitor center with local information.

Birdwatchers will want to ask for directions to places where burrowing owls can be seen right in town. Twenty-four miles north of Davenport is historic Fort Spokane, described above.

Lodging

Black Bear Motel, 30 Logan, tel. (509) 725-7700, is an older motel with rooms for $29 s, $34 d, along with tent ($8) and RV hookups ($12). **Davenport Motel,** 1205 Morgan, tel. (509) 725-7071, is an attractive and clean place with rooms for $37 s, $41 d. **Harrington B&B,** tel. (509) 253-4728, is 13 miles southwest of Davenport in the minuscule settlement of Harrington. Rates are $55 s or d, including an indoor pool, sauna, period furnishings, and a full breakfast in a century-old home. No kids allowed. Camping is available north of Davenport within Lake Roosevelt National Recreation Area (see under "Lake Roosevelt" in the Grand Coulee Dam and Vicinity section).

Food

Eat at **Cottonwood Restaurant** for dinner, or **Ellie's,** tel. (509) 725-3354, for breakfast served any time of the day. **Old Pioneer Bakery,** tel. (509) 725-4281, has fresh baked breads and sweets, while **Paul's Lincoln County Pharmacy,** tel. (509) 725-7091, is home to a popular soda fountain (with espresso, of course). Twenty miles west of Davenport in the cowtown of Creston is **Deb's Cafe & Lounge** with charbroiled steaks, a big salad bar, and country and western bands every Saturday night. Inside are all sorts of memorabilia from Deb Cobenhaver, a famous bullrider in the 1950s.

Events

Pioneer Days in mid-July is a favorite summer event for Davenport folks and includes parades, a football game, 10-km run, antique car show, arts and crafts booths, and various contests and games, especially a three-on-three basketball tourney. Davenport is also home to the **Lincoln County Fair** in late August, including a bull-a-rama, salmon barbecue, entertainment, and livestock show.

SPOKANE

Spokane's population of 187,000 makes it the largest city between Seattle and Minneapolis and the second-largest city in Washington. Though Spokane is less than half as large as Seattle, and has less of the latter's vertical and horizontal sprawl, the two cities have had much in common from their earliest days: both were leveled by great fires, after which both towns were rebuilt in brick; both cities attribute some of their early growth to outfitting gold and silver miners; both have impressive park systems designed by the same firm; and both cities hosted a world's fair. The legacy of that fair remains as Spokane's centerpiece: the 100-acre Riverfront Park.

Known as the "Lilac City" for its bountiful springtime blooms, Spokane has the same friendly, comfortable atmosphere of a small city in the Midwest. Located just 18 miles from the Idaho border, its tall downtown buildings and spreading suburbs seem an odd apparition among the undeveloped landscape of eastern Washington. The surrounding landscape is a mixture of rich agricultural lands, especially in the Palouse to the south, and piney hills as you head north toward the Selkirk Mountains. Slicing through it all is the Spokane River, or at least the dammed version; seven hydroelectric dams hold back the river waters between its origin at Coeur d'Alene Lake, Idaho, and its junction with the Columbia River near old Fort Spokane.

Spokane weather is much drier than cities east of the Cascades; it gets less than 17 inches of rain a year. Summers days frequently reach into the 80s, and winters are fairly mild, though it does snow.

HISTORY

The name Spokane comes from the Indian word "Spokan," meaning "Sun People." The area around Spokane Falls has been occupied for thousands of years and was a favorite place to fish for salmon each summer. The first white settlers came to this area around 1810—very early in Washington's history—when David Thompson built Spokan House, the first trading post in the state along the Spokan River. (The "e" in Spokane was added later.) The War of 1812 and turbulent times that followed led to abandonment of the post in 1826, and white settlers didn't return until 1838, when Elkanah Walker and Cushing Eels established a Protestant mission that lasted until 1847. Though Spokane County was created in 1859, including all of the land between the Columbia River and Rocky Mountains north of the Snake River, the first permanent settlers didn't arrive at "Spokane Falls" until 1872. The first real settler was James N. Glover, the "Father of Spokane" and a strong proponent of the region's benefits.

Early Years

By 1880, Spokane's population had grown to only 350, and the town competed hotly with neighboring Cheney for the county seat. Vote counters announced Spokane as the winner, but Cheney residents suspected the officials of lying about the results, so they came at night, kidnapped the election official and his records, and proclaimed Cheney the winner of the vote. Spokane's population grew dramatically by the next election—partly due to the arrival of the Northern Pacific Railway—and in 1886 the city had the votes it needed to win the county seat back.

Spokane experienced a tremendous boom following the discovery of fabulously rich silver, lead, and zinc deposits in the nearby Coeur d'Alene area: from a population of 350 in 1880 to almost 20,000 by 1890. The Northern Pacific was the Northwest's first railroad, but its monopoly drove transportation prices sky-high; though eastern Washington was the cheapest place to grow wheat, the farmers paid the highest prices getting it to market. The city of Spokane was so determined to get a second railroad, they gave the land, free of charge, to the Great Northern Railroad Co. to be sure it would pass through town—and to loosen the Northern Pacific's grip on farmers.

As in Seattle and Ellensburg—and most cities in the pioneer West—a devastating fire ripped

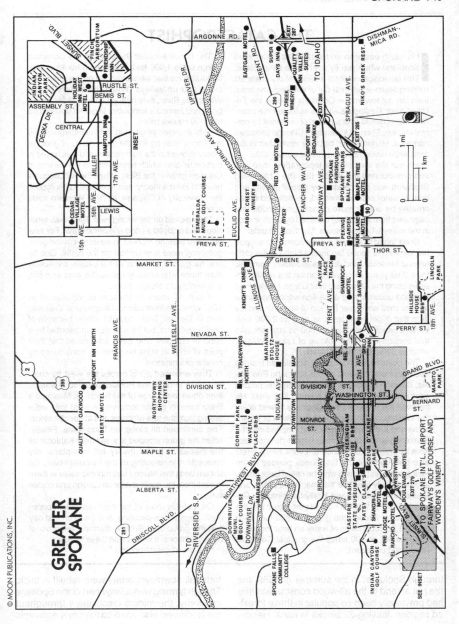

GREATER SPOKANE

© MOON PUBLICATIONS, INC.

THE CATASTROPHIST

It is much easier to understand the Channeled Scabland when you fly over it in a small plane. This geological oddity is a series of dry channels running south-southwest out of the Spokane area, then fan out toward the Columbia River in the Tri-Cities area. Geologists always assumed the channels were created over a period of centuries by normal erosion. Then a University of Chicago professor named J. Harlen Bretz, became interested in the area while visiting Spokane in the early 1920s.

He got the idea from a topographic map and soon formulated the theory that the Channeled Scabland was not created by glacial activity and normal water erosion. Instead, he believed it was created by one or more catastrophic floods that originated from a vast lake dammed by earth and ice in the valley where Missoula, Montana, stands.

Bretz found more and more evidence to support his theory. He found lap marks high on the cliffs around Missoula, and erratics (boulders found far from their place of origin) high on the mountainsides along the Columbia River Gorge. He believed the flood occurred as the Ice Age waned and snow and ice melt went over the top of an earth and ice dam that might have been as high as 2,000 feet. When it broke, it released a 3,000-square mile lake that contained half the volume of Lake Michigan, which is 500 cubic miles of water.

The catastrophic flood Bretz envisioned headed due west from Missoula across the Idaho Panhandle, down the Spokane Valley, where the natural contour of the land turned it south and west. He believed the Palouse River originally flowed down the Washtucna Coulee where the towns of Washtucna and Kahlotus are now, and emptied into the Snake River about 70 miles further downstream from its present confluence at Lyons Ferry. Bretz also believed that the first floods ponded in the Pasco basin and formed what he called Lake Lewis, and eventually filled the Yakima, Walla Walla, and Snake River valleys, and finally bore into the Columbia River at Wallula Gap. He theorized that the floods came through the gap up to 800 feet deep and at 1.66 cubic miles of water an hour for two or three weeks, or 190 times the greatest Columbia River flood on record.

The floods scoured the sides of the Columbia Gorge up to 1,000 feet, and carried boulders embedded in ice that were stranded on the mountainsides and up valleys. When the waters hit the Willamette River, they headed upriver as far as Eugene and formed a temporary lake that covered up to 3,000 square miles.

This sounded pretty wild to his colleagues and went completely against the grain; nearly all geologic theory evolved in the 19th century and was based in part on religion which held strictly to the version of Creation given in the Bible. When the Ivy Leaguers heard of Bretz's theory, some referred to his school, the University of Chicago, as "that Western trade school."

They picked on the wrong man. Bretz was tenacious and enjoyed a good academic brawl. For several summers he worked in eastern Washington, gathering more ammunition for the battle. One by one he gained converts to his cause, especially from those who actually toured the area with him and geologists already there.

It took 42 years for Bretz to be vindicated. In 1965 when the International Geophysical Year was held in Denver, Bretz couldn't attend because of health problems, but he was well represented by a band of disciples who were determined that their point of view at least be seriously considered by on-site examination.

They arranged a trip across the west by chartered bus through the Rockies and into Montana, then down the course of the floods. At Missoula a Bretz believer began lecturing on what they were seeing from the bus windows and at specific stops. This continued all along the flood route. Finally, when the group stopped at a site near Kahlotus all the pieces of Bretz' theory fell into place: dry cataracts, the rerouting of the Palouse River, the stream beds that haven't had running water in them in centuries, the ripple marks on canyon and coulee walls.

On that day most of his most outspoken opponents began back-pedaling, and it was on that day that the group sent Bretz a dramatic telegram of congratulations. It ended with these words:

"We are all catastrophists."

through Spokane. In the summer of 1889, the fire put an end to the all-wood construction that had previously been so popular in these forested regions, leaving 32 blocks in ruins. Henceforth, all downtown areas were rebuilt in brick. Though farming was a large part of the Spokane economy, the mining discoveries throughout the Northwest also sparked the city's economic growth. Several of Spokane's grand old homes belonged to those who made their fortunes from these mines.

World's Fair

The event that put Spokane on the map for most of the country was Expo '74, the city's World's Fair. The theme for the fair, "Celebrating Man's Fresh, New Environment," was a real problem for the developers, since the location chosen was Havermale Island in the middle of the polluted Spokane River, in a dirty, run-down section of town. The governing bodies of Washington and Idaho combined their efforts to clean up the river, while grass and trees were planted and buildings torn down to prepare for the fair. The result was a world-class Expo that won international attention and served to gear up the country for the bicentennial celebration. Spokane is the smallest city to ever host a world's fair.

SIGHTS

Riverfront Park

The site of Expo '74 has been preserved as a striking city park covering over 100 acres in downtown Spokane, with many of the original displays still intact on both sides of the Spokane River. Outdoors, stroll around the flower-bedecked paths, play on the rides, visit Canada Island, or take the gondola over dramatic **Spokane Falls,** illuminated at night. The most-photographed landmark is a tall riverside clock tower that was a part of the Great Northern Railroad depot for many years. Indoors, the five-story-high **IMAX Theater**—one of only 40 in the world—has shows

featuring dazzling, sharp images and stereo sound; call (509) 625-6686 for a schedule.

Riverfront Park boasts the **Spokane Opera House,** home to the Spokane Symphony Orchestra. The **Pavilion** amusement park features the SR-2 Scream Machine, the Dragon Roller Coaster, and other rides for the daring, plus tamer attractions for the kids. Be sure to take a spin on the handcarved 1909 **Looff Carousel**— a National Historical Landmark—on the park's south side. Kids of all ages enjoy the enormous red **Radio Flyer wagon** that doubles as a slide. Also check out the *Joys of Running Together* steel sculptures by David Govedare that race around the park borders.

Take a gondola ride over the Spokane River, park, and falls from the west side of the park, play miniature golf, pet the animals at the petting zoo, ride the park tour train, or try your Tonya Harding maneuvers at the ice-skating rink. The park also includes a restaurant, picnic areas, and more. Bikes, strollers, and other wheeled devices can be rented from **Quinn's,** tel. (509) 456-6545, near the South Howard St. Bridge.

It's possible to buy individual tickets to the various rides and attractions, but your best bet is an all-inclusive park admission of $12 for adults, $11 for kids or seniors. Every weekend 10 a.m.- 6 p.m. May-Sept., Riverfront Park hosts arts and crafts booths. Call (509) 456-4386 or (800) 336-7275 for more information on events at the park.

Historical Buildings

You can't miss the **Spokane County Courthouse** on W. Broadway at Jefferson Street. Built in 1895 and modeled after a pair of French chateaux, the castle-like courthouse seems

rather out of place in busy Spokane. Amazingly, this ornate masterpiece was designed by W.A. Ritchie, a 29-year-old man with no previous design experience; his architectural training came from a correspondence course.

Visit the magnificent sandstone **Cathedral of St. John the Evangelist,** 1125 S. Grand Blvd., tel. (509) 838-4277, to see an impressive example of gothic architecture, complete with stained-glass windows and stone carvings. Forty-nine-bell carillon concerts are held here Thursday at noon; Aeolian-Skinner organ recitals are scheduled regularly (call for times). Take a guided tour on Sunday following morning ser-

vices, or Tuesday, Thursday, and Saturday noon-3 p.m. The bookstore and gift shop inside are open daily; admission is free.

Browne's Addition, on the city's west side along W. Pacific and W. 1st, boasts some of the city's finest homes from the 1890s; stroll through the tree-lined neighborhood and stop at **Patsy Clark's** (see "Food," below) for a drink at the grandest mansion on the block. Nearby you'll find the Cheney Cowles Museum and Campbell House.

Historical Museum
The Eastern Washington State Historical Soci-

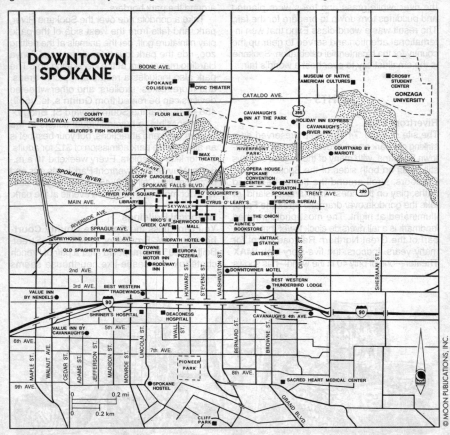

© MOON PUBLICATIONS, INC.

ety houses its extraordinary collection in two buildings at 2316 W. 1st Ave.: the Cheney Cowles Museum and the Campbell House. Both facilities are open Sunday 1-5 p.m., Tues.-Sat. 10 a.m.-5 p.m., and Wednesday evenings till 9 p.m.; tel. (509) 456-3931. Admission to the museum and Campbell House costs $3 for adults, $2 for children and seniors, or $7.50 for families. Get in for half-price on Wednesday. Fascinating half-hour tours of the Campbell House are included in our museum entrance fee.

The **Cheney Cowles Museum** has regional artifacts from the prehistoric to the present, as well as changing contemporary and traditional exhibits in the Fine Arts Gallery. The collection spreads through a number of spacious rooms, with magnificent Indian basketry and other artifacts, exhibits on the fur trappers and early settlers, an electric car, and much more. (Many of the Indian artifacts here are from a collection formerly housed at the now-closed Museum of Native American Culture; a new building is in the works but probably won't open till at least 1997.)

The **Campbell House**, built in 1898 by renowned Spokane architect Kirtland K. Cutter, is a restored Tudor revival style mansion from Spokane's turn-of-the-century "age of elegance." Amasa B. Campbell made his fortune in the lead, zinc, and silver mines of the Coeur d'Alene region and spared no expense on his home. His family lived here until 1924. The home is lavishly furnished with Persian carpets and period antiques. Be sure to check out the basement-level gambling room and safe. Out back is a Japanese style fountain; the Spokane River rolls along directly behind the house.

Bing Crosby

One of America's best-known crooners, Bing Crosby grew up in Spokane and attended Gonzaga College as a pre-law student. (His real name was Harry Lillis Crosby; while still a child, he picked up the nickname from a comic-strip character.) Gonzaga claims that he "left school" just a semester short of his degree "to pursue his singing career," but he was actually kicked out for throwing a piano through a fourth floor window. Nevertheless, Crosby received an honorary doctorate from Gonzaga in 1937, after he had become a star. Crosby gained fame in such films as *White Christmas* and *High Society,* and

his performance in *Going My Way* won an Oscar in 1945. He went on to appear in or narrate 100 films, the last being "Cancel My Reservation" in 1972. Bing died five years later at the age of 74 while playing golf in Spain; a posthumous biography by one of his sons was something less than flattering—to put it mildly.

The **Crosby Student Center** on the campus of Gonzaga University houses a collection of Bing Crosby gold records, trophies (the Oscar is actually a duplicate), awards, pipes, and other memorabilia. The building—originally the Crosby Library—was Bing's gift to his alma mater. A bronze statue of Bing stands outside the student center, and his boyhood home is now the Gonzaga Alumni Association, across the street at E. 508 Sharp. More memorabilia here; also check out photos of Bing and his classmates inside the Administration Building. Bing Crosby souvenirs (coasters, mugs, etc.) are sold in the student center; open daily till midnight in the school year, with more limited summer hours; call (509) 328-4220, ext. 4279, for more information.

Other Collections

Spokane's newest and most light-hearted museum is the **Broadview Dairy Museum,** W. 411 Cataldo, tel. (509) 459-6104, which honors this important Northwest industry with a self-guided tour that includes old butter churns, separators, butter molds, and all parts of the dairy processing story, including how a cow's four stomachs work. Exhibits identify the major breeds of dairy cattle, and a gift shop sells cow paraphernalia. Visitors can watch a seven-minute slide show (shown every half-hour 10:30 a.m.-3:30 p.m.), and get a bird's eye view of the dairy in operation. When I was there, employees were putting caps on plastic milk jugs. The novelty would wear off rather quickly, I'm certain. Open daily 10 a.m.-4 p.m. in the summer, Tues.-Sat. 10 a.m.-4 p.m. in winter; free.

The **Fairchild Heritage Museum** at Fairchild Air Force Base, tel. (509) 247-2100, is open Monday, Wednesday, Friday, and Saturday 10 a.m.-2 p.m. A WW II Women's Air Corps Barracks houses exhibits detailing the base's history and the use of air power in the first and second World Wars. Nearby is a train car housing a B-52 cockpit simulator, used as a mobile pilot-training center for many years. A library is housed in other train cars, and out front are eight historic aircraft, including a B-52D. Fairchild Air Force Base is 10 miles west of Spokane off Hwy. 2.

Gardens

Manito Park and Gardens, W. 4 21st Ave., tel. (509) 625-6622, open daily 8 a.m. to a half-hour before dusk, contains floral and botanical displays, plus a duck pond that makes a delightful picnic spot. The park was created by the famous Olmsted Brothers, who also designed New York's Central Park. Features include the **Gaiser Conservatory,** which houses tropical plants and floral displays (open all year), a formal European-style garden with plantings that change with the seasons (May to early October), and the **Japanese Garden,** a tranquil place to relax. The last of these is supported by Spokane's sister city, Nishinomiya, Japan, and is open April-October. In addition to these, you'll find a rose garden with 150 varieties of roses, and a perennial garden containing native plants.

Stroll through the **John A. Finch Arboretum,** 3404 Woodland Blvd., to see 65 acres of maples, rhododendrons, and ornamental trees along Garden Springs Creek, or walk the interpretive trail lined with signs in Braille and print. Open daily 8 a.m.-4 p.m.; free. Call (509) 625-6655 for more information. Unfortunately, the attractive setting is marred by the rush of I-90 traffic just a few feet to the south.

For a view from the highest point in the city, visit Review Rock at **Cliff Park,** 13th Ave. and Grove St., tel. (509) 456-4381. The rock, a half-acre wide at the base, was once a volcanic island.

Riverside State Park

This delightful park six miles northwest of town has open ponderosa pine forests with a grassy understory, and—as the name suggests—sits along the Spokane River. Access is from Nine Mile Rd. on the north side of the river or several convoluted routes along the south shore. The 7,655-acre park is a popular place for camping, hiking, horseback riding (guided horseback rides are offered by a concessionaire), birdwatching, kayaking (class III rapids), and even ORVing.

A favorite hiking destination is the **"Bowl and Pitcher"** area, where a trail leaves the campground and crosses a suspension bridge to con-

nect with a network of enjoyable paths. These unusual volcanic formations stand along the fast-flowing river and are visible from a dramatic overlook; the resemblance to a bowl and pitcher is vague. Get here by heading northwest from town on Hwy. 291 (Nine Mile Rd.), and turning left onto Rifle Club Rd., then left again on Aubrey L. White Parkway after a half mile. The park entrance and the Bowl and Pitcher are on the right after 1.7 miles.

Another feature of Riverside State Park is the **Spokane House Interpretive Center,** tel. (509) 325-4629, on the site of the first structure built by white men in the Pacific Northwest. Erected in 1810 by the Northwest Fur Company, this fur-trading post sat at the confluence of the Spokane and Little Spokane Rivers. After 16 years of use, the post was moved to a better site at Kettle Falls. No evidence remains of the trading post, but the interpretive center relates its history in a diorama, exhibits, and artifacts. It is located 12 miles northwest of Spokane on Hwy. 291, and a half mile north of the bridge (on the northeast bank); open Wed.-Sun. 10 a.m.-6 p.m. summers only, free.

Mt. Spokane State Park

This 16,000-acre park, 30 miles northeast of the city on Hwy. 206, encompasses 5,881-foot Mt. Spokane and 5,306-foot Mt. Kit Carson. Enjoy hiking, mountain biking, and camping in the summer, downhill or cross-country skiing (see below) in the winter. A narrow, winding road (no RVs) climbs to the summit of Mt. Spokane, where you can stop for a picnic at the CCC-built Vista House. The incredible 360-degree-vista encompasses the entire region, including parts of Idaho, Montana, British Columbia, and Alberta. Dirt roads lead to other areas, and trails crisscross the park offering day hikes for all levels of ability.

Turnbull National Wildlife Refuge

Twenty-one miles south of the city, 17,000-acre Turnbull National Wildlife Refuge, tel. (509) 235-4723, has miles of trails and roads for walking, cross-country skiing, horseback riding, or driving through the protected lake area. This refuge, unlike others in eastern Washington, is not open to hunting; this is strictly an observation-only area, and nature lovers will be rewarded with sightings of grebes, hawks, shorebirds, deer, coyote, owls, badgers, herons, and an occasional bald eagle or peregrine falcon. The refuge is open every day during daylight hours.

Universities and Colleges

Spokane is home to four colleges and universities, along with two community colleges. Sixteen miles southwest of Spokane on Hwy. 904 in Cheney, **Eastern Washington University** enrolls 8,000 undergraduates and 1,600 graduate students in over 100 majors, both on the 350-acre campus and by extension in downtown Spokane. The **Gallery of Art** here has changing exhibits throughout the school year, tel. (509) 359-6200.

One of 28 Jesuit colleges in the U.S., **Gonzaga University,** on Hamilton St. at Centennial Trail, is an independent liberal arts school with 5,000 students and a wide range of degree programs. The law school at Gonzaga is one of three in Washington. The school is best known as the alma mater of Bing Crosby (see above).

Other area schools include the private Whitworth College, a branch of Washington State University, Spokane Community College, and Spokane Falls Community College.

Wineries

Although the Spokane area doesn't have much in the way of vineyards, several local wineries produce wines from grapes grown in Yakima Valley and elsewhere. Most of these offer tours and free tastings. Enjoy a picnic with a bottle of award-winning wine at **Worden's Winery,** W. 7217 45th, tel. (509) 455-7835, located in a log cabin on the outskirts of Spokane. Open daily noon-5 p.m. for tours and tastings.

Latah Creek Wine Cellars, off the I-90 Pines exit at E. 13030 Indiana Ave., tel. (509) 926-0164, features tours, tastings, an art gallery, and a picnic courtyard. The attractive Spanish mission-style winery is open Mon.-Sat. 10 a.m.-5 p.m., Sunday noon-5 p.m. (the winery closes at 4 p.m. in the winter).

Arbor Crest, 4705 N. Fruithill Rd., tel. (509) 927-9894, also has a tasting room and gift shop open daily noon-5 p.m. The building, Cliff House, is a National Historic Site with a magnificent view and parklike grounds.

The small **Caterina Winery** is downtown in the historic Broadview Dairy Building at N. 905 Washington, tel. (509) 328-5069. Open for tours and tasting daily noon-5 p.m. in the summer, and Tues.-Sat. noon-5 p.m. in the winter. **Knipprath Cellars,** S. 163 Lincoln St., tel. (509) 624-9132, is another downtown winery; open Tues.-Sun. 11:30 a.m.-5:30 p.m.

Mountain Dome Winery is Washington's premier producer of sparkling wines and offers tours by appointment only. Call (509) 928-2788 for directions to their winery near Mt. Spokane.

Zoo

Nine miles east of the city at 12600 E. Euclid Ave., just off Pines Rd., **Walk in the Wild,** tel. (509) 924-7220, is a 240-acre zoo and park with nature trails, animal petting area, and weekend trained parrot shows. Though not a world-class zoo, you can see flamingos, eagles, bears, bison, and more. Open daily 10 a.m.-5 p.m., year-round.

ACCOMMODATIONS

See the "Spokane Accommodations" chart for a complete listing of Spokane motels, hotels, and B&Bs. During major summer events such as Lilac Bloomsday Run, Lilac Festival, and Hoopfest, you should make lodging reservations well ahead of your visit to Spokane. If you have the bucks, the finest hotels in town are **Cavanaugh's Inn at the Park** and **West Coast Ridpath Hotel.**

Hostel

The **Hostelling International-Spokane,** 930 S. Lincoln St., tel. (509) 838-5968, is a great place with friendly management, flexible rules, and a delightful porch for hanging out. Separate kitchens for men and women cut down a bit on the social scene, but the lack of a curfew livens things up a bit. Register at the hostel 4-10 p.m. Private rooms for couples are also available. Reservations are advised during the summer, but the hostel generally has space.

Bed and Breakfast

Spokane has two dozen different B&Bs, including several truly outstanding places. The

SPOKANE ACCOMMODATIONS

Accommodations are arranged from least to most expensive. Rates at some lodging places are lower during the winter months. The area code is 509.

HOSTEL

Spokane AYH Hostel; S. 930 Lincoln; tel. 838-5968; $10 pp AYH members, $13 pp nonmembers in dorm rooms, $25 d in private rooms; full kitchen and dining room

BED AND BREAKFASTS

Hillside House B&B; 1729 E. 18th St.; tel. 535-1893; $47 s, $50-55 d; two antique-furnished rooms, shared baths, full breakfast, children okay

Marianna Stoltz House; 427 E. Indiana; tel. 483-4316; $50-59 s, $59-69 d; built in 1908, four antique-furnished guest rooms, shared or private baths, wraparound veranda, full breakfast, no kids

Oslo's B&B; E. 1821 39th Ave.; tel. 838-3175; $50-60s or d; two guest rooms, Norwegian atmosphere, private baths, garden and terrace, full breakfast, no kids under 13

Spokane Room B&B; N. 15405 Edencrest Dr.; tel. 467-9804; $55 s, $65 d; a suite with private bath, deck overlooking garden, full breakfast

Cobblestone B&B Inn; S. 620 Washington; tel. 624-9735; $55 s, $65 d; 1900 inn, front porch, stained glass windows, two guest rooms, shared baths, full breakfast, children okay

Waverly Place B&B; 709 W. Waverly Place; tel. 328-1856; $65-75 s, $65-80 d; 1902 Victorian home, jacuzzi, outdoor pool, wraparound porch, four guest rooms, private or shared baths, children welcome

Fotheringham House B&B; 2128 W. 2nd Ave.; tel. 838-1891; $70-80 s or d; beautiful Victorian home, period furnishings, full breakfast, three guest rooms, shared or private baths, no kids under 13

Love's Victorian B&B; Deer Park (15 miles north); tel. 276-6939; $75-98 s or d; historic 1886 Victorian home, three guest rooms with antiques, jacuzzi, fireplace, private baths, full breakfast

HOTELS AND MOTELS

Ranch Motel; S. 1609 Lewis; tel. 456-8919; $25 s, $29 d; kitchenettes available

Cedar Village Motel; W. 5415 Sunset; tel. 624-2450; $28 s, $34 d; kitchenettes available, local calls 25 cents, quiet out-of-the-way location, free airport shuttle

Starlite Motel; S. 3809 Geiger Blvd.; tel. 747-7186 or (800) 772-7186; $29 s, $35 d; kitchenettes available, local calls 25 cents

Lantern Park Motel; Airway Hts.; tel. 244-3653; $29-31 s, $32-37 d; jacuzzi, kitchenettes available

Calkins' Clinic Center Motel; S. 702 McClellan; tel. 747-6081; $30 s, $32 d; local calls 25 cents

Downtowner Motel; S. 165 Washington; tel. 838-4411; $32 s, $35 d

Motel 6; 1508 S. Rustle St.; tel. 459-6120; $32 s, $38 d; outdoor pool

Maple Tree Motel; 4824 E. Sprague; tel. 535-5810; $33 s or d; kitchenettes available

Shadows Motel & RV Park; N. 9025 Division; tel. 467-6951; $33 s, $38 d; kitchenettes available, local calls 25 cents

Bel Air Motel 7; E. 1303 Sprague Ave.; tel. 535-1677; $33-37 s, $37-39 d; AAA approved

Bell Motel; W. 9030 Sunset Hwy.; tel. 624-0852 or (800) 223-1388; $34 s or d

Boulevard Motel; W. 2905 Sunset; tel. 747-1060; $34 s, $40 d; kitchenettes available

West Wynn Motel; W. 2701 Sunset; tel. 747-3037; $35-43 s or d; indoor pool, jacuzzi, sauna, local calls 25 cents, AAA approved

El Rancho Motel; W. 3000 Sunset; tel. 455-9400; $37 s, $39 d; outdoor pool, kitchenettes available

Shangri-La Motel; W. 2922 Government Way; tel. 747-2066 or (800) 234-4941; $39 s, $41 d; outdoor pool, kitchenettes available, continental breakfast, free airport shuttle, AAA approved

Value Inns by Cavanaugh's; W. 1203 5th Ave.; tel. 624-4142 or (800) 843-4667; $39-42 s, $39-48 d; outdoor pool, jacuzzi, kitchenettes available, local calls 25 cents, free airport shuttle

Valu Inn by Nendel's; W. 1420 2nd Ave.; tel. 838-2026 or (800) 246-6835; $39 s, $48 d; outdoor pool, kitchenettes available, AAA approved

Liberty Motel; N. 6801 Division; tel. 467-6000; $40 s or d

Shamrock Motel; E. 1629 Sprague; tel. 535-0388; $40 s, $45 d; continental breakfast, kitchenettes available

Red Top Motel; E. 7212 Trent; tel. 926-5728 or (800) 447-8202; $42 s or d; outdoor pool, jacuzzi, kitchenettes available

Royal Scot Motel; W. 20 Houston; tel. 467-6672; $42 s or d

Spokane Budget Motel; E. 1234 Sprague; tel. 534-0669; $43 s or d; continental breakfast, kitchenettes available

Towne Center Motor Inn; W. 901 1st Ave.; tel. 747-1041 or (800) 247-1041; $44 s, $50 d; exercise room, steam room, continental breakfast, AAA approved

Eastgate Motel; E. 10625 Trent; tel. 922-4556; $45 s, $48 d; kitchenettes available

Days Inn; N. 1919 Hutchinson Rd.; tel. 926-5399 or (800) 325-2525; $45-57 s, $50-62 d; continental breakfast, AAA approved

Best Western Trade Winds-Downtown; 907 W. 3rd Ave.; tel. 838-2091 or (800) 528-1234; $46-60 s, $65 d; outdoor pool, jacuzzi, sauna, exercise room, pool table, continental breakfast, AAA approved

Spokane Valley Super 8 Motel; N. 2020 Argonne Rd.; tel. 928-4888 or (800) 800-8000; $47 s, $55 d; AAA approved

Best Western Thunderbird Inn; 120 W. 3rd Ave.; tel. 747-2011 or (800) 578-2473; $47 s, $60 d; outdoor pool, exercise room, jacuzzi, AAA approved

Rodeway Inn; W. 827 1st Ave.; tel. 456-8040 or (800) 424-6423; $47-54 s, $54-67 d; outdoor pool, jacuzzi, sauna, kitchenettes available, AAA approved

Apple Tree Inn Motel; N. 9508 Division; tel. 466-3020 or (800) 323-5796; $48 s, $51 d; outdoor pool, kitchenettes available, AAA approved

Park Lane Motel and RV Park; E. 4412 Sprague; tel. 535-1626 or (800) 533-1626; $50 s or d; continental breakfast, sauna, kitchenettes available, free airport shuttle

Friendship Inn Spokane House; W. 4301 Sunset; tel. 838-1471 or (800) 424-4777; $52 s, $57 d; outdoor pool, jacuzzi, sauna, free airport shuttle

Shilo Inn Spokane; E. 923 3rd; tel. 535-9000 or (800) 222-2244; $54 s or d; exercise room, indoor pool, sauna, jacuzzi, free airport shuttle

Suntree 8 Inn; S. 123 Post; tel. 838-8504 or (800) 888-6630; $55 s, $60 d; continental breakfast, local calls 35 cents, free airport shuttle, AAA approved

Super 8 Motel; W. 11102 Westbow; tel. 838-8800 or (800) 800-8000; $55 s, $61 d; indoor pool, jacuzzi, continental breakfast, free airport shuttle, AAA approved

Alpine Motel; 18815 E. Cataldo (10 miles east of Spokane); tel. 928-2700; $57 s, $60 d; outdoor pool, AAA approved

(continues on next page)

SPOKANE ACCOMMODATIONS

(continued)

Best Western Trade Winds-North; 3033 N. Division St.; tel. 326-5500 or (800) 621-8593; $58-64 s, $60-66 d; indoor pool, hot tub, continental breakfast, AAA approved

Cavanaugh's Inn Fourth Avenue; E. 110 4th Ave.; tel. 838-6101 or (800) 843-4667; $60-74 s, $66-74 d; outdoor pool, free airport shuttle, AAA approved

Comfort Inn Broadway; E. 6309 Broadway; tel. 535-7185 or (800) 597-6663; $60-70 s, $65-75 d; outdoor pool, jacuzzi, continental breakfast, kitchenettes available, AAA approved

Holiday Inn Express; N. 801 Division; tel. 328-8505 or (800) 465-4329; $60-75 s, $65-80 d Fri.-Sat.; $50-65 s, $55-72 d Sun.-Thurs.; breakfast buffet, free airport shuttle

Comfort Inn North; 7111 N. Division; tel. 467-7111 or (800) 221-2222; $63 s or d; outdoor pool, kitchenettes available

Quality Inn Oakwood; N. 7919 Division St.; tel. 467-4910 or (800) 228-5151; $63 s, $68 d; indoor pool, jacuzzi, continental breakfast, AAA approved

Hampton Inn Spokane; S. 2010 Assembly Rd.; tel. 747-1100 or (800) 426-7866; $63 s, $73 d; indoor pool, jacuzzi, exercise room, continental breakfast, free airport shuttle, AAA approved

Holiday Inn West; W. 4212 Sunset Blvd.; tel. 747-2021 or (800) 465-4329; $64-70 s, $72-78 d; outdoor pool, tennis court, free airport shuttle, AAA approved

Comfort Inn Valley; 905 N. Sullivan Rd.; tel. 924-3838; $65 s or d; outdoor pool, kitchenettes available, local calls 25 cents

WestCoast Ridpath Hotel; W. 515 Sprague; tel. 838-2711 or (800) 426-0670; $65-75 s, $75-85 d; indoor and outdoor pools, exercise facility, local calls 50 cents, free airport shuttle, AAA approved

Cavanaugh's River Inn; N. 700 Division St.; tel. 326-5577 or (800) 843-4667; $70-95 s, $75-99 d; two outdoor pools, wading pool, jacuzzi, sauna, free airport shuttle, tennis courts, AAA approved

Ramada Inn; Spokane International Airport; tel. 838-5211 or (800) 272-6232; $75 s, $81 d; indoor and outdoor pools, jacuzzi, exercise room, kitchenettes available, free airport shuttle, AAA approved

Courtyard by Mariott; N. 401 Riverpoint Blvd.; tel. 456-7600 or (800) 443-6000; $79-85 s or d Fri.-Sat.; $72 s or d Sun.-Thurs.; indoor pool, jacuzzi, exercise room, free airport shuttle, AAA approved

Cavanaugh's Inn at the Park; W. 303 N. River Dr.; $84-134 s, $94-144 d; tel. 326-8000 or (800) 843-4667; indoor and outdoor pools, wading pool, jacuzzis, sauna, exercise room, kitchenettes available, free airport shuttle, AAA approved (four diamond)

Red Lion Inn; N. 1100 Sullivan Rd.; tel. 924-9000 or (800) 547-8010; $83-93 s, $93-103 d; outdoor pool, jacuzzi, free airport shuttle, exercise room, kitchenettes available, AAA approved

Quality Inn Valley Suites; E. 8923 Mission; tel. 928-5218 or (800) 777-7355; $85-250 s, $95-250 d; indoor pool, jacuzzi, sauna, continental breakfast, kitchenettes available, exercise facility, free airport shuttle, AAA approved

Sheraton-Spokane Hotel; N. 322 Spokane Falls Court; tel. 455-9600 or (800) 848-9600; $98 s, $118 d; indoor pool, exercise room, sauna, jacuzzi, free airport shuttle, AAA approved (four diamond)

best are listed in the chart "Spokane Accommodations"; for a complete account see the city's Yellow Pages. For referrals to B&Bs, call the **Spokane Bed & Breakfast Reservation Service,** tel. (509) 624-3776.

Fotheringham House B&B, tel. (509) 838-1891, across the street from Patsy Clark's (a favorite Spokane restaurant), is an 1891 Victorian home in the historic Browne's Addition part of town. This beautifully restored home was built by the first mayor of incorporated Spokane and has period furnishings, carved woodwork, and tin ceilings in the three guest rooms.

Waverly Place B&B, tel. (509) 328-1856, is located in another Victorian-era home on Corbin Park. Built in 1902, the gorgeous home features hardwood floors, gas chandeliers, a wraparound porch, and an outdoor swimming pool. **Marianna Stoltz House,** tel. (509) 483-4316, a classic American foursquare home constructed in 1908, stands on a tree-lined street near Gonzaga University. A wide veranda, spacious parlor, and antique furnishings add to the grace. Complimentary wine or homemade liqueurs in the evening.

Hillside House B&B, tel. (509) 535-1893, is a cozy country home on Spokane's South Hill near Lincoln Park with two antique-furnished rooms that share a bath. **Love's Victorian B&B** in Deer Park (15 miles north of Spokane), (509) 276-6939, is a delightful old home built in 1886 with three antique-furnished guest rooms and jacuzzi. Great country location near a pond.

Cobblestone B&B Inn, tel. (509) 624-9735, was built in 1900 and features two upstairs guest rooms, a big front porch, stained glass windows, and attractive furnishings.

Oslo's B&B, tel. (509) 838-3175, is a quiet, modern home with two guest rooms and a Norwegian atmosphere (Scandinavian breakfast if desired). In addition to private baths and a garden and large terrace, you'll find a friendly pug dog waiting to greet you (and cry when you leave).

Campgrounds and RV Parks
The closest public campgrounds are in **Riverside State Park,** tel. (509) 456-3964, six miles northwest of town. Riverside tent sites ($10; no RV hookups) are available year-round. Call for details. **Mt. Spokane State Park,** tel. (509) 456-4169, 30 miles northeast of Spokane (also described above), has tent sites for $10; open early May through October. For campsite reservations at both of these state parks, call (800) 452-5687 ($6 extra fee). Reservations are available up to 11 months ahead of time.

Private RV parks include **Alpine RV & Tent Park,** 18815 E. Cataldo, tel. (509) 928-2700; **Peaceful Pines Campground,** a mile southwest of Cheney on Hwy. 904, tel. (509) 235-4966; **Park Lane RV Park,** E. 4412 Sprague, tel. (509) 535-1626; **Ponderosa Hill RV Park,** 7520 Thomas Mallen Rd., tel. (509) 747-9415; **Shad-**

ows Motel & RV Park,** N. 9025 Division, tel. (509) 467-6951; and **Spokane KOA,** 3025 N. Barker Rd., in Otis Orchards, tel. (509) 924-4722.

FOOD AND DRINK

If you like good food, you're in for a treat in Spokane. Folks here eat out a *lot* and support a wide range of restaurants, from corner coffee shops to an elaborate mansion offering a gourmet menu. In addition to the places listed below, there are plenty of cute bistros that cater to the downtown lunch crowd. Walk around a bit and you're sure to come across something interesting.

Breakfast
For all-American breakfast "comfort food" served in an old railroad car, don't miss **Knight's Diner,** N. 2909 Market, tel. (509) 484-0015, a Spokane landmark for 40 years. Sit at the long mahogany counter to watch the chef working a mountain of hash browns and to catch the banter slung by the speedy waitresses. You'll find a cross-section of Spokane folks at this immensely popular, noisy, and hectic morning eatery any day of the week. Another similar Spokane institution is **Frank's Diner,** W. 1516 2nd, tel. (509) 455-7402, offering inexpensive breakfasts and other stick-to-the-ribs food in an antique railcar.

Light Meals and Coffee
Espresso Delicioso, N. 706 Monroe, tel. (509) 326-5958, has a plain exterior in a working class neighborhood, but inside you'll find delightfully creative meals (espresso eggs for breakfast, unique sandwiches for lunch, and seafood, chicken, steak, or pasta for dinner), plus espresso and desserts. This place is on the counter-culture end of the spectrum, with folkish bands most evenings.

McGowan's Cafe, W. 402 Main, tel. (509) 838-0206, serves a good homemade lunch (plus breakfast and dinner Mon.-Sat.) of salads, pastas, healthy soups, and sandwiches. The cafe is in the same building as Spokane's largest book dealer, Auntie's Bookstore, a great place to hang out in the evening.

Another popular downtown sandwich and salad shop is **Domini's,** W. 703 Sprague, tel. (509) 747-2324, in business for 90 years. This family-run place has a great chaotic atmosphere and huge sandwiches with thick slices of meat.

Two Moon Cafe, W. 300 Sprague (across from the train station), tel. (509) 747-6277, gets rave reviews from locals. The Mexican-inspired entrees are a bit pricey, but delicious. Included are calamari steaks, Mexican seafood, salads, pasta, and chicken dishes. Popular for lunch and dinner, but also open for breakfast.

Also well worth a visit for pastas, sandwiches, and salads is **Lindaman's Cafe North,** N. 6412 Monroe, tel. (509) 324-9252.

American Eats

In the Old Flour Mill near Riverfront Park, **Clinkerdagger Restaurant,** 621 W. Mallon Ave., tel. (509) 328-5965, serves up a well-prepared Northwest menu (including fresh seafood) with a view of Spokane Falls.

The Onion, W. 302 Riverside, tel. (509) 624-9965, is a Spokane institution with fast and friendly service, a noisy, convivial atmosphere, and justly famous gourmet burgers, barbecue ribs, fajitas, and salads. Huckleberry milk shakes are another favorite, and beer drinkers will find plenty of offerings and a weekday happy hour. The location is within one of Spokane's classic old buildings, originally the St. Regis Hotel; many of its original furnishings are still present.

For buffet meals, try **Just Like Home,** W. 202 3rd, tel. (509) 747-4500; **Spokane Salad Co.,** W. 430 Main, tel. (509) 456-2577; or **Golden Corral,** N. 7117 Division, tel. (509) 468-1895. **Calgary Steak House,** E. 3040 Sprague, tel. (509) 535-7502, claims to make the most scrumptious steaks in Spokane.

Pizzas and Italian

For pizza, pastas, calzone, and Yugoslavian treats, try the **Europa Pizzeria And Bakery,** 125 S. Wall St., tel. (509) 455-4051. **Cucina! Cucina!,** tel. (509) 838-3388, is a hopping and very noisy Italian spot on the corner of Wall and Main downtown. A bit trendy, but the food is well prepared and includes pizzas made in wood-burning ovens. **Rock City Grill,** W. 505 Riverside, tel. (509) 455-4400, is another very popular Italian eatery with calzone, unusual pizzas (including one with buffalo chicken wings), and such specialties as Wood Oven-roasted Prawns and Veal Parmesan.

A quieter and much smaller Italian place is **Amore Ristorante Pizzeria,** S. 1228 Grand Blvd., tel. (509) 838-8640, where the delicious entrees are heavy on the garlic. Another place with great specials, including a smoked salmon lasagna, is **Luiji's,** N. 113 Bernard, tel. (509) 624-5226.

If you're just looking for a fast slice of New York-style pizza to go ($1.50), drop by **David's Gourmet Pizza,** N. 4 Howard, tel. (509) 838-

Patsy Clark's Restaurant

DIANNE BOUERICE LYONS

6982. The shop isn't much bigger than a bread-box but comes up with all sorts of distinctive pizzas and huge calzone.

For cheap eats, try the **Old Spaghetti Factory,** S. 152 Monroe St., tel. (509) 624-8916. Like its Seattle and Tacoma clones, this converted warehouse features an Italian menu that generally stays under $10; open daily for dinner only.

Asian Food
Excellent Thai cooking (including several off-beat desserts) at **Thai Cafe,** W. 410 Sprague, tel. (509) 838-4783. A showy, Benihana-style Japanese steak, seafood, and sushi place is **Shogun Restaurant,** E. 821 3rd Ave., tel. (509) 534-7777.

Peking Garden, E. 3420 Sprague, tel. (509) 534-2525, is among the city's better Chinese restaurants—and inexpensive to boot. Try the big Mongolian barbecue where you select the food and watch them cook with flair (and flare).

Downtown's **Mustard Seed Cafe,** W. 245 Spokane Falls Blvd., tel. (509) 747-2689, is an airy place with a Japanese and Chinese menu of spring rolls, beef teriyaki, spicy Szechuan shrimp, and other items. Heavy on the grease at times.

More International Places
Enjoy delicious Greek food at **Niko's Greek and Middle Eastern Restaurant** out in the Valley at S. 321 Dishman-Mica Rd., tel. (509) 928-9590, and downtown at W. 725 Riverside, tel. (509) 624-7444. In addition to traditional faves such as spanakopita, lamb dishes, and baklava, the restaurant has a number of Indian specialties. Enjoy belly dancing on Thursday nights in the Valley location.

Marrakesh, W. 2008 Northwest Blvd., tel. (509) 328-9733, serves a different sort of Middle Eastern meal, with five-course Moroccan feasts for $15.

Upstairs Downstairs, on Howard at Main, tel. (509) 747-9830, is a quiet little rustic French restaurant with excellent food and wines, a relaxing atmosphere, and good service. The menu changes with the seasons.

Mexican food is represented by **Azteca,** 200 W. Spokane Falls Blvd., tel. (509) 456-0350; **Coyote Cafe,** W. 702 3rd, tel. (509) 747-8800; **Papagayo's,** 411 N. Division, tel. (509) 483-8346; and **Senior Guillermo's,** E. 7905 Trent,

tel. (509) 924-4304, out in the Valley. Papagayo's also has a lite menu if you're counting calories.

Seafood
Milford's Fish House, N. 719 Monroe St., tel. (509) 326-7251, is Spokane's favorite place for fresh seafood. Be sure to check the fish-of-the-day specials and fresh oysters. Excellent food, friendly service, and an attractive exposed-brick setting. The antique bar has been here since the 1930s. Reservations are strongly advised. **Salty's at the Falls,** N. 510 Lincoln, tel. (509) 327-8888, offers some of the finest summer dining views in town, and a deck overlooking the Spokane River. Try the blackened salmon on Caesar salad.

Food with a View
Ankeny's, atop the Ridpath Hotel at W. 515 Sprague Ave., tel. (509) 838-6311, and **Eagle's Nest,** atop Shilo Inn at E. 923 3rd, tel. (509) 534-1551, both offer top-of-town dining with panoramic vistas across Spokane. **Windows of the Seasons Restaurant,** W. 303 N. River Dr. at Cavanaugh's Inn at the Park, tel. (509) 328-9526, sits along the Spokane River with more grand views. Stop by for a drink at sunset, but eat elsewhere, none of these have dinners worth a special trip. Two other places with a view (and more notable meals) are described above: Salty's at the Falls and Clinkerdagger's.

Pricey Eats
One of the most elegant mansions in the Northwest houses **Patsy Clark's Restaurant,** 2208 W. 2nd St., tel. (509) 838-8300. Patsy came to America in 1870, made millions in the Anaconda copper mines, and commissioned an architect to build him a nice little home—and money was no object. The resulting structure features stained-glass windows from Tiffany's (with over 4,000 pieces), Italian marble, carved wood from England, and an eight-foot-high grandfather clock. Enjoy a dinner of duck, lamb, prime rib, or seafood, or just have a drink from the extensive wine list and pick up the detailed brochure for a self-guided tour of the lavish interior. If you sit down to eat, be prepared to drop at least $30 per person. Patsy's is the sort of place presidents dine (former President Bush did so), though critics are not always as kind. Open daily

for dinner plus Sunday brunch; reservations required.

Bakeries

Spokane town has several good bakeries, including **Au Croissant,** N. 224 Howard, tel. (509) 624-6152, for French and Persian baked goods; **Great Harvest Bread Co.,** W. 816 Sprague, tel. (509) 624-9370, for whole grain breads, monstrous bagels, and sweets; and **Fitzbillies Bagel Bakery,** W. 1325 1st Ave., tel. (509) 747-1834, for fresh bagels in a hang-out atmosphere.

A popular yuppified place with wonderful rustic breads is **Fugazzi,** N. 1 Post St., tel. (509) 624-1133. This is primarily a light lunch cafe, but those who stop by for bread are often enticed to stay for a pasta, soup, or salad.

Brewpubs

Birkebeiner's Brew Pub, W. 35 Main, tel. (509) 458-0854, serves up tangy, fresh-brewed suds in a smoke-free environment. Good pub grub too. **Hale's Ales,** at E. 5634 Commerce, began in Spokane and now has a second brewery in Kirkland. Call ahead for brewery tours, tel. (509) 534-7553.

The food isn't worth bothering with, but **Ft. Spokane Brewery,** W. 401 Spokane Falls Blvd., tel. (509) 838-3809, has beer on tap and live music almost every night, including jazz, Cajun, and rock.

Farmers Market

The **Spokane Market Place** is an outdoor market with fresh produce, seafood, ethnic specialties, and baked goods. Find the market every Saturday, Sunday, and Wednesday 9 a.m.-5 p.m. May-Sept. on the north end of Riverfront Park at the end of the Howard St. bridge.

SHOPPING

Downtown, a series of **skywalks** links 15 blocks of shopping and dining on two levels, including two shopping malls plus large department stores such as Nordstrom, The Bon Marché, and Lamonts. **River Park Square,** at the northeast end of the skywalk at Main and Post, connects to **Sherwood Mall** at Riverside and Stevens. One

old-time shop worth a visit is **Indiana Harness & Saddlery Co.,** E. 3030 Sprague Ave., tel. (509) 535-3400, with Western wear, saddles, cowboy boots and hats, horse tack, and lots more.

The **Flour Mill,** adjacent to the Riverfront Park at W. 621 Mallon, was the most modern mill west of the Mississippi when it was built in 1890; today the restored brick building is home to 22 shops, including galleries, restaurants, gifts, and candy stores. At Wellesley and Division, the **Northtown Mall** has a Sears, JCPenney, Emporium, Mervyn's, and more than a hundred boutiques and other shops.

For a sour taste of the new America, head out North Division to join the long traffic jam past ugly strip malls, shopping centers, and a clutter of neon signs.

RECREATION

Spokane is surrounded by a diversity of recreation opportunities. Located just 33 miles from Spokane is **Coeur d'Alene Lake,** one of the most beautiful in the mountain west with the world's longest floating boardwalk and an 18-hole shoreline golf course that features a floating green. Immediately north of Spokane are the **Selkirk Mountains,** where you'll find all sorts of wild country and a string of small towns along the Pend Oreille River. To the south are the wide open spaces of the Palouse farmlands; to the west lies a massive desert in the Columbia Basin, along with famous Grand Coulee Dam.

Skiing

Thirty miles northeast of town on Hwy. 206 at Mt. Spokane State Park (see above), **Mt. Spokane** offers Alpine skiing, including a 1.5-mile-long run, five chair lifts, and a 2,000-foot vertical drop. Night skiing draws the crowds here, as does the dry snow and 360-degree view of the Cascade, Selkirk, and Rocky Mountains. Other features include ski school and rentals, restaurant, and bar, but no child care. Lift tickets are reasonable: $25 for adults, $20 for youths; adults ski weekdays for just $20. Call (509) 238-6281 for more information, or (509) 238-6223 for the snow report. Bus transportation from Spokane is provided for a fee on weekends.

Stay at **Snowblaze Condominiums,** tel. (509) 238-4543, or **Kirk's Lodge,** tel. (509) 238-9114, near the state park.

Some 30 miles of groomed **cross-country ski trails** are adjacent; get Sno-Park permits at local sporting goods stores before heading up to ski. Other nearby places with cross-country ski trails are **Downriver Golf Course,** tel. (509) 327-5259, **Indian Canyon Golf Course,** tel. (509) 747-5353, and **Hills Resort,** tel. (208) 443-2551 in Priest Lake, Idaho.

Other nearby ski areas include **49° North** near Chewelah (see under "Chewelah" in The Northeast Corner section), along with two Idaho resorts: **Schweitzer Mountain,** 75 miles northeast of Spokane, tel. (800) 831-8810, and **Silver Mountain,** 68 miles east of Spokane, tel. (208) 747-0221.

Other Adventures

Hikers and cyclists should be sure to check out the excellent **Spokane River Centennial Trail,** a nearly level paved path that extends 63 miles along the river from Coeur d'Alene, Idaho, to the confluence of the Spokane and Little Spokane Rivers in Riverside State Park.

Swim at one of more than half-a-dozen outdoor pools around Spokane; call (509) 625-6960 for details. The **YWCA,** W. 829 Broadway, tel. (509) 326-1190, has an indoor pool. More swimming at **Liberty Lake,** near the Idaho border. Contact **Four Season's Outfitting,** tel. (208) 773-0453, for nearby whitewater rafting opportunities.

Northwest Outdoor School, tel. (509) 255-5200, is a Spokane-based operation with a wide range of professionally taught rock climbing and backpacking classes during the summer and fall, and snow-camping classes when winter blows in.

Enjoy a trail ride with **Indian Canyon Riding Stable** at Indian Canyon Park, 4812 W. Canyon Dr., tel. (509) 624-4646.

Spokane is justly proud of its numerous public and private golf courses; more than a dozen can be found in the area, including **Indian Canyon,** S. Assembly and West Dr., tel. (509) 747-5353, one of the top public courses in the U.S. and the site of many major golf tournaments.

EVENTS

The **Lilac Bloomsday Run,** held the first Sunday in May, attracts over 50,000 runners with a downtown 12-km course. It's called the world's largest timed race; all competitors are given finishing times. At the same time, Spokane hosts one of America's largest fitness and running trade shows. Call (509) 838-1579 for more information. After Bloomsday, Spokane blossoms with two weeks of activity called the **Lilac Festival,** culminating in the Armed Forces Day Torchlight Parade on the third Saturday of May. The lilac garden at Manito Park is usually in full bloom for the festival; other events include entertainment, concerts, and an amateur golf tournament.

Another popular May event is a National Off-Road Biking Association **Mountain Bike Race** at Mt. Spokane. For a different sort of racing, cruise out to **Spokane Raceway Park** for drag and stock car races on Saturday nights May-September. Call (509) 244-3663 for details.

Basketball players from all over the Western U.S. descend on Spokane for **Hoopfest** in late June, a weekend of three-on-three basketball games. More than 2,500 teams compete in this double-elimination tournament that spreads over 160 downtown courts. In addition to the hoops, you'll find a food fair and other activities at Riverfront Park. Call (509) 624-2414 for more information.

On the **Fourth of July** Spokane comes to life with food, entertainment, and an open air symphony concert at Riverfront Park. Fireworks follow the classical music. Cheney's mid-July **Rodeo Days** features bronc and bull riding, calf roping, and a parade at one of the largest amateur rodeos in the Northwest.

Pig Out in the Park, on the week before Labor Day, is four days of food, live music, and a beer garden in Riverfront Park. The **Spokane Interstate Fair,** tel. (509) 535-1766, held for nine days in mid-September at the fairgrounds at Broadway and Havana, features big name musical entertainment and a PRCA rodeo.

In late November, **Christmas Tree Elegance** features the lighting of an enormous metallic tree, strolling carolers, carriage rides, and decorations.

ENTERTAINMENT

Nightlife

In recent years, Spokane has become something of a proving ground for the grunge rock scene, with several hot local bands hoping to break out to the national market. Two Spokane clubs where you're likely to hear original rock from such local bands as The Mekons, Budda Ledbelly, or Black Happy are: **The Big Dipper,** S. 171 Washington, tel. (509) 747-8036, and **Mother's Pub,** W. 230 Riverside, tel. (509) 624-9828.

Ft. Spokane Brewery, W. 401 Spokane Falls Blvd., tel. (509) 838-3809, has live music almost every night, including jazz, Cajun, and rock, while **Birkebeiner's Brew Pub,** W. 35 Main, tel. (509) 458-0854, has blues and jazz several times a week in a smoke-free atmosphere.

Country-western music lovers will want to head east to **Chili D's,** S. 152 Browne, tel. (509) 455-9210, for Grand Ole Opry-style music Wed.-Sat. and free dance lessons on Thursday nights.

For a more laid-back experience, stop by **Espresso Delicioso,** N. 706 Monroe, tel. (509) 326-5958, where you'll hear folk and jazz music most evenings, and a popular Celtic jam on Tuesday nights. **O'Doherty's Irish Grille,** W. 525 Spokane Falls Blvd., tel. (509) 747-0322, often has live Irish music.

Hobart's, at E. 110 4th Ave. in Cavanaugh's Fourth Avenue, tel. (509) 838-6101, has jazz most nights. For Top 40, try **Ankeny's** atop the Ridpath Hotel at 515 W. Sprague, nightly except Sunday. Other hotel bars with entertainment include: **Eagle's Nest,** atop Shilo Inn at E. 923 3rd, tel. (509) 534-1551; **Spokane House,** at Friendship Inn, W. 4301 Sunset Hwy., tel. (509) 838-1471; and **Cesare's Lounge,** inside Cavanaugh's Inn at the Park, W. 303 N. River Dr., tel. (509) 326-8000.

Music and Theater

Riverfront Park sponsors concerts and other entertainment during the summer months; call (509) 456-5511 or (800) 336-7275 for a schedule of upcoming events.

The **Spokane Symphony Orchestra**—in existence for more than 50 years—presents classical, pops, and chamber concerts, plus *The Nutcracker* at the Spokane Opera House, 334 W. Spokane Falls Blvd., tel. (509) 624-1200. The symphony has been in existence for more than 50 years. The opera house is also home to music, dance, and dramatic productions throughout the year, including popular Broadway musicals.

Another long-lasting musical group is **Spokane Jazz Orchestra,** tel. (509) 458-0366, established in 1975. This 19-member big band calls itself the oldest continually performing, in-

Spokane Opera House

residence, professional community jazz orchestra in America. Lots of qualifiers on this score, but the music is fun.

The **Spokane Civic Theater,** 1020 N. Howard, hosts performances from drama to comedy year-round; call (509) 325-2507 for schedule and ticket information. Get information on the **Spokane Interplayers Ensemble,** a resident professional theater group, by calling (509) 455-7529.

Spectator Sports

The Northwest League's **Spokane Indians** play Class-A ball at the Interstate Fairgrounds Stadium, on Havana St. between Sprague and Broadway. The stadium, which seats 10,000, was designed for Class-AAA ball, played here until 1982; it's now the classiest ballpark in the league. The Indians play 38 home games each season; call (509) 535-2922 for ticket and schedule information. In the winter months, the **Spokane Chiefs** play tier-one ice hockey at Spokane Veterans Memorial Arena. Concerts, ice shows, rodeos, circuses, and other major events also take place here.

From May to October, take a chance on a horse at the **Playfair Race Course,** Altamont and Main Streets; call (509) 534-0505 for post times and prices. Also in town is the **Spokane Polo Club,** tel. (509) 747-0084, with weekend matches all summer long. Call for details.

Greyhound Park, tel. (800) 828-4880, has summertime dog racing Tues.-Sun. just across the Idaho border in the town of Post Falls.

INFORMATION AND SERVICES

Visit the **Spokane Regional Convention and Visitors Bureau** on the corner of Main and Browne, tel. (509) 747-3230 or (800) 248-3230, for up-to-date information on festivals and events, maps, brochures, and other information. Open Memorial Day through September Mon.-Fri. 8:30 a.m.-5 p.m., Sat.-Sun. 9 a.m.-6 p.m.; and Mon.-Fri. 8:30 a.m.-5 p.m. the rest of the year.

The **area code** for Spokane and all of eastern Washington is 509. Spokane is a major regional center for medicine, and an incredible 11% of the city's employment base works in various types of health care. Medical emergencies can be handled at **Sacred Heart Medical Center,** 101 W. 8th Ave., tel. (509) 455-3131; **Deaconess Medical Center,** 800 W. 5th Ave., tel. (509) 458-5800; **Valley Hospital and Medical Center,** E. 12606 Mission, tel. (509) 924-6650; or **Holy Family Hospital,** N. 5633 Lidgerwood, tel. (509) 482-0111.

Books

The main **public library** is located at W. 906 Main, tel. (509) 838-6757. Half-a-dozen branch libraries are scattered around town, not to mention the local colleges and university libraries.

Book lovers should be sure to stop by **Auntie's Bookstore,** W. 402 Main, tel. (509) 838-0206. This excellent and spacious store has frequent poetry and prose readings, along with a fun game and puzzle shop. **Merlyn's Science Fiction-Fantasy Store,** N. 1 Browne, tel. (509) 624-0957, has books for the sci-fi crowd.

TRANSPORTATION AND TOURS

By Air

Spokane International Airport, just west of town, is served by several major commercial airlines, including **Continental,** tel. (800) 525-0280; **Delta,** tel. (800) 221-1212; **Horizon,** tel. (800) 547-9308; **Northwest Airlines,** tel. (800) 225-2525; and **United,** tel. (800) 241-6522.

By Train

Amtrak's Empire Builder has service to Spokane four days a week from Chicago, Minneapolis, and other Midwest cities, continuing west to Ephrata, Wenatchee, Everett, Edmonds, and Seattle or southwest to Pasco, Wishram, Bingen, Vancouver, and Portland. Eastward departures leave at 5 p.m. on Monday, Wednesday, Friday, and Saturday; westbound trains leave at the ungodly hour of 2:40 a.m. Sunday, Monday, Wednesday, and Friday. Stop by their station at 221 W. 1st St. or call (509) 624-5144 or (800) 872-7245 for fares and specifics.

By Car

Spokane is not as taken with the numbered street system as Seattle and Tacoma, so a good map is a necessity. Spokane addresses can be a little confusing, but rest assured that W. 410 Sprague and 410 W. Sprague are one and the same.

By Bus

Spokane Transit serves downtown Spokane and the Cheney area; call (509) 328-7433 for routes and schedule information, or get a map from the visitors bureau. Fares are 75 cents for adults and youths.

Greyhound provides nationwide connections from their terminal at 1125 W. Sprague; call (509) 624-5251 or (800) 231-2222 for schedule and fares. **Empire Trailways,** tel. (509) 458-0184, and **Northwestern Trailways,** tel. (509) 838-5262 or (800) 366-3830, also offer regional bus connections.

Tours

Karivan Tours, tel. (509) 489-7687, has daily bus tours of Spokane in the summer. Pick up a 20-page **walking tour** of the city at local bookstores or from the visitor information center. Over in Post Falls, Idaho, just 20 miles east of Spokane, are the **Spokane River Queen Cruises,** tel. (208) 773-1611. These cruises depart Templin's Resort Marina daily in the summer months; dinner cruises are also available.

PALOUSE COUNTRY

The Palouse is a broad area of low hills and wide open land; you'll see an occasional fringe of trees, but mostly these hills are nothing but soil—deep and rich. This soil is so rich and the climate so stable that the area, Whitman County particularly, is known as the best wheat-growing area in the world.

Early French fur traders called this area of green grassland *pelouse* (lawn). The name was soon given to the land, the Native Americans who lived here, and the river that runs through it. The Indians rode spotted horses that the white settlers dubbed palouse or palousey horses; "a palousey" eventually became "appaloosa." Today, the national headquarters of the Appaloosa Horse Club is a right across the Washington line in Moscow, Idaho.

Wheat Country

The Palouse begins just south of Spokane and runs south all the way to the Snake River and the Blue Mountains. It is bounded on the east by the Selkirk Mountains in western Idaho, and on the west by the Channeled Scablands. The soil in this area is all loess, meaning it was blown in over the centuries by the steady southwest wind. It is more than 100 feet deep in many places, and as you drive through this part of the state you'll notice that the wind has piled the soil up against the southern ends of buttes, especially in the Channeled Scabland area, while the northern ends are barren and blunt.

The Palouse Country (locals simply call it "the Palouse") is also set apart from the rest of eastern and central Washington by rainfall. The amount of rainfall increases as you travel east in Washington because of the gradual elevation gain.

Wheat isn't the only crop in the region. Peas, soybeans, lawn-grass seed, rape, and a variety of other crops can be seen as you drive south from Spokane toward Pullman and Clarkston. Tourism is not a major factor in most of the small towns here, so expect lower prices for straightforward food, and motels that are plain, clean, and cheap.

Steptoe Butte State Park

Follow the signs from Hwy. 195 and drive to the top of Steptoe Butte State Park, about 50 miles south of Spokane, for panoramic views of the Palouse River farmland and Idaho's mountains to the east. The park has picnic areas, but no water or overnight facilities. Landscape photographers love Steptoe Butte because it serves as a 1,170-foot tripod for photos of the rolling hills of Washington and Idaho's Palouse Country. Almost a perfect pyramid—its original name was Pyramid Peak—it is also a popular place for kite flyers because of the almost-constant wind.

The peak has another distinction: it is the top of a quartzite mountain more than 600 million years old, part of the Selkirk Range rising above the 15 million-year-old basalt that covered the rest of the range. In geological vocabulary, any remnant of an older formation protruding out of a

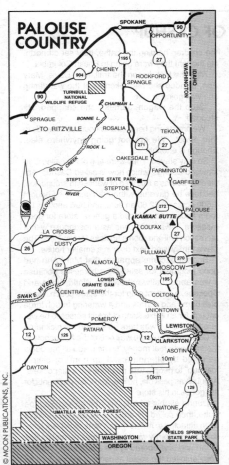

PALOUSE COUNTRY

© MOON PUBLICATIONS, INC.

The state park has a day-use area at the foot of the peak with a well and picnic tables (open year-round). Several publicly and privately owned radio and television antennas bristle from the summit but don't interfere with the views from the road that corkscrews around and around to the summit. The best time to visit Steptoe Butte is early in the morning and late in the evening when the low sunlight defines the rolling Palouse hills and you can see far into Idaho, south to the Blue Mountains of Washington and Oregon, west to the Cascade Range, and north past Spokane into Canada.

The park is east of Hwy. 195 on Hume Road. Follow the signs from the town of Steptoe if you're coming from Spokane; if you're driving north from Colfax and Pullman, the signs for the butte and Hume Rd. are a short distance south of Steptoe. For park information call (509) 549-3551.

Palouse, Garfield, and Oaksdale

Seventeen miles north of Pullman on State Hwy. 27 is Palouse. The small farm community of 900 is home to the **Boomerang Museum,** tel. (509) 878-1309, where you'll find a large collection of old printing equipment, including linotypes and a turn-of-the-century flatbed letter press.

Three-hundred-acre **Kamiak Butte County Park,** four miles southwest of Palouse along Hwy. 27, has camping and picnicking. A steep, one-mile hiking trail leads through evergreen forests to the top of this 3,360-foot butte, providing views of the Palouse Hills.

Minuscule Garfield is home to **New Morning Glass Studio,** tel. (509) 635-1263, where you can watch as fine glass pieces are made. The studio uses the 3,000-year-old "off-hand" technique of glassblowing and provides detailed one-and-a-half-hour tours where visitors can learn the intricacies of glass production. They also offer six-week courses and sell quality glass art for reasonable prices.

Just east of Oaksdale (pop. 400) is **Hanford Castle B&B,** tel. (509) 285-4120, an imposing hilltop Victorian mansion built more than a century ago. On the grounds are a conservatory, an old fountain, and sweeping views of the surrounding wheat fields. The restored mansion features a full breakfast and rooms with private baths and fireplaces.

newer formation now is called a "steptoe." The hill is named for Colonel Edward J. Steptoe, who was soundly defeated in the area in a running battle with the Cayuse Indians on May 17, 1858. It was only with the assistance of the Nez Percé Chief Timothy that Steptoe's men were able to escape down a narrow canyon through the middle of the Cayuse lines. A local storekeeper named James H. "Cashup" Davis (he insisted on "cash up front") built a hotel on the peak around the turn of the century, but it burned in 1911.

THE SAGA OF CASHUP

James Davis was an eccentric Englishman whose exploits made him one of Eastern Washington's most memorable characters. Davis was born in England in 1815. He and his brother, Sevier, decided to go to America in 1840. Unlike most immigrants, they did not travel steerage class. Davis brought with him a fine team of horses, an elegant surrey, a pair of hunting hounds and some expensive hunting rifles, and he wrote that he came to America "from choice and preference and not by accident of birth."

They first settled in Ohio. James married a local woman in 1844 and moved to Wisconsin where they lived for 22 years while they produced 11 children, all of whom survived and all but one of whom moved to Washington. The Davis clan set out across the plains for the Promised Land with the younger children riding in the covered wagon while the older ones walked, almost all the way. They settled near McMinnville in Yamhill County, Oregon, but in 1872 James headed north alone across the Columbia River into Whitman County, Washington Territory, for a homestead.

He found a site near Thornton he liked, staked it and returned for his family. When they arrived at the claim, they found it had been jumped, but Davis only shrugged and went a few miles west and found another he liked as well and staked it. He built a house that was part dugout. The walls were built of virgin bunch grass roots, and he used sacks of flour for the partition between rooms. They stayed there two years while they built up their herd of cattle to more than 100 head. Then he sold them to a man named Long who it is said drove them all the way to the market at St. Louis.

With the cash from the sale, Davis built a 10-room house, the first home in what is now St. John. Davis still wasn't satisfied. In 1875 he sold everything except his transportation and livestock, and with

the children herding the cattle, they set off north. He thought they were going to British Columbia.

After the first day on the trail, Mrs. Davis, Mary Ann, decided she had taken all of the wandering she was going to take.

"Stop the wagon, James!" she snapped. He stopped.

"We are staying here," she announced in words to that effect. "We are not going anywhere else. Enough is enough."

So they stayed. They were at a place called Cottonwood Springs, which now is called Cashup. Apparently he was a little tired of wandering around, too, because he gave up without a fight. They bought 1,600 acres for $2.60 an acre, and built another 10-room house and included a general store for good measure. It was also used as a roadhouse with a recreation hall and rooms upstairs for travelers. The Davis family lived next door in a smaller house.

Soon it became apparent that Mary Ann had good judgment for selecting a homesite because it was about halfway between Walla Walla and Spokane, a perfect stop for the stage coach. Davis built barns and corrals and a watering trough large enough for an entire string of freight horses to be watered at once. It was here he earned the nickname of Cashup because he was one of the few people in the area with real money, so he made all the deals he could by offering "cash up front" or simply "cashup" to people with no money in their pockets. As much as possible, he required cash payments for the goods in his store.

During all this time Davis had owned Steptoe Butte, then called Pyramid Peak, and had always been attracted to it. The Indian wars didn't last long, so the Davis family went back to their normal routine of farming and operating the stage stop and inn. They enjoyed the social aspects of the venture as much as the income it brought.

Colfax

The town of Colfax (pop. 2,800) is county seat for Whitman County, one of the most productive wheat and barley producing counties in the nation. The town was named for Schuyler Colfax, vice president during the first administration of U.S. Grant. On Armistice Day in 1938, high school teams from Colfax and St. John met on a snowy football field; St. John won

14-0. Fifty years later the same players returned for a rematch, albeit in rather different physical condition; this time Colfax won 6-0. The **"Codger Bowl"** of 1988 is memorialized in an unusual 65-foot-high chainsaw-carved pole with the cartoonish faces of football players facing outwards from five columns. It is said to be the largest chainsaw sculpture in the world.

This came to a halt in 1883 when Northern Pacific built a line into the area, putting the stage coaches out of business. It was then that Davis put his next plan into effect: he had always thought the top of the butte would make a fine site for a hotel.

Davis spent around $10,000 building a road and then his two-story hotel on the 3,610-foot peak. He wrote a story for a local paper that told details on the structure. It was 60 feet square with the lower floor being a 40 by 60 foot hall that included a stage and dressing rooms. Also on that level was a kitchen and Davis's private reception room. The upper floor had an unspecified number of bedrooms plus a dance hall. On top was an observatory with a huge telescope strong enough to see Walla Walla on a clear day.

Davis didn't know it at the time, but Steptoe Butte, now named in honor of colonel Edward J. Steptoe, is a significant geological formation. It is the top of a quartzite mountain more than 600 million years old, part of the Selkirk Range, that stands above the basalt, only 15 million years old, that covered the rest of the range. In fact, all over the world similar formations of the remnant of an older formation protruding out of newer material are called "steptoes."

The hotel's popularity didn't last long and Davis lost a lot of money; the local population was too small to support such an extravagant establishment, and the steep roads weren't inviting. As business faded, so did Davis. Now in his 80s, he finally gave up and moved himself to the hotel while Mary Ann stayed in their house in Cashup, where she died in 1894. He told everyone he wanted to be buried on the peak, and even dug his own grave and left a shovel standing beside it. Death came on June 22, 1896. Unfortunately, his wish to be buried on the hill was not granted. He was buried in the community cemetery instead.

The hotel stood for another 15 years, but on March 11, 1911, two boys set fire to it, whether by accident or intent was never determined. Eventually the whole peak was sold at a sheriff's auction for $2,000. It was donated to the state to be used as a state park by the last owner, Virgil McCroskey.

The **Perkins House** at 623 N. Perkins Ave., tel. (509) 397-3712, was built in 1884 by Colfax's first permanent resident, James Perkins. Inside this National Historic Site are antique furniture and household items from the late 19th century. Out back is a log cabin built in 1870. Stop here on the last Sunday in June for an ice cream social. Perkins House is open June-Sept. on Sunday and Thursday 1-5 p.m. Get good steaks, pasta, and seafood, plus the "famous" vinegar pie at **Diana Lee's Grill & Bar,** tel. (509) 397-2770. Swim during the summer months at the outdoor **swimming pool** in Schmuck Park.

Concrete River Days on the second weekend of July includes a parade, food fest, auction, carnival, golf tournament, and live music. The Palouse Empire Fairground near Colfax has rodeos, horse shows, and fairs all summer long, including **Palouse Empire Plowing Bee** in April, and the **Colfax Jr. Rodeo** on Memorial Day weekend. The main event is the four-day **Whitman County Fair** beginning the weekend after Labor Day. It features a rodeo, demonstrations of antique harvesting equipment, a carnival, and all the standard country fair activities.

PULLMAN

Pullman (pop. 24,000) looks like a typical small college town with an abundance of we-deliver pizza joints, along with submarine-sandwich shops and beer-by-the-keg outlets. Prosperous downtown Pullman is an attractive, tidy place with red brick buildings and a wide range of shops. The diverse student body helps make Pullman a surprisingly open and culturally mixed small city. Surrounding Pullman are agricultural lands that make up the heart of the rich Palouse country and contribute to Pullman's reputation as "lentil capital of the world." (Despite this claim, much of the pea and lentil industry is actually based just across the border in Moscow, Idaho.)

History

Pullman was founded by Bolin Farr, who came from Missouri to settle at the confluence of Dry Fork Creek, Missouri Flat Creek, and the south fork of the Palouse in 1876. Thus, the town was first called "Three Forks." By 1881, it had grown—to a population of three. Hoping to attract financial aid from Chicago industrialist George Pullman (of Pullman sleeping-car fame), the citizens decided to name their "city" Pullman. It's still a matter of controversy whether he contributed anything, but the name stuck. A railroad branch extended to the town, the "crossroads of the Palouse," in 1883; by then Pullman had two stores, a hotel, a post office, and a blacksmith shop.

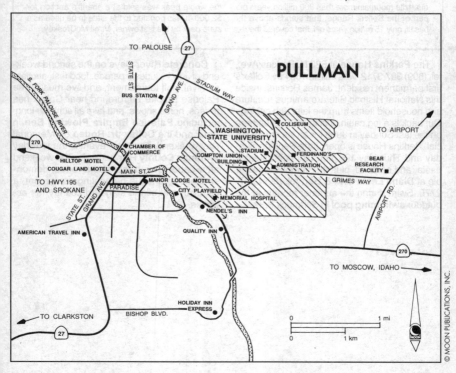

Following the common pattern of the West, two fires devastated the wooden downtown district in 1887 and again in 1890; structures were rebuilt in brick, and many of these buildings are still standing.

In 1892, the Washington Agricultural College opened in Pullman. There were just 21 students that first semester, but the school would grow into Washington State University, and the central focal point for the city. Today, the local economy is dominated by academia; the university employs over 4,700 people.

WASHINGTON STATE UNIVERSITY

Washington State University has a student body of more than 16,000 distributed throughout one graduate school and seven undergraduate colleges offering more than 100 major fields of study. The school is well known as a major agricultural research center, but facilities also include an Electron Microscopy Center, Nuclear Radiation Center, Water Research Center, and International Marketing Program for Agricultural Commodities. Students live in 23 residence halls, in the community, or in 24 fraternities and 14 sororities. For a fine view of the campus and surrounding Palouse landscape, head to the top of the Physical Sciences Building.

CUB

The center of WSU student life is **Compton Union Building,** tel. (509) 335-9444, better known as the "Cub." Inside are all the standard student center stuff: an information desk, a wide range of eating places, a coffeehouse with live music, billiards, bowling, and video games, a post office, a credit union, a florist, a student art gallery, a convenience store, an outdoor recreation center, and even a hotel. The main campus library—**Holland Library**—is located next door.

Ferdinand's Bar

The Food Quality Building is home to Ferdinand's, a soda fountain run by the university's agricultural school, and the campus's most popular tourist attraction. As part of its agricultural research work, the university has maintained a dairy herd for more than 70 years; today, most of the milk produced goes into cheeses and ice cream. The cheese is made at a state-of-the-art plant in the Food Quality Building, and you can watch the operation and a 10-minute cheesy video upstairs from Ferdinand's. The soda fountain has 19 flavors of delicious ice cream, making this a popular stopping place for students and visitors. On football Saturdays, you may have to wait 45 minutes for a cone!

The most famous product at Ferdinand's is **"Cougar Gold,"** a delicious cheddar-like cheese that is only sold in hefty 30-ounce tin cans. This unique method of packaging came about in the 1930s, when researchers were looking for a way to protect cheese from contamination while being stored for long periods (the cheese still needs to be refrigerated). The cheeses are aged for up to a year to develop the proper flavor and texture. Technological advances have meant that plastic wrap now serves the same function, but Cougar Gold and other WSU Creamery cheeses still come in their distinctive tins.

Ferdinand's is open Mon.-Fri. 9:30 a.m.-4:30 p.m., and on special event weekends (such as home football games). You can also mail-order the cheeses by calling Ferdinand's at (509) 335-4014; they aren't cheap—around $12 a tin plus shipping.

Museum of Art

Although not impressive by Seattle standards, the Museum of Art in the Fine Arts Center houses Washington's finest arts exhibition space east of the Cascades with changing exhibits throughout the year. Also here is a permanent collection of works by well-known 19th and 20th century American and European painters, from Goya to Warhol. Some of these works are always on display during the summer. The museum is open Tuesday 10 a.m.-4 p.m. and 7-10 p.m., Wed.-Fri. 10 a.m.-4 p.m., and Sat.-Sun. 1-5 p.m. Docent-led tours are available by request; be sure to ask about other events here, such as musical performances, art talks, and lectures. Call (509) 335-1910 for more information, or (509) 335-6607 for a recorded schedule of events. Small student art galleries on campus can be found elsewhere in the Fine Arts Center and in the Cub.

Other Museums

The **Museum of Anthropology** on the first floor of College Hall, tel. (509) 335-3441, has traveling exhibits from all over the globe and Northwest Indian artifacts (mostly from Snake River sites now inundated by reservoirs). Certainly the most unusual items are the plaster casts of what are purportedly Sasquatch footprints.

My favorite WSU museum is the **Jacklin Collection** inside the Physical Sciences Building. Here you'll discover the largest petrified wood collection in the western states, many of which have been beautifully polished. The collection is open weekdays 8 a.m.-5 p.m. In the entryway are several fun (and maybe even educational) science exhibits to play with.

Connors Museum of Zoology (in the Science Building) claims to have the largest public collection of animals and birds in the Pacific Northwest; not all that interesting unless you enjoy stuffed critters in ancient glass cases. Open by appointment only is the **Drucker Collection of Oriental Art,** tel. (509) 335-3823, in White Hall. It includes oriental furniture, textiles, costumes, and art work. There's also an impressive **Nez Percé Music Archive** in Kimbrough Hall featuring tribal songs by historical Indian leaders, including the voice of Chief Joseph. (You can also hear the recordings in the Kemble A. Stout Music Listening Library on campus.)

In addition to the larger exhibits at WSU, visitors will discover a big herbarium collection in Heald Hall for botanists, collections of fungi and insects in Johnson Hall, and even the Smith Soil Monolith Collection, donated by a pedagogical philanthropist. Get a brochure describing these and other on-campus collections at the Cub information desk.

Bear Research Facility

Don't miss the fenced-in bear research facility along Airport Rd. on the east edge of campus. Directed by Dr. Charles Robbins, the Bear Research, Education, and Conservation Program, tel. (509) 335-1119, is an important facility for research on bruins from all over the world, particularly brown and black bears. This is the only place where adult grizzlies are housed for nutritional, physiological, and ecological research by graduate students and visiting sci-

entists. Generally, the facility houses six grizzlies and four black bears, visible behind a stout fence. Now endangered in the Lower 48, a few grizzlies can still be found in the northern Cascades and the Selkirk Mountains of Washington State. The resident bears were orphaned as cubs and would not have otherwise survived. In the winter, they hibernate in special temperature-controlled dens. Tours are available.

Tours and Information

For free **campus tours,** drop by the University Relations Office in Room 442 of the Administration Building. These walking tours are offered at 1 p.m. Mon.-Fri. all year and last approximately an hour and a half. Call (509) 335-4527 for WSU details.

Public parking is available at a number of lots around campus; get a parking day-pass for a buck and eight pennies from the **Safety Building,** located across from the Cub.

OTHER SIGHTS

Three Forks Pioneer Museum

Roger Rossebo likes to call Three Forks Pioneer Village Museum, the 17-building town on his wheat and pea farm near Pullman, "the Smithsonian of the Palouse." That isn't much of an exaggeration; although all the buildings are chock full of period furniture and decorations, Rossebo still has enough farming implements and other antiques in storage to furnish and decorate the small city he is assembling.

The collection includes one of the first cabins built in the Palouse region, plus more than 15 other historic or recreated structures. A small village green with a picnic area and fountain is near the little red schoolhouse for those who bring a picnic lunch.

To reach Three Forks, go north from Pullman on Hwy. 27 one-half mile and turn left on Albion Road. Drive two miles and turn right at the Three Forks sign onto Anderson Rd., then drive 2.8 miles on the gravel road to the Rossebo farm and museum. Hours are Sunday 9 a.m. to dark May-Sept., or by appointment at other times. Admission is $2 for adults, $1 for students, and kids under 11 are free. For information, call (509) 332-3889.

Parks

Lawson Gardens, on Derby St. near Dilke St., covers 11 acres of land and features a formal rose and flower garden with a reflecting pool and gazebo. On the west side of town, **Sunnyside Park** has hiking trails, picnic areas, tennis and basketball courts, and playgrounds; this is the site of Pullman's annual Fourth of July picnic and fireworks. **Reaney Park** on Reaney Way and Gray Lane has a swimming pool, gazebo, and playground.

ACCOMMODATIONS AND CAMPING

Accommodations

See the "Pullman Accommodations" chart for a complete list of local lodging places. The nicest of these is the historic **Ash Street House B&B,** tel. (509) 332-3638, owned by the chef at Seasons Restaurant, so you know the breakfast will be good. In addition, there are an equal number of motels and B&Bs in Moscow, Idaho, just 10 miles east of Pullman.

The most unusual Pullman lodging place is the Cub Hotel on the WSU campus. It's open only during the school year (closed summers, as well as Thanksgiving and Christmas breaks) and covers two floors in the Compton Union Building.

If you're planning to be in town for WSU football games or graduation, reserve several months, and maybe a year, ahead of time. The busiest time is when the Applecup Game (against arch-rival University of Washington) comes to Pullman. Late folks end up staying in Clarkston and "commuting" to the game.

Campgrounds

Campers can stay at the city-run **Pullman RV Park** at South and Riverview Streets for $10 April-Nov.; for reservations, call (509) 334-4555, ext. 227. **Kamiak Butte County Park,** 13 miles northeast of Pullman on Hwy. 27 has additional camping.

FOOD

The best Pullman place for breakfast and lunch is **Old European Waffles, Cakes, & Teas,** S. 455 Grand Ave., tel. (509) 334-6381. **The Com-**

PULLMAN ACCOMMODATIONS

Accommodations are arranged from least to most expensive. The area code is 509.

Manor Lodge Motel; S.E. 445 Paradise; tel. 334-2511; $22 s or d; kitchenettes available

Cougar Land Motel; W. 120 Main; tel. 334-3535 or (800) 334-3574; $30 s, $34 d; outdoor pool, kitchenettes available

Hilltop Motor Inn; Davis Way at Wawawai Rd.; tel. 334-2555; $31 s, $37 d; quiet location, bungalows

American Travel Inn; 515 S. Grand; tel. 334-3500; $34 s, $38 d; outdoor pool, AAA approved

Country B&B; six miles south of Pullman; tel. 334-4453; $40-55 s or d; continental breakfast

Nendel's Inn; S.E. 915 Main; tel. 332-2646 or (800) 547-0106; $45-50 s or d; outdoor pool, next to noisy railroad tracks

Compton Union Building Hotel; WSU Campus; tel. 334-9444; $45 s, $60 d; on-campus hotel, closed summers and school holidays (Christmas and Thanksgiving breaks)

Ash Street House B&B; N.E. 315 Ash St.; tel. 332-3638; $60 s or d; turn-of-the-century home, four upstairs rooms, gourmet breakfast, children okay

Quality Inn Paradise Creek; S.E. 1050 Bishop; tel. 332-0500 or (800) 669-3212; $52-75 s, $60-83 d; outdoor pool, sauna, jacuzzi, fitness center, breakfast buffet, kitchenettes available, airport shuttle service, AAA approved

Holiday Inn Express; S.E. 1190 Bishop Blvd.; tel. 334-4437 or (800) 465-4329; $64 s or d; indoor pool, jacuzzi, fitness center, free continental breakfast, airport shuttle service, AAA approved

bine, E. 215 Main, tel. (509) 332-1774, is a down-to-earth coffee shop and student hangout. Come here for fresh baked breads and pastries, soups, sandwiches, and espresso.

The cheapest eats around can be found on campus at the Compton Union Building. Here are five different eateries, including a cafeteria and a make-your-own-sandwich deli. Also be sure to check out the ever-popular **Ferdinand's Dairy Bar** at WSU (described above) for delicious ice cream, milk shakes, and cheeses.

All-American
Pete's Bar & Grill, 1100 Bishop Blvd., tel. (509) 334-4200, serves inexpensive burgers, pasta, and chicken and has a big salad bar. **Hilltop Restaurant,** Colfax Hwy., tel. (509) 334-2555, grills fine steaks and has a Sunday brunch and a panoramic city view, but not much in the way of atmosphere. The best steaks anywhere around are across the border at **Lone Jack Steak Co.** in Potlatch, Idaho, tel. (208) 875-1421.

Ethnic and Vegetarian
Enjoy authentic Mexican cuisine—including tasty chimichangas and potent margaritas—at **Alex's Restaurante,** 139 N. Grand Ave., tel. (509) 332-4061. For fine Chinese cooking, head to **Ron's Gourmet Wok,** N. 115 Grand, tel. (509) 332-5863. **Studio 7 Vegetarian Restaurant,** N.E. 720 Thatuna, tel. (509) 332-6863, makes veggie fare. **Mat's Rathouse** throws the finest local pizzas.

Gourmet Fare
Swilly's Cafe, 200 Kamiaken, tel. (509) 334-3395, is a very popular yuppified bistro with excellent lunches and dinners made from the freshest produce, baked goods, seafood, and meats. **Sea Galley Restaurant,** S.E. 1000 Bishop Blvd., tel. (509) 334-7032, is the place for fresh seafood; they also have a big salad bar.

Seasons Restaurant, S.E. 215 Paradise, tel. (509) 334-1410, is Pullman's most elegant dining establishment with a menu that changes with the seasons. A bit pricey, but worth it for an out-on-the-town dinner.

If you don't mind the drive, **Cafe Spudnik,** 215 S. Main in Moscow, Idaho, tel. (208) 882-

9257, makes decidedly different (and very good) dishes such as salmon in pastry puff and gourmet pizzas. Nice atmosphere, and outdoor cafe seating during the summer.

ENTERTAINMENT AND EVENTS

Events
Pullman's annual **Fourth of July** celebration actually covers three towns. It begins in Johnson, 10 miles south of Pullman, where a silly parade features the weirdest and wackiest floats and costumes. Then it's on to Albion, six miles north of Pullman, for a big potluck meal at Community Hall. In the afternoon, head back to Pullman for a barbecue, live music, and after-dark fireworks close to a lentil field.

Pullman's main event is the **National Lentil Festival,** held the third weekend in September. It features a parade, arts and crafts fair, live entertainment, a kids fishing derby, and all sorts of food made from lentils—from lentil lasagna to lentil brownies (much better than it sounds). Be sure to pack your bottle of Beano for this event.

Performances
The 12,000-seat **Beasley Performing Arts Coliseum** at WSU stages events from rock concerts to comedy shows. For a schedule call (509) 335-1514; for tickets call (800) 325-7328. The university has two theaters in Daggy Hall where you can attend Shakespearean plays, student productions, and a summer repertory season in June and July called **Summer Palace.** Call (509) 335-7236 for details.

Established in 1969, the **Washington-Idaho Symphony,** puts on seven productions a year; call (208) 882-6555 for upcoming concerts. You can also hear free **summer outdoor concerts** at Reaney Park on Wednesday evenings from late June to early August.

The **Lionel Hampton/Chevron Jazz Festival** in nearby Moscow is one of the biggest area events. Held the last weekend in February, it features many of the greats in jazz, with past performances by Lionel Hampton, Dizzy Gillespie, and the Marsalis brothers. Call (800) 345-7402 for ticket info.

Dancing and Boozin'

Pete's Bar & Grill, 1100 Bishop Blvd., tel. (509) 334-4200, has live music and dancing for the college crowd. **Rico's Tavern,** E. 200 Main St., tel. (509) 332-6566, is a great rockin' place with blues and jazz bands, imported beers, and homemade wine coolers. **The Cavern,** N.E. 1000 Colorado, tel. (509) 334-5151, often has reggae, jazz, or rock bands.

SPORTS AND RECREATION

Outdoor Recreation Center

Located in the University's Compton Union Building (Cub), the Outdoor Recreation Center offers excellent non-credit classes in kayaking, cross-country skiing, rock climbing, wilderness survival, backpacking, and other subjects. Most of these last one to three days and are open to the public for a fee. The ORC also rents a wide range of equipment to both students and the public, including backpacks, mountain bikes, tents, rafts, canoes, skis, and snowboards. The rental shop is open Mon.-Fri. 8 a.m.-5 p.m.

Rock climbers will love the excellent **climbing wall** in Bohler Gym, open to students and the public every day. Passes can be purchased, or you can take a lesson on Saturday during the school year for only $5. Call the ORC at (509) 335-2651 for more on the climbing wall, rentals, and classes.

Sports

The WSU Cougars field teams in football, basketball, baseball, gymnastics, and track and field; for a schedule of athletic events, call (509) 335-9626 or (800) 462-6847. The 40,000-seat Martin Stadium really rocks when the Cougs play the arch-rival University of Washington Huskies.

Other Recreation

Swimmers will find two outdoor **swimming pools** open in Reaney Park from mid-June to Labor Day (tel. 509-334-4555), along with three more pools (one is Olympic-size) at the University, tel. (509) 335-9666. The university also has a nine-hole golf course and putting green

open to the public. Contact **Whitman County Travel,** tel. (509) 397-4688, for information on all-day archaeological tours of the famous Marmes Rockshelter and other important sites.

INFORMATION AND SERVICES

The **Pullman Chamber of Commerce,** N. 415 Grand Ave., tel. (509) 334-3565 or (800) 365-6948, is open Mon.-Fri. 9 a.m.-5 p.m. and Saturday 10 a.m.-2 p.m. year-round. They have all sorts of local brochures, including a walking tour of historic buildings. If you're crossing the border into Idaho, get info at **Moscow Chamber of Commerce,** 411 S. Main, tel. (208) 882-1800. The **area code** for Pullman and all of eastern Washington is 509; for Moscow, Idaho, it's 208, but it is a local call between the two cities, and you don't need to dial the area code.

For books, visit **Neill Public Library,** N. 210 Grand Ave., tel. (509) 334-4555, or one of the seven on-campus libraries at WSU. **Brused Books,** N. 105 Grand Ave., tel. (509) 334-7898, is a fun place to browse for used books.

TRANSPORTATION

Air Service

Horizon Airlines, tel. (800) 547-9308, has daily service between Moscow-Pullman Airport (in Pullman) and Spokane, Seattle, Boise, and Portland. **Inter-State Aviation,** tel. (800) 653-8420, offers flightseeing and air charter services from Pullman.

Bus Service

Pullman Transit, tel. (509) 332-6535, provides local bus service throughout town Mon.-Fri. only for 35 cents.

Wheatland Express Commuter Bus, tel. (509) 334-2200 or (800) 334-2207, has shuttle bus service between Pullman and Moscow, Idaho, for $1.50 one-way. Buses run Mon.-Sat., and bikes are carried for no extra charge. They also offer tours of the Palouse area.

Link Transportation Services, tel. (208) 882-1223 or (800) 359-4541, provides shuttle bus service from Pullman and Moscow to Spokane Airport for $33 one-way. Connect to virtually any point in the country aboard **Northwestern Stage Lines,** 1002 Nye St., tel. (509) 334-1412 or (800) 366-6975.

PULLMAN VICINITY

Moscow

Although it's across the state line, the town of Moscow, Idaho, is a twin to Pullman. Moscow is just 10 miles away and has a number of attractions worth visiting: the **University of Idaho,** the **Appaloosa Museum and Heritage Center,** and many historic structures, including the **McConnell Mansion.** The country around here rises quickly into forested mountains, quite a change from the rolling grasslands of the Palouse. The weekly

farmers market in downtown Moscow runs all summer long on Saturday from 8 a.m. to 1 p.m.

Uniontown

Tiny Uniontown (pop. 300), a dozen miles south of Pullman, was first settled by German immigrants in the 1880s. Today, agriculture is the main support, as evidenced by the big grain elevator on the north side of town and the rolling farmland all around. Constructed in 1905, **St. Boniface Church** is Washington's oldest Catholic church.

The most distinctive feature—it's pretty hard to miss—is Steve Dahmen's old barn surrounded by a 600-foot fence of **iron wheels.** The wheels came from steam engines, threshing machines, hay rakes, tractors, wagons, and even sewing machines. Stop by to talk to the fence's friendly creator and to sign his guest book.

CLARKSTON AND VICINITY

Clarkston (pop. 7,000) lies in the very southeast corner of Washington along the Snake River, and right across the bridge from its larger neighbor, Lewiston, Idaho. The names reflect two famous explorers who traveled through here almost two centuries ago, Meriweather Lewis and William Clark. Clarkston is in the portion of eastern Washington often referred to as "The Banana Belt," because it has, as early Native Americans put it, "no wind, no snow." Some may take exception to the "no snow" part, but the climate is generally milder than that of other areas east of the Cascades. Clarkston is Washington's most inland seaport, more than 450 miles east of the Pacific via the Columbia River and its chief branch, the Snake.

History

On October 10, 1805, the Lewis and Clark expedition camped here en route to the Pacific. The region's first settlers were cattle ranchers, taking advantage of the nearly endless grazing lands. The Asotin Creek irrigation project of 1895 brought much-needed water to this parched region, and a wagon bridge built in 1896 between Clarkston (originally called Vineland) and Lewiston provided access to Lewiston's railroad. These projects, as well as dams constructed in the

1960s and '70s that turned the wild lower Snake into a navigable waterway, paved the way for agriculture, industry, and population growth. Unfortunately, these dams also destroyed magnificent stretches of wild river and buried countless archaeological sites.

Clarkston's first containerized shipment departed for Japan in 1975; today's primary exports are peas to Europe and paper products to Japan. Despite this, agriculture and forest products, not international shipping, are the mainstay of the city's economy. The largest local employer—by far—is Lewiston's **Potlatch Corporation.** Tours of the Potlatch Corporation's sawmill and paperboard plant are available Monday, Wednesday, and Friday; call (509) 799-1795 for reservations.

SIGHTS

See "River Rafting" under "Recreation," below, for the biggest summertime attraction in the Clarkston area.

Scenic Drives

To reach Pullman and other points north, you need to cross into Lewiston and traverse the

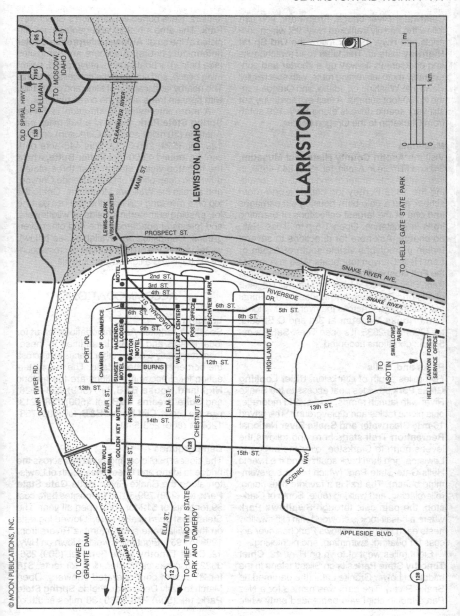

© MOON PUBLICATIONS, INC.

Clearwater River bridge. From here, you can follow the heavily trafficked Hwy. 95, which connects into Hwy. 195, or follow the **Old Spiral Highway** instead. This latter road switchbacks and corkscrews its way up a shorter and considerably more interesting route, with spectacular views into Washington, Idaho, and Oregon from the 2,750-foot summit. A less extraordinary but still very scenic drive is along Hwy. 129 south from Clarkston to the Oregon border.

Museums

Visit the **Asotin County Historical Museum,** 3rd and Filmore in Asotin, tel. (509) 243-4659, to see early Asotin artifacts and buildings, including the 1882 Forgey log cabin, a one-room school, and a pole barn housing old carriages and one of the largest collections of branding irons in existence. Open 1-5 p.m. Tues.-Sat.; no charge. Ask here for directions to several Indian petroglyphs visible south of Asotin or from Hells Canyon tour boats. Also in Asotin is the **Full Gospel Church** in Chief Looking Glass Park. Built in 1889, it is on the National Register of Historic Buildings and houses the original oak pump organ. Across the river in Lewiston is **Luna House Museum** at 3rd and C Streets, tel. (208) 743-2535. It's open Tues.-Sat. 9 a.m.-5 p.m.; donations accepted.

Parks and Trails

Five miles south of Clarkston, **Chief Looking Glass Park** provides boat access to the Snake River with launch ramps, docks, and moorage, plus picnic tables and a playground. The paved 16-mile **Clearwater and Snake River National Recreation Trail** starts here and follows the levees north to Clarkston, over the bridge to Lewiston, and then back south along the river to Hells Gate State Park (which has a big swimming beach). The trail is a favorite bike riding, rollerblading, and walking route. South of Clarkston, the path cuts through **Swallows Park** where a basalt rock is crowded with cliff swallow nests each spring. Swallows Park has river access for boating, swimming, and picnicking.

Eight miles west of town on Hwy. 12, **Chief Timothy State Park** sits on Silcott Island in the middle of Lower Granite Lake (the dammed up Snake River). The park was named for a Nez Percé Indian chief who befriended early white settlers. He is buried in Clarkston's Beachview Park. The area's history and geology are depicted at the small **Alpowai Interpretive Center** (intermittent hours). Also here are campsites (see below), a boat launch, playground, swimming beach, and summertime concession stand. The nearby landscape is of sage and grass hills, with riparian trees along the creek bottoms.

A more interesting destination is **Fields Spring State Park,** four and a half miles past Anatone (30 miles south of Clarkston) on Hwy. 129, tel. (509) 256-3332. This 445-acre park centers around 4,500-foot **Puffer Butte,** where the ridgetop vistas stretch over three states, down the deep gorge of Grand Ronde Canyon, and across the Wallowa Mountains. Get to the top on a mile-long trail from the day-use parking lot, passing summertime fields of wildflowers, and forests of ponderosa pine and other evergreens. Campsites are available (see below); winter visitors will enjoy the miles of cross-country ski trails and a lighted sledding hill.

ACCOMMODATIONS

Lodging

See the "Clarkston Accommodations" chart for local motels and B&Bs. In addition to these, there are nearly a dozen other places just across the border in Lewiston, Idaho. The most interesting local accommodations are the historic **Highland House B&B,** tel. (509) 758-3126, and **Suite Dreams B&B,** tel. (509) 758-8213, plus the scenic **Cliff House B&B,** tel. (509) 758-1267 or (800) 253-5460.

Campgrounds

The closest public campground lies across the bridge to Idaho and three miles south of Lewiston along the Snake River: **Hells Gate State Park,** tel. (208) 799-5015. Campsites here cost $9 for tents or $12 for RVs; open all year. The Steamboat *Jean* is also here; it towed log rafts on the Willamette and Columbia Rivers from 1938 to 1957. Eight miles west of town on Hwy. 12, **Chief Timothy State Park,** tel. (509) 256-3332, also has campsites ($11 for tents, $16 for RVs) with coin-operated showers. Open March to early December. **Fields Spring State Park,** tel. (509) 758-9580, 30 miles south of

CLARKSTON ACCOMMODATIONS

Accommodations are arranged from least to most expensive. Rates may be lower during the winter months. Additional motels are available just across the river in Lewiston, Idaho. The area code is 509.

Aster Motel; 1261 Bridge St.; tel. 758-2509; $23 s, $28 d

Golden Key Motel; 1376 Bridge St.; tel. 758-5566; $26 s, $30 d; outdoor pool, local calls 25 cents

Sunset Motel; 1200 Bridge St.; tel. 758-2517 or (800) 845-5223; $27 s, $32 d; often filled, reserve ahead

Hacienda Lodge; 812 Bridge St.; tel. 758-5583 or (800) 600-5583; $32 s, $38 d

Motel 6; 222 Bridge St.; tel. 758-1631 or (800) 466-8356; $35 s, $41 d; outdoor pool

Highland House B&B; 707 Highland; tel. 758-3126; $35 s, $60-70 d; historic colonial style house, antique furnishings, full English breakfast

Best Western Rivertree Inn; 1257 Bridge St.; tel. 758-9551 or (800) 597-3621; $55-75 s, $60-95 d, outdoor pool, jacuzzi, sauna, exercise room, kitchenettes, free airport shuttle, AAA approved

Quality Inn; 700 Port Dr.; tel. 758-9500 or (800) 228-5151; $57-75 s, $60-75 d; outdoor pool, free airport shuttle, AAA approved

Cliff House B&B; 2000 Westlake Dr., tel. 758-1267 or (800) 253-5460; $60-75 s, $65-75 d; great views, jacuzzi, full breakfast, private bath, no kids under 10

Swallowhaven B&B; 904 22nd Ave.; tel. 758-8357 or (800) 441-8357; $70-100; scenic Snake River views, three guest rooms, private baths, full breakfast

Suite Dreams B&B; 629 Riverview Blvd.; tel. 758-8213; $90 s or d; historic home, river views, large attic suite, full breakfast, no kids under 10

Clarkston on Hwy. 129, has campsites ($10) with coin-operated showers and is open all year. Because it is at 4,000 feet in elevation, Fields Spring offers a cool break on hot summer days. For campsite reservations ($6 extra fee) at both state parks, call (800) 452-5687. The reservations are available up to 11 months ahead of time. Park that land yacht at **Hillview RV Park,** 1224 Bridge St., tel. (509) 758-6299.

FOOD AND SHOPPING

For the best local breakfasts, cross over to Lewiston's **Waffles-N-More,** 1421 Main St., tel. (509) 743-5189. Or sit down for a coffee and big breakfast with the Clarkston locals at **Come Inn Cafe,** 508 Diagonal St., tel. (509) 758-2884. The **Bridge Street Connection,** 1250 Bridge St., tel. (509) 758-3141, is a bit fancier.

Lewiston's bowling alley, **Strike & Spare Bar & Grill** at 244 Thain Rd., tel. (509) 743-8883,

makes good sandwiches and burgers for lunch. Get reasonable family meals at **Southshore Landing** in the Quality Inn, 700 Port Dr., tel. (509) 758-9500.

If you're looking for something more exotic, **Phoenix Mountain Restaurant,** 701 6th St., tel. (509) 758-9618, serves huge portions of Chinese food. Get Mexican meals at **El Sombrero,** 2315 Appleside Blvd., tel. (509) 758-2416.

Fazzari's, 1281 Bridge St., tel. (509) 758-3386, features very good pizza, spaghetti, and sandwiches and is open daily for lunch and dinner. Another popular Italian place is **Tomato Brothers,** 200 Bridge St., tel. (509) 758-7902. **Three Mile Inn,** three miles south of Asotin, tel. (509) 243-4158, has outstanding river views and fine dining, with filet mignon, prime rib, and even Australian lobster tails.

Shopping
Meacham Mills, 1265 Port Way, tel. (509) 758-0412, is a unique family owned flour mill that

uses stones to grind various types of grains. They also sell a variety of gourmet food products. The old Clarkston Airport hanger at 935 Port Way now houses a large **antique mall** with some 100 dealers. It's open Tues.-Saturday.

EVENTS AND ENTERTAINMENT

Events

The small **Asotin County Fair,** held the last weekend in April, features a rodeo, parade, cowboy breakfast, and stock show and sale. Also in late April, the **Dogwood Festival** celebrates spring's flowering dogwoods with concerts, art in the park, and historical walking tours. The **Fourth of July** brings all the usual favorites: fireworks, a parade, and barbecue in the park. Several events in neighboring Lewiston complete the summer calendar: **Lewis Clark Air Festival** in late July, **Hot August Nights** (concerts in the park and antique car show) in late August, **Lewiston Roundup Rodeo and Parade** in early September, and **Nez Percé County Fair** in late September. Mid-December's **Christmas on the Confluence** is a lighted boat parade on the Snake River, departing from Swallows Nest Park in Lewiston.

Music and Art

The best local places for live country music are over in Lewiston at **The Corral,** 1618 Main St., tel. (509) 746-7353, and **Curley's Alibi,** 1702 Main St., tel. (509) 743-0317. **Tomfoolery,** 301 2nd St., tel. (509) 746-2005, also in Lewiston, has rock and pop tunes.

The **Valley Art Center,** 842 6th St., tel. (509) 758-8331, features rotating exhibits and sales and also offers workshops and classes in all media.

RECREATION

River Rafting

Quite a few local companies offer float trips and jetboat excursions through the deepest river gorge in North America, the Snake River's **Hells Canyon,** separating Oregon and Idaho. The canyon lacks the steep cliffs of the Grand Canyon, but is nevertheless an extraordinary place. From the summit of He Devil Peak to the Snake River—five air miles distant—the terrain plummets more than 8,000 feet. (A Nez Percé Indian legend tells how their ancestors were threatened by seven devils. Using a very big stick, Coyote dug out the canyon, leaving the devils in what is now Idaho. Perhaps this could explain some of the right-wing militia mania that festers in parts of that state.)

Approximately 68 miles of the river—from Hells Canyon Dam in Oregon to the Washington border—is a National Wild and Scenic River. This is something of a miracle, since it represented a rare victory for conservationists over the electric power and agricultural interests that have managed to dam up lengthy portions of the Snake River. In 1964, a license was granted to build the High Mountain Sheep Dam in the middle of this undeveloped country. (At least a half-dozen other sites were also considered for additional dams.) After years of litigation, congress finally voted to protect the river in 1975.

The Snake River features several class IV rapids, along with many class II and III rapids. In addition to the wild water of the canyon, along the way you'll see mysterious petroglyphs, an ancient lava flow, abundant wildlife, and rugged canyon scenery. Some outfitters use only inflatable rafts or dories, while the others use jet-powered boats. Most offer overnight trips as well as day trips.

For a complete list of commercial guides and outfitters, contact the Forest Service's **Hells Canyon Office,** three miles south of Clarkston on Hwy. 129, tel. (509) 758-0616. The office is open Mon.-Fri. 7:45-11:30 a.m. and 12:30-4:30 p.m. year-round. For a 24-hour recording of current river conditions and other info, call (509) 758-1957. The **Clarkston Chamber of Commerce,** 502 Bridge St., tel. (509) 758-7712 or (800) 933-2128, also has info on local river-running companies.

It is also possible to run the Snake River yourself if you have the equipment and skills, but you'll need to get permits through a lottery system that requires application in December and January; contact the Clarkston Forest Service office for permit requirements.

Other Recreation

The outdoor public **swimming pool** in the Beachview Park at 2nd and Chestnut is open summers only; call (509) 758-1673 for hours. Several local parks offer Snake River swimming, and the Clearwater River—just over the Idaho border—is a popular summertime innertubing spot. Nearby reservoirs offer a variety of boating opportunities, including windsurfing, and the Snake River is famous for its rainbow trout, bass, steelhead, salmon, and monster sturgeon.

The local public putting-around place is **Swallow's Nest Golf Course,** 1725 Swallow's Nest Loop, tel. (509) 758-8501.

INFORMATION AND SERVICES

For maps or other information contact the **Clarkston Chamber of Commerce,** 502 Bridge St., tel. (509) 758-7712 or (800) 933-2128. Hours are Mon.-Fri. 9 a.m.-5 p.m. year-round. Right across the Hwy. 12 bridge in Lewiston is the **Lewis-Clark Visitor Center,** tel. (208) 746-5172; open March-Oct. only, and daily in the summer.

Out front, you'll find *Tsceminicum,* a large sculpture depicting Nez Percé legends and animals. Lewiston's **chamber of commerce** is at 2207 E. Main St., tel. (208) 743-3531 or (800) 473-3543, and is open weekdays all year.

The Clarkston **area code** is 509; in Lewiston, it's 208. Despite the area code difference, it's a local call from Clarkston to Lewiston, and you don't need to include the area code for these calls. Medical assistance is available at **Tri-State Memorial Hospital,** 1221 Highland Ave. in Clarkston, tel. (509) 758-5511.

TRANSPORTATION

Horizon Airlines, tel. (800) 547-9308, has daily service between Lewiston Airport and Spokane, Seattle, Boise, and Portland. **Empire Airlines,** tel. (800) 392-9233, flies to Boise and Coeur d'Alene, Idaho.

Northwestern Stage Lines, tel. (509) 838-4029 or (800) 366-6975, has bus connections all over the Northwest from the bus stop at Super 8 Motel, 3120 North South Hwy. in Lewiston.

SNAKE RIVER/BLUE MOUNTAINS COUNTRY

As you drive Highway 12 from Clarkston to Walla Walla, the country offers up a hilly palette of grassland, sage, and strip-cropped wheat fields. Harvesting these rolling fields requires special self-leveling combines. The wide, easy highway sails over an easy 2,785-foot pass at Alpowa Summit, and then drops slowly down to the town of Pomeroy on the western side. Not much development out here, just a few weathered homesteads set against the big land and the even larger sky. The Selkirk Mountains of Washington and Idaho are visible to the northeast, and the Blue Mountains of Washington and Oregon occupy the southern horizon.

POMEROY

Thirty-one miles west of Clarkston is the farming town of Pomeroy (pop. 1,400), the county seat—and only real settlement—in Pomeroy County.

It's also the only county seat to have been established by an act of congress. A bitter rift with neighboring Pataha City (now essentially a ghost town) was finally resolved when congress awarded the seat to Pomeroy in 1884. Today Pomeroy is an agricultural center with half-a-dozen big grain elevators in use (or disuse). Not far away is the world's largest producer of Kentucky bluegrass lawn seed, Dye Seed Ranch.

Practicalities

Pioneer Motel, 1201 Main St., tel. (509) 843-1559, has rooms for $32 s, $36 d. Nothing great to eat in Pomeroy, but you might try **Donna's Drive-In** for breakfast and burgers, and **Valentine Ridge Sub Shop** for sandwiches and soups. The city park has an outdoor summer-only swimming pool.

Northwestern Stage Lines, tel. (800) 366-6975, has bus connections from Pomeroy to other parts of the Northwest.

THE NEZ PERCÉ WAR

In 1877, the federal government tried to force the Nez Percé (nay-PUR-say) Indians under Chief White Bird and Chief Joseph onto a reservation so that white ranchers could have their lands in Washington's Blue Mountains and Oregon's Wallowa Valley. The Indians stubbornly refused, and tensions quickly mounted. A few drunk young men killed four whites, and subsequent raids led to the deaths of at least 14 more. The Army retaliated, but was turned back by the Nez Percé. Rather than face government reinforcements, more than 1,000 Nez Percé began an 1,800-mile flight in a desperate bid to reach Canada. A series of running battles followed as the Indians managed to confound the inept Army using their geographic knowledge and battle skills.

East of the newly established Yellowstone National Park in Wyoming, the Indians plotted a masterful escape from two columns of Army forces, feinting a move down the Shoshone River and then heading north along a route that left their pursuers gasping in amazement—straight up the narrow Clarks Fork Canyon, "where rocks on each side came so near together that two horses abreast could hardly pass." Finally, less than 40 miles from the international border with Canada, the Army caught up with the Nez Percé, and after a fierce battle, the tribe was forced to surrender (although 300 did make good their escape).

Chief Joseph's haunting words at the surrender still echo through the years: "Hear me, my chiefs, I am tired; my heart is sick and sad. From where the sun now stands, I will fight no more forever." Despite promises that they would be allowed to return home, the Nez Percé were hustled onto remote reservations in Oklahoma and Washington, while whites remained on their rich ancestral lands. Chief Joseph spent the rest of his life on the Washington's Colville Reservation and died in 1904, reportedly of a broken heart.

Outdoor Recreation

The **Pomeroy District Office** of Umatilla National Forest is on the west end of town at 120 Main St., tel. (509) 843-1891, and is open Mon.-Fri. 7:45 a.m.-4:30 p.m. year-round. Stop here for information on the nearby Wenaha-Tucannon Wilderness, and for the scoop on camping, hiking, and mountain-biking in the area. While here, pick up a map of the 70-mile **Kendall Skyline Drive.** The loop takes you through the Blue Mountains along rough but scenic forest roads.

The closest Forest Service campsite is **Alder Thicket Campground,** 18 miles south of Pomeroy on Forest Rd. 40. No charge (and no running water), and open till closed by snow in the fall. Four other Forest Service campgrounds are within 35 miles of Pomeroy; see the ranger station for specifics.

WENAHA-TUCANNON WILDERNESS

This 177,000-acre wilderness (pronounced "wen-NA-ha two-CAN-un") straddles the Washington and Oregon line within Umatilla (YOU-ma-til-la) National Forest. The wilderness is named for the two major rivers that cut through the Blue Mountains: the Wenaha and the Tucannon. The rugged terrain consists of deep canyons, narrow basaltic ridges, and mountains (2,000 to 6,400 feet in elevation) covered with lodgepole pine and other conifers. Some 200 miles of maintained trails cross the wilderness, with access from all sides, but the area is primarily used by elk hunters.

Hiking Trails

The **Mt. Misery Trail** (No. 3113) starts from the end of Diamond Peak Rd. (42 miles south of Pomeroy) off Forest Rd. 40, at an elevation of 5,900 feet. This 16-mile-long trail follows Horse Ridge for several miles, providing dramatic vistas into the wilderness and good camping spots with nearby springs. A number of loop trips of varying lengths are possible from this trail, or you can simply hike out as far as you want and return back down this relatively easy route. Because of the elevation, snow is likely to cover the trails until mid-June.

A popular lower-elevation path is the five-mile-long **Panjab Trail** (No. 3127) that begins at the end of Forest Rd. 4713, approximately 60 miles south of Dayton. Starting at 2,900 feet in elevation, this path climbs 5.6 miles to the Indian Corral area at an elevation of 5,600 feet. It ends on a ridgetop offering breathtaking vistas, and from here you can continue deeper into the wilderness on several other trails. Because of the lower elevation, this trail is accessible earlier in the summer.

A fine day hike begins from the Teepee Campground, 32 miles south of Dayton at the end of Forest Rd. 4608. The **Oregon Butte Trail** (No. 3134) climbs for three miles into the wilderness—gaining 900 feet as you go—and ends at a fire lookout built in 1931. There's a good campsite on the ridge and a cold spring down the hill a short distance.

For details on other hiking trails, see *100 Hikes in the Inland Northwest* by Rich Landers and Ida Rowe Dolphin (Seattle: The Mountaineers).

LOWER SNAKE RIVER AREA

Reservoir Recreation

The once-mighty Snake River through southeastern Washington is now just a series of placid reservoirs behind massive dams built in the 1960s and '70s. The lakes are popular with boaters, and locks make it possible for barge traffic to travel from the mouth of the Columbia all the way to Clarkston. Farthest east of these in Washington is Lower Granite Dam, which creates Lower Granite Lake. Downstream from here are the others: Little Goose Dam holding back Lake Bryan, Lower Monumental Dam creating Lake Herbert G. West, and Ice Harbor Dam creating Sacajawea Lake.

A number of parks and boat launches provide year-round recreation on these reservoirs. **Wawawai County Park** has camping (fee charged), picnic areas, a playground, rock climbing, and hiking trails. Get here by heading north from Clarkston on Hwy. 195 to tiny Colton, and turning left on Wawawai Road. Follow the road approximately 15 miles to the park; the last stretch is called Wawawai Grade Road. Just south of the park, **Wawawai Landing** has a launch ramp and dock on Lower Granite Lake. **Lower Granite Dam** and reservoir are accessible by driving 25 miles north from Pomeroy. The dam has a visitor center and a fish ladder with underwater windows. The locks are a good

place to watch barges loaded with wheat heading downriver for Portland.

Just west of this dam on Lake Bryan is **Boyer Park and Marina,** with launch ramps, moorage, docks, swimming beach and bathhouse, picnic area, and camping. **Central Ferry State Park,** tel. (509) 549-3551, on Hwy. 127 about 12 miles north of Dodge, features a swimming area with lifeguards, boat launches and docks, bass and catfish fishing, a picnic area, snack bar, showers, and camping in hookup sites ($15). The park is open mid-March to mid-November. Call (800) 452-5687 for campsite reservations ($6 extra fee), available up to 11 months ahead of time.

The **Lower Monumental Dam,** about six miles from Kahlotus on Devils Canyon Rd., has a visitor center, picnic area, and boat dock. **Windust Park,** three miles downstream of the dam on the north shore, has free primitive campsites (open all year), swimming, a picnic area, and boat launch facilities.

Little Goose Dam, tel. (509) 339-2233, the creator of Lake Bryan, is about a mile west of Starbuck on Hwy. 261. Facilities here include a boat dock, fish-viewing area, and visitor center.

For information on Ice Harbor Dam and Lake Sacajawea near the mouth of the Snake River, see under "Sights" in the Tri-Cities section.

Starbuck

Not much here of note, other than the name—now better known as Washington's coffee company extraordinaire. The town was first incorporated in 1906 and has a grain elevator, a few houses, and a cafe, but no Starbucks Coffee. The beautifully rugged sage-covered landscape around here is the sort of place where someone from Wyoming would feel right at home. Cottonwood trees line the Tucannon River, and tumbleweeds pile against barbed wire fences. Just north of Starbuck on Hwy. 261, the road descends to what was once the Snake River—now just a fat reservoir backed up behind the Lower Monumental Dam.

Lyons Ferry State Park

Located in remote and desolate country at the confluence of the Snake and Palouse Rivers, this popular park has good fishing, swimming, and boating. Get here by driving eight miles northwest of Starbuck on Hwy. 261. The campground has out-in-the-sun tent sites ($10) and coin-operated showers; open April to mid-November. Call (509) 646-3252 for more information, or (800) 452-5687 for campsite reservations ($6 extra fee), available up to 11 months ahead of time.

In 1968, Washington State University researchers discovered human bones in what came to be known as the **Marmes Rockshelter**. Carbon-14 dating showed the bones to be at least 10,000 years old, making this one of the earliest known human occupation sites in North America. Unfortunately, the Lower Monumental Dam inundated both this important site and a Palouse Indian burial area; the graves were moved to a nearby hill. A three-quarter-mile trail leads from the campground to the new grave site.

The Army Corps of Engineers has free dispersed camping along the reservoir, approximately two miles north of Starbuck. Near the state park is **Lyons Ferry Hatchery**, tel. (509) 549-3551, where self-guided tours are available. **Lyons Ferry Marina**, tel. (509) 399-2001, has additional campsites, a launch ramp for the Snake River, and a small store. A towering Union Pacific railroad trestle spans the river nearby.

Palouse Falls State Park

About six miles north of Lyons Ferry and another two miles in along a gravel road is Palouse Falls, one of the most incredible waterfalls in Washington state. It's particularly impressive in the spring when the flow reaches a peak. Here, the Palouse River hurdles over a wide semicircle of volcanic rock into an enormous plunge pool almost 200 feet below. The dark basalt and dry sage-and-grass landscape seem stunned by the powerful roar of water in this remote place. On sunny days, you're likely to see a rainbow in the spray. Acrophobics should stay away from the cliff-top overlook that affords views of the pool far below.

The state park has picnic tables and on-the-lawn campsites ($7; open mid-March to early October). Call (800) 452-5687 for campsite reservations ($6 extra fee), available up to 11 months ahead of time. Primitive, unmaintained trails lead to the top of the falls and down into the gorge below. Watch your step if you take these steep and sometimes dangerous paths.

DAYTON

The landscape east of Dayton is a striped blanket of undulating wheat-covered hills, scattered farms, and an over-arching sky. Home to some 2,500 people, the small farming town of Dayton has a Blue Mountains backdrop, a number of interesting historical buildings, and even a four-star restaurant. Lewis and Clark passed through the area in 1806, but the Cayuse Indians had long lived here, using present-day Main Street as a race track for their horses. The town was established in 1871 by Jesse Day (hence the Dayton name) and prospered as a crossroads town and agricultural center. The main business today is the Green Giant/Pillsbury plant where more than a third of the world's asparagus is canned. The plant also processes seed peas. The lazy Touchet (TWO-she) River flows right through town.

Depot Museum

Built in 1881 by the Oregon Railroad & Navigation Company, Dayton's train depot—oldest in the state—is now the town museum. The immaculate and beautifully restored wooden structure originally had quarters for the stationmaster upstairs, with passenger rooms below. Now on the National Register of Historic Places, the museum contains the original depot furnishings and woodstove downstairs, along with a fascinating collection of memorabilia that includes candid turn-of-the-century photos upstairs. The volunteer staff will be happy to offer a half-hour tour of the museum. Admission is $1, and hours are 10 a.m.-5 p.m., Tues.-Saturday. Call (509) 382-2026 for information.

Historic Buildings

Dayton's impressive **Columbia County Courthouse** was built in 1887, making it the oldest in the state of Washington. The recently restored Italianate-style courthouse features a tall central tower capped by wrought iron railings. It is one of more than 80 local buildings listed on the National Register of Historic Places. Pick up a walking tour of the others from the museum, or just saunter down any of the tree-lined streets to enjoy the many turn-of-the-century Victorian homes (many of these remain unrestored).

Lewis and Clark Trail State Park

Five miles west of Dayton, the 37-acre Lewis and Clark Trail State Park, tel. (509) 337-6457, is a choice stopping place for travelers. The best known travelers to camp here were the Lewis and Clark party as they were heading back east in 1806. The park's tall ponderosa pines and cooling waters of the Touchet River are a welcome break from the sizzling summer heat of the encircling wheat fields. A 30-site campground has space for tents and vehicles ($10; no hookups) and is open early May to mid-September; in the off-season you can camp in the day-use area. Coin-operated showers are available in the summer. Call (800) 452-5687 for campsite reservations ($6 extra fee), available up to 11 months ahead of time. There are always fish in the adjacent Touchet River, and you can walk the mile-long nature trail. During the summer, rangers put on historical campfire programs.

Accommodations

There are a surprising number of lodging choices in Dayton. Least expensive is **Dayton Motel,** 110 S. Pine St., tel. (509) 382-4503, for $28 s or d. **Blue Mountain Motel,** 414 W. Main St., tel. (509) 382-3040, charges $32 s or $36 d for its country-style rooms. The **Weinhard Hotel,** 235 E. Main St., tel. (509) 382-4032, offers the finest accommodations in town for $55-99 s or d. (The building was built in 1890 by the nephew of Henry Weinhard, as in Henry Weinhard's Ale.)

Choose from three local bed and breakfasts for homier lodging. **The Purple House B&B,** 415 E. Clay St., tel. (509) 382-3159, is in an historic home filled with Oriental rugs and antiques. It has three guest rooms with private or shared baths, a full European-style breakfast, and an outdoor pool. Rates are $85 s or d in the house, or $125 d in the spacious carriage house.

Baker House B&B, 303 N. 3rd, tel. (509) 382-4764, also has accommodations ($45-90) but may be hard to reach at times.

Campgrounds

The closest public campsites are in Lewis and Clark Trail State Park, described above. The Umatilla National Forest's **Godman Campground** is 25 miles southeast of Dayton on Forest Rd. 26 at an elevation of 6,050 feet. No charge or running water, and it remains open till closed by

snow. At the campground is a trailhead for the West Butte Creek Trail into Wenaha-Tucannon Wilderness Area (see above). **Blue Willow RV Park,** behind the Dayton Motel on S. Pine, tel. (509) 382-2099, has RV campsites for $15.

Food

Nothing special on the breakfast scene, but your best bet for family start-the-day fare is **Panhandler's Restaurant,** 404 W. Main St., tel. (509) 382-4160. For a good breakfast or lunch, try **Weinhard Espresso Cafe,** at 235 E. Main Street. In addition to soups and sandwiches, they offer homemade breads, pastries, and wonderful cheesecakes. For more substantial meals (from sandwiches to steaks), try **Woodshed Tavern,** 250 E. Main St., tel. (509) 382-2004.

Dayton's claim to fame is **Patit Creek Restaurant,** 725 E. Main St., tel. (509) 382-2625, the only four-star French restaurant east of the Cascades. The decor is simple, but the changing menu features regional dishes made from fresh local ingredients. Reservations are strongly advised.

Events

The main local summertime festival is **Dayton Days** on Memorial Day weekend, which includes three days of pari-mutuel horse racing, a rodeo, parade, arts and crafts displays, and dance. There are more local activities—a parade, wine tasting, auction, and dancing—at **Depot Days,** held the third weekend in July. The **Columbia County Fair** comes 'round on the second weekend in September and always includes big name country music, a rodeo, livestock auction, and demolition derby. Each October, the Dayton Historical Society sponsors a tour of the town's finest historic homes for $7.50 per person. Call the museum at (509) 382-2026 for specifics. On the day after Thanksgiving the town erupts in a big display of fireworks, and the celebration continues with hayrides, the arrival of Santa, and caroling at the community tree.

Skiing

Ski Bluewood, 22 miles southeast of Dayton and 52 miles from Walla Walla, offers downhill skiing on 1,125 vertical feet in the Umatilla National Forest. It has the second highest base elevation in Washington (5,670 feet), and because Bluewood is over 300 miles from the coast, conditions here are generally drier than on most Washington slopes. The ski area has two triple chair lifts and a Poma. Slopes cover a spectrum from beginner through expert terrain, and the season generally runs from Thanksgiving to April. Adult rates are $23 on weekends, and $17 on weekdays; call (509) 382-4725 for more information, or (509) 382-2877 for snow conditions.

Information, Services, and Transportation

The **Dayton Chamber of Commerce,** tel. (509) 382-4825 or (800) 882-6299, can be found at 166 E. Main Street. The telephone **area code** for Dayton and all of eastern Washington is 509. The town has an Olympic size outdoor **swimming pool** open summers, as well as a nine-hole **golf course.**

Northwestern Stage Lines tel. (800) 366-6975, has bus connections from Dayton to other parts of the Northwest.

Waitsburg and Dixie

Waitsburg, a small older town 10 miles southwest of Dayton and 21 miles northeast of Walla Walla, is a minor farming center for the area. Built in 1883, the **Bruce Memorial Museum** occupies a gorgeous, antique-filled Victorian home and carriage house. Tours are by appointment only; call (509) 337-6688 or 337-6582 for details. Beyond this, Waitsburg doesn't have much to offer travelers, but lodging is available at the **Waitsburg Motel,** tel. (509) 337-8103.

Tiny Dixie is 10 more miles southeast from Waitsburg. The name came from the three musical Kershaw brothers who once lived here; their favorite song was "Dixie."

WALLA WALLA

As you drive toward Walla Walla from the east, Highway 12 takes you through mile after mile of gently rolling wheat fields growing out of the rich chocolate-brown soil. It's enough to make Midwest farmers drool. The strip-cropped patterns of plowed and fallow land look like cresting waves, with the Blue Mountains bordering the southeast horizon.

If you arrive in the pretty town of Walla Walla on a hot summer day, you'll probably wonder, at least momentarily, if you took a wrong turn somewhere and drove to New England. Walla Walla (29,000 people, plus another 6,500 in neighboring College Place) is an oasis in eastern Washington. Whereas many towns in this part of the state are hot and dry, Walla Walla is a refreshing change. Here, trees have been cultivated for decades and offer much-needed shade and visual relief from the sameness of the eastern Washington landscape; parks are cool and well cared for; old homes and commercial buildings add to the city's elegance. Walla Walla College, Whitman College, and Walla Walla Community College supply the youthful influence, while the big Washington State Penitentiary supplies the most jobs (including lots of inmate work at the prison license-plate factory). Kids will be happy to know that "Lincoln Logs" are made in Walla Walla.

Walla Walla has four distinct seasons, with an average of four days over 100° in summer, two winter days below zero, and about 20 inches of snow. There are nearly 300 sunny days most years. The Walla Walla Valley also enjoys a variation in height that much of eastern Washington lacks; the western end of town lies at 300 feet above sea level, while the Blue Mountain foothills to the east rise to 3,000 feet. The valley enjoys a long growing season with wheat, potatoes, asparagus, peas, alfalfa, grapes, and the famous Walla Walla Sweet Onion the big money crops; livestock and dairy products are also significant parts of the economy.

HISTORY

In 1805, the Lewis and Clark party passed through the Indian hunting grounds at the confluence of the Columbia and Walla Walla Rivers, revealing this land to Anglo eyes for the first time. The first permanent white settler, and first to build a home anywhere in the Northwest, was Dr. Marcus Whitman, a medical missionary who arrived in 1836. His attempts to teach Christian principles to the Cayuse Indians met with little success, and the family was murdered by Cayuse Indians 11 years later (see the special topic "The

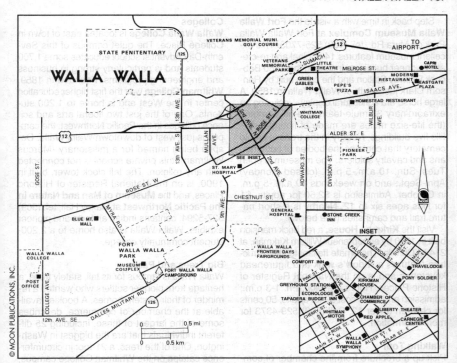

Whitman Massacre"). After this incident, settlers were prevented from occupying these lands, and all Protestant missionaries were pulled out.

There was no further Anglo settlement in the Walla Walla area until after the Indians and whites agreed to the treaties laid out by the Great Council of Walla Walla in 1855. During this three-week gathering, Washington Territorial governor Isaac I. Stevens negotiated treaties between the U.S. and the Nez Percé, Cayuse, Umatilla, Yakama, and Wallawalla tribes. It was another four years before the U.S. Senate finally ratified these treaties, opening the land to settlement.

Steptoeville

In 1856, Col. Edward Steptoe built an army barracks—**Fort Walla Walla**—at Mill Creek to keep the peace. "Steptoeville" rose up around it and was later named Walla Walla, for the Indian word meaning "Many Waters." What had been a Nez Percé trail eventually turned into Walla Walla's Main Street. In 1859, the city was named the

county seat—no small honor, since the county included half of Washington, all of Idaho, and parts of Montana. When gold was discovered in Idaho in the 1860s, prospectors came to Walla Walla for supplies and the town prospered. Like a number of other Northwest cities, Walla Walla suffered a substantial loss when a series of fires swept through the wooden downtown area in the 1880s. Most of the oldest buildings still standing date back to the late 1880s, when the town was rebuilt in brick. Old Fort Walla Walla was finally abandoned by the army in 1910.

SIGHTS

Museums

Walla Walla has a surprising number of historic places to explore, including **Whitman Mission National Historic Site,** seven miles west of Walla Walla (see under "Walla Walla Area," below).

Step back in time with a visit to the **Fort Walla Walla Museum Complex** at Fort Walla Walla Park on Myra Rd., tel. (509) 525-7703. This excellent museum features 14 original and re-created pioneer buildings, including the 1880 Babcock Railway Station and the cabin built by Ransom Clark just south of Walla Walla in 1859. A large horse-era agricultural display—including an extraordinary 33 mule-team side-hill combine (the life-size mules are made of fiberglass)—fills five buildings. Nearby in the trees is an old cemetery that contains the bodies of both Indians and cavalry soldiers. The museum is open Tues.-Sun. 10 a.m.-5 p.m. (closed Monday) April-Sept.; and on weekends 10 a.m.-5 p.m. in October. Admission is $2.50 for adults, $1 for kids ages six to 12. Nearby is a short nature trail and campsites (see below).

Visit the **Kirkman House,** a red brick mansion built in 1880 by entrepreneur William Kirkman, at 214 N. Colville. The ornate Italianate style structure features a widow's walk and figurehead keystones and is on the National Register of Historic Places. Hours are Mon.-Fri. 1-3 p.m.; admission and tours cost $2 for adults, 50 cents for children under 12. Call (509) 529-4373 for more information.

Walking Tour

Pick up a brochure from the chamber of commerce, 29 E. Sumach, for a walking tour of the historic downtown area. Some of the sites you'll pass are the wonderful 1917 **Liberty Theatre,** built on the site of Steptoe's fort at W. Main and Colville, and the **Dacres Hotel,** built in 1899 at W. Main and 4th. The **Reynolds-Day Building,** on Main between 1st and 2nd, was constructed in 1874. Washington's first State Constitutional Convention was held here in 1878. The 1906 **Sheriff's Office** is a classic building with ornate rooftop balustrade. It's hard to miss the 10-story **Whitman Motor Inn,** built in 1928 at 2nd and W. Rose. President Dwight D. Eisenhower spent a night here in 1954 when he was in the area to dedicate nearby McNary Dam. Another piece of trivial history: Founded in 1869, the **Baker Boyer Bank** is the oldest in Washington and one of the few independent banks left in the state. Their seven-story home office at the corner of Main and 2nd Streets was built in 1910 and was the town's first "skyscraper."

Colleges

Walla Walla College is located east of town in College Place. The quiet campus of this Seventh-Day Adventist school educates some 1,700 students and is particularly strong in business and engineering programs. Founded in 1859, **Whitman College** was the first higher education center in the West and is home to 1,200 students. One of the just two liberal arts and science colleges in the Pacific Northwest, the campus is just west of downtown Walla Walla. Despite being named for a missionary (Marcus Whitman), this private school is not connected with any religion. The tall clock tower, built in 1900, is on the National Register of Historic Places, and the **Museum of Man and Nature in the Pacific Northwest** at Maxey Hall, tel. (509) 527-5294, contains Indian artifacts and pioneer exhibits. Walla Walla is also home to a 2,200-student community college.

Big Trees and Parks

Walla Walla is famous for its tall, stately trees, a heritage from pioneer settlers who wanted a reminder of their eastern homes. A booklet, available at the chamber of commerce, describes some of the largest of these, including 25 different individuals that are the biggest in Washington. One of the trees, a 21-foot in circumference catalpa on the Whitman College campus, is the largest in America. The 47-acre **Pioneer Park** contains many more state record trees. Located on Alder St. at Division St., this well-kept city park was originally a cow pasture but now includes—in addition to marvelous forested areas—an aviary, rose garden, duck pond, swimming pool, gazebo, brass cannon, and picnic tables. The overall design for Pioneer Park came from John C. Olmstead, creator of New York's Central Park. **Fort Walla Walla Park** is the largest city park and is home to more tall trees, along with the Fort Walla Walla Museum (described above). Locals claim that **Mountain View Cemetery,** on S. 2nd Ave. near Abbott Rd., is one of the most attractive in the state.

Wineries

Walla Walla Valley is one of Washington state's three official viticultural appellations; the others are Columbia Valley and Yakima Valley. The valley is best known for cabernet sauvignon, merlot, riesling, and chardonnay grapes and is home to six small family-owned wineries. Visit **Woodward Canyon Winery,** tel. (509) 525-4129, about 10 miles west of town in **Lowden,** for a taste of top-quality chardonnay and cabernet. These wines are higher priced than some of the mass-producers', but well worth it; open Mon.-Sat. 10 a.m.-5 p.m., Sunday noon-5 p.m. **L'Ecole No. 41 Winery,** tel. (509) 525-0940, also in Lowden, specializes in semillon and merlot wines and is open Wed.-Sun. 11 a.m.-4 p.m., or by appointment. **Biscuit Ridge Winery,** tel. (509) 529-4986, 11 miles east of Walla Walla in Dixie, features gewürztraminer and pinot noir wines. The tasting room is open daily 10 a.m.-5:30 p.m.

The other three Walla Walla area wineries are open by appointment only: **Patrick M. Paul Vineyards,** 1554 School Ave., tel. (509) 522-1127; **Leonetti Cellar,** 1321 School Ave., tel. (509) 525-1428; and **Waterbrook Winery** in Lowden, tel. (509) 522-1918.

Onion Power

Although wheat is the most important crop in the Walla Walla area, onions are the town's claim to fame. The famous Walla Walla Sweet Onions were developed from Spanish and Italian varieties first brought here in the late 19th century. Careful experimentation by John Arbini in the 1920s produced a sweet-tasting onion that quickly became a favorite of vegetable buyers. Their sweetness is illusory; actually these mild-flavored, juicy, large onions have almost no sugar, but only half the sulfur of other onions. And it's the sulfur that gives onions their strong bite and causes tears. Walla Walla Sweets are best used raw or slightly cooked, in hamburgers, sandwiches, and salads. These onions are so mild that you can bite into one like an apple, and so soft they have to be harvested by hand. Unfortunately, they have a short three- to six-week shelf life and must be stored separately. This means you're likely to only see them in stores from mid-June to mid-August when they are at their best. Today, the "Walla Walla Sweet" label can only be put on onions grown within Walla Walla County in Washington and adjacent Umatilla County in northeastern Oregon. Contact the chamber of commerce at 29 E. Sumach, tel. (509) 525-

0850 or (800) 743-9562, for a list of local shippers, along with a wonderful recipe for roasted Walla Walla Sweets.

ACCOMMODATIONS

See the "Walla Walla Accommodations" chart for a complete listing of local lodging options. A good choice for those on a tight budget is the inexpensive but clean **Tapadera Budget Inn,** tel. (509) 529-2580 or (800) 722-8277. At the higher end of the spectrum are the historic **Whitman Motor Inn,** tel. (509) 525-2200, (800) 237-1495 (in WA), or (800) 237-4436 (out of state), and **Best Western Pony Soldier,** tel. (509) 529-4360 or (800) 634-7669, ext. 25.

Green Gables Inn B&B, tel. (509) 525-5501, is located in a beautiful 1909 arts and crafts style mansion along a tree-lined street. The five guest rooms all have private baths and a mix of antique and modern furnishings; the master suite has a jacuzzi and private deck. A separate carriage house is available for families.

Built in 1883, another excellent B&B, **Stone Creek Inn B&B,** tel. (509) 529-8120, was once home to Washington's last territorial governor, Miles Conway Moore. A National Historic Site, this three-story Victorian mansion is surrounded by four acres of open grounds and has two comfortable guest rooms with private baths.

Campgrounds

Fort Walla Walla Park, 1530 Dalles Military Rd., tel. (509) 525-3770, is a shady, city-run campground with coin-operated showers. Tent sites are $9; RV sites cost $13. Nearby is a privately run place, **Four Seasons RV Resort,** 1440 Dalles Military Rd., tel. (509) 529-6072. More camping at **Lewis and Clark Trail State Park,** 26 miles northeast of Walla Walla (see above under "Dayton" for details.

FOOD

Breakfast and Lunch

Start your day at **Clarette's Restaurant,** 15 S. Touchet, tel. (509) 529-3430, for the best breakfasts in Walla Walla. At lunchtime, your options increase considerably. **Merchants Ltd.,** 21 E.

WALLA WALLA ACCOMMODATIONS

Accommodations are arranged from least to most expensive. Rates may be lower during the winter months. The area code is 509.

Tapadera Budget Inn; 211 N. 2nd Ave.; tel. 529-2580 or (800) 722-8277; $31 s, $38 d

Colonial Motel; 2279 E. Isaacs; tel. 529-1220; $32 s, $38 d; outdoor pool, local calls 25 cents

Capri Motel; 2003 Melrose; tel. 525-1130; $32 s, $42 d; outdoor pool, kitchenette available

EconoLodge; 305 N. 2nd Ave.; tel. 529-4410 or (800) 446-6900; $34 s, $38 d; outdoor pool, kitchenettes available

City Center Motel; 627 W. Main; tel. 529-2660 or (800) 453-3160; $47 s, $49 d; outdoor pool

Super 8 Motel; 2315 Eastgate St. N; tel. 525-8800 or (800) 800-8000; $47 s, $51 d; outdoor pool, jacuzzi

Walla Walla Travelodge; 421 E. Main St.; tel. 529-4940 or (800) 255-3050; $52 s, $58 d; outdoor pool, AAA approved

Whitman Motor Inn; 107 N. 2nd Ave.; tel. 525-2200, (800) 237-1495 (in WA), or (800) 237-4436 (out of state); $55 s, $62 d; historic hotel, outdoor pool, AAA approved

Comfort Inn; 520 N. 2nd Ave.; tel. 525-2522 or (800) 221-2222; $62 s, $61-68 d; pool, sauna, jacuzzi, continental breakfast, kitchenettes available, AAA approved

Best Western Pony Soldier Motor Inn; 325 E. Main St.; tel. 529-4360 or (800) 634-7669, ext. 25; $65-70 s, $70-75 d; outdoor pool, free continental breakfast, jacuzzi, sauna, exercise room, kitchenettes available, AAA approved

Stone Creek Inn B&B; 720 Bryant; tel. 529-8120; $95-125 d; historic Victorian mansion, spacious grounds, two antique-furnished guest rooms, full breakfast, no kids under 12, bikes available

Green Gables Inn B&B; 922 Bonsella; tel. 525-5501; $75-100 s or d in the main house, or $160 for up to four in the carriage house; 1909 mansion with antiques, six guest rooms, wraparound porch, fireplaces, full breakfast, AAA approved

Main, tel. (509) 525-0900, is a great deli with a lunch buffet that includes homemade soups, fresh salads, and baked goods. You can also get charged up with an espresso here. Also of note for lunch is **Cookie Tree,** 23 S. Spokane, tel. (509) 522-4826, with homemade breads and pastries.

American
Jacobi's Cafe, 416 N. Second, tel. (509) 525-2677, is housed in the old Northern Pacific Railroad depot and adjacent railroad dining car. The big menu includes steaks, Mexican food, and various kinds of seafood, soups, and sandwiches, but the students come for the microbrews, local wines, and espresso. The **Homestead Restaurant,** 1528 Isaacs, tel. (509) 522-0345, serves three meals daily from a varied menu that includes steaks, seafood, sautes, and vegetarian selections.

Fast Food
Although Walla Walla has all the standard fast-food eateries (out on Wilbur and Isaacs), you'd do far better visiting **The Ice Burg,** 616 W. Birch, tel. (509) 529-1793. This popular drive-in makes great hamburgers and shakes. Out in College Place, **The Scoop,** 328 S. College Ave., tel. (509) 525-8276, also stirs up more milk shakes (the milk comes from the Walla Walla College Dairy), along with meatless veggie-burgers.

International
The Walla Walla area has a rich Italian heritage. One example is **Pastime Cafe,** 215 W. Main, tel. (509) 525-0873, where the big old-time Italian meals—lasagna, ravioli, and spaghetti—are still cranked out, just as they have been since 1927. For a pizza, stop by **Pepe's Pizza,** 1533 Isaacs, tel. (509) 529-2550. They also deliver. Another good place for pizza is **Lorenzo's,** 1415 Plaza

Way, tel. (509) 529-6333, where the salad bar is the best around.

Looking for big Mexican meals and great margaritas? Head to **El Sombrero's** at Oak and N. 2nd, tel. (509) 522-4984. The **Modern Restaurant,** 2200 Melrose Ave. at the Eastgate Plaza, tel. (509) 525-8662, specializes in Cantonese cuisine, with inexpensive lunch specials and a Sunday brunch.

Bakers and Grocers
Although Walla Walla has the big chain grocers, one place is more noteworthy: **Andy's Market,** 1117 S. College Ave., tel. (509) 529-1003, out in College Place. Because of the Seventh-Day Adventist college nearby, this large market is almost entirely vegetarian. You'll find a few frozen meat items (but no pork), lots of frozen and canned "vegemeat" products, bulk foods, and deliciously earthy breads. Not far away, at 166 N. College Ave., is **Rodger's Bakery,** tel. (509) 522-2738, with breads, bagels, breadsticks, and hot soups. **John's Wheatland Bakery,** 1828 E. Isaacs, tel. (509) 522-2253, is another excellent bake shop that uses fresh local ingredients.

EVENTS

A popular event with photographers is the **Walla Walla Balloon Stampede,** held at Howard-Tietan Park in mid-May; after the 50 or so balloons go up, enjoy the arts and crafts displays and demonstrations. The **Wings Over Walla Walla Air Faire** is held mid-June at the airport. Then comes a big **Fourth of July** at Pioneer Park, followed by the **Walla Walla Sweet Onion Harvest Festival** and **Mountain Man Rendezvous** a week later. Labor Day weekend brings the **Walla Walla Frontier Days Fair & Rodeo** at the fairgrounds on Orchard St., with horse racing, an evening rodeo, concerts, and educational exhibits. The **Italian Heritage Celebration** in early October is the place to be if you speak Italian.

ARTS AND ENTERTAINMENT

The **Walla Walla Symphony Orchestra,** 3 W. Alder, tel. (509) 529-8020, has been performing since 1907 with 100 amateur and professional musicians and is the oldest continuous sym-

phony west of the Mississippi. Performances are given Oct.-May. Founded in 1944, the **Walla Walla Little Theatre,** 1130 E. Sumach, tel. (509) 529-3683, is a community theater that produces four plays each season. **Harper Joy Theatre** at Whitman College, 345 Boyer, tel. (509) 527-5180, also stages several productions each year, and the local community college puts on **Outdoor Summer Theater** musical productions at Fort Walla Walla amphitheater during July.

Art buffs will want to visit the **Clyde and Mary Harris Gallery,** tel. (509) 527-2561, at Walla Walla College. Other galleries include the **Sheehan Gallery** at Whitman College, tel. (509) 527-5111; and **Carnegie Art Center,** 109 S. Palouse, tel. (509) 525-4270.

For live music of the rock and roll variety, dance on down to **19th Hole Restaurant & Lounge,** 201 E. Rees, tel. (509) 522-1109. **Barnaby's Pub,** 405 Wellington, tel. (509) 525-7142, is the place for country and western music in Walla Walla.

SPORTS AND RECREATION

For information on hiking and camping in the Blue Mountains of Umatilla National Forest (much of which lies in Oregon), visit the **Walla Walla Ranger Station** on W. Rose St., tel. (509) 522-6290. The **Wenaha-Tucannon Wilderness Area** within the Umatilla is described on under "Snake River/Blue Mountains Country."

Memorial Golf Course, off Hwy. 12, is an 18-hole course open to the public; tel. (509) 527-4507. The closest winter downhill place is Ski Bluewood (see "Skiing" under "Dayton" in the Snake River/Blue Mountains Country section).

Cycling
Enjoy the **bike path** from Cambridge Dr. to Rooks Park or from 9th and Dalles Military Rd. to Myra Road. For a more adventurous ride, head out scenic Old Milton Highway south of town. It's especially pretty in the fall. Rent bikes from **The Bicycle Barn,** 1503 E. Isaacs, tel. (509) 529-7860, or **Main Street Cycles,** 15 E. Main St., tel. (509) 525-7585. **The Rage,** tel. (509) 529-5283 or (800) 827-8157, has bike tours and offers shuttles into the Blue Mountains that take you uphill and let you roll back down.

Swimming

Outdoor summer-only **swimming pools** can be found in Pioneer Park at Alder and Division Streets; Jefferson Park at 9th Ave. and Malcolm St.; as well as the 50-meter Memorial Pool on Rees Ave. at Sumach Street. Call (509) 527-4527 for pool information. Indoor year-round pools are at the YMCA (tel. 509-525-8863), Whitman College (tel. 509-527-5921), and Walla Walla College (tel. 509-527-2396).

INFORMATION AND SERVICES

For local information, contact the **Walla Walla Chamber of Commerce,** 29 E. Sumach, tel. (509) 525-0850 or (800) 743-9562. Hours are Mon.-Fri. 8:30 a.m.-5 p.m. year-round. The **library** is at 238 E. Alder, tel. (509) 527-4550, and the main **post office** is at 128 N. 2nd, tel. (509) 522-0224. The **Blue Mountain Mall,** 1600 W. Rose St., hosts JCPenney, Sears, Fred Meyer, and upwards of 40 other shops.

Walla Walla's telephone **area code** is 509.

As the main medical hub for southeastern Washington and northeastern Oregon, Walla Walla has two hospitals: **St. Mary Hospital,** 401 W. Poplar St., (509) 525-3320, and **Walla Walla General Hospital,** 1025 S. Second Ave., tel. (509) 525-0480.

TRANSPORTATION

Valley Transit, tel. (509) 525-9140, serves the Walla Walla/College Place area Mon.-Sat. 6:30 a.m.-7 p.m. The fare is just 25 cents anywhere the buses run. Stop by the Transit Center at Main and 4th Streets for a schedule. The **Greyhound Bus Lines** depot is at 315 N. Second, tel. (509) 525-9313. **Northwest Trailways,** tel. (800) 366-3830, also has regional bus service.

Walla Walla Regional Airport on Airport Way has service to Seattle and Portland on **Horizon Air,** tel. (800) 547-9308.

WALLA WALLA AREA

West from Walla Walla lies farming country with a Midwestern look; this could just as well be Nebraska. There are a pair of wineries in tiny Lowden (see "Wineries" under "Sights," above), but not much else of interest to the traveler. Far to the southeast lie rolling tree-covered hills that rise into the Blue Mountains. A blanket of snow covers the summits till late summer.

Whitman Mission

You can get the whole story of Marcus and Narcissa Whitman's pioneer mission on the Oregon Trail at the **Whitman Mission National Historic Site,** seven miles west of Walla Walla on Hwy. 12, tel. (509) 522-6360. None of the original buildings remain, but you can walk the self-guiding trails to the mission site, grave, monument, and locations of the first house, blacksmith shop, and grist mill. Maintained by the National Park Service, the visitor center here is open daily 8 a.m.-4:30 p.m. (except Thanksgiving, Christmas, and New Year's); admission costs $2 for adults, $4 for families, and free for kids under 17.

Inside the visitor center you'll find a diorama of the Whitman mission, plus artifacts found here and a fine exhibit about the Cayuse tribe. An ornate tomahawk on display belonged to Chief Tomahas and is believed to be the weapon he used to murder Dr. Whitman (see the special topic "The Whitman Massacre" for more on this sad story). Be sure to walk up the hill to the Whitman Memorial, a 27-foot-tall obelisk overlooking this lonely place. Come here on a late fall day with the clouds overhead, the brown grass at your feet, great blue herons on the shore of the pond, and a chill west wind to really appreciate the peaceful wildness that both the Cayuse and the Whitmans loved. A section of the Oregon Trail (used until 1844) passes right through the Whitman Mission site.

Fort Walla Walla

The tiny settlement of **Wallula** stands along the east shore of Lake Wallula, the Columbia River reservoir created by McNary Dam. A plaque here commemorates one of the earliest garrisons in the Northwest. In 1818, the Northwest Fur Company established **Fort Nez Percé** at the junction of the Walla Walla and Columbia Rivers. The fort soon became a center for fur trade in the region. Fearing Indian attacks, the company built two strong outer walls and armed the men heavily; it was soon being called the "Gibraltar of the Columbia." In 1821, the British-owned Hudson's Bay Company took over the business, later renaming it Fort Walla Walla. The fears of Indian attacks intensified, and in 1856 the company abandoned the fort rather than risking destruction. The fort's commander ordered the black powder and shot balls be dumped into the Columbia River to keep them out of Cayuse hands. Shortly after his men abandoned the fort, Indian warriors burned it to the ground.

Two years later a new Fort Walla Walla rose, but this time as a U.S. Army military garrison farther up the river. This fort would eventually become the center around which the city of Walla Walla grew. The original fort site later grew into the town of Wallula, but in the late 1940s, construction began on the McNary Dam downstream along the Columbia River. After its completion, the old town and fort site were inundated, and the town's residents moved to higher ground.

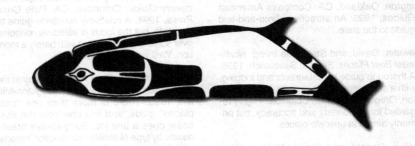

BOOKLIST

DESCRIPTION AND TRAVEL

Begoun, Paula, Stephanie Bell, and Elizabeth Janda. *Best Places To Kiss In The Northwest.* Seattle: Beginning Press, 1995. A silly title and sappy sweet writing, but a fun guide to romantic hideaways, intimate restaurants, viewpoints, gardens, and more in Oregon, Washington, and British Columbia.

Bergman, Ann, and Rose Williamson. *Going Places: Family Getaways in the Pacific Northwest.* Seattle: Northwest Parent Publishing, Inc., 1995. A useful guide to family-friendly places, with tips on travel with kids.

Chasan, Daniel Jack, Matthew Chasan, and John Doerper; photos by Bruce Hinds. *Washington.* Oakland, CA: Compass American Guides, 1995. An attractive photo-and-text guide to the state.

Brewster, David, and Stephanie Irving. *Northwest Best Places.* Seattle: Sasquatch, 1995. A thorough guide to restaurants and lodging, with a smattering of things to do, in Washington, Oregon, and British Columbia. Highly regarded for its honesty and accuracy, but primarily aimed at upscale places.

Holden, Ronald, and Glenda Holden. *Wine Country of Washington.* Holden Pacific, Inc., 1989. Detailed information on Washington wineries.

Ingle, Elaine C. *Washington State Traveler's Affordable Accommodations: Washington State.* Wenatchee, WA: Cottage Computer Publishing, 1995. A very useful guide to motels, B&Bs, and other lodgings throughout the state.

Irving, Stephanie. *Seattle Best Places.* Seattle: Sasquatch, 1996. A complete guide to restaurants, hotels, shopping, sights, and things to do in and around Seattle.

Irving, Stephanie, and Nancy Leson. *Northwest Cheap Sleeps.* Seattle: Sasquatch, 1995. A guide to budget lodging places and other attractions in Washington, Oregon, and British Columbia.

Jones, Phillip N., ed. *Columbia River Gorge: A Complete Guide.* Seattle: The Mountaineers, 1992. Complete information on hiking, climbing, windsurfing, bicycling, and other activities in the Gorge.

Litman, Todd, and Suzanne Kort. *Washington off the Beaten Path.* Old Saybrook, CT: The Globe Pequot Press, 1993. A tour of Washington's out-of-the-way and little-know places.

Martin, Don, and Betty Martin. *Washington Discovery Guide.* Columbia, CA: Pine Cone Press, 1994. A relatively complete guide to the state, but the focus is selective, skipping over some important areas with barely a mention. Well written, but odd.

McFarlane, Marilyn. *Best Places to Stay in the Pacific Northwest.* New York: Houghton-Mifflin, 1995. There is more than one "best places" guide, and this one from the east coast does a fine job. Easy-to-use breakdowns by type of facility—destination resorts, island getaways, ski lodges—make vacation planning a breeze.

McRae, Bill, and Judy Jewell. *Pacific Northwest.* Oakland, CA: Lonely Planet, 1995. A regional guide to Oregon, Washington, and Idaho.

Robinson, Kathryn, and Stephanie Irving. *Seattle Cheap Eats.* Seattle: Sasquatch Books, 1993. Helpful reviews of more than 300 inexpensive restaurants, cafes, and dives around Seattle. A fine book for budget travelers in search of good eats.

Seattle Access. New York: Access Press, 1995. The best overall guide to the city of Seattle, with up-to-date information and helpful maps. Easy to use.

Washington State Lodging & Travel Guide. Published annually, this very complete book lists nearly every lodging place in the state. Available from the Washington State Tourism Development Division, tel. (800) 544-1800, or visitor centers around the state.

Welke, Elton. *Places to go with Children around Puget Sound*. San Francisco: Chronicle Books, 1994. State parks, fish hatcheries, museums, and attractions that appeal to all ages.

HIKING AND CLIMBING

Adkison, Ron. *The Hiker's Guide to Washington*. Helena, Montana: Falcon Press Publishing Co., 1993. Seventy-five of Washington's most popular hikes, from Hurricane Ridge to Mt. Spokane, along with lesser-known trails in wilderness areas; maps included.

Beckey, Fred. *Cascade Alpine Guide: Climbing and High Routes*. Seattle: The Mountaineers, 1995. Four volumes of very detailed Cascade climbing routes, plus historical information and photos.

Burton, Joan. *Best Hikes with Children in Western Washington and the Cascades*. Seattle: The Mountaineers, 1988. Having kids doesn't have to mean the end of your days on the trail. Ninety hikes from one to seven miles, all featuring lakes, waterfalls, views, or other points of interest that will motivate kids of all ages.

Hooper, David. *Exploring Washington's Wild Olympic Coast*. Seattle: The Mountaineers, 1993. A fine guide to hiking the coastal strip of the northern Olympic Peninsula from Neah Bay to Queets.

Judd, Ron C., and Dan A. Nelson. *Pacific Northwest Hiking*. San Francisco: Foghorn Press, 1995. Useful descriptions of hundreds of trails throughout Washington and Oregon.

Landers, Rich, and Ida Rowe Dolphin. *100 Hikes in the Inland Northwest*. Seattle: The Mountaineers, 1987. Descriptions, photos, and maps of hikes in eastern Washington plus parts of Idaho, Montana, and Oregon.

Manning, Harvey and Penny Manning. *Walks & Hikes in the Foothills and Lowlands Around Puget Sound*. Seattle: The Mountaineers, 1995. Descriptions and photos of hikes from Bellingham around the sound to the Olympic Peninsula.

Spring, Ira, and Harvey Manning. *50 Hikes in Mount Rainier National Park*. Seattle: The Mountaineers, 1988. Maps, descriptions, and photos of 50 Mt. Rainier hikes.

Spring, Ira, and Harvey Manning. *100 Hikes in Washington's North Cascades: Glacier Peak Region*. Seattle: The Mountaineers, 1995. Lesser-known areas of Glacier Peak Wilderness from Darrington to Wenatchee and Lake Chelan; maps, photos, trail descriptions.

Spring, Ira, and Harvey Manning. *100 Hikes in Washington's North Cascades: National Park Region*. Seattle: The Mountaineers, 1994.

Spring, Ira, and Harvey Manning. *100 Hikes in Washington's South Cascades and Olympics*. Seattle: The Mountaineers, 1992.

Spring, Ira, and Harvey Manning. *Fifty-Five Hikes in Central Washington*. Seattle: The Mountaineers, 1990.

Spring, Vicky, Ira Spring, and Harvey Manning. *100 Hikes in Washington's Alpine Lakes*. Seattle: The Mountaineers, 1993.

Sterling, E.M. *Best Short Hikes in Washington's North Cascades and San Juan Islands*. Seattle: The Mountaineers, 1994.

Sterling, E.M. *Best Short Hikes in Washington's South Cascades and Olympics*. Seattle: The Mountaineers, 1995.

Sutliff, Mary. *Teanaway County: A Hiking and Scrambling Guide to Washington's Central Cascades.* Seattle: Signpost Books, 1980. Descriptions and photos of hikes from Lake Kachess to Blewett Pass.

Whitney, Stephen R. *A Field Guide to the Cascades and Olympics.* Seattle: The Mountaineers, 1983.

Whitney, Stephen R. *Nature Walks in & around Seattle.* Seattle: The Mountaineers, 1987. Short nature walks at 25 parks and natural areas between Redmond and Federal Way. Great for families, nature photographers, or a quick escape to the outdoors.

Wood, Robert L. *Olympic Mountains Trail Guide.* Seattle: The Mountaineers, 1991. Detailed trail descriptions, maps, and photos of national park and national forest trails on the Olympic Peninsula.

HISTORY

Bennett, Robert A. *Walla Walla: Portrait of a Western Town 1804-1899.* Walla Walla: Pioneer Press Books, 1980. Indians, treaties, trails, and Walla Walla's beginnings in Washington Territory days. The three-book series features excellent historical photos and drawings and informative, interesting text.

Bennett, Robert A. *Walla Walla: A Town Built to be a City 1900-1919.* Walla Walla: Pioneer Press Books, 1982. Early automobiles, aviation, Chinese community, street cars, and over 400 photos celebrating Walla Walla's turn-of-the-century growth spurt.

Bennett, Robert A. *Walla Walla: A Nice Place to Raise a Family 1920-1949.* Walla Walla: Pioneer Press Books, 1988. WW II, a new airport, the rise of the canning industry, and Walla Walla's emergence as a modern city.

Blankenship, Russell. *And there were Men.* New York: Knopf, 1942. Some of Washington's most famous eccentrics are discussed.

Brewster, David, and David M. Buerge. *Washingtonians: A Biographical Portrait of the State.* Seattle: Sasquatch Books, 1988. This ambitious Centennial project presents Washington's history in a series of insightful biographies. Enjoyable reading.

Chevigny, Hector. *Russian America.* New York: The Viking Press. 1965. This is a very readable account of the Russian years, and the complete story of Anna Petrovna is one of the saddest from the Northwest.

Cook, Warren L. *Flood Tide of Empire: Spain and the Pacific Northwest, 1543-1819.* New Haven: Yale University Press. 1973. This is a thorough book, perhaps best known for being the first to tell of Spanish efforts to stop the Lewis and Clark expedition.

Dodds, Gordon B. *The American Northwest: A History of Oregon and Washington.* Arlington Heights, Illinois: The Forum Press, Inc., 1986. A comprehensive history of the Northwest from 15,000 B.C. to the present, with emphasis on the people and their politics.

Fiege, Bennye. *The Story of Soap Lake.* Soap Lake, WA: Soap Lake Chamber of Commerce, 1976. Photos and text describing Soap Lake's heyday.

Kirk, Ruth, and Carmela Alexander. *Exploring Washington's Past: A Road Guide to History.* Seattle: University of Washington Press, 1995. A town-by-town description of hundreds of historical sights around the state.

Lambert, Dale A. *The Pacific Northwest: Past, Present, and Future.* Wenatchee, WA: Directed Media, Inc., 1986. A very readable, well-illustrated textbook on Pacific Northwest history.

Lampman, Ben Hur. *Centralia: Tragedy and Trial.* Seattle: reproduced by The Shorey Book Store, originally published by the American Legion, 1920. The American Legion's story of the Centralia Massacre.

LeWarne, Charles P. *Washington State*. Seattle: University of Washington Press, 1993. A detailed and profusely illustrated Washington history textbook covering pre-history through modern times.

LeWarne, Charles P. *Utopias on Puget Sound, 1885-1915*. Seattle: University of Washington Press. 1995. The history of five communal experiments: Home, Burley, Freeland, Equality, and Port Angeles.

Lewis, William S., and Naojiro Murakami. *Ranald MacDonald: The Narrative of His Life, 1824-1894*. Portland: Oregon Historical Society Press, 1990. The incredible story of a man almost unknown in America but revered in Japan whose daring exploits helped open Japan to the outside world.

McCoy, Keith. *The Mount Adams Country: Forgotten Corner of the Columbia River Gorge*. White Salmon, Washington: Pahto Publications, 1987. History of the Mt. Adams area from pre-Indians, Lewis and Clark, and early pioneers to modern-day climbers, the CCC, and Bigfoot. Interesting reading and numerous photographs assembled by a lifetime Mt. Adams-area resident.

Martinson, Arthur D. *Wilderness above the Sound: The Story of Mount Rainier National Park*. Niwot, CO: Rinehart, Roberts Publications, Inc., 1994. An enjoyable history covering the mountain's discovery, early ascents, and development of the national park, illustrated with lots of historical photos.

Portman, Sally. *The Smiling Country: A History of the Methow Valley*. Winthrop, WA: Sun Mountain Resorts, 1993. The fascinating story of how Methow Valley was transformed from gold rush to tourist rush.

Ross, Alexander. *Adventures of the First Settlers on the Oregon or Columbia River, 1810-1813*. Lincoln: University of Nebraska Press, 1986. A reprint of Ross's original eyewitness account of John Jacob Astor's 1810 expedition from New York to the Columbia River aboard the Tonquin. Fascinating and lively, the book describes the fur-trade existence as it happened, based on Ross' original journal entries.

Ruby, Robert H., and John A. Brown. *A Guide to the Indian Tribes of the Pacific Northwest*. Norman, Oklahoma: University of Oklahoma Press, 1986. History, location, numbers, culture, and contemporary life of over 150 Indian tribes of the Pacific Northwest. An excellent reference tool.

Ruby, Robert H., and John A. Brown. *The Chinook Indians: Traders of the Lower Columbia River*. Norman, Oklahoma: University of Oklahoma Press, 1988. Comprehensive history of the relationship between whites and the Indians of the lower Columbia Valley, from fur trading to modern-day legal battles.

Ruby, Robert H., and John A. Brown. *Indians of the Pacific Northwest; A History*. Norman, Oklahoma: University of Oklahoma Press, 1981.

Schwantes, Carlos, et al. *Washington: Images of a State's Heritage*. Spokane: Melior Publications, 1988. A comprehensive pictorial history of the state, covering early Native American life through the eruption of Mt. St. Helens and Bill Gates' Microsoft. Rarely seen photos and historic drawings highlight the easily digestible text.

Scott, James W., and Ronald L. DeLorme. *Historical Atlas of Washington*. Norman, Oklahoma: University of Oklahoma Press, 1988. Very informative atlas depicting the many faces of Washington in map form, from the earliest explorers to the present day.

Seattle, Chief. *Who Can Sell the Air?* Summertown, TN: The Book Publishing Co. The words of Chief Seattle, including his legendary homages to the natural world.

Shepherd, Donald, and Robert F. Slatzer. *Bing Crosby: The Hollow Man*. New York: St. Martins Press, 1981. The contrasting life of an American family man and private jerk.

Speidel, William C. *Sons of the Profits*. Seattle: Nettle Creek Publishing Co., 1967. An irreverent history of Seattle's growth between 1851-1901.

Spranger, Michael S. *The Columbia Gorge: A Unique American Treasure*. Pullman: Washington State University, 1985. History, geology, sights, development, maps, and photos of the Gorge. Interesting reading for visitors and researchers alike.

The Great Seattle Fire. Seattle: reproduced by The Shorey Book Store, 1965. A fascinating collection of original documents and news clippings describing the Seattle fire of 1889.

Swan, James G. *The Northwest Coast Or, Three Years' Residence in Washington Territory. 1857*. Seattle: University of Washington Press, 1972. A fascinating report of life on the frontier with both whites and Native Americans depicted.

Winthrop, Theodore. *The Canoe and the Saddle*. Portland: Binfords & Mort. nd. The first book written (1863) about the Washington Territory.

Wood, Robert L. *Across the Olympic Mountains; the Press Expedition, 1889-1890*. Seattle: The Mountaineers. 1967. The interesting story of the most famous early exploration of Olympic National Park.

NATURAL SCIENCES

Alt, David D., and Donald W. Hyndman. *Roadside Geology of Washington*. Missoula, MT: Mountain Press Publishing Co., 1984. A great book for anyone with an interest in geology, with easy-to-understand descriptions of how volcanoes, glaciers, floods, and other processes shaped the state's topography over the eons.

Angell, Tony, and Kenneth C. Balcomb III. *Marine Birds and Mammals of Puget Sound*. Seattle: University of Washington Press, 1984. Habits and habitats of western Washington birds and marine mammals.

Kozloff, Eugene N. *Plants and Animals of the Pacific Northwest*. Seattle: University of Washington Press, 1976. The most thorough, and illustrated, book of its kind.

Kozloff, Eugene N. *Seashore Life of the Northern Pacific Coast*. Seattle: University of Washington Press, 1983.

Mosher, Milton M., and Knut Lunnum. *Trees of Washington*. Pullman, WA: Washington State University Cooperative Extension, 1992. A 40-page guide to the state's trees, with distribution maps, identification keys, and lots of details.

OUTDOOR RECREATION

Furrer, Werner. *Water Trails of Washington*. Edmonds, WA: Signpost Books, 1979. Maps and descriptions of Washington rivers for kayaks and canoes.

Kaysing, Bill. *Great Hot Springs Of The West*. Santa Barbara, California: Capra Press, 1994. A complete guide to well-known and obscure hot springs from Washington to Colorado, complete with maps, facilities, and clothing requirements; plenty of photos.

Kirkendall, Tom. *Mountain Bike Adventures in Washington's North Cascades & Olympics*. Seattle: The Mountaineers, 1989.

Kirkendall, Tom, and Vicky Spring. *Cross-Country Ski Trails No. 1: Washington's North Cascades*. Seattle: The Mountaineers, 1988. Descriptions and photos of more than 80 ski trails.

Kirkendall, Tom, and Vicky Spring. *Cross-Country Ski Trails No. 2: Washington's South Cascades and Olympics*. Seattle: The Mountaineers, 1988. Descriptions and photos of more than 80 ski trails.

Kirkendall, Tom, and Vicky Spring. *Bicycling the Pacific Coast: A Complete Route Guide, Canada to Mexico*. Seattle: The Mountaineers, 1990.

Morava, Lillian B. *Camper's Guide to Washington Parks, Lakes, Forests, and Beaches.* Houston, TX: Gulf Publishing Co., 1995. The photos are amateurish, and the descriptions are basic, but the book includes some campgrounds missed by other books.

Mueller, Marge, and Ted Mueller. *North Puget Sound: Afoot & Afloat.* Seattle: The Mountaineers, 1995. Painstakingly detailed guide to North Puget Sound, from Point Roberts to Whidbey Island and west to Neah Bay, helpful to both boaters and landlubbers. Boat launches, parks, points of interest, plus photos and maps.

Mueller, Marge, and Ted Mueller. *The San Juan Islands: Afoot & Afloat.* Seattle: The Mountaineers, 1995. Thorough guide to "the big four" and numerous lesser islands in the San Juan chain. Boating, biking, sightseeing, and more, with maps and photos. Books by these prolific authors are always well written and very helpful.

Mueller, Marge, and Ted Mueller. *The San Juan Islands Essential Guide.* Seattle: The Mountaineers, 1994. Yet another in the in-depth series, this time with a nuts-and-bolts focus on lodging, restaurants, shopping, tours, and other activities in the San Juans.

Mueller, Marge, and Ted Mueller. *Washington's State Parks.* Seattle: Mountaineers, 1993. A very detailed guide to all of the state parks that shows each park's facilities, history, and activities.

Mueller, Marge, and Ted Mueller. *Exploring Washington's Wild Areas.* Seattle: Mountaineers, 1994. This book provides an overview of Washington's wilderness areas and national parks, with brief descriptions of hiking and climbing in each. An excellent introduction to these wild places. Nicely illustrated, too.

North, Douglass A. *Washington Whitewater I.* Seattle: The Mountaineers, 1992. Seventeen whitewater trips on the Cascades' most popular rivers for paddlers and rafters; every detail is covered, from put-ins and take-outs to camping, scenery, and special hazards.

Perry, John, and Jane Greverus Perry. *The Sierra Club Guide to the National Areas of Oregon and Washington.* San Francisco: Sierra Club Books, 1983. Features, activities, camping, boating, and more in national forests, parks, and beaches.

Sheely, Terry W. *The Northwest Sportsman Almanac.* Edmonds: Alaska Northwest Books, 1988. A beautiful and thorough book, loaded with superb color photographs and artwork as well as exhaustive coverage of hunting, fishing, camp cooking, shellfishing, woodlore, and more in the northwest U.S. and Canada.

Stienstra, Tom. *Pacific Northwest Camping.* San Francisco: Foghorn Press, 1996. No better guide to Washington's campgrounds! Over 1,500 campgrounds, from boat-in island sites to RV parks, state parks to wilderness areas.

Washburne, Randel. *Kayaking Puget Sound, the San Juans, and the Gulf Islands.* Seattle: The Mountaineers, 1990. Destinations, routes, ratings, and launching info.

Washburne, Randel. *The Coastal Kayaker's Manual; A Complete Guide to Skills, Gear and Sea Sense.* Old Saybrook, CT., Globe Pequot Press, 1993. A how-to and why-to book that is essential to the beginner.

Wert, Fred. *Washington's Rail Trails.* Seattle: Mountaineers, 1992. A guide to all the abandoned railroads that are being made into trails.

Williams, Chuck. *Mount St. Helens National Volcanic Monument.* Seattle: The Mountaineers, 1988. Great pocket guide for post-eruption hikers, sightseers, and skiers; photos, history, and detailed trail descriptions.

Woods, Erin, and Bill Woods. *Bicycling the Backroads.* Seattle: The Mountaineers, 1988-94. Three volumes—Around Puget Sound, Of Northwest Washington, and Of Southwest Washington—provide in-depth information on bike routes, terrain, elevation gain, and points of interest, plus explicit directions and plenty of maps.

INDEX

Page numbers in **bold** indicate the primary reference; *italicized* page numbers refer to information in charts, maps, and special topics.

ABOUT THE AUTHOR

Born in Georgia, Don Pitcher grew up all over the East Coast—from Florida to Maine—but moved west to attend college. He received a master's degree in fire ecology from the University of California at Berkeley and has worked seasonally for the Forest Service, Park Service, and Alaska Department of Fish and Game as a trail crew foreman, wilderness ranger, and fisheries biologist, and even spent a summer locating spotted owls.

Don's love of travel and the outdoors led him to work on various guidebooks as both a writer and photographer. In addition to taking over this volume from the previous authors, he wrote *Wyoming Handbook* and *Berkeley Inside/Out*, and co-authored *Alaska-Yukon Handbook*. He also photographed a book on Wyoming and a forthcoming book on Alaska (both published by Compass American Guides). His photos have appeared in numerous other books, calendars, cards, magazines, and ads. Don bases his travels around the world from his Alaska home.

MOON TRAVEL HANDBOOKS: THE IDEAL TRAVELING COMPANIONS

Moon Travel Handbooks provide focused, comprehensive coverage of distinct destinations all over the world. Our goal is to give travelers all the background and practical information they'll need for an extraordinary travel experience.

Every Handbook begins with an in-depth essay about the land, the people, their history, art, politics, and social concerns—an entire bookcase of cultural insight and introductory information in one portable volume. We also provide accurate, up-to-date coverage of all the practicalities: language, currency, transportation, accommodations, food, and entertainment. And Moon's maps are legendary, covering not only cities and highways, but parks and trails that are often difficult to find in other sources.

Below are highlights of Moon's North America and Hawaii Travel Handbook series. Our complete list of Handbooks, covering North America and Hawaii, Mexico, Central America and the Caribbean, and Asia and the Pacific, is on the order form on the accompanying pages. To purchase Moon Travel Handbooks, please check your local bookstore or order by phone: (800) 345-5473 Monday-Friday 8 a.m.-5 p.m. PST.

MOON OVER NORTH AMERICA
THE NORTH AMERICA AND HAWAII TRAVEL HANDBOOK SERIES

> "Moon's greatest achievements may be the individual state books
> they offer. . . . Moon not only digs up little-discovered attractions,
> but also offers thumbnail sketches of the culture and state politics
> of regions that rarely make national headlines."
> —*The Millennium Whole Earth Catalog*

ALASKA-YUKON HANDBOOK
by Deke Castleman and Don Pitcher, 460 pages, **$14.95**
"Exceptionally rich in local culture, history, and reviews of natural attractions. . . . One of the most extensive pocket references. . . . An essential guide!"   — *The Midwest Book Review*

ALBERTA AND THE NORTHWEST TERRITORIES
by Nadina Purdon and Andrew Hempstead, 466 pages, **$17.95**
"*Alberta and the Northwest Territories Handbook* provides strong coverage of one of the most rugged territories in Canada."
—*The Bookwatch*

ARIZONA TRAVELER'S HANDBOOK
by Bill Weir and Robert Blake, 448 pages, $17.95
"If you don't own this book already, buy it immediately"
—*Arizona Republic*

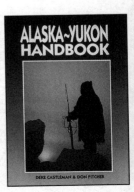

ATLANTIC CANADA HANDBOOK
by Nan Drosdick and Mark Morris, 436 pages, **$17.95**
Like a corner of Europe, Canada's eastern seacoast provinces boast Irish brogue, Scottish kilts, Highland flings, and a rich heritage of British influence. *Atlantic Canada Handbook* provides extensive coverage of this region, including New Brunswick, Nova Scotia, Newfoundland, and Prince Edward Island. While there are many guides to Canada, none offers the detailed regional coverage of this comprehensive handbook.

BIG ISLAND OF HAWAII HANDBOOK
by J.D. Bisignani, 349 pages, **$13.95**
"The best general guidebooks available"   —*Hawaii Magazine*

BRITISH COLUMBIA HANDBOOK
by Jane King, 375 pages, **$15.95**
"Deftly balances the conventional and the unconventional, for both city lovers and nature lovers."
    —*Reference and Research Book News*

COLORADO HANDBOOK
by Stephen Metzger, 470 pages, **$18.95**
"Hotel rooms in the Aspen area, in the height of winter sports season, for $20-$30? . . . who but a relentless researcher from Moon could find it?"   —*The New York Daily News*

GEORGIA HANDBOOK
by Kap Stann, 350 pages, **$17.95**
". . . everything you need to know to enjoy a journey through Georgia."   —*Southern Book Trade*

HAWAII HANDBOOK
by J.D. Bisignani, 1004 pages, **$19.95**
Winner: Grand Excellence and Best Guidebook Awards, Hawaii Visitors' Bureau
"No one since Michener has told us so much about our 50th state."   —*Playboy*

HONOLULU-WAIKIKI HANDBOOK
by J.D. Bisignani, 365 pages, **$14.95**
"The best general guidebooks available."   —*Hawaii Magazine*

IDAHO HANDBOOK
by Bill Loftus, 282 pages, **$14.95**
"Well-organized, engagingly written, tightly edited, and chock-full of interesting facts about localities, backcountry destinations, traveler accommodations, and cultural and natural history."
    —*Sierra Magazine*

KAUAI HANDBOOK
by J.D. Bisignani, 274 pages, **$13.95**
"This slender guide is tightly crammed. . . . The information provided is staggering."   —*Hawaii Magazine*

MAUI HANDBOOK
by J.D. Bisignani, 393 pages, **$14.95**

Winner: Best Guidebook Award, Hawaii Visitors' Bureau
"*Maui Handbook* should be in every couple's suitcase. It
intelligently discusses Maui's history and culture, and you can
trust the author's recommendations for best beaches, restaurants,
and excursions." —*Bride's Magazine*

MONTANA HANDBOOK
by W.C. McRae and Judy Jewell, 466 pages, **$17.95**

"Well-organized, engagingly written, tightly edited, and chock-full
of interesting facts about localities, backcountry destinations,
traveler accommodations, and cultural and natural history."
—*Sierra Magazine*

NEVADA HANDBOOK
by Deke Castleman, 473 pages, **$16.95**

"Veteran travel writer Deke Castleman says he covered more
than 10,000 miles in his research for this book and it shows."
—*Nevada Magazine*

NEW MEXICO HANDBOOK
by Stephen Metzger, 322 pages, **$14.95**

"The best current guide and travel book to all of New Mexico"
—*New Mexico Book League*

NORTHERN CALIFORNIA HANDBOOK
by Kim Weir, 779 pages, **$19.95**

"That rarest of travel books–both a practical guide to the region
and a map of its soul." —*San Francisco Chronicle*

OREGON HANDBOOK
by Stuart Warren
and Ted Long Ishikawa, 520 pages, **$16.95**

". . . perhaps the most definitive tourist guide to the state ever
published." —*The Oregonian*

TEXAS HANDBOOK
by Joe Cummings, 598 pages, **$17.95**

"Reveals a Texas with a diversity of people and culture that is as
breathtaking as that of the land itself."
—*Planet Newspaper,* Australia

"I've read a bunch of Texas guidebooks, and this is the best one."
—*Joe Bob Briggs*

UTAH HANDBOOK
by Bill Weir and Robert Blake, 458 pages, **$16.95**

"What Moon Publications has given us—at long last—is a one-
volume, easy to digest, up-to-date, practical, factual guide to all
things Utahan. . . . This is the best handbook of its kind I've yet
encountered." —*The Salt Lake Tribune*

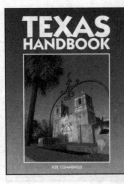

WASHINGTON HANDBOOK
by Don Pitcher, 800 pages, **$19.95**

"Departs from the general guidebook format by offering information on how to cope with the rainy days and where to take the children. . . . This is a great book, informational, fun to read, and a good one to keep."
—*Travel Publishing News*

WYOMING HANDBOOK
by Don Pitcher, 495 pages, **$14.95**

"Wanna know the real dirt on Calamity Jane, white Indians, and the tacky Cheyenne gunslingers? All here. And all fun."
—*The New York Daily News*

Hit The Road With Moon Travel Handbooks

ROAD TRIP USA
Cross-Country Adventures on America's Two-Lane Highways
by Jamie Jensen, 800 pages, **$22.50**

This 800-page Handbook covers the entire United States with 11 intersecting routes, allowing travelers to create their own cross-country driving adventures. Of the featured routes, six run west to east from coast to coast, and five run north to south from Canada to Mexico.

Packed with both practical information and entertaining sidebars, *Road Trip USA* celebrates the spontaneity and culture of the American highway without sacrificing the essential comforts of bed and bread. In addition to engaging commentary on literally thousands of sights and diversions, readers will find such essential information as the locations of diners with the best apple pie and the call letters of good radio stations on lonely stretches of road.

The World Wide Web edition of *Road Trip USA* has been generating excitement on the Internet for over a year. The *Road Trip* exhibit includes a map with hundreds of original entries and links to local Internet sites. WWW explorers are encouraged to participate in the exhibit by contributing their own travel tips on small towns, roadside attractions, regional foods, and interesting places to stay. Visit *Road Trip USA* online at: **http://www.moon.com/rdtrip.html**

MOONBELT

A new concept in moneybelts. Made of heavy-duty Cordura nylon, the Moonbelt offers maximum protection for your money and important papers. This pouch, designed for all-weather comfort, slips under your shirt or waistband, rendering it virtually undetectable and inaccessible to pickpockets. It features a one-inch high-test quick-release buckle so there's no more fumbling around for the strap or repeated adjustments. This handy plastic buckle opens and closes with a touch but won't come undone until you want it to. Moonbelts accommodate traveler's checks, passports, cash, photos, etc. Size 5 x 9 inches. Available in black only. **$8.95**

MOON TRAVEL HANDBOOKS

NORTH AMERICA AND HAWAII

Alaska-Yukon Handbook (0161) $14.95
Alberta and the Northwest Territories Handbook (0676) $17.95
Arizona Traveler's Handbook (0714) $17.95
Atlantic Canada Handbook (0072) $17.95
Big Island of Hawaii Handbook (0064) $13.95
British Columbia Handbook (0145) $15.95
Colorado Handbook (0447) $18.95
Georgia Handbook (0390) $17.95
Hawaii Handbook (0005) $19.95
Honolulu-Waikiki Handbook (0587) $14.95
Idaho Handbook (0617) $14.95
Kauai Handbook (0013) $13.95
Maui Handbook (0579) $14.95
Montana Handbook (0498) $17.95
Nevada Handbook (0641) $16.95
New Mexico Handbook (0153) $14.95
Northern California Handbook (3840) $19.95
Oregon Handbook (0102) $16.95
Road Trip USA (0366) $22.50
Texas Handbook (0633) $17.95
Utah Handbook (0684) $16.95
Washington Handbook (0455) $19.95
Wyoming Handbook (3980) $14.95

ASIA AND THE PACIFIC

Australia Handbook (0722) $21.95
Bali Handbook (0730) $19.95
Bangkok Handbook (0595) $13.95
Fiji Islands Handbook (0382) $13.95
Hong Kong Handbook (0560) $15.95
Indonesia Handbook (0625) $25.00
Japan Handbook (3700) $22.50
Micronesia Handbook (0773) $14.95
Nepal Handbook (0412) $18.95
New Zealand Handbook (0331) $19.95
Outback Australia Handbook (0471) $18.95
Pakistan Handbook (0692) $22.50
Philippines Handbook (0048) $17.95

Southeast Asia Handbook (0021) $21.95
South Korea Handbook (3204) $14.95
South Pacific Handbook (0404) $22.95
Tahiti-Polynesia Handbook (0374) $13.95
Thailand Handbook (0420) $19.95
Tibet Handbook (3905) $30.00
Vietnam, Cambodia & Laos Handbook (0293) $18.95

MEXICO

Baja Handbook (0528) $15.95
Cabo Handbook (0285) $14.95
Cancún Handbook (0501) $13.95
Central Mexico Handbook (0234) $15.95
Mexico Handbook (0315) $21.95
Northern Mexico Handbook (0226) $16.95
Pacific Mexico Handbook (0323) $16.95
Puerto Vallarta Handbook (0250) $14.95
Yucatán Peninsula Handbook (0242) $15.95

CENTRAL AMERICA AND THE CARIBBEAN

Belize Handbook (0307) $15.95
Caribbean Handbook (0277) $16.95
Costa Rica Handbook (0358) $18.95
Jamaica Handbook (0706) $15.95

INTERNATIONAL

Egypt Handbook (3891) $18.95
Moon Handbook (0668) $10.00
Moscow-St. Petersburg Handbook (3913) $13.95
Staying Healthy in Asia, Africa, and Latin America (0269) . . . $11.95
The Practical Nomad (0765) $13.95

PERIPLUS TRAVEL MAPS

All maps $7.95 each

Bali	Jakarta	Phuket/S. Thailand
Bandung/W. Java	E. Java	Sabah
Bangkok/C. Thailand	Java	Sarawak
Batam/Bintan	Kuala Lumpur	Singapore
Cambodia	Ko Samui/S. Thailand	Vietnam
Chiangmai/N. Thailand	Lombok	Yogyakarta/C. Java
Hong Kong	N. Sumatra	
Indonesia	Penang	

WHERE TO BUY MOON TRAVEL HANDBOOKS

BOOKSTORES AND LIBRARIES: Moon Travel Handbooks are sold worldwide. Please contact our sales manager for a list of wholesalers and distributors in your area.

TRAVELERS: We would like to have Moon Travel Handbooks available throughout the world. Please ask your bookstore to write or call us for ordering information. If your bookstore will not order our guides for you, please contact us for a free catalogue.

> Moon Publications, Inc.
> P.O. Box 3040
> Chico, CA 95927-3040 U.S.A.
> tel.: (800) 345-5473
> fax: (916) 345-6751
> e-mail: travel@moon.com

IMPORTANT ORDERING INFORMATION

PRICES: All prices are subject to change. We always ship the most current edition. We will let you know if there is a price increase on the book you order.

SHIPPING AND HANDLING OPTIONS: Domestic UPS or USPS first class (allow 10 working days for delivery): $3.50 for the first item, 50 cents for each additional item.

EXCEPTIONS: *Tibet Handbook, Mexico Handbook,* and *Indonesia Handbook* shipping $4.50; $1.00 for each additional *Tibet Handbook, Mexico Handbook,* or *Indonesia Handbook.*

Moonbelt shipping is $1.50 for one, 50 cents for each additional belt.

Add $2.00 for same-day handling.

UPS 2nd Day Air or Printed Airmail requires a special quote.

International Surface Bookrate 8-12 weeks delivery: $3.00 for the first item, $1.00 for each additional item. Note: Moon Publications cannot guarantee international surface bookrate shipping. Moon recommends sending international orders via air mail, which requires a special quote.

FOREIGN ORDERS: Orders that originate outside the U.S.A. must be paid for with an international money order, a check in U.S. currency drawn on a major U.S. bank based in the U.S.A., or Visa or MasterCard.

TELEPHONE ORDERS: We accept Visa or MasterCard payments. Minimum order is US$15. Call in your order: (800) 345-5473, 8 a.m.-5 p.m. Pacific standard time.

ORDER FORM

Prices are subject to change without notice. Be sure to call (800) 345-5473 8 a.m.–5 p.m. PST
for current prices and editions or for the name of the bookstore nearest you
that carries Moon Travel Handbooks.
(See important ordering information on preceding page.)

Name: _____ Date: _____

Street: _____

City: _____ Daytime Phone: _____

State or Country: _____ Zip Code: _____

QUANTITY	TITLE	PRICE

Taxable Total _____

Sales Tax (7.25%) for California Residents _____

Shipping & Handling _____

TOTAL _____

Ship: ☐ UPS (no P.O. Boxes) ☐ 1st class ☐ International surface mail

Ship to: ☐ address above ☐ other _____

Make checks payable to: **MOON PUBLICATIONS, INC.**, P.O. Box 3040, Chico, CA 95927-3040 U.S.A.
We accept Visa and MasterCard. **To Order**: Call in your Visa or MasterCard number, or send a written order with your Visa or MasterCard number and expiration date clearly written.

Card Number: ☐ **Visa** ☐ **MasterCard**

☐ ☐ ☐ ☐ ☐ ☐ ☐ ☐ ☐ ☐ ☐ ☐ ☐ ☐ ☐ ☐

Exact Name on Card: _____

Expiration date: _____

Signature: _____